THE ESSENTIAL

BIBLE

HANDBOOK

THE ESSENTIAL
BIBLE
HANDBOOK

Abingdon Press
Nashville

This book is printed on acid-free paper.

Library of Congress Cataloging-in-Publication Data applied for.

Scripture quotations marked (NIV) are taken from the Holy Bible, NEW INTERNATIONAL VERSION®. Copyright © 1973, 1978, 1984 by International Bible Society. All rights reserved throughout the world Used by permission of International Bible Society..

Scripture quotations marked (CEV) are from the Contemporary English Version © 1991, 1992, 1995 by American Bible Society. Used by permission.

Scripture quotations marked (KJV) are from the King James or Authorized Version of the Bible.

All scriptures quotations unless otherwise noted are taken from the New Revised Standard Version of the Bible, copyrighted 1989, Division of Christian Education of the National Council of the Churches of Christ in the United States of America. Used by permission. All rights reserved.

Scripture quotations marked (RSV) are taken from the Revised Standard Version of the Bible, copyright 1971 [2nd edition, 1971] by the Division of Christian Education of the National Council of the Churches of Christ in the United States of America. Used by permission. All rights reserved.

ISBN 978-1-426-70059-0

09 10 11 12 13 14 15 16 17 18—10 9 8 7 6 5 4 3 2 1

MANUFACTURED IN THE UNITED STATES OF AMERICA

CONTENTS

NEW TESTAMENT

ADDITIONAL TOOLS

THE HISTORY OF THE BIBLE

A LIBRARY TAKES SHAPE

The Bible is actually a collection, a library, of many writings. The story of the writing, editing, collecting, and preservation of the Bible is as fascinating as a detective story.

Like a detective story, there are many clues to the Bible's development. Some of these clues may seem tedious and trivial, it is not always easy to see the main direction that is present among the lists of names and all the places and dates. But a general overview is not hard to manage, and it adds immensely to our appreciation of this literature that we claim as Scripture.

Both the Old and New Testaments began as stories circulated by word of mouth. People who lived a nomadic life had little use for written language. Israel's identity grew out of centuries of a wandering existence, with no single place as home and no written records. Storytelling was an art form; and the masters passed on the stories of Abraham and Sarah, Isaac and Rebekah, Jacob and Rachel, Joseph, Moses and Miriam, Joshua, Deborah, and Gideon.

A great surge of writing down old stories seems to have taken place during the times of kings David and Solomon (around 1000 to 922 B.C.). Scholars think that the oral traditions were in danger of being lost when Israel seemed securely based as a nation with political boundaries. David might also have felt that the old stories would give him more backing for his monarchy.

This golden age of Israel's kingdom gave rise to writing about its contemporary experiences as well. First and Second Samuel reveal an insider's view of the royal court during the reigns of Saul and David. Many of the Psalms were probably written during this same period.

THE OLD TESTAMENT

This two-step process—spoken and written—characterizes most of the books of the Old Testament. As time went by, each of the three main sections of the Old Testament came to be accepted as religious standards—they were *canon* (the word *canon* originally meant a measuring reed; the idea here is a standard or authority) for Jewish faith.

Our Story

All of what appears in the Old Testament hinges on the first five books, which form a unit known as the *Torah*. Often referred to as *Law*, Torah is primarily the remembered foundational events of God's people Israel. How this people began, how they survived and came to be a nation—this long, dramatic story is tied to the creation and then sinful fall of the world.

Our Challenge

Centuries after the Exodus and the conquest of the land, Israel faced a series of political crises. During that period of time, the people lost half their kingdom, ten of their tribes, and all their independence. But it was not as though Israel had no choices. At least sixteen persons spoke up through those trying times, calling the leaders and the people to stay true to their God. These *prophets* saw that true spiritual loyalty and justice were the only ways for Israel to maintain its standing. Prophetic writings expose the continual challenge to all peoples who claim trust in God.

Our Reflections

Much of Israel's history was unsettled as the people wandered, fled, fought, and wept over their nation. But during the height of the kingdom of Israel, a number of pieces were composed and recorded. These writings cover such topics as hymns for worship (the Psalms), wisdom (Proverbs), history (Chronicles), and romantic love (Song of Songs). The *Writings* offer both a look at the times and an affirmation of those human elements common to all ages. By A.D. 90, the Jews had closed their canon by recognizing the authority of the Writings—the Psalms, Job, Ecclesiastes, Song of Songs, and the rest.

THE NEW TESTAMENT

The Jewish Scriptures were the only scriptures for Jesus and his disciples and for the first generation of the church. Soon, however, Christians began to realize that they had some important needs that were not dealt with in the Jewish Scriptures. Motivated to meet these needs, a number of Christians in the first two generations wrote letters, gospels, and sermons that were circulated among the churches. We can distinguish in the New Testament writings a reflection of the three purposes guiding the New Testament.

1. Getting the Word Out

The earliest Christians, steeped in the Jewish tradition, knew well the power of word of mouth. They also realized that word of mouth was not as effective in the Roman Empire, which increasingly relied on writing. The authority of the spoken word was less accurate and was not as reliable as time passed. Writing, then, preserved the common aspects of the Jesus story.

However, the Christian message was more than a story. This Christian message declared a universal need for all humankind to repent and trust in God through Christ. And why trust in Christ? Because of what Jesus Christ did: his teaching, preaching, and healing; his suffering and death; his resurrection and ascension; and his relationship with future believers. The four Gospels contain most of this material.

2. Fighting Fires

Believe it or not, disagreement among believers took place within the first few years of the Christian movement. Individual preferences and the longstanding differences between Jews and Gentiles created controversies almost immediately. People disagreed about what ideas to believe and what actions were acceptable. The apostle Paul responded to such difficulties by writing letters to various congregations. Perhaps it can be comforting to us to remember that the first Christian writings were spurred by church fights.

3. Guarding the Beliefs

Obviously not everyone who came into contact with this new religious movement agreed with it. Many Jews were not persuaded that Jesus was the long-awaited Messiah. Other persons who became

Christians sometimes followed ideas by teachers who interpreted the faith a little too differently. Then there was the Roman government, wary of another movement from such a trouble-making province. These pressures from within and without led New Testament writers to clarify their faith as Christians.

Gospels

One important part of the New Testament consists of stories of Jesus and his influence while on earth and what that influence calls forth from humanity. We have four versions, each offering a distinctive emphasis: Matthew, Mark, Luke, and John. These books are called Gospels because they tell the *good news* of Jesus Christ

History of the Early Church

The writer of Luke did not stop at Jesus. He also provided a document describing activities of the first generation of people after Jesus. The Book of Acts covers the period from the day of Pentecost through Paul's mission to the Gentiles and his eventual imprisonment.

Correspondence

Just as family and friends keep in touch today, so the young congregations had contact with one another. Several church leaders wrote to numerous audiences— Paul was the most prolific writer—covering many theological and practical topics.

Finale

As a rousing but mysterious culmination to our Scriptures, the Book of Revelation ends the New Testament. Revelation symbolically explains God's purposes through Christ for the fullness of time and creation.

OLD AND NEW

Somehow, believers in the Jewish religious community and the fledgling Christian church trusted in the authority of certain writings. Despite all the stories of hate, murder, war, revenge, and infidelity to God and to fellow human beings, Jews and Christians accepted certain writings as unique and special. Christians added books to the Jewish list. They did so not to oppose, but to continue, what they saw going on in the Hebrew Bible.

Christians believed that Jesus Christ gave an unsurpassable fulfillment to the story of God, which Israel had remembered from Abraham through the rebuilding of the Temple. Jesus was a Jew who referred to Scripture constantly and saw his ministry in its terms (see Matthew 5:17-20). Thus, the Hebrew Bible became the Christian one as well. The writings that we now call the New Testament depend heavily on events and ideas from the Old Testament. Indeed, the New Testament and its proclamation could not exist without the witness of Jewish Scripture. That fact should not surprise us. After all, Christians believed that the God whom they knew as the Father of the Lord Jesus Christ was the very same God who called Israel into being.

One distinguished Bible scholar explains the unity of the Bible this way:

"The Bible . . . has a unity like that of a great drama. It moves from beginning to end, from creation to new creation. The story deals with people's hopes and fears, their joy and anguish, their ambitions and failures. There is a great deal of diversity in the Bible: different authors, different historical situations, different kinds of theological expression. But underlying all this great variety is the dynamic movement, similar to the plot of a drama, which binds the whole together. The biblical drama, however, is unique in that God appears in the cast. Not only is God the Author who stands behind the scenes prompting and directing the drama but God enters onto the stage of history as the Chief Actor—the protagonist. The biblical plot is the working out of God's purpose for the creation in spite of all efforts to oppose it.

The denouement is reached, according to the conviction of the Christian community, when the crucifixion and resurrection of Jesus of Nazareth are proclaimed as the sign of God's decisive victory. In the light of this climactic event the earlier stages of the story are understood with a deeper and larger meaning" (*The Unfolding Drama of the Bible*, by Bernhard W. Anderson [Fortress Press, 1988], pages 14-15)

THE AUTHORITY OF THE BIBLE

THE BREATH OF GOD

The most common appeal to the Bible's authority has been by the concept of *inspiration*. For the most part, the Bible does not directly speak about inspiration. One verse, however, is often quoted: "All scripture is inspired by God and is useful for teaching, for reproof, for correction, and for training in righteousness" (2 Timothy 3:16). The word *inspired* in this passage is the Greek *theopneustos*, which literally is *God-winded* or *God-breathed*. It follows a verse referring to "the sacred writings" (verse 15), that is, the Hebrew Bible and possibly some of Paul's letters as well. There is more than one way to speak about inspiration. We can identify four basic ways to think of the inspiration of the Bible.

1. One view holds that every *word* of the Bible is totally inspired by God and contains truth free from error. The assumption here is that God effectively persuaded all biblical writers to put down just the correct words, all the time.

2. Another way to speak of inspiration is to say that it applies to the *ideas* and *concepts* but not to the actual words of the Bible.

3. Still other Christians have argued that God inspired not words or ideas but *individual people*. These folks then wrote what they did using the language and thought forms of their culture.

4. Yet another view of inspiration is that God inspired the *community* that produced, preserved, and passed on the writings we call Scripture.

So, inspiration can be defined as all the words, all the ideas, all the writers, or all the believers who kept the writings as Scripture. Each of these positions has its advocates, its strengths, and its critics. Not all Christians agree on how to describe the God-breathed nature of the Bible. But Christians do agree that Scripture is inspired by God. God is the ultimate source or origin of Scripture.

MORE ON THE BIBLE'S AUTHORITY

Inspiration has not been the only way that Christians have understood God's involvement in the Bible. We can identify three other ways to talk about the authority of Scripture.

1. Probably the most popular of these three takes particular biblical events as the norm for what God is doing and what God is like. God acted in a special way to call Abram, to save Israel from the Egyptians, to preserve the Hebrews through exile, and to save all humanity through Jesus' death and resurrection. This *salvation history* is one basis of the Bible's authority. God is revealed through the events of salvation history recorded in the Bible.

2. Another view of authority became popular during the Protestant Reformation. Martin Luther, among others, said Jesus Christ is the ultimate standard of authority. This *Christocentric* view says that even the Old Testament has to be read in light of Jesus. Anything that disagrees with the

words or spirit of Jesus does not have equal authority with Jesus. The Bible is Scripture because of him.

3. Another position focuses on what happens to the person reading the Bible rather than on the Bible itself. The authority of Scripture here is in what happens to a person today to change his or her life as he or she reads the Bible. What is important is the moment of realizing the point and the claim that God makes as we listen to Scripture. This is a form of *existentialism*.

WORD OF GOD

Each of these ways of claiming the authority of the Bible makes some sense. The Bible does have a sense of being inspired. It does assemble around certain pivotal, saving events. It does call readers to hear and make decisions in the present moment. It does center in a decisive way around Jesus Christ. There is something true and valid about each of these approaches. But even taking them all together, does that tell the whole story about what we can believe about the Bible? Or is something still missing?

There is—and we must look back to the Bible itself to find it. We are chasing a slippery eel now, one that the Bible calls the *Word* of God. The Hebrew term for *word* (*dabar*) means not only word but also deed or thing. It usually refers to some kind of action or event. So, the Word of God is divine action, God busy doing something. And that something is making God known, communicating what God is like and what God's purposes are. This concept is fundamental to the witness of both Old and New Testaments.

By the Word of God, creation appeared, Israel was guided, Jesus was raised. By the Word of God, prophets spoke, Mary trusted,

Saul became Paul, and Luther changed the world. By the Word of God, people who have never heard the gospel can read the Bible and be stirred to claim faith.

The Word of God, then, is another helpful way to talk about the Bible's authority as Scripture. The Bible itself is not the Word, but in and through the Bible we hear the Word. Reformers in the sixteenth century also claimed that we hear the Word through preaching, as a sermon reveals the meaning of a biblical passage for the listeners.

The Bible, as the necessary conduit through which the Word of God flows to us, has two aspects: one human and one divine. The Bible is full of the words of real human beings located in particular times and settings. *And* the Bible carries divine freight. Through it God's Word says something more than what human culture alone can generate.

This approach is another way of reminding ourselves that nothing can contain or limit God. No theory of the Bible's authority can express all that is true about the Word of God. For it is carried into our life by the Holy Spirit, who "blows where it chooses, and you hear the sound of it, but you do not know where it comes from or where it goes" (John 3:8a).

SCRIPTURE'S APPEAL

For more than two thousand years these writings have been at the heart of something almost unexplainable. People all around the world have listened to those words, have said *Yes* to the Spirit's tug, and have become different because of it. Through it all, yesterday and today, those who follow find out in their souls what Scripture declares to all who will listen: that we live by the love, the goodness, the grace of a living, present God.

THE CENTRALITY
OF SCRIPTURE

When we try to understand God's message to us and to live life in accordance with the will of God, we turn to the *Scripture* and *tradition* of the church for guidance, to our own *experience* for verification, and to our *reason* for the tools with which to bring Scripture, tradition, and experience together.

SCRIPTURE

In many ways the Bible is like a patchwork quilt. It comes to us having been written by many persons in many different times. And yet the multicolored patches form one garment. The experiences that prompted the writing of the Bible were so important to those who lived, told, and wrote about them that it became and remains today a sacred text.

The Bible is sacred because it contains the Word of God. The Bible has stories of history, just as it has poetry and moral and ethical instruction. But the Bible is more than interesting history, beautiful poetry, and important moral lessons. The Bible is sacred because God has chosen to use it as a means of communicating with us.

We might summarize the centrality of the Scripture in these ways:

Scripture is central because in and through it we meet God. To be sure, Scripture is the record of how others have met God. We read of Moses meeting God in the burning bush that was not consumed; of Ruth meeting God in a crisis point in her life; of Paul meeting God on the road to Damascus. But as we read, study, and meditate upon Scripture, God meets us there too and shares the divine nature with us.

Scripture is central because in it God shares with us the divine plan. The world often seems chaotic to us. Events we experience may make no sense to us. We look for a deeper meaning to life than the simple biological cycle of birth and death. Scripture teaches us that God has ordered the world for God's own purposes. God has appeared in the world in Jesus of Nazareth "reconciling the world to himself" (2 Corinthians 5:19).

Scripture is central because through it we understand God's nature. "God so loved the world . . ." is the way John describes God's nature (John 3:16). The God revealed in Jesus Christ is unique among the gods that have been worshiped by humankind throughout its long history. When the volcano erupts on Hawaii, the Christian does not interpret this to mean that the goddess Pele is unhappy with humankind. Terrible things happen in the world, but we know from Scripture that God's nature is love and that "all things work together for good for those who love God" (Romans 8:28).

Scripture is central because in it we find all that is necessary for holy living. Holy living is living that is graced by the spiritual gifts of faith, hope, and love. Through the Scripture we gain the spiritual strength required to live in harmony with God's purposes. All persons seek answers to the questions of life: How do I know what is right and wrong? To which goals should I devote my life and energy? How can I fulfill my potential? These are questions the Bible takes seriously and for which it offers answers.

For these reasons the Bible has the central place in our lives and is the basis for all our worship as Christians. If we look closely at the hymns we sing and the prayers we pray, we will find that they all are centered in the biblical message.

THE RECEIVED TRADITION

When Jesus went to the synagogue he read from the Hebrew Scriptures. While these Scriptures were considered sacred texts, they were also part of the tradition into which Jesus was born. So it is with us. Scripture is both sacred text and part of our tradition. The Bible is part of the world into which we are born. It is part of our tradition.

In the church, tradition has enriched the experience of us all. The hymns, prayers, and creeds of the church, while centered in Scripture, have become part of our tradition. When we affirm the creeds, we share across the centuries with those who found in the Scripture the central ideas of the faith now embodied in those timeless statements of faith. We remember the stories of our fathers and mothers in the faith and draw strength from their examples. We sing the great hymns of the church and rejoice in the traditions that help make us who we are.

Tradition helps us reach beyond the weaknesses of the church in the present and recover the richness of faith expressed in earlier generations. For example, John Wesley believed that the full message of Scripture, especially the idea of scriptural holiness, was not being taught in the church of his time. He offended many church leaders of his day by his method and style of preaching. His conviction about the meaning of Scripture led to an emphasis on holiness of heart and life in the Methodist societies in England and, eventually, in the Methodist movement in North America. Wesley did not reject tradition. Rather he reached beyond his own day to an earlier tradition that for him led to a more fulfilling understanding of the Word of God. The tradition of the church can also enrich our lives and our faith and can help us understand the Scripture for our own time.

EXPERIENCE

Scripture and tradition present us with an understanding of the world. But surely one of the most important tasks of life, if not *the* most important task, is to develop beliefs that are genuinely our own. Our personal experience is a vital part of that development.

The specifically religious experience seems to be universal, but not all religious experiences are alike. For the Christian, the authentic religious experience must be in harmony with the gospel. When we believe God is speaking to us, what we hear must be tested against the basic message of the Scripture. If what we hear is different from the message of Scripture, that is a red flag that something is out of kilter. Upon further examination, we may discover that our understanding of Scripture is faulty; or, alternatively, we may discover that some aspect of our personal experience is "out of sync" with the core of the gospel.

Scripture and tradition serve as the bearers of a priceless message. But the message may remain mere information unless it is verified by personal experience. Scripture and tradition may teach us that God is love; but if we do not experience

God's love as a reality in our lives, those teachings will be difficult to believe. When we do experience God's love as a reality, our spirits resonate with the witness of Scripture and tradition.

REASON

God has given us minds and the power of reason by which we may understand our world and our place in it. Reason is that part of us through which we are able to plan ahead, to learn from mistakes, to understand meanings, and to apply ethical standards to our living. The power of reason has made it possible for persons to walk on the moon, to improve the quality of food products, to discover the basis of disease, and to establish institutions that provide healing and support for persons in special need.

The very fact that we speak of the Scripture as God's Word implies that God chooses to address us as rational beings. Words are uniquely products of rationality. Without reason it would not be possible to hear or to respond to God's Word. Nor would it be possible to examine our lives and our traditions in the light of Scripture.

When we read Scripture, we are enabled by reason to consider the time and place in which the particular passage was written and to reflect on the people and the situation to which it was first addressed.

Reason helps us determine the unique relevance of that Scripture for us and for our time. For while God's truth is timeless, every generation must discover how to apply that truth in its time and place. Surely the fundamental truth of the Scripture is that God is love and that we are called to be in loving relationships. It is through reason that we are able to determine just what it means to act lovingly toward the other.

SUMMARY

The life of the Christian is to be lived in response to the gracious love of God. We learn of that love in the Scripture, especially in the Gospel story of the birth, life, ministry, suffering, death, and resurrection of Jesus of Nazareth. We are supported in our faith by the witness of all those who have gone before us and who have shaped the tradition we have received. In our lives, when we know the empowerment of love, we verify in our own experience the truth of the Christian message. In reading the Scripture, in responding to the tradition, and in interpreting our experience we employ the power of reason.

But in all things, reason, experience, and tradition are focused on what God has made known in Scripture.

MAJOR THEMES
IN SCRIPTURE

Where do we look for major themes in *Scripture*? How will we know what is major when we find it?

Our first guide is *tradition*, which simply means what the church has taught with some consistency throughout its history.

We also use *reason* as we examine Scripture and tradition. We ask questions, challenge conventional answers, and balance rival conclusions.

Finally, we find that our beliefs interact with our *experience*. How does a belief influence our experience? How do our experiences reflect on a belief?

The scriptural themes outlined here have stood the test of hundreds of years of experience in the tradition of the church. They have been tested by reason and lived out in experience.

GOD: CREATOR AND REDEEMER

This Good World

A foundation for everything else we believe is our faith in God as Creator. We and our world owe our existence to the constant flow of the creative and sustaining energy of God. Indeed, now that we are learning more about the mysteries of space, we may say that whatever other worlds may exist out there, whatever extraterrestrial creatures may live in whatever strange worlds, they, too, owe their existence to the same God we acknowledge as "maker of heaven and

earth, and of all things visible and invisible" (The Nicene Creed).

The Bible begins with two stories of Creation: Genesis 1:1–2:4a and 2:4b-25. Over and over in Genesis 1 we find the words: "And God saw that it was good." We are impressed that, no matter how bad things may look, the world we live in is fundamentally good. The profound importance and value of the relationship between male and female and the integrity of human sexuality are stressed (Genesis 1:27-31; 2:21-25).

Psalm 8 is a moving affirmation of the wonder of creation and our place in it, acknowledging our dependence upon our Creator.

In a poem of haunting beauty the prophet Isaiah sings of the wonder of God's being and the intimacy of God's presence with us (Isaiah 40).

The Human Creature: Special and Spoiled

We humans are a part of creation. Contemporary concern with ecology reminds us of this fact. True, we are given "dominion" over the rest of creation (Genesis 1:26, 28), which surely means that we are to respect and use our world for our common good.

But we are also different from the rest of creation. We are made "in the image of God" (Genesis 1:27). Tradition has identified this image in many ways. One basic understanding is that we are created with a special relationship to God, a relationship of responsibility and response-ability, as one scholar put it. Rooted in this relationship are the creative gifts that make human life beautiful, gifts that we all share in some measure.

We are special—and always will be. But we have spoiled it. The story of Creation continues into the story of the Fall (Genesis 3). Adam and Eve, endowed with the freedom to respond to God's will, choose to go their own way. That's precisely *our* story.

What was their sin? Basically, pride, self-will. And note: we all exercise the same proud self-will (Romans 3:23).

The consequence is alienation. First, from God, against whom we have rebelled; then from nature: we are driven out of the Garden. And tragically, from each other: man from woman, later brother from brother (as Cain from Abel, Genesis 4:1-8).

God's Concern for Humanity: Covenant

The bad news is our rebellion. The good news is God's response. God is troubled by our misbehavior and must deal with it. But God never gives up on us (Genesis 6:1-8). Our Creator is also our Redeemer.

One of the most beautiful insights of the Old Testament is that God takes the initiative to form a covenant, a contract, with humanity. Essentially what God says is this: I really do love you and do not want to let you go on the way you are. If you will just listen to me and obey me, I will see that you receive the blessings I really intend for you.

So God made a covenant with Abraham (Genesis 12:1-3; 22:15-18); and renewed it with Moses (Exodus 2:24; 3). We note that this covenant, made with Israel, is also for the good of "all the families of the earth."

Jeremiah dreamed of a "new covenant," a spiritual deepening of God's redeeming relationship with humanity (Jeremiah 31:31-34).

The new covenant is given a still deeper meaning by Jesus. On the eve of his death, he established a new form of this covenant with his disciples and through them with us (Matthew 26:26-29; Mark 14:22-25; Luke 22:17-19; also 1 Corinthians 11:23-26).

The term *new covenant* is familiar to us as "New Testament."

God of Goodness and Mercy

The God who is revealed to us in the Old Testament is marked by a very special character. The God of Israel is different from the gods of Israel's neighbors and the gods worshiped in other civilizations. Yahweh, as Israel's God is named, is a holy God and demands holiness of the chosen people. Moreover, God demands exclusive loyalty and worship. That is what is meant when it is said that God is "jealous."

But the wonder of the divine character deepens: this holy God is also a God of mercy. God loves the human creatures; that is why God enters into a covenant to redeem them. And this quality of mercy, translated also as "steadfast love," is the deepest mark of the divine character.

The joining of goodness and mercy is affirmed consistently. When God demands obedience, the promise of mercy is offered as well (see Exodus 20:4-6; Deuteronomy 7:6-11).

The psalmist sings of God's mercy, "steadfast love," and invites us to rejoice in this faith (Psalm 100).

One of the loveliest expressions of God's love is found in the writings of Hosea. His wife had cheated on him, as we have been unfaithful to God. But Hosea could not stop loving his wife and realized that, in much the same way, God cannot give us up.

God Is Love

It is in Jesus Christ that the love of God is most fully revealed and expressed. This is our distinctive Christian belief.

Jesus, of course, was brought up as a Jew believing in the mercy of God. In his own teaching Jesus reaffirmed this faith and added a new dimension to it. Not only does God love us disobedient humans, but God actively seeks us in our erring ways.

So Jesus told the story of the shepherd who "goes after" his lost sheep, the woman sweeping her house to "search carefully" for her lost savings. And the story that everyone loves: the prodigal son whose return is celebrated by the father who "was filled with compassion; he ran and put his arms around him and kissed him" (Luke 15).

These stories were told in response to the frequent criticism aimed at Jesus. He deliberately sought out the social outcast, the disinherited. His response on another such occasion is direct and powerful: "The Son of Man came to seek out and to save the lost" (Luke 19:10).

The followers of Jesus deepened this striking statement by saying, that not only did Jesus teach the seeking love of God, Jesus is himself the expression of God's outgoing, saving love. John 3:16, perhaps the most loved verse in the New Testament, affirms such faith very clearly. Verse 17 states the purpose of God's radical action: not to condemn but to save.

The Triune God

We have just said something that is new in Scripture: we have spoken of God as Father and God as Son. The writers of the Old Testament could not have said this. Only in the New Testament is such a faith affirmed.

The Hebrew faith is strictly monotheistic. There is only one God, the God of Israel. Jesus and his disciples, of course, believed this.

The Christian church clings to the belief in one God. But the church also recognizes

that God is experienced in more than one way. The early Christians sensed that, in Jesus, God was approaching them in a special way. And after Jesus died and rose again, they began to say, "God sent his Son." The God whom they knew as Father had come to them as Son.

Already they were stretching their faith about the one God. But more was to follow. Soon they would experience God as Holy Spirit; and they would have to find new language to use about God.

The writers of the New Testament did not develop a full-blown doctrine of the Trinity. But they used language that suggested the creeds that would follow: Matthew 28:19; 2 Corinthians 13:14. They gave us the raw material out of which later generations of Christians formed the doctrine of the Trinity: One God in Three Persons.

THE PERSON AND WORK OF CHRIST

Incarnation

The startling statement of John 3:16-17 raises two questions about Jesus. Who was he? And what did he do? The answers given in the New Testament grew into two of the great doctrines of the church: Incarnation and Atonement.

Incarnation means that in Jesus of Nazareth God entered human history in a unique way. God became a human being. God was incarnate—enfleshed—in Jesus.

Every writer of the New Testament affirmed this statement about Incarnation. They did so in different ways and with different images: in the Gospel stories about what Jesus said and did, in sermons recorded in Acts, in reflection on who Jesus was in the Epistles, and in the great vision of a new world found in Revelation. Each document, in its own way, affirms

Jesus as *Lord* (the word used for God in the Old Testament) and *Christ* (Messiah).

Perhaps the most eloquent statement of this faith is in what is known as the Prologue to John's Gospel (John 1:1-18). The central affirmation is in verse 14: The Word (which in verse 1 is identified with God) became flesh (an authentic human being).

And if we ask—as we must—what God intends by this mysterious venture, the answer is in verses 17 and 18. Jesus Christ opens up a new way to relate to God (not law but grace). Jesus Christ has made God fully known.

Atonement

The second question is: What did Jesus do? The answer to that question is expressed in the doctrine of the Atonement.

Atonement means the restoration of our relationship with God. We have been at odds; now we may be at one. And the radical assertion of our faith is that this restoration is not our doing; it is God's act on our behalf.

The suffering and death of Jesus is the central deed of Atonement. All through the New Testament is the recognition of Jesus' death on the cross as the saving act of God. In this death God does what is necessary to restore our relationship with God and to heal our relationship with other people.

Several images of Atonement are used by the writers of the New Testament. One is *expiation* (Romans 3:25; 1 John 2:2; 4:9-10). This difficult term means something like cleansing from evil so a person will be able to approach God. Another image is the legal term *justification*. We are guilty. We know it, but cannot do anything about our guilt. God takes on our guilt and freely forgives us (John 3:16-17; Romans 5:8) Ephesians 1:7 adds *redemption*, as in buying slaves out of bondage. Perhaps the

most beautiful image is *reconciliation*. We are alienated from God and defensive about it. God, whom we have offended, makes the advances to us, to break down our defensiveness and to heal the relationship. Second Corinthians 5:19 is the direct statement of this remarkable affirmation.

Resurrection

The work of Jesus does not end with his death. Crucifixion issues in Resurrection. Here again is a central unanimous witness of the writers of the New Testament.

The Gospels tell the story. Each writer tells it in his own way and recounts events as he recalls them. But the witness is clear: God raised Jesus from the dead.

The sermons recorded in Acts reaffirm this faith (Acts 2:24, 32; 17:31). The emphasis is always that "God raised him up." Resurrection is not the bubbling up of human potential. It is God's redeeming act: the winning of life over death.

The same refrain runs through the Epistles. In 1 Corinthians 15:3-8, Paul gives the earliest written account of the event on which our faith is based. And he reasons decisively from this event. The argument is complicated but the conclusion is clear: our hope is solidly based on God's victory over death in the resurrection of Jesus.

Paul draws a helpful inference from this faith. The same energy by which God raised Jesus from the dead is available to us to enable us to defeat the deadly influences that would ruin our lives and to achieve a new quality of life. (Romans 8:11 is one statement of this.)

The Healing of Humanity: Amazing Grace

Reflection on what we have said about the person and work of Jesus Christ will make it clear that all this is God's redeeming action on our behalf. It is the expression of divine grace: the outgoing, sacrificial love of God.

The Creator and Redeemer moves continually toward humanity at ever deeper levels. What was first glimpsed in the covenant (God's concern for humanity), what was sung about by poets and prophets (the divine mercy), is now fully expressed in the self-giving, suffering love of God, given in Jesus Christ.

This amazing grace is the sole basis of our hope for healing. Acceptance of this grace-full gift is the key to release from our guilt and its frustrations, release into free and glad living. A careful reading of Romans 3:23-25 will yield a strong statement of this faith. (See also Ephesians 2:8-9).

John Wesley recovered a beautiful term to express the mystery of God's free gift of love. He spoke of "prevenient grace." That means the love that seeks us out when we are lost (as the shepherd searching for the sheep). It means that, even when we are angry and alienated, God tries to win us back (reconciliation). Even when we are unaware of it, God is trying to get through to us. And when we finally do accept the gift, we sense that it is because God has consistently been trying to persuade us to do so.

Justification by Faith

We admit, however reluctantly, that we are sinners. We not only do wrong things, we are the kind of people who are capable of stupid and destructive thoughts and actions. How can we be forgiven, not just for our mistakes but for our stance?

The Christian reply is the radical doctrine known as *justification by faith*: we are forgiven by accepting God's freely offered gift of grace. Unfortunately, we tend to hide this unexpected, maybe even

uncomfortable, answer in a list of duties and obligations. So our practice becomes an attempt to earn forgiveness by obeying the supposed requirements. Periodically, then, the startling affirmation of free grace has to be recovered. That was a prime aspect of the Protestant Reformation. Martin Luther rediscovered Paul's amazing statement in Romans 3:28. That verse became the watchword of the Reformation and of every Protestant church that emerged from the Reformation.

Faith, then, is the acceptance of God's gift. Trying to earn God's favor is frustrating; it ties us up in knots. The answer, rather, is to open ourselves to God, who has already been trying to reach us; and we trust the steadfast love that we know as grace.

Faith and Works

Paul was quite specific: we are justified by faith "apart from works prescribed by the law" (Romans 3:28). Luther underscored it, saying, "by faith alone." This statement of belief raises an interesting question. Does that mean that, once we are saved, we may behave as we please?

This question seems to have arisen right at the beginning of Paul's ministry. So in one of his earliest letters, to the Galatians, he had to write quite firmly. We are free from the harsh dominance of the law; but we are not freed in order to do as we please. We are released into the deeper law of love (Galatians 5:13-15).

James stressed the importance of living out our faith in works. James put it bluntly: "Show me your faith apart from your works, and I by my works will show you my faith" (2:18).

Surely it is not either/or. Faith draws us into faithfulness. But we must be clear that obedience is not a grim effort to earn forgiveness. Our works of love are a glad response to God's freely given love.

THE HOLY SPIRIT AND THE CHURCH

The Spirit of Power, Truth, Love

Our Christian life begins with forgiveness. Where do we go from here? We feel the imperative to love. But how do we go about that? At this point the New Testament offers us a gracious new resource: the presence and power of the Holy Spirit.

Pentecost was the occasion of a definitive experience in the lives of the disciples (Acts 2:1-4). Jesus had promised them that, after he left, the Holy Spirit would come to them (Acts 1:4-5; John 16:7). And, he added, they would "receive power" (Acts 1:8). We believe we share the same promise: God can be present to us, at the deepest level of our being, to heal, motivate, and stimulate our growth.

John records Jesus as speaking of the Spirit in an impressive series of images (John 14:15-17, 25-26; 15:26-27; 16:7-15). The Holy Spirit is the Spirit of Truth who will lead us into further truth, the Counselor who will stimulate and sustain our growth.

Paul writes extensively of the "gifts of the Spirit" (1 Corinthians 12) and more intimately of the "fruit of the Spirit" (Galatians 5:22). The principal gift or fruit of the Spirit is the capacity to love (1 Corinthians 13).

The Community of the Spirit

This account of Christian experience is still incomplete. It is personal, but it cannot be solitary. We individuals do not live alone; we need community. And the New Testament offers a special fulfillment of that need: the church.

Where Paul writes most extensively of the Spirit, he writes also of the Church (1 Corinthians 11-14). We tend to think of "joining" the church. Paul speaks as if we are "called into" the church to form a community of the Spirit.

The phrase *the body of Christ* is perhaps the best-known image for the church (1 Corinthians 12). As individuals we are bound together in an organic union. We have many different gifts of the Spirit, all of which are essential to the total life of the community. We live and work together "for the common good" (verse 7). So "there is one body and one Spirit" (Ephesians 4:4; read also 4:1-16).

The earliest forms of congregational organization and practice were simple; but as the church grew, they became more complex. Always, however, the function of the church was clear, and still is: first, to nurture our Christian experience ("building up the body of Christ"); and at the same time to equip us "for the work of ministry" (Ephesians 4:12).

The Sacraments

From the beginning of their new life in Christ, Christians met together for fellowship and worship (Acts 2:42, 46; Hebrews 10:23-25). They began with practices already familiar to them, in the life of the synagogues, and gradually gave them new meaning.

Some forms of worship quickly gained special importance, and came to be known as *sacraments* (also known in some church traditions as *ordinances*). There are differences about just what should be called a sacrament, but most Protestants recognize two, perhaps because they are definitely rooted in the New Testament itself.

Baptism was a Jewish practice, as we see in the ministry of John the Baptizer and

Jesus' acceptance of the rite (Matthew 3; Mark 1:4-11; Luke 3:2-22; John 1:6-8, 19-34). However, baptism in the name of Jesus (Acts 2:38) and in the name of the Trinity (Matthew 28:19) gave the rite an entirely new meaning. Fundamentally, baptism is the sign of the saving grace of God at work in our lives, and of our entry into the community of the Spirit.

Holy Communion is the second sacrament (or ordinance) of the church, instituted by Jesus himself at the Last Supper. The story is told in the Gospels and in Paul's even earlier record (1 Corinthians 11:23-25). This Lord's Supper, or Eucharist as it is also known, has become the central act of Christian worship. The whole Christian gospel is affirmed in this sacrament: all that we mean by Incarnation, Atonement, justification, sanctification, and the hope of eternal life.

The People of God

Another image of the church is *the people of God* (1 Peter 2:9-10). This image, of course, reflects back on the understanding of Israel as God's chosen people; and affirms that as Christians we are called to be the newly constituted people of God.

The Greek word for people is *laos*. From this comes our word *laity*, and this word indicates exactly what is meant by the church. The church is not the clergy, or the conference, or the synod, not any institutional form. The church is the people of God. Two phrases help us understand what that means.

The priesthood of believers is a great phrase from the Protestant Reformation. It affirms that every person can come directly to God in faith. Every believer is a priest.

The ministry of the laity means that the laity are the ministers of Christ in secular society. The work of the body of Christ in the world is done by the "members" of the body. The ministry of Christ to society is carried out by the people, the laity, "ordained" to this ministry by their baptism.

What is our responsibility in society? In a word—a demanding word—to love our neighbors. So Jesus tells the searching story of the good Samaritan (Luke 10:25-37). Paul also endorses the central importance of love (Galatians 5:13-15; Romans 13:8-10). We are called to the continuing task of finding ways to implement this "royal law."

DIMENSIONS OF HOPE

The Kingdom of God

One of the impressive marks of the teaching of Jesus is his extensive use of the term "the kingdom of God." However, its meaning turns out to be complicated. Some persons have tried to identify the church as the kingdom. Others have thought of the kingdom as a just social order. Neither interpretation seems to fit the evidence.

The word *kingdom* means rule or reign. Two consistent aspects of God's sovereignty are that God does rule over the universe and over history, whether we admit it or not; but the full effect of God's rule depends on our accepting and obeying it.

So the burden of the prophets' message was that, though Israel theoretically acknowledged God as their King, their habitual disobedience could only end in disaster (Amos 7:7-9).

Jesus adds a new note; he affirms that in his own presence and ministry, the rule of God is present in a new way (dramatically stated in Luke 17:20-21). Jesus asserts this in a series of sayings about the end and outcome of history that are quite troubling (see Mark 13).

In the meantime, we have to come to terms with the sovereignty of God. Perhaps the best simple word is Jesus' exhortation: Let it be the top priority of your life to be ruled by God (see Matthew 6:33).

The Coming Kingdom

The writers of Scripture (Old and New Testaments) are remarkably confident that, no matter how we humans behave, God will ultimately assert the divine rule. The God who established the covenant will be faithful to that commitment. And ultimately, not only Israel but "all the families of the earth" will be blessed (Genesis 12:1-3).

This belief is expressed in the prophet Isaiah's beautiful vision of the messianic kingdom. No matter how disobedient we humans may be, God is faithful and will establish a rule of goodness and mercy (Isaiah 2:1-4; 9:2-7). This vision has fascinated us ever since it was first promised. Will it happen by historical progress? Or is it to be realized only "beyond history"? The ultimate answer is in the hands of God, and we therefore can be confident of the answer.

The Revelation to John is another beautiful, though often puzzling, statement of God's ultimate rule. We must be careful not to use it as a basis for predicting history, as we use charts and graphs to predict the weather. The heart of John's vision is the assurance that no matter what happens in history, God will ultimately affirm the divine sovereignty.

Handel makes us sing it: "He shall reign for ever and ever" (see Revelation 11:15). John assures us that we dare hope to be part of that kingdom: "They [God's people] will reign forever and ever" (Revelation 22:5).

Our Father's House

The question of our personal destiny is basic to our human experience. What happens to us when we die?

In the New Testament our faith is personalized. Jesus joined the Pharisees in affirming the resurrection (Mark 12:18-27). His further personal reflections have become a treasured part of our belief: "In my Father's house there are many dwelling places. . . . I go to prepare a place for you. . . . I will come again and will take you to myself" (John 14:2-3; see also verse 27).

Paul, trained as a Pharisee, also believed in the resurrection of the dead (Acts 23:6; 26:8). Then he added a Christian dimension by affirming that the resurrection of Jesus is the decisive evidence for the validity of such faith (1 Corinthians 15:12-20).

Paul personalized our hope in his thoughtful insight that we will be endowed with a "spiritual body" for the transcendent life in our Father's house (1 Corinthians 15:35-38, 42-44). But our hope is not simply personal; the house itself will be transformed. So John envisioned "a new heaven and a new earth" (Revelation 21:1). Paul put it even more daringly: the entire cosmos will be released into the fulfillment of God's eternal purpose. (Romans 8:18-25).

CANONIZATION AND TRANSLATION

THE PROCESS OF CANONIZATION

What is a canon of Scripture? Why is it important? How did we get it?

The word *canon* comes from a Greek word that means "measuring reed." When we use the word in connection with Scripture, we mean that these books are a measure, or standard, for faith and life.

Canonization is the process by which these particular books came to be regarded as a standard. The canon of Scripture, our Bible, was developed by the people of God in response to the need of the church.

The Scripture of Jesus and the first-century church was the Hebrew Scripture, what Christians call the Old Testament. For nearly one hundred years, the Hebrew Scripture was the sufficient canon for the church. Then people began to ask questions: Is this enough? What about Jesus? How do we live out our new faith in a world that tempts us to be unfaithful?

Paul's letters were the first part of our New Testament to be written. Because the letters helped answer questions about faith and life, they were saved, copied, collected. By A.D. 95, some Christians were using Paul's letters as Scripture.

Many accounts were written to record what Jesus said and did, and what Jesus' life, death, and resurrection mean for Christians. We know of about a dozen Gospels that were written in these early years, but only Matthew, Mark, Luke, and John ever had any real status as Gospels in the church. Other Christian writings also appeared—letters, sermons, apocalypses, teachings.

So why did the church decide to develop a New Testament? No one woke up one morning and decided the church needed a canon. Rather, the canon developed in response to pressures from outside the church and from felt needs from the inside.

The canon developed in part because of needs and pressures inside the church. What was right belief? The church defined right belief in "The Rule of Faith"—what we would call creeds. Writings that helped define and support the Rule of Faith became standards, or canons.

They were known as apostolic because they preserved the teaching and the tradition of the apostles. This process was the positive side of canonization.

The canon developed in part because of pressures from outside. Many books were written that claimed to be Christian teaching. Someone, somehow, had to decide if these books contained the apostolic teaching. This process was the negative side of canonization. Sometime around A.D. 150, a man named Marcion drew up a list of books that he defined as a canon. His list included ten letters of Paul and the Gospel of Luke. He rejected the Old Testament because he thought the Creator was not the God of Jesus Christ. When Marcion's list appeared, the church had to think seriously about which books were authoritative.

The church did not respond by calling together a committee to decide. No one had the power to do that. But there was universal agreement on several points in response to Marcion. First, the church believed that the God of the Old Testament was also the God of Jesus Christ. Therefore, the Old Testament was authoritative for faith and life in the church. Second, there was a move toward four Gospels as a standard for faith. Third, other letters were held to be as authoritative as those of Paul. These included what we call First Peter and First John—and for some churches books such as Barnabas, First Clement, and Hermas.

Irenaeus, a bishop in southern France (about A.D. 185) was the first writer to indicate there was a "New Testament," that is, a recognized collection of writings equal in authority and value to the Old Testament. But Irenaeus's collection still did not include all the books we list in our New Testament. Books such as Hebrews, James, Second Peter, Jude, and Revelation were found on some lists of the canon and not on others.

Then came an event that may have been decisive for the process of canonization. In A.D. 303, during the last great persecution, the emperor Diocletian ordered that all the Scriptures be destroyed and anyone who did not surrender the Scriptures was to be killed. Now the question of the canon became personal. Which books were sacred enough to die for?

After Diocletian's persecution, church councils began to define the canon. The oldest known list of New Testament books exactly like ours today was included in a letter Bishop Athanasius of Alexandria sent to his churches in 367. A council held in Rome in 382 gave a complete list of the canonical books of both the Old Testament and the New Testament.

The books we call the Apocrypha were included as a part of the canon for much of the church's history. At the time of the Protestant Reformation, Luther declared the books of the Apocrypha as secondary and not to be counted equal with the authoritative ones. The Roman Catholic Council of Trent in 1546 declared the Apocrypha to be an authoritative part of the canon. Protestants in general have looked on the Apocrypha as secondary and, until recently, did not include it in printed Bibles. In the last thirty years, Protestants have shown more interest in the books of the Apocrypha, without considering them authoritative.

ENGLISH VERSIONS OF THE BIBLE

Translations of parts of the Bible into the Anglo-Saxon language appeared as early as A.D. 700, but the first complete Bible in English did not appear until 1382. John Wycliffe translated the Bible to put it into the hands of the laity. His was the only English Bible in use for over 150 years. Wycliffe's Bible was based on the Latin and did not use any older texts.

Between 1525 and 1535, William Tyndale's translation appeared. Tyndale had the advantage of access to Greek and Hebrew manuscripts, including Erasmus's Greek New Testament of 1514. Tyndale also had the advantage of the printing press, which made it possible to spread copies of the Bible far and wide at a relatively cheap price. Tyndale's Bible had a great influence on the King James Bible and on the development of English as a literary language. Tyndale was killed before he finished translating the entire Bible.

The first complete printed English Bible was that of Miles Coverdale (1535) who used Tyndale's translation as the foundation of his own. Other early English Bibles based on Tyndale's work were the Matthew Bible (1537), the Great Bible, so called because of its size (1539), the Geneva Bible (1560), and the Bishop's Bible (1568). The Geneva Bible was widely read among the people, while the Great Bible was usually read in church. The Douai version of 1610–11 was a Roman Catholic translation from Latin into English.

The King James Bible of 1611 is one of the masterpieces of English literature. It was translated from Greek and Hebrew, with the Bishop's Bible as the standard of translation. In spite of its rank as a treasure of the English language and the love it has stirred for over 350 years, the King James Version also has its weaknesses. One Greek or Hebrew word was translated several different ways. Parallel passages in the Gospels were translated differently, so it was hard to see relationships. Sometimes a translation obscured the meaning of a verse. The Greek and Hebrew texts used by the translators were not as good as texts we know today.

The English Revised Version (1881–85) and the American Standard Version (1901) were revisions aimed at correcting the more obvious mistakes of the King James. These versions used better Greek texts than the King James Version. In spite of having a more accurate text, these versions were widely criticized for daring to revise the Authorized (King James) Version.

The Revised Standard Version (1946, 1952) was a revision based on superior Greek texts, new knowledge of the Greek vocabulary and grammar of the New Testament, and the changes in the English language between 1611 and 1946. It soon became the authorized Bible of much of American Christianity.

The New Revised Standard Version recognizes changes in biblical scholarship and in the English language since 1952. Scholars know more about ancient languages. There are more-and older manuscripts from which to work. The discovery of the Dead Sea Scrolls, for example, meant that for some books of the Old Testament, we now have manuscripts one thousand years older than any previously used. It is important that the Bible be translated accurately from the best ancient texts. In addition, the English language has changed rapidly in the last fifty years. Words have changed in meaning; new words have appeared. So a standard translation needs to keep up with modern as well as with ancient languages. The New Revised Standard Version is, as nearly as possible, a literal translation of early manuscripts. It is also a free translation wherever necessary to be sure the meaning in English is the same as in Greek or Hebrew.

The New International Version (1978) is an entirely new translation developed by a large team of scholars on behalf of the evangelical Christian community. Widely praised for both its scholarship and readability, the NIV has won acceptance among a very wide readership.

The Good News Bible: Today's English Version (first published in 1966 and revised in 1976 and 1992) and the Contemporary English Version (1995) are popular examples of translations that are more free than the NRSV or NIV. The TEV and CEV are both designed to make the biblical text easily understood by English-speaking readers regardless of their religious or educational backgrounds. To that end, both the TEV and CEV avoid the use of theological jargon.

Paraphrased versions of the Bible take considerable liberty in rendering the biblical text into everyday English in an effort to communicate spiritual truths. Paraphrases try to express the basic, underlying meaning rather than the exact words and phrases of the original biblical text. Because they are so easily understood, paraphrased versions of the Bible can be very useful to newcomers to the Bible, especially when used in tandem with a translation that follows the original text more strictly. Two of the best known paraphrases are *The Living Bible* (1971) by Kenneth Taylor and *The Message: The Bible in Contemporary Language* (2002) by Eugene Peterson.

THE HOLY SPIRIT

The story of canonization and translation of the Bible may appear to be only a record of reaction to outside events, taking votes, deciding what is authoritatively God's Word, and what is not. The story is all of that, of course. It is also a story of careful scholarship, of treasure hunts for ancient manuscripts, and of much time spent in dictionaries.

But the story of canonization and translation also has another layer of meaning, one that is far more profound than the public story. The church has always believed it embarked on the process of canonization and translation under the guidance of the Holy Spirit. We believe God inspired the writing of the Scriptures. We believe God inspired the process of selection of the books that would become Scripture. We believe God was at work in the studies of grammar, vocabulary, and ancient manuscripts that led to the translation of Scripture into the language of the people.

How God worked in those arenas we do not understand. When we try to describe God's actions, words fall short. We disagree with one another over what inspiration means. But we believe, with all our differences, that God was active in the process.

HOW TO STUDY
A BIBLE PASSAGE

The Bible is the church's book. Therefore we call the Bible *Scripture*. The Bible is the authoritative guidebook for the church. But many people in the church have trouble claiming the Bible as their own: "It's hard to understand"; "It's so complex that we're intimidated."

How can you get past those roadblocks? How can you recover your own foundational book? Part of the answer is to learn how to study Bible passages in some depth. It is not a simple matter. But almost anyone can improve his or her skill by working at it. Once you learn questions to ask about a Bible passage and where to look for help in answering those questions, you are off and running. The more passages you examine and the more you become familiar with tools of Bible study, the more skillful you will become in unlocking the message of the Bible.

WHAT IS THE BIBLE PASSAGE YOU ARE STUDYING?

You may have selected a passage for any one of a hundred reasons. Maybe you saw a biblical quotation on a billboard or in a book or on a website. Maybe a passage you heard in church has stuck in your mind. Maybe somebody in your neighborhood or at school or at work asked you (or told you) something about a passage. Maybe you've been searching the Bible for a particular topic and a concordance has directed you to the passage at hand. Or maybe you are trying to read through a book of the Bible and you've found you need to break up the reading into smaller blocks.

Is it a very short passage, say, a few verses? Is it a longer passage, say, an entire chapter? There are no hard and fast rules about the proper length of a Bible passage to study. But as a rule of thumb, you might ask: "Do I have a complete thought here?" Sometimes a complete thought is encapsulated in a single verse. Sometimes the paragraph or stanza breaks will give you clues. Sometimes you need a whole chapter to have a complete thought. Sometimes the flow of a story will tell you where to begin and end. (It would not make sense, for instance, to study only half a parable of Jesus.) Make the best judgment you can and press on. Later steps will help you know whether you have set the boundaries of a passage fairly.

READ THE PASSAGE CAREFULLY, WORD-FOR-WORD

The most important step in any type of Bible study is to read the text itself as if you were seeing it for the first time.

Take as an example Jesus' parable of the good Samaritan (Luke 10:29-37). Who is the neighbor in this story? Most people would answer, "the man who was beaten and left half dead." From that answer it is easy to generalize that our neighbor is anyone in need. That principle may be sound, but it misses some of the punch in this parable. Look at the text again. The neighbor is actually the Samaritan who rescued the beaten man. Think how that idea, a Jew accepting aid from a despised Samaritan, must have shocked Jewish ears. It would be bad enough to be left helpless but even worse to be utterly dependent on the compassion of one's enemy, or so the situation must have seemed to Jesus' listeners. The message about neighbor-love is richer than most of us suppose. And we miss that deeper meaning unless we carefully discover what the biblical text really says.

So as you read the passage, jot down any words or phrases that catch your eye as a potential key to what the passage is saying. Include any terms that you are not familiar with.

INVESTIGATE THE KEY TERMS

Many of the terms used in the Bible are deceptive. You think you know what they mean, but you may miss the richer connotations of the original Hebrew or Greek. So a theological wordbook is an essential Bible study tool. One of the best recent volumes is *The Westminster Theological Wordbook of the Bible*, ed. Donald Gowan (Westminster John Knox Press, 2003).

Take an example. Under the entry for *know*, *knowledge* you find that the Hebrew term translated as *know* means much more than intellectual knowledge. It means to *have experience of* something or someone. To know God, then, means much more than to know information or theories about God; it means that you intimately experience God in your life.

The world the Bible describes is in many respects an unfamiliar world. It is strange because it is so different from our contemporary world. As a careful reader you will not want to gloss over that

unfamiliar character, to assume too quickly that you know what was going on in those ancient days. Bible dictionaries can help. More like small-scale encyclopedias than traditional dictionaries, Bible dictionaries have a wealth of information about the people, events, ideas, and books of the Bible.

Examine the *Pharisees* as one example. Many people have an image of the Pharisees as the bad guys. But a quick look in a Bible dictionary reveals that the Pharisees were in many respects the moral and religious exemplars of their society. Many among them were much like the pillars of our Christian churches today— thoroughly respectable, good, decent, and God-fearing people, the heroes of their society. The Gospel stories sound a little different once you realize that Jesus' warnings against Pharisees in his day may fit some of our church members rather well!

CLARIFY THE LITERARY CONTEXT

Here you need to answer two questions: "What biblical material immediately *precedes* the passage you are studying? What biblical material immediately *follows* the passage?" As a general rule, the longer the passage you are studying, the more material before and after you will want to read. If your focus is on a few verses, read at least the surrounding chapter. If your focus is on a whole chapter, read at least the chapter before and the chapter after.

Make a note of what is going on in the surrounding context. Suppose, for instance, that you have focused on 1 Corinthians 11:27. This verse is misunderstood by some people to mean that they must be morally and spiritually perfect if they are to partake of Holy Communion. And so they forego what is meant to be a means of grace. But a careful look at the surrounding verses (17-34) reveals that Paul was addressing a situation in which some people were making gluttons and drunkards of themselves while others went hungry. His point was that all who partake of the Lord's meal should take care to share the food and drink. He wanted the Corinthian Christians to recognize that the Lord's Supper should be celebrated with a sense of unity and mutual care.

Take as another example the thirteenth chapter of that same letter to the Corinthians. Because of the sheer eloquence of the language, this chapter is frequently lifted out of its context and plopped down in a wedding ceremony or on a greeting card. But suppose you want to take a serious look at what God is saying here through the Apostle Paul. Look at chapter twelve; Paul is talking about gifts of the Holy Spirit and the Christian community as the body of Christ. Now look at chapter fourteen; Paul is still talking about gifts of the Holy Spirit. Chapter thirteen appears in the middle. What does that context imply? At the very least, it reminds us that love—the kind of love that Paul is talking about—is a *gift* from God, not a human achievement. And the context suggests that this gift of love is what somehow *enables* Christians to behave appropriately as members of the body of Christ. Apart from the gift of love we neither use the other spiritual gifts properly nor live in a healthy community of believers.

CLARIFY THE CANONICAL CONTEXT

Canon refers to the books officially recognized as part of the Bible. Asking about the canonical context means asking where the particular passage being studied is located in the Bible as a whole. What connections does this passage have to other places in the Bible? The more familiar you are with the sweep of the entire Bible, of course, the easier this step becomes. For instance, if you know something about the original Exodus from Egypt, you are more likely to appreciate what it meant for the Babylonian exiles 750 years later to be part of a new Exodus, initiated by God, back to the land of Israel. Or to take another example, if you remember the account of the Tower of Babel, you are likely to recognize the reversal in the story of Pentecost. In one case, languages were multiplied and confusion reigned. In the other case, a variety of languages became the occasion for a wondrous common understanding of God's power and purpose.

A couple of Bible study tools can help even beginners make connections between the passage under study and the rest of the Bible. First, check the cross-references in the Bible itself. Often the connecting passage illumines or is illumined by the passage you are studying. For instance, the cross-reference for Luke 3:4-6 will direct you to the source of the Old Testament quotation: Isaiah 40:3-5. And if you look up the cross-reference for Jesus' words from the cross in the Gospel of Matthew chapter 27, verse 46, you will find that Jesus was quoting from the opening of Psalm 22. Another example: the meaning of Jesus' Last Supper with his disciples recorded in Luke 22 is deepened if you recognize the linkage to the Old Testament Passover—and the cross-reference will point you to Exodus 12.

Another basic tool for Bible study that you can use to locate your passage in the wider biblical message is a concordance. Many people use a concordance only when they want to look up a half-remembered verse that keeps nagging their memory. But a concordance has a systematic place in Bible study, too. Suppose you want to study a theme such as *redemption* (because it cropped up in a passage you were reading). A concordance will tell you where to find other references to redemption in the Bible.

CLARIFY THE HISTORICAL AND GEOGRAPHICAL CONTEXT

Our understanding of any important document is enhanced by knowing something about the situation in which it was written. Take Martin Luther King Jr.'s famous "Letter from a Birmingham Jail." We have a better grasp of that message if we know something about the man who wrote it, what was going on in Birmingham and where Birmingham is located, the history of the Civil Rights movement, and so on.

Similarly, our understanding of a Bible passage is enhanced by answering such questions as: Who wrote this? When? Where? What was going on at the time? Suppose that you are reading a passage from the Book of Jeremiah. You need to know that Jeremiah was a prophet whose career spanned forty years (about 626–586 B.C.) and that the empire of Babylonia was about to crush Jeremiah's people of Judah and haul them away as captives. You need to know that, though his contemporaries dismissed him as a doomsayer and traitor, history proved Jeremiah right.

You can find this sort of background information in lots of places. But three types of study tools are easy to use and affordable. Bible *handbooks* help keep you from losing sight of the forest while in the trees. They typically present a thumbnail sketch of the content and historical context

of each book of the Bible. (Most versions also include essays on all sorts of background material on various subjects from ancient measures, weights, money, and calendars to ancient manuscripts to archaeology.) General *introductions* to the Old Testament or New Testament weave more history into the explanations about the content and development of the Scriptures than is found in Bible handbooks. But the use is similar: to get a sense of the big picture within which a particular passage is located. Another resource that can help is an *atlas* or *mapbook* of Bible lands. Even a quick look at a map can help you place a biblical passage in a geographic location and therefore make better sense of it.

STATE THE ORIGINAL MEANING OF THE PASSAGE

For most of us, writing something down helps because it forces us to pull our thoughts together for review. So, take some time to digest everything you have learned about the passage you are studying. Then set down on paper what you think was the intended meaning of the passage for its original readers or listeners. Try not to jump ahead and apply the passage to *your* situation. First, be sure you have a clear sense of the meaning in the *original, ancient* situation.

WHAT DOES THE PASSAGE MEAN TODAY?

Finally, you are ready for the "payoff" of in-depth Bible study. You want to figure out what the passage means for Christian readers today, for you. *After* you have wrestled with the passage to clarify its original meaning, you need to ask yourself:

"How is the world I live in (the big world and your little corner of it) like the world described in the Bible? What are the bedrock similarities underneath the differences?" To answer that, you will need to answer some additional questions. "In what ways am I and the other people in my world similar to the original audience? Do we share some essential needs across the centuries? Are we prone to similar faults that need correcting? Do we face the same kind of anxieties about life and death and human worth? Are we facing social problems similar to what ancient Israel and the early Christian church faced? Do we carry similar responsibilities for the moral health of families and communities?" Once you identify some ways in which contemporary people and situations are similar to the people and situations in the Bible passage, you will recognize that the Bible addresses *you* as well as its ancient audience.

Let's look at a few examples. Take Genesis 1–2. How is the world you and others live in like the world described in the Bible? What needs, problems, and issues do you face that are spoken to in this text? For one thing, we face an environmental crisis. To recover the true meaning of having *dominion* (as distinct from *domination*) would be no small gift today. Likewise, the report that Adam was placed in the garden to *till* (cultivate) and *keep* (protect) it carries implications for the way we treat the natural world. And the story of man and woman who are fit as *helper* and *partner* speaks to our age's confusion about the roles and worth of men and women.

Read Amos 5:10-15, 21-24. It sounds like a litany of contemporary social problems: a breakdown of the judicial system, exploitation of the poor, bribery of public officials. The prophet Amos contended that God is concerned about

social justice, that religious piety cannot make up for indifference to the well-being of the *whole* community. What does that imply for the behavior of Christians today?

Look at Jesus' parable of the workers in the vineyard in Matthew 20:1-16. Who are today's equivalent of the workers who toiled all day? Who are today's equivalent of those who worked just one hour? The tough—but absolutely essential—part of Bible study is to be ruthlessly honest about who you identify with in the Bible passage. Many middle-class people in Christian churches are offended by this story because they identify with the workers who toiled all day. We, like those workers, demand fairness and so find God's gracious goodness a bitter pill to swallow. So we find this parable a challenge to rethink the way we interpret reality and our place in it.

Finally, look at 1 Corinthians 8. The issue surrounded meat, sold in the marketplace, which was left over from pagan sacrifices. Hardly the sort of thing that comes up in most congregations today! But think for a moment: do we face modern equivalents of eating meat offered to idols, things not wrong in themselves but a cause of a brother or sister falling? Then Paul's counsel to the Corinthians addresses us, too.

Gleaning the message that a Bible passage holds for us today is risky. But you can minimize that risk by repeatedly asking: "Is the message I see in this passage really compatible with the original message?" It's one thing to extend the message of a text to address modern parallels. But it's quite another to dismiss or violate the original intent of a passage. Beyond that check, we can only trust Paul's advice to the Christians at Philippi: "work out your own salvation with fear and trembling; for God is at work in you, both to will and to work for his good pleasure" (Philippians 2:12-13).

A SHORT PLAN FOR STUDYING BIBLE PASSAGES

1. What is the Bible passage you want to examine?

2. Read the passage carefully, word-for-word. Jot down any words or phrases that catch your eye as potential keys to what the passage is saying. Make a note of terms that are new to you.

3. Look up the key terms in a theological wordbook or a dictionary of the Bible. Keep a record of what you find.

4. Clarify the literary context of the passage. What biblical material immediately precedes and follows the passage you are studying?

5. Clarify the canonical context. Where is this passage located in the Bible as a whole? What connections does the passage have to other parts of the Bible?

6. Clarify the historical and geographical context. What was going on at the time the passage was written? Write down what you find out about the author, date of writing, place of origin or destination, historical events, issues, and problems.

7. State the original meaning of the passage. Clarity and accuracy here are crucial to the success of the final step.

8. Explain what the passage means for Christian readers today. How is our situation like that of the persons who first heard the biblical passage? What needs, hopes, and fears do we share in common across the centuries that allow us to appropriate the ancient Word for our lives? What are the issues we face (or should face) that are equivalent to the issues faced in the Bible passages?

THE GEOGRAPHY
OF PALESTINE

Since the time of the Greek historian Herodotus (fifth century B.C.), the name Palestine, among other names, has designated much of the territory along the eastern coast of the Mediterranean Sea.

Under British rule by mandate of the League of Nations (1922–47), Palestine meant roughly the territory south of Mount Hermon as far as the Sinai desert and from the Mediterranean Sea to the Jordan River. The land east of the Jordan to the Syrian and Arabian deserts was called Transjordan or the Hashemite Kingdom of Jordan. Transjordan will be included in this discussion of the geography of Palestine.

The traditional boundaries of Palestine embrace a territory about the size of Vermont, around ten thousand square miles. From Dan to Beersheba is about 145 air miles. In times of expansion, as under King David, when Israelite territory took in southern and central Syria, including Damascus, and reached to the Red Sea on the south, the north-south distance was some 350 air miles. East-west the territory measured about 95 miles.

Palestine lies between the cradles of ancient civilizations: the Tigris-Euphrates river valley (modern Iraq) to the northeast and Egypt to the southwest. Palestine is a land bridge over which the traders and armies of the world have traveled. International commerce gave it prosperity in times of peace, and armies reduced it to ashes in times of war.

The land stretching from the Persian Gulf northwestward up the Tigris-Euphrates valley, through Syria, and down the Phoenician coast to the Sinai desert has been called "the Fertile Crescent." Here there was water enough to sustain settled life and to support international trade, travel, and the movement of armies.

The geography of Palestine is very complex. The mountains, valleys, gorges (rifts), and plateaus run mainly north-south, but also northeast to southwest, northwest to southeast, and in some cases east-west.

With elevations ranging from about 9,200 feet above sea level at the crest of Mount Hermon to about 1,300 feet below sea level at the Dead Sea, climates and flora and fauna vary widely. Houses of mud or even sun-dried brick with straw roofs were adequate in the warm climate of the Jordan Valley. But stone houses roofed with beams of wood overlaid with branches and clay mixed with small stones and furnished with braziers for heating in winter were needed in the hill country. Because of its great diversity of land, climate, peoples, and natural life, Palestine has always been the world in miniature.

THE COASTAL PLAIN

Reaching from Tyre in the north to Gaza in the south, the Coastal Plain is some 130 miles long. It is narrow in the north and broadens out in the south. Some parts of the plain were only lightly settled in biblical times. On the southern end were the five Philistine cities (Gaza, Ashdod, Ashkelon, Gath, Ekron).

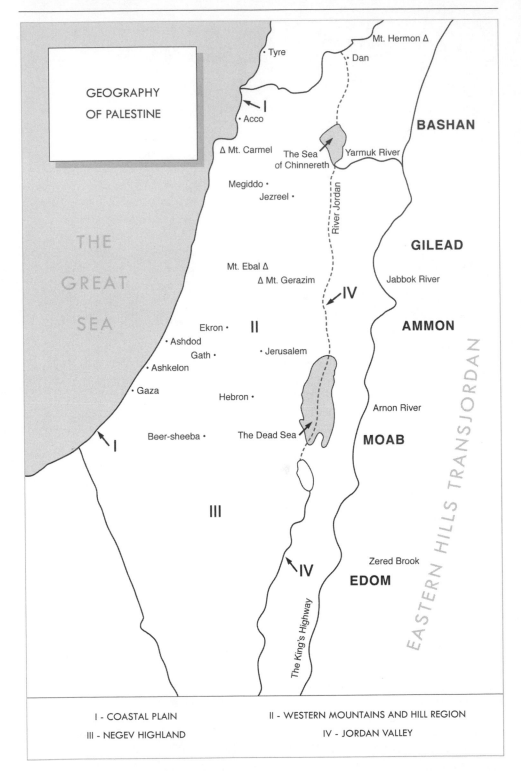

GEOGRAPHY
OF PALESTINE

Mt. Hermon Δ

· Tyre
· Dan

· Acco

BASHAN

Δ Mt. Carmel

The Sea
of Chinnereth   Yarmuk River

Megiddo ·

· Jezreel ·

THE

GREAT

SEA

River Jordan

GILEAD

Mt. Ebal Δ
Δ Mt. Gerazim

Jabbok River

IV

Ekron ·   II

· Ashdod

Gath ·   · Jerusalem

· Ashkelon

· Gaza

Hebron ·

AMMON

Arnon River

Beer-sheeba ·   The Dead Sea

MOAB

EASTERN HILLS TRANSJORDAN

III

IV   Zered Brook

EDOM

The King's Highway

I - COASTAL PLAIN   II - WESTERN MOUNTAINS AND HILL REGION

III - NEGEV HIGHLAND   IV - JORDAN VALLEY

South of Tyre the only good natural harbor is at Acco (modern Haifa), just north of Mount Carmel. Herod the Great constructed an artificial harbor at Caesarea (22–10 B.C.) by building a huge breakwater and semicircular seawall into the Mediterranean Sea. Because of the lack of natural harbors, the Hebrews never ventured westward as did the Phoenicians to the north. Commerce by caravans through their territory moved mostly along the Coastal Plain, as did the armies of the ancient world.

THE LOW HILL COUNTRY

Known in Hebrew as the *Shephelah*, meaning "lowland," this area lies between the Coastal Plain and the mountains of Judea. Wide valleys, suited to agriculture, reach among the low limestone hills. The area was a battleground between the Hebrews and the Philistines on the Coastal Plain and offered suitable sites for fortified cities of the contending peoples.

THE CENTRAL MOUNTAINS

Palestine consists largely of the southern foothills of the Lebanon Mountains. In Lebanon the mountains rise some 6,000 feet above sea level (except for the 9,200 foot Mount Hermon), descend to about 2,000 feet in Samaria (except for the 3,083 and 2,889 foot peaks of Ebal and Gerizim), rise to around 2,600 feet at Jerusalem, and finally fall away to the barren ridges and dunes of the steppe land south of Beersheba (the Negeb). The limestone mountains, once largely forested, are now mostly barren, with patches of reforestation here and there and pockets of agriculture (olives, figs, wheat, grape vines).

Breaking the north-south mountains and running northwest-southeast are the fertile, near–sea-level plains of Megiddo and Jezreel, the latter dropping quickly to the low Jordan Valley. East-west valleys in Samaria (at Dothan and Shechem) and in Judah (at Aijalon, Sorek, and Elah) offer routes from the Coastal Plain into the mountain areas.

THE JORDAN VALLEY

The Jordan Valley is part of the largest geological fault on earth. It begins in Syria and extends into eastern Africa. In the Rift are the Huleh Valley, the Sea of Galilee (Lake Tiberias), the Jordan Valley, the Dead Sea, the Arabah Plain, and the Gulf of Aqabah. The Sea of Galilee is about 695 feet below sea level and the Dead Sea about 1,300 feet below. The average width of the Jordan Valley is about ten miles.

The water of the Sea of Galilee is fresh, but that of the Dead Sea has a high mineral content (sodium chloride, potash, bromine, phosphate, magnesium, calcium, potassium) and is without marine life. Between the Sea of Galilee and the Dead Sea, a distance of only about sixty-five miles, the Jordan River's snake-like bed actually meanders for some two hundred miles. In ancient times this area was a jungle and the lair of wild animals. Some tributary rivers flow into the Jordan from the east, and several fjords in the Jordan have made east-west travel and commerce possible.

THE TRANSJORDAN PLATEAU

This territory is divided by four main east-west streams (the Yarmuk, the Jabbok, the Arnon, and the Zered) making five definite zones. These are (from north to south) Bashan, Gilead, Ammon, Moab, and Edom.

Bashan is good pasture land, with abundant black basalt for house building.

Gilead, heavily forested in ancient times, also offers good pasture land. Its trees apparently produced a sort of medicinal "balm" valued in antiquity (Jeremiah 8:22).

Ammon forms the center of the eastern highlands, with its capital city at the headwater of the Jabbok River (Rabbah, now Amman). The Ammonites and the Hebrews were often locked in bitter warfare.

Moab, on whose plains Israel camped before entering the Promised Land (Numbers 35:1; Deuteronomy 1:5), is somewhat high (at points over 3,000 feet) and comparatively well watered. Moab has produced wheat and barley and sheep and goats and was sometimes prosperous when there was a famine in Judah (Ruth 1:1). Hostility broke out frequently through the centuries between the Hebrews and the Moabites.

Edom, meaning "red" because of the reddish sandstone of the area, was a source of copper in antiquity. Its wise men were noted for their wisdom (Jeremiah 49:7; Obadiah 1:8). The inhabitants depended largely for their sustenance on the caravans that passed through their borders.

The "King's Highway," a major public road and international caravan route, ran the full length of the Transjordan Plateau from Damascus in the north to the Gulf of Aqabah in the south and brought wealth to the towns and areas through which it passed.

In latitude, Palestine falls in a line with Georgia (United States). In general its climate has two seasons: a rainy winter, with snow in the Lebanon Mountains and occasionally in Jerusalem, and a long, dry summer. The early (or "former") rains, which soften the ground for plowing, fall in October and November. The heavy rains come in December-February. And the late (or "latter") rains, which ripen the crops, descend in March and April.

The rain clouds come from the west. Annual rainfall often reaches sixty inches in parts of Lebanon, forty inches in upper Galilee, twenty-six inches at Jerusalem, ten to fifteen inches in the region between Hebron and Beersheba, eight inches in the Negeb to the south, and five inches in southern Transjordan.

If rains do not come at the right time in the right amounts, crops fail and famine may result (1 Kings 17:1; 18:1-2). Prayers for rain and rain-inducing ceremonies (Zechariah 10:1; Joel 2:23) were an important part of Israel's religious and economic life. The prophets of Israel strongly contended that the Lord Yahweh, not the Canaanite Baal, controlled the rains and the crops the rains nourished (Amos 4:7-8; Hosea 2:5, 8; Jeremiah 5:23-24).

By our standards Palestine is a land poorly endowed, on the whole. The central portion of the country consists of limestone hills and mountains without much depth of soil. Harbors along its coast are few and inadequate. The cut-up, rocky, and generally arid ground doomed its inhabitants to hard labor for a minimal level of existence.

But more devastating than lack of water and good soil for the life of Palestine's people has been the almost incessant warfare and destruction the country's location and physical character have brought. Since Palestine forms a land bridge between the great civilizations of the Middle East, it was inevitable that it should be at the mercy of their peoples in times of international expansion and conflict. Alliance with one or another of the dominant powers, in order to gain security, often ended in Palestine's destruction along with that of its defeated ally. In addition, in times of famine marauding peoples from the desert to the east and south of Transjordan pressed with devastating results into the more fertile corridor to the west.

The great diversity in the surface of Palestine has always made political, economic, religious, and social unification difficult. Thus a common front against external enemies was often hindered by local squabbles and indifference.

To summarize, security, water, bread, and cultural, political, and religious unity have been dominant problems of this little land.

The ancient Hebrews looked on their land as "a good land" (Deuteronomy 8:7-8). Compared to the desert areas in which Israel wandered for a generation in the time of Moses, the characterization is justified. But life on this international bridge has always been difficult and insecure. The Promised Land was no Garden of Eden; hence, seers and prophets looked forward to the coming of that Garden in the latter days.

OLD TESTAMENT

CHAPTERS, VERSES, AND WORDS IN THE OLD TESTAMENT

Biblical Book	Number of Chapters	Number of Verses	Number of Words
Law			
Genesis	50	1,533	38,267
Exodus	40	1,213	32,692
Leviticus	27	859	24,546
Numbers	36	1,288	32,902
Deuteronomy	34	958	28,461
History			
Joshua	24	658	18,858
Judges	21	618	18,976
Ruth	4	85	2,578
1 Samuel	31	810	25,061
2 Samuel	24	695	20,612
1 Kings	22	816	24,524
2 Kings	25	719	23,532
1 Chronicles	29	941	20,369
2 Chronicles	36	822	26,074
Ezra	10	280	7,441
Nehemiah	13	406	10,483
Esther	10	167	5,637
Poetry			
Job	42	1,070	10,102
Psalms	150	2,461	43,743
Proverbs	31	915	15,043
Ecclesiastes	12	222	5,584
Song of Solomon	8	117	2,661
Major Prophets			
Isaiah	66	1,292	37,044
Jeremiah	52	1,364	42,659
Lamentations	5	154	3,415
Ezekiel	48	1,273	39,407
Daniel	12	357	11,606

Biblical Book	Number of Chapters	Number of Verses	Number of Words
Minor Prophets			
Hosea	14	197	5,175
Joel	3	73	2,034
Amos	9	146	4,217
Obadiah	1	21	670
Jonah	4	48	1,321
Micah	7	105	3,153
Nahum	3	47	1,285
Habakkuk	3	56	1,476
Zephaniah	3	53	1,617
Haggai	2	38	1,131
Zechariah	14	211	6,444
Malachi	4	55	1,782
Totals	929	23,138	602,582

Figures for the chapters, verses, and words are based on the *Synopsis of the Books of the Bible in the Authorized Version of 1611* (Philadelphia: National Bible Press, n.d.).

OLD TESTAMENT CHRONOLOGY

Because of the fragmentary nature of available literary and archaeological sources, dates are approximate.

? Creation

? Flood

2000–1500 B.C.? The Patriarchs (Abraham, Isaac, Jacob, Joseph)

1300 B.C.? The Exodus from Egypt

1200–1020? B.C. The Judges

1020–1000 B.C.? King Saul

1000–960 B.C.? King David

960–930 B.C.? King Solomon

930–922 B.C.? Division of the Kingdom

Kings of Judah	Kings of Israel
Rehoboam 922–915	922–90 1 Jeroboam I
Abijam 915–913	
Asa 913–873	
	901–900 Nadab
	900–877 Baasha
	877–876 Elah
	876 Zimri
	876–872 Tibni[1][2]
	876–869 Omri
Jehoshaphat 873–849[1]	
	869–850 Ahab
Jehoram 849–843	850–849 Ahaziah
	849–843 Joram
Ahaziah 843–842	843–815 Jehu
Athaliah 842–837 (queen)	
Jehoash 837–800	
	815–802 Jehoahaz
Amaziah 800–783	802–786 Joash
	786–746 Jeroboam I

1. Including coregency years
2. Rival rule

930–922 B.C.? Division of the Kingdom

Azariah/Uzziah 783–742[1]	
	746–745 Zechariah
	745 Shallum
	745–737 Menahem
Jotham 742–735[1]	
	737–736 Pekahiah
Ahaz 735–715[1]	736–732 Pekah
	732–724 Hoshea
Hezekiah 715–687	722 B.C. Fall of Samaria (the Northern Kingdom) to Assyria
Manasseh 687–642	
Amon 642–640	
Josiah 640–609	
Jehoahaz 609	
Jehoiakim 609–598	
Jehoiachin 598–587	
Zedekiah 587	

597 B.C. First deportation of Judah

587 B.C. Fall of Judah (the Southern Kingdom) to Babylonia. Second deportation of Judah.

538–539 B.C. Cyrus, King of Persia, decrees that the Jews may return to Judah and rebuild the Temple. The Jews return under the direction of Sheshbazzar.

520 B.C. Zerubbabel, the new governor of the Persian province Yehud (formerly central Judah) attempts to rebuild the Temple. Local opposition thwarts these efforts.

516/515 B.C. By decree of Darius I, work continues on the Temple, which is completed and dedicated.

458 B.C. With a commission from Artaxerxes I, Ezra goes to Jerusalem to establish pentateuchal law as the law in the province of Judea and to regulate temple worship (some scholars date this event and all of Ezra's ministry to 398 B.C. and after).

458/457 B.C. Ezra reads the law publicly and launches a formal inquiry into mixed marriages.

445 B.C. Artaxerxes I appoints Nehemiah governor of Judah.

445–433 B.C. Nehemiah serves as governor of Judah, rebuilds Jerusalem's city walls, and enlarges the city's population.

433? B.C. or later Nehemiah returns to Judah and initiates various religious reforms.

---

1. Including coregency years
2. Rival rule

GENESIS

OUTLINE OF GENESIS

1. Trials and successes
   (39:1–41:57)
2. Joseph's family in Egypt
   (42:1–45:28)
3. Jacob's migration to Egypt
   (46:1–47:31)
4. Jacob's death (48:1–50:14)
5. Joseph's last years (50:15-26)

INTRODUCTION

The book of Genesis is a book about how the universe, the earth and its creatures, faith, and the community of faith all began. At its heart, however, Genesis is a statement of faith. The stories in this book testify that all reality begins with God and that nothing exists except by the will and power of God. These stories tell us that, if we push each question of "Why?" or "How?" about our world to its ultimate end, the answer must be: God.

The book of Genesis is also about relationships. From "the beginning" relationships are established between God and creation and among the different parts of creation. No part exists in isolation. The relationship that receives the most attention in Genesis is the relationship between God and the community of faith. This community was born in the relationship established between God and Abraham, and it continues to this day.

Title, Date, and Authorship

The Hebrew title of Genesis comes from the first word in the text, which means "in the beginning (of)," and the name Genesis comes from the title in the Septuagint (the oldest Greek translation of the Old Testament). Genesis is part of the Pentateuch, the first five books of the Old Testament, which is also called the Torah ("law"). These books are traditionally referred to as the "five books of Moses."

The close association of Moses with the law and the specific records he did write (see, for example, Exodus 17:14) have helped to foster the idea that Moses wrote the Pentateuch. Most scholars agree, however, that Moses was not the author of the Pentateuch. Indeed, there is much evidence within the books themselves that more than one person contributed to them.

The sources and writers of the Pentateuch, and of Genesis in particular, are still the objects of much study and debate. There are, however, some generally accepted opinions about how the books came about:

(1) Before much of the material in these books was written it was preserved in oral form. This is the "oral tradition," the stories, history, laws, prayers, and poems that were passed from one generation to the next before they were written down and collected.

(2) Four sources of this tradition are found in the Pentateuch. Each source has a characteristic style, language, and perspective that (in many cases) allow it to be identified. There is no definite agreement concerning which parts of the Scripture belong to which source, and some commentators find more than four sources within the text.

(3) The four most widely accepted sources are called J, E, P, and D. "J" gets its name from the characteristic use of *Yahweh* as the name for God in this source. "E" uses the name *Elohim* (divine being) for God. "P" stands for "priestly" because much of the material from this source focuses on the interests of priests and on the sanctuary. "D" stands for Deuteronomist and is associated with much of the material in the book of Deuteronomy. J, E, and P are found in the book of Genesis.

(4) The writers who put together each of these sources probably used both oral and

written material, much of which was ancient even in their day. Exact dates for J, E, P, and D are not known, nor do we know exactly when the book of Genesis was put into the form we know today. Estimates have been made, however, about the general dates for these sources. J perhaps took shape during the reigns of King David and King Solomon (1000–922 B.C.), E may have developed during the eighth century B.C., P may come from the time of the exile (587–539 B.C.) or soon after, and D in its earliest form probably comes from approximately 650 B.C.

(5) Some scholars believe that one person collected these various sources (and other material, for example, from The Book of the Wars of the LORD, Numbers 21:14) and formed them into the books we have today. Others believe that the collection and formation was done over a number of years by more than one person.

(6) Genesis and the other books of the Pentateuch were put together sometime during or after the Jewish exile in Babylon (587–539 B.C.). The process of writing and organizing the text may have continued for a long time, but the process was completed before 250 B.C. when the Septuagint translation of the Old Testament was begun.

The Content of Genesis

The content of Genesis can be divided into three broad sections: the primeval history (Creation through the tower of Babel), the patriarchal history (Abraham, Isaac, and Jacob), and the story of Joseph.

Each of these sections is a collection of different kinds of materials such as stories, genealogical lists, prayers, and poems. The biggest part of Genesis is taken up with stories about particular people in specific circumstances and times. These stories, however, also have an application and a point beyond the individual lives involved. Genesis is like a "family history" for the community of faith.

Though we use the word *history* in relation to the events described in Genesis, we do not mean history in our modern sense of the word. The writers of Genesis did not produce objective, footnoted, cross-referenced documents with specific dates for the people and events they describe. They had a very definite perspective from which they wrote the book, and this perspective is that all reality, and specifically the reality of the community of faith, is grounded in the will and power of God. They wrote a theological history that seeks to preserve the experiences, remembrances, and beliefs of this earliest community.

This is not to say, however, that what they wrote is not true or historical. The trend of archaeological and other historical research in recent years has been to illuminate more fully this ancient world and to confirm the scriptural account. To be sure, many questions remain unanswered, and, to our twenty-first–century minds hungry for facts on which to base our beliefs, there may never be enough answers. The writers of Genesis, however, are calling us beyond this issue to larger questions that they do indeed answer: How did this world come to be? What is our place in the world? How did the community of faith begin?

GENESIS 1

Introduction to This Chapter

Genesis 1:1–2:4a is the story of Creation as told in the priestly (P) tradition (see the Introduction on page 8). This story is told in stately, rhythmical, and dignified language and is similar to a liturgy that might be used in a worship service.

This account is based, to some extent, on the "science" of its day that assumed that the universe is divided into three parts: the heavens, the earth, and the underworld. This story of Creation also has some similarities to accounts of Creation from other cultures in the ancient Near East, particularly that of Mesopotamia. Genesis 1:1, however, goes beyond any ancient or modern scientific or cultural explanation for Creation. The writer declares that everything, all reality, depends on the sovereign will and power of God for its existence. Nothing is independent or self-sustaining, but all is dependent upon the Creator.

Here is an outline of this section.

I. From the Beginning to the First Day (1:1-5)
II. The Second Day (1:6-8)
III. The Third Day (1:9-13)
IV. The Fourth Day (1:14-19)
V. The Fifth Day (1:20-23)
VI. The Sixth Day (1:24-31)
VII. The Seventh Day (2:1-4a)

The Message of Genesis 1

The people who put together the book of Genesis and those who arranged the Bible realized that the testimony of Genesis 1:1 is the ground upon which

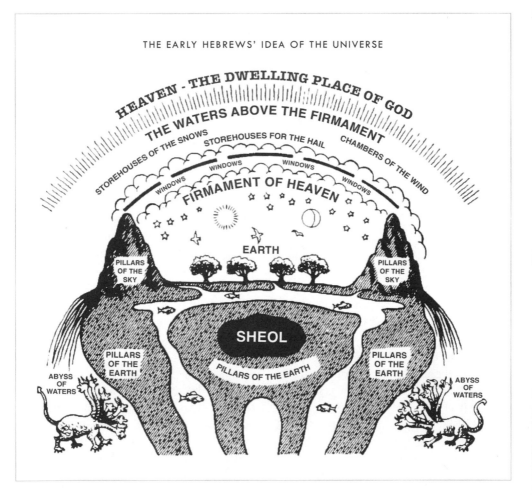

THE EARLY HEBREWS' IDEA OF THE UNIVERSE

everything else in the Bible builds. It is appropriate that the witness of the community of faith should open with "the beginning."

What does Genesis 1 tell us about how the world was created and for what purpose?

- Old Testament tradition declares that God's wisdom and God's word existed before Creation and are the means of Creation. The prologue to the Gospel of John (John 1:1-18) affirms this and declares that Christ is the wisdom and word behind Creation.

- The act of creation belongs to God alone. The verb "to create" that is used in Genesis 1 is applied only to God, never to anything or anyone else.

- Creation is a concrete expression of God's will.

- All creation is unified under and obedient to God's will. This is the established order that God pronounces as "good."

- This "good" not only conforms with God's will but is also beautiful and pleasing.

- Human beings, who are created in the image of God, are entrusted with dominion on earth as God's representatives in God's service. The greatest example of such service is found in the life of Jesus, who, as the image of God (2 Corinthians 4:4) came to serve humankind and creation.

- Human beings and the rest of creation are not divine but are sacred and are blessed.

GENESIS 2–3

Introduction to These Chapters

This story of Creation comes from the Yahwist (also called "J"; see the Introduction). J's account of Creation focuses on the first human beings and explores their relationship to God.

Here is an outline of Genesis 2–3.
I. The Garden and the First Living Being (2:4b-17)
II. The Creation of Woman (2:18-24)
III. A Choice Is Made (3:1-13)
IV. Consequences of the Choice (3:14-24)

The Message of Genesis 2–3

The story of Creation in Genesis 2–3 focuses on the place of human beings in God's created order. Human beings are not created in isolation but are made to live in communion with the earth and its creatures, with one another, and with God. What does this story tell us about the relationship between the Creator and humankind?

- Human beings are created to live in harmonious relationship with God, with one another, and with the rest of creation.

- Human beings are created with the capacity to understand and obey God's laws.

- Human beings are given a vocation and are given limits on how they may use God's creation. These limits, if respected, will lead to well-being.

- Fear, anxiety, and shame come from a failure to trust God and to obey the limits that God sets for human existence.

- Sin is related to the desire of humans to grasp the power of God.

- Brokenness in creation is related to human sin. This brokenness includes the alienation that exists among people and between people and God.

- There is no freedom or security for humankind apart from God.

GENESIS 4:1–6:4

Introduction to These Chapters

The story of humankind continues outside the Garden of Eden. This part of the story explores how the relationship of human beings to one another affects their relationship to God.

These chapters may be outlined as follows.

I. Cain and Abel (4:1-16)
II. Family of Cain and the Birth of Seth (4:17-26)
III. From Adam to Noah (5:1-32)
IV. The Nephilim (6:1-4)

The Message of Genesis 4:1–6:4

The stories of Adam, Eve, Cain, and Abel tell us that these persons are not only our physical ancestors but our spiritual ancestors as well. We can see ourselves in them and learn more about our relationship to God through their stories.

The stories in Genesis 4:1–6:4 testify that God is both judge and redeemer. What do these chapters tell us about sinful humankind's relationship to this God who both condemns and protects?

- The story of Cain and Abel shows us that our relationships with one another affect our relationship to God. We cannot be false to each other without also being false to God.

- We can, may, and shall master sin. We are created to "do well" before God, but this requires great effort and constant diligence. Sin is an intimate enemy who resides on our doorstep and seeks us out.

- We and the earth suffer the consequences of our sin.

- God controls the spirit or breath of life and moves to assert this control whenever human or divine beings overstep their limits.

  - Despite human sin, God has not given up on creation. God is in relationship to humankind and is available to those who call upon the name of the Lord.

GENESIS 6–9

Introduction to These Chapters

Genesis 6:5–9:29 tells the story of the great Flood and of God's covenant with Noah following the Flood. Noah is remembered and honored in the Bible as a man of uncommon righteousness whose

THE GENEALOGIES IN GENESIS 4–5

ADAM-EVE

ABEL   CAIN   SETH

ENOCH   ENOSH

IRAD   KENAN

MEHUJAEL   MAHALALEL

METHUSHAEL   JARED

LAMECH   ENOCH

JABAL JUBAL TUBAL-CAIN NAAMAH   METHUSELAH

LAMECH

NOAH

HAM   SHEM   JAPHETH

obedience to God saved humankind from complete destruction (see also Ezekiel 14:14, 20; Hebrews 11:7).

The story of the Flood as it stands today in the text is a combination of ancient Israelite traditions. The historians P and J (see the Introduction) both contributed material to this final version. Other ancient cultures (for example, the Sumerians of Mesopotamia and natives of North America) also have stories of a great world flood that few human beings survived.

Despite some similarities between the Mesopotamian stories and the Israelite stories, however, one major difference stands out. In the Mesopotamian versions (such as the Babylonian Gilgamesh Epic), the flood comes seemingly at the whim of the gods and humankind survives only through the pity of one god. In the Israelite version, both the Flood and the survival of humankind are by the will and power of God, the Lord of Creation.

Here is an outline of Genesis 6–9.
I. Reasons for the Flood (6:5-8)
II. Preparations for the Flood (6:9–7:10)
III. The Flood (7:11-24)
IV. Dry Land Appears (8:1-19)
V. Offering and Promise (8:20-22)
VI. Blessing and Covenant (9:1-17)
VII. The Curse of Canaan (9:18-29)

The Message of Genesis 6–9

The story of the flood and its aftermath clearly shows that human sin and the capacity of humankind for evil continue to affect human history. What does this story tell us about the relationship between human history and human sin?

- Human sin and the capacity of humankind for evil continue to affect human history because sin affects the

relationship between humankind and God.

- A fundamental witness in the community of faith is that God judges and is active in human history. Creation has not just been turned loose to work out its own destiny.

- God acts in human history to accomplish the righteous purposes for which the world was created.

- Human sin affects the course by which these righteous purposes are achieved, but sin will not ultimately block God's purposes.

- God's judgment is mixed with grace.

- Humankind owes its existence to God's grace, not to its own merit.

GENESIS 10–11

Introduction to These Chapters

Genesis 10–11 begins with an overview of how the world's families spread from Noah's family and divided themselves into distinct peoples (10:1–11:9). Attention is then focused on the family of Abraham, through which will come the Israelite people (11:10-32).

Here is an outline of these chapters.
I. The Descendants of Noah (10:1-32)
II. The Tower of Babel (11:1-9)
III. The Descendants of Shem to Abram (11:10-32)

The Message of Genesis 10–11

The genealogies of Genesis 10–11 serve as a bridge between the primeval time in human history and what we call historical time. These family lists also serve as a bridge between the peoples of the world at large and the family of Israel in particular. The historians of Genesis leave no doubt that all the families of the earth are interrelated. They also indicate that something special is about to happen with this one particular family, and thus set the stage for God's call of Abraham. With this call, the pessimism of Genesis 11:1-9 is tempered with hope. In the midst of the confusion and alienation of humankind, God selects a particular people, a particular man with whom to initiate a special relationship. What do these chapters tell us about the continuing relationship between God and humankind?

- All peoples and nations owe their existence to God's grace and God's plans for creation.

- All begin with God's blessing and promise.

- Even so, people still seek equality with God (compare the "fruit of the tree of knowledge" story in Genesis 2–3 with the story of the Tower of Babel in Genesis 11:1-9).

- Despite human presumption and disobedience, God's purposes ultimately will not be thwarted.

- In the midst of a universal movement away from the Creator, God acts to create a people through whom God's original intentions for creation may be realized.

GENESIS 12

Introduction to This Chapter

This chapter is a turning point in the narrative of the book of Genesis. The story of the human family in Genesis has gradually narrowed its focus from all the world's families (Genesis 10:1-32), to one particular family (Genesis 11:10-32), then to one particular man (12:1).

Chapter 12 has two main parts.

  I. God Calls Abraham (12:1-9)
 II. Abraham and Sarah in Egypt (12:10-20)

The Message of Genesis 12

Abraham and his family leave Egypt richer than when they came, though not out of merit or faithfulness. Only God's intervention and faithfulness to the divine promises save the family that will one day become the people of Israel.

What does this chapter tell us about God and about humankind, represented by Abraham?

- God does not necessarily choose perfect people to fulfill God's purposes in the world.

- Abraham is both faithful and faithless. He is the father not only of all who believe in God but also of all who sometimes fail in belief and in trust.

- God acts to keep the divine promises and purposes alive.

GENESIS 13–15

Introduction to These Chapters

Abraham returns to the Promised Land where his journey of faith continues. These chapters may be divided into three main parts.

   I. Abraham and Lot Part Ways (13:1-18)
  II. War with the Kings of the East (14:1-24)
 III. God's Covenant with Abraham (15:1-21)

The Message of Genesis 13–15

Abraham is remembered by later generations as a man of extraordinary faith (see, for example, Hebrews 11:8, 17). What does Abraham's life tell us about living a life of faith?

- Abraham is not a man of perfect faith, but God chooses him anyway and does not give up on Abraham even in his moments of doubt.

- God brings Abraham outside his tent (Genesis 15:5) and forces him to see another perspective on his situation. God is the Lord of the universe, the one who made and set the stars in their places. The vastness of God's power is offered in contrast to the smallness of Abraham's trust. God challenges Abraham to expand his vision.

- Abraham responds to God's challenge with trust (Genesis 15:6). By this we know that trust is essential to righteousness, to merit before God.

- To be in covenant with God requires patience as well as trust. This covenant relationship also requires a recognition that real security lies not in kings or goods or in the best pastures, but in God.

- Acceptance of God's promises requires not only trust but also an external response. Abraham moved to Hebron, built an altar, turned down the reward from the King of Sodom, and participated in the covenant ceremony. He put his faith and trust in God into action.

GENESIS 16–18

Introduction to These Chapters

These chapters tell of more waiting and more frustration for Abraham and Sarah and of God's continued assurances that the great promises made so many years before will come true. They may be outlined as follows.

I. Hagar and Ishmael (16:1-16)
II. The Covenant of Circumcision (17:1-27)
III. Promises and Punishment (18:1-33)
  A. Promises and laughter (18:1-15)
  B. Intercession for Sodom and Gomorrah (18:16-33)

The Message of Genesis 16–18

The stories in the book of Genesis tell us about people, such as Abraham, Sarah, Hagar, and Lot, and they tell us what these people are like. What do these stories reveal to us about what God is like?

- God is the Redeemer who saves Hagar and Ishmael from death.

- God is the Creator who overcomes both physical and spiritual barrenness and who brings life where there is no life.

- God is the Partner who establishes a redeeming relationship with Abraham, with Ishmael, and (eventually) with Isaac.

- God is the Judge who deals with human sin and who acts to establish divine justice and righteousness in the world.

- God is the patient Teacher who leads and is revealed to the chosen people.

GENESIS 19–20

Introduction to These Chapters

Chapter 19 deals with the fate of Sodom and Gomorrah and of Lot's family. Chapter 20 tells about how Abraham and Sarah try to fool Abimelech, the king of Gerar. These two chapters may be outlined as follows.

I. Sodom and Gomorrah Destroyed (19:1-29)
II. Lot's Descendants (19:30-38)
III. Abraham, Sarah, and Abimelech (20:1-18)
II. Hagar and Ishmael Are Banished (21:8-21)
III. Abraham's Covenant with Abimelech (21:22-34)
IV. God Tests Abraham (22:1-24)
V. The Death of Sarah (23:1-20)

The Message of Genesis 19–20

Over and over again, the stories in Genesis bear witness to certain truths about God's relationship to the world and to the chosen people. In chapters 19–20, we see that God acts to maintain justice and righteousness in the world and to safeguard the destiny of Abraham and Sarah. What else do these chapters reveal to us?

- God has chosen the family of Abraham and Sarah with whom to have a special and redeeming relationship.

- God guides and protects the covenant family.

- God makes accommodation for human weakness, even within the covenant family.

- God judges and punishes human sin.

- God brings good out of evil for those who will listen to and obey God's voice.

GENESIS 21–23

Introduction to These Chapters

These chapters open with the birth of Isaac and close with the death of Sarah. In between these events lie episodes of conflict and of trial for Abraham and his family.

These three chapters may be outlined as follows.

I. The Birth of Isaac (21:1-7)

The Message of Genesis 21–23

In chapter 21 God answers the question posed in Genesis 18:14. Indeed, nothing is too hard for God, who brings life where there is no life. The promised child has arrived. In chapter 23, Abraham buys property in the Promised Land and is no longer a landless sojourner. His possession of this relatively small plot of land both symbolizes and seals the promise that God made concerning the whole land of Canaan (see Genesis 12:5-7). In between these two great events is the story of how God tests Abraham. What does this story tell us about God, Abraham, and faith?

- God calls, tests, and provides for the covenant family (see also 1 Corinthians 10:13).

- Abraham hears, answers, and obeys.

- Faith is a recognition and acceptance of the promise, the test, and the providential care of God (see also Hebrews 11:1).

- Why does God test Abraham, and what does this mean for us?

- Perhaps God tests Abraham because of his wavering and doubt in the past (see, for example, Genesis 17:17). The test will prove whether Abraham can still trust God even if he must give up Isaac, who is the tangible evidence of the truth of God's word as well as his beloved son.

- This kind of test is perhaps one that must be faced by everyone who claims to follow God's word. Each of us is called to face this terrifying summons. Can we accept God as both the one who tests and the one who provides? Can we trust the promises in the face of seeming contradiction and disaster?

GENESIS 24–26

Introduction to These Chapters

In order for God's promises concerning Abraham's descendants to be fulfilled (see, for example, Genesis 13:16) Isaac must have a wife. As has been true in the past, God takes a hand in seeing that events work out as they should. This section also reports the death of Abraham, the birth of Jacob and Esau, and the blessing of Isaac.

Genesis 24–26 may be outlined as follows.

I. Isaac and Rebekah (24:1-67)
II. The Death of Abraham (25:1-18)
III. Birth and Rivalry of Jacob and Esau (25:19-34)
IV. The Blessings of Isaac (26:1-35)

The Message of Genesis 24–26

God continues to act to protect the destiny of the covenant family. Even so, the members of this special family are human beings who, at times, fail God and one another. In these chapters we are told about the end of Abraham's life and about the continuation of the covenant family into the second and third generations. What do these stories show us about the relationships within this very special family?

• Abraham's life is not one of unbroken faith. He has his moments of doubt and weakness. Through the years,

however, his faith proves to be stronger than his doubt.

• Abraham, Isaac, Rebekah, Esau, and Jacob do not always live within God's will.

• Though God's blessings and promises bring material prosperity for Abraham (see also Genesis 24:1) and Isaac, these circumstances do not guarantee them a happy family life. Strife and misunderstanding are evident even in the chosen family.

• The family somehow holds together and moves on into the future with God's help and guidance.

GENESIS 27–29

Introduction to These Chapters

This portion of the Genesis narrative continues the stories about Isaac, Jacob, and Esau.

These chapters may be outlined as follows.

I. Jacob Receives Isaac's Blessing (27:1-40)
II. Jacob Must Flee (27:41-46)
III. Jacob's Dream at Bethel (28:1-22)
IV. Jacob Marries Leah and Rachel (29:1-35)

The Message of Genesis 27–29

These chapters reveal that the members of the covenant family are still often in conflict with one another, even in this third generation. Jacob especially is a man of conflict. At one time or another he is at odds with Esau, Isaac, Laban, Leah, and also eventually with Rachel (see Genesis 30:1-2). Yet these stories leave no doubt that Jacob is also a man in a special relationship with God.

- Jacob and Rebekah lie and cheat to get what they want from Isaac. They take matters into their own hands to see that the promises of Genesis 25:23 are fulfilled. Even later prophets use Jacob's behavior as a negative example in their preaching (see Hosea 12:2-4).

- Jacob becomes a fugitive who is outside the protection and comfort of his family and who is without anyone to offer him hospitality. It is when he is most isolated and vulnerable that God comes to meet him (Genesis 28:10-17).

- We do not know why God chooses Jacob to inherit the promises given to Abraham and Isaac. We only know that Jacob is to play an important role in God's plans for humankind and that Jacob's life is in God's care.

- Jacob is the blessed one. Like his father and grandfather before him, however, he must wait for the fulfillment of God's word to him.

- God does grant Jacob success, though why he has been chosen remains a mystery. The family of Jacob becomes the people of Israel, who are a source of blessing for all the families of the earth (see also Genesis 12:1-3).

- The story of Jacob's life (which continues through Genesis 50:1) shows that God's purposes in the world will be fulfilled, though we do not know how or why.

GENESIS 30–32

Introduction to These Chapters

Jacob has eleven children and prosperous flocks before God finally calls him to return to Canaan. These events are described in chapters 30–32, which may be outlined as follows.

  I. Jacob Prospers (30:1-43)
     A. God sends Leah and Rachel children (30:1-24)
     B. Jacob grows rich (30:25-43)
  II. Jacob Leaves for Canaan (31:1-55)
 III. Jacob Wrestles with "a Man" (32:1-32)

The Message of Genesis 30–32

Jacob serves his time as an exile from his homeland. He eventually leaves for home with a new relationship to God, with wives and children born into the covenant family, and with material riches. Even so, none of this was accomplished easily because he and his family faced barrenness, family conflicts, and legal questions that had to be resolved. It is Jacob's relationship with God, however, which gives meaning to all these struggles. What can we say about this relationship?

- God knows Jacob and has plans for him even before his birth (see Genesis 25:23-26).

- God calls and Jacob responds, though not always with the utmost faith (see Genesis 28:10-22; 32:1-8).

- God's name reveals something about what God is like, and God is known to Jacob as the God of Abraham and the Fear of Isaac. God is not distant but establishes a close relationship with Jacob's family. Thus, Jacob knows God in a personal way. He even has a new name, Israel (he who strives with God), which symbolizes this kinship.

- Jacob gives his name to his descendants, the people of Israel. They, too, know God in a very personal way. They, too, struggle with God and are blessed by God.

- Jacob comes out of his encounter with God with a new name but also with a limp. He is blessed but also weaker. From the story of Jacob's life and the history of the people of Israel, we may see that having a personal relationship with God does not necessarily lead to a life free of conflict. Instead we see that the relationship itself may bring new responsibilities, risks, and costs. New Testament teachings about discipleship reflect this same theme of blessing/cost (see, for example, Mark 8:34-35; 10:35-45).

GENESIS 33–36

Introduction to These Chapters

These chapters close the second large section of material in the book of Genesis that began in Genesis 12:1 with the call of Abraham. The story of the patriarchs Abraham, Isaac, and Jacob is followed by the story of Joseph (Genesis 37–50).

These chapters may be outlined as follows.

I. Jacob and Esau Are Reconciled (33:1-20)
II. Shechem and Dinah (34:1-31)
III. Jacob Comes to Mamre (35:1-29)
IV. The Descendants of Esau (36:1-43)

The Message of Genesis 33–36

This part of Jacob's story shows us that the call to be in relationship with God does not exclude other relationships. Jacob and the covenant family must still live with one another and with the rest of the world, despite their differences. Esau is Jacob's brother but is still very different. The

Canaanites are close neighbors but are also very different. Given the realities of these differences in everyday life, how is the covenant family supposed to live in the world?

- The chosen people must maintain proper ritual and worship to affirm their faith and separate themselves from the worship of false gods.

- The chosen people must recognize the special nature of God's call to them. They do not define their own identity. Rather, God calls them and gives them an identity in which their old ways and habits may not always apply (see also Ephesians 4:22-25; Hebrews 11:8-16).

- The chosen people must trust God. They must accept the fact that they live in a world of life and death, of joy and grief, even as they continue their journey with God.

- The covenant community must recognize that God is the God of all peoples. The stories about Esau, his reconciliation with Jacob, and his prosperity testify that God is also in relationship with him. We see that God cares for the chosen people in a special way but does not neglect the others. There are other sheep that are not of this fold (see John 10:16).

GENESIS 37–40

Introduction to These Chapters

Chapters 37–50 form the last large section in the book of Genesis. This section is introduced as the story of the family of Jacob (Genesis 37:2), which continues the story left off in Genesis

COVENANT IN THE OLD TESTAMENT

In general, a covenant is a solemn promise between two partners that is sealed with an oath and/or symbolic action. The Old Testament speaks of different types of covenants, which vary according to the covenant partners and the types of promises made in the covenant agreement. In some cases, the covenant is between two individuals who pledge loyalty and friendship to one another (see, for example, 1 Samuel 18:3; 20:12-17) or who pledge to respect one another's territorial rights (see, for example, Genesis 21:22-24; 26:26-31). Leaders make covenants with groups of people who agree to carry out certain obligations (see, for example, Joshua 24:25; 2 Kings 11:4-8). Even the covenants that may be said to have such secular concerns, however, bind the partners in a sacred obligation because God is called as a witness to the promises made (as in Genesis 31:49-50).

The most important kind of covenant in the Old Testament is that made between God and individuals or between God and a group of people. These sacred covenants are the foundation upon which the community of faith was built. Though we may speak of *the* covenant, there are in fact many covenants made by God in the Old Testament. Each of these covenants was part of the larger covenant relationship that God established with the people of Israel. The primary expression of this covenant relationship is found in the Ten Commandments, but these commandments were only part of the whole covenant process. Beginning in Genesis, the Old Testament shows us how the covenant relationship between God and the chosen people began and how it developed over the centuries. The following Scriptures highlight this process of growth and change:

- Genesis 9:8-17—God makes a covenant with Noah on behalf of all the creatures of the earth for all time. God is responsible for keeping the covenant promises, and humankind has only to accept this gift and to remember and understand the meaning of the sign of the rainbow.
- Genesis 12:1-3—Though the word *covenant* is not used in this text, God and Abraham establish a relationship in which each has obligations to the other. These promises and obligations are for both the present and the future. God promises Abraham many descendants and great blessings. Abraham must respond with faith and obedience.
- Genesis 15:5-18—In this text we see how the covenant agreement between God and Abraham is formally ratified. Abraham provides the animals for sacrifice and responds in faith to God's promises. God promises Abraham an heir, many descendants, and a homeland.
- Genesis 17:1-14—Abraham receives the covenant promises on behalf of his descendants as God establishes an everlasting covenant with these future generations. God and people are forever bound to one another.
- Exodus 6:2-8—By the time of this Scripture, generations have passed in which Abraham's descendants have become slaves in Egypt, but God has not forgotten the covenant promises. The covenant relationship is renewed when God promises the people of Israel that "I will take you as my people, and I will be your God."
- Exodus 19:5-6; 20:1-17—God declares to Moses that the people of Israel are to be God's special possession or treasured possession. The covenant relationship between God and Israel involves responsibilities as well as privileges, however. For the people of God to keep the covenant means that they must live righteously before God and obey God's laws. The most distinctive expression of these laws is found in the Ten Commandments. These commandments define the responsibilities of the people toward God and toward one another.

COVENANT IN THE OLD TESTAMENT (CONT.)

- 2 Samuel 7—While the term *covenant* does not appear in this passage, the promises made by God to David are covenant-like. The language of covenant between God and David appears explicitly in 2 Samuel 23:5; Psalm 89:3-4, 28, 34; 2 Chronicles 21:7; and Jeremiah 33:19-26.
- Jeremiah 31:31-34—After many more generations have passed, God reveals to Jeremiah a new development in the covenant relationship. The covenant made in the time of Moses has been broken time and again by the people of Israel. They have worshiped other gods, have been false to one another, and have failed to trust in God. Thus, in future days God will make a new covenant with the chosen people that will be internal instead of external. The covenant laws will be part of their inward nature and not just an external code by which they live. The people's hearts, which are believed to be the wellsprings of human character, will be imprinted with the saving knowledge of God.

The Old Testament tells us that, in the beginning, God called one man and made a covenant with one man. Through Abraham's faith and God's steadfast love a community of faith was born. This community was and is a covenant community, for it was created by and is sustained by God's covenant. Though this covenant has changed through time to serve God's purposes, the basic promise remains the same: I will be their God, and they shall be my people.

35:29. Most of this history focuses on Joseph, the eldest son of Jacob and Rachel. Jacob's favoritism toward Joseph causes his brothers to become jealous, and this leads to Joseph being sold into slavery in Egypt. Through his natural abilities and God's providential care, Joseph survives and rises to a position of great power in Egypt. This position in turn leads to a reconciliation with his family and to their rescue from famine in Canaan.

Here is an outline of Genesis 37–40.

I. Joseph Sold into Slavery (37:1-36)
II. Judah and Tamar (38:1-30)
III. Joseph in Potiphar's Household (39:1-23)
IV. Joseph in Prison (40:1-23)

The Message of Genesis 37–40

The story of Joseph is like a short novel with elements of suspense, intrigue, misfortune, mystery, and love. We see the family of Jacob living in a very real world of family conflicts and natural calamities that dramatically affect their lives. Working in and through all of this, however, is the overriding purpose and will of God. What does Joseph's story tell us about God's activity in the world?

- The storyteller never lets the reader forget that God is the key player in all of this, even though God's presence is not always clearly seen.

- Human failings and frailties cannot be denied, but they do not determine the final outcome in the history of the covenant family.

- Like the stories of the patriarchs before it, the story of Joseph shows us the further working out of God's purposes in the world. Other people in the world who come in contact with the chosen people can be blessed by their presence.

```
          FAMILY TREE OF THE
       PATRIARCHS AND MATRIARCHS

                      TERAH
         ┌─────────────┼──────────────┐
     HARAN         MILCAH = NAHOR    SARAH = ABRAHAM = HAGAR
    ┌────┴───┐                       ┌───┴──┐    │
  ISCAH    LOT      SEVEN BROTHERS + BETHEL          ISHMAEL
         ┌───┴───┐                 ┌────┴───┐
       MOAB   AMMON   LABAN    REBEKAH   =   ISAAC
              ┌───┴───┐              │
            LEAH   RACHEL            │
                          ┌──────────┴────┐
                    JACOB = LEAH        ESAU
                          REUBEN
                          SIMEON
                          ISSACHAR
                          ZEBULUN
                          LEVI
                          JUDAH
                        = ZILPAH
                          GAD
                          ASHER
                        = BILHA
                          DAN
                          NAPHTALI
                        = RACHEL
                          BENJAMIN
                          JOSEPH
                      ┌──────┴──────┐
                   EPHRAIM     MANASSEH
```

GENESIS 41–43

Introduction to These Chapters

In these chapters Joseph rises to a position of great power in Egypt and comes in contact with his family once again.

These three chapters may be outlined as follows.

I. Joseph Interprets Pharaoh's Dreams (41:1-57)

II. Joseph's Brothers Come to Egypt (42:1-38)

III. Joseph's Brothers Return to Egypt (43:1-34)

The Message of Genesis 41–43

The story of Joseph shows us human nature both at its best and at its worst. We are not given an idealized picture of the covenant family but are allowed to see them as people of the real world who are sometimes caught in difficult circumstances and who are sometimes at odds with one another. The most important thing about them, however, is their relationship with God, and how they live within that relationship. This relationship is not always as smooth or as strong as it could be, however. What does this story tell us about their feelings and actions toward one another and about their personal relationship to God?

- Joseph is wise and discerning but also manipulative and deceptive. At times he is overcome by feelings of both joy and anxiety. Above all, he is open to God's revelation.

- Joseph's brothers are jealous, angry, heartless, and deceptive. Later they are stricken with guilt and believe that God's judgment has finally caught up with them. Even in the midst of this situation, however, they can find reasons to be merry.

- Jacob is fearful and resigned to grief, though later he has reason to rejoice.

This story thus reveals the strong and often conflicting emotions that influence the lives of Jacob and his sons. How does God work into all this?

- God works through people, through their weaknesses as well as their strengths, to accomplish God's divine purposes for the world.

- God is greater than the strongest earthly power.

- God rules the natural world.

- God's wisdom is available to human beings who are open and responsive.

- God's wisdom and power are greater than any human wisdom or power.

GENESIS 44–47

Introduction to These Chapters

In these chapters, Joseph is finally reconciled with his brothers and is reunited with his father, Jacob.

Here is an outline of Genesis 44–47.

I. The Final Test of Joseph's Brothers (44:1-34)
II. Reconciliation (45:1-28)
III. Jacob's Migration to Egypt (46:1-34)
IV. The Family of Jacob Prospers in Egypt (47:1-26)
V. The Death of Jacob (47:27-31)

The Message of Genesis 44–47

Sometimes even those people who are in relationship with God cannot immediately see the ways of God in everything that happens to them. In Joseph's case, it took years for him to understand the full significance of his slavery and exile from his family. With the coming of his brothers to Egypt, he finally saw how God's purposes were being fulfilled in his life. What does Joseph's life tell us about God's purposes and how they are fulfilled?

- God's purposes in the world are saving purposes.

- God can bring good out of evil, life out of death.

- God works through people to accomplish these purposes.

- The covenant family has been chosen to play a special role in God's plan for the world. In this case, Joseph saves the lives of not only his family but of thousands of other people as well.

- God's saving purposes include not only spiritual necessities (an abiding relationship with God Almighty) but physical necessities as well (food, water, and a safe place to live).

- God's purposes for the covenant family do not end in Egypt. Many survivors will bear God's promises and purposes into the future.

GENESIS 48–50

Introduction to These Chapters

The book of Genesis ends with the deaths of Jacob and Joseph. In these three chapters, relationships among the members of the covenant family are defined and future roles are revealed. All of this looks toward the future, toward the day when the family of Jacob will leave Egypt as a great multitude of people and will establish themselves in the Promised Land.

Here is an outline of chapters 48–50.

I. Jacob Adopts and Blesses Joseph's Sons (48:1-22)
II. Jacob's Farewell Address (49:1-33)
III. The Burial of Jacob (50:1-21)
IV. The Death of Joseph (50:22-26)

The Message of Genesis 48–50

Joseph testifies about the power of God's presence in his life and in the world at large (see Genesis 50:20). This testimony is the fundamental message of the story of Joseph and of the book of Genesis as a whole. Thus Joseph tells us that God plans good for the world, even in the face of human evil. What do Joseph and Genesis tell us about this good?

- The goodness and blessings of God are built into creation (see, for example, Genesis 1:1).

- God remains faithful to the ancient covenant promises, which are passed from one generation of the covenant family to the next (see Genesis 50:24).

- God brings good out of evil and brings life out of death (see, for example, Genesis 21:5-7; also Psalm 40:5, 17; Romans 8:28).

- God uses people to help bring about good in the world (see, for example, Genesis 12:1-3; 45:5). This good is part of the fulfillment of God's ultimate purposes for creation and for the community of faith.

CONCLUSION TO GENESIS

The book of Genesis shows us that the earth and its creatures exist because of the will and power of God. Likewise, Genesis tells us that the community of faith was born because God desired to have a people with whom to dwell in a mutually fulfilling relationship. This community began when Abraham answered God's call to journey to a new land and to live in a faithful relationship with God (see Genesis 12:1-4). God made a covenant with Abraham (see Genesis 15:1) to establish this special relationship. The covenant promises were not just for Abraham, however, because God renewed the covenant with Isaac (see Genesis 26:1-5) and with Jacob (see Genesis 28:10-17). The covenant was for both the present and the future, and it was not just for one person but for a whole people. The promises and responsibilities of the covenant were carried forward by each succeeding generation. Abraham was but one man, but through him God sought and eventually gained a faithful community with whom to abide.

The covenant is the foundation of the relationship between God and the community of faith, both in the past and in the present. It is important, then, to understand what the covenant is, how it began, and how it developed in the Old Testament.

EXODUS

OUTLINE OF EXODUS

I. Early Life and Call of Moses (1:1–4:31)
  A. The rise of Egyptian oppression (1:1-22)
  B. The birth and development of Moses (2:1-22)
  C. The call of Moses (2:23–4:17)
  D. Moses returns to Egypt (4:18-31)

II. Moses, Aaron, and Pharaoh (5:1–7:7)
  A. Moses and Aaron meet Pharaoh (5:1-9)
  B. The effects of Pharaoh's response (5:10-21)
  C. God reassures Moses (5:22–6:13)
  D. Genealogy of Israel (6:14-27)
  E. Call of Moses and Aaron summarized (6:28–7:7)

III. The Plagues and the Passover (7:8–12:36)
  A. God's contest with Pharaoh (7:8–11:10)
  B. Preparation for the Exodus (12:1-36)

IV. Beginning of the Exodus (12:37–15:21)
  A. The departure (12:37-42)
  B. Rules relating to the Exodus (12:43–13:16)

  C. Journey through the Red Sea (13:17–15:21)

V. In the Wilderness (15:22–18:27)
  A. God's provisions in the wilderness (15:22–17:7)
  B. Conflict with the Amalekites (17:8-16)
  C. Jethro's visit (18:1-27)

VI. Establishing a Covenant (19:1–24:11)
  A. Moses and Israel before God (19:1-25)
  B. The Ten Commandments (20:1-17)
  C. Moses the mediator (20:18-21)
  D. Laws of the covenant (20:22–23:19)
  E. Closing exhortations (23:20-33)
  F. The covenant enacted (24:1-11)

VII. Moses Receives God's Directives (24:12–27:19)
  A. Moses and God (24:12-18)
  B. Planning the tabernacle (25:1–27:19)

VIII. Instructions for the Tabernacle (27:20–31:18)
  A. Oil for the eternal lamp (27:20-21)
  B. The priestly garments (28:1-43)
  C. Ordaining the priests and altar (29:1-37)
  D. Establishing the tabernacle service (29:38–31:18)

IX. Breaking and Renewal of the Covenant (32:1–34:35)
A. The golden calf (32:1-35)
B. Moses receives reassurance (33:1-23)
C. Moses returns to the mountain (34:1-35)

X. Construction of the Tabernacle (35:1–40:38)
A. Assembling men and materials (35:1–36:7)
B. Constructing the various parts (36:8–39:31)
C. Inspection and approval (39:32-43)
D. Construction and consecration (40:1-33)
E. God's acceptance and residence (40:34-38)

INTRODUCTION

Historical Background

The book of Exodus concerns events in the history of the people of Israel that likely took place sometime between 1450 and 1200 B.C. The events follow the Genesis account of the entry of Jacob (Israel) and his descendants into Egypt.

Hundreds of years after Jacob entered Egypt, his descendants had been enslaved. Exodus is the story of how these enslaved people were delivered from the Egyptian bondage. Deliverance was not accomplished by the power of human beings. It was the result of the hand of God in the affairs of humankind. It involved confrontation between the God of the Hebrews and the ruler of Egypt, the pharaoh. The confrontation ended in a dramatic defeat for Pharaoh.

The story also involves the development of a special relationship between God and the children of Israel. This relationship is based on a mutual agreement called a covenant. As a result of the establishment of the covenant, the book closes with God coming to dwell among the slaves who have been freed.

The Name of the Book

Exodus means "the going out." The English word comes from the name for the book in the Greek translation called, the Septuagint. The Hebrew title is *Shemot*, meaning "names." It is taken from the first phrase in the book, "These are the names of." Naming books in this way was a common ancient practice.

The Literary History of the Book

Traditionally, the book was considered a single work written by Moses. A careful analysis has led many scholars to observe differing elements in Exodus which they attribute to several sources: J (Yahwist), E (Elohist), and D (Deuteronomist). It is believed that these were finally combined by P (Priestly writer) during the Babylonian exile. A base of Mosaic material underlies these sources.

The Content of the Book

Chapters 1–5: The book of Exodus opens with the descendants of the twelve sons of Jacob enslaved in Egypt. Pharaoh orders that all Hebrew male children shall be slain at birth. Moses is born and concealed. He is set adrift on a river and is found by the daughter of Pharaoh. The princess has him brought up in the royal court.

As a young man Moses, seeing an Egyptian smiting a Hebrew, kills the Egyptian. He flees for his life to Midian in the Sinai wilderness. There he meets and marries Zipporah, the daughter of a Midianite priest named Jethro. As Moses tends Jethro's flock, God appears to him in a burning bush on Mount Horeb. God commissions Moses to deliver Israel. Moses is reluctant to accept the commission. God gives Moses confirmatory signs: God changes the rod of Moses into a serpent, then back to a rod; God makes Moses' hand leprous, then cures it.

Aaron, Moses' brother, is appointed first assistant. Moses and Aaron, in the name of God, ask Pharaoh to permit the people to go into the wilderness for three days to hold a sacrificial feast to their God. Pharaoh refuses, then increases the burdens of the Israelites.

Chapters 6–10: There follows now a series of plagues. At the height of each plague, Pharaoh promises to let the people go. As soon as the plague ends, he refuses to honor his pledge. The following are the ten plagues: water turned to blood, plague of frogs, of gnats, of flies, of fatally diseased livestock, of boils, of hail, of locusts, of thick darkness, and the slaying of the firstborn.

Chapters 11–15: As the angel of death passes through Egypt slaying the firstborn, the Hebrew slaves make a hasty departure. At this point, the P author institutes the festival of the Passover and gives directions for its observance. Led by God, who appears to them in a pillar of cloud by day and in a pillar of fire by night, the Israelites proceed to the Red Sea. Pharaoh pursues and the Israelites murmur against Moses. At this point, God intervenes. The waters of the Red Sea are parted, the Israelites cross over in safety, and the host of the Egyptians is drowned.

The journey from the sea to Mount Sinai follows. It is a series of crises. The people of Israel are unable to drink the bitter waters of Marah, and in their thirst they again murmur against Moses. Moses casts a tree into the waters, and the waters are made sweet.

Chapters 16–19: The Israelites now wander through the wilderness of Sin. The people complain of lack of food. God sends quails and manna daily to feed the people. On the sixth day of the week they gather a double portion, for on the seventh day there is to be no gathering.

From the wilderness of Sin, the Israelites proceed to Rephidim, where there is a lack of water. The people complain. Moses strikes the rock and abundant water flows.

The Israelites are attacked in Rephidim by Amalek. Moses, meanwhile, ascends a hill. As long as he holds aloft his hand, Israel prevails; and when he lets his hand down, Amalek prevails. Aaron and Hur hold Moses' hand up until Joshua completely routs Amalek.

Jethro, Moses' father-in-law, comes to visit him. He finds that all of Moses' time is consumed in acting as judge in all kinds of petty disputes. He counsels Moses to appoint a minor judiciary to settle unimportant cases, and himself to judge only the most important.

From Rephidim, the Israelites proceed to the Wilderness of Sinai, where they encamp before the mountain. Moses meets God on the mountain. Through Moses, God commands the people to obey. If they do so, they will prosper. They agree to do so. With Mount Sinai in a state of volcanic eruption, with the people warned not to approach the mountain lest they be destroyed by God, Moses ascends the mountain for secret conversation with God.

Chapter 20:1-20: The Ten Commandments. Some biblical scholars believe the commandments were first written down during the time of David. However, Egypt, the land where Moses lived, was a world acquainted with writing. The moral intensity and the spirit, if not the actual form, certainly go back to a period much before the Israelite monarchy.

The germ of this morality goes back to the Mosaic period.

Chapters 20:21–23:19: The Covenant Code. This code is divisible as follows: 20:21-26, guidelines for worship; 21:1-11, rules about mundane issues of everyday life; 21:12-17, laws involving the death penalty; 21:18-27, laws about violent assault; 21:28–22:4, laws about livestock; 22:5-17, laws about restitution; 22:18-31, miscellaneous laws; 23:1-9, laws safeguarding justice; 23:10-19, sabbath, sabbatical year, and annual festivals.

Chapter 24: Sacrifices are made to God. The covenant is read to the people by Moses. They promise obedience. Moses ascends the mountain a second time, this time for forty days.

Chapters 25–31: This section is surely the work of P. It contains technical instructions regarding the building of the ark, table of showbread (bread of Presence), and lampstand, the curtains of the tabernacle, its boards and bars, the veil, the screen, the altar of burnt offering, and the perpetual lamp. Aaron and his sons are appointed priests. A description is given of their priestly garments. God gives Moses the two stone tablets.

Chapters 32–34: While Moses is on the mountain, the people begin to murmur. Aaron makes them a golden calf to which they offer sacrifices. God is very angry, and is placated by Moses. When Moses comes down from the mountain, he breaks the tablets, destroys the golden calf, strews it upon the water, and makes the people drink it. The sons of Levi put to death the apostates.

God tells the people to march on and behave. God withdraws from among the people, but when Moses remonstrates, God returns. Moses again ascends Mount Sinai and the two tablets are renewed.

Chapters 35–40: When Moses comes down from the mountain, he transmits to the people the instructions of God regarding the building of the ark. The people all contribute gifts to carry out this project. There follows now a detailed description of the building of the ark of the covenant and the tabernacle (the tent of meeting), curtains, veil and screen, boards and bars, lampstand, and so forth. This description of the building of the ark and tabernacle corresponds to the instructions given in chapters 25 through 31.

In chapter 40, the work is completed. A cloud covers the tent of meeting and the glory of God fills the tabernacle. When the cloud is taken up, the Israelites march on; when it abides over the tent, they pause.

What the Book of Exodus Teaches

The book of Exodus teaches that by the victory over Pharaoh, the God of the Hebrews was shown to be indeed the God of all heaven and earth, and the great lover of the chosen people Israel. Having delivered them from bondage, God providentially supplied their physical needs. And God gave them guidelines for living that would allow them to exist forever in a special relationship of covenantal love.

The core of the covenant, the Ten Commandments, was summed up by Jesus as love for God and love for one's neighbor (Matthew 22:37-40). The theme of deliverance from slavery permeates the New Testament. The deliverance, however, is from spiritual bondage.

The theme of the presence of God based on a covenant relationship is also carried into the New Testament. A new covenant is established by the atoning sacrifice of Christ. People are able to have fellowship with God and to experience God's abiding presence because they have been purified by the blood of Christ. They thereby become "a chosen people, a royal priesthood, a holy nation, a people belonging to God, that you may declare the praises of him who called you out of darkness into his wonderful light" (1 Peter 2:9, NIV).

EXODUS 1–4

Introduction to These Chapters

Chapters 1–4 serve several purposes in the story of the Exodus. Chapter 1 provides a direct connection with Genesis 46–50. The chapter also explains why Egypt began to oppress the people of Israel. Chapter 2 narrates the early life of Moses in Egypt. Moses would have remained in Egypt except for the initiative of God.

Chapter 3 records the call of God to Moses. Chapter 4 records the two signs given to Moses. It also explains how Aaron, Moses' brother, became his spokesman. The section closes with the account of Moses' meeting with Aaron and their journey back to Egypt.

Here is an outline of chapters 1–4.

I. The Rise of Egyptian Oppression (1:1-22)
- A. The cause of the oppression (1:1-7)
- B. The nature of the oppression (1:8-14)
- C. The background for Moses' birth (1:15-22)

II. The Birth and Development of Moses (2:1-22)
- A. Birth and infancy (2:1-10)
- B. A youth sensitive to oppression (2:11-15a)
- C. A sojourner in a foreign land (2:15b-22)

III. The Call of Moses (2:23–4:17)
- A. Activity on earth and in heaven (2:23-25)
- B. Moses meets God at Horeb (2:26–3:22)
- C. God equips Moses for service (4:1-17)

IV. Moses Returns to Egypt (4:18-31)

The Message of Exodus 1–4

The beginning of any book is important for understanding everything that follows. This is especially true of the books in our Bible, for they were written by Spirit-inspired authors.

While Exodus is a book by itself, it is also a part of a larger work—the Pentateuch (the first five books of the Old Testament). The opening section reaches back to connect the reader with the story of Jacob's family and their entrance into Egypt. It also looks forward to the Exodus under Moses' leadership and the establishment of the covenant at Mount Sinai. Entwined in the story are truths about God and God's relationship to the people.

- God's ways are not human ways.

- God is aware of oppressors and the oppressed, although the oppressed are often unaware of God's activities.

- God may call and equip particular people to serve in special ways.

- God may provide signs to confirm divine activity, but words are God's basic means of communicating with the chosen people.

- God may provide a helper for a servant, to cover a lack of ability or confidence.

- Difficulties and hardships in life may be the preparation for greater service to God later on.

- When God acts on behalf of the people, it is proper to honor God with worship.

EXODUS 5:1–7:7

Introduction to These Chapters

In this section three important events occur: (1) Moses and Aaron first meet Pharaoh; (2) Pharaoh first receives God's demands through God's spokesmen; and (3) Moses and Aaron realize that their God-given task will be difficult from the very beginning.

This section also contains a selective genealogy. It locates Moses and Aaron in the stream of the national history, as members of the tribe of Levi. The tribe of Levi was the very one chosen by God to be the spiritual leaders of the nation.

Here is an outline of these chapters.

I. Moses and Aaron Meet Pharaoh (5:1-9)
II. The Effects of Pharaoh's Response (5:10-21)
III. God Reassures Moses (5:22–6:13)
IV. Genealogy of Israel (6:14-27)
V. Call of Moses and Aaron Summarized (6:28–7:7)

The Message of Exodus 5:1–7:7

This section shows God's faithfulness to the people. God is steadfast of purpose and will bring those plans to success. But God's will is hampered by the attitudes of various individuals and groups. Even those God is determined to help do not understand God's ways.

What do these events suggest about God and people?

- The Lord has a genuine concern for the oppressed, and God's power to save is boundless.

- Human resolve, like Pharaoh's, may stand directly opposed to the resolve of the Lord.

- Human inconsistency contrasts with the consistency of God. Human praise easily turns to criticism and complaint, not because God is not at work but because things do not proceed the way people had expected.

- God's leaders can be badly affected by the complaints of those they are trying to help.

- The cure for despair in God's servant is to remember that God's purposes will be fulfilled even though the time may be long until they are accomplished.

EXODUS 7:8–12:36

Introduction to These Chapters

This part of Exodus records the dramatic contest between Pharaoh (and the gods of Egypt) and the Lord God. God's servant Moses is Pharaoh's visible opponent. Behind the scenes is the invisible but all-powerful Lord.

The confrontation between Egypt's ruler and Israel's God begins with an account of miracles performed by Moses. These fail to convince Pharaoh of the gravity of his situation. So God begins to afflict Egypt with the ten plagues. During the first nine plagues Pharaoh refuses to let the people of Israel go. His refusal sets the stage for the last of the plagues, the death of the firstborn.

To commemorate the great tenth plague and the Exodus that follows, God orders the Hebrews to institute the Passover service, and to consider the month of their deliverance as the first month of their year.

Here is an outline of chapters 7:8–12:36.

I. God's Contest with Pharaoh (7:8–11:10)
  A. Miracles of Moses (7:8-13)
  B. The ten plagues (7:14–11:10)
    1. Water turned to blood (7:14-24)

2. Frogs (7:25–8:15)
3. Gnats (8:16-19)
4. Flies (8:20-32)
5. Livestock epidemic (9:1-7)
6. Boils (9:8-12)
7. Hailstorm (9:13-35)
8. Locusts (10:1-20)
9. Darkness (10:21-29)
10. Warning of the final plague (11:1-10)
II. Preparation for the Exodus (12:1-36)
  A. The Passover established (12:1-28)
  B. The death of the firstborn (12:29-36)

The Message of Exodus 7:8–12:36

The struggle between Pharaoh and the God of the Hebrews is a story more of calamity than of hope. It contains many sobering spiritual lessons. It also provides encouragement for the disadvantaged and exploited. Consider the following.

- Different people respond in different ways to the evidence of divine power that God provides.

- God possesses ultimate power over nature and human life.

- One's choices may affect many other people.

- God often sends warning of imminent danger so those who will heed the warning may escape disaster.

- The stubbornness of the wicked highlights God's patience and the fairness of God's judgments.

- Sometimes a cry of apparent penitence comes not from regret of wrongdoing, but from fear of punishment.

EXODUS 12:37–15:21

Introduction to These Chapters

This section provides a transition from the Israelite sojourn in Egypt to the wilderness sojourn, from Egyptian bondage to desert wandering. It opens with the departure of the Israelites from the land of Goshen.

Chapter 13 opens with a further emphasis on the Passover. Then the story continues into chapter 14. The route of the Exodus before the crossing of the Red Sea is traced. And the pursuit of the Egyptian army is detailed. The crisis of the approaching Egyptians is solved with the parting of the waters and the crossing of the sea. Egypt's utter defeat follows, as the waters roll over them.

With Israel safe on the far side and the pursuing army destroyed, the song of victory sung on the shore of the sea is recorded in chapter 15.

Here is an outline of Exodus 12:37–15:21.

I. The Departure (12:37-42)
II. Rules Relating to the Exodus (12:43–13:16)
  A. Rules for the Passover (12:43–13:2)
  B. The feast of Unleavened Bread (13:3-10)
  C. Rules relating to the firstborn (13:11-16)
III. Journey Through the Red Sea (13:17–15:21)
  A. Assurance of God's leading (13:17–14:4)
  B. Pharaoh's pursuit (14:5-18)
  C. God's deliverance (14:19-30)
  D. The victory song (15:1-21)

The Message of Exodus 12:37–15:21

The memorials instituted at the Exodus, the way of God's leading, and the theme of Israel's rejoicing also provide instructive

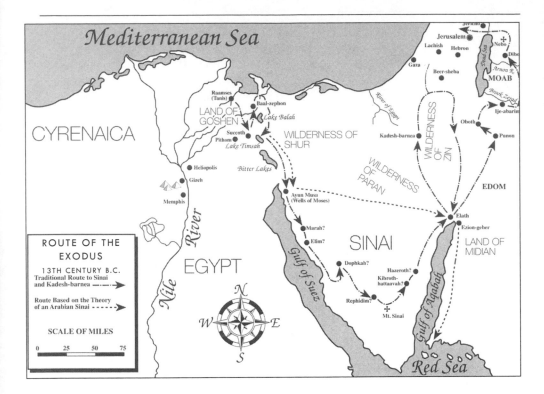

Route of the Exodus map showing the Mediterranean Sea, Cyrenaica, Egypt, Land of Goshen, Wilderness of Shur, Sinai, Land of Midian, Edom, Moab, and the Red Sea with marked locations including Raamses (Tanis), Baal-zephon, Succoth, Pithom, Heliopolis, Gizeh, Memphis, Ayun Musa (Wells of Moses), Marah?, Elim?, Dophkah?, Rephidim?, Mt. Sinai, Hazeroth?, Kibroth-hattaavah?, Kadesh-barnea, Elath, Ezion-geber, Punon, Oboth, Ije-abarim, Nebo, Jerusalem, Jericho, Lachish, Hebron, Gaza, Beer-sheba.

ROUTE OF THE EXODUS

13TH CENTURY B.C.
Traditional Route to Sinai
and Kadesh-barnea

Route Based on the Theory
of an Arabian Sinai

SCALE OF MILES

0   25   50   75

lessons. Consider the following ideas reflected by this section.

- The meaning of religious celebration must never be subordinated to its ritual.

- God's people should ever remember, as nations, as families, and as individuals, the debt of gratitude that is owed to God.

- God can turn our limited material resources into the celebration of God's power if we choose to submit to God's will.

- God always leads us as we would choose to be led if at the beginning we could see the end of the road along which we were being led.

- As with Pharaoh, people sometimes learn sobering lessons from life only

to forget them and return to greater presumption.

- Fear of tomorrow involves a lack of confidence in the God of yesterday.

- There are no insurmountable obstacles or impassable barriers with God.

- It is appropriate to show respect for God's appointed workers on earth.

- True appreciation for God's blessings shows in selfless praise to God.

EXODUS 15:22–18:27

Introduction to These Chapters

After the triumph at the sea, the newly freed slaves and Moses, their leader, travel on into the wilderness. The journey is difficult. It is to lead to Mount Sinai, but along the way they face several crises. In each crisis, God provides for their needs, but it is a time of testing.

Chapter 15 records the crisis over water at Marah. Chapter 16 reports the problem of adequate food. At Rephidim, water is once again a problem, and here they fight with the Amalekites (chapter 17). Even the problem of overwork confronts Moses, who receives helpful advice on a solution from his father-in-law. Their meeting is recorded in chapter 18.

Here is an outline of Exodus 15:22–18:27.

I. God's Provisions in the Wilderness (15:22–17:7)
   A. Water in the wilderness (15:22-27)
   B. Food in the wilderness (16:1-36)
   C. Water from the rock (17:1-7)
II. Conflict with the Amalekites (17:8-16)
III. Jethro's Visit (18:1-27)

The Message of Exodus 15:22–18:27

This part of the book of Exodus charts the descent of the people of Israel from the mountaintop through the valley. The excitement and exaltation of being saved from the Egyptian army soon gave way to the harsh realities of wilderness existence. Words of praise turned to muttering and murmuring.

Difficult as the journey to Mount Sinai was, however, there were compensations. An oasis here and there made the journey bearable. Victory over a nomadic enemy raised spirits. And the visit of a man well acquainted with life in the desert brought advice certain to make easier the daily life of the people. These experiences of the people of Israel suggest the following truths for people today.

- Followers of the Lord can expect both mountaintops and valleys of experience in life.

- It is better to trust God in difficult circumstances than to test God.

- Oases of serenity, like the palm trees and still waters of Elim, restore the soul.

- Leaders, particularly spiritual leaders, need all the support and good advice that they can get.

- Fellowship with others of kindred spirit brings joy and blessings to those who share it.

EXODUS 19:1–24:11

Introduction to These Chapters

This part of the book of Exodus contains the very heart of the Old Testament. Exodus 19–20 describes the establishment of a covenant between the Lord and Israel. Through Moses, God has led to the foot of the holy mountain the company of slaves who were so miraculously freed from Egyptian bondage. God's purpose is to establish a covenant, a special relationship with them. And both God and the people are free to choose whether or not to enter into it.

The heart of this covenant is the Ten Commandments (also known as the Decalogue). The Ten Commandments are the basis for relationships among the people of Israel. These include their relationships with God and with one another.

However, specific rules and laws are necessary for a nation. These are provided in chapters 21–23. They are like an appendix to the Decalogue. They are followed in chapter 24 by the report of the acceptance of God's covenant by the people of Israel.

Here is an outline of Exodus 19:1–24:11.

I. Moses and Israel Before God (19:1-25)

II. The Ten Commandments (20:1-17)

III. Moses the Mediator (20:18-21)

IV. Laws of the Covenant (20:22–23:19)
   A. Concerning the altar (20:22-26)

NUMBERING OF THE COMMANDMENTS IN EXODUS 20

There are considerable differences among various Christian denominations and Jews about how to number the Commandments. That is because there are features of the text that permit or tend toward different numberings. For example, what some traditions call the Prologue is seen as the First Commandment in the Jewish tradition. That seems less strange when one realizes that the actual title for the Commandments is "the ten words," and the first word God speaks is "I am the Lord your God. . . ." Such a numeration serves to place greater weight on the opening sentence as the beginning and foundation of what follows.

In some numberings no separation is made between not worshiping other gods and not making or worshiping idols. These may be understood as distinctive and separate prohibitions, but the plural "them" in the sentence "You shall not bow down to them . . ." syntactically can only refer back to the "other gods" of the First Commandment. Elsewhere the reference to bowing down and worshiping regularly refers to "other gods," not images (see below).

Finally, one has to ask how it is possible to end up with ten commandments if the prohibitions against having other gods and making and worshiping images are construed as one. A count often is usually accomplished by noting that in the Deuteronomic version, the conjunction "and" or "neither," which is used to separate each of the commandments of the second table, occurs between the two prohibitions against coveting (Deut 5:21a and 21b), suggesting that these are to be regarded as two separate commandments.

Commandment	Denomination			
	Jewish	Anglican, Reformed, and other Christian	Orthodox	Catholic, Lutheran
I am the Lord your God	1	preface	1	1
You shall have no other gods before me	2	1		
You shall not make for yourself an idol		2	2	
You shall not make wrongful use of the name of the Lord your God	3	3	3	2
Remember the Sabbath and keep it holy	4	4	4	3
Honor your father and your mother	5	5	5	4
You shall not murder (or kill)	6	6	6	5
You shall not commit adultery	7	7	7	6
You shall not steal	8	8	8	7
You shall not bear false witness against your neighbor	9	9	9	8
You shall not covet your neighbor's wife	10	10	10	9
You shall not covet anything that belongs to your neighbor				10

B. Concerning slaves (21:1-11)
C. Concerning offenses (21:12-17)
D. Concerning bodily injuries (21:18-36)
E. Concerning property damage (22:1-17)
F. Miscellaneous laws (22:18-31)
G. Concerning ethical behavior (23:1-9)
H. Concerning the religious calendar (23:10-19)
V. Closing Exhortations (23:20-33)
VI. The Covenant Enacted (24:1-11)

The Message of Exodus 19:1–24:11

The experiences of the Israelites in these chapters are overwhelming to consider. The presence of God was beyond human language to describe. The sights and sounds that attended God's theophany (appearance or manifestation) would strike fear in any person of any age. And the transition from being abject slaves to chosen people by means of the covenant must have been almost beyond comprehension. But the book of the covenant has the ring of the normal world.

From their experiences the following observations may be made.

- God's spiritual laws are not instruments of slavery, but the constitution of freedom.

- God's ideals for the chosen people transcend their highest thoughts.

- Holy living encompasses every aspect of human behavior.

- God's compassion is to be reflected by the chosen people.

EXODUS 24:12–27:19

Introduction to These Chapters

The events at the mountain continue in this part of the book of Exodus. After the elders of Israel commune and feast on the mountainside, God calls Moses up the mountain to receive a copy of the Ten Commandments. Joshua, his aide, accompanies him. Aaron and Hur remain behind in charge of the people.

Moses spends forty days within the cloud of glory at the top of the mountain. On the mountain he receives the tables of stone on which the Ten Commandments are inscribed. He also receives instructions on how to construct and furnish the tent, or tabernacle. This structure is called a sanctuary. In it the priests are to present sacrifices and offerings to God. It is also to be God's house, so that God can dwell in the midst of the people of Israel. In chapters 25–27, specific plans for the structure are given to Moses.

Here is an outline of Exodus 24:12–27:19.

I. Moses and God (24:12-18)
II. Planning the Tabernacle (25:1–27:19)
A. Acquiring the materials (25:1-9)
B. The tent and its furnishings (25:10–26:37)
C. The courtyard of the tabernacle (27:1-19)

The Message of Exodus 24:12–27:19

This part of Exodus begins with the announcement to Moses that God will give the tablets of stone to him on the holy mountain. The tablets are to be kept as a precious possession by the people of Israel. A place is needed in which to keep them.

The ark is to be the box for safekeeping the tablets. But the ark needs a place in

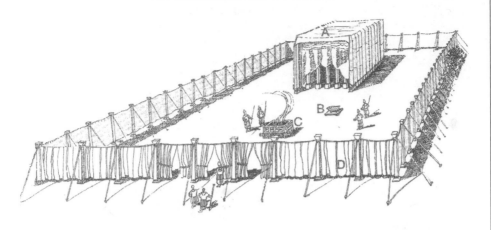

THE TABERNACLE AND ITS COURTS

A. THE TABERNACLE
B. BRONZE LAVER
C. ALTAR OF BURNT OFFERINGS
D. LINEN CURTAINS SURROUNDING THE COURTYARD

which to be kept. Since God intends to dwell among the people, and needs a tent, the ark will be kept in it. Not only does the ark contain God's revealed law and commandments, God intends to speak with Moses from above it. Further, the lid of the ark becomes the mercy seat, where atonement can be realized.

So God's tabernacle and its courtyard are planned for several of God's purposes, all for the good of the chosen people. From this section we can see that:

- God is constant. The tables of stone convey the sense of permanence.

- Even physical structures can witness to the glory of God.

- God desires offerings freely given to advance the Kingdom.

- God is honored by works of artistic

precision and beauty created for God's glory.

- It is better to follow God's pattern than to serve personal whim or convenience.

EXODUS 27:20–31:18

Introduction to These Chapters

In this section of the book of Exodus, God continues to instruct Moses on the establishment of the sanctuary. First the tending of the lamps is mentioned. Then the appearance of the priests' garments is described in careful detail. They are all to be distinctly beautiful, but the garments of the high priest are to be extra special. They are to reflect the holy office Aaron will fill, bearing the spiritual responsibility for the whole congregation.

Moses also receives directions on ordination procedures. The priests are to be sanctified, as well as the altar of burnt offering.

Two altars are used in the tabernacle service, so they are described next. The first is an altar of burnt offering for sacrifices, to be set in the courtyard of the tabernacle. The other is the altar of incense, to be placed within the tent. Only a certain incense is to be burned on it, so the recipe for it is given in this section.

Since these instructions deal with the plans for the tabernacle, Moses is told how to finance its maintenance. The funds needed are to come through a half-shekel tax on adult men.

Water for ceremonial washings is also needed, so Moses is given directions for a laver. The recipes for anointing oil and incense are given next. The craftsmen who are to see to all the preparations of God's tent are named.

Then, near the end of this section, God repeats the command to keep the sabbath. God ends the revelation by presenting to Moses the two tables of the testimony.

Here is an outline of Exodus 27:20–31:18.

I. Oil for the Eternal Lamp (27:20-21)
II. The Priestly Garments (28:1-43)
III. Ordaining the Priests and Altar (29:1-37)
   A. Ordaining the priests (29:1-36a)
   B. Consecrating the altar (29:36b-37)
IV. Establishing the Tabernacle Service (29:38–31:18)
   A. The set daily sacrifices (29:38-46)
   B. The altar of incense (30:1-10)
   C. The sanctuary tax (30:11-16)
   D. The laver (30:17-21)
   E. The sacred anointing oil (30:22-33)
   F. The special incense (30:34-38)
   G. The craftsmen selected (31:1-11)
   H. Observe the seventh day (31:12-17)
   I. The end of the instructions (31:18)

The Message of Exodus 27:20–31:18

Eventually God finishes this revelation. The next step is to bring the message down from the mountaintop of inspiration into the valley of application where the people are. The message is God's; Moses is the medium for the message. From this section these truths emerge:

- God offers the people the opportunity to give the best that they own to God's work.

- Continually burning lamps and ever-ascending incense suggest that God welcomes constant offerings of praise and gratitude.

- Daily morning and evening sacrifices speak of the regularity of devotion to God.

- The difference between sacred and secular should be respected.

- No person is superior to any other in the sight of God.

- When God calls individuals to serve, God also gives them the qualifications to serve.

EXODUS 32–34

Introduction to These Chapters

This part of Exodus records Israel's breaking of the covenant by making the golden calf, and the renewal of the covenant. The incident of the golden calf begins even as Moses talks with God on the mountaintop.

Here is an outline for Exodus 32–34.

I. The Golden Calf (32:1-35)
   A. The making of the calf (32:1-6)
   B. Dialogue between the Lord and Moses (32:7-14)
   C. Moses back in the camp (32:15-35)
II. Moses Receives Reassurance (33:1-23)
   A. The people's reaction (33:1-6)
   B. Moses meets with the Lord (33:7-23)
III. Moses Returns to the Mountain (34:1-35)
   A. The Lord is revealed to Moses (34:1-9)
   B. God's promises (34:10-11)
   C. God's commandments (34:12-28)
   D. Moses reflects God's glory (34:29-35)

The Message of Exodus 32–34

This section of the book of Exodus illustrates human tendencies to sin and the divine inclination to forgive. Impatient people fall easily into ungodly behavior. God abhors rebellion among the people, but can be touched with sincere repentance that leads to reconciliation.

- Patience is an essential virtue for God's people.

- Sometimes outrage is an appropriate reaction to idolatrous and immoral behavior.

- Sometimes wayward people need an intercessor, a go-between, who is willing to put life and reputation on the line in order to bring reconciliation.

- Ruptured relations can be restored when the basis for renewed relationships is spelled out.

- Our relationship to God should show on our face and be revealed in our actions.

- If we are enticed by something that will threaten our relationship with the Lord, we must do away with it.

- Good leadership is better than good excuses.

EXODUS 35–40

Introduction to These Chapters

This final section of the book of Exodus describes the construction of the tabernacle according to the instructions given to Moses on Mount Sinai (Exodus 25:1–31:11). Two men, Bezalel and Oholiab, lead out in the work God has outlined. They give keen attention to every detail. When they are through Moses examines every item to be sure it is properly done. He commends the workers and erects the tabernacle, which is then filled with the glory of God's presence.

Here is an outline for Exodus 35–40.

I. Assembling Men and Materials (35:1–36:7)
II. Constructing the Various Parts (36:8–39:31)
III. Inspection and Approval (39:32-43)
IV. Construction and Consecration (40:1-33)
V. God's Acceptance and Residence (40:34-38)

The Message of Exodus 35–40

There is great satisfaction in the completion of a project properly done. This is especially true when it is a project accomplished cooperatively by a group of people. It is also especially true when the people share the same motivations and goals.

Moses and the people of Israel at Mount Sinai shared the sense of satisfaction at the completion of the tabernacle. That reward of satisfaction at a job well done was multiplied by the Lord's approval of their work. The greatest reward was the evidence of God's continued presence with them.

- God loves cheerful givers.

- Material gifts to worthy causes should not be offered as a substitute for personal involvement.

- There is great satisfaction in working together.

- To do the best job possible we must be willing to give attention even to minor details.

- God forgives the penitent and restores them to the joy of sharing and serving.

LEVITICUS

OUTLINE OF LEVITICUS

INTRODUCTION

The book of Leviticus is the third of the five books of Moses. The name comes from the Vulgate, an early Latin translation. But the Vulgate is based on the earlier Greek translation, the Septuagint. The Greek title means *The [Book] of the Levites* because it contains so much instruction of value to the priestly family of Israel, the Levites.

The Purpose of the Book

The purpose of Leviticus is to help the people of Israel be the holy people of God. God is holy, and God requires a people with a high level of holiness.

Historical Background

The book of Leviticus, like much of Exodus before it, is set at the base of Mount Sinai. It continues the instructions of the Lord to Moses for the people of Israel.

The book of Exodus closes with the tabernacle erected. The Lord's presence indicated approval, for the glory of the Lord filled the tabernacle. The instructions in Leviticus relate to the use of the tabernacle. It is God's dwelling place among the people of Israel. But it is also a sanctuary for worship and atonement. The regulations in Leviticus are intended to help the people live holy lives according to the covenant relationship.

In Leviticus God speaks to Moses from the tent of meeting, the place where God's presence is manifested and where God communicates with the people.

Literary Background

According to tradition, the first five books of the Bible, including Leviticus, were written by Moses. There is doubtless a core of materials in Leviticus from Moses. The current form of the book is probably an expansion on the basic Mosaic material.

Leviticus as it now stands is likely the result of priestly editors (P). These devout men were at work before and during the Babylonian exile (about 650–550 B.C.). They collected, preserved, edited, and arranged the ancient laws and traditions. Their purpose was to make certain that God's people never again aroused the wrath of the Lord against them by ignoring the call to be holy people.

The ritual regulations of Leviticus were followed during the Second Temple period (515 B.C. to A.D. 70). But they were viewed as having been in effect during the period of the tabernacle. They were understood as God's revelation to Moses at Mount Sinai.

The Content of the Book of Leviticus

Chapters 1–7: These chapters contain laws and directions pertaining to sacrifices. Included here are directions for burnt offerings, meal offerings, peace offerings, and sin offerings. Also included is a manual of priestly directions, describing the function of the priest in the sacrifice.

Chapters 8–9: In accordance with the instructions in Exodus 29:1, Aaron and his sons are consecrated priests. In chapter 9, Aaron offers official sacrifice.

Chapter 10: Nadab and Abihu, sons of Aaron, offer strange fire to the Lord and are immediately killed. This injected piece of narrative serves to emphasize the holiness of God and the importance of precise ritual .

Chapters 11–16: This section deals with laws of purification and atonement. Chapter 11 provides a list of clean and unclean animals. Then follows in chapter 12 a set of rules for purification of women after childbirth.

Chapters 13 and 14 are concerned with the tests for leprosy, purification of the leper, and the treatment of the incurable leper, his clothes, and his home. Chapter 15 is concerned with activities that result in ceremonial uncleanness: sexual intercourse, menstruation, and so forth.

Chapter 16 gives a detailed description of the ceremonies of the Day of Atonement.

Chapters 17–26: This section is known as the Holiness Code. The theme that runs through this section is "You shall be holy unto me." In its present form, this code was probably written in the Babylonian exile by a priest and intended for the layperson. It likely existed as an independent collection of laws until it was incorporated into the book.

The principle of holiness is partly ceremonial and partly moral. The author intends that Israel, as the chosen people, shall be set apart for the service of God, and distinguished from all other peoples by the attribute of holiness. The code begins (chapter 17) with laws concerning the slaughter of beasts and the prohibition of eating meat with blood. Chapter 18 specifies sexual relations that are unlawful.

Chapter 19 contains some of the loftiest ethical precepts in the Old Testament. Provision is made for charity for the poor and the alien. Also, there are laws regarding kindly treatment for employees. The famous expression "You shall love your neighbor as yourself" appears here. The ethic of the Ten Commandments is here given renewed expression.

Chapter 20 forbids Molech worship (that is, sacrifice of children). There follow laws about prohibited sexual behaviors; general rules regarding cleanness; general precepts for the priests (chapters 21–22); laws concerning religious festivals (23:1–24:9); and the law of the sabbatical year and the year of jubilee (chapter 25). The taking of interest is forbidden and provision is made for the redemption of servants.

The concluding chapter (chapter 26) lists the blessings that will be showered upon Israel if God's words are obeyed. Then follows a list of the curses that will result from disobedience. In conclusion, mercy is promised to the repentant sinner.

Chapter 27: Laws concerning vows and tithes.

The Concept of God in Leviticus

Leviticus teaches that everything in Israel belongs to God. God owns all land. God reserves only a small portion, that on which the Temple stands. Israelites are permitted to use all other land, but must pay taxes to God, that is, tithes of crops to the priests.

The sabbatical year and the jubilee year are likewise based on this conception of God as the possessor of all land and the owner of all time. God allows the people to use time freely, but reserves a fraction of time, that is, the sabbath and the festival days. It is a sin to take this time which God has reserved and use it for one's private business.

God owns all souls. God allows the parents to redeem the firstborn with an animal offering. Each man redeems his own soul by payment of one third of a shekel per year. Beyond this, the priests, by devoting themselves exclusively to the service of God, redeem all Israel. The conception of God in Leviticus is that of a supreme ruler, and Israel is a theocracy.

Because God is ruler, God must be paid taxes and fines. Sacrifices are both public and private. The public sacrifices are offered at appointed times as part of the official cult. Private sacrifices are offered both as taxes and as fines.

Leviticus and the New Testament

The teachings of Leviticus were an integral part of the world of Jesus. Religious Jews were intent on the correct observance of the sabbath, ceremonial washings, keeping the set feasts, paying the Temple tax, tithing, and the like. The Gospels testify to the controversies that arose between Jesus and other Jewish teachers over the meaning of such things.

Leviticus focuses upon sin, guilt, and atoning sacrifices carried out by the Levitical priesthood. The New Testament writers understood the life and death of Jesus as the full realization of the purposes of Leviticus. Jesus was the once-and-for-all-time sufficient sacrifice for sin. His blood opened a way for believers into the most holy place, God's presence in heaven itself. And Christ was the true high priest. The connections between Christ and Leviticus are most clearly spelled out in the letter to the Hebrews.

LEVITICUS 1:1–6:7

Introduction to These Chapters

All of the book of Leviticus is set at the foot of Mount Sinai. The covenant between God and the people has been established and the tabernacle has been constructed and dedicated.

Here is an outline of chapters 1:1–6:7.
I. Animal Burnt Offerings (1:1-17)
II. Cereal Offerings (2:1-16)
III. Peace Offerings (3:1-17)

IV. Sins Committed Unwittingly (4:1-35)
V. Guilt Offerings (5:1–6:7)

God's presence among the people is visible in the cloud above the tabernacle by day and in the fire by night (Exodus 40:34-38). The presence of God among the people must be reassuring to them, but it could also be threatening. For the Lord is a holy God, and the people are prone to sin, to be unholy. In order for such people to be in God's presence, a means for purifying them is needed.

Purification is made possible through the sacrificial system. The death of an innocent animal victim as a substitute for the errant person atones for the sin. In this way God's command could be fulfilled: "You shall be holy, for I the LORD your God am holy" (Leviticus 19:2).

Leviticus provides the details for the operation of the sacrificial system. These chapters are a part of the first section of Leviticus, which contains rules and regulations for several different offerings. They include burnt offerings, meal offerings, peace offerings, and sin offerings.

The Message of Leviticus 1:1–6:7

Leviticus provides details on the religious practices the Israelites were to follow at the tabernacle. According to Leviticus 1:1, God spoke to Moses about these things in the tabernacle, not on the holy mountain. The information revealed in the tent of meeting was needed by Israel so that the people might worship God properly at the tabernacle. The rituals provided the means by which God's people might be holy. What do the regulations in Leviticus 1:1–6:7 reveal about the problem of human sin for God and for the people? What are the guiding principles God has provided to the people for handling the problem of sin?

- God considers sin a major human problem.

- Sin is common to everyone, from the most holy (the high priest) to the most lowly (one of the common people).

- People may sin against God and against others.

- God has provided a means by which persons who sin can be forgiven.

- The basic means by which sin can be forgiven is through the sacrifice of a substitute acceptable to God.

- Sacrifices to God may be freely given or required.

- Confession of sin is a part of the means of obtaining forgiveness.

- A breach of faith may require restoring to injured persons the value of their property plus an additional amount of compensation before forgiveness is possible.

LEVITICUS 6:8–7:38

Introduction to These Chapters

This section continues the rules and regulations that governed certain cultic rituals of ancient Israel. The activities centered on the tabernacle. They were carried on in the courtyard, within the sacred enclosure, but not within the tent of meeting proper.

The previous section provided instruction primarily to the people of Israel (see Leviticus 1:2; 4:2). In this section, the rules and regulations are addressed particularly to Aaron and his sons (Leviticus 6:8, 24). The focus of the regulations is still on the burnt offering, the cereal offering, the sin offering, the guilt offering, and the peace offering.

Various general matters relating to sacrifices are also included near the end of this section. These can be identified by the words, "Speak to the people of Israel."

Verses 37-38 of chapter 7 close the section of instruction on the burnt offering, cereal offering, sin offering, guilt offering, and peace offering. This concludes the first major portion of Leviticus.

Here is an outline of Leviticus 6:8–7:38.

I. Instructions for the Priests (6:8–7:18)
   A. Concerning the burnt offering (6:8-13)
   B. Concerning the cereal offering (6:14-23)
   C. Concerning the sin offering (6:24-30)
   D. Concerning the guilt offering (7:1-10)
   E. Concerning the peace offering (7:11-18)
II. Maintaining Ritual Purity (7:19-21)
III. Instructions for Everyone (7:22-36)
   A. Prohibiting eating fat and blood (7:22-27)
   B. Specifying the priestly portions (7:28-36)
IV. Final Statement of Authorization (7:37-38)

The Message of Leviticus 6:8–7:38

God's people together form one community. Within that community some members have special functions and responsibilities, such as the priests in ancient Israel. What principles at work in ancient Israel should be at work among God's people today?

- God's people who fulfill special functions in the community may enjoy certain benefits and privileges.

- People in special positions bear greater responsibilities.

- Careful obedience is required of all God's people.

- That which is holy and good can be changed into an abomination before God.

- Holiness can be contagious.

- Persons who knowingly reject God's will have no place among God's people.

- The good of the entire community of God requires that all its members gladly serve the Lord.

LEVITICUS 8–10

Introduction to These Chapters

The rules and regulations of the Mosaic cult were provided in Leviticus 1:1–7. These rules and regulations for sacrifices at the tabernacle could only begin with the consecration of Aaron to the position of high priest. It was the responsibility of Moses to install Aaron and his sons in office.

Moses had received instructions concerning the ordination of Aaron while he was conferring with God atop Mount Sinai (Exodus 29:1-37). Before carrying out the ordination, however, he had to complete the construction of the tabernacle (Exodus 40:1). When it was completed, at its doorway he received instructions from the Lord concerning sacrifices. Now everything was ready except for the ordination of the priests to serve in the sanctuary.

Chapter 8 of Leviticus gives a detailed account of how carefully Moses followed the instructions of the Lord for the ordination. Chapter 9 is an account of Aaron's first sacrifices after his ordination.

Chapter 10 records two errors committed by Aaron's sons as they began to function in their priestly offices. The first was a deadly sin. The second was a minor breach of the regulations.

Here is an outline of chapters 8–10.

I. Preparations for the Ordination (8:1-9)
   A. General preparations (8:1-4)
   B. Preparation of Aaron and his sons (8:5-9)
II. The Anointing of Aaron (8:10-13)
III. The Ordination Sacrifices Offered (8:14-36)
   A. The sin offering (8:14-17)
   B. The burnt offering (8:18-21)
   C. The ordination offering (8:22-29)
   D. Related activities (8:30-36)
IV. Aaron Acts as High Priest (9:1-24)
   A. The directions of Moses (9:1-7)
   B. Aaron officiates at the offerings (9:8-21)
   C. Blessings attend the service (9:22-24)
V. The Danger of Priestly Errors (10:1-20)
   A. Nadab and Abihu (10:1-7)
   B. Admonitions for priests (10:8-11)
   C. Eleazar and Ithamar (10:12-20)

The Message of Leviticus 8–10

The tabernacle had been completed and erected. The rules and regulations for the offering of sacrifices had been established. The ordination of Aaron and his sons as priests initiated the new system of worship. What does this section reveal about the nature of God and God's will for humans?

- God may introduce changes in the way we are to worship. Here the patriarchal pattern was superseded by the Mosaic ritual.

- In every age, God desires a holy people who will worship appropriately.

- A consecrated person will listen for God's direction, serve with dedicated hands, and walk humbly with the Lord.

- God's commands are not to be treated lightly. To know what to do and how to do it must be followed by obedience rather than rebellion.

- It is appropriate to train individuals for particular services for the Lord and to ordain them to those special ministries.

LEVITICUS 11–15

Introduction to These Chapters

With the sanctuary sanctified and the priesthood consecrated, this section of Leviticus is concerned with maintaining ritual purity. The priests are to distinguish between the holy and the common, and between the unclean and the clean. They are also to teach the people of Israel about these things (Leviticus 10:10-11).

Uncleanness is not a physical matter. It is a spiritual concept. Ritually impure or unclean people would pollute the holy sanctuary by entering it. Thus, instruction on the clean and the unclean naturally follows the previous section.

First clean and unclean animals are identified. Then follow rules for purification of women after childbirth. Chapters 13 and 14 are concerned with the tests for leprosy, purification of the leper, and the treatment of the incurable leper, his clothes, and his home. Chapter 15 deals with ceremonial uncleanness caused by sexual intercourse, menstruation, and related matters.

Here is an outline of chapters 11–15.

I. Clean and Unclean Animals (11:1-47)
   A. Large land animals (11:1-8)
   B. Water animals (11:9-12)
   C. Winged animals (11:13-19)
   D. Winged insects (11:20-23)
   E. Uncleanness by contact (11:24-40)
   F. The call to holiness (11:41-47)
II. Uncleanness from Childbirth (12:1-8)
III. Uncleanness from Leprosy (13:1–14:57)
   A. Confirmation of infection (13:1-44)
   B. Isolation of the infected (13:45-46)
   C. Infected garments (13:47-59)
   D. Reestablishing ritual cleanness (14:1-32)
   E. Infected houses (14:33-57)
IV. Uncleanness from Bodily Discharges (15:1-33)
   A. Bodily discharges from men (15:1-18)
   B. Bodily discharges from women (15:19-30)
   C. Summary statements (15:31-33)

The Message of Leviticus 11–15

God, who is holy, desires a holy people. Because the people are liable to personal defilement, God provided instruction to alert them to sources of uncleanness. God also established the steps to be taken for a defiled person to be cleansed from the defilement. These instructions testify to God's deep concern for the welfare of the chosen people.

This section suggests the following insights about God and God's demands on the people.

- The holiness of God is an awesome reality.

- In the process of daily living, people can become impure and inadmissible to God's presence.

- God desires human holiness to enable fellowship between people and God.

- In every age, God has provided the means by which people can be purified and fit to stand in God's presence.

- One of God's people who is defiled and outside the community is to be mourned like one dead.

- God's people must provide the way for the cleansed outcast to be restored to the community.

LEVITICUS 16

Introduction to This Chapter

All of Leviticus to this point has had a more or less direct connection with worship at the tabernacle. The cultic ritual required sacrifices. The regulations for the several types of sacrifices were provided in chapters 1–7. The sacrificial system required priests. To fill that need, Aaron and his sons were chosen to be priests. The ordination of Aaron and his sons was reported in chapters 8–10. Ritual impurity could threaten the holiness of the camp. It also prevented the unclean person from participating in the sacred rituals of the tabernacle worship services.

Chapters 11–15 dealt with a variety of causes for ritual impurity and the required remedies. But the holiness of God was so absolute that the entire people of Israel needed an annual spiritual cleansing. This cleansing was required so that Israel might approach a level of holiness like the holiness of God. The national purification was accomplished through the profound rituals of the Day of Atonement. The Day of Atonement is the focus of this chapter.

Here is an outline of chapter 16.

I. Preparations Required of Aaron (16:1-5)
II. General Instructions About Offerings (16:6-10)
III. Specific Instructions About Offerings (16:11-22)
   A. The priestly atonement offering (16:11-14)
   B. Atonement offering for the people (16:15-19)
   C. The offering of the goat for Azazel (16:20-22)
IV. Completion of the Offerings (16:23-28)
V. The Day of Atonement in Summary (16:29-34)

The Message of Leviticus 16

The Day of Atonement is often called Yom Kippur. The name is derived from the Hebrew name for the day. It is referred to as *the Fast* in the New Testament (Acts 27:9). The feature of fasting on the day became even more important after the destruction of the Temple in A.D. 70. It remains a day of repentance and fasting for Jews today.

The teaching of Leviticus 16 about the Day of Atonement is the capstone of the instruction on how an unclean people can be made ritually pure. Such purity was absolutely essential if God, who is holy, was to dwell with them. This chapter suggests the following meaning for today.

- In every age, God is concerned about the purity of the people.

- In every age people sin, are impure, and are unworthy to stand alone in the presence of the Holy One.

- Before establishing the covenant with Moses, God allowed the patriarchs to make atonement for their families.

- Through Moses, God established the Day of Atonement as an annual day of special cleansing for the people of Israel.

- Christians believe that Christ fulfilled the Day of Atonement once and for all to secure eternal, rather than annual, redemption (Hebrews 9:11-14).

- Those cleansed by the blood of Christ can confidently draw near to the Holy One, even into heaven itself (Hebrews 10:19-25).

LEVITICUS 17–20

Introduction to These Chapters

The instruction on the rituals of the Day of Atonement brought the first half of Leviticus to a climax. Of all the rituals intended to purify the people of Israel from their transgressions, sins, and uncleannesses, the rituals of the Day of Atonement were the most important. Now the compiler of the book turns the readers' attention to related matters.

Biblical scholars call Leviticus 17–26 the "Holiness Code" or the "Law of Holiness." It is a manual for holy living for the people of Israel. These chapters emphasize the holiness of God several times, along with the demand that the people of Israel also be holy. (See Leviticus 19:2; 20:26.)

The purpose of the laws was to separate Israel's practices from the practices of the Canaanites and other pagan peoples. This code and its related materials may be divided into three parts: chapters 17–20, chapters 21–24, and chapters 25–27.

Leviticus 17 is concerned with the sacredness of blood and the slaughter of animals. Leviticus 18 deals with the sanctity of marriage and with sexual

behavior. Leviticus 19 is a collection of various rules of conduct. Chapter 20 lists transgressions that are punishable by death.

Here is an outline of chapters 17–20.

I. Sacrifices Apart from the Tabernacle (17:1-9)
   A. The peace offering (17:1-7)
   B. The burnt offering (17:8-9)
II. Proper disposal of blood (17:10-16)
III. Unholy Sexual Relations (18:1-30)
   A. Introductory warning (18:1-5)
   B. Sex with close relatives (18:6-18)
   C. Other sexual defilements (18:19-23)
   D. Closing warning (18:24-30)
IV. Practical Rules for Living (19:1–20:27)
   A. Honor your parents and God (19:1-8)
   B. Be considerate of others (19:9-17)
   C. Show consideration for property (19:18-25)
   D. Beware of practices that profane (19:26-31)
   E. Show respect to others (19:32-37)
   F. Beware of spiritual adultery (20:1-9)
   G. Beware of physical sexual sins (20:10-21)
   H. The distinctions of holy living (20:22-27)

The Message of Leviticus 17–20

The call to holy living is practical rather than simply a nice idea. Practical applications for today may be seen in the following suggestions.

- All who eat meat today, whether hunters or shoppers, should appreciate the sanctity of the life that is in the blood; there should be no indiscriminate killing and no waste.

- Sexual perversions are still an abomination to God, even if a permissive society allows them.

- Spiritual perversions, such as witchcraft, astrology, and spiritualism are prohibited practices for the people of God.

- Honoring one's parents, obeying God, respecting others, and showing a genuine concern for their welfare are still part of God's prescription for holy living.

LEVITICUS 21–24

Introduction to These Chapters

The Holiness Code continues in these chapters. Chapter 21 provides instructions to assure the holiness of the priesthood. Chapter 22 contains rules for the priests about the offerings. Chapter 23 contains a calendar of Israel's religious festivals. These holy days must be properly observed.

Chapter 24 deals with the light in the tabernacle and the bread of the Presence. Both are related to the Holy Place, where the priest enters each day.

Here is an outline of chapters 21–24.

I. Special Rules for Priests (21:1–22:33)
  A. Mourning and marriage for priests (21:1-9)
  B. For the high priest (21:10-15)
  C. Rules related to permanent defects (21:16-24)
  D. Who may eat the priestly portion (22:1-16)
  E. Acceptable sacrificial animals (22:17-33)
II. Rules for Observing the Festivals (23:1-44)
  A. The sabbath (23:1-3)
  B. The Passover (23:4-8)

C. The offering of first fruits (23:9-14)
D. Pentecost (23:15-22)
E. Rosh Hashanah and Yom Kippur (23:23-32)
F. The Feast of Booths (23:33-44)
III. Rules for the Tabernacle (24:1-9)
IV. How to Deal with Blasphemers (24:10-23)

The Message of Leviticus 21–24

Chapters 21 and 22 are addressed to the priests, to Aaron and his sons. Chapters 23 and 24 are addressed to the people of Israel. But holiness is a national concern. The priests have their functions to fulfill, and the people have their responsibilities. So when the camp is in danger of coming under the wrath of God because of blasphemy against God's name, the entire people of Israel join in executing the blasphemer. These chapters continue to emphasize God's demand for holiness in the chosen people. They suggest the following principles.

- The first fruits of our increase should be devoted to God's service.

- God's people are called to find time to honor the Lord at special times and seasons.

- One of God's people who reviles God's holy name is a matter of concern to the whole community of faith.

LEVITICUS 25–27

Introduction to These Chapters

The sabbatical year, the year of jubilee, and the related law of redemption of property make up chapter 25. Chapter 26 is the concluding section of the Holiness

Code. That long document aimed at instructing the people of Israel in holy living began at chapter 17.

Chapter 26 expresses the conditional promises of God. Holy living brings blessings; living contrary to God's demands for holiness brings calamities.

The final chapter of Leviticus is an appendix. The focus of the appendix is on religious vows.

Here is an outline of chapters 25–27.

I. The Sabbatical and Jubilee Years (25:1-55)
   A. The sabbatical year (25:1-7)
   B. The jubilee year (25:8-12)
   C. Concerning these years (25:13-55)
      1. Property transfers (25:13-17)
      2. Attitudes toward the sabbatical year (25:18-22)
      3. Redemption of property (25:23-38)
      4. Redemption of people (25:39-55)
II. The Promise of Blessings or Calamities (26:1-46)
   A. Preliminary statement (26:1-2)
   B. Blessings promised for obedience (26:3-15)
   C. Calamities promised for disobedience (26:16-45)
   D. Final statement (26:46)
III. Supplement: Redeeming Religious Vows (27:1-34)
   A. Special vows (27:1-13)
   B. Special dedications (27:14-29)
   C. Redeeming the tithe (27:30-34)

THE SABBATICAL AND JUBILEE YEARS (25:1-55)

Every seventh day is the sabbath. Every seventh year is a sabbatical year. Every fiftieth year is a jubilee year.

The Sabbatical Year (25:1-7)

During each sabbatical year the land is to lie fallow. As people rest during the weekly sabbath, so the land is to rest through the sabbatical year. It is a sabbath to the LORD because the land belongs to God (verse 23).

Produce that comes up voluntarily cannot be harvested for storage. It can be eaten by the poor and by wild animals (Exodus 23:10-11). Some understand verses 6-7 as allowing the owner's household to also eat spontaneous produce, but not to harvest it for storage.

Verses 19-20, however, indicate the Lord's provision for the landowner in the sabbatical year. Out of the abundance of the sixth year's crop they have ample food for the seventh year.

Deuteronomy 15:1-11 associates the remission of debts with the sabbatical year. Some interpreters connect the freeing of slaves with it (Exodus 21:2).

The Jubilee Year (25:8-12)

The jubilee year is to start with the blowing of the trumpet (shofar) on the Day of Atonement. Our word jubilee comes from the Hebrew yobel, an earlier name for the ram's horn trumpet.

The land is to rest during the jubilee year as during a sabbatical year. It follows a sabbatical year. Thus for two years in a row crops cannot be stored or sold. But stored food and volunteer produce can be eaten.

The liberty proclaimed throughout the land (verse 10) is release from debt and the freedom to return to the family property. This verse is quoted on the Liberty Bell.

THE SABBATICAL AND JUBILEE YEARS (25:1-55; CONT.)

Property Transfers (25:13-17)

Property must be returned to the original owners or their heirs in the jubilee year. No compensation is given for this restoration. To prevent abuse, however, added rules are given. Fields are leased on a cash crop basis according to the years remaining until a jubilee.

Attitude Toward the Sabbatical Year (25:18-22)

Observance of the sabbatical and jubilee years by the people of Israel is an expression of their trust in the provisions of the Lord. By observing these special years, they can be confident of remaining on the land. To ignore the statutes and ordinances is to court disaster (Leviticus 26:34).

Redemption of Property (25:23-38)

In the eyes of the Lord, the people of Israel are not owners of the land; God is. The people are to God as friendly foreigners (strangers) and temporary settlers (aliens) on the land.

A change of ownership of property is possible only for a limited time. Eventually the return of the land to the original owners has to be granted.

Even though a year of jubilee is not at hand, the people of Israel are to help one another recover lost family property. Assistance is to be offered without thought of profit.

The houses and land of the Levites are treated differently because God did not give the Levites a section of land as their tribal territory. (See Numbers 35:2-7 and Joshua 21:1-42.) Instead, God assigned them certain cities with adjacent pasture and agricultural lands.

Redemption of People (25:39-55)

Since the Lord has freed the people of Israel from slavery in Egypt, they are not to be enslaved again. However, in hard times an Israelite can become a hired servant to a fellow Israelite. He and his family live with his employer while in service. But his service is to be for a limited time only.

Non-Israelite slaves can be acquired and owned forever. They need not be freed in the jubilee year. As with other property, they can be inherited.

Verses 47-55 deal with an Israelite who enters bondage under a non-Israelite. Perpetual slavery is forbidden in such cases. Apparently the non-Israelite slaveholder is informed of Israel's rules on slavery at the time the arrangement is made. An Israelite is to be freed in the jubilee year.

This section encourages the redemption of such an Israelite slave from his non-Israelite master. This might be done through kin or by the slave's efforts. The redeemed slave is to serve his redeemer until the value of the redemption has been repaid, or until a jubilee year has arrived.

The Message of Leviticus 25–27

The people of Israel observed weekly and annual holy days. The seventh and fiftieth years also had religious significance. These observances recognized that God was the ultimate owner of the land and the people. God intended the people to be free from slavery so they might serve under the covenant.

To keep the covenant meant blessings. To refuse to keep it meant curses and calamities. But because of the promises made to the forefathers, God would not completely destroy the people. A remnant would be saved. God's people, including that restored remnant, could redeem holy things. But the first fruits belonged to the Lord.

From these chapters the following truths emerge.

- The earth is the Lord's; people are to be good stewards of it.

- The person who exploits the poor is under the condemnation of the Lord.

- The poor are to be treated with respect and helped by the more affluent.

- Do not exploit like slaves people who serve you.

- God blesses those who are faithfully obedient.

- God will eventually bring calamity on the people who rebel.

- If you vow or dedicate something to the Lord, you must honor your commitment as something holy.

NUMBERS

OUTLINE OF NUMBERS

INTRODUCTION

The book of Numbers is the fourth book in the series often called the five books of Moses (Genesis–Deuteronomy). Numbers continues the historical narrative that began at Exodus 1:1.

In the original Hebrew, the name of this book is actually *In the wilderness* (NRSV) or *desert* (NIV). This name fits the contents of the book well, since the book of Numbers narrates events during the time of the Israelites' wilderness wanderings. The English title, Numbers, was given to this book because its earliest words have to do with the numbers of people in the census taken by Moses (chapter 1).

The Content of the Book

The book of Numbers may be divided into three parts: (1) the Israelites prepare to depart from Mount Sinai, chapters 1–10; (2) the Israelites journey to Kadesh, chapters 11–21; and (3) the Israelites approach the land of Canaan, chapters 22–36.

Numbers 1 continues the narrative that began in the book of Exodus. The people of Israel have left Egypt, journeyed to Sinai, and are receiving instructions about life and worship in the Promised Land. These instructions begin with the Ten Commandments (Exodus 19:1-20) and continue through the tenth chapter of Numbers, when the people finally pull up stakes and continue their journey to the Promised Land.

The Date of Numbers

The book of Numbers is part of the Pentateuch, or the five books of Moses. This group of narratives was written over a period of many years (900–500 B.C.) and was compiled in its final form sometime during the Exile.

Major Themes in Numbers

Theological themes in Numbers include the people's murmuring against Moses while they are wandering in the wilderness, God's continued presence with them during this time, the people's disobedience and lack of trust in God, and what the covenant relationship promises the people and what it requires of them.

NUMBERS 1–2

Introduction to These Chapters

The name Numbers is a fitting title for this book, since right at its beginning, in chapter 1, God commands Moses to number the people. In chapters 1 and 2, Moses numbers all the people of Israel except the Levites, and the arrangements

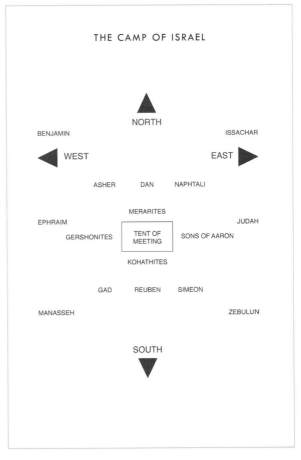

THE CAMP OF ISRAEL

NORTH

BENJAMIN   ISSACHAR

WEST   EAST

ASHER   DAN   NAPHTALI

MERARITES

EPHRAIM   JUDAH

GERSHONITES   TENT OF   SONS OF AARON
                    MEETING

KOHATHITES

GAD   REUBEN   SIMEON

MANASSEH   ZEBULUN

SOUTH

are given for how the people are to be located when they encamp and when they march. In both these sections, the people of Israel are classified by tribes.

Here is an outline of chapters 1 and 2.

I. Moses Takes a Census (1:1-54)
   A. Introduction (1:1-16)
   B. The tribes are counted (1:17-46)
   C. Responsibilities of the Levites (1:47-54)
II. The Position of the Camps (2:1-34)
   A. The camp of Judah (2:1-9)
   B. The camp of Reuben (2:10-16)
   C. The camp of the Levites (2:17)
   D. The camp of Ephraim (2:18-24)
   E. The camp of Dan (2:25-31)
   F. Conclusion (2:32-34)

The Message of Numbers 1–2

These chapters introduce us to a very important phase in the history of the Israelites. The wilderness experience was formative for the Hebrew faith. Although the people do not actually set out on their journey until chapter 10, in these early chapters we see how they begin their preparations. What can we learn about God and God's relationship to the people?

- God is with the people from beginning to end. The book of Numbers begins with the words "The LORD spoke . . . ," setting the stage for what will happen in the rest of the book.

- Moses and Aaron, along with the heads of each tribe, do not hesitate to do what God asks. They fulfill God's command on the same day it is given.

- Those in charge of the religious dimension of Israelite life are set apart from the rest of the people. They are not counted among those persons able to bear arms.

- There is an organized quality about the life of the Israelites during their time in the wilderness. This organization is under the leadership of God, through Moses.

NUMBERS 3–6

Introduction to These Chapters

In these four chapters, the Israelites are still preparing for their wilderness journey. Since the Levites were excluded from the census taken in chapter 1, they are counted by themselves in chapters 3 and 4. Other material in this section includes laws concerning such matters as adultery and living as a Nazirite.

Here is an outline of these chapters.

I. The Duties of the Levites (3:1-51)
   A. Introduction (3:1-4)
   B. The leadership of Aaron (3:5-10)
   C. The Levites belong to God (3:11-13)
   D. The census of the Levites (3:14-39)
   E. A second census (3:40-51)
II. A Third Census Is Taken (4:1-49)
   A. Instructions about the tent of meeting (4:1-33)
   B. Results of the census (4:34-49)
III. Laws and Instructions (5:1–6:21)
   A. The sanctity of the camp (5:1-4)
   B. Law concerning restitution (5:5-10)
   C. Law concerning adultery (5:11-31)
   D. Nazirite law (6:1-21)
IV. Aaron's Blessing on the People (6:22-27)

The Message of Numbers 3–6

In these chapters, the people of Israel are still preparing for their wilderness journey that they will undertake beginning in chapter

10. In this section we read about everything from a census to rules and regulations regarding life in community. What can we learn about God and about God's chosen people from the material in these chapters?

- Ever since Israel's earliest days, certain people have been set apart by God as having religious responsibilities and a special relationship to God.

- God can make demands and expect obedience to those demands.

- Living in community required a certain amount of organization, including designated leaders and rules that must be followed for order to be maintained.

- Wherever the people went in their wilderness journey, God was with them.

NUMBERS 7:1–10:10

Introduction to These Chapters

This section of the book of Numbers contains a tribe-by-tribe listing of offerings brought by tribal leaders to the service of dedication of the tabernacle, a service of consecration for the Levites, who have the priestly responsibilities in the tabernacle, and further preparations for the wilderness journey. This is the last section that describes preparation for the journey. At the end of chapter 9 (actually, at 10:11), the Israelites set out on their journey through the wilderness.

Here is an outline of Numbers 7:1–10:10.

    I. Consecration of the Tabernacle (7:1-89)
        A. The leaders arrive in wagons (7:1-9)

        B. The dedication of the altar (7:10-89)
    II. Consecration of the Levites (8:1-26)
        A. The lighting of the lamps (8:1-4)
        B. The ceremony of purification (8:5-22)
        C. The Levites' duties are assigned (8:23-26)
    III. Miscellaneous Laws (9:1–10:10)
        A. Laws concerning the Passover (9:1-14)
        B. The departure from Sinai (9:15–10:10)

The Message of Numbers 7:1–10:10

These chapters contain the final preparations the people of Israel made before they left Mount Sinai. What can we learn from this material about God and about God's relationships with the chosen people?

- Certain persons in Israel were set apart by God for special services.

- God expects and requires a certain portion in return for what God does on behalf of the people.

- God is the ultimate source of authority about rules and regulations of Israel's life and faith.

- Israelites and sojourners alike can participate in the feasts and festivals of Israelite faith.

- God's presence abides with the Israelites while they journey through the wilderness.

NUMBERS 10:11–12:16

Introduction to These Chapters

Here the Israelites begin their march, journeying in the wilderness for the next forty years. The section opens with a description of all the last-minute preparations. So many people embarking on a journey at the same time, accompanied by the presence of God, must have been an impressive sight. The contrast is vivid when, immediately after they set out, the people begin murmuring against Moses. They are unhappy, and their unhappiness results in dissension among the leaders.

Here is an outline of these chapters.

I. The Israelites Journey to Kadesh (10:11-36)
   A. Introduction (10:11-12)
   B. The order of march (10:13-28)
   C. The Israelites set out (10:29-36)
II. The Israelites Murmur in the Wilderness (11:1-35)
   A. The fire of the Lord (11:1-3)
   B. The people crave manna and meat (11:4-15)
   C. The leadership of Moses (11:16-30)
   D. The people eat meat (11:31-35)
III. Miriam Is Punished (12:1-16)
   A. Miriam and Aaron speak against Moses (12:1-8)
   B. Miriam becomes leprous (12:9-16)

The Message of Numbers 10:11–12:16

In these chapters, the people finally embark on their journey through the wilderness toward the Promised Land. Several important themes surface in these chapters, and will continue to appear throughout the wilderness journey.

- All details of the journey are at the command of God, through Moses.

- There is an orderliness about the journey that is also ordained by God and necessary to keep the people together in community on such a long and arduous trip.

- God is present with the people as they depart, and remains with them throughout the journey.

- God is willing to provide help to Moses as he chafes under the burden of leadership that has been given to him.

- Greed and complaining bring punishment from God.

NUMBERS 13–16

Introduction to These Chapters

In this section a group of spies among the camp undertake a reconnaissance mission to spy out the land of Canaan. After receiving advice to the contrary, the Israelites decide to attack anyway, and the results are disastrous. This section also contains some cultic regulations and a story about an uprising against Moses.

Here is an outline of Numbers 13–16.

I. The Israelites Spy on Canaan (13:1-33)
   A. The spies are designated (13:1-16)
   B. Moses instructs the spies (13:17-24)
   C. The spies report (13:25-33)
II. The Israelites Attack Canaan (14:1-45)
   A. The people respond to the report (14:1-10)
   B. Dialogue between Moses and God (14:11-38)
   C. The results of the attack (14:39-45)
III. Laws Concerning Offerings (15:1-41)
   A. Cereal and drink offerings (15:1-16)
   B. Offering of the first fruits (15:17-21)

C. Laws concerning atonement
(15:22-31)
D. Penalty for violating the sabbath
(15:32-36)
E. The Israelites are to wear tassels
(15:37-41)
IV. Korah Rebels Against Moses
(16:1-50)
A. Korah and others revolt (16:1-15)
B. Korah and others are punished
(16:16-35)
C. Appendix (16:36-50)

The Message of Numbers 13–16

The events and stories narrated in this section intrigue us, and sometimes we are shocked at their contents. In order to understand their true meaning for the Israelite people at that time, we need to understand what was happening among the people during those troubled times. These stories give us some insights into the nature of Israel's God and the relationship between God and the chosen people.

- The first report brought back by the spies argued against the taking of Canaan, the Promised Land. The story's point is that the land was promised by God. By hesitating to enter the land, the people were demonstrating their faithlessness in God.

- Even the leadership of Moses and Aaron was sometimes not enough to support the people during this difficult time of wilderness wandering.

- God became angry with the people on account of their lack of trust. However, when Moses interceded on their behalf, God repented of the decision to choose another people in their place.

- God's mercy does not take the place

of God's judgment, however. The people are to be punished for their faithlessness.

- According to ancient justice, a man's family was to be punished for his sin. Also, the early Israelites believed that all circumstances were attributable directly to God, as punishment for disobedience. So, although we may be shocked at the fate of the families of Dathan and Abiram, in Israelite thought their fate was easily explained.

NUMBERS 17–21

Introduction to These Chapters

These five chapters contain a variety of material, including information about the Levites, legislation concerning contact with the dead, and further narratives about the wilderness journey.

Chapters 17–21 may be outlined as follows.
I. Aaron's Rod Blossoms (17:1-13)
II. Duties of the Priests and Levites
(18:1-32)
A. The Aaronites and Levites are different (18:1-7)
B. Portions for the priests and Levites (18:8-32)
III. Laws of Purification (19:1-22)
A. The ritual of the red heifer
(19:1-10)
B. Water is used for cleansing
(19:11-22)
IV. The Israelites Leave Kadesh
(20:1-29)
A. Water flows from the rock
(20:1-13)
B. Passage through Edom
(20:14-21)
C. The death of Aaron (20:22-29)
V. The Itinerary (21:1-13)

VI. Israel Defeats the Amorites
(21:14-35)

The Message of Numbers 17–21
- God sometimes designates an individual or individuals, such as Moses and Aaron, and provides them with special skills to support them in positions of authority over others.

- The office of the priesthood involves special responsibilities that include bearing the burden of the sins and mistakes of others within the congregation.

- Unbelief is not tolerated among the people of God. Unbelief can cause punishment, although God can repent of that decision if persuaded that the people will change their ways.

NUMBERS 22–24

Introduction to These Chapters

These three chapters include the story of Balaam and Balak, as well as four oracles delivered by Balaam the seer. The story takes place in the plains of Moab, while the Israelites were making preparations to enter that territory.

Here is an outline of Numbers 22–24.
I. Balak Summons Balaam the Seer
(22:1-40)
  A. Balak sends for Balaam twice
(22:1-20)
  B. Balaam's talking donkey
(22:21-40)
II. Four Oracles of Balaam
(22:41–24:25)
  A. Introduction and first oracle
(22:41–23:10)
  B. Introduction and second oracle
(23:11-24)

C. Introduction and third oracle
(23:25–24:9)
D. Introduction and fourth oracle
(24:10-25)

The Message of Numbers 22–24
- God can use foreigners (non-Israelites) to communicate with the chosen people and to fulfill the divine purposes.

- Balaam is firm in his conviction (despite financial incentives) that he must do and say only what God intends. This resolve speaks to his firm faith.

- Sometimes humans, because of their stubbornness, cannot see the obvious truth in a situation.

- Israel is a nation chosen by God and set aside for a special relationship with God. Nothing Israel can do is sinful enough to remove that basic relationship.

- God, unlike human beings, who are subject to change, is constant and immovable.

NUMBERS 25–27

Introduction to These Chapters

In this section we find further stories related to the territory of Moab, an account of a second census taken by Moses and Eleazar, and a discussion of the laws regarding inheritance of property by women. At the end of this section, Joshua is commissioned by God to take the place of Moses in the conquest of the Promised Land.

Numbers 25–27 may be outlined as follows.

I. Disobedience in Moab (25:1-18)

II. Moses Takes Another Census (26:1-65)

  A. Introduction (26:1-4)

  B. The census (26:5-51)

  C. Land allotments (26:52-56)

  D. Census of the Levites (26:57-65)

III. The Daughters of Zelophehad (27:1-11)

IV. Joshua Succeeds Moses (27:12-23)

The Message of Numbers 25–27

- God will not hesitate to punish the people for their apostasy (worshiping other gods). Yoking oneself to another god will bring judgment.

- The slight decrease in the number of the Israelites during the wilderness sojourn testifies to God's presence with them and ability to sustain them despite heavy odds.

- The law in Israel is constantly being revised according to individual circumstances. Although some basic regulations are fixed, in its detail it can be changed or reinterpreted as situations arise that are ambiguous.

- The (impending) death of Moses does not mean the end of leadership of the people. God replaces Moses with Joshua, in order that the people not be left like sheep without a shepherd.

NUMBERS 28–31

Introduction to These Chapters

Numbers 28–31 contains instructions concerning offerings, regulations related to the making of vows, especially by women, and an account of a holy war between the people of Israel and the Midianites.

Chapters 28–31 may be outlined as follows.

I. Regulations Concerning Offerings (28:1–29:40)

  A. Burnt offerings (28:1-15)

  B. Feast of Unleavened Bread (28:16-31)

  C. Other festivals (29:1-40)

II. Vows Made by Women (30:1-16)

III. The Israelites Conquer Midian (31:1-54)

  A. Report of the war (31:1-12)

  B. Ceremonial purification (31:13-24)

  C. Distribution of booty (31:25-54)

The Message of Numbers 28–31

- Feasts, festivals, offerings, and sacrifices were all part of the ritual that had to be observed by the Israelites in order to maintain a proper relationship with God.

- Women were considered to be of less value than men in the patriarchal society of Israel. However, once spoken and heard, a legitimate vow (whether made by a man or a woman) must be kept at all costs.

- Worship of foreign gods was not tolerated among the Israelites.

NUMBERS 32–36

Introduction to These Chapters

These chapters include a description of the land allotment east of the Jordan River, a summary of Israel's wilderness wanderings from the time the people left Egypt, a description of the ideal boundary lines in the land of Canaan, a description of the cities the Levites were to inhabit as well as the cities of refuge, and regulations about the inheritance of property.

Here is an outline of these chapters.

I. The Territory of Reuben and Gad (32:1-42)
   A. Introduction and speech of Moses (32:1-15)
   B. Tribal allotments (32:16-42)
II. The Israelites' Journey (33:1-56)
   A. Introduction (33:1-4)
   B. From Rameses to Sinai (33:5-15)
   C. From Sinai to Kadesh-barnea (33:16-36)
   D. From Kadesh-barnea to the Jordan (33:37-49)
   E. Final instructions (33:50-56)
III. The Boundaries of the Land (34:1-29)
IV. The Cities of Refuge (35:1-54)
   A. Cities given to the Levites (35:1-8)
   B. Cities of refuge described (35:9-15)
   C. Laws concerning killing (35:16-34)
V. Inheritance of Property (36:1-13)

The Message of Numbers 32–36

• Tribal unity was very important for the early Israelites. Thus, the tribes who wanted to settle east of the Jordan River had to first promise that they would join the other tribes in the task at hand before going off on their own. A unified Israel was needed for the conquest of the Promised Land to take place successfully.

• Once the Israelites entered the land of Canaan, it was important that their religious lives remained pure and not tarnished by the cultic rituals of the Canaanites. Worship of other gods in any form was not tolerated by the God of Israel.

• Murder is a crime that offends not only the people involved, but God as well.

DEUTERONOMY

OUTLINE OF DEUTERONOMY

INTRODUCTION

Deuteronomy is the last of the five books of Moses, also called the *Torah*. The book of Deuteronomy concludes with the death of Moses on Mount Nebo, right before the Israelites enter the Promised Land.

The narrative in Deuteronomy picks up where the book of Numbers leaves off. The Israelites are encamped in the territory of Moab, and are waiting to cross over the Jordan River and conquer the Promised Land. Because Moses knows he will not be allowed to cross over the Jordan, he takes this opportunity to say some final words to the congregation before his death.

Deuteronomy is essentially three separate addresses by Moses (chapters 1–4, 5–28, and 29–30). The overall theme of the book is *law* (the name Deuteronomy actually means "second law").

Moses' sermons begin with a review of the events in the lives of the Israelites since the time they left Egypt (chapters 1–4). Moses continues with a discussion of the Ten Commandments (chapters 5–6). The third portion of what Moses has to say involves how to live in a right relationship with God after the people are settled in their new land (chapters 7–30). The final four chapters in Deuteronomy describe the final days of Moses' life.

Deuteronomy (or portions of this book) was probably the book of the law found by King Josiah in the Temple in 621 B.C. This discovery led to vast reform of Israel's religious life (see 2 Kings 22:1-23).

DEUTERONOMY 1–3

Introduction to These Chapters

These three chapters that open the book of Deuteronomy are essentially a historical review of the events that have happened in the life of the Israelites since they left Egypt. This history forms the first portion of the series of (three) sermons Moses preaches to the congregation before his death.

Chapters 1–3 may be outlined as follows.

  I. Part One (1:1-46)
    A. Introduction (1:1-18)
    B. From Horeb to Kadesh (1:19-46)
  II. Part Two (2:1-37)
    A. From Kadesh to the kingdom of Sihon (2:1-25)
    B. The Israelites defeat Sihon (2:26-37)
  III. Part Three (3:1-29)
    A. The Israelites defeat Bashan (3:1-11)
    B. Allotment of eastern territory (3:12-22)
    C. Moses will not cross over (3:23-29)

The Message of Deuteronomy 1–3

- The unity among the twelve tribes is a crucial factor in the success of the conquest of the Promised Land. Therefore, it is very important that all the tribes (even Reuben, Gad, and Manasseh) participate in the conquest together.

- God fights on behalf of the chosen people through their conquest of Canaan. God is behind all these events, directing the people through the leadership of Moses.

- God is different from the gods of surrounding nations. God's mighty deeds speak on behalf of God's ability to guide the people through these experiences.

- At times the promise of the land flowing with milk and honey looks as though it is in jeopardy. However, God will fulfill this promise.

- The Israelites do not always understand how this promise is to be fulfilled. However, their lack of understanding should not result in a lack of faith. All events are proceeding at the will and direction of their God.

DEUTERONOMY 4–7

Introduction to These Chapters

These four chapters in Deuteronomy are crucial in the history of the chosen people. The section begins with the conclusion to Moses' first speech that began in chapter 1. Next comes a long description of the nature of God and why God demands obedience from the chosen people. This exhortation is followed by the Ten Commandments, which form the heart of Israelite law and faith.

THE TEN COMMANDMENTS IN DEUTERONOMY 5

Verse 1 contains a new introduction. The words "Hear, O Israel" are found frequently in the book of Deuteronomy, as Moses exhorts the people to listen to his words of advice.

Verse 2 calls the Sinai experience a *covenant* between God and the chosen people. Moses points out that he has been serving as a mediator between God and the people.

Verses 6-21 contain the Ten Commandments, with an introduction in verse 6. The first half of the commandments are explained; the second half are brief and to the point. This account is very similar to the first account of the Ten Commandments, found in Exodus 20:2-17.

In verse 6, the words "I am the LORD your God" introduce the speaker as the same God who brought the people out of Egypt some years earlier. In general, the commandments are related both to God (the first five) and to other human beings (the last five).

Verse 7 is the first commandment, against having other gods. This is the most important commandment, and is thus first among the ten. The commandment assumes that there are other gods for other nations, but that there is only one God for the nation of Israel.

Verses 8-10 contain the second commandment, which is related to the first. This same subject (making graven images) is addressed in Deuteronomy 4:15-18. The third commandment (found in verse 11) protects God's name. God's name cannot be used for evil purposes (such as magic or divination).

Verses 12-15 concern observation of the sabbath, and include a lengthy explanation. But the explanation does not give the reason the sabbath is holy; rather, it explains exactly who cannot work on that day. No cultic ritual is specified for the sabbath day.

In the Exodus version of the Decalogue, the observation of the sabbath day is related to God's creation of the earth. Since God created the earth in six days and rested on the seventh, God's chosen people should also rest on the seventh day (see Exodus 20:11). In the present passage, resting on the seventh day is related to the psychological need human beings have for rest.

The commandment concerning honoring one's father and mother is based on the idea of an extended family—a prevailing concept in early Israelite society. In the extended family, contact with one's parents continued well beyond the teen years, unlike the situation in the nuclear family of today's American society. Note that this commandment has a positive rather than a negative orientation. The addition to this commandment is not an explanation; it is a promise.

Verse 17 rules out all forms of unlawful homicide, including vengeance killing, demanding respect for the value of each human life.

The commandment in verse 18 prohibits adultery. According to Israelite custom, a man could have intercourse with his household slaves and be within the law. On the other hand, any other sexual relationships outside of marriage were prohibited by the commandment in verse 18.

The commandment against stealing (verse 19) may have originally prohibited specifically the stealing of persons, but as the commandment stands it is meant to safeguard all of the neighbor's property and possessions.

Verse 20 prohibits false witness against one's neighbor. The testimony of witnesses was very important in early Israelite society, since witnesses were required to convict a person of crimes such as murder.

In verse 21, the verb translated *covet* means both to desire inordinately and to take.

Verses 22-33 contain concluding statements related to the Ten Commandments. First, the point is restated that Moses served as a mediator between God and the people when the Ten Commandments were received. The people were quite willing for Moses to intercede on their behalf, because they thought that no one could see the face of God and live (see Exodus 33:20).

The second point these verses make is that Moses was the one designated to interpret the law for the people as well as to report on what the law says (verse 31).

Chapters 4–7 may be outlined as follows.

I. Conclusion to Moses' First Address (4:1-43)
   A. Moses appeals for obedience (4:1-14)
   B. The character of God (4:15-40)
   C. Cities of refuge (4:41-43)
II. Moses' Second Address Begins (4:44–7:26)
   A. Introduction (4:44-49)
   B. The Ten Commandments (5:1-33)
   C. Moses explains the first commandment (6:1-25)
   D. Keeping the commandments (7:1-26)

The Message of Deuteronomy 4–7

- Obedience to the commandments is a very important prerequisite for a successful life in the Promised Land.

- Just as God remained with the people throughout their long wilderness journey, God will remain with them as they enter this next phase of their history.

- The worship of idols in any form is not tolerated by the God of Israel. This issue is especially important because the people are about to enter Canaan with its corrupting influences.

- The laws by which Israel was to live included regulations about relationships between people and people, as well as between people and God.

- In every situation in which the people found themselves, they were to do their best to determine the will of God, and to do it.

- The covenant made earlier with the patriarchs still holds true for the Israelites, and will continue to determine the actions of God on their behalf.

DEUTERONOMY 8–11

Introduction to These Chapters

These chapters are concerned with how the Israelites are to live in their new land, and how they are to remain in relationship with God when their circumstances change. This material is in the form of a sermon; it continues the address Moses is giving to the people of Israel before he dies and they cross the Jordan into the Promised Land.

Here is an outline of Deuteronomy 8–11.

I. Moses Warns Against Pride (8:1-20)
   A. God's actions in the past (8:1-10)
   B. Future prosperity (8:11-20)
II. God's Attitude toward Israel (9:1–10:11)
   A. God's presence with Israel (9:1-5)
   B. God's presence in history (9:6–10:11)
III. God's Requirements (10:12–11:32)
   A. God demands faithfulness and obedience (10:12-22)
   B. God wants loyalty to the covenant (11:1-25)
   C. A blessing and a curse (11:26-32)

The Message of Deuteronomy 8–11

- A successful life in the land of Canaan depends on the people's obedience to the commandments, and on their refraining from being corrupted by the influences of Canaanite religious practices.

- God will continue to act on Israel's behalf; the proof is in what God has accomplished in the past.

- At times God tests the quality of Israel's faith by causing the chosen people to endure suffering.

- The Israelites must never think that victory over an enemy is their own doing. They must always realize that God's hand is at work on their behalf.

- God will never forsake the covenant made with the patriarchs.

- The people of Israel constantly have a choice before them. They can choose either blessing or curse.

DEUTERONOMY 12–15

Introduction to These Chapters

These chapters are central to the message of the book of Deuteronomy. Chapter 12 focuses on the centralization of worship in the sanctuary. This section also includes more exhortation concerning the worship of other gods, and advice on how to live once the people become settled in their new land.

Deuteronomy 12–15 may be outlined as follows.

I. Worship Regulations (12:1-32)
   A. Where to bring burnt offerings (12:1-14)
   B. Appropriate animal sacrifices (12:15-28)
   C. Conclusion (12:29-32)
II. Serving Other Gods (13:1-18)
   A. Dealing with false prophets (13:1-5)
   B. Dealing with others (13:6-18)
III. Clean and Unclean Foods (14:1-29)
   A. What the people may eat (14:1-20)
   B. Annual offerings to God (14:21-29)
IV. Living in Community (15:1-23)
   A. The year of jubilee (15:1-11)

   B. Regulations about slaves (15:12-23)

The Message of Deuteronomy 12–15

- There is only one sanctuary in which it is appropriate for Israelites to worship God. This phenomenon of centralized worship was the most effective way to guard against the pagan influences the people would inevitably encounter as they settled in the land of Canaan.

- No enticement from any person or group of persons should influence an Israelite to worship any other god besides Yahweh, Israel's God.

- Those who encourage others to forsake God and follow other gods are to be cut off from the community.

- Special provisions are made for certain members of Israelite society, so their needs are cared for. The Israelites who have land and can produce food must share their goods with those who are less fortunate.

DEUTERONOMY 16–19

Introduction to These Chapters

These four chapters continue the long sermonic section related to laws and regulations that will govern the people as they settle in the land of Canaan. The present section includes regulations concerning the observance of feasts and festivals, the administration of justice, the rights of the Levites, the proper worship of God, and the cities of refuge.

Here is an outline of these chapters.

I. Festival Celebrations (16:1-22)
   A. The feast of the Passover (16:1-8)
   B. The feast of Weeks (16:9-12)
   C. The feast of Booths (16:13-15)

D. Summary statements (16:16-22)
II. Laws Concerning Justice (17:1-20)
   A. Concerning idolatry (17:1-7)
   B. Concerning difficult cases (17:8-13)
   C. Concerning the king (17:14-20)
III. Treatment of the Priests (18:1-22)
IV. Cities of Refuge (19:1-21)
   A. The cities are established (19:1-14)
   B. The testimony of witnesses (19:15-21)

The Message of Deuteronomy 16–19

- Certain festivals were designated for the Israelites to observe, in commemoration of their history and of God's involvement in it on their behalf.

- A central sanctuary was set aside for the purpose of guarding against the possibility of pagan influences from the surrounding Canaanite culture once the Israelites were settled in the land of Canaan.

- Certain Canaanite practices were specifically prohibited, such as child sacrifice, boiling a kid in its mother's milk, and various forms of divination.

- The law of retaliation was set up to preserve a proper balance in society, not to promote harsh judgment and punishment among its members.

DEUTERONOMY 20–23

Introduction to These Chapters

These chapters continue Moses' exhortation concerning regulations of the settled life in Canaan. This section contains regulations regarding holy war, laws concerning murder, laws concerning treatment of the Levites, and many other miscellaneous rules and regulations.

Deuteronomy 20–23 may be outlined as follows.

I. Regulations Concerning Holy War (20:1-20)
II. Other Laws and Regulations (21:1–23:25)
   A. Concerning murder (21:1-9)
   B. Concerning holy war (21:10-14)
   C. Concerning family matters (21:15-23)
   D. Concerning fellow Israelites (22:1-4)
   E. Miscellaneous laws (22:5-12)
   F. Concerning sexual relations (22:13-30)
   G. Concerning exclusions from the assembly (23:1-8)
   H. Miscellaneous laws (23:9-25)

The Message of Deuteronomy 20–23

- Israel's God, who accompanied the people when they left Egypt, will accompany them during the conquest of the Promised Land as well.

- The numbers of soldiers that participate in the various battles that make up the conquest of the Promised Land are not important. What is important is the presence of God with the people as they go to war.

- Many rules and regulations were necessary to enable a successful settled life in the land of Canaan.

- Some of Israel's laws were strictly religious; others were humanitarian and helped the Israelites live harmoniously with one another.

- Participation in the congregational worship of God was a privilege that was not granted to everyone.

DEUTERONOMY 24–27

Introduction to These Chapters

These chapters deal with laws related to humanitarian matters. These laws cover such matters as divorce; making loans; treatment of slaves, widows, and sojourners; and personal disagreements. A major portion of Moses' second sermon (which began at chapter 5) is concluded in chapter 26. Chapter 27 describes a ceremony at which the covenant between God and Israel is renewed.

Here is an outline of Deuteronomy 24–27.
I. Miscellaneous Laws (24:1–25:19)
II. Concluding Statements (26:1-19)
III. A Covenant Ceremony (27:1-26)
  A. Introduction (27:1-14)
  B. Ritual of the curse (27:15-26)

The Message of Deuteronomy 24–27

- God intends to take care of the unfortunate members of Israelite society, so laws are provided that protect their welfare.

- Individuals within the community are responsible for their own sins.

- Sometimes Israelite law, which was set up to maintain balance and harmonious living conditions in the community, sounds harsh to our modern ears.

- Israel's history is a part of what the people have become.

- The Israelites by this time have come to believe that God is the only God, who designated them as the chosen people.

DEUTERONOMY 28–30

Introduction to These Chapters

Deuteronomy 28–30 contains the third and final sermon of Moses to the people before they cross the Jordan into the Promised Land. First, however, Moses concludes his earlier sermon, begun in chapter 5. Then he proceeds to exhort the people to obey the covenant made with God, and warns them of the punishment that they will incur if they do not obey.

Deuteronomy 28–30 may be outlined as follows.
I. Conclusion (to Moses' Second Sermon) (28:1-68)
  A. The blessings and their explanations (28:1-14)
  B. The curses and their explanations (28:15-46)
  C. God summons the enemy (28:47-68)
II. Moses' Third Address (29:1–30:20)
  A. A description of the covenant (29:1-29)
  B. Israel in exile (30:1-10)
  C. The people have a choice (30:11-20)

The Message of Deuteronomy 28–30

- Blessings and curses are both options for the Israelites, depending on their response to the covenant.

- Events are seen as a direct result of the people's disregard for the covenant.

- Disobedience of the commandments will have disastrous results; obedience will bring a life of peace and prosperity.

- God's actions in the past on Israel's behalf are proof that God will continue to act on behalf of the chosen people in the future.

DEUTERONOMY 31–34

Introduction to These Chapters

Moses has now concluded his third sermon. These last four chapters in the book of Deuteronomy narrate the events during the final days of Moses' life. As they have been all through the book of Deuteronomy, the Israelites are encamped just east of the Jordan River, waiting to cross over into the Promised Land. These chapters contain Moses' final exhortation to obedience, a psalm contrasting God's faithfulness with the people's disobedience, Moses' final blessing on the people, and the story of Moses' death on Mount Nebo.

Here is an outline of these chapters.

I. Moses' Final Words to the People (31:1-29)
   A. Moses encourages the people (31:1-13)
   B. Joshua is commissioned (31:14-29)
II. The Song of Moses (31:30–32:47)
III. Moses Ascends Mount Nebo (32:48-52)
IV. Moses Blesses the People (33:1-29)
V. The Death of Moses (34:1-12)

The Message of Deuteronomy 31–34

• Receiving the land of promise is imminent for the Israelites. The taking of this land represents the fulfillment of God's promise of land made to the patriarchs.

• The people are to enter into the conquest of Canaan, sure in the knowledge that their God is with them.

• After the death of Moses, God will not leave the people without a leader. God will appoint another leader (Joshua) to take his place.

• The God of Israel will not tolerate the worship of any other gods. This idol-worship will be a temptation for the people as they become settled and complacent in their new land.

• God represents stability and dependability in the face of the faithlessness and disobedience of the chosen people.

JOSHUA

OUTLINE OF JOSHUA

INTRODUCTION

The sixth book of our Bible is named for Joshua, the central figure in its story. That story is the story of Israel's conquest of Canaan. Joshua is a great leader in these events, yet he is not a hero in the usual sense. Joshua does not accomplish great deeds by his own ability. Instead, Joshua appears as God's instrument. It is God who is the real hero here.

Jews have traditionally classed Joshua as the first of the books called the Former Prophets (Joshua–2 Kings). These are not prophetic books as we know them, but they received the name for two reasons: (1) After a time, people began to call all great religious leaders prophets, and (2) these books reflect a prophetic view of history.

Christians, on the other hand, usually class Joshua as a historical book, because Joshua tells the history of Israel's conquest and settlement of the Promised Land. More than that, though, this book tells of God's action in and through specific historical events. Joshua gives us both history and a religious interpretation of that history.

Relationship to Other Biblical Books

The book of Joshua stands as an essential part of the whole historical sequence sweeping from Genesis to Nehemiah. As one portion of the ongoing story of God's action in Israel's history, Joshua has strong ties to many biblical books. In Joshua we see God's fulfillment of the Genesis promises to Abraham. Joshua carries forth the themes of law and covenant so basic to the book of Exodus. Sometimes the man Joshua even appears as a parallel to the Exodus leader, Moses. The Psalms often mention the conquest story in poetic praise of God for mighty acts. As mentioned before, Joshua shares a religious viewpoint with many of the prophets. The book has its closest ties, however, with a literary unit that runs from Deuteronomy through Second Kings. Style and theology show that this whole epic was probably written or compiled by one school of writers who maintained a standard outlook and formula for expression. So, Joshua does not stand alone; it is part of a much larger biblical picture.

Authorship

The book is now a well-organized whole, but there are signs that the author(s) used many older sources for his work. He has blended together many stories, some of them ancient tribal traditions whose originators are unknown. This blending has left a few contradictions. For instance in 4:8, twelve stones are carried out of the Jordan. But in 4:9, twelve stones are set up in the river. Either way, the writer still makes his point. His concern to glorify God comes through.

Theology

The book of Joshua shows us a God of unlimited power, justice, and grace. God acts in historical events of this world. Israel is God's chosen instrument in the world. Obedience to God's command gives Israel success; disobedience brings failure. God's promises are true and worthy of trust. The covenant is both God's gracious gift and Israel's moral responsibility.

For special reasons, God wants Israel to possess the land of Canaan. God has promised it and works with the faithful people to bring this about. The conquest is thus a gift, not Joshua's nor Israel's achievement. God's will for the people is freedom and self-determination, and God follows through to give Israel a homeland.

Most of us probably find little quarrel with such a theology. Yet underneath there are some problems. One has been the over-simplification of the "obedience equals success" theory. Some have taken this belief to mean that (1) we can win God's favor by good works, or (2) that every misfortune is proof of sin. Seeing these problems, many have supposed that the writer was a shallow thinker. Perhaps he had not even considered the problem of innocent suffering. So they have written him off. But perhaps the writer was speaking only of the nation's long-term well-being, not of individual short-term events.

Another problem that often bothers readers of Joshua is the picture they see of God as a God of violence and bloodshed, a God who seems to advocate pure mayhem if it suits the divine purposes. Since this is not the God we know through Jesus, many simply dismiss Joshua as primitive religious fanaticism. Others suggest that Israel's religious understanding had just not developed far enough to see God as a God of consistent love toward everyone. But we must remember that peace was always offered before a town was destroyed. The writer may actually be expressing a much deeper thought: that this God is one who works through the people and institutions of this world as they are, good or evil. God uses war, even though it is evil, because God works with what is here, not what we might wish were here.

Dates

In Joshua there are two dates to consider: the date of the events and the date when the writer(s) wrote them down.

The date of the events themselves is fairly clear. After the Exodus from Egypt and the wilderness wanderings, Israel finally established a home in Canaan. This probably happened in the late thirteenth century B.C.

The date of writing or compiling is more complex. We cannot tell how old the ancient sources may be. Many scholars believe that the final composition of all of the books from Deuteronomy through 2 Kings—including the book of Joshua—took place during the time of the monarchy (particularly during the reign of Hezekiah or Josiah) or perhaps during the Babylonian Exile. In any case, the final version of the book of Joshua likely appeared several hundred years after the events it describes. The writers or compilers were determined to tie the story together, to preserve the nation's history, and to interpret that history in the light of faith.

Historical Value

With such a time lapse between the events and the final book we might expect some information gaps, some fuzziness on details. And we do find them in Joshua. So how much historical fact can we expect from this book? Our answer, given the circumstances, is: a surprising amount.

Because of information from Judges 1 and other sources, scholars formerly thought that the conquest was really a slow infiltration, with each tribe working more or less alone. Some tribes may not even have left Canaan for Egypt at all. This is very different from the concentrated campaigns we see in Joshua. So scholars supposed that Joshua was an idealized version of the process. More recent archaeological evidence, however, has shown a massive destruction of Canaanite cites in the thirteenth century. It appears that a concerted effort may have occurred and that Joshua may well be more accurate than previously assumed. For now, we cannot know exactly how quickly or how closely the tribes worked. That need not, however, keep us from understanding the author's main point: the saving, freeing action of God in the history of a faithful, obedient people.

JOSHUA 1–2

Introduction to These Chapters

From the very first verse the author makes it clear that the book of Joshua is a continuation of Israel's great historical narrative. He takes up precisely where the book of Deuteronomy ends, with the death of Moses. Moses has led the people to God's Promised Land. Now the conquest of that land is about to begin.

In the same first verse the author brings in the name of Joshua. Joshua is to take up where Moses left off. Here and in the following ten verses is the author's introduction. It is an introduction that ensures a smooth transition from the last book to this one. In it the author shows that human leadership is changing, but God's purposes and position of command are not.

Following the introduction we find some ancient traditions concerning the conquest itself, including the story of a specific incident through which God worked to help Israel toward its first victory. Throughout these verses, as throughout the book, God is at the center. It is God who promises, commands, and aids the people. Joshua is God's instrument for the task at hand.

Here is an outline of these chapters.

I. Joshua Assumes Command (1:1-11)
II. The Transjordan Tribes Pledge Aid (1:12-18)
III. The Spies (2:1-24)

The Message of Joshua 1–2

In even this short passage we find many of the basic ideas that run through Deuteronomy–2 Kings. We see a God active in history, a God who commands and leads the people, a God who is working to fulfill the promises made to Israel. We see God offering help and strength from the very onset of a difficult struggle. But God's help is conditional; it depends on the people's faithfulness and obedience to the law. The people's success also depends upon their working together. The achievement of good is a cooperative process. It requires cooperation of the people with each other and with God. Only thus can a strong, successful nation be formed and endure.

To us in our time this passage reiterates a timeless biblical message. The almighty God cares for us, will strengthen and guide us, and will fulfill the promises made to us. We, however, bear a part of the responsibility for our own success. We must obey God and work cooperatively with others. God gives the law, not simply to assert authority, but to guide us and to keep us in fellowship with God. If we disobey, we will be going against the grain of life, so we can only fall into difficulty and failure. The tragic stories of many

individuals and nations who have made their own rules attest to this wisdom from the ancient past.

JOSHUA 3–5

Introduction to These Chapters

Now Israel is ready to take the big step. The people will cross the Jordan and invade the land of Canaan. The crossing itself is a miraculous one, a never-to-be-forgotten event. God's power continues to work in this latest stage of the people's struggle for freedom. God is still acting to fulfill the promise.

These chapters, like the previous ones, contain traces of many traditions. The author has skillfully joined them to tell as completely as possible the story of one of the greatest events in Israel's history.

Like all of Joshua, however, this is more than a story. As striking as the events themselves is the attitude the author conveys. At each step we see the people's reverence, obedience, and worship. The author is very concerned that we recognize the importance of these attitudes. This is the work of a person who is trying to preserve and enhance his own people's reverence and faith.

We can see in these chapters some of the writer's other concerns, too. We will note his interest in ritual, his interest in preserving and magnifying liturgical forms, his concern for remembrance of historical events and God's actions in them, and his special interest in the law. The writer wants us to know how Israel came into possession of the land, but he also wants us to learn a religious outlook on all of history. He wants us to see the power and love of God at work in the lives of the chosen people.

Here is an outline of chapters 3–5.

The Message of Joshua 3–5

The message of the crossing is simple enough: God has unlimited power. God cares for the people, and will help them if they will remain obedient and reverent. Ritual is an important element of that obedience and reverence. Historical memories are also important because they remind us of God's great acts in the past and inspire awe, trust, and reverence in the present. Both remembrance and ritual help bind us to our fellow believers.

We today sometimes forget the vital role ritual can play in keeping us aware of God's greatness and trustworthiness. Certainly, ritual can be empty show. But if it is entered into with the heart, ritual can strengthen our faith. It can bind us in more trusting, more obedient fellowship with the almighty, loving God and with God's children.

JOSHUA 6–8

Introduction to These Chapters

Now the conquest begins. These chapters chronicle the first two battles, those at Jericho and Ai. The well-known battle of Jericho was a tremendous success. The battle at Ai was a very different story—a story of sin and discovery, and a story of defeat and eventual victory.

The material in these chapters comes from several different sources, some of them probably quite ancient. We find here many double versions of events. Sometimes these versions do not agree in every detail. Some stories may have become blurred or confused by age, yet they carry important memories of God's action in a crucial era of Israel's life. These the author has woven into a powerful narrative of both history and faith.

The author's main points remain as in previous passages: God's almighty power and the importance of obedience.

Here is an outline of chapters 6–8.

The Message of Joshua 6–8

Obedience—total, complete obedience—that is the key. Achan's disobedience ruined Israel's attack on Ai. Correction of this sinful situation made success possible. The writer never wavers from this basic point: When Israel is obedient, God will bring success. If Israel disobeys, failure will ensue.

We may offer some objections to the writer's simple formula. Life is sometimes more complicated than the writer would make it appear. Still the kernel of truth is there. Sin breaks people's relationship with God. They then have no access to this strength when they need it. There is no substitute for living as God has told us to live.

JOSHUA 9–12

Introduction to These Chapters

After spectacular successes at Jericho and Ai, Joshua moves on to conquer the rest of God's Promised Land. Chapters 9 through 12 tell the story of that conquest.

Joshua now faces a more complicated situation. It is no longer a matter of fighting one city at a time. Word of Israel's military feats has spread. Canaanite leaders recognize the grave threat facing them. So, they begin to join together for defense.

One group coalesces in the south and one in the north. Joshua will have to deal with both these larger coalitions. In addition one city, acting independently, tries a different strategy, a combination of treachery and diplomacy. This complicates matters slightly, but God helps Joshua through it all to eventual victory.

In these four chapters the writer paints a rather majestic picture of Israel sweeping over Canaan by God's great power. The story is told quickly. The victories are complete. A brief note in chapter 11, however, states that the war took a long time. Naturally, it would. Yet the writer has chosen to compress the action so he can bring out his point, the mighty and irresistible power of God that has given Israel the land of promise.

As in previous chapters, the writer has used several sources. Many of these may be very old and carry excellent historical memories. Some may have become confused over time. This much we know: Israel did overcome the Canaanites and did settle in Palestine, there to remain until 587 B.C.

Here is an outline of Joshua 9–12.
I. Treaty with the Gibeonites (9:1-27)
II. Southern Campaigns (10:1-43)
III. Northern Campaigns (11:1-23)
IV. Conclusion (12:1-24)

The Message of Joshua 9–12

Power and gift—if one had to characterize the message of Joshua 9–12 in a few words, these two would do it well. The stories of swift, total conquest show God's tremendous power working at every turn. The miracles, the sudden victorious attacks, and the enemies' panic emphasize God's unlimited force. Gift, while that word never appears in the text, is a central point of the stories. The Promised Land has been conquered, not by Joshua's brilliance nor by Israel's strength, but by the power of God. Israel has not earned the land; it is a gift from God. So the meaning is this: The almighty God cares for the people, fights for them, and will give them the gifts that have been promised to them. For their part, they must remember that what they have is not theirs by merit, but as a gift from God. That core message is as valid for us today as it was thousands of years ago.

JOSHUA 13–21

Introduction to These Chapters

The main battles are over. Joshua and his people have general control of the Promised Land. Now it is time to settle down. Chapters 13–21 tell how the twelve tribes, by lot, obtained their portions. The author gives detailed listings of cities and boundaries assigned. Chapters 20 and 21 also detail the establishment of two special kinds of cities. In the land distribution, as in the battles before, God is the commander and supervisor.

The material in these chapters comes from many sources. It is even more of a jumble in spots than we have found in previous chapters. The lists of towns and boundaries come from various times and appear to have been updated here and there along the way. So, we cannot be sure exactly what lands the tribes received at the actual time of conquest. The lists do give us a general idea, however.

One question has bothered scholars: Did the tribes really distribute the land by lot as described, or do the lists merely reflect geographical realities—the places where each tribe eventually chose to settle? The boundaries as given probably do reflect some natural settlement patterns and population shifts over the centuries. The fact, however, that the text gives us two

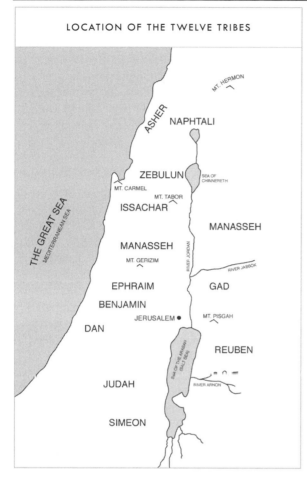

LOCATION OF THE TWELVE TRIBES

MT. HERMON

ASHER

NAPHTALI

ZEBULUN

SEA OF CHINNERETH

MT. CARMEL

MT. TABOR

ISSACHAR

MANASSEH

MANASSEH

MT. GERIZIM

RIVER JORDAN

RIVER JABBOK

EPHRAIM

GAD

BENJAMIN

JERUSALEM ●

MT. PISGAH

DAN

REUBEN

Sea OF THE ARABAH (SALT SEA)

JUDAH

RIVER ARNON

SIMEON

THE GREAT SEA

MEDITERRANEAN SEA

The tribe of Levi is called by God to serve as priests. They have no specific territory but are assigned certain cities throughout Israel. Joseph also receives no allotment. However, two of Joseph's sons, Manasseh and Ephraim, receive shares. The total of territories thus remains at twelve.

These chapters show God's people working together at God's command to form a cohesive nation. The author, writing in exile, was especially concerned with the tribes sticking together. His attention to the details of ancient land holdings, as those details had come down to him, may also reflect his exilic setting. After all, if the people were soon to return home, it might be important to remind everyone just who was supposed to own what. It would also help to maintain hope if people could remember that God had given them this land. The boundaries the writer describes are, of course, ideal ones. Israel very seldom controlled territory that actually matched this description.

accounts of a distribution at two different sites suggests that some sort of initial planned distribution did take place under the leadership of Joshua.

These chapters include another small problem, that of the twelve tribes. Here and in many other Old Testament books, the number twelve is highly significant. Yet we can find differing lists of tribal names. The twelve tribes that receive territories here are: Reuben, Gad, Judah, Benjamin, Simeon, Asher, Dan, Zebulun, Issachar, Naphtali, Manasseh, and Ephraim. But Levi and Joseph were two of Jacob's twelve sons. What about them?

These chapters may be outlined as follows.

I. Land Still Unconquered (13:1-7)
II. Inheritance of the Transjordan Tribes (13:8-33)
III. Division Among Remaining Tribes (14:1–19:51)
IV. Special Cities and Conclusion (20:1–21:45)

The Message of Joshua 13–21

By following God's commands, Israel was able to establish an orderly, cohesive nation. Fair division of land, plus establishment of Levitical cities and cities of refuge, reduced the probability of internal quarrels. The tribes could live together in peace and, with that internal peace, would gain strength to face external foes. Most important, these institutions that would make the nation strong came from God. God, even now, was still providing for the people.

More generally, the message is that God does want the people to live in peace. God not only wants this, but works to help it happen. God provides institutions and processes that make it easier to get along together. Our part is to obey commands and to use the institutions and rules God has given to develop a good communal life.

JOSHUA 22–24

Introduction to These Chapters

These chapters mark the end—the end of Israel's conquest period, the end of Joshua's life, and the end of the book of Joshua. The largest battles are over. The tribes from east of the Jordan can go home. The remaining tribes can move to their assigned territories. The people can work in peace to build a new nation. And yet, misunderstanding of one event, the building of an altar, threatens to undo everything. The matter is settled, however, and the nation remains intact.

This is obviously a crucial point in Israel's history, a time for reflection and stock-taking. We find these attitudes in two farewell addresses given by Joshua. They wrap up all that Israel's experience and Joshua's own example have taught throughout the book. In the first address Joshua pleads with the people to obey God so they may continue to prosper in God's strength. In the second he leads the people

in a covenant renewal, a conscious pledge to continue serving God alone. This end is a new beginning, the start of a new phase of nationhood. It is a phase to be lived, like past phases, in faithful obedience.

This section, like the rest of Joshua, has been woven together from several sources. Some are probably ancient remembrances handed down over the centuries. What the various writers have done with these remembrances reflects the special concerns of the periods in which those writers lived. One important period was the time of King Josiah (640–609 B.C.). A second major period was the Exile (587–538 B.C.). Idolatry, intermingling with Canaanites, and ritual correctness were major concerns from Josiah's time on. The tragic consequences of faithlessness and God's geographically limitless presence were significant ideas during the Exile. Other themes, like national unity and Israel's covenant with God, were important in many periods.

The book climaxes with Joshua's dramatic challenge to covenant renewal at Shechem. This climax is an extremely effective way of placing before readers the book's central point: the importance of obedience and faithfulness.

Here is an outline of these chapters.
I. Departure of the Transjordan Tribes (22:1-34)
II. Farewell Address (23:1-16)
III. Covenant at Shechem (24:1-28)
IV. Three Burials (24:29-33)

The Message of Joshua 22–24

These chapters, especially Joshua's speeches, pound away at a basic point: God is the power that protects and saves you. If you remain faithful to God you will have success; if you do not, you will reap disaster. Joshua's challenge to the people at Shechem invites all to join in the congregation's affirmation: "we also will serve the LORD, for he is our God" (24:18).

The warnings about the temptations of idolatry are all too poignant. Israel too often compromised its allegiance to God and went after idols. Even when overt idolatry had been controlled, faithlessness continued. Finally, the nation collapsed. Yet the call was still there. The people could still return to God. They could again affirm with Joshua: ". . . as for me and my household, we will serve the LORD." The writer hoped that his people would do just that.

As for us, we have the glad and the sad experiences of Israel to learn from. We, too, are tempted to turn from God. But we, like Israel, can also respond to the challenge. We can choose this day, and every day, whom we will serve.

JUDGES

OUTLINE OF JUDGES

INTRODUCTION

Name

The title refers to this book's main characters, the judges. The Hebrew concept of "judge" differs somewhat, however, from our American use of the word. The biblical persons called judges were tribal or national leaders. Often they were military commanders. Sometimes they settled disputes or offered advice. They gained their leadership positions informally or by popular acclaim. Many judges displayed exceptional wisdom, unusual skill in organization, or personal charisma. These were individuals in whom the people could see God's Spirit at work. It was this divine spirit that gave the judges their talents. Since Israel had no king or other central political figure, the judges played an important role in Israel's survival. They provided administrative and military leadership to a new, loosely organized nation.

Classification

Jews consider this book the second of the "former prophets." And, like the book of Joshua, it does exhibit a prophetic viewpoint. Christians, however, usually call this a historical book because it deals directly with the history of Israel and forms part of the epic historical work that includes most of Deuteronomy through 2 Kings.

Author

Who wrote the book of Judges? That is a complicated question. Scholars believe that the book grew over several centuries. It includes stories, conveying kernels of genuine historical memory, which are much older than the book as a whole. Most scholars believe that the crucial writing, compiling, and editing of the book of Joshua—like the surrounding books of Deuteronomy through 2 Kings—took place over generations during the time of King Hezekiah (eighth century B.C.), King Josiah (seventh century B.C.), and sometime during and after the exile of Judah to Babylon (sixth–fifth century B.C.).

Style

The style of Judges varies because so many people contributed to it. We find earthiness and a sense of humor mixed with judgmental comments and dry connecting paragraphs. Still, throughout the book we can see one obvious formula repeated over and over, as described in the NRSV: "The Israelites did what was evil in the sight of the LORD, and the LORD gave them over to . . ." and "the Israelites cried out to the LORD and the LORD raised up a deliverer . . ." and "the land had rest"; or as phrased in the NIV, "the Israelites did evil in the eyes of the LORD, and the LORD handed them over to . . ." and "the Israelites cried out to the LORD and the LORD raised up a deliverer . . ." and "the land had peace." With this formula the later writers or editors tied the string of stories together and made a theological point all at the same time.

Purpose

The writers' purpose was, of course, to preserve Israel's history. But it was more than that—they wanted to convey the lessons of history, to show the nation what it must do to survive and prosper. These writers wanted to encourage faithfulness and obedience in a people who could easily go astray. They wanted to warn the people of the consequences of disobedience and to remind them that God could be depended upon, no matter what the danger.

The Times

What were the times like? Since the book grew over so many centuries we have to deal with several different times. First is the time of the judges themselves, 1200–1050 B.C. This was just after Joshua's conquest of Palestine and before Israel chose its first king. The time was a very unsettled one. Israel still had to fight to maintain its hold on the land. The nation was only loosely organized. It was surrounded by enemies, all trying to move into or regain land that Israel held. There was Ammon east of the Jordan, there was a Canaanite confederation in north-central Palestine, there were Philistines on the west, Moabites to the southeast, and Midianite nomads who ranged to the east and south of Israel.

Israel was frequently at war with these enemies. Unity among the tribes was essential. But Israel had no king. God was to be their only ruler. So, in times of special need, divinely inspired judges took on specific leadership tasks.

The religious situation under the judges was one of alternating faith and faithlessness. When they were faithful, the people depended upon God for protection and leadership. They recognized God's spirit working through the judges. The tribes periodically met to worship God at central sanctuaries, including Shiloh, Bethel, Gilgal, and Mizpah. Some individuals had home worship centers as well. Nonetheless, this was a primitive time. Faith and worship often went awry. Superstition ran high, and divination was a common practice. Idolatry crept in. Ethics were not the highest. We find many cases of sexual laxity, treachery, thievery, and violence here. Low morality was common and was sometimes approved or taken for granted.

The time of the seventh- and eighth-century compilations was more organized. But Israel had fallen into gross idolatry. So concern focuses on pagan influence and idol worship.

By the time of the exilic editor, Israel's land had been destroyed. The defeated Jews feared that God had rejected them or was powerless to help them. This editor used the stories of the judges to show that an all-powerful God would continue to fight for Israel if the people would only respond in obedience.

Theological Perspective

The main theological points in Judges are the same as those of Joshua. The writer emphasizes God's power, desire to help Israel, and faithfulness in fulfilling promises, and the importance of obedience. If the people will obey, God will defend them and enable them to prosper. If they do not obey, disaster will befall.

Here, as in Joshua, we encounter a problem with violence. These stories frequently show God as an advocate of bloodshed. Why should the biblical writers portray God this way? One reason lies in human nature. It is very easy in time of war to assume that God hates the enemy as much as we do. Ancient peoples were no different from ourselves in that respect. They gleefully reported every detail of the foe's defeat and attributed it all to a vengeful God. Second, we must consider that early Israel may not yet have come to recognize God's love for all people. Very old stories tend to think of God's love for Israel alone. Third, a concern for preserving historical material or a reluctance to get into complex questions of God's character may have led a later, more sophisticated editor to let the ancient stories stand without revision or comment. A fourth possibility is that the writer saw God using the world as it is, not the world as we might wish it to be. In a violent world, God is shown moving in violent events toward long-term goals.

Conclusion

Judges, then, is not a simple book. It is an important one, though. It provides both vital historical information and a religious perspective on God's acts in history. This perspective is one that we need to consider in thinking through our own faith.

JUDGES 1:1–2:5

Introduction to This Passage

"After the death of Joshua . . ."—with his first words the writer links this book to the preceding one in his series. We know that the history begun in Joshua is now continuing in the book of Judges.

Next we find a curious question in verse 1: "Who shall go up first for us against the Canaanites?" (NRSV; NIV = "Who will be the first to go up and fight for us against the Canaanites?"). The book of Joshua has just told us all about Israel's conquest of Palestine. Why now this question of who will go first to fight? There are two possibilities. One is that this is a different version of the basic conquest, one in which Joshua is not a major hero. The second possibility is that after Joshua's conquest the land was still not completely under Israel's control. Joshua 14–19 suggests this kind of situation. These stories, then, would be the stories of each tribe's efforts to take control of its territory. Whatever the case, we begin with a recognition that Israel had to fight for the land. As the book goes on we realize that Israel must continue to fight to maintain its possession.

Judges 1:1–2:5 is a complicated mixture of material. We find here some duplicates from Joshua and some passages that differ from the Joshua narrative. One big difference is that now the tribes are working separately rather than as a unit. Another is that there is no one leader. Only a tribe, Judah, is mentioned as leading the way. We also find some differences in the areas conquered. The battles may have taken place after Joshua, or the differences may be due to variations in ancient memories.

The purpose of this section is to preserve as much information as possible, to provide a transition from the book of Joshua, and to establish this writer's unique interpretation of Israel's history in this period.

The outline of this section has just two parts:

   I. Many a Battle (1:1-36)
   II. Departure from Gilgal (2:1-5)

The Message of Judges 1:1–2:5

These verses are clearly a warning against the temptations of faithlessness and disobedience. The writer insists that God is faithful but that the people have not been faithful to God. They failed to complete the task of conquest God had assigned them. That failure would lead to idolatry and eventual ruin.

This is one variation of the message that the writer(s) emphasizes throughout this history. Our success follows obedience; our failure follows disobedience. We today may recognize that all disaster is not necessarily the result of faithlessness. Yet, much of our misery, whether personal, national, or global, stems from someone's failure to live as God has intended. Perhaps we, like Israel, need to recognize the danger of our ways—and weep.

JUDGES 2:6–3:6

Introduction to This Passage

Another introduction—that's what we find in Judges 2:6–3:6. In the preceding section the writer had introduced us to the book of Judges. He had made a clear transition from the book of Joshua. He had told us of Joshua's death. Now here we find Joshua again. It looks like Judges 2:6–3:6 was the opening of an earlier version of the book. The final editor kept what he had and added an introduction of his own (1:1–2:5) before it.

The 2:6–3:6 introduction has two parts. Verses 6-10 form a connecting link to the book of Joshua by reviewing Joshua's death and burial. The accounts of this hero's tribal dismissal and death echo Joshua 24:28-31. In 2:11–3:6 someone has written a summary of what we will find in the book of Judges. It is a story of faithlessness and disaster, yet an affirmation of God's desire to save Israel if only the people will turn to God. This writer explains the role of the judges and how God used them to help Israel. The section concludes with two lists of non-Israelite peoples whose continued presence in Palestine contributed to Israel's downfall.

The material in these chapters obviously comes from several sources. We find numerous repetitions and variations. The writer apparently wanted to save every tradition, and did so despite the inconsistencies this created.

Within this material we find some important theological concepts. The writer outlines for us a pattern of events that will recur throughout the book. He sees the period of the judges as a repeating cycle of defection, oppression, prayer, and deliverance. Here and throughout the book he uses a set formula to begin a story, as seen in 2:11: "Then the Israelites did what was evil in the sight of the LORD" (NRSV; NIV = "the Israelites did evil in the eyes of the LORD"). The main point of the writer's whole historical epic comes through clearly in Judges: If the people obey God, they will prosper; if not, they will suffer. The writer (or several writers) also tries in these chapters to explain a theological puzzle, the problem of why God ever allowed these alien peoples to remain in the land when their presence caused so much trouble. In Joshua the answer was

that Israel itself failed to rout the inhabitants. Israel thereby disobeyed God's command and suffered accordingly. In Judges 2:20-22 and 3:1-6 the writer provides additional explanations for the disastrous situation.

Here is an outline of this brief, but complex, section of Judges:

    I. Joshua Dies (2:6-10)
    II. Israel's Infidelity (2:11-23)
    III. Israel Among the Nations (3:1-6)

The Message of Judges 2:6–3:6

This short passage carries several messages from several hands. The first and most prominent is the story of the later generations' spiritual infidelity and the suffering it caused. The second is God's effort to help. The third includes the explanations of why God allowed corrupting alien influences to remain within Israel: to punish, to test, to teach, or to bring the people back.

These verses speak of our frailty and of the weakness of second-hand religion. We, like the ancient Israelites, live among unbelievers. Our neighbors have values and practices that differ drastically from the biblical ideal. It is easy for us to accept their ways. It is easy to ignore God's commands. In the midst of these temptations, we need help. Unfortunately, it may take some suffering to make us realize that we need firsthand experience of God's power in our lives. That experience is one that we can only get through repentance and obedience.

JUDGES 3:7–31

Introduction to This Chapter

Israel had established itself in Palestine. Still, the nations on every side continually pressed. Some wanted to recover territory Israel had wrested from them. All wanted to extend their holdings as far as they could. So Israel's claim to the land was often threatened. Power shifted from time to time and place to place. Sometimes Israel held its own; sometimes it didn't. The writers set out to explain these changing fortunes from their own unique theological perspective. These events were not just political or military affairs; they were reflections of Israel's relationship with God.

With Judges 3:7-31 we begin the actual stories of the judges. These verses contain three ancient stories of men who saved Israel from encroaching enemies. None of the men is especially well-known today. Other biblical heroes have overshadowed them in the popular mind. This is due, at least in part, to the fact that these accounts are so short. The first is brief and tells only the basic facts plus their interpretation. The third is just one verse long. Only the second carries enough detail to really be a story.

Israel's Judges

1. Othniel	8. Jair
2. Ehud	9. Jephthah
3. Shamgar	10. Ibzan
4. Deborah	11. Elon
5. Gideon	12. Abdon
6. Abimelech	13. Samson
7. Tola	14. Samuel

The first and second stories follow the writer's characteristic formula. They begin with the people of Israel doing evil before God. They worship idols. The Lord becomes angry and sells them into servitude. When the people cry to God for help, a deliverer is provided. The third story, being only a single verse, lacks the full formula. Yet, packed in among the others, it seems to follow the pattern.

Inclusion of these brief accounts shows the writer's determination to preserve all the historical material available. The repeated formula shows his concern to interpret the stories in theological terms.

The writer uses these and subsequent stories to show how Israel is supposed to relate to God. Here we begin a book-long series of examples where faithlessness breeds disaster while return to God brings salvation and peace. God is Israel's king and commander. Trust and obedience to this divine king is Israel's key to survival and success.

Here is an outline of these three accounts:

  I. Othniel (3:7-11)
  II. Ehud (3:12-30)
  III. Shamgar (3:31)

The Message of Judges 3:7-31

This is a message of history. God has saved the people many times. No matter how often they sin and suffer, when they turn to God they will be saved. People of the Exile knew suffering. The writer offers them the evidence of history to show that there is hope. No matter what Israel's sins (and they have been serious), God can still raise up a deliverer.

The United States is currently the world's only superpower. Still, our country could one day fall either from external conquest or from internal weakness. The message of Judges is that there is hope for a nation, even a nation in deep trouble, if that nation will turn to the Lord.

For individuals, too, the message holds. No matter what the sin or the suffering, God can help, if we will only ask for help.

JUDGES 4–5

Introduction to These Chapters

CONTENT

These chapters tell the story of two judges, Deborah and Barak. Deborah is the leader and organizer; Barak is the military commander who carries out Israel's battle for freedom.

The place is Israel's northern territory. Enemies are confining Israel to the hills and denying access to the more prosperous plain areas.

The time is the twelfth century B.C., probably around 1125. Archaeologists have discovered that Taanach, which figures prominently in the story, was destroyed about that time.

The enemy is a coalition of Canaanite kings or of Canaanites and Sea Peoples. These kings have strong armies with horses, iron chariots, and plenty of weapons. Israel is militarily weak and does not even know yet how to work with iron.

The problem, on the surface, is the oppression of these Canaanites. The people of Israel live in fear, shrinking back into the hills to avoid confrontation with the aggressive foe. Back roads are unsafe, caravans are unable to travel into Israel, farmers can scarcely work their land. But the underlying problem, as always in Judges, is Israel's faithlessness to God. Idolatry again has raised its ugly head, and Israel is suffering because of it.

The solution comes when the people finally call to God for help. God does respond by sending help, through Deborah and Barak. These two persons rouse the oppressed people to action. They call upon all the tribes of Israel to form an army. Some, but significantly not all, of the tribes respond. The day of battle comes. The weak, untrained tribesmen face their enemy. Then God, by storm and flood, destroys that enemy, giving Israel freedom and peace.

STRUCTURE

These chapters contain two versions of the same story. Chapter 4 is a prose account. Chapter 5 is a poem. That poem is one of the oldest pieces of Hebrew literature we have. It may well have been composed at the time of the event. The prose version of chapter 4 may be a combination of two battle stories, one about a victory over Jabin and one about a victory over Sisera.

The two chapters tell essentially the same story, but they disagree on a few details. In chapter 4 Jabin is king of Canaan, and Sisera is his general. Chapter 5 does not mention Jabin at all. Instead, we find the kings of Canaan, who are led by Sisera. Jabin appears in Joshua 11:1 as king of Hazor. His mention at this earlier time is one reason for suspecting that he does not quite fit into the Deborah story. His absence from chapter 5 supports that suspicion.

A second difference in detail is the scene of battle. In chapter 4 the battle is at the foot of Mount Tabor. In chapter 5 the battle is at Taanach.

A third difference between the two accounts concerns who fought the battle. Chapter 4 mentions only the tribes of Zebulun and Naphtali. Chapter 5, however, gives these two special credit but indicates that other tribes also helped.

Despite these minor differences, each version makes the same point: God, through Deborah and Barak, saves Israel.

PURPOSE

The writer's general purpose in including these chapters was to preserve Israel's history and to inspire courage and faith, especially in times of oppression. The poem in chapter 5, however, originally had some additional purposes. In the days before writing was common, it served as a teaching tool. It may also have served as a form of popular entertainment. But its most important function was probably to arouse enthusiasm and encourage action when Israelite armies again gathered to face a common enemy. This thrilling story of courage and victory would motivate the assembled recruits to bravery in the coming battle.

STYLE

Both these versions provide detailed, colorful accounts of events. Both are good examples of storytelling art, though perhaps the poem is a bit more dramatic. The writers build suspense, help listeners identify with Israel's cause and its heroes, and teach well their main points: the power and trustworthiness of God, the need for courage and faith, and the importance of cooperation.

A MORAL PROBLEM

In both these pieces, modern readers may find a common Old Testament problem. These stories reveal, even applaud, bloodthirstiness, vengefulness, and deceit. Jael is praised for her treachery and murder. Chapter 5 glories in the misery Sisera's mother experiences as she waits in vain for her son's return. These attitudes are foreign to us and must be recognized as such. Even God's chosen people did not fully understand God in those early days, nor perhaps do we yet.

Here is an outline of these chapters.

I. The Oppression (4:1-3)
II. Deborah and Barak Plan (4:4-9)
III. The Victory (4:10-24)
IV. The Song of Deborah (5:1-31)

The Message of Judges 4–5

This passage carries the message that God is powerful and will save if Israel will trust and obey. It also emphasizes two additional, though not unique, messages: (1) the importance of cooperation among God's people, and (2) the praiseworthiness of courage in carrying out God's will.

We, like the people of ancient Israel, need to rely on God's power if we are to succeed. On the other hand, we must recognize that courageous action on our part may be needed to implement God's plan for helping us.

JUDGES 6–8

Introduction to These Chapters

These are the stories of Gideon. Like many other Israelite judges, Gideon is a great military leader. But in other ways he is a different kind of judge. He does not exemplify the faithful, courageous servant of God. He comes from a Baal-worshiping family and town, he is reluctant to accept God's call, he questions God's concern, and he is slow to believe God's promises. Later he proves headstrong, overly aggressive, and self-serving. He recognizes that God alone must be king, yet sets himself up as a formal leader. His work does save Israel, but others of his actions set Israel up for further disaster. As a judge Gideon is not an unqualified success.

TIME

Archaeological findings place Gideon about fifty years before Deborah, that is, around 1175 B.C. The final editor may have been unaware that the stories were out of order. Some commentators, however, see an alternating pattern of good and not-so-good judges within the book as a whole. This could explain Gideon's appearance after Deborah.

Many of these stories show signs of great antiquity. Though they have been passed down and edited over generations, some of the materials may carry surprisingly accurate reflections of the conditions and events they describe.

PLACE

These stories center in the territory of Manasseh in northern Palestine.

THE ENEMY

The enemy in these stories is Midian, a nomadic tribe based east of the Jordan. Allied with Midian are Amalekite nomads and possibly others.

STRUCTURE

This is a series of stories joined together to form a continuous narrative. There are at least two strands of traditions here. The strands are so thoroughly mingled, however, that one cannot untangle them with any certainty; they may account for the varying descriptions we find of Gideon's character. At one time he is timid, at another extremely aggressive. Sometimes he is faithful and obedient to God; at other times he questions or ignores God. Some of the early stories are very hero-oriented. Other stories emphasize God's action, with Gideon as God's instrument.

Apparently not all the storytellers held the same picture of Gideon, nor did they have the same point to make. The final editor has taken care to use the stories to show the importance of recognizing God's kingship and saving power.

Here is an outline of these chapters.

I. Problems with the Midianites (6:1-6)
II. Gideon's Call (6:7-32)
III. Invasion and Uncertainty (6:33-40)
IV. Preparations (7:1-15)
V. Attack and Victory (7:16–8:21)
VI. The Story Ends (8:22-35)

The Message of Judges 6–8

This section's major message is the basic theme: God is the supreme authority,

God is powerful, and God will save if the people will trust and obey. The story offers both a positive example (God's victory over Midian) and a negative example (the eventual ruin that comes from Gideon's and Israel's failure to keep God in the place of honor).

There is another message, however, that is not stated directly. That is the idea that God can use not just good people but badly flawed ones as well. Gideon was originally fearful, lacking in faith, and doubtful that God even cared. Later he overstepped his commission and grasped at authority beyond his right. Yet God had used Gideon to save Israel.

With all our scientific and technical accomplishments, it is easy for modern people to forget that it is not our own cleverness but the power of God that saves and sustains us. God is the world's supreme authority. Human attempts to usurp that authority can only lead us to disaster. Nevertheless, God will work with us as we are, flaws and all. The story of Gideon stands for us as an affirmation of God's powerful goodness and as a warning against the temptation of self-glorification.

JUDGES 9

Introduction to This Chapter

This story is different from most others in the book in that it is not a story about a judge. This is the story of a man who would lead, not by God's appointment, but at his own initiative. It is the story of Abimelech, Gideon's son. Gideon had refused the people's offer to crown him king. Abimelech was not so scrupulous. Although God was supposed to be Israel's only ruler, Abimelech set out to become a king. Abimelech was usurping God's authority, and he reaped a tragic harvest for his sin.

The story takes place in and around Shechem. Abimelech's mother was a Shechemite, so this was Abimelech's birthplace. It had a large Canaanite population and was an important center for Baal worship.

Shechem was centrally located in northern Israel and sat at the pass between Mount Ebal and Mount Gerizim. That made it an excellent place to establish a city-state. From there one could extend power in several directions. Abimelech may have had grand plans for an ever-enlarging kingdom.

Abimelech's lunge for power probably took place sometime between 1175 and 1150 B.C. We do not know when the original stories were first composed, but they could be quite old. Scholars can detect at least two strands of tradition within the present story, but the strands are thoroughly tied together now. The story probably appeared in the seventh-century history. From there it would take its place in the post exilic history that we have today.

Chapter 9 does not begin with the usual formula concerning the Israelites doing evil, their crying out, and the Lord sending a deliverer. The evil is obvious, but here there is no deliverer, so the formula would not fit. The story does support attitudes and goals consistent with the rest of the book of Judges and even the larger context of Deuteronomy through 2 Kings, however. The writer is openly contemptuous of Abimelech and carefully points out both his sins and his punishment.

Here is an outline of this chapter.

I. Kings of Shechem (9:1-6)
II. Jotham's Fable (9:7-21)
III. Quarrel and Rebellion (9:22-41)
IV. The Outcome (9:42-57)

The Message of Judges 9

Throughout the book of Judges the main message has been that those who trust and obey God, who affirm God's authority, will remain safe and prosperous. Here we see the negative side of that message. The writer presents Abimelech as a bad example. This young man has grasped at power, power that only God may exercise or confer. For this and related sins, Abimelech dies.

In today's technologically advanced, scientifically minded world, many people find it hard to recognize God's activity. It is easy to assume that we are in charge of things. Forgetting that this is God's world, we begin to make our own rules and behave however we choose toward other people and toward the environment. When we do this we can reap only disaster. No one—not Abimelech, not his modern counterparts—can get away with usurping God's authority.

JUDGES 10–12

Introduction to These Chapters

Here we find accounts of six lesser-known judges. The editor apparently knew very little about these men. Perhaps few significant events occurred in their times. The story of just one, Jephthah, is told in detail. He is the only one who faced and put down oppression. The others ruled in peace, apparently serving mainly as administrators. They saved Israel, not from outside evil, but from internal disorder.

These judges served after the death of Abimelech. It was probably around the middle of the twelfth century B.C.

These chapters contain a mixture of old stories, historical notes, and editorial comments. The notes about five of the judges are very short. There is no mention of the people doing evil or of any oppression. The usual opening and closing formulas are absent. Those formulas do occur, however, in the Jephthah story. There we see again that the Israelites did evil which angered the Lord and then they cried out to the Lord. When they did, Jephthah was available to help them.

Here is an outline of these chapters:

I. Tola (10:1-2)
II. Jair (10:3-5)
III. Jephthah (10:6–12:7)
IV. Ibzan (12:8-10)
V. Elon (12:11-12)
VI. Abdon (12:13-15)

The Message of Judges 10–12

The basic message of the Jephthah story is the familiar Judges theme: when people sin, they suffer; when they turn to God, God can and will save them. The message of the remaining notices is an implicit rather than an explicit variation of this basic theme. The brief notes with little comment suggest that during these years the people did not sin and thus were able to live peacefully under a God-given judge. These notes also suggest that good administration is a gift of God just as much as is a more dramatic military victory.

To us these passages may be saying that God provides for the chosen people in many ways. When necessary God may save us in a dramatic way from our enemies. At other times God may keep us safe by the gift of good, steady leadership. Whatever the situation, the blessings of safety, freedom, and peace come from a good, powerful, and caring God. They are available to us when we remain faithful and obedient.

JUDGES 13–16

Introduction to These Chapters

These are the stories of Samson. Samson was a man chosen before birth to be God's instrument in freeing Israel. He was not what we would consider a perfect candidate. He was headstrong, hot-tempered, not very smart, and unwilling or unable to learn from his mistakes. He had a weakness for women and blundered into all sorts of trouble. Yet, in God's Spirit, this man had magnificent physical strength. God used that strength to subdue large numbers of the foreigners who were ruling over Israel.

PALESTINE DURING THE ERA OF THE JUDGES

The stories take place in Judah, in southern Dan, and in the southern Philistine territory near the Mediterranean Sea. Samson's home is on the border between Judah and Dan, about fourteen miles west of Jerusalem.

The enemy Israel faces is Philistia. The Philistines had entered Palestine around 1200 B.C. They had settled along the seacoast, then proceeded to push progressively inland. Slowly they inched ever farther into Israel's territory. By the time of Samson (1150–1100 B.C.) the Philistines had apparently moved into much of southern Palestine. At first they were not heavy-handedly oppressive, but in later years Israel would frequently have to fight off Philistine armies. The memory of these violent encounters may have added to the storytellers' obvious glee in relating their tales of Philistine defeat.

These chapters include several stories and even an ancient poem or victory song. Unlike some parts of Judges, this section contains very little editorial comment. That may be because the stories were so old and so well-known that they were set in the public mind. The editor would not feel so free to add his own comments. The cycle does begin, however, with the standard formula, concerning the Israelites doing evil before in the sight of God. The rest of the formula, "the people cried . . . and the LORD raised up a judge," is missing.

The incidents recorded here are excellent examples of ancient storytelling. They are highly entertaining, suspenseful, and skillfully constructed so that climactic events are set up in advance yet held back just enough to retain the listener's attention. As in most folk literature, we find here some very effective exaggeration. Samson's feats of strength and the number of Philistines killed are fantastic. Yet the exaggeration does not mean that the stories lack historical roots. It simply means that the storytellers playfully poked their listeners in the ribs a little to make the point stick.

Modern readers may be somewhat surprised to find here a biblical hero whose morals are distressingly low. Samson's visits to prostitutes and wanton murder of innocent men in Ashkelon do not match our expectations of a religious figure. What's more, the writers and editors do not criticize Samson's behavior. We must, however, consider the times in which Samson lived. Apparently this behavior was not unusual. And, because the stories were so firmly set, later editors neither condemned nor brushed over Samson's brutality and looseness. Instead they allowed his imperfections to focus the spotlight completely on God's power. In effect they said, "Here is a man in all his weakness. See how God has been able to use him."

Here is an outline of these chapters.

I. The Story Begins (13:1-25)
II. A Stormy Marriage (14:1–15:8)
III. Confrontation with the Philistines (15:9-20)
IV. Temptations, Defeat, and Victory (16:1-31)

The Message of Judges 13–16

The Samson stories provide yet another variation on the basic message that God is the source of saving strength for Israel. Samson is not a hero in himself. In fact, on his own he is a bumbling, hot-tempered fool. Yet God can use a man like Samson to free the people.

The stories also illustrate a converse message. Breaking the covenant relationship with God cuts one off from God's strength. Samson, in allowing his hair to be cut, broke his Nazirite vow. He broke his relationship with God and lost the strength that came from God.

The story's dramatic ending offers another basic message: When people turn and call upon God, God does come to them and save them.

Beneath the human interest and excitement of the Samson tales the writer has given us once again his essential theological word: If we remain in right relationship with God, God will strengthen and save us. If not, we will suffer. Modern people, as much as their ancient counterparts, need to recognize these basic truths if we, collectively and as individuals, are to survive.

JUDGES 17–18

Introduction to These Chapters

These and the remaining chapters form a kind of appendix to the book of Judges. They are historical reminiscences from the same general time period, but they do not narrate stories of particular judges. The stories lack the usual formula. There is no note of Israel's sin, of outside oppression, of a cry for help, or of God's provision for a hero-judge to save the people. These chapters are simply additional bits of history that the editor apparently did not want to leave out.

The story in chapters 17–18 seems to have been composed for a particular purpose: to explain why for many years Levitical priests maintained an illegitimate sanctuary in Dan. The story's development involves events in the lives of a man from Ephraim, a Levite from Judah, and a large portion of the tribe of Dan. These three elements converge because of some religious paraphernalia. As the tale unfolds, the Ephraimite sets up a worship center and hires the Levite to tend it. At that point, the Ephraimite loses the worship center to thieving Danites, who are in the process of moving to new territory. Like many portions of Judges, this is a good example of ancient storytelling.

These events take place around 1100–1050 B.C. At that time Philistine pressure was squeezing the Danites out of their allotted territory. The religious and social situation reflected here suggests that the story itself may come from a time near the events described.

The story's age could help explain a factor that may seem odd to modern readers. That is the biblical storyteller's apparent unconcern for the morality (or immorality) of his characters. The story tells of theft, image-making (which is expressly forbidden and roundly criticized in other texts), and the slaughter of innocent people. The storyteller makes no explicit comment on any of this. Neither does any editor. Only the story itself and two brief bits of editorial information offer any possible hint of justice for these wrongs. Such an attitude could reflect the less-sensitive morality of an earlier age. By the time the editors incorporated this material it would be so entrenched in the popular mind that additional comment would be difficult, and perhaps unnecessary, to include.

On the surface, these chapters do little to promote the writer's particular theological concerns, but he apparently chose to preserve them, basically unaltered, as part of his people's heritage.

Here is an outline of these chapters.

I. Micah's Story (17:1-13)
II. The Danites' Move (18:1-13)
III. The Danites and Micah Clash (18:14-26)
IV. Settlement at Laish (18:27-31)

The Message of Judges 17–18

Listeners or readers are left to determine the meaning of this material for themselves. Listeners of a later time would probably take an "isn't it too bad?" attitude toward the setting up of images and independent sanctuaries. Yet, there are only two historical notes that might vaguely suggest editorial disapproval.

The story does, however, imply a basic message, consistent with Deuteronomy through 2 Kings, that the person who sins will eventually suffer. That is clearly what happens in Micah's case. He originally steals some silver. In the end, his silver idols are stolen from him. The case of the Danites is not so certain. It depends on whether or not that brief mention of the "captivity" was meant to suggest a punishment.

The modern reader can perhaps take from Judges 17–18 this thought: that evil tends to bring evil back to the perpetrator. Recompense may not always be immediate or obvious, but wrong actions set in motion other wrongs that can eventually come back to us.

JUDGES 19–21

Introduction to These Chapters

This section, along with chapters 17–18, forms an appendix to the book of Judges. The story belongs to the Judges time period. This is not, however, the story of a judge. It is the story of an evil event that led to civil war and the near devastation of the tribe of Benjamin. Even though it is not the usual "judge" story, the writer has apparently preserved this account in order to offer as complete an historical record as possible.

These chapters include several distinct traditions and editorial notes. In some spots we can see that a later editor or storyteller needed to give his listeners extra information to explain points of a very old tale. The final editor, however, has skillfully woven the parts together to form an exciting and coherent narrative.

The story lacks the usual formula noting Israel's sin, the oppression it brought, Israel's cry for help, and God's gift of a judge. This standard structure would not fit the situation at all. Instead, it begins and ends with the simple comment, "In those days there was no king in Israel" (NRSV; NIV = "Israel had no king").

We do find here, as in many ancient tales, some skillful storytelling techniques, including occasional exaggeration for effect. Still, much of this material deals with a real historical event. Certainly the story accurately depicts Israel's political situation at the time. We see here a leaderless people divided, tribe against tribe, trying to wrestle with major problems of justice, order, and unity. Mob action, unaided by previously formed policies or institutions, leads Israel to the brink of disaster.

The story, ancient and reworked as it is, offers a curious mix of moral attitudes. The lack of hospitality, the threat of homosexual attack on a guest, the gang rape and murder receive the label "abomination." The authors and editors, however, say nothing about the offering of two women to placate the mob, the slaughter of women and children in Jabesh-gilead, or the kidnapping of wives for the Benjaminites. We would hesitate to draw conclusions about Israel's morality from this story, except to say that it offers an interesting peek into the development of moral sensitivity. Later editors' hesitation to change or comment on the story does not necessarily mean that they shared the story's earlier attitudes.

Here is an outline of these chapters.

I. The Levite's Story (19:1-30)

II. Israel's Response (20:1-48)

III. Making Peace Again (21:1-25)

The Message of Judges 19–21

The writer gives no explicit interpretation to this story. Rather, the story itself shows a problem and points to a solution. The problem is how to provide justice and still maintain unity within the people of God. Israel's rather fumbling answer here was to provide justice, then find a way to heal the breach made in the process. Punish, then forgive and aid in recovery was their solution. Through all this, even though the tribes were disorganized and leaderless, they received support from their true king, God.

This message was especially important for Israel in the time of the Exile. Leaderless and broken, angry with each other and throwing blame right and left, the people needed to know that God could heal and unite their tribes once more.

Today, in our families and in our world, we face the double need to enforce right behavior while maintaining unity. We hope to find less brutal methods than Israel did for accomplishing this. Nevertheless, as we walk that tightrope between righteous indignation and healing forgiveness, we can rest assured of God's aid and support. God, in infinite power, can mend the breaks in our fractured world.

RUTH

OUTLINE OF RUTH

INTRODUCTION

The book of Ruth is a historical short story. It is a love story of the conventional man-woman kind. But it is also a love story in a broader sense. This Old Testament book is a story of many good people who love and care for each other. And, beneath it all, this is a love story about God.

In Ruth, love and concern are everywhere. There is not an unkind person or a villain in the piece. There are only ordinary people showing love to family members and, beyond the family, to strangers. In this superb tale we meet unforgettable characters like Naomi, a grieving widow who looks after the interests of her daughters-in-law; Ruth, who leaves home and risks her safety to care for Naomi; and Boaz, who shows kindness to the foreigner, Ruth, and eventually marries her. Behind the scenes, guiding and protecting, we see a God whose love is stronger and broader than many humans may have suspected.

Purpose and Date

Ruth is intended to be both entertaining and instructive. One of the book's major purposes is to show that God wants people to live in self-giving love. But the author apparently had another, more specific, purpose: to deal with the problem of how Israel should relate to foreigners. Over and over the author reminds us that Ruth is from Moab, that she is a foreigner. Yet she and the other characters treat each other with love. In that light Ruth is a love story with wide social significance—a story of love between nations and groups, between people with differences who share the same parent-child relationship with God.

This second purpose probably arose from the historical situation in which the author lived. Both the language and content suggest that the story as it now stands comes from 450–250 B.C. This was a time after the Exile when Nehemiah and others were trying very hard to preserve Israel's unity and purity by limiting the people's relationships with outsiders. They strictly enforced the traditional rule forbidding intermarriage with foreigners (Nehemiah 10:28-31). They emphasized the law in Deuteronomy 23:3 that forbids foreigners from fully entering the Israelite community. Some saw foreigners as evil, inferior, or both. To many, God seemed to be God of Israel alone. Ruth's author opposed this exclusivism. But instead of writing a diatribe, he wrote a brilliantly gentle story—a story in which a loving Moabite woman marries an Israelite and eventually becomes the ancestress of Israel's greatest king.

The story itself may be a very old one. Its cultural details accurately reflect the Judges period. It contains many ancient words as well. So it seems likely that the author has taken a beloved old story and used it to make an effective point about a situation in his own time.

While most commentators agree on the book's purpose, a few do not place the author in the post exilic time period. Some scholars argue that much of the language could come from the monarchic period, and that concern for inclusiveness could have arisen before the Exile. If this were the case, Ruth's date of composition could be set at the time of Jehoshaphat's reform in the second quarter of the ninth century B.C. However, these arguments do not seem compelling. Instead, the exilic setting still seems the more likely one.

Theology

God, in the book of Ruth, is a God who actively cares for people. However, God works in the shadows. Occasionally God's presence is noted directly. More often, though, we hear of God through the blessings and prayers of the story's characters.

The author assumes that God is behind the good things that happen—the famine's end, the "luck" that brings Ruth to Boaz's field, and so forth. We are led to feel that God is working toward good even when evil seems dominant.

In this story God acts most often through people. They are ordinary people in ordinary circumstances. Yet they are good people, good as God is good. They live in imitation of God and, in so doing, fulfill the plans of God.

Redemption is a key concept in the story of Ruth. The words translated as *redeem* and *redeemer* are used more than twenty times in this short book. On the surface, redemption in ancient Israel referred to recovery (usually through a financial payment) of people or property or prestige lost because of poverty, war, or some other cause. Redemption in this story clearly carries that meaning, but it suggests also a larger meaning of a promised redemption for the whole people of God.

The happy ending makes one final theological point: that God will reward righteous, godly living. This is no rigid legalism, however. The author suggests that happiness will eventually come to those who love and give. The greatest happiness comes to those who love and give beyond what is legally required.

The Author

We know nothing about the author of Ruth except what we can guess from the story itself. We assume that the writer lived after the Exile and opposed the exclusiveness of that period. We can see that he preferred a subtle but effective approach, rather than direct confrontation, to make his point. He was surely a person of great sensitivity.

He was also one of the world's greatest storytellers. Ruth contains scarcely a wasted word. The plot is clear and concise. The writer has spiced his story with small but significant human details and peopled it with skillfully drawn characters. He even takes care to use archaic language in the older people's dialogue. Suspense builds steadily toward the final resolution. Then our author neatly ties the story up with an all-around happy ending. This is the work of a real master!

Place in the Canon

Ruth was not originally part of the great history that encompasses most of Deuteronomy through 2 Kings. In the Hebrew Bible Ruth appears in the third section, among the Writings. Greek and Latin versions placed Ruth after Judges, probably because the story is set in the Judges period. Modern Bibles retain this later positioning. Today, Jewish people read the book of Ruth during the Feast of Weeks, an ancient celebration of the grain harvest.

RUTH 1–2

Introduction to These Chapters

Ruth's author moves quickly and directly into his story. In just five verses he sets the scene, introduces two or three main characters, and sets up the problem. In the remaining verses, he shows us more about the characters' personalities, leads us to identify with them, moves the plot along, and begins to hint at the possibility of a happy ending.

An outline of this section would include:

I. Moab (1:1-18)
II. Bethlehem (1:19-22)
III. Gleaning (2:1-23)

The Message of Ruth 1–2

The message of these chapters is tied in with the message of the entire story. One part of that message is that righteous living—righteousness beyond the ordinary—brings happiness. Here we see the first steps in that process. Ruth has cared for Naomi. Now, in her need, Ruth has come to the field of an extraordinarily kind man. Moreover, this is a man in whom Naomi sees the possibility for more permanent help.

We also see here the beginnings of another message. Repeatedly the author reminds us that Ruth is a foreigner, and repeatedly we are shown that she is an unusually good person. Boaz, an obviously upright man, treats her with special kindness. Thus we learn that foreigners are not vile creatures to be avoided, but human beings with whom we can give and receive love.

These messages speak, not just to the past, but to our lives today. On a personal level, Ruth challenges us to live lives that go beyond the mediocrity of niceness. Through his story the author reminds us that real goodness is worth striving for. On both the personal and wider social levels, we who still live amidst racial prejudice and international suspicion need Ruth's second message. We need Ruth's reminder that surface differences do not negate our common humanity nor our capacity to share love.

RUTH 3–4

Introduction to These Chapters

Now tension builds as the story moves through a series of hurdles to what listeners hope will be a happy ending. Naomi and Ruth take a large, but calculated risk; Boaz, though willing to help the women, must get by a legal obstacle. For a time, that legality nearly ruins the hoped-for solution. But, in the end, goodness triumphs, and "they all live happily ever after." Thus the writer skillfully develops his story to climax and resolution.

Someone, either the basic author or a later editor, has added a genealogy to the happy ending. The list follows Ruth's descendants down to King David. This information is not necessary to the plot but serves to underline the author's message that God accepts foreigners and that Israel should do so too. After all, if David had a Moabite great-grandmother, can Moabites be all that bad?

These chapters can be divided into three parts:

I. Naomi's Plan (3:1-18)
II. A Slight Hitch (4:1-12)
III. Conclusion (4:13-22)

The Message of Ruth 3–4

The book's double message carries through to its conclusion. Here, as in earlier chapters, we see that (1) goodness brings eventual happiness, and (2) God accepts other peoples and wants Israel to do the same. Underneath everything we see the hand of God caring for the people, leading them toward joy.

It is easy for modern Christians to be drawn into the selfishness, the mediocrity, the prejudice, and the cynicism of the world around us. A book like Ruth reminds us again that more-than-conventional goodness is worthwhile, that prejudice and exclusiveness are not God's ways, and that God really does care and work toward our happiness. We need that reminder. Thank God for giving it to us in this exquisite little story!

NAMED WOMEN OF THE BIBLE

Adah, wife of Lamech (Gen 4:19-23)
Adah, wife of Esau (Gen 26:34; 36:2)
Aholibamah/Oholibamah (Gen 36:2-25)
Anah (Gen 36:2, 18, 25)
Anna (Luke 2:36-38)
Asenath (Gen 41:45-50; 46:20)
Bashemath/Basemeth/Basmath (Gen 26:34; 36:10; 36:3, 4, 13)
Bilhah (Gen 29:29; 30:3-5, 7; 35:22, 25; 37:2; 46:25; 1 Chr 4:29; 7:13)
Deborah (Gen 24:59; 35:8)
Dinah (Gen 34)
Elisheba (Exod 6:23)
Elizabeth (Luke 1:5-80)
Eve (Gen 2; 3; 2 Cor 11:3; 1 Tim 2:13)
Hagar (Gen 16; 21:9-17; 25:12; Gal 4:24-25)
Herodias (Matt 14:3-12; Mark 6:14-24; Luke 3:19-20)
Iscah (Gen 11:29)
Jemima (Job 42:14)
Joanna (Luke 8:1-3; 23:55; 24:10)
Jochebed (Exod 1; 2: 1-11; 6:20; Num 26:59; Heb 11 :23)
Judith (Gen 26:34)
Keren-Happuch (Job 1:2; 42:14)
Keturah (Gen 25:1-6; 1 Chr 1:32, 33)
Kezia (Job 42:14)
Leah (Gen 29; 30; 49:31; Ruth 4:11)
Macchah (Gen 22:24)
Mahalah/Mahalath (Gen 28:9)
Martha (Luke 10:38-41; John 11; 12:1-3)
Mary (Matt 1:2; 12:46; Luke 1:2; John 2:1-11; 19:25; Acts 1:14)
Mary Magdalene (Matt 27:56, 61; 28:1; Mark 15:40, 47; 16:1-19; Luke 8:2; 24:10; John 11; 12:1-3)

Mary, mother of James and Joseph (Matt 27:55-61; Mark 15:40, 47; 16:1; Luke 24:10)
Mary of Bethany (Luke 10:38-41; John 11; 12:1-3)
Matred (Gen 36:39; 1 Chr 1:50)
Mehetabel (Gen 36:39; 1 Chr 1 :50)
Milcah (Gen 11:29; 22:20, 23; 24:15, 24, 47)
Miriam (Exod 15:20, 21; Num 12:1-15; 20:1; 26:59; Deut 24:9; Micah 6:4)
Naamah (Gen 4:22)
Puah (Exod 1:15)
Rachel (Gen 29; 30; 31; 33:1, 2, 7; 35:16-26; 46:19, 22, 25; 48:7; Ruth 4:11; 1 Sam 10:2; Jer 31:15; Matt 2:18)
Rahab (Josh 2:1, 3; 6:17-25; Matt 1:5; Heb 1:31)
Rebekah/Rebecca (Gen 22:23; 24; 25:20-28; 26:6-35; 27; 28:5; 29:12; 35:8; 49:31; Rom 9:6-16)
Reumah (Gen 22:24)
Ruth (book of Ruth, Matt 1:5)
Salome, daughter of Herodias (Matt 14:6-11; Mark 6:22-28)
Salome the disciple (Mark 15:40, 41)
Sarah/Sarai/Sara (Gen 11:29-32; 12:5-17; 16:1-8; 17:15-21; 18; 20:2-18; 21:1-12; 23:1-19; 24:36-37; 25:10, 12; 49:31; Isa 51:2; Rom 4:19; 9:9; Heb 11:11; 1 Pet 3:6)
Serah (Gen 46:17; 1 Chr 7:30)
Shelomith (Lev 24:10-13)
Shiphrah (Exod 1: 15)
Shua (Gen 38:1, 2; 1 Chr 7:32)
Susanna (Luke 8:2, 3)
Tamar (Gen 38:6-30; Ruth 4:12; 1 Chr 2:4; Matt 1:3)
Timna (Gen 36:12, 22; 1 Chr 1:39)
Zillah (Gen 4:19-23)
Zilpah (Gen 29:24; 30:9, 10; 35:26; 37:2; 46:18)
Zipporah (Exod 2:21-22; 4:24-25; 18:1-6)

UNNAMED WOMEN OF THE BIBLE

Cain's wife (Gen 4:17)
Cainan's daughters (Gen 5:12-14)
Daughters of Jerusalem (Luke 23:28)
Daughters of Men (Gen 6:1-8)
Daughters of Putiel (Exod 6:25)
Daughters of Reuel (Exod 2:15-22)
Enoch's daughters (Gen 5:21-24)
Enos's daughters (Gen 5:9-11)
Jairus's daughter (Matt 9:18-25; Mark 5:21-43; Luke 8:41-56)
Jared's daughters (Gen 5:18-20)
Jesus' sisters (Matt 13:55-56; Mark 6:3)
Job's wife (Job 2:9, 10; 19:17; 31:10)
Lamech's daughters (Gen 5:28-31)
Lot's daughters (Gen 19:12-17, 30-38)
Lot's wife (Gen 19:15-26; Luke 17:29-33)
Mahaleel's daughters (Gen 5:15-17)
Methuselah's daughters (Gen 5:25-27)
Noah's wife, sons' wives (Gen 6:18; 7:1, 7, 13; 8:16,18)
Peter's mother-in-law (Matt 8:14-18; Mark 1:29 34; Luke 4:38-41)
Peter's wife (Matt 8:14-18; Mark 1:29-34; Luke 4:38-41)
Pharaoh's daughter (Exod 2:5-10; Acts 7:21; Heb 11:24)
Pilate's wife (Matt 27:19)
Potiphar's Wife (Gen 39)
Priestly daughters (Lev 21:9)

Seth's daughters (Gen 5:6-8)
Shaul's mother (Gen 46:10; Exod 6:15)
Shem's daughters (Gen 11:10-32)
Stooped woman healed by Jesus (Luke 13:11-13)
Syro-Phoenician woman (Matt 15:21-28; Mark 7:24-30)
Tabernacle women (Exod 38:8)
Widow of Nain (Luke 7:11-18)
Widow of Zarephath (1 Kgs 17:8-24; Luke 4:25, 26)
Widow with two mites (Mark 12:41-44; Luke 21:1-4)
Wife sold for debt (Matt 18:25; Luke 17:3-4)
Wise-hearted women (Exod 35:22-29)
Woman of Samaria John 4)
Woman taken L'1 adultery (Deut 17:5-6; John 8:1-11)
Woman who responded to a healing (Luke 11:27-28)
Woman who sinned yet loved much (Luke 7:36-50)
Woman with the hemorrhage (Matt 9:20-22; Mark 5:25-34; Luke 8:43-48)
Women at Peter's denial (Matt 26:69-71; Mark 14:66-69; Luke 22:56-59; John 18:16-17)
Women at the cross (Matt 27:55)

FIRST AND SECOND SAMUEL

OUTLINE OF 1 AND 2 SAMUEL

1 Samuel

I. Samuel's Birth and Call (1:1–4:1a)
  A. Samuel's miraculous birth (1:1-28)
  B. Hannah's hymn of thanksgiving (2:1-11)
  C. Eli's wicked sons (2:12-25)
  D. Judgment against the family of Eli (2:26-36)
  E. God's revelation to Samuel (3:1–4:1a)

II. The Ark of the Covenant Narratives (4:1b–7:2)
  A. The Philistines' capture of the ark (4:1b-11)
  B. Eli's death (4:12-22)
  C. The ark's terrors among the Philistines (5:1-12)
  D. The Philistines' return of the ark (6:1-7:2)

III. Israel's Move to Monarchy (7:3–12:25)
  A. Samuel's leadership of Israel (7:3-17)
  B. Israel's demand for a king (8:1-22)
  C. Samuel's secret anointing of Saul (9:1–10:16)
  D. Saul's accession—a second account (10:17-27)
  E. Saul's rescue of Jabesh-gilead (11:1-15)

  F. Samuel's final address (12:1-25)

IV. Saul's Rule over Israel (13:1–15:35)
  A. Escalation of the Philistine threat (13:1-7a)
  B. Saul's cultic offense (13:7b-15a)
  C. Israel against the Philistines (13:15b–14:52)
    1. Jonathan's victory at Michmash (13:15b–14:23)
    2. Jonathan's disobedience of Saul (14:24-46)
    3. Saul's victories (14:47-48)
    4. Saul's family (14:49-52)
  D. A second account of Saul's rejection (15:1-35)

V. Saul's Demise and David's Rise (16:1–30:31)
  A. God's choice of David (16:1-13)
  B. David's appointment to Saul's court (16:14-23)
  C. David's victory over Goliath (17:1-54)
  D. David's introduction (17:55–18:5)
  E. Saul's jealousy of David (18:6-16)
  F. David marries Saul's daughter (18:17-30)
  G. Saul's plot to kill David (19:1-24)
  H. Jonathan's help for David (20:1-42)
  I. David's escape to the priest at Nob (21:1-9)
  J. David's move to Gath (21:10-15)

K. David moves on to Adullam (22:1-5)

L. Saul's massacre of the priests at Nob (22:6-23)

M. David's stay at Keilah (23:1-13)

N. David's reluctance to kill Saul (23:14–24:22)

O. David's courtship of Abigail (25:1-44)

P. David spares Saul a second time (26:1-25)

Q. David's service to the Philistines (27:1–28:2)

R. Saul meets with Samuel's spirit (28:3-25)

S. Dismissal from service (29:1-11)

T. David's revenge on the Amalekites (30:1-31)

VI. Saul's Death (31:1-13)

2 Samuel

I. David Mourns Saul and Jonathan (1:1-27)

A. David's wrath against the Amalekites (1:1-16)

B. David's lament for Saul and Jonathan (1:17-27)

II. David's Reign Over Judah (2:1–4:12)

A. David's reign at Hebron (2:1-11)

B. Abner's killing of Asahel (2:12-32)

C. Warfare between Judah and Israel (3:1)

D. David's sons (3:2-5)

E. Abner's defection to David (3:6-39)

F. Ishbosheth's murder (4:1-12)

III. David Is King Over All Israel (5:1–12:31)

A. Israel's elders name David king (5:1-5)

B. David names Jerusalem as his capital (5:6-16)

C. David's war against the Philistines (5:17-25)

D. David's transfer of the ark to Jerusalem (6:1-23)

E. God's covenant with David (7:1-29)

F. David's military conquests (8:1-18)

G. David's concern for Mephibosheth (9:1-13)

H. David wars against Ammon and Aram (10:1-19)

I. David's sin with Bathsheba (11:1–12:31)

IV. David's domestic crises (13:1–20:26)

A. Tamar's rape (13:1-22)

B. Absalom's revenge (13:23-38)

C. Absalom's return (14:1-33)

D. Absalom's revolt (15:1-37)

E. Absalom enters Jerusalem (16:1-23)

F. Ahithophel's counsel rejected (17:1-23)

G. Absalom's death (17:24–19:8a)

H. David's return to Jerusalem (19:8b-43)

I. Sheba's rebellion (20:1-26)

V. Other Events in David's Reign (21:1–24:25)

A. Famine and David's response (21:1-14)

B. War with the Philistines (21:15-22)

C. David's hymn of praise (22:1-51)

D. David's second song (23:1-7)

E. David's warriors (23:8-39)

F. A census, a plague, and an altar (24:1-25)

INTRODUCTION

The Content of 1 and 2 Samuel

The books of 1 and 2 Samuel contain narratives that highlight selected events in Israelite history from the end of the period of the judges (about 1020 B.C.) until shortly before the death of King David (about 961 B.C.). The opening three chapters of 1 Samuel recount the miraculous birth of Samuel and his timely entry into the priestly service of God. Samuel quickly becomes the major transitional figure in early Israel who oversees the political move by the tribes of Israel from governance by judges to rule by kings.

Despite probable reservations, Samuel anoints Saul as Israel's first king, in response to pleas from a frightened and threatened Israel. Although Saul manages to slow the Philistine aggression on Israelite territory, he lacks the military strength to deal them the final knockout blow. Perhaps even more discouraging to Saul, God turns against him (albeit for just causes), and turns in the direction of David. Saul's jealousy and envy of David prompt the ill-fated king to plot the murder of this young and popular warrior. Understandably, this drives David into flight and hiding. As his relentless pursuit of David continues, Saul becomes increasingly unable to wage war successfully with the Philistines. Desperate for guidance, he turns to a deceased Samuel, by way of a medium, only to learn of his impending death. The very next day, the Philistines rout Saul's army and wound the king. To avoid torture and humiliation at the hands of his enemies, Saul falls upon his own sword. First Samuel ends with an act of kindness by the men of Jabesh, when they stealthily remove the bodies of Saul and Jonathan from public display on the walls of Beth-shan and provide appropriate burials.

Second Samuel provides an account of David's reign, first over the southern tribes of Judah, then over the combined southern and northern tribes. David more than justifies his reputation as a great warrior by conquering not only the Philistines, but also the Syrians, the Amorites, the Amalekites, and many other neighboring tribes. At the height of his career, David controls most of the territories from Syria (Aram) in the north to Elath in the south, and all the lands west and just east of the Jordan River. At no other time in her history would Israel's empire reach such broad limits!

But, for all David's accomplishments as a king and as a warrior, he seems unable to manage his personal and domestic life with the same expertise. His adulterous affair with Bathsheba brings suffering and death to innocent persons. His mishandling of his sons, Amnon and Absalom, leads to rebellion and to his temporary abdication of his royal throne in Jerusalem.

Even though David does quell Absalom's rebellion and regain his throne quickly, the latter years of his reign seethe with internal political conflicts. He faces the difficult question of succession to his throne, as well as subversive mistrust from many factions within the northern tribes. Second Samuel concludes with an act of contrition, when David erects an altar to God for having sinned in the taking of a census. This final act, however, connects the books of 1 and 2 Samuel to the book of 1 Kings, because the site of David's altar becomes the very site upon which King Solomon builds the famous Temple.

The stories of the Hebrew monarchy continue in 1 and 2 Kings, where Solomon succeeds David as king of Israel. But the exciting stories of Samuel, Saul, and David, and the early formative days of the

Israelite monarchy, come to an end. The books of 1 and 2 Samuel are virtually unmatched in the Old Testament for their exciting action and for the pathos of real human experiences. Perhaps the writers of the Old Testament sensed a measure of the glory of these days when they repeatedly invested David's reign with nostalgic glory. These exciting days of early Israelite monarchy, energized by the personalities of Samuel, Saul, and David, are what 1 and 2 Samuel are all about.

The Place of 1 and 2 Samuel in the Old Testament

In the Hebrew Scriptures, 1 and 2 Samuel belong to a group of books designated as the Former Prophets. Included within this canonical division are the books of Joshua, Judges, 1 and 2 Samuel, and 1 and 2 Kings. These narratives provide accounts of the Israelites from their entry into Canaan (about 1240 B.C.) until their deportation at the hands of the Assyrians (722 B.C.) and the Neo-Babylonians (587 B.C.). The expression "Former Prophets" distinguishes these books from other biblical books called the Latter Prophets: Isaiah, Jeremiah, and Ezekiel, plus the twelve minor prophets.

That the rabbis or scribes who arranged and named these collections identified the books of Joshua, Judges, Samuel, and Kings as Former Prophets is interesting. It is clear that the personalities and functions of the characters in the Former Prophets are rather dissimilar to the classical Old Testament prophets such as Isaiah and Jeremiah. Saul and David are political leaders first, and spokesmen for God second. Yet, perhaps the rabbis recognized that the essential characteristic of a judge, a king, and a prophet is that special spiritual empowerment from God known as the charismatic endowment—that is, the Spirit of the Lord. These famous characters

derive their keen insights and their outstanding leadership capacities from God's imparted strength, not from their own innate abilities. The intended chronological meaning of *former* as distinct from *latter* is unclear, but the theological continuity between the two sections clearly indicates the biblical view that God spoke to the people through a variety of persons.

Originally in early Hebrew manuscripts, 1 and 2 Samuel formed a single book on a single scroll. When the rabbis added vowels to the texts, the size of the book increased, so that a single scroll was too large to accommodate 1 and 2 Samuel as a single book. So the book was divided. About the third or second century B.C., Greek versions of the Old Testament (known as the Septuagint) combined 1 and 2 Samuel with 1 and 2 Kings, and designated the entire collection as the books of Kingdoms. Exactly when these scrolls were first separated into four books in Hebrew is unclear, since the Greek and Latin versions, while combining them as books of the Kingdoms, divide them onto scrolls almost exactly as 1 and 2 Samuel and 1 and 2 Kings are divided and now appear in English translations. The division of 1 and 2 Samuel following the death of Saul is appropriate for two reasons. First, these books precede the great reign of King David. Second, this division follows other Old Testament divisions. For example, the Pentateuch closes with the death of Moses rather than the more natural recapture of the Promised Land.

The name of the two books, 1 and 2 Samuel, is interesting since David is clearly the main character in one and one-half of these books. Although we cannot be certain, it seems reasonable that the writers and collectors of this material assigned it Samuel's name because he played such an important role in moving Israel from one historical period, the era of judges, to another age, the monarchy. Samuel anoints Saul king over Israel, provides council for as well as critique of his rule, then anoints David as king when Saul sins against God. Samuel's influence on subsequent Hebrew history is considerable. And it is appropriate that the books recounting this history bear his name.

The Authorship of 1 and 2 Samuel

The authorship of 1 and 2 Samuel is complicated and controversial. The title of the books probably reflects the name of their first major character, Samuel, rather than designating actual authorship. Also, the reference in 1 Chronicles 29:29 to an unknown source, the Chronicles of Samuel, the Chronicles of Nathan, and the Chronicles of God probably refers to a set of documents, now lost, on which the books of Samuel and Chronicles are based, not to the Old Testament books themselves. Complicating matters further, we can hardly help noticing the duplications in these stories. (1) There are two accounts of how Saul becomes king (compare 1 Samuel 9:1–10:16 with 1 Samuel 10:17-27). (2) There are two accounts of how David enters Saul's service (compare 16:14-23 with 17:1-58). (3) There are two accounts of Saul's sin against God (compare 13:7b-15a with 15:1-35). In addition to these duplications, there are more general differences in points of view (pro-monarchy versus anti-monarchy). These factors seem to suggest that more than one writer's material has been combined into the present books of 1 and 2 Samuel. But who were these writers?

Most likely an anonymous author, or perhaps a group of authors, writing during the Babylonian Exile of the Jews (587–538 B.C.), brought together several earlier sources and wrote a history of Israel from the settlement in Canaan (13th century B.C.) until the deportation by the Neo-Babylonians (587 B.C.). The author is often referred to as the *Deuteronomistic Historian*. This historian used different sources, both written and oral, which reflected different points of view or presented different accounts of the same incident.

Two reasons may be given why an ancient writer might have used stories that present different accounts of the same event. (1) Differences in factual details were less important than the overall theological message these different accounts presented. (2) The writer may have believed that each version contained some elements of truth. Thus, to have omitted one version would have resulted in a misrepresentation of the event. In view of these considerations, we must not fault the writer for using more than one account, nor should we judge his writing in light of our own standards of coherence and consistency today.

The historian believed that the history of Israel reflected Israel's apostasy. Apostasy, the worship of other gods, was among the most serious sins a person or nation could commit. It violated the first commandment. Such sin had been forbidden in Deuteronomy 30:15-20. Israel's plight at the hands of the Assyrians and Neo-Babylonians was the direct result of her years of repeated sin. The Exile was God's punishment of the Israelites. To document the justice of God's punishment, the writer retells the history of Israel, clearly showing how king after king allowed the people to fall victim to apostasy. The often-used phrase, "They did what was evil in the sight of the LORD," usually refers to the king's apostasy.

Among the sources used by the historian are the following: (1) the ark narratives (1 Samuel 4:1–7:2; 2 Samuel 6:1–7), (2) the Saul stories (1 Samuel 9:1–10:16; 11; 13–14), (3) the court history of David (2 Samuel 9; 1 Kings 2). In addition to these three larger, more clearly recognizable blocks of material, the writer used stories about Samuel's childhood (1 Samuel 1–3), David's early days (1 Samuel 16), and various hymns and lists. The writer arranged these sources, added his own comments, and superimposed an interpretative perspective to reflect his own theological point of view. As the commentary unfolds, these particular sources will be discussed further, with explanations about how the writer shaped the material to reflect his particular point of view.

Israel's History During These Years

Although the precise details of Israel's history during the years of Samuel, Saul, and David are difficult for us to reconstruct today, the Bible does supply us with a reliable outline of the sequence of events. As indicated above, these books bear the unmistakable imprint of the historian's work. His concern to provide a theological interpretation of history limited his discussions of the economic, political, and cultural aspects of monarchical history. Even so, most scholars feel that these biblical accounts can help us reconstruct an accurate history of this early period.

As we move into the later reigns of David and Solomon, our history becomes even more detailed due to more reliable sources. Also, we can now make use of archaeological investigations of sites such as Shiloh, Megiddo, Gilbeah, Arad, Hazor, and Gezer.

The chronological limits for the period described in 1 and 2 Samuel extend from approximately 1030–1025 B.C. (Samuel, Saul) until 960 B.C. (David's death).

During this fifty- to sixty-year period, the political organization of Israel changed from a loosely assembled group of semi-nomadic tribes and small Canaanite city-states to a relatively large urban state with all of the distinguishing features, such as a common religion, a standing army, a capital city, and cumbersome governmental bureaucracy.

As David's empire stabilized, manufacturing and international trade began to emerge. The young nation, Israel, flexed its territorial muscles with no Egyptians and no Assyrians to limit its appetite. Under David's leadership, Israel extended its sphere of influence from the Euphrates River in the north to Elath in the south at the Gulf of Aqaba, and from the Transjordan to the Mediterranean Sea. Israel had truly come of age! But how did Israel get to this point in history? What roles did Samuel and Saul play in the formation of this new state?

During the last quarter of the eleventh century, when Samuel came into prominence as a judge, the word *Israel* referred to a loosely organized group of tribes living in Canaan and in the Transjordan. These tribes functioned independently, except perhaps during times of severe political crisis.

Several leading Old Testament scholars believe that some of these tribes periodically assembled to worship God and to celebrate a common historical heritage (Deuteronomy 26:5 and following). Although there may well have been other sanctuaries these tribes used, the sites of Shiloh and Shechem are mentioned most often as the locations of fall and spring festivals. This common religion could have served as an initial source of unity and attraction during times of peace. What does seem clear is that originally semi-nomadic tribes infiltrated Canaan and gradually became dominant politically, at least in certain regions in the central hill country and in the valleys to the north. Yet they were not the only intruders into Palestine.

Following their expulsion from Egypt around 1200 B.C., the Philistines relocated in the sparsely settled coastal regions in southwestern Canaan (Gaza, Ashdod, Ekron). Over the next half-century, these highly skilled warriors needed and desired additional territory, then occupied by Canaanites and by the tribes of Israel. Their strong centralized government more naturally lent itself to military aggressiveness than did the loose tribal confederacy system among the Israelites.

Soon after their occupation, the Philistines gained control of the iron industry in Palestine and forced the Israelites into dependency for the purchase of manufactured wares as well as the service on these wares (1 Samuel 13:19-21). Archaic Israelite weaponry was no match for Philistine chariots, spears, and daggers of iron. With increasing frequency the Philistines pushed northward toward the fertile valleys of Esdraelon and the occupied hill country in central Canaan. Meanwhile, Israel also began to expand beyond earlier occupied territories. An inevitable collision ensued in the central hill country, resulting in numerous battles between the tribes of Israel and the Philistines.

A principal battle in the conflict occurred at Aphek, resulting in a decisive victory for the Philistines and a devastating loss for Israel. Since the Philistines seem to have possessed superior military skills, as well as controlling the available iron supply, they indeed posed a serious threat to the continued survival of Israel. Even worse, the defeat at Aphek not only cost Israel valuable territory, but the Philistines also captured the famous ark of the Covenant.

To provide more effective centralized leadership, Samuel anointed Saul of Gibeah as king. Unlike his predecessors (the judges), Saul did not disband his army once the Philistine threat was temporarily checked, but instead retained it, and monarchy became a permanent institution. Saul's relatively brief reign was characterized by almost constant warfare with one hostile tribe or another. He was also plagued with internal dissension, recalcitrant tribes (Gibeonites), and his uncontrollable jealousy of David. As if these military and psychological problems were not a sufficient depressant, Saul also had to cope with the loss of support from Samuel, climaxing in a deep estrangement between the two men, with God in full support of Samuel.

The length of Saul's reign is unclear (1 Samuel 13:1), as is the extent of his new kingdom. Most of his power was centered in the territories of Benjamin, Ephraim, and Gilead. Yet he apparently had considerable support in both Galilee and Judah. Saul's reign ended with his disastrous defeat by the Philistines and his death by his own hand. Since so much of the Saul material is shaped by pro-Davidic writers, this very able ruler probably receives less credit than he actually deserves.

David's reign propelled Israel to her greatest heights of national and international prominence. The tribes in the loose arrangement of the older confederacy quickly attached themselves to this young, vigorous leader who offered safety and security. Within a very few years after becoming king of Judah at Hebron, David accepted a mandate to rule all Israel. He lost no time in conquering the Philistines completely, and then he restricted their territory to the southwest portions of his country. The Philistine menace to Israel was ended permanently.

Next, David moved quickly to bring

additional territories under his control, including Syria, Edom, Moab, Amnon, and others. The previously unconquered Jebusite city of Jerusalem was conquered and named capital of a united country, Israel. David's once small mercenary army had, by this time, swollen to considerable size, with volunteers from many other tribes and segments of society. Israel was now a nation like other nations, in virtually every sense of the word.

But Israelite monarchy was not without its critics, and many of the tribes that had come to David in times of military emergency longed for their independence in times of peace. Also, prophetic voices warned of the potential danger of idolatry inherent within the institution of kingship itself. Even within the royal palace greed, jealousy, and political intrigue darkened the glory of David's reign. Personal weakness of King David heightened his internal discord. But due to excellent support from his loyal subjects, as well as misdeeds of others, David managed to retain his throne and calm his critics.

Yet, the latter days of David's reign were still filled with bitter intrigue and subversion in the matter of succession. Which of David's remaining sons was to follow him as king? The outcome of this palace soap opera must remain unresolved until 1 Kings.

David left a legacy in Israelite history that is yet to be equaled. While it may be true that international politics certainly favored David's territorial expansion, David will always stand out as the central figure in Israelite monarchy. In Jerusalem even today the tomb of David stands in honor of Israel's greatest king.

Major Theological Themes in
1 and 2 Samuel

The material in 1 and 2 Samuel has been shaped and edited according to the theological beliefs of the historian. Theological intentions outweigh factual accuracy in his portrayal of the history of Israel. Yet he is a true historian in the very best sense of that term. He is an interpreter of events occurring in day-to-day affairs. From the writer's point of view, Israel's entire history, from settlement to exile, is replete with apostasy.

Using Deuteronomy 30:15-20 as his theological norm, the writer documents repeated instances where Israel worshiped other gods. He focuses on apostasy to the extent of ignoring other historical factors such as economic and political circumstances. Other than David, Hezekiah, and Josiah, few of Israel's and Judah's rulers upheld the first commandment: "You shall have no other gods before me" (Exodus 20:3). God's punishment for their sins should have come as no surprise to Israel, for prophet after prophet announced the approaching judgment of God (Isaiah 2:6-22; Amos 2:4-5, 6-7).

And upon whom should blame be placed for the catastrophe of 587 B.C.? The writer clearly places responsibility on the shoulders of the rulers. Israel's and Judah's kings committed evil in the sight of the Lord. And as the kings worshiped foreign gods, so did the general population. As the Lord of history, God will not long tolerate repeated violations of the commandments. Even powerful nations such as Babylon and Assyria move to the Lord's beat.

This panoramic view of Israel's place within world history clearly acknowledged the writer's faith in God as the ruler of history. And the particular history of Israel constituted a graphic, if tragic, witness to God's powerful arm. Just as many an individual discovers that personal sin does not long go unpunished, so too does Israel experience God's judgment resulting from this collective sin. For the writer, the final word in Israel's history was not national political political strength or weakness, economic prosperity or poverty, or any other conventional standard. For him, Israel's history, as measured by obedience to God's word, was clearly sinful. And this disobedience intensified during the monarchy.

A second set of theological themes in 1 and 2 Samuel focuses on different forms of divine revelation. The writer interpreted Israel's history as displaying God's awesome presence, both for deliverance and for judgment. But in addition to this more general revelation for the nation, particular individuals also received God's word: Samuel (1 Samuel 3:1–4:1a), Nathan (2 Samuel 7:4-16), and David. Through disclosures to these special persons, God's will was revealed to Israel and Judah.

Yet a third form in which Israel discerned God's presence was in the famous ark of the covenant, first attended by Eli at Shiloh, then later by David in Jerusalem. Certainly for the tribes of the north, the ark represented the dynamic presence of God. The Philistines who captured this holy relic quickly learned of its power. The havoc it wrought in the cities of Ashdod and Ekron attested to God's anger.

A fourth form of personal revelation appearing in 1 and 2 Samuel is God's special form of empowering a leader through the charismatic endowment—the indwelling of God's spirit. Samuel, and the judges who ruled before him, received this power, and delivered Israel out of the hands of its aggressors. Initially Saul experienced God's imparted strength in a powerful way, and successfully rescued Jabesh. But his later disobedience angered the Lord, who retracted the gift and gave it to David instead.

God's covenant with David provides yet another theological theme of great importance in 1 and 2 Samuel. In 2 Samuel 7:1, Nathan tells David that the Lord does not desire a house (temple), but instead will build David a "house." In return for David's loyal and devoted service, God agrees to establish David as one of the world's great rulers, whose fame will reach foreign capitals; to provide David and his country peace and security; and to perpetuate the Davidic dynasty forever.

The Davidic covenant provided a theological justification for monarchy and quieted objections from conservative elements in the north. Kingship was now a legitimate institution. David was elevated to a theological stature comparable to figures such as Abraham and Moses.

A fourth theological theme in these two books is the nature of servanthood. What does it mean to be a true servant of the Lord? Judging from the stories and characters in 1 and 2 Samuel, three traits are essential: (1) obedience to God's word, (2) a sense of morality (even if imperfect in execution), and (3) a loyalty to God. Samuel and David both exhibited these qualities, as did many other Old Testament figures. Human perfection (freedom from sin) is not a prerequisite for servanthood, but consciousness of God's expectation does clearly distinguish God's person.

Finally, we should add a word on the nature of the early Hebrew conception of the afterlife—Sheol. As is clear from 1 Samuel 28:3-25, deceased persons all go to Sheol, a dark, dismal place somewhere below the surface of the earth where one engages in little or no activity, nor desires to do so. A doctrine of heaven as a future reward for the faithful is not yet a tenet of religious faith. Divine retribution plays no role in a person's post-death sojourn. But it is clear that death, even at this stage of Hebrew thought, is not a terminal experience. All persons end up in Sheol.

1 SAMUEL 1–3

Introduction to These Chapters

The opening three chapters in 1 Samuel present accounts of three closely related incidents: (1) the miraculous and timely birth of Samuel, (2) the moral decadence of the house of Eli, priest at Shiloh, and (3) the prophetic call of Samuel, elevating him into God's service. Originally, these stories arose and circulated independently. But the writer has carefully blended them together, forming a continuous and coherent narrative.

Here is an outline of 1 Samuel 1–3.
I. Samuel's Miraculous Birth (1:1-28)
II. Hannah's Hymn of Thanksgiving (2:1-11)
III. Eli's Wicked Sons (2:12-25)
IV. Judgment Against the Family of Eli (2:26-36)
V. God's Revelation to Samuel (3:1–4:1a)

The Message of 1 Samuel 1–3

These opening chapters of 1 Samuel raise several important theological issues. These issues are embedded in the narratives in such a way that they reflect particular theological convictions; they are not included as doctrine. In early Israel theology was primarily an activity, not a set of dogmatic propositions.

The issues raised include (1) the close connection between religion and politics; (2) the mysterious nature of divine revelation; (3) the nature of sin; (4) divine determinism; (5) God's special help for the helpless; and (6) divine retribution.

1 SAMUEL 4–6

Introduction to These Chapters

With no transition the historian leaves the stories about Samuel's emerging leadership of Israel and jumps to several humorous episodes featuring the famous ark. Such an abrupt break in consecutive narratives suggests that the historian has shifted to a source different from the one he followed in chapters 1–3.

Yet there is some continuity between 1–3 and 4–6, with the capture of the ark and its portentous departure from Shiloh. Perhaps this removal of God's presence prepares the way for God's termination of the Elide priesthood and its former leadership of Israel at Shiloh.

Hophni and Phinehas die quickly and with little attention or comment. And Eli suffers a fatal fall upon learning that the ark has been captured. As for Shiloh, it seems to vanish as the central cultic site among the northern tribes, only to be mentioned later by prophets as having been the object of God's punishment.

These three chapters describe the serious threat the Philistines pose to Israelite sovereignty over the land. Israel will have no easy time dispelling these aggressors from Hebrew territory.

Here is an outline of chapters 4–6.
I. The Philistines' Capture of the Ark (4:1b-11)
II. Eli's Death (4:12-22)
III. The Ark's Terrors Among the Philistines (5:1-12)
IV. The Philistines' Return of the Ark (6:1–7:2)

The Message of 1 Samuel 4–6

The theme of these chapters is God's awesome power. When the Philistines captured the ark of the covenant, they thought they had captured a valuable prize. But God almost immediately turned their celebration into mourning. God humiliated Dagon (their god), sent a pestilence of rats, and caused an outbreak of plague. God's power completely overwhelmed the stunned Philistines. While they had heard of God's earlier destruction of Pharaoh's armies, they had no notion of the terrible chaos God could cause. They learned very quickly what it meant to offend God.

But the Philistines are not the only ones in these chapters to feel the sting of God's whip. When the men of Beth-shemesh were careless with the newly returned ark, God lashed out at them, and many of their number were killed. Even God's own people cowered in awe of this mighty God, Yahweh.

Yahweh's awesome power is a theme repeated and illustrated countless times in the Old Testament. God unleashed the plagues upon Egypt, brought down the mighty walls of Jericho, and caused the sun to stand still. But even further, God created the world and all that is therein! And after realizing that human sin was here to stay, God began devising powerful and effective ways of redemption. The entire Bible, from Genesis to Revelation, witnesses to God's awesome power that can be destructive as well as redemptive.

1 SAMUEL 7–12

Introduction to These Chapters

Almost as abruptly as the narrator switched to the ark narrative in 4:1b, he shifts back to the Samuel stories at 7:3 and continues his account of Samuel's leadership in Israel. Chronologically, several years have lapsed between events in 4:1 and 7:3. Samuel is now an adult and is the undisputed religious and political leader of all Israel. He functions both as a judge (7:15) and as a seer (9:1–10:16), roles that reflect different sources or traditions.

With these chapters, the writer begins to intertwine two different accounts of the origin of monarchy. Some scholars refer to

these as the pro-monarchy account and the anti-monarchy account, reflective of their attitude toward kingship. In the commentary section, these strands of tradition will be identified where appropriate.

Here is an outline of these chapters.
I. Samuel's Leadership of Israel (7:3-17)
II. Israel's Demand for a King (8:1-22)
III. Samuel's Secret Anointing of Saul (9:1–10:16)
IV. Saul's Accession—A Second Account (10:17-27)
V. Saul's Rescue of Jabesh-gilead (11:1-15)
VI. Samuel's Final Address (12:1-25)

The Message of 1 Samuel 7–12

Three important theological themes may be found in these chapters: (1) kingship as a form of apostasy, (2) charismatic endowment, and (3) forms of divine guidance.

Samuel's principal objection to kingship is the threat of the sin of apostasy. The first commandment (Exodus 20:3) specifically prohibits the worship of any gods other than the Lord. Generally in the Old Testament, this prohibition pertains to the gods of neighboring tribes who rival Yahweh for Israel's allegiance. But Samuel envisions kingship as a more serious threat. He fears that Israel will deify her monarchs. Israel is a theological community, called by God for special service. Her leaders must stand second to the Lord, not replace the Lord.

Charismatic endowment is the indwelling of God's Spirit. Following his secret anointing, Saul receives God's Spirit (19:6, 9), enabling him to excel in strength, courage, and valor. This same spiritual endowment enlivened the judges, such as Samson and Gideon, and enabled them to perform gallant acts of heroism. The purpose of this gift to God's chosen leaders was to provide leadership at crucial moments in Israelite history, and was an experience that demanded moral accountability.

Throughout the Old Testament, God employs many forms of guidance. The patriarchs and the judges provided leadership for God's people. Now, with the emergence of kingship, God introduces a new form of leadership for Israel. Divine guidance is not limited to priests and prophets, although they play important roles in communicating God's word. Both Saul and David are recipients of God's Spirit. Their successes and failures reflect active divine guidance or punishment.

1 SAMUEL 13–15

Introduction to These Chapters

With his kingship now formalized, Saul turns his attention toward the immediate threat posed by the Philistines. Evidently, since their previous victory at Aphek (4:10), the Philistines have moved quickly to occupy Israelite territory in the central hill country. Israel's fragile political situation is becoming increasingly uneasy. To complicate matters even further, the Edomites, the Moabites, and the Ammonites are also encroaching upon Israelite soil. Not a moment too soon, Saul initiates a series of bold attacks against Israel's enemies (14:47-48) and stifles, for the moment at least, these aggressors. But Saul's days are filled with warfare and he lives constantly with his boots on his feet.

Here is an outline of these chapters.

I. Escalation of the Philistine Threat (13:1-7a)

II. Saul's Cultic Offense (13:7b-15a)

III. Israel Against the Philistines (13:15b–14:52)

IV. A Second Account of Saul's Rejection (15:1-35)

The Message of 1 Samuel 13–15

The two prominent theological issues arising within these chapters deal with two human responses to God's word: obedience and disobedience. These opposites form the basis of divine blessing or divine judgment. Saul has received the gift of God's spirit (charismatic endowment), which sanctions his reign as king and strengthens him for extraordinary leadership. Unfortunately, Saul's disobedience causes God to withdraw this blessing and dispense judgment. Samuel's few words on these matters are very insightful into faith and our response.

In 1 Samuel 13:7b-15a, Saul commits a breach of religious law by usurping priestly functions not available to him: He cultically blesses his army prior to battle, and fails to execute God's orders to destroy completely all of the Amalekites. The fact that Saul's motives are, in both cases, reasonable and appropriate is beside the point; Saul has disobeyed God's commandments. As consequences of his disobedience, Saul loses his charismatic endowment, loses his claim on the throne of Israel, and loses Samuel's support. These punishments are truly high prices to pay, but Saul's sins are serious. Disobedience to God's word carries severe punishment.

By contrast, obedience to the word of the Lord leads to divine blessing. In fact, Samuel's poignant couplet in 15:22 anticipates the great moral claims of the prophets: To obey is better than sacrifice.

1 SAMUEL 16–20

Introduction to These Chapters

Either because Saul usurps powers reserved for priests or because he fails to follow the prescription of holy war, he proves himself an unacceptable leader for the people of God. God rescinds his charismatic endowment. As Saul's successor, God chooses David, the youngest son of Jesse. David's rise to power is filled with dangers and setbacks, but David eventually confirms God's approval and Samuel's anointing. First Samuel 16–20 recounts how this path begins.

Here is an outline of these chapters.

I. God's Choice of David (16:1-13)
II. David's Appointment to Saul's Court (16:14-23)
III. David's Victory over Goliath (17:1-54)
IV. David and Saul's Family (17:55–18:30)
V. Saul's Plot to Kill David (19:1-24)
VI. Jonathan's Help for David (20:1-42)

The Message of 1 Samuel 16–20

The two themes in these chapters that are the most significant, theologically, are: (1) God saves by faith, not by sword or spear (17:46); and (2) ecstatic behavior of prophets (19:24).

The story of David and Goliath illustrates the universal literary motif of the weak humiliating the strong. But David is more than merely a weak man; he is a man of God. He is absolutely confident that the Lord, through him, can destroy this pagan adversary. David's strength, therefore, comes from his faith in the Lord rather than in military weaponry or combat experience. The message is clear: God's people need to put their faith (trust) in the Lord, not in things of war. This faith brings a power that is even stronger than giants. Israel needed to hear this message, and, like David, draw her strength from the Lord.

When David slips away from Saul by night, he flees to Samuel and the prophets at Ramah (19:18-24). Saul sends his messengers to retrieve David, but the messengers fall victim to the spell of God's spirit and begin to prophesy. The same experience befalls the messengers a second and a third time. Finally, Saul himself goes in search of David, and finds himself subject to the same spiritual endowment and its resulting unusual behavior. Saul disrobes and immediately begins to prophesy.

Manifestation of religious zeal in the Old Testament has long been identified with the phenomenon of prophecy. God's spirit frequently caused its recipients to act in unusual ways (see Ezekiel 37:1-4).

1 SAMUEL 21–24

Introduction to These Chapters

From the national prominence and acclaim as Saul's celebrated warrior, David has to flee for his life. He becomes a fugitive overnight. Saul pursues David with an unrelenting vengeance that is fueled by paranoia and by an evil spirit from the Lord. Humor and pathos permeate these narratives, and they represent excellent examples of ancient Israelite literature.

Here is an outline of these chapters.

I. David's Escape to the Priest at Nob (21:1-9)
II. David's Move to Gath (21:10-15)
III. David Moves on to Adullam (22:1-5)
IV. Saul's Massacre of the Priests at Nob (22:6-23)
V. David's Stay at Keilah (23:1-13)
VI. David's Reluctance to Kill Saul (23:14–24:22)

The Message of 1 Samuel 21–24

Two important theological issues emerge from studying 1 Samuel 21–24: (1) Human needs take priority over religious regulation, and (2) reverence is to be shown the servants of God.

In 21:1-6, David deceives Ahimelech, a priest at Nob, into providing him with food and weapons. Ostensibly, David has embarked on a secret mission and requires help from Ahimelech for himself and his men. Actually, however, David wants the supplies for himself, as he flees from Saul. Also, David appropriates holy bread, usually reserved for the priests. David must escape Saul's assassination plot, and he must secure food before fleeing to safety. Thus David's misconduct is a necessary step in avoiding death at the hands of Saul. Human needs clearly take priority over the regulations of cultic law. In the New Testament, three of the Gospel writers include the story of Jesus plucking grain on the sabbath (Matthew 12:1-14; Mark 2:23–3:6; Luke 6:1-11), placing human need above the sabbath laws. Jesus even invokes David's actions in the Nob incident as precedent for his own behavior. Hungry people cannot hear the word of God—on the sabbath or at any other time.

The second major theological theme in these chapters is reverence for the servants of God. Such individuals, whether they are prophets, priests, or kings, are considered sacrosanct. David offers sanctuary to Abiathar, the refugee priest from Nob; he avoids killing Saul, God's anointed king. David almost always uses the priests to consult the Lord prior to military activity. He handles the ark with great care when he brings the sacred object into Jerusalem. David shows respect for God's servants.

1 SAMUEL 25–31

Introduction to These Chapters

This section is bracketed by the deaths of two important leaders in early Israelite history, Samuel (25:1) and Saul (31:4).

Here is an outline of these chapters.

I. David's Courtship of Abigail (25:1-44)
II. David Spares Saul a Second Time (26:1-25)
III. David's Service to the Philistines (27:1–28:2)
IV. Saul Meets with Samuel's Spirit (28:3-25)
V. Saul's Dismissal from Service (29:1-11)
VI. David's Revenge on the Amalekites (30:1-31)
VII. Saul's Death (31:1-13)

The Message of 1 Samuel 25–31

Three issues emerge from studying 1 Samuel 25–31: (1) divine guidance of the affairs of history, (2) the many forms of divine revelation, and (3) justice among God's people.

David was open to divine guidance. He has good reason to avenge Nabal's insult, yet he listens to Abigail's wise words urging restraint. She tells him to avoid incurring bloodguilt and that God, not David, will take care of Nabal. In a second incident, David refuses to allow Abishai to kill Saul, and explains that God will deal with the king. And, David consults the Lord in the matter of revenge against the Amalekites (30:7). David's faith in soliciting divine guidance distinguishes him from King Saul.

There are many forms of divine revelation. In 28:6-7 Saul seeks a word from the Lord by three traditional forms of revelation in the Old Testament: (1) dreams (Genesis 37:5-11), (2) casting of lots (1 Samuel 14:41), and (3) prophets (Amos 3:7). These are all acceptable types of solicitation of the divine will.

There is justice among the people of God. Following David's successful retaliation against the Amalekites (chapter 30), he is urged to limit the spoils to the men who participated actively in the effort. David refuses, and insists that all his soldiers share in the prizes of victory (30:24), regardless of their level of involvement. In fact, David even extends his generosity to other tribal leaders of Judah as well. David's actions reflect his belief that it is God who gives him victory, not his own military might. Therefore, these prizes of war belong to God, and ought to be divided fairly among all of the people of God.

2 SAMUEL 1–4

Introduction to These Chapters

The opening four chapters in 2 Samuel cover events from Saul's death to the assassination of Ishbosheth, his son. Between these two deaths, much of importance occurs for David, for Judah, and for Israel.

Most of the literary problems that occurred in 1 Samuel are absent in 2 Samuel. Although the writer does employ different sources, he harmonizes them in such a way as to produce a continuous narrative of David's reign.

Here is an outline of these chapters.
I. David Mourns Saul and Jonathan (1:1-27)
II. David's Reign at Hebron (2:1-11)
III. Abner's Killing of Asahel (2:12-32)
IV. Abner's Defection to David (3:1-39)
V. Ishbosheth's Murder (4:1-12)

The Message of 2 Samuel 1–4

Two important issues arise in these four chapters: (1) Proper and improper motives for punishment, and (2) the nature of David's faith.

There are proper and improper motives for punishment. When Abner must, for

reasons of self-defense, slay Asahel, he incurs the bloodguilt obligation from Joab and Asishai. Their motive in taking Abner's life is clearly revenge (3:7). Yet, what Abner does is a matter of necessity. He does not plot Asahel's assassination, nor brutally stalk him out of malice. He even tries to persuade him to abandon his pursuit.

But Joab, on the other hand, seems motivated by jealousy. His crime against Abner is a mean and despicable act that is beyond even David's capacity to punish. Unprovoked vengeance is truly an unacceptable motive for punishment. The Lord may excuse revenge as a reprisal for clearly criminal behavior, but Joab clearly goes too far in this case.

David's faith in God is of a special nature. David's faith in the Lord manifests itself in several actions that combine creed and conduct. First, David always consults the Lord prior to a major decision. He allows the Lord to exercise leadership. Second, David respects the Lord's prerogatives in dealing with evil. He avoids taking the lives of Saul and Joab, even though he has sufficient reason. Third, he has a profound respect for human life, and refrains from taking it whenever possible. Life is sacred and must be honored.

David's faith serves as an appropriate model for persons today who are struggling to discover what it means to live according to God's will.

2 SAMUEL 5–8

Introduction to These Chapters

In 2 Samuel 5–8, David keeps his rendezvous with destiny. Ishbosheth is now dead and there are no further hindrances to block his ascendancy to the throne. The elders of Israel come to Hebron and anoint David as their king, and the United

Monarchy is formed. This united nation will last for three-quarters of a century (about 1000 until 922 B.C.), until it breaks apart during the early months of Rehoboam's (Solomon's son) reign.

Here is an outline of these chapters.

I. David's Rule over All Israel (5:1-16)
II. David's War Against the Philistines (5:17-25)
III. David's Transfer of the Ark to Jerusalem (6:1-23)
IV. God's Covenant with David (7:1-29)
V. David's Military Conquests (8:1-18)

The Message of 2 Samuel 5–8

Three major issues emerge from a study of 2 Samuel 5–8: (1) the nature of the Davidic covenant, (2) worship in Israel, and (3) the unlimited nature of God's freedom.

The Davidic covenant contains three promises. First, it distinguishes David as one of the great kings of all the earth. Second, it establishes the Israelites in Palestine and gives them rest and peace. Third, it establishes a dynasty for David so that his descendants will rule over the people of God forever. The fulfillment of these promises has made David an important ruler in the history of Israel. For the biblical writer, this covenant serves two purposes. First, it explains why David did not build the Temple. And second, it provides a theological sanction for kingship.

Worship can be a form of celebration. When David and his band of companions retrieve the ark from Kiriath-jearim (Baale-judah), they march toward Jerusalem in a festive procession. Music and dance are interspersed with sacrificial offerings. This activity illustrates the joyous and emotive nature of worship. The people have something to celebrate, and they give full vent to their joy. Worship is, truly, celebration.

God's freedom is unlimited. By refusing to allow David to build a house, God indicates that there are no limits to the divine freedom to move about. The moment God became institutionalized, God's spontaneity would disappear. The message is that human attempts to limit God will fail.

2 SAMUEL 9–12

Introduction to These Chapters

The action in 2 Samuel 9–12 is an interplay between David's personal behavior (his active concern for Mephibosheth and his adultery with Bathsheba) and his military activity against Aram and Ammon. He satisfied his covenant obligation to Jonathan by honoring and endowing his son, Mephibosheth, with a fealty. In his adulterous relationship with Bathsheba, he exhibits flagrant abuse of his royal power. David pays a very high price for their sin, since its effects continue to trouble him the rest of his days. On another front, David brings his military career to a successful conclusion with battles against Aram and Ammon. Both kingdoms are soundly defeated and are incorporated within David's large and wealthy empire. But it is David's domestic scene that next forms the arena of turmoil.

Here is an outline of these chapters.

I. David's Concern for Mephibosheth (9:1-13)
II. David Wars Against Ammon and Aram (10:1-19)
III. David's Sin with Bathsheba (11:1–12:31)

The Message of 2 Samuel 9–12

Two important issues emerge from 2 Samuel 9–12:

(1) David's obligation to God, and (2) the results of sin.

David satisfies his covenant obligations. He brings Mephibosheth, Jonathan's son, to the royal palace in Jerusalem and bestows great honor and kindness upon him. Jonathan and David had made a covenant (1 Samuel 20:12-17). So David is fulfilling much more than a legal obligation to Mephibosheth. He is fulfilling his word of promise sworn to his beloved friend Jonathan.

Sin results in both punishment and forgiveness. David commits adultery with Bathsheba, and to cover up his mistake he orders the death of Uriah, her husband. These actions violate God's commandments, they violate Israelite morality, and they even violate civil codes. Moreover, these sins are an abuse of royal power—exactly the sort of thing Samuel feared (1 Samuel 8:10-18).

David's sin affects several persons— Uriah, the child, Joab, Nathan, and others. Most of all, the sin angers God. For that David must be punished.

David's sins must be expiated. One of the more troublesome issues in this section is the image of a vengeful God requiring the life of an innocent child. In early Israel, the concept of expiation involved satisfaction of obligation to God. When a person sinned against the Lord, certain means existed to obtain forgiveness. Particularly in the case of shedding innocent blood, the blood of the perpetrator was required in return. But substitutions were permissible, and the biblical story here presents the child, conceived in sin, as an alternative to the king. Thus, from an ancient perspective, David's sins were atoned for, fairly, by the life of his son.

2 SAMUEL 13–16

Introduction to These Chapters

Second Samuel 13–16 contains some of the most morally debased material in the Old Testament. The strife that divides the royal family is created not only by personal rivalries within David's house, but also by divine judgment. This is the fulfillment of Nathan's oracle.

Here is an outline of these chapters.
I. Tamar's Rape (13:1-22)
II. Absalom's Revenge (13:23-38)
III. Absalom's Return (14:1-33)
IV. Absalom's Revolt (15:1-37)
V. Absalom Enters Jerusalem (16:1-23)

The Message of 2 Samuel 13–16

Two important issues emerge from 2 Samuel 13–16:
(1) the nature of David's faith in God, and (2) the fulfillment of prophecy.

Faith in the Lord differs from faith in human counsel. When David orders Abiathar and Zadok to return the ark to Jerusalem, he prepares himself to accept God's will. This kind of trust has characterized all of David's early career, when he consulted the Lord prior to nearly every venture. Yet, at the time David is submissive to God's leadership, he actively does all within his power to act prudently. This is faith as active submission.

By contrast, Absalom relies on his own emotions and on the wise counsel of others, never once on God. He is a perfect contrast with his father. The object of his trust leads him to death.

Nathan's prophecy is fulfilled. Nathan's oracle announced that David's house would be continually ravaged by the sword, and that a member of his own house would have intercourse with his concubines, in full view of all Jerusalem. Both these announcements came to pass

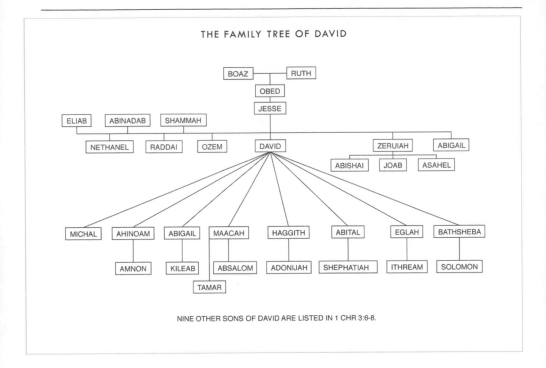

THE FAMILY TREE OF DAVID

NINE OTHER SONS OF DAVID ARE LISTED IN 1 CHR 3:6-8.

exactly as described. The biblical writer believes firmly that what God declared through the mouth of Nathan the prophet has come to pass in David's household.

2 SAMUEL 17–20

Introduction to These Chapters

In 2 Samuel 17–20, David's struggle with Absalom comes to a tragic climax with the battle in the Ephraim forest. Most scholars regard this section as being of considerable historical value. The intimate details of David's moods, Absalom's faulty decisions, and the stern reprimands of Joab all suggest a source very close to the events themselves.

Here is an outline of 2 Samuel 17–20.

   I. Ahithophel's Counsel Rejected (17:1-23)

  II. Absalom's Death (17:24–19:8a)

 III. David's Return to Jerusalem (19:8b-43)

 IV. Sheba's Rebellion (20:1-26)

The Message of 2 Samuel 17–20

God is active in history, responding to sincere prayers. Just as David flees Jerusalem in the wake of Absalom's revolt, he learns that Ahithophel, one of his advisors, has joined the rebellion. David prays that the Lord turn his counsel into disaster (15:31). In 17:14, God answers David's prayer. Absalom chooses to follow Hushai's advice to delay attacking David rather than heed the proposal of Ahithophel to continue pursuit immediately.

The writer makes the point that this delay was not the result of human calculation. From a theological perspective, Absalom's revolt may be considered a part of God's judgment against David for the Bathsheba affair. Therefore, the revolt is a necessary component in God's plan. But yet, because of David's great faith, the Lord does not intend to allow David to die or his dynasty to fall into the wrong hands. So Absalom's rebellion is doomed to failure, even from the outset. God controls the direction of history.

David's love for Absalom is unconditional. When David learns of Absalom's death, he weeps uncontrollably. This reaction shows a father's sincere and unconditional love for his son. Absalom had done little to earn David's love. His cruel revenge against his brother Amnon, his devious undermining of his father's judicial system, his impatience for power, and finally his revolt all display contempt rather than love. And yet, David loved him deeply. David's love for Absalom was unconditional. Perhaps this same kind of love is reflected in John 3:16, and in God's love for us.

2 SAMUEL 21–24

Introduction to These Chapters

The final four chapters in 2 Samuel form an appendix to David's long and successful reign. These chapters consist of several different literary types: hymns, lists, hero legends, and historical narratives.

Here is an outline of these chapters.
I. A Famine and David's Response (21:1-14)
II. War with the Philistines (21:15-22)
III. David's Hymn of Praise (22:1-51)
IV. David's Second Song (23:1-7)
V. David's Warriors (23:8-39)
VI. A Census, a Plague, and an Altar (24:1-25)

The Message of 2 Samuel 21–24

The first theme in 2 Samuel 21–24 concerns the relationship between God and the laws of nature. In 2 Samuel 21:1-14, the writer describes a severe and lengthy famine that afflicts Israel because Saul had violated an early agreement with the Gibeonites by murdering many of their number. In order to atone for Saul's bloodguilt, David turns over to the Gibeonites two of Saul's sons and five of his grandsons. Similarly, in chapter 24, God sends an angel with a terrible pestilence as punishment for David's census. Both stories reflect ancient Israel's belief that God controls the immediate cause. All aspects of the natural order are subject to God's will. On the other hand, our modern scientific perspective explains such events differently. In reading the biblical material, we must learn to withhold judgments about nonscientific descriptions of natural events.

The second major theological issue is the merging of religious faith and political leadership. Throughout the accounts of David's reign, the biblical writer has emphasized David's faith. He always consults the Lord before engaging in battle. He provides a haven of safety for Abiathar, the refugee priest from Nob. He refrains from personal violence against Saul and other adversaries. And even when he sins, he is quick to repent and to seek God's forgiveness. From the perspective of the biblical writer, these qualities of faith prompt God to reward David by granting him and his descendants success as military/political leaders. In the person of the king, religious faith and political leadership must come together in synthesis.

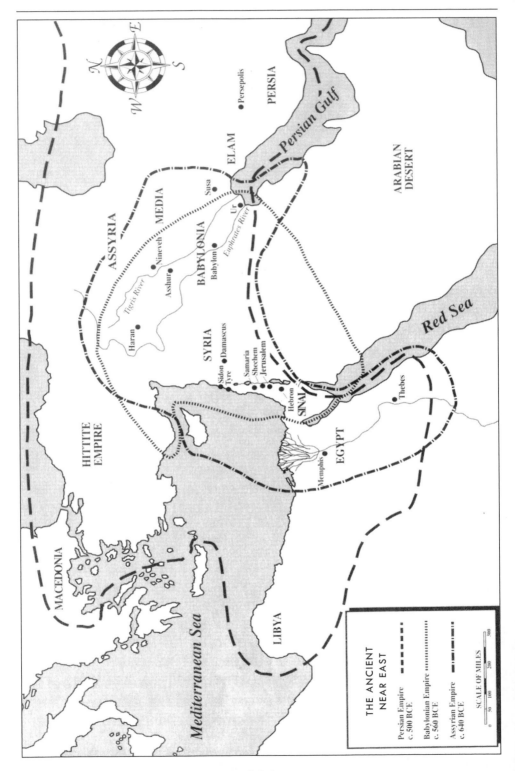

THE ANCIENT
NEAR EAST

Persian Empire
c. 500 BCE

Babylonian Empire
c. 560 BCE

Assyrian Empire
c. 640 BCE

SCALE OF MILES

0   50   100   200   400

FIRST AND SECOND KINGS

OUTLINE OF 1 AND 2 KINGS

A. The reigns of Abijam, Asa, and
   Nadab (15:1-28)
B. Baasha, Elah, Zimri, and Omri
   (15:29–16:28)
C. Ahab becomes king (16:29-34)

VII. **The Reign of Ahab (17:1–19:21)**
A. Elijah, Ahab, and Jezebel
   (17:1–19:3)
   1. Elijah and the famine from
      God (17:1-24)
   2. Elijah and the prophets of Baal
      (18:1–19:3)
B. Elijah and Elisha (19:4-21)

VIII. **Ahab and Ahaziah (20:1–22:53)**
A. Ahab's wars with Syria (20:1-43)
B. Naboth's vineyard (21:1-29)
C. Ahab, Jehoshaphat, and Ahaziah
   (22:1-53)

2 Kings
I. **Ahaziah and Jehoram (1:1–3:27)**
A. The reign of Ahaziah (1:1-18)
B. Elisha succeeds Elijah (2:1-25)
C. The reign of Jehoram (Joram) of
   Israel (3:1-27)

II. **The Work of the Prophet Elisha
    (4:1–7:20)**
A. The widow's jar of oil (4:1-7)
B. The Shunammite's son is raised
   (4:8-37)
C. Elisha and the pot of death
   (4:38-41)
D. The abundance of loaves and
   grain (4:42-44)
E. Naaman's leprosy is cured
   (5:1-27)
F. Elisha and the floating axe-head
   (6:1-7)
G. Elisha saved from the Syrian
   army (6:8-23)
H. Syrian siege of Samaria
   (6:24–7:20)

III. **The End of Ahab; Jehu Begins to
     Reign (8:1–10:36)**
A. Elisha, Hazael, and Jehoram
   (8:1-24)
B. Ahaziah reigns, Jehu revolts
   (8:25–9:29)
C. The death of Jezebel (9:30-37)
D. The reign of Jehu (10:1-36)

IV. **More Kings of Judah and Israel
    (11:1–14:29)**
A. The reign of Queen Athaliah
   (11:1-21)
B. The reign of Jehoash (Joash) in
   Judah (12:1-21)
C. The reign of Jehoahaz (13:1-9)
D. The reign of Joash (Jehoash) in
   Israel (13:10-25)
E. The reign of Amaziah (14:1-22)
F. The reign of Jeroboam II
   (14:23-29)

V. **The Final Days of Israel
   (15:1–17:41)**
A. Stability in Judah, chaos in Israel
   (15:1-38)
   1. Azariah (Uzziah), Zechariah,
      Shallum (15:1-16)
   2. Menahem, Pekahiah, Pekah,
      Jotham (15:17-38)
B. The reign of Ahaz (16:1-20)
C. The reign of Hoshea (17:1-41)

VI. **The Reign of King Hezekiah
    (18:1–20:21)**
A. The beginning of Hezekiah's
   reign (18:1-12)
B. Assyria attacks Judah (18:13-37)
C. Hezekiah and Isaiah
   (19:1–20:21)

VII. **Manasseh, Amon, Josiah, and
     Jehoahaz (21:1–23:37)**
A. The reign of Manasseh (21:1-18)
B. The reign of Amon (21:19-26)
C. The reign of Josiah (22:1–23:30)

1. The book of the law is found (22:1-20)
2. Josiah's religious reform (23:1-30)
D. The reign of Jehoahaz (23:31-37)

VIII. The Last of the Kings of Judah (24:1–25:30)

A. The reign of Jehoiakim (24:1-7)
B. The reign of Jehoiachin (24:8-17)
C. The reign of Zedekiah (24:18–25:21)
  1. Zedekiah begins his reign (24:18-20)
  2. The second siege of Jerusalem (25:1-7)
  3. The destruction of Jerusalem (25:8-21)
D. The governorship of Gedaliah (25:22-26)
E. King Jehoiachin in exile (25:27-30)

INTRODUCTION

The books of 1 and 2 Kings are part of a history of Israel which begins in Deuteronomy and runs through 2 Kings. The books of Joshua, Judges, 1 and 2 Samuel, and 1 and 2 Kings tell of Israel's settlement in Canaan, of the creation of the state of Israel, of the division of greater Israel into two kingdoms, and of the destruction of these kingdoms by Assyria and Babylon.

Content of First and Second Kings

First and Second Kings were originally one book in Hebrew. The Septuagint (the oldest Greek translation of the Old Testament) put Kings together with Samuel and divided them into "the four books of Reigns/Kingdoms." The books of Samuel and Kings were later separated in both the Hebrew and Christian Bibles. In the Hebrew Bible, 1 and 2 Kings are included in the Former Prophets (Joshua, Judges, 1 and 2 Samuel, and 1 and 2 Kings).

First Kings begins in the last years of King David, and 2 Kings ends during the Exile (in approximately 560 B.C.). The content of Kings may be divided into three major sections:

(1) the history of greater Israel from the end of David's reign through Solomon's reign (1 Kings 1–11),

(2) the history of Israel and Judah to the fall of Israel (1 Kings 12–2 Kings 17),

(3) the history of Judah into the Babylonian Exile (2 Kings 18–25).

In Kings the word *Israel* has three different meanings. During the reigns of David and Solomon, *Israel* refers to the covenant community (the original twelve tribes) that is united in the nation Israel. After the division of the nation, *Israel* refers to the Northern Kingdom and *Judah* refers to the Southern Kingdom. Even after the division and after the destruction of the Northern Kingdom, however, *Israel* or *the people of Israel* are often used to refer to all the chosen people, both south and north.

The history of the divided kingdoms is organized according to the careers of their kings. In the books of Kings, each king is judged by the same standard and is either praised or condemned according to how he lived up to this standard. The historian's standard of judgment is whether the king practices pure worship of God and whether the worship rituals are held in the Jerusalem Temple. Most of the kings are condemned because they allow, or even encourage, the worship of foreign gods. Many of them also build shrines to God away from the Temple, which draws the people away from the Temple for worship.

The Chronology of 1 and 2 Kings

The books of Kings do not give specific dates for the reign of each king. Rather, the reigns are coordinated with one another so that the years of one king are used to establish the years of another (see, for example, 1 Kings 15:25).

This method of dating is not always accurate. Differences exist between these dates and the dates figured by considering only the years of Judean kings or of Israelite kings. In addition, Assyrian and Babylonian documents mention Israelite and Judean kings. Dates from these records do not always match those given in Kings. (For example, from the revolution of Jehu in Israel to the fall of Israel to Assyria is 170 years by the coordinated method, 165 years by the dates for Judean kings, 143 years and 7 months by the dates for Israelite kings, and 121 years according to Assyrian records.)

The coordinated system of dating used in Kings is not completely unreliable, but the dates must be compared to dates given in other historical sources. This is why various Old Testament commentaries do not all give the same dates for the kings of Judah and Israel.

The Writer of 1 and 2 Kings

The books of Kings are the conclusion to the history of the people of Israel which begins in Deuteronomy. The historian(s) who wrote these books are known as the Deuteronomistic historians. They combined parts of many historical records within an interpretive framework to produce the document we have today.

Crucial writing, editing, and compiling of this document took place over generations during the reigns of King Hezekiah (eighth century B.C.) and King Josiah (seventh century B.C.) and sometime after Judah's defeat by Babylon in 587 B.C. when many Jews were taken into exile in Babylon (but before the fall of Babylon in 538 B.C.). These historians may have been

priests or prophets who had access to the records of Israel's history kept in the palace and the Temple. The Jews may have taken some of these records with them when they went into exile.

The viewpoint of Kings is that God acts to bless those who are faithful to the covenant and to punish those who disobey the covenant. These actions are in accordance with the law, which is spelled out in Deuteronomy. The writers emphasize that the people of Israel must be faithful to the covenant relationship. In practical terms, this means that the people must not worship other gods nor contaminate their worship of God with foreign practices. All shrines outside of Jerusalem must be destroyed and all worship conducted within the Temple in Jerusalem. In the books of Kings, all the Judean and Israelite kings are strictly judged as to how they lived up to their covenant responsibilities. All idolatry and tolerance of foreign religious influences is condemned.

The Historical Sources Behind Kings

The writers of the books of Kings used many reference materials to get information about the history of Israel. Among these materials were official records from the administrations of King David and King Solomon. One of these documents is recorded in 2 Samuel 9–20 and 1 Kings 1–2 and is known as the "History of the Throne Succession." This history is believed to be an eyewitness account from the end of David's reign and the beginning of Solomon's reign.

Three historical reference books are mentioned by name in the books of Kings: The Book of the Acts of Solomon, The Book of the Chronicles of the Kings of Israel, and The Book of the Chronicles of the Kings of Judah. The book about

Solomon was a collection of stories about Solomon's wisdom and of information from palace and Temple archives. The chronicles of the kings of Israel and of Judah were also official records from the palace archives. These books told of the deeds of each king or queen and of what happened during their rule. The writers of Kings invite their readers to look into these other books for more information on the monarchy and also to confirm what is written in Kings. Unfortunately, these three valuable books are lost to us except for the parts that are preserved in Kings.

The writers of Kings also used stories about the kings, queens, prophets, priests, and others from this time in Israel's history. They included, for example, stories about the ark of the covenant (see 1 Samuel 4:1b–7:2), about the Queen of Sheba (see 1 Kings 10:1-13), and about Elijah and Elisha (see 1 Kings 19).

The historians who wrote Deuteronomy, Joshua, Judges, 1 and 2 Samuel, and 1 and 2 Kings used many different resources to produce the document we have today. They used straightforward historical reports as well as history in story form. These historical narratives are told with an awareness of their value as stories as well as an appreciation for the history that they preserve.

Old Testament Historical Narrative

In broad terms, history is defined as what has happened in the past or, in particular, as an account of what has happened in the past. A narrative is a story that, in its simplest form, is a chronological account of more than one past event which also tells of causes and effects. Thus, a narrative can be history that is told as a story. Such stories are common in the Old Testament and are found in the books of 1 and 2 Kings (for example, 1 Kings 19:1-21; 2 Kings 4:8-37).

Old Testament stories are different from other historical narratives, however, because they are sacred stories. These stories are told in the belief that all of life exists because of, and is subject to, God's will. In the Old Testament there is a recognition that some things are holy and others are not, but all life is held to be sacred. Old Testament historical narratives are told within the context of such faith. Because of this faith, Old Testament history is not just a list or report of events. Old Testament history describes events and people and also interprets them according to their causes and effects. God's will is seen as the ultimate source of all causes and effects within human history.

Old Testament historical narrative tells the story of Israel's life as a people who live in relationship to God. The chosen people are the particular subjects of these stories. The broader focus of these stories, however, is the relationship between God and all of creation. The result of this relationship is revelation. God is revealed to humankind. The Old Testament writers do not give us theological lectures about the nature and being of God. Rather, they tell us who God is by telling us how God acts.

The Old Testament writers do not try to convince us to believe their stories by giving us a lot of information about the setting or about the feelings and thoughts of the characters. Most of the time their narratives do not use many details. This reflects the fact that, in many cases, the stories were passed on by word-of-mouth for generations before they were written.

The goal of any narrative is communication. What the writer or speaker knows or sees must be communicated to the reader or listener. The result of narrative is that the readers or listeners see, recognize, and understand something, perhaps something with which they have had no personal experience. The writers of Old Testament stories seek such communication with their readers. Their stories seek to communicate the same basic testimony: History is the will of a just God who knows us and cares about us. The writers want us to understand that our lives are contained in an order that is moving toward God's end.

Old Testament historical narratives witness to the fact that the world and everyone in it belong to God. They ask us to believe that we live in an ordered world which is moving toward a desired goal. The sacred stories of the Old Testament not only offer the pleasure of a well-told story. They teach, encourage, and sustain the community of faith.

1 KINGS 1–2

Introduction to These Chapters

The books of Kings begin during the last years of King David. First Kings 1–2 is part of "The History of the Throne Succession," which is found in 2 Samuel 9–20 and 1 Kings 1–2. The first two chapters of Kings are an introduction to the story of Solomon's reign. First and Second Chronicles also tell about the reigns of David, Solomon, and the other kings of Judah.

David had a long and successful reign. After the death of Saul, the tribes of Israel united under David's leadership and proclaimed him king. They defeated the Philistines, who had been a threat to Israel for many years, and also dealt with their other aggressive neighbors.

David made Jerusalem the political and spiritual center of life in Israel. The ark of the covenant was given an honored place in the new capital.

Under David's military leadership, Israelite territory grew enormously. During this time, the nation of Israel was the dominant power in the ancient Near East.

Though David was undoubtedly a great king and an exceptional man, the end of his life and reign was troubled. As he became older and more feeble the question of who would succeed him as ruler of Israel led to intrigue and violence. This conflict grew out of longstanding disagreements within the nation as well as from the immediate pressures of deciding who would take David's place.

No precedent had been set in Israel for a king's son to succeed him on the throne. Saul and David were both charismatic military heroes. They were leaders among the people who were elected as king through divine benediction and popular acclamation. At the end of David's reign there was still some support for the view that Israel should be led by a charismatic leader whom the Lord would designate as the rightful ruler. In the days of the tribal league, the leaders of Israel were those on whom the people believed the spirit of the Lord rested. A king's son following him in office was more typical of other nations' governments than of Israel. Some Israelites believed that the old, traditional ways were best, and they were distrustful of the strong central power claimed by the king.

There were tensions within the government, the military, the religious establishment, and the royal household. Those who, in the past, had supported Saul against David had little loyalty to David's house despite David's attempts at reconciliation. There was still some resentment among the tribes of Israel at the growing power of the central government and the resulting loss of tribal independence. A proper judicial system had not been established. Because of this there was discontent among the people at the delays in hearing cases and handing down judgments.

The task of holding onto Israel's territory and defending its boundaries placed a great burden on the Israelite military. The fighting force was made up of David's personal professional troops and citizen militiamen from each of the tribes. These militiamen apparently served on a rotating basis with each tribe sending its share of able-bodied fighting men. As the years went by, Israelite citizens became increasingly reluctant to keep up these military duties that took manpower away from the demands of everyday life.

Within the royal household itself there was jealousy and maneuvering for power. David's wife Bathsheba and his two eldest sons, Adonijah and Solomon, were deeply involved in the struggle for the throne. David did not set up an orderly procedure for one of his sons to take his place. He apparently did little to deal with the intrigue even within his own house until the issue of his successor was pressed upon him.

This is the complex and volatile situation with which 1 Kings opens.

Here is an outline of these chapters.

I. David's Feeble Condition (1:1-4)
II. Adonijah Makes His Move (1:5-10)
III. Solomon Becomes King (1:11-40)
IV. Adonijah Accepts Defeat (1:41-53)
V. The Death of David (2:1-12)
VI. Adonijah, Abiathar, Joab, and Shimei (2:13-46)

The Message of 1 Kings 1–2

The basis for David's instructions to Solomon concerning his kingship (see 1 Kings 2:1-4) is found in Deuteronomy 4:40-45; 17:14-20; and 2 Samuel 7:12-17. According to Deuteronomy, what are the standards for the ideal king?

- If the king keeps God's statutes and ordinances, the king and the people will prosper in the Promised Land.

- The king must be a native Israelite.

- Military alliances, marriage, and the pursuit of riches must be limited because these can lead the king and the people away from God.

- The king must study the law of Moses.

- The king must fear God.

- The king must keep the law and the statutes and ordinances by which the law is applied to daily life.

- The king must not be proud in relation to the people. Everyone is under the law, including the king.

- The king is God's servant on behalf of the people.

- If the king abides by all these standards, he may reign in peace and his descendants will rule after him.

The promises given the king in the Mosaic law are conditional. Peace, stability, and prosperity are related to faithfulness to the covenant requirements. King David applies the conditional aspects of the promises in Deuteronomy to the promises made in 2 Samuel when he speaks to Solomon. In 2 Samuel God promises to punish the king's sins but not to destroy David's dynasty (2 Samuel 7:16).

In later years, God's promises concerning the permanent establishment of a king in David's line are taken for granted by kings and people alike while the conditional aspects of the covenant are largely ignored. Solomon himself fails to abide by all the standards set out in Deuteronomy. Old Testament hopes for the restoration and renewal of the people of Israel come to focus on a messiah who is in the line of David or is an ideal king in the tradition of David (see, for example, Micah 5:2-4). Though David's descendants are no longer on the throne of Judah after 587 B.C., the New Testament claim is that Jesus is born into the family of David to establish an everlasting kingdom.

1 KINGS 3–4

Introduction to These Chapters

First Kings 3–11 tells of the reign of Solomon. This account is based, in part, on "the Book of the Acts of Solomon" (see 1 Kings 11:41). Chapters 3–4 introduce the history of Solomon's reign by telling of the divine gift of wisdom by which he governs.

These chapters may be outlined as follows.

I. Solomon Receives Wisdom (3:1-15)
II. Judgment Between Two Mothers (3:16-28)
III. The Organization of Solomon's Kingdom (4:1-28)
IV. The Fame of Solomon's Wisdom (4:29-34)

The Message of 1 Kings 3–4

First Kings 3:12 says that Solomon is given "a wise and discerning mind" (NRSV; NIV = "heart"). According to the Old Testament, what is wisdom?

- Part of wisdom is understanding, which is practical judgment rather than theoretical understanding.

- Wisdom is action as well as thought, skill as well as perception.

- Wisdom comes from a person's heart as well as mind. The heart is the source of a person's character, the wellspring of hopes, fears, attitudes, motives, and beliefs.

- Wisdom is gained through experience and through study.

- Fear of God is the beginning of true wisdom (see Proverbs 9:10). Fear of God is reverence and awe for God's holiness and a recognition of one's

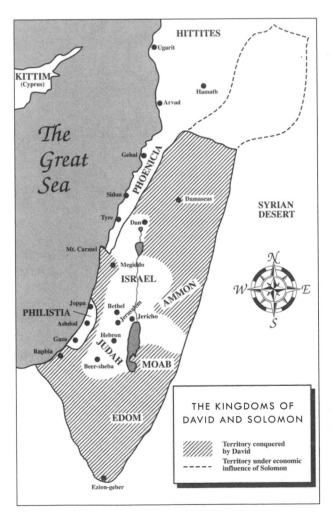

The Great Sea

THE KINGDOMS OF DAVID AND SOLOMON

///// Territory conquered by David
----- Territory under economic influence of Solomon

humbleness in relation to God. Thus a proper appreciation of one's place in the divine order is necessary for wisdom.

- The human capacity for wisdom and wisdom itself are gifts from God.

- Wisdom begins with one's relationship to and faith in God.

- Because wisdom begins with and rests on faith, wisdom has an ethical aspect which includes uprightness and honesty.

- Wisdom is to be applied in the experience and mastery of life and its problems.

1 KINGS 5–8

Introduction to These Chapters

Chapters 5–8 tell about Solomon's alliance with King Hiram of Tyre and about

the building of the Temple and Solomon's palace (see also 2 Chronicles 2–7).

In addition to his wisdom, Solomon is well known for the development of commerce in Israel and for the building of the Temple in Jerusalem. Both of these goals are achieved, in part, through Solomon's abilities as a statesman. His foreign policy includes alliances with other states through marriage with foreign noblewomen (see, for example, 1 Kings 3:1) and through treaties. One of the most important treaties is made with the Phoenician king, Hiram of Tyre.

The Phoenician city-states controlled the Palestinian coast in what is now Lebanon from Mount Carmel northward for about 130 miles. They were a great seafaring trading power. They sold timber from their mountains, worked bronze, iron, glass, gold, and ivory, and were famous for dying cloth a prized purple color with an extract from sea snails. Their trading colonies eventually extended to the

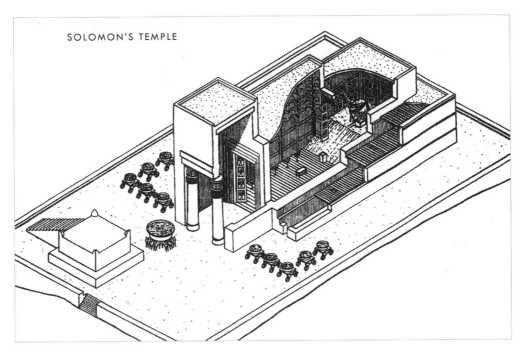

SOLOMON'S TEMPLE

Atlantic coasts of Spain and Morocco. (See Ezekiel 27:1-24 for a description of Tyre's trading empire).

Israel forms the land bridge between Mesopotamia, Egypt, and Arabia, and thus holds the principal land trade routes from one to the other. Tyre (and other Phoenician city-states) controls shipping routes in the eastern Mediterranean. The combination of these two powers is an advantage to both Solomon and Hiram.

Here is an outline of 1 Kings 5–8.

I. Agreement Between Solomon and Hiram (5:1-18)
II. Building the Temple (6:1-38)
III. Solomon's Palace (7:1-12)
IV. Temple Furnishings Are Built (7:13-51)
V. Dedication of the Temple (8:1-66)
  A. The ark and God's glory (8:1-11)
  B. Solomon addresses the people (8:12-21)
  C. Solomon's prayer on behalf of Israel (8:22-53)
  D. Benediction and charge to the people (8:54-61)
  E. Conclusion of the dedication feast (8:62-66)

The Message of 1 Kings 5–8

The Temple in Jerusalem is the center of religious and national life in Israel from the construction of the First Temple by Solomon in 955 B.C. to the destruction of Herod's Temple in A.D. 70. Though the Babylonians destroyed Solomon's Temple in 587 B.C., the Jews who remained in Judah during the Babylonian Exile continued to hold rituals and offer sacrifices in the Temple ruins. The Second Temple was completed in 515 B.C., and remodeled and expanded by King Herod (37–34 B.C.).

During these years, what role does the Temple play in the life of Israel?

- Israel is a theocracy rather than a secular state. Thus, the Temple is the center of national as well as religious life in Israel.

- The Temple is the "House of God" and, as such, is the site of God's special presence in and with Israel.

- The Temple is the place toward which the prayers of the faithful are directed.

- The Temple is the focal point of religious ritual and sacrifice. Daily sacrifices are offered, and there are special rituals and sacrifices on the sabbath and on each of the annual religious festivals.

Centuries after its destruction, the Temple remains a potent symbol of God's special presence in Jerusalem and with God's people. All that remains of either Temple is part of the southwestern retaining wall of Herod's Temple. This is the Western or "Wailing" Wall to which the faithful still come to pray in recognition of the tradition of prayer and worship that began on that site almost three thousand years ago.

1 KINGS 9–11

Introduction to These Chapters

These chapters tell of Solomon's reign, both his triumphs and his failures, after the Temple is built. The opening verses of chapter 9 set the standard by which the king is to be judged. The episodes that follow tell how well he lived up to this standard.

Here is an outline of these chapters.

I. God Appears to Solomon (9:1-9)
II. Building and Commercial Activities (9:10-28)
  A. Part of Galilee given to Hiram (9:10-14)

B. Solomon's fortress- and store-
cities (9:15-25)
C. Solomon's trading fleet (9:26-28)
III. Solomon and the Queen of Sheba
(10:1-13)
IV. Wealth and Business Activities
(10:14-29)
V. Solomon's Idolatry and Its
Consequences (11:1-43)
A. Foreign wives and idolatry (11:1-
13)
B. Solomon's adversaries (11:14-43)

The Message of 1 Kings 9–11

Any evaluation of Solomon's reign must
include the changes, both positive and
negative, that come about in Israel during
this time.

- Most of the territory gained by David
is held and consolidated into the
Israelite state.

- Many civil, military, and religious
construction projects, including the
Temple in Jerusalem, are completed
in all areas of the country.

- Trade and commerce increase
dramatically.

- Wisdom, music, and literature flourish.

- Many people enjoy a newfound
prosperity.

- Class differences also widen. Many
poor people do not share in the new
prosperity.

- The people endure forced labor and
heavy taxes.

- The state rather than the covenant is
now the focal point of national
obligation.

- Solomon officially introduces foreign
cults into Israel.

The problems of idolatry and social
injustice are evident in Solomon's reign,
and these problems continue to plague both
Israel and Judah.

At the heart of the matter seems to be
the desire of the people of Israel to "be like
all the nations." Time and again the king
and the people give in to the pull of
worshiping their neighbors' gods and to
accumulating power and riches like their
neighbors. They struggle to maintain their
calling as God's chosen people. It is one
thing to make a covenant with God when
you are a poor, powerless band of ex-
slaves. Living out this covenant
relationship when you are more in control
of your life is more difficult.

1 KINGS 12–14

Introduction to These Chapters

Long-held differences of opinion, old
rivalries, and tensions between the tribes
come to a head after Solomon's death. One
last chance for the United Kingdom to
survive is wasted by Solomon's son,
Rehoboam. Israel becomes two nations that
are sometimes at war with one another and
sometimes at peace, though both are weaker
in comparison to the United Kingdom. The
new nation of Israel survives until 722 B.C.
when it is absorbed into the Assyrian
empire. The nation of Judah survives until
597 B.C. when it is taken over by Babylonia.

These chapters may be outlined as
follows.
I. Greater Israel Is Divided (12:1-33)
A. Rehoboam will not relent
(12:1-24)
B. Jeroboam sets up his kingdom
(12:25-33)
II. A Judean Prophet Condemns
Jeroboam (13:1-34)
III. The End of Jeroboam's Reign
(14:1-20)

THE
KINGDOMS
OF ISRAEL
AND JUDAH

SCALE OF MILES
0   10   20   30   40

Testament say about the wrath of God?

- The understanding of God's wrath is determined by faith in a divine, personal God rather than in an impersonal, irrational force.

- God's wrath is a process or emotion in God as it is in human beings. God's wrath is distinguished from human anger by its power and scope.

- The objects of God's wrath are individuals and nations (both Israel and others).

- God's wrath is aroused by sin (such as idolatry, injustice, arrogance, and wickedness), which opposes God's holy will.

- God's wrath is exercised in relation to and in balance with divine justice, zeal, and love.

- The aim of God's wrath is the establishment of holiness. It is not just punishment, but is to set things right in the world.

IV. The Reign of Rehoboam (14:21-30)

The Message of 1 Kings 12–14

Jeroboam is designated by God through the prophet Ahijah to be king of Israel. The new king betrays this trust, however, by promoting idol worship, and he falls far short of the standards set for the kings of Israel (see "The Message of 1 Kings 1–2"). Instead, Jeroboam sets a standard for disobedience to which future Israelite kings are compared (see, for example, 2 Kings 15:8-9). Jeroboam's sin provokes God to anger or wrath. What does the Old

1 KINGS 15–16

Introduction to These Chapters

These chapters tell about the reigns of the kings of Israel and Judah from Jeroboam and Abijam to Omri and Asa (1 Kings 15:1–16:28), and they begin the report of the reign of King Ahab of Israel (1 Kings 16:29-34).

They may be outlined as follows.
I. The Reign of Abijam (15:1-8)
II. The Reign of Asa (15:9-24)
III. The Reign of Nadab (15:25-28)

IV. The Reign of Baasha (15:29–16:7)
V. The Reign of Elah (16:8-14)
VI. The Reign of Zimri (16:15-20)
VII. The Reign of Omri (16:21-28)
VIII. Ahab Becomes King (16:29-34)

The Message of 1 Kings 15–16

Omri and his descendants bring Israel a measure of internal stability, strength in relation to her neighbors, and economic prosperity. There is a darker side of his reign, however, that the writers of Kings touch on only indirectly when they refer to Omri's idolatry (verses 25-26). Israel becomes stronger in some ways, but she is weaker in her relationship with God and in the quality of life for many of her inhabitants.

Economic and religious abuses plague both Israel and Judah until the end of their lives as nations. Indeed, later prophets such as Amos and Jeremiah link the failure of economic and social justice to the failure of the people and their leaders to live up to the responsibilities of their faith.

What is the relationship between justice and righteousness (or, between daily life and faith)?

- In the Old Testament, justice and righteousness are inseparable.

- Righteousness is being in right relationship to God.

- Justice is the maintenance of this right relationship.

- This right relationship is founded on the covenant made between God and the chosen people.

- Covenant law defines the way this relationship is to be put into practice in daily life. This includes the relationship between people and God as well as the relationships people have with one another.

- No one, neither king nor commoner, is outside of the obligations of the law.

- The covenant and the law would not exist without God's mercy and grace. Therefore, mercy and grace are necessary parts of justice and righteousness.

1 KINGS 17–19

Introduction to These Chapters

Much of the material about the reign of Ahab focuses on the prophet Elijah and on the religious situation in Israel during this time. Chapters 17–19 tell stories about Elijah's prophetic activities and about his relationship with Ahab and Jezebel. The end of chapter 19 tells about Elisha's call to prophesy.

Here is an outline of these chapters.

I. Elijah, Ahab, and Jezebel
   (17:1–19:3)
   A. Elijah and the famine from God
      (17:1-24)
   B. Elijah and the prophets of Baal
      (18:1–19:3)
II. Elijah and Elisha (19:4-21)

The Message of 1 Kings 17–19

These chapters show us two different parts of Elijah's life as a prophet. There are times when, as God's representative to the people of Israel, he brings life out of death (chapter 17) and he demonstrates God's power over creation (chapter 18). There are also times, however, when Elijah feels afraid and weak and is overwhelmed by the forces working against him (chapter 19). Such contrasts are typical of the lives of many Old Testament prophets. They are called and compelled to speak God's word and to demonstrate God's power, but they do not always feel successful in their work.

What do these stories about Elijah tell us about the life and ministry of a prophet?

- Prophets speak at God's direction within specific historical situations.

- Prophetic messages are not just theoretical, but are related to life and death issues in the lives of God's people.

- The purpose of prophetic speech and actions is to make known God's will and to begin the process of carrying out God's will.

- The prophetic call is not to be taken lightly. The prophet can face personal opposition and threat as well as opposition to the prophetic word.

- God calls to prophesy even those people who feel unprepared or who feel that they have failed in their assigned task.

- God prepares the prophet for his or her task and watches over the prophet's life.

1 KINGS 20–22

Introduction to These Chapters

These last chapters in First Kings tell about the last years of Ahab's reign and the beginning of the reign of his son, Ahaziah. They may be outlined as follows.

I. Ahab's Wars With Syria (20:1-43)
II. Naboth's Vineyard (21:1-29)
III. Ahab, Jehoshaphat, and Ahaziah (22:1-53)
   A. Ahab's war against Syria (22:1-40)
   B. Jehoshaphat and Ahaziah (22:41-53)

The Message of 1 Kings 20–22

The historical record of the books of Kings is history with a purpose; it is history told within the context of faith. The people who wrote Kings based their historical record on the belief that the creative will of God is behind all reality. Thus, events in history are not random or irrational but are related to the will and purposes of God.

Part of God's will is to be known by people (see, for example, 1 Kings 20:13, 28). What is knowledge of God, according to the Old Testament?

- Knowledge is not only mental understanding but also involves the heart (as the source of a person's character) and the will (as the means of action in daily life).

- One of the goals of human life is to know what God is like and what God requires.

- People may know God through God's activities in the world and through God's relationships with individuals.

- People may know God through God's word spoken by a prophet.

- Knowledge of God requires understanding and practice of God's will.

- Knowledge of God includes an active recognition and acknowledgment of God's power, grace, and claim on human devotion.

2 KINGS 1–3

Introduction to These Chapters

Second Kings picks up where First Kings left off in the reign of Ahaziah of Israel. Chapter 1 tells of Ahaziah's premature death, chapter 2 tells how Elisha takes over Elijah's prophetic ministry, and chapter 3 reports on Israel's and Judah's war with Moab.

Here is an outline of these chapters.

I. The Reign of Ahaziah (1:1-18)
II. Elisha Succeeds Elijah (2:1-25)
III. The Reign of Jehoram (Joram) of Israel (3:1-27)

The Message of 2 Kings 1–3

Elisha inherits Elijah's prophetic spirit and begins his own prophetic ministry after Elijah is carried away into heaven. This prophetic Spirit is a portion of God's Spirit that is granted to them. This Spirit is a sign of their authority as prophets and the true substance of their ministries. They are vessels for the communication of God's Spirit on earth. What does the Old Testament tell us about God's Spirit?

- God's Spirit is a creative, life-giving, and personal force.

- This Spirit expresses God's nature and presence. It is a means by which God's nature is communicated to human beings.

- God's Spirit expresses both God's will and God's work to accomplish the divine purposes in the world.

- The Spirit of God is evident in the actions of human history.

- This Spirit is granted by God to those who are receptive and who are called by God for a special task.

- To be filled with the Spirit of the Lord is to have a divine gift for leadership as well as extraordinary insight.

- God gives such a gift not only to the prophets but also to other charismatic

leaders among God's people (for example, Gideon, David, and Saul).

- God's Spirit also works in and through ordinary people for the inspiration and perfection of the community of faith.

- Both God's immediate and ultimate purposes for the world are accomplished through the ones who possess this gift.

2 KINGS 4–7

Introduction to These Chapters

These chapters contain stories about the wonders worked by the prophet Elisha both in the lives of individuals and in the political and military world. These stories testify to Elisha's power and authority as a prophet. They may be outlined as follows.

I. The Widow's Jar of Oil (4:1 7)
II. The Shunammite's Son Is Raised (4:8-37)
III. Elisha and the Pot of Death (4:38-41)
IV. The Abundance of Loaves and Grain (4:42-44)
V. Naaman's Leprosy Is Cured (5:1-27)
VI. Elisha and the Floating Axe-Head (6:1-7)
VII. Elisha Saved from the Syrian Army (6:8-23)
VIII. Syrian Siege of Samaria (6:24–7:20)

The Message of 2 Kings 4–7

The stories in these chapters about wonders worked by Elisha fulfill different purposes as Scripture. They are, first of all, dramatic and entertaining narratives. They also testify to Elisha's power and authority as a prophet. Working wonders is not, in and of itself, however, the mark of a true prophet (see, for example, Deuteronomy

13:1-5). What qualities distinguish a true prophet from a false one?

- True prophets wait on God's word and do not proclaim their limited human imaginings (see Jeremiah 23:21; Ezekiel 13:3).

- True prophets are receptive to the visible world and the (normally) invisible world of God's reality (see 2 Kings 6:15-17).

- True prophets are watchmen among the people of Israel who guard the covenant and who raise an alarm when Israel's faith falls short of the covenant (see Ezekiel 3:16-21).

- The wonders and signs that true prophets perform promote faith and are in the service of life among God's people (see 2 Kings 4:1-7). Their words "do good to one who walks uprightly" (NRSV) or, as rendered in the NIV, "do good to him whose ways are upright" (see Micah 2:7).

- True prophets do not accept money for favorable messages (see 2 Kings 5:1).

- True prophets announce God's word of punishment as well as of salvation (see Isaiah 10:20-27).

- True prophets are ethically and spiritually righteous in their personal lives (see Micah 3:5-8).

- The word of a true prophet is confirmed by God, though perhaps not immediately (see Ezekiel 12:21-25).

2 KINGS 8–10

Introduction to These Chapters

Chapters 8–10 tell about the end of the house of Ahab in Israel and the establishment of the house of Jehu. The prophet Elisha plays a key role in bringing about Jehu's revolution and in bringing a change of rulers in Syria. The historians of Kings regard all these events as fulfillment of earlier prophecies that condemn the family of Ahab and promise its extinction. These prophecies are fulfilled, however, at a terrible cost to the nation both in terms of lives and leadership lost and in terms of political and military stability lost.

These chapters may be outlined as follows.

I. Elisha, Hazael, and Jehoram (8:1-24)
   A. Elisha and the Shunammite Woman (8:1-6)
   B. Elisha and the Revolt of Hazael in Syria (8:7-15)
   C. The Reign of Jehoram (Joram) in Judah (8:16-24)
II. Ahaziah Reigns, Jehu Revolts (8:25–9:29)
III. The Death of Jezebel (9:30-37)
IV. The Reign of Jehu (10:1-36)

The Message of 2 Kings 8–10

Of all the persistent issues raised in the Scripture, perhaps none is more difficult to deal with than that of divinely ordained bloodshed. The books of Kings have their fair share of prophetic proclamations (see, for example, 1 Kings 14:7-13; 2 Kings 8:10-13) and prophetic actions (see, for example, 1 Kings 18:40) that result in people's deaths. How are we to understand these events?

Some aspects of this issue are based on the belief that guilt or sin affects a whole social group, especially the family. The sin of one member contaminates the rest and makes them a potential source of evil which must be eliminated (see, for example, the laws of Exodus 20:5 and Deuteronomy 5:9-10, and their application in Numbers 16:31-33, Joshua 7:24-25, 2 Samuel 21:3-9, and 1 Kings 21:21).

Such vengeance is also based on the belief that God is righteous and just and that God will maintain righteousness and justice within human history. Sin will be punished and wrongs set right.

This is not, however, the only word on how sin and wrongdoing are handled in the community of faith (see, for example, Deuteronomy 24:16; 2 Kings 14:6; also Jeremiah 23:1; 31:29-30; Ezekiel 13:1; 14:9; 18:2-4). These other laws and prophetic oracles uphold individual rather than corporate responsibility for wrongdoing.

Scripture also shows us that even those who are divinely ordained for leadership must live under the law and are subject to condemnation for taking judgment too far. The prophet Hosea, for example, condemns the brutality and bloodshed of Jehu's reign (see 1 Kings 19:15-17; 2 Kings 9–10; Hosea 1:4). Though designated king of Israel by God, Jehu goes too far in his zeal to secure the throne and to eliminate any opposition to his rule. In this case we may say that God's will ordained the change of leadership in Israel, but that human free will unfortunately made the suffering of innocent people a part of the change (see also 2 Kings 8:10-13).

From our present perspective, we may acknowledge the element of human free will at work in both the good things and the terrible things that happen in human history. Though history is moving toward God's ultimately redemptive ends, the innocent and the guilty alike still suffer. We may also acknowledge that we have the benefit of God's revelation in Jesus Christ, who teaches that we are to love our enemies and pray for those who abuse us (see Luke 6:27-31), and that we are each responsible before God for our lives (see Luke 16:19-31).

2 KINGS 11–14

Introduction to These Chapters

These chapters cover the reigns of Athaliah, Jehoash, and Amaziah in Judah and Jehoahaz, Jehoash, and Jeroboam II in Israel. They may be outlined as follows.

I. The Reign of Queen Athaliah (11:1-21)
II. The Reign of Jehoash (Joash) in Judah (12:1-21)
III. The Reign of Jehoahaz (13:1-9)
IV. The Reign of Joash (Jehoash) in Israel (13:10-25)
V. The Reign of Amaziah (14:1-22)
VI. The Reign of Jeroboam II (14:23-29)

The Message of 2 Kings 11–14

In any type of Bible study, there is a need to use all of the biblical record for any given period in biblical history or for any particular biblical teaching. Different books in the Bible inform and supplement one another. Beginning with this period in Israel's history, however, it is especially important to realize that the historical books of the Old Testament do not cover all that is happening in the life of the chosen people at any one time. Certainly the writers of 1 and 2 Kings do not claim that their record of Israel's history is exhaustive.

In addition to the history in Chronicles, several prophetic books supplement our information on the years in the life of Israel covered by the books of Kings.

- Jeremiah and Ezekiel present other points of view on the issue of corporate and individual guilt (compare 1 Kings 21:20-24 with Jeremiah 31:29-30; Ezekiel 18:1-32).

- Hosea and Amos tell of religious and social corruption in the time of prosperity and security enjoyed by Israel during the reign of Jeroboam II.

- Micah and Isaiah speak of the need for Judah to trust God during the trouble with Assyria.

- Jonah tells of God's forgiveness offered to the people of Nineveh, the capital of Assyria, while Nahum celebrates the destruction of Nineveh.

- Isaiah, Jeremiah, Ezekiel, and Micah offer messages both of punishment and of salvation for the people of Israel from the time of King Uzziah to the Exile in Babylon.

- We must always remember to take any one text within the context of all Scripture, and not to isolate any one message or viewpoint from the whole.

2 KINGS 15–17

Introduction to These Chapters

These chapters tell of the events leading up to the destruction of Israel by Assyria and of the final days of Israel's life as a nation. They may be outlined as follows.
I. Stability in Judah, Chaos in Israel (15:1-38)
   A. The Reign of Azariah (Uzziah) (15:1-7)
   B. The Reign of Zechariah (15:8-12)
   C. The Reign of Shallum (15:13-16)
   D. The Reign of Menahem (15:17-22)
   E. The Reign of Pekahiah (15:23-26)
   F. The Reign of Pekah (15:27-31)
   G. The Reign of Jotham (15:32-38)
II. The Reign of Ahaz (16:1-20)
III. The Reign of Hoshea (17:1-41)

The Message of 2 Kings 15–17

The writers of Kings condemn national leaders in Israel and Judah for failing to live by the covenant relationship established between God and the people of Israel. The covenant is also the basis for judgment of Israel and Judah by the prophets of this time. The prophets announce God's message of punishment to both nations for their economic corruption, social injustice, and religious perversion. From the perspective of the prophets and the historians, the fruit of such sin is death. This is not just physical death but also death as a society and as a chosen people.

Israel "died" as a nation in 722 B.C. Judah "died" in 587 B.C. To better understand how and why this happened, we need to understand something of the nature of sin itself as well as the specific failures of God's people in Israel and Judah. What does the Old Testament tell us about the sins of Israel and Judah?

- In broad terms, sin is personal alienation from God.

- Sins of any kind are sins against God.

- The covenant is part of God's revealed will.

- The covenant and God's saving acts on Israel's behalf are the standard against which the people are judged.

- Covenant law governs how the people of Israel are to live; all life is to be ordered by God's law.

- The people of Israel and Judah are guilty of crimes against God and against one another.

- Prophecy and history alike show that God's people must and do suffer the consequences of their sin. Second Kings 17:15 sums up the situation: "They went after false idols, and became false" (NRSV; NIV, "worthless").

2 KINGS 18–20

Introduction to These Chapters

Chapters 18–20 tell about the reign of King Hezekiah of Judah. Hezekiah and Josiah (2 Kings 22–23) are the only Judean kings to receive substantial praise from the writers of Kings. Though Hezekiah's reign is not without its troubles, he, like Josiah, is a religious reformer who moves to bring his country back to a more pure worship of God.

Here is an outline of these chapters.
I. The Beginning of Hezekiah's Reign (18:1-12)
II. Assyria Attacks Judah (18:13-37)
III. Hezekiah and Isaiah (19:1–20:21)
    A. Jerusalem escapes destruction (19:1-37)
    B. Hezekiah's illness (20:1-11)
    C. Judah and Babylon (20:12-19)
    D. The end of Hezekiah's reign (20:20-21)

The Message of 2 Kings 18–20

The biblical record shows that God uses other peoples as tools of punishment against the people of Israel when God's chosen people have been disobedient to the covenant relationship. For example, God uses Syria (see 2 Kings 8:10-13), Assyria (see Amos 3:9-11), and Babylon (see Jeremiah 21:1-10). These tools of punishment, however, are not themselves above judgment (see, for example, Nahum 1:15; 3:18-19; Jeremiah 50:29-30).

Prophetic announcements of punishment and God's actions against Israel and against other nations are all related to particular historical circumstances. In each case there is a crisis of faith and of faithfulness to the covenant in the life of the people of Israel. These texts show how the people of Israel and other peoples of the earth are in relationship with God, though they may not always be aware of this relationship.

What do these texts tell us about God's relationship to the peoples of the earth?

• God is the Lord of all peoples.

• God rules the affairs of all humankind.

• Human pride and strength always give way before God's strength.

• God's will is revealed to the people of Israel, in part, through the words of the prophets.

• The word of God spoken by the prophets affects not only Israel but other nations as well.

• The people of Israel must choose to obey God and live or disobey and die.

• God's long-term will for human history is for a loving and redeeming relationship with all peoples.

2 KINGS 21–23

Introduction to These Chapters

Second Kings 21–23 covers the reigns of Manasseh, Amon, and Josiah. The writers of Kings emphasize the contrast between the religious policies of Manasseh and Amon on the one hand, and Josiah on the other. Manasseh and Amon are condemned as the worst kings ever to reign in Judah. Josiah is praised as the most faithful king.

Biblical sources for this time in the history of Judah are 2 Kings 21–23; 2 Chronicles 33–35; Jeremiah 1–6; Nahum; Habakkuk; and Zephaniah. Assyrian and Babylonian records also provide information about these countries' dealings with Judah.

Here is an outline of 2 Kings 21–23.
I. The Reign of Manasseh (21:1-18)

THE ESSENTIAL BIBLE HANDBOOK

II. The Reign of Amon (21:19-26)
III. The Reign of Josiah (22:1–23:30)
   A. The book of the law is found
    (22:1-20)
   B. Josiah's religious reform
    (23:1-30)
IV. The reign of Jehoahaz (23:31-37)

The Message of 2 Kings 21–23

The people of Judah are apparently not deeply committed to Josiah's reform efforts, because religious unfaithfulness and social injustice are never fully eliminated even during his lifetime (see the prophecies of Jeremiah 1–6). After his death, the people are disillusioned and increasingly disobedient to God's word (see, for example, Jeremiah 7:1–8:3). It was not enough to purify the rituals of worship and sacrifice of pagan influences and to centralize these services in the Temple to safeguard their purity.

The lack of permanent success in the reform movement illustrates the fact that faith is more than ritual. Amos (750 B.C.) and Micah (743–687 B.C.) had already proclaimed this truth to the people of Israel and of Judah (see Amos 5:21-24; Micah 6:6-8). The destruction of Israel in 722 B.C. and the coming destruction of Judah in 597 and 587 B.C. witness to the fact that the covenant relationship requires more of God's people than correct ritual. According to the prophets, what does God require?

- Ritual is important, but it cannot take the place of a right relationship with God and with other people.

- What is required for a righteous life is clearly shown in the covenant and law of Israel.

- Proper worship must go hand in hand with justice and righteousness in daily life.

- The merciful and just relationship God has with people defines the relationship that people have with one another.

- A person's inward and outward life must be in harmony.

2 KINGS 24–25

Introduction to These Chapters

The history of Kings ends in approximately 560 B.C., with Judah at the mercy of the Babylonians. Jerusalem is destroyed, thousands of Judeans are exiled in Babylon, and the people who remain in the ravaged land are at odds with one another. The last four verses of 2 Kings 25 add a footnote of hope concerning Judah's future based on the improved treatment of the exiled King Jehoiachin by the Babylonians.

The books of 2 Kings, 2 Chronicles, Jeremiah, and Ezekiel deal with this time in the history of the people of Judah. Official records of the Babylonian kings, called the Babylonian Chronicles, also provide valuable information about Babylonia's dealings with Judah.

Chapters 24–25 may be outlined as follows.

  I. The Reign of Jehoiakim (24:1-7)
 II. The Reign of Jehoiachin (24:8-17)
III. The Reign of Zedekiah
   (24:18–25:21)
   A. Zedekiah begins his reign
    (24:18-20)
   B. The second siege of Jerusalem
    (25:1-7)
   C. The destruction of Jerusalem
    (25:8-21)
IV. The Governorship of Gedaliah
   (25:22-26)
 V. King Jehoiachin in Exile (25:27-30)

The Message of 2 Kings 24–25

The writers of 1 and 2 Kings explain the changing fortunes of the people of Israel by how faithful they and their leaders are to God. The writers believe very strongly in the concept of reward and punishment: Loyalty to God brings success and disloyalty brings disaster (as, for example, in Deuteronomy 28:1). They testify to the workings of God in history and about the intimate relationship between God and the destiny of the chosen people. The historians of Kings have an awareness of a future for God's people in which the people will have another chance to be faithful and obedient.

We must, however, turn to the prophets of this time to find the true measure of Israel's hope for the future. Jeremiah and Ezekiel are often remembered for their messages of punishment for God's people. They also, however, speak of a time when God and God's people will live in harmony and righteousness with one another. They are able to do this because they know that Israel's covenant with God is both the basis for her punishment and the ground of her hope. God is just but also merciful. According to their prophecies, what sort of future may the people of Israel expect?

- The exile, though long and bitter, is not permanent.

- Atonement will have been made for Israel's sins.

- A remnant of the people will survive destruction.

- The people of Israel may look forward to peace, security, and fruitfulness in their homeland and to a renewed relationship with God.

- The message of judgment is, in the long run, a message of salvation.

FIRST AND SECOND CHRONICLES

2 Chronicles

I. **The Building of the Temple (1:1–7:22)**
 A. Solomon's reign initiated with worship (1:1-6)
 B. Solomon's worship and God's presence (1:7-13)
 C. God's blessings on Solomon (1:14-17)
 D. Preparations to build the Temple (2:1–3:2)
 E. Temple measurements and description (3:3–4:22)
 F. The Temple finished (5:1)
 G. The ark of the covenant to the Temple (5:2–6:1)
 H. Solomon's prayer of dedication (6:2-42)
 I. The closing ceremonies (7:1-11)
 J. God's reply to Solomon's prayer (7:12-22)

II. **The Greatness of Solomon (8:1–9:31)**

III. **The Division of the Kingdom (10:1–11:4)**
 A. Rehoboam's response to the people (10:1-15)
 B. Separation of the northern tribes (10:16-19)
 C. Failure to quell the rebellion (11:1-4)

IV. **The Reign of Rehoboam (11:5–12:16)**

V. **The Reign of Abijah (13:1-22)**

VI. **The Reign of Asa (14:1–16:14)**

VII. **The Reign of Jehoshaphat (17:1–20:37)**
 A. Jehoshaphat's piety and prosperity (17:1-6)

 B. Jehoshaphat, the religious educator (17:7-9)
 C. Jehoshaphat's greatness (17:10-19)
 D. Jehoshaphat's alliance with Ahab (18:1–19:3)
 E. Jehoshaphat's judicial system (19:4-11)
 F. Jehoshaphat's victory (20:1-30)
 G. Jehoshaphat's last days (20:31-34)
 H. The wreck of merchant ships (20:35-37)

VIII. **Jehoram's Reign (21:1-20)**

IX. **Ahaziah's Reign (22:1-9)**

X. **Athaliah Reigns; Jehoiada Revolts (22:10–23:21)**
 A. Prince Joash hidden from Athaliah (22:10-12)
 B. Conspiracy and covenant (23:1-21)

XI. **The Reign of Joash (24:1-27)**

XII. **The Reign of Amaziah (25:1-28)**

XIII. **The Reign of Uzziah (26:1-23)**

XIV. **The Reign of Jotham (27:1-9)**

XV. **The Reign of Ahaz (28:1-27)**

XVI. **The Reign of Hezekiah (29:1–32:33)**
 A. Restoration of Temple worship (29:1-36)
 B. The renewal of Israel (30:1-27)
 C. Renewal of right religious practices (31:1-21)
 D. The threat from Assyria (32:1-23)
 E. The close of Hezekiah's reign (32:24-33)

INTRODUCTION

The Hebrew title of these books is "Events of the Days." The name "Chronicles" actually came from Jerome, the fourth/fifth-century A.D. Christian biblical scholar and translator of the Bible into Latin, who viewed these books as a "chronicle of all of sacred history." The Hebrews put Chronicles at the end of their Bible because it was a later addition to all that had been said and written.

Following written histories and records of his people, the writer of Chronicles recast them with the fresh viewpoint and attitudes that experience had brought to Israel. He applied them to the needs of his times and of all times.

The Historical Period Covered

The Chronicles cover the period of Judah's history as a kingdom. First, however, the books trace the background of world history from Adam to Jacob, the ancestor of Israel. They trace Jacob's descendants to the end of the reign of Israel's first king, Saul. The main story of Chronicles begins with the reign of David, approximately 1000 B.C., and continues to the last king, Zedekiah, and the fall of Jerusalem, 587 B.C. During these more than 400 years, the world political powers were Egypt, to the south of Judah; and Assyria, in the north, until 625 B.C. when Babylonia, to the east, replaced Assyria as a world power.

Chronicles' Interpretation of History

The Chronicler wrote his book with the conviction that God is the creator and controller of nature, and the ruler over history. History, under God, is a matter of divine selection and of development by divine revelation. Through the generations, God prepared and selected Israel as the chosen people. Of all Israel, God chose the tribe of Judah to be its leader (1 Chronicles 28:4). And in all Judah, God chose Jerusalem (2 Chronicles 6:6). From the descendants of Israel God chose David and his heirs to rule the people. God chose David's son, Solomon, to build a temple: the house of the Lord. Chronicles is a history of the Temple.

Chronicles records the history of the kings of David's dynasty and of the people of Israel in relation to the Temple and what it represents: God's rule and presence and purpose, the law and commandments, God's covenant with, and compassion for, the chosen people (and always the power of God's righteousness). For Chronicles, all that happened before Moses was prehistory. Moses, followed by Joshua, established Israel as a theocracy, a God-ruled people. The period of David followed by Solomon, who duplicated Moses and Joshua, was seen by the Chronicler as the fulfillment of God's kingdom on earth. The kings in David's line were God's stewards. When they were faithful, God blessed them. When they were unfaithful, God punished them. If they repented and returned to God, they were pardoned.

The Chronicler's Purpose

The Chronicler writes to inform his readers, through the story of their nation, how God's judgment works. He writes to urge them to be faithful worshipers at the Temple, to keep the covenant, the law and commandments, and to do what is right in the eyes of the Lord. He writes to warn them that what happened to their ancestors and to their nation as the result of faithlessness can happen again to them. He also writes to encourage them that, despite the Exile and the loss of their kingdom and David's dynasty of kings, there is yet hope for them. The people can sincerely hope for a renewal of those good days through faithfulness to God, who is faithful to them in return.

Date

The date of composition of Chronicles is, as the work itself states, after the return from exile (537 B.C.). First Chronicles mentions money coined not before 515 B.C. (1 Chronicles 29:7). It takes David's lineage to the sixth generation after Zerubbabel, who was governor of Jerusalem under Darius at the end of the sixth century B.C. (1 Chronicles 3:19-24). Scholars believe that Chronicles was written after Ezra-Nehemiah was written (as one book), but the book of Nehemiah records the high priests down to Jaddua, who was high priest at the time of Alexander of Macedonia (late fourth century B.C.). Jaddua expressed goals and a zeal similar to those of the Chronicles, which uses the late Hebrew of that century. All this evidence indicates that the

Chronicler wrote his work shortly after 350 B.C.

Author

The author does not name himself. Like Ezra-Nehemiah, Chronicles has a structure and a theology that emphasize counsel, covenant-making, purification of the land and people, and renewal of the Temple ritual. This similarity is due to its author belonging to the same community and epoch. Nevertheless, there are marked differences in vocabulary and in attitudes toward non-Jews. The Chronicler places a strong emphasis, lacking in Ezra-Nehemiah, on the Levites, their importance and tasks. Because the author writes in Levitical preaching style, and because he speaks more highly of the Levites than of the priests, many have thought the author may have been a Levite. The special place he gives to music among the Levites may mean he was also a musician. Another distinguishing characteristic is that, while Ezra and Nehemiah advocated a separate community made up of Judeans who had returned from exile, Chronicles takes a more inclusive stance. The Chronicler emphasizes the spiritual potential of a wider religious community of all Israel, including those in the northern region.

One Book

Chronicles is one book with four sections: (1) the introduction, the genealogies (1 Chronicles 1–9); (2) the story of King David and plans for the Temple (1 Chronicles 10–29); (3) the story of King Solomon and the building of the Temple (2 Chronicles 1–9); and (4) the stories of the kings of Judah (2 Chronicles 10–36). The book was divided into 1 and 2 Chronicles simply because it was too long to go on one papyrus roll; each half fit neatly on one roll.

Sources

The Chronicler refers to a variety of sourcebooks about the kings of Israel and of Judah, including 1 and 2 Samuel and 1 and 2 Kings. About half of the Chronicles' verses are quoted from them. The phrase *parallel to* in this commentary refers to passages that are copies verbatim or are partly quoted, or are on the same subject but written differently. References to books of seers and prophets are to their appearances in Samuel and Kings (or, in one instance, in Isaiah). There being no division by chapters and books, the sections of a book were referred to by the persons storied in them, just as Paul, in Romans 11:2, refers to what was written *in Elijah* (the Greek is *in*, not *of*) when he refers to 1 Kings 19:1. Genealogies from Genesis through 2 Kings are used, as well as military records and censuses, lists of Levites and of prominent families, local and family records and reminiscences, and oral tradition. The author of Chronicles uses the Psalms freely and borrows phrases from the prophets. It is probable that some additions have been made by a later editor. This seems to be the case when references about priests are added that do not quite fit the text.

1 CHRONICLES 1–5

Introduction to These Chapters

Beginning with Adam, Chronicles follows a selective genealogy of those lines that lead down to Jacob, renamed Israel. Then the Chronicler takes the sons of Jacob and their genealogies. Jacob's sons (except, in place of Joseph, Joseph's two sons) are the tribes of Israel, and Chronicles traces the genealogy of each. The list begins with Judah and then moves to Simeon, which, the only tribe south of Judah, became absorbed into Judah. It then traces the tribes who were allocated land east of the Dead Sea and of the Jordan River: Reuben, Gad, and the eastern part of Manasseh.

Here is an outline of these chapters.

I. From Adam to Jacob (1:1-34)
II. The Descendants of Esau (1:35-54)
III. The Sons of Israel (2:1-2)
IV. The Lineage of Judah (2:3-55)
V. The Line of David (3:1-24)
   A. The family of David (3:1-9)
   B. The kings of Judah (3:10-15)
   C. The royal descendants without a throne (3:16-24)
VI. More Descendants of Judah (4:1-23)
VII. The Descendants of Simeon (4:24-43)
VIII. The Descendants of Reuben (5:1-10)
IX. The Descendants of Gad (5:11-17)
X. The Eastern Israelites (5:18-22)
XI. The Eastern Half of Manasseh (5:23-26)

The Message of 1 Chronicles 1–5

God is in charge of the creation. Down through the generations, persons are selected to carry out God's purpose. Most people in each generation are only names when they are gone. Some achieve fame for a time, but it is lost. Some violate the rules that society makes. Some are considered "outsiders." But God uses generation after generation to build toward the goal of a people of God's own choosing, and toward a splendor among those who obey God's law and trust in God.

Whatever may have happened to all the descendants of Adam, it was his descendant Jacob, called Israel, whom God found acceptable to be the ancestor of the chosen people. All Israel's descendants and all those who were brought into relationship with them were God's people. Among them, God chose David to set up a society that would be the ideal society. Whatever David's descendants were like in the royal line of kings, each had the potential of maintaining a God-obeying and God-trusting society.

Each of us, in our time, has the potential of receiving the way of God and passing it on to the next generation.

1 CHRONICLES 6:1–9:34

Introduction to These Chapters

Here the Chronicler's attention is on the Levites, who were the caretakers of Israel's religious life. Special attention is given to the Levites who were priests and to those who were singers at worship services. Space is also given to their distribution among the various tribes of Israel.

Then follow genealogies of the six tribes who made up the main body of northern Israel. The last list is of the tribe of Benjamin, which furnished Israel with its first king, with whose family the genealogical lists end.

The genealogies are carried down to a period in history when the inhabitants of Jerusalem, having been exiled by the Chaldean conqueror Nebuchadnezzar, were allowed to return by the Persian emperor Cyrus. Therefore, the Chronicler lists by families the citizens who had returned to Jerusalem from exile.

Here is an outline of these chapters.

I. The Family of Levi (6:1-81)
II. The Descendants of Issachar (7:1-5)
III. The Descendants of Benjamin (7:6-12)
IV. The Descendants of Naphtali (7:13)
V. The Descendants of Manasseh (7:14-19)
VI. The Family of Ephraim (7:20-29)
VII. The Descendants of Asher (7:30-40)
VIII. The Family of Benjamin (8:1-40)
IX. The Exile and After (9:1-34)

The Message of 1 Chronicles 6:1–9:34

Generations come and go. God's rule remains. Among the people of God are many who are forgotten or are known only through their relationships to the heads of families. Others are known only by their connection with some kind of service or by their residence in some particular place. Very few have been part of legends in popular tradition. Nevertheless, they are all part of the process of history that God ordains. The fact that they are God's chosen people, however, does not save them from disaster, destruction, or the complete loss of the land to which God led them, if they are unfaithful to God.

Still and all, God's choice of this people, the land God gave them for possession, God's purpose, God's rule and commandments, all remain for the people to return to.

The message still applies. Our value is in our participation, during our short time on earth, in the process of history toward the fulfillment of God's purpose. God never fails. We fail by failing God. We can return to God and resume our place in God's care and guidance.

1 CHRONICLES 9:35–12:40

Introduction to These Chapters

This section starts with a brief narrative of the death of Saul, whose unfaithfulness made God put him and his line out of the way. David is pictured as the architect, under God's design, of that kingdom. He ascends the throne, captures Jerusalem, is surrounded by loyal warriors, and, endorsed by ever-increasing popular support, is crowned king of Israel.

David is a very talented, able leader of men, a good organizer and administrator, a folk hero; but mostly, for the Chronicler, a culmination in God's design for his people.

Here is an outline of this section.

I. King Saul (9:35–10:14)
II. David's Kingship (11:1–12:40)
   A. The Choice of All Israel (11:1-3)
   B. David's Capture of Jerusalem (11:4-9)
   C. David's Warriors (11:10-47)
      1. The chiefs of David's mighty men (11:10-14)
      2. The daring loyalty of three (11:15-19)
      3. Exploits of Abishai and Benaiah (11:20-25)
      4. The list of war heroes (11:26-47)
   D. David's Supporters (12:1-22)
      1. Early supporters at Ziklag (12:1-7)
      2. Supporters at the stronghold (12:8-18)
      3. Manassite deserters to David (12:19-22)
   E. David's Coronation at Hebron (12:23-40)

The Message of 1 Chronicles 9:35–12:40

The passage begins with the family tree of Saul. Generations come and go. God's righteous purpose endures, and by it human life stands or falls. By failing God, unfaithful to him, Saul fell.

The passage continues with the people's choice of David. This choice began when David was an outlaw chief because the king, Saul, wished to kill him on account of his great popularity with the people. It shows how group after group of warriors joined David until the time came when all of Israel was for him. It points out that the army's choice of their leader, David, was also all the people's choice, and it was God's choice. It emphasizes that the king is chosen by God, and that he is entrusted with God's rule of the people.

The continuing message of this section of Chronicles is that God rules history in righteousness, and he chooses those who will be faithful to his righteousness. God does not protect those who are unfaithful from the consequences of their own actions. He allows the course of human conflict to punish them. God does not support human choices that are contrary to his will. He does support human choices that carry out his choice. God honors those who are daring and courageous to do his will.

God's choice is for the solidarity of his people. As they join together to do God's will and to support his choice, God will bless them so that they may live together in unity and greatness.

1 CHRONICLES 13–20

Introduction to These Chapters

The ark of the covenant, representing the presence of God, was the focus of all Israel in its journey to, and its establishment in, the land of Canaan. David recognizes this and wishes to bring the ark from the sanctuary where it rests in Kiriath-jearim to his capital, Jerusalem. The journey of the ark to Jerusalem is made in two stages (chapters 13 and 15). Between these two stages, David has three proofs that he has God's blessing: (1) King Hiram of Phoenicia sends him materials to build his palace, (2) he is blessed with many children, and (3) he is able, by his military victories, to establish himself as a power in the region (chapter 14).

Here is an outline of chapters 13–20.

I. Bringing the Ark from Kiriath-jearim (13:1-14)
II. David's House and Home (14:1-7)
III. Victories over the Philistines (14:8-15)
IV. The Ark of God in Zion (15:1–16:43)

A. Bringing the ark to Zion (15:1-29)

B. Worship at the ark of the Lord (16:1-43)

V. David's Desire to Build a Temple (17:1-15)

VI. David's Prayer (17:16-27)

VII. The House of David (18:1–20:8)

A. David's conquests (18:1-13)

B. David's government (18:14-17)

C. Campaign against the Ammonites (19:1–20:3)

D. David's heroes against the Philistines (20:4-8)

The Message of 1 Chronicles 13–20

This portion of 1 Chronicles is about a three-way relationship between God, David, and the people. What David does is related to the worship and will of God, and to God's people. David's major concern is to get the ark of God, the symbol of God's presence, into Jerusalem. He fails at first, but tries again and succeeds. He leads the people in celebrating God in songs of thanksgiving and praise. His desire to build a temple to God in his capital is thwarted because his nation is surrounded by enemies, and the land has no rest. By the power of God he overwhelms his enemies and extends the rule of Israel over its neighbors.

The message of this portion is:

- Bring to the center of life that which makes us aware of God's presence and power.

- Give God the credit for all that is good in life.

- If you have failed to center your attention on God, seek a deeper awareness of God.

- Celebrate the joy of God's presence with God's people in song, prayer, thanksgiving, and praise.

- Put foremost in life the desire to worship God.

- Seek God's guidance in every undertaking.

- Put your life in God's hands. If you have a goal for God's glory that you are unable to achieve, prepare the way for someone else to achieve it.

- Let your actions be directed by God, dependent on God, and dedicated to God.

- Whatever of value comes to you, donate it to God.

- Manage your affairs responsibly for God's glory.

- Remember those who have been kind and helpful to you, and pass on the kindness.

1 CHRONICLES 21:1–23:1

Introduction to These Chapters

David wishes to build the Temple as the crowning act of his reign (chapter 17), but his attention has been turned to the conquest of enemies (chapters 18–21). Chapter 21 is related to his military campaigns. He wishes to make a census of all Israel, including conquered lands, to discover the number of men capable of military service.

A national epidemic follows the census. This disaster, and David's reaction to it, becomes the occasion by which David discovers where the Temple will be built. He gathers and prepares material and workmen for the building and charges and advises Solomon and Israel's leadership on the building of the Temple (chapter 22).

Here is an outline of these chapters.

I. The Military Census (21:1–22:1)

A. David's census (21:1-6)

B. Israel's punishment (21:7-14)
C. David's penitent plea (21:15-17)
D. The threshing floor of Ornan (21:18–22:1)
II. Preparing for the Temple of the Lord (22:2–23:1)
A. Materials and workers (22:2-5)
B. David's charge to Solomon (22:6-16)
C. Charge to the leaders of Israel (22:17–23:1)

The Message of 1 Chronicles 21:1–23:1

David follows an impulse, without consulting God, to take a military census of Israel. God is displeased and punishes Israel. David is distressed that others are suffering when he alone is to blame. He prays for forgiveness. God forgives. Forgiveness restores the relationship, but does not free the wrongdoer from the results of his wrong. A man of decision and action, David is prevented by God's will from building the Temple himself, but does all he can to prepare his successor-son, Solomon, and the leaders of his country to build the Temple.

The message says to all people in all periods:

- Live daily in complete dependence on God.

- Be ready to admit and repent of mistakes.

- Regret not that you suffer for wrong you have done, but that the wrong separates you from God.

- Prefer that you, not others, suffer for your wrongdoing.

- Make the worship of God your first concern.

- Willingly share your ideas, plans, and hopes with others who can carry them out.

- Urge others who are leaders in society to keep God's commandments and be faithful to God.

1 CHRONICLES 23:2–26:32

Introduction to These Chapters

The last part of 1 Chronicles deals with the end of David's reign. It omits the personal and political events recorded in 1 Kings 1–2. It reports mostly what relates to the worship of God in the Temple. It makes pointedly clear that it was David who organized the Levites for the Temple service, although scholars believe that this organization was much later. Mixed into these lists is the division of priests, as well as of Levites, into twenty-four courses. The Temple duties rotate through the year among these courses so that there is continual worship of God, each division coming in to relieve the previous week's division, following the rituals prescribed in the Books of the Law.

Here is an outline of these chapters.
I. David's Organization of the Levites (23:2-6)
II. The Families of Temple Levites (23:7-32)
III. The Descendants of Aaron (24:1-19)
IV. The Rest of the Levites (24:20-31)
V. The Levite Musicians (25:1-31)
VI. The Gatekeepers (26:1-19)
VII. Treasury Keepers (26:20-28)
VIII. Officers and Judges (26:29-32)

The Message of 1 Chronicles 23:2–26:32

According to this portion, King David, near the end of his life, and for the sake of his people, put his kingdom's house in order. His first concern was for the Temple and the worship of God. For that reason he gave primary attention to the organization of the Levites, the people whose hereditary responsibility it was to guide the religious life of Israel. He organized and appointed them in twenty-four divisions of priests and non-priest Levites so that religious service was continuous. Thus the ideal kingdom had an ideal religious order with priests, musicians to lead in worship, gatekeepers to guard the temple, and judges and officers to interpret and apply the holy law.

The Chronicler's message was intended to show to the people of his time what the ideal theocratic state should be. Applicable to all time are his ideals that the people of God should:

- live together in a well-ordered religious life.

- in all things give pre-eminence to the worship of God.

- let praise and thanksgiving be paramount in worship.

- make music a large part of worship, singing to the Lord, playing instruments to praise God and to arouse spiritual fervor, devotion, and understanding.

- share religious duties, all taking turns.

- have persons among them who, as students of God's law, are able to administer and interpret it for the people in order to maintain right human relationships.

- pass on the responsibilities of the religious life as a heritage from generation to generation.

1 CHRONICLES 27–29

Introduction to These Chapters

Chapters 23–26 are germane to the Chronicler's theme: the organization of worship for the Temple soon to be built. They contain the Chronicler's record of the persons who assist in worship—the Levites—and their tasks. Chapter 27 is a digression about general military and civil administration of David's reign. Nevertheless, it carries forward the record of orderliness in the ideal kingdom.

Chapters 28 and 29 return to the main theme, the preparation for the construction of the Temple. The setting is given for Solomon's prosperous succession as King David dies.

These chapters may be outlined as follows.

I. David's Administration (27:1-34)
   A. David's military arrangements (27:1-24)
   B. Stewards of the king's property (27:25-31)
   C. The king's associates (27:31-34)
II. David's Final Arrangements (28:1–29:25)
   A. David's farewell to the leaders (28:1-8)
   B. David's advice to Solomon (28:9-10)
   C. Details of the Temple plan (28:11-19)
   D. David's encouragement of Solomon (28:20-21)
   E. David's appeal to Israel's leaders (29:1-9)
   F. David's prayer (29:10-19)
   G. Celebration (29:20-22)
   H. Solomon's anointing as king (29:23-25)
III. David's Death (29:26-30)

The Message of 1 Chronicles 27–29

In chapter 27 the Chronicler depicts an orderly, stable society. In chapters 28 and 29 he gives David's public statement of faith in God's greatness, power, glory, victory, and majesty, and his confidence in a people who are faithful to God. David charges his son, Solomon, and the people to carry out his plans for a great temple for the worship of God. Consecrating their gifts and themselves to God, the people have great joy.

The message to the people of God is:

- Let your house be in order. Manage responsibly what is entrusted to you.

- Recognize the brevity and finiteness of life and that the rule of God, whom your spiritual ancestors worshiped, is over all creation forever.

- Recognize that all you have is from God and belongs to God. Consecrate it to God, using it and your life, as faithful stewards, for the glory of God.

- Follow responsibly the vocation God has given you.

- In humility and joy, praise God's greatness, power, and glory, with thanksgiving for God's goodness.

- Worship and celebrate God faithfully and publicly.

- Seek God, study God's Word, and understand and obey the commandments.

- Serve God wholeheartedly, freely, and joyously.

- Trust in God and live courageously. Let nothing dismay you or deter you from doing God's will persistently.

- Let your motives and plans be pure in God's sight.

- Do what you can to guide, inspire, and support others in their work for God.

- Help those who do God's work and accept their help.

2 CHRONICLES 1:1–5:1

Introduction to These Chapters

The first four chapters of 2 Chronicles detail the building and the structure of the Temple. Brief attention is given to Solomon's other public works, his wisdom, and his wealth.

Here is an outline of these chapters.
  I. Solomon's Reign Initiated with Worship (1:1-6)
 II. Solomon's Worship and God's Promise (1:7-13)
III. God's Blessing on Solomon (1:14-17)
 IV. Preparations to Build the Temple (2:1–3:2)
  V. The Temple Measurements and Description (3:3–4:22)
     A. The Temple and nave (3:3-7)
     B. The Most Holy Place (3:8-14)
     C. The pillars (3:15-17)
     D. More Temple furnishings (4:1-22)
 VI. The Temple Finished (5:1)

The Message of 2 Chronicles 1:1–5:1

From Solomon's construction of the Temple the Chronicler draws a lesson for his times.

- Solomon's reign was an ideal for Israel, growing as it did out of David's glorious reign.

- Solomon, like his father, David, was God's instrument for the benefit of God's people.

- What Solomon did was because of God's blessing.

- God is too great to be localized in the Temple.

- The place for all interest, all honor, all care, and all lavishing of gifts is the

Temple of the Lord. (Nothing else is worth recording.)

The message of this passage remains:

- Look only to the best in the past as a pattern for the present.

- Never look to a leader, or to any person, as the ultimate for your life; reserve that place for God.

- Any good that human beings do, they do as an instrument of God's purpose, and such persons are to be esteemed only as long as they carry out God's purpose.

- God chooses and uses persons on behalf of the chosen people, and never for themselves.

- No one can do good except by God's blessing.

- It is impossible to contain God in a definition, formula, description, or conceptualization of the human mind. God is greater than the universe, and so is greater than anything human beings can create.

- The focus of all our interest, honor, care, time, gifts, and abilities must be that which glorifies God. The worship of God cannot be a sideline; it must be the mainline of our lives.

2 CHRONICLES 5:2–7:22

Introduction to These Chapters

The summit of the Chronicles is reached in this passage. First Chronicles 1–9 was the approach: the generations from Adam to David. The story of David was the ascent to the summit: David's bringing the ark of the covenant of the Lord to Jerusalem and making everything ready for building a magnificent Temple in which to house it. Even Solomon's building of the Temple was preparation for the great event: worship in the Temple. That is what these chapters are about.

Here is an outline of these chapters.
I. The Ark of the Covenant to the Temple (5:2–6:1)
II. Solomon's Prayer of Dedication (6:2-42)
III. The Closing Ceremonies (7:1-11)
IV. God's Reply to Solomon's Prayer (7:12-22)

The Message of 2 Chronicles 5:2–7:22

This section of 2 Chronicles is about the celebration when the ark of the covenant is brought and lodged in the newly built, magnificent Temple. Both Solomon's dedicatory prayer and God's response carry counsel that emphasizes the relationship of Israel and Israel's king with God. The key words are *seek* and *forsake*. If you do not seek, you are forsaking God. If you do not forsake God, it is because you are seeking God. The message for all times is:

- Set aside a place and time for prayer and praise as a covenant people.

- Worship in the congregation with music and joy.

- God's presence is not to be taken lightly, but to be taken with profound awe and a sincere heart.

- Live openly before God, who knows all our thoughts and motives.

- Interpersonal and intergroup problems can be solved at the altar of God, as can all political, civil, and physical problems.

- At the altar, forgiveness for wrongdoing can be received.

- Pray for faithfulness to God and obedience to the law.

- Invite God into your life and expect a response.

- Tune your life to God's presence so that you may be a living witness for God to all people.

2 CHRONICLES 8–9

Introduction to These Chapters

Solomon's fame, his building and taking of cities, his cities of stone houses, his chariots and horsemen, his wealth, his merchandising and importing on Phoenician ships, fetching great quantities of gold, his enslavement of non-Israelite people for building projects, his complete internal control of the land, the amazement at his wisdom and wealth (shown by the Queen of Sheba and by neighboring kings), his pageantry, prosperity, his brilliant court, the constant scent of sacrifices at his great Temple: All these the Chronicler records in order to picture a fame and respect such as Israel has never known before and will never know again in its long history.

Solomon's glory is a reflection of his having built the Temple. The Temple is evidence that he truly honors and worships God and obeys the commandments. Solomon, Jerusalem, and Israel, like David, are rewarded for putting God and righteousness first.

Here is an outline of these chapters.

I. Solomon, Builder and Despot (8:1-10)
II. Temple Worship (8:11-16)
III. Greatness of Solomon (8:17–9:28)
   A. Solomon's enterprise (8:17-18)
   B. Queen of Sheba (9:1-12)
   C. Solomon's wealth (9:13-21)
   D. Solomon's wealth, wisdom, and power (9:22-28)
IV. Solomon's End (9:29-31)

The Message of 2 Chronicles 8–9

This section of 2 Chronicles is a counsel to leaders of God's people and, by implication, to all of God's people to:

- Make the first business of life whatever pertains to the worship of God.

- Make the second business of life wisely, responsibly, and practically to administer whatever is under your charge.

- Use all the resources available to you to carry out these responsibilities.

- Maintain awe for the sacred.

- Worship God faithfully in public worship.

- Remember that what you do, what you say, and what you are show what is really important to you in life. No one is without a reputation. Let your reputation glorify God, not you.

- Let God be foremost in your life.

- Use for God what you receive.

- Make God your point of reference.

- Rejoice in the abundance of riches with which God has endowed this world.

To add New Testament perspective to this message:

- Remember that God is Spirit, unbound to place or form, and so to be worshiped in spirit and truth (John 4:23).

- Understand that life in Christ, who called his followers to forsake all they have, is not dependent on possessions nor expectant of physical rewards.

- Worship as Jesus worshiped, for this will lead to a deep love for God and for all people.

2 CHRONICLES 10–13

Introduction to These Chapters

Rehoboam inherits the wealth and power of his father, Solomon. He quickly squanders them by offending and turning the majority of the nation's tribes against him, and turning God against him by forsaking God's law. The first failure brings about invasion by the Egyptian king. Only repentance saves Rehoboam's kingdom. Abijah succeeds Rehoboam. Facing great odds in battle, he and his people rely on God and are victorious.

Here is an outline of these chapters.

I. The Division of the Kingdom (10:1–11:14)
   A. Rehoboam's response to the people (10:1-15)
   B. Separation of the northern tribes (10:16-19)
   C. Failure to quell the rebellion (11:1-4)
II. Rehoboam's Good Three Years (11:5-23)
   A. Rehoboam as military builder (11:5-12)
   B. Faithful Israelites in Jerusalem (11:13-17)
   C. Rehoboam's big family (11:18-23)
III. Egyptian Invasion of Judah (12:1-12)
IV. The End of Rehoboam (12:13-16)
V. The Reign of Abijah (13:1-22)
   A. Abijah's confrontation with Jeroboam (13:1-12)
   B. The battle (13:13-20)
   C. The rest of Abijah's reign (13:20-22)

The Message of 2 Chronicles 10–13

The stories of Rehoboam and Abijah show the good that goes with faithfulness to God, and the trouble that attends failure to obey. Rehoboam has success when he is true to God, but trouble when he forsakes God. Abijah triumphs over Jeroboam, the northern Israelite king, because Abijah's people rely on God, whereas Jeroboam and his people forsake God.

Aspects of this message can be applied today.

- Listen to those who have complaints. Be kind to them.

- Listen to wise and mature counsel; do not depend on the shallow counsel of your contemporaries.

- Be conciliatory, not arrogant, in your dealings.

- Do not enter into any struggle to assert yourself, but only follow God's direction.

- Deal wisely with whatever is entrusted to you.

- Do not go along with those who forsake their faith, but keep company with those who worship God.

- Beware lest, when all seems well with you, you abandon God and neglect the law.

- When you suffer from wrong you have done, humble yourself, accept God's punishment as your due, repent, and seek God.

- In the conflicts and struggles of life, be sure of which side you are on. Do not be on the side of those who, in rebellion against God, rely on substitutes for God.

- Whatever your strengths or weaknesses, put all your trust in the Lord, rely on God, and call to God for help.

2 CHRONICLES 14–16

Introduction to These Chapters

This section narrates the reforms of King Asa, fifth king of Judah in the line of David. He tries to restore Judah to the worship of God and to destroy the worship of pagan gods. His peaceful reign is interrupted by an invading Ethiopian-Libyan army, but he is victorious because he and his people rely on the Lord. When Baasha, the king of Israel, wages war against Judah, Asa relies on the king of Syria instead of on the Lord. For this he is condemned, and is punished with illness.

Careful students of the accounts have suggested the following chronology of Asa's reign. During his first fifteen years he engages in reform. In his fifteenth year, Judah is invaded by Zerah, the Cushite (NIV; NRSV = Ethiopian). In his sixteenth year, he engages in war with Israel under King Baasha and makes a treaty with Ben-hadad, king of Syria.

Here is an outline of these chapters.

I. King Asa's Reforms (14:1-8)
II. The Ethiopian Invasion (14:9–15:19)
   A. Overwhelming the invaders (14:9-15)
   B. Azariah's sermon of encouragement (15:1-7)
   C. The covenant celebration (15:8-15)
   D. Asa's zeal for the house of the Lord (15:16-19)
III. War with Baasha and Its Consequences (16:1-10)
   A. Border struggles with Israel (16:1-6)
   B. Hanani's sermon of condemnation (16:7-10)
IV. Asa's End (16:11-14)

The Message of 2 Chronicles 14–16

King Asa is eager to strengthen his people's faithfulness to the God of their ancestors. This makes it possible for God to defeat the otherwise overwhelming army of invaders. When, however, Asa relies on a foreign king to help in war, and on physicians to help in sickness rather than turning to God, he is condemned for not seeking God. In this account the Chronicler is repeating his message to his readers.

It is a reminder that God sees and knows everyone's motives.

It assures all whose hearts are blameless toward God and who seek God that:

- God is with them while they are with God.

- They will have peace and rest.

- God protects those who trust and obey.

- There is great joy in uniting with others in loyalty to God and in worshiping God.

It encourages all who do right and good to:

- Turn away from alien religion.

- Seek God with all their heart and with all their soul.

- Keep true to their inherited faith with its laws and its commandments.

- Act vigorously in the disciplines of faith.

- Fear no foe, no matter how great, as long as they rely on God.

It warns them:

- Do not put reliance on humanity instead of on God, for even if it helps for a while, in the long run you will have continual distress.

- If you forsake God, you separate yourself from God's help.

2 CHRONICLES 17–20

Introduction to These Chapters

For the Chronicler, Jehoshaphat is one of the greater kings in the line of David. The writer chooses episodes in this king's career that show how his reign was good. The mishaps that do occur in his reign are mainly due to participating in enterprises of evil kings of northern Israel. Jehoshaphat tries to outweigh these mistakes by more vigorous actions for the education and justice of his people, and these actions are approved of by God. As with Asa, God triumphs over the king's enemies when he and the people rely on God.

Here is an outline of these chapters.

I. Jehoshaphat's Piety and Prosperity (17:1-6)
II. Jehoshaphat, the Religious Educator (17:7-9)
III. Jehoshaphat's Greatness (17:10-19)
IV. Jehoshaphat's Alliance with Ahab (18:1–19:3)
  A. A marriage and military alliance (18:1-3)
  B. Micaiah and the false prophets (18:4-27)
  C. The battle with Ramoth-gilead (18:28-34)
  D. Jehoshaphat scolded (19:1-3)
V. Jehoshaphat's Judicial System (19:4-11)

VI. Jehoshaphat's Victory (20:1-30)
  A. The incursion into Judah (20:1-4)
  B. Prayer and oracle of assurance (20:5-17)
  C. Praise, victory, and blessing (20:18-30)
VII. Jehoshaphat's Last Days (20:31-34)
VIII. The Wreck of Merchant Ships (20:35-37)

The Message of 2 Chronicles 17–20

Jehoshaphat tries to get all the people of Judah to be faithful to God and to understand and keep the law. But whenever he is in a military or commercial venture, he relies on an unfaithful king (of northern Israel) instead of on God, and he fails. Whenever he calls on God, he is helped. Through this story, the Chronicler counsels his readers as follows:

- Those who walk courageously in God's way, and do what is right in the sight of the Lord, are blessed so that their faithfulness is a witness to all.

- Those who keep company with, and go along with, persons who are not loyal to God, instead of with God, will face disastrous consequences.

God's people must be instructed in and understand the law of God. Therefore:

- Avoid the counsel of those who say what they think you want to hear, promising success no matter what you do. Follow the counsel of those whose faithfulness to God and God's word is sure.

- Do not say what you think will be pleasing, or whatever the majority is saying. Say, with the courage of your convictions, what God would have you say.

- Join with people who seek God, confident that God will help. You are powerless, but God can help you face every problem and crisis without fear.

- Worship, praise, sing thanksgiving to God, and join in celebrating God's greatness and goodness.

- Act boldly against wrong, against anything that draws people away from God.

- Believe firmly in God and in those who speak for God, and you will be steady and not fail.

2 CHRONICLES 21–24

Introduction to These Chapters

These chapters cover the reigns of Jehoram, Ahaziah, and Joash. Athaliah, as queen mother and ruler during the early childhood of Joash, represents apostasy and evil. Jehoiada as priest, son-in-law to King Ahaziah, and protector of Joash, represents faithfulness and good. All their activities demonstrate the Chronicler's teaching that faithlessness to God ends in suffering and loss of freedom; faithfulness restores peace and prosperity.

After the good reign of Jehoshaphat, Jehoram's and Ahaziah's are negative; only Joash's is positive. The Chronicler shows, through these three reigns, that God's promise of the everlasting establishment of David's line is conditioned on faithfulness to God on the part of David's descendants. Under Athaliah, David's line is almost wiped out. Joash alone redeems it, restores the worship of God, and becomes a type of David, who restored Israel after the failure of Saul. Nevertheless, Joash, like Asa and Jehoshaphat, both good kings, comes to grief when he fails in faithfulness to God.

Here is an outline of these chapters.

I. Jehoram's Reign (21:1-20)
    A. Jehoram's evil (21:1-7)
    B. Results of Jehoram's evil (21:8-20)
II. Ahaziah's Reign (22:1-9)
III. Athaliah Reigns; Jehoiada Revolts (22:10–23:21)
    A. Prince Joash hidden from Athaliah (22:10-12)
    B. Conspiracy and covenant (23:1-21)
IV. The Reign of Joash (24:1-27)
    A. Early years of Joash (24:1-3)
    B. Funds to repair the Temple (24:4-14)
    C. Forsaking the house of the Lord (24:15-22)
    D. The results of faithlessness (24:23-27)

The Message of 2 Chronicles 21–24

These stories of four sovereigns of Judah differ in their situations and relationships according to the circumstances of the times. They are judged, however, by unchanging, universal realities, which are, according to Chronicles:

- Forsake God and God forsakes you.

- Nevertheless, God will warn you when you go wrong.

- If you heed the warning and turn back to God, God forgives and helps you.

- If you refuse the warning, you face disaster.

- If you harm God's messenger, God will punish you.

- If you rely on God, God will defeat overwhelming odds against you and save you.

- If you rely on persons or forces not of God, they will fail you.

- If you trust God and those who speak for God, you will succeed.

These principles are illustrated by character types:

- The purely selfish, like Jehoram, are despised by the people.

- Others, like Ahaziah, desire only pleasure with their own kind and ignore God, the law, and the people. They end up isolated and defeated.

- Some, like Athaliah, who assert their will at any cost to others, end up resented by all.

- People like Jehoiada, with courage and wisdom to lead society against evil, end up full of honors.

- Unstable persons, like Joash, under good guidance support good works, but under evil influence neglect faith and lose their way.

2 CHRONICLES 25–28

Introduction to These Chapters

These chapters interpret the reigns of the tenth through thirteenth kings in David's dynasty, kings of Judah: Amaziah, Uzziah, Jotham, and Ahaz. Like all the preceding reigns, these are judged in light of God's overrule. Ideally, all Israel is God's people, God's kingdom is based in Jerusalem, and all the kings of Judah are inheritors of the promise to David. Thus these kings are blessed when they are faithful to God, punished when they are unfaithful, condemned when they fail to rely on God, but forgiven when they repent. The Chronicler is careful to note that every success or failure in each reign

is caused by the king's goodness or badness. He gives Amaziah and Uzziah a mixed score, Jotham a casually favorable evaluation, and Ahaz a negative one.

Here is an outline of these chapters.

I. The Reign of Amaziah (25:1-28)
A. Amaziah's qualified rightness (25:1-4)
B. Amaziah's military activities (25:5-13)
C. Amaziah worships Edomite gods (25:14-16)
D. Amaziah's conflict with Israel (25:17-24)
E. Amaziah's end (25:25-28)

II. The Reign of Uzziah (26:1-23)
A. Uzziah's good beginning (26:1-5)
B. Uzziah's strength in foreign affairs (26:6-8)
C. Uzziah's strength in domestic affairs (26:9-15)
D. Uzziah's pride and his leprosy (26:16-21)
E. Uzziah's end (26:22-23)

III. The Reign of Jotham (27:1-9)

IV. The Reign of Ahaz (28:1-27)
A. The evil religious practices of Ahaz (28:1-4)
B. Judah's defeat by Syria and Israel (28:5-7)
C. Return of the captives to Judah (28:8-15)
D. Judah's affliction by Assyria (28:16-21)
E. Increasing apostasy and end of Ahaz (28:22-27)

The Message of 2 Chronicles 25–28

Four kings of Judah in succession start their reigns with the opportunities and possibilities that come with responsibility. According to the Chronicler, Amaziah, Uzziah, and Jotham obey God, but personal pride brings reverses to Amaziah and suffering to Uzziah. Ahaz, on the other hand, ignores God, depends on the ways of the world, and brings his nation to disaster.

The Chronicler wrote these accounts to help his readers understand why a great people of God could, by abandoning God, become separated from God and from their land. This account is also a reminder that, whatever they do, they can inherit God's promise and plan for them through repentance and return.

The message, applicable to all readers, is:

- Life is a responsibility to do what is right in the eyes of the Lord.

- People unfaithful to God are not to be relied on.

- Pride is non-reliance on God and leads to self-destruction.

- The abominable practices of the nations are to be strictly avoided.

- To worship, support, or follow substitutes for the God in whom our ancestors believed brings disaster.

- The counsel of God's messengers is to be heeded.

- Trust in God brings success to all undertakings.

- Persons should not take advantage of wrongdoers, but should remember their own sin and guilt.

- Enemies in distress should be treated with compassion since they also are in God's care.

- No one should be punished for the guilt of another.

2 CHRONICLES 29–32

Introduction to These Chapters

These chapters are the Chronicler's message of assurance and hope to his readers. In the story of Ahaz (chapter 28), the Chronicler showed what happened to a nation whose people and leaders were unfaithful to God: collapse and captivity. His readers were living in the aftermath of such a collapse. These chapters show what happens to a nation whose people and leader return to faithfulness in worship. This gives hope to his readers that restoration can happen again.

These chapters may be outlined as follows.

I. Restoration of Temple Worship (29:1-36)
    A. Hezekiah's good reign (29:1-2)
    B. The cleansing of the Temple (29:3-19)
    C. Reinstitution of Temple worship (29:20-36)
II. The Renewal of Israel (30:1-27)
    A. Invitation to all Israel to return (30:1-12)
    B. The unity of God's people (30:13-27)
III. Renewal of Right Religious Practices (31:1-21)
    A. Destruction of pagan religion (31:1)
    B. Contributions to the Temple service (31:2-10)
    C. Organization of the priests and Levites (31:11-19)
    D. Hezekiah's service to the house of God (31:20-21)
IV. The Threat from Assyria (32:1-23)
V. The Close of Hezekiah's Reign (32:24-33)

The Message of 2 Chronicles 29–32

The Chronicler uses the story of Hezekiah to portray the ideal religious society and to show how to achieve such a society.

Although applied to Judah and Israel, this account has counsel for every believer in God:

- to keep a clean and whole heart; to be faithful in the worship of God; to keep God's law and commandments; to seek God in all of life; to pray.

For every congregation:

- to make the worship of God the priority and preference in life. Worship must always be consistent with loyalty to God, refusing every substitute for God, everything that would take away from the glorification of God.

- to invite all to join in the worship of God, and to accept all and pray for the forgiveness of all fellow worshipers.

- to worship in unity, wholeheartedly, using song and music to praise God, rejoicing together.

- to bring tithes and offerings gladly for the support of those who are consecrated to the service of God.

For the people of God when threatened by disbelievers who would destroy their society of faith:

- to be ready to defend the faith vigorously.

- to trust in God courageously.

- to ignore propaganda designed to weaken faith in God or to equate God with the gods and religions devised by the peoples of the earth.

2 CHRONICLES 33–36

Introduction to These Chapters

These closing chapters of the Chronicles recapitulate, through the stories of the kings Manasseh and Josiah, the great goodness of faithfulness to God, the law, and the Temple, and the great evil of faithlessness to God, the law, and the Temple. The brief review of the last kings of Judah is like a descent into gloom, ending in tragedy, with a last faint glimmer of hope. The tragedy is that despite the promises of God, the ideal of the kingdom of David and Solomon, the messages from God through the prophets have not prevailed. In the end, the faithlessness of kings and people leads inevitably to doom. The last word, however, is that there will be yet another chance for restoration.

Here is an outline of these chapters.

I. Manasseh and Amon (33:1-25)
   A. Manasseh's seduction of Judah (33:1-9)
   B. Manasseh's humiliation and reform (33:10-17)
   C. The sum of Manasseh's life (33:18-20)
   D. Amon's short, evil reign (33:21-25)
II. Josiah's Faithfulness (34:1-33)
   A. Josiah's purging of Judah (34:1-13)
   B. The discovery of the Book of the Law (34:14-21)
   C. The judgment on Judah (34:22-28)
   D. The covenant made by Josiah (34:29-33)
III. Josiah's Celebration of the Passover (35:1-19)
IV. The Death of Josiah (35:20-27)
V. The Last of the Kings of Judah (36:1-21)
   A. Jehoahaz and Egypt (36:1-4)
   B. Jehoiakim, Jehoiachin, and Babylon (36:5-10)
   C. Zedekiah's and Judah's unfaithfulness (36:11-16)
   D. Destruction and exile of the people (36:17-21)
VI. Cyrus of Persia: Hope for Jerusalem (36:22-23)

The Message of 2 Chronicles 33–36

The theme of the books of Chronicles is repeated: God sends spokesmen to warn the people of wrong. If heeded, God will forgive and bless; if not and they forsake God, destruction is inevitable, and God's promise cannot be realized. The last kings slip back into evildoing so that the Temple and Jerusalem are destroyed, and the people exiled.

Chronicles uses history to:

- warn against popular lifestyles that are really only a reversion to primitive paganism.

- warn against all that opposes, or substitutes for, God.

- assure that God has compassion for the people. That compassion, however, does not save them in spite of themselves. They must respond to God positively, not negatively.

- assure that God judges and punishes those unfaithful to the law, but forgives those who humble themselves.

- assure that to return to God means to seek God, worship God, and keep the law in total commitment.

- remind us that God will not protect from harm those who do wrong and lead others away from God.

- remind us that those who are faithful to God and deal justly are blessed by God and honored by people.

- remind us that there is joy in community of praise to God.

- counsel a pledge (covenant) with others to be faithful to God, to seriously keep the law and commandments.

- counsel support of God's word and God's house.

- counsel attention to those who speak for God.

- counsel trust in and obedience to God despite social pressures and despite political expediency.

EZRA

INTRODUCTION

Except for the books of Ezra and Nehemiah, our knowledge of the Israelite people in those formative years immediately following the Babylonian Exile would be virtually nil. We would know nothing of the return from the Exile, almost nothing of the rebuilding of the Temple and those who inspired this work, and nothing of the Samaritan opposition which began here, but lingered and festered for centuries afterward (see John 4:9).

We would have no information about the repopulation of Jerusalem and the reconstruction of the city walls. We would know nothing of the reforms under Nehemiah and Ezra, which rid the Israelite religion of pagan influences and protected it from foreign divinities. Most importantly, we would have no knowledge of Ezra's reading of the law to the people and of their acceptance of it as God's authoritative word, which, if our understanding of that event is correct, marks the true beginning both of Judaism as a religion and the formation of the Jewish Bible. The books of Ezra and Nehemiah, then, command a place of special honor among the books of the Bible.

The Origin of the Book

When first written, and for centuries afterward, Ezra and Nehemiah stood as one book, called Ezra. Not until the time of Origen (third century) do we have evidence that the book had been divided into two parts. The Book of Ezra-Nehemiah is related to the books of 1 and 2 Chronicles, which originally stood as one book, called The Chronicles. The relationship, in fact, is so close that many scholars until recently believed that all four of these books were originally one book. Recent scholarly studies have concluded, particularly in light of theological differences in the books, that Ezra-Nehemiah and Chronicles are separate literary works. For instance, the theme of retribution is prevalent in Chronicles but almost entirely absent in Ezra-Nehemiah. Also, Chronicles presents a much more welcoming attitude toward the northern tribes of Israel than does Ezra-Nehemiah. Third, Chronicles places greater emphasis upon the Davidic

monarchy. Fourth, Chronicles has much to say about Jacob (always called Israel) and de-emphasizes the Exodus, while Ezra-Nehemiah includes both Abraham and the Exodus. Finally, in Chronicles Israel includes all twelve tribes, while in Ezra-Nehemiah Israel is restricted to Judah and Benjamin.

Who Came First: Ezra or Nehemiah?

The careful reader of the books of Ezra and Nehemiah may well become confused. Events that at first glance seem to be connected with the story just read appear, upon closer reflection, to be related instead to a story told elsewhere in the book. Episodes are related out of chronological sequence, and similar types of action are told one after the other although the events themselves may have happened years, or even decades, apart.

One of the most baffling problems of chronology is whether Ezra or Nehemiah came to Jerusalem first. The present order of the material leaves the impression that Ezra did. Ezra left Babylonia in the seventh year of the reign of King Artaxerxes (Ezra 7:1, 6-7); thirteen years later Nehemiah returned to Jerusalem (Nehemiah 1:1; 2:1); the two men were there together for an undetermined length of time (Nehemiah 8:1, 9).

However, there are many indications that Nehemiah returned to Jerusalem before Ezra did. For example:

(1) When Nehemiah returned to Jerusalem, he found the city to be sparsely settled (Nehemiah 7:4), and he had to take measures to repopulate it (Nehemiah 11:1-2). By the time Ezra arrived, however, Jerusalem seems to have had a large number of people living in it (Ezra 10:1).

(2) Nehemiah had to rebuild the city wall after he arrived (Nehemiah 2:11-12, 16-17). In Ezra's day, the wall seems to have been already standing (Ezra 9:9).

(3) Nehemiah had to appoint people to act as Temple treasurers (Nehemiah 13:13), whereas a group of priests was already acting in that capacity when Ezra first arrived (Ezra 8:33).

(4) Eliashib was the high priest at the time of Nehemiah (Nehemiah 3:1, 20), whereas Jehohanan, the son of Eliashib (or perhaps the grandson; see Nehemiah 12:10-11 and 13:28) seems to have been the high priest at the time of Ezra (Ezra 10:6).

(5) None of the persons who returned to Jerusalem with Ezra (Ezra 8:1-20), nor any of their children, are reported to have assisted Nehemiah in the rebuilding of the wall (Nehemiah 3:1-32). Nehemiah 2:17-18 gives the impression that all the people were eager to help. It seems especially incredible that those who returned with Ezra would not have helped in that project had they been there at the time the work was being done.

(6) Ezra left Babylon with the law book in his hand (Ezra 7:6, 14, 25). He was eager to teach the law to the people (Ezra 7:10), and he had full authority to command obedience to it (Ezra 7:25-26). Why, then, would he wait thirteen years, until Nehemiah arrived (Nehemiah 8:9), to do so? The more natural explanation is that Nehemiah had preceded Ezra to Jerusalem.

There are other reasons, too, for believing Nehemiah returned to Jerusalem before Ezra did, including supporting evidence from an archaeological find (discussed in the Introduction to Nehemiah). None of these arguments is conclusive, not even all of them together, but they certainly point in that direction.

But if Nehemiah actually preceded Ezra, why are we told that Ezra returned the seventh year of Artaxerxes, and Nehemiah the twentieth? The answer seems to lie in the fact that three Persian monarchs ruled under the name Artaxerxes. If we assume Nehemiah returned the twentieth year of Artaxerxes I (465–424 B.C.), and Ezra the seventh year of Artaxerxes II (404–358 B.C.), that would place Nehemiah's arrival in 445 and Ezra's in 397.

Historical Background

The Babylonian Empire had only one great leader—its founder and first king, Nebuchadnezzar. At Nebuchadnezzar's death in 562 B.C., there was no strong leader to take his place. After two weak kings, Nabonidus came to the Babylonian throne. Though he reigned in name some sixteen years (555–539 B.C.), his son, Belshazzar, was the actual ruler most of that time. In 539 Cyrus, the Elamite king whose political shrewdness far outmatched that of either Nabonidus or Belshazzar, wrested the empire from their hands with hardly a drop of blood shed.

Cyrus was a more enlightened ruler than the kings of Babylon had been. Nebuchadnezzar's policy, followed by all his successors, was to take the leaders of the conquered nations into exile in order to minimize the risk of insurrection. Cyrus's philosophy was different. He believed people are easiest to rule when they are happy, and they are happy when they are allowed to live in their own land and worship their own gods. Shortly after his takeover of the empire, therefore, Cyrus issued an edict allowing the exiles within his empire to return to their homelands and rebuild their temples. Among those enjoying this privilege were the exiles from Judah.

EZRA 1–2

Introduction to These Chapters

In these first two chapters of the book of Ezra, the writer has provided several different kinds of information. The book opens with a decree issued by Cyrus, king of Persia. These chapters also contain lists of returnees from the Exile, names of cities in Judah, names of Temple servants, and a list of miscellaneous persons not included on any of the other lists.

Here is an outline of these chapters.

I. The Proclamation of Cyrus (1:1-4)
II. Gifts for the Temple (1:5-11)
III. A Census of Those Returning (2:1-20)
IV. Names of Cities in Judah (2:21-35)
V. Names of Temple Servants (2:36-58)
VI. Names of Others Are Listed (2:59-63)
VII. Conclusion (2:64-70)

The Message of Ezra 1–2

- God takes the initiative to redeem those God has punished. The people could not save themselves. Cyrus was stirred into action by God's initiative.

- God uses people when they do not worship the Lord as their God. Cyrus was an Elamite, not an Israelite, and he worshiped the Persian god. Yet, when God stirred up his spirit, Cyrus obeyed.

- God can turn despair into excitement, and hopelessness into exhilaration. We cannot miss the thrill and anticipation that pervade these chapters. At long last, the people's dream will come true. God has acted again! The second Exodus is here.

EZRA 3–4

Introduction to These Chapters

Chapters 3 and 4 tell of the reinstituting of the religious ceremonies at Jerusalem and about the first attempts at rebuilding the Temple. Here is an outline of Ezra 3–4.

I. The Rebuilding Begun (3:1-13)
   A. Altar rebuilt and offerings reinstituted (3:1-6)
   B. Laying the Temple foundation (3:7-13)
II. Opposition Stops the Rebuilding (4:1-24)
   A. Opposition from Cyrus to Darius (4:1-5)
   B. Later opposition (4:6-24)

The Message of Ezra 3–4

- Sometimes we speak of doing the lesser of two evils. What we do seems right and necessary under the circumstances, yet we know even as we do it that it is less than the ideal solution. Because it is the lesser of two evils rather than the right thing to do, it often comes back to haunt us. That is the lesson of Ezra 3–4.

- Zerubbabel and Jeshua did what seemed to be absolutely necessary to do at the time. Had they allowed the Samaritans (the people of the land) to join with them in rebuilding the Temple, the pure religion of Israel might have become polluted, even to the point of losing its distinctiveness. And Judaism would have become just another religion, hardly distinguishable from the neighboring pagan religions.

- Later, Nehemiah and Ezra would follow this same practice of excluding non-Jews both from their religious community and from their individual families. Once again the policy seemed necessary at the time, but once again it was the lesser of two evils. Hidden within this policy were the seeds of those attitudes of self-righteousness, exclusiveness, and legalism which Jesus condemned in the Pharisees of his day (see Matthew 23:1). The lesser of two evils became a way of life, and led finally to a diseased religion.

- If the work that is attempted is divinely inspired, no amount of human opposition can prevent its completion.

- What may seem rebellious and wicked (4:12) to those in authority may actually be God's will.

EZRA 5–6

Introduction to These Chapters

Chapter 5 picks up the story left at 4:5. In Chapter 6 the Temple is completed, and it closes with a celebration of the Passover and unleavened bread.

Here is an outline of Ezra 5–6.
I. Work on the Temple Is Resumed (5:1-17)
    A. The work resumed (5:1-2)
    B. An investigation of the work (5:3-5)
    C. Tattenai's letter to Darius (5:6-17)
II. The Temple Is Completed (6:1-22)
    A. The decree of Cyrus is found (6:1-5)
    B. Darius's reply to Tattenai (6:6-12)
    C. The Temple is completed and dedicated (6:13-18)
    D. The Passover is celebrated (6:19-22)

The Message of Ezra 5–6

- The author never dreamed that his words would become a part of the Jewish and Christian Scriptures. He wrote in order to help the people of his own day understand how God works through the currents of history to accomplish the divine will. In so doing, however, he left that same message for untold generations to come.

- It was not Darius who, on his own, decreed that the Temple be rebuilt, but the Lord, the God of Israel and the God of the whole world, who "turned the heart of the king" (NRSV; "changed the attitude," NIV) to be favorable toward the Israelites (6:22). In the same way, God had stirred up the spirit of Cyrus to let the people return to their land (1:1).

- Haggai and Zechariah goaded the people to rebuild the Temple not because of nationalistic fervor, but because they prophesied at the bidding of and in the name of God.

- Haggai and Zechariah not only spoke God's words of judgment (as, for example, in Haggai 1:3-6), but also worked beside the people, helping them to rebuild the Temple.

- It was not by chance that the work on the Temple prospered, but it was because the hand of God was in it.

- The Temple was completed not because of the skill of the workers or the determination of the people, but because of the command of God.

- We often explain the events of the world by referring to human motivations and human deeds. But Ezra reminds us of a deeper cause— the God who plants the desires in our hearts and calls us into action.

EZRA 7–8

Introduction to These Chapters

Chapter 7 begins the second major part of the book of Ezra. Here we are introduced to the man Ezra for the first time. We shall be occupied with the work of Ezra for the remainder of the book, and we shall also find a part of his story in the book of Nehemiah (Nehemiah 8–10).

Later rabbis would look back on Ezra as the greatest man of his age. Although modern scholars find reason to doubt some of the achievements his admirers have attributed to him, certainly Ezra was a towering figure of his day, and of extreme importance in setting the direction of post exilic Judaism.

Here is an outline of Ezra 7–8.

I. Ezra's Genealogy and Qualifications (7:1-6)
II. Ezra's Arrival in Jerusalem (7:7-10)
III. The Letter from Artaxerxes (7:11-28)
IV. Those Returning with Ezra (8:1-20)
V. Final Preparations for the Trip (8:21-30)
VI. Ezra's Arrival in Jerusalem (8:31-36)

The Message of Ezra 7–8

There are many lessons for us in these chapters of Ezra, but two stand out in particular.

- "Ezra had set his heart to study the law of the LORD, and to do it . . ." (7:10). How often we fail here! It is not that we don't study the Bible. Many of us enjoy reading the stories of the great heroes of our faith. But how many times do these stories stir us into action? How often does studying the Bible lead our Sunday school class into a special community project? Ezra made it plain that studying God's law is not enough; we must also do it. Ezra is not alone in this emphasis. (See Deuteronomy 5:1; 11:32; 26:16). The Gospel writers (Matthew 7:24-27) and the rest of the New Testament writers (James 1:25, for example) are equally insistent that studying the Bible is not enough; discipleship requires action. Put quite simply, Bible study that does not result in action is contrary to what the Bible teaches.

- It is instructive to compare the names of those returning with Ezra (8:2-14) with the names of those who returned earlier with Zerubbabel (2:2-20). Of the eleven families who traveled with Ezra, eight of them were descendants of those who had gone back with Zerubbabel (the numbers are thirteen and ten, respectively, if Zattu and Bani are counted). That is 72.7 per cent (or 76.9 per cent counting Zattu and Bani). What better evidence could there be for the truth of Proverbs 22:6, "Train up a child in the way he should go, and when he is old he will not depart from it"? (See also Deuteronomy 6:4-9, 20-25; 11:18-21.) Faith produces faith, generation after generation.

EZRA 9–10

Introduction to these Chapters

In these chapters Ezra requires all the men of Israel who have married foreign women to put away these families. The requirement sounds harsh, intolerant, and narrow-minded. Why would Ezra make this requirement? What was wrong with marrying a non-Israelite?

Ezra's actions arose from a concern for religious purity. Israel had been called to be a holy people, a people set apart from the other nations (Exodus 19:3-8). Ezra knew that when an Israelite married a non-Israelite, the danger of apostasy was very real. Even King Solomon had been led into idolatry by his foreign wives (1 Kings 11:1-11). If it could happen to him, it could happen to anybody. The law, therefore, expressly forbade the marrying of the peoples of the land (Deuteronomy 7:1-4). When Ezra discovered that this law had not been kept, he set into motion practices designed to correct the situation, which he found intolerable. Ezra's memoirs may have dealt with other improprieties as well, but this is the only one of Ezra's reforms the book of Ezra has preserved for us.

Here is an outline of these chapters.

I. The Problem Stated (9:1-2)
II. Ezra Sits Appalled (9:3-5)
III. Ezra's Prayer (9:6-15)
IV. The Response of the People (10:1-5)
V. Ezra's Proclamation and the Assembly (10:6-15)
VI. The Search and the Reform (10:16-44)

The Message of Ezra 9–10

When Ezra put his reform into effect, he faced the same problem we face when we try to take the Bible seriously. He was to see that the people obeyed the laws of God (7:26). Yet the law had been given centuries earlier. Could a law written for one age be valid in another?

The law said that the Israelites were not to intermarry with the Hittites, the Girgashites, the Amorites, the Canaanites, the Perizzites, the Hivites, and the Jebusites (Deuteronomy 7:1-2). But in Ezra's day these people were not the problem. Some of those nations no longer existed. The problem now lay with the Samaritans, the peoples of the land, those who worshiped God in the same manner in which the pagan gods were worshiped.

Was the law to be interpreted as being static? Was it to be carried out literally, with no room for interpretation? Or was the law flexible enough that it could be applied to a new situation? Ezra thought that it was. To the list of nations given in the law, he added the Ammonites, Moabites, and Egyptians (9:1).

Today we face the same question. How are we to interpret the Bible? Is the Bible a static book, to be followed literally, with no room for interpretation? If so, what do we do with such passages as Matthew 5:29-30 or Luke 14:26? Do we ignore them? Do we pretend Jesus never said them? Or can we follow the meaning and intent of the passage without obeying it literally?

There is no question about what Ezra would do: The spirit, not the letter, of the law must be carried out. Nor is there any question what Jesus would do. The law was not forever fixed. It could be, and should be, altered on occasion (see Matthew 5).

NEHEMIAH

OUTLINE OF NEHEMIAH

INTRODUCTION

Nehemiah the Man

Nehemiah has not claimed the attention through the centuries that Ezra has. Yet he, too, was a towering figure of his day, and is mentioned in two books of the Apocrypha. In fact, when ben Sirach set out to "praise famous men," he mentioned the deeds of Nehemiah, but not those of Ezra (Ecclesiasticus 44:1; 49:13).

A story about Nehemiah not in the Protestant Bible, found in 2 Maccabees 1:18-36, and 2 Maccabees 2:13, says Nehemiah founded a library and collected the books about the kings, the prophets, and the writings of David. This undoubtedly is a reference to the books of Samuel, Kings, and Psalms. Just as Ezra was responsible for preserving the Law, Nehemiah preserved much of the rest of the Hebrew Bible. This is our only hint of such activity on the part of Nehemiah, however, and it is found in a book not considered to be historically reliable.

Like Ezra, Nehemiah has left us his memoirs, though scholars disagree on exactly how much and which portions of the book of Nehemiah come from Nehemiah himself. Nehemiah was a man of action, passionately devoted to living by the law of God. In the book that bears his name, we'll find Nehemiah building the city wall and putting into effect several religious reforms. In some ways he was a more likeable person than Ezra, but he, too, could be stern and demanding.

The Dates of Nehemiah and Ezra

The introduction to the book of Ezra states that one of the problems of Old Testament scholarship is trying to decide who returned to Jerusalem first—Ezra or Nehemiah. Probably Nehemiah did, and reasons for this are given in the introduction to Ezra. It was also stated there that archaeological evidence supported this claim. Here is that evidence.

In the fifth century B.C., there was a Jewish community on Elephantine Island in Egypt. Among the materials found there, left by this community, was a letter dated in the seventeenth year of Darius II, which would be 407 B.C. The letter is addressed to Delaiah and Shelemiah, sons of Sanballat, whom the letter identifies as the governor of Samaria. Since the letter was sent to the governor's sons, it is reasonable to assume that Sanballat was getting up in years, and had turned over to his sons the responsibility of governing the land.

This fits well with our belief that Nehemiah came to Jerusalem in 445 B.C, the twentieth year of Artaxerxes I (see Nehemiah 1:1; 2:1). For one of Nehemiah's most persistent foes was named Sanballat. And although Nehemiah never refers to him as governor, it is obvious that Sanballat was in a position of authority. He was a young and vigorous leader when Nehemiah was there.

Thirty-eight years later, in 407 (when the Elephantine letter was written), Sanballat was too old to govern, but kept the title of governor, and ruled through his sons.

The same letter refers to Jehohanan as the high priest at the time of the destruction of the Elephantine temple in 410 B.C. That information fits well with our belief that Ezra returned to Jerusalem, not in the seventh year of Artaxerxes I, but in the seventh year of Artaxerxes II, that is, in 397 B.C. For Ezra 10:6 indicates that Ezra went to the chamber of Jehohanan, the son of Eliashib, where he spent the night. Now, Eliashib was the high priest in 445 B.C., during the time of Nehemiah (Nehemiah 3:1, 20). If he had become high priest at a young age, he could have continued in that post for another thirty years or so. Then Jehohanan, his son, could have become high priest, and would have been in office at the time of the destruction of the Elephantine temple in 410 and when Ezra arrived in Jerusalem in 397. Thus the archaeological evidence fits the theory that Nehemiah preceded Ezra in returning to Jerusalem. At the same time, it destroys the contrary theory that Ezra returned first.

What leaves the question open, however, is the fact that archaeology is not infallible. Whereas the evidence cited above would support the conclusions to which we have come, other archaeological evidence indicates that there was a second Sanballat, who served as governor of Samaria during the reign of Artaxerxes II. If these are the Sanballat and the Artaxerxes referred to in the Book of Nehemiah, then Nehemiah came to Jerusalem not in 445, but in 384. And that reopens the possibility that Ezra preceded Nehemiah. It seems best, until more definite information can be obtained, to stay with the earlier dates.

NEHEMIAH 1–2

Introduction to These Chapters

The memoirs of Nehemiah begin at 1:1 and continue through 7:5, excluding, perhaps, the list of workers in chapter 3.

Here is an outline of Nehemiah 1–2.
I. Nehemiah Hears Distressing News (1:1-11a)
II. Permission to Go to Jerusalem (1:11b–2:8)
III. Nehemiah Challenges the People (2:9-20)
 A. The arrival and inspection (2:9-16)
 B. The challenge and responses (2:17-20)

The Message of Nehemiah 1–2

Nehemiah had a multi-faceted personality. Many of his traits are worthy of emulation.

- He was a man of feelings, and he was not afraid to express them. When told of the plight of Jerusalem and the people there, he wept for days (see 1:4).

- He was a man of prayer. He fasted and prayed, and laid his concerns before God (1:4-11; 2:4).

- He was a man of confession. When detailing the sins of his people, he included himself as one of the sinners (1:6-7).

- He was a man of spiritual discipline. His prayer in Chapter 1 shows an intimate knowledge of the books of Moses. He obviously read them frequently (1.7-10).

- He was a man of courage. He was afraid when questioned by Artaxerxes, but he did not let his fear keep him from doing what he knew he must (2:2-3). Nor did he let the threats of Sanballat, Tobiah, and Geshem keep him from building the wall (2:19-20).

- He was a man of wisdom. He knew what to say in order to get the desired results (2:5 with the king; 2:17-18 with the people of Jerusalem).

- He was a man of faith. He knew that his success was due to God (2:8, 18, 20).

- He was a man of action. He gathered the facts first (2:12-15), but then was ready to go to work to get the job done (2:17-18, 20).

NEHEMIAH 3–4

Introduction to These Chapters

In these two chapters we see a determined Nehemiah organizing his people, beginning the work he came to do, and defending his efforts against those who opposed him. Equally as determined, yet doomed to failure, are those who try to frustrate Nehemiah's work.

Here is a brief outline of these chapters.

I. The Work Begins (3:1-32)

II. Opposition and Countermeasures (4:1-23)

The Message of Nehemiah 3–4

- Perhaps the greatest lesson to be learned from these chapters is the interlocking nature of faith and works. No one was more convinced than Nehemiah that the hand of the Lord was upon God's people. Yet, though "we prayed to our God," Nehemiah also "set a guard as a protection . . . day and night" (4:9). And though Nehemiah knew "our God will fight for us" (4:20), he also took precautions to make sure the work got done and his people were protected. He was a man of faith; but he was also a man of action.

- Another lesson we need to learn is how to come together as one. When the wall needed rebuilding, it was not just the common people who came to work. All the people of Judah came, regardless of status, regardless of position. Priests and Levites, goldsmiths and servants, rich and poor labored side by side. And though some internal problems appeared later, there is no hint of them here. The people were one. They believed God was calling upon them to do this great work, and they were determined to do it.

NEHEMIAH 5

Introduction to This Chapter

Once again we come to a section of material that is out of chronological sequence. In the first place, it is inconceivable that Nehemiah would stop to have a "great assembly" (NRSV) or "large meeting" (NIV) (5:7) of his people in the midst of the tense situation described in chapter 4. Second, chapter 5 seems to be an insertion, for the story left hanging at the end of chapter 4 is picked up again in chapter 6. Third, neither Sanballat nor any other adversary is mentioned in chapter 5. The situation described here seems to come from a time when Sanballat is no longer a threat. Fourth, the famine and the sins resulting from it tie in well with the situation described in chapter 13, during Nehemiah's second stint as governor of Judah. And finally, it is evident from 5:14 that the entire episode comes from Nehemiah's second term, for the entire twelve years of his first term as governor are spoken of in the past tense.

Probably the author chose to relate this story here because it suited his purposes. He is showing the difficulties encountered by the restored community. So far he has emphasized problems from without. Now he wants to show that Nehemiah had internal problems, too.

Here is an outline of chapter 5.

I. An Internal Problem (5:1-5)

II. Nehemiah Acts; the People Respond (5:6-13)

III. Nehemiah's Unselfishness as Governor (5:14-19)

The Message of Nehemiah 5

- As we read the opening verses of chapter 5, our sympathies are drawn instinctively to the poor. Their land is being wrested from them, and their families are being torn asunder by the merciless policies of the nobles and officials. We applaud the quick and decisive actions which Nehemiah took to correct the situation.

• Extraordinary circumstances require extraordinary measures. The difficulty is to know when the old is no longer usable, and what is needed to replace it. The one who is able to discern these things, and to convince others to try the new, is the one we refer to as a leader.

• In chapter 4, the people of Israel were united. Together they determined to build the wall regardless of the jeers and threats of Sanballat. They gave it their all; they did what was necessary; they got the job done. But in chapter 5 there is no longer unity. Instead, there is division, bickering, and exploitation of one another. Instead of fighting a common foe, they are fighting one another. Had it not been for Nehemiah and the strong leadership he exerted, everything the people of God stood for might have been lost. A community can cope with external threats; it may even be made stronger because of them. But let the people begin to fight among themselves, and the battle is lost.

NEHEMIAH 6–7

Introduction to These Chapters

Chapter 6 resumes the story of chapter 4. Some lapse of time is evident, however. Chapter 4 ends with the builders sleeping with their clothes on in order to be ready for either work or battle, whereas chapter 6 begins with the wall completed except for putting the doors in the gates. Nehemiah's enemies make their final attempts to prevent the finishing of the wall, but again they fail, and the wall is completed.

In chapter 7, Nehemiah's concern is to populate the city now that the wall is finished.

Here is an outline of these chapters.

I. Plots Against Nehemiah's Life (6:1-14)
   A. "Let us meet together" (6:1-4)
   B. "It is reported . . ." (6:5-9)
   C. "They are coming to kill you" (6:10-14)
II. The Walls Are Completed (6:15-19)
III. Getting Started in Jerusalem (7:1-73a)
   A. Leaders appointed and people counted (7:1-69)
   B. The people settle in their towns (7:70-73a)

The Message of Nehemiah 6–7

• Before Jesus sent out his disciples on their missionary journey, he called them together to invest them with certain powers and to give them final instructions (Matthew 10:1). Among the charges he gave to them was this one: "Be wise as serpents" (NRSV) or "shrewd as snakes" (NIV) and "innocent as doves"(Matthew 10:16). Nehemiah would have known exactly what Jesus meant. That was his strategy in dealing with Sanballat and Tobiah.

• It is not always easy to be wise as serpents; sometimes it is even harder to be innocent as doves. But Nehemiah gives us a helpful model so that we might understand more clearly how to put Jesus' words into action.

• It would have been easy for Nehemiah to have considered his job done once the walls were built. That, after all, was the task he was sent to Jerusalem to do. But though that was a great achievement, and one in which Nehemiah undoubtedly took great pride, he knew he could not stop there; there was still a job to do.

Nehemiah heard God's call, after the wall was built, to repopulate the city. If we do not hear God challenging us to go a step further, is God not speaking, or are we not hearing?

NEHEMIAH 8–10

Introduction to These Chapters

Anyone reading through the book of Nehemiah for the first time will not be prepared for what comes in chapter 8. After seven chapters of Nehemiah's determination to finish the wall in spite of problems and difficulties, both external and internal, suddenly we are back to the story of Ezra. Nehemiah will not appear again until chapter 11. There are two exceptions—Nehemiah is mentioned in 8:9 and 10:1.

The resumption of the Ezra story here in the book of Nehemiah has puzzled readers and fascinated commentators for centuries. The obvious question is, Why? Why does Ezra suddenly appear as the main character in a book that up to this point has not even mentioned him? Does this portion of the Ezra story belong here? Or did it get misplaced? If the latter, was it misplaced accidentally or on purpose? And if on purpose, we are back to the question, Why? What reason did the author (or some later editor) have for putting a portion of the Ezra story here?

Does this portion of the Ezra story belong here? The answer is almost certainly, No. If Nehemiah arrived in Jerusalem in 445 B.C., and Ezra in 397, then it would have been impossible for Ezra to read the law of Moses to the people immediately following the fifty-two days it took to repair the wall. But even if we say that Ezra came to Jerusalem during the seventh year of Artaxerxes I, in 458, we are left with an unanswerable problem. Why

would Ezra, who was sent to Jerusalem to teach the law to the people, wait thirteen years to do so? He is represented as coming to Jerusalem carrying the law of God in his hand (Ezra 7:25) and eager to get started teaching it (Ezra 7:10). It is unlike Ezra to put off the task closest to his heart. It seems best, then, to say that this portion of the Ezra story has been misplaced. It probably originally followed Ezra 8.

We can only guess about who put the story here, and why. Most probably, the author (or, perhaps, a later editor) placed the Ezra material here. Earlier, the author rearranged some material because it suited his purpose to do so (see Ezra 4:6-24). And once again his theological interests dictated that he place this story here. He wanted to show that the people who settled in the restored city had committed themselves to living by God's laws. The people are listed in chapter 7; they hear the word read in chapter 8; they repent in chapter 9; and they "set their seal" to the covenant in chapter 10. They are then ready to populate Jerusalem in chapter 11.

Here is an outline of these chapters.

I. Reading of the Law (7:73b–8:12)
II. The Feast of Booths Observed (8:13-18)
III. A Day of Repentance (9:1-37)
   A. Confession and praise (9:1-5)
   B. Ezra's prayer (9:6-37)
IV. The Covenant Renewed (9:38–10:39)

The Message of Nehemiah 8–10

- Ezra knew the importance of having interpreters available to help the people understand what the Scriptures said (Nehemiah 8:8). In the same way, interpreters can help us as we read the Scripture.

- The people who came together to study God's laws with Ezra understood quite well that what the law commanded, they were to do (see Nehemiah 8:14-16). We need to understand the Bible in the same way.

- The prayer attributed to Ezra (Nehemiah 9:6-37) points out the grace of God in dealing with the people. Although grace is primarily a New Testament word, the *concept* is as old as the first sinners who knew themselves forgiven of their sins. We, like the children of Israel, often refuse to obey. But God is ready to forgive, is slow to anger, and is abounding in steadfast love (9:16, 26). Of course, God will punish, if we continue to disobey, but the purpose of the divine punishment is always to bring us to repentance (9:29-30).

- Some have felt the concerns of Nehemiah 10:30-39 to be of little consequence. They do not constitute "the weightier matters of the law" of which Jesus spoke (Matthew 23:23). But the situation Nehemiah faced was different. The Gospels report that in Jesus' day some of the Pharisees had become masters of the details of the law; in Nehemiah's day, the people were neglecting these details altogether. Nehemiah was determined that they would "not neglect the house of our God" (10:39). We need to hear these words again today. For, though we frequently give lip service to the weightier matters, we often neglect doing even the simplest tasks for the house of God.

NEHEMIAH 11–12

Introduction to These Chapters

Chapter 11 continues the story which was left hanging in chapter 7. Very quickly,

however, the history is again interrupted by a series of lists (11:3–12:26), and when it resumes in 12:27, we are once again surprised. For here we read of the dedication of the wall, an event we might have expected to find much earlier.

Here is an outline of these chapters.

I. Nehemiah's Plan to Populate Jerusalem (11:1-2)
II. Those Living in Jerusalem and Judah (11:3-36)
III. Post exilic Priests and Levites (12:1-26)
IV. The Dedication of the Wall (12:27-43)
V. According to the Command of David (12:44-47)

The Message of Nehemiah 11–12

There are several messages for us today in these chapters of Nehemiah.

- When Nehemiah needed some people to populate Jerusalem, he asked the people to cast lots to see who would go. Some have criticized Nehemiah for this, saying he was shifting the blame from himself to God so the people would not get angry at him. But it could be that Nehemiah sincerely believed that those who lived in Jerusalem should be divinely chosen. In the same way, we today would benefit by seeking divine guidance before we make major decisions.

- Sometimes it bothers us to hear that a later editor took what a biblical writer wrote, and altered it or moved it to a different place in the book. That sounds too much like tampering with God's Word. However, these later editors were people of God, too. Their concern was that God's Word come through loud and clear. Sometimes they felt they could enhance the hearing of God's Word by moving one section of material to another place. God could work through these people as well as the original writers.

• One of the most thrilling aspects of the dedication of the city wall is the note of joy and thanksgiving that comes through time and time again in chapter 12. Note verses 27, 31, 38, 40, and especially verse 43. No one could miss the note of joy in this verse. It is repeated like the refrain of a musical masterpiece. We, too, need to recapture the note of joy in our celebrations.

NEHEMIAH 13

Introduction to This Chapter

The first three verses of this chapter belong with verses 44-47 of chapter 12. These verses continue the idealized picture of the Jewish cultic system with which chapter 12 concludes. Then we are told of the reforms Nehemiah put into effect. The chapter closes with a summary of Nehemiah's work and a prayer for God's favor.

Here is an outline of chapter 13.

I. Separation from Foreigners (13:1-3)
II. The Cleansing of the Temple (13:4-9)
III. The Restoration of the Levites (13:10-14)
IV. Enforcement of the Sabbath Laws (13:15-22)
V. Purification from Foreign Influence (13:23-29)
VI. Nehemiah's Accomplishments (13:30-31)

The Message of Nehemiah 13

Chapter 13 gives us an example to follow, a question to ponder, and a warning to remember.

• Many of us become righteously indignant when we see someone being mistreated, but few of us do anything about it. It is easy to diagnose the problem and point an accusing finger. It is easy to feel sympathy for the one wronged. But after all that has been done, the wrong still remains. Nehemiah did not just bewail the offense; he took action calculated to put an end to it and to reestablish the right. We may not approve of all of Nehemiah's methods, but at least he reminds us that more is required of us than words and sympathetic feelings. Nehemiah has given us an example to follow.

• Some express dismay over Nehemiah's religious intolerance. Should not our religion be open-minded and generous-spirited? Should we not respect and welcome every human attempt to find God's will? Shall we consider every human understanding of God equally valid? Can we mix our Christian concept of God with another, and still have what God has revealed to us through Jesus Christ? Will a tolerant religion result in a watered-down religion? That is at least a question to ponder.

• The forces of evil once defeated are not forever destroyed. If Nehemiah did not know that before he returned to Jerusalem, he surely learned it while there. His two terms as governor of Judah were full of defeated enemies rising up again, and battles won having to be refought. What was true in Nehemiah's day is true today. A nation once reformed cannot be assumed to stay that way. Nor can the church. Nor can our personal lives.

ESTHER

OUTLINE OF ESTHER

I. Esther Becomes Queen (1:1–2:23)
  A. King Ahasuerus gives three banquets (1:1-9)
  B. Queen Vashti is deposed (1:10-22)
  C. Esther selected as the new queen (2:1-18)
  D. Mordecai notifies the king of danger (2:19-23)

II. Haman's Plot and Esther's Determination (3:1–4:17)
  A. Haman's plot against the Jews (3:1-15)
    1. Haman's promotion, Mordecai's defiance (3:1-4)
    2. Haman's retaliation (3:5-15)
  B. Esther sees the king (4:1-17)

III. Haman's Humiliation (5:1–6:14)
  A. Esther's first banquet (5:1-8)
  B. Haman's plot against Mordecai (5:9-14)
  C. Mordecai is honored (6:1-14)
    1. The king decides to honor Mordecai (6:1-6a)
    2. Haman describes the perfect honor (6:6b-9)
    3. Haman is humiliated (6:10-14)

IV. Haman Loses His Life (7:1-10)
  A. Haman is accused (7:1-6)
  B. Haman pleads for his life (7:7-8)
  C. A third accusation (7:9-10)

V. The Feast of Purim (8:1–10:3)
  A. A second royal edict (8:1-17)
  B. The slaughter of the enemies (9:1-15)
  C. The celebration of Purim (9:16-32)
  D. The greatness of Mordecai (10:1-3)

INTRODUCTION

The book of Esther is intensely interesting and masterfully told. Esther must have been especially interesting to the Jews in exile during Persian rule. For in the midst of the humiliation known only to a conquered people scattered throughout an alien empire, here is the story of a Jewish woman who became queen of that empire. And it is the story of a crafty Jewish man who turned the tables on the second most powerful person in the kingdom, and eventually took that man's place as second in command. It is the story of the "divine reversal" of fortunes, God protecting the chosen people and bringing to ruin those who sought to harm them.

The book of Esther has been much beloved by Jews over the centuries. Scores of hand-copied texts have survived from the Middle Ages, more than for any other book in the Old Testament. Medieval Jewish scholars produced more commentaries on Esther than on any other book in the Hebrew Bible except the books of Moses (Genesis through Deuteronomy). It was often said Esther ranked second in importance only to the Torah because it was the book that kept the Jews alive. It was a clarion call to fight back against enemy aggression. The Jews had been inspired by this call, not just during the days of the Persian Empire, but throughout the centuries. Some said Esther was even more important than the Torah, for Judaism could exist without the Torah, but it would have been exterminated without the book of Esther.

But this book, beloved though it is, has also been an embarrassment to sensitive Jews and Christians. Nowhere in its ten chapters is God ever mentioned. Nor are prayer, worship, or any of the great religious festivals mentioned. The great themes of the Old Testament are lacking— themes such as the Exodus from Egypt, the receiving of the Ten Commandments, and the making of the covenant. Even the great virtues taught in the rest of the Bible are missing. Instead, we have a story in which vengeance plays a primary role.

The secular nature of the book and the ethics it espouses have been matters of concern from the beginning. Even at the council of Jamnia in A.D. 90, when Esther was officially adopted as part of the Hebrew Bible, some rabbis objected. And some Christians resisted its inclusion in the Christian Bible until the Council of Carthage in A.D. 397. Luther, at the time of the Protestant Reformation, said he wished Esther had never been written, and not a few Christians today raise the question of why such a book is included in the Bible. Yet it is not entirely fair to characterize the book as secular.

God Plays an Important Role

We spoke earlier of the "divine reversal" of the fortunes of the characters in the story of Esther. The story is full of coincidences, quirks of fate, and little ironies that make for delightful reading. But when it is read on a different level, the book is a powerful statement about God's activity and the working out of the divine will even in those situations when God is silent, and seems to be nowhere about. The fact that God is not mentioned in the story does not mean God was not active in the proceedings.

Additions to the Text

The book of Esther comes to us in three editions, one in Hebrew and two in Greek. The Hebrew version is the shortest and the earliest. But it was one of the Greek versions, the so-called "B text," that found its way from the (Greek) Septuagint to the (Latin) Vulgate, and from there into use by Christians until the time of the Reformation. Today, Roman Catholics and the Orthodox Churches still use the longer version of the story, while Protestants use the shorter version, and consider the Additions to Esther as part of the Apocrypha.

History or Short Story?

The book of Esther has been interpreted in three ways. Some think of it as a record of historical events that took place while the Jews were in exile and Ahasuerus was king. Whereas this is certainly possible, none of the events in the book can be verified by non-biblical sources, and many of them contradict what we know from our knowledge of history. Ahasuerus is the only character in the story whose historical reality is certain, and there is some disagreement even there as to which king is meant.

Most Old Testament scholars hold to a second possibility, namely that the Book of Esther was written not as history, but as a short story, or a historical novel.

The third possibility is to regard Esther as a mythical story describing the conflict between the gods of Babylon and the gods of Elam. Esther could represent the Babylonian goddess Ishtar, and Mordecai the Babylonian god Marduk. Similarly, Haman and his wife, Zeresh, could represent the Elamite god Humman and his wife Seres, while Vashti, the deposed queen, could represent Mashti, the Elamite goddess.

Theoretically, any of the above interpretations of Esther is possible. A large majority of Old Testament scholars, however, favor the second interpretation. Esther is a short story, written to amuse, to instill a sense of pride into a defeated people, and to assure in an ever-so-subtle way that God does not leave the course of history in the hands of those who rely only upon the sword.

ESTHER 1–2

Introduction to These Chapters

In the longer, Greek version of the story of Esther, used by the Roman and Eastern sectors of the church, the book begins with a dream in which God's plans are revealed to Mordecai. In the version of Esther that appears in the Protestant Bible, the story begins with a banquet given by Ahasuerus, King of Persia. The story moves on to show why Queen Vashti was deposed, and how Esther was chosen as Vashti's replacement. Finally, we learn of Mordecai's good deed toward the king, and the fact that Mordecai's deed was recorded in the king's chronicles.

Here is an outline of these chapters.

I. King Ahasuerus Gives Three Banquets (1:1-9)
II. Queen Vashti Is Deposed (1:10-22)
III. Esther Is Selected as the New Queen (2:1-18)
IV. Mordecai Notifies the King of Danger (2:19-23)

The Message of Esther 1–2

• Chapter 1 is replete with the signs of royalty and the opulence that goes with it. Twenty-one of the twenty-two verses in chapter 1 contain one or more of thirteen words which denote royalty (including king, queen, kingdom, royal, reign, majesty, crown, palace, and throne). The twenty-one verses use these words a total of fifty-seven times. The one verse that does not contain such a word (verse 6) describes the opulence of the king's palace, and notes the royal colors of the furnishings (white, blue, and purple). The splendor and unquestioned authority of the king seem to be evident everywhere. Yet throughout the story that follows, the king is portrayed as one who is sometimes disobeyed, who cannot make decisions on his own, and who is easily manipulated by those around him.

• Vashti was a brave woman. It took courage to refuse the king's command. She knew she would pay severely for her disobedience. Yet there were principles that stood higher with her than her good standing with the king. She would not degrade herself and all women by letting herself become an object to be gawked at.

• It was undoubtedly intended as a compliment when it was said of Esther that she found favor in the eyes of all who saw her (2:15). Yet, how did she accomplish this? By keeping her heritage and her religion a secret, by ignoring Jewish customs, Jewish food laws, and Jewish worship practices.

ESTHER 3–4

Introduction to These Chapters

The villain in the story is introduced in chapter 3, and immediately a conflict develops. That conflict leads to the decision to annihilate all the Jews in the kingdom. This in turn leads to a series of communications between Mordecai and Esther, and a decision on what must be done to stop the slaughter.

Here is an outline of these chapters.

I. Haman's Plot Against the Jews (3:1-15)
   A. Haman's Promotion, Mordecai's Defiance (3:1-4)
   B. Haman's Retaliation (3:5-15)
II. Esther Sees the King (4:1-17)

The Message of Esther 3–4

These chapters speak to us of the cost of integrity, the importance of good leaders, the necessity of action, and the choice of reward.

- Mordecai refused to bow to Haman. He knew the risk he was taking in defying the king's orders, but some things are more important than personal safety. Personal integrity is one of them.

- If an elected official does not act according to our wishes, we can replace that person at the next election. The people in the Persian Empire were not so fortunate; they had no way to replace their king. Ahasuerus was a weak king, but all the more dangerous because of it. For he was easily manipulated by the unscrupulous Haman. How important it is to have the right leaders!

- The story of Esther could have had a very different ending. What if

Mordecai had wailed in the streets of Susa, but nothing more? What if he had not devised a plan of action and convinced Esther to approach the king? The pogrom would have taken place. There are times to mourn and times to go into action. Fortunately, Mordecai knew when to end one and to begin the other.

- From our earliest days we have been taught, "Honesty is the best policy." What we have to learn on our own is that honesty can be risky. Esther was fully aware of the risks when she told Ahasuerus the truth about herself. Things turned out well for Esther, but that is no guarantee they always will. Honesty is indeed the best policy; but in terms of earthly reward, dishonesty may pay the higher dividends. Where does our interest lie—in material gain that soon fades away or in spiritual gain that fulfills eternity?

ESTHER 5–6

Introduction to These Chapters

Chapter 5 continues the narrative of chapter 4 and sets the stage for chapter 6, one of the most delightful parts of the story. Here is an outline of these chapters.

I. Esther's First Banquet (5:1-8)
II. Haman's Plot Against Mordecai (5:9-14)
III. Mordecai Is Honored (6:1-14)
   A. The king decides to honor Mordecai (6:1-6a)
   B. Haman describes the perfect honor (6:6b-9)
   C. Haman is humiliated (6:10-14)

The Message of Esther 5–6

- Jesus once counseled his disciples to "be wise as serpents and innocent as doves" (Matthew 10:16). Esther was following that procedure in these chapters. She matched her wits against those of the king, and she won. Yet, all the while she acted in proper deference to the king. There is a lesson here for those who find themselves having to deal with an authoritarian person who acts on whims.

• Haman had every reason to be happy—every reason except one. He had riches; he had many sons; he was second in command in the kingdom; he had twice been invited to dine with the king and queen—yet, still, there was Mordecai. He was so obsessed with his hatred for Mordecai that "all this does me no good." In the same way, we sometimes let one disappointment blind us to all the reasons we have to be thankful.

• Paul gave the Christians in Rome good advice when he warned against thinking of ourselves more highly than we should (Romans 12:3). Had Haman followed that simple principle, and not assumed that he was the one the king wanted to honor, he would have saved himself much embarrassment.

ESTHER 7

Introduction to This Chapter

The downfall of Haman, begun in 6:10, comes to its climax in 7:10. Verses 1-2 of chapter 8 perhaps should be included in chapter 7. Though the action centers around Haman, the emergent hero is Mordecai, and the movement of the plot is plainly in the direction of Mordecai's elevation to second in command. Here is an outline of these chapters.

I. Haman Is Accused (7:1-6)
II. Haman Pleads for His Life (7:7-8)
III. A Third Accusation Against Haman (7:9-10)

The Message of Esther 7

• The message of Esther 7 is a series of questions. How we answer these questions depends upon what we see as important—people, money, convenience, opportunity. Where do we as Christians stand? See Matthew 6:33.

ESTHER 8–10

Introduction to These Chapters

Except for one detail, chapter 7 would have made a fine closing for the book of Esther. Mordecai was victorious in his battle with Haman, and Esther was triumphant in her bout with possible death. One element of the story remains, however—the scheduled slaughter of the Jews is still on the royal calendar. Chapter 8 is concerned with resolving that one detail.

Chapters 9 and 10 include what many scholars believe to be a series of additions to the book. Chapter 9 is necessary to the story if it is true that the purpose of the book was to explain the origin of the festival of *Purim*. Chapter 10 glories in the greatness attained by Mordecai.

Here is an outline of these chapters.

I. A Second Royal Edict (8:1-17)
II. The Slaughter of the Enemies (9:1-15)
III. The Celebration of Purim (9:16-32)
IV. The Greatness of Mordecai (10:1-3)

The Message of Esther 8–10

• The edict of Mordecai in 8:11-12 is almost the exact counterpart of

Haman's edict in 3:13. The *lex talionis* said one should take a life for a life, an eye for an eye, a tooth for a tooth, or a hand for a hand (see Exodus 21:23-25; Leviticus 24:19-20; Deuteronomy 19:21). That is what Mordecai is doing here—he is matching Haman's edict point for point. The Law of Talion first arose, as far as we know, with Hammurabi. Its purpose was to make sure that revenge did not go beyond the bounds of justice.

According to the biblical text, Esther was not satisfied with the Law of Talion. Her request of Ahasuerus was that the Jews be allowed to go beyond the one-day limit imposed upon them by Mordecai's edict (9:13). When her request was granted, the Jews slew 300 more people in Susa the next day.

Jesus was not satisfied with the Law of Talion, either. But how different his dissatisfaction was! "You have heard that it was said, 'an eye for an eye and a tooth for a tooth.' But I say to you . . . if any one strikes you on the right cheek, turn the other also" (Matthew 5:38-39).

- The author of 10:1-3 undoubtedly believed the high point of the book was Mordecai's elevation to second in command in the kingdom. Followers of Jesus are more apt to think the story reaches its climax when Mordecai, unlike his predecessor, unlike the king under whom he served, and unlike most high-ranking officials from that day to this, used his power not to serve himself, but to seek the welfare of all his people. That is a fine note on which to end the book.

J O B

OUTLINE OF JOB

1. Yahweh's response to Job (38:1–39:30)
2. Yahweh's challenge to Job (40:1-2)
3. Job's unyielding response (40:3-5)
   B. God's second speech (40:6–42:6)
   1. Yahweh's speech (40:6–41:34)
   2. Job's submissive response (42:1-6)

VIII. Prose Epilogue (42:7-17)

A. God's response to Job's friends (42:7-9)
B. Restoration of Job's fortune (42:10-17)

INTRODUCTION

The moment you open the book of Job, you enter a mysterious world. Strange words and phrases bombard your senses. A shady character named Satan challenges God. An old man curses his sores and calls the Lord a variety of ancient names. When God speaks, it's not in any manner we recognize. The divine voice is heard over the roar of a whirling dust storm.

In spite of this alien nature—or perhaps because of it—the book of Job has a magnetic quality. When Rabbi Kushner wrote his best-selling book *When Bad Things Happen to Good People* several years ago, he began with an interpretation of Job. In so doing, he continued a millennia-old tradition: When people suffer, they turn to the experiences and wisdom found in this ancient book. In journeying with Job as he wrestles with cruel and unexplainable pain, people encounter God in a new and different way.

This same opportunity is open to us. If God is to speak to us in this manner, though, our eyes must first grow accustomed to the unfamiliar world of Job.

Job: The Man and the Legend

Job was the central character in a popular story circulated in the ancient Middle East (the region around the Mediterranean Sea that included Egypt, the Sinai peninsula, and Canaan). Job was a wealthy man living in Uz, which possibly was the ancient country of Edom, an area east of Palestine in the Syrian desert. He was a semi-tragic figure in that he encountered intense—and undeserved—hardships. He lost possessions and health, and became a social outcast. Throughout these sufferings, brought on as a result of a heavenly dispute, Job did not "curse God." In the end, consequently, his possessions, health, and status were restored.

The biblical writers were well acquainted with this story. References to Job were made by Ezekiel (14:14, 20) and James (5:11).

As was the custom in ancient Middle Eastern literature, the name signifies the nature and action of the character. *Job* has been traced to a variety of meanings stemming from both Hebrew and Arabic roots: one who is at war with God; one born to be persecuted; and the repentant one are possible interpretations.

How the Book Was Written

As Israel lived with its neighbors, it was natural that ideas and experiences of those countries found their way into Israelite culture. The Hebrew sages reflected upon these impressions within the context of their faith in the Lord (Yahweh). The result was the Wisdom Literature found in the Old Testament. This literature is philosophical, with an emphasis upon teaching: Ecclesiastes, Proverbs, several psalms (1, 34, and 92, for example), and parts of other books.

Job is included in this wisdom tradition. In the early sixth century B.C. the

Babylonians enslaved the citizens of Judah and deported the useful ones to Babylon. This period of biblical history, known as the Exile, was traumatic, causing a crisis of faith for those who believed in God's providential care.

It was against this historical backdrop that the book of Job was written. A wise man/poet of Judah found the ancient legend to be an appropriate vehicle by which to examine faith in God in light of the national catastrophe. The tale he appropriated and edited may be found in the prose portions at the beginning and the end of the book (1:1–2:13; 42:7-17). The first part describes Job's sufferings and his virtuous character, while the last portion depicts the restoration of Job's fortunes. The poetic section in between reveals the poet's painful crisis of faith.

The exception to this is the section containing Elihu's speeches. These chapters (32:1–37:24) are viewed by many scholars as being foreign to the original poem. They were probably penned by a later hand.

The Theme of the Book

It is popular to say that the central thrust of the book of Job is dealing with the question, "Why do the righteous suffer if there is a loving God?" This is actually, however, a sub-theme. The major motif instead is the larger question, "What is the nature of faith—how are we to relate to God?"

The poet verbalizes, through the mouths of Job's friends, the popular theology of ancient Israel. Put simply, this theology is: Do good, and God will reward you; do evil, and God will punish you. This is the idea of divine retribution.

Job's replies to his friends, on the other hand, refute this simplistic theology. He stubbornly maintains his righteousness,

asserting that his suffering cannot be based on anything he did. If Job is correct, then the theology of his friends—and of the ancient Hebrews to some degree—has become bankrupt.

Stripped of such an easy view of faith and the world, how, then, can one approach God? This theme is a reflection of the times in which the poet wrote. The nation was in shambles. The old principles and certainties had been turned upside down. Through the words of Job the poet searches for a faith that will discover God in the midst of fear and chaos.

The Structure and Text of Job

The bulk of the poetry section—the part sandwiched between the prose beginning and ending—consists of the dialogue between Job and three "friends" who come to console him: Eliphaz, Bildad, and Zophar. The conversation follows a set form: Eliphaz speaks, Job replies, Bildad speaks, Job replies; Zophar speaks, Job replies.

This forms a cycle of speeches, and there are three such cycles. (The third cycle, 22:1–27:23, is not complete, containing only the speeches of Eliphaz and Bildad, along with Job's replies.) Preceding and following this series of speeches, Job gives a pair of eloquent soliloquies regarding his suffering (3; 29:1–31:40). A fourth friend, Elihu, follows Job's last soliloquy. Instead of conversing with Job, he makes a long series of speeches (32:6–37:24).

The poetry section concludes with the dialogue between God and Job. God makes two speeches, with Job responding to each. With this conversation the conflict is resolved, leading to the prose conclusion.

The Hebrew text of this poetry section is very poor in places. As can be seen in the footnotes in the NRSV, translators in many instances had to make educated guesses regarding the meaning of a word or phrase. In addition, the third cycle of conversation between Job and his friends appears abrupt and illogical in places. This cycle contains fragments of other speeches.

Types of Literature Found in Job

Just as an epic novel may use different types of literature (adventure, romance, mystery), so does the author of Job. The poet, standing in the Hebrew wisdom tradition, employed different literary forms that were well recognized by his audience.

The first, and most obvious, was that of the *narrative*. In the prose sections the author adapted the ancient story of Job. This storytelling style was the basic vehicle by which God's interaction with the Hebrew people was transmitted.

The poem itself has the characteristics of a *legal document*. The dialogue between Job and his friends has the flavor of a debate. In addition, Job often appeals for a judge to decide between himself and the one who is responsible for his unjust treatment—God (9:33). Finally, with the debate with his friends ended, Job calls for God to enter the courtroom and state the divine case against him.

The third major type of literature employed was the *lament*. Several of the Psalms (such as 22, 39, 77, 88, 102) employ this form, wherein a sufferer expresses powerful emotions to God and cries out for help. The poet used this throughout his work, most poignantly in Job's two soliloquies.

A Hint on Reading the Book of Job

To enter Job's world is to enter an environment alien to us. Consequently, while it is important to get a clear understanding of a passage, at times this is impossible. Ancient ways of looking at the world, corruptions in the text of Job, and uncertain Hebrew words and phrases assure us of this.

Using another instrument—your own experience—will help you deal with such a limitation. Read Job with one eye on his world and another on your own world. Read the book with an understanding of your own pain and the pain of those around you. Ask yourself if the words you find on Job's lips or on his friends' have ever been on your own.

The gap between Job's world and ours—made by the centuries that have passed since the poet first scratched on parchment—is enormous. Reading the book with your own experiences just under the surface will help bridge that gap. By doing this you will share the poet's wrestling with the Lord, and his ultimate victory will be yours as well.

JOB 1–2

Introduction to These Chapters

These two prose chapters dramatically set the stage for the rest of the book. Presenting Job's "rise and fall," they contain the first part of the ancient legend of the righteous sufferer. The poet relates the legend up to the point where Job silently sits in the ashes with his friends (2:13). This provides the springboard from which the poet launches into his theological reflections. It is not until the latter verses of chapter 42 that he picks up the tale again, bringing the book to a conclusion.

As in a movie dramatizing a fable from Greek or Roman mythology, the action alternates between earthly and heavenly arenas. No sooner is Job introduced than the scene switches to an other-worldly palace. There God enters into a heated exchange with Satan, the end result being a wager as to whether or not Job fears God for nothing (1:9). After two sets of trials, Job has not cursed God (2:5, 9), and it appears as if the Almighty has won.

Such drama not only seems alien to us, but it is also foreign to the rest of the Old Testament. Nowhere else can be found such detailed heavenly theatrics. The crux of our uneasiness lies in the affront to our theological sensitivity. Can God lose control and be influenced by Satan? Does God allow intense suffering, just to settle a bet? How does this square with our belief in a compassionate, just God?

When we ask ourselves such questions, we must remember that the story of Job was drawn not from Israel but from other lands in the ancient Middle East, countries that did not share the Hebrew faith. The legend was entrenched in the religion of these nations, a religion that included the belief in several gods. The strongest of these deities ruled, and a heavenly "palace" scene, with the great god reviewing the others and losing his temper, was very believable. The Hebrew poet, following the Wisdom style, screened the story through his eyes of faith. Nonetheless, the sense of the unusual remains in reading these chapters.

Perhaps the best we can do in reading these chapters is to remember the author's purpose. These verses are introductory. Although we may gain some theological insights, they should not be pressed. The Hebrew writer, in breathtaking fashion, has simply prepared us for the real theological issue: the relationship between God and a suffering humanity.

Here is an outline of chapters 1–2.

I. Job's Prosperity and Righteousness (1:1-5)
II. The Testing of Job (1:6–2:10)
  A. The first series of hardships (1:6-22)
  B. The second series of hardships (2:1-10)
III. The Introduction of Job's Friends (2:11-13)

The Message of Job 1–2

Often, when we find ourselves suffering, we ask, "Is there a purpose behind this pain?" Our assumption is that God has a benevolent plan, either to teach us something or to accomplish a greater good.

These two chapters explode such thinking. Job's suffering being based on a bet makes the thought of a wise plan behind pain ludicrous. Perhaps the author is saying: "Don't look for rhyme or reason behind your pain. It can't be understood!"

Just as the tale of God's wager with Satan (*the Adversary* or *the Accuser*) undermines such thinking, it also offers a thread of hope for us. In the dialogue with the Adversary, we see God's emotional side. The Lord passionately loves Job; a proud parent's words are found in 1:8 and 2:3. "Have you considered my servant Job? There is no one like him on the earth."

Only a God who can become passionately involved with persons can speak to us in our pain. The Lord's love for Job ultimately produces a whirlwind visitation (chapters 38–41)—a stupendous event, considering the curses Job has hurled against the Almighty in the preceding chapters. And Christians are convinced that God's passion for us produced an even greater visitation—the life, death, and resurrection of Jesus the Christ.

Connected to this are Job's reactions in these two chapters. As noted in the commentary on 2:10, there is a subtle change in his mood. With continued suffering and the lessening of a hope for an easy way out, Job begins slipping into despair. He is about to embark on a journey that will lead him onto a spiritual cross. His cries—like ours—will strike deep into God's heart. God will leave neither Job nor us hanging there alone.

JOB 3

Introduction to This Chapter

If the first two chapters set the stage for the rest of the book, then chapter 3 is the opening scene. For seven days and nights Job and his friends have sat in silence (2:13). Job now breaks the stillness. His words set in motion a series of dialogues that, while exploring the nature of faith, will become surprisingly heated.

What he says here contrasts starkly with his pious utterances in chapter 2. His speech takes the form of a lament. There are no blessings here. Instead, he curses his life, questions the justice of existence, hints at God's hardness, and bemoans his wretchedness.

Such surprising, angry cries allow us to catch a glimpse inside Job. The days and nights of silence have provided him an opportunity to reflect on things. When he speaks, he could do so in the manner of the grieving psalmist, who started with lamenting and ended with praising (see Psalm 77). Judging from his words in chapter 2, this would have been logical. His reflection, however, drives away piety. He begins somewhat reservedly, with a curse upon the day he was born, and ends in total despair. For Job, there will be no easy way out, no lapse into traditional theology. He will be expressing himself without inhibition.

In addition to this psychological value of Job's speech, there is also a structural one. Imagine he is speaking in a courtroom. He is the prosecuting attorney. God is the defendant. Job's words in chapter 3 can then be seen as the opening argument for the prosecution. He indirectly asserts that he is suffering far more than he should, hinting that God is the cause (3:23b). He also directly questions God's justice: Why is light given to those in misery? (3:20). It is interesting to note that Job ends the conversation with his friends by entering into a monologue much more extensive than this one (see xhapters 29–31). This latter speech is his closing argument, after which he rests his case.

Correspondingly, as will be seen in the following chapters, this first monologue has a dramatic effect upon Job's friends. They turn from being comforters to assuming the duties of "defense lawyers." God's character has been assailed, and they take it upon themselves to rally to the defense. Accusations and arguments increasingly take the place of compassion.

Had Job's speech been a continuation of his earlier piety, then his friends would have remained in sympathy with him. He challenges God's justice, however, and the debate begins.

Two other points should be noted regarding this chapter. First, it is written in poetic verse. Chapter 3 begins the author's original work, a poetic masterpiece that will continue—with the exception of 32:1-5 and of some questionable passages—until the closing verses. In Hebrew, this poetry, as in English verse, follows unmistakable patterns, such as in line length and meter.

Second, the chapter appears to be intact, with the possible exception of verse 16. Many commentators believe it is misplaced, having originally followed verse 11.

Here is an outline of chapter 3.

I. Cursing the Day of His Birth (3:1-10)
II. Wishing for an Early Death (3:11-19)
III. Is Living Better Than Dying? (3:20-23)
IV. Crying Out in Pain (3:24-26)

The Message of Job 3

Lurking just below the surface of these verses is a question that must be addressed: Is your faith adequate to help you in times of trouble?

Job, at first, found his faith helping him quite nicely. His belief in God, a belief that had rewarded him in so many ways, was a safe retreat. When everything was first taken from him, he could utter the traditional pronouncement, "Blessed be the name of the LORD"(1:21).

The cursing and the intensifying anger we find in chapter 3, however, show us that his faith was ultimately inadequate. After seven days and nights of silence, when he waited for God's deliverance and it never came, he gave in to the seething emotions inside him. The lament that came from his mouth was, in the final analysis, a lament over the death of his old theology.

What happens if our pain does not go away? Indeed, what happens if, as in Job's case, it multiplies? It is obvious. Our certainties waver, our fervency wanes. If Job—blameless and upright (1:1)—stumbled, so will we.

The answer to the question posed by this chapter is: In the face of sustained pain, our faith will crumble. Our only hope is that out of the ruins a new faith will arise. Emerging from the other side of intense suffering, it will restore our confidence and enable us to live fully once more.

Job eventually reached such a new plateau: However, as the following chapters witness, it was a long and painful process. We, too, can find new strength, if we are willing to pay the price. The first step is acknowledging the limits of the faith we have today.

JOB 4–7

Introduction to These Chapters

This section begins with Eliphaz's response to what Job said in chapter 3. This reply inaugurates the first cycle of dialogues between Job and his comforters. In each cycle Eliphaz will converse first with Job, since he is the eldest friend. Conversations between Job and Bildad, then Zophar, will follow.

In chapter 3 Job, though expressing bewilderment and strong anger, restrains himself. He could lash out more vehemently, but he does not. It is as if he were testing the waters with his strong feelings.

Likewise, Eliphaz shows restraint in his first address. He is responding, in chapters 4 and 5, to Job's belief that his suffering is unjust and undeserved. Such a thought is contradictory to the major tenet agreed to by all three friends: God makes the wicked suffer and blesses the righteous with health and peace. Instead of harshly debating the sufferer, however, Eliphaz begins timidly and compassionately: "If one ventures a word with you, will you be offended?" (4:2). In addition, throughout his speech the friend never directly accuses Job of wrongdoing, and he ends by painting a happy picture of what Job might eventually enjoy.

Such courtesies cannot conceal Eliphaz's disagreement with Job's sentiments, however. The friend is concerned with doing two things in this speech. First, he defends the traditional belief of suffering being the punishment of a just God. He does this by offering what he believes to be certain undeniable theological facts. Second, to support these truths, he wants Job to recognize the authority by which he speaks: divine revelation (4:12-21) and experience/reason (4:8a; 5:27).

Job's response is predictable. He feels that his friends will argue and not console. This serves to deepen both his anger and his despair. He begins by doing something he was afraid to do in his earlier lament: directly blaming God (6:4). His anger then swells, first against his friends, then against his own life. Finally, he turns back to God, lashing out against the divine injustice.

In these chapters, then, we witness Job's worst fears being realized. His last hope of support—the three men who are with him when everyone else has fled—is shaken. It appears that they are not going to accept Job as he is, but will try to change him. Faced with this realization, Job now confronts an existence deprived of even the faintest flicker of light. Job is alone.

Here is an outline of chapters 4–7.

I. Eliphaz's First Speech (4:1–5:27)
   A. Courteous introduction (4:1-6)
   B. The wicked suffer (4:7-11)
   C. God's purity shows our impurity (4:12-21)
   D. God does not help the wicked (5:1-16)
   E. Be humble and trust God (5:17-27)
II. Job's Reply (6:1–7:21)
   A. Anger at God (6:1-13)
   B. Anger at his friends (6:14-30)
   C. Despair over his life (7:1-6)
   D. A blasphemous "prayer" (7:7-21)

The Message of Job 4–7

These chapters carry further the message of chapter 3. There we saw that in the face of sustained pain, our faith will crumble. Here the poet makes it more specific. As if to make sure we do not miss this point, he shows us that in the face of sustained pain, we will abandon our old way of praying.

Eliphaz does nothing more than reinforce the theology that is now meaningless to Job. The sufferer at first reacts angrily. Then, in chapter 7, he makes a last-ditch effort to regain his sanity. Humbly he begins a prayer (7:7). No sooner are the traditional words out of his mouth, however, than he abandons the attempt (7:11). They sound as hollow to him as the theology Eliphaz preaches—the theology Job once believed.

When we are at a crisis in our faith due to suffering, how do we pray? We first start, like Job, with the familiar. Perhaps we recite prayers we've memorized, such as the Lord's Prayer. Maybe we begin with comfortable phrases such as, "Dear Lord, please help me . . ." But how long does our tradition sustain us?

When our tradition disintegrates, we start praying in a different language. Instead of praising and beseeching, our prayers are filled with accusing. Why isn't God helping us?

Paradoxically, talking to God in this way is the ultimate expression of faith. It takes seriously the covenantal relationship we have with our Creator. When we honestly expose ourselves, we trust that God can hear us and then act for us.

JOB 8–10

Introduction to These Chapters

Eliphaz's speech (chapters 4–5) laid the foundation for the remaining discourses of the friends. In a sense, it serves as an overview of what we will hear them telling Job. All three will defend God's reputation of being just. They will do this by citing the suffering of the wicked and the prosperity of the blameless, the focal point of the traditional theology they espouse. These men are not clones of each other, though. The quirks of their individual personalities distinguish them. Contrasting Bildad and Eliphaz is a good example.

In chapter 8 Bildad makes his appearance. His discourse starkly contrasts with that of Eliphaz in both style and tone. The elder friend began courteously (4:2), then gently built his argument to the point where he thought Job could be nudged into repenting (5:27). Bildad dispenses with such civilities. He chastises and attempts to scare Job in his introduction, a six-verse "sermon." He then bullies Job by appealing to tradition (verses 8-10), before finally painting the traditional picture of the wicked's destruction. Instead of being a kindly teacher, he embodies a fiery preacher.

Unintentionally, these first two friends have become the classic police interrogation team. One is "nice" while the other is "mean." Bildad's white-hot anger at the sufferer's refusal to change allows him to assume such a role. His rage is so intense that he can only blurt out a few sentences before he must sit down: Eliphaz's speech covered two chapters while Bildad's fills only one.

Job's response to such fire and brimstone is easy to guess. If Eliphaz's tenderness did not quell the sufferer's rage at the Almighty, Bildad's bluntness will only serve to intensify it. Thus far Job has claimed that God is unjust solely in dealing with him. He has made accusations of being selected as God's target (7:20). In light of Bildad's harangue, Job takes yet another step toward blasphemy: God is not only unjust to him, but allows the wicked to control the earth (9:24). Job waves yet another red flag in front of his comforters.

Job prefaces this outburst, however, by making a profound theological point. Eliphaz has said that God's righteousness makes all people, by comparison, sinful (4:17). Job begins his address by drawing the logical conclusion: "How can a mortal be righteous" (9:2 NIV; NRSV, "just") "before God?" Since people have no claim whatsoever upon God, then humanity is at the Almighty's mercy. This realization will serve as the basis for a repeated plea throughout the book for an umpire (9:33) who will hold the divine power in check.

Here is an outline of chapters 8–10:

I. Bildad's First Speech (8:1-22)
   A. Chastisement of Job (8:1-2)
   B. God's justice regarding Job (8:3-7)
   C. God's punishment of the wicked (8:8-19)
   D. Job's only hope (8:20-22)
II. Job's Reply (9:1–10:22)
   A. God's overwhelming power (9:1-10)
   B. God's consequent injustice (9:11-35)
   C. Job's accusatory prayer (10:1-22)

The Message of Job 8–10

Job is traveling down a road leading him farther and farther from his theological home. He grew up with an all-powerful, all-knowing God. We have seen in these chapters that the sufferer has reached the point of rejecting such a God. *Rejecting* is actually too mild a term: Job is *rebelling* violently. Behind the epithets hurled at God in chapters 9–10 is Job's feeling that this Almighty Being can turn maliciously capricious.

This raises the question for us: What kind of a God do we look for to help us? Our initial wish may be for a deity Job used to be at home with—the "immortal, invisible, God only wise" type. Perhaps we will find, like Job, that a God totally absolute is, in some respects, incapable of giving us what we need.

What kind of God do we need, then? It is the God Job will find at the end of his journey. He is beginning to see a faint form when he desires an umpire (9:33). He wants to be able to talk face-to-face with

God. He wants to ask God questions and understand the answers. In other words, Job wants a God who is compassionately accessible.

When we endure a tragedy, only some of the pain is physical or emotional. The other part is spiritual. We ask our own "whys." "Why are you doing this to me, God?" "Why don't things make sense any more?" We do not hear any answers because our old God is gone and the new one is not yet clearly present. The fact that we cry, however, shows that we are in transition. Our suffering has caused us to leave home and embark upon a dangerous journey. We are afraid. But we are walking beside Job.

JOB 11–14

Introduction to These Chapters

The first speeches of the friends serve to introduce us to their personalities. While all three agree with the orthodox view of divine reward/punishment, they vary in how they try to persuade Job. Eliphaz boldly claims direct revelation, while Bildad appeals to tradition.

In this third friend's introductory speech, Zophar brandishes yet another weapon in the war to defeat Job's arrogance: knowledge. He refers to the "secrets of wisdom" (11:6), and mentions the "deep things of God" (11:7 NRSV; NIV, "the mysteries of God"). He closes his short address with a very logical if . . . then sermon (11:13-20).

Knowing a lot about things and little about people, Zophar bluntly and perhaps blindly tramples on Job's feelings. He sees Job's outcries only as a base for theological debate, callously calling them a "multitude of words" (11:2 NRSV; NIV, "all these words") and "babble"(11:3 NRSV; NIV, "idle talk"). He scolds Job by

saying that the sufferer deserves more than what God has delivered (11:6c). He discounts the horror his friend is enduring when he blithely tells him, "You will forget" (11:16). Zophar is totally incapable of understanding the depth of human suffering.

Job's response serves as a watershed point in the book. Reflecting its importance, it encompasses three chapters (12–14)—the longest speech in the dialogue section.

In this discourse, Job makes a two-part move. He first (chapters 12–13) breaks completely from his friends. It should be noted that in his response to Bildad, he did not lash out at his comforters. It was as if he still hoped they would turn from arguing to consoling. Given Zophar's stinging insensitivity, though, Job now realizes that they are as cold and immovable as granite.

The structure of chapters 12 and 13 reflects this sad realization. Both chapters share a framework that is unlike any other in terms of expressing pure anger and anguish:

- insult of friends (12:2-5; 13:1-2)

- assertion (12:6; 13:3)

- renewed insult of friends (12:7-12; 13:4-12)

- return to assertion (12:13-25; 13:13-27)

Job cannot contain his hurt. He is trying to get his ideas across, but his emotions get in the way. By his continual return to raging at his friends, he is severing all bonds with them.

Just as he turns away from the three men, in chapter 14 he turns toward God. He realizes that his only hope is with the Almighty, yet this deity is the cause of his suffering. Timidly—hesitantly—he alternates between talking to himself and addressing God:

- statement (verses 1-2)

- prayer (verses 3-6)

- statement (verses 7-12)

- prayer (verses 13-17)

- statement (verses 18-19a)

- accusation (verses 19b-20)

- statement (verses 21-22)

In his remaining speeches Job will continue speaking to his friends. But—with rare exception (19:21-22)—he will speak only to dismiss them. His struggle will be with God.

Here is an outline of the content of chapters 11–14:

I. Zophar's First Speech (11:1-20)
   A. Condemnation of Job (11:1-6)
   B. God's knowledge and justice (11:7-12)
   C. "If . . . then" sermon (11:13-20)
II. Job's Response (12:1–14:22)
   A. God's whimsical rule (12:1-25)
   B. Plea for confrontation with God (13:1-27)
   C. Lament and prayer (13:28–14:22)

The Message of Job 11–14

How does one talk to a sufferer? This is a relevant question, now that all three friends have had opportunities to address Job. Job's reply to the last comforter gives a sharp answer, forged from fire that grew hotter with each word he heard.

Do not defend God! The companions, insulted by Job's blasphemies, try to "justify" God's dealings with him. On a theological level, this is absurd: If God is all-powerful, why is human defense necessary? On a personal level, this is insulting: Job's feelings, and his value as a person, are degraded. If the men had kept alive their affection for Job, and had spoken from the compassion of their hearts instead of from the callousness of their brains, then the sufferer would not be alone in his pain.

But he is alone, and this raises for him—and for us—another question: How does one approach a mysterious God? Feeling forsaken by his friends, and feeling that God is hounding him, Job could have ended things after 13:12. Something within him refuses to yield, however.

That something is a distant hope that God is more loving and just than his friends. He refuses to believe that God is as he fears. With timidity and fright he dares to hope. Once he starts, the floodgates open. The faint wish for an arbiter, entertained in 9:33, he now expands into a gigantic scene; it is as if he is saying to himself, "What if I can confront God in a courtroom, and talk face-to-face with the Lord?" Carried away, he continues hoping: "What if God remembers me after I die, restores things the way they were, and allows me to live again?"

Certainly in our pain our friends—with the best of intentions—may nonetheless make our lives even more miserable. Confronted with this, dare to hope that God may break through and surprise you with the unexpected. Look at your situation and allow yourself to fantasize. Disregarding reality, what words would you like to hear? What things would you like to have happen? Whom would you like to see?

This in no way is "pie in the sky" daydreaming. You will still spend most of your time anxious and depressed. But allowing yourself to hope, even briefly, is not just healthy. It communicates to the shadowy God your special, personal needs. And that hope may be the vehicle by which the Lord will come to you.

JOB 15–17

Introduction to These Chapters

These chapters inaugurate the second cycle of discourses in Job.

This second set of conversations between Job and the three comforters contrasts starkly with the first. The difference may be summed up in one sentence: The two sides have given up on each other. Throughout the earlier chapters, each speaker wanted the other to change. The friends tried to persuade Job to confess his sins and repent. Job wanted his companions to stop giving him theology lectures and start showing compassion.

In the series of speeches beginning with chapter 15, there is a realization that neither side will budge. It would be more accurate to call these speeches "monologues" rather than conversations. The men are not concerned so much with listening to as with talking past each other.

Eliphaz's second speech is a good example of this practice of talking past each other. Gone are the courtesies opening his first words to Job (4:1–5:27). Gone are the gentle nudgings and the hopeful conclusion. In their place are a brutal attack on Job's character and a ponderous discourse on the fate of the wicked. There is no doubt in his mind that Job is now beyond help. He is a sinner who will never repent. Thus, the friend, who had been characterized as the most compassionate, turns to prattling callously the dogma of divine reward/punishment.

Job has already realized that his friends will be useful only as tormentors. His reply in chapters 16 and 17 reflects this revelation. Much as he did in his last address (chapters 12–14), he alternates between attacking them, on the one hand, and reflecting/praying, on the other. This switching back and forth makes his reply

to Eliphaz somewhat difficult to follow, since it is unclear to whom Job is speaking: to his friends, to himself, or to God.

This difficult structure reflects the rage he still directs at his friends, who he feels have betrayed him. It also reflects the chaos in Job's heart. He is buffeted by swirling emotions, making a neat, systematic speech impossible. Job is a despairing, confused man, and his sometimes befuddled words in chapters 16 and 17 demonstrate this.

The sufferer, though, has not totally given up. Throughout his earlier speeches he had expressed a vague hope. He wished for an arbiter (9:33) who would hold God in check. He also longed for a court date with God (13:3, 18-27). Similarly, in his speech here, he expresses the hope of having a witness in heaven who can testify to God regarding his character (16:19). Job's hope still rests in his belief in his innocence and in his confidence that God is acting unjustly.

In turning to critical considerations of these chapters, two verses seem out of place: 16:20 and 17:12. Both verses criticize the friends, and both abruptly appear in the middle of passages dealing with other matters. While some scholars judge them to have originally occurred elsewhere (possibly after 17:2), it is important to note, as seen above, that throughout this speech Job alternates his audience. Thus such verses could be seen as "asides," where he purposely interrupts his train of thought, looks at his friends, and lashes out at them.

Here is an outline of chapters 15–17.

I. Eliphaz's Second Speech (15:1-35)
   A. Insult of Job (15:1-6)
   B. Condemnation of Job's arrogance (15:7-16)
   C. The fate of the wicked (15:17-35)
II. Job's Reply (16:1–17:16)
   A. Outrage at his friends (16:1-6)

B. Outrage at God (16:7-14)
C. Despairing cry for hope
(16:15–17:5)
D. Concluding lament (17:6-16)

The Message of Job 15–17

These chapters give insight as to the effects of pain in our lives.

Suffering causes us to be angry. Although this may sound simplistic, it is important. Job unbridles his rage. Directed at both God and his friends, it provides a source of emotional energy. It drives him until he can posit hope in a divine witness.

Often we repress our natural feelings of anger. Perhaps by tapping those feelings we may find, like Job, strength to endure until we can hope again.

Suffering causes us to explore the nature of faith. The faith of Eliphaz and his companions insulates them from the reality of the world—as represented by the wretched Job. They have irrelevant answers for all relevant questions. Job's faith, on the other hand, challenges him to discard worn out views. Faith for him is a quest for a new vision of the Almighty.

We are faced with a decision. Will our faith insulate us from pain? Or will it challenge us to seek new answers that incorporate even senseless suffering?

Suffering causes us to see things more realistically. Eliphaz has no difficulty labeling the wicked. He also does not hesitate claiming that God always punishes them. He makes such declarations from a pain-free context. Job sees just the opposite. Having been cast as a sinner in the eyes of his friends, he knows that such labels can be deceptive. He also sees quite clearly that some of the most wicked of all people escape God's wrath.

Comfort makes us view things in a skewed way. When we run up against the hard, painful wall of suffering, though, reality confronts us.

JOB 18–19

Introduction to These Chapters

Bildad's first speech (chapter 8) to Job was biting. A fiery preacher by nature, this friend tried to persuade the sufferer through a "hellfire-and-brimstone" sermon.

As noted in the previous section, the second cycle of speeches is characterized by each side realizing that the other will not change. They consequently give up on each other. In Bildad's second speech (chapter 18), he retires his preaching role: Job will never repent.

Bildad, freed from needing to help Job see the light, now expresses himself freely. What he attempts is simple: Put Job in his proper place. He criticizes the sufferer for questioning the wisdom of him and the other two (18:2-4). He then fills the rest of his speech with several images descriptive of the fate of the wicked. These images, though, are but slightly veiled references to Job. His anger burns deeply, and one can almost detect glee in his voice as he paints the picture of destruction.

Bildad shows himself as a pedantic and bitter man. There is little new in the address. On the contrary, in addition to harping again on the theme of divine punishment, he uses phrases similar to those in his first speech. He also cuts the speech short, as he did his first one. His anger, or the fact that he runs out of images, contributes to this.

Job's response (chapter 19) is both predictable and surprising. He responds to Bildad's insults with insults of his own (verses 2-3 and 28-29). He also continues indexing how God is pursuing him, a theme in his previous speech (16:11-14).

What is new in this discourse is that in the middle of it he collapses. His anger at his friends and at God had been enough to drive him in his defiance. But now we hear,

"Have pity on me, have pity on me, O you my friends" (19:21a).

As he recalls how all have forsaken him, it is simply too much. His pride breaks, and he beseeches the three men—the ones who are his fiercest tormentors. He still needs human company.

It is important to note that as he tries to persuade them, he once again voices a heavenly hope. He expresses confidence in an emerging Redeemer, or vindicator (19:25). Earlier, he had hoped for an arbiter (9:33) who could restrain God's power. He next dreamed of a witness who could vouch for him (16:19). Now, he looks toward a Redeemer who can administer justice.

In terms of text-critical consideration, Bildad's speech is fairly clear, while Job's contains murky passages: Verses 4, 17, 20, and 26-27 are very difficult to understand. Their structure, along with their phrases, is so complicated that an accurate interpretation is impossible. They reflect the mind of a depressed and anxious man.

Here is an outline of chapters 18–19.

I. Bildad's Second Speech (18:1-21)
 A. Rebuke of Job (18:1-4)
 B. The fate of the wicked (18:5-21)
II. Job's Reply (19:1-29)
 A. Rebuke of friends (19:1-6)
 B. Lament of God's injustice (19:7-20)
 C. Expression of hope (19:21-29)

The Message of Job 18–19

In contrast to the companions, Job is dynamic. Bildad spews out his anger, uses hackneyed phrases, and sits down. Job, on the other hand, explores his feelings and his faith. He talks not in traditional phrases but in new expressions. He can flash fire, or he can cry for mercy. His hurt has pushed him into an openness that makes him more fully human than his friends.

Job, near death, is more alive than his comfortable companions.

We are the most genuinely spiritual when we feel we have nothing to lose. Seeking security so much that we confront present suffering with old beliefs turns us into stiff, cardboard, Bildad-like people. It is liberating knowing that only something new will save us. We filter things through new feelings, radical thoughts, emerging beliefs. Like Job we appear jumbled, confused, and inconsistent. But only then can we appreciate and appropriate God's grace.

There is a constant in our search for help: We cannot escape our need for human companionship. It should not be surprising to see Job beseeching men who respond to him with the compassion of a wall. Loneliness multiplies suffering. Silence makes us focus upon ourselves. Perhaps tormentors like Job's companions—and like friends who do not understand our situations—provide inadvertent help simply by drawing us out of private musings. Even uncompassionate companionship is better than none.

Similarly, more important than even companionship is maintaining integrity. In any crisis, there are things we call our own: feelings, beliefs, thoughts, actions. Open to our own reflection, they are still part of us. To diminish or abandon any of them cuts us off from the one thing that anchors us, namely, our sense of who we are.

JOB 20–21

Introduction to These Chapters

Zophar painted an academic portrait of himself in his first speech (chapter 11). It was a caricature of a highly intellectual man with little ability to understand or deal with human emotions. His second speech (chapter 20) deepens this picture's lines and colors.

Job has just made a final, impassioned appeal to his friends. Dropping his pride, he asked them for mercy (19:21). For Zophar to respond in the manner Job wants, he needs to know the language of compassion. He answers, instead, in a dialect well known to him: "My thoughts urge me" (NRSV; NIV, "prompt me") "to answer . . ." (20:2a); "a spirit beyond my understanding answers me" (20:3b NRSV; NIV, "my understanding inspires me to reply").

His words come from the mind, a mind severed from the heart.

Zophar has not heard Job's appeal. He has, rather, been thinking of Job's earlier speech (chapters 16–17), where the sufferer has accused God of injustice. His speech, thus, is an intellectual response concerned—once again—with defending God's honor.

In a move worthy of his academic skill, he subtly tags a new twist onto the doctrine of divine punishment. Instead of merely proclaiming the horrible fate of the wicked, he suggests that such sinners may actually enjoy a somewhat nice life. It may thus appear that they go unpunished, as Job noted in 12:14-24. However, they will encounter God's justice, and their fate will be a nightmare: "Though his pride reaches to the heavens, and his head reaches to the clouds, he will perish forever like his own dung" (20:6-7a NIV).

Although throughout his speech there are veiled references to Job, Zophar does not lash out at his hurting friend. Gone is the introductory insult characteristic of earlier speeches. Zophar is giving a cool, restrained, dispassionate response.

Job's answer (chapter 21), at first, also appears restrained. This is deceiving. His speech drips with sarcasm, barely covering his deep hurt at his friends' callousness. For example, there is no overt insult of his friends at the beginning of the speech. He

says, "Listen carefully to my words, and let this be your consolation" (21:2).

The message is clear: "You can console me best by simply being quiet and listening!"

Job spends most of his speech directly contradicting Zophar's defense of God's justice. He has little difficulty citing examples where there is no punishment befitting a wicked person's deeds. The phrases he uses, though, are taken from verses in Psalms and Proverbs that depict the punishment of the wicked: 21:13 (Psalm 31:17); 21:14 (Psalm 25:2); 21:15 (Psalm 2:11-12); 21:17a (Proverbs 24:20); 21:17b (Proverbs 24:16); 21:18 (Psalm 1:4). Twisting these phrases of his friends, phrases rooted in Wisdom Literature, shows the utter disgust Job has for those who try to justify God at all costs.

Here is an outline of chapters 20–21.

I. Zophar's Second Speech (20:1-29)
   A. Introductory remarks (20:1-3)
   B. Brief prosperity of the wicked (20:4-29)
II. Job's Reply (21:1-34)
   A. Introductory remarks (21:1-6)
   B. Long-term prosperity of the wicked (21:7-34)

The Message of Job 20–21

It is impossible not to be impressed by the sustained coldness of Job's companions. Zophar must work at ignoring the sufferer's earlier pleas for compassion. To respond to those pleas with a cold theological discourse betrays a basic fact about how a comfortable friend may relate to a suffering one.

At the deepest level, a comforter prefers to stay on safe ground when relating to a sufferer. Zophar grasps at straws when he suggests the "delayed" punishment of the wicked. It makes little sense, as Job points out. It keeps him, though, from being swept into his friend's quagmire. Likewise, a person relating to you in your pain may very well, eventually, say absurd things. He or she will believe them. Those beliefs help preserve the person's sanity.

The statements made by the comforter may appear as "mockings" to the sufferer. Zophar's comments, at best, are just insensitive. They are not directly insulting to Job. Yet, the sufferer hears them as ridicule (21:3). Job knows the real issue: "Will you leave your comfortable world and sit with me awhile?" Zophar's intellectualism is absurd to Job. It says that Zophar does not take Job's situation seriously. Even if he did, he would not—could not— forsake his beliefs to join the sufferer. The whole scene is repugnant.

When you encounter pain, you have enough to worry about. Friends should realize that their attempts to cheer you up, to help you see the light, will not be heard rationally by you. The comments will be filtered through ears that want to hear the footsteps of one daring to venture defenselessly onto your turf.

The beginning of compassion is when the comforter believes he or she can learn from the sufferer. Job sees things around him clearly. His simple insights concerning the escape of the wicked from divine punishment are part of the vision that will eventually lead to a closer, more honest relationship with the Almighty. If Zophar had listened to them, he, too, might have gained a stronger and more realistic faith.

The one approaching you in your pain should not be frightened. Rather, he or she should be willing to listen to your story, your view. By listening instead of lecturing, you may both discover the new face of God.

JOB 22–24

Introduction to These Chapters

Each of the first two series of speeches had its own motif. It is impossible, however, to generalize about the speeches found in the third group (chapters 22–27). The conversations in this cycle are fragmented, presenting many difficulties.

Eliphaz's third speech and Job's reply, chapters 22–24, are the most nearly complete that will be found. If the rest of the conversations in the third cycle were similar to this interchange, a tendency would surface. In trying to prove their belief in divine reward of the righteous and punishment of the wicked, the friends grow increasingly absurd and contradictory. Job, meanwhile, continues expressing his thoughts and feelings straightforwardly.

Eliphaz sermonizes in chapter 22, a style he used in his first address (chapters 4–5). Whereas in that earlier homily he was poised and self-confident, though, this last speech reveals no such composure. His rapidly unraveling argument reflects this.

He begins by baldly asserting God's independence from persons—no one can claim anything from the Almighty (verses 2-4). He asserts this so strongly that his later exhortation to Job to agree with God and accept instruction (verses 21-22) makes little sense. How can a good person honestly expect anything from a God who is so untouchable? Eliphaz's defense of God's mysterious ways blows up in his face.

Perhaps the most dramatic—and absurd—example of the friend's failing logic is his description of Job's sins (verses 6-9). Eliphaz is picking up on Zophar's traditional definition of wickedness in terms of social and economic oppression (20:19). But he carries this to a ridiculous extreme in claiming that Job has sinned by hurting his neighbors. This has absolutely no basis in fact; indeed, Eliphaz himself had earlier praised Job's concern for the weak (4:3-4). It appears as if this friend is searching for anything that can make Job repent.

The overall impression is that Eliphaz appears frantic, grasping at straws. He may actually be preaching this last sermon more to himself than to Job. In the face of confused reasoning, the sheer intensity of his words may comfort him.

Job seems remarkably undisturbed by his friend's deterioration. Indeed, he ignores Eliphaz's speech altogether. In chapter 23 he alternates between lamenting and hoping, similar to his speech in chapter 14. This gives way, in 24:1-17, to complaining about God's cold, unjust ways. Job, realizing that nothing his friends are going to say will surprise him, is more concerned with faithfully expressing the cries of his soul. It is as if Eliphaz had never spoken.

Here is an outline of chapters 22–24.

I. Eliphaz's Third Speech (22:1-30)
   A. Rebuke of Job (22:1-9)
   B. Punishment of the wicked (22:10-20)
   C. Exhortation to Job (22:21-30)
II. Job's Response (23:1–24:17)
   A. Hope for a court date with God (23:1-17)
   B. Reflection on God's injustice (24:1-17)
III. Friend's Fragment (24:18-25)

The Message of Job 22–24

Eliphaz's blustery speech is humorous. His arguments, stretched as they are to their absurd limits, provide comic relief. But through that humor the poet subtly slices apart the three friends' traditional theology.

Trying to understand human pain by focusing on God's raw power is absurd. Eliphaz elevates the Almighty to such a point that God appears mysteriously whimsical. No human can affect God one way or the other. God causes everything, the bad as well as the good; the only thing humans can do is merely accept it. God must have a reason behind causing suffering, a reason known only to God.

In giving this simplistic solution, the pillar supporting faith crumbles. We need to know that somehow God is profoundly affected by us. We need to feel that we can, in some fashion, change God's thinking and acting. Without the assurance that we are taken seriously by God, our rituals become meaningless and our praying becomes prattling.

Part of our hurt in suffering is believing that God does not care. Job cannot sustain hope because of the fear in the back of his mind that God is distanced from human problems. That is why he perpetually falls into pits of depression. Similarly, in confronting pain we periodically feel as if God has turned a cold heart to us. We don't seem important. Our problems and hurts are meaningless to the Almighty. If only God cared, we wouldn't hurt so much.

Part of our hope lies in trusting that there can be a new, warm relationship with God. Job never gives up. His passion for God sustains him, giving him brief respites from despair: "Oh, that I knew where I might find him, that I might come even to his dwelling!" Even though despair outweighs hope ten to one in Job, the fire of his brief, passionate surges will ultimately cause a whirlwind encounter with the Lord.

Suffering is suffocating. It can appear that there is no way out. Allowing yourself to believe that there is one who cares deeply for you may be hard to do. But in such times of hoping, you give yourself room to breathe. And you are better prepared when the Lord comes to you in your own whirlwind.

JOB 25–27

Introduction to These Chapters

These chapters report the last interchange between Job and the three friends. A poem about wisdom (chapter 28) follows it, before Job finally delivers a long summary monologue (chapters 29–31).

This section is extremely difficult to read because of abrupt, unannounced changes in speakers. Also contributing to the difficulty is the presence of several corrupt and unclear verses. One thing, however, seems evident. Since this is the last exchange between Job and the friends, both sides state things in blunt, emotion-laden terms.

The themes of the friends, for example, are nothing new. They underscore human weakness/divine greatness (25:2-6; 26:5-14), and they rehash the doctrine of the just punishment of the wicked (27:7-23). Their words, though, are concise, with fewer—yet more concrete—images. Bildad illustrates this when he describes human frailty by parodying Psalm 8:4: "How much less a mortal, who is a maggot, and a human being, who is a worm" (25:6).

For his part, Job spits heavy sarcasm at the "comfort" his friends have given him (26:2-4). He then defiantly concludes by swearing—in God's name—that he will never agree with what his companions have professed (27:2-6). Job says, "I hold fast my righteousness, and will not let it go; my heart does not reproach me for any of my days" (27:6).

The speeches in these chapters seem somewhat jumbled. Perhaps the verses were accidentally misplaced during book compilation or perhaps a pious editor tried to make Job appear more traditional by attributing to him some of his friends' orthodox theology.

Here is an outline of chapters 25–27.
I. Bildad's Third Speech (25:1-6)
II. Job's Response to Bildad (26:1-4)
III. Friend's Fragment (26:5-14)
IV. Job's Fragment (27:1-6)
V. Friend's Fragment (27:7-23)

The Message of Job 25–27

Progressively, the friends have grown more abrasive as they have attempted to justify their theology. Bildad's lofty depiction of God, and the accompanying degradation of humanity, is a poignant example. The intent is to argue, not to comfort.

Such insensitivity underscores the fact that the sufferer needs to know that he or she is important. Job wants to be respected for his thoughts and struggles. Behind this is his need to know that somehow his pain really does make a difference, that it does matter to somebody. To die slowly, believing that such death is natural and inconsequential, is perhaps worse than the physical pain.

The sufferer faces life sarcastically when he or she is degraded. Sarcasm allows a person to voice anger while laughing at the absurdity of the world. Reading Job's hot, sarcastic reply to Bildad, one can almost sense Job's bitter laughter. Such laughter is his way of putting his companions in their place. It is his way of saying that he does not deserve the harsh treatment inflicted upon him.

Behind the sarcasm is an affirmation of *integrity*. His friends' constant debating does not soften Job. On the contrary, it makes him see his own situation more clearly. He does not have the answers as to why he is suffering. He is only sure that he has done nothing to warrant it. This surety grows in him and gives rise to his powerful proclamation of innocence in 27:2-6.

Such integrity is perhaps our only light while going through the darkest night. It takes strength to say, with Job, "Until I die, I will not put away my integrity from me" (27:5b NRSV; NIV, "I will not deny . . ."). In the very act of saying that, though, we have given God an open invitation.

JOB 28

Introduction to This Chapter

Chapter 28, upon first reading, seems out of place. It completely interrupts the drama that has been unfolding in the prior twenty-seven chapters. It does not advance the dialogue between Job and his friends, nor does it promote Job's summary speech that follows (chapters 29–31).

The poet probably intended it this way, however. He has inserted an "aside," a brief rest from the intense, heated dialogue.

This intermission takes the form of a beautifully mysterious twenty-eight–verse poem reflecting on wisdom. Seeking wisdom refers to seeking to understand the mysteries of the world. Because of the problem of unexplained suffering, this takes a special twist in the book of Job. Here wisdom refers to understanding God's interaction with humans and discerning our proper response.

The poet, in chapter 28, takes an extremely pessimistic view regarding this subject. Job's friends have appeared foolish in their clumsy attempts at explaining, in traditional theological terms, Job's suffering. The poet explains their buffoonery. After praising human ingenuity in the opening verses, he asks if humans can also be ingenious in understanding life's perplexities (that is, pain). The poet answers with an emphatic no: "Mortals do

not know the way to it" (NRSV; NIV, "comprehend its worth") "and it is not found in the land of the living" (28:13).

Such a statement serves to let us know—if we have not already guessed—where the poet stands in the debate between Job and the three men. The friends, thinking they are wise, are theologically bankrupt. Job, though, is seeking the source of wisdom: God. "God understands the way to it [wisdom], and he knows its place" (28:23 NRSV; NIV, "he alone knows where it dwells").

Because he does not have answers, and because he is seeking to ask God questions, Job is actually the wise man!

It is important to make two additional observations. First, this chapter reflects the international flavor of the book, and can best be understood against the backdrop of the entire ancient Middle Eastern world. In several places (see 3:8; 7:12; 26:12-13) the poet alludes to myths and legends that originated in lands outside Palestine. Now, in chapter 28, he refers to mining technology and materials alien to Hebrew culture. Silver, gold, copper, and sapphires, for example, were found in other places in Mesopotamia—such as in the mines of Egypt.

Second, this poem should not be viewed as part of a speech by Job. The character of these verses is cool, restrained, dispassionate. Job's speeches, on the other hand, soar to the heights of hope or drop to the depths of despair; they brim with emotion. Moreover, even though the sentiments of chapter 28 are not alien to Job's views, they are not the same, either. Indeed, the chapter contains striking similarities to the Lord's speeches from the whirlwind (chapters 38–41). It is best, all things considered, to view chapter 28 as a direct statement to us by the poet. It is the only place in the book where we can hear his words directly.

Here is an outline of chapter 28.

I. Human Ingenuity Regarding Treasures (28:1-11)
II. Human Limitations Regarding Wisdom (28:12-22)
III. God's Supremacy (28:23-28)

The Message of Job 28

What is wisdom for us? This chapter reveals that it is not something that can be attained. It is not arriving at answers, as Job's friends vainly attempted. Rather, it is an ongoing process of asking questions. These are questions at the jagged edge of our faith. They are the queries that cannot be resolved, that agitate us and perhaps make us uncomfortable with our religious certainties. "How can I relate to God when nothing makes sense anymore?" "Where can I find God when the world looks so cold and lonely?" "How can I believe in God when there doesn't appear to be any future for me?"

Accept your limitations. Doubtless the ancient wise men thought they could discover anything if they sufficiently contemplated the world around them through the eyes of philosophy. The image of miners seeking treasures may have been symbolic of this. Our technology seduces us into a similar line of thought. All we need is the right data for the computer. Both the ancient and modern minds are wrong. We are vulnerable to life experiences that will make us question our answers and force us to ask unanswerable questions. To acknowledge this limitation opens us to life in a new way.

Allow the answers to come from God. Atheists are people who confront life-wrenching questions and respond that God cannot exist. Job-like people encounter the same questions and affirm that answers rest ultimately with the Creator. Those answers are not given in trite, simplistic phrases.

Rather, they bypass the mind. The Spirit touches our spirits. Hearts discover the Presence that produces an unexplainable calm.

JOB 29–31

Introduction to These Chapters

God is on trial for alleged abuse of power, such as in causing the innocent to suffer and allowing the wicked to go free. Job is the prosecuting attorney; his speech in chapter 3 is the opening statement by the prosecution. God's defense attorneys are Job's three friends. With the exception of the preceding chapter, the book of Job has so far occupied itself with presenting arguments between these two sides.

Completing this analogy, chapters 29–31 are the closing statements for the prosecution. Like a skilled lawyer making a final speech before a jury, Job—in carefully summarizing his argument—deftly laces emotion with reason.

He presses two points. First, God has callously and maliciously abused him. In chapter 29 he paints a beautiful, almost idyllic picture of the intimate relationship the Lord and Job once shared. In the following chapter he then shows how, without any provocation whatsoever, God turned on him. This same God changed into an enemy. Reading these two passages, one is touched by Job's deep hurt at this betrayal by God, his closest friend.

Second, Job is careful to prove, beyond any shadow of doubt, that he has done nothing to cause this vicious treatment. It was mentioned in the prose section (1:1-5) that Job was vigilant in his piety, careful never to sin. Throughout his debate with his friends, furthermore, he claimed innocence (see 23:1-7; 27:5-6). Now, in chapter 31, he goes one step further. Claiming to have led a spotless life, he meticulously—and somewhat tediously—reviews several different ways of sinning. He states unequivocally that he is blameless in each respect.

This speech closes the dialogue section of the book. Following Elihu's discourses (chapters 32–37), Job's closing arguments will be answered by God.

Here is an outline of chapters 29–31.

I. Job's Past Happiness (29:1-25)
II. Job's Present Suffering (30:1-31)
III. Job's Oath of Innocence (31:1-34)
IV. Job's Challenge to God (31:35-37)
V. Renewal of Job's Innocence (31:38-40)

The Message of Job 29–31

Living "the good life" does not mean God is blessing us. Job, in recalling his happy past, equates God's friendship with status in society and protection from harm. Similarly, when we find things happily prosperous, we consider such fortune a nice sign from God.

Because Job encounters suffering, though, does not mean that God has abandoned him. On the contrary, it is precisely Job's righteousness that brings on his pain. Likewise, losing what once was fulfilling to us does not mean we have lost favor with God. Rather, it means that our relationship with the Lord is entering a new phase, a phase of challenge and perhaps growth.

Certainty of our righteousness enables us to confront suffering. The exhaustiveness of chapter 31 shows how important this is for Job. Knowing that he has done nothing to bring on his pain is vital to him. Once he is assured of that, he opens his heart to God, talking to the Almighty in honest, angry, blunt terms.

We need not be as exhaustive as Job. Christ has shown us the reality of grace. Knowing we are forgiven frees us to talk to God openly. The first thing we can ask is, "God, if I have not done anything to deserve this pain, then why am I seemingly being punished?"

Getting God's attention opens the door for God's entrance. Job knocks loudly when he lays down his challenge for a court date. As seen in the closing chapters of the book, this draws the Lord into a whirlwind appearance.

How do we get God's attention? Perhaps by crying over the injustice of a situation. Perhaps by whispering prayers of angry desperation in the middle of the night. Perhaps by daring God as boldly as Job does.

JOB 32–34

Introduction to These Chapters

The section of Job covered by chapters 32–37 surprises us. It is natural to assume that, following Job's fiery challenge to God in chapter 31, we would find the Lord's reply. That response is delayed, however. Instead, a brash young man named Elihu explodes upon the scene.

His appearance is explained in chapter 32. He is the youngest of the men with Job, so it is proper that he speak last. The reason he speaks at all is that Job's friends have done such a bad job in dealing with the sufferer. Job is still proclaiming his righteousness, so it is up to Elihu to set him straight.

If one word describes his character, it is *arrogance*. To him, things are right or wrong, cut and dried. Consequently, filled with the angry idealism of youth, he spits out sentences in rapid, machine gun–like fashion. He is confident that if Job and the three friends are sufficiently bombarded by his insights, then things will be resolved.

Such haughtiness broods just under the surface of his two opening speeches, chapters 33 and 34. He turns first to Job (chapter 33). In a condescending manner, he tells Job the error of his ways: God is speaking to the sufferer through the suffering, so Job should be quiet and listen. He next turns to the three friends (chapter 34). In an equally condescending tone, he criticizes their inability to silence Job. He also preaches a homily to them concerning God's unfathomable justice—as if they had never heard of it.

The other side of arrogance is anger, and it is possible to see Elihu's righteous indignation building to a boiling point in the short span of these two speeches. He addresses Job courteously enough in the opening verses of chapter 33. However, by the end of his second address his temper has gotten the best of him. Talking to the friends, he states: "Would that Job were tried to the limit, because his answers are those of the wicked!" (34:36). Job's three companions never gave him a drop of comfort. Elihu will give even less.

Most scholars think that these chapters were penned by someone other than the poet who wrote the rest of the book. There are many reasons for this. One has already been seen, namely, that the Elihu section seems to intrude upon the action already taking place. Another factor is that the language in these chapters is often different from the rest of Job. Terms in Aramean, a dialect similar to Hebrew, punctuate this fourth friend's addresses. Perhaps most convincing of all, Elihu is never mentioned elsewhere in Job. He is conspicuously absent when the others are introduced (2:11). He is also omitted in the epilogue (42:7-9), when Job's friends are ordered to repent.

It is probably best to see the character of Elihu as an attempt by later generations to answer Job's blasphemies. Elihu is the spokesman for Jewish orthodoxy, the view upholding the doctrine of divine rewarding

of the good and punishing of the bad.

Here is an outline of chapters 32–34.

I. Introduction of Elihu (32:1-5)
II. Elihu's Poetic Introduction (32:6-22)
III. Elihu's First Speech (33:1-33)
    A. Invitation to Job (33:1-7)
    B. Job's sin (33:8-11)
    C. God's saving actions (33:12-30)
    D. Admonition to Job (33:31-33)
IV. Elihu's Second Speech (34:1-37)
    A. Job's arrogance (34:1-9)
    B. God's impartiality (34:10-30)
    C. Condemnation of Job (34:31-37)

The Message of Job 32–34

To experience salvation, we need a mediator between God and ourselves. Such a being not only speaks to God on our behalf, which is Job's view. This mediator also speaks to us on behalf of God. Just as God discovers us anew through the words of the mediator, so do we discover God and the divine mandates for our lives.

Salvation means making changes in our lives. To be forgiven does not mean sitting back and enjoying free grace. The experience of salvation comes with a price tag. It means hearing God's commands for doing things differently in our lives, and then carrying out those changes. We hear the mediator's words to us in different ways. Elihu suggests that such words may come to us through dreams or through suffering (33:14-22). Other avenues may be meditation, prayer, or Scripture reading. However, without one essential ingredient, all these methods leave things open to a subjective interpretation by the individual. A person must seek the counsel of other persons who have heard the mediator's voice.

We should be careful if we tell someone else "the way it is." Elihu comes off as an angry adolescent. Intervening in a situation where a person is behaving destructively requires sensitivity. To intervene with Elihu's spirit may accentuate destructiveness.

God does not need defending! This is a recurring message in Job, but it must be emphasized again in turning to Elihu. His address to Job's friends in chapter 34 stems from his perception that God has been insulted by their inability to silence the sufferer. But does the angry arrogance of an Elihu make God appear any better?

JOB 35–37

Introduction to These Chapters

Elihu's earlier words, as seen in Part 13, were more or less introductory. They afforded us a glimpse into the heart of this angry, self-righteous man. They also afforded Elihu an opportunity to criticize Job and Job's friends.

In turning to his final two speeches (35:1-16; 36:1–37:24), Elihu appears to be purposely assuming the title "God's lawyer." He seems conscious (35:14) of Job's long speech (chapters 29–31), which summarized the sufferer's case against God and challenged the Almighty to appear in court. Accordingly, he claims that he still has something to say on God's behalf (36:2). That something is his own summary speech, where he tries to state God's case in such a way that there can be no doubt of the Lord's vindication.

He believes he can seal victory by silencing Job. He employs a two-pronged strategy. First, he beats down Job by pounding him with assertions of God's overwhelming power and God's overwhelming detachment from human dependency (chapter 35). Having thus shown Job that he has no claim on God's attention, Elihu launches into the second strategic part (chapters 36–37). Here he painstakingly shows Job how God is the great teacher. Everything that happens in history and in nature has behind it some lesson God is trying to impart. The best Job can do is stop rebelling against God and start listening to what the Lord is saying.

In this defense of the deity, Elihu says little that is new. The theme of God's transcending otherness has been played before (4:17-21; 11:7-12), as has the concept of God causing suffering so that people may learn (5:17-18). The manner in which he preaches, though, is unique. He carefully examines things and forms convincing arguments. In chapters 36 and 37, for example, he exhaustively looks at nature, extracting specific lessons that God is imparting. Such a style reflects his self-perception: He indeed is the Lord's articulate attorney.

Compared to his earlier speeches, his addresses here exhibit less self-consciousness and more self-confidence. He is not apologizing for his entrance, nor is he needing to assert or explain his authority. Although the arrogance remains (see 36:2-4), it is greatly diminished. Elihu is gradually forgetting himself as he speaks, with the result being a final discourse that is not only powerful but also hauntingly beautiful.

Here is an outline of Job 35–37.
I. Elihu's Third Speech (35:1-16)
   A. Definition of Job's sin (35:1-4)
   B. God's independence from humanity (35:5-13)
   C. Condemnation of Job (35:14-16)
II. Elihu's Fourth Speech (36:1–37:24)
   A. Arrogant introduction (36:1-4)
   B. God teaches us through pain (36:5-25)
   C. God teaches us through nature (36:26–37:22)
   D. Concluding praise and warning (37:23-24)

The Message of Job 35–37

These speeches raise two immediate questions. The answers to them show the deep rift between the orthodox Elihu and the suffering, exploring Job.

Does God control nature and history with a teaching hand? Elihu's response is an emphatic Yes! There is no doubt in his mind that everything that happens to people—from a chariot accident to an earthquake to a war—is carefully orchestrated by the teaching God. Suffering is thus easy to explain. God gives it to us purposely; we should patiently bear it, searching for the moral behind it.

Job is not so sure. He has questioned why things happen. His conclusion is that there can be no justifiable reason for many of the unfair happenings around him. He has accused God of insensitivity. He is on the verge of believing that God relates to creation in a manner different from the all-powerful, cut-and-dried view espoused by Elihu.

Does God operate within an airtight legal system? Once again, Elihu answers with a strenuous affirmation. God holds the scales. If people do not toe the line precisely, they are punished severely. Even when sinners cry out for help, God turns a deaf ear; if they had first been penitent, they would have earned God's favor (35:9-13).

Job refuses to believe this. God cannot wear a blindfold while holding the scales. Human pain must take priority over impartial laws. A suffering creation must sway the Lord so as to bend those divine mandates. This is, after all, part of Job's reasoning behind doing something as fantastic as challenging God to court.

JOB 38–39

Introduction to These Chapters

"Then the LORD answered Job out of the whirlwind" (38:1). With this introduction,

God steps into the drama. The Lord will make two speeches, the first of which appears in these chapters.

This divine appearance is both surprising and humorous. Picture Job's righteous friends. Everything they believe rules out such a phenomenon. For Elihu especially (chapters 32–37), such an appearance is incomprehensible. In his thinking, if God were to appear to anyone, it should be to himself, the righteous one—not to the blaspheming Job. But a whirling dust storm arises, and out of it blasts the divine voice—directed to a man covered with sores, wishing for death.

The utterances from the storm seem harsh at first. Earlier, the sufferer had hurled invectives and challenges at God. It is unthinkable, then, that placid words would flow from the Lord's lips when the whirlwind finally stirs. The rage of the exploding dust symbolizes the turbulent feelings of the Almighty.

At the eye of the storm is the divine need to turn the tables on Job. Job has dared to question God. Now it is God's turn to question Job. The Lord's speech in chapters 38 and 39 is, for the most part, a series of rhetorical inquiries. The subject is creation/nature. Where was Job when God created the earth? And where is Job when God cares for the beasts of the wilderness? Such questions are not meant to be answered. They are meant to build in Job a healthy respect for the Lord.

It is a mistake, however, to let such abrasiveness overshadow the main point of the whirlwind: the healing of the fragmented, wounded relationship between Job and God. A lover cannot easily stay away from the beloved; if that happens, the love is not true. Similarly, God cannot stay away from this special person. The suffering and loneliness—of God as well as of Job—have been long enough. It is time to deal with the hurtful words and painful experiences. It is time to move on in their relationship—to a deeper, more intimate plateau.

In reading God's two addresses, one precaution must be observed. The reader should not look through the lenses of twenty-first–century logic. If we were writing the book, then the Lord's speeches would deal with Job's earlier questions. We find, though, no such replies. Consequently, some readers reject chapters 38–41 (partially or totally) as not authentic.

Dismissal on such grounds does injustice to the poet's work. He thought in categories different from ours. He also wrote from a faith-centered, relationship-oriented perspective. It is important to remember that the purpose of the whirlwind speeches is to restore a relationship. They are not delivered by a professor. They are spoken by a lover.

Here is an outline of these chapters.

I. God's Command to Job (38:1-3)
II. God's Control of Creation (38:4-15)
III. God's Knowledge of Creation (38:16-38)
IV. God's Care for Creatures (38:39–39:30)

The Message of Job 38–39

God is a person, not an idea. An idea does not speak from a whirlwind. An idea does not have a proper name. An idea cannot hold a conversation.

In reading the book of Job, it is easy to forget this. Given our intellectual bent, we look for philosophical solutions to suffering. Deducing trite formulas ("God gives us pain to teach us a lesson"), we ignore the real message of the biblical writer. The answer to the problem of pain is found not in an idea but in a person. That person is the Lord, who confronts us with the very real possibility of a life-changing relationship.

A relationship with this person involves respect as well as intimacy. Sometimes, in a love relationship, one person takes the other for granted. That individual loses sight of the special nature of the beloved. At such a time, the blinded person must regain the feeling of awe, of respect, for the other.

This is Job's problem. His openness with God shows that he has little difficulty being intimate. What he needs, however, is to recover respect. God's speech is nothing less than an attempt to make him realize this. To take God for granted is death. To express all sorts of feelings to God, while respecting God's "otherness"—that is life.

Appreciation of creation leads to a greater respect for God. One of the curses of our modern mindset is the ease with which we lose our wonder of the world around us. Science and technology explain things away and give us tools for mastery. Genes and computer chips make us gods.

Such an attitude was not only unthinkable to the poet—it was idolatrous. The author of Job was in faithful, simple awe of the world we so easily dismiss. Everything seemed fresh and mysterious. Everything pointed to the greatness of God. It is little wonder that he chose this theme for the speech intended to instill respect in the irreverent Job.

Listening to these verses of praise penned by the poet may help call us back to our root relationship. Rekindling childlike awe of a God who carefully calls the sun to rise each day is essential. It is the beginning of appreciating the God who makes the sun rise on the unjust as well as the just. It is the beginning of respecting the God who sent Jesus.

JOB 40–41

Introduction to These Chapters

The authenticity of this section, containing the Lord's second speech, has been questioned by some. One reason for this is the feeling that the second address is unnecessary. Job is silenced at the end of the Lord's first confrontation with him. Since the blasphemer is quieted, why should there be another speech?

This question misses the point. God's intent is not to force a strangled, silent submission. Rather, the Lord wants to renew a healthy, more intimate relationship. The first speech obviously does not do this (see Job's response in 40:4-5), so God tries again. The address found in these two chapters thus is vital.

At first glance, the strategy appears similar to that found in chapters 38–39. God makes forceful statements and asks questions to which Job cannot respond. It is as if God is trying to elicit a response of humiliation from the sufferer.

There is a subtle twist, though. The Lord focuses on two specific parts of Creation: the *Behemoth* (40:15-24) and the *Leviathan* (41:1-34). The description of the former pinpoints the awesome creative power of God. The description of the latter details God's powerful subduing of evil so that creation may truly be considered good.

Such scrutiny of the creative act produces a lasting effect. The final impression of the speech unmistakably paints God's portrait in positive, warm colors. Even with suffering, the world around Job points to a God who painstakingly ensures that good will triumph.

Since these two creatures play such a vital role in the Lord's second speech, they should be examined. *Behemoth* has been most commonly identified as either an elephant or a hippopotamus. Such mammoth creatures inspired awe in the ancient world; they were signs pointing to the power of the Creator. In later Jewish literature (2 Esdras 6:49-52), Behemoth is depicted as a mythical monster, the land counterpart to Leviathan.

In Hebrew, *Leviathan* (also known as *Rahab*) suggests "coil," as in the coils of a serpent. It has been identified as a crocodile. However, the term has mythological roots. According to ancient myths, Leviathan was a strong sea serpent, symbolic of evil and chaos. This monster had to be subdued by the creator-god in order for creation to prosper.

This myth was taken over by biblical writers to symbolize God's power. Psalm 74:12-14, for instance, refers to God crushing the Leviathan, described as a dragon with several heads. Such symbolism is important to the writer of Job. He has alluded throughout to the myth (3:8; 7:12; 9:13; 26:12-13). Now he uses it to conclude God's speech.

Focusing on such beasts appears to be a strange way of renewing the relationship with Job. It does not seem very personal. It should be noted, though, that such intimacy with God comes only within the context of "fear," or awe before God. God the Creator, who makes colossal giants, suggests the Lord's otherness to Job. God the lover, who slays the dragon so that creation will survive, suggests the Lord's protection of Job. Taken together, Job comes into a new understanding—and appreciation—of God.

Here is an outline of chapters 40–41.

I. God's Challenge to Job (40:1-2)

II. Job's Refusal to Answer (40:3-5)

III. God's Second Speech (40:6–41:34)

    A. God's command to Job (40:6-7)

    B. God's power over people (40:8-14)

    C. God's creation of Behemoth (40:15-24)

    D. God's defeat of Leviathan (41:1-34)

The Message of Job 40–41

The hurting person is part of the Lord's creation. Early in the speech God subtly reminds Job that he is a creature, not a god; "Look at Behemoth, which I made just as I made you" (40:15a). Challenging God could place Job above the created order. Such a position sets him up for self-salvation and isolation. The first thing God must do is remind Job of his proper place in the scheme of things.

God the Creator is trustworthy. Job had argued against God's sense of justice. To him, human affairs appeared to be a matter of chance, without any just, benevolent, guiding hand. God directly confronts this.

Such news is gospel for sufferers. Loneliness and bewilderment accompany pain. To whom can we turn? In whom can we trust? It can only be someone who has been proven worthy. The account of the defeat of pain, of the defeat of the Leviathan in our lives, points to God.

God the Creator deals with a hurting creation in personal ways. In the final analysis, the most important thing about the whirlwind speeches is the whirlwind. The content, though helpful, is not as essential as God's active presence. The Lord freely engages Job, one-on-one. There are no angels or other intermediaries. God and the sufferer meet face-to-face. As the Lord met Leviathan to subdue him, so does the Lord meet Job, to heal him.

The hope of the sufferer is that in the midst of hurt a whirlwind will arise. Job discovered a God who answered him, personally, in the roar of a storm. We, too, can be confident that the Lord will personally, specially, talk to us when we face a dark world. From the mighty whirlwind we will perhaps hear God's warm, clear voice.

JOB 42

Introduction to This Chapter

The action prior to this chapter highlighted the Lord's passionate attempts to restore a relationship with Job. The two preceding chapters contain the second whirlwind speech, which details God's creative power and benevolent care.

The question opening this chapter is thus, What will Job do? His previous response was in short, clipped, angry sentences (40:3-5). Will this one be any different? Will the Lord's second speech produce better results?

The opening verses of chapter 42 answer this. Job admits to rashness. He confesses that he spoke without really knowing all the facts. He praises God. And he concludes his speech promising humility: "Therefore I despise myself, and repent in dust and ashes" (verse 6).

This response must be placed in perspective. The friends had relentlessly dogged Job, trying to beat him into submission. Their only reward was frustration. Now God speaks. In only a fraction of the length of the friends' speeches, the Lord echoes their basic sentiments (that is, divine power and justice). Then Job repents.

Why does God do what the friends couldn't? Because the Lord speaks to Job's feelings, not his thoughts. Without coercion (who can coerce God?), and with no ulterior motive, the Almighty personally appears and passionately speaks. Job is moved. He admits that this was what drew him to repent: "I had heard of you by the hearing of the ear, but now my eye sees you" (verse 5).

Job sees God reaching out, trying to ease his suffering and restore a love relationship. Behind the Lord's words are the whisperings of a lover. His reply is but a passionate praise to that lover.

The remainder of chapter 42 consists of the prose epilogue. This is the conclusion of the tale appropriated by the poet.

In this ending, two very important things happen. First, God criticizes Job's friends, commanding them to beseech Job's intercession (verses 7-9). Following this, the Lord restores Job's fortunes (verses 10-17).

These events show that the conclusion of the book is not just a happy one. It is also a surprising, turning-the-tables one. Throughout, the book has portrayed the friends as the righteous ones. They had health and wealth. They talked about God in terms of statements, not questions. Job, on the other hand, was the complete opposite. The loss of his comfort and well-being seemingly pointed to the shambles of his spiritual life. His speech was filled with angry oaths against God. Yet, in the end, this man was justified by the Lord, and the others chastised. Why?

It is a tribute to the genius of the author that he concludes the book by dramatically answering the question that began it. The friends epitomize the smug theology of ancient Israel: God blesses the righteous and punishes the wicked. Job, conversely, symbolizes the person who is honest with herself or himself, and who seeks new ways of relating to the Lord. Who is right? The book's conclusion givers the author's answer. The one who asks questions, seeking and struggling through a passionate faith, is the one the Lord blesses.

Here is an outline of Job 42.

I. Job's Response to God's Second Speech (42:1-6)

II. Prose Epilogue (42:7-17)
    A. God's rebuke of Job's friends (42:7-9)
    B. God's restoration of Job's fortune (42:10-17)

The Message of Job 42

The Lord never gives up. The fact that Job moves from cursing to praising shows this. God relentlessly pursues Job. The Lord visits him in a whirlwind. God puts together an elaborate speech. When that fails, the Lord constructs another. Finally, the ice in Job's heart melts. Overwhelmed by the Almighty's persistence, he returns the Lord's love.

Suffering produces an emptiness of the heart. The person in pain has little ability to open up to the world. Like Job in his first response to God, the sufferer turns inward. Such a person needs someone to intervene, to give a vision of hope, to love. God in the whirlwind is such a person. Our greatest challenge in helping a sufferer is to reflect that aggressive love. Our greatest challenge as a sufferer is to accept it.

God is the lover who vindicates the beloved. The restoration of Job's fortunes testifies to the worthiness of his life. This comes in the light of his friends' savage attempts to find evil and guilt in him. Because he holds fast to his integrity, he is not abandoned to an angry, lonely death. God says, by making the restoration, that the reward of such integrity is happiness. There is no sad ending.

It is too simplistic to say that the Lord will bless the sufferer. It is more to the point to say that as the sufferer struggles, calling out to God, then that person eventually discovers a new dimension. Job's integrity pushed him to a greater honesty with himself and with God. It allowed him an opportunity for a new exploration of faith. Our integrity, likewise, prepares us for a new life. That life comes from God, who vindicates our pain with a passionate love.

The new life discovered in suffering is nothing less than the kingdom of God. The closing verses of the book are deceptive. In listing Job's new fortune, they mention two radical things. Job's family and friends discover a new faith in God, and the daughters born to him are accorded equality with men. Such events point to more than a happy ending. They point to this realization: Wherever the sufferer encounters God, life will never be the same again. It will take on earthshaking proportions.

Perhaps this is the last—and best—word Job gives to the sufferer. In the enduring of pain, with honesty and with questioning, the sufferer catches a glimpse of the Kingdom. Words like faith, forgiveness, justice, and hope are no longer well-worn cliches. They are life-changing realities. Even if the suffering leads to death, the new life is still affirmed. That is because God—from the whirlwind of our lives—will never stop confronting us until we say, with Job, "I had heard of you by the hearing of the ear, but now my eye sees you (42:5).

PSALMS

OUTLINE OF PSALMS

I. **Book I: Psalms 1–41**
   A. Some Philosophic Problems
      (Psalms 1–10)
      1. Two Lifestyles
      2. A Coronation Hymn
      3. God Is a Shield
      4. Inner Peace
      5. A Straight Pathway
      6. Justice and Mercy
      7. Let Justice Be Done
      8. How Majestic Is Your Name
      9. Evil Enemies
      10. Poverty and Suffering
   B. What Is God Really Like?
      (Psalms 11–20)
      11. God's Law and Order
      12. God's Precious Words
      13. God's Steadfast Love
      14. God Is!
      15. The Presence of God
      16. God's Presence Is Joy
      17. God Hears People
      18. God's King Triumphs
      19. God's Universal Law
      20. God Helps People
   C. Confidence and Serenity
      (Psalms 21–31)
      21. Prayers for the King
      22. Yet Will I Believe
      23. The Lord Is My Shepherd
      24. The King of Glory
      25. Teach Me, O Lord
      26. Test Me, O Lord
      27. A Courtroom Drama
      28. The Lord Is a Refuge

29. The Voice of Thunder
30. The Lord Is Gracious
31. My Times Are in Your Hand
   D. The Pursuit of Happiness
      (Psalms 32–41)
      32. Freedom from Guilt
      33. Secure in the Lord
      34. The Good Life
      35. Delight in Salvation
      36. Excellent Loving-kindness
      37. The Heart's Desire
      38. The Price of Suffering
      39. Uncommon Despair
      40. A New Song on My Lips
      41. Joy of Service

II. **Book II: Psalm 42–72**
   A. Despair, Praise, and Wisdom
      (Psalms 42–51)
      42. Loneliness and Despair
      43. Send Out Your Light
      44. Why Sleepest Thou?
      45. A Royal Wedding
      46. A Hymn of Faith
      47. King of Kings
      48. Zion, the Holy Mountain
      49. God and Mammon
      50. The Nature of Sacrifice
      51. Whiter Than Snow
   B. In God Will I Trust
      (Psalms 52–61)
      52. Coping with Treachery
      53. God Is!
      54. A Cry for Help
      55. God Sustains Us
      56. I Trust in God
      57. Shadow of Your Wings
      58. The God Who Judges

59. God Is My Fortress
60. A National Crisis
61. God Will Listen
C. Gratitude and Praise
(Psalms 62–72)
62. Power Belongs to God
63. Thirsting for God
64. The Righteous Rejoice
65. Thanksgiving Day
66. Truly God Has Listened
67. God's Face Shines
68. Twelve Little Poems
69. God Will Save Zion
70. O Lord, Do Not Tarry
71. Do Not Forsake Me
72. A Moral Testament

III. Book III: Psalms 73–89
A. Is the Covenant in Doubt?
(Psalms 73–80)
73. Is Life Unfair?
74. Has God Forgotten Us?
75. God Judges with Equity
76. An Angry God
77. Is God's Love Steadfast?
78. God in History
79. Jerusalem Is in Ruins
80. Restore Us, O God
B. Songs of Sorrow (Psalms 81–89)
81. Israel Would Not Listen
82. The Heavenly Council
83. Middle East Conflict
84. Longing for Your Home
85. Revive Us Again
86. There Is None Like God
87. The City of God
88. Down to the Pit
89. Broken Promises?

IV. Book IV: Psalms 90–106
A. The Lord Reigns (Psalms 90–98)
90. A Heart of Wisdom
91. God Is the Most High
92. Thy Works Are Great
93. God's Decrees Are Sure
94. Judge of the Earth

95. Sing to the Lord
96. Declare God's Glory
97. Lord of All the Earth
98. The Victory of Our God
B. God Endures Forever
(Psalms 99–106)
99. Holy Is the Lord
100. Make a Joyful Noise
101. Loyalty and Justice
102. Enthroned Forever
103. Blessed Be the Lord
104. God's Creation
105. How God Saved Israel
106. National Guilt

V. Book V: Psalms 107–150
A. Advice for the Righteous
(Psalms 107–114)
107. God Fills the Hungry
108. A Steadfast Heart
109. False Accusations
110. At God's Right Hand
111. God Redeems the Nation
112. Blessed Generosity
113. God Lifts the Needy
114. Historic Moments
B. Gifts from God
(Psalms 115–122)
115. God Is in the Heavens
116. God Hears a Prayer
117. All Nations Praise God
118. An Abundance of Gifts
119. God's Moral Law
120. Woe Is Me
121. I Lift Up My Eyes
122. A Prayer for Peace
C. Hope in the Lord
(Psalms 123–130)
123. Enough of Contempt
124. God Is on Our Side
125. Zion Abides Forever
126. God Will Be Faithful
127. Without God All Is in Vain
128. Living in Fear of God
129. A Curse on the Wicked
130. A Cry from the Depths

INTRODUCTION

Few other books of the Bible, except perhaps the Gospels, have influenced religious experience with quite the effect of the Psalms. Their poetry includes some of the richest language in the literary world, incomparable in power and loveliness. Reflecting on the quality and character of the Psalms, we are aware of their effects on countless generations who have turned to them for personal guidance. We cannot underestimate the strength in these beautiful lines, whether it be to find consolation in loneliness, despair, grief, and pain or to acquire knowledge and inspiration from moments of meditation.

Unlike other books of the Bible which are addressed to humanity and deal with the subjects of law, history, prophecy, wisdom, and instruction, the Psalms are addressed to God or are written about God.

Within these 150 poems, a systematic theology is not evident. Nor is there any historical continuity or unifying religious theme. Nevertheless, throughout the Psalms, on virtually every page, the assumption is stated or implied that God exists, and that concept is never in doubt.

The core of the entire book is the wonderful awareness of God's presence. The deepest yearnings of the soul for an intimate, personal, and right relationship with God are apparent. In those yearnings the broadest range of human emotion is evident. Psalmists are dealing with deepest despair and highest elation, profound grief and supreme joy, utmost sorrow and greatest gladness. But they are also dealing with profoundly important moral and ethical principles. Throughout these poems, deepest respect for the law is apparent. It actually becomes the ethical ideal of the people of God's choosing.

At the same time the Psalms relate the story of the Israelite nation, its high moments of exultation and supreme glory and its grim days of calamity and national disaster. The episodes have a timeless quality about them, appropriate to any period of history including the present. The glowing appeal of these stories is the almost continuous conquest of despair and the heart-warming victory of hope. As personal, devotional resources, these beautiful poems are most valued as deep springs of refreshment and renewal and marvelous sources of comfort.

Psalm and Music

The psalmists have created a great book of hymns which affirms both awesome power and tender personal intimacy as important traits of a monotheistic God. Each psalm is superb lyric poetry that was, at one time, set to music. The people for whom the writers composed and recorded the poems are God's people who have drawn on the qualities of power and intimacy in those great hymns for twenty-five hundred years.

Pipes, reeds, percussion, and strings such as the psaltery and lute were used. The English word *psalm* is derived from the Greek *psalmos* which meant the twanging or strumming of a stringed instrument. Verses 1-3 of Psalm 81 describe the degree to which music and poetry were related in Israel's early life:

> Sing aloud to God our strength;
>   shout for joy to the God of Jacob!
> Raise a song, sound the tambourine,
>   the sweet lyre with the harp.
> Blow the trumpet at the new moon,
>   at the full moon, on our festal day.

Among the very early Hebrew peoples, hymns and songs were memorized in religious training and during social activities of community life. In this way, their best-loved poetry was passed from generation to generation. Bible scholars generally believe that some of the present collection of psalms was accumulated by means of this oral tradition over a period of many centuries.

From the earliest periods in Israel's history religious experiences were at the center of community life. Singing was a part of those activities. Psalms were sung during festivals, on national holidays and high holy days, and during pilgrimages to Jerusalem. As the Hebrews made their customary pilgrimages, they sang psalms of praise.

Titles of some of the psalms contain specific references to choirmasters and to Temple singers such as the Sons of Korah and Asaph. Hymns and anthems were used regularly by the early Hebrews as aids to worship, beginning a tradition that has endured to our time.

In one important sense the individual psalms are prayers, and in recognition of this attribute they are incorporated into denominational prayer books and psalters. The Psalter in the hymnals of most churches contains selected psalms usually printed as responsive readings. Also, frequent use is made of entire psalms or individual verses or sentences in hymns, canticles, collects, and other prayers and acts of praise.

Hymns in use in most Christian denominations include psalms which have been rephrased in rhyme to conform to the meter of traditional hymn tunes. Note how the lovely lines of the Twenty-third Psalm (King James Version) have been rearranged to fit one of several tunes in common use:

> The LORD is my shepherd, I shall not want;
> He maketh me to lie down in green pastures.
> He leadeth me beside the still waters;
> The Lord's my shepherd, I'll not want,
> He makes me down to lie
> in pastures green; he leadeth me
> The quiet waters by. . . .

The Authorship of the Psalms

Authorship of the Psalms is in dispute among biblical scholars, as is the question of by whom and when they were accumulated from the oral tradition. It is true that the Hebrew texts ascribe much of the poetry to David. Biblical scholars have suggested that some of the psalms attributed to David may be poems written by others for David or about him, or written using his literary style. Some scholarly opinion places authorship of many psalms much later in Israel's history, perhaps after the Babylonian captivity and up to the time of the Maccabean era. Recent evidence shows, however, that a number of the psalms may have been written or recorded at earlier dates than scholars has previously thought. In their original forms, many can be shown to date from the monarchical period of Saul, David, and Solomon.

Regardless of who the authors of these psalms were, there is no doubt that David is still the central human figure in the Psalms. His strong relationship with and his virtually unswerving devotion to God dominate the stories throughout the book.

Purposes of the Psalms

The Psalms were put into their present arrangement sometime before the era of the Maccabees (165 B.C.), probably 300–200 B.C. By the time of the Christian era, all of the Psalter had actually been incorporated into the Hebrew Bible, and before too long thereafter into the earliest Christian Bibles as well. Two purposes seem to have been served by including the Psalms in the Bible: public worship and personal devotion. In the first instance, psalms have important liturgical uses in religious services. Introductory statements above the biblical text of a number of psalms include specific instructions as to how the poem is to be used in worship or in celebration. Although the meaning of many of the words in those introductory statements is obscure, there is little doubt that they were directions given to the congregation to enable proper participation in the service.

A second purpose served by the Psalms was private, personal devotion. The Twenty-third Psalm was evidently not used anywhere in liturgy among the people of Israel. But as a quiet, devotional, personal prayer it is incomparable. This and other psalms of comfort and confidence have shown unusual power in bringing people into a unique personal experience with the living God.

Literary Structure of the Psalms

The reader's enjoyment and understanding of the Psalms will surely be enhanced by some understanding of their literary structure. We should remember that the individual psalms are poetry despite the fact that they do not appear to have any rhyme. The original Hebrew did not have rhyme either; it depended upon stress during recitation in order to achieve poetic quality. It might be helpful to try reading some psalms aloud, accenting certain words to assess the psalms as poetry. The structure of the poetry is quite simple; it is comprised of line, verse, and stanza. The verses are usually numbered. When a verse has two distinct subjects or if its two parts are obviously related to two different stanzas, references to one of the parts in this and other commentaries will use the small letters *a* or *b* to represent the first or second part of a verse. Occasionally, verses will take the form of a beatitude, the first word of which is *blessed, happy*, or an equivalent.

As in all literature identified as poetry, psalms possess rhythm, meter, and a certain lyric quality. But these traits are not always evident. Translations have often sacrificed the original Hebrew metered stress and rhythm in order to achieve greater faithfulness in meaning.

Literary devices most commonly employed in the writing and the translating of the Psalms are word pictures, figures of speech, and parallelisms of three types. The first is *synonymous*, in which the idea expressed in one line is repeated with different words in the line that follows:

> The snares of death encompassed me;
> the pangs of Sheol laid hold on me.
> (Psalm 116:3)

The NIV reads:

> The cords of death entangle me,
> the anguish of the grave came upon me.

A second type of Hebrew parallelism is *antithesis*, in which the subject of the first line is followed in the next line by a thought that expresses an opposite or contrary idea:

My flesh and my heart may fail,
  but God is the strength of my heart
  and my portion forever.
(Psalm 73:26 NIV and NRSV)

The third type of parallelism is *complementary*, in which the idea expressed in the second line complements or in some way adds to the thought in the first line:

But I trusted in your steadfast love;
  my heart shall rejoice in your salvation.
(Psalm 13:5)

Abundant use of extraordinary and colorful figures of speech gives all the psalms special beauty and their lovely, lyrical quality. Often used is the *metaphor*:

He makes the clouds his chariot,
  and rides on the wings of the wind.
(Psalm 104:3 NIV)

in which things used in comparisons are quite different.

Also often used is the *simile*: "He is like a tree planted by streams of water" (Psalm 1:3 NIV), in which different words or things are compared and introduced by the words *like* or *as*.

The psalms also contain some *hyperbole*:

Have they no knowledge, all the evildoers
Who eat up my people as they eat bread. . . ?
(Psalm 14:4)

which is clearly deliberate exaggeration in order to emphasize a point.

Many of the psalms, especially the laments, are written in similar format. The psalms begin with a cry for help accompanied by a description of the cause of anguish. Often the cause is a false accusation but it can also be threats of murder, terrible illness, mental distress, or even national calamities. A declaration of trust usually follows along with an expression of confidence that God will intervene. The final words of these poems are thanksgiving for deliverance.

Within the text of a number of psalms, the word *selah* occurs repeatedly. It does not appear to have any literary significance and it has no known meaning in Hebrew. Some students of early music surmise that it may have been an instruction for singing, perhaps to indicate a pause in the liturgy or to allow the introduction of some special feature into the ritual.

The Plan of the Commentary

The general plan of this commentary is a treatment of individual psalms in numeric sequence from 1 to 150. For convenience, they are divided into sixteen parts. Because the poems do not follow a story plot nor any particular order by subject, the attempt to treat each part as having a general theme may seem somewhat artificial. On the other hand, one can find affinities among some of the psalms in each part. The introductory sentences for each of the sixteen parts provide some ideas about ways of focusing one's thoughts on a small group of poems which may be studied and understood in one sitting. The arrangement may also be useful for private devotions and for the preparation of teaching materials for lessons on the Bible.

PSALMS 1–10

Introduction to These Psalms

The authors of the psalms were deeply religious thinkers and supremely confident believers in God. Their beliefs were touched with a sense of awe and wonder in the presence of the Almighty. So it was that in the act of wondering, the deepest questions about the nature of God, humanity, and the world came to light.

Part One of the book of Psalms (1–10) deals with some traditional religious and philosophic questions: good and evil, justice and mercy, anxiety and happiness, as well as the sources of moral law. Also raised are interesting questions about the divine right of kings, the majesty of God, the nature of grace, and whether or not people can approach God directly as an intimate friend.

The importance of a philosophic attitude cannot be dismissed easily. We gain immeasurable insight by asking searching, penetrating questions. In our study of this part of Psalms the questions are the same as those which have perplexed Christians for centuries.

The Message of Psalms 1–10

Part One of the book of Psalms describes the most important questions with which religious people of the ancient Near East were confronted. The language of the individual psalms provides interesting insight into the cultural surroundings in which the authors lived as well as the social and political environment in which their religious faith was being developed and tested. Those questions and the answers which emerged seem hardly different from those of our contemporary civilization.

- What are the characteristics of the righteous?

- Does God's universal sovereignty apply to all nations, even the heathen?

HOW MAJESTIC IS YOUR NAME (PSALM 8)

Here is a glorious hymn of Creation, clearly a poetic paraphrase of Genesis 1. It opens with words ascribing majesty to God's name throughout the universe. The word *name* had a connotation much broader than simply a title. It was, for Israel, the mighty presence of God revealed in the natural world. Appropriately, therefore, this psalm was sung at eventide when the glorious Middle Eastern night sky was revealed by the advancing darkness.

Verse 2 reveals one of the more unique paradoxes of God's character. It is the appointment of lowly, weak, non-warlike personalities to the most monumental and world-shaking tasks. The babes and infants are, figuratively, just such persons. Moses and Jesus, born in poverty and laid in humble baskets and mangers, became the makers of civilization. It is they who "silence the enemy" (NRSV) or "foe" (NIV).

Verses 3-8 are a profound meditation about the nature of the humanity God has created. It begins with words of wonder about God's magnificent physical universe. The psalmist's solo monologue then turns to the crucial question of Psalms: "What is man" (NIV; NRSV, "human beings") "that you are mindful of him?" And at once a flood of phrases provides an answer. God has given power to the people to dominate the world. How perceptive of the psalmist to recognize that dominion and power as evidence of God's grace by the addition of verse 9. It is a repetition of verse 1 and is fitting indeed. It symbolizes the humility that ought to characterize the acceptance of all the responsibility God has given to humanity. To have such a feeling would seem appropriate to today's people as well.

- Can the faithful person be confident that God will be a shield against danger?

- Will God vindicate the falsely accused?

- Will God relieve the repentant sinner from the distress of acute illness?

- Can faithful people be assured of God's justice?

- Will people be humble even when God has given them almost unlimited power over all the earth?

- Why do the wicked prosper and flourish while the righteous suffer?

PSALMS 11–20

Introduction to These Psalms

In this part of the book of Psalms, the titles give David credit as the author. His lovely poetry contains vivid word pictures of what God is really like. David's profound depths of faith made God a spiritual reality and that reality is never in doubt, even during the darkest hours of tragedy and despair.

The words in these poems are uttered with such simple and yet forceful conviction. Little wonder that many of the concepts expressed in this group of psalms have found their way into the most significant theological beliefs about the nature of God. Study of this cluster of the Psalms will be helped by considering the way God chooses to make manifest the divine nature in the affairs of the nations and their people.

The Message of Psalms 11–20

The general theme in this part is the nature of God. These ten psalms contain a noteworthy collection of lustrous ideas about Israel's God and what the people and the king thought their God was like. David had unfailing faith and was very secure in his belief that he knew the living God. He relates these convictions in ways that show how the character of God was revealed to him again and again.

- God is a good listener.

- God is always at the side of Israel's king; this enables him to be triumphant.

- God creates and sustains the universe. The creation includes humanity, which is given special dominion over the creatures of God's natural world.

- God is the author of the principles of law and order by which society is governed.

- God is love and that love is steadfast, abiding forever against all onslaughts.

- Even though fools may believe there is no God, faithful people know that God exists.

- God's presence is something that people can feel when they are near to it.

- There is joy just being in that presence.

- God is especially attentive to persons who have been given a divine mandate to rule.

PSALMS 21–31

Introduction to These Psalms

The Psalms are sources of comfort and help in our dealings with difficult and trying circumstances. But they are also appropriate for periods of quiet contemplation when personal affinity with God is the heart's desire. The great value in moments of untroubled meditation is the opportunity to cultivate a serene and spiritual lifestyle.

Most of the psalms in this group of eleven lend themselves quite well to thoughtful study of ways to live confidently in the security of God's steadfast love. The Twenty-third Psalm is exemplary. It is the principal psalm of confidence and comfort. Other psalms in this group will also be helpful as one grapples with situations of illness, injustice, and false accusations as well as tribulations of spiritual and mental anguish. Reading Psalm 21, we can rejoice with the king, visualizing the righteous among us in positions of leadership to be the calm and confident beloved of God.

The Message of Psalms 21–31

This part of the Psalms emphasizes a point made earlier in the previous section that God is entirely trustworthy. Writers and recorders of these psalms stress the confidence we can all have in God's reliability. From this assurance we gain convictions, taking comfort that we can live life serenely.

- A righteous king of Israel is favored by the Lord.

- In the midst of serious affliction, a faithful person will still trust in God.

- God heals the afflicted.

- We can be serene and confident knowing that the Lord is our shepherd.

- Who is the king of glory? God is the King of glory!

- Who may enter the sanctuary? Those whose hands are clean and whose hearts are pure.

- Being in God's loving and forgiving presence is among life's greatest pleasures.

- God participates in the human effort to secure justice.

YET WILL I BELIEVE (PSALM 22)

This long poem has traditionally been read by Christians at Good Friday services. The first line, the fourth of the seven last words of Christ on the cross, suggests why. Elsewhere within the first section of this psalm (verses 1-21), other phrases are vivid reminders of events leading up to the crucifixion. For this reason the psalm has been interpreted by some as prophetic of the passion and death of Jesus.

The psalm opens with four stanzas arranged antiphonally, the first being the agonized call for help, the second (verses 3-5) a testimony of praise and trust. In the third stanza the psalmist resumes the lament which has all the characteristics of the days following Palm Sunday. In stanza four, we read a prayer of thanks and a plea for assistance.

A second array of four stanzas completes the first section. Here a picture of total deterioration is painted, the finality of death is certain. The bulls (verse 12) are probably wild oxen or bison from the grasslands of Bashan, a region east of the Sea of Galilee. Verses 14-15 depict a state of complete physical degeneration. The words are spoken with a sense of utter hopelessness and futility. In the following stanza, the psalmist's condition seems to be even worse. Wild dogs (hyenas, perhaps) have now begun an attack. The imagery of pierced feet and hands suggests intense pain. Death cannot be too far off now; the psalmist watches hopelessly as enemies gamble for his clothing. The final verses (19-21) of the first section are an earnest prayer for deliverance.

Some dispute exists among scholars as to whether the second section (verses 22-31) is actually a separate psalm. The argument in favor of the single-psalm theory is quite compelling, especially if one agrees that God did answer the earnest prayer for deliverance. That being so, the remainder of the psalm is a glorious hymn of praise and thanksgiving. What makes this story so appealing is that the psalmist is thinking not just of himself but of other people as well. The hope is that people who have been similarly afflicted shall also be healed. In what may be understood as a broad and most unselfish outlook on the whole world, the psalmist prays that all the nations of the world and generations not yet born shall become the people of God and be delivered from all adversity.

THE LORD IS MY SHEPHERD (PSALM 23)

None of the psalms is more beloved than this one. From the earliest religious experiences of childhood (memorizing Bible verses among them) to the hearing of elegies during Christian burial, the Twenty-third Psalm is there. Reasons for its attractiveness are not hard to find. One is its graceful simplicity. Few poems say so much in so few words. Other reasons appear in the train of thought as the poetry progresses.

To say and think, "The Lord is my shepherd," is to establish personal, intimate affinity with God. It is to enter a right relationship, the advantages of which are feelings of perfect peace and contentment and of not being in need of or in want for anything. Lying down in green pastures and walking beside still waters are lovely word pictures, representing the actions of sheep in the presence of the good shepherd who cares very deeply. This is the God to whom we have entrusted ourselves and who provides peaceful nights and uncluttered days, despite the difficulties which life holds. It is the same God who nurtures the renewal of life, especially the inner personality. When the soul is restored, we are not just refurbished for the day's work. We are renewed in the deepest recesses of the mind and spirit and open completely to the closest association with the mind of God.

The intimate presence of the living God is further dramatized as the shepherd (verse 3) is given the role of counselor and teacher, leading the sheep along the right pathway. And the shepherd does this for his name's sake, which seems to say that this is done so that others may know of the good things happening when relations are right between the shepherd and the sheep.

In verse 4, the psalmist dwells further on the shepherd's care; this time it is watchfulness when the sheep are in peril. The shepherd, using the tools of his trade (rod and staff), protects the sheep from deadly perils lurking along the edges of steep, rocky ravines lining the grazing lands. The imagery is wonderfully tender. The psalmist has had a brush with death—an accident or illness perhaps. But the good shepherd has kept him from the valley of shadows.

In the last stanza (verses 5-6) the shepherd is now the host, preparing a banquet. But an odd circumstance prevails. The psalmist must sit down to dine with enemies! In numerous other psalms, enemies are to be feared, distrusted, and often violently dealt with. But here God (the host) is bringing opponents together. Reconciling foes is one more evidence of grace.

In the tradition of the times, a guest was anointed with aromatic oils (verse 5) and the drinking cup was continuously filled to overflowing. That word picture is one of contentment and peace. The psalmist is so filled with the joyous presence of God that he knows that all the days ahead shall be as idyllic as this one.

- The psalmist's portrayal of death is being sent to Sheol, a land where God never goes.

- God speaks to the nations by means of the forces of nature, thunderstorms being especially dramatic.

- God may appear to be angry at times but that anger is only temporary.

- To feel that one's life and times are in God's hands is to capture the essence of perfect serenity.

PSALMS 32–41

Introduction to These Psalms

Among the important human rights elaborated in the American Declaration of Independence is the pursuit of happiness. This right was equally important to Israel when this magnificent collection of poems was being created. Psalms 32–41 deal generally with the state of being happy. While God had not promised a continuous condition of bliss or life forever in the

Garden of Eden, Israel understood that the covenant did not preclude enjoying life, free from anguish and suffering. But, as the world has discovered, and as did the people of Israel, true happiness is not the same as pleasure and bliss.

Happiness or blessedness is reflected differently in these lines. Psalm 32 opens with a beatitude. What could make people any happier than to know that their sins are forgiven?

The Message of Psalm 32–41

Happiness is blessedness in the language of most of the psalms in this part. And the pursuit of a state of blessedness (bliss) on earth was an essential characteristic of early Israel's religious experience. It is inappropriate, however, to equate the state of blessedness with constant pleasure and freedom from the necessary constraints of community and national life. Happiness is shown to be a state in which the godly life of moral restraints is lived with joy.

• Happy is the person who is free from the worry caused by guilt.

• Happy is the nation whose security is in God. Happy is the community which can praise God.

• Happy are the people who fear the Lord.

• Happy is the person who can be proved to be innocent of false accusations.

• Happy are those who are faithful to God and have complete freedom from worry.

• Happy are the people who have maintained their faith at the price of suffering.

• Happy is one who has experienced God's loving salvation and deliverance.

• Happy is the person who knows the joy of helping others.

PSALMS 42–51

Introduction to These Psalms

These ten songs exhibit remarkable diversity in both style and mood. This section opens with three poignant poems of deepest despair. Then the mood is abruptly

---

A HYMN OF FAITH (PSALM 46)

This powerful poem was the inspiration for Martin Luther's great Christian hymn "A Mighty Fortress Is Our God." The psalm is a composition of three stanzas, beginning with a declaration of complete trust in God even if cataclysmic changes (earthquakes and floods) should occur in the earth. By citing potential disasters of such proportions, the psalmist may be imagining the end of the world, although that concept (eschatology) is rarely introduced into the Psalms.

The second stanza of this hymn reveals the psalmist's continued affirmation of trust. The river (verse 4) is doubtless the river of life which flows from Zion, God's earthly home. The nation of Israel, which is fortunate to have God dwelling in its midst, can feel very secure even though other nations are tottering and crumbling. A congregational response (verse 7) completes the stanza. It reveals a strong sense of national security. The line is a wonderful statement of trust.

In the last stanza the congregation is invited to think about the deeds God has done, with power and authority, to bring eternal peace. Then, with one of the great literary gems of history (verse 10), the psalmist sings God's words, "Be still, and know that I am God." It is a stirring moment. The hymn closes with the congregational refrain, a repetition of verse 7.

WHITER THAN SNOW (PSALM 51)

This is one of the great penitential psalms of Christendom. It is useful in ritual as a prayer of cleansing and forgiveness. Apparently it is based on Nathan's rebuke of David following the episode with Uriah and Bathsheba (2 Samuel 12:1-14). David prays for mercy and petitions God to wash away his sins. He is very much aware of his sinful nature and, having repented, he voices his approval of God's judgment. The sin of his mother (verse 5) is not a condemnation of her; it is an acknowledgment of the pervasiveness of sin, which Christian tradition speaks about as original sin.

As the prayer continues David recognizes the importance of truth in his heart and seeks God's wisdom in order to find the truth. Again he begs for God's cleansing power, hoping to become whiter than snow. Hyssop was evidently a plant grown regionally which had some uses in the rites of purification. It was also used medicinally. The prayer goes on to include a request that bones be healed. This is probably said figuratively. In all likelihood, David's mental image of himself was of a person badly broken in spirit by shame.

With verses 10-12, the psalm takes on a new mood of joy. It is as if David feels deeply the forgiving presence of God and a wonderful new sense of having been washed clean and restored to favor. In consequence of God's merciful act of deliverance, David promises to teach others the moral precepts which are now governing his new life (verses 13-14).

David concludes this prayer with three of the psalm's most beautiful lines. They could have been composed only by a very humble person who loved God intensely and who had been made completely whole by the depth of the purification experience.

The concluding lines (verses 18-19) about rebuilding Jerusalem were evidently added during the compiling of the Psalter long after the destruction of the Temple and the Babylonian captivity.

earthly dwelling-place on Mount Zion. The last three poems offer instruction in matters of wealth, sacrifice, repentance, and renewal.

The Message of Psalms 42—51

This group of psalms exhibits wide diversity in both style and approach. It does not seem to have a theme around which a single message might be written. There is, however, an interesting mixture of biblical history and ethical teachings. Admonitions, proverbs, prayers, and ritual sentences are included, as are some very lovely verses worth memorizing as gems of biblical literature.

- Lonely and desolate people may find strength to endure their trials by waiting patiently for God.

- Pray earnestly for light and truth as guideposts to living.

- If it seems that God has forgotten when national disaster strikes, it may be that through the ordeals faith will be made stronger.

- The wedding of a king is the occasion for remembrance of the king's obligation and the importance of perpetuating the house and lineage of David.

- Trusting that God is a fortress sustains people even though the earth may undergo cataclysms.

- Israel's traditions held that God is the governor of the entire universe. The seat of government is Zion.

- Wealth cannot enable one to live forever. Those whose confidence is in wealth rather than God will surely die.

altered with a song of exquisite beauty about a royal wedding. Following this are three majestic hymns of praise that speak to God's mighty powers of creation, God's sovereignty over all the world, and an

- God does not require of Israel that animals be sacrificed. God requires only loyalty and thanksgiving.

- People who trust God and repent of their sins may be wholly cleansed. Understanding God's moral precepts is essential to such purification.

PSALMS 52–61

Introduction to These Psalms

The theme of these psalms is the determination to trust God regardless of events. Even in the most difficult circumstances the writers provide some hint of God's ultimate goodness. The historic inclinations toward hope and trust are deeply embedded in the Hebrew consciousness, and revealed in rich variety in these psalms.

The Message of Psalms 52–61

Throughout these psalms, trust in God is the dominant theme. That trust is the pillar of Israel's religious beliefs and experiences and it is fundamental to a king's performance of royal obligations in peace or war. These poems demonstrate that trust in God is also essential to personal security and peace of mind.

- God can be trusted to judge the wicked regardless of their prestige, power, and wealth.

- Israel discovered that God did fulfill promises to destroy evil.

- God can be trusted to provide unfailing support for the king.

- How difficult it is to forget insults and injuries. Not to forget implies that one cannot quite trust God.

- Psalms of lament almost invariably include a statement of trust and confidence in God.

- God can be trusted to judge with equity.

- God is always a trustworthy refuge.

PSALMS 62–72

Introduction to These Psalms

The psalms in this part are stories of joys and sorrows. But they all imply or reveal trust in God and gratitude for God's faithfulness. Psalms of gratitude often contain remembrance of pain, suffering, or alienation from God. But they also tell of one's appreciation for deliverance, for reconciliation, for fulfillment of the obligations of the covenant, and for steadfast love. In some of these psalms, feelings of gratitude are expressed as pure joy and delight. Israel used the psalms of gratitude during its great festivals celebrating the harvests, the coming of the new year, and covenant renewal.

The Message of Psalms 62–72

The love of God in the hearts of the early Israelite peoples is seldom reflected any more joyously than in this group of psalms, where gratitude and thanksgiving are the dominant themes. The people accepted what life offered them because they understood clearly that their existence was in accord with God's intentions. These poems reveal a deep sense of gratitude that grew among them as they came to understand more fully what the special relationship with God meant to them.

- God's nature is more reliable than human nature.

- Thank God for the special care that is provided for the reigning monarch.

- Thank God for shielding the people from enemies who lurk all around.

- Thank God for a radiant presence in the Temple.

- Thank God for being a good listener.

- Thank God for administering divine justice.

- Thank God for a homeland for the chosen people.

- Thank God for instituting an earthly home on Mount Zion and for living there among the people of Israel.

PSALMS 73–80

Introduction to These Psalms

The covenant between God and Israel is cited a number of times in the Psalms. To emphasize its importance in Israel's history we shall use the covenant as the central theme of this group of psalms. It was crucial to the life and times of the people who were the actors in these poetic dramas. All the psalms in this part are songs of Asaph. They are probably from a collection used by Temple singers. Asaph is identified as one of David's chief musicians.

The Message of Psalms 73–80

Commentary on this group of psalms has focused on the covenant and the historic manifestations of God's faithfulness to it. There were occasions in Israel's history when serious doubts about God's faithfulness arose, particularly in times of national disaster. These psalms offer a rich source of inspiration as the prayers and pleas of the nation of Israel are answered, often in dramatic and exciting ways, by God's intervention into its history.

- Though life seems unfair, God works to restore equity.

- There are times in human events when God seems to have forgotten the people.

- God's anger may be justified under certain circumstances.

- God has entered directly into Israel's history on many occasions. The actions were sometimes destructive but seemed always to cleanse.

- God rejected Israel a number of times when she violated the law and the covenant.

- God was often blamed for the great national disasters that befell the nation of Israel.

PSALMS 81–89

Introduction to These Psalms

The psalms in this group are almost all songs of deep sorrow that arise typically because of alienation from God, the power of sin, and the actions of the ungodly. Despite the mood of despondency which characterizes these psalms, each has an important element of hope which emerges again and again. It is a remarkable cultural trait of the people of Israel. Hope is invariably expressed as an expectation for a better life, not in heaven but here on earth. It is a means of dealing with sorrow. Psalms 84 and 87 are exceptions to the general theme of sorrow.

The Message of Psalms 81–89

With two exceptions, this group of psalms deals with sorrowful situations seeming to range from mild melancholy to absolute resignation. The volatility of human nature is set over against the equanimity and faithfulness of God. Yet even those divine traits are brought into question by the dire circumstances portrayed in these dramatic poems. The general theme of the message is that Israel must bear sorrow as a condition of its existence and perhaps even of its destiny. Yet Israel is never without hope.

- Sorrow is the consequence of doubting God's capacity to act in human affairs.

- Corruption among officials in the heavenly council causes sorrow on earth.

- Sorrow has been the fate of Middle Eastern countries in constant conflict with each other.

- Sorrow may inspire efforts to renew a right relationship with God.

- Despite sorrow of the most abject kind, in the presence of God one can attain a lightened heart.

- Some situations seem to produce a kind of sorrow that is totally devoid of hope.

- Sorrow virtually devoid of hope because of unanswered prayer may be somewhat consoled by simply asking God to remember.

PSALMS 90–98

Introduction to These Psalms

These psalms are hymns of wonder, praise, and thanksgiving. Their lines are sources of inspiration to people everywhere. They are addressed to the Lord who reigns over all the earth. Some of the richest language in Christian hymnody and liturgy is derived from these psalms. Some of the great hymns of Christendom are based on the familiar texts of these psalms. Isaac Watts's "O God, Our Help in Ages Past" uses Psalm 90's majestic lines.

The Message of Psalms 90–98

The central theme of this cluster of psalms is the kingship of God. Four of these psalms (93; 96; 97; 98) are directly concerned with the enthronement ritual. The others have features about them that relate to the concept of God as the monarch, reigning over all the earth. Much of the literature is dramatic and written with imagination and high emotion. But the message is clear and decisive.

- Israel's God is God above all gods

- Israel's God is the Most High.

- Israel's God is a teacher of wisdom.

- Israel's God is a God of the covenant.

- Israel's God is utterly reliable.

- Israel's God judges the peoples of the earth.

- Israel's God created the world.

- Israel's God is a God of victory.

PSALMS 99–106

Introduction to These Psalms

These psalms are lyric poetry dealing with praise, thanksgiving, and history. While some deep sorrow appears, the prevailing mood is joy and celebration. A predominant theme is that God endures. Time, in the vision of God, had no beginning and will have no end. To the people of Israel, the quality of timelessness was a beacon of hope. Just as God had brought them through their tumultuous history, as the poignant memories in the

MAKE A JOYFUL NOISE (PSALM 100)

People of all creeds, generation after generation, have treasured these beautiful sentences as their entrance into the vital experiences of sacred worship. The theme of this beloved liturgical poem is God's faithfulness and enduring, steadfast love. These majestic lines show how the characteristics of faithfulness and love foster the deepest gratitude in the hearts of the people.

Following the call to worship (verses 1-2), the psalmist sings a song of wisdom (verse 3). It reminds us that God is God above all other gods, that God created us, and that God cares for us as the shepherd cares for the sheep. These concepts are in the bedrock of Israel's religion.

Verse 4 is a ritual invitation to enter the inner precincts of the Temple to experience the actual presence of God. There, praise and thanksgiving may seem more personal. The second song of wisdom (verse 5) centers on God's enduring goodness, faithfulness, and constant love.

lines of these psalms reveal, so God will shepherd countless of their generations yet unborn. An enduring God to lean on gives Israel hope in the face of hostility.

The Message of Psalms 99–106

One recurrent theme in these psalms is the enduring faithfulness of God. A second theme is the reverence Israel feels, deep within its national character, for the integrity of the covenants made with God. Despite their repeated failures, these people have never permanently rejected the outstretched hand of God. Perhaps this is because God is everlasting and unchangeable, the refuge to which the people may return again and again.

BLESSED BE THE LORD (PSALM 103)

This psalm is one of the great masterpieces of world literature. It is a song of thanksgiving, sung by an individual of deep spiritual insight. The author is assumed to be David, although different opinions exist in the scholarly community. Yet only a person with the intellectual stature and artistic creativity of someone like David could have written such a magnificent testimony.

A beatitude sung as a call to praise opens the psalm. It is addressed inwardly rather than to a group and expresses gratitude for God's fulfillment of every need (verses 1-5).

The psalmist then sings a longer stanza of praise and thanksgiving (verses 6-18). Its verses are among the more memorable in the Psalter. They are addressed to the congregation as reminders of God's generosity and goodness to Israel. God's attributes of grace, mercy, and steadfast love are described by the most quotable phrases of incomparable beauty. The ideas appearing in some of the lines seem remarkably similar to New Testament expressions. Verses 10 and 12 read much like some Christian definitions of the gifts of grace and forgiveness. As noted above in the introduction to this part of the Psalter, the general theme is the enduring nature of God. In verses 15-18 it is contrasted to the transitory condition of humanity in lines of exquisite grace. Imagine the countless numbers of God's people who have achieved serenity in the face of death with the companionship of these words.

In the final stanza the psalmist returns to the literary style of the beatitude. The scope of the blessings is all-encompassing. It ranges from the council of heaven to the servant world of humanity to everything in creation and even to the depths of a human soul (verse 22).

- God's steadfast love endures forever.

- God's justice is everlasting.

- God's grace, mercy, and faithfulness endure forever.

- God is King forever.

- God will keep a covenant with Israel forever.

PSALMS 107–114

Introduction to These Psalms

The basic credo of Socrates, the intellectual giant of early Greek philosophy, was to live well. This meant living in accord with truth. Living well in the tradition of Israel's covenant relationship with God is to live righteously. The general theme addressed in this group of psalms is advice on the art of living righteously.

The Message of Psalms 107–114

The psalms in this group are upbeat, poetically attractive, and filled with the earthly manifestation of Israel's generous God. The general theme of sound advice for righteous people is explicit in most of these psalms. Where it is not so evident, the characteristics of God may well serve as models of behavior.

- A formula for living well is to admit one's sin, resolve to avoid it, and trust in God.

- God cares for the hungry and we must do the same.

- God sustains the righteous who may be falsely accused of criminal activity.

- The fear of the Lord is the beginning of wisdom.

- We benefit from dealing justly with others.

- Benefits result from diligent study; God sheds light on our study of the ways of the Lord.

- A God of extraordinary majesty and power ministers to the oppressed. Can righteous people do less?

PSALMS 115–122

Introduction to These Psalms

The psalms in this part reveal deep feelings of genuine appreciation for God's gifts. The bounty is unlimited and of unusual variety. Israel's survival as a political presence in the world is understood to be the consequence of God's consistent intercession across centuries of turmoil.

I LIFT UP MY EYES (PSALM 121)

This psalm is among the best-loved of the entire Psalter. Within the cultural inheritance of all humanity there is an attachment to the hills, places to which we repair for refreshment and renewal. But the psalmist professes a dependence on the Lord for help and, in the remainder of the psalm, provides several reasons why.

In verse 1 the psalmist may have been speaking of the hills of Jerusalem, perhaps Mount Zion. The psalmist's confidence is in God, the Creator. The shade in verse 5 is protection against the blazing Middle Eastern sun. The potential harm from both the sun and the moon is a remnant of pre-Israelite mythology.

The final stanza professes trust and confidence. The psalmist proclaims that God's constant watchfulness is a precious gift.

The Message of Psalms 115–122

Throughout the commentary on these psalms, the emphasis is placed on the inexhaustible supply of riches which God makes available to Israel. Material wealth was conspicuously absent from Israel's needs. Their concerns went far deeper into spiritual hunger, which God ably satisfied. With one exception (Psalm 120), the psalms in this group describe some magnificent gifts.

- God has given the earth for the people to use.

- God gives physical and spiritual health to the people.

- God gives military victories to Israel.

- God gives the keystone of the Kingdom to the world.

- God gives light to a world in darkness.

- God gives moral law to society.

- God gives grace, mercy, and steadfast love.

- God gives people the capacity to trust.

PSALMS 123–130

Introduction to These Psalms

The psalms in this part are lovely songs of trust and confidence. The ultimate consequence of complete trust and confidence is hope. Even when Israel was in the midst of disasters, the capacity to hope enabled the nation to reject the irrational behavior of despair. A most appealing statement of trust is found in Paul's letter to the Romans: If God is for

---

A CRY FROM THE DEPTHS (PSALM 130)

Interpreters of this psalm are not in agreement about whom the psalmist is representing. Some have suggested it to be Israel. Others think it is an individual in deep distress. Its use in Christian liturgy as a psalm of penitence makes the latter interpretation more appropriate to this commentary. The opening cry (verse 1) comes from the "depths," a metaphor relating terrible distress to being in the watery deeps. From such a void, the psalmist implores God to listen (verse 2). The cry comes from an admitted sinner; yet if God kept a record (marked "sins" NIV; "iniquities" NRSV) no one would be found faultless. For such a one as this sinner, hope lies in God's willingness to forgive (verse 4). So the psalmist "waits" (verse 5) and the waiting is done even more diligently than that of the night watchman who awaits the morning (verse 6).

The climax of this petition for mercy is the expression of confidence and hope. Even though it may have been stimulated by emotional fervor, the petition speaks eloquently to circumstances in Israel's history.

---

us, who is against us? That question is a fitting introduction to a cluster of short poems which stress an intimate affiliation with God's gift of hope.

The Message of Psalms 123–130

These psalms deal with concerns of the nation and God's role in mediating the disturbances. In faithfulness to the covenant, God responds and gives Israel hope. The episodes in these psalms generally provide some rationale for Israel's maintenance of a climate of expectancy.

- There is a limit to Israel's tolerance of its enemies.

- Israel expects victory because God is with the people.

- The presence of God liberates the

people from persecution and frees them from fear.

- God will restore Israel again and again.

- God-fearing people will live successfully.

- Unless God is present nothing of value can be accomplished.

- God does punish the wicked.

- Peace for Israel is not beyond hope.

PSALMS 131–140

Introduction to These Psalms

In this part of the Psalms God's attribute of grace tends to predominate. Although evidence of this gift has not been lacking in many of the psalms already discussed, we shall attempt to highlight it here. We do this because of its special importance to individual persons harboring anxieties and depression.

The Message of Psalms 131–140

The repetitive use of "Bless the LORD" in this group of psalms is to emphasize Israel's faithfulness. The blessing is also spoken with some expectation that God's grace will be manifested in all that transpires.

- God's grace enables one to accept life as it unfolds.

- God's grace informs the actions of kings.

- God's grace is manifested by the divine presence in Jerusalem on Mount Zion.

NO ESCAPE FROM GOD (PSALM 139)

This is one of the great devotional psalms as well as a priceless literary gem circulated well beyond the Psalter. This psalm can best be understood as a very private prayer in which God and the reader are very much alone. The content differs sharply from the other psalms in this group. It does not deal with history or God's actions in Israel's behalf. On the contrary, this psalm is fully contemporary for any era and the text is largely self-explanatory.

The first stanza (verses 1-6) is an acknowledgment of God's immediate awareness of the psalmist's thoughts. Human comprehension of powers of this kind is impossible. Divine foreknowledge of every thought makes it impossible to hide from God's presence (verses 7-12). The idea that God can go to Sheol contradicts the general belief that Sheol (NRSV; NIV= depths) is a place God does not visit. The wings of the morning (NRSV) or dawn (NIV) is a metaphor of the Canaanite mythological winged goddess of dawn.

In verses 13-18 the psalmist muses on the wonders of God's creation of the human form. The language is not only beautiful but surprisingly accurate. Verses 15-16 are uncommonly perceptive in their treatment of God's creative processes through millennia of biological development. Verses 19-22 are the psalmist's vigorous reaction to enemies who are known to be God's enemies as well. This lovely psalm closes with a prayer for guidance.

- God's grace is manifested to Israel by the saving acts in the nation's history.

- God's grace provides steadfast love for Israel.

- God's grace has enabled Israel to bear its burdens, even the most calamitous.

- God's grace sustains the lowly as well as kings.

- Grace allows for private time to commune with God.

PSALMS 141–150

Introduction to These Psalms

The psalms in this final part are chiefly songs of loving adoration, praise, and thanksgiving. They are addressed to God, who gave diligent oversight to the preservation of Israel as a nation. This oversight continues in our time despite gaps of hundreds of years. These psalms are not formal Hallel songs of praise (see Psalm 113–118; 136), but they acknowledge God as the exhilarating core around which all of Israel's life swirls. The last five psalms (146–150) are identified as the *hallelujah psalms* because of the frequency of the words "Praise the LORD."

The Message of Psalms 141–150

The invitation to praise the Lord appears throughout the Psalms a hundred times or more. Praise is the predominant way Israel expressed its faithfulness to God. It seems appropriate that the last chapters of the Psalter are given over to extensive praise (Hallelujah).

- Praise God for moral guidance.
- Praise God for mercy and for salvation.
- Praise God for always being near in times of need.
- Praise God for grace and compassion.
- Praise God for freeing prisoners, healing the sick, and lifting the oppressed.
- Praise God for the care of widows and orphans.
- Praise God for bounteous harvests.
- Praise God for the special care of Israel.

CONCORDANCE OF FAMILIAR PHRASES IN THE PSALMS

All your words are true; / all your righteous laws are eternal. (119:160 NIV)

The sum of your word is truth; / and every one of your righteous ordinances endures forever. (119:160 NRSV)

As far as the east is from the west, / so far has he removed our transgressions from us. (103:12 NIV)

As far as the east is from the west, / so far he removes our transgressions from us. (103:12 NRSV)

Better is one day in your courts / than a thousand elsewhere. (84:10 NIV)

For a day in your courts is better / than a thousand elsewhere. (84:10 NRSV)

Bless the LORD, O my soul. (103:1 NRSV)

Praise the LORD, O my soul. (103:1 NIV)

Cast your cares on the LORD. (55:22 NIV)

Cast your burden on the LORD. (55:22 NRSV)

The cattle on a thousand hills. (50:10 NIV and NRSV)

Create in me a pure heart, O God. (51:10 NIV)

Create in me a clean heart, O God. (51:10 NRSV)

The days of our life are seventy years. (90:10 NRSV)

The length of our days is seventy years. (90:10 NIV)

Deep calls to deep. (42:7 NIV and NRSV)

Do not put your trust in princes. (146:3 NIV and NRSV)

Down to the sea in ships. (107:23 NRSV)

Out on the sea in ships. (107:23 NIV)

The fear of the LORD is the beginning of wisdom. (111:10 NIV and NRSV)

"Flee like a bird to your mountain." (11:1 NIV)

"Flee like a bird to the mountains." (11:1 NRSV)

The fool says in his heart, / "There is no God." (14:1 NIV)

Fools say in their hearts, "There is no God." (14:1 NRSV)

For a thousand years in your sight / are like a day that has just gone by, / or like a watch in the night. (90:4 NIV)

For a thousand years in your sight / are like yesterday when it is past, / or like a watch in the night. (90:4 NRSV)

For as high as the heavens are above the earth, / so great is his love for those who fear him. (103:11 NIV)

For as the heavens are high above the earth, / so great is his steadfast love toward those who fear him. (103:11 NRSV)

From everlasting to everlasting / the LORD's love is with those who fear him. (103:17 NIV)

The steadfast love of the LORD / is from everlasting to everlasting/ on those who fear him. (103:17 NRSV)

From everlasting to everlasting you are God. (90:2 NIV and NRSV)

God is our refuge and strength, / a very present help in trouble. (46:1 NRSV)

God is our refuge and strength, / an ever-present help in trouble. (46:1 NIV)

The God of Jacob is our fortress. (46:7 NIV)

The God of Jacob is our refuge. (46:7 NRSV)

Great is the LORD, and greatly to be praised. (145:3 NRSV)

Great is the LORD and most worthy of praise. (145:3 NIV)

He alone is my rock and my salvation; / he is my fortress, I will never be shaken. (62:2 NIV)

CONCORDANCE OF FAMILIAR PHRASES IN THE PSALMS (CONT.)

He alone is my rock and my salvation, / my fortress; I shall never be shaken. (62:2 NRSV)

He who keeps Israel will neither slumber nor sleep. (121:4 NRSV)

Indeed, he who watches over Israel / will neither slumber nor sleep. (121:4 NIV)

The heavens declare the glory of God. (19:1 NIV)

The heavens are telling the glory of God. (19:1 NRSV)

Hide me in the shadow of your wings. (17:8 NIV and NRSV)

How good and pleasant it is / when brothers live together in unity! (133:1 NIV)

How very good and pleasant it is / when kindred live together in unity! (133:1 NRSV)

How sweet are your words to my taste, / sweeter than honey to my mouth! (119:103 NIV and NRSV)

I lift up my eyes to the hills. (121:1 NIV and NRSV)

I rejoiced with those who said to me, / "Let us go to the house of the LORD." (122:1 NIV)

I was glad when they said to me, / "Let us go to the house of the LORD!" (122:1 NRSV)

If I rise on the wings of the dawn . . . (139:9 NIV)

If I take the wings of the morning . . . (139:9 NRSV)

If the LORD had not been on our side . . . (124:1 NIV)

If it had not been the LORD who was on our side . . . (124:1 NRSV)

It is good to praise the LORD. (92:1 NIV)

It is good to give thanks to the LORD. (92:1 NRSV)

Keep me as the apple of your eye. (17:8 NIV)

Guard me as the apple of the eye. (17:8 NRSV)

The law of the LORD is perfect. (19:7 NIV and NRSV)

Lead me in the way everlasting. (139:24 NIV and NRSV)

Lead me to the rock that is higher than I. (61:2 NIV and NRSV)

Let the words of my mouth and the meditation of my heart / be acceptable to you. (19:14 NRSV)

May the words of my mouth and the meditation of my heart / be pleasing in your sight. (19:14 NIV)

The LORD is king! Let the earth rejoice. (97:1 NRSV)

The LORD reigns, let the earth be glad. (97:1 NIV)

The LORD is merciful and gracious, / slow to anger and abounding in steadfast love. (103:8 NRSV)

The LORD is compassionate and gracious, / slow to anger, abounding in love. (103:8 NIV)

The LORD is in his holy temple. (11:4 NIV and NRSV)

The LORD will keep you from all harm. (121:7 NIV)

The LORD will keep you from all evil. (121:7 NRSV)

May the peoples praise you, O God. (67:3 NIV)

Let the peoples praise you, O God. (67:3 NRSV)

Make a joyful noise to God, all the earth. (66:1 NRSV)

Shout with joy to God, all the earth! (66:1 NIV)

May God be gracious to us and bless us / and make his face shine upon us. (67:1 NIV)

May God be gracious to us and bless us / and make his face to shine upon us. (67:1 NRSV)

My cup overflows. (23:5 NIV and NRSV)

My God, my God, why have you forsaken me? (22:1 NIV and NRSV)

My soul waits for the Lord. (130:6 NIV and NRSV)

My times are in your hands. (31:15 NIV)

CONCORDANCE OF FAMILIAR PHRASES IN THE PSALMS (CONT.)

My times are in your hand. (31:15 NRSV)

"Oh, that I had the wings of a dove!" (55:6 NIV)

"O that I had wings like a dove!" (55:6 NRSV)

Our help is in the name of the LORD, / the Maker of heaven and earth. (124:8 NIV)

Our help is in the name of the LORD, / who made heaven and earth. (124:8 NRSV)

Out of the depths I cry to you, O LORD. (130:1 NIV and NRSV)

Out of the mouths of babes and infants . . . (8:2 NRSV)

From the lips of children and infants . . . (8:2 NIV)

Search me, O God, and know my heart. (139:23 NIV and NRSV)

Send forth your light and your truth. (43:3 NIV)

O send out your light and your truth. (43:3 NRSV)

The stone that the builders rejected / has become the chief cornerstone. (118:22 NRSV)

The stone the builders rejected / has become the capstone. (118:22 NIV)

Teach me your decrees. (119:135 NIV)

Teach me your statutes. (119:135 NRSV)

Teach us to number our days aright, / that we may gain a heart of wisdom. (90:12 NIV)

So teach us to count our days / that we may gain a wise heart. (90:12 NRSV)

They were at their wits' end. (107:27 NIV)

[They] were at their wits' end. (107:27 NRSV)

Unless the LORD builds the house, / its builders labor in vain. (127:1 NIV)

Unless the LORD builds the house, / those who build it labor in vain. (127:1 NRSV)

Wash me, and I will be whiter than snow. (51:7 NIV)

Wash me, and I shall be whiter than snow. (51:7 NRSV)

Where can I go from your Spirit? (139:7 NIV)

Where can I go from your spirit? (139:7 NRSV)

Your word is a lamp to my feet / and a light for my path. (119:105 NIV)

Your word is a lamp to my feet / and a light to my path. (119:105 NRSV)

PROVERBS

INTRODUCTION TO WISDOM LITERATURE

Proverbs, Job, and Ecclesiastes belong to a particular group of books within the Hebrew Bible commonly known as Wisdom Literature. Members of the Roman Catholic community add two additional wisdom books to their biblical canon, Sirach and the Wisdom of Solomon. The early church included Psalms and Song of Solomon among the poetical books of the Old Testament, bringing the number to seven.

The designation of these books as Wisdom Literature stems from the central theme of these writings, namely the theme of wisdom as the goal of all human activity. Wisdom, or being wise, refers to several different kinds of knowledge or expertise that may be achieved in different ways and may be exhibited in diverse forms. Accordingly, the wisdom books appear quite different in literary styles, ethical values, and theological themes.

The final versions seem to have been the literary product of a special class of persons in early Israel, known as the sages or wise men. This professional group spent considerable energy discovering the meaning and values of human existence within a divine moral order. They also collected, organized, and wrote down the adages and proverbial lore of previous generations.

Human existence, as perceived by the sage, is comprehensible only within the limits of wisdom. Happiness and well-being come only to the persons who discover and exercise wisdom. The literary results of these practical insights into life and its meaning come down to us in the Wisdom Literature of the Old Testament.

What Does Wisdom Mean?

The Hebrew term for wisdom is *hokmah*. Across the many centuries of ancient Israelite history, this term amassed a broad range of meanings, so many in fact that a single simple definition is almost impossible to formulate. Generally, wisdom may be said to refer to five types of human activities: (1) technical skill, (2) political insight, (3) moral knowledge, (4) a gift of divine revelation, and (5) superior knowledge, broadly speaking. Probably it is best not to assume an evolutionary pattern of historical growth for the concept of wisdom, since many of these different meanings probably functioned simultaneously in early Israel.

First, the term wisdom is applied to persons who exhibit expert technical skill in some area of craftsmanship or construction. In Exodus 35:30-35, Bezalel, a wise craftsman filled with God's Spirit, is adept at working with gold, silver, bronze, and with stones. Similarly, Oholiab has extraordinary talent with fabrics. Elsewhere other persons highly skilled in some technical vocation are identified as wise: farmers (Isaiah 28:23-29), professional mourners (Jeremiah 9:17), and entrepreneurs (Ezekiel 28:4-5).

Verification of the wisdom of these persons came by the empirical method; firsthand experience and direct observation validated their wisdom. While Bezalel's skill is clearly the result of long experience and training, the capacity for this expertise is viewed by the biblical writer as a gift from God. Thus a secular talent was not distinguished from a theological interpretation.

Second, wisdom is also used to characterize persons who provided astute political advice. Ahithophel, a trusted political adviser to King David who turned traitor to participate in Absalom's ill-fated revolt, is considered wise (2 Samuel 16: 23). An anonymous wise woman from Tekoa aids Joab in convincing David to recall his son Absalom from exile (2 Samuel 14:1-20). Certainly this political astuteness applied to King Solomon as well (1 Kings 4:29).

Third, a wise person is one with keen moral insight (Proverbs 1:2). These persons have knowledge of the divinely established pattern of cause and effect, and such knowledge clearly enables them to attain worldly success and to avoid the disasters of folly. The particular values associated with this moral insight enable a person to achieve happiness and to prosper materially in this life. These virtues can be learned, but must be taught too, since they are not altogether natural. In a word, wisdom morality is an ethic that relies on human reason and moral effort to master the game of life. It has a definite utilitarian nature and determines moral worth on the basis of consequences.

The entire value system and the means of achieving it have a definite theological foundation in the notions of Creation theology and the concept of the fear of the Lord. Both of these themes will be discussed further in the introduction to Proverbs; it is sufficient here to stress that morality was never viewed as an end in itself, nor held apart from religious faith. The ultimate purpose of right conduct was to satisfy a person's obligation to God. Moral right was right only because God declared it to be right.

Fourth, in Proverbs 1:20-33 and 9:1-6 the concept of wisdom is personified and depicted as a female prophet. She boldly extends the Lord's gift of life to those who respond affirmatively to her call, and utters God's judgment upon all who shun her counsel. Wisdom is understood here too as the gift of divine revelation. In 8:22-31 the idea is personified and depicted as a darling child, playing as God creates the world.

Finally, wisdom is used to designate a broader, more inclusive quality than denoted by the four preceding special abilities, namely superior knowledge. King Solomon (1 Kings 4:29-34) serves as the prime model for such a wise person in the Old Testament. The tremendous breadth of his knowledge ranged from judicial matters to zoology, from moral conduct to literary genius. Apart from moral excellence or even the religious element in wisdom as God's gift, a wise person in the Old Testament is the person who is simply smarter than the average individual— smarter in every way.

The Theology of Wisdom Literature

The theological realm operative for the sage differs remarkably from that found in the Pentateuch, the historical books, and the prophets. Even within the Old Testament itself, notably Jeremiah 18:18 and Ezekiel 7:26, attention is called to the differences among the priest, the prophet, and the sage. The law or instruction of the priest as well as the word of the prophet both reflect a belief that divine revelation somehow was not a part of the natural order of things, and often intruded into history. God and nature were related as Creator and created, but even so, sharp differences still existed between them. And Israel's history, in particular as interpreted by Israel's historians, was understandable only from a theological point of view—history and revelation.

By contrast, the sage's world lay in the realm of concrete human experience and individual ethical values as means to a happy, successful life. Formal religious practices and priestly Torah were part of another world for the sage. Even the word of the prophet fell outside the sage's sphere of operation. For the person of wisdom, divine revelation came through a moral order open to reason, experience, and reflection. For every human action, there was an obvious consequence. Successful living came about precisely because a person knew this pattern and operated within its limits.

Since this moral system had been established by God, faith became the keen awareness of this order, indeed a profound respect (fear of the Lord) for its operations. Reason and human experience were fully capable of perceiving and understanding the will of God. No special instruction or divinely inspired word were necessary. The sage lived in a different world, and his literary expressions stand in bold relief to the work of priests, prophets, and historians.

From Whence Did Wisdom Come?

Across the long years of her national history, Israel witnessed the rise and development of three classes of religious leaders: the priest, the prophet, and the wise man or sage (see Jeremiah 18:18). Each of these three groups communicated God's words in distinctive ways. The priest issued law or instruction, the prophet spoke oracles of judgment or salvation, and the sage offered counsel. Many scholars now believe that the sages were a professional class in Israel, and that much of our biblical Wisdom Literature derives from their work, either directly or indirectly.

The sages seem to have been a learned class of persons who were highly regarded for their practical and perceptive insights into morality, politics, and psychology. They produced an elitist code of ethics (now found in Proverbs) that assumed a high level of economic well-being and social development. The values they promoted were aimed at self-actualization and happiness through obedience to the divinely established moral order. Highly individualistic and utilitarian, the sages concerned themselves with how persons could best succeed in society as it existed at that time and how they could best transmit the wisdom.

However, not all the Wisdom Literature originated with these learned sages in the national state during the monarchy. The beginnings of this kind of knowledge dated far back into the early stages of Israelite history. Many of the proverbial sayings later collected by the sages first began as folklore, as riddles, and as pithy sayings told for amusement as well as for erudition.

Cultures throughout the world claim long literary histories for proverbs. Perhaps such sayings were passed along for generations from parent to child, or by singers of tales. Clearly, the imperative-style instructional material originated in the family unit, with the father taking primary responsibility for his child's moral education. Encapsulating these fundamental insights of nature and of human behavior into literary forms, the ancient Israelites carefully nurtured a tradition of proverbs that eventually became a part of a body of material preserved and enriched by the sages. It is entirely possible that some of the sayings of the Old Testament date back to these early periods.

Yet a third source for the Old Testament wisdom material was the theological community in ancient Israel. Whether or not such persons in the community were vocationally distinctive, or were perhaps even sages, cannot be determined. But many Israelite proverbs bear an unmistakable religious imprint (10:22). Such sayings reflect a deep faith in God as the moral force in human society.

Other sayings attest to divine guidance in the affairs of persons (Proverbs 16:9). But perhaps the most telling evidence that secular wisdom was closely related to Israelite faith is the crucial declaration that the fear of the Lord is the beginning of wisdom (Proverbs 1:7). At precisely what point in Israelite history these sayings underwent this immersion in theology is uncertain. It is also difficult to identify the social circles or institutions out of which the proverbs came. Perhaps some sages who experienced their moral teachings through two-line proverbial sayings also expressed their faith through the same literary form.

The majority of proverbial sayings and other longer pieces within the Wisdom Literature originated from within these three circles. Even so, King Solomon must be mentioned also in any discussion of sources for wisdom. Whether he penned as many proverbs himself as mentioned in 1 Kings 4:32, or whether he patronized learned sages in some type of royal school, Solomon must be credited with bringing Israelite wisdom into prominence.

With King Solomon, wisdom became the special province of the royal court. Training and instruction passed from the home to the school; the style became didactic and the tone persuasive. Certainly,

as Israelite culture flourished under the monarchy, a new pride grew in the human intellect. Thus the coming of age marked the real birth of the professional sage.

OUTLINE OF PROVERBS

I. **A Father's Instruction (1:1–4:27)**
   A. Superscription (1:1)
   B. The purpose of Proverbs (1:2-7)
   C. Avoiding the ways of sinners (1:8-19)
   D. Wisdom's prophetic announcement (1:20-33)
   E. The benefits of wisdom (2:1-22)
   F. The Benefits of Faith (3:1-12)
   G. The wisdom of God (3:13-20)
   H. Moral instruction (3:21-35)
   I. A father's instruction (4:1-27)

II. **Moral Values of the Wise (5:1–9:18)**
   A. Avoiding temptations from women (5:1-23)
   B. Instructions against wrong conduct (6:1-35)
   C. Instructions to avoid adultery (7:1-27)
   D. Wisdom's second announcement (8:1-36)
   E. Wisdom and folly contrasted (9:1-18)

III. **The Proverbs of Solomon (10:1–22:16)**
   A. Group one (10:1-32)
   B. Group two (11:1-31)
   C. Group three (12:1-28)
   D. Group four (13:1-25)
   E. Group five (14:1-35)
   F. Group six (15:1-33)
   G. Group seven (16:1-33)
   H. Group eight (17:1-28)
   I. Group nine (18:1-24)
   J. Group ten (19:1-29)

INTRODUCTION

The book of Proverbs presents a wide range of moral instructions, dressed in the literary styles of proverbial sayings and brief poems. The six sections within the book were written over many centuries, by many hands, and under vastly different circumstances. But beneath the watchful eye of post exilic editors, these many diverse sayings were assembled, edited, and offered confidently as a guide to a happy, fulfilling, and prosperous life.

The Content of Proverbs

The range of ethical teachings is as broad as human experience itself. This anthology presents advice on conduct such as proper sexual behavior, industriousness, effective communication, loyalty, friendship, and abstinence from intoxicants.

Many sayings reflect a strong religious belief, encouraging faith and obedience to the Lord's will. Yet other sayings probe the mysteries of God's revelations in the strange world of nature or within the perplexing nexus of human relationships. Some sayings reflect the regularity and predictability of the natural order. All these sayings are preserved precisely because they work well, because they have been tested in the vast crucible of human experience, and because they have all stood the test of time. They present a high standard of conduct. The writers are confident in their belief that God rewards the righteous person and punishes the evildoer.

Certainly the book of Proverbs is a manual of instruction, but even more, it is a profound synthesis of early faith and human reason. For the sages who coined the proverbs and edited the sayings composing the book of Proverbs, there was no greater act of piety than the apprehension and enactment of moral virtue. The goal of moral knowledge was an instrumental goal, useful in conforming to God's will as exhibited in the natural and moral order. The book of Proverbs is a fitting legacy to this very different model of religious faith. Moral conduct was indeed an appropriate expression of faith in God.

Structure and Organization

The book of Proverbs can be divided into six sections, based on internal headings and clear changes in literary style and ethical/religious content: (1) Introduction (1:1–9:18); (2) The Proverbs of Solomon (10:1–22:16); (3) The Sayings of the Wise (22:17–24:22); (4) Supplement to the Sayings of the Wise (24:23-34); (5) The Proverbs of Solomon II (25:1–29:27); and (6) Four Appendices (30:1–31:31). Analysis of these sections suggests to scholars that Proverbs consists of various strands of material that originally existed independently of one another. Variations in literary style alone indicate separate authors, different settings and dates, and distinct purposes. For these reasons, Proverbs has aptly been characterized as an anthology.

Just as one finds no transitional elements between the six separate sections, other than the superscript headings, there is little effort made to link or group individual sayings within respective units. Especially in 10:1–22:16, this style can lead to a certain monotony.

Authorship and Date

Tradition ascribes principal authorship of the book of Proverbs to King Solomon, the son of David, King of Israel. In part, this belief is based on the superscriptions in the book itself (1:1, 10:1, and 25:1). Also, Solomon is alleged to have composed three thousand proverbs (1 Kings 4:29-34) and numerous songs, and to have been wise in greater measure than the sands of the seashore. However, internal literary divisions and subject analysis suggest that many persons composed the sayings and poems in Proverbs. In fact, even Proverbs itself mentions the authors Agur (30:1) and Lemuel (31:1). Still other sayings were collected by the men of Hezekiah (25:1).

While King Solomon could easily have written and collected thousands of proverbs (since he was probably responsible for promoting and nurturing the wisdom tradition in his royal court), the style, vocabulary, and theme of many sayings in chapters 1–9, 22:17–24:22, and 30–31 indicate authors and dates other than King Solomon. Yet because of Solomon's undisputed contributions to Israelite wisdom, the compilers of the Hebrew Bible were proper in honoring Solomon by the dedicatory superscription in 1:1.

The authorship of proverbial sayings stemmed from three major centers: the Royal Wisdom School (founded by Solomon and nurtured during the monarchy), folk tradition, and the theological community. Still other sayings arose from anonymous individuals in ancient Israel, and became part of an ever-increasing repository of collective knowledge available to the community. Also, we believe that a Hebrew sage borrowed substantial material from the Egyptian source known as Instructions of Amenemope. And from within the book of Proverbs, we have the materials ascribed to Agur (30:1) and Lemuel (31:1).

Because of the very nature of proverbial sayings as true and universal insight into human existence, they truly became the property of the entire community. The legacy of Proverbs is not, therefore, a legacy of a particular scribe or king, but the legacy of an entire nation. Proverbs is an anthology of the ancient Israelite wisdom tradition.

The problem of assigning dates to either individual sayings or the collections of sayings is also difficult. Careful study of comparative Wisdom Literature from Egypt, Mesopotamia, and Ugarit has led Old Testament scholars to rethink earlier notions about the dating of certain literary forms and themes. A post exilic date for Proverbs 1–9, for example, is no longer a necessary conclusion; there are parallel materials that are clearly from the tenth or ninth centuries.

Scholars also no longer maintain the notion that the two-line proverbial saying is a later development (or corruption) of the one-line unit. Further complicating the dating issue is the absence of specific historical references. As indicated earlier, the superscriptions are more reflective of special patronage than of actual Solomonic authorship. The difficulties of dating notwithstanding, the meaning of most proverbial sayings is relatively clear and timeless.

Although it is likely that most of the six sections of Proverbs were in existence by the latter part of the fourth century, differences in the arrangement of certain sections of Proverbs in the Greek translation of the Old Testament suggest that the book itself was not finalized until the late Hellenistic period. It is also entirely possible that a few sayings were added during that late phase of development, as suggested by Aramaic and Greek loan words

Theological Themes in Proverbs

The book of Proverbs pivots on the axis of five major theological themes: (1) divine retribution, (2) the fear of the Lord, (3) moral conduct, (4) divine revelation, and (5) creation orders. Many other theological themes surface in Proverbs as well, as is to be expected in such an eclectic work. From time to time, certain themes may even appear to contradict one another. There are repetitions of themes, comparisons, contrasts, analogies, puns, and so forth. But most of the proverbs relate to the five themes mentioned above.

Divine retribution is the idea that the Lord rewards the person of faith and righteousness, and punishes the apostate person and the evildoer. A detailed analysis of appropriate Old Testament texts reflects variation in both the means of retribution and the timing of a divine response. For example, in Genesis 18:22-33, because God is just (righteous), Abraham can persuade God to consider carefully judgment against Sodom. Even so, once Lot and his family escape, Sodom is destroyed; retribution is directly executed

by God and is relatively swift. Elsewhere, in Habakkuk, God admonishes the prophet to wait and have faith (Habakkuk 2:3). The editor(s) of the extended historical works in Deuteronomy through 2 Kings clearly feels that the Exile is a just punishment for Israel because of their apostasy. Isaiah and Jeremiah both view "history" as the realm where God operates.

While theological refinements indicate differences in the ways and means of retribution, the Old Testament most certainly views both history and nature as locales where the Lord rewards the righteous and punishes the evildoers. In Proverbs, however, divine retribution occurs through the operation of the moral order (11:8, 11). The law of act-consequence operates without exception: Evil acts bring their own punishment (1:8-19). Of course, this innate moral system of the universe is the creation of God, and as such it surely operates under God's will. But retribution for the sages does not involve suspensions of the ordinary scheme of nature or intrusion into history. Each human act contains intrinsically the seeds of its own consequence; this is retribution for the sage.

"The fear of the Lord" is an expression used by the sage to refer to religious faith. In fact, for the sage, the ultimate level of human knowledge or insight brings a person to an acute consciousness of God's natural and social order. Human reason always requires the empowering of faith to function properly. Just as the natural order is governed by certain laws (such as gravity and inertia), so too is the social or moral order governed by act-consequence. The dangers occurring from ignoring this "order" of things are clear and foreboding. But the benefits of wisdom are success and fulfillment. True respect for this sovereign moral order of the universe is known as the fear of the Lord.

Logically following from the notion of the fear of the Lord is a strongly rigid moral code. The panoply of ethical values displayed in Proverbs was encoded into the universe by God. Therefore, conformity yields success! Right behavior, as prescribed by the divine moral order, brings prosperity, just as wrong behavior brings worldly failure. Thus morality for the sage was measured by consequences; utility became the guide to what God expected. Specifically, the sages warn against association with evil companions (1:8-19), consorting with harlots (7:10-23), drunkenness (23:29-35), and so forth. They commend industry, proper communication, etiquette, honesty, friendship, and above all, the fear of the Lord.

Fourth, the sages perceived God's presence in ways that were different from the concepts of revelation advanced by priests and prophets. The sages began, theologically, at a different point in their quest for divine knowledge; they began with general human experience in nature, and moved analogically to the realm of human morality. They observed the orderly operations of nature: the regular seasons, gravity, growth, mating patterns, and so forth. By analogy, human interrelationships exhibited similar patterns of predictability, because the same divine laws of act-consequence that animated nature also structured human existence. The will of the Lord was clearly evident in the created order. Righteousness, loyalty, and prudence were God's moral expectations as preserved in experience.

Fifth, Creation for the sages assumes a different theological meaning than it does for the authors of the Pentateuch. Creation in Proverbs marks the establishment of both a natural and a moral order. It does not provide a historical framework for human sin and divine redemption. Creation here means regularity, predictability, causation, comprehensibility. Creation reflects the moral nature of the universe; the world and human existence are not indifferent moral concerns, precisely because God implanted a moral fabric within the scheme of the universe. To discover Creation is to discover God's moral will. The notion of divine Creation is a resounding affirmation of the meaning of human existence; life has value because God created it so.

PROVERBS 1–4

Introduction to These Chapters

Here is an outline of Proverbs 1–4

I. Superscription (1:1)

II. The Purpose of Proverbs (1:2-7)

III. Avoiding the Ways of Sinners (1:8-19)

IV. Wisdom's Prophetic Announcement (1:20-33)

V. The Benefits of Wisdom (2:1-22)

VI. The Benefits of Faith (3:1-12)

VII. The Wisdom of God (3:13-20)

VIII. Moral Instruction (3:21-35)

IX. A Father's Instruction (4:1-27)

The Message of Proverbs 1–4

The openly religious nature of these beginning chapters may well surprise the reader who is more accustomed to the practical morality in the sayings of 10:1–22:16. Although absent from chapters 1–4 are references to the great traditions of the Exodus, election, law, and kingship, Proverbs nonetheless attests to the belief that God established a moral order at Creation, and that life is abundant only with proper regard for this order. The faith of a sage may be different from the faith of a priest or a prophet, but all three groups still affirm the notions of God, of divine revelation, and of human responsibility.

Chapter 2 clearly structures human

intellectual knowledge and morality within the realm of religious faith (verses 5-9). Wisdom and understanding, insight and morality (verses 2-3), are not ends in themselves. The goal of reason is not knowledge for the sake of knowledge. The true object of human knowledge and morality is a proper understanding of God and of the orders of creation. True insight into human existence is impossible apart from faith, and is meaningless without this faith. True insight is insight into how God's world operates and how humankind is intended to fit into this operation.

With this faith, both true understanding and right conduct become clear. Expressed differently, knowledge and morality both lead persons to knowledge of God and follow from the knowledge of God. Perhaps this relationship defies rational comprehension, but ultimately faith, the fear of the Lord, is both the effect and the cause of knowledge and morality.

The second major theme found in Proverbs 1–4 is the delicate balance between human effort and divine grace. Although this problem may seem more at home in the letters of Paul and in the life of the earliest Christian communities, works versus grace was also a matter of concern to the Old Testament sage.

The sage clearly advocated personal morality, knowledge of act-consequence, and mastery over nature. While these goals were assuredly unattainable apart from faith (3:5), they do seem to be the consequence of human effort. In 4:13-18, wisdom produces life itself! Yet, verses 5-8 suggest that such effort should be secondary and that God supplies the cause of right conduct.

Perhaps the sage feels the dynamic tension between faith and works, and believes that somehow they come together with one nourishing the other. Human righteousness leads to the fear of God and

yet, at the same time, proceeds from it. Only in theological analysis are they separable; in actual practice, faith and human effort are synthesized as opposite poles on a magnetic field. They energize each other.

PROVERBS 5–9

Introduction to These Chapters

Chapters 5–9 continue the moral teachings begun in chapters 2–4. The principal genre continues to be the instruction, and the style consists of synonymous and synthetic parallelism. In addition to the instruction, these chapters contain a numerical saying (6:16-19), two poems personifying wisdom (8:1-36 and 9:1-6), and an expanded poem detailing the dangers of adultery (chapter 7).

These chapters may be outlined as follows.

I. Avoiding Temptations from Women (5:1-23)
II. Instructions Against Wrong Conduct (6:1-35)
III. Instructions to Avoid Adultery (7:1-27)
IV. Wisdom's Second Announcement (8:1-36)
V. Wisdom and Folly Contrasted (9:1-18)

The Message of Proverbs 5–9

Proverbs 5–9 contains several major themes that are of great significance in the religious life of ancient Israel. The sages made serious attempts to define specific behavior that surely led to disaster: fornication, adultery, unwise debt assumption, indolence and lack of advanced planning and preparation, lying, stirring up dissension, and so forth. These chapters also introduce the important notion of individual responsibility (9:12). Proverbs 6:20-35 contrasts the life-giving light of wisdom with the fateful end of

THE "HEART" IN THE OLD TESTAMENT

The Hebrew term for "heart," often translated as "mind," is easily misunderstood in English translation. In both languages, the heart can simply be the organ in one's chest. But of greater interest biblically is its metaphorical use for the internal wellspring of the acting self. In the modern West, heart and head are often opposed as the loci of feeling and thinking, respectively. But the ancient Hebrews used "heart" comprehensively to indicate the inner person, the "I" that is the locus of a person's will, thought (Prov 16:1, 9; 19:21), and feeling (Prov 14:10, 13; 17:22). Thus all of a person's actions (Prov 15:13; 2 Sam 7:3), especially speech (Prov 16:23), flow from the heart, expressing its content, whether good or bad (Gen 6:5; 8:21; Sir 37:17-18; Matt 12:33-35; 18:18-19). Scripture can use related terms, such as "belly" and "kidneys" Jer 11:20; 17:10) in much the same way as "heart" (cf. John 7:38 NRSV footnote).

Most important, one's basic disposition toward God is a matter of the "heart" (Prov 3:5; 19:3; Deut 6:5; 1 Sam 12:20). Like a deep well, the heart has a hidden depth (Prov 20:5). Its deepest depths, what modern psychologists might call the subconscious or the unconscious, only God can plumb (Prov 25:2-3), though hidden even from the heart's owner and friends: "The heart is devious above all else, and beyond cure—who can understand it? I the Lord test the mind and search the heart" (Jer 17:9-10 NRSV and NIV collated; cf. Prov 21:2; 15:11).

When seeking to replace Saul, the Lord finds in David "a man after his own heart" (1 Sam 13:14 NRSV). But even the seer Samuel is not able to recognize the Lord's chosen, because mortals "look on the outward appearance, but the LORD looks on the heart" (1 Sam 16:7). In Proverbs, since the heart is the locus of wisdom, it often is used to suggest wisdom. Those who are not wise "lack heart" (Prov 7:7; 10:13).

We can understand the absolute urgency of the admonition in Prov 4:23: "Above all else, guard your heart" (NIV). This is a fundamental precept, like Socrates' "know thyself"; but it goes beyond Socrates in depth and scope. For Israel, all human hearts are inescapably related to the one Lord, whether in loving service, in uncertain vacillation (1 Kgs 18:21; Ps 86:11), or in grievous rebellion (Prov 19:3). Thus in a prayer that plumbs anthropological depths, the psalmist, wary of personal sin and self-deception, concludes, "Search me, O God, and know my heart" (Ps 139:23). Augustine understood the biblical heart well: "Our hearts are restless until they find their rest in thee." And when the prophets anticipate God's final renewal of a wounded and disobedient human race, they do it in terms of the heart, as it is the hidden seed of the new humanity: "A new heart I will give you, and a new spirit I will put within you. . . . I will put my spirit within you, and make you follow my statutes . . . and you shall be my people, and I will be your God" (Ezek 36:26-28; see also Ps 51:7-11; Jer 24:7; 31:33).

Even though the heart can represent the whole person in its "mental," inner aspect (what my heart thinks is what I think), there is in the admonition to guard one's heart an awareness of the mysterious reflexivity that humans possess: I can look at myself and make even my inmost self the object of care, reflection, improvement, and betterment. Some commentators have looked upon guarding the heart (Prov 4:23) as equivalent to keeping it from sin. The admonition is more comprehensive than that, but certainly does not exclude it, as is evident from Prov 4:24.

folly. These themes reinforce the notion that, for the sage, religious belief and proper moral conduct are inseparable.

Another theme emerging from these chapters is the relationship between Wisdom and Creation. In chapter 8 Wisdom describes herself as being present when God was creating the world (8:22-23). Then Wisdom turned and became available to humans, as a source of ultimate understanding, giving persons insight into the mysteries of God.

PROVERBS 10–14

Introduction to These Chapters

Chapter 10 begins a new section of Proverbs, distinct from chapters 1–9. It begins with a new superscription in verse 1. Also, there is a change in style from extended poems, instructions, and shorter poems to two-line sayings characterized by parallelism.

The Message of Proverbs 10–14

Few new theological insights emerge in this section. Rather, righteousness is defined by many new examples, and the way of folly receives judgment. Specific virtues—honesty in court, compassion for the poor, judicious speech, hard work, patience—characterize the righteous person. The rewards of this proper conduct are divine favor, longevity, community esteem, prosperity, and peace of mind. This proper morality arises from faith (the fear of the Lord).

This connection between creed and conduct is reciprocal—one cannot function effectively without the other. Undergirding this effort to instill morality, the sages affirm over and over again the principle of divine retribution—the Lord rewards the righteous and punishes the wicked, here on earth. Divine judgment (or reward) is not postponed.

PROVERBS 15–18

Introduction to These Chapters

These chapters continue the collection of short, two-line sayings that began in chapter 10. All the proverbs in this section are attributed to Solomon.

The Message of Proverbs 15–18

In chapter 16, God's name appears in eight of the first nine sayings. Three of these eight sayings (verses 1, 4, and 9) affirm the notion of divine determinism (that is, the idea that earthly events occur according to God's will, for some higher purpose). See especially verse 4a.

Later in the same chapter, verse 33 states that even the sacred lots fall at the Lord's will. Collectively, these four sayings argue for more than divine foreknowledge; they insist that there is a causal relationship between events on earth and God's will. Human existence falls under divine control. Human beings are not the makers of history, but history's recipients.

Clearly, divine determinism eliminates the reality of human freedom (see Deuteronomy 30:15; Proverbs 12:11). Human guilt is also called into question. That is, how can God hold persons responsible unless they have the freedom and ability to do something other than what they did? Yet, according to Proverbs 16, we have no real part to play in the events that befall us. This is indeed a paradox! Both divine determinism and human freedom can be documented in the Old Testament.

PROVERBS 19:1–22:16

Introduction to These Chapters

These chapters continue the sayings under the heading Proverbs of Solomon.

The Message of Proverbs 19:1–22:16

For the sages, kingship seems to be both socially and morally necessary, and it has political and military value as well. Moreover, the king is subject to divine providence, just as all other human beings are (see 20:18). Kings, too, are subject to the operations of the moral order of divine retribution. Therefore, it is particularly wrong for a king to be perverse (see 16:12). Kings are required to administer justice in legal dealings (16:10) and to always be fair and above reproach.

As organizers and maintainers of social order, kings are necessary. Without their wise leadership, society would deteriorate into chaos and anarchy. Sages establish high standards of conduct for kings and make them responsible for their own behavior, just like everyone else. Along with the power of the king comes responsibility, for the king sets the pace for moral excellence.

PROVERBS 22:17–24:34

Introduction to These Chapters

Since the publication in 1923 of the Egyptian Instructions of Amenemope, biblical scholars have noted numerous parallels, both in form and in theme, between Proverbs 22:17–24:22 and the Egyptian document. Similarities in the introduction, in the expanded style of the standard two-line indicative saying, the almost precise count of thirty sayings, and the thematic content have led scholars to conclude that a Hebrew sage probably borrowed Amenemope's material to include in his own work.

Minor revisions were necessary to accomodate Israelite religion, and a few words were changed here and there. Such a practice among ancient Near Eastern sages was not uncommon, as many other such parallels exist among Egyptian, Mesopotamian, and Israelite wisdom materials. The international context of the wisdom movement brought together scribes from many nations. There was considerable exchange of ideas and literary styles, and there were lively debates.

During the monarchy and afterwards, Israel was doubtless a participant in these interchanges. It is, therefore, neither surprising nor dishonest that one sage borrows material from another sage. After all, wisdom's gifts were universal, bound neither by political boundaries nor by religious loyalties.

Here is an outline of this section.
I. Introduction (22:17-21)
II. The Thirty Sayings (22:22–24:34)
  A. Group one (22:22-29)
  B. Group two (23:1-35)
  C. Group three (24:1-34)

The Message of Proverbs 22:17–24:34

Most Old Testament scholars concur that Proverbs is a manual for ethical instruction. The sayings were collected and presented in order that generations of students might learn to distinguish righteousness and wisdom from evil and folly. Much of the material appears here because of its practical nature. It gives sound advice or teaches valuable lessons. Youth, especially, can be and should be taught right behavior—it does not come naturally.

There are also many sayings in Proverbs that emphasize purity of intent, rather than merely outward consequence. In 16:2, the Lord is described as weighing the spirit (NRSV), which means understanding the true motives of the heart (NIV). In 20:12 God created not only the outward senses, but the inward spirit as well. In 21:2 the Lord weighs the heart. Outward behavior is only one criterion for ethical evaluation—motive must also be taken into account in determining the virtue of an act.

In short, the ethics of Proverbs are much more complex and sophisticated than might be imagined. The Israelite sages established several criteria for assessing the moral worth (or worthlessness) of human behavior. Traditional categories of philosophical ethics must be used with caution in analyzing Proverbs. The sayings in Proverbs come from many hands, reflect many ethical criteria, and urge many patterns of conduct deemed "wise." Both the ends and the means are important elements in righteous conduct.

Israel and Judah. Divine leadership came through the mouth of prophets, called aside to deliver a unique word. Then in the Wisdom Literature, the sages claimed God's will could be discerned through the natural and moral orders. Righteous conduct always met divine approval while folly ended in divine judgment.

PROVERBS 25–29

Introduction to These Chapters

These chapters contain more proverbs of Solomon. They may be outlined as follows.

  I. Superscription (25:1)
  II. Group One (25:2-28)
  III. Group Two (26:1-28)
  IV. Group Three (27:1-27)
  V. Group Four (28:1-28)
  VI. Group Five (29:1-27)

The Message of Proverbs 25–29

The message of this section of Proverbs is based on the general assumption that God is revealed in various ways, including the law (28:4, 7 ,9), prophecy (29:18), and the teachings of wisdom (1:20-33).

The law (Hebrew Torah) generally refers to the Pentateuch, or the first five books in the Old Testament. Because of its traditional authority in Jewish thought, the Law occupies a position of supremacy in the canon. The concepts of election (God's special choice of Israel as a means of grace) and the Exodus (freedom and redemption) provided ancient Israel with a sense of theological identity and purpose. The laws the people received at Mount Sinai distinguished them from other peoples, and provided a means by which they satisfied their obligation to the Lord.

In the prophetic literature, Israel's theologians recorded their interpretations of God's operations in the histories of

PROVERBS 30–31

Introduction to These Chapters

Here is a brief outline of these chapters.
  I. The Words of Agur (30:1-9)
  II. Instructions and Numerical Sayings (30:10-33)
  III. The Words of Lemuel (31:1-9)
  IV. The Ideal Wife (31:10-31)

The Message of Proverbs 30–31

In a book that serves as the standard for divine retribution in the Old Testament, the words of Agur appear shocking and certainly out of place. To question wisdom's disclosure of divine knowledge, including the paths of moral righteousness, strikes at the very heart of wisdom theology.

Agur confesses his ignorance of wisdom, that is, the knowledge that comes from God. But even more disturbing is his belief that other persons are likewise ignorant. No one really has journeyed up to heaven and returned! No one can collect the winds and hold them in a clenched fist. No one can except God. Such knowledge is not possible for humans—not even the sages.

In many respects, we share Agur's doubts. Often, our actual experiences do not confirm wisdom theology and its notion of retribution. Job and Ecclesiastes had difficulty reconciling the experience of human suffering with wisdom's doctrine of retribution.

But Agur did not have the last word, for the final verses (30:5-9) respond well to his doubts. Only within the embrace of faith can one find understanding to confront (if not explain) human limitations on the knowledge of God's ways. Belief in divine retribution is a confession of faith, not a description of empirical facts. Agur's objections are offset by the only refutation possible—a confession of faith. For within faith, the Lord provides comfort and promise.

ECCLESIASTES

OUTLINE OF ECCLESIASTES

INTRODUCTION

The book of Ecclesiastes is certainly one of the most fascinating books in the Old Testament. Yet, when one begins reading, one may well wonder exactly how such a book came to be included in the Old Testament. After all, the author does not believe in divine retribution. He feels that there is no real profit to be gained from work on earth. And even worse, divine revelation is altogether scarce—if available at all. This material certainly differs radically from Proverbs and from most other books in the Old Testament.

Yet, for all of its differences, this small book contains some of the most intriguing reading in the Bible. The issues of doubt and pessimism it raises are issues that many persons confront day after day. The book truthfully concedes that goodness is not always rewarded tangibly, and evildoers are not always punished. Scarcely a thoughtful person has not wondered on occasion whether human existence has any real meaning or purpose. But the inclusion of Ecclesiastes within the biblical canon suggests that the content is worthy of examination.

The Author of the Book

According to the superscription (1:1), the book belongs to "Qoheleth, the son of David, king in Jerusalem." The word *Qoheleth* means one who speaks in an assembly, referring to a function rather than to a specific person. If the Hebrew word refers to a position rather than to a proper name, it should be translated as the *Speaker*. When Martin Luther translated this book, he translated Qoheleth as the

Preacher. The NRSV and NIV translations prefer to call him the *Teacher*.

Moreover, it is clear that the author assumes the identity of King Solomon, since he was the only son of David who was ever king in Jerusalem. To be sure, this Solomonic pseudonym is appropriate in view of Solomon's patronage of wisdom in his royal court. To affix such a famous name to a book guaranteed almost instant acceptance among the scribes, and was not really considered plagiarism at that time.

What, really, do we know about Qoheleth? In terms of concrete biographical data, we know nothing. But judging from the style and content of his writing, this person had extensive training in the wisdom tradition, and quite possibly was a sage himself. He writes with an almost intimate knowledge of basic wisdom notions such as retribution, morality, the righteous versus the wicked, proper speech, and so forth. He quotes many traditional proverbs, and occasionally adds his own peculiar words of scepticism. Also, in the conclusion, the final editors refer to Qoheleth as having taught knowledge and arranged proverbs with great care (12:9).

Here is a sage who has carefully weighed his real-life experience against his wisdom theology only to find the latter wanting. As the years pass, his pessimism deepens about the possibilities of human knowledge of God, including divine retribution. Finally, as he reaches his mature years, he submits his final legacy—his profound words of doubt—vanity of vanities, everything is vanity!

For the most part, this book represents Qoheleth's memoirs. Perhaps the superscription (1:1) and the conclusion (12:9-13) belong to another writer, and various proverbs from the wisdom tradition may have been included. But the great majority of the book belongs to Qoheleth.

The Date of the Book

The date of Ecclesiastes is approximately 250 B.C. The book contains numerous Aramaic words from the post exilic era, shows considerable influence from Greek philosophy, and displays a full knowledge (and rejection) of mature wisdom theology.

On the other hand, a Qoheleth scroll found at Qumran indicates the inclusion of the book in the canon by mid-second century B.C. There are no concrete historical allusions in the book that reflect its date. So most scholars concur in dating the book after 300 B.C. but before 150 B.C.

Theological Themes in the Book

Ecclesiastes lacks a clear pattern of thematic development or even of logical consistency. Most efforts to trace the development of a common theme (such as vanity) are futile. The book contains too many tangents, overt contradictions, and repetitions. It is even difficult to prepare a basic outline of the book.

Qoheleth has compiled this book over a number of years, and several themes have been examined and reexamined from different points of view. This technique gives the work a certain redundancy and even outright contradictoriness. Traditional proverbs are juxtaposed with pessimistic conclusions drawn from experience (1:14-18). Poems precede narratives (1:1-11; 3:1-9).

But the rough, uneven style of the book reflects Qoheleth's perception of the rough, uneven, undirected nature of human existence. It is vain, he concludes, to try to understand the purpose and value of human existence. Instead, one should enjoy life as God gives it. Likewise, it is of no profit to try to discern a logical structure to his book. As Qoheleth advises persons to enjoy life and reap whatever benefits come along (2:24-26), so would he advise readers to examine his book, draw whatever lessons they may find appropriate, and not expect to solve the mysteries of human existence by studying the pages of his reflections.

The basic theological ideas in Qoheleth's book challenge wisdom ideas in Proverbs, such as divine retribution, divine revelation communicated through the natural and moral order, wisdom as providing the way of understanding and succeeding in life, and our unique and exalted place in God's created order.

Qoheleth can find nothing in his experience to validate these ideas. Instead, he urges persons to enjoy life, accept their work as self-rewarding, and not expect complete understanding of God's ways. Morality—like faith—should be unconditional, that is, not based on anticipated rewards (or punishment). For life, even with all its perplexities, is still vastly superior to the alternative, death.

ECCLESIASTES 1–3

Introduction to These Chapters

The first three chapters of Ecclesiastes may be divided into five parts.

I. Superscription (1:1)
II. Vanity of Vanities (1:2-11)
III. Search for Meaning and Value (1:12–2:26)
IV. Times and Seasons (3:1-15)
V. Human Mortality and Divine Justice (3:16-22)

The Message of Ecclesiastes 1–3

Four major theological themes emerge from the first three chapters in Ecclesiastes: (1) Human existence is devoid of any real meaning, purpose, or value; (2) God has predetermined nature and history, so that persons have no contributions to make, apart from mechanistic compliance; (3) God has chosen to conceal God's will from persons; and (4) human beings and animals share a common fate—death.

When Qoheleth proclaims boldly that all is meaningless ("vanity," literally *breath* or *vapor*) (1:2), he states a thesis that he then supports by way of real-life experiences in the remaining chapters. Qoheleth pursues the meaning of human existence by means of traditionally accepted ways—power, pleasure, wisdom, religion, and so forth—but yet all ways lead to the same conclusion: All is vanity. Human reason and experience contrast sharply with traditional Hebrew faith, especially wisdom theology (see Proverbs 1:20-33).

Qoheleth discovers several reasons why the traditional ways do not lead to genuine insight into a meaningful existence. First, God has ordered and structured the creation in such a rigorous fashion that everything happens according to a preset plan. In fact, this orderly creation is so structured that persons, too, are intimate parts of the grand design, playing only the role assigned to them by God. They make no real contribution to the operations of a mechanistic world order. Our roles are minimal and are of little significance (1:13-14).

Second, all existence is vanity because God has chosen to conceal the divine purpose from the mind of humans (3:11). In other words, there is no revelation! Human beings know that God created the world, and that God made everything beautiful, but further insights into God's will and purpose remain hidden.

Finally, Qoheleth probes the traditional Hebrew belief in divine retribution—the notion that God distinguishes between the righteous and the wicked and treats them accordingly. But Qoheleth concludes that such distinctions do not occur in real life (3:16). He finds even the judicial system fraught with injustice; this is the ultimate irony. The traditional explanation that innocent suffering is only a test (3:18) fails Qoheleth's logic. And with no substantial life beyond death, persons' fates are the same as that of the beast—namely death. Both spirits go down to the earth. And divine retribution goes unfulfilled.

Qoheleth challenges traditional Hebrew faith on the basis of his human experience, and he concludes that wisdom theology has claimed more than it can verify. God and God's ways remain a mystery to this ancient sage, and human existence is not altogether a happy situation. But never once does Qoheleth deny or even doubt God's existence. Even with all the contradictions and perplexities of human existence, the reality of God remains beyond question. Not much can be known about God or God's purpose on earth, but God's existence cannot be questioned. The challenge of Qoheleth is directed at what persons have claimed about God rather than at God's existence.

ECCLESIASTES 4–8

Introduction to These Chapters

Ecclesiastes 4–8 may be divided into the following parts.

I. Social Injustice (4:1-3)
II. Better This Than That (4:4-16)
III. Miscellaneous Observations (5:1-20)
IV. More Vanities on Earth (6:1-12)
V. Wisdom and the Wise (7:1-29)
VI. The Plight of Human Finitude (8:1-17)

The Message of Ecclesiastes 4–8

Qoheleth concludes that not even wisdom can enable persons to discover God's scheme of things on earth. In 7:24,

he laments that such ultimate meaning is "far off, and very deep" (NRSV; NIV, "most profound"). In 8:17, he observes that regardless of how much one works at it, one cannot discover God's work. Persons must learn to live without any real sense of meaning, purpose, or value—at least not such as the sages in Proverbs claimed could be known. So, Qoheleth asks, what is good for one to do, faced with this limited knowledge? Give up and die? Certainly not! What Qoheleth recommends is practical morality, centering in these chapters around five behaviors: (1) enjoying companionship of friends (4:9-12); (2) paying proper attention to religious observances, including the vows one makes before God (5:1-7); (3) maintaining moderation in all things (7:15-18); (4) respecting the authority and power of the king (8:2-9); and (5) enjoying life, including one's toil, for that is God's gift (8:15).

Although there are no absolute guarantees that these behaviors will result in happiness and prosperity, they do enable most persons to endure an otherwise meaningless and oppressive existence. Life offers few rewards, so one should take advantage of the few benefits available, such as friendship, good food, good drink, and whatever wealth one may acquire. For even as perplexing as life is, it is still much better than death.

ECCLESIASTES 9–12

Introduction to These Chapters

Chapters 9–12 may be outlined as follows.

I. One Fate Comes to All (9:1-3)
II. Life Is Superior to Death (9:4-10)
III. Time and Chance (9:11-12)
IV. Wisdom's Limited Value (9:13-18)
V. Miscellaneous Sayings (10:1-20)

The Message of Ecclesiastes 9–12

After considerable thought, carefully weighing his experience and his tradition, Qoheleth concludes that persons know very little about God's will or God's ways (8:16–9:2). He has no confidence in reason's perception of the created order, including divine retribution (9:2-3). While God has prearranged nature so that we have seasons and times, one cannot be certain what they are or what lies ahead. This pervasive scepticism leaves Qoheleth insecure about exactly what and how much persons can know about the operations of the world.

This scepticism would paralyze some persons, as far as any real activity is concerned. But not Qoheleth. Although life is replete with uncertainties, and granted that our knowledge is very limited, Qoheleth urges us to go ahead with life, enjoy what pleasures we can (9:7-9), be venturesome in our commercial activities (11:1), diversify our economic interests (11:2), and enjoy our youthful days.

We never know what sort of rewards may come our way. Life still offers much more than death offers. To act decisively in the face of existential uncertainty is to display courage and deep resolve. To act without certainty that clear and knowable consequences will result is to forego human weakness. To live under the cloud of divine mystery is to live alone and in isolation from God. But at least it is to live rather than to die.

SONG OF SOLOMON

OUTLINE OF SONG OF SOLOMON

INTRODUCTION

From A.D. 90 at the Council of Jamnia, where Jewish rabbis met to establish the Hebrew canon, the Song of Solomon has evoked the broadest range of human reaction. At Jamnia, Rabbi Akiba is reported to have called this little book the Holy of Holies, referring to its special place in Hebrew life. Some Christians revered it as an allegory about Christ and his love for the church, while other Christians reacted negatively to its sensual, erotic imagery.

Other students of the Bible, both Jewish and Christian, condemned the book for the lack of a single reference to God in any verse. Yet others prized the work for its profound insight into love and human physical attraction. Imaginations have been taxed beyond their limits in an effort to identify the lovers and to untangle the seemingly disjointed sequence of love songs. But even with all of its mystery and ambiguities, Song of Solomon was included in the canon. Today, it presents one of the most eloquent and moving tributes to love in all of literature.

The Name of the Book

The name derived from the first words in the Hebrew text is literally *Song of*

Songs, suggesting an idiom for the superlative (the best of the best). In English translations of the Bible, Protestants typically call the book *Song of Solomon*, perhaps because his name appears six times in the text. In Roman Catholic versions the book is called *Canticles* or *Canticle of Canticles* (again, an idiom for the superlative).

The Date of the Writing

A specific date for Song of Solomon is difficult to determine, because there are few reliable historical references in the book and because the songs seem to reflect more than a single author. Solomon's name appears six times in the book: 1:5; 3:7, 9, 11; 8:11-12. Most of the instances suggest Solomon's fame or his reputation as a singer. Or they even identify him as the beloved, but do not actually identify him as the author.

Elsewhere, Tirzah, the tenth-century capital of the Northern Kingdom, is mentioned in parallelism to Jerusalem (6:4). Perhaps, however, the most important evidence for dating the material is the appearance of foreign terms, such as a Persian word for garden in 4:12 and a Greek word, palanquin, in 3:9. Many words and syntactical elements in Song of Solomon are unique in the Old Testament. In view of all these factors, most scholars cautiously assign a date for final composition to the fourth or third century B.C. This date allows for the inclusion of several songs that may date much earlier, possibly as far back as the tenth or ninth century, as suggested by the Tirzah-Jerusalem parallel.

The Author of the Book

Likewise, it is difficult to identify the author of Song of Solomon. The superscription (1:1) ascribes these songs to Solomon; however, the Hebrew preposition used, taken by some scholars as indicating authorship, may actually have several other meanings: for Solomon, to Solomon, or about Solomon. Clearly, as the patron sage of wisdom in Israel, Solomon is the honoree, and is probably the pseudonymous lover and bridegroom. After all, the author of 1 Kings 4:32 refers to King Solomon as the composer of over one thousand songs. Finally, the book's inclusion in the Hebrew canon is generally attributed to its association with Solomon, although other reasons probably contributed also.

The book has the literary nature of an anthology rather than a continuous poetic narrative or hymn. There are too many logical inconsistencies, contradictions, and repetitions for the book to be from a single hand. So it is unlikely that Solomon could have written the entire book.

Interpretations of the Book

Due to the numerous literary and thematic complications in Song of Solomon, interpretations have been many and diverse. Basically, these different interpretations may be divided into four groups: allegorical, dramatic, liturgical, and secular.

The allegorical interpretation flourished among many Jews and early Christians, but has few adherents today. The rabbis saw the book as an expression of the intimate covenant relationship between God and Israel (see also Genesis 15:1; Jeremiah 31:31-34). Drawing on the motif of human marriage as symbolizing these covenants, early rabbis saw in Song of Solomon many images that had been developed by prophets such as Hosea and Jeremiah. Later, Christians such as Origen and Augustine saw the book as an allegory of Christ and his bride, the church. These multi-level interpretations disregarded the human aspect of love, opting instead to symbolize the entire book as meaningful only on another, more spiritual level.

A second interpretation relates Song of Solomon to certain Greek tragedies. Some scholars identify two characters while other scholars find three roles—a king, his beloved, and a shepherd. A chorus serves as background. Some type of plot emerges that pits the king against a shepherd lad for the affections of a young maiden. The drama is incomplete because the dramatic struggle has been left out of the present book.

A third view sees Song of Solomon as a series of Judean wedding songs, similar to certain songs and marriage celebrations among Syrian peasants. The bride and groom assume the identities of king and queen and celebrate the beauty of their physical natures in preparation for their wedding.

Finally, the book may be seen as a collection of secular love poetry, celebrating the eternal bliss of physical love. What we find is a moving testimony to that fundamental passion that moves the very souls of men and women, drawing them together in a moment of sheer passion. Such a strong physical attraction lies at the heart of any loving relationship.

The Content of the Book

These songs have been collected and edited much as an anthology. Many of them reflect a rural or pastoral setting; still other songs display signs of cult and ritual. Together, they form an anthology of love songs and love poems that affirm the pure goodness of physical passion.

Absent from Song of Solomon are the great theological traditions in the Old Testament, such as the covenants with Abraham, with Moses, and with David.

There is not a single reference to the Exodus, to the law, or to divine revelation. In fact, there is no mention of God at all. Retribution (or the absence thereof) occupies not a single line. Instead, we have in this book an affirmation of the uninhibited joy of physical love between a man and a woman. This is nature at its best—unashamed, undefiled, and uncorrupted by society's norms.

SONG OF SOLOMON 1–4

Introduction to These Chapters

These chapters may be outlined as follows.

The Message of Song of Solomon 1–4

The central theme in Song of Solomon is love romantic love between a man and woman who unite in marriage. Quite possibly, selections from this book were used originally as parts of marriage rites, or were ritual texts in a religious ceremony. Whatever their original settings in life, they have been collected into a larger book and now form a lyrical celebration of human love. Ancient Near Eastern literature abounds with love poetry from all walks of life; in fact, Syrian love songs such as these punctuate many phases of rural life including courtship and marriage.

From the outset, this book is replete with the celebration of strong physical attraction. The sexual imagery in Song of Solomon is too obvious to be overlooked. References to actual lovemaking (2:6; 8:3) leave no doubt that the relationship is (or is about to be) consummated. There are other allusions to sexual activity, such as pasturing flocks (6:2), eating fruit (4:16), and so forth. The imagery of the latch, the bolt, and a head wet with dew (5:2-6) are vivid and clear. Yet, this material is not sensual or erotic in any negative, immoral sense of those terms. Instead, readers are offered the open and unashamed expression of sheer delight in the physical aspects of love.

When the king-lover offers his impression of his beloved's physical body, one does not recoil or cringe. The reader knows that there is nobleness in such affirmations. Nature has endowed men and women with bodies, with sensory organs, and with minds to relate to and understand these elements.

One cannot help being impressed by the free and open words of affection these two lovers express toward each another. They do not play games with each other. They do not suppress their real feelings out of some false sense of modesty. True, the woman defers to custom when she withholds public affection for her beloved (8:1). But elsewhere, her words and her actions clearly convey her feelings to her beloved. And likewise, he publicly celebrates his love for her. He prizes her beauty, he extols her virtue, and he praises her charms.

Song of Solomon sets a high standard for the expression of physical love. It pays tribute to the grandeur of sexuality without being pornographic. Sexuality complements a relationship of serious and mature love; in fact, loving sexuality is the intended design by which our species is continued. Sexuality is both natural and necessary, but it is to occur within the relational context of love.

SONG OF SOLOMON 5–8

Introduction to These Chapters

These chapters may be outlined as follows.

   I. The Missing Lover II (5:2-8)
  II. The Look of the Lover (5:9-16)
 III. The Beloved Is Discovered (6:1-3)
 IV. The Maiden's Extraordinary Beauty (6:4-10)
  V. The Nut Orchard (6:11-12)
 VI. In Praise of the Shulammite Maiden (6:13–7:9)
 VII. Love in the Garden (7:10-13)
VIII. Love in the Chamber (8:1-4)
 IX. The Strength of Love (8:5-7)
  X. The Maiden Cares for Herself (8:8-10)
 XI. Solomon's Vineyard (8:11-12)
XII. Conclusion: Call and Response (8:13-14)

The Message of Song of Solomon 5–8

Continuing human love is the primary focus of the book. Serious students will discover that human sexuality, while important, is not the only factor in the relationship of love. Serious and mature love, as exists between the man and his beautiful bride, entails fidelity. In 8:6-7, the maiden enjoins her lover to wear her as a seal about his arm and around his neck. Love has bound them together, and each has a claim of fidelity upon the other.

A strong marriage is nurtured by faithfulness of both partners. They will neither need nor want an affectionate relationship with another person. As the maiden says in 8:6, love is as strong as death. A sense of fidelity dissipates the danger of jealousy. The bonds of love bind the relationship together so tightly that none can break it apart. As seen in 6:3, "I am my beloved's and my beloved is mine" (NRSV; NIV "I am my lover's and my lover is mine").

Serious and mature love is nurtured also by a deep concern for the well-being of each other. The "missing lover" theme may have been part of the ritual of wedding love that prompted some of these songs. But the distress of the maiden at the sudden and inexplicable disappearance of her beloved reflects her genuine concern. Her sense of loneliness and concern override her fear of danger at night, as she frantically searches for him throughout the city.

Even when she is victimized (5:7) by the watchmen, she does not waver in her concern for her beloved. She urges her attendants to continue the search and, when they find him, to assure him of her love.

It is abundantly clear from their song that the maiden has reserved her most intimate affections for her lover. She has not been promiscuous. He describes her garden as locked and her fountain as sealed (4:12). In 7:13, the fruits she has stored likely refer to her sexuality. In every respect, this beautiful and stately maiden has not allowed herself to be used, opting instead to wait and reserve her deepest expressions of love for one who truly honors them.

Serious and mature love between two adults is fully reciprocal. It is clear that both persons are deeply attracted to each other. Their feelings are mutual, and their trust invites open and free expression of this love. Each one offers praise and respect for the other. Each one finds joy in the other's embrace. Each one longs for that special moment of union, when they become as one in sexual embrace. There is no doubt in the mind of one as to the feelings or motives of the other.

ISAIAH

OUTLINE OF ISAIAH

4. Restoration of Judah (29:1-8)
5. Miscellaneous oracles (29:9-24)
6. Oracles concerning Egypt (30:1-17)
7. Restoration of Judah (30:18-26)
8. Oracle against Assyria (30:27-33)
9. Oracle against Egypt (31:1-3)
10. Oracle against Sennacherib (31:4-9)
11. The future of Judah (32:1-8)
12. Oracle against Judah's women (32:9-14)
13. Outpouring of the Spirit (32:15-20)
E. Post exilic oracles (33:1–35:10)
   1. Prophetic liturgy (33:1-24)
   2. Judgment on God's enemies (34:1-17)
   3. Restoration of Zion (35:1-10)
F. Historical appendix (36:1–39:8)
   1. Attack on Jerusalem (36:1-22)
   2. Isaiah advises Hezekiah (37:1-38)
   3. Hezekiah's illness (38:1-22)
   4. Merodach-baladan and Hezekiah (39:1-8)

II. Prophecies from the Exilic Period (40:1–55:13)
A. God acts in history (40:1–48:22)
   1. Call to announce God's coming (40:1-11)
   2. God the Creator (40:12-31)
   3. Trial of the nations (41:1-29)
   4. First servant song (42:1-4)
   5. Oracle of restoration (42:5-17)
   6. Israel's judgment and redemption (42:18–43:7)
   7. Israel's Restoration (43:8–44:8)
   8. Against Idolatry (44:9-23)
   9. Commission of Cyrus (44:24–45:13)
   10. Miscellaneous oracles (45:14–46:13)

11. Lament over Babylon (47:1-15)
12. God's actions in history (48:1-22)
B. Restoration of Israel (49:1–55:13)
   1. Second servant song (49:1-6)
   2. Return and restoration (49:7-26)
   3. Covenant with Israel (50:1-3)
   4. Third servant song (50:4-11)
   5. Salvation for Abraham's descendants (51:1-16)
   6. Kingship of God (51:17–52:12)
   7. Fourth servant song (52:13–53:12)
   8. Assurance of Israel's restoration (54:1-17)
   9. Song of triumph (55:1-13)

III. Prophecies from the Post Exilic Period (56:1-66:24)
A. Miscellaneous oracles (56:1–59:21)
   1. Keeping the sabbath (56:1-8)
   2. Oracle against leaders (56:9-12)
   3. Oracle against idolatry (57:1-13)
   4. Consolation for Israel (57:14-21)
   5. What the Lord desires (58:1-14)
   6. Call to repentance (59:1-21)
B. The glory of Jerusalem (60:1–62:12)
   1. Jerusalem's restoration (60:1-22)
   2. The prophet's mission to Zion (61:1-11)
   3. Zion is vindicated (62:1-12)
C. Concluding oracles (63:1–66:24)
   1. God's vengeance (63:1-6)
   2. The prophet petitions God (63:7–64:12)
   3. God answers (65:1-25)
   4. Final oracles (66:1-24)

INTRODUCTION

The prophet Isaiah was the son of Amoz, as the first verse in the book tells us. We know little or nothing about Isaiah's personal life. From reading Isaiah 6:1-8, some conclude that Isaiah was a priest in the Temple before he was called to prophesy. Isaiah's name means *Yahweh gives salvation*.

Chapters 1–39 are a collection of prophecies from the ministry of Isaiah the prophet. The later chapters in the book come from a later period, and were probably spoken and recorded by disciples of Isaiah the prophet.

Isaiah was a prophet of the Southern Kingdom (Judah). He directed his message to Judah, and especially Jerusalem, between 742 and 687 B.C. During this time, the Southern Kingdom was under the domination of Assyria, to the northeast. The Northern Kingdom (Israel) had ceased to exist as an independent nation about 722 B.C., when it fell to the Assyrians.

The first 39 chapters of Isaiah are divided into six main parts: the prophet's memoirs (chapters 1–12), oracles concerning Judah and its neighbors (chapters 13–23), the Isaiah Apocalypse (chapters 24–27), oracles concerning Egypt (chapters 28–32), post exilic oracles (chapters 33–35), and a historical appendix (chapters 36–39).

Throughout chapters 1–39 Isaiah preaches a message of social justice, faith in God, rewards for the obedient, and judgment on the unfaithful. With this message Isaiah stands in the tradition of his contemporaries (Hosea, Micah, and Amos).

We know almost nothing about the prophet who wrote chapters 40–55 in the book of Isaiah. Because this prophet's words are included within the Old Testament book we call Isaiah, he has been given the name Second Isaiah, or Deutero-Isaiah. As we will see when we examine his prophecies, Second Isaiah stands in the tradition of the prophet Isaiah. Their messages are interrelated.

Whereas the prophet Isaiah lived and worked in Judah, Second Isaiah was a prophet of the Exile. Although the book never states this explicitly, Second Isaiah probably ministered to the people while they were in exile in Babylon. The book contains many references to Babylon and to circumstances that existed there (see chapter 47, for example). In addition, the prophet speaks often of returning home to Judah. In fact, Second Isaiah's prophecies begin and end on that subject. (See 40:3-5 and 55:12-13.)

The Babylonian Exile began with the fall of Jerusalem in 587 B.C. The inhabitants were captured and taken to Babylon, where they lived until King Cyrus of Persia defeated Babylon in 539 B.C. Second Isaiah's prophecies were directed to those exiles, and were delivered shortly before their return to Judah in 538 B.C.

Second Isaiah has two main parts: oracles about God's activity in history (chapters 40–48), and prophecies about the future restoration of Judah (chapters 49–55).

The message of Second Isaiah's prophecies fits the historical circumstances of prophet and people well. The people are in exile. Cyrus is about to appear on the scene and release them, after fifty years of bondage in Babylon. In this context, the prophet preaches a message of trust in God and hope for an imminent return to their homeland.

Chapters 56–66 form the third major portion of Isaiah. Many commentators maintain that this final section was written by yet a third prophet, a disciple of Second Isaiah in Jerusalem during the early years of the restoration. This unknown prophet is often called Third Isaiah.

Chapters 56–66 can be dated most probably sometime during the fourth century B.C. Five main characteristics suggest a late date for these prophecies. First, these chapters share many words and themes with the words of the prophets Haggai and Zechariah, who also lived and worked during the fourth century B.C. Second, spread throughout these chapters is an interest in eschatology, or the events surrounding the last days. In general, eschatology is an interest of later biblical writers.

Third, this prophet seems to take the content and themes of Second Isaiah and expand on them, adding his own interpretations. For example, the idea of making preparations to return to the homeland, central to the message of Second Isaiah, is taken up and altered slightly in chapters 56–66. There it is the persons inside the gates of Jerusalem who are to make preparations for those who are yet to return (not the exiles in Babylon, who are addressed in chapters 40–55).

Fourth, the themes of cultic worship and ritual, virtually absent in the prophecies of Second Isaiah, play a major role in the theology of chapters 56–66. And fifth, these final chapters emphasize the universality of the message of salvation, which is largely a later phenomenon in the Scripture.

Chapters 60–62 form the heart of this prophet's message. The rest of the oracles in this third portion of Isaiah are a mixture of the prophet's own words and prophecies adapted from other places in the Scripture.

ISAIAH 1–2

Introduction to These Chapters

Isaiah 1 contains a group of oracles that serve to introduce the rest of the book. Most of the elements found throughout Isaiah's prophecies are alluded to in this first chapter. Isaiah 2 begins with a short section describing the coming age (verses 2-5), and continues with a longer oracle on the day of the Lord.

Here is an outline of Isaiah 1 and 2.

I. Introductory Oracles (1:1-31)
   A. Superscription (1:1)
   B. Oracle to rebellious people (1:2-3)
   C. Oracle to a sinful nation (1:4-9)
   D. Concerning religious practices (1:10-20)
   E. The fate of Jerusalem (1:21-28)
   F. Judah's faithlessness (1:29-31)
II. Oracles Concerning the Day of the Lord (2:1-22)
   A. Second superscription (2:1)
   B. The coming age (2:2-5)
   C. The day of the Lord (2:6-22)
      1. Judgment on idolatry (2:6-11)
      2. Judah's punishment (2:12-17)
      3. Judgment on idolatry (2:18-22)

The Message of Isaiah 1–2

What do these introductory chapters to Isaiah's message tell us about what God is like?

- God is a God who speaks through specific persons (Isaiah the prophet) to specific circumstances (what was happening in Judah in Isaiah's time).

- God can be disappointed in and angry at the behavior of the people of Judah.

- God can show displeasure at disobedience and rebellion. The consequences can be severe.

- God will not bring about utter destruction. At least a few survivors will remain.

- God is not pleased with ritual obligations performed in a context of disobedience or without justice.

- Obedience will bring about rewards. Rebellion will bring about punishment.

- The making of and worship of idols is a fruitless enterprise in God's eyes.

- God's ultimate goal is the restoration of Jerusalem as the faithful city—a reign of peace.

ISAIAH 3–5

Introduction to These Chapters

Isaiah 3–5 contains oracles concerning Judah and Jerusalem, an allegory about a

---

SONG OF THE VINEYARD (ISAIAH 5:1-7)

The song of the vineyard is one of the most beautiful poetic passages in the Old Testament. It is an allegory about a vineyard and its owner, and it teaches us about the relationship between God and the people of Israel.

The poem may have been composed in honor of a special occasion in Israel, perhaps a feast or some other kind of religious celebration. The prophet asks his audience to imagine themselves in the middle of a crowded street in Jerusalem. The singer gets the attention of those around him and then begins to sing the song. The first part of verse 1 introduces the song. Unfortunately, the audience is not told who the singer's friend is, and neither are we.

The owner of the vineyard took great pains to take care of it the proper way. Because the vineyard was on a hill, it probably received plenty of sunlight, and we know that the soil was fertile. All these factors would seem to point toward a bountiful harvest. Indeed, this is what the owner expected, since he went to the trouble of building a watchtower in the middle of the vineyard (rather than a temporary structure to use just during the time of harvest). However, at the end of verse 2 we read of the owner's great disappointment. He asks himself, why are the grapes so small and sour (wild)? Jeremiah 31:30 indicates what happens when one tries to eat wild grapes.

What went wrong? The singer asks the crowd this question in verses 3 and 4, just as the singer's friend (the owner of the vineyard) must have asked himself. In these verses, however, the song begins to shift in orientation. Now the owner of the vineyard begins to speak. The audience probably begins to realize at this point, as do we, that this song is more than just a story about a vineyard that didnt produce.

In traditional biblical imagery, the vineyard is a metaphor for the people of Israel, and the owner of the vineyard represents God. Matthew uses these same symbols in his parable of the wicked tenants. (See Matthew 21:33-44.) So in verse 4, the owner of the vineyard (God) is asking the people to judge what more he could have done for the vineyard (the people of Israel). The only possible answer was, "nothing more." In effect, the people of Judah are being asked to pass judgment on themselves. They are sour, wild grapes. They are a grave disappointment.

In verses 5-7 God reveals the punishment for the people's failure. The people, represented by the vineyard, will be removed, devoured, trampled on, and ignored. God will break down the wall around the vineyard, leaving it undefended, just as the people will be left undefended. Their enemies will trample them.

Just in case the audience missed the point of the allegory, verse 7 makes the comparison very clear. "The vineyard of the LORD" is the house of Israel. Just as the owner of the vineyard looked for juicy, sweet grapes, God looked for justice and righteousness from the people. Just as the vineyard owner was disappointed in the results of his effort, so God is disappointed in the response of the people. Justice and righteousness are important concepts in the prophetic tradition. (See Amos 5:24, for example.) Justice refers to the way persons behave, and righteousness refers to the relationship between persons and God.

vineyard, and a series of woe oracles.
These chapters can be outlined as follows.

    I. God's Judgment on Jerusalem
       (3:1–4:1)
      A. The collapse of the city (3:1-11)
      B. God and Jerusalem's leaders
         (3:12-15)
      C. The women of Jerusalem
         (3:16–4:1)
    II. Restoration of Jerusalem (4:2-6)
   III. Song of the Vineyard (5:1-7)
   IV. Woe Oracles (5:8-23)
      A. First woe (5:8-10)
      B. Second woe (5:11-17)
      C. Third woe (5:18-19)
      D. Fourth woe (5:20)
      E. Fifth woe (5:21)
      F. Sixth woe (5:22-23)
    V. Judgment on Judah (5:24-30)

The Message of Isaiah 3–5

- God was active in Israel's early
  history, God was active in Isaiah's
  time, and God is active now. God has
  the power to summon the forces of
  heaven and earth.

- Trouble and unrest in the
  political/social circumstances of
  Jerusalem are symptomatic of trouble
  in the relationship between God and
  the people.

- Being in a right relationship with God
  means being in right relationships
  with other human beings and with
  ourselves.

- God will ensure that a remnant of
  survivors remains after destruction.

- God can be disappointed in the
  response on the part of the people.
  Disappointment due to the sin of the
  people will bring punishment.

- God uses other nations (such as
  Assyria) as a means of punishment.

ISAIAH 6

Introduction to This Chapter

Isaiah 6 contains the call of the prophet.
Using vivid imagery and majestic
language, the prophet narrates his
experience in the Temple in Jerusalem,
when God commissioned him to prophesy
to the people of Judah.

Here is an outline of Isaiah 6.

    I. The Vision of the Prophet (6:1-4)
   II. The Prophet Is Commissioned (6:5-13)
      A. Initial response (6:5)
      B. The prophet is cleansed (6:6-8)
      C. The message is conveyed (6:9-13)

THE VISION OF THE PROPHET (ISAIAH 6:1-13)

The first few words in verse 1 date the occurrence of Isaiah's call. The year that Uzziah, king of Judah, died was 742 B.C. Isaiah introduces the description of his vision with the words "I saw." These words are commonly used to introduce visions in the prophetic literature, confirming that God is the source.

The prophetic literature contains many reports of many visions. But very rarely does a prophetic vision involve the image of God. The prophet Ezekiel also sees God enthroned, and gives more details of God's appearance than Isaiah does. (See Ezekiel 1:26-28.)

In Isaiah's vision, God is seated upon a throne, probably a reference to the ark of the covenant. The prophet's brief description of God is intended to convey majesty and power. God is "high and exalted" (NIV; NRSV, "lofty"). God's garment is so large that it fills the whole Temple. God is larger than (human) life.

THE VISION OF THE PROPHET (ISAIAH 6:1-13; CONT.)

Verse 2 describes the seraphim that hover over God. They represent the linking of heaven and earth in the vision. These winged creatures, which were serpents of some kind, probably corresponded to the Uraei, serpents who protected God in Egyptian mythology. These seraphim had six wings apiece. Two of these wings covered the seraph's face, two of them covered its feet (a euphemism for genitals), and two were used for flying.

Verse 3 repeats the song of praise that one seraph sings to another. In the Hebrew language, repetition is one way to add emphasis to a statement or idea. This song of praise begins by repeating the word "holy" three times. By saying that God is holy, holy, holy, the song is praising God as holy to the infinite degree. The same kind of threefold repetition for emphasis is found in Jeremiah 7:4.

Yahweh Sabaoth in Hebrew (NIV, "the LORD Almighty" NRSV, "the LORD of Hosts") is the cultic name for God that was used in Temple worship. The name signifies God's power over heaven and earth.

The exact meaning and origin of the word *Sabaoth* is uncertain. The original reference may have been to the armies of Israel and/or Judah. In this case, the God of hosts would have been the God who led the Israelite and Judean armies in battle. Or perhaps the word is more abstract, and simply means all-powerful. The origin of the term, whether Canaanite (pre-Israelite) or Israelite, is also unclear.

"The whole earth is full of his glory" brings the power of God to an earthly level. God's glory means God's dignity and respect. In the priestly tradition, the glory of God was thought to be hidden behind the cloud (see Exodus 16:10). This same concept appears in the New Testament when the shepherds encounter the angels who tell them the good news of Jesus' birth (see Luke 2:9). The earth as full of God's glory is mentioned as a hope of the psalmist at the end of Psalm 72 (verse 19).

The song of praise sung by the seraph had a profound effect. It caused the foundations of the Temple to tremble. That powerful image is also part of the final vision in the book of Amos (see Amos 9:1-4). In addition to the shaking of the foundations, the Temple was filled with smoke. The smoke shielded the eyes of the prophet from the image of God, which was important since no one can look at the face of God and live. (See Exodus 33:20.) Smoke and fire are often used as symbols to indicate the presence of God, called a *theophany*.

In verse 5 the prophet speaks in the first person. His response seems somewhat surprising at first. Why would a vision of God cause the prophet to say, "Woe is me"? Why did the prophet not respond joyfully to being in the presence of God? Since he is a "man of unclean lips," the prophet cannot stand in the presence of God or join in the song of praise. We know from the cultic regulations in the book of Leviticus that unclean things (and persons) are an abomination to God. (See Leviticus 11:24-45.) The prophet immediately becomes aware of his guilt and the guilt of his people, and he responds accordingly.

One of the seraphim takes a burning coal from the altar, using a pair of tongs. He touches the mouth of the prophet, his unclean lips, with the burning coal. This act of purification on the part of the seraph takes away the prophet's sin and guilt. Symbolically, the guilt of the whole people is taken away. After this purification, the prophet is free to respond and to be used for God's purposes.

Verse 8 gives the prophet's response. The questions God asks sound similar to the words used when Moses was commissioned to lead the people out of Egypt. (See Exodus 3:10.) The prophet assumes God's questions are directed to him.

THE VISION OF THE PROPHET (ISAIAH 6:1-13; CONT.)

Without hesitation, the prophet responds positively. "Here am I" is a common response to requests and commands made by God. Abraham had a similar response when God put him to the test (see Genesis 22:1). In most of the other prophetic call narratives, there is initial hesitation on the part of the prophet when he is confronted with the task. (See Exodus 4:10; Jeremiah 1:6.) This tradition of initial hesitation makes it all the more remarkable that Isaiah responds quickly and positively. His claim to be a man of unclean lips, sometimes said to indicate hesitation, is really an admission of guilt. Besides, it was uttered before the actual call was issued.

Now God tells the prophet what the essence of his message will be. The people are commanded to hear, and see, but for all their efforts they will be unsuccessful (verse 9). These words are quoted by Jesus in the tenth chapter of Matthew. Note the way God instructs Isaiah to speak to "this people." The tone sounds bitter and angry.

Verse 10 continues the message. The heart of the people will become fat, so that it will beat more sluggishly. Their ears and eyes will be closed. In various ways, then, the senses of the people will be dulled to the ways of God, and the words of the prophet.

Why would God charge Isaiah to dull the senses of the people? A careful reading shows that the words in these verses describe the effect of the prophet's activity, not the content of the message he is to convey. God will punish the people through the vehicle of the prophet.

In verse 11 Isaiah raises the question, "How long, O Lord?" This question is a formula used often in the laments of the Old Testament, especially in the psalms of lament (Psalm 13:1, for example). With this question, the prophet is not asking how long he will be prophesying this message to the people. Instead, he is asking how long the people's senses will be dulled. The answer comes immediately—until the message is received and responded to. But then it will be too late. Destruction will have already taken place.

Verse 12 refers to the future exile of Judah to Babylon, which occurred in 587 B.C.

Verse 13 sounds a note of hope. One tenth of the population will survive the destruction. However, even that remnant will be destroyed again, like a tree stump that begins to grow new shoots which are then destroyed, but not totally. Just enough growth is left so that the stump can eventually grow into a new tree. The last part of verse 13 is awkward and difficult to translate.

Taken as a whole, Isaiah 6:1-13 functions as an introduction to the major section that follows, about the Syro-Ephraimitic War (through 9:6). As we read this section of Isaiah we are struck with the courage of this prophet. Far from hesitating to fulfill his calling, the prophet offers to be the messenger almost before he is asked. He is not afraid to be in God's presence. Nor is he afraid to proclaim God's message, difficult as it is to hear.

The Message of Isaiah 6

- God does not hesitate to use the prophet as a vehicle to proclaim the message. Nor does God hesitate to carry out the punishment that has been set.

- Once purified (forgiven), a formerly sinful human being can now speak on God's behalf.

- God leaves an element of hope with the prophet. Destruction will not be complete; a stump will remain as the beginning of a new tree.

ISAIAH 7–9

Introduction to These Chapters

Isaiah 7–9 is a series of oracles, most of which are related in some way to the Syro-

Ephraimitic War. In 734–732 B.C., Syria, Judah, and Israel were involved in skirmishes connected to the advancing Assyrian threat. Pekah, king of Israel (the Northern Kingdom), and Rezin, king of Syria (to the north), allied with each other in an effort to stand against the Assyrians. They tried to convince Ahaz, king of Judah (the Southern Kingdom), to join with them in their alliance. Eventually Rezin and Pekah besieged Jerusalem, but could not subdue the city. Ahaz, against the advice of Isaiah, chose to ally with Tiglath-Pileser, the Assyrian king. The Assyrians subsequently defeated both Syria and Israel.

Against this background we have Isaiah 7–9. Here is an outline of these chapters.

I. The Syro-Ephraimitic War (7:1–8:22)
  A. The sign of Shear-Jashub (7:1-9)
  B. The sign of Immanuel (7:10-17)
  C. Further threats (7:18-25)
  D. The sign of Maher-Shalal-hash-baz (8:1-4)
  E. Miscellaneous oracles (8:5-10)
  F. Binding the testimony (8:11-22)
II. The Messianic King (9:1-7)
III. Judgment on Ephraim (9:8-21)
  A. Pride brings punishment (9:8-12)
  B. The leaders are corrupt (9:13-17)
  C. Immorality among the people (9:18-21)

THE SIGN OF IMMANUEL (ISAIAH 7:10-17)

This famous passage has an especially important place in the history of the Christian tradition. The Gospel of Matthew quotes 7:14 as a prophecy fulfilled with the birth of Jesus (see Matthew 1:18-25).

Verse 10 begins with the word "again," showing a continuity in the narrative with what has preceded. God tells Ahaz to ask for a sign, so that he might believe in the message God is sending him. God agrees to anything, whether it is "in the deepest depths or in the highest heights" (NIV; NRSV, "as deep as Sheol or high as heaven"). But Ahaz refuses to test God (verse 12).

When verse 13 begins the prophet himself is speaking, since he speaks of God in the third person. Isaiah's impatience with Ahaz shows through here. It is bad enough, according to Isaiah, that Ahaz is stubborn when it comes to dealing with other persons. But it is even worse to be stubborn in one's dealings with God! God will give you a sign anyway, whether you want it or not. Note that Isaiah calls God "my God." This label indicates that the prophet realizes Ahaz has already made his decision. He now has no right to call God "my God."

Verse 14 tells of a young woman or virgin who will bear a son named "Immanuel." The Hebrew word translated "young woman" means a girl of marriageable age. This same word is used in Genesis 24:43 to refer to Rebekah and in Exodus 2:8 to refer to Moses' sister. The Septuagint (the Greek translation of the Old Testament) translates this word as *parthenos* (virgin), and Matthew 1:23 interprets the word in Isaiah 7:14 to mean a virgin. Clearly, the Matthean quotation of Isaiah 7:14 assumes that this passage is a prophecy about the birth of Jesus. However, Matthew re-interprets 7:14 into a special set of circumstances.

By naming her son Immanuel, this woman shows her trust in God. Verse 14 describes what this child will be like and what will happen to him when he is old enough to distinguish between good and evil. What does it mean that Immanuel will eat cream and honey? In 7:22, cream and honey designate a time of plenty, for those who survived the devastation. Thus, cream and honey are the food for times of salvation. Before that time, however, there will be devastation to Syria and Israel (Ephraim). Verse 17 continues the threat, applying it to Judah as well.

The Message of Isaiah 7–9

These chapters are some of the most important in all of the Old Testament prophetic literature. What message do they contain about God and God's relationship to the world?

- The house of David is God's chosen house. God is willing to work through the prophet to bring about the downfall of the Davidic dynasty, for the ultimate goal of a restored community.

- Sometimes God wants to be put to the test. When Ahaz would not cooperate, the downfall of the Southern Kingdom came one step closer.

- If King Ahaz had trusted God rather than becoming involved in political maneuvers with Assyria, he could have saved himself and his kingdom.

- God, although resolved to punish the people for their disobedience, holds out hope for restoration. To think of a day when humankind will live an abundant life helps us to live through the dark times in our lives. That same hope helped Ahaz through times of despair.

- God is the Lord of hosts, the mighty God. Isaiah used Yahweh Sabaoth ("LORD Almighty" or "LORD of hosts") to remind his audience that God is all-powerful. The power of God is our assurance of ultimate restoration.

- God knew that the people of Judah would not heed the warnings they were given. God sent Isaiah to harden their hearts rather than to change their minds. In that way, destruction would surely happen, causing the people to repent and change their ways.

ISAIAH 10–12

Introduction to These Chapters

Isaiah 10–12 are the final three chapters in the first portion of the book. They contain a collection of various kinds of prophetic oracles, including a messianic oracle, a woe oracle, and an oracle of promise.

Here is an outline of these chapters.
I. Miscellaneous Oracles (10:1-34)
  A. No justice among the people (10:1-4)
  B. Judgment on Assyria (10:5-19)
  C. Remnant of Israel (10:20-23)
  D. Oracle of promise (10:24-27)
  E. The Assyrian threat (10:28-34)
II. Oracles Concerning the Messiah (11:1-16)
  A. The messianic king (11:1-9)
  B. The messianic age (11:10-16)
III. Concluding Songs (12:1-6)
  A. A song of deliverance (12:1-3)
  B. A song of thanksgiving (12:4-6)

The Message of Isaiah 10–12

- God's people have been disobedient. God will not hesitate to punish them, nor will God hesitate to restore them again in the future.

- God intends to use Assyria as an instrument to bring about the destruction of Judah.

- God sent Isaiah to harden the hearts of the people, in order to bring about their repentance and restoration.

- God will watch over the people by (ultimately) destroying their enemies.

- God will use the future messianic king to bring about justice, righteousness, and an era of peace. This king will depend on God for support in his mission.

THE MESSIANIC KING (ISAIAH 11:1-9)

Chapter 11 discusses the messiah as the one who will bring about future salvation. Verses 1-9 describe the messianic king in language similar to that in chapter 9.

The messiah is described as a shoot that will grow out of "the stump of Jesse," who is the father of King David (see 1 Samuel 16:1). The image places the future messiah in the Davidic line. The messiah will have various gifts that will enable him to rule wisely: wisdom, understanding, counsel, might, knowledge, and fear of the Lord. Fear of God refers to obedience, or good behavior.

Verses 3-5 expand on the idea of ruling wisely by describing how this king will make judgments during his rule. He will judge with righteousness. In so doing he will be the champion of the poor and lowly. He will be able to smite those who do evil by his words alone.

"Faithfulness [will be] the sash around his waist" (NIV; NRSV, "belt around his loins") worn as his innermost layer of clothing so it remains close to him.

Verses 6-9 describe an idyllic future life that will be free from danger, brought about by the messianic king's rule of peace. Beasts that are normally enemies will live side-by-side in a peaceful manner. Verse 6 says "and a little child shall lead them." If a young child can supervise a group of animals such as the ones listed, the situation must be peaceful.

ISAIAH 13–16

Introduction to These Chapters

These four chapters begin the second major section of the book of Isaiah, chapters 13–23. These chapters contain mainly Isaiah's oracles concerning foreign nations.

Here is an outline of chapters 13–16.
I. Oracle Against Babylon (13:1-22)
   A. God summons the armies (13:1-5)
   B. The day of the Lord (13:6-16)
   C. God stirs up the Medes (13:17-22)
II. Oracle Against Babylon's King (14:1-23)
   A. Return from exile (14:1-2)
   B. Taunt song to Babylon's king (14:3-23)
III. Oracle Against Assyria (14:24-27)
IV. Oracle Against Philistia (14:28-32)
V. Oracle Against Moab (15:1–16:14)
   A. Raid on Moab (15:1-9)
   B. Fate of the Moabites (16:1-5)
   C. Destruction of Moab (16:6-14)

The Message of Isaiah 13–16

- God uses other nations as instruments to bring about the ultimate fate of the people of Israel/Judah.

- The power and might of a foreign nation does not always assure its position as a leader.

- Ultimate doom is not in store for Israel, as long as the people recognize the absolute authority of God.

- The suffering Israel had to endure was for the ultimate goal of restoration as the people of God.

ISAIAH 17–20

Introduction to These Chapters

Chapters 17–20 continue the theme of oracles against foreign nations. Most of the speeches in this section focus on Egypt (chapters 18–20). These oracles concerning Egypt are preceded by an oracle against Damascus and a warning against idolatry.

Here is an outline of chapters 17–20.

I. Oracle Against Damascus (17:1-6)
   A. The fate of Damascus (17:1-3)
   B. The fate of Jacob (17:4-6)
II. Oracle Against Idolatry (17:7-14)
   A. The people will turn to God (17:7-9)
   B. Punishment for idolatry (17:10-11)
   C. A storm brews (17:12-14)
III. Oracles Concerning Egypt (18:1–20:6)
   A. First oracle against Egypt (18:1-7)
   B. Second oracle against Egypt (19:1-15)
   C. Conversion of Egypt and Assyria (19:16-25)
   D. Third oracle against Egypt (20:1-6)

The Message of Isaiah 17–20

Most of the material in these four chapters focuses on the nation of Egypt and what will happen to that nation at some time in the future. What do these oracles tell us about Israel's God? about the people of Israel? about Egypt?

- God's judgment on sin and disobedience extends far beyond the limits of God's own people. God will punish other nations as well.

- Because God is active in history, we can never be certain of the future. Nor can we control it.

- God will not act in history until the time is right. God can be a spectator of historical events if that is appropriate in God's eyes.

- God will listen to supplications made not only by the people of Israel, but by the people of other nations as well. God has the power to change the course of history.

ISAIAH 21–23

Introduction to These Chapters

This section begins with an oracle against Babylon, followed by messages to other nations such as Edom, Arabia, and Sidon (a city). Isaiah 21–23 concludes a larger section of the book (chapters 13–23) in which most of the prophet's oracles against foreign nations are contained.

Here is an outline of chapters 21–23.

I. Oracle Against Babylon (21:1-10)
II. Oracle Against Edom (21:11-12)
III. Oracle Against Arabia (21:13-17)
IV. Warning to Jerusalem (22:1-14)
V. Oracle Against Shebna (22:15-25)
VI. Oracle Against Tyre and Sidon (23:1-18)

The Message of Isaiah 21–23

- God acts for the purpose of calling the people to repentance. When they do not respond appropriately, God will punish them again.

- There can be no rest, no escape from God's judgment, until there is trust in God.

- God's judgment can come upon foreign nations just as it comes upon God's own people. Final judgment will involve everyone.

- Fortifications and an abundance of weapons cannot compensate for a failure to trust in God.

ISAIAH 24–27

Introduction to These Chapters

Chapters 24–27 of the book of Isaiah are usually called the *Isaiah Apocalypse*. Their content is primarily eschatological (relating to events at the end of time). Various kinds of prophetic literature are

---

FUTURE DELIVERANCE (ISAIAH 27:2-6)

This song about a vineyard is in contrast to the song of the vineyard found in Isaiah 5:1-7. Verse 2 forms the introduction to the song, using the familiar words in that day. Verse 3 indicates that God is speaking in the first person. Rather than destroying the vineyard (as in Isaiah 5:5-6), God will protect the vineyard from outside harm. God will water this vineyard (verse 3), rather than commanding the clouds not to rain on it (see 5:6). According to verse 4, God is not angry with the yield of this vineyard. There are no thorns and briars to battle. As a result, this vineyard will not be destroyed. As far as outside enemies are concerned (nations other than Israel, the vineyard), they will need to make peace with God. The repetition in verse 5 is for emphasis.

Israel and Jacob will, at some time in the future, blossom again. At that time the original promise made to Abraham will be fulfilled (see Genesis 12:1-3).

---

found in these chapters, such as apocalyptic poetry, eschatological prophecies, oracles of judgment, and oracles of salvation.

Most commentators agree that the Isaiah Apocalypse was not the work of the prophet Isaiah. Various suggestions have been made for the date of this section. Whereas the prophet Isaiah is most often concerned with the judgment God is about to bring upon Judah, the events spoken of in chapters 24–27 are on a worldwide scale. Concern for the events that will take place at the end of time is characteristic of the theology of later Judaism, perhaps dating these chapters to 400 or 300 B.C.

Many of the prophecies in these chapters concern a certain city, whose identity is uncertain. Commentators have suggested such cities as Carthage, Babylon, and Samaria, but no one knows for certain. That is unfortunate, since the identification of the city might tell us something about the origin and date of these prophecies.

Here is an outline of chapters 24–27.
  I. Total Destruction (24:1-13)
 III. Future Deliverance (24:14-16)
 III. Total Destruction (24:17-23)
 IV. Thanksgiving Song (25:1-5)

  V. Eschatological Oracles (25:6-12)
 VI. Victory Song (26:1-6)
 VII. Future Restoration (26:7-19)
VIII. Future Judgment (26:20–27:1)
 IX. Future Deliverance (27:2-11)
  X. Concluding Oracle (27:12-13)

The Message of Isaiah 24–27

Within the book of Isaiah, these chapters stand apart from the rest of the book. What message do they convey about God and about humankind?

- No matter how desperate the situation, there is always room for hope in the future of a restored Jerusalem.

- The people must rely on their trust in God to help them through times of despair.

- One day in the future, God will judge the rulers of Israel's enemies. They will have to pay for their actions.

- We cannot always predict or understand what miracles God will perform on our behalf.

- Trust in God will provide for the people strength they did not know they had.

- Human beings can only accomplish so much. After that they must trust that God's power will work effectively.

ISAIAH 28–30

Introduction to These Chapters

Most of chapters 28–35 consists of oracles concerning Judah (the Southern Kingdom) and Israel (the Northern Kingdom, here called Ephraim). Chapters 28–30 contain an oracle about Samaria's religious leaders, an oracle about the political leaders in Jerusalem, a parable, an oracle about the future restoration of Judah, and a group of oracles about hypocrisy in the religious practices of the people.

Here is an outline of chapters 28–30.
  I. Oracles Against Religious Leaders (28:1-13)
     A. Oracle concerning Ephraim (28:1-4)
     B. God's future blessing (28:5-6)
     C. Oracle concerning Judah (28:7-13)
  II. Oracles Against Political Leaders (28:14-22)
  III. Parable of the Farmer (28:23-29)
  IV. Restoration of Judah (29:1-8)
  V. Miscellaneous Oracles (29:9-24)
  VI. Oracles Concerning Egypt (30:1-17)
     A. Ambassadors sent to Egypt (30:1-7)
     B. Judah's alliance with Egypt (30:8-17)
  VII. Restoration of Judah (30:18-26)
  VIII. Oracle Against Assyria (30:27-33)

The Message of Isaiah 28–30

- The restored world in the future is the same world that exists now. It is the people who will be changed.

- In the face of danger, appealing to military might will do no good. The people must rely on God.

- Obedience to God requires trust in God.

- We may not always understand God's purposes.

- Hope helps us endure the trials of this world.

- Asking what is God's will is the best way to make plans, no matter what the task.

- When the people see what God can do, they will have no choice but to behave.

ISAIAH 31–33

Introduction to These Chapters

Chapters 31–33 continue the series of oracles concerning Egypt and others that began in chapter 28. This present section includes oracles concerning Egypt, Assyria, the women of Judah, and the future age of justice, as well as a section describing the coming of the Spirit, and a prophetic liturgy (in chapter 33).

Here is an outline of chapters 31–33.
  I. Oracles Concerning Egypt and Others (31:1–32:20)
     A. Oracle against Egypt (31:1-3)
     B. Oracle against Sennacherib (31:4-9)
     C. The future of Judah (32:1-8)
     D. Oracle against Judah's women (32:9-14)
     E. Outpouring of the Spirit (32:15-20)
  II. Prophetic Liturgy (33:1-24)
     A. Part one (33:1-6)
     B. Part two (33:7-16)
     C. Part three (33:17-24)

The Message of Isaiah 31–33

- Humankind can hope for peace, if persons will repent and return to God.

- God is capable of actions that seem to be impossible.

- Our actions should be directed first to God and then on behalf of one another.

- In the glorious future that God promised to bring about, the prophet believed that society would be different from the way it was in his day.

- Those who can remember days of darkness and despair are better able to look toward a bright future.

ISAIAH 34–35

Introduction to These Chapters

These two short chapters form a conclusion to the series of oracles in Isaiah 28–33, in the same way that chapters 24–27 conclude chapters 13–23. The material in this section concerns the fate of the enemies of Judah and the final restoration of Jerusalem.

Because much of the language and imagery in these two chapters is similar to that of chapters 40–55, the work of Second Isaiah, many commentators consider these chapters to have been originally part of Second Isaiah's prophecies. We have no way of knowing for certain.

Here is an outline of chapters 34–35.

I. Judgment on God's Enemies (34:1-17)
   A. God will judge the world (34:1-4)
   B. God will punish Edom (34:5-17)
II. Restoration of Zion (35:1-10)

The Message of Isaiah 34–35

- Failure to get along with its neighbors caused Judah to look to God for help and protection.

- God will have revenge on those nations who deal unjustly with God's people.

- God will come to save those who believe, even though they may have suffered in the past.

ISAIAH 36–39

Introduction to These Chapters

Chapters 36–39 are the only lengthy narrative section in the book of Isaiah. Much of the material found in these chapters is found also in 2 Kings 18–20. Most commentators think that the narrative in 2 Kings was written first, and portions of it were used in Isaiah 36–39.

Chapter 39 contains a number of references to the Exile into Babylon, and so is a transitional chapter in the book as a whole (chapters 40–55 come from the time of the Babylonian Exile).

Here is an outline of Isaiah 36–39.

I. Attack on Jerusalem (36:1-22)
   A. Do not rely on Egypt (36:1-12)
   B. Rabshakeh's speech to Jerusalem (36:13-20)
   C. The people's response (36:21-22)
II. Isaiah Advises Hezekiah (37:1-38)
   A. Hezekiah goes to the Temple (37:1-7)
   B. Hezekiah is challenged again (37:8-20)
   C. Isaiah responds (37:21-29)
   D. Hezekiah is reassured (37:30-35)
   E. The Assyrians are defeated (37:36-38)
III. Hezekiah's Illness (38:1-22)
   A. God responds with a sign (38:1-8)

B. Hezekiah's song (38:9-20)

C. Concluding verses (38:21-22)

IV. Merodach-baladan and Hezekiah (39:1-8)

The Message of Isaiah 36–39

- Human beings are dependent upon God in times of despair or physical illness.

- Praise and thanksgiving are an appropriate response when one is renewed after a time of tragedy.

- Arrogance on the part of human beings will be punished.

ISAIAH 40

Introduction to This Chapter

Chapter 40 begins the work of the prophet of the Exile. The message of this chapter is the heart of the message of the next fifteen chapters, which makes chapter 40 an appropriate introduction to the prophet's work.

Here is an outline of chapter 40.

I. Call to Announce God's Coming (40:1-11)

A. First cry (40:1-2)

B. Second cry (40:3-5)

C. The prophet's call (40:6-8)

D. Third cry (40:9-11)

II. God the Creator (40:12-31)

A. Concerning the nations (40:12-17)

B. Concerning princes and rulers (40:18-24)

C. Concerning the heavenly host (40:25-26)

D. Concerning the exiles (40:27-31)

The Message of Isaiah 40

- The exiled people were turning away from God, because they thought God

---

CALL TO ANNOUNCE GOD'S COMING (ISAIAH 40:1-11)

Because this section begins the words of another prophet, we might expect a superscription or introduction, like that found in Isaiah 1:1. It is typical of this prophet that he tells us nothing about his date or his circumstances. Instead, this prophet's words begin with the cry "Comfort, comfort my people." The repetition of the word *comfort* is characteristic of the language of this prophet. Repeating an imperative verb indicates the urgency of the prophet's message. Similar repetitions occur in 51:9; 52:1, 11. "My people" and "your God" are phrases often used to describe the covenant between God and the chosen people (see Exodus 19, for example). "Your God" indicates that the prophet is speaking on God's behalf.

Verse 2 summarizes the message of this prophet. Israel's time of punishment is ended. In other words, the Exile in Babylon is soon to come to an end. Israel's sin is forgiven by God. That the prophet speaks of these events in the past indicates his certainty of what he is proclaiming. In other words, he is so convinced of the imminent end of the Babylonian Exile that he speaks of the event as though it has already happened. This belief is a highlight of this prophet's message.

The people have already received double the punishment they might have had. In other words, in the prophet's mind (and God's) the people have suffered more than enough. Now their suffering is about to end.

The second cry is spoken by an unidentified person to an unidentified audience. This voice commands that it is now time to "prepare the way of the LORD" in the wilderness (desert). This verse and the two that follow it are quoted directly in Luke 3:4-6. However, in Luke and the other Gospels, the words "in the wilderness" are taken as an identification of the location of the voice,

CALL TO ANNOUNCE GOD'S COMING (ISAIAH 40:1-11; CONT.)

rather than the place where the highway was to be built. Somewhere in the tradition (between the formation of Old and New Testaments) the exact meaning of this cry altered slightly. However, its essential message remains the same: It is time for a highway to be built on which the exiles will make their journey home. "The way of the LORD" is an important concept in the prophecies of Second Isaiah (see 42:16; 43:16, 19; 48:17; 49:11; 51:10).

Verse 4 mentions valleys that will be lifted up and mountains that will be leveled, symbolizing obstacles that might be put in the way of the returning exiles. "The glory of the LORD" will be revealed to everyone at the same time. The phrase "the mouth of the LORD has spoken" concludes this part of the chapter.

Verses 6-8 correspond to the call of the prophet that appears in most prophetic books. As a matter of fact, the only information we have about Second Isaiah comes to us in these three verses. They are introduced by a second voice, who says, "Cry out!" Again, we are not told who is speaking. Here, however, we do know who is addressed by the voice—the prophet himself.

The second phrase in verse 6 tells us the prophet's answer to the cry: "What shall I cry?" It is addressed to the unknown speaker. Ordinarily when prophets are called they voice some initial objections to their call, usually related to their own incapabilities. Here, the prophet's objection relates to the message he is called to proclaim. It appears to be unnecessary and futile, since human life is transitory. However, verse 8 answers the prophet's objection. Yes, it is true that human life is fleeting. But the message is important nevertheless, because "the word of our God will stand forever." This word is a reference to the promises God has made to the people in the past.

Most commentators agree that the last phrase in verse 7 is a gloss, or a comment by a later reader. Glosses such as this one indicate what persons throughout the Old Testament tradition thought was important enough to need to be commented on or explained.

The addressee in the third cry in verses 9-11 is specified as "Zion, herald of good tidings" (NRSV; NIV, "You who bring good tidings to Zion"). The herald is commanded to go up on a high mountain to proclaim a message of deliverance. Again, the prophet has the attitude that the message to be proclaimed concerns an event that has already taken place. The return from the Exile is described in terms of what God will do to bring it about. God's "arm" symbolizes might or power, which will be used on the people's behalf. Verse 11 describes the other side of God. God is mighty, but tender and nurturing as well. From beginning to end, Second Isaiah's message presupposes that none of this would be happening if it were not for God.

had forsaken them. In the face of this attitude of despair, the prophet proclaims his message of comfort and hope.

- The promise of deliverance the prophet brings is closely related to the fact that God has forgiven the sins of the people.

- Just as God once delivered the Israelites from the hand of the Egyptians at the Red Sea, God will again prepare a way for the chosen people to escape their bondage and return home.

- In response to what God is about to do for the people, they will renew their trust in God.

- God is both Creator and lord of history. Both these aspects of God are important to Second Isaiah's message.

ISAIAH 41:1—44:23

Introduction to These Chapters

These four chapters contain a series of speeches concerning the nations, the first of four servant songs, and a series of oracles concerning Judah's restoration.

Here is an outline of these chapters.

I. Trial of the Nations (41:1-29)
- A. God stirs up Cyrus (41:1-5)
- B. The making of idols (41:6-7)
- C. Oracle of assurance (41:8-13)
- D. Oracle of assurance (41:14-16)
- E. God the Creator (41:17-20)
- F. The nations on trial (41:21-29)

II. First Servant Song (42:1-4)

III. Oracle of Restoration (42:5-17)
- A. God is victorious (42:5-9)
- B. Call to praise (42:10-13)
- C. The lord of history (42:14-17)

IV. Israel's Judgment and Redemption (42:18—43:7)
- A. Concerning the blind and deaf (42:18-25)
- B. Redemption of Israel (43:1-7)

V. Israel's Restoration (43:8—44:8)
- A. The nations on trial (43:8-15)
- B. Proclamation of salvation (43:16-21)
- C. Israel on trial (43:22-28)
- D. Oracle of salvation (44:1-5)
- E. The nations on trial (44:6-8)

VI. Against Idolatry (44:9-20)

VII. Concluding Words (44:21-23)

The Message of Isaiah 41:1—44:23

- In the person and work of Cyrus, king of Persia, we can see the hand of Yahweh, the God of Israel.

- The people are in despair, thinking that their God has forsaken them. Just at the height of their despair, Second Isaiah's message of hope breaks through.

- God's divinity is shown by the involvement God has had in history. No other gods can make this claim.

FIRST SERVANT SONG (ISAIAH 42:1-4)

This passage is the first of four servant songs found in Second Isaiah's prophecies. The other three songs are 49:1-6; 50:4-11; and 52:13—53:12. There are several very important things the prophet does not tell us in these songs: the identity of the servant, the nature of the task, and the circumstances of the servant's commissioning. The first issue is probably the most significant; commentators have written volumes discussing the identity of the servant. Is it Israel? Is it the prophet? Is it King Cyrus? Is it some other unknown person? We must realize that the servant's identity will remain hidden to us; perhaps that was the prophet's intention. What is most important is the message.

In verse 1 God is speaking about the servant, the one God chose and now upholds. God's commissioning of this servant is similar to the call of a prophet, except that the servant was apparently given his task in public. (God speaks to a group of people in verse 1, asking them to witness the event.)

Verses 1-4 tell us three things the servant will do: he will "bring forth justice to the nations," he will "faithfully bring forth justice," and he will establish "justice in the earth." All these phrases are variations on the theme of bringing justice. According to verse 4, bringing justice means that God's law (teaching) will be known and obeyed by everyone.

Verse 4 could also be translated "He will not burn dimly or be bruised." Such a translation suggests an allusion to future suffering the servant will have to endure.

- The people of Israel, summoned by the prophet, respond to God's promise in joy and celebration.

- At times the people have been blind and deaf to God's message.

ISAIAH 44:24–48:22

Introduction to These Chapters

This section begins with the so-called Cyrus Oracle (which actually starts at 44:28). Also included in these chapters are two calls to praise, a trial speech, more material concerning idol worship, a lament over Babylon's fate, and various miscellaneous oracles.

Here is an outline of Isaiah 44:24–48:22
I. Commission of Cyrus (44:24–45:13)
    A. Introduction (44:24-28)
    B. The Cyrus oracle (45:1-7)
    C. Concluding call to praise (45:8)
    D. The power of God (45:9-13)
II. Miscellaneous Oracles (45:14–46:13)
    A. Oracles concerning the nations (45:14-25)
    B. Address to Israel (46:1-4)
    C. Against idol worship (46:5-8)
    D. Oracle of deliverance (46:9-13)
III. Lament over Babylon (47:1-15)
IV. God's Actions in History (48:1-22)
    A. Oracle of deliverance (48:1-11)
    B. Oracle of deliverance (48:12-17)
    C. Peace like a river (48:18-19)
    D. Release from Babylon (48:20-22)

The Message of Isaiah 44:24–48:22

These chapters conclude the first half of Second Isaiah's prophecies. What can we learn from the material included in chapters 45–48 about God and about the chosen people?

- God has chosen Cyrus, a heathen king, to accomplish great things on behalf of the chosen people.

- God is seen as protector and supporter of the people of Israel, in contrast to the Babylonian gods, who must be carried by their people.

- Second Isaiah proclaims a message that is positive and hopeful in its entirety.

- God's goal in releasing the people from their captivity involves not just the people of Israel, but people from all over the earth.

ISAIAH 49:1–52:12

Introduction to These Chapters

Chapters 49–52 begin the second half of Second Isaiah's prophecies. In this section are two servant songs, several calls to praise, some miscellaneous oracles, and a call to depart from Babylon. Whereas chapters 40–48 are composed of numerous short oracles and speeches, the second half of Second Isaiah contains units that are, for the most part, longer and more complex.

Here is an outline of chapters 49–52.
I. Second Servant Song (49:1-6)
II. Return and Restoration (49:7-26)
    A. Day of salvation (49:7-12)
    B. Call to praise (49:13)
    C. God's love for Israel (49:14-26)
III. Covenant with Israel (50:1-3)
IV. Third Servant Song (50:4-11)
V. Salvation for Abraham's Descendants (51:1-16)
    A. Future deliverance (51:1-8)
    B. Awake! Awake! (51:9-16)
VI. Kingship of God (51:17–52:12)
    A. Restoration of Jerusalem (51:17-23)
    B. Awake! Awake! (52:1-2)
    C. Fate of Israel's enemies (52:3-6)
    D. Future restoration (52:7-12)

SECOND SERVANT SONG (ISAIAH 49:1-6)

This servant song is the second of four; the others are found in 42:1-4; 50:4-11; and 52:13 –53:12. In this song, the servant speaks in the first person and addresses the "coastlands" (NRSV; NIV, "islands") and peoples from afar, in other words, the Gentiles. Like the first servant song, this one speaks of God's commissioning of the servant and the servant's mission. (See Jeremiah 1:5.)

Like the prophet Jeremiah, the servant was called by God while he was still inside his mother's womb. Also like the prophets, the servant's call has to do with the words he speaks. His mouth is "like a sharp sword"—the words that come from it will not always be easy to hear, but they will reach their destination. The same thing is said about the words of a prophet in Jeremiah 23:29. The second part of verse 2 indicates that during at least some of his mission the servant worked in secret.

Verse 3 explains the reason for God's commissioning of the servant—so that God might be glorified. In a response similar to that of the prophets when they are called, the servant hesitates, saying that thus far his work has been in vain. He seems to be reassuring himself in the second half of verse 4. God is still with him, protecting him and guiding him as he works.

Verses 5 and 6 contrast Israel in the past with the restored land. Verse 5 introduces the saying with a series of phrases describing God's calling of the servant. Verse 6 expands the servant's mission from Israel "to the nations," "to the ends of the earth."

The Message of Isaiah 49:1–52:12

What do these chapters tell us about God and about God's relationship to the people in exile?

- God is in control of history and everything that happens in history.

- God maintained (and will continue to maintain) a close relationship with the people, even though they do not deserve God's continued protection.

- God remains faithful to the covenant formerly established with the people of Israel.

THIRD SERVANT SONG (ISAIAH 50:4-9)

As is the case with the servant song in 49:1-6, this song points out the similarities between the mission of the servant and the ministry of Israel's prophets. The servant speaks in the first person, addressing the people of Israel.

In verse 4, the servant says that God "has given me a tongue of a teacher"—in other words, the servant knows how to communicate the message he is given to proclaim. He proclaims this message to the weary exiles who are in need of words of comfort. "Morning by morning" means that God tells the servant not only what to say, but also when to say it.

The servant was obedient, and did what God told him to do (verse 5). However, the people did not respond positively to the message. The fact that the servant had to suffer physical abuse at the hands of his audience did not deter him from accomplishing his mission. Why? Because God is on the side of the servant (verse 7). His sincere conviction is symbolized by his setting his face like stone.

In verses 8-9, the servant uses legal process to convince his audience that God is on his side. Those who oppose the servant are summoned to state their case. The fact that they are silent proves the truth of the servant's conviction.

- The servant is able to continue his mission, even though it seems to be unprofitable, because he is assured of the continuing presence of God.

- Persons who do not treat the people of God with justice and righteousness will be punished for their attitude.

- That God intends to uphold the covenant obligations with the people is evidenced by the fact that God has kept the promises made earlier to Abraham.

ISAIAH 52:13–55:13

Introduction to These Chapters

Chapters 53–55 are the final three chapters in the book of Second Isaiah, the prophet of the Babylonian Exile. They are followed by a collection of prophecies from the post exilic period, from the hand of an anonymous prophet called Third Isaiah (chapters 56–66). Isaiah 53–55 includes the fourth servant song, a call to praise, a proclamation of salvation, a conclusion to the book, and other miscellaneous oracles.

Here is an outline of these chapters.

I. Fourth Servant Song (52:13–53:12)
   A. God speaks (52:13-15)
   B. Others speak (53:1-10)
   C. God speaks (53:11-12)
II. Assurance of Israel's Restoration (54:1-17)
   A. Summons to sing (54:1-10)
   B. Future salvation (54:11-17)
III. Song of Triumph (55:1-13)
   A. Restoration of Judah (55:1-5)
   B. Epilogue (55:6-13)

FOURTH SERVANT SONG (ISAIAH 52:13–53:12)

The fourth servant song is one of the most well-known passages in Scripture. The fourth song should be read in the context of the first three songs (see 42:1-4; 49:1-6; and 50:4-11) and should be seen as the climax of the message proclaimed in these earlier songs. This fourth song is divided into three parts, according to who is speaking. The song includes three verses from chapter 52 and all of chapter 53.

The fourth servant song begins with a speech by God. The concluding words (verses 11b-12 of chapter 53) are also spoken by God. These introductory and concluding words form the frame for the speech by an unidentified group of people (53:1-11a).

God opens the speech in verses 13-15 with a description of the servant as "exalted and lifted up." The description is introduced by the words "See, my servant." These same words, uttered by God, are used to introduce the first servant song in Isaiah 42:1-4. The description of the servant's high status stands in direct contrast to his physical appearance, which God describes in verse 14. His appearance was so marred that he looked almost inhuman.

The meaning of the Hebrew verb in verse 15 is uncertain (NIV, "sprinkle"; NRSV, "startle"). When it is used elsewhere in the Old Testament it means to leap; perhaps here nations will leap, figuratively, as a result of being startled. The reaction of kings and nations to the servant's accomplishments and his physical appearance is reminiscent again of the first servant song in 42:1-4.

The last two lines of verse 15 make clear that the mission of the servant is unique. Nothing like this has ever happened before. These words are quoted directly in Romans 15:21, where Paul is discussing the newness of the gospel message.

FOURTH SERVANT SONG (ISAIAH 52:13–53:12; CONT.)

In 53:1-10, a group of people begin describing the servant's life history and lamenting his current situation. They begin by stating that he grew up in relatively normal circumstances. He did not stand out so that he would be noticed by others. "Like a young plant" is language similar to that used in many messianic prophecies. For example, Isaiah 11:1 speaks of a shoot from the stump of Jesse. (See also Jeremiah 23:5.)

In verse 3 the description of the servant moves from his appearance to his humiliation. Using language that reminds us of the lament psalms, this unidentified group of people portray the servant's whole life as dominated by suffering. Many of the words used in verse 3 have uncertain meanings, but the general tone and message are clear. The servant has been humiliated and rejected by his community.

Verses 4-6 turn our attention to the attitude that persons had about this servant. Whereas in verse 3 the servant was rejected, in verse 4 the speakers seem to come to the realization that his humiliation was actually on their behalf. "Borne our infirmities" might also be translated "borne our sickness"; "carried our sorrows" (NIV; NRSV, "diseases") might be translated "carried our pains."

After coming to the realization that the servant's humiliation and rejection were for their sake, these persons respond by a kind of confession that they have turned away from God (verse 6). The servant, in his own quiet way, has atoned for these sins.

The idea of suffering in silence is continued in verses 7-9. Even though the servant was "oppressed" and "afflicted," he did not open his mouth to complain. He is likened to a lamb who is being taken to be slaughtered. Verses 7 and 8 make the point that even in the face of violence perpetrated by others ("stricken"; "cut off") the servant did not waver.

The second half of verse 8 and all of verse 9 describe the death and burial of the servant. He was buried with evildoers, thus continuing the atmosphere of suffering and shame that surrounded him. "And with the rich in his death" (NIV, verse 9) might also be translated "and his tomb with evildoers." This latter translation makes better sense since it parallels the first phrase in the verse.

Verses 10-12 describe the servant's deliverance from his former state. God, who was involved in the servant's situation from the beginning (verse 10), has intervened and turned his circumstances around. But what does God's intervention really mean? Was the servant resurrected from the dead? The text is vague at this point. It is clear, however, that as a result of the change in his circumstances the servant will prosper in the future. "We shall see his offspring" is a Hebrew way of saying that he will live a full life. A large family was a sign of prosperity and God's blessings.

God is speaking in the first person in 53:11-12, as in the introductory words in verses 13-15 of chapter 52. Thus the fourth servant song begins and ends with what God has to proclaim. The last part of verse 12 summarizes the servant's mission. "He bore the sin of many, and made intercession for the transgressors."

The Message of Isaiah 53–55

These are important chapters in Isaiah, since they contain the fourth servant song and they also conclude a major section of the book. They provide insight into the message of chapters 40–55.

- God can work wonders through unlikely persons.

- Proclaiming God's word is not always an easy task. Sometimes suffering is the result.

- God's will is not always clear to us, but God can accomplish whatever is intended.

- Trust in God will bring its own rewards, even though it is difficult to recognize what those rewards will be.

- God will love us steadfastly, and will not forsake us. The covenant assures us of God's continued presence.

- God's thoughts and ways are not our thoughts and ways.

- A return to restored Jerusalem is a return to a right relationship with God.

ISAIAH 56–59

Introduction to These Chapters

Isaiah 56–59 begins the third major portion of the book of Isaiah. This third section is a collection of prophecies from the post exilic period (after the return from Exile in 538 B.C.). In these first four chapters the prophet speaks against the nation's political leaders and against the practices of idolatry, and he offers a poem of consolation and a summons to repent.

Here is an outline of these chapters.

  I. Keeping the Sabbath (56:1-8)
  II. Oracle Against Leaders (56:9-12)
  III. Oracle Against Idolatry (57:1-13)
  IV. Consolation for Israel (57:14-21)
  V. What the Lord Desires (58:1-14)
  VI. Call to Repentance (59:1-21)

The Message of Isaiah 56–59

These chapters are more difficult to read and interpret than some others in the book of Isaiah. What can we learn from them about God and God's people?

- Some rituals and regulations are useful and pleasing to God if they are performed in the right spirit.

- Worship of God is available to everyone.

- Community leaders have an obligation to guide the people with integrity. Punishment results if that obligation is not taken seriously.

- Sometimes the deeds and virtues of the righteous go unnoticed.

- God's anger is not endless; forgiveness is possible.

- Justice and righteousness are more pleasing to God than fasting or other rituals, especially if the right attitude does not accompany the performance of ritual.

- There are times when the nation as a whole needs to repent and ask God's forgiveness.

ISAIAH 60–62

Introduction to These Chapters

Chapters 60–62 are similar in content and themes to chapters 40–55. These chapters are inspiring and uplifting. They speak of a glorious future for God's people as they inhabit a restored Jerusalem.

Here is an outline of chapters 60–62.

  I. Jerusalem's Restoration (60:1-22)
    A. Zion will arise (60:1-3)
    B. The people will return (60:4-9)
    C. Jerusalem will be restored (60:10-16)
    D. Future salvation (60:17-22)
  II. The Prophet's Mission to Zion (61:1-11)
    A. The Spirit of the Lord (61:1-3)
    B. God will bring salvation (61:4-11)
  III. Zion Is Vindicated (62:1-12)
    A. A new name for Zion (62:1-5)
    B. The watchmen prepare (62:6-12)

The Message of Isaiah 60–62

- God's people can shed light on the rest of the world.

- God will be glorified by the return of the people.

- With the blessing of God, the chosen people will stand out among all other people.

- God's blessing can change circumstances dramatically.

- God can bring about radical changes by a mere utterance.

ISAIAH 63–66

Introduction to These Chapters

These chapters form the conclusion to the prophecies in the third portion of the book of Isaiah, and to the book of Isaiah as a whole. They contain an oracle proclaiming God's vengeance, an intercessory psalm, an oracle giving God's answer to the request, and several unrelated concluding oracles.

Here is an outline of Isaiah 63–66.
I. God's Vengeance (63:1-6)
II. The Prophet Petitions God (63:7–64:12)
    A. The Exodus from Egypt (63:7-14)
    B. The prophet's request (63:15–64:12)
III. God Answers (65:1-25)
    A. The people rebelled (65:1-7)
    B. God's servants (65:8-16)
    C. New heavens and a new earth (65:17-25)
IV. Final Oracles (66:1-24)
    A. Worship in the Temple (66:1-6)
    B. Jerusalem will rejoice (66:7-16)
    C. The glory of God (66:17-24)

The Message of Isaiah 63–66

These concluding chapters of the book of Isaiah draw together many of the themes that are found throughout the book as a whole.

- God has the capability and the willingness to punish the people if they disobey.

- God's steadfast love is available to those who would become God's people.

- When the people suffer, God suffers.

- God's actions on behalf of the people in the past show God's intentions to protect the chosen people now and in the future.

- Some cultic ritual is abhorrent to God.

- God will distinguish between the righteous, deserving salvation, and the evil, deserving punishment.

- The transformation of heaven and earth is the ultimate intention of God.

JEREMIAH

OUTLINE OF JEREMIAH

A. Biographical narratives about
   Jeremiah (26:1–29:32; 32:1-44;
   34:1–45:5)
   1. Jeremiah's Temple sermon
      (26:1-24)
   2. Oracles Concerning the king
      of Babylon (27:1-22)
   3. Jeremiah's confrontation with
      Hananiah (28:1-17)
   4. Jeremiah's letters to Babylon
      (29:1-32)
   5. Jeremiah's purchase of a field
      (32:1-44)
   6. Oracles to Zedekiah and to
      Jerusalem (34:1-22)
   7. The sign of the Rechabites
      (35:1-19)
   8. The scroll of Jeremiah (36:1-32)
   9. Jeremiah is arrested (37:1-21)
   10. Jeremiah insists on surrender
       (38:1-28)
   11. The fall of Jerusalem (39:1-18)
   12. Gedaliah appointed governor
       (40:1-16)
   13. Report of Gedaliah's murder
       (41:1-18)
   14. The flight to Egypt
       (42:1–43:7)
   15. Sign act against Egypt (43:8-13)
   16. Israel's idolatry in Egypt
       (44:1-30)
   17. Oracle to Baruch (45:1-5)
B. The Book of Consolation
   (30:1–31:40; 33:1-26)

**IV. Oracles Against Foreign Nations
(46:1–51:64)**
A. Oracles against nations other than
   Babylon (46:1–49:39)
   1. Oracles against Egypt
      (46:1-28)
   2. Oracle against the Philistines
      (47:1-7)
   3. Oracles against Moab (48:1-47)
   4. Oracle against the Ammonites
      (49:1-6)

5. Oracle against Edom (49:7-22)
6. Oracle against Damascus
   (49:23-27)
7. Oracle against Kedar and
   Hazor (49:28-33)
8. Oracle against Elam (49:34-39)
B. Oracles against Babylon
   (45:1–51:64)

V. Israel Is Taken into Exile (52:1-34)

INTRODUCTION

The prophetic ministry of Jeremiah began
in 627 B.C. during the reign of the Judean
king Josiah (640–609 B.C.) when Jeremiah
was only a youth. His ministry continued
until around 580 B.C. and ended in Egypt.

Jeremiah was one of the major prophets of
ancient Israel. Much of his life and many of
his words are recorded in the Old Testament
book that bears his name. His personal story
is interwoven with his prophecy and with the
story of the people of Israel.

The years of Jeremiah's ministry
were turbulent and tragic years for
Israel. Jeremiah's prophecy must be seen
against this background. He addressed
specific circumstances in the life of
Israel, and he delivered God's messages
concerning these circumstances.

Historical Background

After the death of King Solomon, the
kingdom of Israel was divided into Israel
in the north and Judah in the south. (Israel
sometimes means specifically the Northern
Kingdom. Israel can also mean the people
of Israel, which includes all the chosen
people in the north and in the south.) The
Northern Kingdom was conquered by
Assyria in 722 B.C.

When Assyria's power declined, King
Josiah of Judah extended his power into
parts of the Northern Kingdom. Josiah also

initiated a religious reform in Judah. This reform sought to rid Israelite faith and practice of the pagan rituals that had been introduced in years past. Worship was purified and centralized into the Temple in Jerusalem. Shrines and sanctuaries in outlying areas were closed.

Josiah's reign ended when he was killed in battle at Megiddo in 609 B.C. His son, Jehoahaz, took his place but was deposed by the Egyptians, who put Jehoahaz's brother, Jehoiakim (Eliakim), on the throne. The religious reforms of Josiah were soon forgotten.

During this time, Babylonia was becoming a world power. By 603 B.C., Jehoiakim and Judah were under Babylonian control. Jehoiakim tried to break away from Babylon in 601 B.C. to establish Judah as an independent state once again.

In December 598 B.C., the Babylonian army besieged Jerusalem. Jehoiakim was killed and his son, Jehoiachin, soon surrendered the city. Hundreds of Israelites were deported to Babylon, including the king, his court, priests, artisans, and other leading citizens. Zedekiah, the uncle of Jehoiachin, was made king under Babylonian control.

Judah rebelled in 588 B.C. and, once again, Babylonian forces attacked Jerusalem. The city fell in 587 B.C. after an eighteen-month siege. More Israelites were deported and the city was destroyed.

King Nebuchadnezzar of Babylon appointed Gedaliah, a member of a prominent Judean family, as provincial governor. Gedaliah was assassinated in 582 B.C. by a zealous member of the Judean royal family. Fearing reprisals from the Babylonians for Gedaliah's death, some Israelites fled to Egypt. Jeremiah was forced to go with them. More captives were taken from Judah to Babylon, and the hardship of those left in Judah increased.

In 539 B.C., Persia defeated Babylonia.

Cyrus, the Persian king, gave the exiled Israelites permission to return to Judah. Jeremiah did not live to see this return. His prophecy, however, helped pave the way for Israel's survival as a community of faith by dealing with Israel's disaster within the context of faith.

Important Dates for the Book of Jeremiah

722 B.C.	Northern Kingdom absorbed by Assyria
687–642 B.C.	Manasseh king of Judah
642–640 B.C.	Amon king of Judah
640–609 B.C.	Josiah king of Judah
627 B.C.	Jeremiah called to prophesy
612 B.C.	Babylonians conquer the Assyrian capital
609 B.C.	Jehoahaz, king of Judah, deposed by Egypt
609–598 B.C.	Jehoiakim king of Judah
605 B.C.	Babylonians defeat Egyptians and Assyrians at Carchemish; extend influence over Judah
601 B.C.	Jehoiakim rebels against Babylon
598–597 B.C.	Babylonian siege of Jerusalem; Jehoiakim killed
598–597 B.C.	Jehoiachin king of Judah; Jerusalem surrenders; many Israelites deported to Babylon
597–587 B.C.	Jedekiah king of Judah
588–587 B.C.	Judah rebels; Babylonian siege of Jerusalem; Jerusalem destroyed; more Israelites deported
587–582 B.C.	Gedaliah appointed governor of Judah
582 B.C.	Gedaliah assassinated, Jeremiah forced into exile in Egypt

(Note concerning dates: Remember that some dates are known precisely and others are only approximate. Historical sources will frequently vary as much as a year or two in giving some dates. Most ancient documents have been lost or destroyed, so there are not many sources of information other than the Bible for this time in history. This situation is complicated by the fact that ancient systems of dating do not correspond to our present calendar. Also, not all ancient dating systems are alike. Keep these factors in mind as you study the history of Israel, especially when you find references which give differing dates for the same event.)

Jeremiah the Man

Jeremiah was born into a priestly family sometime around 645 B.C. His father, Hilkiah, was a descendant of the priest Abiathar who had been banished to his ancestral home in Anathoth by King Solomon. (See 1 Kings 2:26-27.)

In a priestly family, Jeremiah was taught Israel's ancient traditions and the words of Israel's prophets. We do not know whether he received formal training as a priest.

At his call to prophesy, Jeremiah calls himself a "boy" (NRSV; NIV, "child"). This may or may not mean that he was a very young man. It may merely indicate that he felt himself too immature for the task God assigned to him. He must have been a relatively young man at the time, though, because his recorded ministry spanned forty-seven years.

At first Jeremiah tried to escape the claim of God's call. He must have understood the burden and personal cost of fulfilling such a call. In later years, he expressed contempt for those people who embraced the office of prophet without appreciating the gravity of it. At times,

Jeremiah hated his calling and longed to quit his duties as God's spokesman. He even confronted God with the terrible burdens he bore for God's sake. But he could not push God's word away.

To fulfill his duties, Jeremiah had to forgo a wife and children of his own. He had to suffer hatred, misunderstanding, and physical abuse. At times his life was threatened. His message of judgment against Israel often disagreed with popular belief and official theology.

Though Jeremiah is often remembered as a sorrowful and gloomy man, he also offered words of hope and comfort to Israel. He was commissioned by God not only put "to pluck up" and "to tear down" but also "to build and to plant."

Jeremiah the Book

The book of Jeremiah is a collection of different kinds of material. It contains prophetic oracles from Jeremiah's public preaching, prayers, stories about Jeremiah, vision reports, sermons, laments, and historical narratives. Some of the book is prose and some is poetry.

The collection was started during Jeremiah's ministry and was finished sometime after 560 B.C. Baruch, Jeremiah's friend and scribe, wrote much of the material in the collection. Jeremiah may have had other disciples or scribes who helped record his words and life.

The book has the following sections:

(1) Oracles Against Judah and Jerusalem, 1:1–25:14

(2) Biographical Narratives, chapters 26–29; 32; 34–45

(3) Oracles of Consolation and Hope, chapters 30–31; 33

(4) Oracles Against Foreign Nations, 25:15-38; chapters 46–51

(5) Historical Appendix, chapter 52

A Word of Caution

Keep in mind that the book of Jeremiah is the record of material which, for the most part, was originally spoken instead of written. These oracles, sermons, and laments were delivered over a period of approximately forty-seven years. Their present written order and relationships are not always in chronological order. Where possible, the historical circumstances in which the material was spoken will be identified.

Kings During Jeremiah's Ministry: 627–580 B.C.

Name of King	Reign Begins
Josiah	640 B.C.
Jehoahaz	609 B.C.
Jehoiakim	609 B.C.
Jehoiachin	598 B.C.
Zedekiah	597 B.C.
Gedaliah (governor)	587 B.C.

JEREMIAH 1

Introduction to This Chapter

Chapter 1 introduces Jeremiah and establishes his authority as a prophet. We are told where he comes from, how long his ministry lasts, and how God calls him. The chapter closes with two vision reports that further explain Jeremiah's prophetic duties. Here is an outline of the chapter.

   I. Introduction (1:1-3)
  II. Jeremiah's Call to Prophesy (1:4-10)
 III. Vision of a Rod of Almond (1:11-12)
 IV. Vision of a Boiling Pot (1:13-19)

The Message of Jeremiah 1

In chapter 1, Jeremiah is introduced, called, commissioned, strengthened, and sent out to speak God's word. This sets the stage for the rest of the book. What does this chapter tell us about the ministry of a prophet?

- Prophets speak at God's direction within specific historical situations. Their words are related to life (-and-death) issues and are not just theoretical.

- God calls even those who feel unprepared.

- This call is not to be taken lightly. The prophet must expect personal opposition and opposition to his prophecy.

- The prophetic word is a creative force because it is God's word.

- God prepares the prophet for the prophetic task and watches over the prophet's life.

JEREMIAH 2–4

Introduction to These Chapters

These chapters contain oracles against Israel that list Israel's sins and announce the punishment to come. In the middle of these announcements of judgment are oracles calling for repentance and return to the blessings of the Lord. Prophets did not usually deliver long, prepared sermons. Rather, they spoke brief messages as the occasion and word of God demanded.

The oracles from Jeremiah 2:1–6 are probably from the time of the reign of King Josiah (640–609 B.C.).

Here is an outline of chapters 2–4:
   I. Oracles Against Unfaithful Israel (2:1-37)
     A. When Israel was devoted to God (2:1-3)
     B. God's faithfulness (2:4-13)
     C. Israel a slave of foreigners (2:14-19)
     D. Israel degenerate and shamed (2:20-28)

E. Israel rejected God's correction
(2:29-37)

II. Oracles Calling Israel to Repent
(3:1–4:4)

  A. Israel called from her harlotry
(3:1-5)

  B. Judah called to acknowledge her
guilt (3:6-20)

  C. Israel must admit her shame
(3:21–4:4)

III. Oracles About the Foe from the
North (4:5-31)

  A. The alarm raised in Judah
(4:5-10)

  B. Armies will sweep over
Jerusalem (4:11-18)

  C. Jeremiah laments the disaster
(4:19-22)

  D. Vision of the Desolation to Come
(4:23-31)

The Message of Jeremiah 2–4

Even during the time of national
religious reform by King Josiah, Jeremiah
has much to say against the ways of his
people. He holds their present idolatry and
disobedience up to the light of the past.
Their past relationship with God could
show them the way into a blessed future.
Their present ways could only lead to
destruction for Israel and for the earth.

What must the people of Israel do to
gain new life in the Lord?

- Remember the past: God's saving
actions and the promises which God
and Israel made to one another in the
wilderness.

- Confess their sins of idolatry and
wickedness.

- Return to the covenant relationship in
"truth, justice, and righteousness," not
just in ritual.

JEREMIAH 5:1–8:3

Introduction to These Chapters

Chapters 5 and 6 contain oracles
announcing the corruptions for which
Israel is judged. Chapter 7 begins with a
sermon that Jeremiah preaches in the
Temple in Jerusalem. The last half of the
chapter lists abuses in worship of which
the people are guilty. Here is an outline of
these chapters:

I. The Search for Truth and Justice in
Israel Is Futile (5:1-31)

  A. Jeremiah is to search for a
faithful man (5:1-6)

  B. God has no choice but to judge
(5:7-11)

  C. Consequences of ignoring God's
word (5:12-17)

  D. A word of hope (5:18-19)

  E. The foolish do not fear the Lord
(5:20-31)

II. The Foe from the North Approaches
(6:1-30)

  A. Oracles of war against Jerusalem
(6:1-8)

  B. No one will listen to the word of
God (6:9-12)

  C. The people sin (6:13-21)

  D. The foe from the north strikes
terror (6:22-26)

  E. Jeremiah to test God's people
(6:27-30)

III. Oracles Concerning the Temple
(7:1–8:3)

  A. Jeremiah's Temple sermon
(7:1-15)

  B. Oracle against idolatrous worship
(7:16–8:3)

The Message of Jeremiah 5:1–8:3

Judgment is announced on Israel for
specific reasons. The people of Israel have
known what is expected of them all along.
God has not just suddenly changed the

Law. Jeremiah proclaims that Israel must count on God's justice as well as on God's blessing.

On what foundation are Jeremiah's announcements of judgment against Israel based?

- Israel has failed to live up to its part of the relationship.

- The people take God's presence with them for granted even as they turn away from righteousness.

- Their lives are not directed by knowledge of God or of God's will.

- Truth, justice, and righteousness are lacking in Israel. Therefore, God is justified in punishing Israel.

JEREMIAH 8:4–10:25

Introduction to These Chapters

The first three verses of chapter 8 conclude the oracle that begins in Jeremiah 7:29. Chapters 8:4–10:25 are a collection of prophetic oracles, laments, and prayers that were probably delivered during the reign of King Jehoiakim (609–598 B.C.). Here is an outline of the content of these chapters:

I. Oracles Against Israel and a Lament for Her Fate (8:4–9:1)
  A. The unnaturalness of sin (8:4-12)
  B. God and Israel are disappointed (8:13-17)
  C. The people's sickness (8:18–9:1)
II. Lamentations Over the People of Israel (9:2-26)
  A. Justice demands punishment for sins (9:2-9)
  B. Lament and interpretation (9:10-16)
  C. Funeral lament for Zion (9:17-22)

D. The mark of those who know God (9:23-26)
III. Oracles Against Idols and a Plea for Mercy (10:1-25)
  A. Comparing lifeless idols to God (10:1-16)
  B. Oracle to those living under siege (10:17-22)
  C. Prayer for mercy (10:23-25)

The Message of Jeremiah 8:4–10:25

The prophecies and prayers of chapters 8–10 warn that those who ignore God's instruction (see, for example, 8:9) are doomed to lose their way in sin (see 10:23).

What are God's instructions to Israel (see 9:23-26)?

- Human knowledge, power, and wealth offer neither real security nor cause for pride.

- The goal of life should be to know and understand what God is like and what God requires.

- Knowledge of God requires understanding and practice of God's will.

- God practices steadfast love, justice, and righteousness, and so must the people of God.

- Physical symbols (such as circumcision) and ritual (such as worship) are empty without wholehearted commitment to God's will.

JEREMIAH 11–15

Introduction to These Chapters

This section contains laments, prayers, oracles, and a report of a sign act that

Jeremiah is commanded to perform. The first two of Jeremiah's personal laments tell of Jeremiah's inner struggles with his prophetic office and the oppression he lives under.

Here is an outline of these chapters:

I. Jeremiah and the Covenant (11:1-17)
II. Jeremiah Laments His Fate (11:18–12:6)
III. Lamentation for Judah (12:7-17)
   A. God laments Judah's fate (12:7-13)
   B. God offers hope for other nations (12:14-17)
IV. Pride and Sin Bring Punishment (13:1-27)
   A. The sign of the linen waistcloth (13:1-11)
   B. A proverb is reinterpreted (13:12-14)
   C. A plea for repentance (13:15-17)
   D. Oracle against Jerusalem's shame (13:18-27)
V. Lamentation over Judah (14:1–15:9)
   A. Lament and prayer because of drought (14:1-12)
   B. Oracle against false prophets (14:13-16)
   C. Lament, prayer, God's response (14:17–15:9)
VI. Jeremiah's Second Personal Lament (15:10-21)

The Message of Jeremiah 11–15

Despite the years of Jeremiah's prophetic warnings, Judah continues to live in false pride, sin, and shame. What do the oracles of chapters 11–15 tell us about the relationship among God, Jeremiah, and Judah at this time?

- God mourns for "the beloved of my soul" but will not turn aside the "sword of the LORD" that must punish Judah.

- Jeremiah grows weary, angry, and fearful in his duties to Israel.

- The people sometimes turn to God in times of acute distress. Most of the time, however, they fail to follow their covenant responsibilities while still counting on God to uphold them.

JEREMIAH 16–19

Introduction to These Chapters

These chapters tell of physical symbols of Judah's fate (18:1-12; 19:1-15) and of a personal symbol (16:1-13). Jeremiah is again driven to voice his complaints to God because of the continuing opposition to his message and the plots against his life (Jeremiah 17:14-18; 18:18-23). Here is an outline of these chapters:

I. Jeremiah's Life Is to Be a Symbol (16:1-21)
   A. Jeremiah is not to have a family (16:1-13)
   B. Oracle of eventual deliverance (16:14-15)
   C. There will be no refuge for Israel (16:16-18)
   D. All nations will turn to God (16:19-21)
II. Oracles Against Backsliders (17:1-13)
III. Jeremiah Prays for Vindication (17:14-18)
IV. Teachings About the Sabbath (17:19-27)
V. A Sign and a Lament (18:1-23)
   A. The sign of the potter's vessel (18:1-12)
   B. Oracle against Israel's stubbornness (18:13-17)
   C. Jeremiah laments opposition (18:18-23)
VI. A Sign of Judah's Fate (19:1-15)

THE POTTER AND THE CLAY
(JEREMIAH 18:1-12)

The shaping of a vessel in the potter's hands illustrates the power of God to shape human destiny. This image is similar to that of God shaping Adam in the Garden of Eden (Genesis 2:7). In contrast to the clay of the potter, which has no will of its own, Israel does have a choice in how she is shaped. If Israel chooses evil, God, the master potter, will shape evil against her.

The workshop Jeremiah visited probably consisted of a room where the potter sat at his wheel forming vessels and where pots awaiting finishing were stored. The wheel may have been made of a pair of stones, one on top of the other. A cone-shaped protrusion on the bottom stone fit into a socket on the top one. A small room for storing pots ready for firing would have been next to the kiln. The area around the kiln and workshop probably contained a well or basin for water, piles of new clay being weathered, and piles of shards (scrap pottery), ashes, and slag.

Potters played a major role in Israelite society. Their importance is reflected in the many Old Testament references to the potters' craft and vessels.

The Message of Jeremiah 16–19

The prophet's life is taken over by the Word he must declare. Jeremiah is called to act as well as to speak. What do prophetic sign acts accomplish?

- Sign acts get people's attention.

- These acts give the prophet an opportunity to explain the action and to explain how God's Word applies to it.

- The sign acts give people visual as well as verbal food for thought. They encourage people to look for God's truth even when it comes in surprising ways.

- Sign acts set in motion the accomplishment of God's Word because they have creative power just like the prophetic word.

JEREMIAH 20–22

Introduction to These Chapters

Jeremiah 20:1-6 describes the consequences of Jeremiah's word and actions in chapter 19. The remainder of chapter 20 contains two more of Jeremiah's personal laments. This concludes the group of oracles that come, in general, from the time of King Jehoiakim. Chapters 21–25 are oracles from the reign of King Zedekiah (597–587 B.C.).

Here is an outline of chapters 20–22:

I. Jeremiah's Suffering and Lamentation (20:1-18)
  A. Jeremiah is beaten and confined (20:1-6)
  B. Jeremiah accuses God (20:7-13)
  C. Jeremiah laments his birth (20:14-18)
II. Oracle Against Zedekiah and Jerusalem (21:1-10)
III. Oracles About the Royal House (21:11–22:30)
  A. Oracle to the king of Judah (21:11-14)
  B. Oracle to the king (22:1-9)
  C. Oracle concerning King Shallum (22:10-12)

D. Oracle concerning King Jehoiakim (22:13-19)
E. Oracle concerning Jerusalem (22:20-23)
F. Oracle concerning King Jehoiachin (22:24-30)

The Message of Jeremiah 20–22

These chapters deal with issues of authority: Who is really in charge in Israel? These oracles and laments answer that God is in charge.

- Jeremiah may complain bitterly to God about his duties and the consequences of these duties. Nevertheless, God knew Jeremiah and appointed him a prophet even before his birth. Jeremiah is bound to speak God's Word.

- The kings of Judah are not the ultimate authority over God's people. Their office is a trust and a responsibility from God, to whom they must answer for their actions.

- Even pagan kings serve God's purposes. King Nebuchadnezzar of Babylon is God's instrument of punishment against Judah.

- No one, high or low, is outside of God's authority. In particular, people to whom much power is entrusted are held strictly accountable for the use of that power.

JEREMIAH 23–25

Introduction to These Chapters

After the sweeping condemnations of Zedekiah, Jehoiakim, and Jehoiachin, Jeremiah offers an oracle of hope concerning future leaders. The rest of the material in this section (23:9–25:38)

contains oracles and a vision report that announce judgment on other groups of leaders—false prophets, the remnant in Jerusalem, the people of Israel, and other nations. Here is an outline of these chapters:

I. A Hopeful Oracle About Future Leaders (23:1-8)
II. Oracles Concerning the Prophets (23:9-40)
    A. Both prophet and priest are wicked (23:9-12)
    B. Evil deeds of Jerusalem's prophets (23:13-15)
    C. False prophets denounced (23:16-22)
    D. The false prophets' lying dreams (23:23-32)
    E. The burden of the Lord (23:33-40)
III. The Vision of the Basket of Figs (24:1-10)
IV. Oracle About the Seventy-year Exile (25:1-14)
V. Oracle Concerning the Nations (25:15-38)

The Message of Jeremiah 23–25

Jeremiah offers two notes of hope in these oracles. First, Israel may look forward to a future day when a truly righteous king will rule over them (compare Isaiah 11:1; Zechariah 3:8). Second, the nation which punishes Israel will itself be punished after seventy years. His message is not entirely gloomy.

In the meantime, sin must be dealt with, especially the sins of the false prophets, priests, and other dishonest leaders. Oracles of judgment are declarations of God's punishment for sin. The basis for such declarations by Jeremiah and by other prophets is found in the nature of sin itself. What may we learn from this about sin?

- In broad terms, the Bible sees sin as personal alienation from God. Sins of any kind are, first of all, sins against God.

- The Old Testament understanding of ritual, moral, and spiritual sins rests on the recognition of God's own moral being.

- Through what is sinful in relation to the will and being of God, we understand what is sinful in relation to one another. Because of this, our sins against one another affect our relationship to God.

- According to the Old Testament prophets, the standard of moral good is God's revealed will. Sins against this standard are a violation of the covenant relationship that has been established between God and God's people.

JEREMIAH 26–28

Introduction to These Chapters

Jeremiah 26:1 begins a series of chapters (26–45) that contain biographical information about Jeremiah. Much of this material is drawn from Jeremiah's memoirs that were written by his scribe, Baruch (see Jeremiah 36:1-4).

Chapters 26–28 tell of Jeremiah's conflict with Judean religious leaders—the priests and especially the prophets. Each chapter is dated according to the reign of the king of Judah at the time, and each chapter comes from a different time.

Here is an outline of chapters 26–28:
I. Jeremiah's Temple Sermon (26:1-24)
   A. Summary of the sermon (26:1-6)
   B. Report of Jeremiah's arrest and trial (26:7-24)

II. Oracles Concerning the King of Babylon (27:1-22)
   A. Report of the sign of the yoke (27:1-11)
   B. Oracle against false prophecy (27:12-15)
   C. Oracle against false prophecy (27:16-22)

III. Jeremiah's Confrontation with Hananiah (28:1-17)
   A. Hananiah disputes Jeremiah's prophecy (28:1-11)
   B. Oracle against Hananiah (28:12-17)

The Message of Jeremiah 26–28

Jeremiah's message to the people of Israel at the beginning of the reign of Jehoiakim (609–598 B.C.) holds out the possibility of escape from punishment. God would relent if the people of Israel would repent (26:3). By the time of the reign of Zedekiah, however, the only alternative to destruction the people have is to serve the king of Babylon (27:8).

What has happened to bring about this change?

- Neither the king nor many of the people listen to Jeremiah's warnings.

- They recognize the power of his words but they do not believe his message and they want him out of the way.

- False prophets and unreliable leaders continue to be a problem in Israel.

- God expects the people to know a false prophet from a true one. The people are held responsible for choosing to believe lies rather than recognizing God's Word spoken by the true prophet.

- The people have failed to recognize and obey the true Word. They must recognize and obey the Word even before the test of time has proven the Word.

JEREMIAH 29–31

Introduction to These Chapters

Chapter 29 continues the reports of Jeremiah's confrontations with religious leaders. The leaders named in this chapter are exiles living in Babylon.

Chapters 30–31 are often called the Book of Consolation. The oracles here deal with the future restoration of Israel and Judah.

Here is an outline of these chapters:

I. Jeremiah's Letters to Babylon (29:1-32)
  A. Letter to the exiles (29:1-23)

A NEW COVENANT (JEREMIAH 31:31-34)

These verses had great influence on the New Testament. They are quoted in Hebrews 8:8-12; 10:16-17, and are behind the words about the cup of the Lord's Supper in 1 Corinthians 11:25. The new covenant is referred to in other New Testament passages (for example, 2 Corinthians 3:5-6), and it influenced the distinction between the Old and New Testaments. Among Christians, this passage about the new covenant may be the best known and most misunderstood passage in the book of Jeremiah. The new covenant does not cancel or replace God's covenant with Judaism in favor of future Christians. When Jeremiah speaks of the new covenant, he has in mind a renewed relationship between God and Israel. The day will come, Jeremiah promises, when God will inscribe the Torah (law or right instruction) upon the hearts of all the people. This new covenant is one of the inner being. The people's hearts, the wellsprings of human character, will be imprinted with the saving knowledge of God.

B. Jeremiah's dispute with Shemaiah (29:24-32)

II. The Book of Consolation (30:1–31:40)
  A. The restoration of Israel and Judah (30:1–31:1)
  B. Oracles concerning future abundance (31:2-22)
  C. Oracles concerning the new covenant (31:23-40)

The Message of Jeremiah 29–31

Jeremiah's messages to the people of Israel, both in Jerusalem and in exile, are not completely filled with promises of doom. The oracles in these chapters show that God's plans for Israel go beyond punishment to a more fulfilling future. What are these promises of hope?

- The exile is not permanent. After seventy years the people will be able to go home.

- In the meantime, they can live their normal lives in the confidence that God has not forgotten them.

- Their new lives after their restoration will be fruitful and happy.

- God's new covenant with them will bring an inward change and a new knowledge of God.

JEREMIAH 32–34

Introduction to These Chapters

These chapters pick up the biographical material on Jeremiah from chapter 29. The incidents and oracles here are from the time of Zedekiah.

Chapter 32 comes from 588/587

B.C. and tells of Jeremiah's purchase of land in Anathoth. Chapter 33 also comes from this time and is an appendix to the Book of Consolation. Chapter 34 comes from perhaps late 598 or early 588 B.C., near the time of or during a Babylonian siege of Jerusalem.

Here is an outline of these chapters:

I. Jeremiah's Purchase of a Field (32:1-44)
   A. Jeremiah buys the field (32:1-15)
   B. Jeremiah prays about the siege (32:16-25)
   C. God answers Jeremiah's prayer (32:26-44)
II. Appendix to the Book of Consolation (33:1-26)
III. Oracles to Zedekiah and to Jerusalem (34:1-22)
   A. Oracle to Zedekiah (34:1-7)
   B. Oracle concerning slavery in Jerusalem (34:8-22)

The Message of Jeremiah 32–34

In Jeremiah 32:27 God asks a question: "See, I am the LORD, the God of all flesh; is anything too hard for me?" Jeremiah shows that nothing is too hard for God and that God is free to work God's will in all of the earth.

- In the midst of war and despair, God has Jeremiah purchase a field as a sign that Judah will one day be restored and productive.

- In the midst of the false confidence and evil doings of the people and their leaders, God proclaims their punishment.

- The masters of slaves in Jerusalem think they are in control and may take their slaves back into service as they please. They will discover, however, that God is a master greater than they are, and they will be punished for breaking their covenant with God.

- In spite of all the terrible sins of the people of Israel, God declares that sin can be forgiven and that guilt can be cleansed.

JEREMIAH 35–37

Introduction to These Chapters

Chapter 35 tells how Jeremiah uses the Rechabites as a living sign concerning faithfulness to religious principles. Chapter 36 is an important source of information about the process by which Jeremiah's words and works were collected and written down. Chapter 37 begins the series of chapters that take Jeremiah from the siege of 587 B.C. through his prophecies in Egypt (chapters 37–44).

Chapters 35 (approximately 601 B.C.) and 36 (605–604 B.C.) are from the time of King Jehoiakim. Chapter 37 (588 B.C.) is from the time of King Zedekiah.

Here is an outline of these chapters:

I. The Sign of the Rechabites (35:1-19)
II. The Scroll of Jeremiah (36:1-32)
   A. Jeremiah's oracles written on a scroll (36:1-8)
   B. Baruch reads the scroll to the people (36:9-10)
   C. Baruch reads the scroll to the princes (36:11-19)
   D. The scroll is read to the king (36:20-26)
   E. Another scroll is made (36:27-32)
III. Jeremiah Is Arrested (37:1-21)
   A. Oracle to Zedekiah (37:1-10)
   B. Jeremiah is arrested and imprisoned (37:11-21)

The Message of Jeremiah 35–37

The oracles and events of chapters 35–37 show that God's Word will survive and will be confirmed.

- In the midst of rebellious and unfaithful Jerusalem, Jeremiah finds the Rechabites. Their lives are living, daily testimony to their faith and their tradition. They are an example to Israel of faithfulness to religious principles.

- Even though the king burns the record of Jeremiah's words, another scroll is made. God's Word through Jeremiah has survived to this day.

- History bears out the true prophetic word.

- God watches over Jeremiah so that Jeremiah may continue to proclaim God's Word to Israel.

JEREMIAH 38–40

Introduction to These Chapters

Chapters 38–40 continue the story of Jerusalem under siege and tell what happens to Jeremiah after the city falls. In chapter 38, Jeremiah is almost killed by Zedekiah's advisors who favor the rebellion against Babylon. Chapter 39 describes the fall of Jerusalem. Chapter 40 begins a narrative (chapters 40–41) that reports on Jeremiah's relationship to the governor of Judah appointed by Nebuchadnezzar in 587 B.C.

Here is an outline of these chapters:

I. Jeremiah Insists on Surrender (38:1-28)
   A. Jeremiah in the cistern (38:1-13)
   B. Oracles to Zedekiah (38:14-28)
II. The Fall of Jerusalem (39:1-18)
   A. Report of defeat and exile (39:1-10)
   B. Jeremiah and the Babylonians (39:11-18)
III. Gedaliah Appointed Governor (40:1-16)

A. Jeremiah remains with Gedaliah (40:1-6)
B. Report of Gedaliah's administration (40:7-16)

The Message of Jeremiah 38–40

God's promises of defeat for Israel are realized as the Babylonians take Jerusalem in 587 B.C. By this time Jeremiah has been prophesying for about forty years. During this time he has suffered physical abuse and mental and emotional anguish. What does Jeremiah do as his announcements of punishment for Israel are fulfilled?

- In spite of continued threats and abuse, Jeremiah still proclaims the unpopular message of punishment.

- He continues to offer hope to those who submit to God's judgment and trust in God.

- He chooses to stay in his ruined homeland. His duties to Israel are not over because he continues to care for the welfare of his people.

JEREMIAH 41–45

Introduction to These Chapters

These chapters take Jeremiah from his defeated homeland into unwilling exile in Egypt. After Gedaliah's assassination (chapter 41), the commanders of the remaining Israelite forces come to Jeremiah and seek a word from God through him (chapter 42). They decide not to obey Jeremiah's message but rather flee to Egypt, taking Jeremiah with them. In Egypt, Jeremiah continues his prophecy (chapter 44). The prophecies against Israel end with a look back at God's promises of difficulties and of deliverance (chapter 45).

Here is an outline of chapters 41–45:

I. Report of Gedaliah's Murder (41:1-18)
   A. Gedaliah and others are killed (41:1-3)
   B. Some pilgrims are spared (41:4-9)
   C. Ishmael escapes (41:10-18)
II. The Flight to Egypt (42:1–43:7)
   A. The people seek an oracle (42:1-6)
   B. Jeremiah warns against Egypt (42:7-22)
   C. Jeremiah taken to Egypt (43:1-7)
III. Sign Act Against Egypt (43:8-13)
IV. Israel's Idolatry in Egypt (44:1-30)
   A. Oracle against the refugees (44:1-14)
   B. Oracle against idolatry (44:15-30)
V. Oracle to Baruch (45:1-5)

The Message of Jeremiah 41–45

The oracle in Jeremiah 45:2-5 comes at the end of the long narrative about Jeremiah's life and ministry (chapters 26–45). This oracle helps to put the lives of God's servants into perspective.

- The book of Jeremiah shows that, from the beginning of Jeremiah's life to the end, God's message to Israel is put before personal considerations.

- Though prophets, kings, or ordinary people may desire "great things," God's purposes are the only truly great things.

- God's purposes will always be accomplished.

JEREMIAH 46–49

Introduction to These Chapters

Chapters 46–49 are a collection of oracles against nations other than Israel.

Some of the nations addressed in these oracles are also listed in the oracle in Jeremiah 25:19-26. Jeremiah 25:19-38 may have introduced the collection of oracles in chapters 46–49 at one stage in the collection of Jeremiah's work.

The oracles themselves have few references to historical events and they do not mention specific kings (though the introductions in 46:2, 13 and 47:1 do give some historical references). The collection may not have been included in the scroll of Jeremiah's words that was made by Baruch. A later collector may have brought these oracles together. At some time in the editorial process, the collection was put at the end of Jeremiah's memoirs.

Unlike Jeremiah's oracles against Israel, the oracles in chapters 46–51 contain verses apparently borrowed from other Old Testament books, especially Isaiah and Obadiah. So parts of these oracles may have come from a later writer rather than from Jeremiah.

The nations are soundly condemned to punishment, but Egypt, Moab, Ammon, and Elam are promised future restoration. The day of the Lord (see Jeremiah 25:33; 46:10) is a day of defeat for other nations as well as for Israel. All flesh must drink the cup of God's wrath. This is not accomplished in one twenty-four–hour day. Each nation in turn feels the consequences of God's judgment. Each has magnified itself against God, has set itself against God's purposes, and has trusted in power and riches. Even Babylon, who deals out God's punishment to Israel and to these others, will face judgment (chapters 50–51).

The prophetic message is always that human might must give way to God. Those in power are brought low, and the death they dealt to others is dealt to them as God's purposes are worked out in human history.

Here is an outline of chapters 46–49:

I. Oracles Against Egypt (46:1-28)
  A. Oracle to Pharaoh's army (46:1-12)
  B. Oracle about Nebuchadnezzar in Egypt (46:13-26)
  C. Consolation for Israel (46:27-28)
II. Oracle Against the Philistines (47:1-7)
III. Oracles Against Moab (48:1-47)
IV. Oracle Against the Ammonites (49:1-6)
V. Oracle Against Edom (49:7-22)
VI. Oracle Against Damascus (49:23-27)
VII. Oracle Against Kedar and Hazor (49:28-33)
VIII. Oracle Against Elam (49:34-39)

The Message of Jeremiah 46–49

These oracles against the nations are related to a particular time in the history of Israel and of Israel's neighbors. However, they are more than just reactions to historical circumstances. These oracles have a larger perspective, as do all the oracles in Jeremiah. They describe Israel's and the other nations' relationship to God. What, then, do these oracles tell us about God's dealings with human beings? What do they tell us about what God is like?

- God's nature and will are revealed through the words and actions of the prophet.

- God acts in self-revelation to Israel and to other nations.

- God is the Lord of all peoples.

- God rules and judges the affairs and history of all humankind.

- Israel has sinned and is punished for these sins.

- Israel must choose to obey God and live or disobey and die.

- God wants to be in relationship with all people.

- God's will is for a loving and redeeming relationship with people. This relationship with Israel is realized in the new covenant.

JEREMIAH 50–52

Introduction to These Chapters

These last chapters in the book of Jeremiah contain oracles against Babylon (Jeremiah 50:1–51:64) and a historical narrative about Judah and Babylon from 588 B.C. to 560 B.C. (Jeremiah 52).

Here is an outline of chapters 50–52:

I. Oracles Against Babylon (50:1–51:64)
  A. God's judgment announced (50:1-46)
  B. Evil is coming to Babylon (51:1-58)
  C. Report of a sign act (51:59-64)
II. Israel Is Taken Into Exile (52:1-34)
  A. Jerusalem falls (52:1-11)
  B. The spoils of war (52:12-27)
  C. Israel in Exile (52:28-34)

The Message of Jeremiah 50–52

The oracles concerning Babylon in the book of Jeremiah treat Babylon as a necessary and timely instrument in God's hands. What does Jeremiah teach us about King Nebuchadnezzar's relationship to God and about Babylon's role in God's plan for history?

- Nebuchadnezzar is God's servant and holds power over other nations at God's discretion.

- God uses Nebuchadnezzar and his armies to discipline Israel and her neighbors.

- Nebuchadnezzar is not above judgment himself.

- The kings of Babylon, like the kings of Judah, are subject to God's plan for human history and to God's judgment.

- The military power of Babylon's kings may be useful to God for a time, but they too will eventually be defeated.

If Babylon may only look toward future defeat, toward what may Israel look?

- Israel's sins will be pardoned and the people will sin no more.

- The people will return to their land and live in plenty.

- Israel will be at "rest"; war will be over, the land and people will be fruitful, and the people will have a new peace of mind and contentment coming from a close relationship with God.

CONCLUSION

Jeremiah was a prophet, one who has been called by God. He was called to speak to the people of Israel in the context of a particular historical situation. During the years of Jeremiah's prophecy, Israel faced the end of life as an independent nation. Jeremiah brought the people a word that interpeted what was happening to them in light of God's demands and promises. The focal point of these demands and promises was the covenant.

Jeremiah spoke to the people about their relationship to God established in the covenant at Sinai. The covenant was more than just part of Israel's history. Their identity as a people was bound up in the covenant relationship with God. By this relationship and the memory of the Sinai experience, Israel was to find her way.

Jeremiah called on Israel to remember the past as the basis for interpreting the present and anticipating the future. The explanation for the tragedy of the people of Israel lay in God's sovereign power, justice, and faithfulness. The covenant agreement was both the basis for their punishment and the ground of their hope.

A new community would be established, based on a new covenant, a new saving act by God on Israel's behalf. Israel had shown her inability to abide by the old covenant, but the relationship to God established in the old covenant was not completely broken. On the basis of God's past loving-kindness and justice this new covenant would be established.

The new covenant of faith would be an inward and personal relationship to God. The people would have a new heart engraved with God's statutes. Through the people's intimate knowledge of God, the new community would be born.

Jeremiah struggled and suffered with his people through the long years of his prophetic ministry. The punishment he proclaimed came to pass. The new covenant he announced took root and flowered in the coming of Jesus Christ.

LAMENTATIONS

OUTLINE OF LAMENTATIONS

INTRODUCTION

The book of Lamentations is a series of five poems that mourn the ruin of Jerusalem and the suffering of her people. These poems were written in response to the destruction of the city by the Babylonians in 587 B.C. Hundreds of people, including the king and his court, were either killed or were deported to Babylon. Details of the siege and its aftermath are found in the books of Jeremiah and 2 Kings. The book of Lamentations records the emotional, psychological, and religious impact of this loss on the people of Israel.

The five poems voice the people's grief and sorrow and express their horror at what happened to them and to their homeland. The poems also acknowledge God as the power behind Israel's downfall. They ask, *What is the meaning of this tragedy?*

The Author of Lamentations

The poems of Lamentations are the work of a single author. Both Jewish and Christian tradition at one time named Jeremiah as this author. This view was, in part, based on 2 Chronicles 35:25. However, the general view today is that Chronicles refers to laments Jeremiah wrote that are not in the book of Lamentations. We do not know the name of the person who wrote Lamentations.

The events described in Lamentations are seen from the perspective of someone living in Judah from 587 B.C. to 538 B.C. when the exiles were given permission to return to Judah. These were harsh years for Judah, a time of economic hardship and spiritual reassessment. The people struggled to feed themselves and to come to terms with what had happened to them. The poems of Lamentations were composed over a period of years during this time.

All the poems were probably written or adapted for use in public worship services on days of fasting and mourning. In particular, these poems would have been used at the annual service held in remembrance of Jerusalem's destruction. An editor (who may or may not be the author) collected the poems and put them in order. Perhaps these laments were once part of a larger collection of worship materials.

The Form of the Poems

The five poems in Lamentations are laments, as the title suggests. Such poems are frequently found elsewhere in the Old Testament, since one-third of the Old Testament is poetry. Psalms, Proverbs, Song of Solomon, Lamentations, Obadiah, Micah, Nahum, Habakkuk, and Zephaniah are almost entirely poetry. The greater parts of Job, Isaiah, Hosea, Joel, and Amos are poetry, and Jeremiah is about one-half poetry.

Four of the five laments (chapters 1–4) are acrostic poems. In an acrostic poem, each of the twenty-two letters of the Hebrew alphabet appears in order at the beginning of each line or stanza. In English, we would compose an acrostic poem with the first line beginning with A, the second with B, the third with C, and so on. Such a form helps someone in memorizing a poem. This form also helps its writer express the completeness of grief and despair or of hope and faith. It lets the poet express "everything from A to Z," so to speak. Lamentations 5 is not an acrostic poem, but it does have twenty-two lines.

Laments express the sorrow or despair of individuals (for example, Jeremiah 11:18–12:6) and of whole communities (for example, Lamentations 5). Sometimes a community is personified as an individual (for example, Lamentations 1:18-19). Having one voice speak for the community expresses the tragedy on a personal level for each member of that community.

Laments are written in response to a disaster or the threat of a disaster. They usually have these parts:

1. The situation of the lamenter is described
2. Sin is confessed
3. God is called on to act on behalf of the lamenter
4. Faith in God is affirmed
5. God is praised

Funeral laments, often accompanied by music, are composed for the dead (see, for example, 2 Samuel 1:18-27). The dead are eulogized, and their passing is mourned, or, in the case of an enemy, a death is celebrated. Funeral laments also offer consolation to those who are grieving. The poems of Lamentations mourn for the people of Israel individually and as a community.

Lamentations in the Church

By the end of the second century B.C., Lamentations was included in the part of the Hebrew Scripture known as the *Writings*. After its inclusion in the Hebrew Bible, it became part of the Christian Old Testament.

Because the poems of Lamentations are regarded as sacred Scripture by both Christians and Jews, the poems became more than a defeated community's remembrance and reflection. The poems provide expressions of sorrow that have been and will be used by other mourners. Lamentations also gives us plenty of "food for thought" on how faith in God relates to what happens to God's people in this world.

In Jewish tradition and practice, Lamentations is read during the public mourning in the Hebrew month of Ab (July/August). This mourning commemorates the fall of Jerusalem in 587 B.C. Lamentations is also read by Jews every Friday afternoon at the Wailing Wall in the old city of Jerusalem.

In Christian congregations, Lamentations is traditionally read during Holy Week to reflect on the sufferings of Jesus before his crucifixion.

LAMENTATIONS 1–5

Introduction to These Chapters

The book of Lamentations shows how the worshiping community of Judah tried to deal with its suffering after the catastrophe of 587 B.C. In later years, Jewish rabbinical philosophers concluded that suffering serves divine purposes: it purifies, it teaches, and it is an agency of God's plan. The poems of Lamentations reflect a similar view of suffering. The people of Judah, though once rebellious, are now ready to confront their tragedy and find their way back to God.

Here is an outline of the book of Lamentations:

I. Jerusalem Laments Her Miserable State (1:1-22)
II. Lament over the Anger of the Lord (2:1-22)
III. Personal Lament and Prayer (3:1-66)
IV. Lamentation over the Siege of Jerusalem (4:1-22)
V. A Communal Plea for Mercy (5:1-22)

The Message of Lamentations 1–5

The poems of Lamentations came from Israel's attempts to find meaning in her suffering at the hands of the Babylonians. What does Israel discover in this search?

- The people of Israel have sinned and must confess their sin.

- Their suffering is a punishment from God for sin.

- Yet, they still have a relationship and a future with God.

- Though the Temple is gone, the people may seek God in public and private prayer and in worship.

- They may call on God for help because God's justice includes both punishment and mercy.

CONCLUSION

The book of Lamentations is full of complaints, to be sure. However, its aims are not limited to a description of suffering. These poems are an expression of Israel's humbleness and repentance in the face of a terrible national tragedy. The people of Israel, as individuals and as a community, had suffered in ways most of us can scarcely imagine. The poems of Lamentations helped them cope with this suffering because they could voice their pain together through the poetry. As a Jewish proverb says, "The one who suffers alone suffers most."

Israel never forgot her suffering and loss. The future brought other such times to God's people, but Israel's faith was not destroyed. The people of Israel came to recognize that what Jeremiah said was true: God's ultimate redemptive purposes for God's people will be fulfilled.

EZEKIEL

OUTLINE OF EZEKIEL

INTRODUCTION

Ezekiel was a prophet of Israel whose ministry and words are recorded in the book which bears his name. His call to prophesy came in 593 B.C. when he was living in exile in Babylonia. He fulfilled his prophetic duties in exile and probably never returned to his homeland.

The events of 597 B.C. had thrown Israel into a crisis that was both political and spiritual. With their humiliation and defeat at the hands of the Babylonians the people of Israel began to question God's power to control events in history. They also questioned God's faithfulness to the promises made to Israel in the past.

Ezekiel dealt with these disturbing questions. His prophecies answered these questions according to God's power, justice, and mercy. Ezekiel's prophecy showed the people of Israel how to understand what had happened to them and how to find their way into the future as God's chosen people.

Ezekiel the Book

The book of Ezekiel is a collection of prophetic speeches and vision reports. Ezekiel's speeches (also called oracles) are announcements (through the prophet) of

ISRAEL AFTER SOLOMON IN THE CONTEXT OF WORLD EMPIRES

After the death of King Solomon, the United Kingdom of Israel was divided into Israel in the north and judah in the South. (Israel sometimes means specifically the Northern Kingdom. Israel can also mean *the people of Israel*, which includes both the northern and the southern kingdoms.) The Northern Kingdom was conquered by Assyria in 722 B.C.

When Assyria's power declined, King Josiah of Judah (640–609 B.C.) extended his power into parts of the Northern Kingdom. Josiah's reign ended when he was killed in a battle with the Egyptians at Megiddo in 609 B.C. His son, Jehoahaz, took his place as king, but the Egyptians took him to Egypt and put his brother, Jehoiakim, on the throne in Judah.

During this time, Egypt and Babylonia were fighting over what was left of the Assyrian Empire. In 605 B.C. the Babylonians defeated the Egyptians in a key battle at Carchemish, and Judah then came under Babylonian influence. Daniel and his friends are said to have been taken into exile in Babylonia at this time (see Daniel 1:1).

King Jehoiakim tried to break away from Babylonian control in 601 B.C. to establish Judah as an independent state once again. In December 598 B.C., the Babylonian army besieged Jerusalem. Jehoiakim was killed and his son, Jehoiachin, soon surrendered the city. Hundreds of Israelites were taken as prisoners to Babylon, including the king, his court, priests, artisans, and other leading citizens. Ezekiel was in this group of exiles. Zedekiah, Jehoiachin's uncle, was made king under Babylonian control.

Judah rebelled in 588 B.C., and, once again, Babylonian forces attacked Jerusalem. The city fell in 587 B.C. after an eighteen-month siege. More Israelites were taken to Babylon and Jerusalem was destroyed.

King Nebuchadnezzar of Babylon appointed Gedaliah, a member of a prominent Judean family, as governor of Judah. Gedaliah was killed in 582 B.C. by a zealous member of the Judean royal family. More captives were taken from Judah to Babylon, and the hardships of those left in Judah increased.

In 539 B.C. Persia defeated Babylonia. Cyrus, the Persian king, gave the exiled Israelites permission to return to Judah. The Israelites continued to live under Persian rule until Persia was defeated by the Greeks under Alexander the Great in 334 B.C.

Judah rebelled against Greek rule in 165 B.C. and was an independent nation until Roman legions captured Jerusalem in 63 B.C.

God's word for Israel. Ezekiel announces judgment and punishment for Israel's sins. He also announces God's promises of restoration and salvation for the people.

The collection of Ezekiel's prophecies may be divided into three major sections. Chapters 1–24 are mainly announcements of judgment against Jerusalem from 593 B.C. (the time of Ezekiel's call to prophesy) to 587 B.C. (the destruction of Jerusalem). Chapters 25–32 are announcements of judgment against foreign nations from approximately 587–585 B.C. (except 29:17-21, from 571 B.C.). Chapters 33–48 are prophecies about the future restoration of Israel, which come after 587 B.C.

Ezekiel's prophecies were collected and preserved, either orally or in writing. This was probably first done by Ezekiel himself and a group of his followers. This collection was eventually organized and edited into the form we know today.

Ezekiel the Man

Ezekiel was born into a priestly family and may have been trained for the

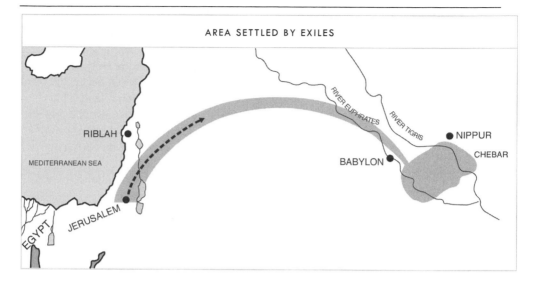

AREA SETTLED BY EXILES

priesthood. He was probably taken from Jerusalem to Babylon in 597 B.C. along with other Temple priests. We do not know how old he was at the time, but he may have been a young adult. As far as we know he spent the rest of his life in Babylonia.

Once in Babylon, Ezekiel settled with other exiles in a village away from the capital and lived in humble circumstances. His wife went with him into exile. She died in Babylonia, leaving Ezekiel numb and speechless with grief.

The spectacular vision in which Ezekiel was called to prophesy (see Ezekiel 1:1–3:15) reflects the strength and turbulance of his prophetic ministry. The power and thunder of God's might echo in Ezekiel's life and words. Ezekiel showed self-discipline and strong emotion as he fulfilled the duties God set before him. He was both stern and passionate in his commitment to proclaim and to act out God's word for Israel.

Ezekiel's ministry did not come without a personal cost to the prophet. He suffered misunderstanding and sometimes outright hostility for the message he brought. His actions at times may have seemed bizarre to his fellow exiles. Even his wife's death and the great loss he felt were used by God as part of his message. He shared physically and emotionally in the despair and hardship of exiled Israelites.

Ezekiel was more than just a "fellow sufferer," however. His message about Israel's sin and its consequences helped the people of Israel make sense out of what had happened to them. Ezekiel provided answers to the inevitable questions of "Why?" and "Where do we go from here?"

EZEKIEL 1–3

Introduction to These Chapters

Ezekiel 1–3 introduces the book and establishes Ezekiel's authority as a prophet. These chapters describe the visions in which God calls Ezekiel to prophesy and commissions Ezekiel as a watchman for Israel.

Here is an outline of these chapters.
I. Vision of the Glory of the Lord (1:1-28)
  A. Introduction (1:1-3)
  B. Signs of God's presence (1:4)

C. The living creatures (1:5-14)

D. The wheel within a wheel (1:15-25)

E. The glory of the Lord (1:26-28)

II. God Commissions Ezekiel as a Messenger (2:1–3:27)

A. Ezekiel's task (2:1-7)

B. Ezekiel accepts his task (2:8–3:3)

C. Ezekiel is fortified (3:4-11)

D. The effects of the vision (3:12-15)

E. Ezekiel's commission as a watchman (3:16-21)

F. Ezekiel is bound by God's word (3:22-27)

The Message of Ezekiel 1–3

The vision reports of Ezekiel 1–3 establish the perspective that Ezekiel's message comes from God. What do these visions tell us about God's word and its relationship to God's people?

- Genesis 1 tells us that God's word has creative power. According to Old Testament tradition, this creative power extends to God's word spoken by the prophet. The prophetic word about the future is not spoken to speculate about or to predict the future but to make known God's word for the future. The prophetic word acts to make things happen.

- The Israelites believed that oracles and demonstrations of God's words possessed a power that set in motion the accomplishment of God's word. Language was seen as a dynamic force that could affect the physical world. Thus, the prophetic future began with the spoken word or symbolic action of the prophet on God's behalf.

- In the past, the people of Israel knew their homeland as God's land. They knew God's special presence in Jerusalem and in the Holy of Holies in the Temple. Yet, God meets Ezekiel in an unclean, foreign land. This shows God's willingness and power to meet the people wherever they are. God shows Ezekiel and, through Ezekiel, shows Israel that God is free to act and to be in relationship with Israel anywhere.

- Each individual is responsible for recognizing God's truth as it comes through the prophet. Individual salvation as well as the salvation of Israel as a whole is at stake in Ezekiel's message.

EZEKIEL 4–7

Introduction to These Chapters

Ezekiel 4–7 contains reports of symbolic actions and announcements of judgment. Ezekiel acts out the coming siege of Jerusalem and tells the people the cost of their sin.

Here is an outline of these chapters.

I. Hardships of the Siege (4:1-17)

II. The Sword of the Lord (5:1-17)

III. Judgment on Idolatry (6:1-14)

IV. The Day of the Lord (7:1-27)

A. The coming judgment (7:1-9)

B. What will happen in Jerusalem (7:10-23a)

C. The people are judged (7:23b-27)

The Message of Ezekiel 4–7

- The Israelites' subjugation to the Babylonians, their exile, and the coming destruction of Jerusalem are not random acts of fate. These tragedies are logical and faithful consequences of their failure to live under the Law.

- The Law is at work, and, therefore, God is at work in their lives.

- God is revealed to Israel even in judgment.

EZEKIEL 8–11

Introduction to These Chapters

On approximately September 1718, 592 B.C., Ezekiel is transported from Babylon to Jerusalem in a vision. Chapters 8–11 tell of this vision.

Here is an outline of these chapters.

I. Abominations in the Temple (8:1-18)
  A. From Tel-Abib to the Temple (8:1-4)
  B. The image of jealousy (8:5-6)
  C. Elders caught in idol worship (8:7-13)
  D. More abominations (8:14-18)
II. The Guilty Are Killed (9:1-11)
III. God Leaves the Temple (10:1-22)
IV. Prophecies of Judgment and Promise (11:1-25)
  A. Prophecy against wicked counselors (11:1-12)
  B. A word of hope (11:13-21)
  C. God's glory leaves Jerusalem (11:22-25)

The Message of Ezekiel 8–11

With this vision Ezekiel and the exiles are allowed to see the consequences of sin within their beloved Temple and home city. Jerusalem and the Temple are the centers of their spiritual and physical yearnings for home. Yet, God shows them that they may not count on even this sacred ground from now on. Above all, the prophet and people are shown God's freedom to act according to the divine will. What does this vision tell us about the freedom of God?

- God's presence in the Temple is not guaranteed. God will leave the Temple and the city because of human sin.

- God will meet the exiles in a land far from their traditional place of worship. God is now the sanctuary for their prayers and obedience.

- Israel must endure disaster as the consequence of sin but will not be completely rejected. God is free both to judge and to redeem. Therefore, the people of Israel will be recreated with new hearts and spirits.

EZEKIEL 12–15

Introduction to These Chapters

Chapters 12–15 contain reports of symbolic actions and oracles addressed to the exiles and to those still in Jerusalem.

Here is an outline of these chapters.

I. Israel Is a Rebellious House (12:1-28)
  A. They shall go into exile (12:1-16)
  B. The fearfulness of the siege (12:17-20)
  C. False sayings (12:21-28)
II. Condemnation of False Prophets (13:1-23)
  A. Foxes among the ruins (13:1-9)
  B. A whitewashed wall (13:10-16)
  C. False prophecy and magic (13:17-23)
III. Idolatry and Individual Responsibility (14:1-23)
  A. Idols lead to alienation (14:1-11)
  B. Individual responsibility (14:12-23)
IV. Parable of the Vine (15:1-8)

The Message of Ezekiel 12–15

This section opens with Ezekiel acting out for the exiles what they have already experienced in their journey from Jerusalem to Babylon. They must understand that they have not seen the last of such journeys. They must also be made to see what has happened and what will happen to Israel in the light of God's justice.

These chapters give examples of sin among the exiles and those in Jerusalem. Such examples build a case against Israel which makes sense according to the covenant that made them God's people. The basic terms of this covenant are stated in the Ten Commandments (see Exodus 20; Deuteronomy 5) and are expanded in other Scripture (see Exodus 21–23; Leviticus 26; Deuteronomy 28).

What does Ezekiel tell the exiles about God's intentions to be true to the covenant promises of judgment and of hope?

- The vine—Israel—has produced sinful fruit and has abandoned the Creator, the source of life for the vine.

- Israel cannot rely on past promises or glory to save her now.

- Israel cannot ignore or postpone the word of judgment.

EZEKIEL 16–19

Introduction to These Chapters

Ezekiel 16–19 shows us some of the creative ways in which Ezekiel delivered his prophetic message. Chapters 16–17 are allegories. The oracles in chapter 18 use Israelite legal forms and traditions. Chapter 19 is a funeral lament.

Here is an outline of Ezekiel 16–19.

I. Allegory of Unfaithful Jerusalem (16:1-63)
   A. The unfaithful wife (16:1-43)
   B. The corrupt sister (16:44-58)
   C. Hope in the covenant (16:59-63)
II. Allegory of the Eagles (17:1-24)
III. The Soul That Sins Shall Die (18:1-32)
   A. Individual responsibility for sin (18:1-24)
   B. Turn and live (18:25-32)
IV. A Lamentation for Israel's Leaders (19:1-14)
   A. The young lions (19:1-9)
   B. The withered vine (19:10-14)

The Message of Ezekiel 16–19

Ezekiel tells the people of Israel that they must fully face and accept the depths to which they have fallen. The realities of sin and death are not to be avoided. Only in this hard and narrow way can they find life.

- The people have disgraced themselves and God's holy name, and they should be ashamed.

- Each person must examine his or her own life and make the decision to turn away from sin.

- New hope and strength will not come from earthly rulers, because they have been overwhelmed.

- Israel's history as a people has been one of rebellion and sin. Only God's patience and mercy have kept the thread of salvation running through their long history of disobedience.

- God's ultimate will is to save even those people who have sinned and have been unfaithful.

EZEKIEL 20–24

Introduction to These Chapters

These chapters conclude the part of Ezekiel's prophecies comes for the most part between 593 and 587 B.C. (chapters 1–24). Chapters 20–23 tell the history of Israel's sins and of the consequences of these sins. Chapter 24 announces an end to this history of rebellion against God. This last chapter shows the depth of Ezekiel's commitment to his calling in a time of both personal and national tragedy.

Here is an outline of these chapters.

I. A History of Rebellion (20:1-49)
II. The Sword of the Lord (21:1-32)
III. The Sins of Jerusalem (22:1-31)
IV. The Allegory of Two Sisters (23:1-49)
V. The Siege of Jerusalem (24:1-27)
   A. The pot of boiling flesh (24:1-14)
   B. The death of Ezekiel's wife (24:15-27)

The Message of Ezekiel 20–24

In early 588 B.C., at the beginning of the end for the city of Jerusalem, Ezekiel must also bear the loss of his beloved wife. He remains true to his calling, however, and submits his grief to the purposes of God's word. What does Ezekiel's life as a man and a prophet tell us?

- The prophet is not exempt from pain. He is a messenger and a witness who suffers along with his people under God's judgment.

- Because the prophet also bears God's judgment, his life becomes a symbol of hope. That God speaks through a witness who is himself under judgment shows that God has not abandoned the people called by God's name.

- God's servants must have the capacity and willingness to listen, to speak, to care, to feel, and to suffer for the sake of God's word.

EZEKIEL 25–28

Introduction to These Chapters

Ezekiel 25–28 is a collection of announcements of judgment against foreign nations. The nations are condemned because they have been involved in Israel's rebellion against Babylon or because they have taken advantage of Judah's desperate situation for their own gain. Most of these oracles are from around 587 B.C.

Here is an outline of these chapters.

I. Ammon, Moab, Edom, and Philistia (25:1-17)
   A. Against Ammon (25:1-7)
   B. Against Moab (25:8-11)
   C. Against Edom (25:12-14)
   D. Against the Philistines (25:15-17)
II. Against Tyre (26:1–28:19)
   A. Tyre will be given to Babylon (26:1-21)
   B. Lamentation over Tyre (27:1-36)
   C. Judgment and hope (28:1-19)
      1. The end of a proud king (28:1-10)
      2. Lament for the King of Tyre (28:11-19)
III. Judgment Against Sidon (28:20-26)

The Message of Ezekiel 25–28

These oracles against the nations are related to the political and military realities that the people of Israel faced in their life as a nation. God's people live in history, not apart from it. These oracles point to a larger perspective than just particular historical circumstances, however. They point to God as the Lord of all peoples who commands the powers of life and death.

- God judges and rules the destiny of humankind.

- Human pride and earthly power and might must always yield to God's power and will.

- God gives human beings wonderful gifts (for example, the wisdom to master life). But the gifts must always be used according to God's laws, and the giver must always be acknowledged as the ultimate source of power.

- God's nature and will are revealed to Israel and to other nations through the prophetic word.

- In their punishment and in their restoration the people of Israel will be a witness to God's power and will come to a new knowledge of God.

EZEKIEL 29–32

Introduction to These Chapters

Chapters 29–32 are a series of announcements of judgment against Egypt. Ezekiel strongly condemns Egypt because of Egypt's pride, and because Egypt encouraged Israel to rebel against Babylon.

Here is an outline of these chapters.
I. Prophecy Against the Pharaoh (29:1-21)
II. The Day of the Lord (30:1-26)
III. Allegory of Pharaoh as a Cedar Tree (31:1-18)
IV. Lamentations over Egypt (32:1-32)
  A. Lament over Pharaoh (32:1-16)
  B. Egypt sent down to the pit (32:17-32)

The Message of Ezekiel 29–32

Ezekiel's prophecies serve more than one purpose within his ministry. The laments and oracles against Egypt show these different purposes. The prophetic word teaches new knowledge of God and of God's ways, reproaches wrongdoers, tells God's intentions for the future, and acts to begin the process of accomplishing God's will. What do these oracles and laments teach Israel and Egypt?

- There is no earthly power to which Israel may look to avoid dealing with God.

- There is no avenue of escape for anyone from God's will.

- All peoples are under the constraints of divine justice.

- Divine justice follows a person into the world after death.

EZEKIEL 33–39

Introduction to These Chapters

Chapters 33–39 in the book of Ezekiel come from the period of time after the destruction of Jerusalem in 587 B.C. The material in these chapters speaks of the siege of Jerusalem and of the Exile. These prophecies also look forward to the restoration of the homeland of Israel's people.

Here is an outline of these chapters.
I. Responsibility of Prophet and People (33:1-33)
  A. Responsibility and judgment (33:1-20)
  B. Jerusalem has fallen (33:21-22)
  C. Possessiveness and sin (33:23-29)
  D. The exiles do not hear (33:30-33)

The Message of Ezekiel 33–39

The prophet Jeremiah had told
Israel of a foe from the north that
would be the agent of God's
judgment. In Jeremiah and Ezekiel's time
this foe was Babylon. Ezekiel foresees a
time when another foe from the north will
come against the reunited people of Israel.
This foe is from the mountains of Asia
Minor in the area of Meshech-Tubal, a
nation with whom Israel had dealings in
the past (see Ezekiel 32:26). At an
unnamed time in the future the power of
God will bring this foe into battle with
Israel. This is really God's battle, however,
for the forces of nature and cosmic terror
rather than Israelite warriors are decisive in
Gog's defeat.

The people of Israel did return to their
homeland under the direction of the
Persian king Cyrus in 539 B.C. They lived
under Persian rule until the Greeks
defeated Persia and became the dominant
world power. The cataclysmic battle with
Gog has yet to take place in Israel.

THE VALLEY OF DRY BONES (EZEKIEL 37:1-14)

This vision probably comes from a time after the
fall of Jerusalem in 587 B.C. but before the exiles
fully understand that they may yet live despite their
sin (see Ezekiel 33:10).

The very dry bones show that death has long
since triumphed in the visionary valley to which
Ezekiel is taken. The dead lie here in disgrace
because they did not receive a proper burial.

Ezekiel speaks two words to the bones. The first
word gives the bones human form again (verses 7-8).
The second word gives them the breath of life and
makes them fully human (verses 9-10). The Hebrew
word for "breath" may also be translated "spirit"
(verses 1, 14) or "wind" (verse 9). This is literal
breath and is also the life force which is the hallmark
of a human being (see also Genesis 2:7).

The bones represent the people of Israel who see
death on all sides and have given up hope for the
future. Ezekiel's message to them is that God will
raise them from their graves of exile and of despair.
The issue of life and death is always in God's hands
and God has declared that Israel will live.

The Revelation to John casts a battle
with the forces of Gog in the future under
different circumstances (see Revelation
20:7-10). Thus, precise identification of
Gog or of the time of this great battle
either in the past or the future is uncertain.

What conclusions can we draw from the
prophecies of Ezekiel concerning the
future for the people of God?

- During the years of Ezekiel's
  prophecy the people of Israel had
  only God's word to turn to. Their
  political, economic, and military
  power were gone. Their land was
  devastated and under foreign control.

- The prophetic word from Ezekiel and
  other prophets was that God was
  watching over God's word to perform
  it (see also Jeremiah 1:11-12).

- God's word for Israel was one of both judgment and redemption.

- Answers to their questions about the past and the future were in God's word to them.

- The tension between judgment and promise, good and evil would be resolved in God's future.

- The people of Israel had been set apart as the people of God. They, as representatives of God's kingdom on earth, would be triumphant.

EZEKIEL 40–48

Introduction to These Chapters

In Ezekiel 40–48 the prophet is shown the restored Temple and the renewed land of Israel. The content of this entire final vision may be outlined as follows:

I. The Dimensions of the Temple (40:1–42:20)
   A. The Temple's gates and courts (40:1–41:4)
   B. A description of the Temple (41:5-26)
   C. The chambers and the walls (42:1-20)
II. God's Glory Returns to the Temple (43:1-12)
III. The Altar and Temple Regulations (43:13–44:31)
IV. Land Use and Community Regulations (45:1–46:24)
   A. Creation of a Holy District (45:1-25)
   B. Regulations for Prince and Priests (46:1-24)
V. The Sacred River (47:1-12)
VI. The Boundaries of the New Israel (47:13–48:35)

Here is an outline of Ezekiel 40–44.

I. The Dimensions of the Temple (40:1–42:20)
   A. The Temple's gates and courts (40:1–41:4)
   B. A description of the Temple (41:5-26)
   C. The chambers and the walls (42:1-20)
II. God's Glory Returns to the Temple (43:1-12)
III. The Altar and Temple Regulations (43:13–44:31)

The Message of Ezekiel 40–44

When the people of Israel are once again reunited in their homeland, the necessities of daily living must be provided for. These necessities include the rituals of worship and celebration. The instructions in Ezekiel 40–44 provide the basis on which Israel could become a worshiping community again.

- Keeping in mind the abominations described in Ezekiel 8, these instructions provide protection for what is holy and sacred.

- The holy and sacred is identified with and authenticated by the presence of God.

- Shared ritual can bring the community of faith together and provide common ground on which they all may meet.

EZEKIEL 45–48

Introduction to These Chapters

Chapters 45–48 include a description of land distribution, a long list of regulations concerning the prince, the observance of festivals, and the habits of the priests, and a description of the boundaries of the new Israel.

Here is an outline of these chapters.

I. Creation of a Holy District (45:1-25)
II. Regulations for Prince and Priests (46:1-24)
III. The River and the Boundaries of Israel (47:1-23)
   A. The sacred river (47:1-12)
   B. The boundaries of the new Israel (47:13-23)
IV. Division of the Land and City (48:1-35)

The Message of Ezekiel 45–48

The new name of Jerusalem ("The LORD Is There") is a symbol of the renewed relationship between God and the people of God. Now they may once again dwell together. Ezekiel 40–48 gives a structure by which the people are to live out their relationship with God. The purpose behind this structure can be seen in the regulations about religious festivals. Through these rituals and ceremonies the people of Israel are to:

- maintain the purity of God's sanctuary,

- remember how God called them out of slavery to be God's people, and

- celebrate the bounty of the land which God gave them.

This new life is not the creation of the people. Rather, it comes from God and is God's gracious gift. This life-giving gift is symbolized in the river that flows from the Temple (God's dwelling) out into the land.

- Both the people and the land are transformed by God's gift.

- This new reality is not other-worldly. It is based on Israel's historical experience with God.

- The new life is to be lived in this world in real time.

- This transformation goes beyond normal expectations of fruitfulness and security, however, because Israel's new life is like a return to paradise (see Genesis 1–2). These expectations have not yet been fulfilled in human history (see Revelation 22:1-5).

CONCLUSIONS

Ezekiel's idealized Israel was not created when the exiles were allowed to return home in 539 B.C. Many of them stayed in Babylonia, where, in later years, the Babylonian-Israelite community became an influential force in world Judaism.

The instructions for the new Israel do, however, offer a perspective from which the community of faith is to be set up in the Promised Land:

- God is to be Israel's sanctuary.

- All life must center on and flow from God.

- The land and its bounty are to be shared equally, even with foreigners.

From an even broader perspective, Ezekiel shows the people of God how they may move successfully into the future:

- They must recognize and honestly accept the failures of the past.

- They must pass through the stages of recognition, acceptance, grief, and repentance in order to move into new life.

- They must recommit themselves to live under the covenant.

- They must be open to God's new creation in them and through them.

As a prophet, Ezekiel calls into question people's assumptions about God and about what it means to live a life of faith. He proclaims that God's future for the community of faith comes through recollection, reconciliation, and expectation. Above all, Ezekiel demands that God's people, both then and now, accept God's reality and God's future for their lives.

DANIEL

OUTLINE OF DANIEL

I. **Daniel and His Friends in Babylon (1:1–6:28)**
   A. Daniel, Shadrach, Meshach, and Abednego (1:1-21)
   B. Nebuchadnezzar's dream of a great image (2:1-49)
   C. The fiery furnace (3:1-30)
   D. Story of Nebuchadnezzar's madness (4:1-37)
   E. Story of the handwriting on the wall (5:1-31)
   F. Daniel in the lions' den (6:1-28)

II. **Daniel's Visions (7:1–12:13)**
   A. Vision of four beasts (7:1-28)
   B. Vision of the ram and the he-goat (8:1-27)
   C. Daniel's prayer (9:1-27)
   D. Vision by the great river (10:1–11:1)
   E. Revelation of the future (11:2-45)
   F. The time of the end (12:1-13)

INTRODUCTION

Like Ezekiel, Daniel was an exile caught up in the struggle between mighty Babylon and tiny Judah.

The book of Daniel tells of events in Daniel's life as an exile and tells of visions that came to Daniel from God. The overall perspective of these visions and stories is that underlying all earthly reality is God's reality. That is, both history and time are subject to God's control; and no one—king, captive, or peasant, those who are wise or are unknowing, angelic prince or human being—may escape the influence of God's dominion.

Daniel the Book

The book of Daniel is a collection of stories and vision reports. Chapters 1–6 are stories about Daniel and his friends in Babylon. Chapters 7–12 tell of Daniel's visions.

Part of the book is written in Hebrew, the language of Israel (Daniel 1:1–2:4a and 8:1–12:13). The rest of the book is written in Aramaic (Daniel 2:4b–7:28), a language closely related to Hebrew and which functioned as the international language in Mesopotamia in the late Babylonian and Persian periods.

The stories and visions in the Aramaic chapters demonstrate that God is Lord of all peoples and that God's power is greater than the power of any earthly ruler. The Hebrew chapters place Daniel and his friends in Babylon and tell how world events will affect Jerusalem and God's chosen people.

Through dramatic and sometimes obscure symbolism the vision reports in Daniel reveal some of God's plan for "the end of the age." Because of this, these visions have been called *apocalyptic* (from a Greek word meaning *revelation*) and *eschatological* (from a Greek word meaning *end*).

The book contains stories told by Daniel and stories told about him. Daniel

7:1 says that Daniel himself wrote an account of one of his visions. Daniel may have written others or he may have dictated these accounts to a scribe. The Israelites took their sacred writings with them into exile and they continued in Babylon to practice their scribal traditions of recording history (for example, Jeremiah 52), prophecy (for example, Ezekiel 20), and hymns (for example, Psalm 137).

These stories and vision reports could have been recorded in part during Daniel's lifetime and then collected and arranged in their present form after his death.

Historical Circumstances

Who wrote the book of Daniel and when it was written are matters of dispute, however. Many of the earliest Jewish and Christian interpreters of Daniel believed Daniel to be a prophet and accepted the book as Scripture that came from the Exile.

Later interpreters believed that the book of Daniel was written during the Maccabean period, which was the second century B.C. (approximately 170–165) in Palestine. They believed that Daniel best reflects the conflict of that time between the Jews and the Greek tyrant Antiochus IV. In this case, Daniel would have been written by someone using Daniel's name and holding Daniel up as an example of a pious and wise man from the past. This would make the book of Daniel prophecy "after the fact." The purpose of such prophecy would have been to instruct and encourage the Jews in their struggle against Greek oppression.

Recent discoveries in the fields of ancient Near Eastern history, archaeology, and language suggest that the book of Daniel did originate in the Babylonian Exile. Current scholarship, however, is still divided between the views that Daniel came out of Babylon in the fifth or sixth century B.C. and that the book came from Judah in the third or second century B.C.

Whenever Daniel was written, it is obvious that the book came out of a community under stress. In the face of warfare and oppression, the community of God's people naturally would ask, "What does all this mean?" In answering this question, Daniel offers God's people a particular way to look at the world. Daniel's perspective is that all reality, both earthly and heavenly, is under God's dominion. Therefore, God's people may face the world and the future with confidence.

The additions to the book of Daniel are stories, a prayer, and a hymn. They are found in Daniel in the Septuagint, a Greek translation of the Old Testament that was begun in the third century B.C. in Egypt. These additions are accepted as Scripture by the Roman Catholic Church but are assigned to the Apocrypha by the Protestant Church.

Daniel the Man

What we know of Daniel's personal background comes from Daniel 1:3-4.

Daniel was from an honored and privileged Israelite family. This may be one of the reasons that he was taken to Babylon. In 598 B.C. and 587 B.C. the Babylonians took many Israelite leaders and artisans into exile. When he went to live in Babylon, Daniel was probably in his late teens. He was a well-educated, intelligent, and handsome young man.

Like most upper-class Israelite boys of his time, Daniel's education probably began at home, where he was taught the history of his people and of God's covenant with Israel. He was probably also instructed in the ethical conduct of life as well as in reading and writing.

During his time in Babylon, Daniel

learned the Babylonian language and script and was probably taught Babylonian history as well. He became an able administrator in the governments of Babylon and Persia and led a prosperous life.

The Israelites brought their sacred writings with them into exile, and Daniel continued to study them. He also observed the personal rituals of his faith, such as prayer, meditation, and fasting.

Daniel knew about dreams and about their interpretation. He had visions from God concerning great mysteries. He was a man of courage and conviction. Though he knew how to flourish in a pagan society, he also continued to live out his faith in God.

Indeed, the fundamental fact about Daniel is his reliance on God. Daniel was an outstanding man who is renowned to later generations for his wisdom and courage. Yet, it is to God that Daniel gave the praise and credit for all his accomplishments.

VISIONS IN DANIEL			
CHAPTER 2	CHAPTER 7	CHAPTER 8	CHAPTERS 10–12
The Great Image	The Four Beasts	Ram and He-Goat	A Word for Latter Days
Gold (Babylon, Daniel 2:38)	Lion (Daniel 7:4)		
Silver (Media-Persia? Daniel 2:39)	Bear (Daniel 7:5)	Ram (Media-Persia, Daniel 8:20)	Persia (Daniel 11:2)
Bronze (Greece? Daniel 2:39)	Leopard (Daniel 7:6)	Goat (Greece, Daniel 8:21)	Greece (Daniel 11:3-4; also 11:5-45?)
Iron/Clay (Rome? Daniel 2:40)	Indescribable Beast (Daniel 7:7-8)		Rome (or *the western coastlands* in the NIV and *Kittim* in the NRSV) (coming to power, Daniel 11:29-30; "The end of the days," Daniel 12:1-13)
Supernatural Stone/God's Kingdom (Daniel 2:44)	Kingdom of the Son of Man and of the Saints (Daniel 7:13-14)		

DANIEL 1–3

Introduction to These Chapters

Daniel 1–3 is a collection of stories about Daniel and his Jewish friends in King Nebuchadnezzar's court. Chapter 1 introduces the Hebrew youths and explains when and how they came to Babylon. Chapter 2 tells of Daniel's role in interpreting a dream for Nebuchadnezzar. Chapter 3 is the story of Shadrach, Meshach, and Abednego in the fiery furnace.

Here is an outline of these chapters.

I. Daniel and His Friends (1:1-21)
   A. Introduction (1:1-2)
   B. The youths get special treatment (1:3-7)
   C. The Hebrew youths are tested (1:8-16)
   D. The Hebrew youths excel in wisdom (1:17-21)
II. Nebuchadnezzar's Vision (2:1-49)
   A. Nebuchadnezzar has a dream (2:1-11)
   B. The Hebrew youths seek God's help (2:12-23)
   C. Daniel tells Nebuchadnezzar's dream (2:24-35)
   D. The interpretation of the dream (2:36-45)
   E. Outcome for Daniel and his friends (2:46-49)
III. The Fiery Furnace (3:1-30)
   A. Nebuchadnezzar's image of gold (3:1-2)
   B. The summons to worship the image (3:3-7)
   C. Accusations against the Jews (3:8-12)
   D. The youths refuse the king's order (3:13-18)
   E. Four men walk in the fire (3:19-25)
   F. The faithful youths are rewarded (3:26-30)

The Message of Daniel 1–3

Daniel 1 introduces the time, setting, and circumstances for the book of Daniel. This chapter establishes the high character and faithfulness of Daniel and his friends. Chapters 2–3 also testify to their devotion to God and to the rewards that follow. These are very personal stories of faith and of conflict.

These are more than exciting stories, however. These stories have a larger perspective than just the individuals involved. God's action and will are in each one. What do these stories tell us about God?

- God is Lord of all peoples and is greater than all human power.
- God's rule is eternal.
- God directs the course of human history.
- God is present in a foreign land as well as in Jerusalem.
- God is in relationship to all peoples.
- God reveals mysteries to believers and to nonbelievers. The believer is a source of knowledge to the nonbeliever.
- God's faithful servants are rewarded.
- God's wisdom is available to those who earnestly seek it.

These qualities of God's nature and action are proclaimed throughout the book of Daniel.

DANIEL 4–6

Introduction to These Chapters

Daniel 4–6 tells of Daniel's dealings with three different kings—Nebuchadnezzar, Belshazzar, and Darius.

In each case, Daniel's God-given wisdom and devotion are tested and proved.

Here is an outline of these chapters.

I. Signs and Wonders Shown (4:1-37)
  A. Nebuchadnezzar praises God (4:1-3)
  B. The dream (4:4-18)
  C. The interpretation (4:19-27)
  D. The fulfillment (4:28-33)
  E. Nebuchadnezzar's restoration (4:34-37)
II. The Handwriting on the Wall (5:1-31)
  A. Belshazzar's feast (5:1-2)
  B. A hand writes on the wall (5:3-9)
  C. Daniel interprets the writing (5:10-16)
  D. Daniel condemns the king (5:17-23)
  E. The message (5:24-28)
  F. The end for Babylonia (5:29-31)
III. Daniel in the Lions' Den (6:1-28)
  A. Daniel's place under Darius (6:1-3)
  B. The plot (6:4-9)
  C. Daniel is trapped (6:10-13)
  D. Daniel's night in the lions' den (6:14-18)
  E. Daniel's rescue (6:19-24)
  F. Daniel prospers (6:25-28)

The Message of Daniel 4–6

The stories in Daniel 4–6 show Daniel in very dramatic circumstances. Within these circumstances he shows us a life well-lived before God. Daniel's testimony comes out of how he lives and from his reaction to the circumstances in which he finds himself. These stories tell us a lot about the proper relationship between an individual and God.

- God can use dreams to communicate with human beings, both the faithful and the nonbeliever.

- For the truth of the dream to be revealed, a person must have realistic perspective on the universe. This perspective is that God is in control.

- To be fully human means to be in proper relationship with God.

- Public praise and confession are part of an individual's relationship to God. The community of faith and the world at large can learn of God through such confession and praise.

- God uses both human beings and heavenly beings to bring about God's will for the world.

- Individual lives as well as great historic events are under God's control.

- Righteousness is required of God's servants even in the face of death.

- Sin is bondage. Righteousness is true freedom.

- Faithfulness is rewarded.

CONCLUSIONS ON DANIEL 1–6

These are very personal, dramatic stories. They involve particular people in specific real-life situations. Yet, these particular people and circumstances reflect a wider and longer-range view of reality. Their stories always point the listener and the reader to God as the fundamental factor in all reality.

- God is shown to be at work in individual lives and in the course of world events, though individuals are still free to choose between sin and righteousness.

- Heaven and earth are related, and earthly events have their divine dimension. This dimension is God's will, which is worked throughout heaven and earth.

- God's people can be faithful to God and still thrive in an alien culture.

- Daniel's exile and his position in Babylonia are used by God for good.

- Human power is temporary and limited; God's power is eternal and without limit.

DANIEL 7–9

Introduction to These Chapters

Chapters 7–9 of Daniel contain four vision reports. With the vision in chapter 7 the focus of the book shifts from Daniel's time in Babylon to future times in the world at large. Chapters 1–6 center on people and events from the Exile. Chapters 7–12 involve cosmic principalities and powers as well.

Here is an outline of chapters 7–9.

I. Vision of Four Beasts (7:1-28)
   A. Daniel has a dream (7:1)
   B. The four beasts (7:2-8)
   C. The heavenly court (7:9-10)
   D. Judgment on the beasts (7:11-12)
   E. One like a son of man (7:13-14)
   F. The vision is interpreted (7:15-18)
   G. More about the fourth beast (7:19-22)
   H. Persecution and triumph (7:23-28)
II. Vision of the Ram and the He-Goat (8:1-27)
   A. Introduction (8:1-2)
   B. The ram (8:3-4)
   C. The he-goat (8:5-8)

   D. The destructive little horn (8:9-12)
   E. The sanctuary is desolate (8:13-14)
   F. A heavenly interpreter (8:15-19)
   G. More about the little horn (8:20-26)
   H. Conclusion (8:27)
III. Daniel's Prayer (9:1-27)
   A. Introduction (9:1-3)
   B. The prayer (9:4-19)
     1. Confession (9:4-6)
     2. The case against Israel (9:7-14)
     3. Plea for mercy (9:15-10)
   C. Gabriel answers Daniel's prayer (9:20-27)

The Message of Daniel 7–9

The symbols and message of Daniel 7–9 are not easily understood. Attempts to pin down every reference will end in frustration. Yet, visions are granted for the benefit of the community of faith. What then can we learn from this material that does not yield its secrets easily?

- God is in control of history and of human destiny. No one lives outside of God's dominion.

- God has a plan for history in which righteousness will overcome sin.

- God's people will suffer but will be victorious in the end. They will share in God's coming kingdom.

- The future may be known to some extent, but the final timetable is in God's hands.

- A well-lived, well-disciplined life of faith which includes prayer brings ultimate rewards.

DANIEL 10–12

Introduction to These Chapters

Chapters 10–12 tell of a vision for days yet to come. Daniel 10:1–11:1 introduces the vision and Daniel's heavenly messenger. Daniel 11:2–12:4 reports the message of the vision. Daniel 12:5-13 concludes the vision and gives a personal message for Daniel concerning his future.

Here is an outline of these chapters.

I. Vision by the Great River (10:1–11:1)
   A. Daniel in mourning (10:1-3)
   B. Daniel sees the vision (10:4-9)
   C. Daniel is strengthened (10:10-17)
   D. Heavenly conflict (10:18–11:1)
II. Revelation of the Future (11:2-45)
   A. Kings of Persia and Greece (11:2-4)
   B. The north and the south (11:5-6)
   C. The south against the north (11:7-9)
   D. The north victorious (11:10-16)
   E. The king of the north meets defeat (11:17-19)
   F. The king of a few days (11:20)
   G. A contemptible person (11:21-24)
   H. The appointed end is yet to come (11:25-28)
   I. Jerusalem suffers (11:29-31)
   J. Jewish revolt (11:32-35)
   K. The arrogant tyrant (11:36-39)
   L. The end of the tyrant (11:40-45)
III. The Time of the End (12:1-13)
   A. Deliverance from a time of trouble (12:1)
   B. Resurrection of the dead (12:2-3)
   C. The vision is sealed (12:4)
   D. How long? (12:5-7)
   E. What shall be the issue? (12:8-10)
   F. Days of the appointed end (12:11-12)
   G. Daniel's place at the end of days (12:13)

The Message of Daniel 10–12

Daniel 10–12 deals with history, people, and time in ways that are not easily interpreted. We may not fully understand the outcome of all we have read. We will miss great value in the text, however, if we only try to figure out how to match the prophecy with past or future events and times. The timeless meaning of these texts and the motivation that produced them must not be overlooked.

Daniel was written, in part, so that we who came after Daniel would know more of God through him. Daniel requires us to remember our past, to know to what authority we must ultimately answer, and to allow the truth of the past to guide us into the future.

At the end of chapter 12 Daniel is told to go on with his life in trust. What do these chapters tell us about going on with our lives?

- We must trust in God and have confidence in the final outcome of God's plan for the world.

- We must be disciplined in the laws and practice of our faith.

- We must maintain an openness to God's revelation.

- We must witness to our experience of God's truth.

- We must be ready for the end but not preoccupied with it.

- We must spend time in acts of charity.

- We must persist in our duty even if the Master does not come at the expected time.

PROPHECY IN THE DIVIDED KINGDOM

THE ORIGIN AND DEVELOPMENT OF PROPHECY: AN OVERVIEW

The Hebrew word most frequently translated as "prophet" in the Old Testament is *nabi*. Before the establishment of the monarchy in Israel, the word *nabi* denoted two quite different vocations. Aaron was called the *nabi* of Moses, meaning that Aaron served as Moses' mouthpiece or spokesperson. A *nabi* was also a member of a group of holy persons who displayed ecstatic or trancelike behavior accompanied by flutes, tambourines, and lyres. In the former sense, the *nabi* was one who spoke on behalf of another. In the latter sense, the *nabi* was one who might be called "possessed"—but possessed by the Spirit of God.

With the establishment of the monarchy, there arose a need for a *nabi* who, called by God, would serve as God's mouthpiece in criticism of the king. As *nabi* (or prophet, in English) Samuel anointed Saul king and later rebuked Saul for his failure to live up to his royal office. In the next generation the prophet Nathan dramatically took King David to task for his treatment of Uriah and Bathsheba. Both Samuel and Nathan had close relationships with monarchs, yet these prophets also stood over and against the kings. The Spirit of God called Samuel and Nathan to speak on behalf of the Lord, and thus as prophets they called the kings to account. From this time forward, the role of the *nabi* was to render the judgment of God in periods of great social and political change.

When the United Kingdom over which David and Solomon had ruled was divided in 922 B.C., Jeroboam I became ruler of Israel, the Northern Kingdom. Turbulence and political chaos ensued for the next two centuries until Israel finally fell to the Assyrian Empire. Even when Israel appeared to be at peace, there was an underlying sense of unease. Elijah and Elisha were active in Israel in the ninth century B.C.; and Amos and Hosea spoke there a century later, beginning the classical period in Old Testament prophecy. Meanwhile, in the south, the eighth-century B.C. prophets Isaiah and Micah successfully worked to keep Judah alive as its northern sister fell. In the next century, around 626 B.C., Jeremiah was called to prophesy to Judah. His long career spanned Judah's reform, relapse into apostasy, and defeat. Jerusalem was destroyed in 5876 B.C., and the leading citizens were deported to Babylonia. The last of the great classical prophets, Ezekiel and Second Isaiah (Isaiah 40–55), preached to the exiles in Babylonia.

PROPHECY IN ISRAEL

The story of Elijah begins abruptly in the book of First Kings. No introduction or transition prepares us for his entrance on the stage of Israelite history. We move suddenly from a stereotyped schema of reigns in the Divided Kingdom to the Elijah cycle (1 Kings 17–19; 21), which hits like a flash of lightning. Appearing without warning, the prophet confronts the Israelite king Ahab.

The historian of First and Second Kings flatly condemns every single one of the northern monarchs. If we were to grade them based on the information we have in these books, they would all be given an F. (Of the southern or Judean kings, a handful would receive passing grades.) Why this condemnation? It goes back to Jeroboam I, the first northern king, who led the secession from the union and in so doing set up altars in Dan and Bethel (the northern and southern limits of his kingdom). The golden calves at these sanctuaries were dangerous in that they resembled the Canaanite idols to the god Baal. Jeroboam I also instituted a new priesthood and a new calendar of festivals, as well as a new capital in Shechem. The obvious reason for these developments was to keep the Israelites away from Jerusalem, the southern capital and the site of the Temple. The northern populace included many foreign, Canaanite peoples, whom Jeroboam wished to appease. Israel also had much wealth due to treaties with foreign peoples and control of vital trade routes. In Solomon's time these treaties had been sealed by marriages with foreign princesses. As a result, Solomon's harem had been huge. These princesses had brought their retinues and their religious cults with them. In 1 Kings 11:1-10, Solomon's many wives are blamed for turning his heart away from God, which led to the subsequent division of the kingdom after his death.

None of the northern kings tore down the altars at Dan and Bethel, and many of these kings continued the practice of intermarrying with foreign princesses. Also characteristic of the Northern Kingdom was its dynastic instability. That is, while Judah held with the Davidic line and a relatively orderly system of inheritance, Israel's throne

was ruled by strong men from the army whose designated successors were often assassinated by yet other strong men. After three violent deaths of kings in the first fifty years of the Northern Kingdom, stability came for a time under a man named Omri. Omri sealed an alliance with the king of the Sidonians by marrying his son Ahab to the king's daughter Jezebel. Omri also built a new capital at Samaria at considerable cost.

Ahab's reign (869 B.C.–850 B.C.) was one of wealth and stability, but the lot of the peasantry deteriorated. Small farmers were forced to mortgage their land and faced the prospect of eviction or enslavement to the wealthy. Ahab had no concern for covenant law, and his wife Jezebel became devoted to the extermination of the worship of God altogether.

Jezebel was extraordinarily devoted to her god, Baal. She sought to make the cult of Baal and the goddess Asherah the official religion of the nation. Ahab did nothing to stop her, and Jezebel executed all who dared to oppose her (1 Kings 18:4). The prophets of God either capitulated or were driven underground, with the exception of Elijah, a Gileadite from near the desert's edge. While Ahab regarded Elijah as the "troubler of Israel," Elijah rightly countered that it was the king himself (along with his wife) who brought trouble: Because of the king's apostasy, God had declared holy war on the now pagan state of Israel. The Omri dynasty came to an end with the assassination of Ahab's son Jehoram by Jehu in 842 B.C. Jehu also exterminated all those connected with Ahab's court. Jezebel was thrown from a window to her death; and the cult of Baal was, at least officially, thrown out of Israel (2 Kings 9–10).

In the century following this purge, Amos and Hosea spoke, with different emphases, on behalf of the covenant tradition. Unlike Elijah, they were prophets of the written word and are known not as much for their actions as for their preaching. The historical context at the time of Amos (750 B.C.) was one of peace and prosperity. Under Jeroboam II (786–746 B.C.), the northern frontier of Israel was expanded at the expense of Syria; and this able military leader forged close ties with Judah. Thus the major trade routes along the coastal plain flourished. Tolls from caravans and tariffs from trade brought great wealth into both countries. It appeared that another "Golden Age," rivaling that of Solomon, had dawned in Israel. Luxury (evidenced by the buildings and ivory inlays unearthed at Samaria in the twentieth century) and security marked the lot of the upper classes. Yet both Amos and Hosea insisted that underneath this fine veneer a dry rot had taken hold of Israel.

Morally, socially, religiously, and politically, the Northern Kingdom in the eighth century B.C. was in fact on the eve of destruction. The nation's prosperity was due to syncretism, that is, to involvement with many religious practices that led to neglect of the covenant tradition. A class of professional prophets had arisen, men employed by the crown, whose role was to support the status quo. Patriotism and complacency made them unable to criticize the state. Indeed, it appears that the material success of the kingdom was understood as the blessing of God on that nation. All is materially well, they seemed to think, and the nation is enjoying divine favor; therefore, we must be in the right.

Amos, called by God to go from Judah to Israel and prophesy, addressed the official cult at Bethel with words of judgment and fury. He was one who saw clearly the social and political sins of the upper classes. He spoke movingly and passionately on behalf of the poor, calling Israel to task for the oppression of the weak. Amos spoke of the coming destruction of the north and attempted by the harshness of his message to turn the

tide—but to no avail. Hosea, on the other hand, emphasized the religious and moral decay evident in Israel's abandonment of the worship of God. Hosea not only saw the reign of Jeroboam II, he also saw anarchy in the years that followed Jeroboam's death as five kings seized the throne by violence. Israel no longer seemed able to hold together as a nation.

Meanwhile, in the east, Assyria was on the rise. Tiglath-pileser III, the Assyrian king, coveted Israel as a bridge to Egypt and the Mediterranean. His policy was to conquer a nation and then to deport its inhabitants to break up any resistance. He invaded in 734 B.C. and made Israel an Assyrian vassal. When Israel's last king, Hoshea, withheld tribute, the new Assyrian king, Sargon, laid siege to Samaria and eventually subdued the city in 722 B.C. Sargon deported thousands of Israel's inhabitants. These famous "Lost Tribes" of Israel dwindled into obscurity. Foreigners from Mesopotamia were resettled in the land, mixing with those who remained. The people of the region later came to be known as the Samaritans.

PROPHECY IN JUDAH

Judah escaped the calamity that befell Israel only because her king, Ahaz, signed away his liberty and made Judah a vassal state of the Assyrian empire. Micah, preaching in the Southern Kingdom from before 722 B.C. to 701 B.C., was convinced that his country was not immune to the sickness and destruction that had befallen the North. It seemed to Micah that Jerusalem was just as bad as Samaria and, in spite of its Davidic line, equally under judgment. Despite its vassal status, Judah revolted against Assyria in 705 B.C. under King Hezekiah (715–687 B.C.). The fierce Assyrian king Sennacherib invaded Judah in 701 B.C. He stopped short of taking

Jerusalem but destroyed the countryside. His warring armies burned a path home, possibly through Micah's hometown of Moresheth.

With his humble peasant origins, Micah was incensed by the false sense of security that prevailed in Jerusalem, the City of David and the site of court intrigue and aristocratic privilege. The people felt no fear of danger. Had not God promised that he would establish David's throne forever (2 Samuel 7)? Micah declared flatly that Jerusalem would fall and be left a heap of ruins (Micah 3:12). Micah's stern words disturbed Hezekiah's conscience and moved him to make reforms. For a time foreign cults were removed and economic abuses were corrected. But as we will see, Hezekiah's reform was short-lived.

Manasseh, the most evil and most compromising of Judean kings, ruled from 687 to 642 B.C. He mandated the abominable Assyrian practices: human sacrifice, sacred prostitution, magic, and divination, such that the Temple itself was utterly defiled by pagan rites. It was the preaching of Jeremiah (called to be a prophet around 627 B.C.) that helped bring about massive reforms under King Josiah, who reigned from 640 to 609 B.C. Among other things, Josiah acted to repair the Temple in Jerusalem. During this project, "the book of the law of the LORD given through Moses" (2 Chronicles 34:14), a portion of what we now know as Deuteronomy, was discovered. King Josiah led his people in renewing their commitment to God's law. King Josiah died in 609 B.C., however, and the old problems soon resurfaced. During his long prophetic ministry, Jeremiah saw the eventual fall of Judah to a new power that arose in the east: Babylonia. When Assyria fell to Babylonia in 612 B.C., Jeremiah became convinced that the conquest of Judah would follow not for political reasons, but because God would use Babylonia to mete out his judgment on a sinful Judah.

The last three southern kings—Jehoiakim, Jehoiachin, and Zedekiah—abandoned Josiah's reform. They also refused to pay tribute to Babylonia, and the mighty Nebuchadnezzar (reigned 605–562 B.C.) countered with reprisals. The first, in 597 B.C., resulted in a deportation of the leading citizens to Babylonia. Jeremiah, seeing the catastrophe as God's judgment, advocated nonresistance to Babylonia. As a result, the war party in Jerusalem had him imprisoned, thrown into a cistern, and finally placed under house arrest in the palace. The last king of Judah, Zedekiah, broke his treaty with Nebuchadnezzar and vainly looked to Egypt for support in his rebellion. This time Nebuchadnezzar invaded Judah and destroyed Jerusalem. Zedekiah was forced to witness the death of his sons; then he was blinded and taken to Babylonia in chains. In the end, yet more of Jerusalem's inhabitants were deported.

After the fall of Jerusalem, Jeremiah's message changed. He went from offering oracles of doom to giving oracles of hope, return, and a new covenant. His last letters, written to the exiles in Babylonia, are known as the "Book of Consolation" (Jeremiah 30–31).

The connection between prophecy and political crisis is close indeed. The prophets pleaded, cajoled, and threatened in order to shake the complacency of those kings and citizens who felt that God's covenant did not really matter and that nothing of consequence would follow from their evil deeds. The classical prophets serve to remind us not only of God's mighty acts in history but also of the dangers that social, political, and religious compromise bring. The prophets were called by God to speak God's words to God's people. The prophets meant to disturb and disrupt and thereby to open the hearts of the people to God.

The Prophets of Israel and Judah and their Kings

Prophet	King
Samuel	Saul
Nathan	David
Gad	David
Ahijah	Solomon, Jeroboam I
Iddo	Solomon, Rehoboam, Abijam
Shemaiah	Rehoboam
Azariah	Asa
Hanani	Asa
Jehu	Jehoshaphat, Baasha
Jahaziel	Jehoshaphat
Eliezer	Jehoshaphat
Elijah	Ahab, Ahaziah, Jehoram
Micaiah	Ahab
Elisha	Ahaziah, Jehoram, Jehu, Jehoahaz, Jehoash
Zechariah	Joash
Isaiah	Uzziah, Jotham, Ahaz, Hezekiah
Hosea	Uzziah, Jotham, Ahaz, Hezekiah, Jeroboam II
Amos	Uzziah, Jeroboam II
Jonah	Jeroboam II
Micah	Jotham, Ahaz, Hezekiah
Oded	Pekah
Huldah	Josiah
Zephaniah	Josiah
Jeremiah	Josiah, Jehoahaz, Jehoiakim, Jehoiachin, Zedekiah
Uriah	Jehoiakim
Ezekiel	none named
Daniel	Jehoiakim, Nebuchadnezzar of Babylon, Belshazzar, Darius the Mede, Cyrus of Persia
Haggai	Darius of Persia
Zechariah	Darius of Persia
Obadiah	none named
Joel	none named
Nahum	none named
Habakkuk	none named
Malachi	none named

HOSEA

OUTLINE OF HOSEA

INTRODUCTION

Hosea's name occurs in the title and in the heading of this book. The name Hosea does appear in other places in the Hebrew Scriptures (see 2 Kings 15:30; 1 Chronicles 27:20). He is identified as the son of Beeri. We know very little about him except that he was probably fairly young when he began his ministry, as he was of marriageable age. His career spanned nearly a quarter of a century of Israel's most difficult history.

Hosea's work began during the peaceful years of Jeroboam II (786–746 B.C.). His work concludes sometime around the time of the horrendous defeat of Israel by the Assyrians in 722 B.C.

Ironically, even Israel's peaceful years were disrupted both by internal and external developments. Internally Jeroboam's own son Zechariah (746–745 B.C.) succeeded to the throne. Within six months Shallum ben Jabesh gained the throne by assassinating Zechariah. The internal politics of Israel quickly became marred by conspiracy and murder. Shallum was himself assassinated within a month by Menahem (745–737 B.C.) (see 2 Kings 15:8-16). Given the fact of Assyrian expansion and the grave threat that expansion posed for

Israel, Menahem expediently decided to become a vassal state to the Assyrian ruler Tiglath-pileser III. Israel had to pay an enormous tax as tribute to the Assyrians (see 2 Kings 15:19). The palace intrigue continued with the rapid accession of Pekahiah (737–736 B.C.). Pekah ben Ramaliah (736–732 B.C.) then seized the throne. He very soon attempted to form an alliance against the detested Assyrians. Israel attempted to force her southern sister nation, Judah, into the alliance by means of a war. The Syro-Ephraimitic war forms a part of the backdrop against which Hosea must be read.

In Assyria, Shalmaneser (727–722 B.C.) succeeded Tiglath-pileser. Hoshea, the king of Israel, foolishly withheld the payment required from vassal states. Angered by the foolhardy challenge, the Assyrians made Hoshea Shalmaneser's captive (Hosea 13:10). The capital city was besieged; Israel's armies were soundly defeated. The northern kingdom of Israel collapsed in 722 B.C.

Hosea used various metaphors to describe the relationship which existed between God and Israel as the people of God. The most frequently used metaphor is that of the unfaithful wife as harlot. Harlotry characterized the people of God. Hosea spoke to his own people. Throughout his work he showed familiarity with major centers of Israel's land: Samaria (7:1; 8:5; 10:5, 7), Bethel (4:15; 5:8; 10:5; 12:4), and Gilgal (4:15; 9:15; 12:11).

The book can be easily divided into two major sections. The first part centers on the prophet's experience with marriage and family (chapters 1–3). The second part consists of loosely joined material that defies simple attempts to organize or outline (chapters 4–14).

HOSEA 1–3

Introduction to These Chapters

These three chapters may be outlined as follows.

I. Superscription/Title (1:1)
II. Gomer and the Children (1:2-9)
III. Restoration Promised (1:10–2:1)
IV. Unfaithfulness and Punishment (2:2-13)
V. Restoration and Redemption (2:14-23)
VI. The Restoration of Gomer (3:1-5)

The Message of Hosea 1–3

The first three chapters of Hosea are a remarkable narrative of the stubborn and long-suffering love of God. What are some of the truths we learn from these chapters?

- Nothing can stop God's love.

- When God gives an instruction, a man or a woman must obey.

- Marriage is a sacred institution.

- We can learn of God's feelings by praying.

- God is not far removed from our lives; God is close and feels the pain of faithlessness and sin.

- God refuses to be divorced from the realities of human life.

- The reality of God allows us to interpret the events of our lives.

- God can use even the worst circumstances for good.

- God sets the example for all people to follow.

HOSEA 4–5

Introduction to These Chapters

Chapter 4 begins the second major part of Hosea's work. With but two exceptions (chapter 11, in which Hosea presents the wonderful image of the tender and loving father, and 14:3-9, in which Hosea presents a bright vision of the future) the balance of the book presents little more than a people and a nation in catastrophe and collapse. Judgment is the characteristic tone and intent of chapters 4 and 5. Here is an outline of these chapters.

I. The Lord's Controversy with Israel (4:1-19)
   A. God's controversy (4:1-3)
   B. The case against the priests (4:4-10)
   C. The case against the cult (4:11-14)
   D. Ephraim is joined to idols (4:15-19)
II. The Treachery of Ephraim (5:1-15)
   A. A despicable treachery (5:1-7)
   B. War between brothers (5:8-14)
   C. The threat of an absent God (5:15)

The Message of Hosea 4–5

In these two chapters we have heard both the prophet and the Lord speak to a people caught up in false worship, to leaders who have lost their integrity and have made little more of religion than a way to make a living, and to nations who cannot see God at work in history. Through it all the prophet seeks to secure repentance; God seeks repentance and a genuine return to the ways of God's choosing. What can we learn from these chapters?

- Following unworthy teachers has tragic results.

- Sins are both by omission and commission; we either neglect to do what ought to be done, or we deliberately do what we ought not do.

- Social morality and theological beliefs are intertwined.

- There is an ecology to sin; when God's will is broken, the entire creation suffers.

- Preoccupation with sensual thinking prevents wisdom.

- God seeks wholehearted commitment to God's purposes.

- Doing religious things is not necessarily the same as wholehearted commitment to God.

- War between brothers is both sin and judgment.

- God can and will work in history in order to secure commitment to God's purpose.

- Without the assurance of God's presence in history, we are left with little more than our own resources to deal with the terrors and realities of history.

- With God's presence we can endure history's best and worst.

HOSEA 6–8

Introduction to These Chapters

The catastrophe and tragedy of unsuccessful warfare should make the nation aware of the need for repentance. In this sense, the people should see the relationship between the events of history and their relationship with God. However, the depth of awareness is shallow. Israel not only continues turning from God,

Israel runs the peril of losing its identity altogether as the people of God. A death sentence cannot be far removed from apostasy and loss of identity.

Here is an outline of chapters 6–8.

I. Shallow Repentance and Intrigue (6:1–7:7)
  A. A litany of repentance (6:1-3)
  B. God rejects shallow repentance (6:4-6)
  C. Varieties of faithlessness (6:7–7:2)
  D. The kings have fallen (7:3-7)
II. Israel Loses Its Identity (7:8-16)
III. Israel's Death Sentence (8:1-14)

The Message of Hosea 6–8

Chapters 6 through 8 treat the political collapse of Israel. With the sounds and sights of destruction and chaos, and the threat of lost national identity, Hosea graphically captures Israel's dilemma. But even though God intends to use history as a means by which to punish Israel, still the same God holds out hope. The people may still return. They cannot return through shallow, ritualistic rites of sacrifice and memorized litanies. They can only return through a thoroughgoing repentance and confession to God.

What can we learn from these chapters?

- Sin has its awful consequences (7:9).

- The consequences of sin are not arbitrary; they are the natural outcome of given actions.

- God seeks and desires heartfelt and sincere repentance that is more than mere ritual. True repentance is a deep and ethical process.

- Any nation will decline when its leaders are morally corrupt.

- In large measure we will become like those with whom we associate.

- Identity once lost is very difficult to regain.

- While external enemies may pose a threat, any individual or nation must beware the peril of internal chaos, discord, and sinfulness that will destroy as well.

- God desires a right attitude and behavior rather than religious activity.

HOSEA 9:1–11:11

Introduction to These Chapters

Hosea continues the indictment of the nation of Israel for its apostasy, evidenced by its crass worship rituals and its profligate sensuality. Though the people are convinced that their cultic worship makes a difference, Hosea presses home his truth. There can be no legitimate worship unless it is worship of the God of the covenant. Since the prophecies stress the widespread and active cultic worship, they were probably first uttered in a time of relative peace, perhaps after the events of 733 B.C. (See "The Love of God," p. 347)

However, against the backdrop of continued national apostasy that warrants all the punishment God can bring to bear on Israel, Hosea addresses a profound theological question. His argument in part echoes Amos's argument that since the nation violated the covenant, the nation deserves just punishment. The law of God demands just consequences.

But what of the love of God? Surely the Hebrew people remembered God's love in the Exodus, in the wilderness, and in the period of the conquest. But is the love of God equal to the sinfulness of the people? Hosea dares to address this question in chapter 11 through the sensitive and powerful images of the father and his wayward son.

Here is an outline of Hosea 9:1–11:11.

I. Ephraim's Idolatry and Punishment (9:1-17)
  A. From celebration to grief (9:1-6)
  B. A fool for God's sake (9:7-9)
  C. A deadly attraction (9:10-17)
II. Israel's King; Bethel's Idol (10:1-15)
  A. Life without king or cult (10:1-8)
  B. Israel's iniquity (10:9-15)
III. The Love of God (11:1-11)
  A. Israel the child (11:1-7)
  B. God the Father (11:8-9)
  C. God's promise of a homecoming (11:10-11)

The Message of Hosea 9:1–11:11

The emotions of these chapters range from the white-hot wrath of a rejected God

---

THE LOVE OF GOD (HOSEA 11:1-11)

How can any people survive if all they have is the haunting specter of an absent God who has abandoned them to the horrors of history? In one sense, the law of God has been justly fulfilled. The people have sinned grievously. Now they suffer the only appropriate punishment. God's patience has worn through. Now God acts through history to execute the just punishment. But in another sense, Hosea cannot leave the issue alone. Is God's love equal to the demand of the law? Modern readers need to see the incredible courage of Hosea in asking such an important question.

Hosea portrays God in the person of a loving father. The oracle recovers the love of God from Israel's historical memory in verses 1-4; pictures the present love of God in verses 5-7; appropriates the love of God in the present suffering in verses 8-9; and finally portrays God's love in the future in verse 11.

Father is a powerful image. God had been described as the father of the tribe (Exodus 4:22; Isaiah 1:2; Jeremiah 3:19, 22). God's love stirred God's saving act in the Exodus from Egypt. But the nation quickly turned from God in rebellion. One can hear the heartbrokenness of God in the review of history. Hosea uses the word *heal* to describe God's saving acts in history. The connection between God and Israel is historical and moral. The relationship was conferred by love. It should have been confirmed by maintenance of covenant responsibility. Hosea is unafraid to picture God with very human feelings, sympathies, and gentleness.

The present crisis (described in verses 5-7) reflects either actual refugees or a political policy of seeking alliances with the enemy. Some kind of a military disaster has already occurred. Hosea may be referring to the Assyrian campaign of 733 B.C. But even with the facts of history and current events facing them with bare truth, still the people stubbornly refuse to repent.

Hosea then portrays God expressing to Israel/Ephraim God's own tortured soul (verse 8). Admah and Zeboiim are towns that had been totally destroyed along with Sodom and Gomorrah (Genesis 10:19; 14:2, 8). In God's own soul wrath gives way to compassion. There follows a triple denial of wrath's finality. "I will not execute my fierce anger; I will not again destroy . . . I will not come in wrath" (verse 9). God does have feelings like those of human beings. But God's action is utterly unlike human behavior. Hosea's words describe; but they do not define or limit God's action.

Verses 10-11, which describe a promised homecoming, may be additions by a later editor. They refer to the future in which God will restore to the land exiles who have languished in foreign lands. Under no circumstances can the return be the accomplishment of the exiles themselves. The return will be yet another gift of a gracious God.

---

to the compassionate feelings of a loving father. The events range from the horrors of warfare waged on pregnant women and little children to the promise of a return to a beloved homeland. What can we learn from these chapters?

- Blessings of harvest and bounty are from God.

- Buildings and institutions do not endure; moral discernment and obedience to the covenant prevail.

- The root of sin is lack of trust in God.

- Exclusive trust in the power of military might is a sin against God.

- Religious leaders have the obligation of prophetic ministry—declaring God's interpretation of events and moral expectations.

- Sometimes the feeling of faith is less important than the execution of responsibility and duty to God.

- History is God's workshop.

- In Israel's history is the memory of God's loving action on behalf of all humanity.

- God's relationship with people is both historic and moral.

- God's own soul is torn by faithless people and nations.

HOSEA 11:12–14:9

Introduction to These Chapters

Following the touching image of a caring, compassionate father and the promise of a return home, the final section of Hosea once again utters a series of oracles that speak of Israel's evil and eventual doom. When the word of grace is finally spoken, it is a severe grace that emerges from God's love.

Here is an outline of 11:12–14:9
I. Israel's Evil and Doom (11:12–12:14)
   A. Israel at the Jabbok (11:12–12:6)
   B. Israel's crisis of identity (12:7-14)
II. Toward an Inexorable End (13:1-16)
   A. God against Israel (13:1-8)
   B. Israel's shattered illusions (13:9-16)
III. A Severe Grace (14:1-8)
IV. Instructions to the Reader (14:9)

The Message of Hosea 11:12–14:9

Hosea wrestled long and hard with the apparent paradox between the love and law of God. If the law is paramount then love must be secondary. If love is primary then what is to be done with the law's requirements? Hosea dared to present a God whose heart is tortured by the sinfulness of the nation. Yet, the same God cannot forever turn away from the beloved people. Only due to God's own steadfast love can the people hope for a future. What can we learn from these chapters?

- The love of God overcomes all sin, even the sin of rejecting God's love.

- Genuine repentance is always demanded, and always possible.

- God will go to great lengths seeking and redeeming people.

- Salvation comes from God alone.

- God is not a tradition, but a reality with whom all people must wrestle and come to terms.

- The courageous words of the prophet are worthy of our consideration; history has vindicated the prophet.

JOEL

OUTLINE OF JOEL

INTRODUCTION

The immediate cause for the book is a devastating plague of locusts that threatens to destroy the land and the economy. Like other prophets, Joel takes his cue from real events in the life of the nation. He goes further than the event by interpreting the importance or the meaning of the event to his contemporaries. For Joel the overwhelming swarms of locusts suggest not only an act of God, but also the future activity of God in the life of the nation.

Joel the Man

We know very little about Joel himself. His name, meaning *Yahweh is God*, is not an unusual name, as it occurs elsewhere in the Old Testament (for example, 1 Samuel 8:2; Ezra 10:43). He is the son of Pethuel. His home may have been in the territory traditionally associated with Reuben (see 1 Chronicles 5:4).

Joel is familiar with worship procedures and priests, and he may well have been what is called a Temple prophet. In this sense he shares similar views with Haggai and Zechariah. He shows a familiarity with Jerusalem and the surrounding country.

Date of the Writing

One of the critical questions in interpreting Joel has to do with the date of his writing. He could be assigned to one of two periods. Since some of his words are parallels with other prophets (some 20 verses), either those prophets quoted from him, or he quoted from them. Since there is no mention of national sins that would warrant punishment from God and no mention of large menacing empires (neither Assyria nor Babylon is mentioned), scholars conclude that Joel's work comes at a relatively late time. At least one allusion is to scattered people (3:2), thus implying the Exile as a historical era already past. Therefore, we may date his work sometime during the time period of the fifth century B.C.

The Message of Joel

A careful reading of Joel suggests that the prophet does not blithely cast aside the rich traditions of his predecessors. Rather, he takes their work and reinterprets it for the present moment. Joel stands at a vital moment when the old traditions of the prophets were giving way to the newer apocalyptic thinking. In large measure, he reinterprets the traditional prophetic message with a new freshness for his listeners. Joel seeks the meaning of a current crisis while at the same time straining to see the horizon of God's future. Just as Joel would not arbitrarily do away with tradition, he would not eliminate formal worship services.

One of the central elements in Joel's work is the "*day of the LORD*," mentioned no fewer than five times (see 1:15; 2:1, 11, 31; 3:14). No one can escape from its inevitable disaster. But there is still room for hope, since the opportunity for repentance is always present. God's intention is not merely judgment and punishment, because God always yearns for repentance and acknowledgement by the chosen people.

JOEL 1:1–2:11

Introduction to These Chapters

Chapter 1 and the first eleven verses of chapter 2 provide a fitting introduction to the prophecies of Joel. In this material, the crisis that the people of Israel were enduring in Joel's day is described in detail.

The material may be outlined as follows.

   I. Title (1:1)
   II. A Call for National Lament (1:2-14)
   III. A Terrible Crisis (1:15-20)
   IV. The Day of the Lord (2:1-11)

The Message of Joel 1:1–2:11

Modern readers may find the graphic imagery and the theological considerations to be terribly outdated or even offensive.

Few of us consider natural catastrophe the direct result of a deliberate decision and action by God. Seldom do we hear people even attempt such conclusions. But for the ancient Israelites, the realms of nature and human experience were both within the power and authority of the eternal God. Joel's insight into the larger issues of the time cannot be disregarded. If we are inclined to discount or to scoff at anyone who would see the action of God in natural events, we would be on the way to wisdom when we understand as well that God's creation, all of it, has running through it a moral direction and intention. We ought not scoff at those who see God at work through natural events; they see God caring for them and vitally concerned and personally involved in their lives.

What else can we learn from reading these verses?

- Even prophetic religion at times respects the need for external expressions of worship (1:9, 13-14).

- Disasters or catastrophes can serve to turn people toward God.

- God can use disaster to speak to people.

- In the face of overwhelming and uncontrollable natural events, we become aware of our utter dependence upon God.

- God's intentions are for all people.

- God is not far removed from human history; God is near and involved.

JOEL 2:12–3:21

Introduction to These Chapters

As far as the majority of citizens are concerned, the catastrophe is the problem.

But for the prophet, the stress of the moment is only the beginning. Joel refuses to speak only to what is apparent or obvious, while he will continue with his concern for the present crisis. Joel uses the idea of the day of the Lord to develop an enlarged notion of a future hope. Joel's task is to appropriate faith equal to the demand of the hour and build a faith of sufficient depth for eternity.

Here is an outline of Joel 2:12–3:21.

I. Call for National Repentance (2:12-17)
II. The Promise of Fertility (2:18-27)
III. The Outpouring of the Spirit (2:28-32)
IV. God's Judgment of Oppressors (3:1-21)

The Message of Joel 2:12–3:21

Joel did not interpret the current crisis solely within the context of life's usual demands and expectations. He cast the entire catastrophe within the bounds of God's eternal—both historical and future—purposes. He appropriated much existing prophetic and national liturgical material. In this sense he was certainly not original. However, he shows remarkable skill at reinterpreting traditional material in order to give his people courage for today and hope for tomorrow. What else can we learn from Joel?

- Judgment day will be both blessing and curse.

- What judgment day means depends to some degree upon the attitude and faith of the individual.

- God seeks genuine repentance and not a mere using of religion for immediate ends.

- God yearns for the transformation of God's people into morally sensitive and historically aware people.

- God's spirit is equally available to all, regardless of the distinctions of age, sex, or social/economic class.

- No people, no nation, will escape the judgment of God.

- God, while recognizing and accepting the institutions of religion and worship, is not satisfied with external form.

- A crisis can be used to transform an individual toward the intentions of the eternal.

AMOS

OUTLINE OF AMOS

INTRODUCTION

The prophet Amos is the first of the writing prophets. His work occurs during the long and prosperous reign of Jeroboam II, around 786–746 B.C.

In other prophetic works, the sights of military collapse, natural catastrophe, economic disaster, and foreign intrigue all fill the imagination. Amos ministered during a time remarkably free from external stress. Other prophets had to make sense of disaster, both natural and political. Amos found himself speaking an urgent word to a complacent people long since grown spiritually flabby and morally callous. A sensitive reader can hear the groans of the oppressed, the flippancy of vested interest, and the anguished cries of men and women caught up in a corrupt court without hope. We can even hear the voice of God raging against a nation prematurely confident in the false security of ritual and arrogantly ignorant of the divine will of God. Power and wealth, luxury and licentiousness yield abuses of justice, oppression of the poor, corruption of the innocent, and an intolerance for spiritual forces.

The people to whom Amos addresses his work are a prideful people (6:13-14) and a comfortable people with abundant wealth (3:15; 5:11; 6:4-6). Sinfulness is not restricted to the male population. Women too are addicted to wine (4:1). In a morally insensitive society injustice prevails, but it takes the prophet to name the sin for what it is. The poor are oppressed, sold into slavery (2:6-9; 5:11), and have no recourse through the legal system because the judges themselves are as corrupt as the surrounding culture (5:12).

The tragedy is that even though the prophet speaks, entrenched and vested interests adamantly ignore the divine will for the nation (7:10-14). The discerning prophet speaks a word from God to a people who have lost the sensitivity to the demands of God for their personal and corporate lives. They were filled with optimism. The prophet discerns the moral truth in a time when popular dogma refused to heed anything of the higher calling.

Amos speaks a harsh word against a cold people. Nothing in his work throbs with hope that the nation will repent and, in doing so, save itself. For Amos the requirement of God's law is quite clear: inescapable punishment.

The task would have been sufficient to test anyone's mettle even if the work had been done by personal choice. But Amos, like other individuals summoned by God into God's work, was summoned against his will and quite without his asking for the responsibility. However, Amos felt overwhelmed by the reality of God and the urgency as well as the immediacy of God's will for Israel. He could do nothing else but obey (3:8). The result of his faithfulness is the utterance and compilation of this great prophetic work of social justice.

AMOS 1–2

Introduction to These Chapters

The first two chapters of the book of Amos contain biographical information about the prophet, as well as the first few in a series of oracles delivered against foreign nations.

These two chapters may be outlined as follows.

   I. Title (1:1-2)

  II. Oracles Against the Nations (1:3–2:16)

    A. An oracle against Damascus (1:3-5)

    B. An oracle against Gaza (1:6-8)

    C. An oracle against Tyre (1:9-10)

    D. An oracle against Edom (1:11-12)

    E. An oracle against the Ammonites (1:13-15)

    F. An oracle against Moab (2:1-3)

    G. An oracle against Judah (2:4-5)

    H. An oracle against Israel (2:6-16)

The Message of Amos 1–2

The first two chapters of Amos consist of oracles against sinful nations. Both crimes of war and crimes of social injustice are judged as sinful. Without the sensitive insight and courageous word of the prophet, Israel may well have continued her blithe ignorance of the subtle crimes against her own people. What else can we learn from these chapters?

- God has expectations of minimal levels of morality for all nations.

- When God speaks events are put into motion; something happens.

- No power can long stand when God decides to act against it.

- God is at work in all nations' histories.

- When God needs a spokesperson, God will raise up a prophet.

- God has a special concern for the poor of any land.

- Prophets sometimes have to publicly reject popular religious attitudes and assumptions in order to present God's truth.

- When we are inclined to neglect weaker members of society, we must remember God's compassion and mercy toward us in our own moments of weakness and need.

AMOS 3–4

Introduction to These Chapters

Throughout its history Israel believed that God protected the chosen people in a special way. In Amos's day people clung to that belief. However, the popular notion was taken as a matter of fact and quite irrespective of moral standards. In the following series of oracles, Amos now addresses the election of Israel not as a privilege but as a burden of responsibility.

Here is an outline of these chapters:

I. Peril and Privilege of Election (3:1-15)
   A. Election and responsibility (3:1-8)
   B. Judgment (3:9-11)
   C. A means of judgment (3:12-15)
II. Oracles Against Israel's Excesses (4:1-13)
   A. An oracle against the women (4:1-3)
   B. An oracle against worship (4:4-5)
   C. An oracle about Israel's refusal (4:6-13)

The Message of Amos 3–4

Amos begins this section by unequivocally stating election's peril as well as its promise. Popular religion is concerned mainly with public displays of piety and worship. Amos's argument is that Israel's worship is just as evil as pagan rituals. Each chases after superstition. Each imagines God primarily concerned with right "religious" behavior. Amos differs. Amos holds that God wants individuals and nations to heed divine discipline and return to God's intentions. Amos's contention is that the ultimate measure of any culture has to do with the moral questions raised by and implied by God's purposes.

- God reveals God's purposes to human beings.

- Historical events are not necessarily random.

- God has been patient and long-suffering in attempting to reach the nations. But God's patience has a limit.

- To an extent we do control our futures by making appropriate moral decisions.

- Election as God's chosen carries with it the burden of higher responsibility.

- God is offended by hollow or insincere worship.

- The prophetic stance is always a minority position.

AMOS 5–6

Introduction to These Chapters

National religion offered only a false security of ritual and ceremony. Amos strips away all the pretense of the cultic religion. Even the long-yearned-for day of the Lord, which had traditionally been a hope for glorious vindication of Israel, will yield darkness and gloom. Violation of God's intention evokes a terrible and final end.

Here is an outline of Amos 5–6.

I. Israel's Just Reward for Sin (5:1-27)
   A. The prophet's lament (5:1-3)
   B. God's appeal to Israel (5:4-17)
   C. The day of the Lord (5:18-20)
   D. The noise of ritual (5:21-27)
II. Oracles of an Inevitable Doom (6:1-14)
   A. Oracles against the idle rich (6:1-7)
   B. An oracle of imminent disaster (6:8-14)

THE NOISE OF RITUAL (AMOS 5:21-27)

Earlier Amos characterized the people as loving ritual and ceremony (4:5). Here all subtlety is placed aside. Amos places the habits of worship against the moral expectations in social systems. Amos speaks the harsh word of the Lord against the worship of Israel. Could any word have been more startling and alarming? With some imagination we might see a wide-eyed and shocked people.

The oracle attacks all of the major elements in Israel's worship. Three major feasts marked the liturgical year (see Exodus 23:14-17; 34:18-24): Unleavened Bread/Passover, Feast of Weeks, and the Festival of the Harvest/Succoth. Amos also condemns offerings and sacrifices, as well as praises and songs. With a single utterance the entire worship life of Israel is condemned.

The Lord's condemnation is not an arbitrary judgment that takes its cue from poorly performed worship. The quality of worship takes its cue from the moral substance of the worshiper's life. God's judgment comes when the people hide behind their religion. The people have confused concentrating on the forms of ritual and worship for the critical work of justice and righteousness demanded by God for the ordering of society. The people have been as fickle in their moral lives as a stream bed in the wilderness. In rainy seasons wadis fill to a gushing overflow. In dry seasons they are nothing more than dried-up riverbeds worthless to a parched land. God demands justice and righteousness that flow constantly.

Verse 24 can well be considered the heart of Amos's preaching. "But let justice roll down like waters, and righteousness like an everflowing stream."

In verses 25-27 Amos returns to the motif of God's action in history. Evidently the priests of the sanctuaries had ceased preaching about the saving acts of God in Israel's past. Priests' work focused primarily on the performance of the worshiper through ritual. Amos alludes to a time when Israel's worship was pristine, in the wilderness, before the development of cultic worship centers and rituals. Other prophets also allude to the wilderness (Jeremiah 2:1-2; Hosea 2:14-15).

"Sakkuth" and "Kaiwan" (NRSV) may be derivations of words meaning "shrine" and "pedestal" (NIV). In any case, Amos's use of the terms suggests they are names of or allusions to Assyrian gods.

The reference to the wilderness in verse 27 evokes the memory of God's saving act. The same God will act in judgment against the people of God's own election. The chosen people will be separated from the chosen land.

The Message of Amos 5–6

The oracles in this section are all addressed to a people who have forgotten their primary responsibility as the people of God. National resurgence, military successes, remarkable economic growth with attendant luxuries of fine homes and sumptuous living had all dulled the moral senses. What can we learn from these chapters?

- God wants people to seek God.

- Seeking God is the way to real life.

- The prophetic faith sees the Lord at work in all of history.

- In the Bible the poor are not the problem. Instead, the rich are a problem to the poor.

- Unless moral obligations to the poor and weak are kept, worship becomes little more than noise and empty ceremony.

- God is worshiped through caring social relationships as well as hymns and prayers.

- No sin is as scathingly condemned as the sin of pride.

- Under sufficient stress of history, popular religion will buckle. When it does, the prophet will inform the nation of a larger God in whose hands lies all of history.

AMOS 7

Introduction to This Chapter

Chapter 7 affords a glimpse into the personal life of the prophet. Amos describes visions that have come to him, speaks of an attempted intercession, and then narrates his dramatic confrontation with the royal priest Amaziah.

Here is an outline of this chapter:
I. Judgment and Visions (7:1-9)
   A. Judgment by locusts (7:1-3)
   B. Judgment by fire (7:4-6)
   C. Vision of the plumb line (7:7-9)
II. Conflict and Confrontation (7:10-17)

The Message of Amos 7

The seventh chapter of Amos contains a variety of material: oracles, vision reports, and the dramatic narrative of the confrontation with Amaziah. God will use all these means to make God's will known to Israel. God may even use apparently unqualified individuals to carry God's word to the hearts of people. What else can we learn from the chapter?

- God can use nature to reach the hearts of people.

- Intercessory prayer may affect a person's life.

- A true prophet cares for the people.

- The Bible never understands God in the abstract. In the Bible, God is a being with moral purpose and power.

- God has countless forms of power that can be used to effect faithful response to God's will.

- Against God's measure all humanity falls short.

- God will lift up a prophet in times of national need.

- The prophet's authority rests not in personal character but instead in God's will and instruction.

AMOS 8–9

Introduction to These Chapters

Following the confrontation in Bethel, Amos's prophecy continues with visions of increasing immediacy. The end of Israel is not far off now. The question raised in Amos's thinking is, What will survive? Institutions, government, rituals, and customs may be obliterated by an enemy. What will endure? For Amos the heart of faith will survive: trust in the ultimate power of God, true religion that has moral sensitivity and social obligation as its motives. Amos makes sense of the impending disaster by interpreting it as a means of discipline and not merely an utter doom.

Here is an outline of Amos 8–9.
I. A Vision and an Indictment (8:1-14)
   A. The basket of summer fruit (8:1-3)
   B. An oracle of indictment (8:4-14)
II. The Finality of Israel's Doom (9:1-10)
   A. Vision of the Lord (9:1-4)
   B. A doxology (9:5-6)
   C. God's freedom (9:7-10)
III. A Promise of Restoration (9:11-15)

The Message of Amos 8–9

Over and over again Amos strained to have people understand the moral obligation that rests heavily on God's people. But just as frequently and with equal verve the people rejected the prophet's pleading. The prophet reaches deeply into history and creation in order to re-present a God capable of working through all history, not just Israel's history, and through all creation, not merely in the creative acts for Israel. Amos discerns a freedom that startles us with its implications.

What can we learn about the nature and character of God from these chapters?

- God's judgments may be closer than people think.

- The prophetic urgency for repentance is ridiculed only at individual and national peril.

- God is the God of all history, not just for Israel or any other nation that desires to see itself as chosen.

- Our words and acts of pride may come back to haunt us.

- Worship is of little value if we are preoccupied with how we can pervert justice and amass more fortune.

- When God wreaks judgment no one can escape the presence of God.

- God's sovereignty is absolute; God cannot be obligated by anything that individuals or nations do or say.

- Ultimately God yearns to bless individuals and nations.

- Even the most evil of nations may be included in the ultimate grace of God.

OBADIAH

OUTLINE OF OBADIAH

INTRODUCTION

The prophecy of Obadiah consists of merely twenty-one verses, making it the shortest book in the Old Testament. The work focuses on the historic enemy Edom, and its reprehensible attitude and behavior during the final collapse of Jerusalem.

The name *Obadiah* means *servant of the Lord*. The name is not unique, in that another twelve individuals share it in the Old Testament (see, for instance, 1 Kings 18:3; 1 Chronicles 3:21; Ezra 8:9; Nehemiah 10:5). Other than Obadiah's name we know nothing specific about him. Unlike other prophets, he lists no dates of his work, no family identity, no occupation, and no home territory.

What can we deduce from Obadiah's work? He speaks of the dreadful events that occurred when Jerusalem finally fell to the Babylonians in 587 B.C. and he seethes with anger at Edom's participation in that disaster. Obadiah makes many references to other prophetic works, especially Jeremiah 49:7-22. One possibility is that the work is in part a collection of material assembled from various extant prophetic works that Obadiah re-presented and reinterpreted to his people. Since the work does focus on a single theme of God's justice and judgment, scholars hold that it is the work of one writer who uses other material. While we cannot date Obadiah to a particular year, it appears to have been written while the people languished in exile.

The prophet's attitude parallels that of another exile, who wrote Psalm 137. The last three verses of Psalm 137 are rarely read in Christian worship services. The soul-deep anger, the graphic expression of hate, a yearned-for day when an enemy will have to pay for what was done to innocent people are simply too strong for most of us. But shallow piety and sentimentality were not an option for the pained exiles. The memories ran too deep. We have a record of how deeply the people of God yearned for a day of vindication. The Bible does not blink or flinch at even the harshest of human realities.

The Edomites were descendants of Esau (see Genesis 25:30; 36:1). Like their ancestor, they had little regard for spiritual values. They are never referred to for their gods. They seem to have been a nation with little or no conscience or ideals. Certainly their reprehensible behavior upon the collapse of their neighbor gives stark evidence of a dearth of human decency. In effect, the Edomites displayed an opposite temper from that of the people of Israel, just as Esau had displayed callous shallowness when he sold his birthright for a meal of pottage (see Genesis 25:29-34).

Whatever virtue the Edomites had stemmed from their commercial interests. The nation found itself located at the intersection of many trade routes. From this interest the Edomites developed a shrewd business sense and a wisdom about worldly things (verse 8). Jeremiah also refers to this peculiar wisdom: "Is there no longer wisdom in Teman? Has counsel perished from the prudent? Has their wisdom vanished?" (Jeremiah 49:7).

Topographically Edom found itself in the relatively secure mountainous (and therefore inaccessible) region to the southeast of the Dead Sea. Thus the Edomites enjoyed a relatively secure existence without the international disruptions endured by their northern neighbors. However, the shadow side of this relative calm is that Edom developed an attitude of callous disregard for others as well as a self-sufficiency that rejected the notion of God's protection and providence.

The Message of Obadiah

Since the book concentrates on the long-hated Edomites' doom, why is it included in the Bible? It seems to have small spiritual insight or message. It speaks not a word about sin, mercy, or righteousness. Like the author of Psalm 137, Obadiah believed passionately in the higher values and aspirations of life and of the nation. He had seen all that he held highest and dearest thoroughly demolished, while a hated enemy only scoffed and then participated in the looting and killing. Obadiah's blood boiled, remembering the taunts of the conquerors. But then the scoffing words would not be the last words.

The higher values of life are God's, and they cannot be destroyed. Not only will God have the last word against Edom, but God will have the last word in the lives of all nations. On Obadiah's experience, or one very much like it, another psalmist reflected, "Those who go out weeping, bearing the seed for sowing, shall come home with shouts of joy" (Psalm 126:6).

Obadiah spoke to a defeated and demoralized nation. The arrogant strength of Edom had engulfed the people of God. Are arrogant nations more powerful than God? Obadiah's response is, No! What else can we learn from the prophet Obadiah?

- When God acts, no defense is sufficient.

- Even when God is silent, still God continues to work.

- Pride goes before a fall.

- Eventually and inevitably God will secure victory for the divine purposes in history.

- In God's sight, it is criminal to rejoice over someone else's catastrophe.

- No nation can long endure if it intends to limit God's love or limit its own moral obligations.

JONAH

OUTLINE OF JONAH

I. The Great Refusal (1:1-3)

II. Jonah Punished (1:4-16)

III. Jonah Rescued (1:17–2:10)

IV. The Great Mission (3:1–4:11)
  A. Jonah's obedience (3:1-4)
  B. Nineveh's repentance (3:5-9)
  C. Jonah's rebuke (3:10–4:11)

INTRODUCTION

The book of Jonah is unique. No other book contains such remarkable circumstances, miraculous rescues, human traits, peculiar reversals, or surprises. Because the book is unique, and because it contains what is one of the most quickly recognized stories in the Old Testament, it evokes more discussion and argument than many other books.

In contrast to other prophetic works that are collections of oracles, Jonah contains only one oracle (3:4). With one exception, Amos, all the other prophets pronounce their oracles in the hearing of their own people, in their home territory. Jonah must travel to the heart of the nation to which this oracle is proclaimed.

In Israel's tradition, many of those called to prophesy hesitated and argued with God about the task. Recall Moses arguing that he could not speak well (Exodus 4:10). Elijah, too, resisted God's

summons to further work, citing his lack of support (1 Kings 19:14-18). Jeremiah argued that he was too young to do such work (Jeremiah 1:6). But in each of these instances, the prophet finally succumbed to the will of God.

In Jonah's story, the reluctant prophet does a good deal more than resist with an argument. Jonah actually denies God's claim on him and attempts to flee from God's presence. Indeed, the entire first half of the story is of Jonah's refusal.

The name Jonah does occur in earlier tradition. Second Kings 14:25 lists the name as that of a prophet, the son of Amittai of the region of Gath-hepher. A careful reading of the episode in Kings exhibits the prophet's concern for the expansion of national boundaries, with no further concern for God's will for the king, the social order, or the nation's behavior. He gives evidence of the same attitude of which this prophet Jonah is guilty.

The Nature of the Book

The story itself overflows with peculiar and spectacular phenomena. Had the writer been concerned primarily with a historically reliable series of events, the story would take on a different character. As it is, the story is replete with storytelling devices. It includes elements of various types of ancient literature— folktale, allegory, parable, satire—but the book defies easy categorization. In any case, the book of Jonah is one of the Bible's literary gems, with highly skillful presentation of structure, characters, plot, and style.

Historical Circumstances

Determining the date of the book's composition is very difficult, probably impossible. It could easily have been composed at any time. Another book in the Old Testament, the book of Ruth, shares a similar ambiguity with regard to its date.

The Purpose of the Book

In the mind of the author and his audience, an all-powerful and sovereign God seemed terribly slow to punish the heathen for what they had done to God's chosen nation. Jonah's fear that the heathen might be spared represents a generally held apprehension. Through sensitive and human representation of these foreigners, Jonah forces his listeners to reconsider God's sovereignty. Against a popularly held prejudice that relished the notion of God's punishment of enemies, Jonah lifts up the truth of God's compassion. God's care and compassion are equal to God's wrath and judgment.

In this work Jonah presents the possibility of repentance. The important question is not whether Nineveh could or would repent, but whether or not Israel could or would repent from a narrow, nationalistic view of God.

JONAH 1:1-16

Introduction to This Passage

The book of Jonah begins by introducing the story and setting the scene for the rest of the narrative.

Chapter 1 has two parts.
 I. The Great Refusal (1:1-3)
 II. Jonah Punished (1:4-16)

The Message of Jonah 1:1-16

The remarkable parable of the reluctant prophet reveals God, who intends to accomplish a dual purpose. First, the prophet will learn that he must obey the command of God. Second, the audience will learn through Jonah's experience that God's intention transcends their limited vision of God's sovereignty. The story begins with the word of God. God's word and work are always a moral work. Even a person who attempts to avoid God can be used by God to achieve God's purposes. What can we learn about ourselves and God through this chapter?

- The command of God may threaten our preconceptions and our wishes.

- The path of self-will is always away from God and toward our own destruction.

- Any attempt to flee from either the call of God or the presence of God is futile.

- God will use any means necessary to reveal the divine purposes.

- In every human spirit there is a yearning to know God.

- Sometimes it takes a storm in order to stir the deepest yearnings for God.

- Confession of our identity and our highest calling reveals our basic sinfulness.

- God does not turn from us when we turn from God.

- People do not necessarily have to know God in order to have God know and care for them.

JONAH 1:17–4:11

Introduction to These Chapters

Whenever Israel looked out to the west and saw the Mediterranean Sea, images of monsters were conjured up. The Hebrews were never a seagoing people. The sea therefore represented a great life-threatening force. The writer could hardly have shown Jonah in a worse plight than to be cast overboard in the midst of a raging storm. Perhaps the more imaginative listeners could discern in the story Israel's own story.

As the story of Jonah continues in the following verses, the author utters a prayer in which almost every line echoes a line in the book of Psalms.

Jonah 1:17–4:11 may be outlined as follows.

   I. Jonah Rescued (1:17–2:10)
  II. The Great Mission (3:1–4:11)
      A. Jonah's obedience (3:1-4)
      B. Nineveh's repentance (3:5-9)
      C. Jonah's rebuke (3:10–4:11)

The Message of Jonah 1:17–4:11

Through a parable the author has brought a new insight to a reluctant people.

God's concern and compassion are for all the creation. What else can we learn from this story?

- We can limit God's love and will through our own disobedience.

- When God calls an individual to a specific task, that task cannot be taken lightly.

- The protection and grace we receive in life are gifts and graces from God.

- God respects true repentance, no matter who it comes from.

- God does not want to be known as a small God with limited perspectives and limited concern for persons.

- God wants us to love all creation as God loves all creation.

- We learn of God's revelation through our own experiences and through the character of God.

- Sometimes God's love haunts us as much as it blesses us.

- In the face of life's storms, both believer and pagan are equally in need of God's mercy.

MICAH

OUTLINE OF MICAH

INTRODUCTION

Micah's prophetic ministry came at a time when the states of Israel and Judah were confronted with overwhelming foreign military powers. Internally, Israel was in chaos with betrayal and murder the order of the day within the ruling families. Economic and social injustices were the norm, and pagan worship was tolerated and openly practiced. Micah saw the destruction of Israel and foresaw the destruction of Judah. He gave reasons for these events and linked the present, past, and future of Israel and Judah with God's will and power.

In the midst of destruction and uncertainty, Micah focused on the need for divinely ordained justice and true worship in the lives of God's people. He also proclaimed that a time would come when all would be made right by God. Such a time will come because God's ultimate will is not for destruction but for restoration and relationship with all peoples.

Micah the Man

Micah was from the village of Moresheth (perhaps the same as Moresheth-gath) in the Shephelah region of Judah. The Shephelah is a region of broad valleys and rolling hills that runs from north to south between the coastal plain and the central highlands of Judah. In biblical times it was heavily forested and was also under cultivation. Groves of olives and sycamore figs as well as vineyards were tended here. The chalky hills on the western side of the central valley also provided raw materials for the pottery industry.

The Shephelah is crossed by many valleys running both north-south and east-west. These valleys were well-traveled military and trade routes from the coast into the hill country and from Jerusalem and Samaria into southern Judah. Since Moresheth is on the western edge of the central north-south valley, Micah could observe the comings and goings of travelers (and of invading armies) and hear news of what was happening in Jerusalem and in Israel.

Micah may have been a farmer or a tradesman before his call to prophesy took him to Jerusalem. He identified with and felt a sympathy for the common people of Judah. The rulers of Judah come under sharp attack in his prophecies because they were mistreating the people.

Tekoa, the hometown of the prophet Amos, was not far from Moresheth, and Micah may have heard of the prophecies of Amos in Israel. Micah may also have been in Jerusalem at times and heard the preaching of Isaiah. His calls for justice within Israelite society echo the concern for justice expressed by Amos. His preaching, like that of Isaiah, influenced King Hezekiah of Judah.

Micah may have returned to his home and resumed his life there once his prophetic duties were completed. He was not connected to the priesthood or the royalty, and he had no official standing in the community in Jerusalem which he was called to address. He was apparently a man of humble origins with a gift for eloquent

---

THE FORM OF PROPHETIC ORACLES

Old Testament prophetic speeches are called oracles. Oracles are the revealed word of God. The prophet serves as God's messenger, reporting the word to the people. Prophets used different forms of speech in reporting God's word. These forms include hymns, laments, allegories, and announcements of judgment or of salvation.

In general, oracles that are announcements of judgment have three parts: (1) an introduction or call to attention; (2) a description of sins; and (3) a proclamation of punishment. (Not all oracles of judgment have these parts, and some have the parts in different order.)

Micah 3:9-12 is an example of such an oracle:

(1) call to attention: "Hear this, you leaders . . . and rulers" (verse 9a NIV; NRSV, "rulers . . . and chiefs");

(2) description of sins: "who abhor justice" (verses 9b-11 NRSV) or "who despise justice" (NIV);

(3) proclamation of punishment: "Therefore . . ." (verse 12).

Judgment is announced because of specific failures on the part of the people. Listing these failures shows that God's judgment is rational and just.

Announcements of hope are similar in form to announcements of judgment, though the reasons for God's actions are not always given. (See, for example, Micah 2:12-13.)

The phrase "Thus says the LORD" (NRSV; NIV, "This is what the LORD says") appears often in prophetic oracles. This phrase testifies to the authority of the prophet's words.

---

speech and a willingness to respond to God's call.

Micah the Book

The book of Micah is a collection of prophecies organized around the themes of punishment and hope. Micah's prophecies were first spoken, then written. He perhaps had followers who copied his words onto scrolls. This material was then organized and recopied and an introduction was added. The book went through many copies and possible revisions before it came to its present form. As a result, some of Micah's prophecies may have been lost or left out.

Micah himself may have written down some of his prophecies. The ability to read was apparently common in ancient Israel, and during the Assyrian period writing also became a common skill. So, although Micah was a farmer or tradesman rather than a scribe or priest, he still could probably read and write.

The book of Micah contains two major sections (chapters 1–5 and 6–7) which are each divided into prophecies of punishment (chapters 1–3 and 6:1–7:6) and prophecies of hope (chapters 4–5 and 7:7-20). None of the prophecies are dated, apart from the general dates given in 1:1.

MICAH 1–3

Introduction to These Chapters

Micah 1–5 has two sections: chapters 1–3, containing mostly prophecies of punishment, and chapters 4–5, containing prophecies of hope. These prophecies focus on the leadership of the people of Israel, first to condemn the present leaders and then to look forward to a future time when righteous leaders will rule.

Here is an outline of chapters 1–3.
I. Introduction (1:1)
II. Transgression Will End in Exile (1:2-16)
  A. Oracle against Samaria and Jerusalem (1:2-7)
  B. A lament for Judah (1:8-16)
III. The Fate of the Wicked (2:1-11)
  A. Woe to the wicked (2:1-5)
  B. Oracle against false prophets (2:6-11)
IV. An Oracle of Hope (2:12-13)

V. Against Rulers, Priests, and Prophets (3:1-12)
  A. Against those who practice evil (3:1-4)
  B. Against false prophets (3:5-8)
  C. Oracle against false confidence (3:9-12)

The Message of Micah 1–3

Micah's oracles of judgment against the people of Israel are declarations of God's punishment for sin. The basis for such declarations by Micah and by other Old Testament prophets is found in the nature of sin itself. What does Micah tell us about the nature of sin?

• In broad terms, sin is alienation from God. Sins of any kind are, first of all, sins against God.

• The Old Testament understanding of ritual, moral, and spiritual sin rests on the recognition of God's own moral being.

• Through what is sinful in relation to the will and being of God, we understand what is sinful in relation to one another.

• Because of this, our sins against one another affect our relationship to God.

• According to the Old Testament prophets, the standard of moral good is God's revealed will.

• Sins against this standard are a violation of the covenant relationship that has been established between God and God's people.

• Micah singles out the sins of community leaders—priests, prophets, kings, and other leaders— for special condemnation. He makes it clear that privilege and power come with the responsibility for maintaining justice and righteousness within the community. The failure of leaders to do this brings disaster on everyone.

MICAH 4–7

Introduction to These Chapters

Chapters 4 and 5 contain prophecies of salvation that are the counterpart to the prophecies of judgment in chapters 1–3. Chapter 6 again picks up the theme of judgment. Then, in chapter 7, the book is concluded with affirmations of hope for the future.

Here is an outline of Micah 4–7.

I. God's Judgment Will Lead to Redemption (4:1–5:15)
  A. The splendor of Zion (4:1-5)
  B. A remnant shall be saved (4:6-8)
  C. Pain and exile come before redemption (4:9-13)
  D. Israel's deliverance from Assyria (5:1-6)
  E. Israel will be scattered but not defeated (5:7-9)
  F. God's wrath against idolatry (5:10-15)
II. Announcements of Judgment and Hope (6:1–7:20)
  A. The controversy of the Lord (6:1-5)
  B. What is good before the Lord? (6:6-8)
  C. Oracle against Jerusalem (6:9-16)
  D. A song of woe (7:1-7)
  E. Confessions of faith, prophecies of hope (7:8-20)

WHAT IS GOOD BEFORE THE LORD? (MICAH 6:6-8)

Micah voices questions that the people might ask about how they are to be obedient to God. The questions focus on the sacrificial ritual that was part of Israel's worship. Often the people would go to the priests in the Temple and question them about the appropriate sacrifices for a particular occasion.

Micah takes the questions about the sacrificial system to the extreme of child sacrifice, a practice that was strictly forbidden in Israel. Presenting such an extreme case highlights the answer given in verse 8. Micah asks Israel to remember (as in verse 5) that God "has showed you" (NIV) or "has told you" (NRSV) what is required to live a righteous life. The people cannot plead ignorance of God's will as a defense for their wickedness.

The upholding of justice includes keeping all of the law, which is the basis for life within the community of faith.

"Kindness" (NRSV) or "mercy" (NIV) is loving-kindness or steadfast love. This is not just a feeling but also an attitude and a way of life. God is loving, merciful, and kind, so God's people must be this way toward one another. The relationship that God has with people defines the relationship that people are to have with one another.

"To walk humbly with your God" means to live in communion with God and to do God's will. Human beings must know their proper place in relation to God and live accordingly.

Notice that the questions in verses 6-7 have more to do with the form of faith than with its substance. Ritual is important, and this oracle does not claim to do away with ritual. Rather, Micah says that a person's inward and outward life both must be in order. Ritual cannot take the place of right relationships with God and with others (compare this to Amos 5:21-24).

The Message of Micah 4–7

The prophecies of Micah are filled with contrast. He offers both words of condemnation and words of healing. His messages tell us that God's people must suffer the consequences of sin, and that these consequences can be terrible. Suffering is not the last word, however. God's last word through Micah is one of restoration and hope. The people of God must now live in the tension between their failure and God's promise, ever diligent to know God's way and to walk in it.

What do Micah's prophecies of punishment tell us about Israel's failures?

- The people of Israel and Judah are guilty of crimes against God and against one another.

- The covenant and God's saving acts on Israel's behalf are the standard against which the people are judged.

- God has been faithful to the covenant but Israel has not.

- The law governs how Israel is to live out her covenant responsibilities, and all life is to be ordered by God's law.

- Because the people of Israel have failed in their covenant responsibilities, God will confront them as divine judge and punisher.

- The people of Israel are plagued by their enemies because of their sin.

What do Micah's prophecies of hope tell us about the future of Israel?

- Israel can find hope for the future by looking to her past relationship with God.

- The covenant relationship is both the basis for Israel's punishment and the ground of her hope.

- Israel will be given another chance to walk with God.

- Confession of sin and patient endurance of its consequences are required on the way to new life.

- Israel may look for a future anointed one from God who will lead her into a new age of security and righteousness.

What do Micah's prophecies tell us about what God is like?

- God's nature and will are revealed through the words and actions of the prophet.

- God's nature and will are also revealed in God's past words and actions.

- God intervenes in human history to accomplish the divine will.

- God wants to be in relationship with all peoples. All peoples will one day come to worship and learn of God.

- God's will is for a loving and redeeming relationship with people.

In conclusion, Micah's prophecies tell us that the people of God must, for now, live in the tension between their failure and God's promise. They must be ever diligent to know God's way and to walk in it.

NAHUM

OUTLINE OF NAHUM

INTRODUCTION

The ministry of the prophet Nahum came at a time when Judah had hopes of gaining her independence from her Assyrian overlords. Nahum foresaw Assyria's ruin, and his prophecies celebrate the destruction of the Assyrian capital city of Nineveh.

Nahum had other reasons as well to be confident of Judah's future. King Josiah had begun a series of religious reforms in 621 B.C. which were designed to rid Judah of the influence of foreign cults and bring Israelite life more firmly under the rule of God's law. Thus, Nahum spoke to the people of Jerusalem when forces for positive change were at work for the people of Israel.

Nahum the Man

The record of Nahum's prophecies contains little personal information about him. He is said to have received a vision, that is, the word of God received through revelation and inspiration. This vision was an oracle. The Hebrew word used here for "oracle" literally means a *burden*. Nahum received this oracle about Nineveh which he then announced to the people of Israel.

An oracle is the revealed word of God, and the term *burden* is also used by other prophets to refer to a word concerning punishment and disaster (see Jeremiah 23:33-40). This meaning may come from the belief that the message of a prophet is a burden placed by God on the prophet. The prophet is then to place the burden of God's condemnation on the nation or individual receiving the message.

Nahum probably delivered his prophecies in Jerusalem, perhaps even in the Temple itself. Since all of the prophecies recorded in the book which bears his name concern the fall of Nineveh, he was probably active in his prophetic ministry shortly before 612 B.C. He was called from his home in the countryside to come to the capital city of Jerusalem to speak words of disaster for Nineveh, which were words of hope for Israel.

The Message of Nahum

Nahum briefly touches on Judah's sin that brought Assyria to her door (Nahum 1:12). This sin is dealt with more fully by other prophets, such as Micah and

Jeremiah. Still, the people of Israel must have felt that their sin had been atoned for and that it was time for God to punish their afflictor. On what basis could they have held such a belief and still have received Nahum's prophecies?

- The Assyrians were cruel tyrants.

- Assyria was a source of religious corruption.

- Israel's experience with God had shown that no one may live outside of the power of God.

- God is Lord of the earth and deals with sin wherever it is found.

- God's might is greater than that of the mightiest of human kingdoms.

- Those who commit crimes against other people become God's enemies.

- God is just and is a source of salvation to those who know God and take refuge in God.

- We must realize the suffering that captive peoples experience and ask ourselves how we would feel about our enemies had we been through the same thing.

- We must remember that Nahum's celebration of vengeance is based on the beliefs (which we share) that God is righteous and just and that God will maintain righteousness and justice within human history. God's victory over Assyria was seen as a victory over evil in which God and Israel were vindicated before the world.

- We must take Scripture within the context of all Scripture and not isolate any one message or viewpoint from the whole. For example, the book of Jonah testifies that repentance and forgiveness were also within God's will for Nineveh. Other prophets tell of a time when all nations will live in peace (see, for example, Micah 4:1-4; Isaiah 2:1-4).

HABAKKUK

OUTLINE OF HABAKKUK

I. Introduction to Habakkuk (1:1)

II. A Cry for Help and God's Answer (1:2–2:5)
A. How long? and why? (1:2-11)
B. The righteous shall live by faith (1.12–2.5)

III. Oracles of Woe Concerning the Wicked (2:6-20)

IV. A Prayer of Habakkuk (3:1-19)

INTRODUCTION

The prophet Habakkuk lived during the last quarter of the seventh century B.C. in Judah. His prophecies focus on how God, the righteous, and the wicked relate to one another. He concludes that God is just and all-powerful; therefore, the righteous may look forward to divine vindication and the wicked to divine punishment.

Habakkuk the Man
The book of Habakkuk's prophecies gives no personal information about him. The dates and circumstances of his prophetic ministry must be determined from references within the book. The prophet Habakkuk probably delivered his prophecies around 609–597 B.C. The wicked whom the prophet Habakkuk condemns are probably the Babylonians.

Habakkuk the Book
The book of Habakkuk is a collection of different types of prophetic messages. Habakkuk 1:2–2:5 reports a dialogue between the prophet and God concerning divine justice. Verses 2:6-20 are a collection of announcements of woe against the wicked. Chapter 3 is a hymn of praise and confession of faith in God.

Habakkuk may have spoken his prophecies in the Temple in Jerusalem, perhaps even during worship services in the Temple. His prophecies (in particular the hymn in chapter 3) were probably used many times as part of the worship ritual.

The Message of Habakkuk
Habakkuk's questions to God concerning justice, his oracles of woe against the wicked, and his hymn of praise are all based on the reality of Israel's covenant relationship with God and on the requirement for Israel to live life under the law. The covenant and the law are the foundation upon which rests all of prophetic teaching.

Given this foundation, what does Habakkuk say that the community of faith may expect from God?

- God's people may find answers to their present situation based on past experience and knowledge of God plus new revelation.

- The community of faith may have confidence in God even in the midst of conflict.

- God is the ultimate source of security for all people.

- God's justice will be confirmed and upheld (as in the past) even though the material evidence of this may not yet be seen.

- God will reckon with sin.

- The object of God's wrath is the sinner (either within the community or in other nations) in rebellion against the Creator.

- God is the Lord and master of history.

ZEPHANIAH

OUTLINE OF ZEPHANIAH

INTRODUCTION

Zephaniah's prophetic ministry came during the reign of King Josiah of Judah (640–609 B.C.). Josiah began a program of religious reform in 621 B.C. in connection with his efforts to get out from under the influence of Assyria and to rid Judah of foreign gods (see 2 Kings 22–23). The worship of foreign gods in Judah was a symbol of the power of other nations over Judah and was a violation of the covenant upon which Israel was founded. While repairs were being made in the Temple a book of the law was found and brought to the king. Josiah based much of his reform on this book, which is now part of the book of Deuteronomy. Pagan cults were prohibited and worship services were limited to the Temple in Jerusalem.

Josiah aimed to purify Israelite faith and stop the practice of combining worship of God with worship of foreign gods. The kings who came before Josiah, Manasseh (687–642 B.C.) and Amon (642–640 B.C.), had allowed pagan cults to openly flourish in Judah.

Zephaniah's prophecies probably came before the reforms of 621 B.C. His words may have encouraged Josiah in his reform efforts.

Zephaniah the Man

Zephaniah was a descendant of someone named Hezekiah, who may have been the King of Judah (715–687 B.C.). Zephaniah lived in Jerusalem and probably associated with the upper classes in the city, those with power and wealth. Despite these connections, however, Zephaniah condemned the powerful officials and merchants in Israelite society who abused their positions, and those who were indifferent to God. He declared that God would punish sinners, both in Israel and in foreign countries.

Beyond punishment, Zephaniah saw that God intended to renew the people of Israel and to draw them together as God's people once more.

Zephaniah the Book

Like other prophetic books, Zephaniah is a collection of prophetic messages that were spoken before they were written.

Verses 1:2–2:3 are a prophetic message of doom that focuses on Judah and Jerusalem. Zephaniah 2:4-15 is a collection of oracles against foreign nations. Zephaniah 3:1-13 tells of the sins and coming punishment of Jerusalem. The conclusion, Zephaniah 3:14-20, is an announcement of salvation for the people of Israel.

The Message of Zephaniah

Like the other prophets, Zephaniah's words rest on the foundation of Israel's covenant relationship with God. He declares that Israel has failed to live up to these responsibilities and has forgotten the lessons of history. Zephaniah's prophecies accuse, instruct, remind, and warn the people of Israel.

What does Zephaniah tell God's people?

- Magic, superstition, and idolatry have no place among the people of God.

- No one may ignore God's instruction.

- Crimes which people commit against one another are crimes against God.

- God is the Lord of history, of all nations.

- The Day of the Lord is one of darkness and destruction that is brought on by sin.

- Beyond the time of punishment, God's intentions are for salvation and restoration of the community of faith.

- The key to a righteous life is humility and obedience, calling on the Lord.

- There is time and opportunity for repentance, to seek righteousness and humility before the terrible day.

- Zephaniah's prophecies tell people in the community of faith that their choices are clear: They may live with God or die apart from God.

PROPHETS OF THE
PERSIAN PERIOD

INTRODUCTION

After the Exile a bedraggled remnant of the Jewish people returned to Jerusalem. King Cyrus of the Persian Empire had set them free following his defeat of Judah's Babylonian captors. When the exiles returned home, a sad sight met the people's gaze.

They found a country that had suffered the effects of over fifty years of neglect. Where the great Jerusalem wall had stood, nothing was left but scattered stones. The beautiful Temple that Solomon had built was a heap of charred ruins. All the fine homes had been destroyed. The Babylonians had left only a few poor homes to house people whom they considered to be of no use to them as exiles.

Two men were the leaders of those returning from the Exile. They were Zerubbabel, whom the Persian king Darius appointed governor of the exiles, and Joshua, the high priest. When the people returned, they scattered about the countryside looking for good farmland and for places where they could build their homes. At first the returning Jews also had some zeal regarding the need to rebuild the fallen Temple. However, although they began the reconstruction work on the Temple in earnest, the work eventually slowed to a halt. Many people became more concerned about building fine homes for themselves than about rebuilding the Temple.

The result of the exiles' deliverance from Babylonia was not immediate prosperity, however. Instead, they found that conditions for agriculture in their homeland were bleak. The prophet Joel, who was active during this period of time, proclaimed that the poor agricultural productivity brought on by a fierce locust plague was the result of the sins of the people.

Joel said that it would take more than hard work in the fields and reconstruction of destroyed buildings to restore the land. Repentance and a newfound religious zeal were necessary in order to bring Jerusalem back to its former glory.

Because the poor agricultural conditions required an exhausting amount of energy to improve, the people discovered that they lacked the needed will to restore the Temple. They said that "the time has not yet come to rebuild the LORD's house" (Haggai 1:2). The people had lost sight of God's purpose for them in returning them to Jerusalem.

The prophet Haggai had returned with the exiles from Babylonia. According to Ezra 5:1-2, Haggai and a second prophet, Zechariah, actually inspired the rebuilding of the Temple. These men, like Joel, told the people that their lack of prosperity was the result of neglecting to put God's purposes first. In short order, after the encouragement of Haggai and Zechariah, the Temple was indeed rebuilt.

Another prophet, Malachi, was active in ministry around 450 B.C., a generation after the Temple was rebuilt. The living conditions in Palestine had not become as good as the people had hoped. Consequently, the Jews, who saw themselves as favored by God above all the nations, became discouraged by their weakness. They became lethargic, especially because of their colonial position in the Persian Empire. Many people decided to wait passively for the coming of God's messiah who would free them from all their problems.

Malachi assured the people that the messiah would come, but his coming would mean judgment on all those who were found to be unworthy. The Jews would not be exempt from God's judgment because of their bloodline.

After Malachi's prophetic ministry, Nehemiah led another group of exiles back to reestablish the nation. He also oversaw the rebuilding of the wall of Jerusalem. Later, Ezra returned to Palestine bringing the Law. (Some scholars believe Ezra came first. See the introduction to Ezra for details.)

Haggai and Zechariah

Haggai and Zechariah were contemporaries in Jerusalem. They were active in ministry during one of the lowest points in the history of the Jewish people. Sixty-six years earlier, in 587 B.C., the city of Jerusalem was defeated by the armies of Babylonia, The conquerors desecrated the Temple. and forced a large portion of the Jerusalem population to live in exile in the labor camps of Babylonia. Some of the people escaped the invaders by fleeing to foreign countries. Only a handful remained in the Promised Land, mainly those who were incapable of fleeing or of surviving the forced march to Babylonia. For the fifty years of the Exile, Palestine was little more than an abandoned wasteland.

Fifty years after the beginning of the Exile, the Persian Empire under Cyrus defeated the Babylonians in war. Cyrus then freed the exiles and allowed them to return to their homeland. Once home, some of the exiles set about the task of restoring the Temple. Their efforts were of little avail, however. Most of the people were hard-pressed to eke out a living in their new circumstances. Restoring the Temple, originally built by King Solomon, to its former glory was a task that seemed beyond their ability.

Haggai and Zechariah were prophets of God. They believed something had to be done about the Temple. They did not view poverty and despair as valid reasons to leave the once splendid structure in a state of ruin. The Temple was, after all, a symbol of God's presence among the people. If the Temple was in ruins, there was little hope of restoring national and religious pride. Haggai further proclaimed that material prosperity for the exiles would return if they restored the Temple and used it regularly as a place of worship.

When we read Haggai's prophetic book, we get a glimpse of how one can turn apathy into action. Zechariah's call for repentance, promises of restoration, and messages about the coming day of the Lord also touched the consciences of the people. The prophetic words of Haggai and Zechariah thus did much to spur the people to rebuild the Temple. Largely because of these prophets' energy and enthusiasm, the work of restoring the Temple was completed within four years.

During the time of Haggai and Zechariah, Zerubbabel, a Babylonian Jew, returned to Palestine to become the governor in postexilic Jerusalem at the command of the Persian king Darius I. The prophets Haggai and Zechariah, prompted by disturbances taking place within the Persian Empire, hoped that Judah would be restored to being a national power under Zerubbabel's rule. Being from the line of David, Zerubbabel represented the ideal for a postexilic king of Judah. Some people even hoped that Zerubbabel might be the long-awaited messiah from the line of David. However, a restoration of the kingdom of David did not occur; and the Persian Empire failed to replace Zerubbabel as governor of Judah with another man from the lineage of David.

Zechariah's public prophetic career began about a month before Haggai delivered his final utterances (Haggai 2:10-14, 20-23; Zechariah 1:1), so his prophetic career took place primarily after Haggai's activity as a prophet was over. While Haggai seems to have been more practical, Zechariah was more of a visionary, as is evidenced by his biblical writings. These two men are often overlooked when we study the Bible. This situation is quite ironic, for few people can claim to have revitalized a dispirited nation. Yet that is what these two prophets were able to do. Few people have found such a remarkable balance between faith and action.

JOEL

Joel's ministry seems to have taken place in Jerusalem shortly after the return of the exiles. After their return the exiles found that drought, pestilence, and years of neglect had produced bad agricultural conditions. The book of Joel graphically describes a locust plague that devastated the land. Joel called on the priests of the land to summon the people to fasting and prayer so that the plague might cease. The locust plague is seen as God's judgment on the people. According to Joel, repentance is the key to improving conditions in the land. Joel appealed to the people to repent

of their sin, including their failure to rebuild the Temple.

Little is known about Joel as a person, but his recorded oracles do reveal that he was not only a prophet of doom and gloom. Joel's prophecy includes an aspect of promise as well. Joel announces that beyond the judgment of God is the promise that God will restore "the years that the swarming locust has eaten" (Joel 2:25). God will pour out his spirit on young and old in that day (Joel 2:28-32), a promise remembered by Peter in his sermon immediately following the Pentecost experience (Acts 2:15-21).

MALACHI

Malachi's ministry took place after the Temple was rebuilt and worship was being conducted there on a regular basis. However, the chosen people of God were still a colonial people in the Persian Empire. Even though the Persian rule was relatively benign, it was not a happy time for the chosen people. They had hoped that once the Temple was rebuilt, they would return to their former glory. Yet those high hopes were dashed. Those who had expected Judah to become a new international power as a result of restoring the Temple were sadly disappointed. For several decades after the rebuilding of the Temple, no prophetic voice was heard calling the people back to the fundamentals of faith. It was in such a world that Malachi ministered.

In Malachi's day the Jewish people had some fundamental questions about their religion. Did God love Judah? Were they still God's chosen people? Was there really justice in God's world? Intermarriage with persons outside the faith was common in Malachi's day. With that practice came the risk of mixing the Jewish faith with pagan religious practices and idol worship. These were the kinds of issues that Malachi faced.

Malachi addressed those issues by speaking of the future and foretelling the coming of a messenger who would prepare the way for the coming of the messiah.

It is entirely possible that Malachi, whose name means "my messenger," saw himself as the messenger prophesied in Malachi 3:1-4. Malachi may have seen himself as the one who would help usher in God's day of judgment, a day when God would be like a refiner's fire or like a strong soap.

The prophet accused the people of dishonoring God by placing polluted food on the altar and by offering unworthy sacrifices, such as blind, lame, or sick animals (Malachi 1:8). The people were only going through the motions of their religion. It was clear that they found the whole process boring and wearisome. Malachi suggested that it would be better to close the doors of the Temple than for the people to go on halfheartedly in their religious practices.

The people responded to Malachi's concerns by saying that it was no use going to worship if doing so did not result in tangible benefits. In response to this complaint Malachi suggested that if the people would present a tenth of their income to God and stop robbing God of what was due him, then God would pour out on them a great blessing, and Judah would be a great nation once again (Malachi 3:10-12).

After the time of Malachi, Ezra, a priest and scribe, led a reformation of the Jewish people. Ezra strove to lead the penitent people into a better way of life. Above all else, Ezra was a teacher of the law. He sought to impress the people with the holiness of the law and the blessings to be gained through obedience to it.

Nehemiah served as the governor of Palestine under the Persian rule from 445 to 433 B.C. He organized the community to rebuild the Jerusalem wall. To many people rebuilding the wall seemed like an impossible task, suffering as it was from many decades of neglect. Other people were jealous that Nehemiah would be able to do what they were unable to accomplish. He squarely met his opposition and saw the Jerusalem wall rebuilt in the brief span of fifty-two days. Nehemiah went on to cooperate with Ezra in numerous reforms and especially in the public instruction in the law (Nehemiah 8:9).

The reforms of Ezra and Nehemiah, on which the survival of the Jewish faith was to depend, presupposed the foundational work of the prophet Malachi. Malachi, though termed a "minor prophet," had a major role in God's reformation work among the post exilic Jewish people.

HAGGAI

OUTLINE OF HAGGAI

INTRODUCTION

Historical Background

Haggai's prophetic ministry came in 520 B.C. when the people of Judah were struggling to recover from their long years of domination by Babylon. After Persia defeated Babylon in 539 B.C., King Cyrus of Persia gave permission for the exiles within his empire to return to their respective homelands. He restored the worship of the various sects in the empire, giving permission for the returning Jewish exiles to rebuild the Temple in Jerusalem.

In 538 B.C. some of the Jewish Babylonian exiles returned to Jerusalem, though many stayed behind and continued their lives in Babylon. The people who went back to Jerusalem found the city still in ruins from the siege of 587 B.C. The Temple had been used to some extent during the intervening years but it was basically in ruins, too.

This split between civil authority and religious authority was new for Israel. In the past, the "church" and state had been one under the ultimate authority of God. The king had led the people on God's behalf. Now political and military power were no longer associated with religious power because foreigners held the final civil authority.

In this situation it was especially important that the Temple and the religious structure be restored and maintained, because in this realm lay the preservation and future of the people of Israel.

Cyrus died in 529 B.C. and was succeeded by his son, Cambyses, who ruled until his death in 522 B.C. Darius I then took the Persian throne and faced restlessness and rebellion in his vast empire. This may have seemed to Haggai to be a sign that the end of foreign rule over Judah was at hand. During the Exile, the prophets Ezekiel and Second Isaiah had proclaimed that God would reestablish God's people in Judah and God's rule on the throne in Zion. With Zerubbabel, a descendant of David, already installed as governor, the time was right for Haggai to declare that God's house must be rebuilt in preparation for the coming of a new era.

Haggai the Man

The book of Haggai gives no personal information about him. He is simply called the prophet, one who is called. Jewish tradition states that he was known as a prophet in Babylon during the Exile, so he may have been among those returning to Judah in the years 538–520 B.C. Along with the prophet Zechariah, he became the major force in Jerusalem behind the restoration of the Temple. Serious reconstruction work was begun in 520 B.C. and the new Temple was completed in 515 B.C.

Haggai combined the concerns of prophet and priest. His prophecy brings together the method and inspiration of the prophet and the institutional concerns of the priest. Under the circumstances of his day, the Temple and the proper worship of God were the keys to renewal and regeneration for the Israelite people. The symbols and ritual of their faith had to be maintained as part of their identity as God's chosen people.

Haggai the Book

The record of Haggai's prophecies is a collection of addresses that are dated from the sixth to the ninth months of 520 B.C. The collection also contains information about the results of Haggai's oracles. Haggai himself or an editor/scribe collected and organized the prophet's words.

The book of Haggai is the shortest of the three prophetic books (Haggai, Zechariah, and Malachi) which come from after the Exile. The books of Ezra and Nehemiah also deal with this time in the history of Israel.

The Message of Haggai

Haggai's prophetic ministry came in a particular time and place, and he spoke to a specific need within the community of faith in Judah. His interests may seem narrow and limited, but God's word that came to him was designed to answer the pressing needs of the time. His emphasis on cause-and-effect, that is, "do the right thing and God will bless you," may seem to some readers today to be simplistic, too cut-and-dried.

This does not mean, however, that his prophecies have no wider application. It is true that Haggai does not express the broader concerns for peace, justice, and righteousness that other prophets do. Yet, Haggai's prophecies (indeed, all Scriptures) work within the context of other Scriptures with one perspective balancing and informing the other. (For example, we looked to Isaiah to help us understand the larger perspective of Haggai 2:20-23.)

What can we say then from Haggai's prophecies that would apply beyond the need of the time and place in which he spoke?

- Be obedient to God's word. God is faithful to the ancient promises to Israel. In return for God's steadfast love, the people of God must be faithful to the covenant relationship.

- This covenant relationship between God and Israel involves worship and ritual as well as righteousness and faith in daily life.

- Construction of the Temple has a meaning beyond its physical presence. In its construction the people turn away from their worries and concerns to express their love for and confidence in God.

- God's will, not comfort or prosperity, must be the first priority for people in the community of faith.

- Once these proper priorities are established, God, the master of creation, will see that the people's needs are met.

ZECHARIAH

OUTLINE OF ZECHARIAH

INTRODUCTION

The prophets Zechariah and Haggai were both leaders in reconstruction of the Temple in Jerusalem, which had been in ruins since 587 B.C. Zechariah's prophecies deal with the Temple and its ritual. They are based on the traditions which name Zion and Jerusalem as the places in which God has chosen to dwell in the midst of the people. Zechariah tells that the completion of the Temple will be part of a new age of salvation for the chosen people in God's kingdom.

Zechariah the Man
Though not all of Zechariah's family history is clear, he was probably, like Ezekiel, a prophet from a priestly family.

He was born in exile in Babylon and came to Jerusalem sometime between 538 and 520 B.C.

Zechariah's prophecies show the influence of both priestly and prophetic concerns in his life. As a member of a priestly family, Zechariah would have been taught the precepts of the law, particularly those relating to the priestly duties of sacrifice and ritual. He would have learned how to judge and give opinions in cases involving questions of religious or ritual procedure.

The law and memories of the Temple, its rituals of worship and sacrifice, were handed on to him through his family and the other priests and teachers in exile. The law and the Temple were probably an important part of his life even though he lived far from Jerusalem.

Zechariah may have also listened to the prophetic preaching of Ezekiel and Second Isaiah, who were among the Jewish exiles in Babylon. Some of the prophecies of Zechariah and of Ezekiel express a similar concern for the Temple, its rituals, and its maintenance.

Zechariah was also a visionary prophet who called his people to return to God in preparation for the coming of God's kingdom.

Zechariah the Book

The book of Zechariah is a collection of vision reports and prophetic oracles that may be divided into four sections: (1) Zechariah 1:1-6 is an introduction to the book. (2) Zechariah 1:7–6:15 is a series of eight vision reports. (3) Zechariah 7:1–8:23 is a collection of prophetic oracles concerning ethical living. (4) Zechariah 9:1–14:21 is a collection of oracles condemning other nations and proclaiming God's plans for and actions in history. This last section is believed by scholars to be from a time later than Zechariah's time, probably from the end of the fourth and beginning of the third centuries B.C. These later prophecies are from unknown prophets who could be called Zechariah's spiritual disciples. They elaborate on themes found in chapters 1–8 concerning the future of God's people and of the world. The record of Zechariah's prophecies from chapters 1–8 probably existed as an independent collection until the record of chapters 9–14 was added in the editorial process which brought the book to its final form.

Historical Background

The historical setting and circumstances for Zechariah's prophecy are the same as those of the prophet Haggai. Zechariah moved from Babylon into a discouraging situation in Jerusalem. The territory available to the Israelites had shrunk to an area around Jerusalem about twenty-five miles from north to south. The population was somewhere around 20,000, which was less than half of what it had been before 587 B.C.

Many exiles chose to stay in Babylon because, after three generations there, it was the only home they had known. Many of them were well established in business there as well. Those who did return faced many hardships. The city of Jerusalem was still in ruins. Farmers had endured a series of unsuccessful seasons which left many people destitute.

There was conflict among the people as well. Those who returned from exile saw themselves as the remnant of the true Israel in whom the hopes of the nation rested. Some of those who had stayed in Judah resented the newcomers and their claims to their ancestral land.

There was also conflict between the Israelites and the Samaritans, their neighbors in what had been the Northern Kingdom of Israel. The Samaritan aristocracy wanted to claim Judah as their territory. They may also have been among the group of people from the old territory of Israel whose offers to help with the rebuilding of the Temple were rejected by the leaders in Jerusalem (see Ezra 4:1-3). This rejection increased hostilities between the people in Judah and those in Israel.

There were also religious differences to settle. The returning exiles were ready to rebuild the Temple and claim the prophetic promises of restoration and renewal for God's people. The people who had stayed behind had, in many cases, either abandoned their faith in favor of pagan cults or had mixed worship of God with worship of idols.

In 538 B.C., the Persian king had promised the returnees help in rebuilding the Temple, but this aid never materialized. Indeed, as the years went on and the throne of Persia changed hands, the authorization given to rebuild the Temple was misplaced in the Persian archives. Added to this was the evidence that Persian power over Judah gave no sign of weakening. The people began to wonder about the reality of the promises of restoration. They became preoccupied with their struggles to survive in a hostile situation, and their concern with the Temple faded.

Into this discouraging situation the prophets Haggai and Zechariah stepped with their bold calls for the people of Israel to throw off their doubt and apathy and get to work doing God's will.

ZECHARIAH 1–8

Introduction to These Chapters

These first eight chapters in the book of Zechariah contain prophecies from the mouth of the prophet Zechariah. These prophecies are introduced in the first six verses.

Here is an outline of these chapters.

I. Introduction and Call for Repentance (1:1-6)
II. Zechariah's Eight Night Visions (1:7–6:15)
   A. Vision of divine horsemen (1:7-17)
   B. Vision of four horns and four smiths (1:18-21)
   C. Vision of the measure of Jerusalem (2:1-5)
   D. The return of the exiles (2:6-13)
   E. Vision of Joshua and Satan (3:1-10)
   F. Vision of the lampstand and olive trees (4:1-14)
   G. Vision of a flying scroll (5:1-4)
   H. Vision of a woman in an ephah (5:5-11)
   I. Vision of four chariots (6:1-8)
   J. Instructions concerning the Temple (6:9-15)
III. Announcements and Instructions (7:1–8:23)
   A. Oracle concerning fasting (7:1-7)
   B. God requires righteousness (7:8-14)
   C. Oracles of hope for Judah and Jerusalem (8:1-23)

The Message of Zechariah 1–8

After their exile in Babylon, the people of Israel had to cope with a change in their identity as a people. Their existence was still grounded in their covenant relationship with God; they were still the chosen people. The circumstances in which they lived out this identity had changed, however.

They no longer were a religious community with independent military and political power. After 500 years of living under a monarchy, they had no king.

Though the Persians were relatively lenient masters, the people of Israel were still under the control of foreigners. All they had left was part of their homeland and their relationship with God.

In this time of transition and strain, what did Zechariah tell the people of Israel?

- The people of Israel may have lost their military and political independence, but they have not lost their identity as God's people.

- Even under trying and destitute circumstances, they must maintain the responsibilities which are theirs as God's people.

- God has not abandoned the covenant relationship and they must not abandon it.

- The formalities of ritual and worship are not enough for a righteous life. The ethical and social standards of the covenant must be upheld as well.

- The people must rebuild the Temple.

- The Temple will be the focus of the new age of salvation to come. God's glory will be present in the Temple and with the people.

- With the Temple at the center of life, the people of Israel and of other nations as well will come to God and seek the presence of God.

- The people of Israel will be a source of revelation and blessing to the rest of the world.

- God is at work in history to bring in a new age of righteousness, security, and prosperity for all peoples.

We do not live under the same circumstances as did the people to whom these prophecies were originally addressed. Zechariah's prophecies, however, clearly do apply to how we live out our faith in our own age of uncertainty and strain. He calls the faithful of any age to confident and obedient service to God.

ZECHARIAH 9–14

Introduction to These Chapters

These chapters in the book of Zechariah probably come not from Zechariah himself but from later prophets, perhaps disciples of the prophet Zechariah himself. The style and point of view of these prophecies reflect a later age in Israel's history, though these chapters do continue the conviction expressed in Zechariah's prophecies that God is at work in history to bring about a universal reign of God.

These chapters cannot be dated with any certainty. Scholars have proposed dates ranging from the seventh to the second century B.C. Whatever the international dynamics were, Israel faced internal difficulties as well. Within the Jewish religious community, there were charges that the community leaders failed in their responsibilities to keep the faith alive and to maintain the welfare of the people.

The prophecies of Zechariah 9–14 reflect these civil and religious conflicts. Human history is seen in a more and more pessimistic light. These prophecies focus hopes for the future of God's people on God's actions in judgment and salvation, which will bring about a transformation of the world.

The prophecies of Zechariah 9–14 rest on the foundation of previous prophetic messages. The words of prophets such as Isaiah, Amos, and Hosea are reflected in these last chapters of Zechariah. They especially affirm the Old Testament traditions concerning God's choice of Jerusalem and Zion as God's dwelling among the people of Israel and of the benefits which flow from that choice.

These prophecies do not just give us new interpretations or reapplications of older prophecies, however. They give a more comprehensive and thorough view of the radical transformation of life which will come in the new age.

Zechariah 9–14 also gives a different view of the messiah who is to come. This messiah is in the royal line of David and is to have a universal dominion, but he will rule through humility rather than through force.

These final six chapters in the book of Zechariah contain prophecies from someone (or some group of persons) other than Zechariah the prophet. These prophecies are introduced by the beginning oracle in verses 1-8.

Here is an outline of these chapters.
I. The Restoration of Israel (9:1-8)
II. The Coming of the Future King (9:9-10)
III. The People Will Be Brought Home (9:11-17)
IV. God as Master of Nature and History (10:1-12)
V. Oracles of Judgment Against Rulers (11:1-17)
VI. Oracles on the Day of the Lord (12:1–14:21)
   A. Jerusalem redeemed and cleansed (12:1–13:6)
   B. The refining fire of judgment (13:7-9)
   C. Warfare and victory (14:1-21)
      1. The fate of Jerusalem (14:1-5)
      2. God will be king over all the earth (14:6-15)
      3. All peoples will worship God (14:16-21)

The Message of Zechariah 9–14

These prophecies come from a time of increasing emphasis on the law as the basis

and definition of the community of faith in Israel. Because they were no longer a political or military power, the identity of the people of Israel was bound up in their faith, and their lives were organized around the law.

There was also an increasing awareness of the need to maintain Israel's integrity as a distinct community. This at times led to exclusiveness and withdrawal from the non-Jewish world. However, the community was open to all peoples at the point of obedience to the law. Anyone who was faithful to the covenant and obedient to its laws could be part of the Israelite community of faith. There was a tension within the faith community between exclusivism and universalism.

The prophecies of Zechariah regarding the end times following the day of the Lord make clear that universalism—a unity of faith for all peoples—is the ultimate will of God. This proclamation was influential in New Testament thought and belief.

The prophecies of Zechariah 9–14 also affirm the New Testament beliefs that:

- God cares for those in the faith community.

- The king/messiah to come identifies with the condition of his people and embodies the truth of the new kingdom.

- God's people will face tribulation before the time of the final fulfillment of the new kingdom.

- The people of God will be spiritually renewed.

- All peoples will come to worship God and acknowledge God as Lord of the universe.

The prophecies of Zechariah gave the people of Israel guidance and hope through times of uncertainty, controversy, and crisis. These prophecies, which were the Scriptures of the New Testament church, helped those who knew Jesus and those who came after him more fully understand the meaning of Jesus' life, death, and resurrection.

As Christians we have the benefit of seeing the Old Testament prophecies in their original settings and also knowing the further application of these prophecies by those who wrote the New Testament. By taking into account both the Old and the New we may appropriate the messages of these prophecies for our own lives.

Both the Old and the New Testaments teach us that the present day, though troubled, may be lived in obedience, in confidence, and in faith. Such a faith holds a long-range view of reality, because not only the present day but all the days of the future are firmly in God's hands.

MALACHI

OUTLINE OF MALACHI

INTRODUCTION

The book of Malachi comes from a time when many Jews in Judah were disillusioned with their fate and lax in their faith. The abundant life which they had expected after the completion of the Second Temple in 515 B.C. had not come about. In the face of this disappointment, many of them, including priests, turned away from their religious and moral obligations. The prophecies of Malachi confront the people with their shortcomings and call on them to renew their commitment to God.

Historical Background

Malachi comes from the time between the completion of the Second Temple in 515 B.C. and the arrival of Nehemiah in Jerusalem in 445 B.C. Judah was still a province of Persia under the administration of a Persian governor (the Israelite governor, Zerubbabel, was no longer in power). Despite the high hopes which the returning exiles brought to Jerusalem from Babylon, even the rebuilding of the Temple did not guarantee harmony and prosperity in Judah. There were still many difficulties to be faced and overcome if the people of Israel were to survive as a distinct community.

Both Malachi and Nehemiah tell of the problems which threatened to tear the Jewish community apart and destroy it. Though the Temple ritual was maintained, there was a general feeling in the community that there was no real profit from practicing the faith, and, if there was no profit, why bother? People neglected the sabbath and instead made it a day for business. Businessmen cheated their employees and their customers. Jewish men divorced their Jewish wives to marry foreign women who had no loyalty to Jewish faith.

Economic conditions became so bad that some poor people had to sell themselves and their children into slavery to pay their debts and taxes. During the Exile, agricultural production in Judah had been greatly reduced. There were no large estates and much of the marginal lands went unused. The farms that remained in the highlands were small and not very productive. When the exiles returned to Judah repairs were begun on the agricultural terraces and other farming installations, but progress was slow and crops were poor.

Proper tithes were not paid to the Temple so that priests had to leave their positions in the Temple to earn a living elsewhere. Priests even offered improper sacrifices in the Temple and perverted the law in cases which were brought before them. With such corrupt leadership, public morality was breaking down.

Malachi the Man

Little is known about the prophet whose words are recorded in the book of Malachi. The Hebrew word Malachi means *my messenger*, and it probably is not the personal name of the prophet. Rather, the name of the book of Malachi may have been taken from Malachi 3:1, where "my messenger" is one who prepares the way for the coming of God. The prophet may have identified himself as such a messenger or those who recorded his prophecies may have identified him in this way.

Most Old Testament prophetic books give few details about the life or background of the prophets, and the book of Malachi gives less information than most. This is not surprising, however, because the main concern in prophetic books is not biography but the proclamation of God's word. What we know about Malachi as a person must come from his prophetic announcements.

Malachi was a man who believed that both morality and ritual were important in the life of God's people. He was able to grasp the depth and power of God's feelings for the people of Israel, from fierce anger and judgment to tenderest love

and care. He was a man of courage who accepted God's call to be a messenger. This call put him at odds with the leaders of his community, his neighbors, and perhaps even his friends. Though he must have faced hostility at times, he fulfilled his duties as God's messenger.

Malachi the Book

The central message of Malachi's prophecies is that the people of Israel must remain faithful to their covenant with God. This means that they must obey the requirements of the covenant that are given to Israel in the law. Only through obedience can they find life and peace.

Each major section of the book uses a series of questions and answers to get Malachi's message across to his listeners. This style of prophecy has been called a "prophetic dispute" in which questions are asked (either from God's, the prophet's, or the people's point of view) and then answered by the prophet (see also Isaiah 40:12-17; Micah 2:6-11; Haggai 1:4-6; 2:3-5 for other examples of this form).

These disputes put questions before the people so that they would think about their situation from God's perspective and see themselves in a new light.

The Message of Malachi 1–4

The prophecies of Malachi challenge the people of Israel to examine their lives and their beliefs in the revealing light of God's truth. Malachi declares that their actions and their beliefs must be in harmony. He makes clear that how the people of Israel live out their faith affects every part of their lives. They cannot survive as a divided house when they are constantly practicing evil and expecting good.

The prophecies of Malachi also grant the people the right to question God. They may doubt and question, but they also must be ready for an answer. Those who complain against God or mock God will get an answer whether they like the answer or not.

What kind of answers does Malachi give the community of faith?

- Actions reflect beliefs. A righteous life is one in which faith in God is expressed both internally and externally.

- People's relationships with one another affect their relationship with God. One has to be right for the other to be right.

- Proper ritual (such as sacrifice and tithing) must be maintained to keep the Temple going and to focus the people's loyalty on God.

- There is injustice in the world. God knows this and will deal with it.

- God is the Lord of history. The ultimate goal of history is the coming of God's kingdom.

- God comes to the people as judge and as redeemer. The possibilities for both blessing and curse are built into the covenant relationship, and God has not abandoned that relationship.

- The prophetic word comes to the people so that they might choose obedience and salvation over sin and destruction.

- The prophetic word calls for justice, righteousness, and faithfulness. In this word lies hope for the people of God.

BETWEEN THE TESTAMENTS

INTRODUCTION

The span of time between Ezra and the fall of Jerusalem is called the intertestamental period. For many Christians it is an obscure time. However, an understanding of both the events of history and the writings of the Jews during the period provides a background that enables us to understand Paul's expression, "But when the fullness of time had come, God sent his Son . . ." (Galatians 4:4).

Second Kings closes with the leading Judeans in exile in Babylonia. Their captive king, Jehoiachin, was released from prison and allowed to live in the court of the Babylonian king, Evil-merodach. The year was 561 B.C. Second Chronicles closes with a reference to the decree of Cyrus, king of Persia. Cyrus proclaimed that captive Judeans could return to Jerusalem if they wished. (See 2 Chronicles 36:23.) The year was 538 B.C. Cyrus had conquered the Babylonian Empire and reversed its policies toward captive peoples.

The prophetic words of Jeremiah, Isaiah, and Ezekiel, along with other writings that had been brought to Babylonia, had enabled those in exile to adjust their religion and their lives to their circumstances in Babylonia. But the people also believed that God would return them to Jerusalem. The book of Ezra records the return, but a majority of the people chose to remain in Babylonia. From the time of the Exile onward, Jews were scattered throughout the biblical world. They were called the Jews of the Diaspora. They supported their spiritual homeland both financially and prayerfully while living in foreign lands. Jerusalem, the Holy City, was the special focus of their interest.

The returnees were faced with strong opposition from neighboring peoples. Local nobles from Samaria and the Transjordan saw those who were returning as a threat to their control over the mixed population of the region. A natural antagonism arose between the religious returnees and the permanent inhabitants who were primarily interested in wresting a living from the rocky Judean hills. Despite the local opposition, the Temple in Jerusalem was rebuilt by 515 B.C. The prophets Haggai and Zechariah were active in this effort. The period from 515 B.C. to A.D. 70 is often called the Second Temple period.

The returning Jews did not have a Jewish king to rule over them. Instead, the high priest had the political responsibility. The Jerusalem community continued to be under the authority of the Persian king and his authorized agents. But devout Jews looked toward the time when a king appointed by God would rule them. He would be the Messiah, the anointed one, envisioned in their holy writings.

Nehemiah came with the authority of the Persian throne to rebuild the walls of the city. He also instituted needed social and religious reforms sometime between 445 and 425 B.C. The story of Esther is set in this same period of time. The last of the minor prophets, Malachi, was also active in this period. Before the close of the century, Ezra arrived in Jerusalem, perhaps in association with Nehemiah for a short time.

Ezra carried out religious reforms that purged Judaism of a number of tendencies that had crept in and threatened its survival. He outlawed mixed marriages, and he established the Law (Torah) as the supreme authority and guide for orthodox Jewish faith and practice. (See Ezra 9–10 and Nehemiah 8–10.) A Jewish tradition arose that prophetic inspiration stopped with Ezra and that all the books in our Old Testament had been written by that time. But as we shall see below, the expression of devout religious thought could not be completely halted.

THE HELLENISTIC ERA

Little is known about the Jerusalem Jewish community in the century between Ezra and the arrival of the conquering Greeks. Alexander the Great conquered Palestine in 333 B.C. and the remainder of the Persian empire shortly after that date. His conquest ushered in the Hellenistic era when Greek thought and culture became an influence on and then a threat to Judaism.

Alexander died in 323 B.C., a victim of drink and disease. Soon after his death a dynasty named the Ptolemies gained control of Egypt and Palestine. From 310 to 198 B.C., the Ptolemies permitted the Jews in Palestine considerable freedom. Many Jews lived in Egypt, for Alexander had encouraged them to settle in his new city, Alexandria. Many others migrated there later. Because they came to speak Greek as their usual language, they needed a Greek translation of the Hebrew Bible. This first translation of the Old Testament

was made about 250 B.C. It is called the Septuagint.

The Jews were attracted to other features of Greek life and culture. A tendency to adopt the Greek way of life developed even in Jerusalem. Even members of the ruling priestly families followed this lifestyle. The wealthier members of Jerusalem society were sympathetic to Hellenism, as the adoption of Greek culture is called. A division developed between the Hellenized Jews and those more devout and orthodox.

In 198 B.C., the Greek dynasty in Syria took control of Palestine from the Ptolemies. In 167 B.C., Antiochus IV Epiphanes moved to stamp out orthodox Judaism. His policies were supported by the Hellenized Jews. They included desecrating the Temple of the Lord by sacrificing a pig on the altar and dedicating the Temple to the worship of the Greek god Zeus.

As a result of these policies, pious people revolted against the Syrians. At first the Maccabean revolt was led by an old priest named Matthias; but soon it passed to his son, Judas. By 164 B.C., Judas had recaptured the Temple. It was cleansed and a re-dedication ceremony was observed. The Feast of Hanukkah dates back to this event.

The conflict between the Maccabees and the Hellenizing Jews with Syrian support continued until 160 B.C. By then the leader was another son of Matthias named Jonathan. He was strong enough to establish an independent kingdom, and he functioned as both high priest and king. He was followed by a series of kings known as the Hasmoneans, after the family name; but their kingship was not of the house of David and their priesthood was not of the house of Aaron. Because of this and other religious differences during the Hasmonean period, Judaism developed groups or sects such as the Sadducees, Pharisees, and Essenes. We meet most of these sects in the New Testament.

Due to a struggle for power within the Hasmonean family, Roman forces that had earlier gained control of Syria intervened. Under General Pompey they occupied Jerusalem in 63 B.C.

THE ROMAN ERA

Once Rome had acquired control of Palestine, it never relinquished its domination. The Romans recognized Herod the Great as king of Judea in 37 B.C. His position was dangerous, however, for there was political instability in Rome. By shifting his allegiance at the right time, Herod was able to survive until shortly after the birth of Jesus. Herod died in 4 B.C., and his kingdom was divided among three sons, with Archelaus ruling Judea. The incompetent Archelaus was removed by the Romans, and the area became a province led by a series of procurators. The Jews chafed under Roman rule, and from the time of Pontius Pilate (A.D. 26-36) political unrest threatened the stability of the province. The first Jewish revolt against the Romans broke out in A.D. 66.

The revolt resulted in incredible suffering and bloodshed for the Jews. Jerusalem and the Temple were destroyed by Titus in A.D. 70. A remnant of the Zealots took refuge on a rocky fortress known as Masada, near the Dead Sea. In A.D. 73, Masada fell and the revolt ended.

The (Jewish) Christians had fled from Jerusalem before the siege by the Romans. They took refuge in Pella, across the Jordan River; and in time they disappeared from the historical record. The church had already begun its expansionary movement into the Roman world before the revolt. As a result, it was becoming more and more a Gentile church.

The very existence of Palestinian Judaism was threatened by the defeat. The people of the Diaspora, who had always looked to Jerusalem for spiritual identity and direction, were also threatened. The Temple was gone and with it the cultic rituals. A continued Judaism required drastic modifications.

Only the Pharisees survived the revolt with sufficient strength to face the task. Rabbi Johanan ben Zakkai rose to the occasion. He established, with Roman permission, a community of scholars at Jamnia, near modern Joppa. These scholars began the task of restructuring Judaism for existence without a state and without a temple. The Law (Torah) and their traditions (Oral Law) became even more important, and prayer and the synagogue took the place of sacrifice and the Temple. But the destruction of Jerusalem was destined to lead to a widening gulf between the Jews and Christians, the synagogue and the church.

The rift between the two was well established by the close of the first century A.D. This point marks the close of the period between the testaments, for the New Testament was complete. The Revelation to John is believed to have been written by A.D. 95.

THE LITERATURE BETWEEN THE TESTAMENTS

A definite change of atmosphere comes between the Old and the New Testaments. For example, angels and demons are only rarely mentioned in the Old Testament, but they appear more frequently in the New Testament. The New Testament shows a greater interest in life after death, in individual prayer, in the last days, and in the nearness of God to individuals in the community of faith. The writings of the period between the testaments help us to close the gap between the two. The time from Ezra to Jesus was definitely not a silent period, as we shall see.

The works of Ezra and Nehemiah were the last Old Testament books written, and the tradition arose that the spirit of prophetic inspiration left Israel at that time. Since in this view no more revelation could be expected, there was nothing left to do but to interpret and apply the prophetic revelation that had already been received. A group of scribes who copied the sacred texts and sages who studied and interpreted them developed. They believed that their interpretations and expansions were just as inspired as the written word. The contributions of this group developed into what came to be called the Oral Law. The purpose of these interpretations was to enable the devout to keep the written law (Torah). By the time of Jesus, the process had made it possible for the Pharisees to "make void the word of God" by their traditions. (See Matthew 15:1-6.)

The suppression of the prophetic impulse that some of the devout felt, however, could not be complete. After Ezra, religious works were produced among the Jews. These include the Apocrypha, the Pseudepigrapha, the Dead Sea Scrolls, and to a lesser degree, the writings of Philo and Josephus.

THE APOCRYPHA

The Apocrypha is a collection of books that were a part of the first translation of the Hebrew Bible into Greek, known as the Septuagint. These books are not found in the Hebrew Bible. They did not meet the standards for acceptance as authoritative Scripture that the Jews held at the close of the intertestamental period. The Apocrypha continued to be kept in the Latin Vulgate. Since the Protestant Reformation in the sixteenth century, they have not been in Protestant Bibles. The Apocrypha can still be found in the Old Testament section of Roman Catholic Bibles.

The Apocrypha includes some additions to biblical books, such as Susanna, the Prayer of Azariah and the Song of the Three Jews, and Bel and the Dragon. These stories illustrate the wisdom of Daniel. There is also an addition to Esther. The addition consists of pious expressions about God, because the book does not mention God otherwise. First Esdras contains material similar to the biblical Ezra. Two short stories in the Apocrypha are named Tobit and Judith. Two historical books, First and Second Maccabees, tell about that revolt and the early Hasmonean kingdom. The Wisdom of Solomon and Ecclesiasticus are classed as Wisdom Literature. Some of the books are short compositions: Baruch, the Letter of Jeremiah, the Prayer of Manasseh, and Second Esdras. Second Esdras represents a type of literature that we call apocalyptic.

The collection of books in the Apocrypha fall into several literary types, but all of them are inherently religious in nature. These books reflect the religious and cultural concerns of the Jews in Palestine in the period from about 200 B.C. onward. The best way to become acquainted with these important writings is to read the Apocrypha. In reading these books you will discover the religious concepts that were most important to the authors.

- You will discover an interest in angels and demons. These spiritual beings are only mentioned in the Old Testament, but in the Apocrypha they appear as important intermediaries between God and persons, or Satan and persons. Several of the angels appear with names, such as Michael, Raphael, and Gabriel.

- You will discover concern with life after death. The Old Testament does not give much space to this concern. In the intertestamental period pious people who looked for justice in this world and found none were drawn to the concept of life after death. To them it seemed logical that a just and merciful God would see to it that the inequities of this life were righted in an afterlife. This was also a period of religious martyrdom, especially during the Maccabean revolt. Such martyrdom for the faith was directly associated with the idea of life after death and the Resurrection.

- You will discover an interest in eschatology. The *eschaton* is the "last days," the end of time. This idea is connected with the Messianic Age. The Apocrypha goes far beyond the Hebrew prophets in developing ideas about the end time. To the authors of the apocryphal books, there was no hope in this present world. Evil was so rampant and persons so rebellious that there was no hope of reformation. Instead, God must surely intervene. God would bring this evil, present age to a close and usher in a new and glorious age through the messiah. There would be a new age with justice, righteousness, and peace.

- You will discover that the biblical concept of wisdom was further developed. For example, Proverbs 1:20-33 presents wisdom as a woman who can help the individual find knowledge and the fear of the Lord. In the Apocrypha, wisdom is a bridge

between God and persons. This idea sets the stage for the appearance of Jesus as the Word (John 1:1-18).

- You will discover that in the intertestamental period, a much greater emphasis is placed on the importance and significance of individual prayer to God than in the Old Testament.

- You will discover that the Apocrypha also stresses the importance of almsgiving. This giving of charity or the sharing of one's material blessings with the less fortunate became a fundamental characteristic of later Judaism and Christianity.

We think of the books mentioned above when we hear the word *apocryphal* today. The word comes from a Greek expression meaning *concealed, hidden*. The hidden books were to be kept from public view. According to 2 Esdras 14:44-48, they were to be given to "the wise among your people." Twenty-four books could be made public, the passage states, to be read by "the worthy and the unworthy" alike. The twenty-four are the books in our Old Testament, arranged according to the Jewish system of counting them. So the apocryphal books were first considered as fit only for the wise. Later, when they were not considered acceptable as Scripture by the Jews and certain Christian groups, the books came to be thought of as false or heretical. Protestants usually read the Apocrypha for information about pre-Christian Judaism but not for establishing theological doctrines. Catholics base some doctrines on the Apocrypha.

PSEUDEPIGRAPHA

In the period between the testaments, many other books were written by Jews that are not counted among the books in the canon or the Apocrypha. They are lumped together as a class and called the Pseudepigrapha by Protestants. *Pseudepigrapha* means *written under an assumed name*. Some of the books are written as if Moses, Isaiah, Enoch, and Adam were the authors.

The Pseudepigrapha contains legends about biblical characters. These writings include: The Testaments of the Twelve Patriarchs, The Book of Jubilees, The Lives of the Prophets, The Testament of Job, and The Life of Adam and Eve.

A group of psalms is called The Psalms of Solomon. Another work called The Sibylline Oracles was supposedly written by mysterious prophetesses known as the Sibyls. Two works are based on the Maccabean Revolt. An account filled with legend is called Third Maccabees, while a book of popular philosophy is known as Fourth Maccabees.

By far the largest part of the Pseudepigrapha is made up of apocalypses. An apocalypse is a book that "reveals secrets." The most familiar apocalypse for modern Christians is the book of Revelation in our New Testament.

APOCALYPTIC LITERATURE

Apocalypses were tracts for hard times. They were intended to provide a word of hope, but the revelation was veiled to all but those who were skilled in understanding. They were written with much symbolism, and that symbolism was rooted in earlier apocalyptic sections of the Old Testament. Examples of apocalyptic literature in the writings of the prophets include Isaiah 24–27, Ezekiel 37, Daniel 7–12, Joel 3, and Zechariah 9–14.

Apocalypses are written in times of crisis, including the difficult times in which

the Old Testament prophets mentioned above lived. The Jews who wrote the apocalypses in the intertestamental period lived in one of the most trying times in Jewish history. Because the prophetic spirit was considered silent, each author wrote under the name of some great Old Testament figure. By taking the standpoint of someone in the distant past, the authors were able to "predict" the events of their own time. They gave the message of God's ultimate triumph over the present world order of evil. Through visions and allegories they revealed not only the secrets of the moment that had been determined long ago in heaven, but also the future. Their message was that God will crush all opposition, destroy evil forever, and create a new and blessed (messianic) age where all God's people will be released from oppression and reign in glory.

OTHER WRITINGS OF THE PERIOD

Philo Judaeus was a Jew who lived in Alexandria from about 20 B.C. to A.D. 45. His commentary on Genesis attempts to reconcile Greek philosophy and Judaism. He also wanted learned Greeks to recognize that all their wisdom had its origins in the teachings of Moses. This he explained in his *Life of Moses*. Philo explained God's relation to this imperfect world by means of an intermediary. This was the *Logos*, or Word, the chief instrument of God's activity. This idea strongly affected early Christian thought, expressed especially in John 1:1-18.

About the time of Philo, the scribes of Qumran were copying their biblical scrolls and writing their sectarian documents along the northwest shore of the Dead Sea.

Joseph Mattathias lived from A.D. 37/38 to 100. His four works were *The Jewish War, The Antiquities of the Jews*, an autobiography, and a tract against all slanderers of the Jews entitled *Against Apion*. Because he became an advisor to the Roman army during the revolt of the Jews in A.D. 66–73, he is known to us by the name of his Roman patron added to a Roman form of his own name: Flavius Josephus. Because he was considered a traitor by the Jews of the time, his work survived only in Christian circles. His writings illuminate the period in which the church was born and in which the New Testament was written.

NEW TESTAMENT

CHAPTERS, VERSES, AND WORDS IN THE NEW TESTAMENT

Biblical Book	Number of Chapters	Number of Verses	Number of Words
Gospels			
Matthew	28	1,071	23,684
Mark	16	678	15,171
Luke	24	1,151	25,944
John	21	879	19,099
History			
Acts	28	1,007	24,250
Pauline Letters			
Romans	16	433	9,447
1 Corinthians	16	437	9,489
2 Corinthians	13	257	6,092
Galatians	6	149	3,098
Ephesians	6	155	3,039
Philippians	4	104	2,002
Colossians	4	95	1,998
1 Thessalonians	5	89	1,857
2 Thessalonians	3	47	1,042
1 Timothy	6	113	2,269
2 Timothy	4	83	1,703
Titus	3	46	921
Philemon	1	25	445
General or Catholic Letters			
Hebrews	13	303	6,913
James	5	108	2,309
1 Peter	5	105	2,482
2 Peter	3	61	1,559
1 John	5	105	2,523
2 John	1	13	303
3 John	1	14	299
Jude	1	25	613
Apocalypse			
Revelation	22	404	1,200
Totals	**260**	**7,957**	**169,751**

NEW TESTAMENT CHRONOLOGY

Because of the fragmentary nature of available literary and archaeological sources, many of the dates are approximate.

Major Events

4 B.C.	Jesus born? Herod the Great dies.
A.D. 28–33	Jesus' one-year ministry *within* this period?
A.D. 30?	Jesus' crucifixion, death, and resurrection.
A.D. 40?	Paul's conversion/call on the road to Damascus (Acts 9).
A.D. 41–44	Herod Agrippa I rules Judea; apostles persecuted (Acts 12); James executed. A.D. 44
A.D. 44	Herod Agrippa I dies (Acts 12:20-23).
A.D. 51–53	Paul in Corinth.
A.D. 63–64?	Paul's execution in Rome?
A.D. 66	First Jewish Revolt begins.
A.D. 70	Jerusalem destroyed.
A.D. 95	Domitian emperor of Rome; localized persecutions in Asia Minor. John of Patmos writes Revelation?
A.D. 112	Trajan emperor of Rome; localized persecutions in Asia Minor under Pliny the Younger.

Roman Emperors	Political Leader in Galilee	Political Leader in Judea
Augustus 31 B.C.–A.D. 14	Herod the Great 37–4 B.C.	Archelaus 4 B.C.–A.D. 6
Tiberius A.D. 14–37	Herod Antipas 4 B.C.–A.D. 40	Roman procurators A.D. 6–41 (Pontius Pilate in office A.D. 26–36)
Caligula A.D. 37–41	Agrippa I A.D. 40–44	Agrippa I A.D. 41–44
Claudius A.D. 41–54	Agrippa II A.D. 54–93	Roman procurators, A.D. 44–66 (Felix in office A.D. 52–60 [Acts 23–24]; Festus in office A.D. 61–62 [Acts 25–26])

Nero A.D. 54–68
Galba, Otho, Vitellius A.D. 68–69
Vespasian A.D. 69–79
Titus A.D. 79–81
Domitian A.D. 81–96
Nerva A.D. 96–98
Trajan A.D. 98–117

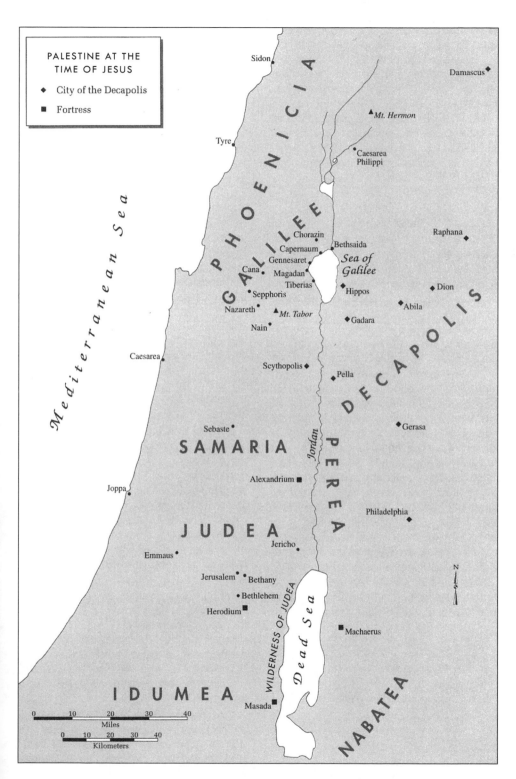

PALESTINE AT THE TIME OF JESUS

◆ City of the Decapolis
■ Fortress

Mediterranean Sea

Sidon
Damascus

Mt. Hermon

PHOENICIA

Tyre

Caesarea Philippi

GALILEE

Chorazin
Capernaum   Bethsaida
Gennesaret   Sea of
Cana Magadan   Galilee
Sepphoris Tiberias
Nazareth   Hippos
Mt. Tabor
Nain   Gadara

Raphana

Dion
Abila

DECAPOLIS

Caesarea

Scythopolis ◆
Pella

Sebaste

SAMARIA   Gerasa

Jordan

Alexandrium ■   PEREA

Joppa

JUDEA

Jericho   Philadelphia

Emmaus

Jerusalem Bethany
Bethlehem
Herodium ■   Dead Sea

WILDERNESS OF JUDEA

IDUMEA   Machaerus ■

Masada ■

NABATEA

N

0   10   20   30   40
Miles

0   10   20   30   40
Kilometers

407

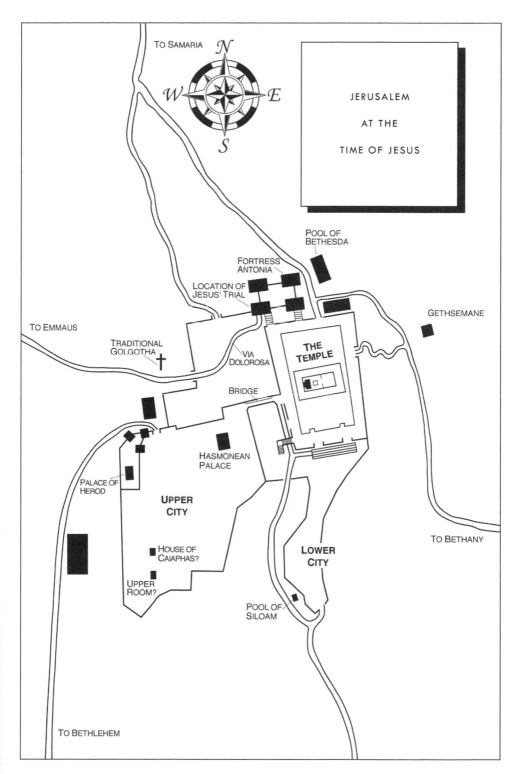

JERUSALEM

AT THE

TIME OF JESUS

TO SAMARIA

N

W E

S

POOL OF
BETHESDA

FORTRESS
ANTONIA

LOCATION OF
JESUS' TRIAL

GETHSEMANE

TO EMMAUS

TRADITIONAL
GOLGOTHA

VIA
DOLOROSA

THE
TEMPLE

BRIDGE

HASMONEAN
PALACE

PALACE OF
HEROD

UPPER
CITY

TO BETHANY

HOUSE OF
CAIAPHAS?

LOWER
CITY

UPPER
ROOM?

POOL OF
SILOAM

TO BETHLEHEM

MATTHEW

OUTLINE OF MATTHEW

8. Healing the epileptic boy
(17:14-21)
9. Prediction of the Passion
(17:22-23)
10. The Temple tax (17:24-27)
B. Church discipline (18:1–19:2)

VI. Judgment (19:3–26:2)
A. Jesus goes to Jerusalem
(19:3–23:39)
1. Demands and rewards
(19:3–20:28)
2. Jesus heals two blind men
(20:29-34)
3. Events in Jerusalem
(21:1–23:39)
B. Teaching about the end of the age
(24:1–26:2)
1. Signs of the end (24:15-28)
2. Parables of judgment
(25:1-46)
3. Summary (26:1-2)

VII. The Passion of Jesus (26:3–27:66)
A. Conspiracy of priests and elders
(26:3-5)
B. Anointing at Bethany (26:6-13)
C. Judas's betrayal to the chief
priests (26:14-16)
D. The Last Supper (26:17-29)
E. The garden of Gethsemane
(26:36-46)
F. Jesus' arrest (26:47-56)
G. Hearing before the Sanhedrin
(26:57-68)
H. Peter's denial (26:69-75)
I. Jesus before Pilate (27:1-26)
J. Jesus is mocked and scourged
(27:27-31)
K. The Crucifixion (27:51-54)
L. The entombment (27:57-61)
M. A guard placed at the tomb
(27:62-66)

VIII. Resurrection (28:1-20)
A. At the tomb (28:1-10)

B. The guard tries a cover-up
(28:11-15)
C. The Great Commission
(28:16-20)

INTRODUCTION

The title of the first book in the New Testament tells us the most important thing we need to know about it. The Gospel According to Matthew is a book of *good news* about Jesus the Christ. A history book, a book of teachings, a manual for Christian disciples—Matthew is all of these. But above all it proclaims that Jesus is Emmanuel, God with us (1:23); that Jesus is the Christ, the Son of the living God (16:16). Matthew is the first of four such books in the New Testament. We call the first three of these *synoptic* Gospels because they give us parallel accounts of the life and teachings of Jesus, and his death and resurrection.

When we are aware of the sources of the Gospel of Matthew, its singular structure, and some of its distinguishing features, we can better understand and appreciate this book.

Sources

Matthew cannot be called the author of the first Gospel in the sense that he wrote the book himself. It would be more accurate to speak of him as the *redactor* or *editor*. Whoever Matthew was, he compiled the book from several sources already in existence. To say this in no way diminishes the value of the book, for its importance lies in the arrangement of the material to serve Matthew's purposes. Most New Testament scholars now believe that Matthew gathered the contents of his Gospel from four principal sources: (1) the Gospel of Mark, (2) a collection of the teachings of Jesus, more than likely from an earlier document, also known to Luke but apparently not to

Mark, which has long since disappeared, (3) a source from which Matthew gathered material appearing only in his Gospel, some of which may have come from the oral tradition of Israel, and (4) the Hebrew Scriptures, what we call the Old Testament. We will see how Matthew used these sources as we consider the structure of his Gospel and the purposes it served.

Structure

Matthew has been called "The Teacher's Gospel," not surprisingly, because nowhere else are the teachings of Jesus so helpfully and memorably arranged for teachers. Chapters 3–25 are divided into five "books," calling to mind the first five books of the Old Testament, which are called the five books of Moses, and also the division of the book of Psalms into five books. The narrative transcribed from Mark forms the "vertebrae" of the Gospel of Matthew (chapters 3–4, 8–9, 11–12, 14–17, 19–23). Into this arrangement Matthew introduces five blocks of teachings or sayings of Jesus, so placed to serve as commentaries on the unfolding story of Jesus' ministry (chapters 5–7, 10, 13, 18, and 24–25). As the outline clearly reveals, in each book Matthew recounts a sequence of events in the ministry of Jesus, followed by a collection of sayings, parables, or instructions appropriate to what is happening in Jesus' own life, and in the life of the first-century church for which Matthew wrote.

The genealogy, preparations for Jesus' coming, and the stories of his birth and infancy introduce the Gospel (chapters 1–2). The Passion narrative and the Resurrection stories conclude the Gospel (chapters 27–28). All the material in the first two chapters is unique to Matthew. (Luke's genealogy differs from Matthew's in significant ways.) The Passion-Resurrection narrative almost certainly circulated among early Christians, first as oral tradition, and perhaps even before Mark's Gospel as a written document.

Against the skyline of Matthew's Gospel a number of towering peaks rise up from which the whole Gospel takes its special meaning. Five in particular provide the distinctive character of this work.

The Christ

At the very beginning an announcement is made to Joseph in his dream as to who Jesus is and why he is coming: "You are to give him the name Jesus, because he will save his people from their sins . . . and they will call him Immanuel—which means, 'God with us' " (NIV, 1:21, 23). Or, as phrased in the NRSV, "You are to name him Jesus, for he will save his people from their sins . . . and they shall name him Emmanuel."

Peter's confession, "You are the Christ" (16:16 NIV; NRSV, "Messiah"), puts into words the faith out of which Matthew speaks. *Christ* is from the Greek *Christos*, meaning God's anointed or chosen one, sometimes called *messiah* from the Jewish word for the one who was to rule at the end of the age.

At the end of the episode where Peter fails to walk on the water and Jesus pulls him into the boat, Matthew writes, "And those in the boat worshiped him, saying, 'Truly you are the Son of God' "(14:33). The word *worshiped* and the designation *Son of God* convey the understanding of Jesus as the Christ. The same word is used at the very end of the Gospel on the mountain in Galilee when the risen Christ appears to the disciples: "When they saw him. they worshiped him" (28:17). The identification of Jesus with the Christ of God puts the authentication of God on everything that Jesus says and does in the Gospel.

Fulfillment

More than any of the other Evangelists (Gospel writers), Matthew goes to unceasing lengths to establish that Jesus came to fulfill holy prophecy. Repeatedly we come upon the statement, "This was to fulfill what was spoken through the prophet . . ." (NIV; for example, 8:17; 21:4). Matthew brings more than sixty quotations from the Old Testament into his Gospel, anchoring the good news of the coming of the Christ deeply in the soil of Jewish hopes and expectations. Jesus says in the Sermon on the Mount, "I have come not to abolish [the law and the prophets] but to fulfill [them]" (5:17). A close study of the way Matthew uses Scripture reveals that frequently he bends prophecy to accord with events happening to Jesus. And one strongly suspects that he sometimes bends the report of what takes place in order that it agree with prophecy. One can see this most vividly in 21:2-6, the story of the triumphal entry into Jerusalem, where the story seems to have Jesus riding two beasts into the Holy City because the prophecy appears that way in Zechariah 9:9. But whatever distortions may lie in Matthew's use of the Old Testament, the effect of his vision is to weave an unbreakable strand around Jesus and his Jewish predecessors, binding them in faith, hope, and covenant.

Apocalyptic

The stress which the Evangelist puts on the apocalyptic Christ is unmistakable. Apocalyptic faith believes that at the heavenly-appointed time God will overthrow the ruler of this present age of darkness and evil and establish the eternal rule of blessedness. Matthew identifies Jesus the Christ with this figure of Jewish apocalyptic expectation. With Matthew the center of history lies in the future, at the day of judgment, of which Matthew gives us

glimpses in Chapters 24–25. Throughout the Gospel are recurring references to darkness, "where there will be weeping and gnashing of teeth" (25:30). The heavy news of Matthew's Gospel to the church for which it was written was that the apocalypse is coming soon. Said John the Baptist, "Even now the ax is lying at the root of the trees" (3:10).

The Church

Apocalyptic emphasis notwithstanding, Matthew shows no less concern for the church, an institution within which people must be disciplined to live now. Matthew leaves no doubt that Jesus the risen Lord is present in the community of believers. At the heart of the chapter on church discipline and administration Jesus promises in Chapter 18, verse 20, "Where two or three are gathered in my name, I am there among them" (NRSV; NIV, "Where two or three come together in my name, there am I with them"). At his final appearance to his disciples Jesus promises to those who have taken up God's mission, "I am with you always, to the end of the age" (28:20). Matthew is the only one of the four Evangelists to use the Greek word *ekklesia*, meaning *church*—a people who are called out of society to a life in covenant with each other and with their risen Lord. In fact, Chapter 18 is a manual of discipline for church members who were living between the appearing of Christ and the day of judgment.

Ethical Righteousness

The Gospel of Matthew might well be called a summons to righteousness. Among the Beatitudes is this blessing, "Blessed are those who hunger and thirst for righteousness" (5:6), and the more explicit, "Blessed are those who are persecuted for righteousness' sake" (5:10 NRSV; NIV, "because of righteousness"). Later in the Sermon on the Mount Jesus commands, "Seek first his kingdom and his righteousness" (NIV, 6:33). Righteousness means being faithful to the covenant that binds the church to God. It means being right with God. Throughout the Gospel Matthew stresses the importance of ethical obedience to the higher righteousness (5:20). It was to fulfill all righteousness that Jesus was baptized (3:15).

Setting

We do not know who wrote (compiled) this Gospel. It is improbable that Matthew the tax collector and disciple could be the author, although his memories could be scattered through these pages. Of some things we may be sure. This Gospel is the work of a Jewish Christian, one who brings the faith and traditions of Israel to the new covenant. The book was prepared for a congregation (or congregations) of Jewish Christians in a time of controversy between the followers of Christ and the Jewish religious establishment of the late first century. Sometime between the fall of Jerusalem to the Romans in A.D. 70 and the end of the century, Christians were expelled from the synagogues. The intensity of the conflict between Jesus and the scribes and Pharisees, apparent in this Gospel, may indeed reflect the conflict between Jews and Christians in the bitter years between 70 and 100. Apocalyptic fervor was strong in northern Palestine. This invites the speculation that Matthew may have been written for Christians in one or more of the cities of Syria. One cannot be more precise as to date and location. What is beyond any question is that this Gospel comes out of the crucible of the first century when the followers of Christ faced both persecution and apocalyptic judgment. The Gospel prepared for them has not ceased to be good news for us, their descendants in the crucible of the twenty-first century.

MATTHEW 1–2

Introduction to These Chapters

Chapters 1 and 2 form a prelude to the Gospel of Matthew. Like a prelude or overture to a music drama, the principal themes we will hear throughout the drama are sounded in clear statement. Before the curtain even rises on the life of Jesus, the evangelist gives an announcement of what the Gospel is all about: Jesus the Christ, Emmanuel of God, has come in fulfillment of the promises God made to Israel, beginning with Abraham. He comes not only as the royal heir of David but with salvation for the whole world. These are the ruling themes of Matthew's Gospel. The evangelist heralds these themes by means of a genealogy, a divine annunciation of the holy birth, the story of Jesus' birth, attended by a heavenly epiphany, the appearing of magi from beyond Israel to worship, and by God's special providence for him who is to be the Son of the living God (16:16).

Here is an outline of these chapters:

I. Genealogy (1:1-17)
II. Annunciation and Conception (1:18-25)
III. The Birth of Jesus (2:1-12)
IV. Flight Into Egypt and Return (2:13-23)

The Message of Matthew 1–2

Chapters 1 and 2 of Matthew's Gospel do more than just prepare for what follows. The prelude itself announces good news. This above all: in a world often inhospitable to our hopes and dreams, where we feel frightened and lonely here and now, and threatened by what may happen in the future, in this world God is with us. Jesus the Christ comes even yet to forgive people the sins that burden their lives. To the familiar question, "What's in a name?" Matthew answers: In the name of Jesus is

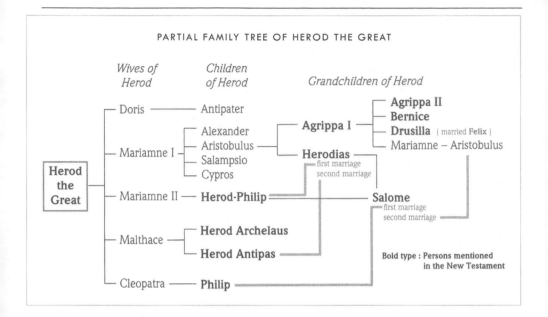

PARTIAL FAMILY TREE OF HEROD THE GREAT

Wives of Herod — *Children of Herod* — *Grandchildren of Herod*

Herod the Great

- Doris — Antipater
- Mariamne I
  - Alexander
  - Aristobulus — Agrippa I
    - Agrippa II
    - Bernice
    - Drusilla (married Felix)
    - Mariamne – Aristobulus
  - Salampsio
  - Cypros
  - Herodias
    - first marriage
    - second marriage
- Mariamne II — Herod-Philip
- Salome
  - first marriage
  - second marriage
- Malthace
  - Herod Archelaus
  - Herod Antipas
- Cleopatra — Philip

Bold type : Persons mentioned in the New Testament

God's presence and God's forgiveness.

The birth story speaks to our imagination in two ways. The magi can be examples for us. They made a long and perilous journey to come to the Christ, following a strange and unfamiliar star. So must be many human journeys to the Christ. The question they asked upon arriving in Jerusalem is a universal one: "Where is he who has been born . . .?" We identify with them in asking, Where will we find the one with power to save?

Dark shadows also fall upon these pages, peopled with those who sought the young child's life. The shadows did not flee away when Herod and Archelaeus vanished from the scene. Sometimes the message of the Gospel comes in the form of questions we are compelled to answer. Little children remain vulnerable to the world's evil; what sanctuaries can we find to which they may be taken for safety? How disturbing, if we are honest with ourselves, to realize that most human beings are strange compounds of both Joseph and Herod. The Gospel is asking, How is it with us?

MATTHEW 3–4

Introduction to These Chapters

With chapter 3 Matthew begins the first of five so-called books into which he divides his Gospel. Chapters 3 and 4 contain the narrative account of the beginning of Jesus' ministry; chapters 5 through 7 include the teaching discourse on discipleship, what we call the Sermon on the Mount.

Here is an outline of chapters 3–4:

    I. Preaching of John the Baptist (3:1-4)

    II. Crowds Are Baptized (3:5-6)

    III. Challenge to the Pharisees and Sadducees (3:7-10)

    IV. John's Announcement (3:11-12)

    V. Jesus Is Baptized (3:13-17)

    VI. Jesus' Temptation (4:1-11)

    VII. John's Arrest (4:12-16)

    VIII. Jesus Comes Preaching (4:17)

    IX. Jesus Calls His First Disciples (4:18-22)

    X. Teaching, Preaching, and Healing (4:23-25)

The Message of Matthew 3–4

Both John the Baptist and Jesus began their ministry preaching, "Repent, for the kingdom of heaven is at hand." The message is both proclamation and prescription. There is a maxim by which authentic Christian preaching can be identified: the imperative is in the indicative. In other words, because God has sent Jesus the Christ among us to be the way, the truth, and the life (indicative), we ought to turn around and follow him (imperative). Repentance is not only necessary, but possible, on account of what God has done.

In John's indictment of the Pharisees and Sadducees we would not expect to find much of a word for Christians today. The setting and the dynamics seem poles apart. But by our very assumption that we are not like the Pharisees, do we not give ourselves away? Sometimes we think we have the best family ties, we keep the commandments, we are members of the church in good standing, and we pray faithfully. Put all that boasting together and it comes out sounding like, "We have Abraham as our Father." Self-righteousness may be the most dangerous of sins; it blinds us to our real need of a new heart.

We live in an age that understands and responds to endorsements. Advertisers know the value of finding a "big name" to endorse the products they sell. Matthew knew how important it was that Jesus the Christ have unquestioned credentials. None could appeal to a higher credential than a voice from heaven saying, "You are my beloved Son." The truth to which that voice bore witness remains for us today.

MATTHEW 5–7

Introduction to These Chapters

Chapters 5–7 form the teaching discourse in Matthew's first section. This

The Lord's Prayer in Matthew and Luke		
	Matt 6:9-13	Luke 11:2-4
Address	*Our* Father *who is in the heavens*	Father
1st divine petition	May your name be sanctified	May your name be sanctified
2nd divine petition	May your kingdom come	May your kingdom come
3rd divine petition	*May your will be done; as in heaven, so on earth*	
1st human petition	Give us *this day* our necessary bread	Give us each day our necessary bread
2nd human petition	And forgive us our *debts*, as we also *have forgiven* those indebted to us	And forgive us our sins, for we ourselves forgive everyone indebted to us
3rd human petition	And lead us not into temptation, *but rescue us from the evil one*	And lead us not into temptation

THE BEATITUDES (MATTHEW 5:3-12)

A beatitude is a blessing. "How happy!" in God's sight are those to whom Jesus refers—the poor in spirit, the mourners, the meek, and the others.

"Those who mourn" (verse 4) are those who grieve for the sins and sorrows of the world. God will console them in the new age.

"Blessed are the meek" (verse 5) has been called Jesus' incredible beatitude. The beatitude does not take the usual sense of our word *meek*. It signifies not weakness, but one who is aware of his or her own limitations. Because they have this awareness, the meek know how much they must depend on God.

Instead of Luke's single word "hunger" (Luke 6:21), Matthew includes "and thirst for righteousness" (verse 6), making it a blessing for all who yearn for an upright life. Those who seek goodness with all their hearts will be satisfied in the time of God's promised rule.

Only those who show "mercy" to others can receive God's mercy (verse 7), because divine mercy cannot enter a heart that is not itself merciful.

The "pure in heart" (verse 8) are not the morally perfect. They are the ones who seek above all else to come before God. You will find God if you search with all your heart (see Deuteronomy 4:29).

"Peace" in the biblical sense is more than just the absence of conflict. It is harmony and well-being, both within oneself and among all people. Because these qualities are what God wants for all creation, we become true sons and daughters of God when we strive for peace (verse 9). The ancient Jewish word *shalom* (peace), used 172 times in the Old Testament, has no single English equivalent that captures its full meaning.

The kingdom of heaven belongs to those who have suffered for the sake of God's righteousness (verse 10).

In verse 11 Jesus speaks in direct address to the disciples. They will be persecuted because they are loyal to him, and disciples are not above their master. But they are to rejoice, because in the kingdom of heaven they will find blessing.

The Beatitudes are instructions in how to live the Christian life. They are also promises about the kingdom of heaven, both now and in the age to come. While there is much universal wisdom and morality in the Beatitudes, their full meaning comes only from the gospel (good news) of the Christ, God with us.

---

section has come to be known as the Sermon on the Mount, so called because Matthew places the setting for this discourse on a mountain. Whether it was to parallel Moses receiving the law on Mount Sinai is something on which scholars do not agree. Luke 6:17-49 includes some, but not all, of the material in Matthew 5–7. Luke puts the sermon "on a level place," giving rise to the name, the Sermon on the Plain. In Luke Jesus addresses a great multitude. In Matthew he speaks to the disciples alone.

These three chapters constitute the most systematic arrangement of what discipleship means. This is what the disciples are to teach those who become followers of Jesus. The Evangelist places it here immediately following the call of Jesus' first disciples (4:18-22) and the summary of how he went about Galilee teaching in the synagogues (4:23). This is not a "sermon" in the sense we think of sermons, preached from a pulpit in a worship service. It is a summary of what disciples/teachers are to teach and what believers are to do.

Here is an outline of chapters 5–7:

The Message of Matthew 5–7

Doing and being bring their own blessing. We may be tempted sometimes to think of the Beatitudes (5:3-12) as requirements. If we meet them we will be "rewarded." True, Jesus promises comfort, mercy, inheritance, and satisfaction. But to make these rewards our motives for mourning, mercy, hungering for goodness, and all the others is to miss the nature of God's blessing.

The emphasis of the Sermon on the Mount is on the inner condition of the heart (or soul). It is not enough to refrain from murder and adultery. It is not enough to say prayers, give generously, and participate in religious rituals. It is not enough to say, "Lord, Lord" at the proper time and to do good works. What matters is how we feel in our hearts toward God and our reasons for our behavior.

God's mercy and forgiveness are never measured by our deserving. They are unlimited and unqualified. But it happens that where we have refused or failed to forgive those who have trespassed against us, God's forgiveness cannot reach us (6:14). An unforgiving heart is an effective defense against our own forgiveness.

To worry anxiously betrays a lack of confidence in God (6:25). Our worst fears may be realized tomorrow. But in the long run, as expressed in Deuteronomy 33:27, "The eternal God is your refuge, and underneath are the everlasting arms" (NIV). Moses spoke those words to the people of Israel as they stood on the eve of their entrance into the Promised Land. Jesus speaks the words of 6:25-34 to everyone about how to trust the promises of the kingdom of heaven.

THE LORD'S PRAYER (MATTHEW 6:9-15)

The prayer contains seven petitions, the first three (verses 9-10) concerned with God's name, God's kingdom, and God's will. The final four (verses 11-13) are concerned with human needs: daily bread, forgiveness, temptation, and deliverance from evil. Matthew has probably inserted the prayer into Jesus' discourse at this point because it related to the practice of piety.

The first three petitions are really a prayer for the coming of God's kingdom, for the day of universal practice on earth of God's holy will.

We are to ask God for our necessities each day (some translations have it "for the morrow"). This may be seen as a contrast to the acquisitive accumulation of provisions for much time to come.

The petition for forgiveness is contingent upon the petitioners' having forgiven those who sinned against them.

The word translated "temptation" here refers to the terrible time of testing at the end time. We should not assume that God would ever lead a person deliberately into temptation to sin.

The final petition may be a prayer to be saved from the Evil One (Satan).

Matthew has adapted the prayer to liturgical use, adding the doxology at the end (a marginal reading in the NIV and NRSV).

To hear Jesus' words and do them (7:24) is to build life securely against washouts and cyclones, to become men and women for all seasons.

MATTHEW 8–9

Introduction to These Chapters

With chapter 8 Matthew begins the second book of his five-book Gospel. Chapters 8–9 form the narrative portion; chapter 10 contains the teaching discourse on apostleship. Jesus is getting ready to send out his disciples on their mission; the ten incidents of mighty works reported in chapters 8–9 stand as a kind of model or teaching demonstration of what the disciples' healing ministry will be like. The number ten corresponds to the ten wonders performed for the Israelites in Egypt, according to ancient tradition.

The emphasis of these two chapters is on the authority and power of Jesus to heal. The miracles manifest in action the authority with which Jesus spoke in chapters 5–7. One might say these are "credentials" for believing what he taught "on the mountain."

The structure of the narrative is carefully wrought. Ten miracles are reported, in clusters of three, three, and four. Between the first group (8:8-17) and the second (8:28–9:8) we find an interlude (8:18-22) on the requirements for being a disciple. Between the second cluster and the third (9:18-34) Matthew introduces another interlude telling of the calling of Matthew, and the questions that his own disciples and those of John the Baptist asked Jesus.

Here is an outline of chapters 8 and 9:
I. Three Healings (8:1-17)
II. Interlude on Discipleship (8:18-22)
III. A Healing and a Mighty Work (8:23-34)
IV. Healing a Paralytic (9:1-8)
V. Ceremonial Purity and Fasting (9:9-17)
VI. Four Healings (9:18-34)
VII. Summary (9:35-38)

The Message of Matthew 8–9

Matthew arranged his Gospel to include ten so-called miracles at this point. He did that for one reason: to support the faith that Jesus did speak and act with the authority of God. The miracles are not reported to prove that Jesus was a wonder worker, an exorcist, or one with power to control the weather. The mighty works were not in themselves the main purpose or wonder of the incidents. There were many exorcists and magicians of all kinds in the ancient world. But Jesus did these wonderful things always in response to the faith of the afflicted persons or those who brought them to Jesus. Whether we believe the miracle stories as literal accounts of what happened, or as symbolic stories to convey a truth about the spirit and power of one who came in the name of God, they can be for us what they were for the first Christians. They can be images of what God still does for those who come with confidence and trust.

God's power is spiritual. Faith transfigures that power into physical and material effects. This does not mean that we do it all by the act of faith. Sometimes God acts even before persons have faith, as in the calming of the storm, and the healing of the two demoniacs. In these two instances faith followed the mighty works. Nor does it mean that everything will happen just as we want it, even with great faith. It does mean that through faith God can cleanse us, reduce the fevers of life, quiet our fears in the face of life's storms, rebuke the demons that plague us, forgive us so we are no longer paralyzed by our guilt and sins, restore our sight, and lead us out of death into new life.

When the Gadarenes saw the herd of swine plunge into the sea (8:32), they were upset, as well we might expect them to be. To lose a whole herd of animals was to lose one's livelihood. This is not the main point of the story, nor is it even a detail by which we evaluate Jesus. The story raises more troublesome questions. From that day forward Jesus has always disturbed the communities into which he has come. He comes with comfort, as he did for the two demoniacs. But he comes also to change our values, our expectations, and our commitments. When these change, there is no telling how upset we will be, sometimes even begging him to leave our neighborhood (8:34).

MATTHEW 10

Introduction to This Chapter

Chapter 10 contains the teaching discourse of Matthew's second section. The teaching is more sharply focused here than in the more general discourses (chapters 5–7, 13, 18, 24–25): Jesus speaks to the disciples about the mission on which he is about to send them.

Three strands of purpose bind this chapter into a unity: requirements—how they are to carry on the mission (5-15); responses—what they will encounter in the way of welcome and rejection (16-25); and rewards—what consequences they may expect from the mission (26-42).

But beyond this briefing of the disciples about their mission, Jesus addresses the church in the time after the first mission has ended. His words to his disciples are also words to his followers "on mission" in the Apostolic Age after the first disciples have passed on. Also in this chapter is Matthew's list of the twelve disciples.

The rewards Jesus promises are without comparison, but the dangers, difficulties, and distress that his disciples must face are sufficient to discourage all but the most stout-hearted.

Here is an outline of chapter 10:
I. Commissioning the Apostles (10:1-4)
II. Requirements (10:5-15)
III. Responses to Be Expected (10:16-25)
IV. Rewards and Consequences (10:26-42)

The Message of Matthew 10

Being a disciple is a job having few equals: tough things to do; opposition everywhere you go; flogged even in the holy places, if not physically, yet psychologically and emotionally; being hated for Christ's sake; separation from your own family; and maybe a cross as your reward at the end. So what is there to love about it?

I can be certain that the Christ will acknowledge me (call me his disciple) before God. I can be confident that the life I may lose for Jesus' sake will be far outweighed by the life I will find with him. Those rewards are still in effect for anyone who becomes a Christian disciple.

"I have not come to bring peace but a sword" (10:34). This text has been misused across the centuries. People have quoted it in a military context, as though Jesus thereby sanctioned war. But Jesus was not referring to military or political matters. We cannot make ethical decisions about violence by quoting this verse. Jesus knew that loyalty to him would divide families as though a great sword had cleaved the fabric of relationships. Fidelity to Jesus must supercede every other commitment.

A Christian disciple will learn the art of both receiving and giving. These two acts are like the systolic and diastolic beats of the human heart. We are to receive one who comes in the name (that is, in the Spirit, the purpose) of the Lord. We are to receive the prophet (one who speaks for God.) We are to receive the righteous person (the good person with loving intentions). We are also to give, even the humble offering of a cup of water, to someone in need. We receive in order that we may give; we give that others may receive. The cycle of receiving and giving has no closing and no ending.

MATTHEW 11–12

Introduction to These Chapters

The Gospel returns in chapters 11–12 to the narrative of Jesus' ministry as he moves into a new stage of opposition and rejection by the synagogue leaders. Matthew tells us nothing about the results of the apostles' mission, if indeed they have yet gone. It may be that the briefing in chapter 10 looked forward to the Great Commission in Matthew 28:16-20. The "hidden revelation" serves as a general title of the whole of the third section of the Gospel (chapters 11–13).

According to Matthew, Jesus reveals by several disclosures that he is the one who has been anticipated. (11:4-6, 27; 12:6, 8, 28, 41-42). In these two chapters we observe the widening rift between the religious authorities and his new followers (verse 25). All this leads up to chapter 13, where the hidden meaning of the Kingdom is revealed through parables.

In chapter 11 Jesus speaks to the crowds about John the Baptist, who has inquired from prison, "Are you the one who is to come?" (verse 3). Jesus condemns the cities where people have not responded to his revelation, and he invites the crowds to come to him to find rest for their souls (11:29).

Chapter 12 takes us into three controversies with the Pharisees, each of which prompts a repeated indication of who Jesus is (12:8, 18, 23). The concluding verse sums it up: For whoever does the will of my Father in heaven is my brother, and sister, and mother.

Here is an outline of chapters 11–12:
I. Jesus and John the Baptist (11:2-19)
II. Woe to Unrepentant Cities (11:20-24)
III. Self-revelation of Jesus (11:25-30)
IV. Opposition by the Pharisees (12:1-45)
V. Jesus' True Family (12:46-50)

The Message of Matthew 11–12

The beatitude in Matthew 11:6 comes across the centuries independently of the Sermon on the Mount. A blessing awaits the persons who find no offense in Jesus and who are not put off by what different people do in the name of Jesus: giving the blind their sight, giving the lame the power to walk, healing disease, offering new life to the dying (in spirit as well as body), the gift of hearing to the deaf, preaching justice and mercy to the poor. We are blessed if we take no offense at anything the Spirit of Christ continues to do in the world.

Jesus says, "If any want to become my followers, let them deny themselves and take up their cross and follow me" (16:24). He also says, "My yoke is easy, and my burden is light" (11:30). This is a paradox: two opposites that, by logic, cannot both be true. But both statements are true in a way that transcends logic. What Jesus says is this: If you trust my promises, the gospel will fit you. You will be able to carry heavy burdens, even the burden of the cross, with comfort (strength).

Ever since Jesus said that whoever speaks against the Holy Spirit will not be forgiven, people have worried, wondering,

"Have I committed the sin that God will not forgive?" The answer almost invariably is no, not in the sense of there being a particular act or sin that God will not forgive. But it is possible for a person to so close his or her heart to the promptings of God's Holy Spirit that he or she no longer knows the truth. When we reach the point where we call evil good and good evil, then forgiveness will have neither meaning nor healing. It is not that God will not give, rather it is that we cannot receive.

MATTHEW 13

Introduction to This Chapter

Chapter 13 forms the teaching discourse of Matthew's third section. It is the only one of the five teaching sections of the Gospel explicitly directed to the crowds. Seven parables are here, together with interpretations of two of them, and two explanations of why Jesus taught in parables.

Notwithstanding that the parables have their dark side—the seeds that do not germinate, the fire that will consume the weeds, and the bad fish that will be thrown out—the principal emphasis in this chapter is on the Kingdom. When people hear the word and understand it, the gospel brings forth a rich harvest. The Lord will come at the final harvest and gather the faithful into the Kingdom. And that gathering is worth every price one can pay, every exchange that could possibly be made.

A parable is a brief story (such as 13:24-30), a metaphor (13:31-33), or simile (13:44-50) that conveys a truth about life. The parable is an illustration taken from one familiar realm of life whose truth can be applied to another realm. The wheat and the weeds are not really about agriculture, but through that story the listener can see the truth about

good and bad growing together before the time of judgment. The leaven is not really about baking but about the word of God that transforms all of life. The story of the pearl of great value is not about pearl diving but about the supreme value of the parables Jesus used in much of his teaching, especially teaching about the kingdom of God.

Here is an outline of chapter 13:
I. The Sower (13:3-9, 18-23)
II. Why Jesus Taught in Parables (13:10-17, 34-35)
III. The Wheat and the Weeds (13:24-30, 36-43)
IV. The Mustard Seed and the Leaven (13:31-33)
V. The Pearl and the Net (13:44-50)
VI. Scribes Trained for the Kingdom (13:51-52)
VII. Jesus Teaches in His Own Country (13:53-58)

The Message of Matthew 13

When the Word falls into good soil, it brings forth an abundant harvest. The gospel assures me that this will happen in my own life when I receive the Word. It will happen also in whole communities of people. The Word has power when it is given lodging and nurture.

Christians have always had to live with the tension between patience and zeal. When we see evil we are tempted to rush in and pull it up by the roots. At times that may be necessary. But sometimes the wisdom of Jesus dictates that we be patient. Tearing up evil can sometimes destroy fragile goodness trying to take root and grow, especially in a community like the church.

Who would suppose, looking at a tiny mustard seed, that all the potential for a great shrub lies within that seed? So it is with the Word of God. Seemingly fleeting and fragile, yet what transformations it has wrought in the life of the world!

The Lord's power to heal may depend on our will to receive. To the faith of the one who receives is bound the power of the one who gives. When Jesus does not do for us what he has done elsewhere, maybe the reason lies in the offense we take at and give to him.

MATTHEW 14–15

Introduction to These Chapters

Section four of Matthew's Gospel is the charter for the Christian church. In the narrative section (14:1–17:27) Jesus rejects the rule of the Pharisees and Sadducees (15:12-14; 16:1-12), embraces the Gentiles in his ministry (15:21-29), acknowledges that he is the Christ (16:17), ordains Peter as the rock on which he will build his church, and announces his death and resurrection. Chapter 18 is a manual of discipline for church members.

Chapters 14–15 include reports of events leading up to the climactic revelations and announcements of chapter 16. We read first how Herod Antipas murdered John the Baptist. Next comes the account of Jesus feeding more than five thousand people in a lonely place. During another storm on the Sea of Galilee, Jesus comes to the disciples across the water. Again Jesus finds himself in controversies with the Pharisees over ritual cleanliness. Finally, we read a report of feeding four thousand in the region of the Gentiles.

Here is an outline of chapters 14–15:
I. Murder of John the Baptist (14:1-12)
II. Jesus' Miraculous Works (14:13-36)
  A. Feeding the five thousand (14:13-21)
  B. Jesus walks on the water (14:22-27)
  C. Peter's little faith (14:28-33)

  D. Jesus heals many (14:34-36)
III. Controversy Over Ritual Cleanliness (15:1-20)
IV. Encounter with Gentiles (15:21-39)

The Message of Matthew 14–15

How did Jesus perform the miracle of feeding all those people? Was it superhuman power that simply multiplied the bread ten thousand times? Did people share what they had until all had enough? Did a small piece satisfy the hunger of each one because Jesus had broken the loaf? Matthew doesn't tell us. This we do know from nearly two thousand years of history: When Jesus breaks the bread of life to us we are more than satisfied. We are filled with new life, new purpose, new faith. This fulfillment is the continuing miracle.

To frightened, desperate souls, driven by overpowering winds and waves, Jesus somehow still speaks through the tumult. His presence inspires courage, quiets anxiety, gives assurance that whether we live or die we belong to God (Romans 14:8). For days and nights when the winds are against us, this story is a reminder that we are not alone.

At least Peter got out of the boat! When Jesus said, "Come," Peter jumped in the water. He had not reckoned on what it took to walk to Jesus on the water. Presumably he learned. Peter is a model of courage here, if not wisdom and faith.

Jesus' quotation in 15:9 waves a warning flag to us. How convenient it sometimes is to elevate our own self-interest to the level of a doctrine of God!

The nameless Canaanite woman should hold an honored place in the Christian church. She called out to Jesus for help and mercy. And although she was not of the covenant people, he answered her. Her voice still calls from outside our churches in the voices of people not part of the Christian community but in great need of help, mercy, understanding, and faith.

MATTHEW 16–17

Introduction to This Chapter

From the mountain of the temptations (chapter 4) to the Sermon on the Mount (chapters 5–7) to the mountain of the Great Commission (chapter 28), the highest moments of Matthew's Gospel are associated with the highest places. In chapter 17 we ascend with Jesus, Peter, James, and John to another peak of towering importance: the Transfiguration. The epiphany that occurs on that mountain, and Peter's confession of faith that precedes it (chapter 16), mark a decisive turning point in the life and mission of Jesus. These two events provide a key to the central meaning and purpose of the Gospel: the forthright and forceful declaration that Jesus is the Christ, and his validation as God's beloved Son.

These two chapters conclude the narrative part of Matthew's section four on the church. Through the events that happen here Jesus teaches his disciples what it will mean to be an apostle and to minister in the church. They are with him in controversy with the Pharisees and Sadducees learning to beware of the corrupting leaven of their teaching. After Peter's confession, Jesus tells his disciples that he will suffer many things from the elders and chief priests and will be killed. When Peter protests this announcement, Jesus rebukes him as a man who speaks for Satan. The disciples are told that they too must take up the same cross as Jesus. In discovering that they cannot heal an epileptic boy, the disciples learn that healing requires more than a little faith. Finally, Jesus teaches the need to

compromise sometimes in order not to give offense. We can say in all truth that this chapter represents "field education" for the disciples.

Here is an outline of chapters 16–17:

I. Warning of Pharisees and Sadducees (16:1-12)
   A. "Show us a sign" (16:1-4)
   B. The leaven of the Pharisees (16:5-12)
II. Peter's Confession of Faith (16:13-28)
III. The Transfiguration (17:1-13)
IV. Healing the Epileptic Boy (17:14-21)
V. Second Prediction of the Passion (17:22-23)
VI. The Temple Tax (17:24-27)

The Message of Matthew 16–17

"Who do you say that I am?" Jesus asked Peter. Supposedly you know me best. Who am I? Matthew, through his Gospel, sends Jesus' question down the corridors of history to our time and place. Who do we say that Jesus is? As far as our lives are concerned, this is the ultimate question. It does make a difference whether we say that Jesus is one whom we can trust with our sin when we need forgiveness, whose light we can follow in darkness, in whose word we can find comfort when life tumbles in. Blessed are we when we can say: "Jesus is the Christ, Son of the living God!"

What are we putting on the scale to "balance" God's gift of life? Acquisitions, popularity, insulation from the world's pain, the cries of the hungry, the lonely, the desperate, insurance that we will never lose our life for anyone or anything but ourselves? Or are we willing to give up these things if only we could be given back our souls, our freedom to love God and neighbors?

Moments of transfiguration have come to most people when they have seen the surpassing wonder and glory of life. We treasure such "mountaintop experiences." But it is not given to us to live in some mountaintop tabernacle. There is a world down below suffering demonic seizures of every kind. To this world we are called in Christ's name to descend and meet the real test of our faith.

There can be no healing, whether of physical, moral, emotional, or spiritual distress, without faith. Faith alone may not move a mountain to yonder place. But without faith in a power that gives life, nothing will move.

MATTHEW 18

Introduction to This Chapter

From the narrative in chapters 14–17 it is clear that the followers of Christ have been set free from obedience to the Pharisaic law of Israel. But unless their lives are gathered together under some kind of disciplined order and control, moral and spiritual anarchy will be the fruits of their freedom. So Matthew gathers a group of the sayings of Jesus into a manual of church discipline.

Chapter 18 forms the teaching discourse of section four in the Gospel of Matthew. Originally these sayings were addressed to the disciples. Matthew has assembled them as instructions to the leaders of the apostolic church emerging in Matthew's time, late in the first century.

Looking at this chapter as a whole, we discern seven distinguishing marks of the life of a congregation: 1. Living together in humility toward one another (18:4)
2. Seeing the Christ in one another (18:5).
3. Living so as to give no offense to anyone (18:7). 4. Caring for the weak little ones (18:10). 5. Accepting moral/spiritual

discipline by the church (18:17). 6. Praying together in the congregation (18:20).
7. Forgiving one another without limit (18:21-22).

The central theme of the chapter is: who is the greatest in the kingdom of heaven?

Here is an outline of chapter 18:
I. Humble Yourself Like a Child (18:1-4)
II. Whoever Receives a Child (18:5-6)
III. Woe to Those Who Tempt Others (18:7-9)
IV. Care for the Little Ones (18:10-14)
V. Yield to Church Discipline (18:15-19)
VI. Gather in Jesus' Name (18:20)
VII. Forgive Seventy Times Seven (18:21-35)

The Message of Matthew 18

What Matthew wanted church leaders to understand, church members today still need to recognize. How often is one person's behavior an inducement to someone else to follow suit and find himself or herself in trouble? Sensitivity to the weakness and capabilities of other persons is still required for all Christians. Woe to the person who takes sensitivity lightly!

Jesus told us when we pray to go into our room and shut the door (6:6). Private, solitary prayer brings us close to God. But when two or three are gathered in Christ's name to pray, each gives his or her private agenda to all the others, and receives from them enlargement of personal view and correction of selfish direction. People are created for community. And the heart and soul of Christian community is common prayer.

How do we despise each other? We belittle someone else's effort and achievement. We put people down with derogatory comments about their race, nationality, or religion. We spread rumors and innuendos about another's behavior. We despise persons by our cold indifference to anything they do. We make them feel like nothing, worthless. We confirm in their minds what they already feel about themselves: they are insignificant. Jesus spoke a word in season about all of this: See that you do not treat one of the common people with contempt.

How can we go on forgiving and forgiving those who continue to hurt and destroy? Sentimentality is the enemy of true Christian love. Social order requires restraint. But through it all we can and will forgive because we remember how much God has forgiven us.

MATTHEW 19–20

Introduction to These Chapters

Section five of the Gospel of Matthew (chapters 19–25) is commonly called "The Judgment." In it Matthew includes much of what Jesus said about the judgment to come at the end of the age. Chapters 19–23 are narrative, with teaching units added in association with events that were happening to Jesus and the disciples. Chapters 24–25 are the teaching discourse on judgment.

In chapter 19 the Pharisees first confront Jesus with a loaded question about divorce, hoping to confound him in answers contradictory to the law. The final fourteen verses speak about riches and the kingdom of heaven, turning upside down the priorities that people customarily honor.

The longest unit in chapter 20 is a parable about laborers in the vineyard, with its uncomfortable disclosure that the economy of God's grace has an entirely different design from the ways by which we usually order our lives. After a third

prediction of the Passion, the narrative shifts to a discussion of greatness in the Kingdom in which the disciples once again show themselves to be slow learners. Finally, we have the incident of Jesus' healing two blind men in Jericho. This brings us to the eve of Jesus' entrance into Jerusalem.

Here is an outline of chapters 19–20:
I. Jesus Enters Judea (19:1-2)
II. Marriage, Divorce, and Celibacy (19:3-12)
III. Blessing the Children (19:13-15)
IV. Riches and Possessions (19:16-30)
   A. A young man's questions (19:16-22)
   B. Jesus talks about rewards (19:23-30)
V. Parable of the Vineyard (20:1-16)
VI. The Crucifixion and Resurrection (20:17-19)
VII. Jesus' Teaching About Greatness (20:20-28)
VIII. Jesus Heals Two Blind Men (20:29-34)

The Message of Matthew 19–20

Whoever divorces his wife, except for unchastity (marital unfaithfulness), and marries another, commits adultery (19:9). This is a hard saying. It has caused heartache and guilt across the centuries. And it deeply divides the church today. Roughly one out of every two marriages in the United States ends in divorce. And not for unchastity alone. Divorce on the grounds of irreconcilable differences is now granted in most places. Many Christian marriages end in divorce, Matthew 19:9 notwithstanding. What does the passage say to us?

Marriage is a sacred covenant, "till death us do part." It is not to be entered into casually, nor put off lightly. But we are human, with a human nature that overrides the marriage covenant not only by sexual adultery but by selfishness and insensitivity as well. Where this happens people often acknowledge their failure and infidelity, but conclude that continuing a loveless and destructive marriage is a sin greater than divorce. God forgives sin, even the sin of adultery. Jesus said to one taken in adultery, "Go your way, and from now on do not sin again" (John 8:11).

Such argument offers no invitation to take marriage less seriously, or to rationalize our way out of failure. The bond between husband and wife is still the most sacred of all human commitments. Each has to decide how he or she can honor it best.

By the most common lines of human reason, for the householder to pay his laborers as he did is absurd, just as it would be absurd to so disperse a payroll in any company today. But the parable is not really about work and wages. It is an uncommonly effective way of getting our attention, and letting us know that in the economy of God's grace no one earns any more than another. Symbolically speaking, twelve hours of work do not earn any more than one hour. To the thief on the cross (Luke 23:39-43) and the woman who anointed Jesus' feet (Luke 7:37-38) Jesus gave the same full measure that he gave to Peter, James, and John.

Two blind men cried out to Jesus as Lord. These two men suffered no impairment of their spiritual vision. In fact they saw what a 20-20 vision missed: that one was passing by who could give them sight. They followed Jesus up the road and presumably into the city where sighted people were "blind." They were blind to what God had given them to see by faith. Faith has the power to see what sight may withhold. These two nameless men (Mark calls the blind man in his account Bartimaeus) remind us that our greatest handicap may be looking without seeing. Let our eyes be opened.

MATTHEW 21–23

Introduction to These Chapters

Chapters 21–23 continue the narrative portion of the fifth section of the Gospel According to Matthew. They contain the reports of eleven events or confrontations that occurred in Jerusalem during the week that ended with the death of Jesus on the cross. Matthew wants to show how the conflict between Jesus and the authorities led to the Crucifixion. He needs also to encourage the leaders of the early Christian church as they face the same conflict with the Jerusalem authorities of Matthew's time.

We read here the story of the triumphal entry into Jerusalem, followed by the episodes of the cleansing of the Temple and Jesus' healing in that sacred place. The authorities (scribes, Pharisees, Sadducees) precipitate three controversies with Jesus—over Jesus' authority, the poll tax, and resurrection. Jesus provokes a fourth dispute over messiahship and the Son of David. Jesus tells two parables that condemn the leaders of Israel—the two sons and the rejected invitation to the marriage feast. We also find an elaborate allegory here—the story of the wicked tenants—which a later editor has created from a parable of Jesus.

The final verses of chapter 21 are the first report of an actual conspiracy to destroy Jesus. The most bitter and scathing denunciation of the scribes in all the Gospels makes up the greater part of chapter 23, with the seven woes, which condemn these leaders as hypocrites.

Here is an outline of chapters 21–23:

I. The Triumphal Entry (21:1-11)
II. Driving Out the Money Changers (21:12-17)

The Message of Matthew 21–23

Surprisingly, in three chapters of the Gospel exclusively devoted to conflict with some Pharisees, who no longer even exist in our world, we find much that speaks across the centuries to our time and our situation. The party of the Pharisees is long dead. But contemporary culture has borrowed the name pharisaism to describe something that is alive and well. The plumage by which we identify today's "Pharisees" is hypocrisy—the assuming of a false appearance of virtue or goodness. It is not uncommon for people to say yes— sign up for some purpose, name in the newspaper, a show of participation. But when the cameras are turned off, many times these same people become no-shows.There is a pretense of conspicuous piety, but when the echoes of empty phrases have died away, nothing is seen or heard. Keeping up outward appearances can cover extortion and rapacity. Some persons give lip service to the "role models of old" but perpetuate the sins that cost them their lives.

Whether or not Jesus ever blasted a fig tree in quite the way the Gospel reports it, the story nevertheless carries an important message. The purpose of every tree is to bear fruit in its season. The tree that bears no fruit is best cut down. Likewise with faith, or with the church. If it does not bear the fruits of mercy, justice, goodness, and peace, it is worthless.

The parable of the rejected invitation is a warning to everyone who makes light of God's invitation to feast on divine grace and goodness. Lots of things seem more exciting. Do we really need grace all that much? Maybe some other time. Perhaps when we retire. But the commercials offer such wonderful things to make life full. The wheel of fortune spins, and we only go around once. So we make light of it. So what?

Lots of people have nightmares of showing up at a wedding (or some other festival) wearing the wrong clothes. But this may be a "good" nightmare to have if we expect to show up in their number when the saints go marching in. The proper attire for any person who would be at God's reception is garments of praise, justice, peace, and humility, not in some outfit of our own concoction!

How much shall I render to Caesar today, and what do I owe God? No day dawns but that we have to face and answer that question. And we can't always say, "This is for Caesar and that is for God." For more often than not, we render obedience to God through service to institutions and agencies of the civil state. And almost always the best way to serve the state is by fidelity to God.

MATTHEW 24–25

Introduction to These Chapters

These two chapters form the fifth and final teaching discourse in the Gospel. Before working through the many blocks of material that Matthew has gathered here, one should be aware that chapter 24 is an *apocalypse*, a very different kind of literature from anything else in the Gospel. An apocalypse is a writing that purports to disclose or reveal a hidden meaning of events taking place in the world. Such writing almost always points to signs of the end time, whether the end of the world or the culmination of Israel's history. Chapter 24, which is mainly based on the Little Apocalypse of Mark 13:1, is filled with signs of the End. The principal sign of the End will be the sign of the Son of Man in heaven. Then, says the apocalypse, "they will see 'the Son of Man coming on the clouds of heaven'" (24:30).

The challenging problem for students of the Gospel presented by the Little Apocalypse is to know how much of it may be the authentic words of Jesus and how much may be the apocalyptic faith of Matthew or others writing after the destruction of Jerusalem in A.D. 70. Whether Jesus thought of himself as the Son of Man is uncertain. Without question, first-century Christians believed Jesus the Christ would return with power and great glory. Here it may be sufficient to say that while the symbolic language of the apocalypse may not be literally true, it has a meaning that is eternally true.

Chapter 25 includes three extended parables on the Kingdom and the final judgment.

Here is an outline of chapters 24–25:
I. Destruction of the Temple (24:1-2)
II. The Coming Persecution (24:3-14)
   A. False teachers (24:3-8)
   B. A time of tribulation (24:9-14)
III. Signs of the End (24:15-28)
IV. Coming of the Son of Man (24:29-44)
   A. Signs of the Son of Man (24:29-31)
   B. Lessons of the fig tree (24:32-35)
   C The need for watchfulness (24:36-44)

THE JUDGMENT OF THE NATIONS (MATTHEW 25:31-46)

Because Matthew chose this parable as the culmination of Jesus' teaching ministry, and placed it immediately before the beginning of the Passion narrative, we infer that it has unparalleled significance for Jesus and in the understanding of the early church. The parable reveals several things of central importance to the Gospel.

Nowhere are the priorities and commitments of Jesus' life and ministry shown with greater clarity than in the imagery of this parable. The compassion pictured here is expected of every follower of Jesus.

The people—as individuals and as nations—will be judged at the end time by how they responded to the needs of the least of those whom Jesus embraced as brothers and sisters. So the lives we now live become in fact our judgment at the End.

The parable is ambiguous about Jesus and the Son of Man. He does not say, "I am the Son of Man." But the Christians following the Resurrection readily identified with Jesus the Christ the one whom he announces as the heavenly figure coming in glory.

The righteous did these things not because they expected to be rewarded but out of compassion. They did not know that the Son of Man (or Jesus) was manifest in the hungry, the thirsty, the prisoner, or the stranger.

The Message of Matthew 24–25

These chapters have been grossly misused by Christians across the centuries. People have made it a hunting ground for texts supposedly forecasting apocalyptic events in every age since the Resurrection. We abuse the Scriptures when we make them a horoscope of predictions. Chapters 24 and 25 are rather a warning and an invitation. The Gospel warns us about the consequences of infidelity or indifference, and invites us to choose faithfulness and compassion, and to enter into opportunities and responsibilities of the community of faith.

One word catches the essential meaning of these two chapters (at least up to the parable of the Last Judgment): *Watch!* No one knows, not even the Son, when the end time may come. For each of us there comes an end time beyond which lie no tomorrows in this life. Ahead for our nation lies some judgment of history. And for the world, a cataclysm will come from which none may hide. But Jesus bids us watch. And the Gospel tells us how to wait and be ready.

The cry of the maidens shut out of the marriage feast haunts us, because it reminds us that no one improvises a faith in the moment of crisis when it is needed. No one suddenly fills a life with compassion and Christian witness when the account must be rendered.

The parable of the Last Judgment shows us the imperative of love's expectation. It tells how we are to live in response to the love that we know God has for us.

MATTHEW 26

Introduction to This Chapter

Chapters 26 and 27 constitute what has come to be known as the Passion story, the narrative account of Jesus' final days in Jerusalem before his death on the cross. Chapter 26 is the longest chapter in the Gospel; 26 and 27 taken together contain 141 verses, thirteen percent of the whole book. But more important than comparative length is the content of these pages: the conspiracy against Jesus by the high priests and elders; his Last Supper with his disciples; his agony and arrest in Gethsemane; the two trials before Caiaphas and Pilate, which condemned him to death; his torture by the Romans; the Crucifixion on Calvary, and his burial in the tomb. These are the definitive events in the Christian story in which believers ever since have found the primary meaning of their faith.

Chapter 26 begins with Jesus' fourth announcement of the Crucifixion and carries the story through the hearing before Caiaphas and Peter's denial.

Here is an outline of chapter 26:
I. Jesus' Announcement (26:1-2)
II. Conspiracy of Priests and Elders (26:3-5)
III. The Anointing at Bethany (26:6-13)
IV. Judas's Betrayal to the Chief Priests (26:14-16)
V. The Last Supper (26:17-29)
VI. Peter's Promise (26:30-35)
VII. The Garden of Gethsemane (26:36-46)
VIII. Jesus' Arrest (26:47-56)
IX. Hearing Before the Sanhedrin (26:57-68)
X. Peter's Denial (26:69-75)

The Message of Matthew 26

The Lord's Supper is a time to remember the meal Jesus ate with his disciples on the night when he was betrayed. Each time we drink the cup at Communion we receive forgiveness of sins. And we remember Jesus' promise that he will drink the cup anew with us in God's kingdom. That promise and that gift make Communion an occasion no less for joy than for sorrow.

Peter sometimes stands as a mirror in which we see ourselves reflected. "I will never fall away," he fervently proclaims. But in the same night, maybe no more than six hours later, he cries with equal ardor, "I do not know the man." On the mount of Transfiguration Peter wants to build three booths so the disciples and Jesus can stay there, little understanding why Jesus must go down the mountain to his death (17:4). And while Peter sleeps, his master goes far into the valley of the shadow of death, alone! Words echo from the apostle Paul: "So, if you think you are standing firm, be careful that you don't fall!" (NIV 1 Corinthians 10:12).

One of the most pathetic sentences in the entire Gospel occurs in 26:56: "All the disciples deserted him and fled" (26:56). We have read much in this Gospel about the responsibility of true shepherds of the sheep. Here is a frightening picture of sheep abandoning the shepherd! Shepherds need warning about fidelity to shepherding. And who cannot think of shepherds who forsook the sheep? But sheep can also forsake the shepherd and run away. Or, as a preacher once reminded his flock, "Sheep can nibble themselves lost."

MATTHEW 27

Introduction to This Chapter

A succession of ten episodes comprises chapter 27. These have to do with the trial before Pilate, and Jesus' torture and death at the hands of the Romans. The account of Judas's suicide is a powerful reminder of the trail that led to this awful moment. The unexpected appearance of the women on Calvary and at the tomb—none of the disciples were any longer to be seen—is the glimmer of things to come on the first day of the week.

Here is an outline of chapter 27:

I. The Chief Priests Deliver Jesus (27:1-2)
II. The Suicide of Judas Iscariot (27:3-10)
III. Jesus Before Pilate (27:11-23)
IV. Jesus Condemned to Death (27:24-26)
V. Jesus Is Mocked and Scourged (27:27-31)
VI. Jesus' Crucifixion and Death (27:32-50)
VII. Signs at the Crucifixion (27:51-54)
VIII. The Women at Calvary (27:55-56)
IX. The Entombment (27:57-61)
X. A Guard Placed at the Tomb (27:62-66)

The Message of Matthew 27

We find the deepest meaning of the cross not in the physical details of the Passion but beneath, above, within, and beyond Jesus' death on Calvary. It is important to know the literal facts of what happened at Golgotha. But for the meaning of what happened we turn back to Isaiah 53:4-5, 12: "And by his wounds we are healed" (NIV; NRSV, "bruises"). We turn forward to Romans 5:8: "While we were still sinners, Christ died for us"(NIV). We turn upward in our imagination to John 12:31-33: "I, when I am lifted up from the earth, will draw all people to myself." We look inward in faith as did "the two of them" at Emmaus in Luke 24:31: "Their eyes were opened and they recognized him."

The blood of Jesus' death cannot be washed from the hands of Pilate. We can still hear the splash of water in that bowl. The Roman governor's futile gesture comes as a reminder that none can wash their hands of crucifixions, then or now. Forgiveness, possibly. Accountability, certainly!

For nearly two thousand years the Gospel of Matthew has regrettably been the fountainhead of appalling anti-Semitism. From verse 25 in particular people have tried to build a case against the whole Jewish people, contending: "They crucified the Lord." In the same spirit one could say: "The French burned Joan of Arc at the stake." "The English burned Thomas Cranmer." "The Americans hung the witches at Salem." Jesus was crucified at the instigation of certain high priests who feared for their power and at the hands of Roman authorities who viewed Jesus as a political threat. But to attribute such a miscarriage of justice and morality to a whole nation is unconscionable. We grossly misread the Gospel of Matthew when we transfer its religious antipathies to our day.

The symbolic "signs," visible only to the eyes of faith, continue to show what the Crucifixion means. The veil of Temple religion, designed to keep God in the sanctuary and people out, was rent from top to bottom. The whole earth has been shaken by what God did on that hilltop. People no longer need to fear an eternity locked in tombs; the cross/Resurrection has split open our confinement in death. And people of every race and nation still declare: "Truly this is the Son of God."

Against what adversaries did Jesus have to contend in the Passion! He dealt with the envy of the high priests, the timidity of the disciples, and the betrayal of those he trusted. He also encountered Pilate's fears, the soldiers' cruelty, the mocking derision of the people, the insecurity of a Roman governor who tried to "stonewall" the Resurrection. But thanks be to God who gives us the victory (over all these things) through our Lord Jesus Christ.

MATTHEW 28

Introduction to This Chapter

Chapter 28, with its report of the Resurrection, stands not only as the climax in the story of Jesus; it also serves as the keystone in the arch of Matthew's Gospel. All of Matthew's purpose is fulfilled in the short narrative of Resurrection/ Commission.

The Gospel opens with the announcement that Jesus shall be called Emmanuel, God with us (1:23). The very last words of the last chapter reaffirm that proclamation: "I am with you always, to the end of the age" (verse 20). But with us now is the power of the risen Lord.

The beginnings of the mission in the name of Christ appear throughout the Gospel (10:5-8; 22:9-10). That mission is now ratified in the commissioning of the disciples for their mission to the whole world by their risen Lord: "Go . . . and make disciples of all nations" (verse 19).

It is here reported that the disciples "worshiped him" (verse 17). The Greek verb Matthew uses for *worship* is the same verb John uses to report Jesus' words that "the true worshipers will worship the Father in spirit and truth" (John 4:23). The inference is clear that the young Christian church is to bow before its risen Lord even as the faithful have always worshiped Yahweh. Christian worship now takes on a new dimension toward the risen Lord.

"Everything that I have commanded you" (verse 20), the entire teaching of the five discourses or books of Matthew's Gospel, is now authenticated. This is what

COVENANT IN THE NEW TESTAMENT

The prophecy of Jeremiah concerning the new covenant had a great influence on the New Testament and on the way the early Christian church carried out the covenant tradition that was their heritage from Old Testament faith. The distinction between the "old" and "new" covenants also influenced the division of Scripture into the Old and New Testaments (that is, Old and New "Covenants").

Jeremiah declared that the new covenant was to be a new saving act by God on behalf of the people of Israel. Israel had not lived up to the old covenant, but their special relationship to God was not completely broken. They were to receive a new covenant based on God's lovingkindness, faithfulness, and justice. This new covenant was to be one of an inward and personal relationship to God. The people of God would have a new heart, engraved with God's statutes, and through this intimate knowledge of God's saving will, a new covenant community would be born.

The following Scriptures show how the covenant relationship is fulfilled and recreated in the New Testament:

- Luke 1:68-75: Zechariah's prophecy reveals that the coming of the Redeemer is part of God's holy covenant and part of God's promises made to Abraham so many years before.

- Matthew 26:26-28; Mark 14:22-25; Luke 22:17-20: Jesus declares that his shed blood is the blood of the [new] covenant (see also 1 Corinthians 11:25; Exodus 24:8). Thus, the new covenant is ratified by the lifeblood of Jesus. The Last Supper is a covenant ceremony in which Christ and his believers are bound to one another. The bread and the cup seal and commemorate this relationship whenever this sacrament is celebrated.

- John 13:34-35: Members of the new covenant community live under a new commandment of love for one another. This love is to be a sign to the rest of the world that they are Christ's disciples under the new covenant.

- 2 Corinthians 3:4-6; Galatians 3:15-29: Paul declares that it is through the Spirit in Jesus Christ that we who come after Abraham may be heirs to God's promises and ministers under the new covenant. The chosen people were unable to live faithfully under the written code, or old covenant, and brought judgment on themselves. God responded with a new saving act, a new covenant of the Spirit in which God's people find new life as the body of Christ.

- Hebrews 8:6-13; 10:26-36; 12:24; 13:20: The writer of Hebrews declares that Jesus is the means by which God brings the new covenant to humankind. This new covenant is not just new in time but also new in quality, and it is an eternal covenant. The coming of Jesus with this new covenant fulfills, perfects, and replaces the old covenant. Under the new covenant, believers are to live in faith and hope. They are to encourage one another to follow Jesus' commandment of love and to practice good works in their daily lives. They are to meet together regularly to maintain the covenant community. Above all they are to desire that God's will work in and through them to accomplish that which is pleasing to God through Jesus Christ.

the church is to hear, to believe, and to teach to all nations. One might say that by the Resurrection God puts the stamp of divine approval on what Jesus has taught.

Here is an outline of chapter 28:

I. At the Tomb (28:1-10)

   A. Dawn, earthquake, and angel (28:1-4)

B. "He is not here" (28:5-6)
C. "Go and tell his disciples" (28:7-8)
D. Jesus meets the women (28:9-10)
II. The Guard Tries a Cover-up (28:11-15)
III. The Great Commission (28:16-20)

The Message of Matthew 28

Not in this Gospel, nor in any of the other three, do we see the actual Resurrection. This tremendous event marking the beginning of the age to come remains hidden behind a veil of mystery. At the door of the tomb we must walk by faith, not by sight. Recall Jesus' words to Thomas recorded in the Fourth Gospel: "Because you have seen me, you have believed; blessed are those who have not seen and yet believe" (NIV, John 20:29). We are still called to believe where we cannot "prove," as were the women and the disciples in the Gospel story.

"Do not be afraid" (verse 5). Rebirth into new life is still and always a frightening experience to witness or to pass through, no less today than at the tomb of Jesus long ago. As at Jesus' birth where the angel said, "Do not be afraid; for see—I am bringing you good news of great joy" (Luke 2:10), so at the empty tomb God still sends assurance with the message, do not be afraid.

Subconsciously we still sometimes try to find Jesus among the dead—among the pages of history, enclosed within the covers of the Bible, in moral codes. We forget that "He has risen" and comes to us as a living Spirit.

Where, then, can we "find" Jesus? He comes to us when we go into the world on God's mission, making disciples by faithful witness to the gospel, telling others by precept and example what Jesus said and did. This is where Jesus says he will be with us. The risen Christ is not just a universal spirit like the air we breathe. He is "Maker, Defender, Redeemer, and Friend" to all who join him in his passion, his death, and his resurrection. "If we have been united with him like this in his death, we will certainly also be united with him in his resurrection" (NIV, Romans 6:5).

MARK

OUTLINE OF MARK

I. Jesus' Baptism and Early Ministry (1:1-45)
  A. Introduction (1:1)
  B. John the Baptist (1:2-8)
  C. The baptism of Jesus (1:9-11)
  D. The testing of the Messiah (1:12-13)
  E. The theme of Jesus' preaching (1:14-15)
  F. The calling of disciples (1:16-20)
  G. The authority of Jesus over demons (1:21-28)
  H. The healing of Peter's mother-in-law (1:29-31)
  I. Summary (1:32-39)
  J. The leper and the messianic secret (1:40-45)

II. A Ministry of Division and Debate (2:1-28)
  A. Debate over Jesus' sabbath authority (2:1-12)
  B. Jesus and the outcasts (2:13-17)
  C. Controversy over Jesus (2:18-28)

III. Christology and Discipleship (3:1-35)
  A. Controversy over Jesus (3:1-6)
  B. Opposition and success in Galilee (3:7-35)

IV. Jesus the Teacher (4:1-41)
  A. Jesus the teacher of the Kingdom (4:1-34)
  B. Jesus' command over the storm (4:35-41)

V. Three Stories about Jesus (5:1-43)
  A. Victory over the Gerasene demoniac (5:1-20)
  B. Raising of Jairus's daughter (5:21-24a)
  C. Woman with a hemorrhage (5:24b-34)
  D. Jairus's daughter healed (5:35-43)

VI. Rejection and Miracles (6:1-56)
  A. Rejection of Jesus in his hometown (6:1-6)
  B. The mission of the disciples (6:7-13)
  C. The death of John the Baptist (6:14-29)
  D. The Feeding of the five thousand (6:30-44)
  E. Jesus' walking on the sea (6:45-52)
  F. The crowds coming to Jesus (6:53-56)

VII. Christianity and Judaism (7:1-37)
  A. Ritual defilement; the Corban Issue (7:1-23)
  B. The status of the non-Jew (7:24-30)
  C. Healing outside Galilee (7:31-37)

VIII. The Expectations of Discipleship (8:1-9:1)
  A. Feeding of the four thousand (8:1-10)

B. Pharisaic questioning (8:11-13)

C. The disciples' lack of understanding (8:14-21)

D. The man healed in stages (8:22-26)

E. The way of Jesus and his followers (8:27–9:1)

IX. **The Transfiguration of Jesus (9:2-50)**

A. The Transfiguration (9:2-8)

B. The Elijah expectation (9:9-13)

C. Jesus' exorcism (9:14-29)

D. Second prediction of the Passion (9:30-32)

E. Lessons on discipleship (9:33-37)

F. Friends and enemies of Jesus (9:38-41)

G. Admonitions to disciples (9:42-50)

X. **From Galilee to Judea (10:1-52)**

A. Marriage and divorce (10:1-12)

B. Receiving the Kingdom (10:13-16)

C. The prior demand of the Kingdom (10:17-22)

D. The requirements of discipleship (10:23-31)

E. The third prediction of the Passion (10:32-34)

F. The disciples argue over greatness (10:35-45)

G. The seeing blind Bartimaeus (10:46-52)

XI. **Jesus Enters Jerusalem (11:1-33)**

A. Jesus' entrance into the City (11:1-11)

B. Cursing the fig tree (11:12-14)

C. The cleansing of the Temple (11:15-19)

D. The interpretation of the fig tree (11:20-26)

E. The issue of Jesus' authority (11:27-33)

XII. **Jesus and the Authorities (12:1-44)**

A. The allegory of the wicked tenants (12:1-12)

B. Concerning loyalty to Caesar (12:13-17)

C. The issue of resurrection (12:18-27)

D. The greatest commandment (12:28-34)

E. About the Davidic Messiah (12:35-37)

F. Woes against the Scribes (12:38-40)

G. The greatness of the widow's gift (12:41-44)

XIII. **The Synoptic Apocalypse (13:1-37)**

A. The destruction of the Temple (13:1-2)

B. Warnings against false prophets (13:3-8)

C. Expectation of tribulation (13:9-13)

D. The meaning of the tribulation (13:14-23)

E. Signs of the Parousia (13:24-31)

F. Calculating the end time (13:32-37)

XIV. **The Meaning of Jesus' Work (14:1-72)**

A. The anointing of Jesus' body (14:1-9)

B. Judas's intention to betray Jesus (14:10-11)

C. Preparation for the Supper (14:12-16)

D. The Last Supper (14:17-25)

E. Struggle in Gethsemane (14:26-42)

F. Jesus' arrest in the garden (14:43-52)

G. Jesus before the Sanhedrin (14:53-65)

H. Peter's denial (14:66-72)

INTRODUCTION

Authorship, Date, Place of Writing

We do not know who wrote the Gospel of Mark. According to Eusebius (fourth century), Papias, a bishop of the second century, reported the tradition that Mark was composed by (John) Mark based on the recollections of Peter. It does not seem likely today that this tradition is reliable. Mark does not have the character of an eyewitness piece of work; it is, rather, based on oral traditions circulating in the Markan church. The author must remain anonymous, though he must also be given credit for having created the Gospel as a type of literature, since Mark was the first to be written.

The customary date for Mark is around A.D. 70, at about the time of the Jewish revolt against Rome. Of course, no one really knows and the Gospel does not say, but internal indications point to a time when conditions were severe for some Christian communities. And Mark also seems to be aware of the destruction of the Temple in A.D. 70 (see 13:2).

Rome is given in early sources (second century on) as the traditional site of writing, but again the Gospel itself does not say where it originated. Other places have been suggested, such as Syria, Egypt, or Asia Minor. We cannot know for sure, though a reasonable case can still be made for the Roman location. For example, the persecution of Christians at Rome under the lunatic emperor Nero in the sixties could be the source of certain problems reflected in Mark.

Purpose of the Gospel

Why the Gospel was written has to be inferred. Certainly Mark wished to set out the Gospel as he understood it. Beyond that, he likely meant to address the situation posed by hard times for the Christian community. Mark looks at his time apocalyptically. He sees that the suffering now inflicted on the Christians is not accidental but points to the time of the end, when the faithful will experience tribulation.

Other related problems appear, such as false messiahs and false prophets in the church (13:6, 22), coming to terms with the destruction of the Jerusalem Temple (13:1-2), accomplishing the universal mission of the church (13:10), and enduring to the end (13:11-13).

We might further suppose that Mark was responding to the situation in the church when the tradition about Jesus was growing dramatically and probably getting out of bounds. What Mark did was to take a large slice of the oral Jesus tradition and commit it to writing. In this way he fixed its form forever and prevented any further development. In a sense Mark represents the initial effort toward the formation of a canon.

The Synoptic Problem

The first three Gospels are called *synoptic* gospels because of their broad similarity. Following a long period of debate, scholars have concluded that this similarity was not accidental, that Mark was written first and then used independently by both Matthew and Luke. In addition, Matthew and Luke had a second source, which we do not any longer possess, but from which they drew substantial material.

So Mark was written first and served as a source for both Matthew and Luke. The author of Mark, then, even though anonymous, has greatly influenced Christian history and literature. He was certainly a creative figure and, as the church came to recognize, composed a work of inspiration.

Style and Sources

Mark's style of writing is very elementary, even rough. Though his Greek is correct, he writes in a popular fashion, in the way of oral storytelling. His language is not complex and he obviously did not intend to produce a work of high literary merit. Characteristic of his style is the coordinating sentence—lots of "ands" coupled with modest use of subordinating clauses.

There is also a sense of urgency; Mark likes the word *immediately* (NRSV), or *at once* (NIV), for example. Yet Mark's thought is also very subtle, and his theological intention is not always easy to grasp.

As to sources, it is not so apparent that Mark had any beyond the oral material that lay at hand in his community. There has been some success in identifying a collection of miracle stories, perhaps a collection of parables and of Scripture proof-texts. Certainly also the Passion narrative had attained some fixed form before Mark set pen to papyrus, but for the most part Mark had no models to emulate.

THE KINGDOM OF GOD

The Kingdom of God. It is difficult to find an adequate phrase in English to convey the meaning of the Greek *basileia tou theou.* The translation "kingdom of God" is problematic because it conveys the notion of a locale with fixed boundaries. God's *basileia* signifies divine "kingly rule" or "reign," not "kingdom" in a territorial sense. A further difficulty is that it conveys a male monarchical model of rule with the image of God as king. For believers whose government is democratic, and who are conscious of the limitations and dangers of having solely male images of God, "kingdom" is an inadequate term.

In a first-century Palestinian context, the term *basileia* would first call to mind the Roman imperial system of domination and exploitation. Jesus' annunciation of the *basileia* of God offered an alternative vision to that of the empire of Rome. The *basileia* that Jesus announced was one in which there was no more victimization or domination. This *basileia* was already present incipiently in Jesus' healing and liberative practices, his inclusive table sharing, and his domination-free relationships. Jesus' preaching of this *basileia* posed a political threat to the Roman imperial system, for which Jesus was crucified.

With these problems in mind, *basileia* might be translated "rule," "reign," or "realm." While no English phrase adequately captures all that *basileia tou theou* signifies, it is important that whatever the translation, it convey the sense of God's saving power over all creation, already inaugurated in a new way with the incarnation and ministry of Jesus, and continued in the faithful ministry of the believing community, while not yet fully manifest. It is authoritative power and empowerment by God-with-us.

Themes in Mark

Mark 1:15, "The kingdom of God has come near," points to the major Markan theme. The Kingdom in Mark is to be understood apocalyptically; the end approaches and brings with it struggle and hostility. The Markan community sees itself passing through the final hours of tribulation. Suffering is inevitable and must precede the time of the end.

At the same time the apocalyptic outlook carries certain implications for discipleship, another of Mark's major concerns. Through the portrayal of the historical disciples Mark implements his own view. The picture of the disciples is largely negative; they repeatedly fail to understand Jesus or even to remain loyal to him. In the end they abandon him to his fate in the world. One of them denies him; another betrays him.

This picture is so powerful in the Gospel that it cannot be accidental. Mark is evidently campaigning for his own view of discipleship—perhaps against others in his community—a view which insists that following Jesus, who was crucified, necessarily entails the possibility of suffering and sacrifice.

Other matters appear in the Gospel, though more indirectly. Mark's portrayal of Jesus discloses the Markan christology (concept of Christ). The twin titles of *Son of God* and *Son of man* are most characteristic for Mark. They combine with the picture of the suffering one to provide a view of Mark's paradoxical Christ.

It is also apparent from the internal evidence of the Gospel that Mark's community has separated from Judaism. It is probably a community which has its own roots in Judaism but has become of mixed Gentile-Jewish-Christian character. Such issues as sabbath observance, ritual regulations, and the value of the law generally can be seen as having already been determined in the Markan community. These debates with Judaism are not so bitter as, say, in Matthew; in fact, it seems that they are already settled for Mark and his community. What we are hearing in the Gospel appear to be mostly the echoes of those controversies.

Mark also contains the silence-theme, better known as the "messianic secret." A feature of Mark is the repetition of commands by Jesus to those who have been healed to be silent, or, alternatively, to others (including demons) not to disclose Jesus' identity. This peculiarity of Mark has been long recognized to come basically from the author of the Gospel, but there has been no unanimity as to its meaning.

The silence commands are actually of three types: (1) commands to demons (1:25); (2) commands to be silent about healings (1:44-45; 5:43; 7:36-37; 8:26); and (3) commands to be silent about Jesus' identity (1:34; 3:11-12; 8:30). The first— the only clear example—is the oldest of all the types and perhaps even became the inspiration for the others. Originally these commands were simply part of the commanding word of the exorcist by which he gained control over the demons; they had nothing to do with Jesus' identity or with suppression of Jesus' reputation as a healer.

The second two show Mark's handiwork. Jesus urges those whom he has healed to say nothing—there is one exception in 5:19-20—though he is often unsuccessful. At the same time there are many healings in which no injunction to silence is given. Mark is probably trying to put some restraints on the picture of Jesus as a miracle worker. There is no doubt for Mark that Jesus does mighty deeds; yet at the same time there is much more to the story of Jesus. In particular, there is the message of the cross, which unveils the true meaning of Jesus. So it is the paradoxical portrayal of Jesus as the powerful yet suffering one that is underlying the peculiar mixture of silence and openness in Mark.

The identity sayings are similarly motivated. Jesus is pictured as not wishing it known who he is, except at the moment of his own self-disclosure (14:62). Caesarea Philippi is the key scene here (8:27-33). Jesus publicly disclaims any messianic titles until they are given the appropriate meaning—that is, until the suffering role becomes apparent.

MARK 1

Introduction to This Chapter

The beginning of the Gospel of Mark is not a birth story, as in Matthew and Luke. There is little of a purely biographical interest. Yet certainly Mark means to tell his Gospel by rehearsing the ministry of Jesus.

Here is an outline of this section:
   I. Introduction (1:1)
  II. John the Baptist (1:2-8)
 III. The Baptism of Jesus (1:9-11)
 IV. The Testing of the Messiah (1:12-13)
  V. The Theme of Jesus' Preaching (1:14-15)
 VI. The Calling of Disciples (1:16-20)
VII. The Authority of Jesus Over Demons (1:21-28)
VIII. The Healing of Peter's Mother-in-Law (1:29-31)
 IX. Summary (1:32-39)
  X. The Leper and the Messianic Secret (1:40-45)

The Message of Mark 1

Mark's story is not simply a human biography. Certainly Jesus had a human life, but Mark's message is a form of proclamation, a "gospel" (good news). Even the introduction of John the Baptist serves this proclamation, for John functions to announce in advance the gospel, that is, the coming of good news in Jesus.

There is something surprising in that role. John is hardly the first choice of the respectable. He is a scruffy figure, preaching repentance and demanding baptism. That people go out in response to him is no measure of his personal popularity but of God's purpose in history.

Also surprising is the presentation of Jesus. The first thing the messianic king does is to submit himself to the humbling experience of a baptism for sinners. And though he is acclaimed as the messianic king, no one else sees it. He then proceeds to call unlikely disciples, and to astonish with his messianic deeds of healing and exorcism. In such ways is the kingdom of God "at hand."

We can sum up these insights in the following way:

- What constitutes the gospel is not, for Mark, the life of Jesus, but the proclamation-with-passion of Jesus. Yet also for Mark the gospel is a story.

- God's saving activity on our behalf is never predictable but always surprises us.

- What we often consider good news is not necessarily the "gospel of God."

- The Kingdom is present wherever messianic deeds of healing occur.

- There are powers of evil in the world to be combatted in the name of the Kingdom.

MARK 2

Introduction to This Chapter

A new section clearly begins at 2:1, though the theme of controversy continues. This new section extends to 3:6, and constitutes something of a unity in itself. It is likely a pre-Markan collection of stories, with some Markan modifications. Chapter 2 embraces the controversy over the healing of the paralytic and Jesus' forgiveness of sins, the calling of Levi and the attached controversy scene over fellowship with sinners and tax collectors, the issue of fasting, and the sabbath debate. In these scenes Mark is continuing to build up his picture of Jesus' ministry as a time of division and debate. The Kingdom does not come without strife and contention.

Here is an outline of this chapter.
I. Debate over Jesus' Sabbath Authority (2:1-12)
II. Jesus and the Outcasts (2:13-17)
III. Controversy Over Jesus (2:18-28)

The Message of Mark 2

In this chapter Mark details how the coming of the Kingdom is a joyous experience bringing freedom and a wholly new situation. At the same time the Kingdom stirs opposition. For there are those who prefer the comfort of the old ways, and who are not prepared to submit to the risk of something new. So the Kingdom brings both joy and hostility.

This opposition and hostility occupy Mark in this chapter, as he sets out just how the Christian experience of the Kingdom induces enmity. Behind this picture lies Mark's concept of discipleship, which necessarily embraces the possibility of pain and suffering in the service of the crucified one.

We can summarize these insights in the following way.

- Jesus' presence, as the presence of the power of the Kingdom, brings with it the healing grace of the Kingdom. This grace is available to all and especially is grasped by the undeserving and those who have little in the world.

- To submit to the authority of the Son of Man is at the same time to run the risk of rejection in the world.

- The experience of the Kingdom is not unambiguously joyful but also brings with it the challenge of living in the face of hostility and opposition.

- The old ways in the world, such as sabbath observance and fasting, are being set aside in the name of the new freedom of the Kingdom.

MARK 3

Introduction to This Chapter

The controversy scenes which began at 2:1 conclude at 3:6, and a new section is introduced at 3:7. This new section opens with notice again of Jesus' reputation as a healer and its effects, followed by the appointment of the twelve to their mission, the Beelzebul controversy, and the sayings on the unforgivable sin. The section concludes with Jesus acknowledging that a true relationship to him is not familial, but one of following. Mark continues to develop the themes of christology and discipleship.

Here is an outline of this chapter:
I. Controversy over Jesus (3:1-6)
II. Opposition and Success in Galilee (3:7-35)
   A. Jesus' growing reputation (3:7-12)
   B. The choosing of the Twelve (3:13-19a)
   C. Accusations of demonic possession (3:19b-27)
   D. The unforgivable sin (3:28-30)
   E. Jesus' true family (3:31-35)

The Twelve Disciples in Matthew, Mark, Luke, and Acts

Matthew 10	Mark 3	Luke 6	Acts 1
Simon, also known as Peter	Simon (to whom he gave the name Peter)	Simon, whom he named Peter	Peter
Andrew his brother	James son of Zebedee	Andrew his brother	John
James son of Zebedee	John the brother of James (to whom he gave the name Boanerges, that is, Sons of Thunder)	James	James
John his brother	Andrew	John	Andrew
Philip	Philip	Philip	Philip
Bartholomew	Bartholomew	Bartholomew	Thomas
Thomas	Matthew	Matthew	Bartholomew
Matthew the tax collector	Thomas	Thomas	Matthew
James son of Alphaeus	James son of Alphaeus	James son of Alphaeus	James son of Alphaeus
Thaddaeus	Thaddaeus	Simon, who was called the Zealot	Simon the Zealot
Simon the Cananaean	Simon the Cananaean	Judas son of James	Judas son of James
Judas Iscariot, the one who betrayed him	Judas Iscariot who betrayed him	Judas Iscariot who became a traitor	

The Message of Mark 3

In this chapter Mark continues to set out his picture of the controversial Christ, whose Kingdom comes near wherever acts of grace and healing come near. At the same time this Kingdom implies a new circumstance which overturns many of the old ways and causes an eruption of hostility toward the messenger. The scenes of sabbath observance, family rejection, and accusations of demonic possession all make this point with a powerful impression upon the reader.

We may gather together these lessons in the following way.

- Acts of kindness and charity may not produce gratitude when at the same time something cherished must be given up. There were some who valued the observance of the law above the restoration of wholeness to the crippled and the maimed.

- Those who feel themselves called to be disciples must always be prepared to reckon with the possibility that such a life may not be an experience of glory. Even rejection from family members is a possibility.

- To do the will of God is to be Jesus' true family member.

- To be insensitive to the presence of the Kingdom is to suffer such a spiritual blindness that the possibility of restoration is foreclosed.

MARK 4

Introduction to This Chapter

In this chapter Mark develops his picture of Jesus as a teacher. There is not much emphasis in Mark on this teaching role of Jesus; rather, Jesus is for Mark primarily the active healer and miracle worker, and supremely the suffering one. But Jesus does teach in Mark, and although there is nothing like the Sermon on the Mount in Mark, there are parables and various sayings about the Kingdom and about discipleship. That process begins significantly in this chapter, though Mark returns to the dynamic, miraculous Christ at the conclusion (4:35-41).

Here is an outline of chapter 4:

I. Jesus the Teacher of the Kingdom (4:1-34)
   A. The parable of the sower (4:1-20)
   B. Warning words (4:21-25)
   C. The seed growing mysteriously (4:26-29)
   D. The simile of the mustard seed (4:30-32)
   E. The importance of parables (4:33-34)
II. Jesus' Command over the Storm (4:35-41)

The Message of Mark 4

In this chapter Mark has brought before us the Jesus who teaches the Kingdom. The message of the Kingdom lies hidden in Jesus' activity, just as the seed is buried in the ground. And also like the seed, the message of the Kingdom will bring forth eschatological abundance, even if it does not appear to be the case in the present time. From a larger perspective we can summarize these insights in the following way.

- The activity of God's kingdom is often hidden in the world and available only to those who look with the special seeing of faith.

- What often seems to us to be a failure of the Kingdom to manifest itself in the world may turn out to be a surprising, enormous victory.

- None of us should assume that the presence of the Kingdom at work in the world is self-evident; rather, it lies within the ordinary and mundane things of the world. The Kingdom does not show itself apart from the world, but within it.

- The Kingdom is not at humankind's disposal but rather is God's Kingdom to make manifest where and when God will.

- Jesus' saving power, which is the power of the Kingdom, is available not only in the calms of life but even and especially when the storms seem to prevail.

- While salvation is not dependent upon human action, faith is the appropriate human response to the saving action of God.

MARK 5

Introduction to This Chapter

This chapter is taken up with three stories: the exorcism of the Gerasene demoniac, the raising of Jairus's daughter, and the healing of a woman with a hemorrhage. Evidently these stories were of more than ordinary significance to Mark, since he uses considerable space relating them.

Here is an outline of this chapter:
I. Victory Over the Gerasene Demoniac (5:1-20)
II. Raising of Jairus's Daughter (5:21-24a)
III. Woman With a Hemorrhage (5:24b-34)
IV. Jairus's Daughter Healed (5:35-43)

The Message of Mark 5

In this chapter Mark has graphically depicted the overcoming of demonic powers, victory over death, and Jesus' powers of healing. All these are manifestations of the Kingdom as it makes its way in the world. Interwoven in the stories are other typical themes in Mark, such as the invocation of secrecy and the insistence on the response of faith. These themes may be summarized in the following way.

- The Kingdom cannot be deterred even by the power of death; hope is a possibility even in the face of apparent hopelessness.

- God's power is made available at the point where human possibilities are exhausted.

- Miracles are not merely self-evident, objective events in the world but require the response of faith.

- God's mercy is shown not simply to the well-to-do and deserving but especially to those who are down-and-out and without hope in the world.

The Miracles of Jesus

A. Miracles Performed Directly on Persons

1. Exorcisms
#1 Healing the Demoniac in the Synagogue in Capernaum
_____   Mark 1:21-28   Luke 4:31-34   _____

#2 The Gadarene Demoniac(s)
Matt 8:28-34   Mark 5:1-20   Luke 8:26-39   _____

#3 The Syrophoenician (Canaanite) Woman
Matt 15:21-28   Mark 7:24-30   _____ _____

2. Exorcisms/Healings
#4 The Speechless Demoniac
Matt 9:32-34   _____   Luke 11:14-15   _____

#5 On Collusion with Satan
Matt 12:22-30   (cf. Mark 3:22-27)   Luke 11:14-15   _____

#6 Jesus Heals a Boy Possessed by a Spirit
Matt 17:14-21   Mark 9:14-29   Luke 9:37-43a   _____

3. Healings
#7 Jesus Heals a Deaf Man (and Many Others)
_____   Mark 7:31-37   _____ _____

#8 A Blind Man Is Healed at Bethsaida
_____   Mark 8:22-26   _____ _____

#9 Cleansing of the Leper
Matt 8:1-4   Mark 1:40-45   Luke 5:12-16   _____

#10 The Centurion of Capernaum
Matt 8:5-13   _____   Luke 7:1-10   John 4:46b-54

#11 The Healing of Peter's Mother-in-law
Matt 8:14-15   Mark 1:29-31   Luke 4:38-39   _____

#12 The Healing of the Paralytic
Matt 9:1-8   Mark 2:1-12   Luke 5:17-26   _____

#13 (Jairus's Daughter and) the Woman With a Hemorrhage
Matt 9:18-26   Mark 5:21-43   Luke 8:40-56   _____

The Miracles of Jesus (cont.)

#14 Two Blind Men
Matt 9:27-31   (cf. Mark 10:46-52)   (cf. Luke 18:35-43) _____

#15 Healing the Withered Hand
Matt 12:9-14   Mark 3:1-6   Luke 6:6-11   _____

#16 The Healing of the Blind Man/Men
Matt 20:29-34   Mark 10:46-52   Luke 18:35-43   _____

#17 The Healing of the Crippled Woman on the Sabbath
_____   _____   Luke 13:10-17   _____

#18 The Healing of the Man with Dropsy
_____   _____   Luke 14:1-6   _____

#19 The Cleansing of the Ten Lepers
_____   _____   Luke 17:11-19   _____

#20 The Healing at the Pool
_____   _____   _____   John 5:2-7

#21 Jesus Heals the Man Born Blind
_____   _____   _____   John 9:1-41

4. Raising the Dead
#22 Jairus's Daughter (and the Woman with a Hemorrhage)
Matt 9:18-26   Mark 5:21-43   Luke 8:40-56   _____

#23 The Widow's Son at Nain
_____   _____   Luke 7:11-17   _____

#24 The Raising of Lazarus
_____   _____   _____   John 11:1-44

B. Miracles Performed on Nature

5. Sea Miracles
#25 Stilling the Storm
Matt 8:23-27   Mark 4:35-41   Luke 8:22-25   _____

#26 Walking on the Water
Matt 14:22-33   Mark 6:45-52   _____   John 6:16-21

The Miracles of Jesus (cont.)

6. Miraculous Provision
#27 Five Thousand Are Fed
Matt 14:13-21   Mark 6:32-34   Luke 9:10b-17   John 6:1-15

#28 Four Thousand Are Fed
Matt 15:32-39   Mark 8:1-10   _____   _____

#29 Payment of the Temple Tax
Matt 17:24-27   _____   _____   _____

#30 The Miraculous Catch of Fish
(cf. Matt 4:18-22)   (cf. Mark 1:16-20)   Luke 5:1-11   _____

#31 The Marriage at Cana
_____   _____   _____   John 2:1-11

7. Curse Miracles
#32 The Cursing of the Fig Tree; the Fig Tree Is Withered
Matt 21:18-19   Mark 11:12-14   _____   _____

Matt 21:20-22   Mark 11:20-26   _____   _____

Jesus' Miracles: Summary

	Matthew	*Mark*	*Luke*	*John*
Exorcisms	2	3	2	0
Exorcisms/Healings	3	1	2	0
Healings	8	8	10	3
Raising the Dead	1	1	2	1
Sea Miracles	2	2	1	1
Provision Miracles	3	2	2	2
Curse Miracles	1	1	0	0
Totals	20	18	19	7

MARK 6

Introduction to This Chapter

In this chapter the Galilean picture of mixed success and opposition continues, with the rejection theme heightened by the vivid story of John's death. The miracle stories fill out the other side of Mark's paradoxical picture.

Here is an outline of this chapter:

I. Rejection of Jesus in His Hometown (6:1-6)
II. The Mission of the Disciples (6:7-13)
III. The Death of John the Baptist (6:14-29)
IV. The Feeding of the Five Thousand (6:30-44)
V. Jesus' Walking on the Sea (6:45-52)
VI. The Crowds Coming to Jesus (6:53-56)

The Message of Mark 6

In this chapter Mark carries forth the familiar theme of rejection, this time by Jesus' own hometown people. This theme is developed into the idea of worldly hostility, as seen in the story of the death of John. The mission of the disciples shows how any disciple may also expect to suffer rejection. Even so, the powerful Christ is present and provides for all his disciples' needs and comes to them when the storms are rough.

We can summarize these points in the following way.

- What is familiar to us is too easily taken for granted, and we cannot see in it the activity of the divine.

- Only faith can see where the Kingdom is at work in the world.

- To undertake mission in the name of Jesus is to run the risk of rejection in the world.

- There are powers of evil in the world which greet the proclamation of God's rule with death and hostility.

- In the face of adversity Jesus is there to satisfy with his word.

MARK 7

Introduction to This Chapter

Mark now focuses attention on the question of the relationship of the Christian community to Judaism. Here issues as to the binding nature of the oral law arise. In Judaism there existed a long tradition of oral interpretation of the requirements of the law of Moses. This oral law was considered as binding as the written law, at least in certain circles (Pharisaic). The question would have been raised among Jewish Christians as to whether they too must also observe this oral law. These scenes in Mark are meant to answer those concerns.

In addition, the assertion of freedom from the oral law raises the question as to the nature of this new community which Mark represents. The healing stories in this chapter are addressed to such questions.

Here follows an outline of this chapter.

I. Ritual Defilement; the Corban Issue (7:1-23)
II. The Status of the Non-Jew (7:24-30)
III. Healing Outside Galilee (7:31-37)

The Message of Mark 7

In this chapter Mark sets out the new freedom of the Kingdom. This freedom extends especially to the old law and its oral interpretation. Christians are not bound to the law, and do not observe the ritual regulations regarding proper washing, nor even the dietary regulations. Mark's community has obviously separated from Judaism and finds little value in continuing to observe all the old ways. Indeed, the scenes in this chapter show that Mark's church appealed to the Jesus-tradition to undertake a sharp criticism of such things as the oral law of Judaism.

This debate gives rise to the further question of the makeup of this new community that no longer observes the law. Mark does not speak his last word on this issue in this chapter. However, the scenes that take place outside Judea, in Tyre and Sidon and the Decapolis, are symbolic of the new community that is generated by the Kingdom and that does not exist on the basis of national identity or belonging to a certain people.

These insights may be summarized in the following statements.

- The Kingdom gives rise to a new freedom that overturns all the old ways and will not submit to the rule of the law.

- The presence of the Kingdom in Jesus brings into being a new community that is based on the free grace of God, and not on any personal qualities of deserving, family, race, or national pride.

- What matters in the behavior of the members of the new community is not external adherence to a set of regulations but internal matters of thought and intention.

MARK 8

Introduction to This Chapter

This chapter begins with what seems to be a repetition of a former incident, the miraculous feeding story. A somewhat mysterious explanation of the two events follows, preceded by the signs controversy

and followed by a healing story. Then Mark breaks truly new ground with the significant scene occurring at Caesarea Philippi. For the first time the disciples seem to catch on to who Jesus is, though they still have lessons to learn in the meaning of Jesus' messiahship. Discipleship and its expectations are the dominant themes throughout the chapter.

Here is an outline of this chapter:
I. Feeding of the Four Thousand (8:1-10)
II. Pharisaic Questioning (8:11-13)
III. The Disciples' Lack of Understanding (8:14-21)
IV. The Man Healed in Stages (8:22-26)
V. The Way of Jesus and His Followers (8:27–9:1)
    A. Peter's confession at Caesarea Philippi (8:27-30)
    B. First prediction of Jesus' passion (8:31-33)
    C. The meaning of discipleship (8:34–9:1)

The Message of Mark 8

In this chapter Mark has brought his picture to a preliminary climax. The second feeding story, with its accompanying lessons for the disciples, emphasizes the identity question and points to the continuing failure of the disciples to understand. Both Pharisees, who ask for proofs, and the disciples, who ponder why they have no bread, fail to see what is going on around them. The disciples are like the blind man who only came to see in stages. In this way Mark introduces that process of coming-to-see which is disclosed, at least partly, at Caesarea Philippi.

In summary we can develop these themes as follows.

- Understanding of who Jesus is cannot be gained from observation of marvelous events; such events have an ambiguous character that opens them to various interpretations.

- Miracles are called "signs," that is, pointers to something significant, but not proofs. Miracles cannot give a proof for faith, for they require precisely the interpretation of faith in order to be meaningful.

- Jesus is not the Messiah by popular acclamation; as the popular Messiah he was a failure. He was instead the suffering Messiah, the one acknowledged by Peter but still misunderstood.

- There can be no true quality of life which is not prepared to give itself up. Servanthood is the condition for finding life.

MARK 9

Introduction to This Chapter

Mark's story of the Transfiguration opens this section. Following the prediction of the Passion, a contrast is inserted that has in view the coming glory of Jesus. Yet it is not a different Jesus with which Mark wishes to present the reader but still the suffering, crucified one. This is seen in the exorcism story that follows, and in the second prediction of the Passion. The continuing failure of the disciples remains in view in this chapter, as they show themselves unable to deal with the concept of servanthood or of an appropriate faith.

Here is an outline of this chapter:
I. The Transfiguration (9:2-8)
II. The Elijah Expectation (9:9-13)
III. Jesus' Exorcism (9:14-29)
IV. Second Prediction of the Passion (9:30-32)
V. Lessons on Discipleship (9:33-37)
VI. Friends and Enemies of Jesus (9:38-41)
VII. Admonitions to Disciples (9:42-50)

The Message of Mark 9

The dominant theme in this chapter is discipleship. Even the Transfiguration, which opens the chapter, contains lessons for the disciples. They are to see that, though the cross cannot be surmounted, beyond it does lie hope. The Transfiguration gives a glimpse of Jesus in his resplendent glory. If there were no such expectation in Mark, the pervasive emphasis on the cross and the crucified one would cause the story to be depressing.

Again the disciples are taught the importance of servanthood. Yet they continue to misunderstand, even when given special instruction. Their dullness extends to spiritual incompetence. They cannot rouse the demons; they do not even know how to pray. Indeed, their prayerless existence is a sign of their faithlessness.

These insights can be summarized in the following way.

- There is hope beyond the suffering and pain to be found in this world. The God of the cross does not mute that pain but takes it up into the hope of glory.

- To follow Jesus is to learn his way of servanthood.

- To be kind to one's neighbor, who may be like a needy child, is to be kind to Jesus at the same time.

MARK 10

Introduction to This Chapter

In this chapter Jesus makes the transition from Galilee to Judea, on his way to Jerusalem. Yet along the way Jesus does not do anything different. He continues to teach and deliver utterances on the subject of discipleship. The third prediction of the Passion follows, as the cross event comes more and more to the forefront. At the same time the demands of discipleship grow stronger and more urgent. And, paradoxically, the disciples themselves grow even denser in their misunderstanding of that demand.

Here follows an outline of this chapter:

I. Marriage and Divorce (10:1-12)
II. Receiving the Kingdom (10:13-16)
III. The Prior Demand of the Kingdom (10:17-22)
IV. The Requirements of Discipleship (10:23-31)
V, The Third Prediction of the Passion (10:32-34)
VI. The Disciples Argue Over Greatness (10:35-45)
VII. The Seeing Blind Bartimaeus (10:46-52)

The Message of Mark 10

The dominant theme in this chapter is discipleship. Along the way to Jerusalem, Jesus attempts to convey to his disciples the high cost of discipleship. He emphasizes that the new community existing in his name operates according to a standard different from the usual reckoning of the world. In Jesus' community there are no places of rank and preference but all alike are servants.

Wealth and possessions are not guarantees or signs of special favor; they may even get in the way of attaining the Kingdom. And even divorce, practiced everywhere, is not God's best intention for those who aspire to follow Jesus. As usual, the disciples embody all who simply do not grasp this fundamental point about Jesus and his work.

We can sum up these insights in the following way.

- Following the crucified one brings with it a cost that not all are prepared to pay, and many do not even understand.

- In discipleship to Jesus the standards of the world are abandoned; a new standard, the way of servanthood, is taken up as the model of the Kingdom.

- In this new way of discipleship, something fundamental about the nature of God and the structure of the universe is disclosed. The God who appears in the work and words of Jesus is the servant-God, who gains by giving up and rules by dying.

- Jesus' glorious rule is not denied but affirmed only in and through the way of the cross.

MARK 11

Introduction to This Chapter

Jesus comes now to Jerusalem, entering the city to the acclaim of the gathered crowd. The whole scene has overtones of divine determination; Jesus knows his destiny and goes about fulfilling it. The cleansing of the Temple follows, though Mark is careful to separate Jesus from any sort of political activity. The enigmatic fig tree incident brackets the cleansing story, while debate over Jesus' authority, provoked by the cleansing scene, concludes the chapter.

Here is an outline of this chapter:

I. Jesus' Entrance Into the City (11:1-11)
II. Cursing the Fig Tree (11:12-14)

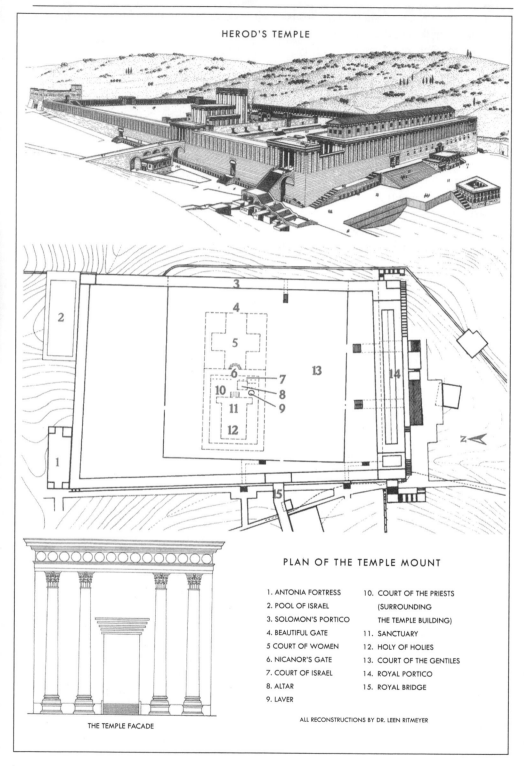

HEROD'S TEMPLE

PLAN OF THE TEMPLE MOUNT

1. ANTONIA FORTRESS
2. POOL OF ISRAEL
3. SOLOMON'S PORTICO
4. BEAUTIFUL GATE
5. COURT OF WOMEN
6. NICANOR'S GATE
7. COURT OF ISRAEL
8. ALTAR
9. LAVER

10. COURT OF THE PRIESTS
    (SURROUNDING
    THE TEMPLE BUILDING)
11. SANCTUARY
12. HOLY OF HOLIES
13. COURT OF THE GENTILES
14. ROYAL PORTICO
15. ROYAL BRIDGE

ALL RECONSTRUCTIONS BY DR. LEEN RITMEYER

THE TEMPLE FACADE

The Message of Mark 11

In this chapter Mark brings Jesus finally to Jerusalem. The entrance into the city has ironic overtones, as the assembled crowd shouts at Jesus its narrowly nationalistic hopes. Jesus is indeed the coming one, but he does not fulfill the role expected of him. Instead of leading an army against the Romans, he enters the city and mounts an assault on the Temple itself. He then offers lessons in the possibilities of faith-in-prayer and debates further with the officials of Judaism. Throughout the chapter the picture of the surprising Messiah dominates. Jesus never seems quite to come up to anyone's expectations.

We can set out the following theses from this chapter.

- What we most seem to hope for from God is an experience of God's glory; especially we want God to embody our nationalistic dreams and aspirations, and we assume that they are God's will for us.

- The possibilities of faith are limitless, but they occur in the context of the experience of the crucified Christ. What is possible for faith has to happen under the sign of the cross, not apart from it.

- The authority of Jesus is not evident merely from his works. No amount of miraculous deeds can demonstrate who he is, and always there remains a decision to be made. That decision is the essence of faith itself.

MARK 12

Introduction to This Chapter

The theme of controversy continues. A series of issues comes up, as Jesus confronts the Jerusalem authorities regarding matters of political and theological significance. Loyalty to Rome is raised in the question of payment of taxes to Caesar, theological orthodoxy appears in the debate over the resurrection, and the rabbinic argument over the heart of the law is at stake in the matter of the Great Commandment. The question of the Davidic descent of the messiah and warnings with lessons about hypocrisy and riches conclude the section.

Here follows an outline of this chapter:

The Message of Mark 12

Controversy marks this chapter. Jesus is engaged in various debates, which follow logically on the question about his authority. At stake is the truth of the gospel, the question of Jesus' true identity, and even more importantly, his role. Mark wishes to show the reader an edifying picture of Jesus outwitting his opponents in the learned center of Judaism. At the same time the lessons are very real for Mark's church in its historical situation.

The traditions in this chapter lead to the following central themes.

THE GREATEST COMMANDMENT
(MARK 12:28-34)

"One of the scribes" (NRSV) or "teachers of the law" (NIV) (verse 28) asks a question that was commonly debated among the lawyers, having to do with which commandment was "the most important" (NIV), or "first of all" (NRSV). So Jesus is here invoked as authority for the Christian community in this ongoing debate. His answer combines Deuteronomy 6:4-5 and Leviticus 19:18.

The first passage is commonly referred to as the *Shema*, from the Hebrew for the first word in the commandment, meaning *hear*. It speaks of *love* (verse 30) toward God with all one's being. Jesus expands the quotation from Deuteronomy by adding "with all your mind." The second (verse 31) speaks of duty to the neighbor: "You shall love your neighbor as yourself" (verse 31). Jesus was not the first to combine these two; other examples appear in pre-Christian Judaism, for example, the Testaments of the Twelve Patriarchs. But the important thing is what is meant in this twofold commandment.

Jesus affirms that "there is no other commandment greater than these" (verse 31), and wins the approval of the scribe (verses 32-33), who seems to know well the prophetic tradition. The scribe's comment that the love commandment is much more important than burnt offerings and sacrifices recalls the critique of the great prophet Amos (see Amos 5:24).

Jesus admires the scribe's wise answer (verse 34), and commends him with, "You are not far from the kingdom of God" (verse 34). The scribe' insight is of the kind that corresponds to the experience of the Kingdom.

This shrinking of the law to the twofold commandment to love God and the neighbor is found throughout the New Testament (see Matthew 22:34-40 and Luke 10:25-28). The word commonly translated "love" is the word *agape*, which describes that attitude of concern for the other person that does not count on rewards or calculate worth. As directed to God, agape expects obedience to God's will. As directed to the neighbor, agape expects caring that does not notice any differences between one human and another.

- There are those who, like historical Israel, have turned away from the gospel. There are consequences of doing so, and each must live with his or her own fate.

- Christians have a responsibility to Caesar, and what is rightfully his must be paid. At the same time there is another ruler and another rule that also have a claim. This claim is the ultimate one, beside which the ways of Caesar fade and cannot be allowed to take precedence.

- To believe in the God of the crucified one is, paradoxically, also to believe in the God of unlimited possibilities. This God of the cross is also God of the living, who gives life even to the dead.

- To accept the burden of discipleship is to render one's will in obedience to God and service to neighbor.

- The role of servant is not enacted in order to gain the approval of fellow human beings.

- God is not interested in our being religious but in our being fully human beings who are turned in servanthood toward the world.

- The measure of giving is not the amount but the devotion the gift expresses.

MARK 13

Introduction to This Chapter

This chapter in Mark is often called the *synoptic apocalypse*, or *little apocalypse*. Certainly this section does not, however, resemble the usual apocalypses, such as Daniel or Revelation. It is evident that Mark wishes to address certain issues with regard to expectation of the end of time, since the material consists of sayings of Jesus on a variety of matters relative to that expectation. But we might more accurately say that this chapter really reflects a great deal of the situation of the Markan church awaiting the Parousia. It therefore provides a strong clue to the historical conditions under which the Gospel of Mark was written.

Here is an outline of this chapter:

   I. The Destruction of the Temple (13:1-2)

  II. Warnings Against False Prophets (13:3-8)

  III. Expectation of Tribulation (13:9-13)

  IV. The Meaning of the Tribulation (13:14-23)

  V. Signs of the Parousia (13:24-31)

  VI. Calculating the End Time (13:32-37)

The Message of Mark 13

In this chapter issues relating to the hope of the ultimate rule of God through Christ have been exposed. The picture is drawn very deliberately by Mark, with appropriate emphasis upon the certainty of that rule that must finally prevail, but also on the reserve expected of faith in seeking out the time of the End. To be sure, there are signs for those who have the eyes to see. The faithful can expect to pass through hard times; false leaders will arise to deceive. And at the Parousia there will be no uncertainty; the appearance of Christ in his eschatological role will be unmistakable. Meanwhile, the task of the faithful community is to proclaim the gospel throughout the world and to conduct its mission with patience and watchfulness.

We may summarize these themes in the following way.

- However it may appear that history is going, however much it may seem that history is gaining the upper hand, it remains the object of Christian hope that God's rule will triumph.

- The community of faith needs to have eyes to perceive false messiahs and false prophets; they are those who betray its hope and proclaim victory where there is still to be trod the way of the cross.

- Speculating over the time of the Parousia is not an appropriate activity for faith; only God knows, and God will bestow this knowledge at the right time.

MARK 14

Introduction to This Chapter

The Passion narrative is introduced by the story of the anointing of Jesus; the familiar themes of the betrayal, the Supper, and the arrest in Gethsemane follow. The disciples' final failure is embodied in their desertion in Gethsemane and especially in Peter's dramatic denial of Jesus. Before that, the trial of Jesus by the Sanhedrin gives opportunity for Mark to set out plainly Jesus' claim to messiahship and the basis for his condemnation. Throughout the section the focus is on the meaning of Jesus and his work in the world.

Here follows an outline of this chapter:

I. The Anointing of Jesus' Body at Bethany (14:1-9)

II. Judas's Intention to Betray Jesus (14:10-11)

III. Preparation for the Supper (14:12-16)

IV. The Last Supper (14:17-25)

V. Struggle in Gethsemane (14:26-42)

VI. Jesus' Arrest in the Garden (14:43-52)

VII. Jesus Before the Sanhedrin (14:53-65)

VIII. Peter's Denial (14:66-72)

The Message of Mark 14

This chapter is deep in theological material. The anointing, the betrayal, the Last Supper, the arrest and appearance before the Sanhedrin, and Peter's denial, all are familiar themes, yet pregnant with meanings that lie at the core of Christian faith. Let us try to summarize some of the leading themes of this chapter.

- Devotion to Jesus has its proper place and expresses gratitude for his passion as a work done "for many."

- The betrayal of Jesus by Judas remains a mystery to faith. Yet we should realize that the other disciples really did not fare a great deal better. Judas's story confronts every Christian with the question as to whether he or she could have persisted in the face of the Passion.

- The sacrament of the Lord's Supper represents Jesus in his passion. Through the elements we are participants in his passion and see ourselves included in the community of the new covenant. This experience occurs in the context of hope for the eschatological rule of God.

- The suffering of Jesus models the suffering which may well come to any

disciple. There is no easy path through the cross.

- Suffering makes clear the reality of Jesus' humanity. It also defines the humanity of disciples.

- The trial of Jesus expresses paradoxes. While he was in the hands of human authorities, in another sense he was beyond their reach. For even though they condemned him, his death ultimately condemned them.

- The denial of Peter suggests that the desire to save ourselves reaches the deepest parts of our selfhood. Peter faced losing his life while trying to save it, as did all the disciples. Somehow they got the lesson backwards.

MARK 15

Introduction to This Chapter

The Passion narrative continues. Jesus is brought before Pilate for trial. After examination Pilate relents, under Jewish pressure, and condemns Jesus. The crucifixion follows. The scene at the cross shows compellingly the terrible anguish of Jesus. He dies uttering an agonizing cry. Certain women are introduced who will appear in the empty tomb story. The body is taken by Joseph of Arimathea and buried. All is darkness, leading to the finale in Chapter 16.

Here is an outline of this chapter:

I. Jesus' Trial before Pilate (15:1-15)

II. The Abuse of Jesus (15:16-20)

III. The Scene of Crucifixion (15:21-39)

IV. The Burial of Jesus (15:40-47)

The Message of Mark 15

This chapter brings to a climax Mark's story of Jesus' passion. It is a powerful portrayal of the reality of Jesus' condemnation, crucifixion, and death. The question profoundly posed by the Passion narrative is whether one can see in this deeply wounded and humiliated figure the very action of God. That is the challenge of faith.

Let us set forth the following themes in summary.

- Jesus' appearance before Pilate raises issues of justice. We can say that Jesus was treated unjustly, but to do so is only to make an interesting observation. What is acutely important in Mark is that this one who suffered unjustly did so in order that all the world, including those who commit injustice, might go free.

- The single most striking thing in Mark's portrayal of the crucifixion is the terrible agony with which Jesus faces his fate and dies. He goes to his death not like, say, Socrates, cheerfully drinking the cup. Jesus' cup was from the start an anguished one. The cost of redemption included a separation in the very being of God.

- From the death scene of Jesus, Mark draws lessons in discipleship. There is no escaping the call to take up the cross, and it may lead to something so humiliating that one can feel severed from God. And no one should count on a miraculous deliverance.

- The story of Jesus' burial offers a tiny shaft of light in the tunnel of darkness. There were a few—some ordinary women, a compassionate member of the Sanhedrin—who clung to their faithfulness and acted out of devotion. The history of the church is like that. Even in the worst of times God has witnesses.

MARK 16

Introduction to This Chapter

Mark now brings his story to its conclusion. It is a strange conclusion. The women mentioned in 15:40 come to anoint the body of Jesus and find the tomb empty. Inside they encounter a young man, who is obviously an angel. He tells them that Jesus has risen, and to go and relate to the disciples that Jesus will meet them in Galilee. The women say nothing but flee out of the tomb in fear and astonishment. The Gospel ends in this seemingly unsatisfactory way, with no appearance of Jesus narrated.

Here is an outline of this chapter:

I. The Women at the Tomb (16:1-8)

II. Problems in the Text of Mark (16:9-20)

The Message of Mark 16

The Markan story of the discovery of the empty tomb is remarkably restrained. Already in that restraint is one of its lessons. For Mark does not encourage any sort of "glory" theology based upon the empty tomb. Certainly the proclamation is central: He is risen, he is not here. But such a proclamation must be taken in the context of faith. The good news of the empty tomb is good news only to faith. There remain other ways to interpret an empty tomb besides the idea of Resurrection.

Let us summarize the insights that this chapter conveys to us.

- The questioning and downcast women show that they have not been alive to God's possibilities in Christ. They continued to live in the realm dominated by death. The idea of a resurrection was too overwhelming for them to comprehend. Even after inspecting the tomb they were obviously not convinced.

- The empty tomb remains a sign for faith. The story of the women at the tomb says that there is hope beyond the cross, even though there is no way past the cross. But only faith can grasp that possibility.

- Faith does rest in part upon the evidence posed by the empty tomb. It is certainly likely that Jesus' tomb was empty, but any number of other interpretations could be put upon that fact. The ultimate ground of faith is the encounter with the present and living Lord.

LUKE

OUTLINE OF LUKE

G. Sensitivity to physical need (9:10-17)

IX. The Nature of Christ (9:18-50)

A. Messiahship affirmed and interpreted (9:18-22)
B. Implications for discipleship (9:23-27)
C. Exaltation and validation of Christ (9:28-36)
D. Evidence of messiahship (9:37-45)
E. Redefining Greatness and community (9:46-50)

X. The Journey to Jerusalem (9:51–18:30)

A. Samaritans resenting and resented (9:51-56)
B. Priorities for discipleship (9:57-62)
C. Sending out of emissaries (10:1-24)
D. The good Samaritan (10:25-37)
E. Visit with Martha and Mary (10:38-42)
F. Commentaries en route (11:1–12:3)
G. Commentaries with the crowd (12:4–13:9)
H. Confrontation over the sabbath (13:10-17)
I. The nature of the kingdom (13:18-30)
J. A Warning and a lament (13:31-35)
K. Teachings at a Pharisee's house (14:1-24)
L. The cost of authentic discipleship (14:25-35)
M. Attitude Toward the lost (15:1-32)
N. Attitude Toward possessions (16:1-31)
O. Directions to disciples (17:1-10)

P. Encounter with the ungrateful (17:11-19)
Q. Suddenness of the Kingdom's coming (17:20-37)
R. Parables on persistence and prayer (18:1-14)
S. Centrality of children (18:15-17)
T. Self-denial essential to discipleship (18:18-30)

XI. The Approach to Jerusalem (18:31–19:44)

A. Warnings of what lay ahead (18:31-34)
B. The visit to Jericho (18:35–19:27)
C. The ascent to Jerusalem (19:28-44)

XII. Ministry in Jerusalem (19:45–21:38)

A. Cleansing the Temple and teaching (19:45–48)
B. His authority questioned (20:1-8)
C. Parable on spiritual irresponsibility (20:9-18)
D. Plotting by questioning (20:19-26)
E. Dialogue on life After death (20:27-40)
F. Commentary on messiahship (20:41-44)
G. Genuineness contrasted with pretense (20:45–21:4)
H. Impermanence of all Except faith (21:5-36)
I. Jesus' daily patterns (21:37-38)

XIII. The Final Hours (22:1–24:1)

A. Covenant of betrayal (22:1-6)
B. The Last Supper (22:7-38)
C. Prayer at Olivet (22:39-46)
D. Betrayal and arrest (22:47-54)
E. Peter's denials (22:55-62)
F. The preliminary hearing (22:63-71)

G. Hearing Before Pilate (23:1-25)
H. Procession to Calvary (23:26-32)
I. Crucifixion (23:33-49)

XIV. The New Beginning (23:50–24:53)
A. Burial and final tributes (23:50–56)
B. The exciting discovery (24:1-12)
C. Appearance on the road (24:13-35)
D. Appearance to the disciples (24:36-43)
E. A commission given (24:44-49)
F. Blessing and Response (24:50-53)
G. The response of his followers (24:52-53)

INTRODUCTION

The Writer of the Gospel

Luke was writing as a non-Jew. Through the Gospel and the Book of Acts he wanted to let the world know that Christ was for all persons—not just for Jews. For Luke was a citizen of the world.

When you pick up this Gospel, remember that you are looking at the first part of a two-part work. The Book of Acts is the second section. Both books appear to have been written by the same author and are addressed to the same unknown individual, Theophilus. At the outset of the Gospel he refers to other narratives "of the events that have been fulfilled among us" (1:1). He indicates his desire to "write an orderly account for you" (1:3 NIV).

In his introduction to Acts Luke states that in the Gospel he dealt with all that Jesus began to do and teach, "until the day when he was taken up" (Acts 1:1-2). Acts is a sequel to Luke and presents what happened after Jesus' ascension through the acts of the apostles and the activity of the Holy Spirit.

In Acts we learn that Luke was actively involved in the life of the early Christian community and was a close companion and coworker of Paul himself (see Acts 16:11-18; 20:5–21:18; 27:1–28:16). In 2 Timothy 4:11 we read "only Luke is with me." In Philemon Paul speaks of Luke as a "fellow worker" (Philemon 24). In Romans Paul speaks of a person named Lucius (Romans 16:21), whom he identifies as his kinsman or fellow countryman. Some think this may be a reference to Luke. We do know from Acts that Luke journeyed with Paul to Rome on what appears to have been Paul's last journey, and that as a prisoner.

Paul also gives us the famous identification of Luke as a physician. In his letter to the Colossians he writes: "Luke, the beloved physician, and Demas greet you" (Colossians 4:14). A physician had a high standing in the first century. Undoubtedly this background has some bearing on what we find included in this Gospel. Luke describes Jesus as a person with unusual understanding of and compassion for persons. Jesus is especially concerned for those in a misunderstood minority or those whose hurts have been overlooked. As a physician, Luke may have had and understood those feelings himself. Out of his own sensitivity, he may have seen this same understanding nature and helpful outreach in Christ (but to a greater degree), and, if so, he wanted others to know it too.

The Content of Luke

The writer never identifies himself as a physician, but this designation is consistent with the concerns revealed in this Gospel. Persons appear to be more important than systems and structures. The extensive account of Jesus' travels through Samaria and his attitude toward Samaritans illustrate these concerns. The prominence Luke gives to women in his narratives is another illustration. Although Luke states his purpose to be the writing of "an orderly account of" what had been heard from eyewitnesses, he seems to have been even more interested in writing "an orderly account of" the nature and compassion of Jesus.

Luke begins at the very beginning. He tells us more about the events surrounding the birth of Jesus than any of the other Gospels. These impressive events are to underline the spiritual importance of the personhood of Jesus. Luke introduces us to John the Baptist and includes the account of his baptizing Jesus with a description which again underlines the spiritual significance of Jesus. To strengthen his case, Luke provides a genealogy that traces the ancestry of Jesus back to David, Abraham, Noah, and Adam—a line of spiritual heroes from the days of Creation.

The narration of the ministry of Jesus begins in his home-town, Nazareth, and the synagogue there. It moves out from there to surrounding areas until ultimately it ends in Jerusalem. Basically Luke describes three phases of ministry and witness: in the area of Galilee (4:1–9:50), en route to Jerusalem (9:51–19:44), and in or near Jerusalem (19:45–21:38). The largest portion of the narrative relates to the ministry en route to Jerusalem. Especially in this portion, we see Jesus encountering many different types of persons, responding to each one in ways appropriate to his or her needs.

This Gospel has other distinctive characteristics. For one thing, the Greek language in which it was written gives evidence of being the best-educated use of Greek in the New Testament, which could be an outgrowth of Luke's mind and training as a physician. Another language characteristic is that Luke records many of the sayings of Jesus as short, pithy statements.

An important characteristic of this Gospel is the attention given to the Holy Spirit. This is an important characteristic of both the Gospel and Acts. There are seventeen references to the Spirit in the Gospel (compared with twelve in Matthew, six in Mark), and fifty-seven references in Acts. The presence and work of the Holy Spirit are prominent especially in the beginning of both books. In Luke the Spirit is related to the stories of Zechariah; Gabriel; and Mary, Elizabeth, and Simeon. Acts begins with the story of Pentecost. From Luke's perspective Jesus and the church lived and ministered through the enablement of the Holy Spirit. Thus it is not surprising to discover that the prayer and devotional experiences of Jesus occupy an important place in Luke.

Among the materials Luke includes that are not in the other Gospels are five miracle events, six parables, including that of the Good Samaritan, and special events such as the story of Zacchaeus, the trial before Herod, the thief on the cross, and the walk to Emmaus.

No one knows the exact date of the writing of this Gospel. The earliest projected date is about A.D. 75, but the prevalent opinion of Bible scholars places its writing later, in the 80s or 90s. It would have been about the same time as Matthew, and after Mark, since it includes much of Mark in its contents.

LUKE 1

Introduction to This Chapter

In a sense this first chapter is an introduction to the entire book. Here you will find stated the person to whom the book is addressed, the reason for its being written, and the background for the birth of

Jesus. Some themes are sounded that will reappear in various forms later in the narrative. Some sensitivities are demonstrated that become the mark of Luke's style. The chapter tells us of the angelic announcements to Zechariah and Elizabeth of the impending birth of their son, John the Baptist, and to Mary of her role as the earthly mother of the messiah.

The chapter may be outlined as follows:

I. The Author's Purpose (1:1-4)
II. The Announcement to Zechariah (1:5-25)
III. The Announcement to Mary (1:26-56)
IV. The Birth of John the Baptist (1:57-80)

The Message of Luke 1

The story of the announcements to Elizabeth and Zechariah and Mary and Joseph suggest two striking discoveries. One discovery is that you can never count God out. The Lord is always doing the unexpected to and through unexpecting, but hopeful, people, open to divine purposes and power. Our God is the God who acts with amazing but fulfilling surprises. The second discovery is that the Almighty never counts us out. God still comes to us, often when we least expect it, with new possibilities for life and new purposes to life.

LUKE 2

Introduction to This Chapter

This chapter brings us the familiar nativity story and also the only stories in the Gospels about the childhood of Jesus. It is a beautiful narrative intended to affirm through its unusual events that God was

---

THE MAGNIFICAT (LUKE 1:46-55)

The verses beginning with 46 through verse 55 compose that Scripture portion known as the Magnificat, which is a Latin word for "magnify" (NRSV) or "glorifies" (NIV) found in the first line. It might be considered the first Christian hymn. This beautiful and memorable passage has some parallel in the Song of Hannah (1 Samuel 2:1-10) as she rejoiced over the birth of her long-desired child, Samuel.

---

moving into the midst of humanity in an unusual way.

Chapter 2 can be outlined as follows:

I. The Birth of Jesus (2:1-21)
II. Presentation and Affirmation (2:22-38)
III. The Childhood of Jesus (2:39-52)

The Message of Luke 2

If there is any central theme to the varied stories in this chapter beyond their common focus on the childhood of Jesus, it is the theme of expectations fulfilled. However, the expectations were not always fulfilled in expected ways.

The shepherds were surprised and surprising as the audience for the regal announcement of the birth of the Messiah. A baby born to a peasant family was hardly the expected way for Christ to arrive. Bethlehem, although the seat of the line of David through which the messiah was to come, was certainly not ready. Yet God acted as predicted and came as promised.

The heavenly host sang. Simeon and Anna rejoiced. Mary and Joseph assumed their spiritual responsibility as parents in a diligent and faithful manner. They became stewards of the spiritual potential of the lad entrusted to their nurture (as we all should do for those entrusted to our parenting). Not fully knowing what the future might hold for Jesus, they recognized him to be

THE BIRTH OF JESUS (LUKE 2:1-21)

Caesar Augustus was the Roman emperor from 26 B.C. to A.D. 14. *Caesar* was the title of the ruler and *Augustus* was the name given him by the Roman Senate after he assumed the office. Previously his name was Gaius Octavius, and he was a nephew of Julius Caesar. Quirinius was appointed governor in A.D. 6 and took a census, or registration of the population, about A.D. 8. Here some confusion exists because Herod the Great, identified by Luke as ruler at this time (1:5), died before Quirinius assumed office. Therefore, there is a historical discrepancy that makes it difficult to identify the exact year of Jesus' birth.

The method of registration of the population as stated here was for each to return to his own town (verse 3) or homeplace of the family group. Bethlehem, meaning *house of bread*, was the ancestral home of the line of David (see 1 Samuel 17:15). Joseph was a descendant of David (3:23, 31), and thus would go to Bethlehem with any family members he had to register. They traveled from Nazareth, a village in Galilee fifteen miles southwest of the Sea of Galilee, where Mary and Joseph had been living (1:26).

Verse 7 reports specifically on the birth of Jesus. "Guest room" would be a better translation than "inn." The norm of that day would have been a peasant house in which family members and their animals slept on different levels in the same structure. In this case, the home of family or friends was so overcrowded that the guest room was full and the only place for the baby was in a feeding trough.

The baby is referred to as the firstborn, thus implying that other children were born later to Mary. Mark names four such brothers and suggests that there were at least two sisters (Mark 6:3).

For shepherds to be with their sheep at night was not unusual in Palestine. Shepherds moved with their flocks from place to place seeking enough plant growth for the sheep to feed on in the midst of dry, arid countryside. These nomadic shepherds might carry tents with them to use for longer stays in one area. However, often they simply camped out in the open. Some of the spiritual insights of the Old Testament were likely received in such a setting (see, for example, Psalm 19:1 and 23).

Once again an angel appears as a messenger (verse 9). Awed by this unexpected, glorious confrontation, the shepherds were frightened, just as were Zechariah (1:12) and Mary (1:29). In all three incidents, the angel first sought to relieve that sense of fear. Here is where the Greek word *gospel* occurs in the text. It means "good news" (verse 10). Interestingly, the good news was that a peasant couple had brought forth a child, whose coming was for each and every wanderer upon the face of the earth, to whom it was first announced. In this child each could find a personal ("to you is born") "Savior" and "Messiah" (NRSV; "Christ," NIV), in whom God would be present .

The anthem of the "heavenly host" (verse 14) is commonly known by the Latin wording *gloria in excelsis*, which states the first line. It affirms that God merits the highest glory for this divine entrance in and among humanity in Jesus. To express "glory" is to offer the highest praise.

As the shepherds went to Bethlehem ("city of David"), the two marks by which they were to identify the Christ child were the cloth wrappings and the manger location (verses 12, 16).

the child of expectation and God's presence and responded accordingly.

Yet in the midst of rejoicing that God has come in Jesus for all humanity, forever testifying that God never abandons us, we are reminded that God often acts differently from our predictions. It may just be that God in wisdom and love sends us not quite what we want but what we actually need, even a new way of understanding where divine values are in contrast to our human wants.

LUKE 3:1–4:13

Introduction to These Chapters

The narrative in this section focuses on two primary events: the baptism of Jesus by John the Baptist, and the temptation of Jesus in the wilderness. These events were important as preparation for the ministry of Jesus and provide an insight into Jesus' own concepts of the nature and purpose of his life. Additionally, a listing of the ancestry of Jesus is provided by Luke to convey not only his background but his spiritual credentials.

The material is organized as follows:
I. John Prepares the Way (3:1 20)
II. The Baptism of Jesus (3:21-22)
III. Ancestral Heritage of Jesus (3:23-38)
IV. Preparatory Temptations (4:1-13)

The Message of Luke 3:1–4:13

The rugged demands of discipleship appear in this passage. For John the Baptist, faithfulness to proclaim the message given him by God led him to a wilderness pulpit. His message would hardly have been cordially received in the community synagogue. He had to pay the price of isolation born out of conviction. This was not unusual for a prophet.

Yet the demands became even more rugged. His faithfulness led to a confrontation and condemnation with royal disregard for moral principle. This would result in his imprisonment and finally his death.

Jesus came to enter into his ministry through the door of baptism. It was an exalted and exalting moment. God was near and the Spirit was received. Jesus had the sanction of divine blessing and royal heritage. Yet from this exaltation he moved immediately into temptation. In the temptation he would have to reject physical comfort, worldly dominance, and self-serving demonstrations of power, to which his credentials would have entitled him.

The invitation to discipleship is freely offered. But the demands of faithfulness can be strenuous.

LUKE 4:14–5:16

Introduction to These Verses

"The Spirit of the Lord is upon me, because he has anointed me . . ." (4:18). These words of Isaiah read by Jesus in his home synagogue can serve also as a theme for the events in this section. Having moved through the initiatory and preparatory events of baptism and temptation, Jesus emerged to begin his ministry as Son of God and Christ or Messiah. He did so by returning to his home area, Galilee (not the area of his birth in Judea). There he publicly affirmed his calling or mission and began to undertake it. His being anointed is given support by what he was able to do and the way people began to respond to him, moving from scepticism to acclaim and allegiance toward him in this opening phase of ministry. This section may be outlined as follows:
I. At Jesus' Home Synagogue (4:14-30)
II. Ministry of Healing (4:31-41)
III. General Ministry in the Area (4:42-44)
IV. Beginnings of Enlistment (5:1-11)
V. Ministry and Meditation (5:12-16)

The Message of Luke 4:14–5:16

Within these verses that describe the beginnings of the ministry of Jesus are found traits that help us sense what was important to Jesus personally and what directions he would take.

We see Jesus' need for spiritual receptivity and replenishment. He obtained this from two sources: corporate worship within his religious tradition and personal, private withdrawal for prayer and pondering. He stood both within his tradition and beyond his tradition. He did not forsake what he inherited, but he also sought and was open to what was beyond it.

Another trait was his willingness and determination to put hands and feet to faith experience. His faith perspective moved him to witness and to caring.

Then the caring took the form of reaching out to those whom society rejected or from whom society stood aloof. Traditional barriers, stigmas, and prejudices were given no heed. Jesus bypassed them and placed human need above traditional distance and rejection. His empathy was strongest for those who received little of such.

Jesus urged his hearers, ancient and modern, to be always open to new possibilities—in achievements and persons. In many times and ways he called upon us to let down our nets again to find marvelous possibilities amid the improbable.

By his therapeutic helpfulness to those victimized by diseases of mind and body, he clearly witnessed to the newly discovered fact that God is on the side of health, not illness. The healing that Jesus brought is an evidence of what God wills and what works for humanity, up to our openness to receive and the limits of our mortality.

LUKE 5:17–6:11

Introduction to These Verses

One of the fundamental controversies Jesus would experience begins to surface in this portion of Luke's account. While we have noted that Jesus showed respect for his Jewish heritage and traditions, we sense that he wished to bring new light to that tradition. We wait to see how he would interface the old and the new. This section of the Gospel will begin to show us the nature of the relationship between the two.

Included are events of healing and activities that were exposed to a critique by the religious authorities of the Jewish tradition, and Jesus' own critique of his actions and intentions. The old and the new meet here in the following areas:

I. Regarding Forgiveness (5:17-32)
II. Regarding Fasting (5:33-35)
III. Regarding Attitudes Toward the New (5:36-39)
IV. Regarding the Sabbath (6:1-11)

The Message of Luke 5:17–6:11

Up to this point in Luke's narrative Jesus has appeared to be in harmony with the inherited Jewish tradition. Also he has received wide acclaim and devotion. Basically, all has been positive.

Now the atmosphere about Jesus changes somewhat. For one thing, his acclaim becomes a mixed blessing. It draws attention to him from the religious authorities. Their attention becomes curiosity, then suspicion, then jealousy, then resentment, then hostility. And the die is cast that will ultimately lead to a cross upon a skull-shaped hill.

All is well until Jesus begins to be, or think, differently or independently. Jesus never seeks to condemn or repudiate the law. He shows it both respect and a high degree of allegiqnce. Yet he sees beyond the law itself to the purposes of God for persons as revealed through the law. This is the new thing that Jesus brings.

Jesus seeks to be faithful to both what has been and what should be. He probably knows well that only time and the Holy Spirit will lead his hearers then, and now, to distinguish what is of passing interest over against what is of eternal purpose in our spiritual heritage and experience. This comes as we "grow in the grace and knowledge of our Lord and Savior Jesus Christ" (2 Peter 3:18), for Jesus came "among us . . . full of grace and truth" (John 1:14).

LUKE 6:12-49

Introduction to These Verses

As this section begins we observe the specific calling of an inner circle of followers to be known as "disciples" or "apostles" and later referred to as "the Twelve." Following this selection process, Jesus taught some basic guidelines to those persons, along with a sizable number of other followers and a multitude of persons curious or seeking assistance. These teachings are a briefer form of a set of teachings recorded in Matthew 5–7 and known familiarly as the Sermon on the Mount. These teachings expand the new perspectives on attitudes and actions that Jesus, as God's spokesman, wished to bring.

The foci of the section are as follows:
I. A Selected and Receptive Audience (6:12-19)
II. The Nature of Happiness (6:20-26)
III. The Nature of Relationships (6:27-42)
IV. The Tests for Sincerity (6:43-49)

The Message of Luke 6:12-49

- Jesus chose twelve of his disciples to form a small group of apostles (meaning ones sent out) for special instruction and support. While Jesus' inner circle was unique because Jesus

is unique, the passage does suggest the importance for Christians of being part of a small group of fellow-believers for purposes of support, spiritual growth, and accountability.

- The "Sermon on the Plain" includes not only blessings for the poor, those who mourn, those who are persecuted, but woes for the comfortable, self-confident, and popular by worldly standards. That gives both comfort and pause to those of us in North American churches.

- Jesus teaches new attitudes and new behaviors—love for one's enemies, doing good in the face of eveil, showing mercy, avoiding judgmental attitudes, and forgiving others—that flow from Jesus' image of God as gracious, generous, and merciful.

LUKE 7:1-35

Introduction to These Verses

Two highly dramatic miracles of healing occur at the beginning of this chapter: the healing of a Roman centurion's servant and the return to life of a widow's son. The public context of these events is as important as the events themselves, because it spreads even more widely abroad the reputation of Jesus among Gentiles and Jews.

Interestingly, these events indirectly result in John the Baptist reentering the narrative to make some inquiries of Jesus. Then Jesus offers an appraisal of John.

The material falls into three parts:
I. Impressive Miracles (7:1-17)
II. John's Query and Jesus' Response (7:18-23)
III. Jesus' Appraisal of John (7:24-35)

The Message of Luke 7:1-35

Caring and conviction are evident in this chapter. We see not only two dramatic episodes of healing but repeated new references to the outreach ministries of Jesus. Then occurs a significant declaration and witness: the mark of God's special servant is not military or political power but love in action through caring. This attitude identifies those who are indeed God's people or Jesus' disciples. It is not so much what is proclaimed in God's name but what is shared of one's self to meet others' needs in God's name that marks the lifestyle of a disciple.

Additionally, there is the importance of conviction. The spiritual conviction and sacrifice of John the Baptist is identified and admired. Jesus goes on to express his own conviction related to where truth lies, and how spiritual sophisticates can still miss the truth God lays at their doorsteps. Informed conviction must stand even though it is rejected or ridiculed.

LUKE 7:36–9:17

Introduction to These Chapters

Jesus' ministry moved into ever-widening circles of expression and expectation. More demands were placed upon him; more persons were exposed to him; more reactions took place around him. As he continued his expanding ministry of deed and word, he also began to interpret the nature of the relationship between his gospel and the world of people and powers around him. He both discussed and modeled what it meant to be in the world but not of the world.

This section develops as follows:

I. Gratitude of the Forgiven (7:36–8:3)
II. The Word Sown in the World (8:4-18)
III. The Wider Family of Jesus (8:19-21)
IV. The Mastery of Christ (8:22-56)
   A. Mastery over physical elements (8:22-39)
   B. Mastery over disease and death (8:40-56)
V. Commission to Minister to the World (9:1-6)
VI. Lingering Recollection of John (9:7-9)
VII. Sensitivity to Physical Need (9:10-17)

The Message of Luke 7:36–9:17

This section unveils for us a Christ who moves out into the world, motivated and directed by the desire and intention to meet human need. The need may be the need for forgiveness, new insight into truth, a sense of belonging, hope amid fear, release from the demonic, healing for illness, or life amid death. Human need becomes the magnet for Jesus' ministry.

And it is the same for all his disciples, ancient and modern. To believe in Christ is to become his disciple—and to join his mission to witness and to heal!

The Parables of Jesus

Patches and wineskins[1]	Luke 5:36-39	Matt 9:16-17	Mark 2:21-22
The blind leading the blind[2]	Luke 6:39-40	Matt 15:14b	
The log in your own eye[2]	Luke 6:41-42	Matt 7:3-4	
Producing good fruit[2]	Luke 6:43-45	Matt 7:16-20	
The two builders / building on a solid foundation	Luke 6:46-49	Matt 7:24-27	
The riddle of the children	Luke 7:31-35	Matt 11:16-19	
The two debtors	Luke 7:41-43		
The lamp	Luke 8:16	Matt 5:14-16	Mark 4:21-22
Seed and the soil and the sower	Luke 8:4-8	Matt 13:3-8	Mark 4:3-9
The good Samaritan	Luke 10:30-35		
The parable of a shameless neighbor	Luke 11 :5-8		
The kingdom divided against Itself[3]	Luke 11:17a	Matt 12:25a	Mark 3:24
The house divided against itself[3]	Luke 11:17b	Matt 12:25b	Mark 3:25
The return of the unclean spirit	Luke 11:24-26	Matt 12:43-45	
The rich fool	Luke 12:16-21		
The returning master	Luke 12:36-38		
The thief in the night / the watchful owner	Luke 12:39-40	Matt 24:43-44	
The good and wicked servants	Luke 12:42-46	Matt 24:45-51	[Mark 13:33-37]
Going before a judge	Luke 12:58-59	Matt 2:25-26	
The barren fig tree	Luke 13:6-9	[Matt 21:20-22	Mark 11:20-25]
The mustard seed	Luke 13:18-19	Matt 13:31-32	Mark 4:30-32
The yeast	Luke 13:20-21	Matt 13:33	
The narrow door	Luke 13:24-30		
Choice of places at table	Luke 14:7-11		
The great supper / great banquet	Luke 14:16-24	Matt 22:1-14	

[1]Although treated as a saying in Matthew and Mark, this passage is described as "a parable" by Luke.

[2]Although treated as a saying in Matthew, this passage is described as "a parable" by Luke.

[3]Although treated as a saying in Matthew and Luke, this passage is described as "a parable" by Mark.

The Parables of Jesus (cont.)

The fool at work	Luke 14:28-30		
The fool at war	Luke 14:31-32		
The lost sheep	Luke 15:3-7	Matt 18:12-14	
The lost coin	Luke 15:8-10		
The prodigal son	Luke 15:11-32		
The dishonest steward	Luke 16:1-9		
The rich man and Lazarus	Luke 16:19-31		
The servant who serves without reward	Luke 17:7-10		
The unjust judge and the persistent widow	Luke 18:1-8		
The Pharisee and the tax collector	Luke 18:9-14		
The talents/the greedy and vengeful king	Luke 19:11-27	Matt 25:14-30	
The wicked tenants / the Lord's Vineyard given to others / vineyard tenants	Luke 20:9-18	Matt 21:33-44	Mark 12:1-11
The fig tree in blooml	Luke 21:29-31	Matt 24:32-35	Mark 13:28-29
The weeds		Matt 13:24-30	
The hidden treasure and the pearl		Matt 13:44-46	
The net		Matt 13:47-48	
The owner of a house		Matt 13:52	
What can defile[4]		Matt 15:10-11	Mark 7:14-15
The unmerciful servant		Matt 18:23-35	
The laborers in the vineyard		Matt 20:1-16	
The two sons		Matt 21:28-32	
The bridesmaids		Matt 25:1-13	
The seed growing of itself			Mark 4:26-29
The watchful servants			Mark 13:33-37

[4]Described as "a parable" by both Matthew (15:15) and Mark (7:17).

LUKE 9:18-50

Introduction to These Verses

This section comes midway in the narrative account of Jesus' ministry prior to the triumphal entry into Jerusalem. It immediately follows the feeding of the multitude (9:12-17), which must have created both awe and curiosity. Jesus' reputation as a teacher and miracle worker had become widespread. So it would have been natural for many to be asking one another, and themselves, what even Herod had asked: "Who is this about whom I hear such things?" (verse 9).

Aware of these questions, Luke attempts now to provide some explicit answers by bringing into his account some events that testify to the nature of Christ. The following themes appear in and through these events:

   I. Messiahship Affirmed and Interpreted (9:18-22)
   II. Implications for Discipleship (9:23-27)
   III. Exaltation and Validation of Christ (9:28-36)
   IV. Evidence of Messiahship (9:37-45)
   V. Redefining Greatness and Community (9:46-50)

The Message of Luke 9:18-50

Divinity and humanity are blended in this section. On the one hand we see the highest affirmations about Jesus: "the Christ of God" (verse 20 NIV), and "This is my Son, my Chosen" (verse 35). We see the astonishment and marvel of the people. We even see the disciples wanting to immerse themselves in this greatness (verse 46).

However, what Jesus tries to unveil is a new definition of divinity. To be God's Son means to enter into the world of God's children. To be glorified means to be called to sacrifice. To be Messiah means to suffer.

Unbelievable these concepts were and distasteful they still are. The credentials of divinity are now to be established by servanthood.

LUKE 9:51–10:42

Introduction to These Chapters

The location of events now began to shift as Jesus set out to go to Jerusalem (9:51). In a sense the atmosphere became more solemn, the teachings more expansive and insistent, and concerns about the future more evident. It was both the end of the beginning and the beginning of the end of Jesus' ministry.

Our first focus relates to the location through which Jesus passed, the area of Samaria and its residents. Then there will also be attention given to the sending out of others in discipleship, as well as a personal visit to the home of friends of Jesus. The outline is as follows:

   I. Samaritans Resenting and Resented (9:51-56)
   II. Priorities for Discipleship (9:57-62)
   III. Sending Out of Emissaries (10:1-24)
   IV. The Good Samaritan (10:25-37)
   V. Visit with Martha and Mary (10:38-42)

The Message of Luke 9:51–10:42

In this section, beginning with the chosen route through Samaria and ending with the choices of Martha and Mary, Jesus is forcing persons to face the questions of priorities. To what are we committed? Then Jesus intends to give a new definition of the priority of loving God and neighbor. It requires seeing and identifying with the unloved in companionship and care. We are to become more sensitive to where human hurt and need exist and become a source of strength and part of the solution to them. We must avoid letting customs or busy-ness rob us of our awareness of this

THE GOOD SAMARITAN (LUKE 10:25-37)

The "lawyer" (verse 25, NRSV; NIV, "an expert in the law") was probably the same as a scribe, that is, a person who studied and interpreted the Jewish law. The Gentile readers would more readily understand the designation of lawyer.

The question asked is also later asked in Luke's account by a "ruler" in 18:18. In Mark's account of this incident the question is, "Which commandment is the first of all?" (Mark 12:28). Jesus was being "tested" by the inquirer as he sought to see whether Jesus would give the accepted and traditional response that such life was obtained through obedience to the law. However, Jesus turned the question back upon the inquirer (verse 26).

The quotations offered by the lawyer (verse 27) included the famous *Shema* (Deuteronomy 6:4-5), a central affirmation in Jewish faith. Additionally, he quoted a sentence from elsewhere in the law (Leviticus 19:18b) about attitude toward one's neighbor. Jesus did not initiate the idea of loving neighbor as self; it was part of the inherited law.

The lawyer sought to "justify" (verse 29) following the first question by asking a second question, seeking clarification of a point as a means of following up the first question.

Jesus' reference to Jerusalem was appropriate in the light of his own journeying in that direction and his hearers' familiarity with that route from Jerusalem to Jericho (verse 30). It was a crooked trail descending over 3,000 feet from the green hills around Jerusalem to the desert wilderness below sea level at Jericho. About halfway down the present roadway are the ruins of a building dating back to Roman times called the Inn of the Good Samaritan. The winding road surrounded by many huge boulders and nearby caves made it a likely place of ambushes by robbers.

A "Levite" (verse 32) was similar to a lay leader in the congregation, assisting the priest in caring for altarware and other physical properties in the place of worship, providing musical leadership, ushering, and teaching. This person had made a commitment to a life of service to God. *Levite* comes from a Hebrew term meaning a person pledged for a debt or vow. Originally they were from the tribe of Levi (descendants of Levi, one of the sons of Jacob) and were charged with the care of the sanctuary. (See Numbers 1:50-53; 3:6-9, 25-37; 4:1-33.)

The central feature and surprise of this story is that a Samaritan (verse 33) showed compassion for the Jewish victim when those of his own background and religious tradition would not. The longstanding enmity between Jews and Samaritans was a consequence of both religious and ethnic conflicts.

He placed oil and wine on his body (verse 34) because of their use in that time as therapeutic ointments.

A denarius (verse 35), a Roman silver coin, was the typical day's wage.

---

calling and these priorities. Our faith must bring an over-arching purpose to our living, a heart to our feeling, and caring hands and feet to our doing.

LUKE 11:1–13:9

Introduction to These Chapters

As Jesus continued to journey toward Jerusalem, the teaching portion of his ministry took on ever-larger dimensions in Luke's account. There were more sayings than events. Geographical surroundings took second place to instructional recollections. There was more that Jesus wanted his followers to know and understand. And this Luke recalls for us in the following format:

I. Commentary on Prayer (11:1-13)

II. On Evil Within (11:14-36)

The Message of Luke 11:1–13:9

As Jesus moves toward Jerusalem and continues his teachings, he invites his followers to utilize prayer as a means of self-awareness and awareness of God's purposes. He pushes his hearers toward authentic lives and genuine spirituality.

Much of what is taught in this section suggests two attitudes that could combat the drift toward spiritual blindness or insensitivity and also shape the priorities for our future lifestyle. One was to weigh carefully values that last against values of the moment. We are to more responsibly weigh moments, words, things, persons, attitudes. Jesus called upon his hearers to raise the question in everything they did and sought as to whether it was something of lasting value—and to be watchful in pursuit of eternal values.

Also, Jesus affirmed that every moment is important. He called upon his disciples to live life aware of the limits of time and opportunity. Their daily choices and achievements were to be governed by the sense that every moment was important and should be used in the best way for the service and purpose of God. The idea is summed up in the word *Watch!* which would be picked up elsewhere in the New Testament. His followers are to be watchful—of time, choices, purposes—in faith. This is not to be watching and waiting but watching and doing.

LUKE 13:10–16:31

Introduction to These Chapters

The journey to Jerusalem continued, as did the teachings of Jesus en route. This section of teachings covers a number of different topics, largely unrelated to each other. These particular teachings were most often stimulated by events or encounters. Thus it is a blending of actions and attitudes, divided as follows:

I. Confrontation over the Sabbath (13:10-17)
II. The Nature of the Kingdom (13:18-30)
III. A Warning and a Lament (13:31-35)
IV. Teachings at a Pharisee's House (14:1-24)
V. The Cost of Authentic Discipleship (14:25-35)
VI. Attitude Toward the Lost (15:1-32)
VII. Attitude Toward Possessions (16:1-31)

The Message of Luke 13:10–16:31

There is a sense in which the plight of the two sons in Luke 15:25-31 sums up the human weaknesses that Jesus addressed in the varied experiences and teachings of this section. The younger son was lost in human relationships—fleeing from a meaningful relationship with his father rather than seeking it, until need prompted him. He was lost in pursuit of possessions and then lost with the loss of possessions. He was lost in self-control, becoming more driven by impulses than committed to priorities. He was lost in values, giving himself to what seemed attractive. The end justified the means. He lost any high purpose or commitment in life. He lost his spiritual values and code for living.

The elder son was lost in spiritual pride and contentment. He was lost in a lack of compassion or a place for repentance.

THE PARABLE OF A FATHER AND TWO SONS (LUKE 15:11-32)

This parable is not just the story of the Prodigal Son, as it is so often called. It is the parable of a father and two sons (verse 11), as is clearly stated at the outset. Both sons were lost, one lost in self-indulgence (verses 12-14) and one in self-centeredness and pride (verses 28-30).

Under the Mosaic law the father, at a time of his choice, would determine and announce a division of his possessions (Deuteronomy 21:15-17). The actual bestowal of these possessions would usually take place at death: but might take place during the father's lifetime. This younger son wanted his portion while his father was still living, and the father granted this wish (verse 12).

"Wild living" (verse 13, NIV; NRSV, "dissolute living") can be translated "reckless or wasteful living." It is from this verse that the designation "prodigal son" arises. A prodigal is primarily not a lost person but a wasteful person.

Under the law, swine meat was not allowed in the Jewish diet (see Leviticus 11:26). The Talmud, or commentary upon the Jewish law, said, "Cursed is the man who tends swine." Thus to feed pigs (verse 15) would be shameful and degrading for a Jew. This indicates how desperate this lad had become. Also it may indicate how insensitive he had become to his own religious tradition and upbringing. The pods (verse 16) may have come from the carob tree.

The key phrase in marking the transition in the direction of the story, and the son's life, is "when he came to himself" (verse 17, NRSV; NIV, "to his senses"). When he got in genuine touch on the inside with who he was and where he had descended, he changed the outside of his life. He feared and felt that his father justifiably might not accept him back as a son. So he prepared a statement in advance of the encounter with his father in which he would seek for only the status of a hired servant (verses 18-19), which was all he felt he deserved.

An embrace and a kiss were customary expressions of warm hospitality toward welcome guests. The father, however, had not waited at the house to bestow these. He had gone out on his own initiative to bestow them before the son's arrival (verse 20). The father interrupted the boy's well-prepared statement (verses 21-22), never allowing him to complete it. The *best robe* would have been one of exquisite craft and quality reserved for very important guests. The *ring* was a symbol of family status, perhaps a signet ring. The *sandals* marked him as a son, rather than a servant or slave. In passing it should be noted that the son was received in this manner even though he had wasted all that the father had given him, which could have been one-third of the father's possessions. Thus the father had had a sizable personal loss through the son's irresponsibility.

While the younger son was lost in his vice, the elder son (verse 25) was lost in his virtue (verse 28). He complained that in contrast to a fatted calf being killed for the banquet honoring his brother's return, not even a baby goat (kid, verse 29) had ever been killed for a meal in his behalf.

Until the father designated otherwise, all he possessed would go to the first-born son, who shared the supervision of it. Thus the father said, "You are always with me, and all that is mine is yours" (verse 31).

The parable ends on the note of rejoicing over that which was lost and is found (verse 32), including the children of God.

To these circumstances all the portions of this section are addressed: the lostness in spiritual traditions that do not allow for healing, in relationships that are not inclusive, in shallow commitments that will not pay a price, in being possessed by possessions, in allowing no place for repentance in others nor seeing the need for it in ourselves. However, the greatest gladness God knows as our heavenly parent is when one of us, children of divine creation, having been dead becomes alive and having been lost is found (15:32).

LUKE 17:1–18:30

Introduction to These Chapters

This section is similar to the two preceding sections in format. It contains additional teachings of Jesus as he continued en route to Jerusalem. The primary focus of Luke continues to be more on what Jesus said than what he did. This focus narrows slightly as Jesus gave more specific directions to his disciples and also unveiled more central principles of the Kingdom.

Luke has organized the material as follows:

I. Directions to Disciples (17:1-10)
II. Encounter with the Ungrateful (17:11-19)
III. Suddenness of the Kingdom's Coming (17:20-37)
IV. Parables on Persistence and Prayer (18:1-14)
V. Centrality of Children (18:15-17)
VI. Self-denial Essential to Discipleship (18:18-30)

The Message of Luke 17:1–18:30

In Luke 17:6 Jesus spoke of how faith even in small quantity could accomplish much. He used the figure of speech of uprooting a tree as an illustration of what

might be accomplished. Faith was there identified as that which makes a difference in one's circumstances or surroundings. It is that which enables something to happen rather than something to be felt.

Although much of the various material in this section is not interrelated, we can find a common approach to these Scripture passages by discovering in them the traits for our life-style that the attitudes and life of faith should bring into existence. Looking panoramically at the passages, we find a call for the following: forgiveness (17:3-4), gratitude (17:11-19), awareness of the Kingdom around us (17:20-21), watchfulness for the day of the Son of Man yet to come (17:22-35), persistence in prayer (18:1-8), contrition (18:13-14), humility and receptivity (18:15-17), and sacrifice and commitment (18:18-30).

Each of us has tendencies within us to block the cultivation and possession of these virtues, such as spiritual stumbling blocks (17:1), hesitancy to forgive (17:3), ingratitude (17:16-18), spiritual indifference (17:27-28), momentary faith (18:8), spiritual pride (18:11-12), superiority (18:15), mixed loyalties (18:22), and possession-centeredness (18:23). Only through that form of faith that opens the door to God's operations and transformations within us, and the practice of faith that tackles the difficult and confronts that within us which is not in harmony with God's purposes for us, can this mountain be removed. Yet it can be, as Jesus affirmed, that what is impossible for human beings is possible for God (18:27).

LUKE 18:31–19:44

Introduction to These Chapters

Both despair and hope are intermingled in this section that records what happened as Jesus drew near to Jerusalem, the object of his pilgrimage. The section begins on a somber note as Jesus made clear his impending rejection, torture, and death. Yet to a blind man came sight and to a rich tax collector a new reason for being and a new style of living—and teaching was imparted on what should be done with what Jesus brought. Then, coming full circle, the section ends on a somber note with tears over Jerusalem's present and future.

The section is divided into three parts:
I. Warnings of What Lay Ahead (18:31-34)
II. The Visit to Jericho (18:35–19:27)
III. The Ascent to Jerusalem (19:28-44)

The Message of Luke 18:31–19:44

Jesus went to Jerusalem out of commitment to God and to people. As this section reveals, Jesus continued to make his witness and carry out his ministry on the way and after he arrived.

Why did he go to Jerusalem? Obviously he knew, in large measure, what awaited him. The largest portion of Luke's narrative relates in some manner to Jerusalem. As early as 9:51 Luke states of Jesus that "he set his face to go to Jerusalem." The remainder of the narrative describes events and sayings that took place on the journey there or while there.

This focus on Jerusalem seems important to Luke because the Messiah was to appear there, according to the prophetic tradition. Keeping the Jerusalem destination in the foreground reinforced the image of Jesus as Messiah.

Toward this city representing the might of God and humanity, Jesus set his face. Practically, Jesus would have known that for his truth to make a big difference in society, it would have to make an impact upon the powers that determined the fate of God's children (such as Zacchaeus). As Messiah he would have to

witness to that fact by his very presence in Jerusalem.

As a Jew who sought to enliven his religious tradition while living out that tradition, making change from within rather than from without, Jesus would make a pilgrimage to Jerusalem, especially to be there for the Passover. And if he had new truth to share about God, he would have to share it where God was seen to dwell. As Paul after him felt about Rome, Jesus could not be content until he had witnessed at Jerusalem.

LUKE 19:45–21:38

Introduction to These Chapters

Jesus has arrived at Jerusalem and entered the city. We now enter with Jesus into the last week in his life. This section includes those passages which report teachings and events that took place during the first half of that week. As to location, the primary focus is the Temple. As for the teachings, they primarily deal with basics, such as the purpose and future of the Temple, the nature of Jesus' authority and role, the nature of life beyond life, and the last days. The section includes the following components:
I. Confrontations in the Temple (19:45–20:8)
II. Parable on Spiritual Irresponsibility (20:9-18)
III. Plotting by Questioning (20:19-26)
IV. Dialogue on Life After Death (20:27-40)
V. Commentary on Messiahship (20:41-44)
VI. Genuineness Contrasted with Pretense (20:45–21:4)
VII. Impermanence of All Except Faith (21:5-36)
VIII. Jesus' Daily Patterns (21:37-38)

COINS IN THE GOSPELS

By New Testament times coins had been in use in Palestine for over six hundred years. The Jews struck currency of their own from the Persian era (fifth century BCE) until the end of the Bar Kochba revolt (135 CE). The currency circulating at Jesus' time would have been a mixture of various denominations of gold, silver, brass, and bronze coins from all parts of the Roman Empire and beyond.

"They paid him thirty silver coins."

Because they were made of the highest grade of silver, shekels and half-shekels struck at the mint at Tyre were accepted by the Jews as the official standard for payments specified in the Bible. Thus the Greek word *argyria* ("silver"), used to describe the money paid to Judas for betraying Jesus (cf. Exod 21:32; Zech 11:12), is believed to refer to the silver Tyrian shekel, worth approximately four denarii. This same coin is probably what Jesus refers to as a *stater* (Matt 17:27), which Peter used to pay the temple tax for Jesus and himself. The coin shown here, struck in 60/59 BCE, pictures the Phoenician deity Melkart as Heracles; the reverse pictures an eagle and reads "Tyre, Holy and Inviolate." The *didrachma,* or "two drachma" (Matt 17:24), a silver coin used to pay the half-shekel temple tax (Exod 30:13), may refer to a silver half-shekel struck at Tyre, essentially the same design as the shekel but half the weight. Shekels and half-shekels of this type were struck at the mint at Tyre from 126 BCE until about 70 CE.

"Render unto Caesar the things that are Caesar's."

The *denarius*, a Roman silver coin, was the typical day's wage. The coin shown, first issued c. 19 CE, pictures Emperor Tiberius (14–37) and reads "Tiberius Caesar, son of the Deified Augustus and himself Augustus." The reverse shows Livia, mother of Tiberius, represented as Pax, goddess of peace, and reads "High Priest." The denarius is mentioned in Matt 20:2; 22:19; Mark 6:37; 12:15; 14:5; Luke 7:41; 10:35; 20:24; and John 6:7; 12:5.

"What woman having ten drachma. . . ."

The *drachma* (Luke 15:8), a Greek silver coin, was approximate in value to the Roman denarius. The coin shown here, from Parthia, has the bust of Orodes I, the Parthian emperor (57-37 BCE) who briefly drove Herod I from Jerusalem; the reverse shows a seated Arsaces (founder of the Parthian Empire) and reads "King of Kings; Arsaces, Benefactor, Righteous one, God Manifest, Lover of the Greeks."

"Take nothing for the journey except a staff— no bread, no bag, no money [chalkon] in your belts."

The Greek term *chalkon* ("copper"; Mark 6:8) could refer to any midsize copper coin.

"Are not five sparrows sold for two assaria?"

Assarion (Matt 10:29; Luke 12:6) is the designation of various copper coins struck outside of Palestine. In NT times, sixteen assaria equaled one denarius. The obverse of the coin pictured here shows Augustus and reads "Deified Augustus, Father", the reverse shows an altar between the letters S(ENATVS) C(ONSVLTO), meaning "By the Consent of the Senate," and reads "Providence."

"A poor widow came and put in two lepta, which are worth a quadrans."

The *quadrans* (Mark 12:42) was a small bronze coin; four quadrans normally equalled an assarion, sixty-four quadrans a denarius. The coin pictured here was struck in Rome about 5 BCE, during the reign of Augustus. The obverse (not pictured) shows an altar; the reverse contains the legend "Apronius Gallus [the overseer of minting operations], maker of gold, silver, and bronze coins."

A *lepton* (or "thin piece" [Mark 12:42; Luke 21:2]), also called a *perutah* by the Jews, was a small copper coin, the coin of least value in circulation. These coins varied greatly in size and value; normally, two lepta equaled one quadrans. The coin pictured, struck in either 8 or 12 CE, shows a palm tree with clusters (obverse), and a wheat head with the legend "Belonging to Caesar" (reverse).

Photographs and text by Dr. E. Jerry Vardaman

The Message of Luke 19:45–21:38

The materials that are recorded in this section of Luke's account have a common locale, the Temple; but they touch on many different subjects. Yet interwoven beneath them all is a consistent attempt on the part of Jesus to encourage his hearers to distinguish the eternal in the midst of the temporal, that which is of true value amid momentary impressiveness.

For instance, Jesus came to the centerpiece of the Jewish spiritual tradition, the Temple, along with multitudes of other faithful pilgrims. Yet he announced the impermanence and even the destruction of the Temple. Thus he proclaimed that one's faith must be centered not in impermanent buildings to house God but in the eternal personhood of God (21:6). While acknowledging an obligation to the governing power, Jesus affirmed an equal obligation to God (20:25). He pointed out that life in God is longer and transcends human relationships (20:38). A widow's sacrificial giving far exceeds in authentic spiritual value the pious customs of the formally religious. Hardship and persecution and participation in calamities await the Christian disciple, but God's providential protection and deliverance will be equally present.

Introduction to These Verses

The net result is a renewed call for watchfulness. This call is not just to be watchful and spiritually prepared for the coming of the Son of Man but also to be watchful for the eternal in the midst of the temporal, and the spiritually genuine in the midst of the synthetic.

LUKE 22:1-54

In this section of Luke's narrative, Jesus moves toward the last mile of the way, and in preparation comes face to face with the realities of his own somber predictions. It is Jesus' last time with his disciples before his arrest and death. It begins with preparations for the last supper, ends at the high priest's house, and includes the following:

I. Covenant of Betrayal (22:1-6)
II. The Last Supper (22:7-38)
III. Prayer at Olivet (22:39-46)
IV. Betrayal and Arrest (22:47-54)

The Message of Luke 22:1-54

Jesus had the ability to use simple images to reveal deep and important truths. He did this often in his teaching, using as object lessons a lamp, a coin, birds, seeds, and even a colt. At this last supper he taught in a memorable way with cup and bread. These simple, everyday items Jesus forever filled with special meaning by injecting himself into them. In this ceremony the material and spiritual came together as tradition and immediacy also merged. These physical items became a part of the bloodstream and cells of those partaking; they became part of those persons.

Just as these items enter into our bodies and become part of us, so Christ enters into us by his spirit and becomes part of us. The Lord's Supper becomes not just communion with a memory but an avenue for a new entrance of Christ into us.

Then through our life Christ moves out into the life of the world. It may be into a night of darkness and struggle as on the Mount of Olives. It may be into a confrontation with principalities and powers and spiritual wickedness, such as awaited the disciples. If we can be watchful, God will send us the resources to strengthen us as we struggle to align our wills with God's purposes for us and allow Christ to live through us.

We are overwhelmed by his gracious acceptance, forgiveness, and promise. They turn us around. Then we move into our world of sinister shadows, frustrated hopes, and sweaty prayers, aware of his presence within us, and of his life to be lived through us, and of his love for others to be shared by us, even as we have received it. And we realize we have been converted.

LUKE 22:55–23:49

Introduction to These Chapters

The day of infamy was at hand. Jesus had entered into the "lonesome valley." He had to walk it all by himself. Separated from the support of the disciples, and away from the supportive crowds, Jesus was alone with accusers and opponents in a legal process with a fixed aim: his death. Then the death march was undertaken and the throes of a criminal execution experienced. It was the last mile of the way, with these markers en route:

I. Peter's Denials (22:55-62)
II. The Preliminary Hearing (22:63-71)
III. Hearing Before Pilate (23:1-25)
IV. Procession to Calvary (23:26-32)
V. Crucifixion (23:33-49)

The Message of Luke 22:55–23:49

The death of a prominent person always has a strange fascination for us. Every detail becomes important. Yet of all such deaths none has equaled the attention given to the death of Jesus. The reason lies beyond the method of his dying. For Luke, and many others, the reason for the fascination with this man's death was that God was in this picture in a unique way. This death was not just that of an itinerant prophet named Jesus but one who was seen as the Christ of God.

Luke's account of the crucifixion tells

us of a God who moves into the midst of life's struggles and needs and into the depth of life's sorrows and injustices. In so doing, the divine style is that of reconciling love expressed through servanthood. Luke wants us to see the cross as a marker erected on this earth of ours to tell us of a God whose concern was for this world and all within it, and who travails with us for it.

At this point Luke would probably also want us to recall the words of Jesus he recorded in 14:27: "Whoever does not carry the cross and follow me cannot be my disciple." The cross requires us to leave our customary ways and hold onto it. We grasp it not just for the comfort and compassion it offers, and we take up the challenge it presents to us. If we adhere to its demands, the cross will change our lives.

LUKE 23:50–24:53

Introduction to These Chapters

This section begins with the solemn removal from the cross and burial of the body of Jesus. Simultaneously, the hopes and spirits of the followers of Jesus had sunk to the ground with that burial.

But on the first day of the week joy came in the morning. The resurrection of Jesus broke down despair and raised up new hopes through the encounters that followed. The result is that the narrative ends finding the disciples with great joy and blessing God. The events of this section are as follows:

I. Burial and Final Tributes (23:50-56)
II. The Exciting Discovery (24:1-12)
III. Appearance on the Road (24:13-35)
IV. Appearance to the Disciples (24:36-43)
V. A Commission Given (24:44-49)
VI. Blessing and Response (24:50-53)

The Message of Luke 23:50–24:53

It was a shattering experience for these women to face an open tomb wherein the body of Jesus no longer lay. If they had not been able to do anything for Jesus during his suffering, at least they could do something for his body in death. But they sought Jesus where he was not to be found, for the miracle had happened. For those of us who have lowered our vision of possibilities to only the expected, the unexpected is a miracle. Yet God brings that miracle to us, as to the women, often enough to make us aware that the unpredictable is a part of life's experiences. This awareness can be our sustenance and hope.

Furthermore, Luke shows us that Christ was to be found in new places. Christ outdistanced any attempt to imprison him in a tomb. He goes before us. As we go out beyond our present lifestyles, our preconditioned expectations of Jesus or any structure that would confine him, there we will find Christ. Luke calls us to a relationship with Christ that is ever moving and not simply waiting, exploring and not simply affirming what we already know.

The last paragraphs of Luke's account point outward. Jesus said, Repentance and forgiveness of sins is to be preached in his name in all nations, beginning from Jerusalem. Then Christ walked with them out of their narrow world toward the wider world. Through his Spirit Christ continues to lead, walking with us and in us. We are the channel through which his risen presence moves into the world.

To summarize, Luke blesses us in his orderly account by unveiling for us a Christ who at personal risk came in love, informed by his words, healed by his touch, hurt with us and then for us. And still, centuries after his death, he remains with us, calling us and enabling us by his risen presence and spirit to do the same for others.

JOHN

OUTLINE OF JOHN

VI. Teaching About the New Passover (13:1–17:26)

   A. Jesus and his disciples (13:1-38)
      1. The Supper and the foot washing (13:1–17:26)
      2. The betrayal of Judas (13:21-38)
   B. Jesus' final teachings (14:1-16:33)
      1. Fellowship with the disciples (14:1-31)
      2. The church with the Father (15:1-27)
      3. Jesus' followers in the world (16:1-33)
   C. Jesus' prayer for his followers (17:1-26)

VII. The Messiah's Death (18:1–20:31)

   A. God's judgment of human sin (18:1–19:42)
      1. Arrest, trial, and suffering (18:1–19:16)
      2. Crucifixion and death (19:17-37)
      3. The burial (19:38-42)
   B. Grace expressed in the Resurrection (20:1-31)
      1. Jesus appears to Mary (20:1-18)
      2. Jesus appears to the disciples (20:19-29)
      3. The signs of Jesus (20:30-31)

VIII. New Life for All Humanity (21:1-25)

   A. Jesus with the disciples beside the sea (21:1-14)
   B. The command to follow Jesus (21:15-25)

INTRODUCTION

The early church symbol for the Gospel of John is the eagle. According to the church scholar Jerome (A.D. 349–420), each New Testament Gospel can be identified with one of the four creatures in the vision of Ezekiel (see Ezekiel 1 and 10). One of the four, the eagle, was thought to best represent the Gospel of John. An eagle soars in the heights with majestic patterns of flight. So John's Gospel soars to heaven and swoops back to earth, telling the story of Jesus the Christ. What is known about this majestic Gospel?

The Uniqueness of John's Gospel

John is the odd one out of the four New Testament Gospels. The first three Gospels are very similar in content. In fact, they are so similar that Matthew, Mark, and Luke must have somehow used each other as they wrote their versions of the good news. But the Gospel of John is very different from these other Gospels. For example, in John's Gospel Jesus offers no parables; he offers long discourses instead of brief sayings and teachings; he does not heal lepers; all miracles are signs of his identity (and not simply acts of mercy).

John is also unique in its use of opposites or contrasts. The Fourth Gospel constantly contrasts light and darkness; miracles and debates with the Jews; Jesus and the disciples with Judaism; and so forth. Embedded in these contrasts is a strong use of symbolism. The Gospel's use of symbolism is not meant to suggest that things did not really happen as presented. Rather, the use of symbolism is an attempt to help the reader penetrate deeper into the significance and meaning of events.

How can the uniqueness of John's Gospel be explained? People, geography, times, and intended purpose influence the writing of any document. These influences are important for understanding the uniqueness of John's Gospel.

The People Behind John's Gospel

The earliest reference to the writer of this Gospel is from the church leader Irenaeus (A.D. 140–203). He states that this Gospel was written in Ephesus by John, the disciple of Jesus. Irenaeus received this information from his teacher, Polycarp (A.D. 70–160), who knew John the apostle personally. But this information must be accepted with some caution, because early church writers have not always been proven correct. Irenaeus was almost certainly referring to John, the son of Zebedee, one of the twelve apostles. Perhaps this John left his masked signature in the Gospel narrative. The Gospel contains several references to a mysterious beloved disciple who seems to be present at important points in the story but is never named (see 13:23-25; 18:15-16; 20:2-10, for example).

However, things are not that simple. A good analysis of the text indicates different styles of writing and word choice. This implies editing and revision by different individuals. Hence, we will probably never know beyond a doubt the true author or authors of John's Gospel. But we are justified in assuming that John the apostle was somehow behind this Gospel (see 21:24). Perhaps John the apostle wrote the first draft and his followers edited "his" Gospel after he died, adding stories and accounts that John had personally told them. In the thinking of the first century, if the apostle John was somehow behind the Gospel, it would be said that John wrote the Gospel.

The Location and Date of John's Gospel

The writing of John's Gospel went through various stages. There are three probable levels of development. The first stage began in Palestine. After Jesus' death, John and the other disciples became leaders among those who believed Jesus was the Christ. We know that John did not immediately leave Palestine (Acts 8:14; Galatians 2:9). During this time in and around Jerusalem, John probably established his own little group of "disciples" or followers. This would have been quite normal. These followers would have been people who not only believed in Jesus but wanted to learn more about Jesus and his teachings.

The second stage was a major move—for unknown reasons—of John to Ephesus. It is very probable that at least some disciples went with him. Ephesus was a major seaport city in western Asia Minor with a large population. Trade was the main industry in Ephesus. It was also the home of a pagan Greek religion devoted to the mother goddess, Artemis (Acts 19:32-34). In this city, an early draft of John's Gospel was probably written. The date of John's arrival in Ephesus and the draft of the Gospel would be after Paul's missionary activity in the city during the 50s. A good estimate for the arrival of John and some of his disciples in Ephesus would be the decade of the 60s.

The third stage is the final writing of John's Gospel. This probably occurred after the death of John. His disciples and followers edited, wrote, and published a final version of the Gospel, holding true to what John had written and taught. The early church understood this Gospel to be John's testimony (21:24) to Jesus Christ. The final edition that we find in our New Testament was probably completed between A.D. 80 and 100.

This brings up an intriguing question. Were John and his disciples aware of the other Gospels during these stages of development? Certainly as an eyewitness and an apostle, John would have drawn from the same basic pool of information that influenced the other Gospel writers.

But it is more likely that John and his disciples never knew the other Gospels in their finished state as we know them today. If they did know the other Gospels, it was probably in some form of a rough draft.

The Structure of John's Gospel

John is a carefully finished account of Jesus' life. Material was chosen and organized with care to announce a central theme: eternal life comes through Jesus Christ and this is God's purpose for humanity. This is accomplished in two ways: First, Jesus is directly related to four major Jewish festivals. Second, *signs* play a very important role, pointing to the central message. For example, there are signs of turning water into wine (2:1-11), healing the sick (4:43-54), feeding the five thousand (6:1-15), and raising Lazarus from the dead (11:1-44). All of these signs point to eternal life through Christ. At the end of the Gospel, the reader is assured that Jesus did additional signs, which the disciples witnessed (20:30). The Gospel also has an introductory chapter, which attempts to prepare the minds of the readers, and a concluding chapter that challenges believers and disciples to follow Jesus (21:22). The structure of John's Gospel is so carefully arranged that it almost certainly reflects the thinking—if not the hand—of John himself.

The Purpose of John's Gospel

This is by far the most important aspect of the Gospel. What was the intention of those behind this writing? What was the deeper purpose of John the apostle? It seems quite clear that the Gospel is meant to help the reader understand the identity of Jesus as the Messiah and the Son of God and to initiate response to him (see 20:31). But what else can we know about the purpose of John's Gospel?

As noted above, this Gospel is written for early church believers. On the one hand, tradition tells us that John the apostle was involved with a particular congregation or church in Ephesus. Perhaps he was associated with several congregations in and outside of this city. But more than likely one community was his home congregation. This particular congregation was the setting for the formation of John's Gospel. Like all other New Testament documents, John was written with a particular living church situation in mind. On the other hand, through this one congregation, the Gospel addresses all humanity and the church universal. This is the complete audience to whom the message is directed. But with the help of this particular congregation, we can better hear what John is saying about Jesus the Christ.

The social structures of the first century make some useful suggestions about church congregations. Beyond the Gentile/Jewish distinction, an Asia Minor church would have been comprised of two groups of believers: Jewish Christians and Hellenistic or Greek-influenced Christians. The Jewish believers would tend to see Christ through the Jewish Torah, or law. The Hellenistic Christians would tend to see Christ through Greek philosophy, culture, and wisdom. It would follow that Jewish converts would have difficulty accepting Jesus as more than a man (that is, divine). The Hellenistic Christians would have difficulty thinking of Jesus as less than divine (that is, human) because of the influence of Greek philosophy.

In the middle of these social groups, John's purpose emerged. He seeks to present a very balanced Christ, who is more than human, as fully God, and yet not less than God, having become fully human. Christ is the true mediator of God and humankind. John then goes on to use

THE PROLOGUE TO THE GOSPEL OF JOHN

A Poetic Confession of God's Word (1:1-5)

The Gospel begins with the same three words as the Old Testament. The start of Genesis reads, "In the beginning . . . God created the heavens and the earth" (Genesis 1:1). The Gospel of John begins, "In the beginning was the Word, and the Word was with God, and the Word was God" (1:1). The analogy is deliberate and meaningful. John is saying poetically, the Word is God and God is the Word. The Word of God and God the Word were there in the beginning. They always were and they always will be.

What is the meaning of *Word*? The Greek term *logos* carries the meaning of personal action. What a significant term for speaking about Jesus the Christ. He not only is the personal expression of God to humanity, but this word is an action, an act. In the beginning, God "acted personally" toward humanity—toward us. God did not simply speak. God acted. God's speech and God's action are synonymous. For God—and based on God's Word—to speak and act toward us is to get personal and to draw near.

The writer then refers to the Word as *He* (verse 2). He was in the beginning with God. Exactly how the action of God gets personal and draws near to humanity is a mystery. This Gospel makes it clear from the start that the Word is divine. Jesus the Word is God. The Word will never be less than God. The Word is God. It is amazing—but this Word draws near to humanity as flesh (see verse 14).

Then we read that all things were made through him (verse 3). This statement has traditionally been understood as *Creation*. In this sense, the reader is again brought back to the Genesis Creation accounts. Not only was the Word present when all things were created, but they were created through, with, and for Him. He is the basis of everything that exists.

It follows that the Word is the purpose of all things. If all things are made or have their being through him, then all things are true, right, and real only in him. He is the reason behind all that is; he is the goal of all things; he is the center of the universe; he is the key to what philosophy calls reality. The universe only makes sense in him. He is the beginning and the end. To say the same thing in a negative manner, without him the creation—and humanity, the peak of creation (see Psalm 8)—would be nothing but chaos, the void, the formless space (Genesis 1:2).

This focus on Jesus the Word continues. Because the Word is life, everything has life in him (verse 4). He alone is life-giving. As life, he is light (see verse 9). Without any light, there would be chaos and darkness. The reassuring truth about the Word of God is that chaos and darkness could not extinguish this light (verse 5). In this way the centrality of the Word for the entire universe is affirmed. And this points us back to the first verse.

The Sign of John the Baptist (1:6-8)

After this awesome beginning, the Gospel refers to a supporting event. Looking back to the Old Testament, God promised through the prophets to tell the people when to expect more complete divine words and actions. The prophet Malachi, writing about 400 B.C., tells about a messenger, or angel, who would prepare the way before the Lord, the same Lord whom you seek. He adds, "The messenger of the covenant in whom you delight" (NRSV; NIV, "whom you desire") "is coming, says the LORD" (Malachi 3:1; see also Isaiah 40:3).

In all four Gospels, this expected messenger is identified as John the Baptist. His task is to indicate God's new action. God keeps the promises and sends a messenger to point out God's drawing near. This messenger is one who is equipped to hear and see God's personal action in Christ. In this manner, John represents all humanity, who are also equipped, or given the gift of faith. But John is a further example to humanity in that he accepts the gift of faith (the "power,"

THE PROLOGUE TO THE GOSPEL OF JOHN (CONT.)

NRSV; NIV, "right," verse 12) and becomes as a child—a child of God. John accepts God's personal action in Christ and accepts his calling to point to and bear witness to the Word.

The Word as the Light of the World (1:9-13)

Now Christ the Word is explained by the analogy of *light* (verse 9). Christ the light does two things. First of all, the true light proclaims the truth of God. The basic truth of the Creation, humanity, the universe, and so forth are all dependent upon the one light of God. Therefore, Christ is the only true light of God that shines in our darkness. At the end of the Gospel, Pilate asks Jesus, "What is truth?" (see John 18:38). But the reader is told at the beginning what is truth—the Word is truth, the true light.

Second, this light enlightens every person. The emphasis is still on the Word. Humanity remains secondary. The Word enlightens because the Word is the key to the universe. The light could do nothing else! As a result, we are enlightened by him. We can know nothing without the enlightening truth. The emphasis remains on the "true light." Without him, everything is out of focus—we must have the light.

This light was already here and was not recognized (verse 10). This is a continuing problem with humanity—the world did not recognize him. Here we are, made through him and for him, and yet we do not know him. How can this be? Something has gone wrong. Rebellion is evident everywhere; we have turned away from the key to all things. Humans created for God have refused to be children of God—we have sought our own will and have run away.

The next verse pushes this theme of rebellion further (verse 11). The rebellion of the creation is very personal. He came to his own, and he was not received. Following the Genesis themes in the Creation accounts, humanity is created for covenant fellowship with God. In this manner, we are created in the image of God. But humanity rebelled, returning the creation to chaos and darkness (much like the symbolism of Adam and Eve being thrown out of the garden). So now when the one through whom all things were created comes home, his own people received him not.

But the Word is the light of all humanity (verses 12-13). Those who accept this truth become "children of God." Notice that these persons are given power, divine power to become children. Why would God give us the power to become children? (This statement anticipates Jesus' conversation with Nicodemus, in John 2:23–3:21.) The power is the gift of faith. Accepting this gift is the beginning of life as a child of God. Thus faith as a child begins with God and comes from God.

A person who accepts the gift of faith no longer acts and thinks from self—or from the side of humanity. The child of God thinks and acts out of God. All the characteristics of a child are meant to be evident in the person who believes. The child of God will trust the Father, accept and obey the will of the Father, experience the greatest joy in being with the Father, and so forth. The child of God seeks the light and runs from the darkness to the safety of the Father. And all this is done by the Father.

This is why John's Gospel begins with heavenly things. Humans are simply asked to become children through Christ, their brother, and to trust the Father. Hence, humanity is born of God (verse 13). In this sense, we are not born of blood (woman), of flesh (lust), or of man (Matthew 16:17; 1 Corinthians 15:50). We are made for God; we are born for God.

God's Word of Grace Becomes Flesh (1:14-18)

These are the last verses of the introduction to the prologue, or opening chapter. They function as a summary of what has already been said.

THE PROLOGUE TO THE GOSPEL OF JOHN (CONT.)

The famous opening verse states the Gospel in miniature (verse 14). This may be the most profound thought and verse in the Christian Bible. It states in a few words what has already been poetically stated and will soon be more fully presented. The Word that was with God in the beginning and for whom all is created becomes flesh. In part, this profound thought is incomprehensible—we cannot comprehend God! But with the help of the prayerful, poetic beginning, perhaps we can apprehend a portion of God's truth.

The word "flesh" refers to humanity in general. The Word became a human being. Out of all the species of creation, the Word became humanity. God freely chose humanity for fellowship with the divine. What a humbling thought! God, in divine freedom, chose to covenant and embrace humanity, speaking on our terms in the flesh so that we could apprehend and hear God's truth.

Dwelling among us carries the Old Testament meaning of *tenting* among us. In Exodus 25:8-9, Israel is instructed by God to make a tent (from the Hebrew word meaning *tabernacle*) so God can dwell among or in the midst of the people. In this sense, God dwells, like the people, in a tent. The Israelites at this time were a nomadic people and home was a tent. In such a tent, God chose to be present with Israel (Joel 2:27; Zechariah 2:10; Ezekiel 43:7). Early Jewish thought also stressed the "Shekinah promise," or God's promise to always dwell with the people. In this sense, John records how the Word became flesh and lived among us, fulfilling God's continued promise to humanity through Israel. And now this is accomplished once and forever.

Because of God's coming to humanity, God's glory is made known. God willingness to come out of love for the rebellious—the true light in our darkness—is "full of grace and truth." When the eyewitnesses beheld the Word in the flesh, when the apostles went to the tabernacle, or tent (the Christ), they saw his glory, the glory of the only Son from the Father. This event of *incarnation* (literally, "in the flesh") is affirmed in the other three Gospels by the event of the Transfiguration (Matthew 17:1-8; Mark 9:2-8; Luke 9:28-36; see also 2 Peter 1:16-17).

The witness of John the Baptist is briefly reintroduced (verse 15). The glorious miracle is that John only knew this truth because it was given to him by God (1:33). His message is clear and straightforward (3:22-36): Jesus is the one who comes after me. He is the glorious "tabernacled" presence. Because of this truth, John's witness can never displace the Word, the light, the Christ. This danger of displacement remains a current one. Too often the witness or formulation of the truth replaces or eclipses the truth. But only by the full presence of the true Word will all receive grace upon grace (verse 16).

The last two verses of the introduction to the prologue state the two occasions when God has drawn close to humanity. This happened first through Moses' establishing the old covenant with the law. After God liberated Israel from Egypt, the law became the guidelines for Israel's covenant response to God. This response was channeled through the old tabernacle experience. The second, more profound, way God drew close to humanity was in the tabernacle of Christ, establishing a new covenant in grace. Now humanity can respond to God in the name of Christ through the permanent tabernacle of the true Word (Hebrews 7:23-25).

How do we really know God? There is an Old Testament theme that flesh cannot see God and live. Moses desired to see God's glory or see God (Exodus 33:18). He was told that this could not happen if his life were to continue (also see Isaiah 6:5). John's Gospel reflects this Jewish understanding. No one has ever seen God (verse 18). But the Son, the Word, the light, the one who tabernacles with us, makes God known.

Jesus' teachings about love and unity to encourage the congregation(s) to seek oneness in Christ (chapters 13–17). This is John's deeper theological purpose.

JOHN 1:1-18

Introduction to These Verses

John's opening chapter contains some of the most profound Christian literature ever produced. Unlike the other Gospels, John begins with eternal things. The intention is not first to establish that Jesus was very human. This Gospel has no interest in family trees or Jewish lineage. The real importance of Jesus the Nazarene lies in his "pre-existence." The starting point of this Gospel is that Jesus existed or lived before the world was created.

In order to speak of these eternal things, the Gospel begins poetically. Because of our inability to speak of truths that are literally out of this world, poetic verse is helpful. As a result, some have argued that this Gospel begins with a hymn. Certainly these verses could well have been an early hymn to the praise of God's salvation plan for humanity. Perhaps these lines were composed by John and inspired through a vision. And perhaps these verses were sung by churches in and around Ephesus.

The prologue may be divided into four parts:
I. A Poetic Confession of God's Word (1:1-5)
II. The Sign of John the Baptist (1:6-8)
III. The Word as the Light of the World (1:9-13)
IV. God's Word of Grace Becomes Flesh (1:14-18)

The Message of John 1:1-18

These verses attempt to prepare readers for what is to come. The gospel, or good news, is that God has come to humanity. God has not left us alone in the darkness but has come to tabernacle with us and rescue us from death and destruction. Here are some truths that stretch our minds at the beginning of this Gospel.

- God acts personally for humanity.
- God sends the Word—spoken and acted.
- All creation has its purpose and existence in God's Word.
- Christ is the light of humanity.
- Christ is the place (the tabernacle) where God is found.
- John the Baptist is a sign of God's true Word.
- God sends humanity the gift of faith through the Holy Spirit.

JOHN 1:19-51

Introduction to These Verses

The remaining verses of chapter 1 are written in narrative style, a more earthly telling of events. After stretching the reader's mind with poetic wonder and truth, the Gospel turns to the actual story of Jesus' life.

This section has two parts:
I. John's Witness to the Word (1:19-34)
II. The First Disciples (1:35-51)

The Message of John 1:19-51

These verses are narrative in style, rather than poetic. They give an account of the work of John the Baptist, and of the calling of Jesus' first disciples. What can we learn from these verses?

- God calls all persons to discipleship.
- Discipleship means abiding in fellowship with others.

- There was a close relationship between John the Baptist and Jesus, as well as among the disciples of each.

- The ministry of Jesus is closely related to tradition and to history.

- The Holy Spirit helps us recognize God.

- God gives us the power to recognize God's promise.

JOHN 2

Introduction to This Chapter

The first "sign" (John's term for miracle) Jesus acts out happens at the wedding celebration in Cana of Galilee, where Jesus changes water into wine. This miracle signifies a new day, a new celebration, a new life established through a new covenant between God and humanity. This new covenant relationship will be worked out between the bridegroom, Jesus (3:29), and his bride, the church. The popular Old Testament metaphor of the marriage relationship as representative of God's covenant with Israel is now redefined, turned around, and reestablished.

The theme of the new covenant and new life is affirmed in the sections that follow.

Chapter 2 has two parts:
I. The New Wine Miracle (2:1-11)
II. Cleansing of the Temple (2:12-25)

The Message of John 2

- Human goals must always be formed in relationship to God's will.

- God held to the covenant with Israel faithfully, despite Israel's unfaithfulness.

- The Holy Spirit serves to unite us with God, after we have been purified through Christ.

JOHN 3

Introduction to This Chapter

Chapter 3 contains the well-known story of Nicodemus, as well as more information about John the Baptist.

Here is an outline of this chapter:
I. Nicodemus and the New Birth (3:1-21)
   A. Nicodemus is introduced (3:1-2)
   B. Earthly things and heavenly things (3:3-15)
   C. God's Love is universal (3:16-21)
II. Testimony of John the Baptist (3:22-36)

The Message of John 3

- As the concluding section of chapter 3 indicates, to see life is to enjoy the same covenant relationship with God that is first a truth between the Father and the Son. To turn away and refuse the gift of faith is to harden one's heart and enjoin the wrath of God.

- God's wrath is not a personal attack by God upon the unbeliever. Rather, God's wrath is the result of running away or distancing oneself from God.

- If to live is Christ, and to die is gain (see Philippians 1:21), then rejection of the Spirit's promptings and the Word of God in Christ can only result in a person's flight into darkness— away from the light. To not choose Christ is to choose the opposite. This is what John's Gospel calls God's wrath.

GOD'S LOVE IS UNIVERSAL (JOHN 3:16-21)

Now Jesus' statements include all humanity. The preceding verses center on Israel. From verse 16, Jesus speaks about a new covenant in Christ that is for all—all the universe.

Jesus begins with a grand statement. Here is the good news of Christianity succinctly stated. Jesus states that God first loved the world, and acted toward it. Notice how the verse begins with God's action and states that God came to the world in general. Only then comes the personal emphasis that whoever believes shall have life. In this manner God came down to us and will lift us up, uniting us forever with the divine. This is God's self-giving and self-sacrificing love that acts. God's Word acts. Now for those who believe because they hear the Spirit, eternal life is assured.

God's action is an action of love. The Son did not come to condemn us. What a positive statement about the world! We are not condemned, but saved. The term "world" (*kosmos* in Greek) refers to the entire universe of created things.

Belief in this personal Word of God to the world is restated in the remaining verses. The imagery of light is again employed. To be out of the light is to be condemned (verse 18). Judgment has occurred by the light. Now we must choose—simply because the light has come. Evil deeds are a sign of not choosing the light. But if we hear the Spirit bearing witness to the Word of God, we will more and more seek the light in response to God (verse 21). This will bear witness that we have chosen the Son when the Word of judgment comes to the world. Here we find in a few verses the new meaning of life.

JOHN 4

Introduction to This Chapter

This chapter tells of the dramatic encounter between Jesus and the woman of Samaria. The second part of the chapter contains a healing miracle. John 4:1 may be outlined as follows:

I. The Samaritan Woman at the Well (4:1-42)

A. Introduction (4:1-6)
B. Jesus asks for water (4:7-15)
C. Jesus is a prophet (4:16-26)
D. The disciples return (4:27-30)
E. Jesus teaches the disciples (4:31-38)
F. Conclusion (4:39-42)

II. A Sign of Life's New Meaning (4:43-54)

A. Introduction (4:43-45)
B. The healing (4:46-54)

THE DISPUTE BETWEEN JEWS AND SAMARITANS

The breach between Jews and Samaritans can be traced to the Assyrian occupation of northern Palestine (721 B.C.), but the most intense rivalry began about 200 B.C. The source of the enmity between the Jews and the Samaritans was a dispute about the correct location of the cultic center (see John 4:20). The Samaritans built a shrine on Mt. Gerizim during the Persian period and claimed that this shrine, not the Jerusalem Temple, was the proper place of worship. The shrine at Mt. Gerizim was destroyed by Jewish troops in 128 B.C., but the schism between Jews and Samaritans continued (see John 4:9).

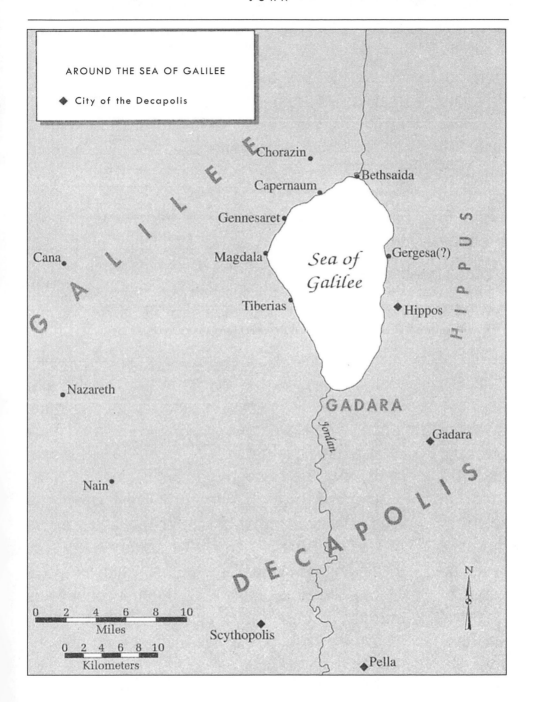

AROUND THE SEA OF GALILEE

◆ City of the Decapolis

GALILEE

Chorazin
Capernaum
Bethsaida
Gennesaret
Cana
Magdala
Sea of
Galilee
Gergesa(?)
HIPPUS
Tiberias
Hippos

Nazareth

GADARA

Jordan

Gadara

DECAPOLIS

Nain

0   2   4   6   8   10
Miles

0   2   4   6   8   10
Kilometers

Scythopolis

Pella

N

The Message of John 4

- Jesus is the living water who quenches human thirst for God.

- The grace of God through Jesus is available to all: male and female; chosen people and rejected people.

- God's spirit is not limited to any physical or cultural location.

JOHN 5

Introduction to This Chapter

In the next several chapters, Jesus is placed against the backdrop of Judaism. Jesus is directly related to four Jewish festivals: Pentecost, Passover, Tabernacles, and Dedication. The writer of John's Gospel has a definite purpose in mind throughout this section. Jesus is presented as the fulfillment of the meaning of these feasts. He is understood and presented as the essence and the completion of all Jewish expectations.

Chapter 5 may be outlined as follows:
I. Healing on the Sabbath (5:1-18)
II. Teachings About Healings (5:19-47)
  A. Relationship between Father and Son (5:19-29)
  B. Testimony about the relationship (5:30-40)
  C. Jesus judges the Jews (5:41-47)

The Message of John 5

Jesus fulfills the meaning of the occasion. By performing a miracle on the sabbath, he becomes the healing truth of a new sabbath that will be completed at his resurrection. This will make him the real life-giver and judge.

The Jewish authorities would have understood these claims as an attempt to usurp the powers of God and claim divinity. By these claims, Jesus asserts the beginning of a new time or that he represented humanity's new historical relationship with God.

JOHN 6

Introduction to This Chapter

This section reports Jesus' activities and teachings as appropriate to Passover. Jesus feeds the large crowd, supplying life's bread; walks on the sea and quells the storms of life; and teaches about his identity as the bread of life. For the Jews, Passover centered on two general themes: God's deliverance of Israel in the past (through Moses) and God's promised deliverance of Israel in the future (through the coming Messiah). Into this situation Jesus arrives. Through his work and teachings, he redefines Passover.

Chapter 6 has three parts:
I. Feeding the Five Thousand (6:1-15)
II. Jesus Walks on the Sea (6:16-21)
III. Jesus the Bread of Life (6:22-71)

The Message of John 6

In this Passover feast, the emphasis falls on Jesus as the bread of life and Jesus' power over chaos. At the previous Passover, he cleansed the Temple. On the next Passover, he will offer himself as a sacrifice for the many. So we see a movement from getting the temple (of his body) ready to now establishing the new element (the unleavened bread) and rationale (defeating the seas of chaos), to finally reconstituting this entire Jewish festival that celebrates God's deliverance of Israel.

During this second Passover, Jesus is established as the bread of life. He is a prophetic Moses figure of the past, and manna, the shewbread that was expected to be a sign of the new messiah's arrival. He is the bread provided by God to reconcile humanity to God. But he is also the future bread of life.

"I AM" SAYINGS

"I am" is Jesus' characteristic formula of self-revelation in John. Many times the "I am" is followed by a noun: "I am the bread of life" (6:35; see 6:48; 6:51); "I am the light of the world" (8:12; 9:5); "I am the gate for the sheep" (10:7, 9); "I am the good shepherd" (10:11, 14); "I am the resurrection and the life" (11:25-26); "I am the way, and the truth, and the life" (14:6); "I am the true vine" (15:1; see also 15:5). These nouns are common symbols from religious and human experience, and the "I am" identifies Jesus as the one who meets basic needs and desires. Other times, as at 4:26, the "I am" is spoken without an accompanying noun (see also 6:10; 8:24, 28, 58; 13:19; 18:5, 6, 8). When Jesus speaks this way, he is making a direct connection with the divine name (as in Exod 3:14, "I AM WHO I AM"), in order to identify himself as the one in whom God is visible and made known (1:18). This usage expresses the conviction of the prologue, "the Word was with God, and the Word was God" (1:1).

JOHN 7–8

Introduction to These Chapters

For the next 153 verses, Jesus is involved with the Jewish feast of Tabernacles. This is a major pilgrimage festival that was celebrated in Jerusalem for eight days in the fall of the year (September/October). Also known as the Festival of Booths or Ingathering, it required that pilgrims actually dwell in booths or branch huts in the vineyards. Because God had provided for the people of Israel during their wilderness wanderings, the people now combine thankfulness for these past blessings with thankfulness for the current fall harvest.

John 7:1–8 may be outlined as follows:
I. The Feast of Tabernacles (7:1-52)
II. The Woman Caught in Adultery (7:53–8:11)
III. Jesus the Light of the World (8:12-59)

The Message of John 7–8

In this section, Jesus is understood and explained through the major themes of the Jewish Feast of Tabernacles. The major themes are the following:

- This festival was intended to bring all Israel together. In the same manner, Jesus is God's Word reconciling all humanity to the Father (Zechariah 14:16).

- The pilgrims gathered in the holy city of Jerusalem, the place were God dwelt in the Temple. It is in the Temple that Jesus teaches, heals, and debates his true identity with the religious officials of Israel.

- The feast celebrated Israel's wilderness wanderings when God provided for their needs. Jesus is God's light who shines in the dark wilderness of life.

- Jesus is the water of life who sends the spirit to replenish humanity.

- This feast celebrated the harvest. Jesus is the beginning of God's true harvest reconciling the Father with humanity.

In John 7:53–8:11, Jesus conveys several truths:

- Jesus does not rank sexual sins as more weighty than other sins. Neither should the church.

- Jesus' counterchallenge, "if any one of you is without sin, let him be the first to throw a stone at her", (NIV) addresses *individuals*, not a mob or undifferentiated crowd, with a call to self-awareness and humility.

- Jesus invites *both* the woman caught in adultery *and* the religious leaders (the scribes and Pharisees) to give up old ways and embrace a new way of thinking and acting.

- *Light* was an important element in celebrating the Feast of Tabernacles. When Jesus declares that he is the light of the world, he is claiming to be the fulfillment of Tabernacles joy.

Light is an image or metaphor for God's activity in the act of creation (Genesis 1:3-4), for God's presence in the wilderness (Exodus 13:21), for God's wisdom and law, and for God's Word. By declaring himself to be the light of the world, Jesus is claiming a very special relationship with God.

- It is important for Christian believers to understand the context for the harsh language in John 8 about "the Jews." Scholars have recognized clues in the Fourth Gospel that indicate an historical shift between the time of Jesus and the time this Gospel was written. After the destruction of the Temple in A.D. 70, the issue of who could rightfully claim and interpret Jewish Scriptures became enormously important, and tension emerged between the larger Jewish community and those Jews who professed faith in Jesus. Sometime in the last quarter-century of the First Century, the latter group was expelled from Jewish synagogues (see 9:22; 12:42; 16:2). The Gospel of John reflects an effort on behalf of Jewish Christians to reclaim their Jewish roots. Hence, this Gospel mentions important Jewish feasts and claims that Jesus is the fulfillment of those feasts. The Evangelist makes comparisons between Jesus, on the one hand, and Abraham, Jacob, and Moses, on the

other. The language of chapter 8 is sometimes unmistakably harsh toward Jewish leaders and power structures. It is important for readers today to recognize that the Johannine Jewish Christians were a largely powerless minority group up against the Jewish establishment. The situation in today's world is entirely different. For one thing, Christians are mostly Gentile, not Jewish, by heritage so we are not in the midst of an intra-family quarrel. Second, the balance of social power has shifted such that Christianity is not at risk because of Judaism. Any use of John 8 by Christians in a crusade against Judaism would be wholly inappropriate. The danger of such misappropriation was horribly evident in the damage inflicted by the Third Reich upon Europe's Jewish population.

JOHN 9–10

Introduction to These Chapters

These two chapters are concerned with themes relating to light, seeing, and the Feast of Dedication. They may be outlined as follows:

I. Jesus Heals a Blind Man (9:1-41)

II. Jesus and the Feast of Dedication (10:1-42)

The Message of John 9–10

- Sin has to do with resistance to Jesus, with refusing to "see" him as the light of the world, as one who does God's works.

- Light can produce both sight and blindness, the latter for those who stare but do not recognize the light's source or power.

- With whom do we identify in the story of the healing of the blind man? Perhaps those of us who are sincere, educated church leaders have some similarities to the religious leaders in the story.

- Scripture and tradition are important, to be sure, to our understanding of God and God's will. But the behavior of the blind man who was healed (see 9:25, 30-33) suggests that our *experience* is a legitimate element in our discernment of what God is doing in any new situation.

Jesus explains that not only does God the good shepherd come to the sheep in the person and word of Jesus, but God eternally covenants with the sheep.

- Jesus is the new Davidic king who will make one sheepfold for all humanity.

- This feast celebrated the rededication of the Temple. Jesus now surpasses the Temple as the place where God dwells. He is God incarnate, rededicating all humanity for dwelling in right relationship to God.

- Between the desecration of the Temple and its rededication, the Jews depended upon God to supply their needs. Now God supplies the shepherd, the light, the water, and the bread for the chosen people living in the caves of wilderness as they await his return and final purification.

- This feast celebrated freedom in worship. Now in Christ all are free to enter the sheepfold through the door.

- Finally, one tradition states that the light in the Temple burned for eight days—hence, the festival of lights. Jesus is the new light that shines in

the darkness and will never be quenched.

JOHN 11:1-54

Introduction to These Verses

This is the second longest narrative in all four Gospels. The longest narrative is the account of Jesus' death. Although this grand event centers on Lazarus, it seems to flow out of and help interpret Jesus' resurrection. In this manner, the resurrection of Lazarus confirms and establishes Jesus' mission and identity. Looking forward, it is precisely his power over death that allows him to redefine and reconstitute the Passover festival. Looking back, this event is a fitting sign that Jesus is the new focal point of all major Jewish festivals.

Here is an outline of John 11:1-54:
I. The Story of Lazarus (11:1-44)
   A. Introduction (11:1-4)
   B. The death of Lazarus (11:5-16)
   C. Jesus arrives in Bethany (11:17-27)
   D. Jesus speaks to Mary (11:28-37)
   E. Lazarus is raised (11:38-44)
II. Jesus' Death; Lazarus's Resurrection (11:45-54)

The Message of John 11:1-54

This event is the focal point of the Fourth Gospel. It is the crowning action of all that has gone before—of Jesus' teachings and healings. Here is the climactic seventh and most nearly perfect sign that has been building since the opening verses.

From here, things move in a different direction. Jesus begins carefully instructing and preparing the disciples for his absence. He redefines the Passover for Judaism and all humanity. There is a plan of salvation;

RESURRECTION LIFE

Is salvation only something for the distant future? What does it have to do with Christians right here and now? Jesus said, "I came that they may have life, and have it abundantly" (John 10:10). Did he mean abundant life on earth? Now or later? Is the abundant life restricted to heaven? Those are questions that sprang up in the early years of the Christian church and spring up for believers even today. The Gospel of John can help us sort out the answers just as it helped the first Christians.

The Fourth Gospel includes three positions about the fullness of salvation. Each is presented as a part of the total picture, but one position in particular is emphasized.

One view locates salvation in the future. Judgment will happen on some future final day in history (see 12:48). On that day there will be a general resurrection of those who have died (see 6:39-40 and 6:54). That time of resurrection will bring a day of reckoning (5:28-29). That event is commonly referred to as the second coming of Christ. We live, as did the first Christians, in the time between Christ's earthly life and his final reappearance as Lord and Judge.

Another perspective found in the Gospel of John locates salvation in the future of individual persons when they die. In some passages, Jesus assures his followers that there is a heavenly home waiting for them (14:2-3). This heavenly realm exists at the same time as the world as we know it. The fullness of salvation is in the future of each individual believer, not in some future event when salvation or judgment will come to everyone at once. This is probably the perspective accepted by most people in our churches today when they think about death and eternal life.

But the Gospel of John puts the heaviest emphasis on a third position. To some degree at least, salvation can be enjoyed here and now by those who have faith in Jesus. *Eternal life* is often spoken of as something Christians possess in their *present* lives (see 3:36; 5:24; 8:47; 17:3). Judgment is described as happening in the present (see 3:18-19; 5:24; 12:31). We are judged according to our response to Christ. Resurrection is not only something far off; in some sense, we are brought from death to life when we believe in Jesus Christ.

That seems to be the point of the raising of Lazarus reported in chapter 11 (as well as demonstrating Jesus' power). When Jesus tells Martha that her brother will rise again, Martha repeats the traditional belief about resurrection on the last day. But Jesus goes on to make a startling claim: "I am the resurrection and the life. Those who believe in me, even though they die, will live, and everyone who lives and believes in me will never die." As if to prove that he is talking about something different and more immediate than Martha's hope in a distant future, Jesus restores Lazarus to life. Resurrection to life is not merely a hope for something far away; it happens when Christ is present among those who believe in him. The Fourth Evangelist does not deny that faith has something to do with salvation that survives death. But his emphasis is on the quality of Christian life *here and now*. There are particular blessings that can be part of a Christian's present life. *Without* saying "ignore tomorrow," this Gospel writer is saying "live for now—in all the fullness Christ offers. Christ comes again when we believe in him!"

there will be delays, but God's plan is being worked out. The new direction begins here at the tomb of Lazarus. This is the "watershed" sign.

Jesus even tells the meaning of this event before it actually happens. In this sense, Lazarus's death is a preview, a window, a foretaste of Jesus' death. In Jesus, death itself will be destroyed. It is asserted here that he has the power to do just this.

JOHN 11:55–12:50

Introduction to These Chapters

Passover has arrived. This is the third Passover recorded in John's Gospel (2:13-25; 6:1-14). The third Passover seems to symbolically express Passover perfection. Certainly at this Passover things are quite different. This Passover is preceded by the raising of Lazarus from the dead and followed by Jesus' steady movement toward his own death and resurrection. In this context Jesus announces that the hour has come for the Son of Man to be glorified (12:23). The remaining half of the Gospel deals with this critical new Passover hour.

Now Jesus is no longer just the radical rabbi teaching new things in the Temple precincts (10:23-24). This hour means that he now becomes the Lamb of God (1:36), who takes away the sins of humanity. With this chapter John concludes the dramatic transition to Jesus as the center of Passover. But these events also mark the final and full rejection of Jesus by the Jews. Up to this point, they are undecided, they are forced to decide who Jesus is. Their rejection is complete, crucifying and burying the one who some thought might be the Messiah. This chapter affirms John's earlier statement in 1:11.

Here is an outline of this section:

I. Jesus Anointed in Bethany (11:55–12:11)
II. Jesus Enters Jerusalem (12:12-19)
III. Greek Interest in Jesus (12:20-26)
IV. Final Public Teachings (12:27-50)

The Message of John 11:55–12:50

The opening three stories theologically set the stage for what is coming. First Jesus is anointed following Lazarus's resurrection, and prior to his own burial and resurrection. Second, entering Jerusalem, he is hailed as king of Israel. He is "crowned" as the messianic representative who will defeat death on behalf of his sheep.

Finally, the Greeks, or Gentiles (that is, all humanity) come to him, signaling that his hour has come. As God confirmed Jesus at his baptism (Mark 1:11), so now the Father confirms the Son. Jesus is ready to act out his title as the lamb of the Passover festival, the one lamb sacrificed for many. The leaders of the Jewish community will not accept Jesus, and they finally reject him. (See comments above under "The Message of John 7–8)".

JOHN 13

Introduction to This Chapter

Jesus instructs the disciples in order to prepare them very carefully for his imminent departure—a departure they do not understand. The writer of John's Gospel tells of two general themes that Jesus emphasizes to his disciples. One has to do with Jesus' work being finished. When he goes to the Father, he will have accomplished the work given him to do. The other theme is that although he will be away, the Holy Spirit will unite them with him and the Spirit will minister to their needs. These two profound truths will stand during the interim period, the time between Jesus' drawing near and his coming again.

Jesus' public ministry now completed, he concentrates his energies on the disciples. They are given his undivided attention. There appear to be no outsiders present as he begins to prepare them for his absence. In his preparation of the disciples, he gives them an important example to follow, an example that summarizes the Gospel's moral meaning.

This chapter has three main parts:
I. The Supper and the Foot Washing (13:1-20)
II. The Betrayal of Judas (13:21-38)
III. The New Commandment (13:31-35)

The Message of John 13

Prior to Jesus' final teachings to the disciples, he acts. He gives them action prior to explanations, a consistent pattern throughout this Gospel.

THE CHURCH AS A SPECIAL COMMUNITY

The word *church* is never used in the Gospel of John. Yet the Fourth Evangelist has much to say about the church. Two of Jesus' speeches are especially relevant: (1) *Jesus* as the Good Shepherd and the Door (10:1-18); and (2) Jesus as the True Vine (15:1-17). From these and other passages. in John, we can decipher three general characteristics or the church.

First, *the church*, the community of believers, *is one because of its unity with Christ* (see 17:11, 20-23). Our unity is modeled after the relationship between Christ and God. We are united with Christ, but not absorbed into him like drops of water in a pond. Out individuality remains. Yet, like individuals in a family, we share a common loyalty and serve a common purpose.

The second distinguishing characteristic of the church is that *the community of believers is one in love*. This is clearest in the "new commandment" from Jesus: "love one another; even as I have loved you . . . you also love one another" (13:34; see also 15:12, 17). The bond of care and concern *among* believers grows out of God's love *for* them. John 3:16 is probably the best known expression of God's love in the entire Bible.

The third characteristic of the church is that it *is where God continues to make himself known*. The church is one way (not necessarily the only way) that God makes himself known in the world. The church is one place where those of us living today can still find God available. God is not limited to our memory of the ancient past or our hope for the far-away future. God is present now in the Christian community—in worship and in service.

First of all, Jesus' followers must live out a life of selfless giving and self-sacrifice, just as Jesus is about to do. We can assume that Jesus' act of footwashing made its greatest impression on the disciples after his death and resurrection.

Second, this love for others is not self-based. It is not dependent upon individual moral fiber and strength. It is an example that comes from Christ and it is empowered by God—just as Christ is empowered by the Father. This power is God's love for humanity through Christ. This godly love is about to be redefined as a work of the Holy Spirit in the disciples.

JOHN 14–15

Introduction to These Chapters

These chapters can be divided into two general themes:
I. Fellowship with the Disciples (14:1-31)
II. The Church with the Father (15:1-27)

The Message of John 14–15

Chapter 14 records Jesus' teachings about his relationship with the disciples after he is glorified. Chapter 15 discusses how believers are to live daily while Jesus is away with the Father. Taken together, these two chapters offer a firsthand account of what Jesus wanted his followers to know just prior to his departure.

JOHN 16–17

Introduction to These Chapters

In chapter 15, Jesus explained to his disciples that they would be

THE HOLY SPIRIT AS THE PARACLETE

The reason the Fourth Evangelist can make such strong claims about Christian living right here and now is found in his understanding of the Holy Spirit. Although the Gospel of John does use the term *Spirit*, his favorite term for the Holy Spirit is *Paraclete*. There are four basic meanings of that special term. Two meanings are drawn from the legal court system of that day. Paraclete may refer to someone called to the side of another to help, like a witness who helps a client in a court case. Hence, one translation of Paraclete is *Advocate*. A related meaning is someone who intercedes or steps in on behalf of, or appeals on behalf, of someone else, sort of like a defense lawyer. Hence, one translation of Paraclete is *Intercessor* (or *Counselor*). A third meaning is someone who comforts and consoles someone else, or gives them strength. Thus, Paraclete is sometimes translated *Comforter*. Finally the term also applies to someone who proclaims or exhorts. That leads to the translation as *Proclaimer*. The Fourth Evangelist may intend to draw upon all four meanings to describe the Holy Spirit. Probably no single English word captures all that he meant.

The Paraclete has a special relationship to Christ. The Paraclete, Jesus says, will come only if Jesus departs (15:26; 16:7). He comes from God the Father (15:26) in response to Jesus' request (14:16) and is sent in Jesus' name (14:26). The Paraclete is called "the Spirit of truth" (14:17; 15:26; 16:13) who glorifies Christ (16:14) and witnesses to Christ (15:26). He will guide the disciples but does not speak on his own behalf (16:13). He will remind the disciples of what Jesus has said (14:26). In short, the Paraclete is the continuing presence of Christ in our midst!

What does that mean for us? Why should we care? Because it is through the Paraclete, or Holy Spirit, that God's revelation first made known in the historical Jesus is made known to persons who live in later times. This is why Christians continue to experience the presence of the *living* Christ after all these years. This is why people in our time still have the experience of being confronted and changed by the reality of Jesus Christ. The Paraclete is not some abstract principle, not some vague oblong blur. The Paraclete is known to us in a *personal* way!

hated as his followers. Now he becomes more explicit as he teaches how this will happen. The outline is as follows:

I. Jesus' Followers in the World (16:1-33)
II. Jesus' Prayer for His Followers (17:1-26)

The Message of John 16–17

Jesus prepared the disciples for his departure in a threefold manner. First, he gave them an example when he washed their feet. Then he taught them and counseled them. And now, finally, he prays for them.

Jesus' entire life is a prayer on behalf of humanity. In a very real way, the words of this prayer are literally the acts of his life. With Christ praying for humanity with a life so lived, and now presented before the Father for eternity, how could Jesus' followers not pray during this interim period while he is away? How could anyone trivialize his sacrificial work by not praying?

JOHN 18–19

Introduction to These Chapters

These two chapters recount the final events of Jesus' life: his arrest, trial, crucifixion, death, and burial. In these chapters, Jesus lives out the new meaning and content of Passover.

Here again Jesus goes before us, as he did in prayer in the previous chapter. But here he goes before us living out a perfect life of worship to the

Father. He is always in control of his life. In this sense, he is the true representative of humanity who takes our place and suffers all the consequences of rebellion. He alone stands before the judge of the universe. He suffers all this. And God speaks loudly and clearly: "No! I cannot accept your rebellion!"

These chapters rehearse Jesus' arrest, trial, crucifixion and death, and burial.

John 18–19 may be outlined as follows:
I. The Arrest (18:1-11)
II. The Trial (18:12-27)
  A. Jesus is taken to Caiaphas (18:12-14)
  B. Jesus is examined (18:15-27)
III. Jesus in the Praetorium (18:28–19:16)
IV. Crucifixion and Death (19:17-37)
V. The Burial (19:38-42)

The Message of John 18–19

Jesus' hour is his time of suffering for humanity. He accomplishes two things.

- From God's side, his hour is the time when the darkness of rebellion and sin in the creation come into direct confrontation with the will of God. He faces it all for us, as God came to humanity in order to bring us into right relationship. In this manner, God judges sin and rebellion, speaking a mighty "No!" to our sickness unto death.

- From the human side, Jesus Christ, being without sin, takes our place and plows a path through our sin and rebellion, leading a way back to the Father. Thus Jesus' arrest, trial, sufferings, crucifixion, and burial complete a life of worship to the Father that humanity was unable to live. Because God descended to us, living out that perfect life of fellowship and worship, Christ now reaches the bottom and is about to ascend with his (and therefore our) perfect humanity.

In the Gospel of John, the encounter between Jesus and Pilate is far more detailed than in Matthew, Mark, or Luke. What do we learn from this encounter?

- When Jesus says "my kingdom is not from this world . . . my kingdom is not from here" (John 18:36 NRSV; NIV, "not of this world . . . my kingdom is from another place"), he is referring to the *source* of his kingdom. The kingdom of which Jesus speaks is clearly *in* and *for* the world, but *comes from* God. This truth grants contemporary Christians perspective about particular claims without rationalizing disengagement from the world.

- Jesus' kingship is about bearing witness to the truth of God—and Jesus himself is the incarnation of that truth. Anyone who has seen Jesus has seen God. Final judgment is not so much about an event at the end of time as it is about our decisions in the present.

- How do we understand our allegiances to God and to country? Who is the sovereign in our lives?

- How do we respond to a sovereignty built not on violence but on suffering love?

JOHN 20

Introduction to This Chapter

The crucifixion cannot be understood apart from the Resurrection. Now that Christ has confronted sin and rebellion for humanity, now that he has suffered and died on our behalf, now that the case has been sent for deliberation, the disciples await the verdict. The news is overwhelming! He lives! This is God's eternal expression of grace following the judgment (the crucifixion) for humanity. This is the essence of the Gospel (Acts 2:23-24; Romans 1:4; 1 Corinthians 15:3-7), and must be seen in light of the ascension (Acts 1:6-11). Together these events are the good news.

Chapter 20 has three parts:
I. Jesus Appears to Mary (20:1-18)
II. Jesus Appears to the Disciples (20:19-29)
III. The Signs of Jesus (20:30-31)

The Message of John 20

The Resurrection is the first half of God's almighty and eternal "Yes!" to humanity; the resurrection and ascension are the full "Yes!" of God to humanity. And this almighty "Yes!" brings us back to where the Gospel began: "In the beginning was the Word, and the Word was with God, and the Word was God" (1:1).

With the Resurrection and the ascension, the Word comes full circle back to where it all began. Christ descended for humanity. Now Christ ascends for humanity. Thus the Resurrection must be seen in the light of the ascension and in the light of the crucifixion.

In the crucifixion, God says, "Absolutely not!" to human rebellion and sin. But the resounding "Yes!" is spoken much louder, much more clearly, and with eternal finality. Christ's resurrection begins the new age of eternal life and peace through the Holy Spirit.

JOHN 21

Introduction to This Chapter

This final chapter is sometimes called the epilogue of John's Gospel. It has two parts:
I. Jesus with the Disciples Beside the Sea (21:1-14)
II. The Command to Follow Jesus (21:15-25)

Some have argued that this chapter is a later editorial addition to the Gospel, suggested by an apparent ending to the book at the conclusion of the previous chapter. Perhaps this account was based upon an incident John once told his disciples, and the disciples added it to the Gospel after John's death. But there is no real evidence to suggest that this section is anything other than a legitimate account of an experience the disciples remembered.

This account is the third post-Resurrection appearance. In this particular appearance, the disciples are given a commission to start working. In this manner, the Gospel of John explains to us how Christ will not leave his church desolate (14:18) but will provide for all its needs as the body of Christ.

The Message of John 21

Here we find the full commission of Jesus' disciples. They are called to bear witness to him at all times and in all places. Needs will be supplied—both spiritual and physical—based on particular calling. In order to bear witness, they must come to know fully who he is and who they are in relation to him. This happens continually and constantly, before, during, and after Jesus speaks the words, Follow me!

ACTS

OUTLINE OF ACTS

1. The controversy is stated (15:1-5)
2. Elders gather; Peter's speech (15:6-11)
3. Description of the Gentile mission (15:12-21)
4. Representatives sent to Antioch (15:22-29)
5. Victory for the Gentile mission (15:30-35)

C. The second missionary journey (15:36–18:22)
1. Paul and Barnabas separate (15:36-41)
2. Derbe and Lystra (16:1-5)
3. Phrygia, Galatia, and Troas (16:6-10)
4. In Philippi (16:11-15)
5. Conflict and arrest (16:16-24)
6. Imprisonment and vindication (16:25-40)
7. To Thessalonica (17:1-9)
8. A narrow escape (17:10-15)
9. Paul in Athens (17:16-21)
10. Paul's speech in the Areopagus (17:22-31)
11. Responses to Paul's speech (17:32-34)
12. Paul in Corinth (18:1-4)
13. Timothy and Silas arrive (18:5-11)
14. More resistance (18:12-17)
15. To Syria and Antioch (18:18-22)

D. The third missionary journey (18:23–21:16)
1. Apollos in Ephesus (18:23-28)
2. Paul in Ephesus (19:1-20)
3. Paul travels on (20:1-6)
4. The raising of Eutychus (20:7-12)
5. Toward Palestine (20:13-38)
6. More ports of call (21:1-16)

E. Paul as a prisoner (21:17–28:31)
1. Paul's arrest and defense (21:17–22:30)

2. Paul's appearance before the Sanhedrin (23:1-11)
3. Paul is transferred to Caesarea (23:12-35)
4. Paul in Caesarea (24:1-27)
5. Paul and Festus (25:1-27)
6. Paul and Agrippa (26:1-32)
7. Voyage to Rome (27:1–28:16)
8. In Rome (28:17-31)

INTRODUCTION

Acts is a daring sequel to the gospel witness of the life and work of Jesus. Acts is the only book that continues the narrative of the work of Jesus through the church and the apostles. Originally the book was part of a larger corpus of material. When the New Testament canon was formed, the first volume, the Gospel of Luke, was placed with the three other Gospels. Acts was placed following the Fourth Gospel. Its placement indicates its function as it links the life of Jesus with the letters of Paul.

The Author of Acts

The author of the book of Acts has traditionally been identified as Luke, the beloved physician (see 2 Timothy 4:11, Colossians 4:14, Philemon verse 24 where Luke is mentioned). The book is addressed to *Theophilus*, which in Greek means "lover of God." Therefore, the work could easily have been intended for a single reader's eye.

On the other hand, the tone of the work is clearly apologetic. The book could easily have been a work intended to place the Christian faith and church in a positive light before the Roman authorities. In that case, Theophilus could have been a patron of the early Christian movement. All attempts at identification of the book's original audience are matters of conjecture, since we simply cannot ascertain for certain the individual or individuals to whom the work is addressed. One thing is certain, however. The work is read by Christians as a stirring account of the initial moments in the life of the Christian movement.

The Date of Acts

Any attempt to date the writing is equally frustrating. No evidence within the book itself gives specific years. The tone of defense and apologetic imply a time when the church was under great stress, possibly persecution. A good number of episodes in the book of Acts give strong encouragement to those under stress. But a specific date simply cannot be determined. Many scholars conclude that the work was written sometime late in the first century.

The Purpose of Acts

Much more important than who the author was, the identity of the individual called Theophilus, or the time of the writing, is the purpose of the work. Obviously, the overriding purpose is that of edification of Christian believers. "It seemed good also to me" (NIV) or "I too decided" (NRSV) (Luke 1:3) implies that corrective with respect to doctrine or tradition was necessary to a degree. Since much of the second half of the work centers on the trial and defense of Paul, the purpose could well have been to defend Paul as representative of all Christianity. One scholar suggests that the book is an attempt to recover the reputation of Paul.

Certainly a reading of Acts gives a different perspective from what Paul's own letters reveal. In Acts, the great apostle strides across the Mediterranean—in sharp contrast to the beleaguered preacher and struggling apostle portrayed in the epistles.

Throughout the work divine guidance is emphasized. The reason is quite clear. The early church impetus toward expansion could not be the result merely of individuals who wanted to direct the fortunes of the believing community. The expansion had to be the result of God's own intention and direction. This in turn gives justification for the mission to the Gentiles. Perhaps no other single purpose is as clear or important in Acts as the legitimacy of the Gentile mission.

The Theology of Acts

Theological concerns to which the writer addresses himself include the expected return of Jesus. Christians felt that Jesus' return was imminent. At any moment all of history could come to its grand conclusion with the return of Jesus. The delay of the return posed a special problem for the early church. Indeed, Acts begins with a scene intended to dispel sky-gazing expectation.

Unlike other writings in the New Testament, the book of Acts contains no systematic presentation of major topics in Christian thinking. At no time is any complete treatise presented regarding God, Jesus, the church, or even the Holy Spirit. Throughout the work passages can be found in which these issues are mentioned. But any organized formulation of theological issues is largely accidental.

The work of the Holy Spirit does occupy a major place in Acts. However, the work of the Spirit is varied and never fits into categories or systems. Some readers may want to find in these pages the Holy Spirit working with pure spontaneity. Indeed, there are moments of spontaneity and ecstasy. However, a good deal of the Holy Spirit's work is challenging, confrontive, directive, and stern. The early church struggled long and hard not only within itself but with its Lord as well with regard to the mission to those outside the law. At every important point in the church's history the Holy Spirit prevails and the church reaches out to its ultimate destination: a universal gospel.

How to Read Acts

Modern readers will face certain difficulties when reading Acts. The reason for this is quite simple. We want to use familiar categories of thought and expression. But Acts is an ancient book and therefore uses ancient customs and conventions. Miracles, for instance, are sprinkled throughout the work—people are healed, both through a touch and by the mere passing of Peter's shadow. A young boy is brought back to life by the apostle Paul. A poisonous snake can do no harm to Paul on Malta. Prisoners are released from prison by earthquake and angels—for the ancient Israelites these incidents are not unusual at all.

Such stories are central in Christian thinking. But for modern readers they are difficult. We must remember to consider the abiding human experience that these peculiar images or categories address. We will be a good deal closer to an appropriate use of the Bible if we can allow the ancient methods to express something that is true in human nature and in God's work with the creation. We must resist the temptation to rationalize everything away for scientific or logical reasons.

Similarly, ancient historical methods include speeches or sermons that were not mere verbatim reports. Composite speeches were common in the ancient world. Again, the writer is not concerned solely with strict reporting of events and statements. Luke's concern is the meaning of events and beliefs contained in the sermons. Another ancient convention is

that of using a specific incident as representative of a larger phenomenon. For instance, there were many more encounters between Christians and Samaritans than the single incident reported by Luke. However, the intention is accomplished. The reader will understand that single events stand for widespread occurrences.

At times the writer does not quote the Hebrew Scriptures exactly. For some readers such incidents are errors and thereby call into question the authority of the Bible. Such a perspective, however, is shortsighted. The writer did not have at his disposal fine libraries with multiple volumes that were cross-indexed. He had only the material at hand, recollections saved through storytelling, his own reminiscences, and the memorized Scriptures. Again, ancient readers would not have balked at slight misquotations of Scripture.

The same insight should be kept in mind with respect to some details that appear either contradictory or incredible. Luke's purpose was not to present a seamless weave of exact history. We can almost see his excitement grow as he tells the dramatic story of how the church grew from a few frightened souls to the victorious faith that reached even Rome itself!

Finally, we must remember that Luke's purpose was to tell the story of the movement of Christianity beyond the bounds of race, tradition, and culture. Therefore, if we attempt to make this work serve as an anvil on which to work out systematic theological formulations, we overstep Luke's intention.

The Meaning of Acts

The development of the book of Acts underscores its purpose. Beginning in Jerusalem with a handful of believers, the gospel moves steadily outward. It travels first from Jerusalem to the Gentile world. Then it moves from Aramaic-speaking converts to Gentile converts. Through the work of Peter and Paul the gospel makes its way to the masses of people populating the entire known world.

When we ask the question, what is the book of Acts about? the answer might well be, *Acts is about the inevitable work of God to spread the gospel of Christ to every corner of the world.*

An image may help. Nearly everyone has stood at the edge of a pond, thrown a stone into the middle of the water, and watched the ripples reach the shoreline. In a way the book of Acts shows the initial splash of the ministry of Jesus. Inevitably, and without regard for resistance, the Holy Spirit propels the gospel into both the far reaches of human imagination and the geographical expanse of the Roman Empire.

ACTS 1–2

Introduction to These Chapters

Three major events form the content of these chapters: the risen Christ (the Resurrection); Christ's ascension; and finally the unprecedented phenomenon of Pentecost.

Here is an outline of chapters 1 and 2:
I. Introduction of the Risen Christ (1:1-5)
II. The Ascension (1:6-11)
III. The Apostles in Jerusalem (1:12-26)
IV. Pentecost (2:1-42)
  A. Introduction (2:1-4)
  B. Mighty work understood by all (2:5-13)
  C. Peter's interpretation and sermon (2:14-36)
  D. Response to the preached word (2:37-42)
V. A Description of the Early Church (2:43-47)

The Message of Acts 1–2

These two chapters recount remarkable events and truths. The power and truth is not restricted to a single historical era. We must ask what the significance of these events is for our generation as well as for the early church. What, then, do these chapters tell us about God and God's work with us?

- Election is by God.

- The task of Christianity is not to passively await Christ's return. Rather, Christians must establish new relationships to the world in which they live.

- The real boundaries are never geographical; they are religious, national, and racial.

- The Holy Spirit sometimes breaks up comfortable and familiar patterns.

- God's summons is both filled with promise and laden with responsibility.

- God's power exceeds even the power of death.

- Christ will return.

- The Holy Spirit is available to all.

- The Christian community is characterized by its care, discipline, and prayer.

ACTS 3–4

Introduction to These Chapters

Chapters 3 and 4 continue with the stories of miraculous works by the apostles. Earlier we saw the vigorous movement attracting large numbers of people. Doubtless there were more events than Luke could possibly include in the text of this single volume. Therefore, he has to use stories that not only illustrate the unprecedented impact of Christ but also represent many other similar events. We will see this technique illustrated in later chapters.

Here is an outline of these chapters:
I. Peter Heals a Lame Man (3:1-10)
II. Peter Preaches (3:11-26)
III. Peter and John Before the High Council (4:1-4)
IV. The Next Day (4:5-7)
V. Peter's Speech (4:8-12)
VI. The Apostles' Release (4:13-22)
VII. Congregational Thanksgiving (4:23-31)
VIII. Exemplary Christian Behavior (4:32-37)

The Message of Acts 3–4

Interpreters of miracles must keep in mind that miracles serve many functions. In Acts salvation is not through miracles but by grace. Miracles are invitations to both repentance and faith. As in the Gospels, they point beyond themselves to larger realities.

What can we learn from these chapters?

- Christians call attention to the remarkable power of God.

- Christian power is not wealth. It is healing power in the name of Jesus Christ.

- Salvation comes through the name of Jesus.

- Prayer asks for sufficient strength for the demand of the hour.

- Prayer is in response to both courage and strength.

- Prayer makes no mention of relieving the Christian community from stress or threat of persecutions.

- Christians show deep care for each other through sharing of goods.

ACTS 5–6

Introduction to These Chapters

The euphoric pictures of the church presented in Acts 2:42, where fellowship and prayer characterize the congregation, and in 4:32-37, where believers share their possessions as there is need, are now shattered by a dreadful narrative of lies, deceptions, and death. Also, in this part of Acts we will see escalating resistance to the movement, though it does not yet assume violent proportions.

Here is an outline of chapters 5 and 6:
I. Ananias and Sapphira Deceive and Lie (5:1-11)
II. Preaching and Healing Continue (5:12-16)
III. Miracles and Resistance (5:17-26)
IV. An Appearance Before the Council (5:27-32)
V. Gamaliel's Wise Counsel (5:33-42)
VI. Cracks in the Foundation (6:1-4)
VII. Selection of Stephen (6:5-15)

The Message of Acts 5–6

In contrast to the ideal image of chapter 4, in chapters 5 and 6 the images of life within the new movement reveal significant discord and conflict.

Many contemporary Christians labor under the idea that in the early years of the church there was a time when all was perfect. Many express a desire to somehow retrieve this ideal state of a pristine movement. A careful reading of any of the Gospels, however, reveals disagreement and pride among the disciples. Luke's narratives in Acts reveal similar stresses. Conflict seems to characterize the human experience in community. Lies, deceptions, feelings of threat, and mixed motives always exist alongside the possibilities of love, compassion, healing, and influence.

Rather than becoming discouraged because we moderns cannot achieve a long-lost perfection, we can draw comfort and courage from the narratives in Acts. The Christian movement has never been perfect. But God has continually been present with and has led the fallible instruments of apostles and converts.

What can we learn from these chapters?

- We cannot deceive others without deceiving God.

- The Holy Spirit gives the gift of perception and insight.

- The presence of the Holy Spirit does not necessarily require spectacular signs and events.

- Wisdom is also a manifestation of the presence of the Holy Spirit.

- We must never underestimate the influence that an individual may have.

- Christian witness is expressed in both word and action.

- God works in fresh and often peculiar ways.

- Wise counsel sometimes is to refrain from immediate and arbitrary resistance.

- When argument fails, violence is frequently the next step.

- Christian witness requires courage since effective preaching usually evokes a response.

- Sometimes only a minority can initially see the implications of any broad-reaching truth.

ACTS 7

Introduction to This Chapter

This chapter recounts the speech and martyrdom of Stephen. Previous confrontations with the High Council—the Sanhedrin—ended first with threats (4:17, 21) and beatings (5:40). This trial will end with a brutal killing. Chapter 7 shows us Stephen's courage in the face of anger, a speech filled with accusations, and a screaming mob.

Here is an outline of chapter 7:
I. Stephen's Speech (7:1-53)
  A. Abraham's story (7:2-8)
  B. Joseph's story (7:9-16)
  C. Transition (7:17)
  D. Moses' story (7:18-43)
  E. Ark of the covenant (7:44-46)
  F. Polemic against the Temple (7:47-50)
  G. A stinging indictment (7:51-53)
II. Stephen's Death by Stoning (7:54-60)

The Message of Acts 7

Strictly speaking, this chapter is Stephen's polemic against the Jews, especially against the importance of the Temple. Luke uses the speech to show how Christians came under attack. More broadly interpreted, however, Stephen's speech reinterprets history. In his interpretation the Jews repeatedly rejected God's overtures.

What learning can we glean from this chapter?

- God repeatedly attempts to reach toward the creation through prophets and apostles.

- God calls men and women for special tasks.

JEWS AND GENTILES IN LUKE AND ACTS

Luke writes for a mixed community of Jewish and Gentile Christians who are struggling to define their identity in relation to those Jews who did not believe in Jesus. He tries to answer the questions, Who are the true people of God? Having their roots in Judaism, how do Christians understand themselves as an institution apart from Judaism? Why have the people of the promise as a whole not accepted the gospel?

There is no agreement among scholars on how Luke answers these questions. In Luke and Acts there are both positive and negative portrayals of Jews. On the positive side, in the Gospel the first followers of Jesus and those who benefit from his healing and exorcisms are Jews. Acts relates the conversion of many Jews (2:41; 4:4; 6:7). There are positive portrayals of Pharisees (Luke 13:31-35; 20:27-39; Acts 5:34-39), and Paul never ceases being one (Acts 23:6-10). On the other hand, there are condemnations of Pharisees and scribes (Luke 11:37-51; 15:1-2; 16:13-15) and accusations of Israel's hardheartedness (Acts 7:51-53; 28:23-31). The Jewish Sanhedrin delivers Jesus to Pilate, and a crowd of Jews demand Jesus' crucifixion while Pilate three times declares him innocent (Luke 22:6623:25; Acts 2:22-23). There is rejection and persecution of Christians by some Jews (Acts 9:23; 12:3, 11; 13:45; 14:2-5).

This ambiguous portrayal has been resolved in various ways by scholars. For some, Luke portrays Israel as having rejected God's plan of salvation. As a result, Israel is excluded from God's promises, which are now fulfilled for those who have accepted them—namely, Gentile Christians, who replace Israel as the people of God. Luke's polemic against the Jews not only serves purposes of self-definition for Gentile Christians but also reflects a specific threat to the community in Luke's day. The problem is much like the one Paul faced in Galatia, where he battled Jewish Christians who advocated full observance of the Mosaic Law. Luke's story of Jesus' controversies with the Pharisees aims to help his community deal with the present conflicts with Law-observant Christians.

A different interpretation is that Luke never portrays Israel as a whole as being rejected by God or in any way replaced. Rather, Luke insists that to the Jews belong the promises made by God through their ancestors (Luke 1:72; Acts 2:39; 7:17; 13:23), and those promises are never revoked. However, they have taken on a new form with the coming of Jesus and the outpouring of the Spirit. The people of God in this new age consist of both Jews and Gentiles who have accepted the gospel. Israel, then, is a divided people: some reject God's plan, just as some have always been disobedient to God's design, while others who believe in Jesus constitute the restored Israel. The latter include those Gentiles who are granted a share in the blessings of Israel through their acceptance of the gospel. Hope is held out for all peoples to become part of the restored Israel.

A further question involves the way contemporary Christians in a post-Holocaust era who are aware of Christian anti-Semitism are to read Luke. When encountering anti-Jewish assertions in Luke, preachers and teachers must clearly represent the historical situation of the early Christians as the backdrop for such thinking. It must be recognized that Luke's statements were made in a context of intra-Jewish conflict and thus take on an entirely different character when they are made by Christians who are no longer Jewish, and when they are applied to the Jewish people as a whole. Christians must clearly denounce as abhorrent all contemporary forms of Christian anti-Judaism.

- God is not restricted to national boundaries or buildings. God is everywhere.

- God is present with the faithful in all circumstances.

- Any significantly different interpretation of history by a minority will threaten the long-held tradition of the majority.

ACTS 8:1–9:31

Introduction to These Chapters

In the opening verses of Acts the apostles are told they will be witnesses in Jerusalem, Judea, Samaria, and all the world. Through various incidents we have seen how the Christian movement began as a small, relatively obscure sect within Judaism. Increasingly, resistance to the rapidly growing movement mounts. Evidently persecution erupts. In these two chapters the localized movement begins its phenomenal expansion into all the world. Here is an outline of Acts 8:1–9:31:

    I. Persecution and Introduction of Saul (8:1-3)
    II. Philip in Samaria (8:4-8)
    III. Simon the Magician (8:9-13)
    IV. Baptism of the Holy Spirit (8:14-25)
    V. Philip and the Ethiopian Eunuch (8:26-40)
    VI. The Conversion of Saul (9:1-31)
       A. On the road to Damascus (9:1-9)
       B. In Damascus (9:10-22)
       C. Escape to Jerusalem (9:23-31)

The Message of Acts 8:1–9:31

In these chapters we have seen Christianity survive a widespread attack. Luke shows not only the broad outline but a specific man set on destroying the movement. For sheer drama these chapters rank high. The power of the

Spirit seen earlier in miracles now manifests itself through the conversion of Christianity's greatest enemy.

What can we learn from these chapters?

- The Holy Spirit works in subtle ways as well as spectacular ways.

- The Holy Spirit's power is far superior to mere magic.

- The power of the Holy Spirit cannot be purchased.

- The Scriptures must be interpreted.

- Christianity yearns to expand itself to other persons and regions.

- Even the most adamant persecutors can be converted.

- No power can ultimately resist the power of God.

- Occasionally Christians will have to trust in the authenticity of conversion and trust formerly detested enemies.

- Persecution has its hour, but God's intention always prevails.

ACTS 9:32–10:48

Introduction to These Verses

This chapter begins a new section in which Peter extends the Christian movement to the Gentiles. Previously, Christianity had transcended traditional boundaries of contempt (Samaritans and eunuchs). Now the movement begins to reach far beyond even the apostles' imagination.

Here is an outline of Acts 9:32–10:48:

    I. Peter at Lydda (9:32-35)
    II. Peter at Joppa (9:36-43)
    III. The Vision of Cornelius (10:1-8)
    IV. Peter's Vision (10:9-16)
    V. The Envoy's Journey (10:17-23)
    VI. Peter Goes to Caesarea (10:24-33)

VII. Peter's Speech (10:34-43)

VIII. The Results of Preaching (10:44-48)

The Message of Acts 9:32–10:48

What can we learn from these chapters?

- Peter's ability to heal others came not from himself but from God through Jesus Christ.

- God leads people to fresh and exciting insights.

- God extends the offer of salvation to all people.

ACTS 11–12

Introduction to These Chapters

Peter's startling insight opens enormous possibilities for the spread of Christianity. However, the expansion of the movement is by no means without hindrance. God's intention will have to struggle mightily against external powers as well as internal dissension and resistance. In these two chapters the Christian mission takes deeper roots in Antioch. This firm foundation will be critical when storms of persecution break against Christianity.

Here is an outline of Acts 11 and 12:

I. Against the Gentile Mission (11:1-17)

II. The Brethren Are Silenced (11:18)

III. A Mission to the Greeks (11:19-26)

IV. Christian Famine Relief (11:27-30)

V. Herod Agrippa's Persecution Begins (12:1-4)

VI. A Miraculous Escape for Peter (12:5-19)

VII. The Death of Herod Agrippa (12:20-23)

The Message of Acts 11–12

What can we learn about God and God's intention from these chapters?

- Initially God's intention may be apparent to only a minority.

- Resistance to God comes not only from without but from within as well.

- Congregations develop as a result of anonymous and obscure people as well as famous and well-known people.

- Christian congregations are related in the mission of God.

- Christians share from their resources to help others.

- Christian witness may involve real risk.

- God protects and sustains the Christian movement and mission.

ACTS 13

Introduction to This Chapter

Beginning with chapter 13, Luke's narrative becomes a description of the mission of Christianity to the Gentiles. Resistance will inevitably develop both from within the Christian church itself and from the external forces of threatened Jewish elements.

Here is an outline of Acts 13:

I. Barnabas and Saul Called to Mission (13:1-5)

II. Encounter with a Magician (13:6-15)

III. Paul's Sermon (13:16-41)

IV. Trouble Brewing (13:42-47)

V. The Mission Continues (13:48-52)

The Message of Acts 13

The first missionary journey begins the great drama of Christianity's expansion to the Gentiles. Along the way Christianity encounters a magician, conspiracy, and hostility. This chapter is bracketed by the Holy Spirit. The Spirit sends the missionaries out, and, at the conclusion, fills them with elation and courage. A more subtle point is that Christianity attracts both critical thinkers and Roman authorities.

What can we learn about God and God's will from this chapter?

- The Holy Spirit stirs churches and individuals to mission.

- Prophets and teachers, uniquely gifted people, are used by God in the congregation.

- New mission and direction require adequate preparation through prayer.

- Christianity is far superior to charlatans and magicians.

- The power of the Resurrection is central to any Christian proclamation.

- God can and does work through obscure and nameless individuals to sustain congregations.

ACTS 14

Introduction to This Chapter

Chapter 13 concluded with the disciples departing from Pisidian Antioch. They were both being threatened by an angry populace and filled with the Holy Spirit. The peculiar juxtaposition of threat and Holy Spirit seems both ironic and appropriate. Luke has cleverly described the mixture of feelings that will occur in the Christian mission. He has hinted at suffering and glory, at the cross and the Resurrection. In the balance of this first journey the same ironies and combination of threat and promise continue.

Here is an outline of chapter 14:
I. A Plot Develops (14:1-5)
II. The Disciples Flee (14:6-7)
III. A Cripple Is Healed (14:8-14)
IV. Paul's Protest (14:15-18)
V. Return to Antioch (14:19-28)

The Message of Acts 14

Luke's presentation of the first journey provides many insights into God's intention and the Christian missionary enterprise. Throughout the narrative there is a tension between Christianity's power and Christianity's suffering. Theologically these two perspectives may be called a theology of glory and a theology of the cross. Sensitive Christians have always recognized the necessary relationship between the two. Certainly Luke keeps the tension in balance. To stress one over the other is to run the risk of a truncated gospel. The church must always recognize the glory of God's victory and the suffering of bearing Christ's cross.

What other insights may we glean from this chapter?

- God is always present with Christians, both in victory and in trial.

- Christian preaching will evoke response. The word will never go forth to return empty (see Isaiah 55:11).

- Christian witness will always require courage.

- Persecution never achieves its intention. New congregations will be formed.

- Christians must learn how to speak to a culture not familiar with biblical narrative and revelation.

- The victory God intends in the Resurrection overshadows suffering (see Romans 8:28, 31-39).

- God's work continues not only through well-known persons, but through anonymous and obscure persons as well.

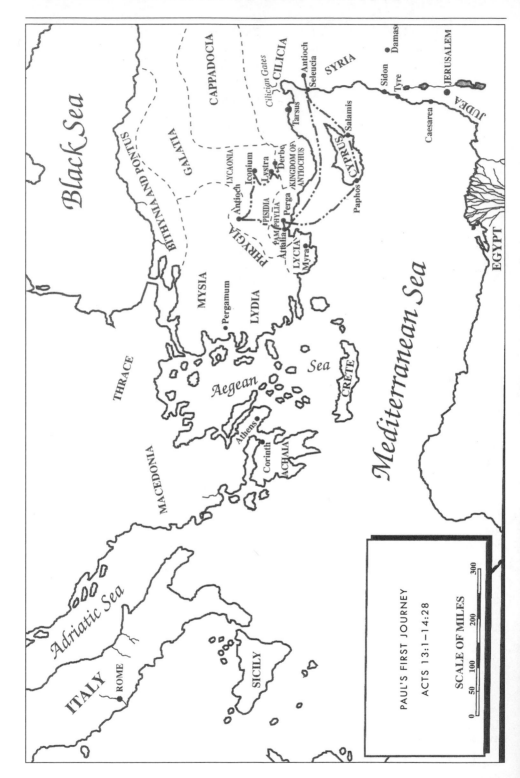

PAUL'S FIRST JOURNEY

ACTS 13:1–14:28

SCALE OF MILES

0   50   100   200   300

Paul's First Journey

Place	What Happened	Background
Antioch, Syria	Paul and Barnabas are set aside for a special preaching mission in territories to the west. (Acts 13:1-3)	Referred to as "Antioch the Beautiful" or Queen of the East," founded by Seleucus I Nicator in honor of his father, Antiochus. Located approximately 20 miles from the Mediterranean, had good access to the sea via the navigable Orontes River. Under Rome, Antioch was the capital of syria, the third city in size in the Empire.
To Seleucia, Syria	Out of that city sailed Paul, Barnabas, and John Mark. (Acts 13:4-5)	Port city far from Syrian Antioch
By sea to Salamis, Cyprus	Paul and Barnabas preached to Jews in the synagogue at Salamis. (Acts 13:5)	Largest port on eastern side of the island, closest to Syria
Across the island to Paphos, Cyprus	Sergius Paulus, the proconsul, converted to the Christian faith. (Acts 13:6-12)	Seaport at the southwest tip of Cyprus, the seat of the island's Roman government. Had a temple to Aphrodite, famous enough to draw visits from numerous pilgrims.
By sea to Perga, Pamphylia	John Mark left them and returned to Jerusalem. (Acts 13:13)	Major city in Pamphylia. Center for the worship of Artemis, a nature goddess.
To Antioch, Pisidia	Rejected in the synagogue, Paul and Barnabas exclaimed, "It was necessary that the word of God should be spoken first to you. Since you reject it . . . we are now turning to the Gentiles" (Acts 13:46). (Acts 13:14-52)	In Asia Minor, became the major metropolis of Pisidia. Founded by Seleucus I Nicator, one of Alexander the Great's right-hand men. A center of Hellenistic influence, commanding the great trade routes between Ephesus and Cilicia.
To Iconium, Phrygia	Paul and Barnabas spent considerable time in this town. They left when they were threatened with stoning. (Acts 14:1-7)	Had been a populous town since early times. Location on a main trade route connecting Ephesus with Syria was decisive factor in its prosperity. Looked to as the capital of Lycaonia by the Greek Empire and later by the Romans.

Paul's First Journey (cont.)

Place	What Happened	Background
Escape to Lystra, Lycaonia	A lame man was healed here, and Paul and Barnabas were hailed as gods. Paul was stoned. (Acts 14:8-20)	Lay some eighteen miles south-southwest of Iconium, on a major Roman road to Antioch, Pisidia. In the Lycaonian part of the province of Galatia.
To Derbe, Lycaonia	Paul made many converts. (Acts 14:21)	An inland city in the southeastern part of Lycaonia in Asia Minor. Sixty miles from Lystra.
Back to Lystra, Lycaonia	Strengthened new converts and the new church, appointed church leaders. (Acts 14:21-23)	
Back to Iconium, Phrygia	Strengthened new converts and the new church, appointed church leaders. (Acts 14:21-23)	
Back to Antioch, Pisidia	Strengthened new converts and the new church, appointed church leaders. (Acts 14:21-23)	
Back to Perga, Pamphylia	Brief stay. Paul and Barnabas preached here. (Acts 14:24-25)	
Then to Attalia, Pamphylia	(Acts 14:25)	A port city of Pamphylia.
By sail to Antioch, Syria	Returned to home base, shared the good news of the Gentiles receiving Christ. Paul and Barnabas settled down with the disciples in Antioch for some time. (Acts 14:26-28)	
Later to Jerusalem, Judea	Controversy over circumcision settled. Apostles and elders decreed that circumcision would not be required of Gentiles as a prerequisite for salvation. (Acts 15:1-35)	Surrounded by deep valleys on all but the north side, easy to defend. Had strong walls as well as the Temple restored by Herod the Great. Other features were the Tower of Antonia, a gymnasium, the palace of Herod, the pool of Bethesda, the pool of Siloam, and a large amphitheater.

The first journey took two years. In that time Paul and Barnabas visited Cyprus, Pamphylia, Phrygia, and Lycaonia.

ACTS 15

Introduction to This Chapter

In this chapter Luke describes the conference in which the issue of the Gentile mission will be resolved. The single subject over which the conflict is waged is the practice of circumcision. The Old Testament tradition insists upon circumcision. The insight of Christianity is, in part at least, that this physical event is not necessary for salvation. In all probability, the hesitation regarding a mission to the Gentiles, who had no Jewish tradition, is far more complex than this one apparent cause. Eating with Gentiles, social relations, and cultural differences are all much more difficult to pinpoint.

Luke portrays the Jerusalem Conference in five separate scenes.

Here is an outline of this chapter:
I. The Controversy Is Stated (15:1-5)
II. Elders Gather; Peter's Speech (15:6-11)
III. Description of the Gentile Mission (15:12-21)
IV. Representatives Sent to Antioch (15:22-29)
V. Victory for the Gentile Mission (15:30-35)

The Message of Acts 15

This chapter presents an account of how the early church made a decision about a potentially divisive issue: the extent to which Gentile converts to Christianity needed to abide by Jewish Law. Luke provides a model for decision making about any important matter. Leaders with diverse experiences are gathered, both sent and welcomed by the larger church (verses 3-4). Testimony is given about what God is doing in a new time and place (verses 7-12). Scripture and tradition are consulted (verses 15-21). The decision in favor of a new practice is guided by the Holy Spirit (verse 28), characterized by unanimity (verses 22, 25), and endorsed by the wider church (verses 30-31).

What else can we learn from this chapter?

- God gives insight to people.

- Insistence on strict adherence to religious ritual places burdens on people, not blessings.

- The congregations of God are sustained and guided by the Holy Spirit.

- Moderation and compromise are acceptable ways of resolving conflict.

- Differences of opinion do not have to cripple a mission; they can serve to expand the scope of mission.

- Luke implies a necessary correlation between earthly and divine authority in the Christian enterprise.

ACTS 15:36–17:15

Introduction to These Chapters

Acts 15:36 begins a description of Paul's second missionary journey that will continue until Acts 18:22. As the Christian mission continues, the gospel makes its advance both territorially and culturally.

Here is an outline of 15:36–17:15:
I. Paul and Barnabas part company (15:36-41)
II. Derbe and Lystra (16:1-5)
III. Phrygia, Galatia, and Troas (16:6-10)
IV. In Philippi (16:11-15)
V. Conflict and Arrest (16:16-24)
VI. Imprisonment and Vindication (16:25-40)
VII. To Thessalonica (17:1-9)
VIII. A Narrow Escape (17:10-15)

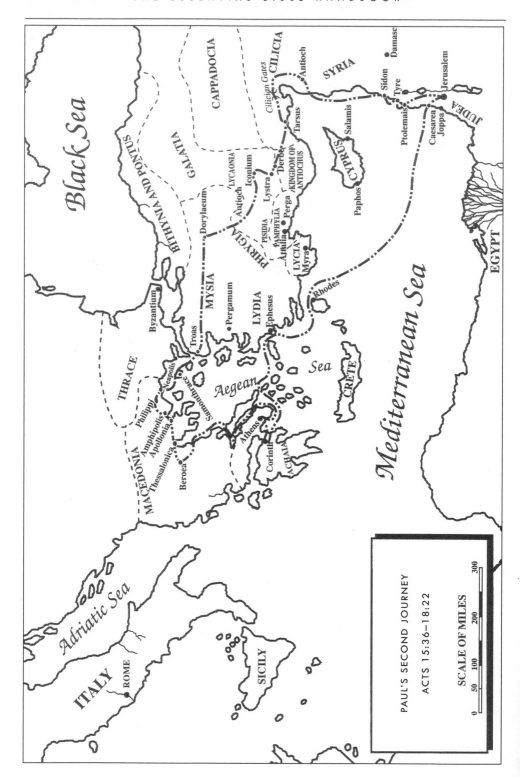

PAUL'S SECOND JOURNEY

ACTS 15:36–18:22

SCALE OF MILES

0   50   100   200   300

The Message of Acts 15:36–17:15

Luke's account of Paul's second missionary journey takes the reader across Asia Minor (through Syria and Cilicia) toward the Asian continent. The Holy Spirit presses the missionaries toward Europe instead. Through careful use of these events, Luke draws attention not only to Paul but also to the continued work of the Holy Spirit through Paul.

Especially significant is the interpretation of the direct intervention of the Holy Spirit when the missionaries intended to revisit established churches. On the surface it must have looked to the frustrated missionaries like a failure of their mission. They could not go where they had planned to go. As a result, the missionaries had to make adjustments and take their work in a completely different direction. We might even say that they had to take a challenging course through the unknown rather than the comfortable path of revisiting well-known territory and familiar people.

What else can we learn from our examination of this section of Acts?

- Paul could make adjustments in his behavior without sacrificing his principles.

- Paul preached to whomever came to hear him. We see that he trusted in his message rather than the numbers of people who listened.

- The gospel of Christ appeals to all classes of society: the high (wealthy women), the low (the servant girl), and the workers (the Philippian jailer).

- Even in the most lonely circumstances, God remains with the faithful.

- God can use what appears to be failure to fulfill the divine purpose.

- The suffering Messiah is authenticated by faithful persons willing to suffer on his behalf.

Paul's Second Journey

Place	What Happened	Background
Antioch, Syria	Paul and Barnabas parted company over Paul's refusal to take John Mark on the second journey. Paul's new missionary partner was Silas. (Acts 15:36-41)	
To Derbe, Lycaonia then to Lystra, Lycaonia	Paul and Silas joined by young Timothy. (Acts 16:1-5)	
Through Phrygian and Galatian region	Prevented by Holy Spirit from preaching in Asia. (Acts 16:6)	

Paul's Second Journey (cont.)

Place	What Happened	Background
Led by the Spirit of Jesus to Troas, Asia	In a vision a Macedonian cried out, "Come over to Macedonia and help us" (Acts 16:9). (Acts 16:6-9)	An important port city in the Roman province of Asia on the Aegean Sea. Strategically located two miles south of the Dardanelles (the strip of water separating Europe from Asia). Roman influence was strong in Troas, as indicated by the presence of a theater, a temple, baths, and an aqueduct.
Straight to Samothrace, To Neapolis, Macedonia; And to Philippi, Macedonia	The gospel first preached in Europe, converts made. Paul and Silas thrown in jail. (Acts 16:11-40)	Named for its conqueror, Philip II of Macedon. Located on a major Roman road (the *Egnatian Way*) that connected Rome and Asia. Enjoyed special citizenship privileges from Rome dating from a decisive battle on the plains of Philippi in 42 B.C.
Through Amphipolis, Macedonia	Traveling on the *Egnatian Way*. (Acts 17:1)	Situated on the Strymon River, astride the thoroughfare known as the *Egnatian Way*. Founded by the Athenians in the fifth century B.C.
To Apollonia, Macedonia		Some twenty-eight miles west of Amphipolis, closer to Thessalonica. Named in honor of the god Apollo.
To Thessalonica, Macedonia	Paul and Silas pressured out of Thessalonica. (Acts 17:1-9)	Built on the site of a more ancient city that had been named for some hot

Paul's Second Journey (cont.)

Place	What Happened	Background
		springs located there, that is, Therme. Located on the *Egnatian Way*. Renamed after the sister of Alexander the Great.
To Beroea, Macedonia	Warmly welcomed by synagogue here. Many converts. People from Thessalonica caused trouble in Beroea. (Acts 17:10-14)	Located about twenty-four miles from the Aegean Sea, approximately fifty miles west of Thessalonica.
To Athens, Achaia (Greece)	Paul left Silas and Timothy behind. Gospel proclaimed here but made few converts. (Acts 17:15-34)	Circled the base of the Acropolis, which dominated the whole area. On the Acropolis were some of the architectural splendors of all time, the Parthenon and the Erechtheum—temples dedicated to gods and goddesses of Greece. Also had a music hall, a stadium, and a theater.
To Corinth, Achaia (Greece)	Paul's ministry here highly successful. Strong church established. Silas and Timothy rejoined Paul here. Paul stayed at least a year and a half. (Acts 18:1-17)	Capital city of the Roman province of Achaia. Acrocorinthus Rock, rising approximately 1800 feet behind the city, served as a stronghold against invaders. Possessed two deepwater ports at the end of the narrow ishthmus connecting mainland Greece with the southern peninsula. Acquired great wealth.
Sailed to Ephesus, Asia	Preaching in the synagogue, Paul was asked to stay longer. (Acts 18:18-21)	An imposing city, its temple of Diana was one of the seven wonders of the

Paul's Second Journey (cont.)

Place	What Happened	Background
		ancient world. Location on the Cayster River just a few miles from the sea and on major highways brought great wealth.
By sea to Caesarea, Palestine; Went "up to Jerusalem"; Went "down to" Antioch, Syria	Paul landed at Caesarea, "went up to Jerusalem" to pay his respects to the church, then traveled to Antioch. (Acts 18:22)	Located on the Mediterranean coast, about twenty-three miles south of Mount Carmel and sixty-four miles northwest of Jerusalem. Built by Herod the Great between 25 and 13 B.C., boasted a temple, a theater, and an amphitheater, and had a complete system of drainage. Capital of Palestine.

ACTS 17:16–18:22

Introduction to These Chapters

Luke now focuses solely on Paul's work in new and challenging mission fields. The issues that had spawned internal resistance have been resolved. The resolution came at a good time, since now the Christian movement begins to evoke more antagonism from a variety of sources. It will need all the internal strength it can muster.

Here is an outline of Acts 17:16–18:22:
I. Paul in Athens (17:16-21)
II. Paul's Speech in the Areopagus (17:22-31)
III. Responses to Paul's Speech (17:32-34)
IV. Paul in Corinth (18:1-4)
V. Timothy and Silas Arrive (18:5-11)
VI. More Resistance (18:12-17)
VII. To Syria and Antioch (18:18-22)

The Message of Acts 17:16–18:22

The second missionary journey focuses primarily on Paul. Even though the Gentile mission has been approved, Paul still continues preaching to Jewish audiences in synagogues. Only after Jews refuse the Christian message does Paul turn primarily to Gentiles. We see that Paul very reluctantly turns away from the Jewish tradition. Indeed, twice during the journey he complies with ancient customs. The triumph of Christianity is accompanied by the tragedy of those who exclude themselves from the gospel.

What can we learn from these chapters?

• God is the God of all Creation.

- In a world where people like to banter about ideas, the truth of Christ needs to be proclaimed. God assures Christians of continued support both by the Holy Spirit and through other faithful people.

- Even though we may not know who they are, other people hold fast to the faith.

- God does not have to be searched for; God is present with all persons.

- Christians do not turn their backs on people—other people turn their backs on Christianity.

ACTS 18:23–19:41

Introduction to These Chapters

Luke here begins his description of Paul's third missionary journey.

Here is an outline of chapters 18:23–19:41:

   I. Apollos in Ephesus (18:23-28)
  II. Paul in Ephesus (19:1-20)
 III. Paul Plans for the Journey to Rome (19:21-22)
 IV. A Riot Started by Demetrius (19:23-41)

The Message of Acts 18:23–19:41

The Christian movement encounters many challenges. Through graphic vignettes Luke tells his readers how the earliest Christians met these challenges. Clearly, he intends to instruct his readers on how they too can effectively give witness when confronted by antagonists or questions.

What can we learn from these verses?

- All Christians have a responsibility to witness.

- God uses helpers as well as major, central figures.

- Actions substantiate Christian claims of power.

- Religion cannot be used in a secondhand way with any great effect.

- Christianity has nothing to do with magic.

- When Christianity begins to address the economy, vested interests will feel threatened.

ACTS 20:1–21:16

Introduction to These Chapters

The description of Paul's third journey runs through 21:16. Luke continues to lift Paul to the heights of authority and power. Christianity still advances in the face of increasingly violent opposition. The riot in Ephesus could not stop Christianity's impact. Increasingly, Paul's work aims toward Jerusalem and eventually Rome itself.

Here is an outline of Acts 20:1–21:16:

   I. Paul Travels On (20:1-6)
  II. The Raising of Eutychus (20:7-12)
 III. Toward Palestine (20:13-38)
 IV. More Ports of Call (21:1-16)

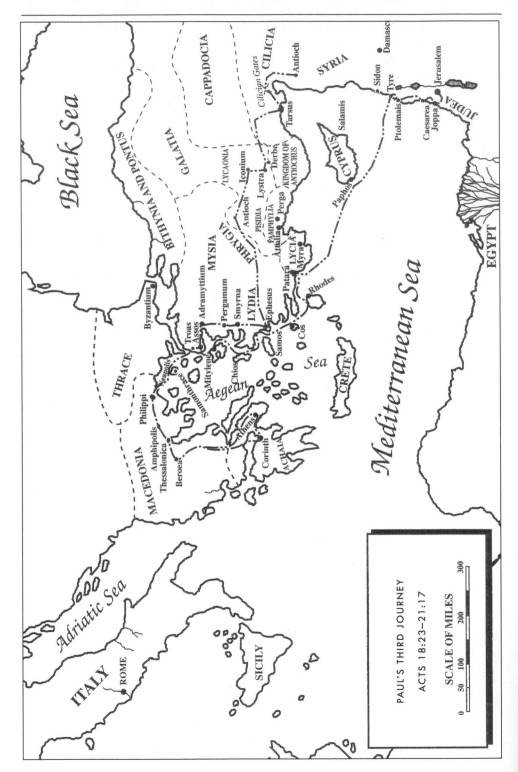

PAUL'S THIRD JOURNEY

ACTS 18:23–21:17

SCALE OF MILES

0 50 100 200 300

Paul's Third Journey

Place	What Happened	Background
Antioch, Syria; To Galatia; Through Phrygia	Paul passed through Galatia and Phrygia, strengthening the converts. (Acts 18:23)	
To Ephesus, Asia	Paul preached to Jews only briefly but for two years to Gentiles in the lecture hall of Tyrannus. Paul's influence felt not only in Ephesus but also in the province of Asia. Paul run out by silversmiths. (Acts 19:1-20:1)	
To Macedonia; Corinth, Achaia, (Greece); Returned through Macedonia; Sailed away from Philippi, Macedonia	Just after the Passover. (Acts 20:1-6)	
To Troas, Asia; By road to Assos, Asia	Here a week. (Acts 20:6-12)	A seaport of Mysia not far from Troas.
To Samos	(Acts 20:13-15)	Island off the eastern coast of Asia Minor.
To Miletus, Asia	Paul met with the elders of Ephesus to bid them farewell. He thought he would not see them again. (Acts 20:15-38)	Seaport located some thirty-six miles south of Ephesus at the mouth of the Menander River, four harbors. Like other cities under Greek influence, a street from the harbor to the city walls (similar to Athens and Corinth). Temples to Apollo and Athena, and a magnificent open-air theater.

Paul's Third Journey (cont.)

Place	What Happened	Background
To Cos, Asia		Island off the southwest tip of Asia (one-day stay).
To Rhodes, Asia		Island at the tip of Asia minor.
To Patara, Lycia		On the Lycian mainland.
To Tyre, Phoenicia	Paul in Tyre for seven days with the Christians there. Warned not to go to Jerusalem (Acts 21:1-6)	An ancient and important port of the Phoenicians. Built on an island to protect it from siege, remained impregnable to attack until Alexander the Great conquered it by building a causeway.
To Ptolemias (or Acre), Palestine	Paul greeted the believers. (Acts 21:7)	Before being named for one of Alexander the Great's generals, was known as Acco or Acre. Located on the Mediterranean coast, eight miles north of Mount Carmel and about twenty-five miles south of Tyre.
To Caesarea, Palestine	Stayed in the house of Philip the evangelist. Paul warned again not to go to Jerusalem. (Acts 21:8-14)	
In spite of warnings, went to Jerusalem	Received warmly by the elders, apostles. A controversy was begun by Asian Jews (Paul's old enemies), and Paul came into the custody of Romans. (Acts 21:15-26:32)	

The Message of Acts 20:1–21:16

During the final leg of the third journey, the story gathers momentum. Paul becomes increasingly anxious to return to Jerusalem. The regions into which he has journeyed exhibit resilient, if obscure, Christian congregations. In large measure, Paul's work has been remarkably successful. Like his Lord, Paul must complete the will of God, which he does in the face of all sorts of resistance, both hostile and friendly.

What can we learn from these chapters?

- Christian witness is a costly demand.

- We often prefer to claim achievement and authority rather than duty and responsibility. But Paul's witness and Luke's reaffirmation state clearly that Christian virtue frequently takes the form of humble obedience.

- Resistance to God's will can be either hostile or friendly.

- Christians need both time alone with God and the support of the believing community for adequate preparation for difficult tasks.

- The faith will sometimes be threatened by heresy.

ACTS 21:17–22:30

Introduction to These Chapters

The previous section concluded with the end of Paul's third missionary journey (21:16). Paul's missions have spread the Christian message to both well-known and obscure places. Barriers have been hurdled. Now it is time to complete the work. In the last part of chapter 21, Luke's narrative gains momentum as Paul begins his final journey, this time to Rome itself.

Here is an outline of Acts 21:17–22:30:

I. Paul in Jerusalem (21:17-26)
II. More Trouble and Arrest (21:27-40)
III. Paul's Speech (22:1-21)
IV. An Outraged Mob (22:22-30)

The Message of Acts 21:17–22:30

Paul returns from his missionary journey with great successes to report. However, the hard-won compromise of the Jerusalem Conference seems nearly forgotten by some and unknown by many more. The same question emerges again: what is the appropriate relationship with the Gentiles? Luke also uses Paul's defense to speak to Christians about another dilemma: the relationship between Christians and Jews.

What can we learn from these chapters?

- Paul's intention is to get to Jerusalem and then to Rome. From the outsider's perspective his arrest implies failure. But God will use this circumstance to get Paul to Rome. The eyes of faith can see God at work even in seemingly unexplainable events.

- Paul can adapt to different expectations without losing his own integrity, even under pressure.

- Christians cannot forget their Jewish heritage without some loss of their own identity as people of biblical faith.

- Paul's genius is that he understands God's love for all people. This truth offends any who want God to love only their own kind.

- The Christian witness may have to survive not only in the face of a hostile, screaming mob but within familiar settings of friends who do not understand the vast implications of God's intention.

ACTS 23–24

Introduction to These Chapters

In these two chapters Paul appears before both Jewish authorities (the Sanhedrin) and Roman authorities. He has sharp dissent with Jews but little conflict that is against Rome.

Here is an outline of Acts 23 and 24:

I. Paul's Defense (23:1-11)
II. A Plot Develops (23:12-15)
III. Paul Is Removed from the Scene (23:16-35)
IV. Paul Is Charged (24:1-9)
V. Paul's Response (24:10-23)
VI. The Verdict Is Delayed (24:24-27)

The Message of Acts 23–24

The apostle Paul now faces the attack of both the official authority (the Sanhedrin) and unofficial resistance (a conspiracy to kill him). As he does in his Gospel, Luke here portrays the Roman Empire in a favorable light, emphasizing Roman concern for the safety of a citizen and a tacit tolerance for the Christian movement. The challenge to Christianity, as Luke reports it, comes from Jewish leaders. And within Christianity itself, as represented by Paul, there is an important link between Jewish tradition and theology and the Christian hope and ethic. (See sidebar entitled "Jews and Gentiles in Luke and Acts" near Acts 7 above.)

What can we learn from these chapters?

- A clear conscience is critical when challenged by evil intent.

- The Christian does not have to grovel at the feet of authority; the Christian is bound by and trusts in higher authority.

- God sustains the faithful in moments of great stress.

- Christians and Jews share a great deal of heritage and hope. The Christian needs to understand the biblical roots of faith.

ACTS 25–26

Introduction to These Chapters

When reading Luke's narrative of the dramatic events surrounding Paul's defense before both Jewish and Roman authorities, we may be tempted to rush quickly on to find out what the results are. How does this end? What happens next? Such questions indicate the skill with which Luke presents the material. We must consciously slow ourselves down sufficiently to ask what Luke is attempting to show or illustrate through these thrilling narratives. What is the purpose of the stories?

Will the encouragement Paul received be enough? For how long can Christians anticipate Roman authority to treat them benevolently? What will happen if the Roman benevolence ends?

What attitude does the writer have toward Roman authority in this narrative? Luke's presentation clearly shows a benevolent attitude toward Roman rule. In no small measure, Luke presses this significant point home to his readers, whether Christian or Roman.

Here is an outline of Acts 25 and 26:

I. The Arrival of Festus (25:1-5)
II. Paul's Appearance in Court (25:6-12)
III. A Defense of Christianity (25:13-27)
IV. Paul's Defense (26:1-23)
V. A Lively Exchange (26:24-32)

The Message of Acts 25–26

The scenes of Paul's trial are at once both thrilling and terrifying. The grandeur of royalty, the flourish and trappings of imperial government, and the authority of

Rome all appear very intimidating. In the midst of all this stands a single figure with little more than the authority of his conversion, the summons to mission, and his experience in the mission field. Yet, through it all, Luke has little question about how events will turn out. The promise of God's presence is no vague or empty hope. God is sufficient for the hour and present in the need of the moment. With this assurance firmly in mind, the Christian can withstand even the most demanding trials.

What else can we learn from these chapters?

- The Christian is concerned with responsibilities and does not necessarily protect reputation or status.

- The Christian's calling has the authority of God behind it.

- The truth of Christ's resurrection will confuse many; but nevertheless it must be proclaimed.

- In the midst of stress, an individual will draw on what is internalized— what is known to be true in personal experience.

- The act of conversion affects the balance of a person's life and may take the Christian to places she or he does not want to go.

ACTS 27–28

Introduction to These Chapters

Chapters 27 and 28 bring the Christian message at long last to Rome, though in a manner different from what Paul had anticipated at the beginning. Luke's narrative has maintained suspense for quite some time now. Trials, narrow escapes, and confrontations all threaten to overwhelm Paul. But God has protected the movement's main spokesman.

In the final narrative Paul takes a perilous journey to Rome. The narrative itself is one of the longest in the entire Bible. It compares with the length and character of the Joseph story in Genesis 37:1–50.

Here is an outline of Acts 27 and 28:
I. The Journey Begins (27:1-8)
II. Bad Omens (27:9-12)
III. Storm, Drifting, and Landfall (27:13-44)
IV. On Malta (28:1-6)
V. A Miraculous Healing (28:7-10)
VI. From Malta to Rome (28:11-16)
VII. In Rome (28:17-31)

The Message of Acts 27–28

Luke's original readers would have realized very quickly that the extended narrative is intended to heighten the drama of Paul and the Christian hope. Through it all God proves faithful to the promise that the intention of God cannot be denied. God would see to it that the message is proclaimed even in Rome. Triumph is implicit throughout. But along with triumph is the tragedy that many who hear the gospel continue to reject it.

Modern Christian readers should be careful that a reading of the book of Acts does not feed the fires of anti-Jewish feeling. As Luke has shown very deliberately and carefully, Christians and Jews share a tremendous heritage. They also share a wonderful hope that God continues to press for the divine purpose to succeed unhindered throughout the whole of creation.

What else can we learn from Acts 27 and 28?

- God's intention can be delayed but not denied altogether.

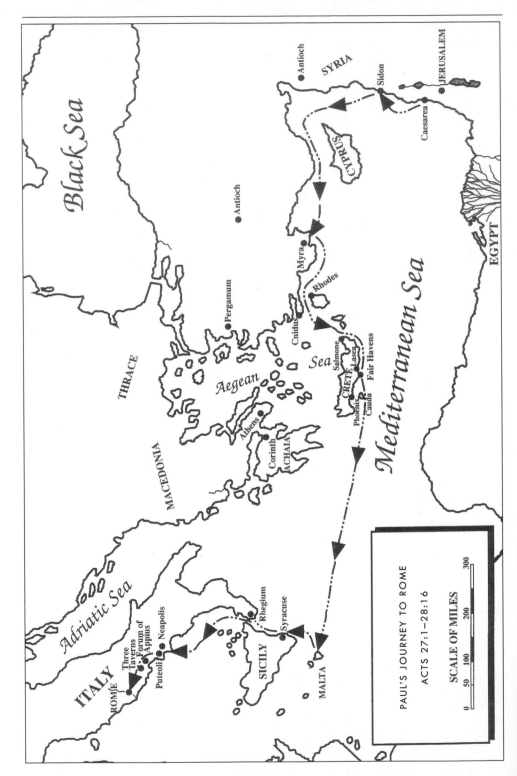

Black Sea

Antioch

SYRIA

Sidon

JERUSALEM

CYPRUS

Caesarea

EGYPT

Antioch

Myra

Rhodes

Pergamum

Cnidus

Salmone

Fair Havens

THRACE

Aegean

Sea

Lasea

CRETE

Phoenix

Cauda

Mediterranean Sea

Athens

Corinth

ACHAIA

MACEDONIA

Adriatic Sea

Rhegium

Syracuse

SICILY

MALTA

Three Taverns

Forum of Appius

Neapolis

Puteoli

ITALY

ROME

PAUL'S JOURNEY TO ROME

ACTS 27:1–28:16

SCALE OF MILES

0   50 100   200   300

- God can and will use different persons to accomplish the divine purposes. In this narrative, even detested soldiers are used to protect the Christian missionary.

The winter storm that Paul encounters provides an occasion for hope. God offers salvation even in the bleakest of circumstances.

- Rejection of the gospel is not the final word.

- Rejection in Acts merely opens up new territory for the gospel message.

ROMANS

VI. Perfectionism and Sanctification (6:1-23)
- A. Sin and baptism (6:1-14)
- B. Sin and lordship (6:15-20)
- C. The issue of sanctification (6:21-23)

VII. Christians and the Law (7:1-25)
- A. The two ages and the law (7:1-6)
- B. The problem with the law (7:7-12)
- C. Sin and Paul's conversion (7:13-25)

VIII. Work of the Holy Spirit (8:1-39)
- A. Flesh and spirit (8:1-17)
  1. Liberation by Christ (8:1-4)
  2. The contrast between flesh and spirit (8:5-9)
  3. The problem of the body (8:10-11)
  4. Spirit and sonship (8:12-17)
- B. Human Suffering (8:17-30)
  1. Spirit, suffering, and hope (8:17-25)
  2. Human vulnerability and weakness (8:26-27)
  3. Providence and predestination (8:28-30)
- C. Principalities and Powers (8:31-39)

IX. The Triumphant Gospel (9:1–11:36)
- A. Introduction (9:1-5)
- B. Election and Israel's fate (9:6-18)
- C. Individual responsibility (9:19-29)
- D. The doctrine of unenlightened zeal (9:30–10:4)
- E. Righteousness by faith alone (10:5-13)
- F. The rejection of the gospel (10:14-21)
- G. God did not reject Israel (11:1-10)
- H. Why Israel rejected the gospel (11:11-24)
- I. The mystery of Israel's Salvation (11:25-32)
- J. Conclusion (11:33-36)

X. Basis for a Christian Ethic (12:1-21)
- A. The theme of the section (12:1-2)
- B. The use of Christian gifts (12:3-8)
- C. The struggle between good and evil (12:9-21)
  1. Guidelines for genuine love (12:9)
  2. Life in the congregation (12:10-13)
  3. Life outside the congregation (12:14-20)
  4. Conclusion (12:21)

XI. Living in the World (13:1–15:13)
- A. Christians and government (13:1-7)
- B. Love and the end times (13:8-10)
- C. Moral alertness in the final days (13:11-14)
- D. Guidelines for the weak and strong (14:1-23)
- E. Accepting outsiders (15:1-6)
- F. Summary statements (15:7-13)

XII. Conclusion (15:14-16:27)
- A. Paul's calling and strategy (15:14-21)
- B. The appeal to participate in mission (15:22-23)
- C. The Jerusalem offering (15:24-29)
- D. First conclusion to the letter (15:30-33)
- E. The role of Phoebe (16:1-2)
- F. Greetings to church leaders (16:3-16)
- G. The conclusion of the book (16:17-27)

INTRODUCTION

Paul's letter to the Romans was probably written from Corinth in the winter of A.D. 56–57. In the letter itself, Paul mentions his host, Gaius of Corinth (16:23), and recommends Phoebe, from the nearby town of Cenchreae (16:1). Thus we may conclude that the letter was written during the three-month period that Paul spent in or around Corinth. This period was just prior to Paul's departure to deliver the Jerusalem offering.

The Form of the Original Letter

Although there are many textual variants related to the final chapters of Romans, it now appears certain that Paul's original letter contained sixteen chapters. The only portions that may not stem from Paul are the closing benediction (16:25-27) and the warning against heretics that breaks up the sequence of greetings (16:17-20). Thus it is essential to take the material from the final chapters into account in considering the purpose and character of Romans.

The Nature and Purpose of Romans

Paul dictated this letter to solicit help from the Roman house churches in the planning and logistical support for a mission to Spain (see 15:24, 28). The theological argument is designed to unify the competitive house churches in Rome so they will be willing and able to cooperate in this effort. The power of the gospel (1:16) to achieve the unification of all nations (15:7-13) provides the imperative for this mission and therefore stands at the heart of Romans.

The Situation in Rome

Although Paul has never been to Rome, he clearly has a firm grasp of the situation there. He mentions in Romans 1:8 that their faith was proclaimed throughout the world. He also mentions in 1:13 that he had often intended to come, which indicates that he had studied and thought about the Roman church situation for a long time. We know that he was a missionary partner for a number of years with Roman refugees, Prisca (Priscilla) and Aquila, mentioned in Acts 18:1-3 and 18:26. That Prisca and Aquila are now back in Rome at the time of writing is indicated by Romans 16:3-5. So we have every reason to believe that Paul had heard frequent reports about the situation in Rome.

It appears that the Roman churches were founded sometime in the decade of the thirties or early forties by anonymous Christian missionaries traveling to Rome. The most likely centers for the earliest congregations were the small Greek-speaking Jewish synagogues whose presence in Rome has been proven by archaeology and other historical research. These synagogues were quite small and local in their background. The synagogues attracted people who had immigrated to Rome from a particular part of the Roman empire. Most of the inscriptions found in these synagogues are in Greek, which indicates that the language used by the Jewish community in Rome was primarily Greek, rather than Latin or Hebrew. Another peculiarity was the lack of a centralized organization for the synagogues. This had a serious consequence for the development both of Judaism and Christianity in Rome.

When conflicts began to emerge between Christian missionaries and their zealous Jewish opponents in the late forties, the Roman authorities had no organization to consult. Concerned about public disorder, the government simply closed all the synagogues and expelled the agitators. This event, the so-called "Edict of Claudius," probably occurred in A.D. 49, which correlates closely with Prisca's and Aquila's arrival in Corinth as refugees when they first met Paul. The result was that the early Christian communities were now forced to discover new leaders and new locations for their common life. The impression of recent scholars is that the Christian groups formed themselves into house churches, at least five in number, with new leaders who had not been affected by the expulsion of the Jewish Christian missionaries.

In the years between 49 and 54 it appears that the Roman house churches developed in distinctive and independent ways, in some instances departing quite drastically from their roots in the synagogues where they had been founded. Charismatic leaders came to the fore in some of these churches and, in several instances at least, well-to-do patrons and patronesses who had means to provide a house became prominent leaders. It was probably during this period that some anti-Semitic tendencies visible in Romans 9–11 began to become prominent. Feelings of superiority on the part of Gentile Christian house churches in relation to Jewish Christian groups began to emerge.

After the death of the emperor Claudius in 54, it appears that the Jewish Christians were allowed to return to Rome and the synagogues were allowed to reopen. It was during this period that conflicts began to arise that are dealt with in the latter chapters of Romans. When the Jewish Christian leaders like Prisca and Aquila began to return, they found that the churches in which they earlier had been members were drastically altered because of new leaders and the new settings of house churches. In all probability the conservative order of worship based on the Jewish prayer book was no longer in effect.

New charismatic forms of worship and new hymns that came from different branches of early Christianity were being used. Conflicts over leadership began to surface when the Gentile Christian leaders of house churches resisted the resumption of leadership roles by Jewish Christian missionaries who were returning. Conflicts involved conservative versus liberal theology, charismatic versus traditional orders of service, Jewish versus Gentile patterns of ethics, different church calendars, and a variety of other issues, not all of which are reflected in Romans itself.

In this situation, the terms "weak" and "strong" were used, probably to indicate the outlook of groups that we would today identify roughly as conservative or liberal. The term "strong" was evidently used by the majority of Gentile Christians who felt strong enough to break free from the Jewish law and calendar. They used the derogatory term "weak" to designate the conservatives who did not feel free to break from the traditional patterns of worship and belief that they had inherited from their Jewish tradition. But the way these terms are used in Romans 14–15 indicates that the conflicts were not simply between Jewish Christian conservatives and Gentile liberal Christians. There is evidence that there were both conservative and liberal Jewish Christians and conservative and liberal Gentile Christians. The situation was quite tangled and the conflicts at the time that Paul wrote the letter, in the winter of A.D. 56–57, appear to have been quite intense.

ROMANS 1:1-15

Introduction to These Verses

Romans is the only Pauline letter addressed to a church that he did not found. This means that Paul has to introduce himself in a way that is very different from his other letters. The first fifteen verses of chapter 1 provide this self-introduction. Paul needs to explain why he is writing and identify who he is. As we know from general experience, first impressions mean a lot. So the way Paul introduces himself and approaches the congregation at Rome will have a great deal to do with how he will be received.

The Address of Romans

The situation of church conflict helps explain the level of tact with which Paul addresses the Roman house churches and also the peculiar address of the letter. In Romans 1:6-7 Paul addresses the Christians in Rome but does not refer to them as a church. These verses contain three fairly distinct identifications of the Christians, which probably reflects Paul's knowledge of how the Christians identified themselves. It is likely that the liberals, or the "strong," identified themselves as "called to belong to Jesus Christ," stressing their election and thus their superior status. The conservatives, or the "weak," probably identified themselves as the ones "called to be saints." This would indicate the high priority given to moral standards, in some instances based on the Old Testament law.

The middle address in the beginning of verse 7 is probably Paul's effort to find a unification formula: "to all God's beloved in Rome." Paul's effort is to find an inclusive basis for the church, a motivation for mutual acceptance. He stresses at this point and throughout the letter that each Christian is unconditionally loved by God, that both conservatives and liberals are recipients of God's grace. In this and in many other ways Paul seeks to find a common ground that will unite the competing house churches and the various leaders now present in Rome. This effort at unification is one of the keys to understanding the first fifteen verses and, indeed, the whole letter.

The introduction of a Pauline letter is a primary place to discover the purpose of writing. While many elaborate theories have been constructed to explain Paul's purpose, it is best to take into account what Paul actually says in these opening verses. In Romans 1:11 he says he wants to see the Romans in order to impart a spiritual gift to strengthen them. This is further explained in 1:15 as preaching the gospel.

Clearly, however, Paul does not wish to give the impression that the Roman house churches lack a legitimate gospel. He says in verse 12 that he wishes to be "mutually encouraged by each other's faith, both yours and mine." That he does not consider their faith deficient is also indicated by verse 8, in which he expresses gratitude that their faith is proclaimed all over the world. Why, then, does Paul wish to preach in Rome? The puzzle is deepened by the fact that Paul mentions his standard missionary procedure in Romans 15:20, not to preach in an area where someone else has witnessed, so that I do not build on someone else's foundation.

There are several clues in this introduction to solve this puzzle. Paul places both his work and the faith of the Roman house churches in a global context. He refers in verse 5 to his apostolic task to bring about the obedience of faith in all nations. There is another expression of this theme in verse 13 in which the work in Rome is set in the context of "the rest of the Gentiles" (NRSV) or "among the other Gentiles" (NIV). In the following verse he states the worldwide horizon of his missionary obligation.

Therefore, we can be certain that Paul's preaching in Rome is directly related to world mission. When Paul returns to this theme in 15:24, we discover what this means. He discloses his plan to establish a Christian mission in Spain, which was then perceived to be the end of the civilized world. Paul hopes to involve the Romans in the planning and support of this mission. This means that Paul's letter to the Romans needs to be understood as a missionary letter. It sets forth the gospel that Paul wishes to preach but also aims at finding common ground between the splintered factions of the Roman house churches so that they will stop fighting with one another and cooperate in this common mission. Church politics and world mission are here closely united.

This section of Romans has two main parts.

I. The Beginning of Paul's Letter (1:1-7)
II. The Announcement of Paul's Mission (1:8-15)

The Message of Romans 1:1-15

Paul's approach is an intriguing model for the way we should interact with each other in the church. Although he is obviously quite concerned about some of the tensions within the congregation and provides a very elaborate theological rationale for how the gospel should be understood, he nevertheless respects their achievements and their viewpoint. Such tact is directly related to the gospel as Paul sets it forth in Romans.

The essence of the gospel relates to the grace of God shown in Jesus Christ. When people internalize God's love they are capable of accepting one another and respecting one another more fully. Rather than seeking to impose their views on others, they learn to respect people with whom they disagree. This kind of tact is as crucial for the life of modern congregations as it was in Paul's time.

The opening verses of Romans call us to reflect on the relationship between

diversity and inclusiveness. Paul mentions in verse 13 that he has been prevented from visiting Rome repeatedly in the past. Both he and the Romans had faced adversity. When we as Christians in the twenty-first century think back on the life of our churches over the past few years, we can remember similar conflicts and adverse circumstances that we have had to surmount. The frequent and often unwilling movement of our people from one community to another produces the kind of pain that the Roman refugees had experienced. Then, as now, such adversity caused groups to become hostile to one another.

From the opening lines of Romans, Paul makes a case for an inclusive gospel. He seeks to include all those in Rome and believes that his gospel is relevant for all the nations. He explicitly includes people of different educational levels and different language backgrounds in his identification of the gospel.

As the argument of Romans will make plain in subsequent chapters, Paul's conviction is that the grace of God holds persons in adversity firmly in the hollow of God's hand. Nothing can separate us from the love of Christ. The gospel of Christ reveals that God's love stands behind us even in the worst of circumstances. This is why Paul speaks of himself as under obligation (Romans 1:14) because the gospel compels him to seek the unity of the church and the unification of the human race. The gospel sets no boundaries, then or now. This is a splendid resource to help us cope with the conflicts between groups and individuals today.

ROMANS 1:16-32

Introduction to These Verses

With Romans 1:16 Paul opens up the

formal argument of his letter. It is very important to keep the purpose of this abstract argument in mind. It clarifies the gospel that he intends to proclaim in Spain. It also has a particular bearing on the Roman house churches, as seen in the emphasis on inclusiveness between Jews and Gentiles. Paul sees in the gospel the basis for unifying the church. This interest is also visible in the opening section of his argument dealing with human idolatry and divine wrath (1:18-32).

While it may strike modern readers as puzzling that Paul would begin on such a negative note, his purpose is to shatter the pretensions dividing the Roman house churches. Before he can make a case that the Christians in Rome are equal in grace, he must first prove that they are equal under wrath. Only when the claims of superiority by the "weak" and the "strong" are destroyed will the Christians in Rome really be in a position to understand fully how the righteous must live by faith alone (1:17). These verses may be divided into two parts.

I. The Gospel as Divine Power (1:16-17)
II. Human Idolatry and Divine Wrath (1:18-32)

The Message of Romans 1:16-32

Nowhere else in the Greco-Roman world or in ancient Judaism does one have so strong an emphasis on the conscious repudiation of the knowledge of God on the part of humankind. Paul's emphasis on suppressing the truth about God as the essence of sin, and his contention that humans tend to confuse themselves with the divine, set him off from his

DEFINING RIGHTEOUSNESS

The peculiarity of the English language and the tradition of translating Romans leads to some difficulties in understanding the term *righteousness*. English provides two different words for what in the original text of Romans was a single family of terms. We speak of *righteousness* and *justification*, both of which have rather different connotations in English.

The difficulty is particularly visible in the thesis of Romans 1:17. Often this verse is translated in the direction of the *righteousness of God* being revealed in the gospel, with the following citation translated as *the just shall live by faith*. The problem is that the word *just* comes from exactly the same stem as the term *righteousness*. When this translation problem is not understood, as is so frequently the case in the Protestant tradition, *justification by faith alone* gets entirely separated from the *righteousness* of God. That is, God's activity in transforming humans is understood as the gift of forgiveness which allows us to be justified, even though we have violated the law. However, we must understand that in Pauline theology, being justified is very different from being righteous. In fact, Paul wishes to speak of humans in this entire letter as being "rightwised," a term from old English that would be better used in place of *justify* in the translation for Romans. To rightwise is to make right, to set one right, and to achieve a transformation in which humans come to reflect the righteousness of God.

contemporaries in the ancient world. The radical side of his idea of a natural revelation consciously perverted by humans can best be explained on the basis of Paul's theology of the cross.

Paul discovered in the Christ event the depth of human perversion and twistedness, and the tendency of humans to reject the truth and to deny its validity for their lives, even to the point of killing the Christ when they had him in their grasp. This idea of a radical and universal fall of humans is what gives Paul's argument its particular sharpness and its relevance for the modern world as well.

ROMANS 2

Introduction to This Chapter

With Romans 2:1-16, we encounter some of the most difficult and hotly disputed lines in Paul's letter to the Romans. Here he deals with issues that are directly relevant to the Roman house churches. The repeated references to judging in verses 1-3 are strongly reminiscent of the tendency that Paul sees in the Roman congregation, which was split between the weak and the strong (Romans 14:1). It is well, therefore, to bring the material of Romans 14:4 and 10 into Paul's argument here. Paul suggests that when humans judge one another they lose sight of the distinction between the creature and the Creator. Also, the reference to despising God's kindness in verse 4 seems to relate quite closely to the material in Romans 14:10: why do you despise your brother?

Here is an outline of this chapter:
I. The Judgmental Spirit (2:1-5)
II. Judgment According to Works (2:6-7)
III. The Relevance of Impartiality (2:8-16)
IV. No Exemption by Religious Status (2:17-29)
   A. Claims of religious superiority (2:17-20)
   B. Rhetorical questions (2:21-23)
   C. No exemption through circumcision (2:25-29)

The Message of Romans 2

The major thrust of this passage is that claims of religious superiority must be abandoned, no matter what their origin. The major challenge in studying this material is to avoid falling into anti-Semitic interpretation.

Many commentators perceive Paul to be arguing against Jews or Judaism in this passage. From the time of the Reformation down, indeed from virtually the time when Christianity became the established religion in the Roman Empire, this has been the major stream of Christian interpretation. The presumed superiority of Christianity over Judaism was seen to be the purpose of Paul's argument. Nothing could be further from the truth. This kind of interpretation simply leaves intact the very form of religious superiority that Paul is trying to overcome in Rome.

The crucial point is that Paul's targets are Christians. Related to this is the point that the argument is perceived to be a friendly one. In fact, Paul goes out of his way in the course of Romans to defend the prerogatives of Jewish Christians. Paul does not wish to attack Jewish culture or the Jewish religion. Rather, he wishes to convince the house churches of Rome that the misuse of the great religious heritage of the Hebrew Scriptures is leading to serious disruptions in the life of the community and to the expression of sinful attitudes and acts between the Christian groups. When Paul lists the boasts of the Jews in 2:17-20, he is attempting to articulate the kind of pride and arrogance that was surfacing in the Jewish Christian churches in Rome, not to make a general case against the Judaism of his day. The "you" in this argument is clearly the Jewish Christian. This passage can be related to modern expressions of religious superiority.

Many of the conflicts within denominations in American experience have also witnessed the expression of arguments based on the fallacious claims of religious superiority. People having different views of the inspiration of Scripture or different attitudes toward disputed public policy issues or toward military service have argued that their own religious perceptions or their own interpretation of Scripture is intrinsically superior to others. It is this kind of situation that Paul's argument in Romans 2:1 tries to overcome.

ROMANS 3:1-20

Introduction to These Verses

The previous argument about universal sin raises the questions that Paul must answer in Romans 3:1-20 to prove his case. He cannot afford to discredit the Jewish faith as such, or the Torah on which that faith is based. He therefore is forced to walk a thin line between acknowledging the truth of the religious tradition in the Hebrew Scriptures, while at the same time arguing that everyone, both Jew and Gentile, is involved in sin in equal measure.

Here is an outline of Romans 3:1-20:
I. Objections Concerning Universal Sin (3:1-2)
II. The Faithfulness of God (3:3-4)
III. The Fairness of God (3:5-8)
IV. The Question of Jewish Advantage (3:9)
V. The Proof From Scripture (3:10-18)
VI. The Conclusion of the Argument (3:19-20)

An important observation concerning the question-and-answer style of this material throws light on how it should be understood. Recent research into this question-and-answer style shows that in the Greco-Roman world it was widely used in the grammar school system. The style of the so-called "friendly interlocutor" was frequently used by a skilled teacher in order to discover loopholes in an argument and to build up a case from common sense. The audience was perceived to be friendly in this kind of instruction. This fits closely the circumstances of Paul, who does not

wish to confront the Roman Christians as enemies or opponents.

The Message of Romans 3:1-20

Paul is dealing here with the most dangerous of Christian vices, self-righteousness. This is the root of Christian arrogance and very frequently the fundamental cause of conflicts between Christian groups. The problem is that persons and groups use their conformity to a certain standard to try to make themselves "righteous." The whole purpose of Paul's argument from 1:18 on is to prove that this cannot work, that this effort in fact is a form of sinful pride, an effort on the part of creatures to make themselves into the Creator, to gain control of their destiny and to dominate others.

Paul is forced to make a very sweeping and hard case, climaxing in 3:20, because he is confronting the kind of conflicts that would later become characteristic of Christian groups, namely self-righteous groups on both right and left claiming their superiority over others, believing that others are damned or lost. They are acting in such a way as to disallow their leadership or their contribution.

Paul's hope is to lead the congregation to see that this terrible perversion of the Christian faith is based on the kind of lie described in Romans 1:25. Whereas the Christian groups in Rome feel certain that they are elect and secure, that they are superior to their competitors, Paul offers a forceful medicine of reality therapy in this argument, ending in 3:20. No human being can be rightwised in God's sight by works of the law.

If Paul's argument were taken seriously today, it would undercut all claims of cultural or religious superiority, providing a realistic basis for mutual respect between denominations, religions, and nations.

SALVATION BY FAITH ALONE (ROMANS 3:21-26)

In this passage we come to what has traditionally been called the heart of Romans. It is in this section that Paul's marvelous declaration of salvation by faith alone is stated. Here he proclaims freedom from the performance principle. The righteousness of God in this passage is perceived as God's victory over sin, manifest in the Christ event. This victory transforms humans by making them acceptable to God, despite their failures and despite their rebellion.

The setting right of the human race through Christ conveys to us the grace of God, which we can never earn. This means that our lives are no longer dependent on what we are able to perform, on our obedience to the law. Salvation is understood here as the faithful response of humans to the love of God, manifest in the Christ event.

What has been understood traditionally as "justification by faith" is a matter of being set right by this unconditional love of God, to be restored to the original righteousness that humans were intended to have from the moment of their creation. To stand under this righteousness is to become righteous. It is also understood by Paul as entering the sphere of divine righteousness, that is, submitting to the lordship of Christ. Thus salvation in this passage is a matter of submitting to the righteousness of God, which means a change of direction toward the service of God in everyday affairs.

Paul means that the transformation of the human race does not come through submission to the law, whether this be the law of the Jewish Torah or the laws of one's social group. The revolutionary quality of the true Christian faith is clearly manifest in this assertion. In most cultures and in many forms of popular Christianity, salvation remains a matter of conforming to certain beliefs or actions. The law takes manifold forms, most of which are not even in the Old Testament. But Paul does not wish to abandon the law except as a cause and means of salvation. He insists that the law and the prophets bear witness to the salvation that comes through faith alone. He contends that we uphold or establish the law by faithfully responding to the final revelation of the law's intent in Christ. But Paul does not mean that we uphold the law in the sense of falling back into conformity. While law can never become a means of salvation, it nevertheless points toward salvation.

Humans are rightwised (justified) by God's grace as a gift. They do not earn it; indeed they cannot earn it. There is no way that humans can merit a new life, because as Paul has stated in 3:23, all humans without exception sin and "fall short of the glory of God." We are accepted by God purely on the basis of God's love revealed in Christ. Nothing we can ever do will ever earn that grace.

ROMANS 3:21–4:25

Introduction to These Chapters

This section of Romans contains the final two arguments that support the thesis set forth earlier in Romans 1:16-17. In 3:21-31 Paul states the positive argument concerning humans being rightwised by faith by the one true God. In 4:1-25 Paul sets forth Abraham as the example of such faith and the ancestor of all faithful persons. The key term in these final two sections is *rightwising*, which is often translated as *justification* or *justify*. There are no less than nineteen references to this concept in 3:21–4:25.

Here is an outline of this section:

I. We Are Rightwised by Faith (3:21-31)
  A. Salvation by faith alone (3:21-26)
  B. Righteousness through faith (3:27-31)
II. Abraham as the Example of Faith (4:1-25)

A. Abraham's faith in God (4:1-8)
B. Abraham's justification (4:9-12)
C. Abraham's promise is fulfilled (4:13-22)
D. The promise to faithful Christians (4:23-25)

The Message of Romans 3:21–4:25

The key sentence in 4:25 places in nuclear form the connection between the life, death, and resurrection of Christ and the transformation of humans into the new righteousness. Christ died "for our trespasses" in the sense that humans discovered their own hostility against God in the death of Jesus. In that death we recognize the depth of human alienation and sin. But we recognize at the same time that we are forgiven at the very moment of Christ's death. He died for the sake of others, guiltlessly, dying in their places so that they might have communicated to them the surpassing grace of God.

Since Christ "was raised for our justification [rightwising]," Paul is affirming that in the Resurrection the death of Christ was confirmed and the truth of the revelation of Christ was revealed. The theme of dying and rising with Christ that will be developed in Romans 6 receives here its first articulation. Under the power of the Christ event, we recognize that our former lives were null and void. We also see that we have the possibility to share in his resurrection by receiving a new life based on grace rather than on our own accomplishments. For Abraham is indeed the ancestor of the faithful of all generations.

The Creator is capable of producing something out of nothing. This is directly correlated with Christian belief in 4:24, in that Christians believe that God produced life out of the death of Christ. The essence of the Christian orientation, therefore, is to believe that God can make something out of nothing. We humans are nothing; our accomplishments amount to nothing. But God restores us to righteousness by gospel power alone. Faith is defined here as a matter of setting trust in that divine power.

ROMANS 5

Introduction to This Chapter

Romans 5:1-11 has an introductory role in the series of amplifications of Paul's basic argument which we find in 5:1–8:39. In particular, we see themes in 5:12-21; 6:1-23; and 8:1-39 introduced for the first time in this section. The restored relationship with God marked by peace provides the basis for future salvation despite all present sufferings. The paradoxical state of the new life is developed throughout chapters 5–8, in that the peaceful relationship with God and fellow humans is set in the context of a world in which the principalities and powers are very much present and effective.

In the second half of chapter 5, Paul sets out the contrasting realms of Adam and Christ.

A number of important themes surface in this chapter: suffering in relation to maturity; peace and reconciliation; the relation between the present experience of justification and the future experience of salvation; the cause of human sin and the role of Adam; and the relation between the old age and the new. Christian realism is at the forefront of this passage.

Chapter 5 may be outlined as follows:
I. Introduction to the Argument (5:1-11)
   A. Peace in the midst of affliction (5:1-2)
   B. Afflictions and sufferings (5:3-5)
   C. Reconciliation with God (5:6-10)

D. Summary statement (5:11)
II. The Realms of Adam and Christ
(5:12-21)
A. Introduction (5:12)
B. Sin in the garden of Eden
(5:13-14)
C. Adam and Christ are compared
(5:15-21)

The Message of Romans 5

In chapter 5 we encounter one of the pervasive themes in Pauline theology, namely the overlapping of the two ages. The age of Adam, marked by sin and death, is counterposed against the sphere of Christ, marked by justification and life. Particularly from verses 15-17, we gain the sense of these two ages in tension, with Christians caught between. We are members of Christ's age but still conscious of the pervasive impact of the old world.

This feature of Pauline thought has manifested itself throughout Romans. His very mission plan to go to Spain seems to have been shaped by this sense of end-time urgency. The thesis of Romans, that the righteousness of God is revealed at the present time, strongly suggests the dawning of a new age. The hope expressed in this passage of the glory of God being manifested in believers breathes the spirit of the fulfillment of history toward which Paul was working. The overlapping of the ages produces an element of tension which is crucial to understanding Pauline thought.

This vital sense of life as a constant struggle is what provides the element of realism that we detect from the opening lines of chapter 5 and which will be the major theme to be traced through the end of chapter 8. Evil is a reality. The old world is still in effect, even though the new world has dawned. The frequent use of battle metaphors in Christian hymns speaks to this underlying truth, that the Christian life of righteousness involves a struggle for righteousness. It involves a constant battle against the old age.

ROMANS 6

Introduction to This Chapter

There are powerful resources for faith in this chapter. Paul's contention is that the old Adam does not prevail. The new life is a reality. Humans are set free from sin and have a relationship in Christ. This is the good news at the heart of Romans.

Romans 6 has three main parts:
I. Sin and Baptism (6:1-14)
II. Sin and Lordship (6:15-20)
III. The Issue of Sanctification (6:21-23)

The Message of Romans 6

Paul is realistic in this chapter. He believes that the Christian life is poised between dying and rising. The baptism that we experience does not abolish the ravages of time. Rather, it places Christians in a formative relationship to past and future events. The past event is the death and resurrection of Christ; the future event is the return of Christ at the end of time and the final gift of glory.

We live between the times, which inserts an undeniable element of tension within the Christian life. It keeps us from ever being satisfied with things as they are, and particularly with our own performance. It counters our tendency toward overconfidence.

The death and resurrection of Christ in the past and the coming triumph of righteousness are the definitive poles of Christian self-identity, far more real to believers than the news events that pour over our consciousness day by day or the trends that our popular prophets perceive.

This tension between faith and world produces a certain skeptical attitude on the part of Christians concerning the world around them. Early Christians had a clear sense of not being defined by the world. One of the reasons they were persecuted was that they seemed constantly to be marching to a different drummer, to have a different sense of time. They were, in fact, poised between dying and rising, caught and enlivened by the tension between the already and the not-yet. Thus they were tough, resilient, and forward-looking. They walked with clear eyes through a world that they knew was obeying a false god. But they were perfectly confident, despite all setbacks and persecutions, of the future that they had to share.

The eternal life referred to in 6:22-23 is an integral part of this robust consciousness. The early Christians realized that while they were already participants in this eternal life, they were still in a dying world. They already had the free gift of God (verse 23). But they recognized that nothing they accomplished in this life would ever be complete until the end of time.

ROMANS 7

Introduction to This Chapter

In this chapter, Paul reaffirms the basic idea of Christians being released from the law (7:6), answering several important objections that could have led to a misunderstanding of Paul's basic idea. He offers a revolutionary perspective on the law, seen in the light of the Christ event, and of Paul's own experience from his conversion through his struggles with the law in the early church.

Each of the issues in Romans 7 had a direct relevance to the Roman house churches. Thus, although the argument appears somewhat abstract and general in places, it had a very practical bearing on

the problems being faced by the congregations in Rome.

Chapter 7 may be outlined as follows:

I. The Two Ages and the Law (7:1-6)
II. The Problem with the Law (7:7-12)
III. Sin and Paul's Conversion (7:13-25)

The Message of Romans 7

The gospel provides a deliverance from the plight of self-defeating zealotism described in Romans 7. The gift of divine righteousness addresses the sense of vulnerability that provides the energy subverting the law. Paul shows, through this argument in Romans 7, that such behavior is a sign of returning to the old age of bondage to the law.

Any good achieved through such struggles for power will turn out to be evil. Only by understanding our lives as based solely on grace is there a possibility of overcoming the power of this attitude in which we oppose the status that others have because we want the status for ourselves and for our group alone. Thus when Paul says at the end of the chapter that "but with my flesh I am a slave to the law of sin" (NRSV) or in the NIV, "but in the sinful nature a slave to the law of sin," he is describing the actual motivational structure of the house churches in Rome, locked in their lethal battle with each other. Such battles are the flat repudiation of genuine faith. The same point could be made about similar battles in the modern world.

The hope for which Paul gives thanks in verse 25 is particularly relevant for persons and nations that discover contradictions between ideals and performance in their own history. Christ alone can deliver us from the past. His life and death reveal the essence of our dilemma. They convey to us an acceptance at so profound a level that we are able to accept ourselves as we are.

PRINCIPALITIES AND POWERS
(ROMANS 8:31-39)

These verses provide a conclusion not only for chapter 8 but for all the material from 5:1 onward. The theme of these verses is that nothing can separate believers from the love of Christ.

Paul provides an elaborate list of the cosmic powers in verses 35-39. In the first century, people believed that the world was dominated by cosmic forces and powers. They personified the idea of evil and of social forces such as economics or government. They believed that there were powers in the heavens ("the heights") and that there were powers below the surface of the earth ("the depth"). They were convinced that every human institution was something of an otherworldly power, capable of exercising an evil, superhuman control.

Human institutions and forces have an external structure, but they also have an internal spirit or ethos. We know this to be the case of the institutions for which we work and the governments that have been established by humans. Each has a different structure, and even those with similar structures have a different kind of spirit, shaped by the persons leading them and shaped by the peculiar history of the institution.

Paul's contention in verses 31-39 is that none of these institutions and forces is capable of separating humans from the love of Christ. Although the world remains fallen and these forces remain a reality, Christians have no need of losing heart. There is a basis for final confidence, a relational foundation for hope in the love of God that is demonstrated to us in that God "did not spare" (NIV) or "withhold" (NRSV) "his own Son, but gave him up for us all" (NIV) or "all of us."

Then we can cease the sinful striving to be the center of the world. This chapter is as relevant to individuals as it is to nations.

ROMANS 8

Introduction to This Chapter

Chapter 8, with its emphasis on life in the Spirit, is the indisputable high point of Romans.

Chapter 8 may be outlined as follows:
I. Flesh and Spirit (8:1-17)
  A. Liberation by Christ (8:1-4)
  B. The contrast between flesh and spirit (8:5-9)
  C. The problem of the body (8:10-11)
  D. Spirit and sonship (8:12-17)
II. Human Suffering (8:17-30)
  A. Spirit, suffering, and hope (8:17-25)
  B. Human vulnerability and weakness (8:26-27)
  C. Providence and predestination (8:28-30)
III. Principalities and Powers (8:31-39)

The Message of Romans 8

The thrilling sequence at the end of chapter 8 affirms not only the triumphant power of God over all human institutions but also the basis of Christian realism and hope. These forces, which are often distorted and cause uncounted evil, and which contribute to the groaning of the whole creation, do not have ultimate power. They are in the process of transformation. And as Christians become agents of righteousness, their task is to work for the transformation of these forces and institutions.

The final transformation, of course, will not occur until the end of time. But in the meantime, Paul recommends an attitude that is the opposite of servility toward the principalities and powers of this world. Christians are not to be frightened of these powers, for they are incapable of separating believers from the love of God. Trusting in the power of the spirit over the flesh, and certain that their relationship with God is secure, contemporary Christians are called to take up this transformation of worldly institutions. If we took the gospel seriously, we too would face adversity with courage and become "more than conquerors through him who loved us."

ROMANS 9–11

Introduction to These Chapters

In Romans 9:1–11 we encounter Paul's discussion of the problem of unbelieving Israel in relation to the triumph of divine righteousness. The key issue for Paul is stated in 9:6, whether the word of God had failed. If the gospel is indeed triumphant, as Paul has argued throughout Romans up to this point, then how does it happen that the first recipients of the gospel did not accept it? If the promise to Abraham was that through Israel all the Gentiles would be blessed, does the refusal of Israel to accept the gospel of Jesus Christ mean that God has taken back the promise? If God's word cannot be relied upon, then the gospel itself is untrue and the mission of Paul rests on a false foundation.

The issues of Jewish unbelief and world conversion are intimately linked in Paul's writings. This is an issue that he must answer in a satisfactory manner in order to make his gospel credible.

Romans 9–11 may be outlined as follows:

I. Introduction (9:1-5)
II. Election and Israel's Fate (9:6-18)
III. Individual Responsibility (9:19-29)
IV. The Doctrine of Unenlightened Zeal (9:30–10:4)
V. Righteousness by Faith Alone (10:5-13)
VI. The Rejection of the Gospel (10:14-21)
VII. God Did Not Reject Israel (11:1-10)
VIII. Why Israel Rejected the Gospel (11:11-24)
IX. The Mystery of Israel's Salvation (11:25-32)
X. Conclusion (11:33-36)

The Message of Romans 9–11

No human theology, even Paul's own, can finally penetrate the "mind of God." There is a need for humility both in the church and in Paul's mission. Yet to this one transcendent God belong all things and persons because they derive ultimately from the same God (see 11:36).

God is glorified when zeal is transformed by the gospel and when the world is thereby reunited. Paul is concerned not only with Jewish zeal, but with Gentile zeal as well. All people in Paul's time as well as our own belong together under the one true and transcendent God, and Paul's confident hope is that they shall one day discover this destiny—together.

ROMANS 12

Introduction to This Chapter

Chapter 12 may be outlined as follows:

I. The Theme of the Section (12:1-2)
II. The Use of Christian Gifts (12:3-8)
III. The Struggle Between Good and Evil (12:9-21)
   A. Guidelines for genuine love (12:9)
   B. Life in the congregation (12:10-13)

C. Life outside the congregation
(12:14-20)

D. Conclusion (12:21)

The Message of Romans 12

This chapter provides a coherent basis for a realistic ethic in the modern world. It calls for an ongoing transformation, not only of moral standards, but also of the world itself. But evil is taken as seriously here as it is in chapter 8, providing a realistic context for the ethic of sacrificial love.

Living sacrifices (12:1) will continue to be required in the ongoing and still unfinished effort to "overcome evil with good" (12:21).

ROMANS 13:1–15:13

Introduction to These Chapters

In these chapters Paul takes up some of the most difficult issues as far as the situation in Rome was concerned. The question of how to relate to the Roman authorities was very touchy and had played a role in the expulsion of Christian leaders during the time of the edict of Claudius. The question of the relation between love and law divided the conservatives from the liberals. The question of how to respond to the anticipated return of Christ and what kind of ethic was required in the end-time period was complex and difficult. Finally, the issues of mutual tolerance between groups in the house churches were highly sensitive. Paul leaves these issues until the latter part of Romans because now there is a sufficient basis to create a compelling argument.

This section may be outlined as follows:

I. Christians and Government (13:1-7)

II. Love and the End Times (13:8-10)

III. Moral Alertness in the Final Days
(13:11-14)

IV. Guidelines for the Weak and Strong
(14:1-23)

V. Accepting Outsiders (15:1-6)

VI. Summary Statements (15:7-13)

The Message of Romans 13:1–15:13

The hope lifted up in this section is for the unification of the world through the gospel. This hope is as relevant for the twenty-first century as it was for the first century.

The centrality of the Gentile mission for the entire letter of Romans is magnificently caught by the series of Scripture quotations that lead up to this final benediction (15:9-12). The hope is that when the gospel is received, all the nations will glorify God, thus fulfilling the destiny of Israel to be a blessing to the world. This goal, if achieved, will help overcome the conflicts that have so long divided the nations. The restoration of righteousness to the world will occur when nations and races begin to praise God in unity, rather than divisively worshiping and glorifying themselves.

ROMANS 15:14–16:27

Introduction to These Chapters

There are two excellent places to discover the purpose of Paul's argument in Romans, the introduction in 1:1-15 and the conclusion, which begins with 15:14 and continues through 16:27.

In a carefully crafted letter like Romans, the conclusion restates the purpose of writing and appeals for the practical application of the argument. We can see from the content of this peroration that Paul writes to promote his mission. The appeal is for cooperation in the missionary activities in which Paul is involved—in Jerusalem, Rome, and Spain.

Skilled in the art of creating forceful letters, Paul uses the element of emotional appeal recommended by the teachers of the ancient world. We sense the pathos particularly at the end of chapter 15, and the element of personal involvement in the greetings of chapter 16.

Here is an outline of this section.

I. Paul's Calling and Strategy (15:14-21)
II. The Appeal to Participate in Mission (15:22-23)
III. The Jerusalem Offering (15:24-29)
IV. First Conclusion to the Letter (15:30-33)
V. The Role of Phoebe (16:1-2)
VI. Greetings to Church Leaders (16:3-16)
VII. The Conclusion of the Book (16:17-27)

The Message of Romans 15:14–16:27

Paul seeks unity by respecting the unique potential of each group and each member within the Christian community. There are resources here for the modern church to recover a sense of its mission of world unification, overcoming unbridled zealotry inside and outside the religious communities, and looking for the final triumph of the gospel over the cancer of human sin.

The obedience of faith (16:26) is the final goal of the gospel, implying submission to the righteousness of God and hence the restoration of planet earth.

FIRST AND SECOND CORINTHIANS

OUTLINE OF 1 AND 2 CORINTHIANS

1 CORINTHIANS

I. Beginning of the Letter (1:1-9)
  A. Address and blessing (1:1-3)
  B. General thanksgiving (1:4-9)

II. Encouragement and Instruction (1:10–6:20)
  A. Church members should be one in Christ (1:10-17)
  B. The centrality of the cross (1:18–2:5)
  C. God's wisdom made known in Christ (2:6-16)
  D. The foundation of Christian maturity (3:1–4:21)
  E. Immoral practices and lifestyles (5:1–6:20)
    1. Incest and excommunication (5:1-13)
    2. Refraining from lawsuits (6:1-11)
    3. Be firm in Christian faith (6:12-20)

III. Answers to Practical Questions (7:1–12:31)
  A. Questions about marriage (7:1-40)
  B. Concerns about food and dietary practices (8:1-13)
  C. Paul's apostolic responsibility (9:1–11:1)

  D. The practice of public worship (11:2–12:31)
    1. Men and women in worship (11:2-16)
    2. Celebrating the Lord's Supper (11:17-34)
    3. Comments about spiritual gifts (12:1-31)

IV. Directives Concerning Important Issues (13:1–15:58)
  A. The superiority of love (13:1-13)
  B. Speaking in tongues (14:1-40)
  C. The meaning of the resurrection of Christ (15:1-58)

V. Paul's Concluding Comments (16:1-24)
  A. Update on collections for the needy (16:1-4)
  B. Travel plans and work of helpers (16:5-18)
  C. Final greetings (16:19-24)

2 CORINTHIANS

I. Beginning of the Letter (1:1-11)
  A. Address and general blessing (1:1-2)
  B. General thanksgiving (1:3-11)

II. Paul's Sincere Concern (1:12–3:3)
  A. Why Paul did not come to Corinth (1:12–2:4)
  B. Paul's apostolic commission (2:5–3:3)

III. The Old and New Covenants (3:4-18)

IV. Paul's Ministry by God's Mercy (4:1–7:4)
   A. Paul an ambassador of Christ (4:1–5:21)
   B. Paul's love of the Corinthians in Christ (6:1-13)
   C. The Corinthians must cling to Christ (6:14–7:4)

V. Appeals for Sincerity in Christ (7:5–9:15)
   A. Paul rejoices in news about them (7:2-16)
   B. Collection for Jerusalem believers (8:1–9:15)

VI. Paul's Authority as an Apostle (10:1–13:10)
   A. Boasting and laboring in the Lord (10:1-18)
   B. Paul is a fool for Christ (11:1–12:13)
   C. Appeal for renewal in Christ (12:14–13:10)

VII. Paul's Concluding Comments (13:11-14)
   A. A final appeal (13:11-13)
   B. A blessing of grace (13:14)

INTRODUCTION

Paul's letters to the Christians at Corinth are fascinating. They are addressed to new believers living in a fast-paced city. They speak of believers' problems that have become very evident in a modern world surprisingly similar to life in the Corinth of long ago. They contain one of the most profound prose passages in the history of literature (1 Corinthians 13). They focus the believer's attention on the essentials of the Christian faith. And they explain the Christian answer to the great human dread that faces all, death and extinction (1 Corinthians 15). Before we look at the text of the letters, we must ask what is known about the city of Corinth, those to whom the letter is addressed, and the author of the letters.

The City of Corinth

Corinth was an important city because of its location. It was situated on a small portion of land that connected the mainland of Greece with the massive peninsula called *Peloponnesus* (constituting southern Greece). This peninsula was the site of the famous Peloponnesian War between Athens and Sparta (421–404 B.C.). Also on the peninsula was Olympia, the ancient religious center of worship where the Olympic games were held in honor of the Greek god Zeus. Corinth was the connecting city on the isthmus between this historically important peninsula and mainland Greece. Athens was less than fifty miles to the east.

The city of Corinth also acted as a land link between the Soronic Gulf on the Aegean Sea and the Gulf of Corinth on the Adriatic side. As a strategic trade route, Corinth would have been very cosmopolitan, bursting with activity. Interesting people, new trends and ideas, plenty of employment opportunities, cultural activities, and athletic contests contributed to life in Corinth. As in any port city of the Roman Empire in the first century, there also would have been a certain amount of crime, licentiousness, and sexual promiscuity evident. Hence, Corinth was in many respects a very "modern" city.

Historically, Corinth thrived from the tenth to the first century B.C. Because

Corinth headed a league of cities (the Achaian League), Rome perceived Corinth as a threat and eventually sacked the city in 146 B.C. One hundred years later Julius Caesar brought many freed Italian slaves to the city, reconstituting its population. According to archaeological inscriptions, this Italian influence remained. Recent excavated city ruins indicate that Latin remained a formal language for the Corinthians. Yet Greek would have been the common language because of local Grecian influences and citizenry.

Apparently Corinth had a fairly strong Jewish population. At various times in Jewish history following the Babylonian Captivity of 586 B.C., Jews from Palestine emigrated throughout the Mediterranean world and beyond. Corinth would have been an attractive city for immigration because of the cosmopolitan population and the strong economy. So it is not surprising that in Corinth Paul met two Jewish converts, Aquila and Priscilla (Acts 18:1-3; 1 Corinthians 16:19), who had been exiled from Rome because of the emperor Claudius's (10 B.C.–A.D. 54) edict, probably issued about A.D. 49. Also, Jewish synagogues have been excavated by archaeologists, indicating a strong and active Jewish population.

Paul the Evangelist

Attempting to establish the movements and activities of Paul the apostle have proven difficult. When and where he traveled and wrote his letters is not always clear. Portions of the Acts of the Apostles and Galatians, along with a few biographical notations from Paul's other letters, are the only pieces of the puzzle available. Paul's primary concern was to tell the good news of Christ. His own welfare and activity were secondary to this concern. Hence we have little evidence for reconstructing his life and activities. It is not clear when he was born or when he died.

However, there is one clear piece of evidence that helps us date Paul's activities with the Christians in Corinth. The evidence is the dates of the Roman proconsul or tribunal in Corinth, Gallio. According to the account of Paul's activities in Acts (18:1-18), Paul's preaching in the Jewish synagogue brought him into serious conflict with the local Jews. Paul was told in a vision to stay in Corinth despite the tension, and he stayed a year and six months (Acts 18:11). The Jews finally brought a lawsuit against Paul (Acts 18:12-17), and Paul was brought before the local Roman tribunal, Gallio.

According to an inscription found at an archaeological excavation in Delphi, Gallio was proconsul in either 51–52 or 52–53. Assuming Paul was in Corinth for almost two years, and considering Gallio's dates as proconsul, Paul must have founded the church in Corinth between the years A.D. 51 to 53 (see also 1 Corinthians 3:5-15). This mission work was done during the latter part of Paul's second missionary journey (A.D. 50–53; see Acts 15:36-41).

The Christian community was comprised of numerous house churches. These cells of Christians included both Gentiles (Acts 18:6) and Jews (1 Corinthians 1:22-24). Sometimes Paul refers to these individual cells in his writings (see, for example, 1 Corinthians 1:16; 16:19). On other occasions, Paul seems to address all the cell groups as the church, suggesting that on occasion all got together—perhaps to hear one of Paul's letters (Romans 16:23; 1 Corinthians 14:23). The number of Christians in Corinth, the number of house churches, and the average number in a house church are almost impossible to estimate. The number of Christian converts was not great. Hence, we could estimate that in a city the size of Corinth (which probably had a population of about 100,000), there were perhaps only about fifty to one hundred converts when Paul wrote his letters. If we very roughly estimate ten persons to a house church, Paul was writing to about five to ten house churches.

While resident in Corinth, Paul supported himself by working at his trade of tent making (Acts 18:1-3). This trade was also referred to as "working with leather" because portable shelters used by shepherds, soldiers, and nomadic peoples were often fashioned from animal skins. It is probable that Paul worked in one of the small shops at the busy and popular bazaar or marketplace in Corinth.

Pursuing his trade, Paul would have come into contact with people from many different trades and with common laborers from the Corinthian work force. As a result, many of Paul's converts probably came from a lower socioeconomic background. Later Paul writes to the Corinth Christians referring to the "low and despised in the world" (NRSV; NIV "the lowly things of this world and the despised things"; 1 Corinthians 1:28) and those who are slaves or free (1 Corinthians 7:21; 12:13). But the church also would have had at least a handful of educated and wealthier individuals (Acts 18:8; Romans 16:23; 1 Corinthians 1:14—Paul probably wrote his letter to the Christians in Rome from Corinth). These wealthier folk would have perhaps supplied the villas and homes where house churches met for worship.

The Social Setting

The first Corinthian house churches experienced some social tensions. First, there were tensions between Jews and Gentiles. Many of the Jews felt that their religious heritage was important for any who believed Jesus of Nazareth was the expected messiah. Hence, they thought that converts had to become Jews before they could become Christians! (See Paul's letter to the Galatians.) But Paul merely emphasizes that Christ is everything and Jewish practices are no longer valid for a right relationship with God.

There were also tensions between social classes. The Christian faith brought together people from various backgrounds and social classes. It was a Roman custom to rank people at communal meals according to social standing in the community. Thus when house churches in Corinth held communal meals, Roman customs intensified the setting. It is not surprising then to find Paul addressing such problems with characteristic keenness and intensity (read 1 Corinthians 11:17-34 with this tension in mind).

There were also tensions over leadership. Paul says at the beginning of his first letter ". . . Each of you says, 'I belong to [NRSV; NIV = "follow"] Paul,' or 'I belong to Apollos,' or 'I belong to Cephas' [Peter], or 'I belong to Christ.' Has Christ been divided?" (1 Corinthians 1:12-13; for Apollos's visit, see Acts 18:27–19:1; 1 Corinthians 3:4-9; 4:6). Paul's question is not surprising considering the situation in Corinth. With many house churches that rarely would have gathered in one place, competition and jostling for superiority would have been a natural development—as is sometimes evident in churches today!

Finally, there were apparently tensions with pagan religious groups in the city. Because the Corinthians seem to have attributed great importance to knowledge or wisdom (Greek, *gnosis*), many scholars have argued that Gnosticism influenced the believers of Corinth (1 Corinthians 1:5, 20-22; 3:18-19; 8:1). Although the source of this influence is not at all clear, there does appear to be a tension between a pagan-type knowledge and Christian wisdom. Perhaps a clearer indication of a Gnostic social tension between Christian believers and pagan religions was a question Paul was asked to address: should believers eat foods dedicated to the gods of pagan religions (1 Corinthians 8:1-13)?

The Letters of Paul

The Corinthians epistles offer us at least two advantages: They are an excellent example of the way in which Paul wrote letters, and they contain what he considered to be the essence of the Christian faith.

Paul's style of writing reflects the Roman habits of his day. His letters normally contain an opening statement of greeting identifying sender and addressee (1 Corinthians 1:1-3). Then follows a general thanksgiving (1 Corinthians 1:4-9). Following these customary rituals, a message is presented that functions as the body of the letter (1 Corinthians 1:10–15:58). Finally an ending or farewell is offered, including comments about activities and intentions of Paul and his companions (1 Corinthians 16:1-24).

For the most part, Paul's letters are always courteous and considerate. They attempt to address the down-to-earth, concrete situations and problems with which the various Christian communities of the Mediterranean world struggled. But at times Paul does become less than gentle with his new converts. He refers to the Galatians as being "foolish" and "bewitched" (Galatians 3:1; his emotion is also expressed in Galatians 4:19). He affectionately refers to the Christians at Thessalonica as children in need of nursing (1 Thessalonians 2:7-8; see also 3:7-8). And to the Corinthians he speaks of his hardship and anxiety for all the churches

that have made him indignant about their fall from the true gospel (2 Corinthians 11:21-29).

What is Paul's understanding of the Christian faith? Because Paul is dealing with complexities of social classes, differing religious backgrounds (Jews and Gentiles), and divided cell groups, he states his understanding of the essential Christian message in the Corinthian epistles.

First of all, Paul emphasizes the resurrection of Christ. Because of Paul's experience on the Damascus road (Acts 9:1-22), he knows Christ is alive. His summary of the gospel to the Christians at the city of Corinth emphasizes that Christ was "raised on the third day" and appeared to many, "he appeared also to me" (1 Corinthians 15:3-8). Because Christ is alive, those who are in Christ are "a new creation" (2 Corinthians 5:17). The theme of Christ's resurrection emanates from every thought and idea Paul struggles to communicate—it leaps from every line of his letters. It is the driving force behind his enthusiasm, his excitement, and his energetic communication of the Christian faith.

Second, Paul emphasizes the work of the Holy Spirit. The Spirit of God is the Spirit of the resurrected and living Christ. Paul deeply and profoundly experiences the Spirit of the living Christ in all his missionary activity following his experience on the Damascus road. He understands the Spirit as the practical experience of Christ working in all of the Christian life. There is no Christian activity without the Spirit (1 Corinthians 1:27-30). This same Spirit not only works within all Christian activity, but the Spirit also gives gifts to individuals for the building up of the community.

For Paul, these two Christian truths cannot be disputed. The living Christ and the work of the Spirit are two necessities of the Christian's faith that will even rescue and reconstitute the fussing Corinthian believers. These two experiential truths are emphasized again and again throughout the Corinthian correspondence. In fact, all the other issues that Paul addresses in his letters to Corinth assume these two intensely practical beliefs.

The Number of Corinthian Letters

How many letters did Paul write to the Corinthians? We have two clear letters in our New Testament, but were there other letters? The question has been raised by Paul's own statements. He refers to his previous letter in the 1 Corinthians epistle (1 Corinthians 5:9-11), which would suggest that 1 Corinthians is not his first letter. Because of the immorality theme of this previous letter (1 Corinthians 5:9), at least a portion of it could be identified with the same theme found in a section of 2 Corinthians (2 Corinthians 6:14–7:1). If this previous letter is contained in 2 Corinthians, then it would follow that 2 Corinthians is comprised of several communications from Paul to the Corinthian churches. Estimates among scholars as to the number of Paul's epistles that possibly have been combined to form 2 Corinthians range from two letters to seven letters.

If shorter communications of Paul have been blended into this letter, on the one hand they probably would have been copied together in order to make them available for all the cell house churches. On the other hand, the more communications that are identified, the more difficult is the editing process. That is to say, someone close to Paul would have sought to blend the writings in a manner that met the needs of the believers in Corinth during the latter half of the first century A.D. and that accurately communicated Paul's teachings. (It does appear that three different writings of Paul can be identified in 2 Corinthians: chapters 1–9, the excerpt in 6:14–7:4, and chapters 10–13.) Over a period of time, these letters would have been viewed as one document. But regardless of how many letters are combined in 2 Corinthians, we will understand the letter as teachings, explanations, and directives of Paul to those at Corinth.

And regardless of how many letters are identified in both 1 and 2 Corinthians, we have before us two outstanding New Testament books attributed to Paul. Throughout the writings, he struggles with every ounce of energy to keep the diverse Corinthian believers on course with regard to the Christian faith.

The Time and Occasion for These Letters

Paul wrote 1 Corinthians from the city of Ephesus (1 Corinthians 16:8). The year was A.D. 54 or 55. Although it had not been long since his departure, Paul received a report from Chloe's people (1 Corinthians 1:11) telling of tensions, rivalries, and general confusion over lifestyles and beliefs. Paul was asked to help sort out the problems. His response was the New Testament letter entitled 1 Corinthians.

Second Corinthians is far more difficult to date. If there is more than one letter from Paul contained in 2 Corinthians, then different occasions and circumstances would have to be identified. However, even if there is more than one letter contained in 2 Corinthians, Paul was writing not long after his 1 Corinthians epistle. Probably about one year later, that is, A.D. 55 or 56, Paul met with Titus in Macedonia and was greatly encouraged because of what he heard about the believers at Corinth (2 Corinthians 7:5-9). This news may have encouraged Paul to dash off a letter telling of his care for the Corinthian believers (chapters 1–9). It was perhaps a little later that Paul received some disturbing news and wrote again, attacking the false apostles (2 Corinthians 11:13).

Paul's Opponents at Corinth

Finally, a word about Paul's opponents in Corinth. In the 1 Corinthians letter, Paul addresses a host of problems. To explain the many problems of sexual relationships (1 Corinthians 4:1-13), marriage (7:1-16), spiritual wisdom (2:6-16), death (chapter 15), and so forth to one particular group of people—or even to one house church— seems improbable. Paul's first letter more accurately reflects various tensions, disagreements, and opinions from any number of groups (including Gnostic groups) that made the young house churches on occasion creak and groan.

However, Paul does refer specifically to some opponents in his second letter (2 Corinthians 10:1-13). He refers to these persons with great sarcasm, calling them "super-apostles" (2 Corinthians 11:5; 12:11). They apparently claimed that Paul did not give the Corinthians proper leadership and authority (2 Corinthians 10:10). Furthermore, Paul refused to accept financial and material support from the

Corinthians (2 Corinthians 11:7-12 and 12:13-15), and now Paul took a collection for the poor (2 Corinthians 12:16-18). Finally, there was a claim about unusual spiritual gifts and experiences (1 Corinthians 12:1-11). Although Paul was probably referring to specific individuals when he called them super-apostles, the problems Paul addressed are too varied to identify a particular group or single resistance to Paul's ministry. Unless some new or unexpected information surfaces, definitive information about Paul's opponents in Corinth will remain lost to antiquity.

Events in the Life of Paul

An overview of Paul's life will help identify the years of relationship and fellowship he enjoyed with the Corinthians. Because Paul was not interested in telling churches about his own importance and career, very little information is available about his life. The primary sources are 2 Corinthians 11:16-33; Galatians 2:1-10; and scattered bits from his other letters. The secondary source is the book of Acts, written by the author of Luke's Gospel. From these sources, we can attempt to reconstruct Paul's years in the following manner.

MAIN EVENTS OF PAUL'S LIFE

Birth of Paul	A.D. 10
Death of Christ	30
Conversion of Paul	31–32
Years in Arabia (Galatians 1:17)	32–34
Damascus and Jerusalem	34–35
Hidden years in Tarsus	35–46
Barnabas brings Paul to Antioch	46–47
Second Jerusalem visit (Acts 15)	47
First missionary journey	47–48
Third Jerusalem visit	49
Second missionary journey	50–53
Paul in residence at Corinth (Acts 18:11)	51–53
Third missionary journey	53–57
Letter of Paul to the Corinthians now lost (1 Corinthians 5:9-11)	53–54
Corinth's letter to Paul (1 Corinthians 7:1; 8:1)	53–54
Report from Chloe's people (1 Corinthians 1:11-12)	54–55
Second Corinthian letter—from Ephesus (First Corinthians)	54–55
Paul briefly visits Corinth (2 Corinthians 2:1)	54–55
Third letter to Corinth (2 Corinthians 10-13)	54–55
Titus meets Paul in Macedonia; report on Corinth (2 Corinthians 2:5-11; 7:6-13)	55–56
Fourth Letter to Corinth (2 Corinthians 1-9)	55–56
Paul's final visit (1 Corinthians 16:1-9; Romans 15:25-27)	56
Jerusalem arrest (Acts 21:27–22:29)	56–57
Trials, journey to Rome, house arrest in Rome (Acts 23:30–28:31)	57–62
Martyrdom in Rome under Nero	62–64

Although these dates are approximate, they suggest two things. First of all, Paul had very little time with the Corinthian believers. His relationship with them, based on visits and letters, lasted only about five years (this was longer, however, than Paul spent with most of his fledgling churches). It is not surprising that the Corinthians would have looked back on Paul's teachings and visits with great fondness in the decades to come. It also would have been natural for them to treasure his letters, holding them in great esteem. This great respect for Paul's letters eventually influenced the universal church to include Paul's writings in the New Testament Scriptures.

Second, Paul's correspondence always addresses and responds to real life situations. On occasion Paul's letters may sound profound and theological—they did to some Corinthians (2 Corinthians 10:10). But this is because Paul attempts to encourage believers to live in thankful response to God's grace in Christ from their particular station in life. This was certainly the situation throughout his sometimes stormy relationship with the believers at Corinth. In this sense, the Corinthian epistles are a wonderful example of ministry for laity and pastors.

The Importance of These Epistles

In Paul's day, Corinth must have been an exciting and very modern place. The problems and difficulties of the first Christians in that fast-paced city of Corinth remain very real issues today. Questions of wisdom, Christian knowledge, lifestyles, death, love, marriage, worship, suffering, and so forth remain very serious issues for believers of all ages. Because Paul boldly addresses these Christian concerns, the Corinthians correspondence is a major help in working through these ever-present Christian issues. Here, perhaps more than anywhere else, Paul achieves a profound balance between doctrinal statement and practical Christian living.

1 CORINTHIANS

1 CORINTHIANS 1:1-9

Introduction to These Verses

As noted in the Introduction, Paul's letters generally follow the Roman custom of letter writing. Paul begins with a courteous greeting, identifying himself and the recipients of his letter. In modern terminology, these opening lines of Paul act as a type of letterhead.

This opening greeting also sets the stage for what is about to happen. As is still the custom in many cultures, it is polite to talk generally as a form of greeting before serious conversation occurs. Paul knows his addressees very well. Yet he does not rush immediately into issues he has on his mind. He is careful to set the stage respectfully and correctly.

These verses can be divided as follows:

I. Address and Blessing (1:1-3)
II. General Thanksgiving (1:4-9)

The Message of 1 Corinthians 1:1-9

Using the normal format of letter writing for his age, Paul clarifies the three parties in his letter. God is the main actor, Paul is the called apostle, and the Corinthians are those called to faith. Everything is initiated by God and sustained by God through Christ. Thus the assurance of the Corinthians is that God will not leave them alone. Although they may have questions and they may be experiencing difficulties in the daily living out of their faith, strength and certainty come from God through the finished work of Christ.

From the beginning, Paul is enthusiastic and full of confidence. But his confidence is not in his own ability to solve the problems in Corinth. Paul's confidence is in God's plan through Christ to bring the Corinthian believers to the end of their spiritual journey—blameless on the day of our Lord Jesus Christ.

1 CORINTHIANS 1:10–2:5

Introduction to These Verses

The Corinthians must have been a very sensitive and explosive group. To this point in the letter Paul has been delicate and quite formal. He has approached the situation cautiously but positively. Now he begins to penetrate more severely. But he does so by continually focusing on Christ. He is seeking to help the Corinthian believers bring everything—all their problems, difficulties, tensions, misunderstandings—to Christ. Paul can help them only if they see everything in the light of Christ. He has already hinted at a problem in his formal introduction:

individual spiritual gifts are meant to benefit the total community (verse 7). Paul now begins to speak more directly.

These verses can be outlined as follows:

I. Church Members Are One in Christ (1:10-17)
II. The Centrality of the Cross (1:18–2:5)

The Message of 1 Corinthians 1:10–2:5

These verses introduce the heart of the letter. Paul knows these believers well. He has lived alongside them and labored with them. He knows their city, their influences, and their habits. Having already heard of existing problems (7:1), and following his careful and full introduction (1:1-9), he now begins to focus their attention on Christ. Bringing them to the point of Christ, he perhaps senses that he will be better able to then instruct and help them with their tensions and problems. So, after this refocusing of their faith on Christ, Paul then diplomatically deals with both their practical questions (7:1–12:31) and theological questions (13:1–15:58).

1 CORINTHIANS 2:6-16

Introduction to These Verses

Up to this point in the letter, Paul has attempted to explain that the wisdom of humanity is of no consequence in the face of God's truth. In fact, human wisdom must be let go, dismissed, released, if the gospel is to be grasped. But once human wisdom is gained, by letting human wisdom die to the gospel, a new, eternally profound wisdom is born.

The Message of 1 Corinthians 2:6-16

This section is perhaps second in importance only to Paul's speaking of love (chapter 13). These verses deal with

a wisdom that comes only from God, that begins with God's action, and that depends upon God's continued self-revealing for clarity and understanding. This divine wisdom requires the entire Godhead. It implies the need and action of the Father, Son, and Holy Spirit for true wisdom and insight. Only as God draws close to humanity—as God becomes totally human—is humanity able to understand, discern, and be guided. Such is the depth of Paul's teaching.

1 CORINTHIANS 3–4

Introduction to These Chapters

Now that he has explained spiritual maturity in Christ (2:6-16), Paul considers the present spiritual level of the Corinthians. To show his sincere fellowship and camaraderie with the Corinthians, he begins by calling them *brothers*. In the past he could not speak to them as mature believers. They were believers in Christ, but they had not yet grown sufficiently in their new spiritual birth. They still maintained old habits, old ideas, human insights, human values, and human understandings. They had not yet really thought about life and death from God's word spoken in Christ. Hence, they were spiritual infants in Christ.

These chapters may be outlined as follows:

I. Paul's Prior Work in Corinth (3:1-19)
II. Christ Is the True Foundation (3:10-23)
III. The Responsibilities of Stewards (4:1-7)
IV. Paul Admonishes the Corinthians (4:8-13)
V. Concluding Admonitions (4:14-21)

The Message of 1 Corinthians 3–4

Now that Paul has addressed their interests about deep spiritual wisdom, he turns to the spiritual status of the Corinthians. He seeks to bring their particular spiritual interests to the truth of Christ. In this manner and from a human perspective, he does not scold the believers at Corinth. Nor does he speak from his own self-asserted authority. His statements about their immaturity and need for growth are based solely on the truth of God spoken in Christ.

1 CORINTHIANS 5–6

Introduction to These Chapters

Attention is now turned toward bad habits and questionable living practices. Paul is here addressing the worst of the Corinthian believers' lifestyles. There are problems that have been reported to Paul (1:11). Later Paul will go on to address questions they have asked him. But first things first. Paul has received disturbing news and information. He must deal with these practical problems that will compromise the gospel and could end up destroying the house churches at Corinth—and therefore the church at Corinth.

These chapters may be outlined as follows:

I. Incest and Excommunication (5:1-13)
II. Refraining from Lawsuits (6:1-11)
III. The Root of These Problems (6:12-20)

The Message of 1 Corinthians 5–6

In this section Paul deals with disturbing information he has received concerning the behavior of some of the Corinthians. The kind of immorality discussed in these verses threatens to destroy both the house churches and the city itself, by compromising the gospel of Jesus Christ. Paul gives both practical and theological advice to the Corinthians on how to respond to these circumstances.

1 CORINTHIANS 7–8

Introduction to These Chapters

Paul has just dealt with reports he has heard from Chloe's people. The reports told of an urgent situation that demanded Paul's immediate attention. Now he can turn to other things. Chloe's people also direct to Paul questions that have surfaced among the Corinthian house churches. Although two of the topics are vaguely related to what Paul has just written—marriage and spiritual gifts—the questions of the Corinthians introduce new topics into the letter.

These chapters can be outlined as follows:

I. Questions about Marriage (7:1-40)
II. Concerns about Dietary Practices (8:1-13)

The Message of 1 Corinthians 7–8

In this section Paul addresses practical matters that were on the minds of the Corinthians. He discusses how to live within the marriage covenant, divorce, what unmarried persons should do (those widowed, divorced, or not yet married), how to relate to an unbeliever, and whether to eat food offered to idols. Paul offers all his advice in the context of serving the resurrected Christ.

1 CORINTHIANS 9:1–11:1

Introduction to These Chapters

Paul has been addressing specific questions that the Corinthian believers directed to him (marriage and food habits).

Before he turns to the area of public worship, Paul speaks of his own charge to care for the spiritual well-being of the Corinthians. Paul perhaps senses that some will take issue with his answers to their questions. So he speaks of his own authority and he gives the believers at Corinth some general encouragement.

The Message of 1 Corinthians 9:1–11:1

The believer's sole task is being a witness, pointing with all of life's living habits to the truth of God in Christ. Thus the true believer pleases all, not for self-glorification, but that all may come to know Christ.

In this manner, they should follow Paul's example. Paul does not mean that they should in any way glorify him. Rather, as Paul centers his life and activities on the living and resurrected Christ, they should do the same. They should imitate Paul in their lifestyle and habits, including food and drink. By following Paul, they will focus their full life on Christ—and not Paul.

1 CORINTHIANS 11:2–12:31

Introduction to These Chapters

The central activity of the believers at Corinth was worship. Paul almost certainly would have received news from Chloe's people about house churches at worship. Perhaps he also has been asked direct questions about women in worship, the celebration of the Lord's Supper, and the place of spiritual gifts.

These chapters may be outlined as follows:

I. Men and Women in Public Worship (11:2-16)
II. Practicing the Lord's Supper (11:17-34)
III. Comments about Spiritual Gifts (12:1-31)

The Message of 1 Corinthians 11:2–12:31

In this section Paul continues to address concerns that have evidently been raised by the Corinthians. Here he discusses the place of women in worship, the celebration of the Lord's Supper, and the varieties of spiritual gifts. Spiritual gifts lead Paul to a

SPIRITUAL GIFTS AND THE BODY OF CHRIST (1 CORINTHIANS 12)

All the different gifts of God come through the same Holy Spirit. The source is the same; the gifts must be seen from God's perspective—not the perspective of humanity. These gifts indicate types of service in the Lord. So gifts and service are bound together just as the Holy Spirit and Christ are bound together. And as Christ and the Spirit are God's message to humanity, so a believer's gifts and service enable a Christian to live out a thankful response to God. For Paul, the threefold God (trinity) means a threefold experience in the life of the believer. This threefold response of gift, service, and thanksgiving is given for one purpose, that of upbuilding the community of faith.

From the source of the Spirit come diverse gifts: "the message" (NIV; NRSV = "utterance") of wisdom and knowledge (verse 8), referring to practical discourses, teaching, and counseling; gifts of faith, or strong members witnessing to the source of the community; healing, both spiritual and physical; gifts of the working of miracles, prophecy, spiritual discernment, various kinds of tongues, and interpretation of tongues (verse 10). These gifts are apparently known by the Corinthian believers. The one Spirit of God gives these gifts, not in accordance with humanity's desires, but in accordance with God's will and for the health of the community.

SPIRITUAL GIFTS AND THE BODY OF CHRIST (1 CORINTHIANS 12; CONT.)

Why does the Spirit give diverse gifts? Paul uses the analogy of the body to explain how the Spirit comes from God and gives gifts to persons in accordance with God's will (not humanity's). A body is unified but has several parts. The many individuals of the body of Christ are not only unified in Christ but receive from Christ through the Spirit an assigned gift and place of service. The Spirit comes from God. Believers baptized into one body drink the same Spirit. This is the unity and diversity of Corinth's house churches.

Paul pushes this analogy further. The nature of a body is a unity of many parts. On the one hand, one part cannot justly say that because it is not some other part of the body it does not belong. Perhaps some house church members in Corinth were arguing and competing over certain tasks and responsibilities within the community. On the other hand, everyone cannot be one part of the body. This would deny the very nature of body. Rather, the body is naturally created and ordered by God.

So it is with the church, the body of Christ. The many are in the one. Parts of the body do not have the natural or spiritual right to discharge or cut off any other part of the body. The parts of the body that have the hidden and most discreet gifts have, in fact, the most important gifts. It is not the most visible gifts that are of the greatest importance to the community, such as speaking in tongues. The showiness of certain gifts indicates that they are the least important. Perhaps Paul is remembering certain individuals who had promoted such thinking among the house churches in Corinth. Paul is quite clear that the lesser gifts receive greater honor in the assemblies and the unpresentable parts are treated with greater modesty (verses 23-24).

God's creation of the body has a beautiful naturalness. The weaker and humbler parts are in fact the stronger because, as with Paul, God is made strong in weakness (2 Corinthians 12:10). This naturalness keeps strife from entering the body. There is no competing or struggling in the body because each part knows its gifts, its place of service, and its means of thankful response to God. The elimination of competition allows for an environment of caring, concern, and building up. What happens to one happens to all—good or bad.

What does all this mean? Paul explains what he has been trying to say in a summary paragraph (verses 27-31). The Corinthian believers are "the body of Christ" collectively and individually (verse 27). Paul now lists God-ordained assignments (see Ephesians 4:11-16): apostles (or preachers), prophets (also proclaimers of the gospel), teachers, miracle workers, healers, helpers, administrators, and those who speak in tongues. Then Paul asks if all could do one task, or if all should be the same. Of course not! They should struggle and seek the greater gifts, or the gifts that have less showiness. According to Paul's ordering, at least some Corinthians sought the lowest gift of all, that of speaking in tongues. Value those higher gifts on my list, says Paul.

---

summary statement concerning the gift God has given to humanity.

1 CORINTHIANS 13

Introduction to This Chapter

Now that Paul has given some practical directives, he can speak with greater freedom and broader theological insight. In this chapter Paul discusses the better way, or the way of love.

The Message of 1 Corinthians 13

For Paul, the greatest way is agape love. This love is first and foremost God's love for humanity. God freely chooses to be in fellowship with humanity in Christ. Humanity deserves nothing, earns nothing, achieves nothing. But God freely

THE SUPERIORITY OF LOVE (1 CORINTHIANS 13:1-13)

The manner in which Paul formulates his "more excellent way" has been called a hymn of love, even though it is prose and not poetry. In the first three verses of this section, he contrasts gifts and other actions of the religious instinct with the gift of love. Paul himself experienced the gift of tongues (14:18), which he has just placed last in his list of spiritual gifts (12:10). So he can rightly use himself as an example. If he speaks in tongues but does not have love, he is nothing more than an annoyance to others. What is Paul attempting to say here? The key to his opening statements and to this whole section is the word *love*.

The Greek word Paul uses for love throughout this chapter is very important. The word *agape* is not a common term in ancient Greek. The more common Greek term is *eros* (sexual desire), which is the root of the term *erotic*. Paul's use of agape for love indicates his concern and intention to communicate a deeper meaning of the term for the Corinthians. Following all that Paul has previously written in his letter to these believers, his understanding of the term *love* comes solely from God.

The "more" or "most excellent way" (12:31) is God's way. God elected Israel to be the chosen people, God's instrument to prepare the way for the plan of salvation. That plan has reached initial completion in Christ, who has defeated the powers of darkness, rebellion, and desertion. Now humanity can freely respond thankfully and worshipfully to God's love. Agape love is given by God for the sake of humanity, risking humanity's rejection and denial.

What then holds and indeed draws humanity to God? For Paul, it is agape, divine love. God's love is more powerful than anything else. This love binds humanity to God through the self-giving love expressed in Christ. The Lord came, suffered, and died so that all persons will now have the opportunity to freely respond to God's love. How powerful is this agape love? It is more powerful than the Corinthians think and can even imagine! It is more powerful than laws, legal requirements, stated obligations, threats, demands—or any other non-loving set of rules or show of force. God risks everything. But the binding force of that agape love is more powerful than anything else in the universe (Romans 8:37-38). Nothing can match the power of God's love. Consequently, humanity is eternally bound to God in Christ through the Spirit.

From humanity's side, agape can only be defined by God's character made known in Christ. Humanity cannot define the term as used by Paul. Perhaps this is why he has chosen such an unusual term to identify and describe the more excellent way. In essence, Paul understands agape as the primary and only real divine attribute (see 1 John 4:8, 16). Then Paul goes on to explain how this agape love should be reflected in the lives of Christian believers.

Paul explains that if believers do not reflect God's love, they do nothing more than make hard, loud sounds (like gongs and cymbals). In the worship gatherings of communities or various house churches, believers should reflect God's agape love among fellow believers. This is far more important than speaking in the tongues of mortals (that is, ordinary speech) and of angels (ecstatic speaking in tongues). Christians are called to reflect the very love of God in their lives. This love has been made known fully in Christ. One of Jesus' primary teachings on this subject is the parable on forgiveness, Matthew 18:21-35.

Even if the Corinthian believers have powers of prophecy but do not reflect divine love, they are empty. Here Paul mentions one of the higher gifts on his list (12:10), a gift relating to the higher mysteries of God's truth. But for Paul, the much deeper mystery and far greater truth—greater than profound prophetic pronouncements—is the mystery that God freely chose humanity for eternal fellowship. As a result, God loves the Corinthians and has acted out that love in the birth, life, death, and resurrection/ascension of Christ.

THE SUPERIORITY OF LOVE (1 CORINTHIANS 13:1-13; CONT.)

Even if the worst possible disasters could happen to a person, nothing is gained without agape love. Paul here uses the term "gain" (verse 3). Regardless of how much the Corinthian believers give away and give up, they cannot add anything to their salvation in Christ. Do not trust in self-sacrifice. Rather, put your trust only in the sacrificial love of Christ.

In verses 4-7 Paul contrasts divine love with human love. The type of agape love made known or revealed in Christ is patient and kind. These expressions of divine love in Christ bear witness to God's attributes of wisdom and grace. This true nature of God made known in Christ should be reflected in the Corinthian believers. Like their God, love in the midst of their community should be patient and kind, certainly not envious, boastful (bragging about achievements), arrogant or proud (of self), stubborn about having its own way or rude (dwelling on feeling hurt).

Nor does this agape love wish evil and misfortune on others. Rather, agape love reflecting God's love for humanity can only sincerely rejoice when others do well or experience good fortune. As the divine love of God has borne all the rebellion of humanity in Christ, so believers should bear and withstand all things. Bear what? Because the general context is one of love in relationships, Paul is speaking here about the attitude and fellowship among the Corinthian believers. Agape love bears or conceals what is pleasing in others. At the same time, agape love believes in others (both in and outside of the fellowship) as children of God, hopes in the ultimate destination of others as eternal dwellers with God, and endures the temptation to regress and live a human eros-type love.

In the last group of verses (verses 8-13), Paul contrasts agape love with other gifts of the Spirit. There is only one divine truth that will endure and never end. It will never end because it is God's free will that is expressed in agape love. God's will is to fellowship with humanity for eternity and Christ has acted out God's will. Nothing can reverse this act. This agape love will never end.

But other things will end. Prophecies will end because God's work at a particular time and place will be fulfilled. Those who speak in tongues will someday stop because of their passing on to full fellowship with God in eternity. The knowledge of God will pass away when God is fully revealed in Christ's second coming.

For now, we are all little children. Paul's use of the term *child* does not reflect immaturity as much as naivete or a sense of not yet being fully aware. Thus speaking, thinking, and reasoning are now done without full awareness and maturity. However, someday the believers in Corinth will outgrow these limitations and restrictions.

To explain this further, Paul uses the contrast of looking in a mirror. Because ancient mirrors were sometimes rather crude, Paul's statement probably had more meaning to the Corinthians than for the reader of Paul's letter today. Nevertheless, the contrast is an enduring one. The limitations of our own body are similar to looking in a dim mirror. But someday, we shall be face to face with God. Now our present knowledge is partial, but someday it will be full. How full will that knowledge be? Our knowledge will be as complete as God's present knowledge of us.

loves humanity. Because God loves humanity, humanity is reconciled to God and freed to live a life of thankful response to God. Loving God means loving one's neighbor.

1 CORINTHIANS 14

Introduction to This Chapter

Now that Paul has established the base of all creation—agape love—he turns to other gifts. These other gifts were probably very interesting to the Corinthians.

The Message of 1 Corinthians 14

In the context of agape love, Paul explains that spiritual gifts are real. They are a part of the Christian experience of faith. But spiritual gifts are also primarily for the building up of the community. These gifts must be traded and shared in the life of the believing community. Only in a secondary sense can they be understood as helpful to individual believers. Within this framework, Paul lists faith gifts and orders them according to value.

1 CORINTHIANS 15

Introduction to This Chapter

Paul now turns to the central event in the life of Christ. Apparently some do not believe in the resurrection of the dead. Paul has gained this information (perhaps again from Chloe's people) and he wants to put right the understanding of those in Corinth. Because of Paul's meeting Jesus on the Damascus road, the resurrected Christ is a reality close to Paul's experience and deep faith. This is a topic he addresses clearly, enthusiastically, and without delay.

The Message of 1 Corinthians 15

Paul explains in this chapter that the heart of the Christian faith is the resurrected Christ. Because he was resurrected, all will live like him and go directly to be with him after the final baptism of death. For those not asleep, they will be instantly changed. All will be made like the resurrected Christ, receiving spiritual/physical, imperishable, and honorable bodies like Christ.

1 CORINTHIANS 16

Introduction to This Chapter

Paul closes his letter in the normal style of the first century. He opened with gracious greetings. Now he closes with kindly words. He tells of his travel plans, the efforts of his helpers, and his concern to raise some money for those less fortunate in Jerusalem who are struggling in the midst of a famine.

This chapter may be outlined as follows:

I. Update of Collections for the Needy (16:1-4)
II. Travel Plans and Work of Helpers (16:5-18)
III. Final Greetings (16:19-24)

The Message of 1 Corinthians 16

In the body of this letter, Paul has given the Corinthians answers to their questions and offered some key directives of his own. Because he knows the believers at Corinth very well, he can write with affection, energy, and strong encouragement. His close relationship with the believers at Corinth encourages him to share his plans for himself and his workers. This letter gives the Corinthians sound directives to focus their attention on Christ. And just as important, it gives them a sense of how Paul is practically living out the faith he proclaims. His witness is meant to inspire the same in the everyday lives of the Corinthians.

THE MEANING OF THE RESURRECTION (1 CORINTHIANS 15)

Paul delivered to the Corinthians what he received from God. The message is not Paul's message, interpretation, or concoction (2:15; Galatians 1:11). God's message to Paul and to the Corinthians through Paul was that "Christ died for our sins." This is in accordance with the only Scriptures the early Christians had available to them, the Old Testament. He was buried. On the third day he was raised from the dead (verse 4). He really was restored to life—and this too was foretold in the Old Testament Scriptures. This is all proven because he appeared to the disciples (especially Cephas, 1:12 and 9:5) alive and well. Here is the essence of Paul's gospel: *died, buried, arisen, appeared.* Following the Old Testament record, God accomplishes everything. God does it all—for humanity.

There is further evidence. Jesus appeared to many more than the disciples. "Five hundred" saw Jesus alive after his death and burial (a possible reference to Pentecost, Acts 1:15 and 2:41). Many of these witnesses are still alive, but some have died. Then Jesus appeared to James, probably referring to Jesus' brother (verse 7; see Galatians 1:19). Paul's reference above to Cephas and the disciples is now expanded to James and apostles or missionaries who teach and preach the gospel. Paul seems to exclude himself from this group, indicating that his call to missionary work came directly from Jesus on the Damascus road.

Now that Paul has created the context or stated the four parts of the gospel, he begins to focus on the resurrection. Christ's resurrection does not depend upon human beliefs and opinions. The fact is that "Christ has been raised from the dead" (verse 20). He is the first harvest, the one who leads the way, the spearhead that opens the path to life before God. All who have died will follow him. Through the rebellion of humanity against God (represented by Adam) came death. This death has now been reversed by the new eternal representative of humanity, Jesus Christ. All are lost in Adam; all are alive in Christ.

Paul's reasoning is logical and Christ-centered. First is Christ the representative of all humanity; then follow those who belong to Christ and are resurrected when he comes; finally, after the rebellion has been defeated, everything is delivered back to God, where it belongs. It is the purpose and mission of Christ to bring everything in the creation back to the Creator. The final victory will be over death, which now temporarily rules. When Christ returns, his resurrection will have its full effect on wayward humanity.

Now that Paul has established the fact of the resurrection, he turns to the nature of the resurrection. Perhaps those who questioned the resurrection did so on the grounds that there could be no practical explanation of a physical body (verse 35). The idea of a spiritual body is not uncommon in Greek thought. But is there a physical body? How will the resurrection of the body occur? What kind of body will people receive?

These are foolish questions, says Paul. Consider such a practical thing as planting a seed. The seed needs to be placed in the ground in order to be transformed into a living plant. Paul's primary emphasis is on transformation, not death. The body of the plant that exists after the transformation is freely assigned by God to each seed. All flesh (and seed) is different. Thus animals, heavenly bodies, earthly bodies and so forth will have their own transformed inheritance (verses 39-40).

These events in creation are not unlike what will happen to human persons. An individual will be sown (or planted, buried in the ground) as a mere seed. When the seed is transformed into a plant, it will be imperishable (no longer in need of burial). The seed of our physical body is sown or buried in dishonor and rebellion (verse 43); it is transformed to glorify God.

Drawing from the Old Testament (Genesis 2:7), Paul explains how the perishable, dishonorable, weakened physical body of humanity (by way of the first human being) became a seed. The next Adam (Jesus Christ) led the way for transforming the physical body of the first Adam into the spiritual/physical plant of the resurrection. But the order must not be confused. First comes the

THE MEANING OF THE RESURRECTION (1 CORINTHIANS 15; CONT.)

seed/body that must be buried or planted in order for the second spiritual/physical body to be harvested. The seed body was fashioned by God from the dust of the earth, from the creation that needs planting. This body is earthly. The second person comes from heaven and is of God. Those individuals who live and trust in the dust of the first man are dust; those who live and trust in the heavenly resurrected man Jesus are of heaven and will be resurrected like him (verse 48).

All humanity is born in the image of God. But because of sin, all persons now have the image of rebellious humanity. But when our present seed-state is buried or planted, believers will be resurrected into the image of the resurrected Christ. This new transformed image will be the image of the man in heaven. Paul concludes this profound section with a definition of the kingdom of God. God's kingdom is not of the dust image, but in the image of the resurrected Christ. Flesh and blood must be planted and transformed. Only in this manner can humanity be made imperishable. For Paul, then, the kingdom of God is defined, based, and established particularly in the resurrection of Christ and generally in the resurrection of humanity.

How is this resurrection going to happen? It is almost as if Paul is raising his voice for a final point. The mystery of it all is before us in Christ. Because Christ will return someday, there will obviously be those who will not have fallen asleep (or died). But we should not worry. Those who have not been planted will be instantly changed from a perishable seed to a resurrected spiritual body like Christ. This will happen in a moment, "in the twinkling of an eye" (verse 52), in the shortest possible span of time. The trumpet sound will signal the return of Christ (Matthew 24:31; Revelation 1:10; 4:1) followed by the resurrection of the dead and the immediate change.

2 CORINTHIANS

2 CORINTHIANS 1:1-11

Introduction to These Verses

As with 1 Corinthians, Paul opens his second Corinthian letter in the traditional manner. He gives his name, the names of those to whom he writes, and he gives a general blessing. Then he adds an extended thanksgiving that expresses Paul's deeper theological perceptions and insights about God, Christ, Paul himself, and the Corinthian community.

There are two main sections of this passage:

I. Address and General Blessing (1:1-2)
II. Thanksgiving (1:3-11)

The Message of 2 Corinthians 1:1-11

In these opening verses, Paul directs the attention of the Corinthian believers to God. After identifying himself and the Corinthians as established in God, he explains affliction, suffering, salvation, and comfort as blessings from God. And Paul speaks from experience here. He had sought to proclaim the gospel on his own. In the key verse of this opening section, Paul testifies that he learned through tremendous frustration to rely not on himself but "on God who raises the dead" (verse 9). Paul wants the Corinthian believers to understand themselves by first focusing their attention on God. After this, he turns to their specific problems, needs, and faith experiences.

2 CORINTHIANS 1:12–3:3

Introduction to These Verses

The content of Paul's second Corinthian epistle is difficult to summarize. (As noted in the Introduction, this may suggest that 2 Corinthians is a composite letter.) His thoughts move back and forth from his concern and love for the Corinthians to Christ's love for the Corinthians. In this manner, Paul succeeds in giving Christ's sustaining love for the community at Corinth a very clear personal accent.

These verses may be outlined as follows:

I. Why Paul Did Not Come to Corinth (1:12–2:4)

II. Paul's Apostolic Commision (2:5–3:3)

The Message of 2 Corinthians 1:12–3:3

In this first section of the letter's main message, Paul carefully explains why he has not come to visit the Corinthians. His beginning point is his commission from God. Paul works very hard at explaining how human concerns pale in the light of God's almighty *Yes!* spoken in Christ to all humanity (1:20). As a result of this overwhelming truth, being called by God means one has to be flexible. Paul's change of plans must be understood as God-centered and not as a result of his own personal desires. Paul's sincere concern for the Corinthians stems from this commonality in the gospel of Christ. The most important truth is that the fragrance of the gospel be made known to all. Now Paul can talk more generally about the new covenant that binds them together.

2 CORINTHIANS 3:4-18

Introduction to These Verses

In this section Paul contrasts the old and the new covenants. His distinction centers on the person and work of Christ.

The Message of 2 Corinthians 3:4-18

This is a very powerful theological section. Paul contrasts the two covenants, arguing that Christ is the basis of the new covenant. He explains that a believer can be confident about God because of Christ. God has acted toward humanity, sending Christ to do what humanity could not do—fulfill the law. Moses, the law, and the old covenant lack permanent splendor and glory. This first covenant was meant to set the stage for the coming of the new covenant. Hence, Christ fulfills the old law (and covenant), giving humanity true freedom for God. Then Christ sends the Spirit to guide and direct believers in using their new freedom in Christ. In this manner, believers are slowly changed into the status of the risen Christ.

2 CORINTHIANS 4:1-7:4

Introduction to These Chapters

Paul now returns to his own ministry and calling. He writes of his faithfulness to the gospel, his hope in Christ, and his continuing work of reconciliation. The emphasis is on God's love and mercy toward Paul. Throughout these verses, Paul is boasting about God's love for humanity made clear in Christ.

These chapters may be outlined as follows:

I. Paul, An Ambassador of Christ (4:1–5:21)

II. Paul's Love of the Corinthians in Christ (6:1-13)

III. The Corinthians Must Cling to Christ (6:14–7:4)

The Message of 2 Corinthians 4:1–7:4

Throughout this section Paul concentrates on his ministry and message. His apostolic ministry is open to God in that he and his fellow workers struggle to present Christ. They are ambassadors for Christ and not individuals of authority and prestige. Their ministry begins with Christ and ends with Christ. Even though they experience hardships, pain, and suffering, they are happy, joyous, and unperturbed. And like Paul, the Corinthian believers should grow and strengthen inwardly and decline outwardly. This hope is in Christ, who establishes them as a new creation through reconciliation.

There is one outstanding feature that Paul emphasizes throughout this section. Perhaps it is a result of Paul's need to defend his apostleship in the midst of some house churches. But Paul's main emphasis is that *God acts first*. God first called Paul, God now sustains Paul and his fellow workers, and God makes promises to all believers. Paul's apostleship is a response to God's act of reconciliation. And all those in Corinth are also called to live in response to God's reconciliation.

2 CORINTHIANS 7:5–9:15

Introduction to These Chapters

Paul now turns to three themes that extend his proclamation of God's reconciling work in Christ. The previous section emphasized his own experiences and apostleship. He reflected on his past and related his experiences to the Corinthian believers. Paul again begins with action—but this time human action that follows the action of God. The action Paul speaks of in this section is future action, but again it is a future action based upon God's action in Christ.

This material may be divided into two main sections:

I. Paul Rejoices in News of the Corinthians (7:5-16)
II. Collection for the Jerusalem Believers (8:1–9:15)

The Message of 2 Corinthians 7:5–9:15

In this section, Paul deals with the ever-present problems of Christian charity. But throughout, Paul consistently chooses to deal with giving only in a theological manner. As a result, giving by believers is not the primary characteristic of a Christian. The primary characteristic—the only characteristic—of a Christian is Christ. Because the Father gave his Son for the reconciliation of humanity, Christian charity and giving are always a response to God. In this way, giving can never become a reason for God loving a believer. Generous giving can only be an obedient, worshipful, and thankful response to God. Thus, in all Christian charity, God is the primary actor. Giving bears witness to God's eternal giving. And Paul refuses to consider charity and Christian giving in any other manner.

2 CORINTHIANS 10:1–12:13

Introduction to These Chapters

There is a clear break in the epistle at this point. These verses indicate a different theme. They leave the plans for an offering and turn to Paul's apostolic work. Paul now begins speaking about himself as "I" and "me" rather than "we." But the most noticeable change in this section is the general circumstances at Corinth. Suddenly there seem to be questions and doubts concerning Paul's apostleship. This type of personal appeal by Paul is not unusual in his letters (Galatians 5:1-12; Ephesians 3:1-19; Philemon 1:19), but such a topic following his encouragement that the Corinthians support the collections for the poor seems out of place. Suddenly the mood is one of distrust rather than encouragement. This has prompted many scholars to argue that chapters 10–13 comprise a different letter. Nevertheless, these chapters will be treated as part of the letter's total content and message.

This material may be outlined as follows:

I. Paul Boasts of Laboring in the Lord (10:1-18)

II. Paul Is a Fool for Christ (11:1-12:13)

The Message of 2 Corinthians 10:1–12:13

In this section Paul focuses on the nature of his ministry and his authority as an apostle. In the face of apparent doubt and suspicion on the part of the Corinthians, Paul makes a personal appeal on behalf of the message he proclaims— the gospel of Jesus Christ.

2 CORINTHIANS 12:14–13:10

Introduction to These Chapters

After all that has been said, Paul makes a final appeal that the Corinthians keep themselves focused on Christ. Paul is prepared to come yet again to visit them, for the third time (verse 14; see also 13:1). Earlier in this epistle, he had mentioned his hesitation in making a third visit, almost certainly the painful visit (1:23 and 2:1). Paul is now bold enough to visit them because he has had the opportunity in letters to make his position clear.

The Message of 2 Corinthians 12:14–13:10

The problems facing the Corinthian believers are the confusion over collections for the poor in Jerusalem and the teachings of false prophets. In these verses, Paul confronts both these problems. First of all, his purpose is to build up the Corinthian house churches. Key to that strenghthening is reestablishing them on the foundation of Christ. There are no ulterior motives

evident in Paul. His intended purpose is to ground the Corinthians thoroughly in Christ.

But how is this building up to be done? There are no apostles or teachers available to help the Corinthians. Possibly there are false prophets or false apostles in their midst. The Corinthians are in need of sound teachings and spiritual help. Knowing that they are not capable of discovering God's truth in Christ by examining the Old Testament (1 Corinthians 1:26-31) and that they are generally immature in the faith (1 Corinthians 3:1-4), Paul tells them to examine themselves in Christ. He throws them back upon the living Christ in prayer. Paul has given the Corinthians an excellent preparation for his imminent visit

2 CORINTHIANS 13:11-14

Introduction to These Verses

In his concluding comments, Paul makes one final request in the hope that things will be right when he visits.

The letter ends as it began, with a general blessing. This was a very common Jewish practice that Paul retained from his Jewish tradition. But Paul's benediction here is unique and noteworthy for several reasons. First of all, it is the most lengthy benediction that has survived the ages.

Second, Paul mentions all three names of the Godhead—*Christ, God,* and the *Holy Spirit* (even though he does not use the term *trinity*, a word not found in the Scriptures).

Third, Paul indicates the role or work of each person in the Godhead. Grace is the divine movement toward humanity expressed in Jesus the Christ. In Christ, humanity hears God's resounding *Yes! I love you!* (1:19-20). God's agape love (1 Corinthians 13:1) is what sends the word of Christ, the Son of the Father. God freely and first chose to have fellowship with humanity. It is God's love that now and forever holds humanity in true existence—in right relationship to God. That which binds together God the Father and God the Son is God the Holy Spirit. This same Holy Spirit unites all the believers and all the house churches of Corinth together in eternal fellowship.

The Message of 2 Corinthians 13:11-14

Paul's final words place all the emphasis on God. Throughout the letter, Paul centers all his attention on Christ. Even in his "boastful" section (chapters 11–12), everything is said for the single purpose of directing the Corinthian believers to God. Now here in his final statement (and in good Jewish tradition), Paul ends where he began: with God. His thanksgiving is always from God to humanity. Yet he does not fail to deal with the problems and stresses and strains of the Corinthians. But he does so by beginning with God, subjecting their difficulties to God's word spoken in Christ, and ending with God. This benediction is a fitting summary to his Corinthian epistles. It recognizes that God has reconciled humanity in Christ once and forever. Individuals are now called to believe and respond to God's love through Christ and in the Holy Spirit.

GALATIANS

OUTLINE OF GALATIANS

INTRODUCTION

The Nature of the Epistle

Galatians presents one of the most spiritually vibrant and concise introductions to the Christian faith in the New Testament. In only a few chapters Paul brings readers examples of his most mature thought. Galatians opens with his defense of his apostleship (1:11–2:10) and his vision for the Gentile mission (2:11-18). Moving to his mystical understanding of being *crucified with Christ* and living *in Christ* (2:19-21), he then concentrates on his central concept of justification by faith (3:1–4:28) and the revelation that there is neither Jew nor Greek, male nor female, slave nor free since all are one in Christ (3:26-29). He completes the epistle with a moving definition of Christian freedom and the role of the Holy Spirit in daily life (5:1–6:16).

In Galatians Paul reveals his passionate concern for the truth of the gospel and the spiritual health of the congregations in Galatia. Skipping over his customary words of praise to a church community, he bluntly goes right to the heart of the problem. He begins the very first chapter with a strong reprimand: "I am astonished that you are so quickly deserting the one who called you" (1:6), and continues throughout the epistle to express his feelings openly. He condemns those who oppose his ministry (1:8-9), sarcastically hopes that those who favor circumcision will slip and cut themselves (5:12), defends his own ministry against all critics (1:11–2:21), uses personal examples to persuade his readers (2:20; 4:12-14; 4:19-20; 6:11), and ends with a testy challenge to his enemies to leave him (and the Galatians) alone in the future (6:17).

Galatians is partially modeled on a type of ancient Greek literature known as an *apologetic letter* that can be traced back at least to the fourth century B.C. In the ancient world an "apology" was not a personal request for forgiveness, but a formal defense in which an author argues against opponents in a fairly predictable form. Paul probably read numerous examples when he studied in Jerusalem (Acts 22:3). Throughout Galatians the outline of such a form is clearly visible: the introduction (1:6-11), the statement of the facts (1:12–2:14), the major proposition (2:15-21), the proofs (3:1–4:31) and the giving of practical advice (5:16–6:10).

It is also possible to see in Galatians how much Paul was influenced by the training he received as a rabbi and a Pharisee. In Galatians he admits rather proudly that he was first in his class in rabbinic studies: "I advanced in Judaism beyond many among my people of the same age" (1:14). In Acts 22:3 Luke records a speech in which Paul relates that he studied under the famous teacher Gamaliel and was educated according to the strict manner of the law. In Chapters 3 and 4 of Galatians he employs arguments from Old Testament Scriptures that move in a kind of logic that was very common in the Judaism he studied in the first century but remains very foreign to readers today. Most of his first-century readers no doubt found his arguments very persuasive, however, and were motivated to accept his reasons for believing in Jesus as the Christ predicted in the Old Testament.

The Author

Bible scholars generally agree that the apostle Paul is certainly the author of Galatians. The very first word in the text is his name, and the argument and style are similar to those in his other authentic letters, especially the much longer Epistle to the Romans. At the end of Galatians he admits that a secretary has actually transcribed the text, but he signs it with his own hand: "See what large letters I make when I am writing with my own hand" (6:11), so that no one will doubt that it is his.

The Galatians

Even though it is certain that the churches of Galatia (1:2) were located somewhere in the general area known in the first century A.D. as Asia Minor (what is now modern Turkey), it is not possible to determine precisely where the people to whom Paul wrote were living. At various times in history the word *Galatia* referred to regions either in the central or the southern part of that area, and it is difficult to know how Paul defined the term. Scholars who think that the letter went to congregations in the Roman province in the south suppose that Paul visited them when he traveled to other nearby cities (Acts 13:14–14:23; 16:1–18:23), but it is impossible to be sure. References elsewhere in the New Testament provide very little concrete information about where Galatia was (Acts 16:6; 18:23; 1 Corinthians 16:1; 2 Timothy 4:10; 1 Peter 1:1). The itineraries given for Paul's travels in Acts are notoriously difficult to coordinate with the information provided in Galatians 1 and 2.

The Occasion

Wherever the Galatia was to which Paul wrote, it is clear that the reason he corresponded with the Christians living there was that they were under severe pressure to abandon the message of faith that he had given to them on a previous visit (1:9; 4:13-20). The opponents with whom Paul is so angry were probably Jewish-Christian missionaries (possibly from Jerusalem, as 2:1-21 seems to imply) who came to Galatia after Paul founded the churches there. Their mission was to bring the Galatians' faith in line with a Christianity that still observed the major principles of the Torah and the traditions of Judaism. In Paul's view what they offered was not merely a fine-tuning but a perversion of the gospel of Christ, a second gospel which was not a gospel at all. The opponents taught a number of things that Paul rejected: that Christians still had to be circumcised to believe in Jesus Christ (2:1-6); that they had to depend on works of the law to be saved (3:1–4:28); and that they had to keep ritual observances of the Jewish calendar (4:10) in order to be true believers in God. Against this point of view, Paul argues that they must return to the true gospel that he originally taught them, that they must not exchange the truth for a lie (2:14) or trade their newfound

freedom for slavery again (4:8-9). Instead they must believe in God's promise in Scripture, visible especially in the life of Abraham and fulfilled in Christ, so that they will live life by faith and faith alone.

The Date

Galatians was probably written during one of Paul's later missionary tours (see Acts 15:36–18:22; 18:24–21:17) between the years 50 and 55 A.D. It is likely that he composed it after he finished the letters to the church in Corinth and just before he began his longer epistle to the Romans. Although church tradition says that he wrote it while he was in the city of Ephesus (see 1 Corinthians 16:8; Acts 19:1-10), it is also possible that it was sent from Macedonia, Antioch, Corinth, or even Rome.

GALATIANS 1:1-5

Introduction to These Verses

Paul begins his letter to the Galatians with his own name and a reference to the fact that he is an apostle appointed by Jesus Christ and God the Father. This is a normal way for him to start a letter (see Romans 1:1; 1 Corinthians 1:1; 2 Corinthians 1:1; Colossians 1:1), although he occasionally adds the title *servant* after his name as well (see Romans 1:1; Philippians 1:1).

Concerning Paul's name, Acts 13:9 reports that Paul was also called Saul, and up to that point in Luke's account he is called nothing else (Acts 9:1-22; 11:25, 30; 13:1-2; also see 22:7, 13). Saul was his Hebrew name and apparently Paul (a Greek spelling of the Roman surname *Paulos*) was his name in the Roman world, where Greek was the most common language.

In Galatians the word *apostle* is especially important because Paul is forced by his opponents to defend his calling as one who is sent by God to preach the good news of Jesus Christ. Apparently Paul's enemies argued that he did not preach the right message (1:6-9), and did not have the proper beginning in the faith (1:13-14) or the correct training to be called a true apostle (1:18-20). What was more, it was well known that at one time he had been a brutal persecutor of the church (1:13; Philippians 3:6). But Paul argues strongly that he is an apostle and that his calling has nothing to do with human standards of judgment but comes directly from God (1:15-17) through Jesus Christ.

The word apostle literally means *one who is sent out,* and refers to a representative, an emissary, or a delegate. Such a person was often commissioned by a king or queen, for example, to represent the royal house in diplomatic negotiations. Although it is difficult to know precisely how people earned the right to use such a title in the early church, it appears that at the very least one had to have a direct commission from the risen Jesus and had to have certain gifts from the Holy Spirit to qualify (see Acts 1:1-26; 1 Corinthians 12:1-11, 29). Galatians and Romans make it clear that Paul was particularly sensitive about this point because his apostolic authority had been challenged. Thus he had to prove that he was a full-fledged apostle and that his commission did come directly from Jesus. He believed that he qualified on several counts.

Although he had not been present at the crucifixion or the Resurrection and had persecuted the church ruthlessly for a time, he had received his commission from Jesus on the Damascus road through a special post-Resurrection appearance. This event obviously made a tremendous impact on his life and work (Acts 9:1-19; 22:3-11; Galatians 1:12).

God has given him a special position among the apostles. His calling was to be the apostle to the Gentiles and to the Jews living in Gentile areas (Acts 13:44-48; Galatians 2:7).

As he says in 2 Corinthians 12:11-13, he had performed the signs of a true apostle: signs, wonders, and mighty works (or miracles).

Even though he had become an apostle after the first disciples and had come so late, in fact, that he could call himself an afterbirth or miscarriage of an apostle, he was an apostle nevertheless (see 1 Corinthians 15:8-10).

The Message of Galatians 1:1-5

- Paul is an apostle of Jesus Christ, and thus he is entrusted with a special mission to preach the good news to others.

- Paul's authority comes directly from God.

GALATIANS 1:6-9

Introduction to These Verses

Paul opens the second section of his letter with words of astonishment about the unfaithfulness of the Galatians to the truth of the gospel. What happened was this: after Paul had set up churches in the area of Galatia by his preaching and teaching of the message about Jesus Christ, Jewish-Christian missionaries came later and presented a different message. Apparently they, like Paul and many others, have been converted to Christianity from the Jewish faith. But, unlike Paul, they believed that one can continue to be a Jew in all ways and be a Christian too, as if the Christian faith were merely tacked on to their earlier beliefs. Paul does not agree. For him the gospel is not an afterthought to Judaism. Although it is based on the Old Testament, it is a new revelation from God and it is distinct because it is based on Jesus Christ, his life, death, and resurrection.

The Message of Galatians 1:6-9

Paul is astonished that the Galatians are deserting the grace of Christ and turning to another gospel. There are those who are troubling the Galatians and perverting the good news of Jesus Christ. Paul argues that there really is not another gospel, since just as Christ is one, all teaching that comes from him is also one. No one, not even an angel, can preach a gospel that is contrary to Paul's, because Paul's gospel was given to him by the risen Jesus himself. Those who do such a thing will be cursed and condemned, because by distorting the truth they have cut themselves off from God the Father and from the grace and peace of Jesus Christ.

GALATIANS 1:10–2:6

Introduction to These Chapters

The third section of Galatians begins Paul's statement of the facts in the defense of his ministry. In basic outline the facts are: his ministry is God's will, not just his own; he learned the gospel from God, not from others; God has changed his life; God prepared him in Arabia; the other apostles accepted his ministry; he now lives in Christ and Christ lives in him.

These verses may be outlined as follows:

I. Paul's Gospel Comes from God (1:10-12)
II. Paul is Called to Be an Apostle (1:13-24)

III. The Jerusalem Conference (2:1-6)

The Message of Galatians 1:10–2:6

- Paul is a servant of God who struggles with the dilemma of pleasing God or preaching a message that will be well received. He opts for the former task.

- Paul sees himself in the tradition of Jesus, the humble servant.

GALATIANS 2:7-21

Introduction to These Verses

In this section of Paul's letter to the Galatians, the Jerusalem Conference is still under way (see 2.1). Here Paul is concerned with ministry to various groups of people, a disagreement with Peter over the relationship between Jews and Gentiles, and the distinction between law and gospel. In the concluding verses of this section Paul reveals much about his own faith in Jesus Christ.

These verses may be outlined as follows:

I. Establishment of Two Ministries (2:7-10)
II. Paul's Run-in with Peter (2:11-21)

The Message of Galatians 2:7-21

- Paul is entrusted with the gospel, to interpret it as best he can and to preach it to his audience.

- Genuine disagreements and differences in interpretation of law and tradition characterized the early church just as they characterize today's church.

- Faith in Jesus Christ is essential if one is to be justified (in right relationship with God).

GALATIANS 3:1-21

Introduction to This Chapter

For Paul, justification by faith alone was the very heart of the gospel of Jesus Christ. Since Paul had been trained as a Pharisee, the revelation that he no longer needed to keep the law fully to be put right with God struck him like a lightning bolt. This knowledge was a miracle to him. Indeed, as he says in Romans 1:16, it was the very power of God for salvation.

Throughout the centuries Christians have often been moved by this same discovery. Martin Luther realized that the whole Roman Catholic system of making people think that they could earn their way into heaven was false; instead, they could be rescued from the power of sin only by faith in Christ. His commentary on Galatians is still exciting reading for those who want to share his discovery. Much later, in 1919, Karl Barth started a second reformation by his study of Paul's concept of justification in Romans. Barth's commentary on Romans opened the door to the neo-orthodox movement in Christian thinking, which still influences the church today.

Paul's understanding of the power of faith in Christ is still significant wherever people believe that you have to earn everything you get and that all should get exactly what they deserve. Throughout the rest of Galatians Paul shows that for Christians, what they get is dependent on what God gives in Christ, and what God gives is motivated by divine promises and love for the chosen people (3:8, 14, 18).

In this part of Galatians Paul shifts his style somewhat and generally abandons personal examples. Now he uses illustrations from the Old Testament and the experiences of the Galatians. In many ways chapters 3 and 4 (along with Romans

3:1 and 4) are some of the most difficult parts of Paul's letters to understand. He believes that if he can prove a point from the Old Testament Scriptures, his readers will be convinced that what he argues is absolutely true.

These passages may be outlined as follows:

I. Have You Really Understood the Gospel? (3:1-5)

II. The Example of Abraham (3:6-9)

III. Rescue from the Curse of the Law (3:10-14)

IV. God Gives a Covenant and a Promise (3:15-21)

The Message of Galatians 3:1-21

- Justification by faith is the heart of the Christian gospel, according to Paul.

- Justification by faith is more important than the Old Testament conception of law.

- The law did have a reason for existence, however. The law existed so that sin would be evident to human beings.

GALATIANS 3:22–4:31

Introduction to These Chapters

In chapter 4 of Galatians, Paul discusses more fully his idea of the law and how it relates to the gospel. Whereas in chapter 3 the discussion focused on the Old Testament concept of law, in this chapter Paul's thoughts center on what that law means when viewed from the perspective of the coming of Christ. Paul also speaks of his dissatisfaction over the spiritual attitude of the Galatians.

This material may be outlined as follows:

The Message of Galatians 3:22–4:31

- This section concentrates on defining Paul's concept of justification by faith alone through examples from the Old Testament Scriptures and the experiences of the Galatian Christians.

- Paul shows that since Abraham, the father of the Jewish faith, received God's promise before circumcision and the Ten Commandments came into the world, faith is superior to the law. Even though the law requires that a punishment or curse be upon those who have not kept it, Christ has taken the curse upon himself to give the promise to those who believe in him.

- An example from legal proceedings demonstrates the same point. Just as a will cannot be broken, so God will not break the contract (covenant) made with Abraham before the law was given.

- The law served a function as a spiritual disciplinarian, but now that faith has come it is no longer needed. Now those who believe have full rights as children of God.

- Paul hopes that the Galatians will remember their affection for him and trust in the gospel. He is worried about them and hopes that they will not need to be reborn in Christ.

GALATIANS 5:1-24

Introduction to This Chapter

Here Paul begins a section in the final portion of his letter which brings exhortation or moral advice to his readers. Many of his letters end in a similar manner (2 Corinthians 13:5-11; Philippians 3:1–4:9; 1 Thessalonians 4:1–5:22).

This chapter may be outlined as follows:

I. For Freedom Christ Has Set Us Free (5:1)
II. Through Love, Faith Liberates Us (5:2-6)
III. An Angry Aside (5:7-12)
IV. Love Calls Us to Serve One Another (5:13-15)
V. The Law of the Spirit (5:16-24)

The Message of Galatians 5:1-24

- In the fifth chapter Paul provides moral advice (exhortation) to his readers and gives some practical examples of how they should live.

- He repeats his understanding of circumcision: Those who practice it are obligated to keep the whole law. Since it is impossible for anyone to be that good, those who try are cut off from Christ. By returning to Christ through the Spirit, the Christian may have hope again.

- The chief characteristic of the Christian faith is not one of restriction but of freedom. Freedom comes from the gift of the Holy Spirit, especially the gift of love which allows a person to give himself or herself away to God and to others.

- The walk with the Spirit is a pilgrimage on the road that has been designed for those who follow God.

FRUIT OF THE SPIRIT (GALATIANS 5:22-24)

In Galatians 5:22-24 Paul turns from the negative to the positive, from life outside the Spirit to the fruit of the Spirit. The language here is connected with church life. The vocabulary of the church is also that of the Holy Spirit.

"Fruit of the Spirit" refers to the idea that in the Spirit the Christian is constantly growing and producing for God's kingdom. It is possible that the language entered the church from the Old Testament (see Psalm 1:3; Proverbs 1:31; 8:19; 11:30; Jeremiah 21:14). It may also have come from Jesus' references to the vine and the branches (John 15:5, 8, 16). Possibly the idea is present that the Holy Spirit plants the seeds in the spirit of the believers and they produce spiritual "fruit" for God. The image of the spiritual fruit is a common one in the New Testament (Matthew 7:15-20; Luke 3:8, 8:15; Romans 7:4; Philippians 1:11; Colossians 1:10; Hebrews 12:11). Many of the qualities included here in Galatians are available to Christians because they are fundamental qualities of God, the one who gives them.

The kind of "love" Paul means specifically is *agape* love, self-giving love, generous love, love that is unlimited and willing to sacrifice for the other person. Love is freedom, in essence, because it lets the self go and is directed only to God and to the other. Agape love is the kind of love that Jesus gave to humanity through his death and resurrection. By following his example Christians can really be free. Love is the first fruit of the Spirit (Galatians 5:22); it is the best gift of the Spirit (1 Corinthians 13:13). Love is the more excellent way. Agape love was such an important thing to the first Christians that it is mentioned more than one hundred times in the New Testament.

"Joy" is a feeling that comes from being close to God and being part of God's plan. It is a response in the Gospels, for example, to Jesus' miraculous birth (Matthew 2:10; Luke 1:14; 2:10) and later to his ministry (Luke 6:22-23; 10:17). Paul connects it with hope (Romans 12:12 and 15:13) and the power of the Holy Spirit (Philippians 2:1-4). He often mentions joy as a constant of the Christian life, even in the midst of great suffering, pain, and persecution, since the Holy Spirit brings hope, peace, and comfort (see 2 Corinthians 2:3; 7:4, 13). Joy is a spiritual fruit Christians may search for and request from God (Psalm 51:1-12).

For *peace* see the promise of Jesus in John 14:25-27.

"Patience" also means *steadfastness, endurance,* or *forbearance.* It points to patience toward God or toward other people. It was considered to be a characteristic of Christ and his servants (2 Corinthians 6:6; Colossians 1:11; 2 Peter 3:15). It can also describe God's own patience (Romans 2:4; 9:22; 1 Timothy 1:16; 1 Peter 3:20). Second Timothy 3:10 says that it was a particularly strong point of Paul's.

The basic meaning of "kindness" is *goodness, uprightness,* or *generosity.* It is a characteristic of God (Romans 2:4; 11:22; Titus 3:4). "Goodness" (NIV; NRSV, "generosity") is similar but can also mean *excellence* or *honesty.* It is a fruit of light (Ephesians 5:9), and something that the Christian can expect through the power of the Spirit (Romans 15:14). Christians, Paul seems to be saying, are easy to spot, because they are kind and gentle people.

"Faithfulness" does not refer to one's beliefs but to a basic characteristic of *fidelity* or *trustworthiness* (see Matthew 23:23; Romans 3:3; Titus 2:10). The Christian is constant in faithfulness to God and God's ways.

"Gentleness" comes from the same Greek word that is translated as *meek* in Matthew 5:5, "blessed are the meek." In the ancient world meek had the meaning *tamed,* and often referred to wild horses that had been trained. Paul may have that image in mind as he thinks of the Christian having all of the wild desires and passions in 5:19-21 tamed under the direction of the Spirit. The same idea is found in Matthew 11:29, where Jesus says, "Take my yoke upon you."

Paul concludes with those things that do not characterize a person led by the Spirit and those that do.

GALATIANS 5:25–6:10

Introduction to These Verses

In this section of his letter Paul turns from the characteristics of individuals to those of the church. These verses briefly summarize how Christians are to behave toward other people, particularly those in the church, in the household of faith.

The Message of Galatians 5:25–6:10

- Paul turns in this section to a practical working out of the fruit of the Spirit in the Christian congregation.

- In order to march in line in the Spirit (5:25), Christians need to keep in mind certain responsibilities to each other. These include correcting each other's faults, bearing other members' burdens, and sharing with teachers and pastors.

- Paul also warns that each Christian must examine himself or herself as an individual before taking on responsibilities in the church. Each person will get the fruit he or she has sowed, either for evil or for good. Christians should seek only to do good to all people, especially to other believers.

GALATIANS 6:11-18

Introduction to These Verses

Paul concludes Galatians with personal words and a summary of some of the main themes of the letter.

These verses may be outlined as follows:

I. My Own Signature (6:11)
II. Walk in the Shadow of the Cross (6:12-16)
III. I Bear the Marks of Jesus (6:17)
IV. The Benediction (6:18)

The Message of Galatians 6:11-18

- Paul concludes his letter by writing the last few lines in his own handwriting. This action enables his readers to know that he wrote the letter. It also gives him an opportunity to express his last thoughts more personally.

- The main argument of the letter (verses 12-16) is that Paul's opponents are not telling the truth

about the law. Real life comes from Christ and his cross. Those who believe in him will have new life.

- The letter ends as it began (1:3). Paul prays that the free gift of Christ in love may be with all of his readers.

EPHESIANS

OUTLINE OF EPHESIANS

INTRODUCTION

Who Wrote Ephesians?

It is nearly impossible to begin a discussion of Ephesians without looking first at the question of authorship. For over 150 years there has been a continuous, sustained debate about the real author of Ephesians, and that debate continues. Some scholars take what the letter says at face value and assume that because Paul is mentioned by name in 1:1 and 3:1 that the apostle Paul must be the author. Many others argue that because of the style, content, and perspective of the letter, someone other than Paul must surely have written it.

All serious students of Ephesians agree that the letter presents difficult problems. The content differs particularly from Romans and Galatians and clearly has different major themes. Whereas justification by faith, freedom from the law, and the question of circumcision are primary issues in Romans and Galatians, they are not of first importance in Ephesians. Ephesians, moreover, has long and complex sentences. Although Paul sometimes uses a lengthy style (see Romans 1:1-7, which is one sentence), generally he does not, and certainly not page after page.

The author of Ephesians also indicates a very reverential attitude toward the apostles, which differs considerably from that in Galatians 1 and 2 and many scholars are convinced that Paul could not have changed his mind so much in a relatively short time.

Those who think that Paul wrote Ephesians argue that it is not unusual for authors to change their style if they are writing at different times in their lives for different readers. In addition, they point out, there are themes in Ephesians which are found throughout Paul's other genuine letters. In their opinion, Paul's style may differ in Ephesians because he is older and because he quotes more Christian hymns and Old Testament Scriptures in that letter.

While these arguments are worth considering, it is most likely, as most scholars argue, that Paul did not write Ephesians. The long, ponderous style is different from his writings anywhere else in the New Testament. The attitude toward the apostles is also very revealing. In Galatians 1:16 Paul says that he did not have to confer with other apostles to receive revelation from God and refers to them as of only reputed importance, who added nothing to him (2:6).

In Ephesians, however, the apostles are people who should be honored. Although the Spirit has revealed the mystery to God's holy apostles and prophets (3:5), and the church was built on them (2:20), the author implies that they were people who received a blessing from God in the past and that he himself was not one of them. It is also unlikely that Paul would call himself a "holy" apostle. In 1 Corinthians 15:8-10 he refers to himself instead as one untimely born, as one of the least of the apostles.

For these and other reasons, it is best to assume that Ephesians was written not during Paul's lifetime, but much later, when the church was an established institution that revered the apostles as figures of the past.

Who wrote the letter then? Over the centuries many suggestions have been made, but it is most likely that Ephesians was written by an unknown Christian who borrowed Paul's name. Perhaps he was a student of Paul's or, more probably, an admirer who respected his memory as a "holy apostle."

In the ancient world it was not unusual for a writer to assume another's name if he thought that the author's ideas were similar to his. It is likely that the New Testament books of James and Jude were written the same way, utilizing the names of apostles to make sure that the letters were widely read.

In a final sense, it may not be critically important who wrote Ephesians. The author of Hebrews is also unknown, but all Christians realize that it contains Christian truth. In a similar way, Ephesians has a great deal to teach us about Christ's church, the unity of his body, and the way Christians should act.

To Whom Was the Letter Written?

We cannot be certain where the original readers of Ephesians lived. The oldest and most reliable manuscripts of Ephesians do not contain any reference at all to those "in Ephesus" (see footnote a in the NIV & NRSV). Moreover, the writer indicates that he does not know his readers (1:15; 3:2-3; 4:21), whereas the apostle Paul was very friendly with them, having conducted a three-year ministry in their city (Acts 18:19-21; 19:1-20; 20:17-38). It is possible, as is often suggested, that Ephesians was a "circular letter" that left the name of the recipients blank and was sent around to many different churches in one area. Although we cannot be certain, it is likely that the letter was sent to congregations throughout western Asia Minor (modern Turkey).

Why Was the Letter Written?

In a strict sense, Ephesians is not a letter, but a style of writing called *rhetoric* in the ancient world. Rhetoric was delivered in speeches or written in tracts to influence the thought and conduct of a general audience. Unlike Paul's letters, Ephesians is not directed toward incidents in a specific church but is written very generally to build the Christian church as a whole (chapters 1–3) and to tell the readers how they should act (chapters 4–6).

The author's writing indicates that his readers are aware of a popular philosophy which was called *Gnosticism*. He appears to be worried that they may be influenced by it so much that they might lose their faith in Christ because of it. Gnosticism was a philosophy that prided itself on the knowledge (*gnosis* in Greek) of those who believed in it. In one popular form of the belief system, followers believed that only they could understand the mystery (see 3:3) of the unknowable God. They thought that there was a whole series of planets and beings in different levels of heaven that controlled human destiny. Sometimes they were given names like "the ruler of the power of the air" (NRSV; NIV "the ruler of the kingdom of the air"; *archons* in Greek, 2:2), "ages," (*aeons*, see 3:9), "rulers and authorities" (3:10). The goal of philosophy and religion, in their opinion, was to return the divine spark that dwells in every human being to "the fullness of God" in the highest heaven (3:19), so that all divine things could be all in all.

The writer of Ephesians counters this kind of thinking with the Christian belief that through Christ, God has overcome all heavenly beings, real or unreal. All things will rest in God who brings the love that surpasses all knowledge.

Ephesians is written to Gentiles, that is, to people who were not born as Jews (see 3:1, 8). The writer refers to them as "aliens" (NRSV; NIV "excluded from citizenship") and "strangers" (NRSV; NIV "foreigners"; 2:12), those "who once were far off" (NRSV; NIV "who once were far away;" 2:13, 17), in order to show them that in Christ their status has been changed and they are now part of the one body of Christ (2:14-18), fellow citizens in the household of God (2:19).

When Was Ephesians Written?

Ephesians was written sometime after Paul's death in A.D. 64–67 (the exact year is not known) and the end of the first century. Since reference is made to it in a letter written about A.D. 96 to Christians in

Rome by the first bishop of that city (Clement I), it is often assumed that Ephesians was completed sometime around A.D. 90.

EPHESIANS 1:1-2

Introduction to These Verses

In these first two verses we encounter the writer of the letter. See the introduction to Ephesians for more information concerning this individual.

The Message of Ephesians 1:1-2

• In the first two verses of chapter 1 the author of Ephesians introduces himself and identifies himself as an apostle. He is called by the will of God and his readers are called saints because they also are set apart for God's special purpose.

• "In Christ" refers to the special closeness that those faithful to him can experience, a spiritual intimacy that indicates that all of God's purpose is realized in him.

• In these verses the writer greets his readers with a typical Christian blessing, extending to them God's special gift in Christ and the peacefulness that comes only from God.

EPHESIANS 1:3-14

Introduction to These Verses

Ephesians 1:3 begins one of the longest sentences in the New Testament. In the Greek, it extends from verse 3 all the way through verse 14! Because of this kind of style the writer of Ephesians has often been accused of writing nearly incomprehensible sentences, connected only by the barest threads of logic. But even though Ephesians is not easy to understand, if the words are allowed to flow as if they were cascading from a wonderfully refreshing waterfall, the pattern of thought becomes very clear. The message is that all things in heaven and on earth have been planned by God in Christ according to God's good will.

These verses may be outlined as follows:

I. Blessed by God (1:3)
II. Chosen by God (1:4)
III. Destined in Love (1:5-6)
IV. Redeemed Through Christ (1:7-8)
V. United in Christ (1:9-12)
VI. Given the Guarantee of the Spirit (1:13-14)

The Message of Ephesians 1:3-14

• God's plan to redeem humanity was established before the foundation of the world.

• God has decided to focus the divine plan for salvation entirely in Christ Jesus. Those who believe in Christ are participating in God's eternal plan.

• In Christ is made known all wisdom and insight and the very mystery of God's plan for the whole universe.

• Believers are assured that all things will be found in Christ. All things are sealed by the Holy Spirit, and believers are given a promise or guarantee that what God has promised will be delivered to them when they become mature Christians.

EPHESIANS 1:15-23

Introduction to These Verses

The third section of Ephesians continues with the author's unusually lengthy sentence

JESUS IS SEATED AT THE RIGHT HAND OF GOD THE FATHER (EPHESIANS 1:19-23)

To sit "at his right hand in the heavenly places" (NRSV; NIV "realms") in verse 20 is a reference to the early Christian belief that after Jesus' death, God raised him up to a place of special prominence and power in heaven. In the Bible, *hand* is a symbol of power and authority (Exodus 13:3; 14:21; Deuteronomy 3:24; Job 19:21). God promises in Psalm 110:1 that only the Messiah will have the ability to sit at the most important place of power, and that his enemies will be put at his feet. Christians believed that place to be given to Jesus (Mark 12:36; Acts 2:25; Hebrews 1:3). The same belief is still expressed today every time worshipers repeat the Apostles' Creed. It is this confidence in Christ's final power that is also expressed in the renowned words of Handel's *Messiah*, "King of kings, and Lord of Lords. And he shall reign for ever and ever. Hallelujah!"

Verse 21 says that Jesus is far above all spiritual powers in authority and might. Since people in the ancient world often believed that there were several different levels of heaven with ascending orders of power, this writer says that Jesus is higher and stronger than any of them. Spiritual powers such as angels, rulers, principalities, powers, authorities cannot intimidate or cause harm to Christians anymore because they have been defeated through Christ's death and resurrection. (See Romans 8:38-39; 1 Corinthians 15:24; Colossians 2:15.) They may have names which strike fear in human hearts, but Jesus' name, because it has been given to him by God, is above every name (Philippians 2:9-11), and it will remain so in this age and all through eternity (the age that is to come).

"God placed all things under his feet" in verse 22 (NIV) is a reference to Psalm 8:6, where it is indicated that all the power of God will be given to those God designates. (See also Psalm 110:1.) Christians knew that this power had been transferred to Christ when he was placed on Gods right hand. (See 1 Corinthians 15:27, Hebrews 2:5-8.)

In the second half of verse 22 and in verse 23, the writer summaries the argument of 1:15-23 by indicating that God has made Jesus head over all things for the church. Head means that Christ is the highest spiritual power, not only on earth, but in the whole cosmos. No one or no thing has been given more power and authority than he has. As it says in 1:10, God unites or sums up all things in the Son. Once again, the closest parallels in the New Testament are found in Colossians. "He is the head of the body, the church; he is the beginning, the firstborn from the dead, so that he might come to have first place in everything" (Colossians 1:18). He is the head of all power and authority (2:10). Christ is not only the head of all spiritual forces, but he is also the head of the church.

The word "church" (*ekklesia* in Greek) appears prominently in Ephesians (3:10, 21; 5:23-32). It always refers to the universal church, not to a congregation in a local area. In its most basic form, ekklesia means *assembly* or *gathering*, but the New Testament often refers to it as the *body of Christ*. *Body* was a common symbol in religious and medical literature at the time Ephesians was written, and the writer appears to be aware of the way it was used. In religious writings it was often said that the universe was like a huge human body with a god as its source or head. Inferior divinities such as authorities and powers were part of the body, but they were under the control of the head. Clearly, the writer is influenced by this kind of thinking since he is determined to demonstrate here that Christ is more powerful than all other spiritual beings. Another metaphor common in the ancient world was used by physicians who understood that muscles, limbs, and organs were controlled by the brain. Since the writer uses physiological terms in Ephesians 4:4 and 15-16 (see Colossians 2:19), he probably has this image in mind as well.

In Ephesians, the writer's use of the concept of the body is similar to that found in Romans 12:4-8, 1 Corinthians 12:12-27, and Colossians 1:18, which points to the unity of all things in Christ. In the Christian church, individual members must not think that they have power independent of Christ or that they are more important than other parts of the body. All members are prized and loved by him and are a part of him. Together they fill up his body as he fills all in all.

construction. Verses 15-23 have only two sentences in the original Greek, the first in verses 15-21 and the second in 22-23.

The Message of Ephesians 1:15-23

- In 1:15-23 the author of Ephesians thanks God for his reader's faith and prays that God will give them a spirit of wisdom and knowledge.

- God has surpassing power, which is demonstrated by raising Jesus from the dead, giving him the highest seat of power in heaven, and making him head over all spiritual forces and over the church.

- Since Christ is over all things and all living beings, everything is summed up and fulfilled in him.

EPHESIANS 2:1-10

Introduction to These Verses

Chapter 2 begins with another long sentence in Greek, this one extending from verse 1 all the way through verse 7, connected only with commas and colons. These verses may be outlined as follows:

I. Delivered from Death (2:1-3)
II. Made Alive Together in Christ (2:4-7)
III. Saved by Faith (2:8-10)

The Message of Ephesians 2:1-10

- In this section the author of Ephesians reminds his readers of the danger they are in from sins and trespasses and from the power of the devil. When people rebel against God and become children of disobedience, they face the possibility of spiritual death. They also have to be careful not to follow the devil, who is known as the "the ruler of the power of the air."

- Although all human beings, whether they are Gentiles or Jews, are sinful by nature and fall under God's judgment, in Christ Jesus they have been forgiven for their sins, they have been given new spiritual life, and they have been delivered from the power of the devil and all the spiritual beings who are in allegiance with him.

- Being put right with God means that Christians are raised up with Christ, made to sit with him on the right hand of power, and given the free gift of forgiveness by God. Those who believe in Christ are his creation and they are made to do good works, to walk in the fruit of the Spirit.

EPHESIANS 2:11-22

Introduction to These Verses

In this section the author of Ephesians demonstrates how the ancient distinction between Jews and Gentiles has been demolished by Jesus Christ.

These verses may be outlined as follows:

I. You Were Once Refugees of Faith (2:11-12)
II. Those Far Away Are Brought Near (2:13)
III. The Wall of Hostility Is Broken Down (2:14-18)
IV. You Are Now Fellow Citizens (2:19)
V. The Foundation and Cornerstone (2:20)
VI. The Living House (2:21-22)

The Message of Ephesians 2:11-22

- The separation caused by circumcision, the sign of the Old Testament covenant, is no longer valid. There is no longer circumcision and uncircumcision.

- Gentiles also are no longer alienated from God as they were at one time. They are not aliens and refugees in God's city anymore but are now full citizens with equal rights and privileges.

- Jesus Christ has broken down the wall between Jews and Gentiles that was symbolized by the wall that kept Gentiles out of the Jerusalem Temple. He has broken down the fence that the law put around the Jews. He has destroyed the hostility that existed between God and humanity. Through his blood, his sacrifice on the cross, Christ has brought peace.

- Gentiles now co-exist as members of one family, brothers and sisters in one household of God. Together they make up a living house that is where God may dwell and truly be worshiped.

EPHESIANS 3:1-13

Introduction to These Verses

In this section the author of Ephesians attempts to link his letter with the life of the apostle Paul and repeats several themes which have already been introduced in the first two chapters.

These verses may be outlined as follows:

I. A Steward of the Mystery (3:1-3)
II. The Message Is Now Revealed (3: 4-6)
III. The Least of the Apostles (3:7-13)

The Message of Ephesians 3:1-13

- The author of Ephesians ties his letter in with the life of the apostle Paul and his imprisonment.

- The author has been given the mystery of God. It was made known

to him by the stewardship of grace. Stewardship refers to God's plan of salvation. The mystery is that God admitted the Gentiles into the family of faith.

- God's uncovering of the mystery has been given only recently. It was not given to the Jews in the past or to those who believed in pagan religions, but only to Christian apostles and prophets. It was even hidden from divine beings who live in the heavens, but now they also know the truth through Christ. Jesus is the one who allows all living creatures to know God and have access to God.

EPHESIANS 3:14-21

Introduction to These Verses

Ephesians 3:14-21 is one of the most beautiful passages in the whole Bible, reaching beyond words to express how wonderful it is to have the Holy Spirit in the inner person of faith. When Christians have Christ in them and are enlivened and motivated by his love, they can only break out in praise about the incomprehensible dimensions of all that God gives.

These verses may be outlined as follows:

I. Empowered Internally by the Spirit (3:14-16)
II. The Dimensions of Faith (3:17-19)
III. A Benediction (3:20-21)

The Message of Ephesians 3:14-21

- The author of Ephesians expresses his praise for the immeasurable power and love of God in Christ. Because God cannot be fully known, the writer can only get on his knees and express gratitude to the one who showers believers with so much love.

- God gives and gives to those who follow Christ. God strengthens the heart and empowers the inner person where spiritual nurturing takes place, so that God may be more fully understood.

- The writer expresses gratitude for all of God's wonderful gifts.

EPHESIANS 4

Introduction to This Chapter

In chapter 4 the author of Ephesians begins the second major section of the letter. This part consists almost entirely of ethical advice, or what is often called exhortation. It was common for ancient writers, Christian and non-Christian, to give this kind of advice to their readers. Examples can be found in every New Testament letter, although they usually are not as long as here.

This chapter may be outlined as follows:

I. Lead a Worthy Life (4:1-3)
II. The Oneness of Faith (4:4-6)
III. The Gifts of the Spirit (4:7-14)
IV. The Way a Body Should Function (4:15-16)
V. Do Not Live as the Gentiles Do (4:17-19)
VI. Be Renewed in the Spirit (4:20-24)
VII. Tell the Truth (4:25)
VIII. Do Not Remain Angry (4:26-27)
IX. Thieves Must Reform (4:28)
X. No Rotten Talk (4:29)
XI. Do Not Grieve the Holy Spirit (4:30)
XII. Be Kindhearted (4:31-32)

The Message of Ephesians 4

- The Spirit has called individuals to particular tasks in the church so that the whole church can grow and be built up in Christ's love.

- The readers of the letter, who are Gentiles, are reminded that they are no longer trapped in their alienation from God or hardness of heart. They have been renewed by the Spirit and have put on Christ. Practical examples are given to illustrate how the new nature is manifested in concrete actions.

EPHESIANS 5:1–6:17

Introduction to These Chapters

The writer gives advice here concerning how to imitate God, how to live successfully in a Christian household, and how to be vigilant in the faith.

These verses may be outlined as follows:

THE ONENESS OF FAITH (EPHESIANS 4:4-6)

In verse 4 the writer returns to subjects he has introduced earlier in the letter, the one Holy Spirit (1:13-14), the one body of Christ (1:22-23; 2:15-16), hope, and calling (1:18). Similar passages are found in Romans 12:4-8; 1 Corinthians 8:6; 12:4-6.

The beautiful expression of the Christian faith found in verses 5-6, "one Lord, one faith, one baptism, one God and Father of all," may be an early example of a Christian creed which later developed into the well-known Nicean Creed and the Apostles' Creed. Unity exists for Christians because of a common faith, a common beginning in that faith (baptism), and the organic oneness of the church, which is the body of Christ Jesus. (See Romans 6:3; 1 Corinthians 12:13; Galatians 3:27.) The unity of faith is found in the solidarity of God as well, one God in three parts: the Father, the Lord Jesus, and the Spirit present in baptism.

I. Be Imitators of God (5:1)
II. Walk in Love (5:2)
III. Put Away All Immorality (5:3-14)
IV. Make the Most of the Time (5:15-17)
V. Get High on the Spirit (5:18-20)
VI. Husbands and Wives (5:21-33)
VII. Children and Parents (6:1-4)
VIII. Slaves and Masters (6:5-9)
IX. Put on the Whole Armor of God (6:10-17)

The Message of Ephesians 5:1–6:17

- Christians must be imitators of Christ, and be grounded in sacrificial love. They should no longer associate with those who are lost in the darkness of sin but should conduct themselves as children illuminated by the light of Christ.

- The writer gives advice on running a household—how husbands and wives should interact, how fathers should treat children, and how masters should treat slaves. All advice is centered in the love of Christ, in the fellowship of the household of faith.

- Christians are also warned to be vigilant in their faith. Even though Christ will be victorious over all spiritual enemies, important battles remain to be fought, and believers are given special equipment of faith so they may stand fast.

EPHESIANS 6:18-24

Introduction to These Verses

In the last seven verses the writer urges his readers to remain alert and prepared for the continuing spiritual battle. They must pray in the Spirit since the Spirit is the one who counsels and strengthens them in all ways. They must also pray for other believers who need God's help. The writer is in special need himself since he is in prison, a representative of Christ even to those who are his captors.

These verses may be outlined as follows:

I. Some Prayers to Offer (6:18-20)
II. Tychicus Brings This Letter (6:21-22)
III. Benediction (6:23-24)

The Message of Ephesians 6:18-24

- The letter closes with words nearly identical to the letter's beginning: peace, faith, and God's forgiveness in Christ are all realized in the eternal, self-giving love of Jesus Christ.

HUSBANDS AND WIVES (EPHESIANS 5:21-33)

Ephesians 5:21-33 is one of the most discussed and most misunderstood passages in the entire New Testament. In some Christian circles it is often taken strictly as a commandment about the order of power in the Christian household. Many Christians believe that the husband must be the head of the household in every way, that he must make all of the final decisions as if God had somehow endowed him with extraordinary wisdom far greater than that given to his wife or children. In many cases this means that he has complete control over all of the spiritual, emotional, and financial resources of the family, and other members of the family are nearly forced to become subservient to him.

Interpretations that insist that husbands must be the controlling head of the house miss the significance of the writer's teaching in Ephesians 5:1. The key verse is 5:21, "Be subject" (NRSV; NIV, "submit") "to one another out of reverence for Christ." Although it says in verses 22-24 that a wife must be subject to her husband, and that he is the head of the family, the whole section is subordinate to the first verse. Wives, according to this passage, are to be subject; they are to obey their husbands. But verse 21 indicates that husbands are also subject to their wives in Christ. There is a mutuality here that is often overlooked.

Frequently Ephesians 5 is cited as an example of the way the Bible makes women appear to be inferior to men. It cannot be denied that biblical writers often shared views commonly held in the ancient world that women were the weaker sex (1 Peter 3:7), that they should be kept in their place in the church (1 Corinthians 11:2-14; 14:34), and even that they were nothing more than property (see, for example, Numbers 5:11-31; Deuteronomy 22:13-21). But Ephesians 5:21-33 goes far beyond these limited principles.

In many ways Ephesians 5 presents a revolutionary perspective about women. Even though this writer accepts the universally held belief in the ancient world that the man was the head of the household, he tells Christian husbands that they have additional burdens which make it impossible for them to mistreat their wives. The wife may be subject to the husband by custom, but spiritually he is also subject to Christ. He cannot do whatever he wants to her, since he must love her as much as Christ loved the church (5:25). Christ clearly loved the church with self-giving love, unbounded love, the kind of love that is willing to die for the other. What is more, the husband is ordered to love his wife as much as he loves his own body (5:28). Here the principle is the same as the second part of the Golden Rule (Matthew 22:39), "You shall love your neighbor as yourself." The husband must now see that his wife is his Christian neighbor and he must love her as one already loved by Jesus Christ.

In this chapter the writer continues to build on his understanding of the body of Christ (1:22-23; 2:14-22; 3:6; 4:4, 15-16). Just as Jews and Gentiles have been reconciled into one body in the church, and are all working and growing together in Christ's love, so the Christian family is also a metaphor for the church (compare 5:30 with 4:2-4). The one body formed by husband and wife (5:31) is similar to the one body made up of all Christians. In a sense, it would not make any difference if verse 22 read, "Husbands, be subject to your wives, as to the Lord," because the mutuality and love demanded would be entirely the same. In a Christian family, as in the church, all members are valued equally, and all members must function together if the family is to be what God intends it to be. There is really only one head of the family, and he is the same one who is the head of the church. Jesus Christ is the Lord of all. He is the one who builds up his church and all relationships grounded in him, through the self-giving love seen in his cross and resurrection.

HUSBANDS AND WIVES (EPHESIANS 5:21-33; CONT.)

The quotation in 5:31 is from Genesis 2:24. Jesus cites it as a basic spiritual principle of marriage in Matthew 19:5. (See 1 Corinthians 6:16.) Men and women are created to exist in complementary and co-equal ways. They are complementary physically, but their intimacy extends far beyond sexual compatibility. They can also have spiritual intimacy, as God intended from the beginning.

In verse 32 the writer uses the word "mystery" to describe the relationship between a Christian wife and husband. The same word is used in 1:9 to describe the union of Jews and Gentiles in the church. The fear of the believer about God's wrath, or the fear of the wife toward her husband, are replaced by the self-giving love of Christ and the unity and fellowship which that love creates.

PHILIPPIANS

OUTLINE OF PHILIPPIANS

INTRODUCTION

The Church at Philippi

According to the book of Acts, Paul founded the church at Philippi on his second missionary journey, probably in A.D. 50. He crossed over the Aegean Sea—from Troas in the province of Asia (modern western Turkey) to Neapolis in Macedonia and on to nearby Philippi—in response to a nighttime vision at Troas (Acts 16:9-10). Silas, Timothy, and possibly Luke (Acts 16:10) were with him.

Philippi, the most important city of the first district of Macedonia in Paul's time (Acts 16:12), had been built (or rebuilt) about the middle of the fourth century B.C. by Philip II of Macedon, the father of Alexander the Great. The city had become part of the Roman Empire after Rome's defeat of the Persians in 168 B.C. After 42 B.C. it was enlarged by Mark Antony and Octavian (Augustus), settled with Roman colonists, made a Roman colony governed by "Italian law," and blessed with all the privileges Rome bestowed on citizens who lived in its colonies.

The city, located in a fertile area fed by copious springs and with gold and silver mines nearby, lay astride the *Via Egnatia*, the main road connecting Rome with Byzantium in the East. The inhabitants were mostly Romans and Macedonian Greeks, with some Jews as well.

The religions of the city were many, centering in the worship of Roman, Greek, and Thracian gods and goddesses, deities from Phrygia and Egypt, and Yahweh of the Jews.

Whether there was a Jewish synagogue at Philippi is uncertain. Acts refers to a place of prayer by the side of a river, where some women had gathered (16:13). Since

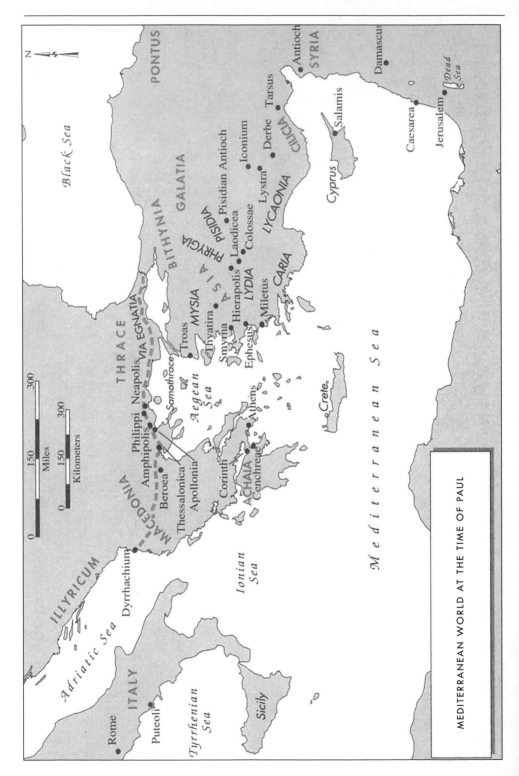

MEDITERRANEAN WORLD AT THE TIME OF PAUL

Jewish synagogues were sometimes built close to water for convenience for ritual washings, a small synagogue may have stood there.

The first convert at Philippi was a Gentile woman, a God-fearer ("worshiper of God," Acts 16:14) called Lydia. Apparently Lydia was a seller at Philippi (and elsewhere) of purple-dyed cloth, made at Thyatira in Lydia (south-central Asia Minor). It may be that the name Lydia means simply "the Lydian," and that she had an unknown personal name. (It is possible, but not probable, that this name was Euodia or Syntyche, and that she was one of the objects of Paul's entreaty in Philippians 4:2-3.) She offered her home to the missionaries as a place of residence and as the gathering place of the fledgling church (Acts 16:15, 40).

Women seem to have had a prominent part in the life and work of the Philippian church, even in the proclamation of the gospel (Philippians 4:3). This role accords with the general status of women in Macedonia, where they played an unusually important role in the political, religious, and social life of the province.

How long the missionaries stayed in Philippi is unknown (according to Acts 16:12), probably a few weeks. The membership, besides Lydia and her household, included the converted jailer and his family (Acts 16:27-34), Epaphroditus (Philippians 2:25), Euodia, Syntyche, and Clement (Philippians 4:2-3). The names indicate that the church was largely Gentile.

Paul's mission at Philippi was terminated as a result of an exorcism that affected the pocketbook of slave owners and led to a hearing before the magistrates and a subsequent beating and imprisonment (Acts 16:16-24). The charge was that the Jewish missionaries were troublemakers who were unlawfully turning Romans into proselytes (Acts 16:20-21). Paul might have revealed his Roman citizenship in order to escape beating and imprisonment without a proper trial before the proconsul of the province, but he did not do so. He may have wished to embarrass the local magistrates and thereby gain a more favorable position for the church (Acts 16:35-39). He later called his treatment at Philippi "shameful" (1 Thessalonians 2:2 NRSV; NIV, "insulted").

Through the missionaries a vigorous church was raised up at Philippi, one that Paul trusted implicitly and one that made a unique contribution to his subsequent ministry (Philippians 1:5, 7; 4:14-16).

Place and Date of Writing

Acts records only three of Paul's prison experiences: at Philippi (16:23-40); at Caesarea (23:35; 24:23, 27); and at Rome (28:16, 20). But Paul speaks of more imprisonments than his opponents had experienced (2 Corinthians 11:23); and Clement, a Roman Christian, wrote (about A.D. 95) that Paul was in prison seven times. Many modern scholars have argued that to the three in Acts we should add one in Ephesus and perhaps one in Corinth.

The arguments are weak for an imprisonment in Corinth, but one at Ephesus is quite possible. First Corinthians 15:32; Acts 20:17-19; 2 Corinthians 1:8-10; and data in Philippians (and Philemon) offer support for such a conclusion.

If Paul was in prison in Ephesus (about A.D. 55), this city's relative closeness to Philippi helps us understand Paul's many exchanges with the Philippian church while he was confined. These exchanges are: news of Paul's arrest reached Philippi (Philippians 4:14); the Philippians sent a gift by Epaphroditus to aid him (2:25; 4:18); news of Epaphroditus's illness is carried back to Philippi (2:26); word comes to Paul and Epaphroditus concerning the Philippians' distress over Epaphroditus's illness (2:26); Paul hopes to send Timothy to Philippi and to receive a report back from him (2:19) and to go to Philippi himself (2:24).

If Paul had written the letter to the Philippians from Rome or Caesarea, so many exchanges with the Philippians while he was in prison seem difficult or unlikely. Journeys between Ephesus and Philippi could be made in about a week, whereas trips between Rome and Philippi (some eight hundred miles) and Caesarea, which is even farther from Philippi, would require a month or more.

Other arguments exist for Ephesus as the place of origin. There was a praetorium (the governor's residence) at Ephesus (Philippians 1:13), and those of "Caesar's" (4:22 NIV; NRSV, "the emperor's household") could mean slaves and freedmen in the governor's service there. Also, the language, style, issues addressed, and concepts of Philippians bear some similarities to those in 1 and 2 Corinthians, letters written at Ephesus or shortly thereafter.

Scholars who argue for Rome or Caesarea as the place of writing of Philippians point out that the Ephesian imprisonment is only hypothetical. The two-year period Paul was in prison both in Caesarea (Acts 24:27) and Rome (Acts 28:30) allows plenty of time for the exchanges with the Philippians noted above. Furthermore, the references in Philippians to the praetorium and Caesar's household connect more naturally with Rome or Caesarea (Acts 23:35). The best reason used by the advocates of Rome as the place of origin is the fact that in Philippians Paul seems to be awaiting a final life-or-death decision (1:20-26; 2:23). He would not have expected a final

decision at Ephesus or Caesarea, since, as a Roman citizen, he had the right of appeal to Caesar's court in Rome.

At present, equally good reasons can be cited in support of Ephesus, Rome, or Caesarea. Fortunately, the exact place of origin is not crucial to an understanding of the message of Philippians.

The Unity of the Letter

There is considerable roughness in the flow of thought in the letter. The sudden outburst in 3:2-3 is surprising. Also, 3:1 seems to connect logically with 4:4, making the intervening material appear intrusive. The farewell and benediction of 4:4-9 could well end the letter. But a long section about Epaphroditus and the Philippians' gift, which would appropriately appear near the beginning of the letter (or at least in connection with 2:19-30), is tacked on. And why doesn't 2:19-30, with its practical concerns, come at the end, according to Paul's usual practice?

Many scholars have concluded that two or three letters were combined into our present letter by someone later than Paul. Their reasons are, in part, the roughness noted above; the likelihood that Paul wrote more than one letter to his favorite church; the fact that 2 Corinthians appears to have been compiled by a later editor from at least two letters addressed to the Corinthians; and a reference by the second-century Christian martyr Polycarp to "letters" written by Paul to the Philippians.

Various attempts, not always agreeing in details, have been made to identify these letters. The hypothesis of two letters usually assigns to the first letter 3:2–4:23 and to the second 1:1–3:1. The hypothesis of three letters goes: letter one—4:10-20; letter two—1:1–3:1; 4:2-9, 21-23; and letter three—3:2–4:1.

Many scholars argue for the unity of the letter. They point out that Paul was writing an informal letter, not a logical treatise. He may have been interrupted in his dictation and begun again without careful consideration of logical sequence. Such breaks in logical sequence appear in other letters he wrote (for example, Romans 16:17-20; 2 Corinthians 2:14-15). Furthermore, why would a later editor arrange the supposed letters in the illogical fashion we find here? And what happened to the original openings and conclusions of the previous letters?

Since scholars have not agreed on the question of the letter's unity, it is best to study the letter as it now is, rather than try to rearrange its "original" parts for chronological consideration.

The Purposes of the Letter

(1) The letter informs the Philippians of Paul's present situation and his prospects for the future (1:12-26; 2:24).

(2) It thanks the Philippians for their gift (1:5; 4:10-20).

(3) It ensures a good reception for Epaphroditus, who was returning with the letter (2:25-30).

(4) It prepares the way for the coming of Timothy (2:19-23).

(5) It assists the Philippians in solving certain problems in the church: persecution by opponents (probably Gentiles and Jews, and possibly legalistic or Gnostic Christians) (1:28-30; 3:2-19); dissension among members (1:27; 2:2-3; 4:2-3)—and helps them move on toward Christian maturity (3:12-21).

PHILIPPIANS 1:1-11

Introduction to These Verses

Writings from prison often have a peculiar potency and glow. Some of them

have influenced the course of human history for good or ill.

One thinks of the diabolical impact of Hitler's prison-begun *Mein Kampf* and the seven hundred vitriolic letters from the federal penitentiary in Atlanta written by Eugene Dennis, the general secretary of the American Communist party.

On the good side are John Bunyan's *Pilgrim's Progress* from the Bedford jail in England; Dietrich Bonhoeffer's letters, essays, poems, and prayers from a Nazi prison; and Olin Stockwell's *Meditations from a Prison Cell,* originally written on the margins of his Bible during his confinement in China by the Communists.

Anwar Sadat, the Egyptian leader, once said, "There are two places where you always find yourself one is prison and the other is war." A prison experience gives a person time to think and often deepens and accelerates the convictions that are brought into a prison cell.

Paul's letter to the Philippians possesses an unearthly radiance. It is his most joyful letter. Through the centuries it has helped millions of people triumph over whatever circumstances have dashed their dreams. They have affirmed with Paul, "I can do all things through him who strengthens me" (4:13 NRSV).

Here is an outline of Philippians 1:1-11:
I. The Greeting (1:1-2)
II. The Thanksgiving and Prayer (1:3-11)

The Message of Philippians 1:1-11

- The opening of this letter is warmly personal and gracious. From almost the first line the Philippians would feel both the graciousness of Paul and the grace and peace of God.

- In the first words Paul's humble sharing of authority in God's service with Timothy and his inclusion of the whole church, with its bishops and deacons, as God's servant people along with Timothy and himself, strikes a democratic and familial note.

- Paul's thankful remembrance of them, in particular for their generous support of his mission, his confidence in them and their future as the special people of God, his tender yearning for them, and his desire to enrich their lives with knowledge and spiritual fruits, all say eloquently "I have you in my heart" (1:7 NIV; NRSV, "you hold me . . .") and "I long for all of you with the affection (NIV; NRSV "compassion") of Christ Jesus" (1:8).

- Paul was a master psychologist. Whenever he could, he accentuated the positive and minimized the negative. He knew that praise and encouragement accomplished more with new Christians than stinging criticism. Sharing was not just a work with him, but a total attitude and way of life. Paul shared and wished his converts to share with him because God shared the gift of the Son.

PHILIPPIANS 1:12-26

Introduction to These Verses

During his imprisonment Paul obviously had been meditating on the effects of his circumstances on the progress of his mission of spreading the gospel in the world. Had his chains put fetters on that gospel? Quite the contrary! (See also 2 Timothy 2:9.) He saw evidence that the gospel was marching on precisely because of his imprisonment.

Undergirding his confidence was his firm belief that "all things work together for good for those who love God, who are called according to his purpose" (Romans 8:28). Paul was overwhelmingly certain that he had been divinely called to spread knowledge of God and the gift of Jesus, the Messiah, everywhere (Acts 26:15-18; Romans 1:1-6; 15:15-16; 2 Corinthians 2:14-16; Ephesians 3:1-13; Colossians 1:24-29). The message contained in the "good news" was: "In Christ God was reconciling the world to himself" (2 Corinthians 5:19). As Christ's ambassador Paul's task was to invite the world to be reconciled to God (2 Corinthians 5:20).

Chains could not defeat God's purpose. Nothing but faithlessness on the part of the ambassador(s) could hinder that purpose (1 Corinthians 4:1-5; 2 Corinthians 4:2; 6:3-10; Philippians 3:12-16). Indeed, suffering was central to being a disciple of Jesus (Matthew 10:16-23; Mark 8:24; Acts 14:22; Romans 8:17). By suffering the ambassadors were toughened, purged, encouraged (Romans 5:3-5), humbled and empowered (2 Corinthians 12:7-10), and made more effective as witnesses (2 Corinthians 4:7-12). Therefore, disciples of Jesus should rejoice in their sufferings (Romans 5:3; 2 Corinthians 12:9; Philippians 4:4; Colossians 1:24; 1 Thessalonians 5:16-18).

This section has three parts:
  I. Paul's Imprisonment (1:12-14)
  II. Paul's Christian Opponents (1:15-18)
  III. The Coming Verdict (1:19-26)

The Message of Philippians 1:12-26

This section of Philippians is rich in meaning for us today.

- From every human point of view Paul's imprisonment was a disaster. It involved personal humiliation and suffering, delay of his plans for evangelizing the West, inconvenience and probably great expense for his associates and for himself, embarrassment for the church before the Jewish and Roman worlds, and much more.

- But by meditation, prayer, and the Holy Spirit's illumination Paul saw not the discouraging negatives of his situation but the heartening positives—all rooted in his conviction that God has a way of bringing good out of evil. He saw Christ's suffering and death as a glory road that he himself was privileged to walk in imitation of his Lord. He speaks later in this letter about his sharing of Christ's sufferings as if it were a splendid station on the path to resurrection life (3:10-11).

- Equally striking is his magnanimous attitude toward the ungrateful and hostile Christian preachers who increased the bitterness of his prison experience. Slight and insult are not commonly known to be inspirers of joy and rejoicing. Where did Paul learn this response if not from Jesus (Matthew 5:11-12)?

- Finally, Paul's calm in the face of death and his loving concern at this time for his much more fortunate readers reveal a source of power not of this world. The text here discloses the agony of his soul in his awful predicament and that he is fully human. He wants the prayers of the Philippians and the Holy Spirit's help (1:19). But he is in no doubt about the outcome: "Christ will be exalted now as always in my body, whether by life or by death" (1:20).

PHILIPPIANS 1:27—2:11

Introduction to These Verses

Up to this point in the letter Paul has been talking mostly about himself—his gratitude toward and love for the Philippians, the content of his prayer for them, how the gospel is being advanced through his imprisonment, the attitudes of Christian leaders toward what has happened to him, and the struggle within him as he faces the coming verdict. The personal pronoun "I" has been prominent.

At 1:27 the pronouns become "you" and "your." Introspection becomes instruction and exhortation. His readers have heard enough about him. He now wants to talk about them: their problems and needs, their attitudes, their opponents, their recent doings, and their responsibilities as citizens of two orders at once (as Christians in the Roman colony at Philippi and as members of the heavenly community—1:27; 3:20). The concern about "you" continues all the way to 4:9. The letter ends (except for the final greetings and benediction) with a section centering on you and I (4:10-20).

This section has two parts:
I. The Threats to Unity (1:27–2:4)
II. Jesus Christ as Source and Pattern (2:5-11)

The Message of Philippians 1:27—2:11

- The appeal to the Philippians for humble service of others, rather than self-aggrandizement, is powerfully reinforced by this magnificent hymn about the attitude and actions of the church's Lord.

- The hymn and the appeal for unity that introduces it glorify what to the Greek mind was largely despised: humility. Philosophers and the highborn regarded humility as servility, and thought it appropriate

JESUS CHRIST AS SOURCE AND PATTERN (PHILIPPIANS 2:5-11)

How did Jesus Christ relate to God and others in attitude and deed so that he became the source and pattern of Christian thought and conduct?

The explanation comes in what most scholars believe is an early Christian hymn in honor of Christ Jesus (2:5-11). This passage seems to have rhythm and strophes (stanzas), though scholars do not agree on the exact number and content of the strophes. It is printed in poetic form in some translations.

We do not know whether the hymn was composed by Paul, by someone associated with him, or quite independently of him in some section of the early church. Whether Paul wrote it or not, he obviously agreed with its view of Jesus Christ and included it in his letter because it says about Jesus what he wanted the Philippians to know about their Lord's attitude (toward himself, toward God, toward others) and his redemptive activity.

The hymn traces Christ's thought and work from his glorious pre-incarnate existence and self-emptying to his earthly experience of humble servitude, and to his subsequent exaltation by God to universal lordship. It stresses the voluntary character of Jesus Christ's self-abnegation, and implies that God rewards those who follow Jesus Christ in renouncing and self-seeking and in acting for the benefit of others.

Some phrases of the hymn deserve special comment:

(1) "Though he was in the form" (NRSV; NIV, "very nature," but cf. footnote) "of God" (verse 6) is subject to various interpretations: that he shared in the divine essence or the divine mode of being; that he shared in the divine glory (John 17:5); or that he bore the image of God, as Adam did (Genesis 1:26-27; 2 Corinthians 4:4; Colossians 1:15).

The phrase does not say flatly that Christ was God—the New Testament normally refers to Jesus Christ as God's Son (Matthew 11:27; John 3:16; Romans 1:3; Galatians 4:4; Hebrews 1:2)—but it implies participation in God's being, attributes, and work, on the analogy of a human son to a father (John 5:17-20; 8:29).

Paul and the early church drew on Jewish and Hellenistic concepts concerning the word of God, the wisdom of God, and the Son of man to emphasize Christ's intimate relationship with God in creation, redemption, and consummation.

(2) "Something to be grasped" (verse 6 NIV; NRSV, "exploited") translates an obscure Greek word that appears only here in the New Testament. It can be understood in two senses in this passage: something not yet possessed but desirable and thus a thing to be grasped at; or something already possessed and thus a thing to be clutched and held on to.

Probably the first meaning is best here. Christ as Son (Word, wisdom, man of heaven [Son of man], last Adam), participating in God's very being, attributes, and work, did not seek to wrest sovereignty over the universe from the Father in an act of rebellion. To grasp at sovereignty would be to make himself independent of the Father, instead of the obedient instrument of his redemptive purpose.

(3) "But emptied himself" (verse 7 NRSV; NIV, "made himself nothing") cannot mean that he gave up his identity as God's Son, but rather possibly his prerogatives as God's Son (omniscience, omnipresence, and glory). Or perhaps the phrase simply means that he poured himself out (for others)—he impoverished himself—instead of seeking to enrich himself. Thus the thought would agree with Paul's statement in 2 Corinthians 8:9: "You know the grace of our Lord Jesus Christ, that though he was rich, yet for your sakes he became poor, so that you through his poverty might become rich" (NIV).

JESUS CHRIST AS SOURCE AND PATTERN (PHILIPPIANS 2:5-11; CONT.)

(4) The phrase "taking the form of a slave" (verse 7 NRSV; NIV, "taking the very nature of a servant"), means full participation in the being, status, and activities of another. In pouring himself out the heavenly Christ became one of us. We are not told what he became a slave to, but it must mean to those things in an evil world that hold human beings in bondage: human limitations, death, sin, the law (Romans 6:1–7), and possibly the evil spirit-beings of which Paul speaks (Romans 8:38-39; Galatians 4:8-9; Colossians 2:15). He could not come into this world without coming under the forces that operate here. This does not mean, however, that he yielded to the pressure of those forces (2 Corinthians 5:21; Hebrews 4:15; 1 John 3:5).

(5) "In human likeness" (verse 7) probably stresses the full humanity of Jesus and means that he was fully like us in his basic constitution and his situation.

Whether the passage means that Jesus took our fallen nature has been much debated. In Romans 8:3, Paul says that God sent "his own Son in the likeness of sinful flesh" (NRSV; NIV, "man"). Did Paul distinguish between perfect, unfallen flesh and sin-dominated flesh and hold that Christ came in the former but not the latter? Possibly so, as some scholars maintain. Others argue that likeness means identity, and say that Christ took the same fallen nature that we ourselves have, and that he remained sinless because he constantly overcame the temptation to sin. New Testament writers stress the complete humanity of Jesus (Luke 2:52; Galatians 4:4; Hebrews 2:17; 4:15; 5:7-9; 1 John 4:2).

(6) "Obedient to the point of death—even death on a cross" (verse 8) expresses the depth to which Christ's self-abnegating attitude and activity brought him. Death on a cross was undoubtedly the most shameful of deaths in Paul's time; it was reserved for slaves, criminals, foreign rebels, and the like.

Why Jesus' death was necessary is not indicated here. Paul deals with that elsewhere (Romans 3:24-26; 2 Corinthians 5:18-21; Galatians 3:13-14). Some scholars argue that Paul's reference to the "servant" ("slave") here is an echo of Isaiah 52:13–53:12, with its teaching about the vicarious, atoning death of the servant of the Lord. But there is no hint of this here.

(7) "God also highly exalted him" (verse 9) indicates that God rewarded him who poured himself out for others. (In the theology of Paul and the church, the exaltation was believed to have occurred through God's act in Jesus' resurrection and ascension—Acts 2:32-33; Romans 1:4). Paul and the church knew that Jesus had taught that whoever humbles himself will be exalted (by God) (Matthew 23:12; Luke 14:11; 18:14) and that this is a principle of God's kingdom. And the implication is strong here that the Philippians who abase themselves and exalt others will likewise be blessed by God.

The reward "given" to Christ—the Greek word suggests a gift of grace—consisted of several elements:

(a) super-exaltation (the literal meaning of the Greek word behind "exalted"), that is, elevation to the highest possible degree of status and authority, possibly meaning higher than he had before his self-emptying;

(b) "the name that is above every name," that is, Lord (meaning the Master, borne also by God in the Old Testament), who is elevated above all so-called gods, lords, principalities, and powers (1 Corinthians 8:5-6; Ephesians 1:20-21; Colossians 2:15) and who possesses all authority in heaven and on earth (Matthew 28:18; 1 Corinthians 15:24-25);

(c) the worship of creation in its totality (heaven, earth, underworld) and the universal confession of the lordship of Jesus Christ (see Revelation 5:13), a worship and confession that bring glory (honor, praise) to God the Father—the ultimate authority (1 Corinthians 15:28) who exalted the Son as the instrument of divine redemption.

only for slaves and lower-class people. It was not a virtue to be cultivated. Humility was viewed quite differently by Jews and Christians, as we know from the Old Testament, the Qumran texts (the Dead Sea Scrolls), and the New Testament.

In Jewish and Christian thought humility is the attitude one should have in the presence of almighty God and God's messengers. To be proud is to be guilty of sin, for it puts self above the honor and obedience due to God and the covenant law. Many persons glory in their wisdom, might, and riches, when they should glory in their understanding of and relationship with God and in their doing what God delights in (Jeremiah 9:23-24). Jesus condemned every sort of pride and exalted the humility of children. He washed the feet of his disciples and enjoined them to do likewise—and even to become the servant (slave) of all (Mark 10:42-44).

Nothing could glorify humility and self-abnegation more than this hymn, written or cited by Paul, about the self-emptying of Christ in behalf of others. Beside it in grandeur is a shorter companion piece about Christ's becoming poor so that we might be made rich (2 Corinthians 8:9).

PHILIPPIANS 2:12-30

Introduction to These Verses

After presenting Christ Jesus as the unselfish, other-minded, self-emptying, obedient, and highly exalted One who became the source and example of the Christian spirit and life, Paul turns to the Philippians' situation in the light of Christ's work. This short section has only two parts:

I. The Philippians' Mission (2:12-18)
II. God's Helpful Servants (2:19-30)

Paul points out that as Jesus Christ was

obedient to the purpose of God through his obedience unto death (2:8), so the Philippians must be obedient—both to Paul and to God's purpose for them (2:12-13). Then Paul returns to thinking about the outcome of his trial and its possible effect on the Philippians.

First he thinks theologically about their situation in the light of his death or survival (2:12-18). Then he thinks in practical terms about their specific needs and what possible help his associates may be able to offer them (2:19-30).

The Message of Philippians 2:12-30

- Paul saw the remedy for the Philippians' shortcomings as being a cooperative working of the Philippians and God: "Work out your own salvation . . . for it is God who is at work in you" (2:12-13).

The first use of the word *work*—in the phrase "for it is God who is at work"—translates a different Greek word, and means "for God continually and mightily energizes you." God is the Great Energizer, with whom the Christian is to cooperate in the achieving of God's good purpose of salvation.

- The passage does not teach the sole efficacy of divine grace and human passivity or the efficacy of human work with God's assistance. The Christian is to work because God has been and is working mightily (in Jesus Christ) for human redemption (see John 5:17). Thus Paul, Timothy, and Epaphroditus are fellow workers and servants (1:22; 2:16, 22, 25, 30). The Philippians' task is to labor side by side with Paul in the gospel (4:3), and to work continually toward the present and future well-being of the Christian community. Then they will shine brightly as stars, holding fast the word of life (2:15-16).

PHILIPPIANS 3

Introduction to This Chapter

One major threat to the church is yet to be considered: false teaching about the way of salvation, advocated by enemies of the cross of Christ (3:18).

If this letter to the Philippians is a unity and not a composite of several letters illogically put together after Paul's time, we must say that Paul's transition to the subject of this pressing danger is very abrupt.

This chapter may be outlined as follows:

I. Introduction (3:1)
II. The True Way to Righteousness (3:2-21)
   A. Renunciation of assets (3:2-8)
   B. Faith-identification with Christ (3:9-11)
   C. Progressing in Christ (3:12-16)
   D. Following models (3:17-21)

The Message of Philippians 3

- Assets from heredity and personal achievements, if trusted in for salvation, are a hindrance to God's favor and blessings. As Paul pointed out so bluntly in his letter to the Galatians, salvation is by faith alone. The bringer of that salvation is Jesus Christ, "who gave himself for our sins to rescue us" (NIV; NRSV, "set us free") "from the present evil age" (Galatians 1:4). "A person is justified not by the works of the law but through faith in Jesus Christ" (Galatians 2:16 NRSV). Self-righteousness comes through human assets and works but not God's righteousness (that is, a right relationship with God).

- If this is so, then all modern religions of achievement must be ineffective. This includes those forms of Protestantism that stress salvation through education and becoming through doing.

- Important also is Paul's position that being "in Christ" during this life brings with it no absolute perfection. We "press on" in the knowledge that that goal is yet to be reached. We are Christians in the making, ever seeking to become actually that which we became ideally at the point of beginning.

PHILIPPIANS 4

Introduction to This Chapter

The letter concludes with some specific counsels, some general exhortations, and an extended word of thanks for the gift the Philippians sent at the hands of Epaphroditus.

Paul has dealt in chapters 2 and 3, on theological and personal grounds, with the serious threats to the health of the Philippian church, arising from the nefarious teaching of the "Divine Men." But some manifestations of the problem still remain, and Paul seeks to deal with these.

Chapter 4 has four parts:

I. Introduction (4:1)
II. Quarrel in the Philippian Church (4:2-9)
III. Thanks for the Philippians' Generosity (4:10-20)
IV. Concluding Greetings and Benediction (4:21-23)

The Message of Philippians 4

Both the theological and the practical dimensions of this letter attest to the versatility of its author. One moment we are in the heavenly places, thinking God's and Christ's thoughts after them (2:5-11); next we are on the earth amid the hassle of contending theologies about the way of salvation (3:2-21). Then we move on to a squabble between two women who apparently were grasping for power in the church. Finally we encounter a sticky problem about how to say thank you for gifts that must be acknowledged but basically are not wanted.

Theologians—and Paul was a masterful one—are not supposed to be practical persons. But here in Philippians is a remarkable blend of theology and ethics, undergirded with sound psychology about how to handle difficult people and situations. Paul knew not only how to raise up churches but how to care for them as well, as would a "nurse" and a "father"

(1 Thessalonians 2:7, 11). Paul's patience with his stumbling and often obnoxious Christian children rivaled that of Moses in the wilderness.

In 4:21-23 there are many jewels, such as: the suggestions for healing divisions within the church, especially the emphases on rejoicing, magnanimity, trust in the Lord, prayer, and thanksgiving; the importance of keeping one's mind on the best values and one's eyes on the finest examples of Christian living; the lesson that contentment in one's situation, no matter how desperate it is, comes from complete trust in the one who gives power to do all things; that generosity to others does not go unnoticed by the God who wants to supply all our needs; and that God's goal for us is peace (health, well-being), now and hereafter.

COLOSSIANS

OUTLINE OF COLOSSIANS

INTRODUCTION

The Church at Colossae

From the fifth century B.C., Colossae (in the Lycus River valley of central Asia Minor, some one hundred miles east of Ephesus) was a populous wool-working and cloth-dyeing center. It lay near the cities of Hierapolis and Laodicea. The three cities, all prosperous, vied with one another in the textile and wool-dyeing industry. They are mentioned together in Colossians 4:13.

The church at Colossae was founded by Epaphras (1:7). He was a Colossian (4:12), who may have been converted by Paul during his long ministry at Ephesus (Acts 19:10) and who represented Paul (1:7) in the evangelization of the three cities of the Lycus valley (4:12-13). Epaphras was in prison with Paul at the time of the writing of this letter (Philemon verse 23). He was the source of Paul's information about the situation in the church at Colossae (1:8).

Paul's Purpose in Writing to the Colossians

Paul had never been to Colossae (1:4, 9), but he felt a responsibility for the church there. Not only had a convert of his founded the church, probably under his direction (1:7), but he knew himself to be God's apostle and priest to the whole Gentile world (Romans 15:16; Colossians 1:24-29). The church at Colossae lay in his special area of evangelization (Romans 15:19-20; 2 Corinthians 10:13-18).

Undoubtedly, when Epaphras described its needs to Paul, he resolved to help by writing this letter.

Several purposes are apparent: (1) Some people, whether members of the church or not, were advocating a "philosophy and empty deceit" (2:8 NRSV; NIV, "hollow and deceptive philosophy"). This attitude threatened to undermine the truth about Jesus Christ long preached by the church, and the way of salvation taught by Paul. Paul was deeply concerned that the church not be turned in a false direction and be subverted both doctrinally and ethically. He wanted it to lead a life "worthy of the Lord, fully pleasing to him, as you bear fruit in every good work and as you grow in the knowledge of God" (1:10 NRSV).

The philosophy involved the worship of angelic, cosmic powers (2:8, 18, 20) in addition to Christ. These were celestial spirits, who apparently were regarded as God's agents in governing the movements of the heavenly bodies. Thus the spirits in some respects controlled human destiny, as astrological thought holds. Their worshipers observed feast days, special seasons, and certain practices to honor and perhaps appease these spirits (2:16-23).

Apparently it was taught that all these powers, along with Christ, constituted God's fullness, that is, the full range of God's attributes and manifestations. Allegiance to Christ was not enough to guarantee salvation. The ruling powers also had to be recognized and pacified.

This philosophy stressed special visions offering secret knowledge of ultimate reality and the way of salvation. Paul thought that such knowledge led to pretensions and self-congratulation (2:18).

The heresy seems to have been a mixture of elements from several sources: Judaism (perhaps like that found in the Dead Sea Scrolls); early Gnosticism (like

that advocated by the "Divine Men"); and Hellenistic astrology and pagan mystery cults. Paul felt that glorifying and pacifying astral powers debased Christ and introduced practices that were a threat to Christian freedom.

(2) Paul meant by the letter to introduce Tychicus, the carrier of the letter, who was to encourage the Colossians in the true way of salvation and inform them about Paul's circumstances (4:7-8).

(3) He wished also to ensure a good reception for Onesimus, the converted runaway slave, who was returning in company with Tychicus to his master at Colossae (4:9).

(4) Epaphras, the founder of the church, apparently was under attack by the heretic philosophers and needed Paul's support. This letter would enhance his standing with the Colossian church (4:12-13).

(5) Paul meant to prepare the way for the visit of John Mark (4:10); and also to urge Archippus, possibly Philemon's son or a resident in Philemon's house (Philemon 1-2), to carry out faithfully some responsibility entrusted to him in the Lord's service (4:17). Since Epaphras was in prison with Paul, it may be that the service he was to perform was to carry on Epaphras's pastoral responsibilities.

(6) Finally, Paul seems to wish to establish his authority and teaching firmly in the Gentile churches, both those founded directly by him and those raised up by his followers (1:7, 23-29; 4:16).

Authorship, Place, and Date

Two positions are widely held today on the question of authorship: (1) Paul, as the letter clearly claims (1:1, 23; 4:18), was the author. As was frequent with Paul (1 Corinthians 16:21; Galatians 6:11; Colossians 4:18; 2 Thessalonians 3:17), he added an authentication in his own handwriting.

In Colossians there is some variation in language, style, and theology from Paul's other letters, due to the special circumstances under which Colossians was written. But the similarities to the other letters are greater than the dissimilarities. Furthermore, strong ties with the letter to Philemon, unquestionably written by Paul, argue for Paul's authorship of Colossians. The two letters have the same senders (Paul and Timothy), greetings from many of the same persons (Aristarchus, Mark, Epaphras, Luke, Demas), and the mention of Archippus. The letters seem to have been written at about the same time and carried to Colossae by Tychicus and Onesimus.

(2) A disciple of Paul wrote the letter to the Colossians in Paul's name. Many facts argue that Paul was not the author. A few are: the use of many words not found elsewhere in Paul's letters; the absence of Paul's characteristic ideas (righteousness, justification by faith alone, the purpose and function of the law); the highly speculative view of Christ, especially in 1:15-20; and the strong emphasis on apostolic tradition as a way of counteracting heresy. Possibly a disciple of Paul, who was thoroughly familiar with Paul's language and thoughts, used his master's authority as a way of meeting heresy sometime after Paul's death.

Since the case against Paul's authorship is not conclusive, the discussion of the letter here will assume the correctness of the letter's own claim. If the letter was written by Paul, the place was Ephesus, Rome, or Caesarea. The date was about A.D. 55–62. If a disciple wrote it, the time was after Paul's death, possibly A.D. 70–90, and the place is unknown.

COLOSSIANS 1:1-14

Introduction to These Verses

These verses are the letter's introduction. They may be outlined as follows:

I. Greetings (1:1-2)
II. Thanksgiving (1:3-8)
III. The Prayer (1:9-14)

The Message of Colossians 1:1-14

This introductory section has several important themes.

First, we learn about Paul, Timothy, and Epaphras and the gospel they preached and by which they lived. Paul had an unshakable conviction that he stood in a chain of command that reached through Jesus Christ to God. Timothy and Epaphras were his Christian brothers and fellow servants (slaves) in conveying to the Colossians and indeed to the whole world the good news Paul had received from God through Jesus Christ. Together they thanked God for the Colossians and prayed continually for their welfare and growth in Christian faith and living.

They regarded the gospel they preached, about the gracious purpose (will) of God to prepare a holy people for membership in the present and future Kingdom by forgiveness of sins and redemption from the bondage of evil powers, as unshakable truth. They saw this gospel as a fruit tree being planted, taking root, and producing fruit (good works) everywhere—obvious testimony to its validity. He (and they) could plainly see that it was transforming persons, remaking homes, lifting and ennobling life here, and forming the outpost of the coming new order.

Second, we learn about the Colossians' response to the hope the gospel held forth. Faith was evoked, and out of it came the deeds of love in the community of believers, a growing faith and love.

Third, we learn about the church's needs: for fuller spiritual understanding of God's will for themselves and the world, for help to live in a way pleasing to God and befitting their relation to the Lord Jesus, for abundant power to overcome their enemies within and without the community of faith, and for an increased sense of privilege in being qualified by God to be members of Christ's kingdom and enjoying its benefits now while awaiting its final coming.

COLOSSIANS 1:15-23

Introduction to These Verses

This is the most important and the most difficult passage in the entire letter to the Colossians. It is shaped in technical language to counter the false teachers' view of Christ.

These false teachers held that Christ was one of the many cosmic powers (spirits) who comprised God's fullness—all of whom needed to be worshiped and appeased. They did not believe about Christ what the writer of 1 Timothy did when he wrote: "There is one mediator between God and men, the man Christ Jesus, who gave himself as a ransom for all" (2:5-6 NIV). In reducing the stature of Christ and his work by making him only one of the many manifestations and agents of God in creation, in the ruling of the cosmos, and in redemption of the world's people, they were robbing Christ of his unique importance. And, they were destroying the Christian faith.

This passage falls into two parts:
I. The Uniqueness of Christ (1:15-20)
II. Application to the Colossians (1:21-23)

THE UNIQUENESS OF CHRIST (COLOSSIANS 1:15-20)

Most scholars agree that in verses 15-20 we have a poetic, rather than a prose, piece about the uniqueness of Christ in creation and redemption. There is a rhythmical quality to the piece, a certain balance and parallelism in the structure of the thought. The lines are gathered into strophes (stanzas); ancient poetic devices of several kinds are used (alliteration, antithesis, and chiasmus).

Because there are many words here not used elsewhere by Paul or rarely used by him, many scholars have suggested that Paul used a poem or a hymn written by someone else before him and adapted it to his purpose in this letter. Others have argued that Paul composed the piece himself, using language and ideas derived largely from others. Whatever the original authorship, structure, and literary history of the piece, it lies before us in all its richness and complexity and dares us to probe its depths. If Paul did not write it entirely in its present form, he obviously agreed with its sublime view of Christ. Since there is today no scholarly agreement on the number of strophes (stanzas) it contains (from two to five have been suggested), the exact contents of each, and what is to be attributed to Paul and what to others before him, we shall take the piece as it lies now and draw from it some of its major affirmations about Christ.

(1) Christ is the unique manifestation of God (verse 15a). An image in the New Testament sense is a true representation of the original. Since Jesus Christ is God's Son (see Romans 5:10; Galatians 4:4), he is a genuine representation of the Father (2 Corinthians 4:4-6). Paul would agree with the author of the gospel of John that whoever has seen Jesus has seen the Father as well (John 14:9).

THE UNIQUENESS OF CHRIST (COLOSSIANS 1:15-20; CONT.)

Behind the idea of someone or something as the image of God are the figure of Adam (Genesis 1:26-27), the concept of wisdom (Proverbs 8:22; Song of Solomon 7:26), the Hellenistic view of the Logos (the Word), and the ancient concept of the divine king as the image of the deity he worshiped and represented.

(2) Christ is prior to and supreme over all created things (verse 15b). "Firstborn" here does not mean the first created of all created beings and things, since the following words indicate that Christ was above the created order and the agent through which creation was accomplished.

The Greek word behind "firstborn" was used in reference to the relation of the Logos to God (in Philo) and in regard to the Messiah (in Hellenistic-Jewish interpretation of Psalm 89:27); and it is compatible with Jewish speculation about wisdom. The word implies both preexistence and superiority.

(3) He was God's agent in the creation of all beings and things and is also creation's goal (verse 16). In Jewish speculation, wisdom was God's agent in creation (Proverbs 3:19; 8:27-31). In their thought about Christ, Christians adopted Old Testament concepts and Jewish (and even some Hellenistic) beliefs where appropriate (John 1:1-5; 1 Corinthians 1:24; Colossians 2:3).

Since whatever principalities, powers, spirits, and angels—good or bad—that exist in the universe owe their existence to God's work in Christ, Christ is Lord over these powers. He is not simply one of them, to be worshiped along with others, as the false teachers maintain.

Christ is creation's goal in the sense that all things are to be united in him at the last (see Ephesians 1:10).

(4) Christ is the bond that holds the universe together (verse 17b). The orderliness, unity, and continuance of the universe are not accidental but are due to the sustaining activity of Christ. The philosophers of Paul's time speculated on what holds the cosmos together. The spirit of God, the Word (Logos), and wisdom were suggested. Here the preexistent Christ is made the cohesive force. (See also Hebrews 1:3.)

(5) Christ is the head of the church, which is his body (verse 18a). Paul frequently speaks of the church as the body of Christ (Romans 12:4-5; 1 Corinthians 10:16-17; 12:12-13, 27). This concept may have come from the church's communion service in which all shared in one loaf, which Jesus had declared to be his body (Mark 14:22; 1 Corinthians 10:16-17).

Here and in 2:19, however, Christ is called "the head of the body, the church," as also in Ephesians 1:22-23 and 4:15-16. Paul's purpose in Colossians in designating Christ as the head and the body (the church) as subordinate to the head is probably to emphasize once more Christ's supremacy. He also wanted to strike again at the Colossian heresy that sought to downgrade Christ.

There would be overtones for the Colossians and the Ephesians in this reference to Christ as the head, since in some Hellenistic thought of the time, Zeus or the Logos was the head of the cosmos (the body). This background would suggest Christ's rulership of the cosmos also.

(6) He is the beginning of the new creation (verse 18b). He is the beginning of the age to come, since he is the firstborn from the dead. Through his death and resurrection others may die and rise through him to the newness of life (1:22; 2:12-13; 3:1-3). He is the firstfruits, guaranteeing the future resurrection of the dead (1 Corinthians 15:20, 23). Here, too, he shows his preeminence.

(7) The divine fullness in its totality dwelt in him (verse 19). The meaning here seems to be that Christ contains and represents all that God is—and that by God's choice.

The heretics thought that God consisted of many powers (aeons), distributed through the universe, and that together they comprised God's totality. Against this view Paul says that in Christ alone the totality of divine powers dwells. God was in Christ (2 Corinthians 5:19), not in some partial way (as the divine might be in many human beings), but in God's fullness.

THE UNIQUENESS OF CHRIST (COLOSSIANS 1:15-20; CONT.)

The church took the popular word and concept of the time, fullness, and used it to express the conviction about the Lord's supremacy over all rivals.

(8) Christ, through his death on the cross, is the means of God's reconciliation of the whole universe (verse 20). Underlying this verse is the assumption that heaven and earth are rifted in a battle of cosmic powers. (See also Romans 8:38-39; Ephesians 1:20-23.) God has begun the establishment of peace and order by the subjugation of the "powers" (NIV; NRSV, "rulers") "and authorities" in Christ's death on the cross (Colossians 2:14-15). Through his resurrection, Christ entered into his kingly rule. At the last day he will complete the subjugation of every rule.

The Message of Colossians 1:15-23

This profound passage, set in lyrical form, places before us the unique claim of the Christian faith: that we know and experience God fully when we know, believe in, and obey Jesus Christ and are members of his church. This claim was offensive to many people in Paul's day, as it still is to adherents of other religions.

Paul placed Jesus Christ at the very center of the universe. Using the highest terms known in Jewish and Hellenistic religious terminology, Paul and some of his fellow Christians painted a cosmic Christ, who was God's agent in the creation of the universe and in bringing into being the new creation (the church). Since he had opened the gate of life to them and was actually making the universe a true cosmos out of the chaos it had become, the highest language they knew seemed appropriate to express their individual and corporate experience of the new life he had brought.

The terms they used were those of the first century, but the faith and experience they describe are common to Christians of every century since.

Christians will always exhaust human language in the attempt to describe what they have found in Jesus Christ.

COLOSSIANS 1:24–2:5

Introduction to These Verses

At the end of the preceding part (1:23), Paul commented about the universal outreach of the gospel. He noted in 1:6 that it was taking root and bearing fruit in the whole world. If Christ's significance is cosmic, then all people will have to be informed concerning his identity and work.

That the gospel had actually reached "every creature under heaven" (1:23) is, of course, an exaggeration. But that it had reached the great centers of the Roman Empire, was spreading out from them, and was being talked about everywhere (even in Caesar's household—Philippians 1:13; 4:22) was fully apparent to Paul.

The spreading of this gospel to the Gentile world was precisely the work God had given him to do (Romans 15:15-16; Galatians 1:16). The shift from "we" to "I" here indicates that Paul is now stressing his unique apostolic responsibility for this work. But in describing his role here he uses the word *servant* (literally, deacon, meaning anyone engaged in service of any sort). Such a term would include Timothy (Philippians 1:1), Epaphras (Colossians 1:7). Tychicus (Colossians 4:7), Apollos (1 Corinthians 3:5), and others (2 Corinthians 11:23). These people were on a common footing in the work of evangelism. Paul had both a unique ministry and a shared ministry.

This section has two main parts:

I. Ministry of Suffering and Proclamation (1:24-29)

II. Paul's Concern for the Colossians (2:1-5)

The Message of Colossians 1:24–2:5

Here we learn a great deal about Paul's understanding of Christian ministry. Some points refer to him alone, some to his associates in ministry, and some to the church as a whole.

- Paul is God-appointed, not self-appointed. He holds a divine office, given to him for the sake of others. His use of "we" (including Timothy) and his commendation of the faithful ministry in Christ of Epaphras (1:7; 4:12-13) and Tychicus (4:7) indicate that they, too, are God-commissioned as fellow servants. However, their role as associates and representatives is different from his.

- His task and theirs is to make the word of God fully known to every person under heaven.

- This word concerns God's hitherto hidden, but now revealed, glorious purpose to save all people through Christ. When Christ comes to dwell in and among them, he becomes for them the hope of a heavenly inheritance.

- God intends to save all people through Christ to his saints (the church), not simply to an elect person or group. Christians understand the revealed mystery and should grow in their understanding of it.

- Suffering in the course of spreading the gospel in the world is part of the minister's calling. It is the consequence of hostility to the proclamation of the gospel, and it hastens the coming of the end time and the realization of the inheritance of the new age.

- Christian ministers are to strive mightily in the power of Christ in proclaiming the gospel and bringing Christians to maturity of life in Christ. They are to protect God's people from false philosophies advanced in beguiling speech.

COLOSSIANS 2:6-23

Introduction to These Verses

Colossians 2:6-7 is a transitional section. It summarizes what Paul has been saying in 1:24–2:5 and introduces what he is about to say in 2:8-15. This section has three parts:

I. Transition (2:6-7)

II. Victory Over the Elemental Spirits (2:8-15)

III. Regulations of the Elemental Spirits (2:16-23)

The Message of Colossians 2:6-23

The message can be summarized under three headings: what the Colossians were saved *from*; what they were saved *by*; and what they were saved to.

What they were saved from. They once lived in "the body of the flesh" (verse 11 NRSV; NIV, "sinful nature"), that is, in a self or personality organized for and directed toward earthly things and hostile to God. They were "dead in trespasses" (verse 13 NRSV; NIV, "dead in your sins"; acts violating God's commands) and, as Gentiles, were both inwardly and outwardly uncircumcised. Death is the state of the person outside Christ (Romans 6:13, 16, 20, 23). They were condemned by the certificate of indebtedness (the IOU of their conscience over their violation of the will of God), which they could not pay off. They were under bondage to cosmic powers and the ascetic rules and regulations associated with their worship (verse 20).

What they were saved by. The savior is "Christ Jesus the Lord" (verse 6), who is the complete embodiment of deity (verse 9). In baptism they died with Christ and "through faith in the power of God" they were raised with Christ (verse 12). All of this was God's doing through the cross of Christ. Through that cross God in Christ broke the hold of the principalities and powers over the lives of the Colossians and by his free forgiveness canceled the IOU.

Human beings are not saved by human wisdom and tradition (verses 8, 22) concerning the cosmic powers or through visions, regulations, and practices their devotees proffer. They are saved only by holding fast to the head (of the church and all cosmic powers—1:18; 2:10).

What they were saved to. The result of their baptismal faith-union with Christ is variously put: fullness of life (verse 9), that is, participation in the same fullness of life (powers, graces) that was in Christ himself; circumcision of the heart (verse 11), that is, humble response to God and the total obedience to God's will that produces inner goodness, not simply outward correctness; freedom from the old sensual nature (verses 11, 23), from guilt before God due to acts of disobedience to God's revealed will (verse 14), and from cramping, ineffective, ascetic, human regulations (verses 16-23); and, above all, union with the one who is the source and nourisher of church/cosmic life and unity (verse 19).

COLOSSIANS 3:1-17

Introduction to These Verses

Up to this point in the letter the supremacy and all-sufficiency of Christ have been asserted as a counter to the claim of the false teachers that other potencies must be recognized and honored by Christians. The writer has made it clear that Christ is all, and in all (3:11).

How, then, will this belief affect the Christian's everyday life in this world? The answer is given in 3:1-17.

These verses may be divided into three parts:

    I. The New Life in Christ (3:1-4)
    II. Putting Off the Old Nature (3:5-11)
    III. Putting On the New Nature (3:12-17)

The Message of Colossians 3:1-17

The thought of Paul's letters oscillates among four centers. Briefly put, they are: *you were*; *you are*; *you must*; *you will be.* It is easy to identify these four centers in 3:1-17 and elsewhere in the letter.

(1) *You were.* You once had your minds set on earthly things: fornication, impurity, passions, evil desire, and covetousness; in these you once walked, when you lived in them (3:7). Your old nature expressed itself in anger, wrath, malice, slander, foul talk, lying, and social divisiveness (3:8-11).

Earlier he had told them that they were living in the dominion of darkness (1:13), separated from God and God's people and hostile in mind, doing evil deeds (1:21), uncircumcised in heart and dead in sin (2:11-13), guilty before God's law (2:14), and under bondage to the elemental spirits (2:20).

The picture of their former lives is similar to that painted in the letter to the Ephesians, chapter 2, where the readers are said to have been without hope and "without God in the world" (verse 12).

(2) *You are*. Whereas you were once dead, you are now alive (2:10, 13) through resurrection with Christ (3:1). You are participating in his resurrection life as a present reality. You are united to the glorified and exalted Christ and are seated with him, though in a hidden way, in God's very presence in heaven (3:1, 3). Your earthly life is also a heavenly life—right now! (See also Ephesians 2:6.)

You have a new nature, which is growing into the likeness of God and coming to full knowledge of God's will (3:10). You are fully forgiven (2:13; 3:13), God's holy and beloved chosen people (3:12), members of a community without racial, religious, or social distinctions (3:11), released from the ascetic regulations imposed by the elemental spirits of the universe (2:20-23), and heirs of a glorious future stored up for you in heaven (1:5, 12).

This all came about through your faith in God and your baptismal identification with Christ in his death on the cross and his resurrection by the power of God (2:11-15).

Salvation for Paul was not just a "someday" experience, but to a large degree a present one.

(3) *You must*. Paul's "therefore" (2:16; 3:5, 12 NIV) links present reality to present obligation. If you are God's transformed chosen ones, you have an obligation to live in a way pleasing to God and to Christ, (1:10; 3:17), to bear the fruit of good works (1:10), to have and exercise the graces that belong to members of Christ's kingdom (1:13; 3:12-17), to grow in knowledge of the truth (1:9-10; 2:2-3; 3:10), and to promote unity in Christ's body, the church (3:11, 14-15).

Maturity in Christ for every person was Paul's driving passion (1:28-29).

(4) *You will be*. While salvation for Paul

was a present reality, it was also for him a future goal. In its final fullness it will be given by Christ at his coming (3:4). Life in the final Kingdom is the "inheritance of the saints in the light" (1:12). Christians and all people will be judged by God and Christ (1:22, 28; 3:6; see Romans 14:10-12; 2 Corinthians 5:10). Their maturity (perfection) in Christ will be supremely important on that day (1:22, 28). Both Paul and the Colossian Christians have the responsibility to promote maturity in the church (1:28-29; 3:12-17, especially verse 16).

The nature of the final salvation is expressed in a few great terms: *inheritance* (promised to God's people in the Old Testament), *light* (the light of God's presence—1:12), *glory* (splendor, radiance from God's presence—1:27; 3:4), and *fullness* of life (2:10).

COLOSSIANS 3:18–4:18

Introduction to These Verses

Though Paul exhorted the Colossian Christians to concentrate attention on heavenly things rather than earthly ones (3:1-4), he did not understand Christianity as a way of fleeing from this world, as countless religious mystics and ascetics have tried to do.

For him Christianity was rather a way of redeeming the world, according to the intention of its Creator and Redeemer (Romans 8:19-22; 12:2; Ephesians 2:1). He rejoiced that Christian communities were being planted throughout the Roman Empire (Colossians 1:5-6) and that they were shining as lights in the world (Philippians 2:15). He recognized the responsibility of Christians to support the God-ordained political authorities and to live as responsible citizens, even to the paying of taxes and other obligations

(Romans 13:1-8a). Proper relations with the neighbor were important to him (Romans 13:8b-10). Likewise important were relationships within Christian households and among Christian workers and churches.

This section of Colossians has four main parts:

I. Rules for the Christian Household (3:18–4:1)
II. Counsels on Prayer and Witnessing (4:2-6)
III. Greetings from Paul and Associates (4:7-17)
IV. Authentication and Benediction (4:18)

Paul's point of view seems to be: Though human life in this world may not continue long (Romans 13:11-14; 1 Corinthians 7:29-31), it is to be lived in all of its dimensions as long as it lasts. It is to be lived according to the pattern ordained by its Creator—a pattern revealed in the Holy Scriptures, in Jesus Christ, in the church's apostolic tradition, in his own inspired experience, and in the best insights of contemporary culture.

The Message of Colossians 3:18–4:18

- Christianity is not just a way of thinking about God and human existence; it is also a way of living in this world. What we do in our time on earth is important to God and determines our destiny.

- Earthly life is to be lived according to the pattern ordained by its Creator; knowledge of God's will is given to those who seek it.

- The kind of life that is appropriate for this world is Christlike life. We are to live in a manner pleasing to him. This way of living is not inevitably in conflict with all prevailing social values, but often affirms and reinforces some of them.

- People of every class and condition are accountable to God/Christ for the way they act toward one another.

- The rights of weak and oppressed people are as important as those of the strong and the privileged.

- Love and just treatment of others are the central ingredients of harmonious and effective domestic life.

- All legitimate work, whatever one's station in life, should be done conscientiously as a service to the Lord Christ, not just to please human masters or employers.

- Persevering and thankful prayer can promote individual and church stability and growth, and can assist fellow Christians in their work of spreading the gospel.

- Careful Christian living and gracious witnessing are the keys to effective evangelizing of the outside world.

- The fellowship of Christian life and service is rich beyond measure. It knows no boundaries of race, class, or gender. It strengthens and encourages the participants, and leads to Christian maturity and full assurance in all the will of God (4:12).

FIRST AND SECOND
THESSALONIANS

OUTLINE OF 1 AND 2 THESSALONIANS

INTRODUCTION

The Church at Thessalonica

Thessalonica, modern Thessaloniki, located at the head of the Thermaic Gulf of the Aegean Sea in Macedonia, was founded about 316 B.C. by Cassander, a general in Alexander the Great's army. He named the city after his wife, the daughter of Philip II and half sister of Alexander.

In 146 B.C., when Macedonia became a Roman province, the city became the capital of the new province. Its location on the Via Egnatia, the famous East-West road, plus its harbor facilities, made it a prosperous trade and political center.

Many religions (advocating the worship of Greek, Roman, and oriental gods, and even Yahweh of the Jews) vied for acceptance and loyalty from the cosmopolitan populace. The Jewish population there was a considerable one. In the Roman period a civic cult praised Roman rulers (especially Julius Caesar and Augustus) and prominent patrons of Rome and exalted the goddess Roma.

The location of the synagogue where Paul preached is unknown. It may have been near an agora (marketplace) close to the harbor area.

Paul, Silvanus (Silas), and Timothy came into this politically and religiously charged atmosphere on Paul's second missionary journey (Acts 17:1-9), after a disastrous experience in Philippi (Acts 16:11-40; 1 Thessalonians 2:2). Paul preached in the synagogue for three sabbaths and evidently remained in the city for some time thereafter. He was there long enough to have worked intensively at his trade (1 Thessalonians 2:9) and to have received financial help more than once from the Philippians (Philippians 4:16). We may guess that he and his companions were there for two or three months.

Paul argued in the synagogue that the Old Testament predicts the coming of a suffering Messiah and that Jesus of Nazareth fulfilled this expectation (Acts 17:3). Some Jews and also many god-fearing Gentiles were convinced, as well as a number of influential women. The Gentiles, male and female, were attracted to Judaism by its worship of one God (monotheism) and its high religious and ethical teaching. However, they did not accept the full yoke of the Jewish law (circumcision, sabbath observance, and the food laws). They were excellent prospects for Paul's law-free gospel about Jesus.

Paul's proclamation about the present and coming rule of Jesus Christ provoked unbelieving and jealous Jews to twist a religious affirmation into a political charge of disloyalty to Caesar and into mob action directed against Paul, his companions, and their host, Jason. When Paul and his associates could not be found, Jason and other Christians were brought before the city authorities and forced to put up money to guarantee the good conduct of their guests. For the good of all, Paul and his companions immediately left the city by night. The infant church was thus put in a precarious position almost from birth.

When Paul arrived at Athens after a mission in Beroea (Acts 17:10-15), he sent Timothy back to Thessalonica to assist the infant congregation and to bring him word of its condition (1 Thessalonians 3:1-5). Paul then crossed over to Corinth and began preaching there. Later Timothy brought a letter to him from the Thessalonians, inquiring about some important matters, to which Paul responded in 1 Thessalonians, chapters 4–5.

First Thessalonians is Paul's joyful reaction to the news of the fidelity of the Thessalonians in spite of their sufferings. It is also Paul's attempt to guide the Thessalonians to a fuller Christian life through a solution to their problems. It is a pastoral letter.

The Problems in the Church at Thessalonica

(1) Persecution by fellow townsmen, probably spearheaded by the unbelieving Jews who had forced Paul from the city (Acts 17:5; 1 Thessalonians 2:14-16; 3:3-4).

(2) Doubts about the integrity of the missionaries, spread probably by the hostile Jews (1 Thessalonians 2:1).

(3) Confusion about the validity of their new faith and experience in the light of Jewish attacks (1 Thessalonians 1:4-10); about the Christian view of the future (the fate of Christians who have died before the coming of Christ, the time of Christ's coming, and Christian activity meanwhile—4:13–5:11); and about the place of suffering in the lives of Christians (3:3-4).

(4) Sexual irregularities (4:3-8), idleness and troublemaking (4:11-12), carelessness (5:1-11), and quarreling (5:13).

Date and Place of Writing

This letter is probably the earliest of the preserved letters of Paul. First Thessalonians dates to A.D. 50 or 51, and was written by Paul from Corinth.

The Occasion and Purpose of 2 Thessalonians

The letter indicates that reports had come to Paul about problems in the church at Thessalonica (3:11) mainly concerning the persecution the church was experiencing, probably from both Jews and Gentiles (1:4-8).

Another problem centered in wrong ideas some Thessalonians had about the coming of Christ. Someone evidently claimed Paul as the authority for the false view that the Day of the Lord had already come (2:2). The practical result of this mistaken view was that some people had quit their daily work. Thus there was a great deal of idleness and meddling in other people's affairs (3:6, 11). Paul had faced the problem of lazy spongers when he was at Thessalonica (3:10), but his instructions went unheeded. Indeed, the situation was much worse.

We can only guess who was teaching church members at Thessalonica that the Day of the Lord had arrived.

There were church members at Corinth who believed that they were enjoying the kingdom of God already (1 Corinthians 4:8). A clear statement in 2 Timothy 2:18 attributes to two false teachers in the church the view that the resurrection is already past. Such a position was held by Gnostic heretics of the late first and second centuries, and may have appeared in embryonic form in the church as early as the time of Paul. It held that the only resurrection there ever will be is release of the spirit from the bondage of flesh, which occurs in baptism and new birth.

Or had the Thessalonians taken too realistically Paul's statement in 1 Thessalonians 5:5, 8 that they were "sons of" (NIV; NRSV, "children of") "the day" and "we belong to the day," as if the day had already broken in? In addition, did the severity of suffering suggest to them that the end-time birth pangs of the new order (see Isaiah 66:7-9) were actually being felt?

It is even possible that a forged letter, claiming Paul's authorship and authority for the view that the Day of the Lord had arrived, was circulating at Thessalonica (2:2). Such a letter would make necessary Paul's repudiation of it and the reference to his handwriting as a way of authenticating his letters in the future (3:17).

Whatever the exact cause of the confusion, Paul felt it important to straighten out the Thessalonians on the significance, time, and consequence of the coming of Christ for present living.

Authorship, Date, and Place of Writing

It is difficult to explain why we have two letters to the Thessalonians that are so alike and yet so different. Second Thessalonians covers many of the same subjects as 1 Thessalonians: notably, thanksgiving for the readers' steadfastness in persecution; a declaration of God's judgment on their persecutors; prayers for their establishment in every good work and word (2 Thessalonians 2:17); teaching about end-time events (eschatology) and about appropriate Christian conduct in the time before the end; and emphasis on Paul's and his associates' authority and on traditional church teaching. And much of the language and phraseology is the same in the two letters.

But there are marked differences. First Thessalonians is warm in tone and filled with personal data; 2 Thessalonians is colder, more formal, and authoritarian. The first letter stresses the unpredictability and suddenness of the coming of Christ; the second offers signs by which one can predict that coming. The second gives information about the lawless one—a kind of speculation about the future that is unparalleled anywhere in the letters of Paul.

Under what circumstances would Paul and his associates write two letters to the Thessalonians so alike, so different, and so close together in time? Many scholars believe that within a few months of the writing of 1 Thessalonians the missionaries, then at Corinth, received new reports about the situation at Thessalonica (2 Thessalonians 3:11). The church members there had not wavered in loyalty to Christ because of persecutions and afflictions (1:4). But serious controversy about the time of the coming of Christ had arisen, provoked by revelations claimed by false teachers and possibly by a letter falsely attributed to Paul. The false teaching that the Day of the Lord had already come had led to serious moral consequences in the church. The missionaries wrote to correct the new situation, which was yet not wholly new. Therefore the similarities and differences in the two letters. The date of writing of 2 Thessalonians, then, would be A.D. 50 or 51.

Other scholars believe that a disciple of Paul (perhaps between A.D. 75 and 90) used 1 Thessalonians as a source of material for a rebuttal of the claim made in the Christian church of that time that Paul believed the Day of the Lord had already arrived. This rebuttal is our 2 Thessalonians. Because of his imitation of Paul's language and ideas, the letters are similar; and, because of his later date, situation, and purpose the letters are different.

1 THESSALONIANS: 1 THESSALONIANS 1

Introduction to This Chapter

The letter begins in the usual Pauline fashion. The writers are Paul, Silvanus (Silas), and Timothy, all three of whom were present at the founding of the church there (Acts 16:1-5; 17:1-15).

The central idea of verses 2-10 may be put as follows: We give thanks for the conclusive evidence that you Thessalonians have a secure place in God's great redemptive plan. This evidence consists of the striking nature of your conversion experience and the character of its fruits.

The Message of 1 Thessalonians 1

This passage must have been highly enlightening and reassuring to the Thessalonians, and it may be so to us. Noteworthy are the following emphases:

- The deep concern of Paul for his beloved children (see 2:11), his constant prayers and his thanksgiving for them, and his unabashed praise of their spiritual state and their witness in the world. The Christian fellowship was obviously very dear to him (2:17; 3:7-9) and ought to be to us.

- The blessed assurance of Christians, that God loves them and has ordained that they should have a place in God's great redemptive plan (verse 4).

- The clear definition of the true nature and results of Christian conversion, which here are presented as the receiving of the word of God through the preaching of Spirit-empowered messengers, deep inner joy inspired by the Holy Spirit, the presence in the Christian of the fruits of the Spirit (faith, love, and hope) and the practical results in daily life to which they lead, the radical change in one's outward manner of life, and the influence of converts on others.

- The strange and wonderful presence in the heart of joy in the midst of affliction.

- The glorious hope for the future, centering in the resurrected Lord, which should be cherished and kept alive by Christians.

1 THESSALONIANS 2:1-16

Introduction to These Verses

Paul's thanksgiving for the Thessalonians was almost completely thrown off track by the section of the letter we now encounter. As he dictated the letter, his joy over the Thessalonians' deep inner transformation (1:5-6) and the striking change in their outward manner of life (1:7-10) became stifled by thoughts about what had happened to the church after his departure.

Grievous troubles for the church had set in. Their fellow countrymen had begun to persecute them (2:14; 3:3-4). Paul's outburst against the Jews (2:14-16) implies that they were instigating the persecution and working through Thessalonian Gentiles to achieve their ends.

What exactly this persecution consisted of we do not know. Were the Jews continuing to press charges, probably of disloyalty to Caesar and Rome (Acts 17:7), before the *politarchs* (the Greek word for *city officials* in Acts 17:6, 8)? In the territory of Macedonia the politarchs were the local, non-Roman magistrates of a free city, who would be anxious to maintain the favor of their Roman benefactors by suppressing any indication of disloyalty to Rome.

More certain is the indication from Paul's remarks here that hostile Jews were spreading lies about Paul and his companions—about their motives, conduct, and the truth of their gospel.

Thus Paul moves quickly in the letter to present evidence that he and his associates are true servants of God. They are entirely above reproach in the conduct of their ministry at Thessalonica and in their attitudes toward and dealings with the Thessalonians after they left there.

This section of the letter has two parts:

I. The Ministry at Thessalonica (2:1-12)
II. Imitators of the Judean Churches (2:13-16)

The Message of 1 Thessalonians 2:1-16

This section, particularly verses 1-12, offers a remarkable portrait of what a Christian minister should be. It should be printed and hung on the wall of every minister's study. Its applicability is obvious, but a few points may be emphasized here, most of them applying to church members as well as clergy:

- The first is courage in the face of opposition. The courage comes from God (verse 2), not from one's own willpower. It would take unbelievable courage, after a vicious beating and imprisonment like Paul and Silas experienced at Philippi, to move just a few miles away to the next town, as the Lord had directed (Matthew 10:23), and brave the prospect of the same kind of treatment all over again. Most of us would probably head for the harbor at Neapolis and board the first ship leaving Macedonia.

- A second point is the resolve to speak not to please human beings but to please God, who tests our hearts (verse 4). Probably the greatest temptation a minister faces today is to avoid controversial subjects and shape sermons, teaching, and comments in such a way that they will evoke assent—and better, flattering response—from hearers. This was the tactic of false preachers in Paul's time (1 Corinthians 2:1-5; 2 Corinthians

2:17; 4:2), and indeed in every time since.

- A third point is the sharing of both the gospel and oneself (verse 8). Unfortunately, many ministers attend to a proper conceptualizing of the content of the gospel (theologizing) and to apt verbalizing of it in worship and think their task well done. But, as Paul points out here, it is the *gospel incarnate in the preacher* that effects change like that described in 1:2-10. What the minister *is* is as important in transforming lives as what the minister *says*. Holy, righteous, blameless, selfless living among those we seek to help gives words divine potency. Theology and words alone are fruitless (1 Corinthians 4:19-20).

- A fourth remark has to do with the economics of preaching. Paul and his associates went to extreme lengths to shield themselves from the charge of cupidity (greed). The trickery, flattery, and polished rhetoric of false apostles in Paul's time were aimed at what the hearers had in their pockets. Nothing much has changed. Though preaching the gospel free of charge (1 Corinthians 9:18) may not be possible or feasible today, the subordination of economic motives is—if transformation of the sort described in 1:2-10 is to take place in our time.

1 THESSALONIANS 2:17–3:13

Introduction to These Verses

The speedy departure by night of Paul and Silas from Thessalonica for Beroea and the subsequent flight of Paul from Beroea to Athens (Acts 17:10-15), as if they were criminals fleeing from the law and justice, were effective ammunition in the hands of Jewish enemies.

Though Silas and Timothy stayed for a while in Macedonia (Silas at Beroea and Timothy possibly at Thessalonica), they must have remained largely in hiding and have made no forward moves in the evangelizing of the province. The opposition's main fury clearly was directed against the leader of the party, Paul, though his associates cannot have escaped hostility. Paul's enemies knew that when one strikes the shepherd, it is not long before the sheep are scattered (see Mark 14:27).

On Paul's instruction, delivered by the Beroeans who escorted him to Athens, Silas and Timothy came to him there (Acts 17:15). With the success of the whole Macedonian venture at stake, Paul finally decided to send both of them back to Macedonia to do what they could to aid the new churches: Silas to Beroea and Timothy to Thessalonica. Paul remained alone in Athens (1 Thessalonians 3:1). While there he had the experience described in Acts 17:16-34.

Again frustrated, this time by cultured despisers of his curious preaching about a resurrected Jewish felon (Acts 17:31-32), he traveled westward to Corinth to attempt another mission. Undoubtedly buoyed up by living and working with a Christian couple named Aquila and Priscilla, he recovered from his loneliness and dejection (1 Corinthians 2:3) and preached persuasively in the synagogue (Acts 18:1-4).

At some point Silas and Timothy arrived in Corinth from Macedonia with good news concerning the churches there (Acts 18:5). Timothy's report about the Thessalonians (1 Thessalonians 3:6) led to Paul's writing our 1 Thessalonians.

This section may be divided into four parts:

The Message of 1 Thessalonians 2:17–3:13

Many striking aspects of Christian faith and experience are evident in this part of the letter:

- The depth of love and concern Christian leaders and laity can have and should have for each other. "We were made orphans by being separated from you," Paul writes (2:17). You are our glory and joy, and "now we really live, since you are standing firm in the Lord" (3;8 NIV). We pray night and day for you. And on the other side, we see the comfort that the Thessalonians' attitude toward Paul and his associates and their constancy in the faith gave the struggling missionaries (3:7). Soul met soul in the Christian encounter, and lives were transformed at their deepest levels.

- The acceptance of suffering as normative in Christian living and the unshakable faith that good will issue from it. Early Christians saw themselves as united with Christ in his suffering and death. Suffering was not simply to be tolerated but to be gloried in. In suffering one develops patience and character, experiences the power of God, bears witness to others of that enabling power, helps carry the burdens of others, is able to comfort others with the comfort one has received, and much more. Paul gloried in his infirmities and weaknesses, because in them God's power is made perfect in weakness (2 Corinthians 12:9). Out of suffering with and for Christ issues resurrection life (2 Corinthians 4:7-12, 14; Philippians 3:10-11; 2 Timothy 2:11). In suffering our outer nature is wasting away, but our inner nature is being renewed day by day (2 Corinthians 4:16). Those who do not suffer cannot be servants of a suffering Lord.

- Evil has a power that seeks to seduce us from faith in and loyalty to Christ and from proclaiming the gospel to the whole world. Paul calls this power *Satan*. Evil is that in life which resists the loving activity of God in the universe. It has been overcome by the power of God, who acted in Christ's death and resurrection to defeat it (Romans 4:25; Colossians 2:15). By faith-identification with Christ in his death and resurrection, we can defeat evil in our lives. As Christians we must be on guard against this evil (1 Corinthians 10:12-13; 1 Thessalonians 3:5, 8).

- Christian life begins with an initial conversion experience—a turning to God from the worship of idols, whatever they may be (1 Thessalonians 1:4-10). But this is just a beginning. There is much yet lacking. Love for other Christians and for all people, even one's enemies, must "increase and abound" (3:12 NRSV; NIV, "overflow"). We must grow into God's likeness until our whole inner selves (thoughts, will, and emotions) will be transformed into readiness for life in God's presence at the coming of the Lord Jesus.

1 THESSALONIANS 4

Introduction to This Chapter

The first half of Paul's letter to the Thessalonians has dealt with his and his companions' personal relationship with the Thessalonians (1:2–3:13). The second half of the letter consists of a discussion of the problems the Thessalonians have, and the way to maturity of life in Christ (4:1–5:24).

In essence, the missionaries are saying to them, Your new Christian faith and life are sound, in spite of what your enemies have charged. Now go on to maturity of life in Christ in full confidence that you are on the right track. Your Christ-taught founders (4:1-2) and your own leaders (5:12) will help you along the way, and God will make you completely holy (5:24). You can and will come out blameless in character and life at the time of Christ's coming (3:13; 5:23). And, together with your Christian dead (4:13-18), you will participate in life in the presence of the Lord (4:17; 5:9-10).

The problems Paul deals with here were suggested by Timothy, who had just returned from Thessalonica, and also may have been raised in a letter Timothy seems to have brought from the church there. Note the word "about" (NIV; NRSV, "concerning") in 4:9, 13; 5:1, by which Paul introduced matters about which the Corinthians wrote him (1 Corinthians 7:1, 25; 8:1; 12:1).

This section may be outlined as follows:
I. Personal Sexual Morality (4:1-8)
II. Love and Work in the Community (4:9-12)
III. Destiny of the Christian Dead (4:13-18)

The Message of 1 Thessalonians 4

Paul's teachings about sex, love of fellow believers, and faithful work for the good of oneself and the community present clear challenges to the church of our time. Here are a few brief remarks about his view of the coming of Christ:

- Paul employs here the picturesque metaphors and symbols of Jewish-Christian apocalyptic: the cry of command, the archangel's call; the trumpet of God; the clouds; the air. Like the language of the books of Daniel and Revelation (the beasts, the trumpets, the bowls, the thrones, the sea of glass, angels and living creatures, a great harlot), Paul's picture of the coming of Christ must be taken as a metaphorical characterization of what cannot be accurately described.

- Paul's belief that the coming of Christ would occur in his generation matches that of Jesus himself (Mark 9:1; 13:28-30). But neither would predict the exact time; both left the time of the coming to God's authority and decision (Mark 13:32; Acts 1:7; 2 Thessalonians 2:1-12).

Jesus even suggested that God might extend the period of grace before Christ's coming (Mark 13:20; Luke 13:6-9; 18:7). God's will is not unalterable, but depends on the character of our response (see Jeremiah 18:7-10). Therefore, the time of the end cannot be predicted. Paul saw a God-ordained restrainer at work, giving opportunity for the spread of the gospel (2 Thessalonians 2:6-7).

Both Jesus and Paul stressed the importance of preparedness for that great event (Matthew 24:42-51; 25:1-13; Romans 13:11-14; 1 Thessalonians 5:1-11). Since God gives people a period of grace, they must seize the opportunity for preparation (by repentance, renewal, diligent proclamation of the gospel, and

Christ-like living). They are not to usurp God's authority over times and dates (Acts 1:7).

- The catching up of dead and living Christians to meet Christ in the air cannot properly be used to form a doctrine of "the rapture" (rescue) of the saints to shield them from a seven-year period of tribulation, as is so often claimed. In the book of Revelation the saints are pictured as going through the end-time tribulations (Revelation 2:10; 6:9-11; 17:6; 18:24; 19:2), not as being rescued from them. And neither here nor in Matthew 24:40-41 is there any suggestion of an ongoing earthly order while the righteous are away in the air. Both Jesus and Paul contemplate the end of the earthly process at the coming of Christ for his final judgment of all people; and they seem to expect thereafter the eternal, heavenly kingdom of God.

1 THESSALONIANS 5

Introduction to This Chapter

Paul's teaching at Thessalonica obviously gave a large place to instruction about the coming of the Lord. But on three points he had not been explicit enough: what would happen to church members who might die before the great event (4:13-18); exactly when it would happen (5:2-3); and what style of life would be appropriate in the meantime (5:4-11).

Paul seems to have thought he had given them adequate instruction on the second and third of these questions (5:1), but Timothy's report and perhaps inquiries in a letter he brought to Paul indicated clearly that he had not done so, or that they had not comprehended what he had said.

Paul's response here about the time of the coming of the Day of the Lord points out its suddenness and unpredictability (5:2-3).

Paul uses several terms for the great end-time event: "the revealing" of the Lord Jesus Christ (1 Corinthians 1:7); his "coming" (literally, his "presence"—1 Corinthians 15:23; 1 Thessalonians 2:19; 2 Thessalonians 2:1, 8); his "appearing" (2 Thessalonians 2:8); and "the day of our Lord Jesus Christ" (1 Corinthians 1:8; 5:5; 2 Corinthians 1:14; Philippians 2:16; 1 Thessalonians 5:2). Neither Paul nor other New Testament writers use the term *second coming*, though Hebrews 9:28 comes close to it. *Second coming* goes back to Justin Martyr in the second century.

As a phrase signifying the end event, "the Day of the Lord" reaches back as far as Amos (eighth century B.C.; see Amos 5:18). In the Old Testament and in Jewish usage it meant the day of God, when God would judge the people and the world and inaugurate the new Kingdom. When Jesus became *Lord* to the church, aspects of the work of God were transferred to him.

This section has four main parts:
I. The Times and the Seasons (5:1-3)
II. While Christians Await the Day (5:4-11)
III. Counsels for Church Life and Worship (5:12-24)
IV. The Conclusion (5:25-28)

The Message of 1 Thessalonians 5

- What sanctification (holiness) means in practical terms is spelled out by Paul in chapters 4 and 5.

- In general terms, it is the process and state of Christian maturity that should follow from the Holy Spirit's work in conversion (1:5-6). It is increasing and abounding in love to one another (3:12).

It is a life worthy of God (2:12), a life characterized by the kind of blamelessness that can stand the test of Christ's judgment at the time of Christ's coming (1:10; 3:13; 4:6; 5:2-3, 9).

- In specific terms, both attitudes and conduct are included. Christian maturity (holiness, sanctification) embraces all that Paul has included in the latter half of his letter: sexual purity, brotherly love (mutual helpfulness and unstinting forgiveness), quiet minding of one's own business, industriousness, mature theological understanding of the Christian situation in the time before the end, spiritual alertness and self-control, respect for church leaders, thankfulness and prayerfulness, gratitude for and effective use of the Holy Spirit's gifts, the ability to discriminate between right and wrong, and power to reject evil and do what is good. All this Paul includes under the category of holiness.

- For Paul, holy persons are not pallid, ascetic recluses who specialize in vague, rapturous inner experiences. Rather, they are persons whose total attitudes and way of life are shaped by the God who dwells in them as the Holy Spirit (4:8). This quality of life is God's gift to those who seek more and more to please God (4:1).

2 THESSALONIANS: 2 THESSALONIANS 1:1–3:18

Introduction to These Chapters
The letter follows the usual outline employed in Paul's letters. The parts need no special treatment here. We shall follow the development of thought, however.

Second Thessalonians has four main parts:

   I. Introduction (1:1-4)
  II. God's Righteous Judgment (1:5-12)
 III. The Coming of Christ (2:1-14)
 IV. Paul's View of Last Things (2:15–3:18)

The Message of 2 Thessalonians 1:1–3:18

- God has a glorious Kingdom in store for the people called through Christ Jesus and the gospel (2:13-14).

- Christian suffering is a means by which God's people become worthy of the kingdom of God (1:5, 11). In suffering, faith, steadfastness, and love they are perfected (1:3-4; 3:5).

- The power of evil (Satan) will be with us to the end, but will ultimately be defeated by the victorious Christ (2:3-8). Evil is a terrifying reality in life. It becomes incarnate in diabolical persons, who lead unrighteous unbelievers into strong delusion and hostility to the truth (2:9-12). Christians can triumph over that power if they pray for one another, persevere in the faith, and do what is right (3:1-5).

- The recompense to be meted out to doers of evil is separation from the presence of God and "from the glory of his might" (1:9 NRSV; NIV, "majesty of his power"), really the continuation of the separation they have brought about by their own unbelief and evil deeds. Here eternal destruction is defined as exclusion from God, who is the giver of life. The recompense of the righteous is rest (relief, as of the relaxation of a taut bowstring—1:7) and life in the presence of the glorious Lord.

- Christian life in this world anticipates the life of the final kingdom of God. God has more in store for us than we have yet realized. While we are people of the day, the day has not yet arrived in all its glory (2:2). Meanwhile, we wait in patience for the fulfilling of God's final purpose.

- Life's responsibilities need to be carried out faithfully while we await the great finale. Laziness, idleness, sponging off of others, and meddling in the affairs of others bring no credit to the church before the world (2 Thessalonians 3:6-12; 1 Thessalonians 4:11-12). The church should discipline such people in love (2 Thessalonians 3:6, 14-15).

FIRST AND SECOND TIMOTHY

OUTLINE OF 1 AND 2 TIMOTHY

3. Theological undergirdings
(2:8-10)
4. A citation from a hymn
(2:11-13)
B. Instructions regarding the teachers
(2:14-26)
  1. Beware of empty arguments
  (2:14)
  2. Set a personal example
  (2:15-19)
  3. Aim at central virtues
  (2:20-23)
  4. Characteristics of the Lord's
  servant (2:24-26)

V. A Call to Courageous Living (3:1-17)

A. Toward an uncertain future (3:1-9)
  1. Times will get more difficult
  (3:1)
  2. Even Christians will waver
  (3:2-5)
  3. False teachers will have their
  day (3:6-9)
B. Remain loyal to the faith (3:10-17)
  1. Timothy has a guide (3:10-14)
  2. Timothy has Scripture
  (3:15-17)

VI. Final Exhortation to Timothy (4:1-22)

A. A final appeal to preach the gospel
(4:1-2)
B. Healthy and unhealthy religion
(4:3-5)
C. An approaching end (4:6-8)
D. Personal words (4:9-18)
E. Closing salutations (4:19-21)
F. A benediction (4:22)

INTRODUCTION TO THE PASTORAL LETTERS

First and Second Timothy and Titus are letters to younger colleagues in ministry written by Paul regarding church administration. The great theologian of the thirteenth century, Thomas Aquinas, observed that the first three letters address pastoral concerns. Thus, the letters to Timothy and Titus are commonly called the Pastoral Epistles.

Date and Authorship of the Pastorals

Modern scholarship has wrestled with authorship. Essentially three alternatives are possible. One is that the letters were written by the apostle Paul very late in his life. Much argument can be made to support this perspective, as there is much in the Pastorals that reflects Paul's authentic teaching.

A second alternative is to attribute authorship of the Pastorals to another writer who is familiar with Paul's writing and who uses Paul's name and authority, but who writes to unique circumstances in a much later time. This may sound peculiar to the modern reader, but in ancient times such pseudonymous writing was quite common.

The third option is to search for pieces or fragments of authentic Pauline writing within the Pastoral Epistles. This third option is sometimes called the "fragment thesis," and it discerns five fragments: Titus 3:12-15; 2 Timothy 4:13-15, 20, 21a; 2 Timothy 4:16-18; 2 Timothy 4:9-12, 22; 2 Timothy 1:16-18; 3:10ff.; 4:1, 2a, 5b, 6-8, 18b, 19, 21b, 22a.

This commentary takes the position that the apostle Paul wrote the Pastoral Epistles. The canon presents the letters to us as Paul's writings. We can imagine the apostle, who is by his own admission now an old man, speaking to a much younger colleague struggling to work both faithfully and effectively in the missionary enterprise of the new Christian movement.

The Background of the Pastorals

What, then, are the Pastoral Epistles? In short, they are the earliest manual of church order that we possess. During the earliest years of the Christian movement, informal gatherings clustered around the person of Jesus. Later, since by nature human beings order themselves into communities and societies, these gatherings formed the primitive church. The Pastoral Epistles are a concerned pastor's response to the demands made on the leadership of Christian churches as those leaders and the churches live out the life of faith in the midst of the real world on which the author looks with tolerance and acceptance.

One aspect of that world, however, was completely unacceptable. Against the Christian faith there emerged various challenges. These heresies did not come from any single perspective or group. The statements against unclean myths and genealogies suggest that the heresies emerged in part from Jewish-Christian traditions. From the Hellenistic/Greek influence came the so-called Gnostic heresies. These heresies were deeply rooted in Greek thought. They included a concern for dualism, a special understanding for only a few who knew more or differently from others, and ethics that were inclined toward the extremely ascetic. The final avenue of heresy was the Marcionite heresy, which because it excluded the Old Testament helped prompt the formulation the New Testament canon.

The Nature of Pastoral Leadership

Throughout the letters the author assumes a developed and reasonably sophisticated church leadership and hierarchy, though the organization of the churches to which Titus is written is not as sophisticated as it is in those to which the letters to Timothy are written. No effort is made to explain how the various functions of church leadership developed. Bishops, elders, presbyters, and deacons all perform the functions of ministry. The leadership is ordained and appointed to various tasks. The details of the various tasks are ignored. Instead, the emphasis is on the character of the pastoral leadership. The selection of officers depends primarily on the moral qualifications of the individual. Under no circumstances should the leader be a new convert.

The leadership at every level must determine what is orthodox and then maintain that orthodoxy in the face of challenges by false doctrine and teachers. The Christian faith developed into a well-formulated body of both thought and practice. No fewer than fifteen references are made to doctrine and/or faith. The church was considered to be "the bulwark" (NRSV) or "foundation" (NIV) "of the truth" (1 Timothy 3:15).

Church leadership is to preach tirelessly with careful self-examination so that the preacher will follow the pattern of sound teaching while guarding the truth. All preachers should handle the truth rightly and set a high example for all to follow. The Christian faith is to evoke a high moral standard in followers that is possible only through a thorough knowledge of the Scriptures and adherence to the sound principles of orthodox faith.

The church's leadership is to be a highly disciplined group adequately supported by the balance of the church. Among the specific tasks of leaders are the public worship services of the church and careful protection of the reputation of the church, as well as careful monitoring of doctrines that should and should not be included in those services. Worship services include reading of Scripture, preaching, and teaching as well as recitation of creeds and singing of hymns and doxologies.

1 TIMOTHY:
1 TIMOTHY 1

Introduction to This Chapter

The Pastoral Epistles, beginning in this first chapter of Timothy, wrestle with the issue of how a Christian must be different in theological and ethical awareness, attitude, and behavior, from the surrounding culture. However, the Christian cannot remain altogether aloof from culture, for the Christian does not live in a vacuum. Therefore, the faith of the earliest Christians is very much like our contemporary faith, a matter of tension between specifically Christian identity and generally cultured and social people.

Paul appropriates a common form of communication familiar to all in the ancient world. When he could not be present with congregations or persons he did the next best thing, he sent a letter via a trusted companion or fellow worker. Paul's letters have a common structure: (1) opening, (2) thanksgiving or blessing, (3) body of the letter, (4) specific instructions, and (5) closing.

Here is an outline of 1 Timothy 1:
I. Address and Greeting (1:1-2)
II. A Warning Against False Teachers (1:3-20)
  A. The spiritual purpose of the gospel (1:3-11)
  B. Ministry and Christian living (1:12-17)
  C. Real authority and power (1:18-20)

The Message of 1 Timothy 1
- The Christian's hope for eternal life is through Jesus Christ.

- Religion and ethics are not foreign to each other; they are vitally related to each other.

- The primary purpose of Bible study is to understand and be apprehended by the salvation of God through Christ.

- The power of God to affect salvation is sufficient even for the most angry and blasphemous individuals or circumstances.

- The truth of Christ's work of salvation is worthy of universal acceptance.

- Christians will always feel tension between their identity as the people of God and as members of culture and society.

- Rejection of biblical faith can result in spiritually shipwrecked lives.

- The Christian faith is a positive faith that leads to life and high moral standards.

1 TIMOTHY 2

Introduction to This Chapter

Chapter 2 begins a section that culminates in 3:15 and essentially deals with how the people of God should behave as "God's household" (NIV) or "the household of God" (NRSV). Chapter 2 addresses the need for maintaining order in public worship.

The issue of appropriate worship was not restricted to the troubled church served by Timothy. Earlier in his own ministry Paul himself had to contend with unruly factions in the Corinthian church.

Here is an outline of this chapter:
I. The Centrality of Prayer (2:1-7)
II. Spiritual Quality Versus Appearance (2:8-15)

The Message of 1 Timothy 2
- Prayer is central in the Christian life.

- Prayers are to be offered for all people.

- Prayer results in an internal tranquillity.

- Public worship is a major part of the Christian life.

- There is but one God, the God revealed through the Old and New Testaments, through history and the person of Jesus Christ.

- In order for prayer to be authentic, an individual must have not merely the posture of prayer but an attitude of prayer. Posture without inner attitude is sheer pretense.

1 TIMOTHY 3

Introduction to This Chapter

Chapter 3 presents and discusses the qualifications and character of church leadership. We will see in this chapter that Paul is very concerned that the church remain secure from criticism or censure from outsiders. Therefore, the quality of character, moral behavior, and teaching ability of church leadership receive strong emphasis.

Here is an outline of 1 Timothy 3.

I. Regarding Bishops or Overseers (3:1-7)
II. Regarding Deacons in the Church (3:8-10)
III. Regarding Women (3:11)
IV. Deacons Have Greater Responsibility (3:12-13)
V. Possible Delay in Visit (3:14-15)
VI. An Excerpt from a Christian Hymn (3:16)

The Message of 1 Timothy 3

In this chapter we have seen Paul describe high moral standards of life to which church leadership should aspire. His concern is that the church remain free from criticism or censure by scoffing outsiders. What else can we learn from this chapter?

- Administrative work should be understood as legitimate ministry.

- Leaders must exhibit concern and not coercion over their charge.

- True character is both an external manifestation and an internal state.

- Ministries of menial tasks are valid, as well as the more highly visible tasks and those of respected greater authorities.

- We can be certain that evil forces do set traps and await our entrapment.

- We need one another in the church to help reinforce our higher calling.

- The *humanity* of Jesus is as much a blessing as is the divinity of Jesus.

1 TIMOTHY 4

Introduction to This Chapter

In the first few verses of the letter Paul alludes to false teachers. Now he will address the threat that the false teachers pose to individuals and to the church as a whole. The major areas of false teaching include: (1) prohibition of marriage, (2) prohibition of certain foods, and (3) an unguarded enthusiasm, and (4) distortion of the resurrection.

Here is an outline of 1 Timothy 4:

I. A Warning Against False Teaching (4:1-5)
II. Words to Timothy About His Teaching (4:6-11)
III. About His Gifts and Authority (4:12-16)

The Message of 1 Timothy 4

The younger preacher finds himself challenged by false teachers. The admonitions of the older apostle imply the image of a timid young minister taken aback by the antagonists in the congregation. What will be the best means by which to undo the potential harm of the false teachers? Public confrontation is not recommended. Instead, Paul points toward the power of personal moral influence in a world that can comprehend only coercion.

True authority is that which emerges from the confluence of personal identity (that is, Timothy's identity as Christian, minister, preacher, and teacher) with the power of God (gained through personal disciplines of study, prayer, and cultivation of spiritual life). Timothy is not instructed to challenge in debate. Nor is he told to humiliate the opponents. What else can we learn from this chapter?

- The power of God can overcome the power of evil.

- Absolute abstinence is not necessarily a Christian response to life.

- The source of the highest attitudes and actions is faith.

- The spiritual life requires discipline, just as athletic endeavor requires physical discipline.

- Physical disciplines have their place for the Christian, but not as ends in themselves.

- The strongest authority a Christian has is the authority of personal life and moral example.

- Scriptures must remain a central part of both public worship and private devotional life.

1 TIMOTHY 5

Introduction to This Chapter

Here is an outline of chapter 5, which is concerned with counsel regarding different classes:

   I. Older Men and Younger Men (5:1)
   II. Older Women (5:2)
   III. Widows (5:3-16)
   IV. Presbyters (5:17-25)

The Message of 1 Timothy 5

First Timothy reveals an imperfect church trying its best to live an authentic witness surrounded by a pagan and sometimes hostile culture. Demands are made on the limited resources of the church by needy people. However, other not-so-needy people make their demands as well. Preachers and would-be preachers are subject to charges of misconduct. Paul responds to the very real demands of a real church.

What else can we learn from this chapter?

- All individuals in the church should be given a measure of respect.

- Christian beliefs and attitudes toward others are learned first in the home.

- Even the most destitute are cared for by God.

- Self-indulgent lives are more a living death than the abundant life God intends for every person.

- Extending hospitality to other Christians is an essential good work to be done by all Christians.

- The church is always under scrutiny by a sometimes hostile surrounding culture.

- Preachers and teachers are entitled to an appropriate payment for their ministry.

- Scriptures are part of the authority to which all Christians should submit their thinking and instruction.

- Good deeds may not be immediately apparent, but they will be known by God.

- Evil deeds may remain hidden for the moment, but they will eventually be known to God.

1 TIMOTHY 6

Introduction to This Chapter

Chapter 6 begins with a discussion concerning slaves. The balance of chapter 6, verses 3-21, picks up the argument that had begun the letter—namely, the false teachers. In the earlier chapter, however, the emphasis had been on the content of the teaching itself. In this final chapter the emphasis is on the character of the teachers themselves.

Here is an outline of chapter 6:

I. Slaves and Relationships with Masters (6:1-2)
II. The Dangers of False Teaching (6:3-10)
III. A Personal Note to Timothy (6:11-16)
IV. Concluding Comments About the Rich (6:17-21)

The Message of 1 Timothy 6

What we believe makes a difference in how we live. Paul understands the vital relationship between what we think and how we act. The false teachers' character forms the major part of the final chapter. In sharp contrast to the questionable character of false teachers, the Christian individual lives an exemplary life.

What else can we learn from this chapter?

- Social status notwithstanding, we are capable of high service in God's name.

- Our Christian faith leads to better work for the glory of God.

- Conflicts over petty issues give stark evidence of a lack of Christian faith.

- The simple gifts of life are to be enjoyed by all Christians.

- Poor moral decisions can lead to shipwrecked lives.

- In circumstances requiring courage the Christian can rely on the same power that gave Jesus the courage to maintain his faith.

- God's authority is greater than any authority on earth

- Wealth in itself can be used for good and charity.

- Dependence on wealth alone may result in missingthe eternal life that only God can give through Christ.

- The blessing of Scripture is for the entire church.

- Diligence and discipline are not options; they are requirements for maintenance of a Christian life.

2 TIMOTHY: 2 TIMOTHY 1

Introduction

Like the first letter to Timothy, the second letter is a personal letter from the older apostle to a younger colleague. The apostle Paul is imprisoned in Rome (1:8,

16; 2:9). Paul can see the end of the journey rapidly approaching (4:6-8). Therefore, he takes a final opportunity to write to the younger minister with instructions and helpful counsel. The tone of the letter is much more personal than the tone of the first letter.

The Ephesian church still wrestles with the problems created by false teachers. Unlike the first letter, the second letter does not spend as much time laying out the various levels of ministry and qualifications of individuals who would execute those responsibilities. Throughout the letter there is a great deal of concern for the highest possible Christian character.

We cannot determine exactly why the first letter to Timothy precedes the second. One clue may be that the first letter is 113 verses longer than the second, which consists of 83 verses. Another clue may be that the second letter contains a farewell scene beginning in 4:6.

Here is an outline of 2 Timothy 1:

I. Greeting (1:1-2)

II. Paul's Reflections (1:3-5)

III. An Appeal (1:6-18)

The Message of 2 Timothy 1

The Christian gospel that both the old apostle and the younger preacher are called to preach is sometimes a scorned and attacked gospel. In this chapter Timothy is summoned to a courageous witness that gives actual life to an ideal. However, the chapter is not mere exhortation to moral effort. Once again, God is characterized as life-giver and sustainer. The model life is possible only because God remains present with the person through the power of the Holy Spirit.

What else can we learn from this chapter?

- All Christians are indebted to others for their faith; we learn from our families; we inherit the tradition.

- Christians need to stir their gifts, lest they become cold and unused.

- The gospel may be potentially embarrassing; however, the gospel is one of power and therefore we should not be ashamed of it.

- God's intention for the creation has been in God's imagination from before time itself.

- Christ has defeated death and the fear of death.

- Trust and responsibility are both God's and ours.

- In times of crisis many may fail; few will sustain courageous moral life.

- We should never overlook the power of one life and the difference that one life can make.

2 TIMOTHY 2

Introduction to This Chapter

Chapter 2 consists of two sets of instructions. The first is a series of instructions regarding Timothy's own disciplines. The second set has to do with Timothy's responsibilities to teachers.

Here is an outline of this chapter:

I. Instructions to Timothy (2:1-13)

   A. Hand on teaching to others (2:1-2)

   B. Be ready for suffering; endure (2:3-7)

   C. Theological undergirding (2:8-10)

   D. A citation from a hymn (2:11-13)

II. Instructions Regarding the Teachers (2:14-26)

A. Beware of empty arguments (2:14)
B. Set a personal example (2:15-19)
C. Aim at central virtues (2:20-23)
D. Characteristics of the Lord's servant (2:24-26)

The Message of 2 Timothy 2

Little did Timothy realize at his ordination that he would someday be appointed to such a difficult church. Threatened by false teachers, he must contend with the apparent authority these false teachers have garnered for themselves. But in the conflict he must keep in mind that his style has as much influence as, if not more than, his doctrinal correctness.

What else can we learn from this chapter?

- The Christian life is a life of discipline and exclusive concentration.

- Embedded in the Christian gospel is suffering for the gospel.

- No matter what the circumstances, God's word cannot be chained or contained.

- God's nature is to remain faithful to God's promises, even through the failure of God's people.

- Against the apparent authority of challenges, God's authority through Christ will prevail.

- In the church we can expect all sorts of people—brighter lights, lesser lights, persons of noble calling, and others of humble gifts.

- Teachers and preachers and other church leaders must have an essential integrity in both method and content.

- People may be drawn to the gospel through our actions rather than our words.

2 TIMOTHY 3

Introduction to This Chapter

Chapter 3 continues the call to courageous living in a time when heretics will have increasing appeal. This section is closely related in thought to 1 Timothy 4:1-5. All of chapter 3 is placed in the context of the last days. The reflections in this chapter are an analysis of the stress that Paul actually sees in the Ephesian church. The current stresses with which Timothy must contend, then, are actual occurrences of what had been predicted in earlier Christian writings.

Here is an outline of this chapter:
I. Toward an Uncertain Future (3:1-9)
   A. Times will get more difficult (3:1)
   B. Even Christians will waver (3:2-5)
   C. False teachers will have their day (3:6-9)
II. Remain Loyal to the Faith (3:10-17)
   A. Timothy has a guide (3:10-14)
   B. Timothy has Scripture (3:15-17)

The Message of 2 Timothy 3

Chapter 3 presents to the younger minister, in no uncertain terms, the environment in which he will be carrying out his ministry. Neither Timothy nor anyone else in the congregation should expect to give witness to the work of God through Christ without evoking an angry response. Paul summons the preacher to examine the hard facts of personal knowledge and experience that are supported by the tradition of the Scriptures.

What can we learn from this chapter?

- The ways people act are symptoms of their separation from God.

- Self-centered people will inevitably exhibit antisocial behavior.

- Lonely and trapped people are prime subjects not only for Christian missionary activity but also for evil intent.

- There is no authority with quite the same power as personal authority based on experience and hard-won moral victories.

- Though evil has its hour, the purposes of God will eventually carry the day.

- The Scriptures are inspired by God.

- The Bible points toward salvation through Christ.

- The Bible gives a firm foundation to the spiritual lives of struggling people.

- The study of Scripture equips us for the tasks of ministry in a sometimes hostile environment that will resent any good, or creative, or higher motive.

2 TIMOTHY 4

Introduction to This Chapter

An overview of the entire letter indicates that either Timothy has given ample reason for Paul to be concerned, or Paul has inferred from correspondence or other communication that the younger preacher is on the verge of conceding defeat to the stresses that abound in the Ephesian church. Earlier Timothy had been urged to "rekindle the gift" (NRSV) or "fan into flame" (NIV) and "not be ashamed" of the gospel (1:6, 8, 13); to "be

strong in the grace" of Christ (2:1-3, 8, 15); and to continue what he had seen and learned from firsthand experience (3:14). In this final chapter, Paul renews the theme that has been developed earlier in his final appeal to Timothy to preach the gospel.

Here is an outline of 2 Timothy 4:

I. A Final Appeal to Preach the Gospel (4:1-2)
II. Healthy and Unhealthy Religion (4:3-5)
III. An Approaching End (4:6-8)
IV. Personal Words (4:9-18)
V. Closing Salutations (4:19-21)
VI. A Benediction (4:22)

The Message of 2 Timothy 4

In this chapter we have heard the intensely personal voice of Paul giving witness to the strength that he has received from God when all those around him had either failed or been unavailable for support. The letter therefore concludes with incontrovertible evidence of the sufficiency of God for Timothy and the entire church.

What else can we learn from this chapter?

- A disciple of Jesus Christ cannot wait for the public to ask for the gospel; there is an urgency to the gospel that cares not a bit about the desires of people.

- In every age there will be people who want a teacher or preacher who says what is comfortable and/or novel.

- The Christian preacher and teacher knows of the eternal truth of God and will therefore not be swayed by temporary whims and fads in thinking.

- Christians have an eternal hope, hope of the kingdom of God.

- God's strength will be sufficient for every need.

TITUS

OUTLINE OF TITUS

I. Greeting (1:1-4)

II. Commands to Titus (1:5-16)
A. Regarding ministry and church officials (1:5-9)
B. A word about opponents (1:10-16)

III. Instructions Concerning Relationships (2:1-15)
A. Dealing with older men (2:1-2)
B. Dealing with older women (2:3-5)
C. Dealing with younger men (2:6-8)
D. Dealing with slaves (2:9-10)
E. What God expects from all Christians (2:11-15)

IV. Living in Society (3:1-15)
A. Responsibility to civil authorities (3:1-2)
B. Reasons/motives for responsibilities (3:3-7)
C. Another "the saying is sure" (3:8)
D. What to avoid (3:9-11)
E. Final personal words and a blessing (3:12-15)

TITUS 1

Introduction to This Chapter

Unlike Timothy, Titus is not mentioned in the book of Acts at all. He is mentioned frequently in Paul's second letter to the Corinthians and Galatians. A Gentile (see Galatians 2:3), he became one of Paul's fellow workers. After his conversion, Paul went to Jerusalem accompanied by Barnabas and Titus (Galatians 2:1-10). When Paul heard of the Corinthian church's refusal to heed his authority, Paul sent Titus to ascertain the condition of the church. Paul would follow later by a prescribed route.

However, Titus was not at the appointed meeting place, Troas (2 Corinthians 2:13). They did meet later in Macedonia (2 Corinthians 7:6). The report Titus brought encouraged Paul, as the hostility that had been reported was no longer apparent. Indeed, the church seemed prepared to heed his authority once again (2 Corinthians 7:9, 13-14). Paul sent Titus back to Corinth to continue the work that had started so auspiciously earlier (2 Corinthians 8:6). The congregation's response to Titus would give evidence of their true Christian character and grace, especially through the contribution that was being collected for the saints in Jerusalem.

Paul had been in Crete on a missionary journey and is now elsewhere (Titus 1:5). Accurate dating of the letter is very difficult. Christian congregations are assumed to be in existence on Crete, since Paul refers to entire families (1:11). In fact, there seem to be many churches in many different cities on the island. Titus's responsibility is to complete the task of organizing these new congregations.

The letter's purpose is similar to the purpose of the letters to Timothy, to elevate the quality of character to Christian standards. We have seen in other epistles the emphasis on the character of teachers and their teaching. In Titus the emphasis is on the character of the people being taught. By any measure, Crete is a difficult situation. Titus would have to compete with a tradition of competition between cities on the island, the fact that the island had been a center for piracy in the Mediterranean, and had been subdued by the Romans, much to the Cretans' dislike. Only since 67 B.C. had the area been a Roman province.

Here is an outline of Titus 1:

I. Greeting (1:1-4)
II. Commands to Titus (1:5-16)
    A. Regarding ministry and church officials (1:5-9)
    B. A word about opponents (1:10-16)

The Message of Titus 1

Titus has been left in an inhospitable place to do a very difficult task. He is to appoint elders who themselves need to aspire to the highest Christian goals and motives, who will assist in correcting the deplorable moral and spiritual conditions in Crete. Against Titus's efforts will be arrayed an intimidating collection of people who consider themselves intellectually and spiritually superior to the paltry efforts of the Christian minister.

However, Paul refuses to allow the circumstances to defeat the Christian missionary enterprise. Instead, Paul takes the circumstances as part of the definition of what the minister's work is.

What else can we learn from this chapter?

- The motive for excellent moral and spiritual character is eternal life.

- Leaders in the church lead by moral example as well as by doctrinal teaching and pulpit eloquence.

- Consciences can become incapable of discerning right from wrong; good from bad; healthy from unhealthy religion.

- Our actions speak at least as loudly as our words.

TITUS 2

Introduction to This Chapter

Set in the context of how the preacher should deal with various elements in the congregation—men, women, and slaves—three themes are developed in Titus 2. The chapter is a recapitulation of and an enlargement upon the directives given in Titus 1. The importance of the family is again emphasized. Throughout the chapter Paul shows the relationship between God's intention and human actions or motives.

One of Paul's recurrent themes is the family (see Ephesians 5:22–6:9; Colossians 3:18–4:1). The family has already been discussed in the Pastorals, especially in 1 Timothy 5:1–6:2. Concern for the family and groups within the church is also expressed in 1 Peter 2:18–3:7, which emphasizes the same theme through an address to slaves (verse 18), wives, and husbands (3:1, 7).

The Greek term translated as "so that" (in the Greek language) occurs six times in this single chapter (verses 4, 5, 8, 10, 12, 14). In each instance the linkage is between God's purpose and human action or attitude. The usage is not apparent in the English translations. Therefore, for the purposes of illustration, a verse-by-verse treatment follows:

Verse 4 ("so that they may encourage" [NRSV] or "then they can train" [NIV]), linking God's intention that the generations can cooperate.

Verse 5 ("so that the word of God may

not be discredited" [NRSV] or "so that no one will malign the word of God" [NIV]), linking God's intention with the younger generation's attitude and action.

Verse 8 (so that the opponents can be shamed), linking God's purpose with the preacher's action.

Verse 10 (so that the teaching of the Savior might adorn all), even teaching by slaves!

Verse 12 (so that we might live), linking incarnation with how we live.

Verse 14 (so that we might live free from the power of death), linking God's promise with human moral effort.

Here is an outline of chapter 2:

I. Dealing with Older Men (2:1-2)
II. Dealing with Older Women (2:3-5)
III. Dealing with Younger Men (2:6-8)
IV. Dealing with Slaves (2:9-10)
V. What God Expects from All Christians (2:11-15)

The Message of Titus 2

The earliest Christian hope had little to do with transforming society or correcting social deficiencies. Instead, the Christian movement concentrated its energies on the identity of individuals as people of worth in the sight of God and people for whom Jesus of Nazareth gave his life. Somewhat disturbing to modern readers is the fact that the Pastoral Letters refuse to tackle the larger moral issues of social injustice to which much contemporary Christian energy is directed. What we often overlook, however, is the incredible power that the earliest Christians attributed to their exemplary behavior and attitude.

What else can we learn from this chapter?

- The older members of the community need to be the wise ones with temperate judgment and insight.

- Older members of any community have an educational responsibility to the younger members.

- In all of our behavior we should be careful not to discredit the name of God.

- We should examine currently popular morality or behavior to see if it corresponds to what has been found fundamentally sound over the course of years.

- All members of the community have a high moral obligation.

- Our behavior embodies and adorns our theological formulations.

- God's intention is always to save.

- Christians live life in the context of eternity and the hope of a returning Christ.

TITUS 3

Introduction to This Chapter

Recall that the letter to Titus begins with concerns about the internal organization of the Christian church on Crete. In chapter 3 the transition has been made between internal organization and external ethical behavior required of Christians in society. In this chapter Titus learns of the relationships, ethical principles, and the motives all Christians should understand in order to be the people of God in the midst of society. Paul addressed similar issues in Romans 13. All of chapter 3 is similar to Romans 12:17–13:7, in that it emphasizes both respecting authority and the Christian duty to be useful citizens.

Here is an outline of chapter 3:

I. Responsibility to Civil Authorities (3:1-2)

II. Reasons/Motives for Responsibilities
(3:3-7)
III. Another "The Saying Is Sure" (3:8)
IV. What to Avoid (3:9-11)
V. Final Personal Words and a Blessing
(3:12-15)

The Message of Titus 3

The letter to Titus begins with instructions to a single preacher and ends with greetings to the entire church. The transition from an individual preacher to the formation and regular gathering of a Christian community is precisely what Titus must make. The transition that will be accomplished is the movement from doctrine to new ethical orientations and a new manner of life. We will be closer to the dynamic life of this letter if we can see not only Titus but also the congregation purposely working to link their thinking with their doing, their theology with their actions in society.

What else can we learn from this chapter?

• The Christian faith is one not only of high spiritual character, but one of humble obedience as well.

• Christians can be compassionate because they can recall a time when they were as bad as the worst they see in society.

• God's gracious work on our behalf is due to God's grace and initiative, not our merit. Even our repentance is not sufficient to merit God's grace.

• Through Christ we become sons and daughters of God and can share in, as well as anticipate, eternal life.

• Christians must be certain that whatever they expect of others, they themselves do.

PHILEMON

OUTLINE OF PHILEMON

I. Introductory Opening (verses 1-3)

II. Thanksgiving (verses 4-7)

III. Paul's Remarkable Request
(verses 8-20)

IV. Final Instructions (verses 21-22)

V. Closing Salutations (verses 23-25)

INTRODUCTION

The letter to Philemon is, like the Pastoral Epistles, a personal letter written by Paul. The immediate reason for the letter is that an escaped slave, Onesimus, is now a trusted helper for the imprisoned apostle. Paul writes to the slave's owner, Philemon, with a remarkable request. Paul wants Philemon not only to refrain from punishing the escaped slave but also to receive him back graciously. At least one interpreter suggests that Paul implies even more than this. According to this interpretation, Paul desires Philemon to release Onesimus from slavery altogether so that Onesimus can stay with Paul as his trusted assistant during the very trying period of Paul's own imprisonment. Most interpreters do not subscribe to such a radical interpretation. Paul writes the letter while in prison (verse 1), probably the period of house

arrest in Rome sometime during the years A.D. 61–63. His other letters are addressed to churches (Romans 1:7; 1 Corinthians 1:2; 2 Corinthians 1:1; Galatians 1:2; Ephesians 1:1; Philippians 1:1; Colossians 1:2; 1 Thessalonians 1:1; 2 Thessalonians 1:1). We have already seen how the Pastoral Epistles, which were written ostensibly to individuals, were also intended for a wider reading.

Paul appropriates from the predominant culture the form of correspondence in common usage at that time. The standard form included: (1) opening: including the sender's name, the recipient's name, a greeting, (2) thanksgiving or blessing, very often with prayers of intercession; (3) body: the actual content/reason for the writing, frequently including future plans; (4) paraenesis (instructions/requests); (5) closing: usually standard forms of benedictions and greetings.

The structure of Philemon is as follows:

I. Opening (verses 1-3): sender, "Paul"; recipient, "Philemon, our dear friend"; greeting, "grace to you and peace from God our Father and the Lord Jesus Christ";

II. Thanksgiving (verses 4-7): "When I remember you in my prayers, I always thank my God . . . I pray that the sharing of your faith become effective when you perceive all the good that we may do for Christ";

III. Body (verses 8-20): "I am appealing to you for my child, Onesimus";

IV. Paraenesis—final instructions (verses 7-22): "welcome him . . . charge that to my account . . . Refresh my heart in Christ . . . prepare a guest room for me";

V. Closing (verses 23-25): greetings, closing benediction.

Modern readers will at once be struck by Paul's seeming lack of concern for the reprehensible but then socially acceptable standard of slavery. Why doesn't the apostle address the issue agressively? The institution of slavery had long since become a major part of the Roman Empire's culture. In fact, slavery had become a predominant means of labor. Roman practice included slaves in nearly every aspect of labor, from the most menial tasks to the higher responsibilities. Wealthy people would often have a large number of slaves that would care for every detail of business and family life. Slaves were frequently managers, accountants, artists, painters, architects, librarians, even doctors. Slavery was intertwined with every aspect of culture. In short, slavery was a fact of life as readily accepted as Roman rule itself. It appears almost incredible to the modern reader, but Paul sees the social and cultural institution as a given, and as such an appropriate place in which the Christian gospel should be lived out (1 Corinthians 7:21-24). To the slaves in Ephesus he charges, "Slaves, obey your earthly masters . . . but like slaves of Christ, doing the will of God from your heart" (Ephesians 6:5-6 NIV).

Paul himself refuses to see slaves as anything but people. They are certainly not mere property (Philemon 10). Granted, slaves still have certain responsibilities to their masters, but by the same token Christian masters also have responsibilities toward their slaves (Ephesians 6:9; Colossians 4:1). In Paul's thinking, the distinction between slave and free man or woman—so strongly marked in Roman society—has begun to fade (1 Corinthians 12:13). To the Galatians Paul asserts, "There is neither Jew nor Greek, slave nor free, male nor female, for you are all one in Christ Jesus" (Galatians 3:28 NIV).

Paul's extraordinary request depends not only upon Philemon's own Christian convictions but also upon the relationship that the two men have. Paul himself characterizes the relationship in warm terms: "fellow worker" (NIV) or "co-worker" (NRSV) (verse 1), "your partner" (verse 17), and in his final instructions requests a guest room to be readied (verse 22). This closeness comes as no surprise, since Philemon had been converted to Christianity through Paul's ministry in Ephesus.

The Message of Philemon

In this extraordinary personal letter, Paul makes an enormous request. He asks Philemon to forgo every societal and legal precedent on behalf of an escaped slave. Paul dares appeal to the highest motive and the deepest commitments in a man who himself has been converted to Christ through Paul's ministry. Paramount in this letter is Paul's trust in the power of agape love, God's love, to dictate to an individual's conscience. What else can we learn from this letter?

- We are not Christian in isolation; we are Christian in community with others.

- Knit together in Christ, each of us is of equal worth before God and in the church.

- The Christian thanks God through constant prayer for other Christians.

- The good that is done by others gives us great joy and comfort.

- Love cannot be coerced; love can only be evoked by the realization that God, whom we know best in Christ Jesus, loves our brothers and sisters as much as God loves us.

- The church depends upon the grace of Christ for its life.

HEBREWS

OUTLINE OF HEBREWS

I. God Speaks Through Christ (1:1–3:6)
  A. God's nature is in the Son (1:1-14)
    1. God speaks to us through a Son (1:1-2)
    2. The Son's nature reflects God (1:3-4)
    3. The Son is superior to angels (1:5-7)
    4. God anointed the Son above all (1:8-9)
    5. The Son is before and beyond creation (1:10-12)
    6. The Son sits at God's right hand (1:13-14)
  B. Jesus made salvation possible (2:1–3:6)
    1. We dare not neglect salvation (2:1-2)
    2. Salvation was made known to us (2:3-4)
    3. The Lord suffered and died for us (2:5-9)
    4. Jesus identified with us (2:10-11)
    5. Jesus witnessed to us (2:12-13)
    6. Jesus' incarnation saves us (2:14-18)
    7. Consider the faithfulness of Jesus (3:1-2)
    8. Jesus is superior to Moses (3:2-6)

II. God Offers Access Through Christ (3:7–5:10)
  A. Do not reject Christ (3:7–4:13)

    1. Israel spoiled its chance (3:7-11)
    2. Let us not spoil our chance (3:12-15)
    3. The people missed God's rest (3:16-19)
    4. God's rest is still available (4:1-2)
    5. God's eternal sabbath rest (4:3-5)
    6. The opportunity remains (4:6-7)
    7. God's rest is greater (4:8-10)
    8. Strive to enter God's rest (4:11)
    9. The Word of God knows us (4:12-13)
  B. Jesus is the perfect high priest (4:14–5:10)
    1. In faith draw near to God (4:14-16)
    2. High priests are appointed (5:1-4)
    3. God appointed Christ high priest (5:5-6)
    4. Jesus is our perfect high priest (5:7-10)

III. Grow Up in Faith and Press On (5:11–6:20)
  A. Grow up in your faith (5:11–6:8)
    1. You should be mature (5:11-14)
    2. Let us go on to maturity (6:1-3)
    3. You cannot begin again (6:4-6)
    4. Land produces good crops or weeds (6:7-8)

B. Be confident in God's promise
(6:9-20)
1. You have done well (6:9-10)
2. Imitate people of faith
(6:11-12)
3. God's promise to Abraham
was sure (6:13-15)
4. God's purpose is doubly sure
(6:16-18)
5. We can be confident (6:18-20)

IV. **Christ Is High Priest for Our
Salvation (7:1–10:39)**
A. Christ is supreme (7:1-28)
1. Who is Melchizedek? (7:1-3)
2. Melchizedek superior to old
priesthood (7:4-10)
3. The Levite priests were
inadequate (7:11-12)
4. There is a better order of
priesthood (7:13-17)
5. A greater hope supersedes the
law (7:18-19)
6. Christ is priest of a better
covenant (7:20-22)
7. Christ is our eternal high priest
(7:23-25)
8. Christ's sacrifice is permanent
(7:26-28)
B. A new covenant (8:1–9:14)
1. High priest in the true
sanctuary (8:1-2)
2. Jesus is not in an earthly
sanctuary (8:3-5)
3. High priest of a better
covenant (8:6-13)
4. The first covenant had earthly
rules (9:1-5)
5. Rituals of the earthly sanctuary
(9:6-10)
6. Jesus, the one effective
sacrifice (9:11-14)
C. Christ's sacrifice purifies us
(9:15–10:18)
1. The new covenant becomes
effective (9:15-17)

2. Old covenant sealed by blood
sacrifice (9:18-22)
3. Christ mediates the new
covenant (9:23-26)
4. Jesus receives those who
repent (9:27-28)
5. Old sacrifices were repeated
(10:1-4)
6. Christ replaced the old
sacrifices (10:5-10)
7. Christ has purified his people
(10:11-14)
8. The new covenant of God's
grace (10:15-18)
D. Persevere in Christ (10:19-39)
1. Jesus has opened the way to
God (10:19-21)
2. Let us draw near with faith
(10:22-23)
3. Let us encourage one another
(10:24-25)
4. Do not spurn Christ's sacrifice
(10:26-31)
5. Recall faith experiences
(10:32-34)
6. Persevere with confidence
(10:35-39)

V. **Live the Life of Faith (11:1–12:29)**
A. Imitate examples of faith
(11:1-40)
1. Faith is confidence in the
expected (11:1-3)
2. By faith Abel and Enoch
pleased God (11:4-6)
3. Noah: heir of righteousness
(11:7)
4. Abraham went out in faith
(11:8-10)
5. Sarah trusted God's promise
(11:11-12)
6. Confidence in things hoped for
(11:13-16)
7. Abraham and Isaac (11:17-19)
8. Isaac, Jacob, and Joseph
trusted God (11:20-22)

9. Moses lived by faith (11:23-28)
10. Israel came to Canaan by faith (11:29-31)
11. Strong leaders and prophets (11:32-34)
12. Faith in times of suffering (11:35-38)
13. Faith in God's promise (11:39-40)
B. Persevere through hardship (12:1-17)
  1. Follow Jesus in faith (12:1-2)
  2. Persevere through suffering (12:3-6)
  3. Discipline leads to righteousness (12:7-11)
  4. Therefore, be strong (12:12 13)
  5. Live in peace and goodness (12:14-17)
C. Come to the joyful city of God (12:18-29)
  1. Yours is not a religion of fear (12:18-21)
  2. Come to the joyful city of God (12:22-24)
  3. Do not refuse God, who calls you (12:25-27)
  4. Worship God with thankfulness (12:28-29)

VI. In Conclusion (13:1-25)
A. Be faithful fellow Christians (13:1-17)
B. Closing of the letter (13:18-21)
C. Postscript (13:22-25)

INTRODUCTION

Hebrews is unique in the New Testament. It has the richest vocabulary, the most eloquent Greek, yet the style of the Jewish rabbis. It quotes the Old Testament most frequently and at greatest length. It has the severest warning and the warmest encouragement for Christians to be faithful.

Hebrews is about Jesus Christ, who he is and what he has done. It is a message of hope, a promise of eternal fellowship with God, conditioned only on our response. It is about God's awesome greatness, perfect righteousness, and grace and love inviting us to respond. Hebrews is a book of action, of persevering movement toward God, into God's presence.

Authorship

Who wrote the letter? We do not know. Shortly after it was written, no one knew. People guessed. We are still guessing.

Some have guessed that Paul wrote the letter. Saying Paul wrote it helped to get Hebrews accepted when Christians were deciding what to include in the New Testament. It was not written by Paul, however. The style, vocabulary, and emphases are not Paul's. Others have guessed it was Barnabas because he encouraged people (Acts 4:36) as Hebrews does. Some have guessed Priscilla because she and her husband, Aquila, instructed a man named Apollos in the gospel (Acts 18:26). Many have guessed Apollos himself, an eloquent man, well versed in Scripture (Acts 18:24) and a leading preacher (1 Corinthians 1:12).

Proof of authorship is not needed to appreciate the value of what has been written. Whoever wrote the letter to the Hebrews was gifted in speech, as well as in vocabulary and style. This anonymous writer knew his contemporary culture and literature. He knew how Jewish rabbis taught. Greek was the universal language of the time, and he knew how Greek authors wrote. From Jewish Scriptures (the Old Testament) he drew symbols and illustrations to press home a message of warning and encouragement for the Christians of his day.

The Audience

To whom was the message sent? Where did they live? We do not know. Again, there have been many guesses such as somewhere in Italy, in Judea, in Egypt. Someone added on the title "To the Hebrews" because the author refers extensively to Hebrew stories and worship in the Old Testament.

All Christians, however, whether of Jewish or pagan background, were accustomed to "search the Scriptures," that is, the Old Testament, to read what it said about the Messiah, Christ. All we know is that the letter was addressed to Christians who needed encouragement. It tells us that they were at one time new and joyful Christians. They have had troubles, however, maybe ridicule or persecution that has disheartened them. They have become lax in the practice of their faith.

Date

When was Hebrews written? A Christian in about A.D. 90 wrote a letter from Rome in which he quoted from Hebrews. About the same time it was being quoted in Alexandria, Egypt. So we know it was written by A.D. 90. How long before? We do not know, except that Timothy, evidently the Apostle Paul's young friend, was still active (13:23). Some scholars argue for the earlier date, that a likely date for the writing of Hebrews is around A.D. 65.

Literary Style

Was Hebrews a letter? We do not know even that. It begins with no greetings, no address, and has no signature. The last chapter reads like the closing of a letter from a Christian leader with words of counsel, a benediction, a postscript with news about coming with Timothy, and with the phrase "Grace be with you all" (13:25 NIV).

The previous parts (twelve chapters in our Bible) read like a lecture or sermon. Was it a sermon—or several short sermons—that someone sent to a group of Christians, attaching a personal note? Was it a tract? In this commentary, it will frequently be referred to as a sermon.

One thing we do know: Hebrews is a masterpiece, a beautiful and intense expression of faith and hope applicable to all Christians.

The Message of Hebrews

There is a triple theme in Hebrews: (1) movement from the inadequate to the adequate, from the imperfect to the perfect, to God; (2) Christ, who alone is supremely sufficient to make that movement possible; and (3) warning and encouragement to persevere in that Christ-enabled movement.

The logic of Hebrews seems to follow this pattern: (1) The assumption is that the business of life, and the desire of all people, is access to God. Everlasting separation from God is the ultimate tragedy. (2) The problem is that sin and indifferent neglect of faith prevent fellowship with God. (3) The need is to break through sin's wall of separation. (4) The solution is Christ. Through Christ we can be forgiven. Through Christ we gain access to God. (5) The responsibility is ours to accept forgiveness, and to move toward communion with God through faithfulness to Christ, who opens the way.

Hebrews is a warning against the neglect of what God has offered in Christ. Rejecting Christ means rejecting God, God's Word, God's spirit, God's grace. It is a warning against drifting off into the inadequacies of pre-Christian Judaism, or into exotic cults or into immorality, or into mere indifference and neglect. But Hebrews is also an encouragement to endure suffering, to persevere in faithfulness to Christ. It is an assurance that God's promise is unfailing, and that Christ is the supreme and only adequate means of our inheriting that promise. That promise is salvation, purification, perfection, "rest" in God's presence forever. The warnings and encouragement interweave with illustrations and arguments that point out Christ's superiority as God's one appointed means of salvation.

Hebrews calls Christ our high priest because, like a priest, he offers a sacrifice on behalf of people. Hebrews uses a story from Genesis (14:17-20) to illustrate Christ's high priesthood. Melchizedek was a priest-king who blessed Abraham, ancestor of the Israelites. Melchizedek was not an Israelite. The story mentions no lineage, birth, or death of Melchizedek. Christ, says Hebrews, is like that (6:20). Using contrast, Hebrews points out the superiority of Christ as the only effective priest for our salvation (7:11, 16, 22; 9:13-14, 23).

The Old Testament in Hebrews

When people became Christians, they inherited the Jewish faith based on the Jewish interpretation of the Old Testament at the time of Jesus. Christians studied the Old Testament and knew it well. The Hebrews sermon shows how Jesus fulfilled the religious hope and faith of the Old Testament. Here are the main elements of Jewish biblical faith emphasized in Hebrews: (1) Stories of the Jews' ancestors are about people of faith in God's righteousness. (2) God called Abraham and promised him and his descendants a great posterity (Genesis 12:1–50). (3) Abraham was met and blessed by Melchizedek, a king-priest (Genesis 14:17-20). (4) Abraham's descendants, the people of Israel, traveled through the Sinai desert country as refugees from Egypt seeking a better country. Led by Moses, they were assured of God's guidance and help.

Nevertheless, they complained (Exodus 15:22-25; 17:1-7; Numbers 14:1; Psalm 95:7-11). (5) God made a covenant with the people of Israel, promising to bring them to a land of rest, and giving them a law to live by. The people promised to obey the law. Moses, their leader, confirmed the covenant by sacrificing oxen and sprinkling the blood on the people (Exodus 24:7-8). (6) Moses constructed a tent of meeting on the pattern God gave him (Exodus 25:8-9; 40:1-11, 16-33). (7) Aaron, brother of Moses, was appointed high priest of the sanctuary. Their tribe, the Levites, was set aside to assist the priests, Aaron's descendants, who conducted religious ceremonies as representatives of the people before God (Exodus 40:12-15). (8) The ceremonies of worship at the tent of meeting included sacrifices of animals, ritually killed. Their blood, the essence of the sacrificed life, was sprinkled as a symbolic cleansing. (9) The most important ceremony took place once a year on the Day of Atonement. On this day only, the high priest entered the Most Holy Place of the tent of meeting carrying the blood of the sacrificed animals, which he sprinkled on the mercy seat (the cover of the box called the ark of the covenant). The mercy seat represented God's presence. The high priest stood before God as a mediator asking God to forgive the people their sins. By this ritual, the sins God's people had committed during the year were said to be forgiven so that their covenant with God might continue (Leviticus 16:1). This ceremony had to be repeated each year. It was preceded by a sin offering to cover the sins of the high priest before he could enter the Most Holy Place. Sin offerings were also made for the sins of the priests. (10) After the death of Moses, Joshua led the people of Israel into Canaan, the promised land of rest (Joshua 1:1-4).

(11) Much later, when the Jewish nation was conquered and many were taken into exile, there developed the hope for a great "Day of the Lord." It would be at the end of time when God would destroy Israel's enemies. The people of earth would unite in worship of God, and righteousness would prevail in the earth.

HEBREWS 1

Introduction to This Chapter

God speaks to us through a Son. The message of Hebrews begins with this fundamental declaration: Through a son God has made the final revelation, completing all the partial revelations of the past. The author quotes Scripture to assure his readers about the ultimate and supreme significance of the Son through whom God discloses the divine mind and purpose.

Here is an outline of chapter 1:

I. God Speaks to Us Through a Son (1:1-2)
II. The Son's Nature Reflects God (1:3-4)
III. The Son Is Superior to Angels (1:5-7)
IV. God Anointed the Son Above All (1:8-9)
V. The Son Is Before and Beyond Creation (1:10-12)
VI. The Son Sits at God's Right Hand (1:13-14)

The Message of Hebrews 1

God's revelation has come in many ways, but the fullest revelation comes through Christ.

The Christian faith is Christ. It is not a system of belief woven about Christ, but Christ himself. In order to warn and encourage Christians concerning their faith in and faithfulness to Christ, the letter to the Hebrews makes clear who and what Christ is, what he has done, does, and will do, and why he is so very important.

To begin with, Christ is, in relation to God, a Son. "Son" implies a priority in relationship, a pre-eminence that can be superseded by no one and by no thing. The Son reflects God and shares God's word of power. Christ is also related to us, as God's message to us for our redemption.

Chapter 1 of Hebrews tells us about the Son:

• He was appointed and anointed by God.

• He was God's instrument in creating the universe.

• He made it possible for us to be purified from sin and that, having done so, he remains in the presence of God.

• As Creator he is superior to all created things; and, although all things decay, he endures forever.

Chapter 1 of Hebrews is like a doorway from the old to the new, from former times when people had only glimpses of God to a full awareness of what God is and what God does and has for us. This chapter prepares us to understand the full message of Hebrews:

• The goal of history is about to be realized.

• The promises of God are about to be fulfilled.

• The purpose of life is about to be consummated in the experience of salvation.

• And all this is made possible through Jesus Christ for those who are faithful to him.

HEBREWS 2:1–3:6

Introduction to These Verses

Having stressed the significance of the Son as the medium of salvation, Hebrews warns readers against neglecting that salvation. It is a grand offer, attested by God. The sermon then explains how Jesus, the glorified Son, identified with and suffered for people in order to free them from sin.

In order to encourage Christian faithfulness, the writer to the Hebrews has affirmed the superiority of Jesus, the Son, over angels. He was given charge of the universe and appointed by God to be high priest, representing the people. Through his incarnation and suffering death, Jesus has atoned for the sins of the people.

Nevertheless, there were many who were inclined to give greater attention to Moses, to whom God gave the holy law and covenant, and to Joshua, the hero, who led God's people into the Promised Land. Therefore, the writer sets out to explain how Jesus goes further than the law and brings people to a truer goal, and is, therefore, much greater than Moses and Joshua. It is through Jesus only, Hebrews says, that people can arrive at the place of rest God intended for them.

Here is an outline of Hebrews 2:1–3:6:

I. We Dare Not Neglect Salvation (2:1-2)

II. Salvation Was Made Known to Us (2:3-4)

III. The Lord Suffered and Died for Us (2:5-9)

IV. Jesus Identified with Us (2:10-11)

V. Jesus Witnessed to Us (2:12-13)

VI. Jesus' Incarnation Saves Us (2:14-18)

VII. Consider the Faithfulness of Jesus (3:1-2)

VIII. Jesus Is Superior to Moses (3:3-6)

The Message of Hebrews 2:1–3:6

This is the heart of the message in Hebrews: God wants to draw us away from our destructive sin. God's offer of salvation is the most serious and urgent opportunity we will ever have. To miss it, to let our lives drift along without accepting it, is the worst tragedy that could happen to us.

The offer of salvation is to wipe away the sins that destroy us and separate us from God. The offer is clear in what Jesus proclaimed through what he was and what he did in his incarnation. He became one with humanity, suffering the common human experiences, even of temptation. In so doing, in sympathy with our human need for God, through his death he broke the barrier our sins had built up between us and God. We have the record of this from the people who knew Jesus personally. In many ways God has continued to verify what Jesus presented to us, especially by the gifts of the Holy Spirit, who carries on God's purpose among us. We can receive this salvation by trusting Jesus Christ, who is uniquely close to God, because he carried through what God appointed him to do.

Moses was a great religious leader, faithful in God's house. Christ, however, is superior to Moses, faithful to God over his house. We can be thankful for all religious leaders who are faithful to God, but as Christ is superior to all, it is to him we must be faithful. Moses foreshadowed what was to come in God's word. But Christ is the perfect word of God to us.

We Christians are God's house. We are God's people. We are, that is, if we hold firmly to our faith.

HEBREWS 3:7–4:13

Introduction to These Verses

The author explains the promise and warning to be found in the story of Israel's faithlessness in the desert (Exodus 15:23-25; 17:2-7; Psalm 95:8-11). The promise is of a goal, a place of arrival God has prepared for the people, called by Hebrews a "rest." The entire argument goes like this:

Those to whom the promise was first made lost it through disobedience.

God's true rest is the eternal sabbath rest.

God's word can discern our real intentions.

Here is an outline of Hebrews 3:7–4:13.
I. Israel Spoiled Its Chance (3:7-11)
II. Let Us Not Spoil Our Chance (3:12-15)
III. The People Missed God's Rest (3:16-19)
IV. God's Rest Is Still Available (4:1-2)
V. God's Eternal Sabbath Rest (4:3-5)
VI. The Opportunity Remains (4:6-7)
VII. God's Rest Is Greater (4:8-10)
VIII. Strive to Enter God's Rest (4:11)
IX. The Word of God Knows Us (4:12-13)

The Message of Hebrews 3:7–4:13

We need to remember what happened to the Israelites when they traveled to the Promised Land of Canaan. Miraculously God had liberated them from slavery, guided them, protected them, and provided for them.

- Nevertheless, when facing difficulties—lack of drinkable water in a desert oasis, the dangers of entering a new land—they did not stop to consider all that God had done and could do for them. They complained, rebelled, were disobedient, and sinned against God.

- Then God knew they were unworthy to enter the rest that was planned for them. They died in the desert.

The same thing, figuratively, could happen to us.

- Through Christ we have been freed from sin, and drawn together and to God.

- If, however, we become careless about our faith, losing the confidence we had when we first believed, we can be deceived by sin and we can drift away from God.

- Then, like the Israelites in the desert, we may never experience the eternal rest God has planned for us.

In Genesis we read that God rested on the seventh day after having created the world. This sabbath rest of God is from the beginning and lasts forever. It is part of God's plan. God not only created the universe, but also set up a goal for the creation. That goal is reached in the ultimate, eternal communion with God's chosen people. Work was not to be an end in itself, but a creative movement toward the rest shared by God with the people. Those first chosen failed to reach it because of disobedience. Nevertheless, God has opened up the possibility of this rest to all who will be faithful. That rest, God's rest, remains for us to enter.

HEBREWS 4:14–5:10

Introduction to These Verses

The admonition in 3:7–4:13 concluded with an urging to enter God's rest. That entry, drawing near to God, is made possible by Jesus' high priestly act. This passage explains how Jesus became our great high priest. The high priest in Israel's sanctuary served as mediator for the people's sins as well as for his own sins before God. High priests were appointed for their task. Jesus was appointed by God, and became the perfect high priest to mediate our sins. He became high priest by humbling himself and suffering in obedience to God. He became like us, except that he did not sin. Hebrews explains this to encourage faithfulness and obedience to Christ as a sure way to draw near to God to receive God's grace and mercy.

Here is an outline of Hebrews 4:14–5:10:

I. In Faith Draw Near to God (4:14-16)
II. High Priests Are Appointed (5:1-4)
III. God Appointed Christ High Priest (5:5-6)
IV. Jesus Is Our Perfect High Priest (5:7-10)

The Message of Hebrews 4:14–5:10

We can have confidence that Christ, as a high priest for us in God's presence, helps us in our spiritual lives because:

- He was appointed by God to relate us to God;

- He was obedient to God, although this meant that he suffered agony in his human incarnation;

- He shared the weakness of human limitations;

- He was tempted, but he passed through this incarnation experience perfectly, and was raised into God's presence;

- He is a perfect high priest, who intercedes for us, because he understands our human problems, so he can relate us to God;

- He will always be our source for eternal salvation. However, we, who are weak, tempted, and lack knowledge, must:

- Hold fast to the faith we have;

- Let it dominate our lives as we keep on drawing closer to God every day;

- Expose our needs to God;

- Accept God's forgiving grace and mercy for daily living;

- Let Christ be the source of our ongoing faith;

- Daily obey what we learn through Jesus Christ.

HEBREWS 5:11–6:8

Introduction to These Verses

The writer of Hebrews pauses abruptly, like a speaker who has lost the listeners' attention, and stops to chide them for their dullness. They may be too immature to understand the message. What is worse, they are immature in their Christianity.

This is the third, and sternest, warning of the sermon. It begins with a scolding. They have been Christians long enough. But there they are, still going over their ABC's of faith, hardly knowing the difference between right and wrong. They dabble in foolish speculations.

Mature persons cannot become immature. They cannot lose their faith and begin over again. People produce what is inside of them, good or bad. In 5:9 the writer has said that Jesus became the source of eternal salvation for all who obey him. There are doubts, however, about the Christians' making use of this source, and hence about their maturing toward eternal salvation.

Here is an outline of Hebrews 5:11–6:8:

I. You Should Be Mature (5:11-14)
II. Let Us Go on to Maturity (6:1-3)
III. You Cannot Begin Again (6:4-6)
IV. Land Produces Good Crops or Weeds (6:7-8)

The Message of Hebrews 5:11–6:8

This passage expresses the writer's concern about the immaturity of the Hebrews' faith. They have been Christians a long time, but have never gone beyond the basics of Christianity. By now they should know enough so that they could teach others, yet they appear not even to understand what the author is trying to say about Christ. Hebrews urges them to go on to maturity, warning them that they run the risk of losing salvation altogether if they continue as they are in a downslide that could bring them in the end to betraying Christ.

The author addresses a general problem among Christians. The passage reminds us:

- The Christian faith is a sharing of the word of God and of the Holy Spirit of God.

- The Christian's life is an experience of the goodness of God illuminated by the heavenly eternal life to come with God.

- Actually, however, many Christians remain immature in faith, spiritually infantile, biblically illiterate, not really understanding the full Christian message.

- It does not make sense for people simply to go over and over again the ABC's of Christianity, which they understand only in terms of their secular background.

- Not to move ahead or grow in Christian faith is to become more apt to fall away from it to the point of neglecting or even rejecting it. This kind of life could even bring one to live in contradiction to Christ and the cross.

- A deliberate rejection of Christ is turning one's back on the saving, liberating possibilities of access to an eternal fellowship with God.

HEBREWS 6:9-20

Introduction to These Verses

These verses close Hebrew's third section of warning and encouragement (6:9-20).

From warning Christians, the sermon abruptly turns to commending and encouraging the Christians. They are not apostate and beyond hope. They must move more assuredly toward the hope that is set before them. They must imitate people of great faith who have lived before them.

Hebrews, in this section, assures Christians that they can rely on the unchangeable promise of God to bless them. But Christians need faith and patience as Abraham had so that they can follow when Jesus leads them to the presence of God.

Here is the outline for Hebrews 6:9-20:

I. You Have Done Well (6:9-10)
II. Imitate People of Faith (6:11-12)
III. God's Promise to Abraham Was Sure (6:13-15)
IV. God's Purpose Is Doubly Sure (6:16-18)
V. We Can Be Confident (6:19-20)

The Message of Hebrews 6:9-20

This passage is a call to Christians to strive toward the realization of a hope that is based on a promise. The promise is God's and therefore absolutely sure. That is because God is constant. As in all of Scripture, God is the given. Life, the result of God's creative action, has meaning only as response to God. God makes that response possible in a promise. God makes that promise realizable through Jesus, who clears the way and shows the way and leads the way to realizing the hope.

Hope is what distinguishes the Christian message. A life that drifts is hopeless. The implication is plain that even a life of effort, if motivated by the desire for pleasure, position, or power, is a life without hope. Such efforts are self-centered, are limited to existence in the world, and are not drawn toward God. They miss the point of life: access to God.

The Message of Hope Is to Christians Who:

- express Christianity in loving service;

- are refugees from this world, seeking God.

It is an appeal to Christians to:

- grow in the hope they live by;

- avoid sluggishness in Christian living;

- imitate those who, by faith and patience, have realized God's promise.

It assures Christians that:

- God will unchangeably carry out the divine purpose and promise to them;

- Jesus helps us come into God's presence.

It tells Christians they can:

- seize the hope God has set before them;

- experience life in God's presence forever.

HEBREWS 7

Introduction to This Chapter

Hebrews 5:9-10 prepares for the fourth and longest lesson about Christ's high priestly action on our behalf. It runs from 6:20, following the warnings and encouragement in 5:11–6:20, to 10:18. Chapter 7 begins the lesson by proving that Jesus is the true, the only, and the needed mediator between human sin and God's righteousness.

The emphasis of the previous paragraph was *hope*. Jesus makes the fulfillment of hope possible. Because hope is for access to God, and human sin makes that access to God impossible, Jesus in his sacrifice has canceled the negating power of sin. In so doing he has made the hope of access to God viable for the sinner. That suggests a priestly function. Jesus was like a high priest, making possible the forgiveness of sins through his priestly act.

High priests, however, had been functioning for centuries as mediators between sinful humankind and a righteous God. Yet people continued to be caught by the clutches of sin. It was necessary to prove that Jesus is more effective because his priesthood is of a higher order. The story of Melchizedek provided the way to prove this fact, by allegory. It proves Jesus to be a greater priest than the Levite priests of the old Israel. As a priest of the new covenant, Jesus replaces the old covenant with a better one. His own sacrifice of himself is eternally effective.

Here is an outline of Hebrews 7:
I. Who Is Melchizedek? (7:1-3)
II. Melchizedek Superior to Old Priesthood (7:4-10)

III. The Levite Priests Were Inadequate (7:11-12)

IV. There Is a Better Order of Priesthood (7:13-17)

V. A Greater Hope Supersedes the Law (7:18-19)

VI. Christ Is Priest of a Better Covenant (7:20-22)

VII. Christ Is Our Eternal High Priest (7:23-25)

VIII. Christ's Sacrifice Is Permanent (7:26-28)

The Message of Hebrews 7

This chapter's message is based on four assumptions:

- God desires communion with human beings.

- Human beings desire to draw near to God, without whom life will never be fulfilled.

- Nevertheless sin, which is rebellion against God's righteousness, separates human beings from God.

- Attempts to break down the barrier of sin and to find access to God have failed.

These attempts have failed because:

- they are devised by a human system;

- they are conducted by human beings;

- human beings are limited by weakness, sin, and death.

However, Jesus Christ is a mediator between our sinful lives and God because:

- he is independent of human limitations;

- through suffering obedience to God he has been made perfect forever, holy, blameless, unstained by sin,

having successfully resisted temptation.

From now on there is no need for any other atonement. Jesus Christ has done it all, what no one else could do.

Hebrews assures Christians that, though human systems and devices fail, those who draw near to God can know that Christ is always there as our mediator making access to God forever possible.

HEBREWS 8:1–9:14

Introduction to These Verses

This passage describes the new covenant between God and humanity, which Jesus, the true high priest, guarantees. It seeks to show that the human institutions of Hebrew religion were a copy, or shadow, of the reality in heaven. Jesus is the true high priest in the true sanctuary.

Here is an outline of this passage:

I. High Priest in the True Sanctuary (8:1-2)

II. Jesus is Not in an Earthly Sanctuary (8:3-5)

III. High Priest of a Better Covenant (8:6-13)

IV. The First Covenant Had Earthly Rules (9:1-5)

V. Rituals of the Earthly Sanctuary (9:6-10)

VI. Jesus, the One Effective Sacrifice (9:11-14)

The Message of Hebrews 8:1–9:14

The great assurance in the Christian life is Jesus. This section of the Hebrews sermon emphasizes the ministry of Jesus as high priest. Jesus serves in a heavenly sanctuary, far more real than an earthly copy of it. Jesus made possible a new covenant, far more effective than the old law and covenant. Jesus made a sacrifice of himself once for all, which makes possible our approach to God, a possibility the old sacrifices of the Hebrew sanctuary did not fulfill.

The passage in Hebrews assumes that our greatest goal in life is fellowship with God. Our religion does not bring about fellowship with God if:

- we think of Jesus as merely a teacher of an earthly religion, no matter how fine it is;

- we place our entire trust in a code of conduct, based on human rules, regulation, and rites, no matter how excellent.

Our faith will arrive at fellowship with God eternally if:

- we trust in Jesus as God's appointed;

- we understand Jesus as our high priest interceding for us in God's presence;

- we accept in our minds and hearts God's will for us as demonstrated in the life and death of Jesus;

- we accept God's full, free pardon of our sins;

- we accept Christ's suffering in our behalf to purify our consciences so that we can serve the living God.

HEBREWS 9:15–10:18

Introduction to These Verses

This is the final section on the high priesthood of Jesus. It goes into greater detail to show how Christ's sacrifice, in contrast to the old and ineffective sacrifices, is the means by which the new covenant God promised is made to work. By his sacrifice we are forgiven and purified forever.

Here is an outline of this passage.

   I. The New Covenant Becomes Effective (9:15-17)
  II. Old Covenant Sealed by Blood Sacrifice (9:18-22)
 III. Christ Mediates the New Covenant (9:23-26)
 IV. Jesus Receives Those Who Repent (9:27-28)
  V. Old Sacrifices Were Repeated (10:1-4)
 VI. Christ Replaced the Old Sacrifices (10:5-10)
VII. Christ Has Purified His People (10:11-14)
VIII. The New Covenant of God's Grace (10:15-18)

The Message of Hebrews 9:15–10:18

This passage is about the new covenant. The old covenant between God and the Hebrew people was inaugurated by the shedding of blood of an animal sacrifice. Because the people kept breaking the covenant, animal sacrifices needed to be repeated annually to restore their relationship with God.

Then Christ came to earth in obedience to God's will for a lasting relationship with humanity. Christ gave his life as a once-for-all sacrifice for people's sins. Having done so, he remains beside God, but will return again to receive the believers who wait for him. Released from the power of sin, those who wait are called to receive the promised inheritance.

- This passage tells us that we, too, have received God's call and have received God's promise of eternal fellowship with God, and can be rid of the sins that obstruct our relationship with God.

- This passage tells us that we can be forever rid of our transgressions against God if we come to Christ eager for communion with God; if we accept the offering of Christ's life and death in our behalf; if we trust Christ as our Redeemer; if we obey God's will for our lives; if we allow God to put in our hearts and minds the law of the new covenant; that is, that we will to live by God's will for fellowship with us.

HEBREWS 10:19-39

Introduction to These Verses

Draw near to God. That is the subject of the sermon. This passage is a call to true worship and faithful endurance. It is the fourth counsel and warning section in the sermon.

The writer of Hebrews has presented Jesus Christ as a high priest mediating on our behalf. He has explained the new covenant as the promise of an undimmed, eternal relationship with God, hope open to all. Now, with the words "Therefore, brothers" (NIV; NRSV = "my friends"), that is, "fellow Christians" (verse 19), the writer turns to encourage readers to draw near to God with faith. A warning is added about the hopelessness for those who disregard and reject Christ's sacrifice for them.

Here is an outline of Hebrews 10:19-39:
I. Jesus Has Opened the Way to God (10:19-21)
II. Let Us Draw Near with Faith (10:22-23)
III. Let Us Encourage One Another (10:24-25)
IV. Do Not Spurn Christ's Sacrifice (10:26-31)
V. Recall Faith Experiences (10:32-34)
VI. Persevere with Confidence (10:35-39)

The Message of Hebrews 10:19-39

In this passage, the author mingles assurances about the effectiveness of Jesus as our high priest with encouragement to be faithful, to draw near to God, to stimulate one another in love and good deeds. The message is also a warning to those who might turn against Christ and deride what he has done for them.

The message warns us:

• to understand that if we deliberately and willfully abandon our faith, if we disparage Christ and mock what he has done, if we flaunt God's gracious love for us, then we condemn ourselves.

The message encourages us:

• to think of a time in our lives when our Christian faith was most buoyant, when we best lived by it unflinchingly, when we witnessed it most clearly, when we endured suffering rather than compromise it;

• to dare to care for those who are derided or persecuted on account of their Christian convictions;

• to focus our attention on Christ and the meaning of his sacrifice for our sins;

• to trust that we are forgiven and made clean;

• to build one another up in faith and hope;

• to do good things for others;

• to be faithful in worshiping and meeting together;

• to live expectantly, confident that the Day of the Lord is coming soon; and most of all,

• to persevere as we move toward God.

HEBREWS 11:1-22

Introduction to These Verses

The eleventh chapter of Hebrews is the fifth and final lesson of the sermon. It is about faith. It is about the goal toward which the life of faithfulness moves.

In this passage, the writer seeks to inspire the readers with great examples of persevering faith. To keep moving on in hope—that is the religion this sermon has proclaimed. Readers are urged to keep on in the same hope that inspired people of faith in times past. They lived by, and moved forward in, hope for what God has promised.

Here is an outline of Hebrews 11:1-22:
I. Faith Is Confidence in the Expected (11:1-3)
II. By Faith Abel and Enoch Pleased God (11:4-6)
III. Noah: Heir of Righteousness (11:7)
IV. Abraham Went Out in Faith (11:8-10)
V. Sarah Trusted God's Promise (11:11-12)
VI. Confidence in Things Hoped For (11:13-16)
VII. Abraham and Isaac (11:17-19)
VIII. Isaac, Jacob, and Joseph Trusted God (11:20-22)

The Message of Hebrews 11:1-22

This passage defines faith in the God who created the universe. The hope of faith is the assurance of what God has planned and promised. The expression of faith is movement toward the fulfillment that God has promised. Faith is faithfulness to God and to Christ, who opens the way to God. Ultimately, faith is the foretaste of the experience of living in God's presence eternally.

The message of this passage is encouragement seen in the faith of persons who trusted in God's promises.

Through these examples, Hebrews says to Christians:

- You cannot depend on the material world; it is imperfect, never permanent, and uncertain.

- You can depend on the existence of God whose word created the world.

- Learn faith from the lives of people who have lived by faith.

HEBREWS 11:23-40

Introduction to These Verses

This passage, gathering momentum as it goes, continues the record of heroes of faith. It covers nearly a thousand years of Jewish history with accounts of courage and commitment. The author's words paint a picture of faith that endures, of people—individuals and an entire nation—whose confidence in God and in where God was leading them made them spurn both the wealth and pleasures offered and the persecution threatened by the world.

Besides persons named in the passage, others, unnamed, are suggestive of Old Testament heroes: Six characteristics of faith strongly mark this series: action, courage, unhesitating choice, identity with the people of God, obedience, and readiness to suffer, endure, and persevere rather than recede from the goal of faith.

Here is an outline of Hebrews 11:23-40:
I. Moses Lived by Faith (11:23-28)
II. Israel Came to Canaan by Faith (11:29-31)
III. Strong Leaders and Prophets (11:32-34)

IV. Faith in Times of Suffering (11:35-38)

V. Faith in God's Promise (11:39-40)

The Message of Hebrews 11:23-40

This section of the faith chapter in Hebrews gives more examples of heroic persons who persevered by faith in God's promise. Great examples for us of faith in action are: Moses, the people of Israel, Rahab, leaders and prophets of Israel, and innumerable men and women who endured suffering rather than giving up or compromising their faith in God's promise for something better and greater ahead. None received the promise in their times. Nevertheless, they had such firm confidence in it that they lived by hope. Now, as God has planned, they, with us, receive the fulfillment of God's promise.

These examples were given as a message for Christians, that we should:

- live by faith;

- never compromise with the world; prefer suffering, homelessness, prison, persecution, death, to losing Christ;

- fearlessly ignore demands of the world that run counter to our faith in God;

- wholly identify with God's people, even if it means leaving the old crowd or being derided by them;

- move fearlessly in the direction of the hope to which God calls us;

- patiently persevere with confidence in God's purpose, trusting in God's power to do great and mighty things.

HEBREWS 12:1-17

Introduction to These Verses

The sermon comes to a close with a fifth and final section of counsel (12:1–13:17). Throughout the eleventh chapter the main intent of the author of Hebrews has been to encourage Christians in their faith by recording the power of faith and faithfulness in the lives of heroes of the past. This encouragement is now focused on the foremost of all faithful ones, Jesus Christ. Looking to him, counsels the writer, you can persevere through hardship toward your God-given goals.

Aware of whatever sufferings the Christians have been through, the author reminds them that they are still alive. They should accept suffering as a discipline God sends to strengthen them. Then they can do their best, and live in peace and thankfulness.

Here is an outline of Hebrews 12:1-17.

I. Follow Jesus in Faith (12:1-2)

II. Persevere Through Suffering (12:3-6)

III. Discipline Leads to Righteousness (12:7-11)

IV. Therefore, Be Strong (12:12-13)

V. Live in Peace and Goodness (12:14-17)

The Message of Hebrews 12:1-17

The writer asks Christians:

- to let past heroes of faith spur us to a life of vigorous faith;

- to resolutely follow the course God sets before us;

- to cast aside anything that hampers total dedication;

- to keep our eyes always on Jesus, who has opened for us the way to God;

FOLLOW THE EXAMPLE OF JESUS (HEBREWS 12:1-2)

For Hebrews, the Christian life is one of movement toward a goal. The writer uses a metaphor, frequent in old Greek writings, of life as a strenuous race. The race course is before us. All around us, as witnesses, is the crowd of heroes who have already run well the race of faith. We, the author included, are the runners, stripped (of sin) for the race. We are determined and we must persevere in the race of faith (the same metaphor is used in Philippians 3:13-14). The race requires endurance, essential in the practice of faith.

The greatest of all expressions of faith is seen in Jesus. He has already run the course. He ran it with perseverance, enduring the cross. He ran with joy. He attained the prize: the seat at the right hand of God (Psalm 110:1). We are to keep our eyes on him, enduring as he did. For us, too, there is the prize, the presence of God.

The heroes of the faith are spoken of as a great "cloud of witnesses." Their lives are a witness to us. Their lives have shown us how to run, how to endure. They, also, are witnesses watching how we run our course. We are watched from above.

Besides the need for endurance is the necessity of laying aside, throwing off, anything that encumbers or hinders us. Like a runner who must put aside any weight, we are to leave off anything, no matter how good or harmless it may seem in itself, that will in any way hamper us or impede the serious business of the Christian life. We must be free to move toward God.

Sin is difficult to get rid of because it "clings so closely." The unusual adjective Hebrews uses to describe sin has been translated in several different ways, but generally it means sins that we find it hard to part with. In other contexts in Greek literature, the word has been used to mean *easily avoided, dangerous,* even *admired*. A very early manuscript of Hebrews uses another word, different by one stroke of the pen in Greek, which means *easily distracting* sin. It must be cast off because it entangles us, trips us up.

The word *race* means *contest, toil, peril*. The English word *agony* comes from the same Greek root. Running a good race is not finding out what one is comfortable with. Running calls for "perseverance," Hebrews' emphasis on endurance.

Jesus is the supreme example to inspire us. Our attention must be fixed on him (verse 2), on no one and on nothing else. He is the "pioneer" of our faith, indeed, the author of our faith. In his earthly course he showed us how to run. He leads the way. He is the "perfecter of our faith" in that he embodies and completes it. Jesus "endured the cross." This is the only time Hebrews specifies the cross. There are clear references to the crucifixion, however (5:8; 6:6; 9:25-28; 13:12), and many references to Jesus' suffering.

The readers had suffered only a little. Greater suffering than any other shall have was Jesus' suffering on the cross, a tortured death as a criminal exposed to public derision. Nevertheless, disregarding the shame, Jesus accepted the shame and torture as a small matter in the light of his goal. That goal could be reached only by way of the cross (5:8). The goal, to cleanse people of sin (9:26) and to open up a way for people to God (10:20-21), was worth the suffering. The goal recalls the declaration of Paul: "For [his] sake I have lost all things. I consider them rubbish, that I may gain Christ" (Philippians 3:8 NIV). The joy sustained him even through suffering itself because it was a suffering self-sacrifice endured for everyone (2:9-10). "Set before him" is the same verb as in "the race that is set before us" (verse 1) and in "the hope set before us" (6:18, NRSV NIV, "offered to us"). His goal is ours.

- to let Christ's example keep us from giving up;

- to accept hardships as disciplines from God to teach us courage;

- to keep remembering that if we endure through painful experiences, we will come to experience peace and goodness;

HEBREWS 12:18-29

Introduction to These Verses

The new covenant is the joyful fulfillment God offers you. Through references to the Old Testament Scriptures, the Hebrews sermon reminds Christians of the joy that comes with obedience to God. It also warns them of the awful consequences of neglecting God's goodness to them. The sermon closes with a call to worship and gratitude.

Here is an outline of Hebrews 12:18-29:
I. Yours Is Not a Religion of Fear (12:18-21)
II. Come to the Joyful City of God (12:22-24)
III. Do Not Refuse God, Who Calls You (12:25-27)
IV. Worship God with Thankfulness (12:28-29)

The Message of Hebrews 12:18-29

In this passage the writer pictures the difference between the old covenant and the new covenant as the difference between Mount Sinai and Mount Zion. Characterizing the old as a religion of fear and the new as one of joy and fellowship with God's perfected people, the writer invites the Christians to receive the new covenant with gratitude and worship. In these verses Hebrews counsels us:

- Do not settle for an earthbound, legalistic religion; instead, join the company of those going on to the joyful fulfillment of God's promise in heaven—to God your judge and Jesus your Savior.

- Keep in mind that the things of this earth are unstable and will all come to an end.

- Accept God's gift of forgiving grace with deep gratitude.

- Worship God's absolute power, greatness, and judgment with awesome reverence.

HEBREWS 13

Introduction to This Chapter

The sermon has ended. Chapter 13 is different, and perhaps does not belong with the rest of the book. Chapter 13 has two parts. The first part (verses 1-17) is Christian counsel. The second part closes the letter.

In the first section, each thought leads briefly into the next. Except for verses 11-14, however, which echo the emphases in the sermon, the counsel to Christians is abruptly different; it is direct and concise.

The second section closes the letter with a benediction in verse 21. Verses 22-25 are an added postscript.

Here is an outline of Hebrews 13:
I. Be Faithful, Fellow Christians (13:1-17)
   A. Care for those in need (13:1-3)
   B. Keep pure and free from greed (13:4-6)
   C. Trust in Christ (13:7-8)
   D. Live by God's grace (13:9-10)
   E. Join Jesus as an outcast (13:11-14)
   F. Praise God, witness, do good, share (13:15-16)

G. Obey your leaders in the faith (13:17)
II. Closing of the Letter (13:18-21)
   A. Pray for us, pray for me (13:18-19)
   B. May Christ work in you (13:20-21)
III. Postscript (13:22-25)
   A. Heed this letter's counsel (13:22)
   B. Timothy and I may come soon (13:23)
   C. Greetings to your leaders (13:24)
   D. God's grace be with you (13:25)

The Message of Hebrews 13

This chapter is a pastoral letter, distinct from, but related to, the sermon that preceded it. It is a letter of counsel to Christians. It includes moral advice about the Christians' relationship to the new covenant with God through Christ. It closes with a request for prayer, a benediction, a doxology, and a postscript. It tells us:

- to care for one another in the Christian fellowship;

- to show hospitality to strangers;

- to extend our caring to all who are in trouble, in prison, or abused for their faith;

- to do all the good we can, sharing what we have;

- to keep marriage sacred, avoiding all extramarital sexual relations;

- to live a life free of love of money; to abhor greed;

- to be content with what we have, trusting in God to provide what we need;

- to maintain the serenity of those who know Christ is ever the same and will never change;

- to imitate the faith of Christian leaders, follow their advice, and pray for them

JAMES

OUTLINE OF JAMES

INTRODUCTION

The Nature of James

James is the first of the books of the New Testament that are referred to as *the general epistles*, since most of these letters were written to general audiences rather than specific congregations. Along with 1 and 2 Peter; 1, 2, and 3 John; and Jude, James was written toward the end of the first century A.D. or the beginning of the second century. At that time, the church was establishing itself as an institution and struggling to help its members establish a consistent code of ethics.

Strictly speaking, James is not a letter, since it is not written to any congregation by name. It is not addressed to particular problems as are 1 and 2 Corinthians, Galatians, and Romans. Rather, it deals with general Christian concerns.

Since James is mainly interested in offering its readers Christian advice, it is usually referred to as a homily. The book fits in with a type of literature commonly known in the ancient world as "exhortation." Advice is given in almost all the New Testament letters, but it is usually accompanied by preaching or teaching as well as references to particular problems faced by a church or a group of churches.

In James, however, nothing but exhortation is presented as the author discusses several main concerns:

- the danger of double-mindedness (1:8; 4:8),

- the danger of pride and arrogance (1:9, 21-23; 2:1-7, 13; 3:1; 4:13-17),

- how to endure in a time of trial (1:2-4, 12-15),

- maintaining equality between the rich and the poor (2:1-7, 14-17; 5:1-6),

- hearing and doing, especially deeds of charity toward the poor (1:22-25; 2:14-26; 4:17),

- the danger of loose talk (1:19; 3:1-12)

Authorship

According to the first verse, the author of the homily is "James, a servant of God and of the Lord Jesus Christ." The New Testament mentions several different men by that name: James, the brother of Jesus (Mark 6:3); James, the son of Alphaeus, one of Jesus' disciples (Luke 6:15); James, the brother of John, one of the sons of Zebedee whom Jesus also called as a disciple (Mark 3:17); James, the father of Judas (not Judas Iscariot; Luke 6:16); James the younger, who was with the women at the cross (Mark 15:40).

Traditionally, it was thought that the author of James was the brother of Jesus who was given the title James the Just. Although he was not a disciple during Jesus' lifetime (Mark 3:21, 31-35; John 7:3-5), he became a leading figure in Jerusalem after Jesus' resurrection. Probably he became the head of the church after Peter left on his first missionary tour (Acts 12:17). Paul mentions him in Galatians 1:19 and 2:9 as one of the pillars of the church (see Acts 15:1) and one who may have opposed certain aspects of his ministry (Acts 2:12).

However, some scholars doubt that James was the true author of the epistle of James. Jesus' name is mentioned only twice throughout the whole work (1:1; 2:1), and nothing is said about his relationship to the author. The homily is written in a highly polished Greek style, one an uneducated fisherman like the brother of Jesus would not be likely to use. According to the Jewish historian Flavius Josephus, James died in A.D. 62. However, the homily clearly reflects the ideas and concerns of a much later period when Hebrews, Jude, and 1 and 2 Peter were also written. Some scholars think that James may have written parts of the original epistle and that the final draft was composed by someone else who used his name to make sure that it would be widely read. However, it is impossible to be sure who the author was.

For reasons that are not completely clear, the Letter of James was not fully accepted by the church until the fourth century. Questions about its authorship must have been raised from the start. Indeed, during the Protestant Reformation, Martin Luther dismissed it as an "epistle of straw," one that was not of primary importance because it was not written by an apostle and because it seemed to run counter to Paul's emphasis upon salvation through grace by faith. But Luther's view was not widely shared by other Reformers. Most readers through the centuries have reached a position like that of the early church fathers, that is, that James and Paul are not in contradiction because they are not dealing with the same point and that James's emphasis upon moral imperative is an important part of Christian identity.

Faith Versus Works

The Letter of James has been of great importance to Christians because it does take up important Christian themes. Scholars note that there are more than thirty-five indirect references to the teaching of Jesus in the epistle, twenty-five of which come from the Sermon on the Mount. The homily also takes up a number of ethical questions that are important in the rest of the New Testament and are significant for believers in any time.

Of particular importance, of course, is the discussion of faith and works that the author carefully develops. Although the apostle Paul argues in Romans 3:1-4 and Galatians 2:1-4 that people are put right with God only through their faith in Jesus Christ and that they cannot earn their salvation by works, the author of James lives in a time when people are content to mouth their beliefs without putting them into practice. It is not enough, he argues, to say that you believe in Jesus Christ, if you are not willing to follow him in the way you live. Christians may be saved by faith, but without the proof of actions and love expressed to one's neighbor in concrete deeds, faith is truly dead.

The Readers

Reference is made in 1:1 to the readers as "the twelve tribes in the Dispersion" (NRSV; NIV, "scattered among the nations"). *Dispersion* is a Jewish term that refers to the fact that the Jewish people lived all over the world, either because they were forced out of Palestine by their enemies or because they chose to live elsewhere. The author probably uses it as a code word for Jewish Christians, but it is impossible to tell where they lived. The church could have been anywhere in the Roman Empire (compare 1 Peter 1:1).

JAMES 1:1

Introduction to This Verse

James starts with a greeting that is similar to that of other letters in the New Testament. In the ancient world most letters began in the same way, with the identification of the writer and his or her credentials, the naming of the person or people who would receive the message, and the greeting. In this case, as was pointed out in the Introduction, the letter format is used to begin a sermon or homily.

The Message of James 1:1

In this opening verse, James introduces himself and gives initial greetings to his readers. He does not indicate who they are, except to refer to them as the twelve tribes in the Dispersion, a title whose meaning is uncertain.

JAMES 1:2-15

Introduction to These Verses

The outline of James's homily is not easy to determine, because even though it contains a number of connected themes, it is not tightly organized. Many of its parts are loosely tied together by the association of similar ideas or words. In 1:2-15, for example, James is mainly concerned to discuss the effects of trials and temptations on the Christian life, although he also introduces here his criticisms of two different types of people within the church—the rich and the double-minded believers.

The Message of James 1:2-15

In this section the author of James indicates that his readers are suffering from trials and temptations that besiege Christians as they try to live a Christian life in the midst of an evil world. Although these trials are not sent by God in any way, they will produce endurance and courage, qualities that will eventually lead to Christian perfection.

The Christian must not be double-minded but must be single-minded in devotion to Christ and his example, remaining humble and not tempted by wealth.

JAMES 1:16-27

Introduction to These Verses

In this section James continues and expands the arguments that he began in 1:5 and 1:13. Here is an outline of this section:

I. Good Gifts from God (1:16-18)
II. Bad Words and the Word (1:19-21)
III. Be Doers and Not Hearers Only (1:22-25)
IV. What Does It Mean to Be Religious? (1:26-27)

The Message of James 1:16-27

In the second half of the first chapter James introduces some of the major themes of his homily:

BE DOERS AND NOT HEARERS ONLY (JAMES 1:22-25)

Verse 22 is one of the main keynotes of James's message to his Christian readers. It is one that will be repeated over and over again throughout the letter (2:2-4, 12, 14, 17, 24, 26). It is summed up in 2:17, where James indicates that if one does nothing more than hear God's word and does not act upon it, then his or her faith is nonproductive and dead in the ground. Common sense and the Scriptures support James's warning: Clearly, a person who says one thing and does another is not a true believer. See Deuteronomy 28:58; 29:29; Matthew 7:12, 24-27; Luke 3:8; Acts 5:1-11; 7:53; Galatians 2:11-18; 6:2 for a few references to the important connection between doing and believing.

- Christians must realize that God has nothing but good gifts for us. God is a God of light, and so illumines believers with God's word.

- The believer must not only hear God's word but must be careful how she or speaks as well. Filthy and angry talk is not appropriate for Christians. It separates them from the righteousness of God.

- Christians must do more than hear God's word. They must act out their faith as well. Those who do not put their faith into action are not being true to themselves or to the Scriptures.

JAMES 2:1-13

Introduction to These Verses

In chapter 2 James identifies a serious lack of Christian fellowship in the church communities to which he is writing. When people come to church dinners they do not observe the equality that Christ's forgiveness brings. If the apostle Paul can write that "there is neither Jew nor Greek, slave nor free, male nor female; for you are all one in Christ Jesus" (Galatians 3:28 NIV), James observes that there are those who clearly believe that some Christians are more "equal" than others. The situation is one that is very easy to understand. When the churches met for fellowship dinners or to celebrate the Lord's Supper, preference was shown to the rich and the famous. They were given seats of special honor, just the kind of seats that Jesus said would not be awarded in his kingdom (Mark 10:37-40), and the poor were put in positions of disgrace. In verse 5

James may be referring to Jesus' teaching in the Beatitudes. There Jesus reminds persons that they cannot treat the poor that way because God has chosen the poor in the world to be rich in faith and heirs of the Kingdom (Matthew 5:3; Luke 6:20, 24-25).

The Message of James 2:1-13

In his fourth section James pinpoints a serious problem that exists in the churches to which he writes. Some of them have forgotten the teaching in the Old Testament and the witness of Jesus that the poor are to receive a special place of honor in God's kingdom. Instead of observing this teaching, some Christians are giving the rich special places in the church and thus denying the oneness of the body of Christ and the fellowship that Jesus' love brings.

In verses 8-13 James reminds his readers that to break the Jewish law in any way means that it is broken in all ways. James advises them to make sure, therefore, that they do not violate the law at all.

JAMES 2:14-26

Introduction to These Verses

This section of James has correctly been seen throughout Christian history as critical for a proper understanding of the author's message. James argues very convincingly that anyone who professes to have faith in Jesus Christ should follow him not only in beliefs but also in actions. Just because people say (verse 14) that they have faith does not mean that they do have it. The proof is in the doing. "Show me your activities," James is saying, "and then I shall really see your faith."

The Message of James 2:14-26

James 2:14-26 is important for a correct understanding of the author's homily.

James knows that it takes more than a statement of belief to make one a believer. Faith must also be backed up by action. People who do not *live* the Christian faith show that they do not really believe in Jesus Christ. Faith without works is dead.

JAMES 3:1-12

Introduction to These Verses

Chapter 3 provides advice for church leaders, especially those who are teachers (3:1, 13), by linking together several proverbial sayings that were well-known in the ancient world.

Teaching was important in the church because it was the way persons became Christians and were taught how they should live in order to follow Christ. Jesus was called a teacher (Mark 4:38; 5:35; 9:17, 38; 13:1; Luke 6:40; John 11:28; 20:16), and the ability to teach was considered to be a gift of the Holy Spirit (1 Corinthians 12:28-29; Colossians 3:16; 1 Timothy 5:17; 2 Timothy 3:16). The first Christians had to be careful because there were people who tried to deceive them through false teaching (1 Timothy 6:3; 2 Timothy 4:3; 1 John 2:26; Jude 1:4).

The Message of James 3:1-12

James 3:1-12 warns Christian readers of the grave responsibilities of being a teacher. Since teachers can influence children and new Christians, they will be judged with greater strictness.

James also warns Christians to beware of the power of the tongue. Although it is only a small organ, it can ruin the whole body and do damage to the church. The tongue has to be controlled so that the individual and the congregation can produce the good results that are expected from them.

JAMES 3:13–4:17

Introduction to These Verses

In this section James examines the danger inherent in jealousy and pride. These verses may be outlined as follows:

I. True Wisdom Versus Jealousy (3:13-18)
II. Friendship with the World (4:1-10)
III. Who Are You to Judge Your Neighbor? (4:11-12)
IV. The Foolishness of Planning Ahead (4:13-17)

The Message of James 3:13–4:17

James loosely connects several important themes: the value of living according to God's wisdom (wisdom from above), the danger of hostility toward God and one's neighbors, and the value of humility as a way of drawing near to God.

He shows how that drawing near can be accomplished in practical terms: by spiritual purification (verse 8), by the avoidance of double standards and conflicting actions (verses 8, 17), by resisting evil (verse 7), by mourning for personal and corporate sins (verse 9), by avoiding character assassination of other people (verses 11-12), and by remembering that only God can control the future (verses 13-16).

JAMES 5:1-6

Introduction to These Verses

In 5:1-6 James intensifies a warning that has been given earlier, namely that those who do not share their wealth are in danger of God's judgment.

In chapter 5 it is not clear whether James is addressing pagan plutocrats who are oppressing poor Christians (verse 6), or writing to a church that has some members in it who have considerable wealth, members whose love of money (1 Timothy 6:10) has choked off their compassion for others. The warning here is similar to the ones given by Jesus (Matthew 6:19-21, 24-33; Luke 6:24; 12:13-21) and those found throughout the Old Testament (Proverbs 11:7; 16:16; 28:6; Ecclesiastes 5:10-12; Amos 4:1-3; 5:10-13; 8:4-6).

The Message of James 5:1-6

In this section James continues to express his concern for the poor, a major theme throughout his writing. Here he warns the rich directly that their wealth is perishable and will not protect them from God's judgment in the last days. They have been able to oppress the poor by holding back wages and living in luxury while others suffered. But the implication is that they will get what they deserve when God's judgment is finally revealed.

JAMES 5:7-11

Introduction to These Verses

James's advice about the need for patience is only loosely connected with the preceding verses. Probably he is thinking that even if poor Christians find themselves oppressed by the rich, they should not despair because they will get their reward when Jesus returns in triumph and judgment.

The Message of James 5:7-11

Advice is given here to the readers of James to be patient in spite of oppression and poverty. The Lord Jesus will come soon to judge all people, and then all persons will receive their deserved reward. As examples of patience James cites the common farmer (who trusts God's plan for growth even though he does not understand the science of growth), the steadfastness of the prophets, and Job, who held on to his belief in God no matter what happened.

JAMES 5:12-20

Introduction to These Verses

This section may be divided into three main parts:

I. Take No Oaths (5:12)
II. Pray for Healing (5:13-18)
III. Correct the Backslider (5:19-20)

The Message of James 5:12-20

The final portion of James is completed with the author's pastoral concern for the weaker members of the church, those who have experienced setbacks, illness, or a loss of faith. James directs them to the power of prayer and indicates his belief that the leaders of the church must play a major role in the healing of the sick and the forgiveness of sins.

FIRST PETER

OUTLINE OF 1 PETER

INTRODUCTION

Type and Style of Writing

Until recently Bible commentators were convinced that 1 Peter, like James and 1 John, was not a genuine letter, but was a tract or a baptismal sermon written for new converts. Now, however, most scholars think that it really is a genuine letter written to real congregations in four different parts of Asia Minor (modern Turkey).

First Peter has the essential elements of a real letter: the naming of the author (1:1), comments to the recipients and wishes for their spiritual health (1:2), inclusion of the name of the church member who delivers it (Silvanus, 5:12), a farewell from the author and others who are with him (5:13), and a peace benediction (5:14).

First Peter differs from personal letters in one respect. It is not sent to just one person or family, but it is written for congregations in five different areas. For this reason it is called a "circular letter" and was meant to be read and passed on to other Christians who were meeting in neighboring homes, cities, or provinces.

The letter, like other New Testament books, contains many different kinds of material. The author quotes or alludes to passages from the Old Testament in order to teach his readers about the Christian faith. The most obvious is 2:21-25, which is closely patterned after Isaiah 53:1, the chapter about the suffering servant. Numerous other passages are also quoted:

Isaiah 40:6-8 in 1:24-25; Isaiah 28:16 in 2:6; Psalm 118:22 in 2:7; Isaiah 8:14 in 2:8; and Psalm 34:12-16 in 3:10-12, to mention just a few.

In addition to the use of Scripture texts, the author of 1 Peter writes in a style that was popular in the first and second centuries called the "rhetorical style." The text is written in a highly polished, literate Greek, makes plays on words, has carefully constructed clauses, and utilizes compound negative words.

Other types of material are also used by the author. The letter is filled with advice given to servants and masters (2:18-20), husbands and wives (3:1-7), church leaders, called "elders" (5:1-4), and Christian believers in general (2:21-25; 3:8-12). First Peter also contains Christian hymns (1:20; 3:18-22), creeds, and prayers developed for new Christians (catechetical teachings).

Major Themes in 1 Peter

First Peter has four major themes that are found throughout the letter: (1) baptism and new birth, (2) encouragement in times of persecution, (3) the church as the true home of believers, and (4) advice for how to live successfully in an alien culture.

Authorship of 1 Peter

Although the first verse is attributed to the apostle Peter and the conclusion of the letter mentions the names of those who were associated with him (see 5:12-13), it is generally agreed that 1 Peter was written by a follower or admirer of Peter who was probably a member of a school or circle that was committed to Peter's teachings. Peter was known in church tradition for his connection with Rome ("Babylon" in 5:13 is a code word for the capital of the Roman Empire; see Revelation 14:8). It was there that Peter died.

The highly literate Greek of 1 Peter is not the kind of language a fisherman from Galilee would be expected to use, and some of the ideas in the letter come from periods that are relatively late in the development of the church. A number of passages show the influence of Paul's letter to the Romans, moreover, and indicate that 1 Peter was written well after the ministry of Paul.

Recipients of the Letter

First Peter 1:1 indicates that the people who received the letter lived in five provinces of Asia Minor (what is now modern Turkey): Pontus, Galatia, Cappadocia, Asia, and Bithynia. The words "to the exiles of the Dispersion" (NRSV; NIV, "God's elect, strangers to the world, scattered throughout") do not necessarily mean that all of the readers were Jews. More likely, the word is used as a sociological term to describe all the Christians in the area, Jews and Gentiles, who felt like refugees in a region where they were persecuted because their cultural upbringing and faith were different.

Date

Because 1 Peter mentions persecution and suffering at the hands of government officials, it is often assumed that the letter was written during one of the periods when the Romans made life difficult for Christians: the reigns of the emperors Nero (54–68), Domitian (81–96), or Trajan (98–117). It is also possible that the persecution mentioned was not official in nature but was of the type that happened from time to time when refugees and unfamiliar religions were introduced into new areas.

Because references to 1 Peter appear in 2 Peter (3:1) and in a writing called The Martyrdom of Polycarp (both written during the second century), 1 Peter was probably sent to Asia Minor sometime at the end of the first century during Domitian's reign.

1 PETER 1:1-2

Introduction to These Verses

The author of the letter identifies himself with Peter, an apostle. According to the Gospels Peter was the spokesperson for the disciples and had his name changed by Jesus from Simon (Matthew 16:16-19). He plays a leading role in the gospel story (see Mark 8:29-30; 9:2; John 20:1-10; 21:15-23) and in Acts (2:14-42; 3:1-26; 9:32–11:19). Paul says in Galatians 2:8 that Peter was entrusted by God with the mission to the circumcised. According to tradition he was persecuted and died as a Christian martyr in Rome (John 21:18-19; 1 Peter 5:1).

The Message of 1 Peter 1:1-2

The author of 1 Peter identifies himself with the apostle Peter, the disciple of Jesus. He writes to people who are political and spiritual refugees, those who are isolated from their neighbors because of their country of origin and their faith in Jesus Christ. He implies that they should not be discouraged since they have been called to their faith by God, made holy by the Spirit, and forgiven through the death of Jesus Christ.

1 PETER 1:3–2:3

Introduction to These Verses

This section of 1 Peter has three main parts:
  I. The Indestructible Faith in Christ (1:3-9)

II. The Witness of the Prophets (1:10-12)
III. Be Holy, as He Is Holy (1:13–2:3)

The Message of 1 Peter 1:3–2:3

This section lists the essentials of the Christian faith and provides encouragement to those who are persecuted. Even though believers are experiencing pain now, they can have confidence in the God who planned their salvation from the beginning, raised Jesus from the dead, and is preparing for the end of history.

1 PETER 2:4–3:12

Introduction to These Chapters

This portion of 1 Peter may be divided into the following parts:
  I. The Living Stone and the Living House (2:4-10)
 II. Good Conduct Removes Alien Status (2:11–3:12)
    A. Set an example to the Gentiles (2:11-12)
    B. Relationships to government (2:13-17)
    C. House servants and masters (2:18-20)
    D. The example of Christ (2:21-25)
    E. Husbands and wives (3:1-7)
    F. Summary (3:8-12)

The Message of 1 Peter 2:4–3:12

This section is constructed around several Old Testament texts and the symbolism of stones and houses. Although the readers are aliens and exiles, politically and spiritually, they can be assured that they are welcome in God's household. This house is built with Christ as the cornerstone and church members as the building blocks. Exhortation is given about the rules believers should follow in politics, master-slave relationships, marriage, and life in general. Above all they must follow Christ's example.

1 PETER 3:13–4:19

Introduction to These Verses

In this section, the author offers reassurance to believers who suffer for doing good, encourages Christians to live by the will of God, and reminds them to be constant in love for one another, "for love covers a multitude of sins" (4:8).

The Message of 1 Peter 3:13–4:19

The author urges his readers to continue with good behavior in spite of their suffering. Christ died for sins once and for all, and preached to the dead spirits, an action that reminds believers of baptism. By acting as Christians they may actually convert some of their accusers. All are reminded to be proud of the name *Christian* and to trust in God.

1 PETER 5:1-11

Introduction to These Verses

In these verses the author summarizes several of the themes that have appeared repeatedly throughout the letter as he gives practical and spiritual advice to church leaders (elders) and those who are either inexperienced in the faith or recent converts (younger). The exhortation is from a pastor to other pastors or church leaders. Those in authority should work with the people of the church and not use their power to dominate the congregation (see Galatians 5:25–6:6). Those who are

members must respect the call of God and be subject to those who have responsibility.

The Message of 1 Peter 5:1-11

In the final chapter the author draws together several themes that have been important throughout the letter: God's call to eternal glory, the need to be subject to one another in the household of faith, and the support God will give believers who are suffering persecution. They must resist the devil, who is behind all this trouble, and must trust in God's strength and love.

1 PETER 5:12-14

Introduction to These Verses

In the final verses the author of 1 Peter reminds his readers why he has written: He is encouraging and testifying the truth about the grace of God. At such a perilous time, as he has stressed throughout the letter, proper Christian conduct is very important. So he turns their attention once more to his advice to stand fast in their faith. For the meaning of exhortation, see the Introduction to James.

The Message of 1 Peter 5:12-14

The final words of 1 Peter mention two of the men who accompanied the apostle Peter and served as his coworkers. One last time believers are urged to conduct themselves as Christians and hold fast to their faith in God. "She who is in Babylon" (verse 13 NIV; NRSV, "sister church") is a symbolic way of sending greetings from the congregation in Rome. The letter ends with a blessing of peace for all those who are in Christ.

SECOND PETER

OUTLINE OF 2 PETER

I. **Greetings (1:1-2)**

II. **Knowledge, Virtue, and Calling (1:3-11)**

III. **Peter's Own Experiences (1:12-21)**

IV. **The Danger of False Prophets (2:1 22)**

V. **Is Christ Really Coming Again? (3:1-18)**

INTRODUCTION

Nature and Style of the Letter

Second Peter, although it claims to have been written by the apostle Peter (1:1, 13-15, 17-19) shortly after the completion of 1 Peter (3:1), clearly comes from a very different environment than that which produced 1 Peter (or the Gospels and Acts, in which Peter played an important role). Along with Jude and Revelation, 2 Peter is one of the latest and most unusual writings of the early Christian church.

Second Peter is now an accepted part of the Bible, but in the early church many Christians doubted its scriptural value. The church leaders Eusebius (A.D. 263–340) and Jerome (A.D. 340–420) both denied that it was Peter's work, and it was not accepted as an inspired writing by the Western church until the last part of the fourth century. In form and style 2 Peter

has common features with later, non-biblical Christian writings often called "pseudepigrapha" (false writings).

Similarities can be found between 2 Peter and second-century Christian books that claimed to represent Peter's thoughts or give the history of his life (the Apocalypse of Peter, the Acts of Peter, the Preaching of Peter, and the Gospel of Peter).

Like James and 1 John, 2 Peter is not a real letter but a sermon, a tract, or an encouraging homily. Its form is very similar to Jewish writings called "testimonials," or "valedictories." A testimonial was a farewell statement or "last will and testament" attributed to a famous person of faith that presented his final advice and predictions for the future (see 2 Peter 1:5-15; 3:3, 7, 10). Knowledgeable readers knew that the person represented in the testimonial had passed away long ago and that the author was really one of his disciples or someone who wanted to gain authority for his own teaching by using a well-known figure's name. Books written after the Old Testament was completed often used this style of writing. Good examples are found in The Testament of Moses, The Testaments of the Twelve Patriarchs, The Testament of Job, and 1 Enoch.

Early Christians did not consider such a practice to be plagiarism but merely a way to spread the master's teaching. For the first believers, attaching Peter's name to 2 Peter pointed to the wonderful tradition that stood behind this new "letter" being circulated in the church.

Sources

Second Peter is made up of a rich tapestry of different sources. It refers to the Old Testament (1:20-21; 2:5-10, 22; 3:8), but does not quote it directly. Extensive use is made of the New Testament letter of Jude, incorporating almost the whole book (most of verses 4-18) in 2:1-18 and 3:1-3. Clearly, the author of 2 Peter had Jude in front of him. As a comparison of the two writings shows, he adapts parts of Jude to address the unique circumstances of the church or churches to which he writes.

The author also draws on Jewish traditions outside the Old Testament (2:4, 11-14), and his work has similarities to Christian letters and books written during the second century (such as 1 and 2 Clement and the *Shepherd of Hermas*).

Clear references are made to the Gospels (compare 2 Peter 1:14 to John 21:18; 2 Peter 1:16-18 to Mark 9:2-13 and other parallels; 2 Peter 2:20 to Matthew 12:45 and Luke 11:26; 2 Peter 3:10 to Matthew 24:43 and Luke 12:39). In referring to the Gospels, the writer bolsters his connection to the apostle Peter.

Second Peter also makes an unusual statement about how difficult it is to understand Paul's writings (3:15-16), even though there is not much in the testimonial that resembles Paul's thought. Here Paul's letters have real authority, perhaps the authority of Scripture, and the author is worried about the way some Christians are misinterpreting them.

He also demonstrates that he is very familiar with pagan religions and philosophies that were popular in the Hellenistic world. Hellenism refers to the Greek culture that influenced most of the civilized world after it was conquered by Alexander the Great in the fourth century B.C. Second Peter uses several Greek words that are not found elsewhere in the Bible but were borrowed from the environment in which the author and his readers lived.

The Situation

Because of the sources the author uses it is likely that he was writing to people who lived outside of Palestine and were influenced both by Jewish tradition and by pagan culture and religion. Verse 4 in chapter 1 indicates why he is writing the testimonial. He is worried that the Christian readers may lose their faith by being influenced by the corruption that is in the world. As 2:1-22 demonstrates, false teachers have come into the church, bringing destructive heresies and the denial of Jesus Christ as Lord (2:1, 20). They are also trying to get Christians to accept a system of conduct that is unchristian and unethical (1:5-8; 2:9-10, 18-22).

A second problem is equally important: 2 Peter's readers are wondering whether Jesus will really come again as the prophets and apostles said he would (3:3-12). The testimonial is written to shore up their faith in and knowledge of Jesus Christ.

Although it is impossible to know for certain where the people who received 2 Peter lived, it is usually assumed that they were in Asia Minor (modern Turkey) or Egypt, places where Hellenistic culture and Judaism were both particularly strong. Because of the variety of temptations they faced (2:2-20), it is often suggested that they lived in a city environment, where any manner of evil could be found any time. Paul addresses similar concerns when he writes to the church in urban Corinth.

Authorship

The author of 2 Peter is an unknown church leader who uses Peter's name to add authority and prestige to the advice he is sending to some churches. It is impossible to know who the author was or where the letter was written. Because 2 Peter has little in common with 1 Peter, there is little evidence to suggest that the author belonged to the same school or circle that influenced the writing of 1 Peter.

Date of the Writing

Bible commentators have suggested possible dates of composition all the way from A.D. 60 (before Peter's death) to 160. Because of 2 Peter's adaptation of Jude, itself one of the last New Testament books, its use of pagan religious terms, and its similarities to Christian writings that were produced in the second century, it must be assigned a relatively late date, somewhere between 100 and 135. Commentators often suggest that 2 Peter was the last book in the New Testament to be written.

2 PETER 1

Introduction to This Chapter

Second Peter 1 may be outlined as follows:

I. Greetings (1:1-2)
II. Knowledge, Virtue, and Calling (1:3-11)
III. Peter's Own Experiences (1:12-21)

The Message of 2 Peter 1

The first part of 2 Peter assures readers that the promises of God and the prophecies of the Old Testament are true. The Lord will come again, and those who have opposed him will be judged. Those who are faithful, however, will be given the eternal Kingdom.

Verses 12-21 are written in the form of a farewell address. The author uses the experiences of the apostle Peter at Jesus' transfiguration to show that the prophecies

about him are not myths, but point to truth seen by Christian witnesses in actual historical events.

2 PETER 2

Introduction to This Chapter

This part of 2 Peter concentrates an attack on the false prophets who are troubling the church. They are the ones who are truly giving their "own interpretation" (1:20), not the word of God.

The Message of 2 Peter 2

Chapter 2 of 2 Peter is a condemnation of the false prophets who are spreading lies in the church and trying to lead the congregation into immoral behavior. Using examples taken from Jude, as well as the illustration of Lot, the author encourages those who are faithful to trust God to rescue them from trial.

2 PETER 3

Introduction to This Chapter

The final chapter urges the readers to maintain their confidence in what they have been taught. No matter what scoffers say, the Lord will come again and the day of judgment will take place.

The Message of 2 Peter 3

The last chapter of 2 Peter reminds believers of the predictions of the apostles and Jesus that the coming and judgment at the last day will surely take place. Not only will all beings on heaven and earth be judged, but a whole new universe will be created, all in God's own good time. Readers are to wait patiently for these events to take place and, in the meantime, give glory to God.

FIRST JOHN

OUTLINE OF 1 JOHN

INTRODUCTION

Style and Main Themes

First John is one of the most beautiful, elegant, and moving books in the New Testament. Through the use of simple and straightforward language (the whole book has a vocabulary of only 303 Greek words), the author introduces readers to the fundamentals of the Christian faith. Indeed, Martin Luther said he had never read a book with such simple, yet expressive, words.

First John is not really a letter, but is more like a tract—a sermon or a guidebook for Christians. The author takes simple themes and shows them from two angles, from a positive and from a negative side, in order to make them easy to understand and give his readers an opportunity to choose between them. Throughout his tract he interweaves discussions about the beginning and the end of time (1 John 1:1; 2:17-18, 24; 3:8), life and death (1:1, 2; 2:18, 25; 3:14-15; 5:11-12, 13); light and darkness (1:5-10; 2:8-11); truth and falsehood (1:6-10; 2:4-5, 21-24, 26-27; 3:7, 18-19; 4:1, 6; 5:20), and love and hatred (1:5; 2:10-12, 15; 3:11-18; 4:7-21; 5:1-5).

Although John uses an uncomplicated style, it is not easy to determine the outline of his message. Because he does not move logically from one point to another but overlaps and interweaves the basic themes like the colors in an exquisite carpet, any outline a commentator provides has to be somewhat artificial. His thinking is not like a law brief that gives evidence in a tightly argued sequence; it is more like a spiral of ideas twisted and turned around one another into a braided strand of pearls. Because he makes it clear in 1:1-5, however, that his basic objective is to bring a fundamental message about Jesus Christ so that his readers might have fellowship with God and eternal life, the outline provided here concentrates on John's desire to bring that message, the major points of the message, and the dangers to the message.

The Situation of 1 John

Like many other books of the New Testament, 1 John was written because of problems created in the church by those who were opposed to the basic truth about Jesus Christ—rival preachers and teachers who tried to lead other believers astray. Scholars are not certain whether there was one group of opponents or more than one that troubled John and the Christians who were members of the church to which he wrote. John pits his own testimony against the message or messages they bring (1:2-3). In 2:18-19 he refers to them as antichrists who "went out from us, but they did not belong to us," as if they were former members of his church who were trying to set up rival congregations. For this reason these opponents are often referred to as secessionists, those who were dividing the Christian fellowship by trying to form new branches of it.

Although it is difficult to know what John's opponents taught, it is likely they told people that Christians did not need to confess their sins to be forgiven (1:8-10; 2:1-2; 5:16-17) and that it was not necessary to accept Jesus as the Son of God to be close to God (2:22-25; 5:9-12). John's lengthy discussions of God's love and the necessity of extending that love to other people indicate that the opponents also failed to emphasize the need for Christian forgiveness and the importance of reaching out to the needy, as God had forgiven and reached out to the church in love through Christ. John knows that his opponents' view of the nature of Jesus Christ is completely wrong. In his tract he is determined to correct that view and show his readers who Jesus really is, teach them what it means to live as Christians, keep them out of the darkness of sin, and lead them to the light of truth and eternal life.

Authorship

The question of authorship in the three epistles of John is extremely complicated, and Bible scholars disagree about the true identity of John. From a superficial point of view, it is clear that 1, 2, and 3 John are closely connected to the Gospel of John. For that reason scholars have traditionally held that the apostle John, the disciple of Jesus, wrote all four books.

Many of the themes are identical, and it is obvious that the purposes in 1 John 1:1-5; 5:11-15 and John 20:30-31 and 21:24-25 are very similar. Early church tradition also attributed Revelation to the same man (Revelation 1:1, 4, 9; 22:8), and it was believed that John wrote all his books from the city of Ephesus.

As early as the third century, however, Origen wrote that some church leaders doubted that all the books were by the apostle. Although Eusebius (fourth century) believed the Gospel of John and 1 John to be authentic, he referred in his writings to the "so-called" second and third epistles of John, which, he said, might be the work of the evangelist or some other writer with the same name. Later, the man who translated the Bible into Latin,

Jerome, said that the author of 1 John was not the same elder (see 2 John 1:1; 3 John 1:1) who wrote 2 and 3 John.

Although some scholars still think that 1, 2, and 3 John, the Gospel of John, and the Revelation to John were all written by the apostle, most modern commentators are agreed that it is not that easy to determine who the authors of all these books were. The most likely solution is that 1, 2, and 3 John were all written over a period of time by the same author, and that this John closely patterned his letters after the Gospel of John, the first draft of which was written by the apostle John. Clearly the epistles were written by someone who felt himself to be spiritually close to the author of the Gospel of John, and it is possible that he was even a student of his.

Most scholars recognize that the disciples who gathered around John the apostle at Ephesus formed a tightly-knit group that worked together to spread the truth about Jesus Christ by writing the last chapter of John's Gospel, the letters of John, and Revelation. It is possible that the epistles of John were written because disagreement arose in the school about the proper interpretation of the Gospel of John, and that the letters of John represent the "official" view of the majority of the members. The letters were thus written to refute the teaching of those who preached a different version and were trying to undermine the congregations established by the apostle and those who followed him. Throughout this commentary the author of the epistles will be referred to as John, even though more than one person may have been involved in writing the letters.

Place and Date

Because of the problems of determining who wrote the three letters, it is also difficult to know where the epistles were written and who received them. They were probably composed in Ephesus, the home base of the Johannine "school," and were sent to churches in Asia Minor (modern Turkey) that the apostle and his disciples founded. Since it is generally agreed that the Gospel of John could not have been written before A.D. 90–100, and possibly even later, the epistles had to have been written sometime in the early part of the second century.

1 JOHN 1:1-4

Introduction to These Verses

First John opens with a long, involved sentence that extends from verse 1 all the way through verse 3. In these verses and in verses 4-5 John declares his purpose for writing his tract: He wants to proclaim the message of truth about Jesus Christ to his readers and testify to it from his own experience.

The Message of 1 John 1:1-4

In the first section of his tract John gives the reason why he is writing: He wants to proclaim the message about Jesus Christ, the Son of God, that he is the word of life. John builds on his readers' knowledge of the Gospel of John and calls them back to the lofty concepts of Jesus' identity introduced there.

The truth found in the Gospel of John is one that John and his colleagues testify to, and their testimony is based on the evidence presented by those who saw it with their own eyes. He wants the members of his church to accept this message because he wants to be sure that they have fellowship with God and with one another.

1 JOHN 1:5-10

Introduction to These Verses

John continues with his introduction of the Christian message he wants his readers to hear. "Message" in Greek is very similar to the word for messenger (*angelos*), which is translated "angel" in English. These words indicate that John and other believers in the church are preaching the Christian message or word about Jesus to his readers through their sermons and through the writing of the letter itself. In 1 John, John makes it clear that he is giving not just an opinion but rather a message directly from God or Jesus himself ("we have heard from him"). As he said in verses 1-4, it is God's own word.

The Message of 1 John 1:5-10

In these verses John defines the message he wishes to proclaim: God is light and in God there is no darkness at all. In this way he argues against his opponents who contend that God may be connected with darkness. In John's view God is light, and so is God's Son, Jesus Christ. Those who believe that they have not sinned and do not need the cross of Christ for the forgiveness of sins are the ones who are really in darkness. John's readers must take care, for if they accept such teaching the word of life will not be in them.

1 JOHN 2

Introduction to This Chapter

This chapter may be outlined as follows:

I. The Danger of Sin (2:1-14)
   A. Do not sin (2:1-6)
   B. Walk in the light (2:7-14)
II. The Danger of the World (2:15-17)
III. The Danger of the Antichrist (2:18-29)

The Message of 1 John 2

In this section John continues the discussion of the nature of sin begun in 1:5-10 and assures his fellow believers that their sins will be forgiven through the death of Jesus on the cross. Jesus himself will be their advocate when they stand before God as Judge.

In order to obtain forgiveness Christians need to live a life of love. If they truly want to walk in the light they must be sure to love one another. They must be certain that the temptations of the world, Satan (the Antichrist), and John's opponents (antichrists) do not destroy their faith.

1 JOHN 3:1–5:5

Introduction to These Verses

This section may be divided into the following parts:

I. What It Means to Be God's Children (3:1-3)
II. Sin Is Not Compatible with Love (3:4-10)
III. Love One Another (3:11-24)
IV. Watch Out for False Prophets (4:1-6)
V. Love Comes from God Through Christ (4:7–5:5)
   A. Love comes from God (4:7-13)
   B. God's love abides in Christ (4:14–5:5)

The Message of 1 John 3:1–5:5

These verses testify to the source of love that believers find in their hearts and experience in their lives: It comes from God. God is love by nature, and those who believe in God can give love to others because God has first given it to them. Anyone who claims to love God but hates other people is a liar, because it is impossible to know God's love without sharing it.

God's love is very powerful because it removes all fear. Opponents, antichrists, the devil, and false spirits are all impotent before God's love. Through Jesus Christ God has defeated all enemies and brings believers victory.

1 JOHN 5:6-10

Introduction to These Verses

In these verses John recapitulates several themes he has mentioned before: he who came (2:28; 3:2), testimony (1:2; 4:14), making God a liar (1:10), belief in Jesus Christ as the Son of God (1:7; 5:5), eternal life (1:1-4), and truth (1:6; 2:4; 3:18-19; 4:6).

The Message of 1 John 5:6-10

John concludes the argument he began in 1:1-4. His message brings the truth about Jesus Christ the Son of God, and only those who believe it can have eternal life. In addition to John's own witness, four other sources of testimony are available: the water, the blood of Christ, the Holy Spirit, and God. The evidence is unshakable: Truly, Jesus is the Son of God.

1 JOHN 5:11-21

Introduction to These Verses

This section has two major parts.
I. The Message Brings Eternal Life (5:11-13)
II. The Message Keeps Persons from Sin (5:14-21)

The Message of 1 John 5:11-21

John's tract concludes with the confidence that believers may pray in Jesus' powerful name and expect their prayers to be answered. Believers can be confident that they will have eternal life even though the rest of the world is in the death grip of the evil one. They must guard against all substitutes for faith in Jesus Christ as the Son of God, and must never worship idols.

SECOND JOHN

OUTLINE OF 2 JOHN

INTRODUCTION

Unlike 1 John, where the author does not identify himself, the writer of 2 John immediately says who he is in the very first verse, where he calls himself "the elder." In Greek the words the elder can be literally translated "the presbyter." For centuries Christians have debated the meaning of this ambiguous title and have tried to determine who the presbyter was. The task is complicated by the fact that *presbyteros* can mean *old man, respected person,* or *a leader in the church* (see Acts 20:17; 1 Timothy 5:17; Titus 1:5; James 5:14;1 Peter 5:1). Suggestions have been made that he was the apostle John in his old age; a man among a group of elders, who were each assigned different geographic areas in the church; a church leader named John who was not a disciple of Jesus and was not acquainted with the apostle John; or, as is most likely, a student of the apostle John who based his letters on the Gospel of John. In 2 and 3 John this John brings the apostle's message to the members of his church and refutes

those who try to preach a different Christ. The title "elder" may indicate that the churches to which he is writing are under his administrative oversight and that he functions somewhat as a bishop.

Recipients

Second John is addressed to "the chosen lady and her children" (NIV) or "the elect lady and her children" (NRSV). While it is not inconceivable that this might be translated as "the chosen Kyria' or "the lady Electa," the much more likely meaning is "the church and its members" or "a local congregation."

Verse 13 indicates that the letter comes from another congregation that contains other children of God. Perhaps John uses symbolic language because he does not want his opponents to know where these churches are if his letter should fall into the wrong hands.

Main Themes

Second John picks up several themes that are prominent in 1 John; truth (verse 2), love (verses 5-6), and the danger of deceivers and the Antichrist (verse 7). This letter appears to be a follow-up of 1 John, and was written at a time when the situation described there had deteriorated. Although some of the children (members) are following the truth, others are still being deceived.

The Message of 2 John

Second John is a letter written by John and members of his church community to another church that is being misled by John's opponents. John warns the members not to accept a lie for the truth and lose their faith. John repeats several themes that were important ones in 1 John (love, truth, abiding in Christ, the commandment of love), and warns his readers not to have contact with deceivers.

THIRD JOHN

OUTLINE OF 3 JOHN

INTRODUCTION

The shortest book in the New Testament, consisting of only 219 Greek words, 3 John, unlike 1 and 2 John, seems to be a personal letter rather than a message or warning to a congregation. Although the author is the same as 2 John ("the elder," verse 1), the epistle is addressed directly to beloved Gaius.

This letter discusses some of the same subjects found in 1 and 2 John (truth, verses 3-4, 12; love, verse 6), but deals more specifically with three individuals. The letter brings encouragement to Gaius, chastises Diotrephes for failing to acknowledge the elder's authority, and praises Demetrius because true believers have testified to the truth of his life and ministry.

The situation is also different from those presumed for 1 and 2 John. Two backgrounds are possible. Either 3 John is a totally independent writing that was sent to someone named Gaius to correct an isolated set of circumstances, or it continues to address the problems already addressed in the previous letters. Most commentators think the second possibility is the more likely. If so, deterioration of the situation described in 1 and 2 John must mean that more people are defecting to John's opponents and that he is getting more and more worried. The circumstances have become so critical that he has given up addressing his readers in general terms and is now being directly critical of one of the chief troublemakers, Diotrephes.

The Message of 3 John

Third John is a personal letter from the elder to a church leader in one of the communities under his pastoral care. He has heard of Gaius's faithfulness from missionaries who have visited the church, and he wants to give him some advice.

He encourages Gaius to continue to offer Christian hospitality to visiting preachers and teachers and to support them when they go on to other churches. He also warns him about Diotrephes, who is completely opposed to the elder's authority. Finally, he praises Demetrius for the manner of his life, which testifies to the truth about Jesus Christ.

JUDE

OUTLINE OF JUDE

I. **Refuting the Ungodly (verses 1-4)**

II. **Do Not Be Like the Ungodly (verses 5-23)**

III. **Closing Doxology (verses 24-25)**

INTRODUCTION

Nature and Style

Jude, like 2 Peter, is sent to an unknown congregation or congregations and concerns the danger of false teachers. The author wants to keep his readers in the Christian fold, so he writes about "the salvation we share" and urges them to "contend for the faith" (verse 3). In verses 15-16 he gives several negative examples from Jewish tradition to show how bad the influence of his opponents is. What Christians are going through, he advises, is not surprising (verses 17-23). Those who understand the predictions of the apostles (verse 7) and are centered in the "Holy Spirit," "love of God,' and "mercy of our Lord Jesus Christ" (verses 20-21) should expect such things. The letter ends with one of the most beautiful benedictions in the New Testament, in which believers are directed to the God and Savior who will never let them fall (verses 24-25).

Jude has some similarities to other New Testament writings. Since it tries to preserve Jewish ethical values against pagan temptations, it is similar to James.

Where it emphasizes the last days and the coming judgment of God, it is like 1 and 2 Peter and Revelation.

The style of the letter indicates that the author has been influenced by both Jewish and Greek thought. Many of his examples (Moses, Michael, Balaam) are from the Old Testament or later Jewish tradition. And his method of Scripture interpretation is similar to that used in the Dead Sea Scrolls. The writer is also dependent on Jewish apocalyptic literature. Apocalyptic writings report mysterious revelations by God and his angels, and portray the divine will for the last days. Mark 13:1 (and parallels in Matthew and Luke) and Revelation provide other New Testament examples. In Jude reference is made to 1 Enoch and The Assumption of Moses (verses 6, 9, 12-16).

The author is also very familiar with Hellenistic Greek ideas, as his polished Greek style, his vocabulary, and his references to Greek religious and philosophical concepts clearly show. Jude must have been written to people in a culture that was strongly influenced by Jewish and Greek thought. The recipients probably lived either in Syria (where Jude may have been well-known), Asia Minor, or Egypt.

Situation

Although the whole letter is written to combat the ungodly persons mentioned in verse 4, it is never clearly said who they really are. Scholars often argue that these persons might have been Gnostic heretics. These heretics thought they had special knowledge (*gnosis*) and liberty from God.

Since the writer of Jude never discusses the meaning of the word *knowledge*, however, as the author of 1 John repeatedly does, and since he is not concerned about elemental spirits or matters of the cosmos (key ideas in Gnostic philosophy) as Ephesians (1:20-21; 3:10, 18) is, it is more likely that Jude's opponents are not Gnostic heretics but church members. Jude indicates that they are involved in church life and regularly take communion (These "are blemishes on your love-feasts," verse 12). Apparently the danger of their interpretation of the Christian faith is that they have misunderstood Jewish apocalyptic writings (verses 15-16) and are misleading the church about the nature of true Christian freedom. Perhaps they misconstrued Paul's teachings about Christian freedom and are urging members to become too libertine in their actions (see verses 4, 10, 11, 15, 16 in comparison with Romans 1:18-32; 3:8; 6:1, 15; Galatians 5:1, 13). Whoever the opponents are, Jude has only the harshest words for them (verses 10-13, 16).

Author

The author calls himself "Jude, a servant of Jesus Christ and brother of James" (verse 1). The implication, accepted by some scholars, is that he is the blood brother of Jesus. But other scholars dispute that claim, since the author of Jude does not identify himself with the apostles and sees them as respected men from the past (verse 17). Jude, however, would have known the apostles well, his brother James being one of them (Acts 12:17; 15:13; 1 Corinthians 15:7; Galatians 1:19; 2:9, 12). It is also unusual that the author of Jude refers to himself as Jesus' *servant*

rather than his *brother*. Jude, along with Jesus, furthermore, was raised in a Jewish Aramaic-speaking environment in Galilee, and would not be familiar with the Hellenistic-Greek ideas that are found in this book.

It may be that the writer of Jude, like James, borrows the name of one of Jesus' brothers in order to increase the value and authority of his own writing. Who he really was remains a mystery.

Date

Because of the similarities of style and content, Jude was probably written around the same time as James, 1 Peter, and 1 John, at the end of the first century or the beginning of the second century.

JUDE 1-4

Introduction to These Verses

Jude begins in the style of a letter, as all the other Catholic Epistles do.

The Message of Jude 1-4

The opening words of Jude bring a typical Christian greeting from the author and supply the reason why he is writing. Opponents are threatening the salvation of the readers, and Jude wants to encourage them to fight against falsehood. Those who have been misleading them have denied Jesus Christ by their words and actions, and they will get their just punishment.

JUDE 5-23

Introduction to These Verses

The second part of Jude is divided into two major sections: (1) Examples are given from the Old Testament and Jewish tradition of ungodly angels and irreverent people. Jude warns that behavior like theirs leads to condemnation (verses 5-16). (2) Advice is also provided not to be like them but to remain in the love of God (verses 17-23).

The Message of Jude 5-23

The main section of Jude is concerned with giving a warning to believers about what happens to those who follow the behavior of the ungodly. A number of examples are given of heavenly and human individuals. In verses 17-23 encouragement is provided to those who hold fast. They will be kept in the love of God in Christ and by their own faithfulness will be able to save others from the punishment of eternal fire (verse 7).

JUDE 24-25

Introduction to These Verses

Jude closes with a beautiful benediction that is often used at the end of services of worship today. The word *doxology* comes from the Greek word for *glory* (*doxa*), which refers to God's weight or value. Doxologies give praise and honor to God, and often express faith when nothing more can be said. Other examples are found in Romans 9:5; 11:36; 2 Corinthians 1:20; Galatians 1:5; Ephesians 1:14.

The Message of Jude 24-25

Jude ends with words of praise for God and Christ. God will keep true believers from falling from salvation. Through Christ God has power and authority over all creatures in heaven and on earth and for all eternity.

REVELATION

OUTLINE OF REVELATION

INTRODUCTION

Nearly three hundred miles north of Jerusalem, along the coastline of the Mediterranean, the land juts sharply to the west on what appears on the map to be an enormous peninsula. The coastline, as it bends west, forms the south edge of modern Turkey—land referred to by geographers as Asia Minor. The coast continues unevenly for nearly three hundred miles before it turns north again.

There, at the northward turn, several islands cluster in the Mediterranean. One of them, thirty miles out, is Patmos—in the first-century Roman Empire a prison island. Rome used Patmos to isolate political prisoners. Sometime between A.D. 81 and 91 a Christian prophet named John was exiled on Patmos. And, while imprisoned on Patmos, John received the inspiration to write the book we know as Revelation.

We know little about John other than what can be deduced from his writing. We know he wrote during a time when the church was young and faced persecution. He clearly had the care and welfare of the church at heart. And he saw, equally as clearly, the peril faced by the church— partly from persecution and partly from a more subtle danger: affluence. And clearest of all, he had searched the Old Testament (the Bible of the early church) for a key to understanding his times. What was clear to his eyes soon crystallized in his mind, preparing him for the visions he was to see and for the immense task of interpreting and explaining them to the church.

The Historical Setting of Revelation

ROME

From the time of Caesar Augustus, the first Roman emperor (27 B.C.–A.D. 14), to Domitian (A.D. 81–96), the Roman Empire reached enormous proportions. It included land from Israel in the south to modern-day England in the north. That expansion took eleven emperors slightly more than 125 years.

Although the Romans tended to rule with an even hand, much depended upon the emotional stability of the emperor. Two, especially, stand out for their instability and violence: Nero (A.D. 54–68) and Domitian. Nero was notoriously vicious and was the first great persecutor of the church. Early tradition accuses him of the deaths of Paul and Peter. The disastrous fire of Rome occurred during his reign and, to counter a pervasive rumor that he had started it, Nero blamed the Christians. Horrible tortures followed. Although the persecutions took place mostly in Rome, word spread and Christians were badly shaken.

Domitian, coming to the throne thirteen years after Nero's death, resumed the violence. Some forms of country-and-emperor worship had accompanied the growth of the empire, but it had never been a life-or-death issue. Domitian took it seriously. One of the main centers of his cult was the city of Smyrna, and we will see in the book of Revelation (2:8-11) that Christians in that place faced a very difficult time.

During the time when Revelation was written, Rome had accompanied its vast political expansion with an equally expansive program of business and economics. As John makes vivid in the later chapters of Revelation, Rome kept a world full of nations, builders, craft guilds, bankers, and merchants well occupied.

Shipping routes spread from Rome in every direction, tying most of the ancient world to its web. From that rich commerce and its exciting variety of goods and opportunities, Christians found an endless supply of subtle enticements.

THE CHURCH

By the time of Domitian, several decisive events had occurred in the church. For one, the Christians who had remained in Jerusalem after Jesus' death had finally left. Within a year after their leaving (A.D. 70), the Jews rebelled against Rome. In retaliation, the Roman army destroyed Jerusalem. From that time on, the early church was cut off from the city of its origin. However, thanks to its kinship with the Jews, it would continue to suffer the aftershocks of persecution aimed at the Jews.

Since Paul's journeys to Asia Minor, that area had responded increasingly well to Christian missionary activity. By A.D. 75, Asia Minor was no longer the mission field, it was the home of the church. The church's roots held more firmly in Asia Minor than anywhere else in the world. Ephesus was its spiritual center, much as Jerusalem had been for the early Christians and for the Jews before them.

The new home was a mixed blessing. Large cities and good ports put the church at the heart of the ancient world. The mission advanced. But advancement brought increased visibility, and when Christians refused to worship the emperor it was even more necessary to make an example of them.

The success of the Christian cause also meant the entry of many Christians into the mainline culture. The subtle temptations of affluence and influence followed. Indeed, John worried as much about that as he did about persecution.

Within the space of two generations, the church had changed its environment from Israel to Asia Minor, had survived the death of nearly all of its founders, and had gone from the exhilaration of rapid expansion to the ravages of unwarranted persecution and the incursion of greed and temptation. By the time John was on Patmos, the worst sides of all those changes enclosed upon the church. To John, things seemed out of control.

John wrote his book to a church that needed to have its apparent chaos put in the larger perspective of God's controlling purposes. Behind the scenes, he wrote, God is even now making the powers of evil accomplish the divine will. History is coming to its end, but it is the end that God has in mind for it. To the Christians who have given in to temptation, John wrote, "Keep the faith. God knows your sins." To those who kept the faith and suffered the consequences, John wrote, "God is in control. Hold on. Endure!"

THE CHURCH BETWEEN TWO CULTURES

During the first century of the Christian church, two great cultures still shaped the thoughts and lives of the people of Asia Minor. Obviously Rome exerted influence. But the area had been dominated by Greece for years before that. Without the resources of mass media, it was not easy for one conquering nation to obliterate the influence of another. It took a great deal of time for the culture of one to replace the other.

For a long time, in Asia Minor, the Greek and Roman cultures coexisted, somewhat like two waves—the first on the shore saturating the sands and then receding, the second overarching and overreaching the first. For a while, although they moved in contrary motion, the two pressed upon the shore simultaneously.

Greek life, lore, and language, first on the shores of Asia Minor, had spread far and soaked deep. The second wave, Rome, rose higher and reached farther, and fell with more oppressive weight.

The Jews had settled in Asia Minor well before the time of Jesus, during the time of Greek control. They spoke Greek. The early Christians, like Paul, spoke Greek. The Gospels were written in a Greek dialect of the common people, called *koine*. All the books of the New Testament were first written in Greek.

The official language of the Roman Empire was Latin. It was the language of the new, higher, and larger wave. And it settled over Asia Minor from the top down. That is, it was the language of the politicians, of administration, and of business.

Most people conducted their daily lives in Greek. And that language, too, had its various levels. Philosophy, religion, and much social life found their natural voices speaking Greek. It was the tongue of the cultural highbrow. But it was also, in some of its dialects, the tongue of the street.

The book of Revelation was not highbrow. John wrote in Greek, not Latin; that is, he wrote in the language of the people and not of the powerful. But he also wrote awkwardly, and was often uncertain about the proper tenses of verbs. His was almost the language of everyday life, of the common folk. In its vitality and color, it was very different from the stern administrative prose of Latin—as different as the clamor of enthusiasm in the streets is from the solemn deliberations of a budget committee.

If we can judge from John's book, then, the early Christians lived between two cultures, not at all members of the dominant class. Nor were they, for the most part, warmly identified with the Greeks. They spoke the language of the common person, not the intellectual, and they worked most closely, at least at first, with the Greek-speaking Jews who had settled in Asia Minor many years before Rome became its captor.

THE EMPERORS OF ROME

The following list of emperors of Rome contains eleven names. In Revelation many references are made through symbolism to the emperors of Rome. Often they refer to the time of Domitian, who ruled during the era in which John wrote. But the references are confusing. For example, he is, at times, considered the seventh emperor.

At other times, it is assumed that Nero, who died in A.D. 68, will arise from the dead and come back to rule, and he will be the eighth emperor. To further confuse the matter, it may also be the case that Domitian is referred to as though he were a second Nero.

We do not know how John kept count. But most scholars agree that he probably did not regard Galba, Otho, and Vitellius as emperors. They each reigned briefly during a time of great confusion, and met unfortunate deaths. None had much to do with shaping the contours of Roman history.

One suggestion for understanding John's references to the seven emperors is to remember that seven is a number for completeness. He may simply have had in mind the entire leadership of Rome up to his time.

Augustus: 27 B.C.–A.D. 14
Tiberius: A.D. 14–37
Caligula: 37–41
Claudius: 41–54
Nero: 54–68
Galba: 68–69
Otho: 69
Vitellius: 69
Vespasian: 69–79
Titus: 79–81
Domitian: 81–96

ASIA MINOR AND THE MEDITERRANEAN SEA

From the maps of the Mediterranean, one can understand the great advantage geography had given Rome. Chapter 18 of the book of Revelation shows us the merchants of the earth, sobbing at the destruction of that enormous city. (In that chapter *Babylon* is John's special code word for Rome.)

But not only do the merchants sob, the shipmasters and seafaring men also cry out in grief. Not that they regret the fate of the Romans as people. They regret the loss of one of their most lucrative markets.

Rome did receive much of its wealth overland. The roads of all the lands around the Mediterranean had been made safe for travel. Roman soldiers guarded them. It was thanks to the Romans that Paul and Silas took their missionary journeys safe from harm.

Rome had also cleared the sea of pirates. The nations of the Mediterranean could export and import. Lively commerce arose, with Rome at its center. In fact, Rome became the economic safety net for the entire region.

By John's time, the commercial interests of Rome reached as far overseas as India—to which Rome exported linen, coral, and metals, and from which were imported silks, perfumes, and jewels. Rome was also a vigorous importer of slaves. When one recalls that John refers to Christians as servants and that the word he used is the ancient word for "slave," one knows John had firsthand experience with the absolute obedience required of slaves.

Not only Rome, but two of the cities to which John sent his letters were also important coastal cities: Smyrna and Ephesus. Like Rome, they shared the wealth gained from a thriving import-export business. In these Roman cities, the wares of the entire known world created unrivaled opulence, for some. John knew the strategic importance of Rome's position at the center of that entire network of buying and selling.

The inland cities to which John wrote in Asia Minor were also strategically located. They were, for the most part, gateway cities—opening to important land routes. Thyatira, for example, lay on a great road that connected the Hermus Valley and the trade centers of the East to the city of Pergamum. Laodicea, considerably south of Thyatira, lay on an important road that began at the coastal city of Ephesus and stretched far into Phrygia. Laodicea may have been the doorkeeper of the most traveled trade route to the West in ancient times.

The area that housed the early church everywhere fed into the Roman overlord of the house. Revelation is not by accident, then, a book about two cities that contest with each other for control of history. The city of Rome, to John's eyes, reached everywhere through and beyond the visible landscape. Only the city of God had hopes of outreaching it.

Who Is John?

The name *John* was not uncommon in Rome, and it was certainly widely used in the church and in its stories: John the Baptist, John the son of Zebedee, John the author of the gospel, John the writer of the epistles, John the author of Revelation. Were some of them the same person? Some traditions said yes, some said no. Of all the writings we have by men named John, the gospel and the epistles seem most similar.

Revelation, however, differs greatly from all the others. It has a different style, different content, and uses a different vocabulary. Most scholars think the writer of Revelation was not the same person who wrote the gospel of John.

But who was he? We don't know who, but we can learn a lot about him from his book. For example, he spoke openly about Christ, even in times when Christians felt immense pressure to worship the emperor. He was faithful during times of persecution—so faithful that the authorities arrested him and exiled him on the island of Patmos.

John was deeply aware of the social and political events of the day. He could grasp their general direction and could measure them by his own rule of faith.

He had a pastor's concern for the churches in Asia Minor. Everything he wrote was directed to those tempted and beleaguered congregations, pointing behind the veil of daily events to the God who was working to save them and to bring history to its end.

He knew the Old Testament well, especially the prophets and the first five books, the Torah. He had pored over those scrolls in search of the key that unlocked the secret of God's work in history. Old Testament images and symbols became the language of his faith, the way he learned to talk about the world and God's will. And he had found particularly important those prophetic writings called *apocalyptic*. Those books used dramatic images, vivid scenery, and extraordinary stories and parables. Expressing itself in each of them is a testimony to God's glory, to the evil of the times, and to God's soon-to-occur intervention in history on behalf of the faithful.

John was first and foremost a Christian prophet. He believed that God had acted to save human beings through Christ. It was through Christ that he saw into the heart of God's purpose, God's plan to form and preserve the church until the end of time.

Finally, John was well-known and respected by the Christians in Asia Minor. His book, possibly the only one of its kind to come from a Christian, had to be accepted on the authority of his name alone.

Revelation: The Word and the Book

John's book is sometimes called *Revelation* and sometimes the *Apocalypse*. Both words come down to the same thing. *Apocalypse* comes from two words in the Greek, one meaning "to remove" and the other meaning "the cover." In Greek myth, Calypso, the daughter of Atlas, dwelt upon an island where she kept Ulysses captive, much as John was held captive on Patmos. *Calypso* means "the concealer." Something that reveals what has been concealed is apocalyptic (*apo* means "to remove"). Therefore, the name that is given to Revelation and to many other books that promise to reveal God's hidden plan is *apocalypse*.

The word *revelation* also comes from two words, the first meaning "to undo" and

APOCALYPTIC LITERATURE

What exactly is an apocalyptic book? It is one that has most of these characteristics:

(1) It bears the name of an important person in religious history. Usually the writings claim to have been written several years earlier, to have been hidden until "just the right time in history" and to have surfaced only recently. Apocalyptic books deal with the present events in a highly symbolic way, therefore, as though the long-dead author had foreseen them much earlier.

(2) It takes the form of a report of visions. The visions usually have remarkably vivid and frequently frightening contents. An apocalypse may contain several visions, each repeating emphases of earlier ones, but repeating them in more intense images.

(3) It uses many symbols, especially combinations of numbers (for example, the number seven meant completeness or perfection to the Jews) or animals or strange creatures that have special meanings.

(4) It emphasizes a present crisis in history. History is portrayed as a struggle between good and evil that now rages toward its final battle. The writer believes the end is near, and encourages the reader to remain faithful even though the force of evil seems almost overwhelming. The writer helps the reader to interpret the signs of the times. Properly read, those signs reveal to the faithful that God is in control.

(5) It holds out hope only in God's intervention. History has strayed beyond the limits of humans to redeem it, and has fallen entirely into the province of evil. Rescue comes only from beyond history, only from God.

(6) It makes many allusions to other books, usually those of prophets or other apocalyptic writers. It can do this because an apocalypse is, from the beginning, a written book—unlike those of Old Testament prophets or those about Jesus, which were first spoken and then later written down by disciples. The author of an apocalypse sits down to write, not with remembered words in his ear, but with books at his elbow. He has had his vision, and he has his reference books to find the words and symbols he needs to describe and interpret them. He writes in a way that other readers of prophecies and apocalypses can well understand.

An apocalypse, then, is a vast and energetic reinterpretation of current events. It tells the news, but not from the standpoint of the powerful whose daily profits make everything seem well to them. It tells the news from the standpoint of those who see the ravages of the poor and the high price morality pays for profit. It reports: These are not the best of times but the worst, and God is coming soon.

the second meaning "veil." A revelation is something that removes the veil and lets us see face-to-face.

More than a word, though, *apocalyptic* is also a form of writing, much as mysteries and romances are forms of writing. The book of Revelation is written in the form of an apocalypse.

The book of Revelation has most of the characteristics shown in the box on page 603. Although it does not claim that its author lived in the past or that it lay hidden long and only recently came to light, it does rely upon striking visions. Combinations of numerical and animal symbols appear on every page. Clearly it describes a crisis of great magnitude occurring in history. It ascribes its authorship to a writer who bears a famous name in the church.

Further, through each vision the writer testifies to God's coming intervention, and to God's presence in the here and now— the evil powers only think they are in control. Allusions to Isaiah, Exodus, Daniel, Ezekiel, Jeremiah, and Zechariah enliven and inform nearly every vision and parable. The book was certainly a written product from the onset; John is often told to write what he sees, and in 1:3 he promises a blessing to those who read the book aloud in church.

The book of Revelation, then, is an apocalypse. It is also a powerful Christian political tract for its time. The book radically rejected the way the Romans saw history. The Romans, at the height of their power, had confidence in their cause. From John's point of view, the very things that supported Rome were the cause of crisis. Wealth and power make for impressive governmental statistics.

And when cities begin taking pride in their religious devotion to empire and emperor, the good stars may seem to be in their ascendancy.

For John, wealth spelled temptation and short-sighted satisfaction with splendor. And power, usually corrupting in itself, in the hands of evil could call bad good and destroy those who dared to say otherwise. But worse, power and wealth combined to entice Christians who wanted somehow to have both the fruits of luxury and the benefits of discipleship. Many submitted, and distorted the gospel so they could enjoy sexual and social license and yet claim to be Christians.

John would not allow secular wealth and power the sole right to interpret history. He wrote against the nation that surrounded him and against the influence it was having on the church. That Rome had its own religion and, at times, forced all to worship at its shrines, only added evidence to a case that, in John's mind, had already reached its verdict.

His book makes the case and reveals the verdict. The courtroom has been behind the scenes of history; but what was hidden is now revealed. And, as in any true court of law, justice is rendered. That is good news for the faithful and bad news for the unfaithful. That is also the theme of John's book: Revelation.

How to Read the Book of Revelation

After reading any other book in the New Testament, Revelation comes as quite a surprise. Its images, bold pictures, and sometimes strident voice may make a reader feel uneasy. Its message is disturbing. The fact that it is unrelenting in its insistence that we pay attention only makes us more uneasy. Add to that its display of violence and carnage, and it is little wonder that Christians turn away from its pages.

But the book can be read with great profit. Through even its stormiest passages come rays of the hope that lies behind the book. John did not intend simply to frighten his readers. He wanted to strengthen them. The way he wrote would not have been unfamiliar to first-century Christians. But, because we do not know their tradition, we often fail to see what John was up to.

The following eight suggestions may help you bear with John's book until you become at ease with it. When you do, it will become easier to see the vision of the light that drove him to decry the world's darkness.

These eight suggestions are not "keys" to the book. They do not pretend that Revelation is a single large and secret code from which we can decipher each jot and tittle of history. They do offer you a way of identifying several of the things John does. When you begin to see how he works, and to recognize the patterns he uses, you may feel encouraged to venture interpretations of your own.

(1) Realize that Revelation, while it is unique in the New Testament, was not unusual in its time. There had been other books like it, some in the Old Testament, and some elsewhere. While no other New Testament books are completely like it, some parts of those books have sections that are similar to Revelation. The most famous of those is called "The Little Apocalypse" and is found in the Gospel of Mark (see Mark 13).

(2) Realize that John did not write in a vacuum. He had a library, and Revelation was written by quoting sources from several other books in his library. Whatever John's visions were, he turned often to his favorite books to help him describe what he saw and to interpret it to his readers. Among his favorite books were these from the Old Testament: Genesis, Exodus, Psalms, Isaiah, Ezekiel, Jeremiah, and Daniel.

(3) Study the outline of Revelation. Notice the patterns in it. There are several sets of sevens—letters to seven churches, seven seals, seven bowls. The number seven is symbolic in the Book of Revelation. It refers to perfection or to completeness. Thus, the seven churches represent not only themselves, but all of the church.

Look at the progression of the book. View it as a single extended sermon, making one point in several ways, each way more dramatic and powerful than the one before.

(4) Think of a stage and all of its apparatus. Imagine John as the playwright. Onstage is the drama of the historical events challenging the first-century church. Backstage is God, who knows the true meaning of those events and who wants the players onstage to understand them as well.

The stage setting, seen by the Christians, is the Greek culture and the Roman government. Because of that, the players interpret the events as though they were all caused by and controlled by the Greeks and Romans.

John's book puts up new scenery. He decorates the stage with important symbols from the Old Testament, symbols that remind the players that God controls history. He puts up scenes of great natural devastation, far beyond what humans could do, to call attention to the God of the creation. The real meaning of history, he wants them to see, comes not from Rome but from God.

As you read Revelation, remember that it was first read by people who saw in the world around them evidence only of Roman power and success. They needed to see scenes that reminded them of God's essential role in history.

(5) Imagine yourself in a time of historical duress, in the presence of great

temptation and evil. What assurances would you want? What signs would you look for? How would you console and encourage your fellow Christians or your children? Which images and stories from your religious tradition would you call on to remind them and yourself that history belongs to God and that it is important to keep the faith? In other words, imagine yourself in the position of John or his readers.

(6) Read the book through without worrying about the precise meaning of all of its signs and symbols. Keep track of its cumulative effect on you. Pay special attention to the effects of such passages as Revelation 21:3-4: "See, the home of God is among mortals. He will dwell with them as their God; they will be his peoples, and God himself will be with them; he will wipe every tear from their eyes. Death will be no more; and mourning and crying and pain will be no more, for the first things have passed away."

(7) Read the Book of Revelation as though it were a series of stories. Don't try at first to force connections. Let the stories stand on their own; think about them; see what connections emerge in your mind.

(8) Don't force premature conclusions about what the book means. Some think it is a detailed prediction of the course of human history. Others think it is a dramatic collection of stories and teachings meant to encourage Christians at all times to be faithful. Others think other things. Christians throughout history have produced a great variety of approaches to this book. So, don't feel rushed to come up with the definitive interpretation.

REVELATION 1:1-8

Introduction to These Verses

A prologue is a brief introduction. In ancient drama, a small speech or event occurred onstage to alert the audience to the significance of the play they would soon see. John uses his prologue to set the stage for the letters, stories, and parables he plans to present.

In the prologue, John tells about the source of his message (an angel), the content and urgency of his message (what must soon take place), and the recipients of his message (the seven churches of Asia Minor).

Several terms that are important to the book of Revelation are mentioned for the first time in the prologue: "revelation," "witness," "angel," "spirit," the number "seven," and the Greek words "alpha" and "omega."

It is well to be alerted now that John has several words he uses frequently. Their meanings become clearer as they occur throughout the book.

The prologue has two parts:
I. The Source of John's Message (1:1-3)
II. Greetings to the Seven Churches (1:4-8)

The Message of Revelation 1:1-8

"Revelation" means to remove the veil, to make visible something that has been hidden. Christ, although hidden from the nations (even though it is through their own blindness that they cannot see him), has been revealed to John. John is to be a prophet and witness, to tell what he has seen. His message is to be read aloud in the seven churches of Asia Minor. The number seven is a symbol for completeness or totality. The letters, therefore, are to be read to all of the churches. What does the prologue affirm?

- That God has been revealed through prophets and angels;

- That God has continued to be known through Christ, who gave John the message of Revelation;

- That Christ is the ruler over all the earth;

- That God is eternal (the Alpha and Omega);

- That we are a kingdom and all priests of God.

REVELATION 1:9-20

Introduction to These Verses

In this part, John tells what happened to him as he received the first vision recorded in his book. He also demonstrates his familiarity with important Jewish symbols—something that would give his work authority with the early Christians, many of whom were converted Jews. It would have meant a good deal to all Christians, however, because the Old Testament was the only Bible of the early church. But most of all, he shows how those traditional symbols could be turned to the service of the Christian church.

John speaks in this part of receiving his message while he was "in the Spirit on the Lord's day." We do not know precisely what kind of an experience that was or how much of his message came to him at that time. In Revelation, he intermingles reports of visions with interpretations and with warnings to his readers to pay attention.

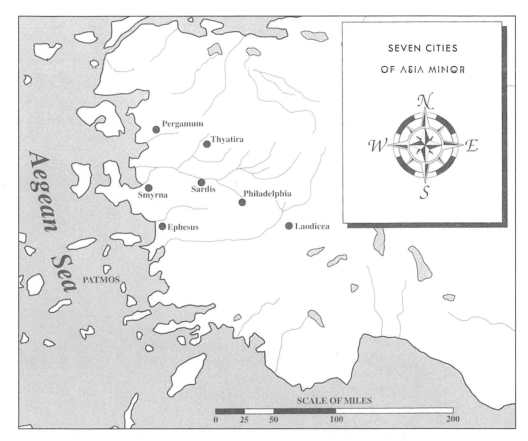

Reports of spellbinding experiences are not rare in the Bible. Nor are books or actions based on visions.

Here is an outline of Revelation 1:9-20:

I. The Call and the Command (1:9-11)

II. The One Like the Son of Man (1:12-16)

III. An Order and an Explanation (1:17-20)

The Message of Revelation 1:9-20

John tells about his imprisonment on the island of Patmos. There, on the Lord's Day, he is told to write a message to the seven churches. The message he writes comes from "one like the Son of Man" (a traditional figure in Old Testament writings, but one whom Christians took to refer to the crucified and risen Christ). What is the meaning of John's vision of "one like the Son of Man"?

- Christ is in the midst of the church.

- Christ is pure and powerful, and will bring justice.

- Death and hell will not have the final word in the lives of believers. Christ holds the key to them both.

- Prophecy concerns both what is and what is to come.

- The church of Christ extends from earth into heaven.

REVELATION 2:1-17

Introduction to These Verses

The letter was an important form of communication in the ancient world. Archaeologists have found evidence of many different kinds of letters. One kind most frequently found is the instructional letter: one that gives advice, teaches, or offers information on important topics.

One reason for the popularity of letters is that, during the first century A.D., the ancient world achieved a very high level of literacy. A much greater percentage of the population could read than was able to during the Middle Ages. Some scholars say there were more readers in first-century Rome than at any time until the modern age.

Christian literature features many letters. Paul's New Testament writings are all letters. But other Christians wrote them as well. We have many examples from bishops and church leaders from throughout the early centuries. When John chose to put part of his book in the form of letters, he knew he had selected a literary form that his readers knew and would take seriously.

John's letters may have been written independently of one another and have been sent to the churches. It is clear that John knew the circumstances of each of the congregations to which he wrote. If he did write each letter separately (perhaps while a prisoner), he later collected them for his book. The book of Revelation, as John indicates in 1:9-10, was written after his time in Patmos. The letters were written under the inspiration of a mighty vision. When John wrote about his vision in its entirety, the letters may have then been restored and put in their place among the visions and inspirations from Patmos.

The order of the letters to the seven churches is no accident. Ephesus, the first mentioned, lies closest to the island of Patmos. Smyrna, the next, rests to the north. From there on, the route connecting these large cities of Asia Minor forms a loop—roughly, the very path one would take traveling on foot to deliver mail. Clearly, John knew the main travel arteries of the area.

He knew the cities and their churches,

as well. Each letter he writes speaks directly to the condition of the church and to the mischief caused by its environment.

The letters all tend to have the same pattern: (1) a statement from the Lord that includes some part of the vision from 1:12-16; (2) praise for what is good and criticism for what is wrong with each congregation (although Sardis and Laodicea receive no praise and Smyrna and Philadelphia receive no criticism); (3) a promise made to those who endure; and (4) A plea to listen to the Spirit's message.

John refers often to those who endure tribulation as "conquerors" (NRSV; NIV, "he who overcomes") and speaks frequently of their crowns. There were two words for crown. One, similar to our word *diadem*, referred to the royal crown and was a symbol of power. The other, the one promised the conquerors, is a wreath of the sort awarded to the victors at games (those who endured to the end).

The coastal churches had the advantage of receiving commercial goods from land and sea. They also caught all the latest gossip, fads, and fancies from everywhere. Each was a cosmopolitan center, welcoming people from every city and shore and used to entertaining ideas from everywhere in the ancient world. All of them housed important temples, and each surrounded Christians with the temptation to average out religious faiths rather than remain committed to one. John, in his letters, addresses those temptations head-on.

Here is an outline of Revelation 2:1-17:

I. The Letter to Ephesus (2:1-7)
II. The Letter to Smyrna (2:8-11)
III. The Letter to Pergamum (2:12-17)

The Letter to Ephesus (2:1-7)

Ephesus was a seaport and one of the great cities of the ancient world. It was rich and politically very important, housing as it did the Roman proconsul for Asia Minor. More important, from John's point of view, it also housed the temple of the goddess Artemis (her temple was one of the seven wonders of the ancient world), the energetic worship of the Roman emperors and empire, and a lively belief in magic among the citizens.

Merge wealth, power, magic, and competing religions, and an environment is created that taxes the faith and obedience of Christians. Add to that several flare-ups, popular and military, against Jews and Jewish Christians, and the temptations increase. Surrounded by symbols of how agreeable and endlessly interesting the secular world can be, yet forced to keep their distance from it, Christians become grudging and cool. Resentment dissolves love.

The message to Ephesus comes from him who stands in the midst of John's vision. It praises the church's endurance, its ability to identify and weed out false apostles, and its patience. The church's love, however, has dwindled—the essential ingredient of the Christian life (1 Corinthians 13:1). The Ephesians are reminded that, if they lack love, they gain nothing.

The threat John makes to the Ephesians is severe. He says, in verse 5, that they must repent of their lovelessness or be removed. To a congregation that had known Paul and now sensed itself as the leading church among the Christians, the threat would have been shocking. Evidently the Ephesians heeded John's warning, for the church remained for some time the leader in Asian Christianity. Some years later, the bishop of Ephesus was acknowledged to be the head of the Asian church.

Verse 7 records a promise to the conquerors. It is a word John uses often. The notion that the Christian life is a form of warfare occurs elsewhere in the Bible. For John, the combat between God and evil was relentless. The military image of conquering and of warfare would be all too familiar to a people who lived under military domination and had seen their homeland destroyed. John holds out the promise that even the least of them can endure and be a conqueror.

John speaks of the "toil" (NRSV; NIV, "hard work") of the Ephesians. Toil comes from a Greek word meaning "to labor to the point of weariness or exhaustion." It derives its meaning from the word for beating or the physical tiredness that comes from the repeated impact of manual labor. Literally, then, when John speaks of the toil of the Christians, he gives us a clue to the extreme demands placed on them. To be faithful exacts great stress; Christians working for the church work to the point of exhaustion.

To their credit, the Ephesians recognize and spurn the Nicolaitans. Who the Nicolaitans were—other than followers of Nicholas, as their name implies—is not known. They may have been one of the many groups that taught that, if one truly believed in Christ, one could indulge in promiscuous sex or pagan religion without sin.

Those who promise to endure through the good times as well as the bad will eat from the tree of life. The tree of life is an important symbol from the Old Testament story of the garden of Eden. The tree and other items from that story appear again in the final chapter of Revelation.

The tree of life symbolizes immortality. Only those who have conquered may eat of it. John knows that, for some, the struggle to endure may become a life-or-death issue. He therefore lifts their sights beyond the immediate to the eternal promise. He changes the scenery here, as he often does, in which people act out their lives,

replacing the seen with the unseen, the visible threats with the invisible truths.

John's use of the tree also shows how he was able to transform the symbols of other religions, and to convert them to a Christian use. Trees had been worshiped as the homes of divine beings or as places where the divine being might be made apparent. Families had sacred trees, which they thought were closely linked with family prosperity. The Greeks had kept certain groves of trees as sacred places. When the Acropolis of Athens was burned and the people feared for their future, the sacred olive tree put forth a new shoot. The people took that as a sign that the future would go well for them. Trees growing over the graves of the dead were thought to carry the life and spirit of the departed one. There is even evidence of an old Athenian law that prescribed punishment for those who cut certain kinds of trees down in cemeteries.

John was writing to Christians who had been born and raised in the midst of the Greek and Roman culture. The mysteries of nature, the kinship of trees to gods and goddesses and families, the tranquillity and worship inspired by the sacred groves—all were familiar features of their environment. John knows that. He uses it now for a wider meaning, changing the scenery, as we have noted, to place the tree now in the garden of Eden, and its meaning in the hope held for the faithful.

The Letter to Smyrna (2:8-11)

Smyrna was also a seaport and therefore a rich and powerful city. John contrasts the city to Christ and Christians.

Smyrna, in 195 B.C., had dedicated a temple to the goddess of Rome. In A.D. 26 it erected a temple to the emperor Tiberius and to the Roman senate. Smyrna competed with Ephesus to be known as the first among the cities of Asia. John, by contrast, wrote for a Christ who was not only first, but last as well. Smyrna was a rich city, but the true riches, according to John, belonged to Christians. The city of Smyrna was bedecked with large buildings and temples, referred to as the crown of Smyrna, but John's Christ promises Christians the crown of life.

John speaks of knowing the poverty of the church at Smyrna. He uses the strong form of the Greek word for poverty. It is not that the Christians at Smyrna had little extra; they had almost nothing at all.

The letter warns of a time of suffering and of an imprisonment lasting ten days. Some of the suffering was caused by Jewish settlers and citizens whose hostility to the Christians continued throughout the century. Imprisonment, however, was a governmental act. One stayed in prison while awaiting trial. For many Christians, the outcome of such trials led directly to death and, promises John, the "crown of life."

John's reference to the "synagogue of Satan" shows that the Christians at Smyrna felt themselves to be fighting for survival on two fronts. There was a large Jewish settlement there, and the hostility between Jews and Christians continued throughout the first century. The situation was worsened by the fact that many of the Christians were converted Jews, some former members of the local synagogues.

John charges the Jews with slandering the Christians. It is true that Jews did take part in some of the persecutions. John's defense is twofold. He claims that Christians are the true Jews—it is they who will receive the crown of life. And he claims that the Jewish synagogue is an expression of evil, not of God.

Part of John's anger at the Jews may arise from the fact that he himself is a Jewish Christian and he weaned himself from the life of the synagogue. Conversion to Christianity also meant being rejected by the Jewish community.

When John uses the phrase "crown of life," he again illustrates how familiar parts of the local environment can be called into the service of his message. The phrase "crown of Smyrna" was common to his readers. The city's buildings, as mentioned above, were considered its crown, its diadem. But crowns were also familiar features of social and religious life. Worshipers of the pagan gods wore crowns of garlands or circlets of flowers. Laurel wreaths were given to the winners of athletic events.

The city of Smyrna had also been compared to the crown of Ariadne. That association would be more important and more compelling for John. In Greek myth, Ariadne had been romanced and then abandoned by Theseus. As Ariadne wept, Venus (the deity of love) came to console Ariadne. Venus also promised her that she would be the bride of Bacchus. She was given a golden crown, placed among the stars, and bore Bacchus a son.

That story was closely associated with religious beliefs that permitted promiscuity. The crown, then, spoke volumes about things that John knew threatened Christian belief—worldly power, pagan religion, and promiscuity. Those may have seemed to some to offer life. He knew the true crown of life came from elsewhere and was offered by someone else.

The crown of life also has a relationship to the crowns of light (also called *nimbuses*) that appear in the works of art depicting Greek deities. Those crowns, which we now call halos, very soon showed up in Christian art as well. This is, possibly, a testimony to the ability of John and others to transform their environment into eloquent symbols of the faith.

The one who "was dead and came to life" promises Christians who conquer all temptations and who face death that the second death, presumably the one following resurrection and judgment, will not hurt them. John uses the phrase "second death" four times. It does not appear elsewhere in the New Testament. It appears again in Revelation 20:6 where John says that those who reign with Christ during the millennium will not experience the second death. It is referred to also in chapters 20 and 21 when the enemies of God are cast into the lake of fire.

The idea of a second death was familiar to the Jews, and probably to John's readers. It helps to distinguish between a death that all must suffer and one that must be suffered only by those who do not receive the benefits of the resurrection.

The crown of life is what makes the difference between the two. Those who endure the first death in faith achieve a crown more glorious than the one that bedecks Smyrna, one that will not tarnish. It is more glorious than the crown of Ariadne, for she dwells only among the stars. The crown of life is given by him who holds the stars in his hands.

The Letter to Pergamum (2:12-17)

Pergamum was the capital of the Roman province of Asia. It was built upon a thousand-foot hill, on which were both temples and the acropolis—a fortress protecting the city. It housed many religious movements alongside its temple dedicated to Caesar Augustus and Rome. Many coins of the era carried pictures of the temple. The imperial cult (the official religion) had its Asian center in Pergamum.

When John refers to Christ as the one with the "double-edged sword" (NIV; NRSV, "two-edged sword"), he is contrasting the power of God's truth to the power of Roman military might. The hill on which the acropolis sat, with its solid and nearly invincible setting and its decorative assortment of temples, John calls "Satan's throne." Those who remained faithful to Christ in the midst of all these symbols of power often paid with their lives as Antipas had. Rome's power took its toll on Christians.

The faithful were called "witnesses," for which another term is "martyrs." "Martyr" soon came to describe those in the early church who told what they had seen and believed about Christ, and who paid the ultimate price: death.

Some Christians at Pergamum had fallen, not to death, but to the practices of other religions. John refers to the teaching of Balaam (see Numbers 31:8), an enemy of Israel who believed that the Israelites would lose God's protection if they could be persuaded to worship idols.

What were the Christians' "stumbling block[s]" (2:14 NRSV)? Eating food sacrificed to idols (which led other, weaker persons to think Christians could also worship idols), immorality, and following the teachings of the Nicolaitans.

Those who remain faithful will receive three rewards: (1) "hidden manna," from the mysterious food by which God fed the Israelites in the desert following their escape from Egypt and the pharaoh. Now the new Moses, Christ, will provide even more. (2) A "white stone." After a jury trial in Roman courts, the defendant would receive either a white stone (innocent) or a black one (guilty). In some cases, the stone meant literally life or death. Believers will gain life. (3) A "new name." Names, in the ancient world, not only referred to a person, they described character. A new name meant a new character, the new person Christ would make out of those who remained faithful.

Names appeared on white stones for another reason in the ancient world. There was a popular superstition that certain mysterious names carried special powers. Followers of some religions carried white stones (called amulets) engraved either with religious names or magical formulas. If the name on the amulet was new, and known only to the holder, the value of it increased enormously. If others learned the name or formula, they could also share in its powers.

John may have used that superstition as an analogy of what God does for the Christian. That is, the new name given believers will not be understood by the world, but it will be a symbol of the power of God to see that person through tribulation and into God's kingdom.

The word *new* is very important in Revelation. The book contains references to a new name, a new Jerusalem, and a new heaven and earth. The word has a special sense. It refers not only to something that is recent but also to something that is new by virtue of its only having recently arrived. In that sense, the new, when it arrives, may be not much different from the old. The word John uses means "fresh"—a matter of a change in quality. It usually implies "better."

The Message of Revelation 2:1-17

In this part, John addresses the churches in the cities on the western coast of Asia Minor. Some of the Christians there have faced pain and imprisonment; all have had to deal with temptations. Some temptations have arisen because the world had filled those cities with enticing novelty. Other temptations arose because of doctrines distorted by members of the church. In the wake of those pressures within and without, John sends the following messages:

- God knows the circumstances faced by every church and every Christian.

- In spite of all trials and temptations, Christians must remain loving and faithful.

- The Christian life is like an endurance race; one must prepare for the long haul.

- Some temptations appear new, but they have been around a long time in one form or another; most of them are forms of a single temptation: to accommodate to the surrounding culture.

- God's promises are long-standing, too; and God will be true to those promises and to all who remain faithful.

- God will strengthen Christians in their times of need and trial.

REVELATION 2:18–3:22

Introduction to These Chapters

The inland churches were not spared either strife or temptation. Three of the four had yielded. One, Thyatira, while generally faithful, had begun a kind of loose-minded tolerance. Its acceptance of a woman named Jezebel signaled not so much a love-inspired openness as an unexamined doctrinal error. Jezebel taught falsely. The idolatry of behavior she inspired led from the way she twisted basic beliefs. Thyatira needed sounder teaching.

Sardis, too, erred because it forgot what it had been taught. Its beliefs forgotten, its works wandered down dangerous pathways. In truth, this hyperactive church spun its wheels in unproductive activity.

Laodicea had wandered farthest. It had turned the faith completely upside down, taking on worldly values, baptizing them, and pretending that made them Christian. Again, a failing in behavior stemmed from a breakdown of careful thought.

Only Philadelphia, whose name means "city of love," received John's praise. Even there, doctrinal issues are at hand, but so far Philadelphia has kept both its heart and its head pure.

The inland churches did not face the welter of novelty that nearly engulfed the coastal churches. But they did not escape problems. For the most part, those problems arose from the entrenched societies of their cities: craft guilds, popular temples, families of great prestige and influence who set the social standards and had done so for generations. Old wealth and power, in spite of the new Roman control, still set much of the stage on which the early church played its first roles in history. And the church had trouble with them as much as it did with new wealth and power. It is difficult to feel secure with a new faith when one is surrounded with contrary institutions that seem to have stood the test of time.

Here is an outline of Revelation 2:18–3:22:

I. The Letter to Thyatira (2:18-29)
II. The Letter to Sardis (3:1-6)
III. The Letter to Philadelphia (3:7-13)
IV. The Letter to Laodicea (3:14-22)

The Letter to Thyatira (2:18-29)

Though it was not the key city in Asia, Thyatira had a thriving business in crafts and trades. As a result, it had numerous trade guilds, among them wool-workers, garment-makers, dyers, leather-workers, tanners, potters, bakers, slave-dealers, and bronze-smiths. Luke, in Acts, names a Lydia who came from Thyatira and was a seller of purple.

Guilds each related to their own gods as well as to the official religion of Rome. Guild meetings could end in worship, drunkenness, sexual license, or all three. For Christians, earning a living through membership in a guild became a crisis of conscience.

Experience with those trades allowed John to forge some very appropriate symbols in his letter to the church at Thyatira. Those close to the metalworkers, for example, would know the importance of burnished brass to warfare, where its highly reflective surface was used to deflect the sun's light and blind the enemy. Here, in a city that prided itself on blinding its enemies, John describes a "Son of God" who, never blinded, sees through one's heart like a fire burning, whose gaze cuts into places others cannot see at all.

The church in Thyatira has been faithful in love and service, and has even improved. But in its midst is a Jezebel. The original Jezebel was the wife of Ahab; her name became proverbial among the Jews for wickedness, much as Hitler's name has become for our age. The woman in Thyatira has great power and is thought by some in that church to be a prophet, like John. But, in fact, she lures Christians into eating meats given to idols—possibly at guild banquets—and into submitting bit by bit to the practices of pagan cults.

The problem of eating food sacrificed to idols (verse 20) was complicated. The early church had honest differences about it. To those who knew God as revealed in Jesus Christ, it was clear that idols were nothing. Consequently, food sacrificed to idols was simply food, nothing more. Most of the guilds had their gods, and when a common meal of guild members was held, food was sacrificed, then eaten. Add to that the dilemma of the Christian who needed guild membership in order to practice a trade, and the eating of such food must have seemed both harmless (to the true Christian) and necessary (to be sociable within the guild). Paul had held that eating such food was, in principle, all right. However, if it led the weaker members of the church to misunderstand and then to believe that worship of idols was allowed, it must be avoided. John does not allow such latitude. It is possible that he disallowed it because it was being supported by Jezebel, whose total doctrine was dangerous. Thus, to give in on one point meant to give the impression that she might be right on others.

The judgment announced by John is wrenching. The reclining bed used for festive dinners with others (guild meals, perhaps) becomes a sickbed for them all. The Christians who follow her must repent or else face the dire fate she faces. What Jezebel announces as the deep things of God, John reveals to be, in truth, the deep things of Satan.

In verses 22-23, John distinguishes between two kinds of followers of Jezebel. Some have been lured by her gradually into wider participation in the pagan cults associated with their guilds. For them, John holds out the hope of repentance. Others, "her children," have fully adopted Jezebel's teachings. For them John pronounces the severest judgment.

To the rest of the Christians at Thyatira, the Son of man promises no more burdens. Their circumstances will be reversed. They, the weak, will have power over the nations. They will be able to shatter resistance to the work of the Son of man. God promises them "the morning star," Venus—in ancient times a symbol of sovereignty.

The word translated "rule" literally means "to shepherd." This is not an image of meekness. Shepherds ruled their flocks with strength and absolute control, breaking away threats, although for the ultimate welfare of the flock.

The Letter to Sardis (3:1-6)

Sardis was an ancient city that had risen in splendor in 560 B.C. and had been in gradual decline ever since. It had great wealth, and its wealth made it irresponsible. Sardis had military might, and that might made it overconfident. Twice, despite its magnificent strategic position, enemies had scaled its walls at night and conquered the city. The guards, foolishly incautious, had left their posts.

John knows that history. He reminds the Christians at Sardis that his message comes from the one who holds seven spirits in his hand. In the early church, as in Judaism, the spirits are viewed as the sources by which God gives life and enlivens the living. The reference to the spirits contrasts with the city of Sardis and its church, who "have a reputation" (NIV; NRSV, "name") of being alive but are dead.

Christians living in a city that had been twice captured by enemies in the dark of night would surely understand allusions to God's coming like a thief in the night. They must remain alert and watchful. Part of watchfulness is remembering. The Greek word for "remember" means more than to entertain a past event in one's mind. It means to let that remembrance bear on one's behavior.

Robes of white symbolize holiness. They will be worn by those whose names remain in the "book of life." Ancient cities used registration books to certify those who had the rights of citizenship. In this case, John reminds those who remain faithful that their names fill, not an earthly register, but God's book of life. In the soft and spoiled city of Sardis, the eventual and true victors are those who awaken, remember, and remain watchful.

John's reference to the book of life would have kindled recollections of different sorts among the Jewish and Greek Christians. Jewish religion used the notion of official lists in several ways. As early as Exodus there are records of official lists and of registrars to make them. Those lists determined who could share in the community's goods. One punishment greatly feared would be to have one's name removed from the list. It meant no more access to food and supplies—almost certainly death.

The book of life gradually came to mean, not the list of citizens of the nation, but of those who were citizens in God's kingdom. Several Jewish and New Testament writings speak of the opening of such books. And, again, to have one's name removed from the book is a grim sentence. But the more positive message is the one conveyed here: Those whose religion deprives them of the rights of earthly citizenship have their names inscribed elsewhere. They are not forgotten.

Greek and Roman cities of John's time also kept lists. Citizens' names were kept according to their class and family. The practice of keeping track of citizens can be seen in the story of Jesus' birth—Mary and Joseph being sent to the city of Bethlehem because he was "descended from the house and family of David" (Luke 2:4). It was the Roman emperor Caesar Augustus who ordered that enrollment of all the people.

In Greek and Roman cities, all new citizens were entered into the records. And, when citizens violated the laws sufficiently, their names were erased. That erasure may have been the fate of those exiled to Patmos with John. In this case, a name on the book gave one the rights of citizenship and the protection of the community. Loss of those rights cost one, if not his life, very likely his livelihood.

Christians of either Greek or Jewish background, then, would know the deprivation of losing their place in the book. Those in Sardis needed especially to

think of that. They had, in effect, traded one book for the other. Inscribing their names so willingly on the registry of secular ways had erased them from the book of life.

The white garments promised those who endure draw attention also to two different notions. Among the Romans, the typical holiday robe was white. On a day celebrating a military triumph, white was the universal color. Dark-colored robes were worn as signs of sorrow and mourning.

If white celebrates the Roman military conqueror, John can make it celebrate the Christian conqueror—the one who overcomes temptation. For him, white stands for purity, not worldly power. He will, later in the book, again depict the martyrs and the other faithful, dressed in white.

Once more, John shows how to take the familiar events about him and rescript them to speak in a new voice, with a new meaning. The military parade transforms into a pageant in heaven. The book of registry becomes a book of life. The conqueror becomes, not the one who overwhelms others, but one who overcomes temptation.

The Letter to Philadelphia (3:7-13)

Its founders expected to use Philadelphia as the gateway to spread the Greek language and culture throughout Asia. It housed many temples, including one to the god Dionysus. Jews had also settled there, and apparently the early church often found itself in conflict with them. John speaks of the Jewish community as Satan's synagogue, testifying to the degree of hostility between Jews and Christians in Philadelphia. Clearly, it was a city of ambition, tradition, religion, and ferment.

Verse 9 appears to promise the conversion of the Jews. John, as a Jewish Christian, believes not that Christianity is a new religion, but that it is the true religion of Abraham and Moses. It had wandered from its true origin. Now Christians represent the recovery of the true tradition. Anchoring that claim is John's deeper belief that it is not nationality but faith in Christ that makes one a true Jew. The irony here comes from John's knowledge of the Old Testament writings, especially the Prophets, which promised that Israel would be a light to the nations and that kings would come to her to see the brightness of her rising. John says instead that Israel will come to the feet of the church to see the fullness of God's love. It is obvious from this and other passages of Revelation that the tensions between Christians and Jews were never far from the surface.

In a city with a proud tradition, John writes to remind the Christians that they, too, have a proud tradition. He connects them with David, anchoring the Christians' claim to be the true children of David and therefore the true Israel. In a city once conceived to be the gateway for spreading Greek culture, the small body of Christians know that, to whatever future really matters, it is Christ who holds the key. And Christ's key opens the door, not only to those now in God's kingdom, but to others, even enemies, who will enter into true worship.

In verse 12 John records a promise to the conquerors: They will be "pillar[s]" in the temple of God. Those who still remembered the Temple in Jerusalem would find that a powerful promise, for that Temple had been the place of pilgrimages for centuries, until its destruction. It would also speak to those who had lived their lives in Rome or its provinces. The priest of the Roman imperial cult each year would erect his own statue in the temple devoted to worshiping the emperor. His name, place of birth, and year of office were recorded. Thus he obtained an enduring place in his temple. The Christians would be not statues, but pillars in the true temple.

John's message is that Christians must believe that Christ holds the key, and Christians must endure. Those who endure will have a crown (again, not the diadem of a king, but the wreath given to those who run the race and see it to its end). They will become pillars of the true temple. The conquerors will wear God's name (belong to God) and be citizens of God's new city. Calling that city the New Jerusalem again asserts the Christians' claim that the church is the true Israel.

The Letter to Laodicea (3:14-22)

Laodicea was one of the richest commercial cities in the world. It contained a famous medical school, a widely known clothing-and-wool industry, and a vast banking enterprise. Among its many medical products, Laodicea manufactured a highly regarded eye salve.

In the presence of this wealth, popular clothing industry, and remarkable eye medicine, John finds a church that has become spiritually poor, naked, and blind. Its affluence has closed its eyes to its own mediocrity. Neither hot nor cold, the Laodiceans' lukewarm religion has spoiled the church's savor.

John calls the Laodicean church "poor," as he had called the church at Smyrna poor. He uses the same strong Greek word in both cases. Here, however, it does not refer to matters of wealth but to matters of the spirit. The Christians at Smyrna had almost no possessions at all; the Laodiceans possessed almost no faith at all. Christ calls the Laodicean church to recover its self-understanding, to see that it must define itself by what comes from Christ, not by what comes from the glamour of wealth that surrounds it. Christ's gold and garments and salve alone mark and heal the faithful.

Those who hear and respond to God's call will find themselves rebuked and disciplined. But they will also find themselves surprisingly transformed into hosts; and Christ himself will come to dine with them. The Greek word translated "eat" may also be translated "to sup" and is the same word used in the phrase the Lord's Supper." It means a long and intimate meal together.

The conquerors, again, are not those who wear crowns like the rulers of the secular world, but those who see the race through to the end. Their crowns connote victory after endurance, not royal power.

The Message of Revelation 2:18–3:22

The letters written to the churches of Asia Minor are meant for all churches. The number seven is a symbolic number meaning all or completeness. The messages to them spoke both to the specific problems of each church and to the church in general.

The churches in the inland cities endured some trials in common with those on the coast. But they also faced some that were peculiar to themselves. To them John sent messages of both general and particular significance. Chief among those messages are the following:

- Christians will face hard times and will also be severely tempted in good times.

- God loves and will strengthen the faithful.

- Not all danger arises from outside the church; distortions of belief and behavior can emerge from within, as well.

- God knows the special circumstances of each church and Christian.

- Immorality is not simply a matter of behavior. It can also stem from a lack of careful thought about the beliefs of the church.

- Those who endure in faith will be rewarded by God.

- Even those outside the church can learn to worship in truth and find favor with God.

- Christians should be watchful for the coming of God.

REVELATION 4–5

Introduction to These Chapters

In this part of the book of Revelation, John shows his command of the apocalyptic books and images already in the Jewish tradition. Remember, the books we call the Old Testament were the Bible of the early church. John shows how, under the inspiration of the Spirit, those books and images gain newer and richer meanings. Images from Ezekiel and Daniel now bear witness to Christ.

John first describes the worship of God in heaven and then, at the heart of that celebration, introduces Christ. Chapter 4 focuses on *God the Creator*; chapter 5 emphasizes *Christ the Redeemer*. Together, they set the stage for the series of judgments and promises that make up the remainder of the book.

This part has two sections:
I. The Heavenly Praise of God (4:1-11)
II. The Scroll and the Lamb (5:1-14)

The Message of Revelation 4–5

John uses images and ideas from other apocalyptic books to interpret and explain his vision. Yet he also turns those images and ideas into a distinctively Christian message. The way he reworked those resources can be seen in his description of worship in heaven. What is the meaning of what he saw?

- God is the center of all true worship.

- The God seen by John is the same God of the Jewish tradition; the rainbow, symbol of God's covenant with Noah, shows that continuity.

- No matter how things appear on earth, God dwells behind the scenes creating the example of true worship.

- God has all power, and is working through events on earth, no matter how things seem.

- God exalts the humble as servants who guide the unfolding of divine history.

- Nothing in the present, on heaven or on earth, has yet achieved its perfection; only Christ has proved completely worthy to God.

REVELATION 6:1–8:5

Introduction to These Chapters

This part begins a series of chapters that describe God's judgment. The seven seals (6:1–8:5), the seven trumpets (8:6–11:19), and the seven bowls (15:1–16:21) all herald greater destruction. These sets of seven do not form a single continuous story line, going from beginning to end, but, more like preachers' illustrations, serve to emphasize a single point in increasingly intensive ways. Therefore, if they seem to conflict with one another in some details, they share in a larger agreement: God acts in history and will bring it to a just and imminent conclusion.

This part, dealing with the seven seals, falls into a pattern that John uses again with the trumpets and bowls. It divides the seven into a pattern of four, two, and one. An interlude usually falls between the middle two and the final item of the seven.

Here is an outline of Revelation 6:1–8:5:

  I. The First Four Seals (6:1-8)
  II. The Fifth and Sixth Seals (6:9-17)
  III. God's People on Earth and in Heaven (7:1-17)
  IV. The Seventh Seal (8:1-5)

The Message of Revelation 6:1–8:5

John sees a stark example of divine judgment. The judgment is not wicked revenge, but justice, a repayment for sin and wickedness. John's vision of the seven seals is told to the seven churches to reassure them that the flow of history is in God's hands and that God is just. He also wants them to understand:

- The judgment human beings experience they often inflict upon themselves—war, famine, and hardship: the affliction of the four horsemen.

- Even the power of kings and other rulers is held at God's permission.

- Ultimately, nothing goes beyond the ability of God to control.

- Christians who suffer death for their beliefs will be especially honored by God.

- God knows and listens carefully to all faithful believers.

REVELATION 8:6–11:19

Introduction to These Chapters

This part of the book of Revelation divides into five parts:

I. The First Four Trumpets (8:6-13)
II. The Fifth and Sixth Trumpets (9:1-21)
III. The Small Scroll (10:1-11)
IV. The Two Martyrs (11:1-14)
V. The Seventh Trumpet (11:15-19)

Again John deals with a set of seven by dividing it into smaller groups of four, two, and one (the first six divide into four and two). And again, he places a long interlude between the sixth and the seventh.

The trumpets, like the seals before them, unleash terrible havoc upon the earth. In the Jewish tradition, trumpets were associated with battle (see Zephaniah 1:15-16), with the approach of the "day of the LORD" (Joel 2:1), and with worship. They were associated especially with the worship on the tenth day prior to the Day of Atonement: the Day of Judgment. Together, the trumpets announce that history and nature belong to God, who judges it, redeems it, and now readies it for entry into the new age.

This part also shows with clarity John's familiarity with and appreciation for Old Testament ideas and Scriptures. He uses them this time in a form of writing that was very common in his time, a form called *typology*. Typology means using familiar types of images and events to quickly communicate new messages and their urgency. One of the most familiar to John's readers was the story of the Exodus and the events leading up to it.

In the Exodus, God delivered the Jews from bondage in Egypt. Pharaoh, king of Egypt, had kept the Jews as slaves. Pharaoh's refusal to release the slaves led to several traumatic events. God created plagues and other afflictions to persuade Pharaoh to let the people go.

Eventually Pharaoh submitted. The Jews went free. The story of that release was repeated by the Jews in special ceremonies every year. For them, God became forever identified as the one who freed them from slavery. And the plagues remained symbols of the extent to which God was able to go in order to set them free.

Because of the power of the Exodus story, John repeats fragments of its themes, and when he does, his readers know enough to fill in the blanks. They know John is talking about the acts carried out by God in preparation for the delivering of the people. Those events remind people that that is the type of thing God does to set the stage for the next, more compelling act—hence, the word *typology*. Among the ingredients from the Exodus story, John uses sudden darkness, locusts, bloodied water, famine, and death.

The Message of Revelation 8:6–11:19

The seven trumpets repeat in many ways the events of the seven seals. John repeats and expands the seven seals for emphasis. He wants to inspire the confidence of believers in God. He uses many familiar and potent symbols to do that.

What meaning does John wish his early readers to find as they read his book?

- God liberates the faithful from bondage.

- The God who liberates them is the same God who liberated the people of Israel from Egypt.

- The dangers to Christians are often those of loyalty to or worship of something other than the true God.

- Not everything has been revealed, and therefore not everything can be known. Although history is in God's hands, beware of those who think they know all they need in order to tell the hour and the day, or to make all of the details plain.

- God remains a mystery; no one knows precisely what God will do. But God's justice can be relied upon.

- Faithful witnesses will not always find the world friendly; but God will not forget them.

REVELATION 12–14

Introduction to These Chapters

To describe this vision, John uses a spectacular parable. The characters in the parable—a dragon, two beasts, a woman, and a child—change meanings from time to time. But they combine to tell a story of gross events, malicious motives, and sometimes frightening peril. The parable also features the stuff of great drama: dramatic rescues, armed conflict, betrayal, and the collapse of a great power.

John doesn't mean this, however, as simply a dramatic presentation. His parable reduces nearly the whole of religious history into a story about beasts and people. He intends that his readers shall find themselves in the story; that they will know where they are in it, and which nations and rulers are being referred to.

The parable has the following outline:

I. The Dragon and the Woman (12:1-6)
II. Satan Is Cast Out of Heaven (12:7-12)
III. The Dragon Pursues the Woman (12:13-17)
IV. The Dragon's Servant: The Beast (13:1-10)
V. A Second Beast Worships the First (13:11-18)
VI. The Martyrs Worship in Heaven (14:1-7)
VII. The Fate of the Unfaithful (14:8-13)
VIII. Judgments Begin (14:14-20)

This parable summarizes John's moment in history: evil on the rampage, with its followers in high worship of it. The church is under duress. But, backstage, God has already begun changing the scenery for the final act. Babylon, the nation that plundered the Temple centuries earlier, is the central symbol of evil and rebellion. It stands for Rome.

The Message of Revelation 12–14

John often speaks to the church in what seem to us to be alarming ways. The parable of the woman, the dragon, and the beasts is an example. He uses the items in his parables in sometimes changing ways, like the shifting color schemes of a kaleidoscope. But always he controls his stories for the purpose of making his central point: God rules history.

He also makes these points through the parable:

- When we look simply at immediate events, we may not see the fullness of God's plan as it unfolds.

- The prophetic books of the Bible and the great story of the Exodus help us see the larger picture of God's work.

- The church, in remaining faithful, will often experience great stress.

- Christians will always face the temptation of worshiping the ideals and idols of their nations.

- God may not be apparent, but God is at work among us.

- The power of evil is great, and must not be underestimated.

- The rule of evil is limited.

- God's blessing is on the faithful.

REVELATION 15–16

Introduction to These Chapters

In this part, John again combines scenes of worship in heaven with scenes of destruction on earth. And again, in the telling of the story, Babylon symbolizes Rome, and by extension, all that Rome has polluted on earth.

John shows his command of typology by putting the story in the form of the Exodus. Typology is a way of telling a story by putting it in the form of a more familiar type of story, or of taking events that are familiar, and using events of that type in a new story. Typologies help readers see the significance of an event by reminding them of other similar events.

In this case, John's story contains many of the ingredients that make the Exodus so memorable. It includes plagues, a sea around which the faithful may gather safely (as the Israelites did about the Red Sea), references to Moses (who led the Israelites through the Red Sea), and a reminder of the tent of witness where the stone tablets bearing the Ten Commandments were kept during the years the people of Israel traveled in the wilderness.

John's story has four sections:
I. The Song of the Conquerors (15:1-4)
II. Presentation of the Bowls of Wrath (15:5-8)
III. Four Bowls of Natural Disaster (16:1-9)
IV. Three Bowls of Warfare (16:10-21)

The word translated "wrath" comes from a root meaning violent movement, something boiling up. The English word *wrath*, closely related to the word *writhe*, means to twist in torment. In John's story, then, God's wrath is the final boiling over of judgment, and the unrepentant are shown in torment.

Two additional points need to be made. First, John seems to have come close to ending his story many times. If one were to total up the destruction delivered upon the earth thus far, the scourges and their aftermaths, surely little would remain for further destruction. If nothing else, the delicate membrane of the earth's ecology would have torn from the excessive pestilence and violence.

It is good for us to remember that John is not telling a single story. He has a single theme, but several stories, each illustrating the theme with great power. His strategy is not to write a chronological history, but rather to write about the meaning of history. And that can be done best by making his point in several ways. As far as he is concerned, his readers must see God's justice as the final force and the driving force in history. And they must believe that it rises above and overreaches any other apparent power in their day. His successive images, stories, and teachings accumulate a weight of persuasiveness that no single part could do by itself.

Second, the brutality of John's images often offends the minds of those who have set their hearts upon a God of love. John's heart was set upon that same God. His use of images almost always comes from a careful use of the Old Testament. He chose the images that his readers would recognize. He used them because he wished to show that he spoke and wrote with the authority of the ancient belief, and to remind his people in sharp ways that his God was no fly-by-night deity. This was the God about whom the ancients had spoken. None other.

In a time of great duress, the images of power were needed to speak to power. But, to John's credit, he never let sheer malice get in the way of justice. And, to the end, he assumed that God's heart was open to those who would worship God in spirit and truth.

The Message of Revelation 15–16

John again describes his vision by using symbols from the book of Exodus. He uses versions of the plagues once visited upon the pharaoh to interpret the meaning of God's action in history. As the plagues spelled disaster for the Egyptians, they spelled hope for the Israelites who were in bondage. Similarly, the plagues now become symbols to speak of the disaster that awaits those who perpetrate evil, and to bring hope to those who wait faithfully for God. And, as in the time of the Exodus where the pharaoh lined up his troops for warfare against God's people, here all of the kings line up their troops for a final battle against God.

For John, this is no simple re-enactment of an old story. He has his own message to send, one that speaks through the old story, but in greater, and graver, terms. What is that message?

- God is active, not passive, in history.

- The same God who delivered the Jews from Egypt is at work to save the faithful from the forces of evil.

- The tent of witness, important for God's original covenant with the people of Israel, remains important; the commandments remain in force.

- God is the ruler of nature as well as of the human world.

- God's justice has to do with all of the nations, not simply with those who have known and worshiped God.

- History is a limited process, and will have an end. Beyond history, and larger than it, is the kingdom of God.

REVELATION 17–18

Introduction to These Chapters

Revelation 17:1–18:24 and 19:1–20:15 tell two stories, but they are meant to stand side by side. In the first story, John tells of an evil woman who rides upon the beast of chapters 13–14. She is given the name of "Babylon." Babylon, to all who knew the Old Testament (and the Greek Old Testament was the Bible of the early Christian church), symbolized great evil. Babylon had pummeled and destroyed Israel, exporting her riches, breaking up her families, and razing her place of worship. It was while in exile following that brutal attack that the psalmist had written, "By the waters of Babylon, there we sat down and there we wept when we remembered Zion" (Psalm 137:1).

But John wants his readers to know that, in his telling of the story, Babylon is used as a symbol. It is Rome he has in mind. The beast he describes offers us some decisive clues in that direction. The seven heads of the beast, he explains, are seven hills—the seven famous hills upon which Rome sat. The seven heads also are the seven kings. Rome had had more than seven kings, but as we shall see, the mathematics of Revelation are not meant to be arithmetic so much as symbolic. As such, they not only denote the rulers of Rome; they have a message to send about them.

The second story (19:1–20:15) works in contrasts. The evil woman (Rome) is compared to the good woman, the church, the bride of Christ.

Here is an outline of these chapters:
I. The Harlot and the Beast (17:1-6)

II. The Harlot and the Beast Explained (17:7-14)
III. The Fate of the Harlot (17:15-18)
IV. The Lament of Heaven (18:1-8)
V. The Lament of the Earth (18:9-19)
VI. The Angel with the Stone (18:20-24)

The Message of Revelation 17–18

This part of Revelation reveals John's sense of the global web of evil. No nation is in it alone; each builds upon and prospers from the production of others— evil or good. Rome was not the first city to use such a web to capture others, and would not be the last. Babylon was a similar city, and had become in Jewish thought the ranking symbol of the evil city. Similarly, the prophetic protest against Babylon became the most striking condemnation of the evil city.

John's message, then, makes brilliant use of the old and familiar symbols to describe a new and unprecedented power. In the process, he also makes clear that the evil nations do does not necessarily unite them. Bound together in order to feed from Babylon's (Rome's) prosperity, the nations disengage quickly when she faces grief.

What is the message of John in this light?

- Even the amassed powers of nations cannot equal the power of God.

- The economic motives that bring nations and people together are not sufficient to keep them together when times are hard; for that, a deeper bond, one of faith, is necessary.

- The symbols and teachings of the church provide the decisive clues to the meaning of events; Scriptures that are in the form of predictions can often help us understand and interpret our present time.

- All worldly power, however awesome it seems in the present, is temporary. Nations rise and fall; only God endures.

- God acts in history and will speak the final word.

REVELATION 19

Introduction to This Chapter

In this part John moves in increasingly wider circles. From the judgment upon Babylon he moves to the judgment upon the beast and false witness, then to the nations they and the woman deluded, including the kings who had lamented the fall of Babylon. It leads to a decisive, but not yet final, battle.

This part communicates its message through a series of rich contrasts. John contrasts the groom (Christ) to the beast, the purity of the bride (the church and the church's martyrs) to the gaudy sinfulness of the harlot, the sanctity of the New Jerusalem with the squalor and spoilage of the degraded city, Babylon.

The point of these verses has as much to do with God as with the church and its martyrs. Ultimately, the issue to be decided is not one between the church and the forces of evil, but between God and the forces of evil. What is at stake for John is the conviction that the world is God's. That is why, so very often in his book, he pauses in his depictions of the turmoil on earth to describe the acts of worship taking place in heaven. The heavenly beings see clearly the God who is the true king and ruler of the universe. It is God who is being belittled by those on earth who claim power for their own, and especially by those who organize cults to worship other gods, and even themselves. John's book vindicates God's ownership. To the opening hymn of Genesis, "In the beginning, God . . . ," he now wishes to add the final verse: "In the end, God."

Here is an outline of this chapter:

I. Voices Rise from Heaven (19:1-5)
II. The Marriage Supper of the Lamb (19:6-10)
III. The Great Battle (19:11-21)

The Message of Revelation 19

This chapter brings the struggle between heaven and earth to the threshold of its conclusion. The battle has been fought and won. There remains, however, the final disposing of the "enemy" and the happy conclusion for the faithful.

In moving to this point, John has gone through three different kinds of events: worship, wedding preparations, and warfare. Although they each would normally be considered quite differently from the others, John has, in fact, a few similar messages he wishes to communicate through those events:

- God, and nothing and no one else, is the subject of John's book and of the lives of Christians.

- God desires to relate closely to those who are faithful.

- The image that best defines how God wishes the church to relate to him is that of the bride. For the faithful, the relationship is to be as celebratory as a wedding and as heartfelt and long-lasting as a covenant between lovers.

- God contains all the powers admired on earth, but in the greatest degree possible. All earthly pretenders to power are trivial compared to God.

- Justice will determine the fate of those who serve God and of those who oppose God's purposes.

REVELATION 20

Introduction to This Chapter

In this part of Revelation, John tells about the final stages through which God subdues evil. Although the time span he discusses lasts more than a thousand years, he condenses it into four brief sections. Further, he uses each of those sections to capsulize one significant event.

This part also continues the story line from chapter 19. The defeat of the beast and its priest/prophet brings Satan, death, and Hades to their final destruction.

The four sections of this part are:

I. The Temporary Binding of Satan (20:1-3)
II. The First Resurrection (20:4-6)
III. Satan's Last Act (20:7-10)
IV. The Death of Death and Hades (20:11-15)

The Message of Revelation 20

In this part, John creates a sequence of scenes that has caused great debate among Christians. That debate has to do with the meaning of the millennium—whether it is literal or symbolic, and whether John thinks that Christ will return to this earth before or after his people reign for one thousand years.

Amid the debates, there are some common themes. Those themes constitute the message of this part of the book:

- While evil seems to move freely, it never moves beyond the ability of God to control it.

- God intends for the faithful to achieve influence among the nations of this world; but that victory is to be the result of God's acts and not of the aggressiveness of God's people. Their task is to remain faithful and to trust God.

THE MEANING AND THE TIMING
OF THE MILLENNIUM

This chapter has led to many differences among Christians. Those differences stem from their understanding of the meaning and the timing of the millennium.

In this chapter, John sees a vision of an angel capturing and binding up Satan. Satan is then thrown into a pit for one thousand years (*millennium* means *one thousand*; hence the millennium refers to a period of one thousand years). The millennium is connected with the resurrection of the martyrs. According to verse 4, the martyrs come to life again to be with Christ during those one thousand years. The remainder of the faithful dead and others come to life only after that.

The question that divides many Christians has to do with the time when Christ will rule on earth. Will he return, raise the Christians from the dead, and rule on earth with them for one thousand years? That is the position held by premillennialists. The "pre" means that Christ comes to rule before the one thousand years start.

Another group believes that John means something different. They say that, for one thousand years, the gospel will triumph. It is after that that the rule of Christ will begin. Because Christ's rule begins after the one thousand years, those who believe this interpretation are called postmillennialists.

Others believe that, like so many other elements in Revelation, the number one thousand is symbolic. Like the numbers ten and one hundred, it stands for completeness or perfection, but now in nearly the most inclusive sense. In that case, the millennium would mean: "the entire time, from the baptism of new believers until their final and complete fellowship with God." That interpretation would not be based on the expectation that a cosmic event might occur. It is, rather, about this time and all times. It means that Christ reigns and saves and fulfills all the time for those who are faithful.

An alternate symbolic interpretation of the number one thousand is that it is whatever time is necessary for the perfecting of or completing of God's purposes.

• Ultimately, evil will be overcome.

• All people must make an account of their lives before God.

• God's victory will be the death of death itself.

REVELATION 21:1–22:5

Introduction to These Verses

After the worship in heaven and the removal of evil from the earth, one would expect God to constitute either a heavenly or an earthly paradise. John sees it otherwise. Conflict, anger, tears, and violence have filled the calendars of both places. Neither is the proper setting for what God chooses to bring about. God plans a "new heaven and a new earth."

This, too, has precedent in the Old Testament. Isaiah had written, "For I am about to create new heavens and a new earth; . . . be glad and rejoice forever in what I am creating; for I am about to create Jerusalem as a joy" (Isaiah 65:17-18).

It is the New Jerusalem, Jerusalem rejoicing, that John now portrays. The New Jerusalem is in every way a contrast to Babylon.

Here is an outline of these verses:
I. A New Heaven and a New Earth (21:1-8)
II. The City of God (21:9-21)

III. The Lamb in the City
(21:22-27)

IV. Eden Restored (22:1-5)

This part is laden with symbols, more than we are able to understand. The meanings of certain gems, the significance of the architecture of the city, the design and geography of its setting—each part is densely compacted with meanings. Yet, without knowing them all, we can take in the larger picture. Above all, we are meant to be swept into the grandeur of the New Jerusalem and the brilliance of its ornamentation. Throughout all the decorative items John has interspersed familiar religious signs and images, so that we can see the New Jerusalem as a fulfillment of all the ancient dreams about God's glory.

The Message of Revelation 21:1–22:5

This part opens before our eyes the grandeur of God's plans for the church. For this to come to pass, however, everything must be made new—heaven and earth. Not that all from the past fades into eternal forgetfulness. It does not. Instead, John collects the bright images of hope from the Old Testament and uses them to explain this new thing God has done. He also shows how, when God uses them, those things become something more and greater than anyone expected.

From the greatest to the smallest, John shows God's acts. The enormous city is created, and yet every small tear is wiped from the martyr's eye. From the heights of the mountain John sees the new city, yet from the memory of the story of the garden of Eden he is able to understand its significance. From the magnificence of its decoration he can sense the elegance of the

---

A NEW HEAVEN AND A NEW EARTH (REVELATION 21:1-8)

John combines two symbols: Jerusalem as the holy dwelling of God and the bride as the one whom God blesses with the divine presence. Neither the old heaven nor the old earth is suitable for the new creation. The new creation outreaches the grasp of either symbol—it is more than a glorified old Jerusalem and more than the simple setting for a wedding. Despite the quantity of its luxury, which John will soon explain, it is the quality of the place that makes it worthy of our attention. It is the place where God chooses to dwell. It is the place of God's personal care for the faithful. It is the place where tears and mourning have vanished and death is no more.

In verse 5, John's pastoral concerns come to the forefront. He draws from what he sees in his vision a message for the people to whom he is writing. As always throughout his book, he has his eyes upon the vision, but his mind and heart rest with the burdened Christians of first-century Asia Minor. The meaning of his vision, translated for those Christians, is found in verses 6-7: "To him who is thirsty I will give to drink without cost from the spring of the water of life. He who overcomes will inherit all this, and I will be his God and he will be my son" (NIV). He follows this rich promise with a warning to the cowardly, faithless, polluted, fornicators, and others that they shall not escape the second death. The moral point of the vision of the new heaven and earth is the same point that John has made throughout the book: Be faithful; God is just and true.

---

city, yet, from the meekness of the Lamb he senses that God is the city's true light.

From these contrasts John derives the message of this chapter. We must always be aware that each thing he presented in his book had a moral to be drawn for his first-century readers, and for us:

- Although we may be overwhelmed with awe at God, God is tender, and knows and cares for our individual pains and grief.

- The symbols we have known and used to understand God and God's kingdom are all essential, but what God offers us goes far beyond them. They are hints, not photographs.

- God's heavenly kingdom is a place where God dwells in the midst of God's people.

- Christ is the bearer of God's light.

REVELATION 22:6-21

Introduction to These Verses

In this part, John presents the final words of the angel of the bowl and of Jesus. He also speaks again to point out the moral and message of all that he has told his readers. The epilogue (final word) interprets the practical meaning of the revelation.

The epilogue has the following parts:
I. The Testimony of Christ (22:6-7)
II. The Testimony of John (22:8-9)
III. The Testimony of the Angel (22:10-11)
IV. The Full Nature of Christ (22:12-16)
V. A Last Invitation and Warning (22:17-19)
VI. A Final Promise and Blessing (22:20-21)

In this last part, John picks up several themes and motifs from the previous chapters. He assumes that his readers have read from beginning to end, and that they will need only to have certain symbols elevated for a moment for their significance to be recalled. So his readers are once more exhorted to keep the words of the prophecy. Again, John tries to worship an angel and is rebuffed. Again comes the warning that the time of the end is near. The symbols of Alpha and Omega, of washed robes, and of gates appear. Warnings are given to fornicators and idolators again. And the root of David is recalled as a metaphor for Jesus. One more time we hear of the bride of Christ, of the call to drink the water of life, of the plagues, and of the tree of life.

Clearly, John intends this as the summary of his sermon as well as a moral exhortation to keep the faith.

The Message of Revelation 22:6-21

In this chapter, John tells his readers how they are to take his book. He also, once more, lets them know what is at stake in the strife they are experiencing. He therefore condenses the message of the entire book into several brief segments, each one holding up a portion of the message he wants all to remember. The message is:

- His readers must live and act in the knowledge that God's kingdom is coming soon.

- John is a prophet, and stands as an equal to all of the other prophets of the Jewish and Christian tradition.

- His words must not be altered, but kept—that is, they must be acted upon.

- The one who gives John his message is Christ.

- God is in Christ, and Christ can be identified with God as the Alpha and Omega, the First and the Last.

- The holy city is like the garden of Eden, containing the water of life.

- The gracious presence of Christ will be with the saints, that is, those who believe and trust in his word.

ADDITIONAL TOOLS

GLOSSARY

A

Aaron: Brother and helper of Moses; first high priest of Israel (see Exodus 28:1-3).

Aaron's rod: The rod, representing the tribe of Levi, budded as a proof of God's will that they should be the priests of Israel.

Ab: The fifth month of the Hebrew calendar.

Abaddon: This term is an alternative name for Sheol, the realm of the dead. It is a dark and cheerless place where one mostly sleeps.

Abarim: A mountainous region at the western edge of the plateau of northern Moab, overlooking the Dead Sea and the Jordan Valley. Mount Nebo is the principal peak and from it Moses viewed the land of Canaan.

Abba: The Aramaic term for father used by Paul.

Abdon: A judge from Ephraim. He provided wise administration in time of peace.

Abel: The younger son of Adam and Eve. His death at the hands of his older brother, Cain (Genesis 4:8-16), came to be considered an anticipation of the death of Christ. Abel was regarded as the first martyr (Matthew 23:35).

Abihu: One of the sons of Aaron. He and his brother Nadab sinned by offering inappropriate sacrifices.

Abimelech: A son of Gideon. Abimelech killed his brothers and set himself up as the king of Shechem.

Abiram: Along with his brother Dathan, he led Korah's rebellion against Moses in the wilderness.

Abomination: Anything that is ritually or ethically offensive to God and to God's people.

Abraham: The founding father of Israel and the father of many nations (see Genesis 17:1-5).

Absalom: A son of David who conspired to overthrow his father, the king; Absalom was slain in the conflict.

Acacia: A tree that grows in Israel, and the wood it produces. Acacia was used to build the ark of the covenant.

Achaia: Roman province comprising most of ancient Greece south of Macedonia. Corinth was the administrative center.

Achan: A man from the tribe of Judah who stole booty devoted to God. Achan's sin caused Joshua's army to lose in its first attempt to capture Ai.

Achor, Valley of: A valley in the northern part of Judah. The name means valley of trouble.

Achsah: The daughter of Caleb and wife of Othniel. Achsah asked for and received rights to a spring for Othniel's land in the Negeb.

Achzib: A town on the border of the Shephelah and central Judah.

Acropolis: A fortress that was well-placed in order to defend cities.

Adar: The twelfth (last) month in the Hebrew calendar.

Admah: One of the cities of the valley, which was destroyed along with Sodom and Gomorrah.

Adonizedek: King of Jersualem, Adonizedek led four other kings in opposing Joshua's conquest of Palestine. Joshua killed him at Makkedah.

Adrammelech: A son of Sennacherib, king of Assyria. He murdered his father in the temple of Nisroch.

Adullam: A city of the Shephelah, originally Canaanite; David took refuge from Saul in a cave near here (see 2 Samuel 23:1); became a fortress city.

Aegean Sea: The body of water leading from the Mediterranean Sea to the Black Sea and washing the shores of turkey (the Roman province of Asia) on the east, Greece on the west, and Macedonia on the north. It was crossed several times by Paul.

Agabus: The prophet who predicted widespread famine (11:28). He spoke with a special gift from the Spirit. Later he predicted that Paul would be bound over to the Romans (21:10-11).

Agape: The Greek for "love" in the sense of an attitude of caring and compassion for the other person without regard to worth or merits. It is not based on emotions but is an act of the will.

Age, ages, age to come: There are two ages: the present age of the created universe in which we live, and the age to come, initiated by Jesus' incarnation, and consummated on his return. Hebrews says that the age to come will supersede the present age.

Agrippa II: Marcus Julius Agrippa (A.D. 27–100). Had Jewish interests but clearly preferred Roman ways. His relationship with his sister was scandalous.

Agur: An anonymous figure in Proverbs 30:1-9 who questions the limits and possibilities of human knowledge.

Ahaz: King of Judah, 735–715 B.C.

Ahimelech: A priest of Israel; a contemporary of David.

Ai: Ancient town approximately two miles southeast of Bethel in the hills north of Jerusalem.

Akkadian: People living in the region between the Tigris and Euphrates rivers before the Babylonians. The Babylonian language is an Akkadian dialect.

Akrabbim: A mountainous region in southern Palestine.

Alamoth: Literally, young women. In the psalm title, it may indicate a song for women's voices.

Alexander: Mentioned in First Timothy 1:19-20. Linked with Hymenaeus as one who had made a shipwreck of his faith. He is often identified with Alexander the coppersmith who had been a witness against Paul.

Alpha and Omega: The first and the last, or the beginning and the end; from the first (alpha) and the last (omega) letters of the Greek alphabet

Amalekites: A desert-dwelling nomadic tribe who are the descendants of Amalek, a grandson of Esau. Members of a nomadic tribe that was descended from Esau. The tribe waged war with the Israelites from time to time during their history.

Amana: A very high mountain in southern Lebanon.

Amariah: The name of several Old Testament men, one of whom was the son of Hezekiah and great-grandfather of Zephaniah.

Amaziah: The name means Yahu is strong. King of Judah in 800-783 B.C. Only twenty-five when he began to reign, he immediately killed those who had assassinated his father (2 Kings 14:5-6). Reconquered Edomite territory and was later assassinated.

Amazis: Pharaoh who took the Egyptian throne from Pharaoh Hophra in 569 B.C.

Amaw: The territory where Balaam was located when he was summoned by Balak, king of Moab.

Amen: A Hebrew word used to end prayers that means "Be it so!"

Amenemopet: An Egyptian author whose collection of instructions served as a source for Proverbs 22:17–24:22.

Amethyst: A purple, transparent quartz crystal.

Amittai: The name means true. Father of the prophet Jonah.

Ammon: Territory in the Transjordan roughly bounded by the river Jabbok on the north and the river Arnon on the south, occupied by a Semitic people known as Ammonites.

Ammonites: A semitic people living in parts of Canaan and east of the Jordan River; Jerusalem was probably an Amorite town before the Israelites settled there; descendants of Canaan.

Amon: King of Judah, 642–640 B.C.

Ampliatus: A man Paul requests the congregation to greet. His identity is unknown.

Amram: A son of Kohath, father of Moses, Aaron, and Miriam.

Amulet: Jewelry that was believed to have magical powers. It was usually worn around the neck to ward off evil.

Anakim: Descendants of Anak, who lived in Canaan prior to the Israelites arrival there. These people were known for their large size.

Ananias: A Christian in Jerusalem who conspired with his wife, Sapphira, to hold back a portion of property. When confronted separately, each died (Acts 5:1, 3, 5). Also, a Christian disciple who helped Paul in Damascus (chapter 9). Also, a Jewish high priest before whom Paul appeared at the end of the third missionary journey (23:2).

Anathoth: Jeremiah's birthplace in the territory of Benjamin, probably the present-day village of Anata, two miles northeast of Jerusalem.

Andronicus: With Junias, an official Paul requests the congregation to greet (see Romans 16:1). Could be a distant relative of Paul.

Angels: Spiritual beings who were thought to be messengers from God (1:20).

Annas: The high priest from A.D. 6/7 to about 15.

Anointing: In the Old Testament, kings and priests were inaugurated by having expensive oil placed on their heads. The word *messiah* means anointed one. In the New Testament, anointing may mean baptism or confirmation.

Antichrist: A term appearing in the New Testament only in Second and Third John for the final, Satan-backed opponent (or opponents) of Christ. Paul refers to him as the man of lawlessness or the lawless one (2 Thessalonians 2:3, 8), whom Christ will destroy at his final advent. Prototypes of this figure are Gog (Ezekiel 38:1-39), Antiochus IV (see below), and Belial (in several books of the intertestamental period.)

Antioch: Hellenistic city in northwest Syria. Ranked with Rome and Alexandria as a major center. Early center for Christian expansion. It was in Antioch that followers of Christ were first known as Christians (11:26).

Antioch of Pisidia: A city in the lake district of southwest Asia Minor. Sometimes called Pisidian Antioch (13:14). Paul preached here to a congregation of Jews and Greek-speaking Gentiles during the first journey.

Antiochus IV: Greek tyrant who ruled Syria and Palestine (175–164 B.C.) and who persecuted the Jews.

Apelles: A man of unknown identity, designated in Romans 16:1 as one approved in Christ.

Apocalyptic: From a Greek word meaning "the unveiling of something hidden" especially of God's hidden purposes for the world, which have been revealed to special persons. The books in which the disclosures are described are called apocalypses.

Apollos: An influential Christian mentioned in Titus. He also appears in Acts and especially in First Corinthians (1:12; 3:4-6, 22; 4:6; 16:12).

Apollyon: A probable reference to the Greek god Apollo, the god of the sun and of prophecy, to whom several Roman emperors were devoted.

Apostasy: Leaving the Christian fellowship; deliberately turning away from Christ and the Christian faith and God's offer of salvation.

Apostle: A messenger or a person sent for a specific message and mission.

Apphia: A Christian woman addressed in Philemon. Because her name appears with Philemon, she is sometimes thought to be Philemon's wife.

Aquila: The husband of Priscilla (also called Prisca); originally he resided in Corinth but was taken by Paul to Ephesus.

Ar: A Moabite city located in the northern part of Moab; perhaps it was the capital of this region.

Arab: From a Hebrew word meaning ambush; it is also translated bandit; generally indicates nomadic tribes living in Arabia.

Arabah: The region in Palestine that extends from the Sea of Galilee south to the Gulf of Aqabah, taking in the Jordan River.

Arabia: From a word meaning desert or steppe, a large peninsula in southwest Asia bordered on the west by the Red Sea and on the east by the Persian Gulf. The northwest portion is often mentioned in Scripture. Its caravan routes carried Arabian goods as well as goods from Africa and India.

Arad: A city in the area of the Negeb, which was conquered by the Israelites during the conquest of Canaan.

Aram: Land of the Arameans, roughly the territory east of the Jordan River and northeast of Palestine around into the upper Tigris-Euphrates valley. The Arameans were a Semitic people (descendants of Shem; see Genesis 10:22-23).

Aramaic: A term used to indicate a group of Semitic dialects that are closely related to Hebrew.

Ararat: A mountainous region in southeastern Turkey and northwestern Iran.

Archelaus: Son of Herod the Great, brother of Herod Antipas. For a while, after the death of his father, Archelaus was tetrarch of Judea; but he committed violence against the Jews. Upon their appeal to Caesar, Archelaus was assigned to Gaul in A.D. 6 (2:22).

Archippus: Paul calls him a fellow soldier in Philemon 1:2. Sometimes interpreted to be Philemon's son.

Areopagus: A hill of nearly 400-foot elevation in Athens, also called Mars Hill. Also the name of the council that met here. Paul spoke to this council when challenged in Athens.

Argob: A territory assigned by Moses to the tribe of Manasseh; its location is uncertain.

Ariel: Another name for Jerusalem. The word means lion of God or hearth of God.

Arimathea: A village twenty miles east of Jaffa in the hill country northwest of Jerusalem. It is mentioned only once in any of the Gospels as the native village of Joseph, who claimed the body of Jesus after the Crucifixion. He was an official of some kind in Arimathea (27:57).

Aristarchus: Is mentioned in Philemon 1:24 but also appears in Acts and Colossians. A Macedonian from Thessalonica who was arrested with Paul in Ephesus (Acts 19:29; 20:4). Tradition holds that he died a martyr's death under Nero in Rome.

Aristobulus: A Christian mentioned by Paul in Romans 16:1; his identity is uncertain.

Ark of the Covenant: The container for the stone tablets of the Law; also thought of as a portable throne for the presence of

God, and the embodiment of God's presence with the people of Israel.

Arnon: A river that flowed from the northeast into the Dead Sea.

Aroer: A city in the Amorite kingdom, east of the Jordan River.

Arpad: A city and minor state in northern Syria. The Bible always mentions it along with Hamath as an example of places destroyed by the Assyrians.

Artemas: Mentioned in Titus 3:12. An early Christian whom Paul intended to send to Crete to relieve Titus, freeing Titus to join Paul in Nicopolis.

Artemis: A goddess of fertility for all living things worshiped in Ephesus and throughout Asia, even as far as Rome. The image associated with her is a meteorite (19:35). The shrines made by Demetrius are probably miniature sanctuaries.

Arvad: An island city-state in northern Syria.

Asaph: A chief musician of David's court. The sons of Asaph may be members of a guild of singers dating from the period of the monarchy.

Ascents: A Song of Ascent; a psalm thatwas sung by pilgrims ascending the slopes of the hill of Zion.

Ashdod: One of the major cities of the Philistines, near the Mediterranean coast north of Ashkelon.

Asher: One of the twelve tribes of Israel.

Asherah: A Semitic goddess or a cult object related to her worship. The King James Version mistranslates the term as "grove."

Asherim: Plural form of the name of the pagan goddess Asherah; it can also mean the idols by which she was represented.

Ashkelon: One of the five main cities of the Philistines, on the Mediterranean coast north of Gaza.

Assayer and Tester: Someone who tests ores for their gold or silver content.

Asshur: Another name for Assyria.

Assyria: A civilization that, along with Babylonia, flourished in Mesopotamia from approximately 2500 B.C. to its defeat by Babylonia in 612 B.C.

Assyrians: The first of the major empires of the Mesopotamian region. The name stems from the name of the major city, Asshur. Famous rulers were Tiglath-pileser III and Shalmaneser. Later the empire was replaced by the Babylonian empire.

Astarte/Ashtoreth (pl. Ashtaroth): A Canaanite goddess used in worship rituals.

Asyncritus: A Christian man who was greeted by Paul in Romans 16:1.

Atharim: A place of uncertain location through which the Israelites moved while under the leadership of Moses; could also mean spies or tracks.

Athens: The capital of modern Greece. It is the major city of the ancient district of Attica. The name is derived from the goddess Athena. Paul spoke here but he did not establish a Christian congregation.

Atonement: Has the general meaning of to be at one. In the Old Testament, used in the sense of removing the effects of sin. Sacrifice is a means of removing the barrier between God and the people that is caused by sin. Sin is forgiven, the barrier removed, and God and people are at one.

Atroth-shophan: A city built by the tribe of Gad; it previously belonged to Sihon, king of the Amorites.

Augustus: The title given by the Roman Senate in 27 B.C. to Gaius Julius Caesar Octavianus, who then was ruler of the Roman Empire. He was emperor at the time of the birth of Jesus.

Aven, Valley of: The name means wickedness. Hosea refers to high places of Aven (10:8). Aven is used in combination with other names to indicate evil.

Avvim: A people living in Canaan before the Israelites arrived; they were destroyed by the Caphtorim.

Azariah: Hebrew name of Abednego, Daniel's friend.

Azazel: A goat (also called the scapegoat) or the one whom it represented, who took the sins removed from the land and people (Leviticus 16:8-10, 26).

Azekah: A city in southern Palestine about fifteen miles northwest of Hebron. Here a rain of hailstones helped Joshua defeat Adonizedek's forces.

Azmon: A city in southern Judah.

B

Baal: A Canaanite fertility God.

Baal-meon: A city in the northern portion of Moab, later inhabited by the tribe of Reuben.

Babylonia: Replaced Assyria as the dominant Mesopotamian civilization in 612 B.C. until its absorption by Persia in 539 B.C.; took control of the Southern Kingdom (Judah) in 598 B.C.

Baca: An imaginary valley of sorrows.

Balaam: A seer asked by Balak, king of Moab, to curse the people of Israel before they entered Canaan.

Balak: King of Moab, opposed the entrance of Israel into the Promised Land.

Balm in Gilead: Resin from the styrax tree, produced especially in the north Transjordan region of Gilead, widely used for medicinal purposes.

Bamah: High place; term used in relation to places of worship on natural or constructed hills.

Bamoth: Location where the Israelites stopped on their way to Moab; located somewhere in the Transjordan.

Bamoth-baal: A longer form of the name Bamoth (see above).

Ban: A decree requiring absolute destruction of everything in a conquered city.

Baptism: A rite of purification using water as symbolic cleansing from sin, practiced by John the Baptist but not by Jesus. In the early church it was the initiatory rite for converts (3:13).

Barabbas: The name of the prisoner whom Pilate released in the form of amnesty when he condemned Jesus to die. Mark and Luke make him out to be an insurrectionist. Matthew says simply that he was a notorious prisoner (27:16).

Barachel: Father of Elihu; his name means God has blessed.

Barak: A judge who, with Deborah, led Israel in defeating Sisera.

Barnabas: An apostle who went with Paul on his first missionary journey.

Bars of Sheol: A poetic designation of the doors, or entrance, to the abode of the dead.

Bartholomew: One of the twelve apostles, according to each of the four lists (Matthew 10:3; Mark 3:18; Luke 6:14; Acts 1:13). Traditionally a missionary to many countries.

Bashan: The region east and northeast of the Sea of Galilee and east of the Jordan River; it was well adapted to growing wheat and cattle and was famous for its groves of oak trees; was taken by the Israelites from the Amorites.

Bath: A unit of liquid measure equal to the amount of an ephah (a dry measure); about five and a half gallons.

Bath-rabbim: An entrance to Heshbon; possibly a gate where there was a pool of water nearby.

Bdellium: A precious stone or perhaps a sticky substance; the term is used to describe manna.

Bear: A constellation of stars containing either the Big Dipper ("Great Bear") or Little Dipper ("Little Bear").

Beelzebul: The chief of the devils or Satan (12:27).

Beer-elim: A city in Moab; the name means well of chiefs.

Beeroth: A city located between the territories of Benjamin and Ephraim.

Beersheba: Major city and religious center in the Negeb; often named as the southern limit of the nation of Israel (see, for example, Judges 20:1)

Behemoth: Commonly identified as either an elephant or hippopotamus. It also has mythological roots, believed to have been the land counterpart of Leviathan, the sea serpent.

Bel: The title of Merodach/Marduk, the state god of Babylon, which means he who possesses, subdues, rules; the title indicates the god's power over a certain place.

Belshazzar: Son and coruler of Nabonidus, who was the last king of the Babylonian Empire (556–539 B.C.).

Ben-Hadad: King of Damascus who followed his father Hazael to the throne in 798 B.C. (2 Kings 13:1).

Benejaakan: A place in the territory of Edom where the Israelites encamped.

Benjaminite: A member of the tribe of Benjamin, the younger son of Jacob and Rachel; brother of Joseph.

Beon: Probably another name for Baal-meon.

Beor: The father of Balaam, the seer who was summoned to curse Israel.

Bernice: The daughter of Agrippa I. Married first to Marcus. When he died, she was betrothed to Marcus's brother Herod. Had incestuous relationship with her brother, Agrippa II.

Berothah: Place on the northern border of Ezekiel's ideal Israel.

Beryl: A sea-green gem.

Bethany: A small village a mile and a half east of Jerusalem, lying on the eastern slope of the Mount of Olives. Bethany was the home of Mary, Martha, and Lazarus whom Jesus raised from the dead (21:17).

Beth-aven: A combination of words meaning house of wickedness and evil. Hosea uses the term as a derogatory reference to the city of Bethel.

Bethel: Town in the hills north of Jerusalem, founded around 2000 B.C. For the Canaanites, it was a sanctuary city dedicated to their god, El. Early in the Judges period, the ark of the covenant was housed here. It was the site of the chief sanctuary for the Northern Kingdom. Amos prophesied here.

Bethezel: A place in southern Judah, near Debir.

Bethhaccherem: Identified with modern Ramet Rahel, two miles south of Jerusalem.

Bethharam: A city of Gad, in the Jordan valley.

Beth-Jeshimoth: A city in Moab.

Beth-le-aphrah: An as yet unidentified city, perhaps belonging to the Philistines.

Bethlehem: (1) A city south of Jerusalem, original home of Micah's Levite, of the Ephraimite Levites concubine, and of Naomi and Boaz. (2) A town of the same name to the north, in Zebulun.

Bethlehem Ephrathah: Bethlehem is a town in the hills six miles south-southwest of Jerusalem; it is the home of King David and the birthplace of Jesus. Ephrathah is a settlement identified with and perhaps part of Bethlehem, also the clan to which the people of Bethlehem belonged.

Beth-millo: A fortress at Shechem.

Bethnimrah: A city of Gad, in the Jordan valley.

Bethphage: A tiny village, a bit farther east than Bethany. It is from Bethphage that Jesus commences his "royal entry" into Jerusalem at the beginning of the Passion week (21:1).

Bethsaida: A village on the northeast shore of the Sea of Galilee. Jesus condemned Bethsaida for her failure to repent. Some evidence indicates this as the scene of the feeding of the multitudes by Jesus (11:21).

Beth-Togarmah: Means House of Togarmah; a region in Asia Minor once part of the Assyrian Empire.

Betrothal: The first stage of the marriage transaction. In the case of Mary and Joseph, Mary was indeed considered Joseph's wife, but he did not know her sexually until after their formal marriage (1:18).

Beyond the River: The name given to the fifth Persian satrapy. The land west of the Euphrates River, including Palestine.

Bezalel: The son of Uri, from the tribe of Judah, appointed by God to oversee the construction of the tabernacle and all its furnishings (Exodus 31:2; 35:30).

Bezer: A city of Reuben that was designated as a city of refuge.

Bildad: One of Job's friends, also known as the Shuhite. His name means either God has loved or son of Hadad.

Bishop: From the Greek word *episkopos* (1 Timothy 3:2; Titus 1:7), meaning overseer. The office of bishop was the highest in the Christian church.

Bitumen: Mineral pitch or asphalt; used as mortar and as caulking for rafts and basket boats.

Blasphemy: Slandering, reproaching, cursing, or showing contempt for God or for something sacred; also, claiming divine qualities for oneself.

Blessed, Blessing: Word formulas through which the power of God was expressed (5:1-11).

Blood: Because blood is life, the sacrificed blood in a religious ritual is considered to have a cleansing power. Symbolically, the blood of Jesus, sacrificed on behalf of humanity, has the power to cleanse the conscience of those who accept Christ as savior.

Boaz: Ruth's protector and second husband.

Book of the Covenant: A law code found in Exodus 21:1-23, probably used by elders who judged court cases (Exodus 24:7).

Booth: A temporary shelter constructed of branches and vines, used in pastures and on battlefields.

Booths, Feast of: One of three major annual festivals of the Israelites. Originally celebrated the closing of the agricultural year; adapted to commemorate the escape from Egypt.

Booty: Possessions of an enemy, taken by the victor after a battle.

Bozrah: Probably the strongest city in northern Edom, a fortress that guarded an important road and the approaches to copper mines in the area.

Bread of the Presence: Twelve loaves of bread, renewed weekly, that were continually in the presence of the Lord. This bread is sometimes referred to as the shewbread (Exodus 25:30; 35:13; 39:36; 40:23; Leviticus 24:5-9).

Breath of the Almighty: Another term for Spirit; all living creatures are dependent upon God's breath.

Bridegroom: A metaphor for Christ as the bridegroom of the church. It is commonly used in connection with the messianic wedding feast, as for example in 25:1-13.

Brook of Egypt: A river flowing across the southern border of Canaan. It is referred to in records of Sargon and Sennacherib.

Brook of the Willows: A river in the region of Moab. The Moabites carried their belongings across this river in flight.

Broom Tree: A desert bush burned for warmth by wandering outcasts.

Burnt offering: A complete burning of the sacrificial animal, which represents the desire of the offerer to be in harmony with God (see especially Leviticus 1:1).

Buz: A tribe and/or territory in northwest Arabia.

Buzite: The designation of someone from the tribe or territory of Buz.

Byword: A name or phrase used as a source of derision and ridicule.

C

Caesar: The family of Julius Caesar. The name became the title as well. Caesar Augustus appears in Luke 2:1; as a title it appears twenty-seven times in the New Testament.

Caesarea: City on the coast of Palestine twenty-three miles from Mt. Carmel.

Caesarea Philippi: City on the southwest slope of Mt. Hermon; here Jesus questioned the disciples regarding his identity. Peter replied that Jesus was the Christ (Mark 8:27).

Caiaphas: Chief priest in the Sanhedrin, the Jewish High Court, at the time of Jesus' trial, according to Matthew 26:57. Another tradition has it that Annas, father-in-law of Caiaphas, was high priest. We have no conclusive evidence. The high priest was appointed by and accountable to Rome.

Cain: The oldest son of Adam and Eve. His sacrifice was less pleasing to God than his brother Abel's. Therefore, he killed Abel.

Caleb: One of the spies who entered Canaan before the Israelite conquest. In the land division he received the city of Hebron.

Caligula: Gaius, great-nephew of the Emperor Tiberius; was Roman emperor from A.D. 37 to 41. He believed he was the incarnation of Jupiter and demanded that his statue be worshiped. He appointed Herod Agrippa king in Palestine.

Calno: A city in Babylon, associated with Carchemish. It was probably located in the northern part of the country.

Canaan: The territory covering, approximately, Palestine west of the Jordan River and part of western Syria.

Canaanites: The people occupying the land of Canaan before the Israelite invasion.

Canneh: Alternate form of Calneh, a city in the Babylonian Empire.

Capernaum: City on the northwest corner of the Sea of Galilee. Jesus made this city his home during his public ministry (4:13). It is thought that Capernaum was also the home of the disciples Peter and Andrew. The synagogue at Capernaum is mentioned in connection with the healing of the centurion's servant (8:5-13).

Caphtor(im): The territory that was home to the Philistines originally. Its location is uncertain.

Cappadocia: A highland province in the territory of eastern Asia Minor.

Carchemish: A city on the Euphrates River that was captured by the Assyrians during the time of Isaiah.

Carmel: See Mount Carmel.

Carnelian: Red quartz, used for jewelry.

Cenchreae: A seaport seven miles east of Corinth on the Aegean Sea. In this city Paul cut his hair in accordance with Jewish tradition (Acts 18:18; also Romans 16:1).

Censer: A shallow container that was used to carry live coals from sacrifices.

Centurion: The Roman officer who commanded a company of 100 infantry in a Roman legion. A centurion supervised the execution of Jesus; he declared Jesus to be a son of God (not a messianic confession), possibly meaning a kind of pagan demigod (27:54). Earlier, Jesus healed a centurion's servant (8:13).

Cephas: The Aramaic name for the apostle Peter. It means rock.

Cereal offering: Flour made from wheat or barley and prepared with oil and frankincense (see especially Leviticus 2:1).

Chalcedony: Quartz, usually gray or milky in color, with a lustrous surface.

Chaldea: A territory in the southern portion of Babylonia during Nebuchadnezzar's reign (604–562 B.C.). Chaldean is sometimes used synonymously with Babylonian.

Chaldean: A person of the southernmost portion of the valley of the Tigris and Euphrates rivers from about the eleventh century B.C. Also the restored Babylonian Empire in the seventh and sixth centuries B.C.

Chambers of the South: A group of stars whose location is uncertain.

Chebar: A river that was a branch of the Euphrates River where Ezekiel received his first vision.

Chemosh: Name or title of the Moabite god; Solomon built a temple to Chemosh (1 Kings 11:7) which Josiah abolished (2 Kings 23:13).

Cherethites: People from the area of the Aegean Sea who settled on the coast of Palestine and became part of King David's mercenary army; they are associated with the Philistines.

Cherubim: Winged creatures who are angelic and spiritual beings, often the guardians of sacred places.

Chiasmus: A form of poetic structure in which words or lines are mentioned in one sequence like ascending stairs and are reversed in order in the following sequence like descending stairs (for example, Isaiah 6:10).

Chilion (Kilion): Naomi's son, Orpah's husband.

Chilmad: A place in Assyria, near modern Baghdad.

Chinnereth, Chinneroth: Sea of Galilee.

Chislev: The ninth month of the Hebrew calendar; our mid-November to mid-December.

Choirmaster: The exact meaning of this term in Hebrew is uncertain; suggests a leader or head of musicians.

Chorazin: A city about two miles north of Capernaum. Jesus upbraided Chorazin and Bethsaida for their unbelief (11:21), promising woe to the cities on the day of judgment.

Christ: The Greek translation of Messiah, the anointed one of God. This was the title affixed by Christians to Jesus, the Christ.

Christ-mysticism: The teaching about the union of believers in Christ.

Chrysoprase: Quartz, apple green in color.

Circumcise: To remove the foreskin from the male genital organ. In Israel, circumcision was a sign of dedication to God and membership in God's people.

Clap one's hands: A way of expressing disgust.

Claudia: A Christian woman mentioned in Second Timothy 4:21. She sent greetings to Timothy. Tradition holds that she was the mother of Linus and may have become the wife of Pudens.

Claudius: Fourth Roman emperor. His full name was Tiberius Claudius Nero Germanius. His reign extended from A.D. 41–54. Named in Acts 11:28 and 18:2; probably identified as Caesar in Acts 17:7.

Cleopas: One of two followers whom the risen Christ accompanied on a journey to Emmaus. The name may be a shortened form of the Greek word *Cleopatros* from which the name Cleopatra comes. Cleopas may have been the father of James.

Close of the Age: That time when the present age will be brought to a decisive end by God and all people, living and dead, and nations will be judged. Then God's new age will begin (28:20).

Cohort: A cohort consists of 600 men, one-tenth of a legion. In Palestine the cohorts had 760 soldiers along with 240 mounted calvary. The cohorts usually protected borders of frontier regions. In Jerusalem the cohort was stationed in the fortress of Antonia.

Consumption: Any disease that causes a wasting of the body (Leviticus 26:16).

Corinth: The chief commercial city and capital of the Roman province of Achaia on the Isthmus of Corinth. The famed temple of Aphrodite with its 1,000 temple prostitutes attests to its immorality. Here the Christian church flourished (Acts 18:1; 19:1; 1 Corinthians 1:2; 2 Corinthians 1:1, 23).

Cornelius: A centurion of the Holian Cohort stationed in Caesarea. He was a God-fearer, a Gentile who worshiped with Jews but was not yet a convert. He was respected by Jews and offered an excellent means by which the gospel could extend from Jews to Gentiles.

Covenant: A solemn promise between two partners that is sealed with an oath and/or a symbolic action. The basic terms of God's covenant with Israel are found in the Ten Commandments (see Exodus 20:1-17; Deuteronomy 5:1-21).

Creed: A statement of beliefs often composed for use in Christian worship.

Crete: Large island in the Mediterranean Sea, southeast of Greece. From here Jews went to Jerusalem (Acts 2:11). Titus was appointed here to supervise and counteract the Judaisers (Titus 1:5-14).

Cubit: A unit for measuring length; approximately eighteen inches.

Cup: A metaphor used by Jesus to signify the experience of suffering and death he would undergo (20:22-23; 26:39). In the Last Supper the cup provides a blessing (26:27)

Curtain of the Temple: The barrier that separated the innermost Holy of Holies in the Temple from the inner and outer courts. It was ripped from top to bottom when Jesus died, symbolic of the end of the former age (27:51).

Cush: Biblical name of two territories: (1) land south of Egypt in the present-day Sudan; also called Ethiopia; (2) land of the Kassites in Mesopotamia; also called Cossaea.

Cushan: May be another name for Midian; based on the presence of tribes descended from Cush, a member of the tribe of Benjamin.

Cushi: The father of the prophet Zephaniah; the name usually means the Ethiopian and refers to a black person from Africa.

Custodian: A person, often a slave, who was responsible for taking children to school and making sure that they were educated and brought up correctly.

Cut Corners of Hair: Ancient heathen practices for mourning the dead included shaving the head, cutting hair at the temples, and cutting the beard; these practices were forbidden to Israelites (see Leviticus 19:27).

Cyprus: Also called Kittim; an island in the Mediterranean Sea approximately forty miles from Asia Minor and sixty miles from Syria; famous for its copper. Paul and Barnabas encountered a magician there (Acts 13:4-12).

Cyrene: A Greek city on the north coast of Africa, home of Simon who was conscripted to carry the cross of Jesus (27:32). A large part of the population were Greek-speaking Jews.

Cyrus: The Persian king who liberated Judah from the domination of Assyria in the sixth century B.C.

D

Dalmatia: The southern portion of Illyricum mentioned in Second Timothy 4:10. The region showed stubborn resistance to Roman rule.

Damascus: A city in Syria northeast of the Sea of Galilee, in an oasis watered by rivers and canals; an important center of commerce and religion (Acts 9:2).

Dan: The northernmost city in Israel. One of the twelve tribes of Israel.

Daniel: An Old Testament prophet living in the second century B.C. His prophecy, Daniel 11:31, was in reality spoken against the king of Syria who set up a statue to Zeus in the Temple in 168 B.C. But it was veiled as a prophecy against the Babylonian King Nebuchadnezzar in the sixth century B.C. Matthew 24:1 cites it as a prophecy against Rome.

Daric: A Persian coin, the first coin mentioned in the Bible.

Darius I: King of Persia, 521–485 B.C.

Darius the Mede: Named in Daniel 5:30 as ruler of the territory of Babylon after Babylon's defeat by the Medes and Persians in 539 B.C. and before the reign of Cyrus of Persia (see Daniel 6:28). His name and identity are not known outside of Scripture.

Dathan: Brother of Abiram; together they led a rebellion against Moses in the wilderness.

David: King of greater Israel, 1010–970 B.C.; founder of royal line; ancestor of Jesus.

Day of Atonement: The annual day of fasting when the high priest atoned for all the sins of Israel (see especially Leviticus 16:1; 23:26-32).

Day of the Lord: From the time of Amos (8th century B.C.) on, it meant the great day when God would judge the world (both Israel and the nations) and inaugurate the new Kingdom (see Amos 5:18-20; Joel 2:30-31). In the New Testament the Lord is the returning Jesus (1 Corinthians 1:8).

Deacon: First mentioned in Acts 6:1-6 as servers. The term stems from the word *diakonia*, meaning work. Deacons served as assistants to bishops/elders (1 Timothy 3:8-13).

Dead Sea Scrolls: These are scriptures found in caves at the northwest end of the Dead Sea between 1947 and 1960. They include many Old Testament books and other writings and date from the late 200s B.C. to A.D. 70.

Decalogue: Another name for the Ten Commandments (Exodus 20:3-17).

Decapolis: Ten Greek cities in the region east of the Jordan from which crowds came to follow Jesus early in his ministry (4:25)

Dedan: Perhaps a settlement of Dedanites living in Edom.

Dedanites: An important commercial and trading people living in the northwest portion of Arabia.

Demas: A coworker with Paul. In Philemon 24 he is identified as a fellow worker.

Demetrius: The leader and chief spokesman for silversmiths in Ephesus. When his livelihood was threatened by Paul's Christian preaching he incited the guild to riot.

Demon: Generally understood to be an agent of the devil (Satan). Demons will be overwhelmed and punished in the final judgment. In the meantime they can be exorcised by confronting them with the name of God (9:28-30; 17:18-20).

Denarius: A Roman silver coin worth one day's labor (20:2, 9-10, 13).

Derbe: A town in central Asia Minor, in the district of Lycaonia. Paul visited here twice, establishing a Christian congregation during the first visit (Acts 14:6, 20). Gaius, one of Paul's disciples, came from Derbe (Acts 20:4).

Desecration: The period when Antiochus placed a statue of Zeus on the altar of the Temple in Jerusalem. It became a symbolic word, referring to any spoiling of a holy place.

Destroyer: The angel of Death who brought about the death of all firstborn in Egypt, with the exception of those in Israelite homes.

Devil: The great adversary of God, believed to entice people away from obedience to God (Matthew 4). God has prepared an eternal fire for the devil and his angels (25:41).

Diatribe: The question-and-answer style of argument; it was designed for the purpose of raising issues with a friendly audience.

Dibon: A city in Moab that later became a possession of the tribe of Gad.

Diotrephes: The opponent of John in Third John 1:9-10.

Dispersion: In the Old Testament it refers to the situation of living in foreign areas outside of Israel and Judah. In the New Testament it can refer to spiritual and/or cultural exile and alienation.

Dividing Wall: A fence, railing, or hedge used for protection. In Ephesians it refers to the wall in the Jerusalem Temple that divided the Gentiles from the Jews.

Divination: The art of identifying the will and intentions of the gods, practiced by diviners; the Babylonians were the first group of people to develop this art to an almost scientific discipline.

Divine Men: Roving teachers, some within the Christian church, around the time of Paul who claimed to be incarnations of a god or god-filled; to possess divine knowledge about the universe and the way of salvation; and to have miraculous powers of perception, speech, and healing. Paul opposed such teachers in his letters to the Corinthians, the Colossians, and the Thessalonians.

Diviners: Those who practice divination.

Doctrine of divine reward/punishment: The orthodox Jewish view, argued by Job's friends, that God rewards the righteous and punishes the wicked. Such a concept explains suffering as the consequence of God's chastisement.

Doctrines: Teachings; instructions.

Dominion: The power of God.

Double-minded: A term used in James to describe unfaithful people who said one thing and did another.

Dove: Often used as a likeness to perfect faith and obedience. Jesus' disciples were to be innocent as doves (Matthew 10:16). The dove was required as sacrificial offering in the Temple in Jesus' time. At Jesus' baptism God's Holy Spirit descended on him like a dove (3:16).

Doxology: A prayer that praises God.

Drusilla: Mentioned in Acts 23:24; third daughter of Agrippa I. Felix, procurator of Judea in A.D. 52–60, fell in love with her and wanted to marry her, and she left her husband for him.

Dumah: Used in Isaiah 21:11, this word may be a variation of the name Edom. The word may also mean silence.

E

East: A designation for countries east of Palestine, including Uz. It was an area known for its scholars.

East Wind: A hot desert wind, or sirocco, that destroys vegetation.

Eber: An ancestor of the Hebrews.

Edom: The land and people to the south and east of Judah, named after a red rock and called the red region.

Edomites: The people of Edom; descended from Esau.

Edrei: The city inhabited by Og, the king of Bashan.

Egypt: A land in northeast Africa along the Nile River; one of the earliest and most powerful civilizations of the ancient Near East.

Ekron: The northernmost of the five main cities of the Philistines; at the head of a valley leading from the coastal plain to Jerusalem.

El Shaddai: An early name for Israel's God, first given to Jacob, translated God Almighty (Exodus 6:3).

Elam: A country in the mountainous region east of the Tigris Valley, the home of the Elamites. Cyrus was king of Elam when he conquered Babylon and formed the Persian Empire.

Elam: A region east of the Euphrates and Tigris rivers on the slopes of the Iranian plateau. Susa was the capital of this region

Eldad: An israelite who prophesied inside the limits of the camp.

Elder: In the New Testament, from the Greek word *presbuteros*; the word can be translated as either an old man or an official of the church. As an official, the position is an ordained clergy with administrative and pastoral duties. The duties of elder and bishop overlap.

Elders: In the Old Testament, grown men who are leaders in their clan, tribe, or community; they represent and maintain the community's customs and laws.

Eleazar: A son of Aaron; father of Phinehas.

Elephantine: An island in the Nile River near Aswan, the home of a Jewish colony during the Babylonian Exile. Important papyri have been discovered there.

Eliab: An Israelite elder who represented the tribe of Zebulun.

Eliakim: The son of Hilkiah; servant in the court of Hezekiah.

Elihu: The name of Job's fourth friend, appearing in Chapters 32-37; the son of Barachel, his name means my God is he.

Elijah (Elias): A prophet in the ninth century B.C. whose return was to be the sign of the appearance of the messiah (16:14; 17:3; 27:47-49).

Eliphaz: The oldest of Job's friends. From the town of Tema, his name possibly means God is fine gold.

Elishah: An island, perhaps Cyprus.

Elizaphan: The leader of the Kohathites in the wilderness.

Elizabeth, Elisabeth: Wife of the priest Zechariah, and mother of John the Baptist. Her name means God is an oath.

Elkosh: Probably a place in southern Judah, though its exact location is unknown; the hometown of the prophet Nahum.

Elul: The sixth month of the Hebrew calendar.

Emim: Ancient inhabitants of the Transjordan, known for their large size.

Emmanuel (Immanuel): A name given to Jesus in Matthew's birth story (1:23). The name recalls the promise foretold by Isaiah (Isaiah 7:14) that God would deliver Israel from her enemies. It means literally God with us.

Emmaus: A town seven miles from Jerusalem. The name means warm springs, but the site is uncertain.

Endor: A village of Palestine south of Mount Tabor.

Endurance: Bearing hardships and difficulties patiently as disciplines from God; the quality of those who are faithful to God.

En-Eglaim: A settlement on the northwest coast of the Dead Sea.

En-gedi: A spring-fed oasis approximately halfway down the western side of the Dead Sea. This site was an extremely important military outpost and source of water for Judean shepherds.

Enoch: Ancient hero of dedicated faith. He was taken up to be with God without having to die.

Epaenetus: A Christian mentioned by Paul in Romans 16:1, where he asks the congregation to greet him. His identity is uncertain.

Epaphras: Mentioned in Philemon 23, he was a native of Colossae responsible for first spreading the gospel to the area of Laodicea and Hierapolis (Colossians 4:12-13). He is identified as a fellow prisoner with Paul.

Ephah: A unit of dry measure, approximately three-eighths to two-thirds of a bushel; also a container which holds this amount.

Ephesus: Large seaport city in the Roman province of Asia, a commercial and religious center. Paul preached here for an extended period of time (Acts 19:8, 10). In the theater a riot broke out, instigated by Demetrius (Acts 19:23-41).

Ephod: A small object consulted by priests to determine the divine will.

Ephraim: One of the twelve tribes of Israel, descended from Joseph's younger son, also used as a name for the Northern Kingdom of Israel.

Ephraim, Mount: See Mount Ephraim.

Epicureanism: A philosophy based on the teachings of Epicurus (342?–270 B.C.). It taught that the gods did not influence the universe or human behavior and that people should avoid pain and excess desire. Followers of Epicurus were often accused of being pleasure seekers.

Epicureans: Followers of a Greek philosophy founded in the fourth century B.C. by Epicurus. In reaction to a stern religion, he believed that the chief goal of life is happiness, free from fear of death or of the gods. He did not believe in the life to come.

Epilogue: Words spoken at the conclusion. Usually a short speech or comment in summary.

Epiphany: From the Greek, meaning manifestation or divine revelation.

Erastus: Another Christian Paul requests the Romans to greet on his behalf in Romans 16:1.

Esarhaddon: Son of Sennacherib, king of Assyria in 681–669 B.C.

Esau: The son of Isaac and Rebekah, the elder twin brother of Jacob and the traditional ancestor of the Edomites.

Eschatology: A teaching about the end of the world, which in the case of Romans implies the triumph of God over evil.

Esdras, First: A book in the Protestant Apocrypha, not found in the Roman Catholic Bible. It retells the story of Ezra, and in some places is better preserved than Ezra.

Essene: This Jewish sect was active from the Maccabean period (160s B.C.) to the Roman destruction of Jerusalem (A.D. 70). This may be the group that authored the Dead Sea Scrolls and lived at Qumran. It has been suggested—although there is no evidence—that John the Baptist and possibly Jesus were associated with this group.

Eternal: That which pertains to the age to come after the present age. It will be forever.

Eternity: A Hebrew term used by Qoheleth in 3:11 to indicate the mystery that persons sense about God's plan or the meaning of the world.

Ethan: Probably a singer in the tradition of Levi.

Ethiopia: The ancient name for the territory south of Egypt, approximately the area of present-day Sudan; also called Cush.

Eubulus: In Second Timothy 4:21 he is one of the Christians who send greetings to Timothy.

Euphrates: One of the major rivers of Mesopotamia, along with the Tigris; the largest river in western Asia, flowing from Turkey to the Persian Gulf.

Evi: A Midianite king killed by the Israelite army.

Evil One: Another term for the devil or Satan.

Exchange of Lordship: The transfer of believers into the realm where Christ is Lord.

Exhort: To offer moral advice or Christian teaching.

Expiation: The act of atoning or making payment for sin.

Ezion-geber: A city in the Arabah where the Israelites encamped on their wilderness journey.

F

Faith: Loyal response to the gospel of unconditional love in Christ.

Fat: A sign of prosperity.

Father: This is the name Jesus used for God. Abba is the Aramaic term that is preserved in our Greek New Testament and is better translated Daddy. Jesus taught his disciples to address God with this term, even though Jews did not even say the name of God because this implied power over the one addressed.

Fear of God: Respecting God's power and acknowledging total dependence upon the Almighty. This phrase designated the proper attitude one should have toward God.

Feast of Dedication: Also called Hanukkah, this feast celebrates the purification of the Temple by the Maccabees in the 160s B.C. It celebrates Jewish freedom to worship their God.

Feast of Tabernacles: Also called Ingathering or Booths, this is a major pilgrimage festival for visiting Jerusalem. The eight-day event celebrates the harvest and God's protection of Israel during the wilderness wanderings.

Feast of Weeks: Also known as Pentecost, an annual one-day festival at the end of the grain harvest (Exodus 23:16; 34:22).

Felix: Antonius Felix, the Roman procurator of Judea in the years A.D. 52–60. He ruled during Paul's final visit to and arrest in Jerusalem.

Field of Blood: According to Matthew 27:8, a burial ground for strangers in Jerusalem, the name based on the incident in Jeremiah 32:6-15. The chief priests bought the field with the mopney Judas returned after the betrayal of Jesus. Luke tells a different story of how the field came to be called Akeldama, field of blood (Acts 1:15-19).

Fire of God: A brush fire or lightning, viewed as a sign of God's displeasure or punishment.

Fish: In the Old Testament, the fish is associated with the freshness of water. The death of fish can contaminate water and once caused a death plague (Exodus 7:21) and a drought (Isaiah 50:2). In the early church, the fish became a sign of Christ. The Greek word for fish, *ichthys*, was understood to mean Jesus Christ, God's son, savior.

Folly: A term used by the sages who wrote Proverbs to describe actions that willfully ignore moral virtue or the natural laws.

Fool: A term used in Wisdom Literature, such as Proverbs, denoting one who does not display proper fear of God.

Freemen: Slaves in the Greco-Roman world who had secured their freedom by purchase or by working to achieve it.

Freewill offering: An offering purely on the impulse of the offerer (Exodus 35:27-29; 36:3; Leviticus 7:16).

Freshets: Temporary streams of water resulting from melting snow or ice.

Friendly interlocutor: The person, often a student or a friend of the speaker, who poses the questions that are used in a diatribe.

Fullness of time: Just the right time when God's plans will finally be realized.

G

Gabriel: An angel or messenger of God, later regarded as an archangel, whose activities are described in First and Second Enoch. He is introduced in the Bible as an interpreter in Daniel 8:16-17.

Gad: The seventh son of Jacob, one of the twelve tribes of Israel, settled land east of the Jordan and west of Ammon.

Gadarenes: Name of the people dwelling in Gadara, a Greek city five miles southeast of the Sea of Galilee. Mentioned in Matthew 8:28 as the scene of Jesus' healing of the demoniacs among the swine who plunged into the sea.

Gaddi: One of the men Moses sent to spy out the land of Canaan; he was from the tribe of Joseph.

Gaddiel: One of the men Moses sent to spy out the land of Canaan; he was from the tribe of Zebulun.

Gaius: A Christian mentioned by Paul in Romans 16:1, among those Paul requests the congregation to greet. He is also mentioned in the letter to the Corinthians (see 1 Corinthians 1:14).

Galatia: A region and Roman province of central Asia Minor (Acts 16:6; 18:23; 1 Corinthians 16:1; Galatians 1:2; 2 Timothy 4:10; 1 Peter 1:1).

Galilee: Northernmost area of Israel. Almost all of Jesus' ministry was in Galilee. Capernaum was a major city in this area.

Gall: A bitter and poisonous herb, mentioned with wormwood in the context of bitterness and tragedy.

Gamad: A city in Syria.

Gamaliel: The grandson of Rabbi Hillel. He counseled moderation in response to Peter (Acts 5:34-39). He was a highly respected Pharisee in the Sanhedrin and was also Paul's teacher (22:3).

Gareb: A suburb or quarter of Jerusalem, possibly on the southwest hill.

Gath: A major Philistine city, northwest of Lachish in the region between the coastal plain and the Shephelah.

Gaza: An important Philistine city in southwestern Palestine; the land gateway for commercial and military traffic between Egypt and Asia.

Geba: A town on the northern border of Judah, six miles northeast of Jerusalem.

Gebal: A Phoenician port city, center of trade and shipbuilding.

Gedaliah: (1) the grandson of King Hezekiah and grandfather of the prophet Zephaniah; (2) Governor of Judah under Babylonian rule, 587–582 B.C.

Gennesaret: Another name sometimes given to the Sea of Galilee (Matthew 14:34); also a fertile valley northwest of the Sea.

Genre: A type of literature. The Christian Gospels are a particular genre that attempts to tell readers who Jesus of Nazareth really was and what he accomplished.

Gentile: The term stems from the Hebrew word meaning nations (other than Israel). In the New Testament it describes peoples other than Jews. This vast population offered Christianity a rich mission field to which the Holy Spirit directed the church.

Gerah: One twentieth of a shekel.

Gerar: An important city and district southwest of Canaan near the Mediterranean coast.

Gerasenes: Persons from Gerasa, a site on the east shore of the Sea of Galilee. Also called Gadarenes in some translations with the site called Gadara.

Gershom: One of the three sons of Levi.

Geshurites: The people who lived in Geshur, a territory in northeastern Palestine.

Gethsemane: The olive grove on the western slope of the Mount of Olives facing Jerusalem to which Jesus retired on the night of the Last Supper, and in which he was arrested. The name means literally an oil plot (Matthew 26:36).

Geuel: One of the men Moses sent to spy out the land of Canaan; he was from the tribe of Gad.

Gibeon: A city of the tribe of Benjamin, six miles southwest of Jerusalem.

Gideon: A leader in the confederacy of Israelite tribes.

Gilead: Name of a territory, a tribe, and possibly a city located east of the Jordan River; famous for its medicinal balm.

Gilgal: A place near Jericho that was the Israelites' first encampment after crossing the Jordan River during their conquest of Canaan.

Girgashites: A Canaanite tribe that was among the peoples dispossessed by the Israelites.

Gittith: A word having to do with instrumental music.

Glory: God's majesty. Literally it refers to one's "weight" or "value."

Glossalalia: The technical term to describe pneumatic or ecstatic utterances, or speaking in tongues. These are unintelligible unless interpreted. Frequently associated with the presence of the Holy Spirit.

Gnostic: A person who believed in Gnosticism.

Gnosticism: This term refers to many groups active during the first centuries of Christianity. Although diverse in beliefs, they generally offered freedom from material pollution through a special saving knowledge (Greek term, *gnosis*). This knowledge offered a special relationship with the god of the universe. A type of gnosticism seems to have been active in Ephesus, where John's Gospel was probably written.

Goah: A suburb of Jerusalem.

God-fearer: A Gentile who worships with Jews but is not yet a convert.

Gog: Named in Ezekiel 39:1 as the leader of evil forces that will rise against the restored Israel; this leader's name and identity are not known outside of Scripture.

Golan: A city of refuge, located in the territory of Bashan.

Golgotha (Calvary): From the Latin *calvaria*, meaning skull. The place outside the wall of Jerusalem where Jesus was executed (Matthew 27:33).

Gomer: Eldest son of Japheth and father of a people from a territory in what is now southern Russia.

Gomorrah: A city destroyed by God along with Sodom for its wickedness, probably now located under the waters of the southern part of the Dead Sea.

Gospel: The Greek word *evangelion* means good news and translates as gospel. The four New Testament Gospels are carefully written (Luke 1:1-4), and each has a particular purpose (John 20:30-31; 21:24-25).

Grace: The unmerited gift of love, conveyed to humans by the life and death and resurrection of Jesus; an important concept in Pauline theology.

Grand Vizier: A prime minister, second in command.

Greco-Roman world: The civilization in the region around the Mediterranean Sea at the time of Paul.

Greek: The language of the New Testament. Common Greek was used by Paul in his writing. Also a term used to describe the European, or Gentile.

Guilt offering: A payment imposed on someone who had inflicted material damage on another person (see especially Leviticus 5:1-7).

H

Hadadrimmon: A pagan fertility god whose seasonal death was mourned by his worshipers.

Hades: From a Greek word meaning abode of the dead. By the time of the New Testament Hades had come to signify a place of punishment (Matthew 11:23). The older Hebrew concept of Sheol was the destination of life after death, but not a place of punishment.

Hadrach: A town in northwestern Lebanon.

Ham: The second son of Noah and the ancestor of the peoples of northeast Africa.

Hamath: An important town in Syria on the Orontes River, taken by the Assyrians and Babylonians.

Hamon Gog: Means multitude of Gog; a valley in the territory of the Transjordan where the dead of Gog's armies will be buried.

Hamonah: City where Gog's forces will be destroyed.

Hananiah: The Hebrew name of Shadrach, one of Daniel's friends.

Hanukkah: A feast celebrated by the Jews in remembrance of the time they regained their Temple in Jerusalem after Antiochus had desecrated it by placing a statue of Zeus on its altar.

Haran: City in northern Mesopotamia in what is now Turkey, to which Abraham's family migrated on their way from Ur to Canaan.

Hauran: A region east of the Jordan River and the Sea of Galilee that marks the northeast limit of Ezekiel's ideal Israel.

Havoth-jair: A group of sixty towns located in the region of Bashan.

Hazael: He seized the Syrian throne in 831 B.C.

Hazar-Enon: A city on the frontier between Palestine and Hamath in Syria.

Hazar-Hatticon: Probably the same place as Hazar-Enon (see above).

Hazeroth: A place where the Israelites encamped during their wilderness journey; Miriam and Aaron disputed with Moses here. Its location in the Sinai wilderness is unknown.

Hazor: May be a place or a group of tribes in the Arabian desert east of Palestine.

Heart: The center of the intellect in Hebrew thought; synonymous with conscience.

Heaven(s): The sky, which serves as a canopy over the cosmic ocean. It was regarded as the crowning glory of God's creation (*see also* Kingdom of Heaven).

Hebrews: In the larger sense, the descendants of Eber; more specifically, the Israelite people.

Hebron: An important city located directly west of the central portion of the Dead Sea, south of Jerusalem. Also the name of one of the sons of Kohath.

Hedges: Thorn hedges or fences constructed to protect vineyards.

Helbon: A city northwest of Damascus, famous for its wine production.

Helech: Possibly a country in southeast Asia Minor.

Hellenism: The term refers to the spread of Greek culture throughout the lands Alexander the Great conquered, including Palestine.

Hellenistic: Of or pertaining to the age of Greek rule. The Hellenes were Greeks, and the Hellenistic age began with the conquest of the civilized world by Alexander the Great in 333 B.C.

Hellenists: Greek-speaking Jews (Acts 6:1; 9:29), as opposed to Jews who spoke Hebrew or Aramaic. A term used to describe foreigners (Acts 2:5-6). Hellenists were in conflict with Jews who spoke Hebrew (Acts 6:1-7).

Hepher: One of the clans within the tribe of Manasseh.

Hermes: A Christian greeted by Paul in Romans 16:1; his identity is unknown.

Hermon, Mount: See Mount Hermon.

Herod Agrippa I: Grandson of Herod the Great. Persecuted the early church (Acts 12:1-23). He killed James and arrested Peter, who was released from jail by an angel.

Herod Antipas: One of the sons of Herod the Great. Antipas was given rule over Galilee and Perea at the death of his father, and ruled from 4 B.C. to A.D. 39.

Herodians: People loyal to the Herods. In 22:16 Matthew pictures them with the Pharisees in opposition to Jesus.

Herodias: The wife of Herod Antipas, but previously married to Philip, her husband's half-brother. Because John the Baptist condemned her for this violation of the marriage law, she prompted her daughter Salome to ask Antipas for the head of John the Baptist (Matthew 14:3-12).

Herodion: A Christian greeted by Paul in Romans 16:1; his identity is unknown.

Herodotus: Fifth-century B.C. Greek historian.

Heshbon: An important city in northern Moab, fifty miles east of Jerusalem; occupied at times by Israelites, Ammonites, and Amorites.

Heshvan: The eighth month in the Hebrew calendar.

Hethlon: A city located on the northern border of Ezekiel's ideal Israel.

Hezekiah: King of Judah, 715–687 B.C.

Higgaion: Literally, a solemn musical sound.

High Places: Canaanite sanctuaries, either open-air or roofed, which were on high hills.

High Priest: This was the head official who performed Temple rituals, especially sacrifices. Traditionally, priests were Levites who received no land (Deuteronomy 10:8-9). During Jesus' time, the high priest was also the head of local government, the collector of taxes, and the one who dealt with ruling powers.

Hin: A liquid measure equal to approximately one gallon.

Hireling: A contracted and compensated worker leading a life of strenuous labor.

Hittites: An Indo-European people who were a great power in Asia Minor from approximately 1650–1200 B.C.; later centers of power were in Hamath and northern Syria; also were among the inhabitants of Canaan.

Hivites: One of the native populations of Canaan before the Israelite settlement; also called Horites.

Hoglah: One of Zelophehad's five daughters.

Holiness: A state of relationship to God in which a person or thing is separated from all that is profane and unclean, completely dedicated to God and suitable for association with God.

Holiness Code: A code of laws found in Leviticus 17:1-26.

Holy of Holies (the Most Holy Place): Smaller of the two rooms in the sactuary of Israel, curtained off at its west end. Shaped like a cube. Restricted to entry by the high priest and then only once a year on the Day of Atonement. Here was kept the ark of the covenant.

Holy ones: Another name for angels.

Holy Place: The larger of the two rooms in the sanctuary of Israel. Rectangular in shape. Restricted to serving priests. Furnished with a table of the bread of Presence, a seven-branched lampstand, and altar of incense.

Holy Sepulchre: The cave where Jesus was buried in the tomb of Joseph of Arimathea. A Church of the Holy Sepulchre now stands above the supposed cave.

Holy Spirit: In the Old Testament the Holy Spirit is believed to be the power and the means of God's activity. Matthew rarely used the word (4:1; 10:20). In other parts of the New Testament the Holy Spirit is associated with God acting through Christ in the church.

Homer: A dry measure equaling about ten ephahs, or about five bushels.

Hope: Confident expectation of access to God, such that it affects one's life direction.

Hophra: Pharaoh of Egypt, 588–569 B.C.

Horeb, Mount: See Mount Horeb.

Horites: (1) Name of a people living in the region of Seir before its occupation by the Edomites; (2) also the name of one of the native population groups of Canaan, sometimes called Hivites.

Hormah: A city of undetermined location; often used to indicate the southern portion of Israel's territory.

Horns of the altar: Projections sticking up from the top four corners of the Temple altar.

Hosanna: The word means literally Save us, we beseech thee. It became a messianic greeting when used by the crowds who cheered Jesus' entrance into Jerusalem (21:9).

Hoshea: Another name for Joshua.

House: (1) God's people (Israel, Christians); (2) the sanctuary built by Moses for worship; (3) the heavenly sanctuary where God is.

House Church: The earliest form of Christian community meeting in the home of a church member. The Roman congregations were house churches.

House of Israel, of Jacob: Jacob, also called Israel, was the son of Isaac and Rebekah, "house of" means his descendants, the people of Israel.

Hur: One of five Midianite kings slain by the Israelite army under Moses.

Hyacinth: A red or cinnamon-colored transparent gemstone.

Hymenaeus: In First Timothy 1:19, he is characterized as having made a shipwreck of his faith. Paul recommends that he be excommunicated from the church. In Second Timothy 2:17-18 he is associated with the Gnostic heretics who hold that the resurrection takes place at the time of Christian baptism.

Hypocrites (Hypocrisy): When Jesus uses the word (Matthew 7:5; 23:13), he refers specifically to the malice and deceptiveness of the persons of whom he speaks, not the more general understanding of our English word, pretending to be something we are not.

Hyssop: A bushy shrub used in purification rites in ancient Israel.

I

I Am: This is the Old Testament name for God given to Moses (Exodus 3:14) and probably is the basis for the Hebrew name for God, Yahweh. The phrase indicates the "mystery" of God (Genesis 32:22-32),suggests equality with God.

Iconium: A city in south central Asia Minor. Visited by Paul and Barnabas on the first journey, where Paul was threatened by both Jews and Gentiles (Acts 13:1-16; 2 Timothy 3:11).

Igal: One of the men Moses sent to spy out the land of Canaan; he was from the tribe of Issachar.

Illyricum: A Roman province located on the eastern coastline of the Adriatic Sea.

Incense: Compounds of gums and spices intended to be burned, or the perfume from such burning.

Isaac: Son of Abraham and Sarah; patriarch of Israel.

Isaiah: One of the major prophets of the eighth century B.C. in Israel, whose words Matthew quotes from Jesus (4:14; 8:17). Other words, attributed to that first Isaiah, are taken from Second Isaiah, the unknown prophet of the Exile in Babylon in the sixth century B.C. (3:3; 12:17).

Ishmaelites: Descendants of Ishmael, the son of Abraham by Hagar; identified as nomadic caravan traders.

Israel: A son of Isaac and Rebekah, also called Jacob, the ancestor of the twelve tribes of Israel; also the name of the Northern Kingdom when greater Israel was divided into Judah in the south and

Israel in the north; its capital was Samaria.

Issachar: One of the twelve tribes of Israel.

Ithamar: One of the sons of Aaron; a priest.

Iyar: The second month of the Hebrew calendar.

Iye-abarim: An Israelite encampment in southern Moab.

Izhar: One of the sons of Kohath; a Levite.

J

Jaar: A village several miles west of Jerusalem.

Jabbok: A tributary of the Jordan River, north of the Dead Sea.

Jacob: Also called Israel, son of Isaac and Rebekah; house of Jacob or house of Israel means his descendants, the people of Israel.

Jahaz: A city in the Transjordan where Sihon, king of the Amorites, was defeated by the Israelites.

Jair: One of the sons of Manasseh.

James: At least three men named James are mentioned in Matthew. (1) James and John, sons of Zebedee, are two of Jesus' most trusted disciples (4:21; 10:2; 17:1; 26:37). (2) According to 13:55 Jesus had a younger brother named James. Although he was not a disciple during Jesus' lifetime, he became an important leader in the Jerusalem church. Paul includes him among those to whom the risen Christ appeared (1 Corinthians 15:7). (3) A James whose mother witnessed the Crucifixion is mentioned in 27:56.

Jamnia, Council of: A meeting of Jewish leaders in A.D. 90 during which several books were admitted to the canon.

Jannas and Jambres: According to Jewish legend the two magicians who challenged Moses and Aaron (Exodus 7:11-12, 22). They are characterized as the opponents to God's truth in Second Timothy 3:8.

Jasper: Possibly the same in Revelation as the modern jasper stone, which is quartz of a red, brown, or yellow color. It may also have been a valuable green jade.

Javan: A territory in the vicinity of Greece; inhabited by the descendants of Java, son of Japheth.

Jazer: An Amorite city in the territory of Gilead.

Jebusites: A clan associated with the Amorites that was in control of Jerusalem before its conquest by David; descendants of Canaan.

Jeduthun: A singer in the tradition of Levi.

Jehoahaz: King of Judah (609 B.C.), carried into captivity to Egypt by Pharaoh Neco.

Jehoiachin: Also called Jeconiah and Coniah, king of Judah (598–597 B.C.), carried into exile by Nebuchadnezzar.

Jehoiakim: King of Judah (609–598 B.C.), son of Josiah and brother of Jehoahaz.

Jehozadak: Father of Joshua (Jeshua) the high priest; carried into exile in Babylon in 587 B.C.

Jemimah: One of the three daughters born to Job when the Lord restored his fortunes; her name means dove or turtledove.

Jephthah: A leader in the confederacy of Israelite tribes.

Jephunneh: The father of Caleb.

Jericho: One of the oldest cities in the world, at the southern end of the Jordan Valley in a key defense position.

Jeroboam: Chosen as the first king of Israel in 922 B.C.

Jerusalem: Chief city in Palestine, sacred to both Jews and Christians. The name implies foundation of shalom/peace. Became a major city due to David's political decisions.

Jesse: Son of Obed; father of David; member of the tribe of Judah.

Jesus: Personal name of the one whom Christians call "the Christ." The chosen one of God. The Jewish form of the name is Joshua or Jehoshuah, and means Yahweh will save (1:21).

Jethro: The father-in-law of Moses, also called Reuel, whose name may mean preeminence (Exodus 3:1; 4:18; 18).

Jew: Biblical term for persons who worshiped Yahweh after the Exile. In the New Testament it is used in contrast to Gentiles, Samaritans, and proselytes.

Jezreel: A fertile valley separating Samaria from Galilee.

Joab: A nephew of David; a brilliant military strategist.

Joah: An official in the court of Hezekiah, sent by Hezekiah to the Assyrians.

Job: The "hero" of the book, living in Uz; the name may mean one who is at war with God, one born to be persecuted, or the repentant one.

John: Brother of James and son of Zebedee, and a fisherman with them, as well as one of the Twelve. Tradition locates him as becoming a leader in the church at Ephesus. The name means God has been gracious.

John the Baptist: A prophet whose father, Zechariah (not the prophet), served in the Temple (Luke 1:5). The Gospel tradition in Matthew and Luke calls John's mother Elizabeth, cousin to Mary the mother of Jesus. John's preaching roused the nation to repentance; multitudes came to the Jordan to be baptized for cleansing. Jesus was baptized by John (3:13-17).

Jonah: Old Testament propet whose name is given to the tale of the prophet who preached in the pagan city of Niveveh. Jesus contrasted the repentance of the people of Nineveh with the lack of response to his own preaching (12:38-42).

Joppa: The city to which Peter was summoned. Some thirty-five miles from Jerusalem, the city offers a small harbor on the Mediterranean Sea. It was destroyed during the Jewish uprising of A.D. 68.

Jordan River: The main river of Palestine; it flows north to south from the Sea of Galilee to the Dead Sea.

Joseph: One of the twelve tribes of Israel; sometimes divided into the half-tribes of Ephraim and Manasseh.

Josephus: (first name Flavius); Jewish historian of the first century. Composed many valuable histories of the Jews.

Joshua: Also called Jeshua; high priest in Jerusalem who came from Babylon with Zerubbabel, helped rebuild the Temple in 520-516 B.C.

Josiah: King of Judah, 642–609 B.C.

Jotbathah: An encampment of the Israelites during their wilderness journey.

Jotham: Regent of Judah, 750–742 B.C.; king of Judah, 742–735 B.C.

Jubilee year: The final year in a cycle of fifty years, in which all slaves were to be released and all property was to be returned to its original owner (see especially Leviticus 25:1; 27).

Judah: The fourth son of Jacob and Leah who was the ancestor of the tribe of Judah; also the name of the Southern Kingdom after greater Israel was divided into Israel in the north and Judah in the south; its capital was Jerusalem.

Judas: One of the twelve disciples. Betrayed Jesus for thirty pieces of silver. The motive for his betrayal has been argued by scholars and others for centuries. Traditions vary as to how he died.

Judea: (1) The territory formerly called Judah in southwest Palestine. It was almost 45 miles square, extending from the Dead Sea to the Mediterranean coast, as far north as Joppa, over to the Jordan River and down to the Dead Sea (2:1; 24:16); (2) Southern part of west Palestine. A small area around Jerusalem governed by Nehemiah after the Exile.

Judgment: Follows after death. God is the ultimate judge. Judgment condemns to eternal separation from God those who have neglected salvation and preferred unrighteousness.

Julius (of the Augustan Cohort): Assigned to guard Paul during the voyage to Rome. He treated Paul well, even allowing him to visit with friends at Sidon. He also protected Paul when other soldiers wanted to kill him.

Junias: An acquaintance of Paul; possibly a fellow prisoner.

Justice: Viewed in terms of helping the weak, punishing the wicked, and blessing the righteous.

Justification by faith: To be set right by the unconditional love of God, restored to the righteousness intended by God.

Justify: The same as "rightwise"; to make right and to transform persons in conformity with divine righteousness.

K

Kadesh: An oasis in the desert of the Sinai peninsula.

Kadesh-barnea: See Kadesh.

Kadmonites: A Semitic people who were nomads or shepherds living in the Syrian Desert between Palestine-Syria and the Euphrates River.

Kain: Another name for the tribe of the Kenites.

Kassites: People originally from the highlands of present-day Iran who settled parts of the Mesopotamian plain in the 17th-16th centuries B.C.

Kedar: An area east and southeast of Israel, part of present-day Jordan and Saudi Arabia.

Kedemoth: A levitical city in the territory of Reuben.

Kenites: A nomadic or seminomadic tribe of metalworkers living generally in southern Judah.

Kenizzites: A people composed of various tribes, including descendants of Caleb, who moved into southern Canaan before the Israelite conquest.

Kerenhappuch: One of the three daughters born to Job when the Lord restored his fortunes; her name means eyeshadow.

Kerioth: The fortified capital city of Moab.

Keziah: One of the three daughters born to Job when the Lord restored his fortunes; her name means cinnamon.

Kingdom of God: Also can be translated as Rule of God or Reign of God. It does not refer to a territory, but to God's dynamic rule as king. By Jesus' day the idea of the Kingdom had taken on apocalyptic or at least eschatological associations in many quarters.

Kingdom of Heaven (Kingdom of God): These two expressions are virtually interchangeable in the Gospels, although Matthew prefers kingdom of heaven to kingdom of God. Jesus spoke, saying the kingdom of heaven had already come (12:28). But the term also refers to the age to come. Wherever God rules in a person's heart or among people now or at the end time—this is what the kingdom of God is like.

King's Highway: A road through Canaan that the Israelites traveled under the leadership of Moses.

Kir: A city in Moab; probably the same location as Kir-hareseth and Kir-heres.

Kiriathaim: A city of Moab that was later possessed by the tribe of Reuben.

Kiriath-huzoth: A city in Moab to which Balaam was taken by Balak.

Kittim: The Hebrew name for the region of Cyprus.

Koa: Exact identity unknown, perhaps Aramean mercenaries in the army of Babylon.

Kohath: The second son of Levi; the grandfather of Miriam, Moses, and Aaron.

Koine: A dialect of Greek. The language of ordinary conversation.

Korah: Great-grandson of Levi; the word may also be the name of a guild of Temple singers dating back to Levi and the priestly, musical traditions.

L

Lachish: A city in Judah halfway between Jerusalem and Gaza; an important military fortress.

Lamentations: Poems used in the ritual of mourning or in times of danger by individuals and the community.

Laodicea: A city of Asia Minor, famous as a center for banking, commerce, and the manufacture of clothes and carpets of native black wool.

Law: The law can refer to several different things: the Ten Commandments; the large body of Jewish legal ordinances and customs called the Torah; the natural order of things; God's rule for living; secular law.

Leannoth: An antiphonal performance by two choral groups.

Leaven: Except in Matthew 13:33 where Jesus likens leaven to the kingdom of heaven, where the good influence of the Kingdom leavens the whole company, leaven has evil connotations in both the Old and New Testaments. Leaven works because of fermentation and it breeds corruption and debases life. In this sense Jesus warned against the leaven of the Pharisees (16:11).

Lebanon: A mountain range running parallel to the eastern Mediterranean coast, also the name of the adjacent coastlands; populated by Canaanites, and the homeland of the Phoenicians.

Legion: The basic unit in the Roman army, consisting of 6,000 men.

Lemuel: A young ruler (or king) whose mother offers him advice on the behavior of kings in Proverbs 31:1-9.

Leper, Leprosy: One of the skin diseases so endemic in that part of the ancient world. The disease causes the skin to erupt in rough, scaly patches; in extreme cases limbs degenerate and drop from the body. A leper was considered unclean. Jesus sent out his disciples to cleanse lepers (10:8). We even see Jesus in a leper's house (26:6).

Leprous disease: A term covering a wide range of skin ailments (see especially Leviticus 13:1-14).

Lepta: Plural of lepton, the smallest coin. It is estimated at one-fourth of a sixteenth of a denarius, about what a workman might expect to earn in a day.

Lethech: A unit of dry measure that equals about 2.5 bushels.

Levi: The son of Jacob who is the ancestor of the tribe of Levi, the priestly tribe of Israel.

Leviathan: A mythological dragon subdued by God at Creation.

Levite: An order in the Israelite cult considered above the laity, but below the priests.

Levites: One of the twelve tribes of Israel; responsible for the functions associated with the tabernacle and worship.

Levitical: Pertaining to the priesthood of Israel—descendants of Levi—and the laws and ceremonies they administered.

Libertinism: Immoral behavior that was motivated by the belief that one has achieved absolute freedom from the law.

Libni: A family of Levite priests who lived in the vicinity of Hebron.

Libya: Area just west of Egypt along the north African coast of the Mediterranean.

Lilies: Probably the name of a tune.

Linus: Mentioned in Second Timothy 4:21. He is one of the Christian men who sends greetings to Timothy. According to tradition he became bishop in Rome.

Little ones: In Matthew 18 Jesus speaks specifically of children for whom the disciples are to have the greatest care and respect. The term can also refer to those new in the faith who need solicitous care.

Logos: The greek term for word. In Greek philosophical thought it referred to the principle of rationality behind the universe by which the universe is ordered and sustained. In the Prologue of the Gospel of John the Logos is the mode of the divine creativity and revelation.

Lord: An intimate Hebrew term for God, stemming from Exodus 4:14. Also translated as Yahweh.

Lotus: An Egyptian water lily, or a thorny Palestinian shrub.

Lucius: A Roman official who was in power during the time of Paul.

Lud: Son of Shem; the plural form (Ludim) may indicate two groups of people, one living in Asia Minor and one in North Africa.

Luke: Companion of Paul; physician; author of the third Gospel and Acts. Gentile by birth. His Gospel is marked by broad concerns: compassion for the poor, concern for women, cosmopolitan interests. He is symbolized by an ox, based on Ezekiel 1:10.

Lydda: City in the plain of Sharon about eleven miles south of Joppa. The site of one of the earliest apostolic miracles, the healing of the cripple (Acts 9:32).

Lyre: A harplike instrument used in worship to praise God.

Lysanias: A subject prince, or tetrarch, of an area northwest of Damascus, about whom little is known.

Lystra: A town in central Asia Minor. Paul and Barnabas fled to this town (Acts 14:6-21). People were friendly until Jews from Antioch and Iconium created further disturbances.

M

Maccabees, First and Second: Books in the Protestant Apocrypha and in the Roman Catholic canon.

Macedonia: Area north of Achaia, modern-day Balkan peninsula. Mountainous region containing the cities of Philippi and Thessalonica. A major land route between east and west.

Magog: The kingdom of Gog; represents any kingdom which challenges God's rule.

Mahalath: Probably the name of a tune.

Mahlah: One of Zelophehad's five daughters.

Mallow: A tasteless, soft plant grown in the wilderness and eaten by the poor.

Malta: An island in the Mediterranean Sea south of Cicily. It is about eighteen miles long and eight miles wide and offers excellent protection for sailing vessels. Paul landed there in mid-October during his voyage to Rome.

Mammon: A term Jesus used in the Sermon on the Mount for wealth, property, or profit. He warned the disciples that they could not serve both God and wealth (Matthew 6:24).

Manasseh: King of Judah (687–642 B.C.).

Manna: Food provided by God for the Israelites during their sojourn in the wilderness (Exodus 16:1).

Marah: The place where the Israelites first found water during their journey in the wilderness (Exodus 15:23).

Marcion: In large measure this reformer of the second century contributed to the formation of the Christian canon. He accepted the Gospel of Luke and Paul's writings, while rejecting the Old Testament.

Marduk: The supreme god of Babylon.

Mareshah: A Canaanite city that became the chief city of the Shephelah region of Judah.

Mark: John Mark of Acts 13:13 who accompanies Paul on missionary work. He abandons Paul and Barnabas at Perga. In Philemon 24 he appears again with the implication that there has been a reconciliation.

Maroth: A town in Judah, possibly the same place as Maarath, which is a village in the hill country.

Martha: Sister of Mary and Lazarus of Bethany. The name means lady or mistress.

Martyr: A witness; one who tells about the nature and significance of Christ. Martyrs gradually came to be identified with those who died because of their faith in Christ.

Mary Magdalene: A woman from Magdala on the west shore of the Sea of Galilee. She apears by name at the Crucifixion (Matthew 27:56) and at the tomb to discover the Resurrection (28:1). Presumably she was in the group of women who followed Jesus. Some legends have it that she was a penitent adulteress. This interpretation is based on the doubtful ending of Mark's Gospel (Mark 16:9).

Maskil: The meaning is uncertain; it may be a meditation.

Massah: A place of encampment of the Israelites while on their wilderness journey. Always associated with Meribah.

Massah and Meribah: A place on Mount Horeb where water was brought forth from a rock (Psalm 81:1).

Master: When used as a title for Jesus it meant chief, one who leads with authority. It is found often in Matthew and serves as the term for the head of the disciples.

Matthias: An apostle chosen to replace Judas. He is believed to have suffered martyrdom.

Mazzaroth: A constellation of stars of uncertain location.

Medad: An Israelite who prophesied inside the camp rather than at the tent of meeting, when the elders were endowed with God's spirit.

Medeba: A city in the Transjordan, near the entrance to the Dead Sea.

THE ESSENTIAL BIBLE HANDBOOK

Medes: Inhabitants of Media, a Mesopotamian territory.

Media: An ancient area extending from the Zagros Mountains to the Caspian Sea, first settled in 1400–1000 B.C., the home of the Medes. Conquered by Cyrus and made a part of the Persian Empire.

Mediator: One who acts as an impartial go-between for two conflicting parties.

Megiddo: An important Canaanite and then Israelite city overlooking the Valley of Jezreel in northern Israel.

Melchizedek: A priest-king in Salem (Jerusalem); a contemporary of Abraham.

Memorial portion: Part of an offering that is most holy and must be eaten in the sanctuary (Leviticus 2:2, 9, 16; 5:12; 6:15; 24:7).

Memphis: A major city in northern Egypt, thirteen miles south of Cairo.

Menorah: Also called a lampstand, a seven-branched candlestick made of pure gold (Exodus 25:31-40).

Mercy seat: A small structure made of gold and located inside the tabernacle; two cherubim were located on top of it.

Meribah: A station on the Israelites' wilderness journey; located in the Wilderness of Zin.

Meribath-Kadesh: A place in the Wilderness of Zin in Kadesh at the southern border of Canaan and the western border of Edom.

Merodach/Marduk: The god of Babylon.

Meshech: A people and a place in Asia Minor between the Black and the Caspian Seas.

Mesopotamia: Literally meaning between rivers, the "cradle of civilization" lies between the Tigris and Euphrates Rivers, now in Iraq; the center of both the Assyrian and the Babylonian empires.

Messiah: The God-appointed king at the end of time and eschatological hope. Literally it means the anointed one, from the Hebrew word meaning to anoint. The suffering messiah was unknown in late Judaism and therefore is the scandal of the New Testament.

Midian: A son of Abraham who was sent eastward to the east country (see Genesis 25:6); the Midianites were nomads, though the land of Midian is generally defined as being in northwest Arabia on the eastern shore of the Gulf of Aqabah.

Midianites: Descendants of Midian, Abraham's son by Keturah.

Migdol: A fortress in northern Egypt.

Miktam: The meaning is uncertain; it may indicate an atonement psalm.

Milcah: One of Zelophehad's five daughters.

Milcom: The Ammonite national god, also called Molech.

Millennium: A thousand-year period of peace and blessedness for the earth, believed by late Jewish and Christian writers to be near at hand. See Revelation 20:1-6.

Millstone: A hard, heavy stone used for grinding grain.

Miriam: Sister of Moses and Aaron, a prophetess (see Exodus 15:20-21).

Mishael: The Hebrew name of Meshach, one of Daniel's three friends.

Mishnah: A collection of oral laws compiled in the second century A.D. It is an extensive summation of the interpretation of the Toral or law of Moses as made over several centuries by the scribes or experts in the law.

Moab: A country east of the Dead Sea and south of the Jordan River.

Molech: A Canaanite deity that required human sacrifices (Leviticus 18:21; 20:2-5).

Moresheth-gath: Possession of Gath; a small village in the foothills southwest of Jerusalem, also called Moresheth; home of the prophet Micah.

Morning Stars: Bright stars visible at dawn, announcing the arrival of the sun. The brightest of these is Venus.

Moserah: A station of the Israelites while on their wilderness journey.

Moses: The one through whom God made the first covenant with Israel at Mount Sinai. Jesus refers to Moses as the giver of the law. In the Transfiguration Moses appears with Elijah, symbolizing the Law and the Prophets (17:3).

Mount Carmel: A prominent mountain at the head of a range of mountains on the coast of Palestine in western Galilee; famous for its beauty and fertility.

Mount Ephraim: In the hill country of central Palestine, the territory given to the tribe of Ephraim, Joseph's son.

Mount Hermon: A mountain situated north of Israel in southern Lebanon, approximately 9,000 feet high.

Mount Horeb: Another name for Mount Sinai. Means desolate region, desert, wilderness.

Mount of Olives: Part of the range of mountains running north and south through Palestine that overlooks Jerusalem to the west. Jesus sat on the Mount of Olives when he delivered the words of the Apocalypse, Matthew 24. The Garden of Gethsemane lies on its lower western slope (26:30).

Mount Paran: In a region also called the Wilderness of Paran, which is roughly south of Canaan, west of Edom, and north of the Sinai.

Mount Perazim: A mountain near the valley of Rephaim.

Mount Seir: A mountain near the Valley of Rephaim.

Mount Sinai: A mountain in the Arabian peninsula where Moses received the Ten Commandments. One name for the mountain of God. Also called Mount Horeb in the Old Testament.

Mount Tabor: Mountain in Palestine southwest of the Sea of Galilee.

Mount Zion: The major hill in Jerusalem, symbolic of Jerusalem; also symbolic of the city of God.

Muth-labben: Probably the name of a tune or a musical instruction.

Mystery: The secret of God's plan for Jews and Gentiles in Christ. The New

Testament writers believed that it was uncovered for the first time through Jesus' life, death, and resurrection. In the ancient world other religious groups believed that they were the only ones who were initiated into God's secrets and, thus, their belief systems were often called "mystery religions."

Mystery Cults: Religions of the late Hellenistic Age (100 B.C.–A.D. 300) that promised union with various deities and eternal life through secret knowledge and rites of initiation.

N

Na'ameh: A region in northwest Arabia, home of Zophar.

Naamathite: A resident of Na'ameh.

Nabonidus: The last king of the Babylonian Empire (from 556–539 B.C.).

Nabopolassar: King of Babylon (626–605 B.C.) and father of Nebuchadnezzar.

Nadab: Brother of Abihu, son of Aaron. See Abihu.

Nahbi: One of the men sent by Moses to spy out the land of Canaan; he was from the tribe of Naphtali.

Nain: A village five miles southeast of Nazareth and twenty-five miles from Capernaum. The name means pleasant because from it there is a lovely view of the Plain of Esdraelon.

Naphtali: One of the twelve tribes of Israel.

Narcissus: A Christian greeted by Paul in Romans 16:1.

Nathan: (1) A son of David, an ancestor of Jesus according to Luke's genealogy; (2) A prophet during the reign of King David.

Natural revelation: The disclosure of God through the natural world, such as seeing divine order in the stars or the seasons.

Nazarene: A name that is used only with reference to Jesus. In Acts it refers to a sect within the Christian movement. When used by a Jew it has a derogatory connotation.

Nazareth: A hill-country village in Galilee, halfway between the Sea of Galilee and the Mediterranean Sea; the home of Mary and Joseph, where Jesus grew to manhood. He was widely known as Jesus of Nazareth (Matthew 26:71). Nazareth was situated not far from a main international highway at Sepphoris.

Nazirites: From the verb meaning to consecrate. These special people let their hair grow, and drank no strong drink or wine. They were sacred persons with a strong loyalty to God. Samson was a Nazirite, which accounted for his need to protect his hair.

Nebuchadnezzar: Also Nebuchadrezzar, King of Babylon (605–562 B.C.) when Judah was defeated and her people taken into exile in 587.

Negeb: A dry region in southern Canaan that runs from the Sinai Peninsula to the Dead Sea; the name sometimes means simply south. In ancient times, it had more vegetation and more settlements than it does now.

Nereus: A Christian whose identity is uncertain; he is greeted by Paul in Romans 16:1.

Nero: Full name Nero Claudius Caesar, mad emperor of Rome in the mid-sixties A.D. After persecuting Christians, he finally died by his own hand.

Nettle: A type of thorny bush or large, prickly weed.

New Year Festival: Also known as Rosh Hashanah, meaning the beginning of the year. Celebrated in the fall, it was a time of sacrifices and trumpet blasts.

Nicolaitans: Possibly the Greek translation for the word Balaam. It means literally followers of Nicholas. It may refer to those who taught that, once saved, Christians were free to do immoral acts without fear of sin.

Nicopolis: The name means City of Victory. Founded by Octavian in 31 B.C., it is the city in which Paul intends to spend the winter (Titus 3:12).

Nile River: The river that flows through the center of Egypt, in which Moses was set afloat (Exodus 1:22; 4:9; 7; 8; 17:5).

Nimbus: Originally a bright cloud that supposedly accompanied the appearance of gods and goddesses. In Christian tradition, a halo or shiny disk over the heads of saints and angels.

Nimrod: A Mesopotamian hero of ancient times who conquered the Babylonians and Assyrians sometime before 1000 B.C.; the land of Nimrod is Assyria.

Nineveh: Capital of Assyria until its fall in 612 B.C.; one of the oldest and greatest cities in Mesopotamia.

Nisan: The first month of the Hebrew calendar.

Noah: Patriarch who, at God's command, built an ark in which he saved his family from the flood.

Nobah: An elder from the tribe of Manasseh who figured prominently in the conquest of Canaan.

Nod: Means wandering; the land of Cain's exile east of Eden; its exact location is unknown.

North: In general, north refers to any invader coming into Israel from the north; major travel routes through Palestine ran north and south between the Mediterranean on the west and the desert on the east.

Nun: The father of Joshua.

O

Oboth: A site in Moab in which the Israelites encamped during their wilderness journey.

Og: A king of Bashan during the time of the conquest of Canaan.

Oholiab: From the tribe of Dan, appointed by God to help Bezalel in the construction of the tabernacle (Exodus 31:6; 35:34; 36:1-2; 38:23).

Oil of Gladness: Oil poured on the head of a king at his coronation. Signified an occasion of celebration, joy, and gladness.

Olivet (Mount of Olives): A ridge of hills east of Jerusalem about a mile from north to south and 200 feet above the site of the Temple. Mentioned in the Old Testament in Second Samuel 15:30 and Zechariah 14:4.

Olympas: A Christian man who was greeted by Paul in Romans 16:1.

Omer: A dry measure that equals about two quarts (Exodus 16:16, 18, 32, 33, 36).

Onesimus: A common slave name meaning useful. He is the escaped slave about whom Paul writes to Philemon. Tradition holds that he became bishop in Ephesus.

Ophir: An area of the Arabian coast of the Red Sea.

Oracle: In general, a divinely inspired message; specifically, a prophetic speech form.

Origen: Third-century Christian scholar and teacher.

Orion: A constellation of stars representing the famous hunter in Greek mythology.

Orphans: A segment of Jewish society that was vulnerable to abuse by the wicked.

Outer darkness: A description of Hades (Hell) to which the sons of the kingdom were cast because they did not believe or were worthless servants (8:12; 22:13; 25:30).

P

Palanquin: A litter, frequently enclosed and used to transport royalty, especially at festive occasions.

Palti: One of the men Moses sentto spy out the land of Canaan; he was a leader in the tribe of Benjamin.

Paphos: A city in southwestern Cyprus. Paul visited there during his first journey (Acts 13:6, 13).

Papyrus: Fragile plants, grown in the Nile, easily destroyed.

Paran, Mount: See Mount Paran.

Parousia: Greek word used in the New Testament to refer to Jesus' coming at the end of time. The New Testament does not speak of Jesus' second coming.

Parthia, Parthians: An ancient country in Western Asia, near modern northeast Iran. Parthian soldiers were famous archers who were greatly feared by the Romans near the Euphrates River.

Passover: The word means to be spared. It is the first of Judaism's great feasts, observed in the spring, commemorating the deliverance from Egypt. The term is used both for the feast and the ritual. Also called the feast of Unleavened Bread (Exodus 12:1–13:16; 23:15).

Pathros: The Land of the South, southern Egypt.

Patmos: A small prison island located in the region west of Asia Minor.

Patriarch: An ancestor in ancient Israel. Especially applied to the earthly heroic ancestors of the Jews, primarily Abraham, Isaac, and Jacob.

Patrobas: A Christian man Paul greets in Romans 16:1.

Pax Romana: Latin meaning Peace of Rome. It described the Roman policy of guaranteeing peace within the borders of the empire. Political rebellion was not tolerated.

Peace offering: An offering that represents the fulfillment of a vow, peace in one's relationship with God, or the celebration of an important event (see especially Leviticus 3:1; 4; 7).

Pekah: A king of Israel from 737–732 B.C.

Peleth: A leader of the tribe of Reuben who participated in Korah's rebellion against Moses.

Pelusium: An important fortress town on Egypt's northern frontier.

Pentecost: The fiftieth day after the Passover observation. For Christians it is the day when the gift of the Holy Spirit came (Acts 2:1). Therefore, Christians reinterpreted the meaning of the celebration in light of the Holy Spirit.

Peor: A mountain in Moab; in biblical literature, an early Canaanite god, Baal-peor.

Perazim, Mount: See Mount Perazim.

Perfection: Consecration to God. Made acceptable to God. Arrival at the place where, cleansed of sin, the faithful are acceptable in the presence of God.

Perga: One of the leading cities in Pamphylia on the southern coast of Asia Minor. Paul and Barnabas visited here during their first journey (Acts 13:13).

Pergamum: A city in Mysia, in western Asia Minor, where the church struggled against the emperor cult. Famous in Hellenistic times as a renowned center for art and learning (Revelation 1:11; 2:12).

Perizzites: One of the native population groups in Canaan living in the central highlands; their exact identity is unknown.

Peroration: The conclusion of an argument, which in the case of Romans is contained in 15:14–16:27.

Persia: A great empire in the ancient Near East from 550 B.C. to 330 B.C.; at its height it stretched from Greece eastward to India and was centered in what is now Iran.

Persis: A Christian woman whom Paul greets in Romans 16:1.

Pestilence: A fatal epidemic or plague.

Pethor: The home of Balaam, who was called by Balak to curse the Israelites.

Phanuel: Father of Anna the prophetess and a member of the tribe of Asher.

Pharaoh: Title of the ruler of ancient Egypt. Also called the king of Egypt.

Pharisee: A very important element in Judaism in New Testament times. Pharisees were legalists; they obeyed the letter of the Law. They did, however, believe in the doctrine of resurrection.

Philadelphia: A city of ancient Asia Minor, a gateway to the East. It was known for its fine grapes, hot springs, and its worship of Dionysus and other gods.

Philemon: The eighteenth book of the New Testament. He is the Christian man to whom Paul writes with the extraordinary request that the escaped slave Onesimus be received as a fellow Christian.

Philip: An apostle listed in Matthew 10:3; Mark 3:18; Luke 6:14; and Acts 1:13. One of the first disciples to be called, he brought Nathaniel to Jesus. He was mentioned in the feeding of the 5,000

(John 6:5-7) and was also an evangelist (Acts 21:8).

Philippi: A city in Macedonia. Paul founded a church here, the first Christian congregation established in Europe (Acts 16:11-40).

Philistia: An area on the southern Mediterranean coast of Palestine. Settled in 1200 B.C.

Philistines: Sea peoples who settled in Philistia; they were fierce fighters who were often at war with Israel.

Philologus: A Christian man greeted by Paul in Romans 16:1.

Phinehas: The son of Eleazar, who was the son of Aaron the priest.

Phlegon: Greeted by Paul in Romans 16:1; his exact identity is uncertain.

Phoebe: A Christian woman who was the deaconness in the church at Cenchreae; Paul recommends her in Romans 16:1.

Phoenicia: A group of city-states on the Mediterranean coast in what is now Lebanon; the Phoenicians were great seafarers, explorers, and traders who thrived from approximately 1200 B.C. to 146 B.C.

Phylactery: A small leather box containing a series of smaller boxes with portions of Scripture on the sides of each box and bound to the wrist or forehead (see Exodus 13:9).

Pibeseth: A city in the Nile Delta.

Pigeon (Dove): The word means literally to moan or moaning bird. The dove was always used as a metaphor for the Spirit of God (Matthew 3:16). Pigeons were also the most common sacrificial offering in the Temple (21:12).

Pipe: A flutelike instrument used in worship to praise God.

Pit: A descriptive term for the grave, commonly used in the Psalms.

Plato/Platonic: A fourth century B.C. Greek philosopher, whose students and their successors created a philosophical system widely popular in the Hellenistic and Roman periods. Platonic views influenced some early Christian writers.

Pledge: A promise that ensures a person's safety and/or prosperity.

Pleiades: A cluster of stars located in the constellation Taurus.

Politarchs: In Macedonia the politarchs were the local, non-Roman magistrates of a free city, who were the instruments of Rome in maintaining law and order.

Pontius Pilate: Roman procurator (governor) of Judea, A.D. 26–36. He condemned Jesus to death (Matthew 27:2-26).

Poor: The easy target of the wicked, open to exploitation and abuse.

Porcius Testus: The Roman procurator of Judea in the years A.D. 60–62; successor to Felix.

Portent: A sign or wonder. Usually one carrying a special meaning or message. In Revelation, a portent carries a message about the meaning of life, especially the future.

Potsherds: Sharp fragments of broken pottery used for cutting and scraping.

Praetorium: The residence of a Roman provincial governor. The Roman Praetorium in Jerusalem was the judgment hall for Jesus' trail before Pilate.

Prefect: A governor or person appointed to a position of authority and command.

Presence: The presence of God in the Holy of Holies in the sanctuary of Israel and in the heavens.

Priests: Ones who were set aside to administer the affairs of the Temple. Chief priests occupied a higher place in the Temple hierarchy, the high priest being chief above all. The chief priests were the ones who actively sought Jesus' death (Matthew 26:3).

Prince of Demons: See Satan or Beelzebul.

Prisca: Wife of Aquila; originally resided in Corinth but was taken by Paul to Ephesus.

Proconsul: A former Roman consul who served as the governor of a province or in command of a Roman army.

Procurators: The procurators or governors ruled over Judea after Archaelaus, son of Herod the great, was deposed for incompetence.

Prologue: This refers to an introduction before the main events. In John's Gospel, the prologue (1:1-18) introduces the various recollections of Jesus' life.

Promise: God's promise to (1) Abraham that his descendants would be a great nation; (2) Israel that they would be guided to a land of rest in rich Canaan; (3) faithful Christians that, through Christ, they will reach eternal rest with God.

Prophecy: An inspired utterance of a prophet, usually declaring the divine will.

Prophesy: Literally, to speak beforehand; to reveal the message of God. In Revelation, it means also to declare the secrets of God.

Prophets: Men who spoke to the nation for God. Jesus called John the Baptist the greatest of them all (Matthew 11:11); he condemned the scribes and Pharisees because they would have shed the blood of the prophets had they lived in the prophets' days. Matthew cites more than thirty texts from the prophets that Jesus fulfilled.

Proselyte: A term originally meaning a foreigner; a person not in his own land. In the New Testament the term is used to describe a convert to Judaism.

Proverb: A two-line saying that uses parallelism to teach a moral lesson or register an observation about the world.

Ptolemais: A city in northern Palestine, north of Mt. Carmel. Modern-day Acre. Paul landed here during his third missionary journey (Acts 21:7).

Ptolemy: The name of all male Egyptian rulers from the time of Alexander the Great (approximately 323 B.C.) until the time of the Roman Empire (approximately 80 B.C.).

Publius: Either the chief native official or high Roman authority on the island of Malta. Paul and his companions were hosted by Publius for three days. One tradition holds that he was later martyred.

Pudens: Mentioned in Second Timothy 4:21; a Roman Christian who sends his greetings to Timothy.

Purification: (1) A priestly act that pronounces a worshiper purified of sin on the basis of a sacrifice made; (2) the result of Jesus' self-sacrifice whereby a sinner is made acceptable to enter the presence of God.

Purim: The Persian word *pur* with the Hebrew plural ending *im*. Refers to the two-day festival in celebration of the victory of Esther and Mordecai over Haman.

Purslane: A small, weedlike plant containing bland juice and used in salads.

Put: A region in northern Africa, probably in present-day Libya.

Q

Qesitah: A small weight of silver used as a form of currency.

Quadrans: Latin for an amount of money, very small, about one sixty-fourth of a denarius.

Quartus: A Christian man who was greeted by Paul in Romans 16:1.

Queen of Heaven: The Babylonian-Assyrian goddess Ishtar, whose worship was possibly introduced into Judah by Manasseh. This cult was popular with women who were restricted to an inferior role in the worship services to God. Offerings included wine and star-shaped or crescent-shaped cakes with the image of the goddess on them.

Queen of the South (Sheba): Matthew makes reference (12:42) to the visit of the Queen of Sheba, south Arabia, to King Solomon (1 Kings 10:1-13) to show that a pagan queen sought wisdom from Solomon. Now something greater than Solomon was here (Christ himself).

Quirinius: The Roman governor of Syria appointed in A.D. 6, who took a census reported by Josephus. However, the date of this census does not appear to agree with the one described by Luke, because Herod, mentioned by Luke as the ruler at the time of Jesus' birth, died in 4 B.C.

Qumran Texts: Qumran is the Arabic name of the place where the Dead Sea Scrolls and a monastery (probably Essene) were discovered after 1947.

R

Raamah: A trading city in southwest Arabia.

Rabbah: The capital of Ammon, the present-day Amman in Jordan.

Rabbinic: Pertaining to the Jewish rabbis, or teachers of the law, who were prominent leaders in Paul's time.

Rachel: Rachel was Jacob's second wife, the mother of Joseph and Benjamin. Many generations after Jacob and Rachel, the slaughter of the children at Bethlehem seemed to Matthew a fulfillment of Rachel's lament in Jeremiah 31:15 (2:16-18).

Rahab: A mythological dragon slain by God at Creation; also a literary synonym for Egypt.

Ram: The name of the clan to which Elihu belonged.

Ramah: A town north of Bethlehem, the traditional site of Rachel's burial. The identification of Rachel with Ramah may well be erroneous (Jeremiah 31:15; Matthew 2:16-18).

Ransom: That which is given to someone so that a sin may be forgiven or covered up.

Raphu: The father of Palti, one of Moses' twelve spies.

Reba: One of the five Midianite kings who were destroyed by the Israelites.

Red Sea: Also known as the sea of reeds, a group of lakes or swamps that may have once existed at the present location of the Suez Canal (Exodus 10:19; 13:18; 15:4, 22; 23:31).

Redeemer: This term refers to one who is responsible for covering the debts of a kinsman or for avenging the death of a family member. Ruth 4:4-6 is a good example of this concept.

Redemption: The act of exchanging one thing for something else. In the Bible as a whole the term refers to God's payment for the high cost of sin. In the New Testament the word refers to the sacrifice of Christ and the way it brings about God's forgiveness.

Rekem: One of the five Midianite kings who were destroyed by the Israelites.

Repentance: A New Testament word for spiritual change of heart, which means turning around or change of mind.

Rephaim: An ethnic term for the pre-Israelite inhabitants of the Transjordan (land east of the Jordan River).

Rest: (1) The land promised to the desert-wandering Israelites. (2) The eternal experience of the presence of God, enabled by Christ.

Reuben: One of the twelve tribes of Israel.

Reuel: The father-in-law of Moses, also called Jethro, whose name means friend of God (Exodus 2:18).

Revelation: Literally, to remove the veil. In the New Testament it means God's self-giving to people as well as the unveiling of certain facts.

Rezin: A king of Syria during Isaiah's time.

Rhodes. A Greek island and city in the southeast portion of the Aegean Sea.

Riblah: An ancient Syrian town north of Damascus, the military highways of Egypt and Mesopotamia crossed here.

Right Teacher: The founder or organizing genius of the community from which the Qumran Texts (Dead Sea Scrolls) came. He apparently lived around the middle of the second century B.C.

Righteousness: A term used by the sages to describe proper moral conduct; also used to designate fairness and fulfillment of contractual obligations.

Righteousness of God: The capacity and will of the Creator to make the creation conform to divine justice and beauty.

Rightwise: To make right, or to achieve a transformation in which humans come to reflect the divine righteousness.

Rimmon: A town in southern Judah.

Root of Bitterness: A symbolic root bearing bitter or poisonous fruit that causes people to sin and thus to turn away from God.

S

Sabbath: From the Hebrew word meaning cessation, desistance. The closing day of a seven-day week. It means rest. In Jewish tradition it includes worship and prayer. Strict observance is required in the Old Testament decalogues (Ten Commandments). For Christians it became the first day of the week.

Sabbatical year: The seventh in a cycle of seven years, in which no harvest is reaped (see especially Leviticus 25:1-7).

Sabeans: Inhabitants of a region in the southern Arabian peninsula, sometimes called Sheba; it was located south of Uz

Sackcloth: A garment made of goat's hair or camel's hair that was often worn as a symbol of mourning.

Sacrifice: Some form of sacrifice is a basic means of communicating with a deity in all religions. For Israel, this was their primary form of worshiping God.

Sadducees: Priestly, aristocratic party in Judaism that emerged after the Maccabean Rebellion. They did not believe in the resurrection, Spirit, or angels, and became opponents of the Pharisees.

Salamis: A major city of Cyprus on the east coast opposite Syria. Paul and Barnabas visited the Jewish community there (Acts 13:5). According to tradition Barnabas was martyred there by a mob stirred up by Syrian Jews.

Salecah: A city located in Bashan; later was possessed by the tribe of Gad.

Salem: An ancient city of which Melchizedek was king at the time of Abraham. Another name for Jerusalem. It means peace.

Salt: An essential in preserving food and thus a necessity of life. Jesus tells his disciples that they are to be the salt of the earth—a requirement for life (Matthew 5:13).

Salt land: An arid region inhabited only by wild, sturdy creatures.

Salt Sea: Another name for the Dead Sea.

Salvation: The word means basically health and well-being on all sides of one's life. In salvation one is rescued from all that threatens peace and security. In New Testament use the word has both a present and a future connotation.

Samaria: The capital city of the Northern Kingdom, Israel. Also the region of the hill country of Palestine. After the deportations of 721 B.C. the Assyrians resettled the area with captives from Babylon, Cuthah, Avva, Hamath, and Sepharvaim (2 Kings 17:24-26).

Samaritans: (1) Descendants of the Israelites who were not deported at the fall of Samaria in 721 B.C.; (2) the non-Israelite pagans who were brought in from other portions of the Assyrian Empire.

Samson: leader in the confederacy of Israelite tribes who single-handedly protected Israel from foreign oppressors.

Samuel: The last political leader in the Israelite confederacy who, as a prophet, selected and ordained Israel's first kings, Saul and David.

Sanctification: An English word for holiness (*see* holiness).

Sanctified: Made holy. Consecrated to God.

Sanhedrin: The seventy-one-member supreme Jewish council during the postexilic period. It was an aristocratic unit until the fall of Jerusalem to the Romans in A.D. 70. This was the group responsible for internal government of the Roman-occupied territory of Palestine (Acts 23:1-10).

Sapphire: A blue, transparent gemstone.

Sarah: Wife of Abraham, mother of Isaac, ancestor of the Israelite people.

Sardis: A Roman city in central Asia Minor. A wealthy commercial center, also a popular location for the worship of various gods of nature.

Sardius: A form of chalcedony, usually deep orange in color.

Sardonyx: A kind of chalcedony with white and brown bands.

Sargon II: King of Assyria from 722–705 B.C. Son of Tiglath-Pileser III. Responsible for the fall of the Northern Kingdom.

Satan: The adversary, or opponent, who challenges God regarding Job's character. One of the sons of God, Satan is an argumentative figure in the book and not necessarily evil.

Satrap: A Persian official, ruler of a satrapy, a governor.

Satyr: A demon, usually represented by a goat, that inhabits waste places (Leviticus 17:7).

Saul: The first king of the united Israel.

Scribes: They were closely identified with the chief priests in the Temple. Jesus links them with the Pharisees in his condemnation (Matthew 12:38; 23).

Sea, Bronze: Also called molten sea (1 Kings 7:23), a large vessel made of cast bronze that may have stood before the altar in the Temple in Jerusalem and perhaps held water in which the priests washed.

Sea of Chinnereth: Another name for the Sea of Galilee.

Sea of Galilee: A freshwater lake in the Jordan River, three and one-half miles long and three miles wide. Around the lake Jesus' Galilean ministry took place. Here lay the towns associated with that ministry: Magdala, Bethsaida, Chorazin. On this lake Jesus sailed with his disciples through the storm (Matthew 8:23-27).

Seba: A kingdom somewhere in Cush (Ethiopia).

Seir, Mount: See Mount Seir.

Selah: A musical term which directs the conductor of a psalm to interrupt the flow of the song with a clash of cymbals.

Seleucus: The name of four of the Greek kings who ruled Syria and, at times, Palestine, from 312 B.C. to 129 B.C., who were part of the Seleucid dynasty.

Semite: Someone who is a descendant of Shem, the son of Noah, or who speaks a

Semitic language (for example, Arabs, Arameans, Assyrians, Babylonians, Canaanites, Hebrews, and Phoenicians).

Senir: In Deuteronomy 3:9, this Amorite term is used to refer to Mount Hermon. The Amorites were probably ancestors of the Hebrews or at least used a similar language.

Sennacherib: King of Assyria from 705–681 B.C.

Septuagint: First version (translation) of the Hebrew Bible into another (Greek) language, about 250 B.C.

Shades: The dead who inhabit Sheol.

Shammua: One of the men sent by Moses to spy out the land of Canaan; he was an elder of the tribe of Reuben.

Shaphat: One of the men sent by Moses to spy out the land of Canaan; he was an elder of the tribe of Simeon.

Shapir: Its exact location is unknown, perhaps a place west of Hebron in the dry hill country of Judah.

Sharezer: In Zechariah its exact meaning is unknown; perhaps part of the name of a pagan god or of an emissary from Bethel.

Sharon: A coastal plain extending from central Palestine northward to Mount Carmel. This was an important agricultural region in ancient Israel.

Shealtiel: Son of King Jehoiachin of Judah, father of Zerubbabel.

Sheba: A country in southwest Arabia; its people were famous traders.

Shebat: The eleventh month in the Hebrew calendar, approximately mid-January to mid-February.

Shechem: Town about forty miles north of Jerusalem, originally Canaanite; became an important Israelite religious and political center.

Sheep: The most commonly mentioned animal in the Bible. The New Testament uses sheep to designate persons. John's Gospel portrays Jesus as the Shepherd who gives his life for the sheep. Jesus is also portrayed as a sheep led to the slaughter (Acts 8:32; Isaiah 53:7).

Sheep Gate: Once a gate on Jerusalem's north city wall near the Temple (Nehemiah 3:1). Sheep for sacrifice were probably brought into the Temple courtyard through this gate.

Shekel: In Old Testament times, a unit of weight, approximately .4 ounces; in New Testament times, a coin of the same weight.

Shekinah: The manifestation of God, or the presence of God, in Jewish tought.

Sheminith: Probably a musical instruction.

Sheol: A term that refers to the realm of the dead. In Hebrew thought, all deceased persons went there.

Shephelah: A foothill district west of the Judean highlands and east of the coastal plain; one of the major geographical divisions of Judah.

Sheshai: The son of Gershom; a grandson of Levi.

Shiggaion: An emotional, passionate song.

Shigionoth: The plural form of a musical term used to define the kind of performance suitable for certain psalms or hymns; may indicate an emotional, enthusiastic, and irregular performance of a song, speech, or writing.

Shiloh: Located eighteen miles north of Jerusalem; a major Israelite shrine was here until its destruction in 1050 B.C.

Shimeites: Descendants of Shemei, the grandson of Levi.

Shinar: A name for Babylonia.

Shittim: A place in Moab northeast of the Dead Sea where the people of Israel camped before crossing the Jordan into Canaan.

Shoa: A people whose exact identity is unknown, perhaps Aramean mercenaries in the army of Babylon.

Shuah: Bildad's tribe, which settled in the northeastern part of the Arabian peninsula.

Shuhite: A member of the tribe of Shuah.

Shulammite: The term is of uncertain origin. It refers to the wife of the king in Song of Solomon who danced before her husband following their marriage. See the commentary on 6:13.

Shushan Eduth: Probably the name of a psalm.

Sibmah: A city inherited by the Reubenites after the defeat of the Amorite king, Sihon.

Sibraim: A place on the northern border of Canaan between Damascus and Hamath.

Sidon: An ancient Phoenician seaport between Tyre and Beirut; an agricultural, fishing, and trading center famous for its purple dye, which was made from the murex shell. Home of the Sidonians, who were known as skilled carpenters and masons.

Sign: Jews in Jesus' day believed God gave outward evidence of divine purpose generally hidden from casual observance. People looked for signs to know God's intention (Matthew 24:3). Jesus warned against seeking for signs (12:39).

Sihon: King of the Amorites, a Canaanite tribe living at times in the mountains of Judah and in an area east of the Jordan around Heshbon and Bashan.

Silver, thirty pieces: The amount of thirty pieces (Matthew 26:15) is from Zechariah 11:12, where the prophet speaks of a worthless shepherd being paid a wage of thirty pieces of silver. This may have been symbolism for Judas, intended by Matthew.

Simeon: One of the twelve tribes of Israel.

Simon: (1) A member of the Zealots, a group of opponents to Roman rule, who became one of the Twelve. (2) Host for a dinner where a woman came in unexpectedly and anointed Jesus with oil. He was a Pharisee. (3) A resident of Cyrene in North Africa. Probably a Jew who came to Jerusalem for the Passover.

Simon, the magician: A man who had impressed Samaritans with his powers (Acts 8:9-24). When he saw the power of the Holy Spirit he wanted the power and offered to buy it. Because of this, the attempt to purchase church office is called simony. Even though a negative connotation is attached to his name, he did become a Christian and was baptized.

Sin: The failure to recognize human limitations, which in Romans is marked by suppressing the truth.

Sin offering: An offering to correct the condition of physical or moral impurity (see especially Leviticus 4:1).

Sinai: See Mount Sinai.

Sirion: Another name for Mount Hermon.

Sisera: A Canaanite king who was slain during Israel's conquest of the Promised Land.

Sivan: The third month of the Hebrew calendar.

Skiffs: Shallow, lightweight boats.

Sky: Believed to be a hard, mirror-like substance separating earth from the heavens.

Smaragdus: A gemstone, light green in color. Possibly an emerald.

Smyrna: A coastal city of Asia Minor, known for its wealth and its natural beauty. It was one of the first cities to engage in worship of the Roman emperor.

Sodi: One of the men Moses sent him to spy out the land of Canaan; he was an elder of the tribe of Zebulun.

Sodom: A very wicked city, destroyed along with Gomorrah, now under the southern part of the Dead Sea.

Sojourner: A person who was not native-born but who was traveling in the land and who enjoyed the privileges of native Israelites (see especially Leviticus 25:1).

Solomon: The son of David and Bathsheba; the builder of the first great Temple in Jerusalem.

Son of Man: Sometimes a title for Jesus (Matthew 17:9; 26:24). In some cases it is a name for the heavenly judge coming at the end time, not identified with Jesus (10:23; 25:31).

Sons of God: An ancient term for divine beings, such as gods or angels.

Sosipater: A Christian man greeted by Paul in Romans 16:1.

Soul: The totality of a human life. According to Hebrews, the soul is the spiritual existence of humankind before God. It lives by means of hope in the future, where God invites it to live in God's presence forever.

Spirit: Two meanings in Job: (1) a night vision or ghost (4:15); and (2) the "wind" that comes from the Breath of God (32:8).

Spirit (Holy Spirit): God's Spirit is sent by the Father and the Son and represents God's presence and activity.

Spoil: Booty taken after an army has defeated a town or city.

Stachys: A Christian man greeted by Paul in Romans 16:1.

Stephen: The first Christian martyr at the hands of the Jews in Jerusalem (Acts 6:1–8:3). The details surrounding his death introduce the figure of Saul (Paul), who witnessed the stoning (Acts 7:58; 8:1).

Stoics: Followers of a philosophy prevalent throughout the Roman Empire. Founded in Athens by Zeno, this philosophy holds that virtue is good and vice is the only evil. Stoics steeled themselves against feeling pain or pleasure, success, or failure. Paul echoes part of this philosophy in Philippians 4:11-12.

Suffering: (1) Christ's suffering involved in his breaking the barrier of human separation from God. (2) Human suffering occasioned in humankind's faithful movement through this world to God.

Sumer/Sumerians: A region in southern Mesopotamia between present-day Baghdad and the Persian Gulf; the Sumerian civilization flourished between 3300 B.C. and 1700 B.C. and was the earliest known society where people could read and write.

Susa: The capital of Elam in southwest Iran; became the winter capital of the kings of Persia; honored by Shiite Muslims as the burial place of Daniel.

Susanna: The name comes from a Hebrew word meaning lily. She was one of the women who ministered to Jesus.

Susi: One of the men sent by Moses to spy out the land of Canaan; he was an elder from the tribe of Manasseh.

Syene: A trading village located at the southern end of Egypt.

Synagogue: The place where the Jewish community gathered to worship and study. Jesus frequently taught in their synagogues (Matthew 12:9; 13:54).

Syria: Area bounded by the Mediterranean, Galilee, and the Arabian Desert. Had great influence on Palestine. Paul's conversion took place here, on the road to Damascus.

T

Taberah: A site of unknown location where the Israelites encamped while on their wilderness journey.

Tabernacle: A portable tent that was carried through the wilderness by the Israelites; God was thought to dwell inside.

Tables of the Covenant: Stone tablets on which were engraved the Ten Commandments.

Tabor, Mount. See Mount Tabor.

Tahpanhes: Also Tehaphnehes; a city on the eastern frontier of northern Egypt.

Talent: In Jesus' time a talent was a unit of weight measurement. It was also a monetary term for 6,000 drachmas, roughly equivalent to $1,000, an extraordinary sum in those days (Matthew 25:14-18).

Talmai: A son of Anak, who lived in Hebron before the Israelites arrived there.

Talmud: The book of oral tradition gathered over several centuries. The Mishnah is part of the Talmud, which was not codified until about the first century A.D.

Tamar: A fortress city in the extreme southeastern part of Judah near the southern end of the Dead Sea.

Tammuz: (1) The Sumerian god of spring vegetation; (2) The fourth month of the Hebrew calendar.

Tarshish: A far-off port that exported fine silver, tin, iron, and lead; perhaps Sardinia or Tartessus in Spain.

Tarsus: A city in Asia Minor, the capital of the province of Cilicia. Located on the Tarsus River, the city is about 6,000 years old. It had a large Jewish element. It was Paul's hometown.

Tax Collector (Publican): The men who collected the poll and land taxes for the Romans. Many were Jews; they were despised for being agents of the hated Roman Empire. Jesus associated with them (Matthew 11:19), ate at their tables (9:11), and declared that they would go into the Kingdom before the chief priests and elders (21:31).

Tebeth: The tenth month of the Hebrew calendar.

Tekoa: A city in the highlands of Judah twelve miles south of Jerusalem.

Tel-Abib: Mound of the flood; a community of exiled Israelites in Babylon; the name comes from the mound on which it was built; the mound was believed to have contained the ruins of a city that was there before the Flood.

Tema: A son of Ishmael (see Genesis 25:15); also the name of a city in northwest Arabia in an oasis at the junction of two important caravan routes.

Teman: Home of the Temanites, a clan descended from Esau; the largest city in central Edom.

Temanite: An inhabitant of the city of Teman.

Temple: A permanent building to replace the tabernacle. First built by Solomon in Jerusalem (1 Kings 5:1–8; 2 Chronicles 2:1–7; Ezekiel 40:1–43). Later rebuilt by Zerubbabel, and finally by Herod, all on the present site of the Dome of the Rock, a Muslim place of worship in Jerusalem.

Tent of meeting: Another name for the tabernacle.

Teraphim: Idols of various kinds; some are used in predicting the future.

Terebinths: A species of gum trees; the turpentine tree of the middle east.

Terrors: A term used in Job to designate the punishment of the wicked; it means those things that wear down and destroy.

Tershish: The place to which Jonah attempted to flee; its location is uncertain.

Tertius: A Christian man to whom Paul dictated the letter to the Romans (see Romans 16:22).

Tetrarch: A ruler of less prominence and territory than a king, usually responsible for a district.

Thebes: The chief city of southern Egypt.

Theophany: An appearance of God, accompanied by awesome sights and sounds such as lightning and thunder (see Exodus 19:16-20).

Theophilus: Person to whom Luke addressed the books of Luke and Acts (Luke 1:3; Acts 1:1). The name means lover of God. The identity of the person is not known.

Thessalonica: An important city in Macedonia. Paul established the church here after beatings in Philippi (Acts 16:22-24; 1 Thessalonians 2:2), and later wrote two letters to the congregation.

Threshing sledge: A heavy weight, pulled by a horse, that rolled over grain.

Thummim: With Urim, items by which persons consulted God about particular questions. Perhaps these were small metal objects.

Thyatira: A city in western Asia Minor. One of Paul's associates may have gone there during a preaching mission in Ephesus (Acts 19:10). There was a strong church in Thyatira (Revelation 2:18-29).

Tiberius: His full name and title was Tiberius Claudius Caesar Augustus, the Roman emperor ruling from A.D. 14–37.

Tigris: One of the major rivers of Mesopotamia, along with the Euphrates; flows from the mountains of Turkey and Iraq over 1,000 miles into the Persian Gulf.

Timothy: Trusted associate and friend of Paul; ranks with the apostles (1 Thessalonians 2:6). Sent by Paul to strengthen Gentile churches (Philippians 2:19), he first appeared as a disciple in Lystra (Acts 16:1).

Tirhakah: An Egyptian king who allied with Hezekiah against Sennacherib.

Tirzah: One of Zelophehad's five daughters.

Tishri: The seventh month of the Hebrew calendar.

Tithe: One-tenth of one's property, donated to support the priesthood.

Titus: Another colleague of Paul whom Paul calls his true child in common faith (Titus 1:4). His assignment was to organize and supervise Cretan churches.

Topaz: A gemstone, usually brown or pink

Topheth (Valley of the Son of Hinnom): A place in the valley of the Son of Hinnom, which runs east and west just south of Jerusalem; associated with pagan worship.

Torah: Hebrew term referring to the law. Its apparent meaning is instruction, or guidance.

Torrent bed: A swift, dangerous stream with a strong current.

Transjordan: Land east of the Jordan River.

Tribulation: A time of serious affliction. Taken from the word describing the place where grain was threshed.

Trophimus: Mentioned in Second Timothy 4:20; an Ephesian whom Paul met at Troas during the journey to Jerusalem (Acts 20:4-5). According to the letter to Timothy, he had been left ill at Miletus.

Truly, truly: According to John's Gospel, this is an expression frequently used by Jesus. It literally means, amen, amen, or absolutely, certainly, or so be it. Jesus uses it in a unique way, offsetting his teachings.

Tryphaena: With Tryphosa, Christian women who were greeted by Paul in Romans 16:1.

Tryphosa: See above.

Tubal: A country in Asia Minor famous for its metal working.

Tychicus: His name appears twice in the Pastorals (2 Timothy 4:12; Titus 3:12) and also in Acts 20:4; Ephesians 6:21; and Colossians 4:7. He is a beloved brother, faithful minister, and fellow slave of Paul. He, along with Onesimus, transported the letter to the Colossians.

Typology: A form of writing that makes the pattern of one event look like the pattern of another event. In the Book of Revelation, John patterns many events after those that occurred in the Exodus.

Tyre: An important trade and port city on the Phoenician coast about twelve miles south of Sidon. In ancient times it was a very important producer of purple dye. Jesus preached here (see Mark 3:8; Luke 6:17). Paul stayed with the small Christian congregation for a week during his voyage to Rome.

Tyropoeon Valley: Valley that divides Ophel from the Upper City of Jerusalem.

U

Ulai: A canal near Susa.

Umpire: A powerful judge arbitrating between two disputing parties.

Universal sin: The doctrine that each person fails to accept and live out the truth about God and human obligations.

Unleavened bread: Bread or cakes baked without yeast.

Uphaz: A place mentioned in the Old Testament as a source of gold; its exact location is unknown.

Ur: Ancient city on the Euphrates River in southern Mesopotamia in present-day Iraq; home of Abraham.

Urbanus: A Christian man who was greeted by Paul in Romans 16:1.

Urim and Thummim: Small objects used in discovering the divine will by casting lots.

Uz: An undefined area east of Palestine in the Syrian Desert.

Uzziah: King of Judah, 783–742 B.C.

Uzziel: One of the sons of Kohath; the grandson of Levi.

V

Valley of Zered: The land surrounding the stream the Israelites crossed at the end of their wilderness wanderings.

Vanity: A term used by Qoheleth to describe the meaninglessness of human existence.

Vault of heaven: Corresponding to sky, this separated earth from heaven.

Vophsi: On of the men Moses sent to spy out the land of Canaan; he was an elder in the tribe of Naphtali.

Votive offering: An offering to God in response to the fulfillment of a wish or vow (Leviticus 7:16; 22:23; 23:38).

Vulgate: Latin translation of the Bible by Jerome in the fourth century.

W

Waistcloth: A loincloth worn either loose like a skirt or pulled between the legs and tucked into the waist.

Watchman: One who stands guard, protecting a person and/or property.

Weaver's shuttle: The part of a loom that passes rapidly back and forth, weaving yarn into cloth.

Whirlwind: A whirling desert dust storm, often accompanying divine appearances.

Wicked: A designation of those who have no fear of God and, consequently, mistreat the powerless.

Widows: A segment of Hebrew society who, because of the lack of male protection, were vulnerable to exploitation and abuse by the wicked.

Wilderness of Shur: A barren region in northeastern Egypt (Exodus 15:22).

Wilderness of Sin: A desert region perhaps in the vicinity of the Sinai peninsula (Exodus 16:1; 17:1).

Wisdom: A term applied to superior intelligence, enabling one to achieve moral insight leading to righteousness.

Wise Men: In the story of Jesus' birth (Matthew 2:1-12), they were probably members of a priestly caste somewhere in Persia who interpreted dreams and observed heavenly signs.

Witness: One who sees and can tell what has been seen, especially one who has seen an important truth. Witness can be a verb (to witness) and refer to the act of telling. It can also be a noun, from which it has two meanings: (1) the person who has seen; (2) the thing that has been seen. In the latter sense, the witness of the martyrs is what they have seen in Jesus; the witness of Jesus is what Jesus has seen and said to God.

Word of God: (1) The Bible (Old Testament). (2) The action of God. (3) Christ as God's communication to human beings. (4) Christ as God's agent of creation.

World: This word has two different meanings in the New Testament. It can refer to the universe or cosmos God created or to the atmosphere of evil and sin that corrupts humanity.

Wormwood: A plant with a bitter taste, often mentioned with gall in the context of bitterness and sorrow.

Wrath: The punishment of those who violate divine righteousness, which in Romans is experienced in everyday life.

Y

Yahweh: The Hebrew name for God, meaning he who is or he who causes to be (see Exodus 3:13-14).

Yom Kippur: The Day of Atonement, in the month of Tishri, or the seventh month, when the high priest entered the Holy of Holies, where the throne of God was, and made atonement for the whole nation. It was a great day of celebration in Judaism.

Z

Zaanan: An unidentified town in western Judah.

Zacchaeus: A tax collector of Jericho with administrative responsibility for other collectors.

Zadok: A priest during the reign of David whose descendants gained control of the priesthood in the Jerusalem Temple.

Zalmunna and Zebah: Midianite kings slain by Gideon, who was avenging the murder of his brothers.

Zarephath: With a name meaning to dye, this was a Phoenician town on the

Mediterranean coast near Sidon where dye was produced.

Zealotism: Fanatical adherence to the perceived will of God, which confuses the distinction between divine and human values.

Zebedee: Husband of Salome and father of James and John, he was also a fisherman.

Zebulun: One of the twelve tribes of Israel.

Zechariah: One of the prophets in the period following the Jews' return from exile. Matthew's interest in Zechariah lies in two passages of his prophecy, which he saw fulfilled in Christ: Zechariah 9:9, quoted in Matthew 21:1-11, and Zechariah 11:7-14, quoted in Matthew 27:3-10.

Zedad: A place on the northern border of Canaan.

Zedekiah: (1) King of Judah (597–587 B.C.); (2) An exile, son of Maaseiah, condemned by Jeremiah for false prophecy.

Zelophehad: An elder from the tribe of Manasseh whose daughters demanded his inheritance at the time of his death.

Zemer: A city in Lebanon.

Zenas: Mentioned in Titus 3:13, a Christian man who lived on Crete. Tradition holds that he was later bishop of Lydda in Palestine and the author of Life of Titus.

Zerubbabel: A Babylonian Jew who was governor of Judah under Darius I.

Zimri: May refer to an Arabian tribe in the incense trade.

Zin: A wilderness north of Paran through which the Israelites traveled on their wilderness journey.

Zion, Mount: See Mount Zion.

Ziphites: A clan of the tribe of Judah.

Zippor: The father of Balak, the king of Moab who summoned Balak to curse the Israelites.

Zipporah: The wife of Moses, daughter of Jethro the priest of Midian (Exodus 2:21; 4:25; 18:2).

Zoar: Town on the southeastern side of the Dead Sea basin; name means little.

Zophar: One of Job's friends, from Na'ameh. His name possibly means singing bird.

GUIDE TO PRONUNCIATION

A

Aaron: AIR-un

Abaddon: AH-ba-don

Abarim: Ah-bah-REEM

Abba: AH-buh

Abednego: Ah-BED-neh-go

Abel: AY-bell

Abihu: Ah-BEE-hoo

Abimelech: Ah-BIH-meh-leck

Abiram: Ah-BEE-ram

Abomination: Ah-bah-mih-NAY-shun

Abraham: AY-brah-ham

Acacia: Ah-KAY-shah

Achaia: Ah-KAY-ah

Achor: Ah-CORE

Achzib: Ahk-ZEEB

Acropolis: Ah-CRAH-poh-liss

Admah: AHD-mah

Adrammelech: AH-druh-MEH-leck

Adramyttium: Ah-drah-MIH-tee-um

Adullam: Ah-DUHL-ahm

Aegean: Ah-GEE-an

Aeneas: Ah-NEE-us

Aenon: EYE-non

Agabus: AH-gah-bus

Agrippa: Ah-GRIP-ah

Agur: AH-gur

Ahasuerus: Ah-hah-zoo-AIR-us

Ahaz: AY-haz

Ahimelech: Ah-HIM-uh-leck

Ahisamach: Ah-HEE-sah-mahk

Ahza: AY-haz

Ai: EYE

Akkadian: Ah-KAY-dee-an

Akrabbim: Ah-krah-BEEM

Alamoth: AL-uh-moth

Alpha: AL-fah

Amalek: AM-ah-lek

Amalekites: Aa-MAA-leh-kites

Amana: Ah-MAH-nah

Amariah: Am-ah-RIGH-ah

Amasis: AM-ah-sis

Amaziah: Aa-mah-ZIGH-ah

Amenemopet: Ah-men-EM-oh-pay

Amethyst: AM-eh-thist

Ammon: AM-mun

Ammonites: AH-moh-nites

Amorite: AA-moh-rite

Amphiatus: Am-piee-AH-tus

Amram: Ahm-RAHM

Amulet: AM-you-let

Anakim: Ah-nah-KEEM

Ananias: Ah-nah-NIGH-us

Anathoth: AN-uh-thothe

Andronicus: An-DROH-nih-kus

Annas: ANN-us

Antichrist: AN-tee-christ

Antioch: AN-tee-ock

Antiochus: An-TIE-oh-kus

Antiochus Epiphanes: An-TIE-oh-kus-Eh-PIH-fah-nees

Apelles: Ah-PELL-us

Apocalyptic: Ah-pah-kah-LIP-tic

Apodictic: Aa-poh-DIK-tik

Apollo: Ah-PAHL-oh

Apollos: Ah-POLL-us

Apollyon: Ah-PAHL-yon

Apostasy: Ah-POS-teh-see

Apphia: AP-fee-ah

Aquila: Ah-KWIH-lah

Arabah: ARE-uh-bah

Arabia: Ah-RAY-bee-ah

Arad: ARE-ad

Aram: AIR-um

Aramaic: Air-ah-MAY-ick

Aram-nahaaraim: AIR-am-Nah-har-uh-EEM

Aram-zobah: AIR-um-ZOH-bah

Arameans: Air-ah-MEE-ans

Ararat: AIR-ah-rat

Archelaus: Ark-keh-LAY-us

Archippus: ARCH-ih-puss

Areopagus: Air-ee-OP-ah-gus

Argob: Ar-GOBE

Ariel: Air-ee-ELL

Arimethea: Aur-im-ah-THE-ah

Arioch: ARE-ee-ock

Aristarchus: Ar-iss-TAR-cus

Aristobulus: Air-iss-TAH-bih-lus

Arnon: ARE-non

Aroer: Ah-ROH-er

Arpachshad: Ar-POCK-shad

Arpad: ARE-pod

Artemas: ARE-teh-mas

Artemis: AHR-teh-miss

Arvad: ARE-vahd

Asaph: AY-staff

Ashdod: ASH-dod

Asher: AA-sher

Asherah: Ah-sheh-RAH

Asherim: Ah-sheh-REEM

Ashkelon: ASH-keh-lon

Ashpenaz: ASH-peh-noz

Assur: ASH-ur

Assyria: Ah-SEER-ee-ah

Astarte: As-TAR-teh

Asyncritus: Ah-SIN-crih-tus

Atad: AY-tad

Ataroth: Ah-tah-ROTHE

Atharim: Ah-thah-REEM

Augustus: Ah-GUS-tus

Aven: Ah-VEN

Avvim: Ah-VEEM

Azariah: As-eh-RYE-ah

Azazel: Ah-zah-ZALE

Azmon: AZ-mon

Azzur: AZZ-ur

B

Baal: Bah-AHL

Baalam: BAY-lam

Baal-meon: Bah-ALL-may-OWN

Baal-peor: Bah-AHL-peh-ORE

Baal-zephon: Bah-AHL-Zeh-FONE

Babylon: BAB-eh-lon

Baca: Bah-KAH

Balaam: BAY-lem

Baladan: BAH-lah-don

Balak: BAY-lak

Bamah: Bah-MAH

Bamoth: Bah-MOTHE

Barabbas: Buh-RRA-bus

Barachel: Bah-rah-KELL

Barachia: Bah-rah-KEE-ah

Barak: Bah-RACK

Barnabas: BAR-nah-bas

Bartimaeus: Bar-tih-MAY-us

Bashan: Bah-SHAHN

Bath-rabbim: Bah-AHTH-rah-BEEM

Beelzebul: Bee-ELL-zeh-bul

Beer-la-hai-roi: BEER-lah-HIGH-roi

Beeroth: Buh-ay-ROTHE

Beersheba: Beer-SHEH-bah

Behemoth: Beh-HEE-moth

Belshazzar: BELL-shah-zar

Benaiah: Beh-NIGH-ah

Beon: Beh-OWN

Beor: Beh-ORE

Berechiah: Beh-reh-KIGH-ah

Berith: Buh-REETH

Berothah: Beh-ROH-thah

Beryl: BEHR-ill

Bethany: BEH-thuh-nee

Beth-eden: Beth-ay-DEN

Bethel: Beth-ELL

Bethesda: Beh-THEHZ-dah

Bethezel: Beth-eh-ZEL

Bethhaccherem: BETH-hah-KIR-um

Bethharam: Beth-hah-RAHM

Beth-jeshimoth: BETH-yeh-shih-MOTHE

Beth-le-aphrah: BETH-leh-ah-FRAH

Bethlehem: BETH-leh-hem

Bethlehem Ephrathah: BETH-leh-hem-eh-FRAH-thah

Bethphage: Beth-FAH-jee

Bethsaida: Beth-SIGH-duh

Beth-Togarmah: BETH-Toh-gar-MAH

Bethuel: BETH-you-ell

Bethzatha: Beth-ZAH-thah

Bezalel: Beh-zah-LALE

Bezer: BEH-zer

Bildad: BILL-dad

Bilhah: BILL-hah

Bithynia: Bih-THIN-ee-ah

Bozrah: BOZ-rah

Buz: BUHZ

Buzi: BU-zye

Buzite: BU-zite

C

Caesar: See-zar

Caesarea-Philippi: Sess-ah-REE-ah-FILL-ih-pie

Caiaphas: KIGH-ah-fas

Caligula: Cah-LIG-you-lah

Cana: KAY-nah

Canaan: KAY-nun

Canaanites: KAY-nuh-nites

Canneh: CAN-neh

Capernaum: Cah-PER-nah-um

Caphtorim: Caf-toh-REEM

Cappadocia: Cah-pah-doh-SEE-ah

Carchemish: CAR-keh-mish

Carmel: Car-MEL

Carnelian: Kar-NEE-lee-an

Casuistic: Kaa-zoo-ISS-tic

Cenchreae: SEN-kree-ah

Censer: SEN-ser

Centurion: Sen-TOR-ee-un

Cephas: SEE-fuss

Chaldeans: Kal-DEE-ans

Chebar: CHAY-bar

Chemosh: CHEH-mosh

Cherethites: CHAIR-eh-thites

Cherubim: CHER-uh-bim

Chilmad: KILL-mad

Chislev: KIZ-lev

Chorazim: KORE-ah-zim

Chorazin: Koh-RAH-zin

Chrysolite: KRIS-oh-light

Chrysoprase: KRIS-oh-prays

Cilicia: Si-LEE-shuh

Circumcision: SUR-kum-shi-zhun

Claudius: CLAH-dee-us

Cleopas: KLEE-oh-pus

Clopas: KLOH-pas

Colossae: Cuh-LOSS-eye

Cornelius: Kor-NEE-lee-us

Cubit: CUE-bit

Cush: KOOSH

Cushan: KOO-shan

Cushi: KOOSH-eye

Cyprus: SIGH-pruss

Cyrene: Sign-REE-nee

Cyrenians: Sigh-REE-nee-ans

D

Dalmanutha: Dal-mah-NOO-thah

Dalmatia: Dal-MAY-shuh

Damascus: Duh-MASK-us

Darius the Mede: Dah-RIE-us the MEED

Dathan: Dah-THAHN

Decalogue: DEH-kuh-log

Decapolis: Dee-CAP-oh-liss

Dedan: DEE-dan

Dedanites: DEH-duh-nites

Demas: DEE-mas

Demetrius: Di-MEE-tree-us

Denarii: Deh-NARE-ee

Denarius: Deh-NARE-ee-us

Desecration: Deh-seh-KRAY-shun

Diblaim: Dib-LIGH-im

Dibon: Dih-BONE

Diotrephes: Die-AH-tref-ays

Doeg: DOH-egg

Domitian: Doh-MIH-shun

Dorcus: DOR-kus

Dothan: DOH-thun

E

Eder: AY-der

Edom: EE-dum

Egypt: EE-gypt

Ekron: EHK-run

El Shaddai: El-shah-DIGH

Elam: EE-lum

Eleazar: Eh-lee-AY-zar

Eliab: EH-lee-ab

Eliezer: Eh-leeh-AY-zer

Elihu: Ee-LIGH-hew

Elijah: Ee-LIGH-jah

Elim: Eh-LEEM

Eliphaz: EH-lih-faz

Elishah: Eh-LIGH-shah

Elisheba: Eh-lee-SHEH-bah

Elizaphan: Eh-lee-ZAH-fahn

Elkosh: EL-kosh

Elohim: Eh-loh-HEEM

Elohist: EH-loh-hist

Elyon: Eh-lee-ON

Emim: Eh-MEEM

Emmanuel: Ih-MAN-yoo-ell

Endor: EN-door

En-eglaim: En-eh-GLAH-eem

En-gedi: En-GED-dee

Enoch: EE-nuck

Enosh: EE-nosh

Epaenetus: Ee-PAY-neh-tus

Epaphras: Ee-PAF-ras

Epaphroditus: Ee-paf-roh-DIGH-tus

Ephah: EE-fah

Ephesus: EH-feh-suss

Ephod: EE-fod

Ephphatha: EFF-fah-thah

Ephraim: EE-frah-eem

Ephraimites: EE-frah-eem-ites

Ephrathah: EFF-ra-thah

Ephron: EFF-ron

Epicurean: Eh-pih-CURE-ee-an

Epilogue: EH-pih-log

Erastus: Eh-RAS-tus

Esarhaddon: Eh-shar-HAD-dun

Esau: EE-saw

Eschatological: Ess-kat-ah-LAH-jih-cal

Ethiopia: Ee-thee-OPE-ee-ah

Eubulus: YOO-buh-lus

Eunuch: YOO-nick

Euodia: Yoo-OH-dee-ah

Euphrates: Yoo-FRAY-tees

Eutychus: YOO-tih-kus

Exhortation: Ex-or-TAY-shun

Ezekiel Ben-adam: Ee-ZEE-kee-al BEN-ah-DAHM

Ezion-geber: EH-zee-own-GEH-ber

Ezrahite: EZ-rah-hite

F

Freshets: FRESH-ets

G

Gadarenes: GAA-deh-reens

Gaius: GAY-us

Galatia: Ga-LAY-shuh

Galilee: GAL-ih-lee

Gamad: GAY-mad

Gamaliel: Ga-MAY-lee-el

Gareb: GAHR-eb

Gaza: GAH-zah

Geba: GAY-bah

Gebal: GAY-ball

Gedaliah: Geh-dah-LIGH-uh

Gedara: GEH-dah-rah

Gedeliah: Geh-dah-LIGH-ah

Gehenna: Guh-HEN-ah

Gennesaret: Geh-NESS-ah-ret

Gentile: JEN-tile

Gerah: GEH-rah

Gerah: Geh-RAH

Gerar: Ger-ARE

Gerasa: GEH-rah-sah

Gerasene: GER-ah-seen

Gergesa: GER-geh-sah

Gerizim: Geh-rih-ZEEM

Gershom: GER-shum

Gethsemane: Geth-SEH-mah-nee

Gezer: GEH-zer

Gibeah: GIH-bee-ah

Gideon: GID-ee-un

Gihon: GEE-hon

Gilead: GIH-lee-ad

Gilgad: GIL-gal

Gittith: GIT-tith

Glossalalia: Gloss-a-LAY-lee-ah

Gnostic: NOSS-tik

Gnosticism: NOSS-tih-siz-um

Goah: GO-ah

Golgotha: GOLE-gah-thah

Gomer: GO-mer

Gomorrah: Guh-MORE-uh

Goshen: GOH-shen

Gozan: GOH-zahn

H

Habakkuk: Hah-BACK-uk

Hadadrimmon: HAH-dad-RIM-on

Hades: HAY-deez

Hadrach: HAD-rack

Hagar: HAY-gar

Hagarites: HAY-guh-rites

Haggai: HAG-eye

Halah: Hah-LAH

Hamath: Hah-MAHTH

Hamonah: Hah-mo-NAH

Hamon-gog: Hay-mahn-GOG

Hamor: Hah-MORE

Hananiah: Han-nah-NIGH-ah

Hanukkah: HAH-nah-kuh

Haran: Hah-RAHN

Hauran: HAWR-ahn

Havilah. HAV-ih-lah

Hazar-enon: Hah-ZAR-eh-NON

Hazar-Hatticon: Ha-ZAR-hah-tee-KAHN

Hazeroth: Hah-zeh-ROTHE

Hazor: Hah-TSORE

Hebron: HEH-brun

Helbon: HEL-bon

Heldai: HEL-die

Helech: HEH-leck

Hellenistic: Heh-leh-NISS-tic

Hermes: HER-meez

Hellenists: HEL-eh-nists

Hermon: Her-MON

Herod: HARE-ud

Herodias: Heh-ROH-dee-as

Herodion: Heh-ROH-dee-on

Heshbon: HESH-bon

Hethlon: HETH-lon

Hezekiah: Heh-zeh-KIGH-ah

Higgaion: HIG-eye-on

Hilkiah: Hil-KIGH-uh

Hinnom: Hih-NOME

Hireling: HIRE-ling

Hittites: HIH-tites

Hivites: HIH-vites

Hobab: HOH-bab

Homer: HO-mer

Hophra: HOFF-rah

Horeb: HOR-ebb

Hormah: HOR-mah

Horonaim: Hore-oh-NAY-yim

Hyacinth: HIGH-ah-sinth

Hymenaeus: High-MEEN-ee-us

I

Iconium: Eye-KO-nee-um

Iddo: ID-oh

Idumeans: Ih-doo-ME-ans

Illyricum: Ih-LEER-ee-cum

Irad: EAR-rad

Isaac. EYE-zik

Isaiah: Eye-ZAY-uh

Ishmael: ISH-may-ell

Ishmaelites: ISH-may-eh-lites

Issachar: IS-oh-kahr

Ithamar: IH-thah-mar

Ivvah: EE-vah

Iye-abarim: EYE-ah-bah-REEM

J

Jaar: Jah-ARE

Jaazaniah: Jah-az-ah-NIGH-ah

Jabal: JAY-bal

Jabin: JAY-bin

Jahaz: JAH-hahz

Jair: Jah-EER

Jambres: JAM-bres

Jannes: JAH-nus

Japheth: JAH-feth

Jared: JAR-ed

Javan: JAH-van

Jazer: JAH-zer

Jebusites: JEB-yoo-sites

Jedaiah: Jeh-DAY-ah

Jeduthun: JED-uh-thun

Jehoahaz: Jeh-HOE-ah-haz

Jehoiachin: Jeh-HOY-ah-kin

Jehoiakim: Jeh-HOY-ah-kim

Jehozadak: Jeh-HOE-zah-dak

Jemimah: Jeh-MY-mah

Jephthah: JEF-thah

Jephunneh: Jeh-FOO-neh

Jericho: JEH-rih-koh

Jeroboam: Jer-oh-BOH-am

Jerusalem: Jeh-ROO-sah-lem

Jeshurun: JEH-shoo-run

Jezebel: JEH-zeh-bell

Jezreel: Jez-REEL

Joash: JOH-ash

Job: JOHB

Jonah: JOH-nuh

Joppa: JAH-puh

Jordan: JORE-dun

Joshua: JOSH-oo-ah

Josiah: Joh-SIGH-ah

Jotbathah: JOT-bah-thah

Jotham: JOH-tham

Jubel: JOO-bal

Judah: JOO-dah

Judaism: JOO-day-iz-um

Judas Iscariot: JOO-das-Iss-CARE-ee-ot

Judea: Joo-DEE-ah

Junias: JOO-nee-as

K

Kabod: Kah-BODE

Kadesh: KAY-desh

Kedar: KAY-dar

Kedemoth: Keh-deh-MOTHE

Kenan: KEN-an

Kenites: KEN-ites

Kephas: KAY-fass

Kerenhappuch: Keh-ren-HAH-puk

Keturah: Keh-TURE-ah

Keziah: Keh-ZIGH-ah

Kiriathaim: Kir-ee-ah-THAH-yim

Kishion: KISH-ee-un

Koa: KO-ah

Kohath: KOH-hath

Koine: Koy-NAY

L

Laban: LAY-ban

Lachish: Lah-KEESH

Lamech: LAH-meck

Laodicea: Lay-oh-dih-SEE-ah

Leannoth: LEE-un-noth

Leaven: LEH-ven

Lemuel: LEM-yoo-el

Levi: LEE-vigh

Leviathan: Luh-VIE-uh-thun

Levite: LEE-vite

Levites: LEE-vites

Levitical: Leh-VIH-tih-kal

Linus: LIGH-nus

Logos: LAW-goss

Lucius: LOO-shus

Lud: LOOD

Lydda: LID-ah

Lyre: LIER

Lystra: LISS-trah

M

Maccabees: MACK-ah-beez

Macedonia: Ma-seh-DO-nee-ah

Machpelah: Mahk-peh-LAH

Magadan: MAH-gah-don

Magdalene: MAG-dah-lehn

Magog: MAH-gog

Mahalalel: Mah-HAH-luh-lel

Mahalath: Mah-hah-LATH

Mahanaim: Mah-hah-NAH-yim

Malachi: MAL-ah-kigh

Malchus: MAHL-kuss

Mammon: MAA-mom

Mamre: MAM-reh

Manasseh: Muh-NASS-eh

Manna: MAN-nah

Marah: MAHR-ah

Marcion: MAR-see-un

Marduk: MAR-duke

Mareshah: Mah-reh-SHAH

Maroth: MAR-oth

Martyr: MAHR-ter

(Mary) Magdalene: MAG-dah-len

Maskil: MAHS-kil

Massah: MASS-ah

Mazzaroth: Mah-zah-ROTHE

Medeba: Meh-deh-BAH

Medes: MEEDS

Media: MEE-dee-ah

Megiddo: Meh-GID-oh

Mehujael: Meh-HOO-jah-el

Melchizedek: Mel-KIZ-eh-deck

Memphis: MEM-fis

Mene: MEN-eh

Menorah: Meh-NOR-ah

Meribah: MEH-rih-bah

Meribath-kadesh: MER-ih-bath-KAH-desh

Merodach: MER-oh-dahk

Meshach: MEE-shack

Meshech: MEE-shek

Mesopotamia: Meh-soh-poh-TAME-ee-ah

Messiah: Meh-SIGH-ah

Methuselah: Meh-THOO-zeh-lah

Methushael: Meh-THOO-shah-el

Midian: MID-ee-an

Midianites: MIH-dee-ah-nites

Migdol: MIG-dole

Miktam: MICK-tam

Milcah: MIL-kah

Milcom: MIL-kahm

Millennium: Mih-LEH-nee-um

Miriam: MIR-ee-am

Mishael: MEE-shah-el

Mizpah: MIZ-pah

Moab: MOH-ab

Molech: MOH-leck

Moresheth: MORE-eh-sheth

Moriah: Moh-RIGH-ah

Moses: MOH-zez

Mount Sinai: Mount SIGH-nigh

Muth-labben: MUTH-lab-un

N

Naamah: NAY-ah-mah

Naamathite: Nah-ah-MAH-thite

Naameh: Nah-ah-MEH

Nabonidus: Nab-boh-NIGH-dus

Nabopolasser: Nab-boh-poh-LASS-er

Nadab: NAY-dab

Nahor: NAY-hor

Nahum: NAY-hum

Nain: NANE or NAY-een

Naphtali: NAFF-tah-lee

Narcissus: Nar-SIH-sus

Nathanael: Nah-THAN-yell

Nazareth: NA-zeh-reth

Nebaioth: Neh-bah-YOTHE

Nebuchadnezzar: Neh-buh-kahd-NEZ-zer

Nebuchadrezzar: Neh-buh-kah-DREZ-zer

Negeb: NEH-geb

Nephilim: Neh-fih-LEEM

Nereus: NEE-ree-us

Nicanor: NIGH-kan-or

Nicolaitans: Nih-koh-LAY-tons

Nicopolis: Nih-KAH-poh-lis

Niger: NIGH-jer

Nimbus: NIM-bus

Nimrod: NIM-rod

Nineveh: NIH-neh-veh

Nisan: Nee-SAHN

Noah: NOH-ah

O

Oboth: Oh-BOTHE

Oholah: Oh-ho-LAH

Oholiab: Oh-HOH-lee-ab

Olympas: Oh-LIM-pas

Onan: OH-nan

Onesimus: Oh-NESS-ih-muss

Onias: Oh-NIGH-us

Ophir: OH-fear

Oracle: OR-ah-cul

Oreb: OR-ebb

Orion: Oh-RYE-un

P

Paddan-aram: PAD-an-AIR-em

Palanquin: PAL-an-keen

Pamphylia: Pam-FILL-ee-ah

Paphos: PAF-ohs

Papyrus: Puh-PIE-russ

Paran: PAR-ahn

Parmenas: PAR-men-as

Parousia: Par-oo-SEE-uh

Parsin: PAR-sin

Parthia: PAHR-thee-ah

Pashhur: PASH-er

Pathros: PATH-ros

Patmos: PAT-moss

Patrobas: PAT-roh-bas

Pekah: PEH-kah

Pelatiah: Pel-eh-TIGH-ah

Peleg: PAY-leg

Pelusium: Pih-LOO-see-um

Peniel: PEH-nee-el

Pentateuch: PEN-tah-tuke

Pentecost: PEN-te-kost

Penuel: PEN-yoo-el

Peor: Pea-ORE

Perga: PER-gah

Pergamum: Per-GAH-mum

Perizim: Pare-eh-ZEEM

Perizzites: PEH-rih-zites

Persis: PER-sis

Pestilence: PEST-eh-lents

Pethuel: Peh-THOO-ell

Phanuel: FAN-yoo-ehl

Pharaoh: FAIR-oh

Pharisees: FARE-eh-seez

Phicol: FIGH-col

Philemon: Figh-LEE-mun

Philistia: Fill-ISS-tee-ah

Philistines: FILL-iss-teens

Philologus: Fih-loh-LOH-gus

Phinehas: Fih-NAY-hass

Phlegon: FLEH-gon

Phoebe: FEE-bee

Phoenicia: Foh-NEE-shah

Phrygia: FRIH-jee-ah

Pibeseth: Pi-BEH-seth

Pishon: PIE-shon

Pisidia: Pih-SIH-dee-ah

Pleiades: PLEE-ah-deez

Politarch: POL-ih-tark

Pontius Pilate: PON-shus-PIE-let

Portent: POR-tent

Potiphar: POH-tih-far

Potiphera: Poh-TIH-fuh-ruh

Praetorium: Pray-TORE-ee-um

Prefect: PREE-fect

Prisca: PRIH-sah

Prochorus: PRO-kor-us

Proconsul: Pro-KON-sul

Prologue: PRO-log

Prophecy: PRAH-feh-see

Prophesy: PRAH-feh-sigh

Proselytes: PRAH-sell-ites

Ptolemais: Tol-eh-MAY-us

Ptolemy: TOH-leh-mee

Puah: POO-ah

Pudens: POO-denz

Purslane: PURS-lin

Put: POOT

Q

Qesitah: Keh-SEE-tah

Quartus: KWAR-tus

Quirinius: Kwih-RIHN-ee-us

R

Raamah: Rah-ah-MAH

Rabbah: Rah-BAH

Rabshakeh: RAHB-sheh-keh

Rachel: RAY-chel

Rahab: RAY-hab

Ram: RAHM

Ramah: Rah-MAH

Rameses: RAM-sees

Rechabites: REH-kah-bites

Regem-melech: REH-gehm-MEH-leck

Rephaim: REH-fah-yim

Rephidim: Reh-fih-DEEM

Reuben: ROO-ben

Rezeph: REH-zeff

Rezin: REH-zin

Rhegium: RAY-jee-um

Rhoda: RO-dah

Rhodes: ROADS

Riblah: RIB-lah

Rimmon: RIM-on

S

Sabeans: Sah-BEE-ans

Sadducees: SAD-yoo-seez

Salecah: Sah-leh-KAH

Salem: SAY-lem

Salim: SAY-lehm

Salome: Sal-OH-may

Samaria: Sah-MARE-ee-ah

Samaritans: Sah-MARE-ih-tons

Samson: SAM-son

Samuel: SAM-yoo-ell

Sanhedrin: San-HEE-drin

Sapphira: Sah-FEER-ah

Sapphire: SAFF-ire

Sarah: SAIR-ah

Sarai: Sah-RIGH

Sardis: SAHR-dis

Sardonyx: Sar-DAH-niks

Satan: SAY-tan

Satrap: SAT-trap

Scythian: SIH-thee-an

Seir: Seh-EER

Selah: Seh-LAH

Seleucus: Seh-LOO-sus

Selucids: Seh-LOO-sids

Senir: Seh-NEER

Sennacherib: Seh-NAA-keh-rib

Sergius Paulus: SER-jee-us-PAH-lus

Shaddai: Shah-DIGH

Shadrach: SHAD-rack

Shaphan: SHAH-fahn

Shaphir: SHAY-fer

Sharezer: Sheh-REE-zer

Shealtiel: Shee-AL-tee-el

Shear-jashub: Sheh-ARE-yah-SHOOB

Sheba: SHEE-bah

Shebat: SHE-bat

Shechem: SHECK-em

Shekel: SHECK-el

Shekinah: Sheh-KIGH-nah

Shelah: Sheh-LAH

Shelomith: Sheh-loh-MITH

Shema: Sheh-MAH

Sheminith: SHEM-uh-nith

Sheol: Sheh-OLE

Shephelah: Sheh-FAY-lah

Shiggaion: SHIG-eye-on

Shiloh: SHIGH-low

Shimeites: SHIM-eh-ites

Shinar: SHIGH-nar

Shiphrah: SHIF-rah

Shittim: SHIH-tim

Shoa: SHOW-ah

Shuah: SHOO-ah

Shuhite: SHOO-hite

Shulammite: SHOO-lah-mite

Shushan Eduth: SHOO-shan-EE-doth

Sibraim: Sib-RAY-im

Sicarius: Sih-CAHR-ree-us

Sidon: SIGH-dun

Sihon: SEE-hun

Siloam: Sih-LOH-am

Silvanus: Sil-VAH-nus

Simeon: SIH-mee-un

Sinai: SIGH-nigh

Sirion: SEER-ee-on

Sisera: SIS-eh-rah

Smaragdus: Smeh-RAG-dus

Smyrna: SMER-nah

Sodom: SOD-um

Solomon: SOL-oh-mon

Sosipater: Sah-SIP-ah-ter

Stachys: STAY-kis

Stoic: STOW-ick

Succoth: SUH-kuth

Sumer: SOO-mer

Susa: SUE-zah

Suzerain: SOO-zeh-rain

Suzerainty: SOO-zeh-rehn-tee

Sychar: SIGH-kar

Syene: Sigh-EEN

Synagogue: SIN-ah-gog

Syntyche: Sin-TIH-kay

Syria: SEAR-ee-ah

T

Tabeel: Tah-buh-ELL

Taberah: Tah-beh-RAH

Tabitha: TAB-ith-ah

Tabor: Tay-BORE

Tahpanhes: TAH-puh-neez

Tamar: TAY-mar

Tammuz: Tah-MUZ

Tarshish: TAR-shish

Tarsus: TAR-sus

Tehaphnehes: Teh-HOFF-neh-hees

Tekel: TEH-kel

Tekoa: Teh-KOE-ah

Tel-abib: Tell-ah-BEEB

Tema: TAY-mah

Teman: TAY-mahn

Temanite: TAY-man-ite

Terah: TER-ah

Teraphim: TER-ah-fim

Terebinths: TER-uh-binths

Tertius: TER-tee-us

Tertullus: Ter-TULL-us

Thebes: THEEBS

Theophilus: Thee-AH-fil-us

Thessalonica: Thess-a-loh-NIGH-kah

Thummim: THOO-mim

Thyatira: Thee-ah-TEE-rah

Tiberius: Tie-BEER-ee-us

Tigris: TIGH-gris

Tigris-Euphrates: TIGH-griss-you-FRAY-tees

Timon: TIM-on

Timothy: TIH-moh-thee

Tirhakah: Tear-hah-KAH

Tirzah: TEER-zah

Titus: TIE-tus

Tobijah: Toh-BEE-jah

Topaz: TOH-paz

Topheth: TOH-feth

Torah: TOH-rah

Trachonitus: Trak-uh-NIGHT-us

Tribulation: Trib-yoo-LAY-shun

Trophimus: TROH-fih-mus

Tryphaena: Treh-FAY-nah

Tryphosa: Treh-FOH-sah

Tubal: TOO-bal

Tubal-Cain: TOO-bal-CAIN

Tychicus: TIK-ih-kus

Typology: Tie-PAH-leh-jee

Tyre: TIRE

U

Ulai: YOO-lie

Uphaz: YOO-faz

Urbanus: Ur-BAN-us

Urim: OOR-im

Uz: UHZ

Uzal: YOO-zal

Uziel: Oo-zee-ELL

Uzziah: Yoo-ZIGH-ah

Uzziel: OO-zee-ell

V

Vitellius: Vih-TELL-ee-us

Y

Yahweh: YAH-way

Yahwist: YAH-wist

Yobel: Yoh-BELL

Yom Kippur: YOME-Kih-POOR

Z

Zaanan: ZAH-eh-nahn

Zacchaeus: Zak-EE-us

Zadok: ZAY-dock

Zarephath: ZARE-eh-FATH

Zebedee: ZEH-buh-dee

Zeboiim: Zeh-BOH-eem

Zebulun: ZEB-you-lun

Zechariah: Zeh-kah-RIGH-ah

Zedad: ZEE-dad

Zedekiah: Zeh-deh-KIGH-uh

Zelophehad: Zeh-LOH-feh-had

Zemer: ZEH-mer

Zenas: ZEE-nas

Zephaniah: Zeh-fah-NIGH-ah

Zerubbabel: Zeh-RUB-ah-bel

Zilpah: ZIL-pah

Zimri: ZIM-ree

Zion: ZYE-un

Ziphites: ZIF-ites

Zipporah: Zih-POH-rah

Zoan: ZOH-an

Zoar: ZOH-ar

Zophar: ZOH-far

JEWISH CALENDAR

The Jews used two kinds of calendars: A *civil* calendar, which contained the official records of kings, childbirth, and contracts; and a *sacred* calendar, from which festivals were computed.

Names of Months	Corresponds With	Number of Days	Month of Civil Year	Month of Sacred Year
Tishri	September–October	30	1st	7th
Heshvan	October–November	29 or 30	2nd	8th
Chislev	November–December	29 or 30	3rd	9th
Tebeth	December–January	29	4th	10th
Shebat	January–February	30	5th	11th
Adar	February–March	29 or 30	6th	12th
Nisan	March–April	30	7th	1st
Iyar	April–May	29	8th	2nd
Sivan	May–June	30	9th	3rd
Tammuz	June–July	29	10th	4th
Ab	July–August	30	11th	5th
*Elul	August–September	29	12th	6th

*Hebrew months were either 29 or 30 days in length. Their year was 354 days, hence shorter than ours. As a result, approximately every three years (7 times in 19 years) an extra 29-day month, *Veadar*, was added between *Adar* and *Nisan*.

JEWISH FEASTS

Feast of	Month on Jewish Calendar	Day	Corresponding Month	References
*Passover (Un-leavened Bread)	Nisan	14-21	March-April	Ex. 12:43–13:10; Matt. 26:17-20
*Pentecost (Firstfruits or Weeks)	Sivan	6 (50 days after Passover)	May-June	Deut. 16:9-12; Acts 2:1
Trumpets, *Rosh Hashanah*	Tishri	1, 2	September-October	Num. 29:1-6
Day of Atonement, Yom Kippur	Tishri	10	September-October	Lev. 23:26–32; Heb. 9:7
*Tabernacles (Booths or Ingathering)	Tishri	15-22	September-October	Neh. 8:13–18; John 7:2
Dedication (Lights), Hanukkah	Chislev	25 (8 days)	November-December	John 10:22
Purim (Lots)	Adar	14, 15	February-March	Esth. 9: 18-32

*The three major feasts for which all males of Israel were required to travel to the Temple in Jerusalem (Exodus 23:14-19).

HOURS OF THE JEWISH DAY

The Jews divided the day into twelve equal parts, beginning at 6:00 A.M. and ending at 6:00 P.M. The New Testament reflects the Roman system of four night watches rather than the Jewish system of three night watches. The first watch for the Jews was 6:00 to 10:00 P.M., the second watch from 10:00 P.M. to 2:00 A.M., and the third watch from 2:00 to 6:00 A.M.

6:00 A.M.	sunrise, end of fourth watch, Mark 16:2
7:00 A.M.	first hour
8:00 A.M.	second hour
9:00 A.M.	third hour, first hour of prayer, Acts 2:15
10:00 A.M.	fourth hour
11:00 A.M.	fifth hour
12:00 P.M.	sixth hour, noon, Matt.
1:00 P.M.	seventh hour, John 4:52
2:00 P.M.	eighth hour
3:00 P.M.	ninth hour, Matt. 27:45, hour of prayer, Acts 3:1
4:00 P.M.	tenth hour, John 1:39
5:00 P.M.	eleventh hour, Matt. 20:6
6:00 P.M.	sunset, beginning of first watch
7:00 P.M.	
8:00 P.M.	
9:00 P.M.	end of first watch, beginning of second watch, Luke 12:38
10:00 P.M.	
11:00 P.M.	
12:00 A.M.	midnight, Acts 16:25, end of second watch, beginning of third watch, Luke 12:38
1:00 A.M.	
2:00 A.M.	
3:00 A.M.	end of third watch, beginning of fourth watch, Matt. 14:25, Mark 6:48, cockcrow, Matt. 26:75, Mark 13:35
4:00 A.M.	
5:00 A.M.	
6:00 A.M.	

UNITS OF MEASURE

Measures of Length

	Rod (reed)	Pace	Cubit	Span	Handbreadth	Finger
Rod (reed)	9 ft. (Ezek. 10.5 ft.)					
Pace	3 paces	3 ft.				
Cubit	6 cubits	2 cubits	1. 5 ft. (Ezek. 18 in.)			
Span	12 spans	4 spans	2 spans	9 in.		
Hand-breadth	36 hand-breadths	12 hand-breadths	6 hand-breadths	3 hand-breadths	3 in.	
Finger	144 fingers	48 fingers	24 fingers	12 fingers	4 fingers	.75 in.

A day's journey = 20 mi.
A sabbath day's journey = 3.637 ft.
Some distance (a little way) = 5 mi.

Mile (Roman) = 4,854 ft.
Stadion (furlong) = 606 ft.
Fathom = 6 ft.

Dry Measures

	Homer	Seah	Ephah	Omer
Homer (kor, measure)	6.524 bu.			
Seah (measure)	3 seahs	2.175 bu.		
Ephah	10 ephahs	3.33 ephahs	.652 bu.	
Omer (sheaf)	100 omers	33.33 omers	10 omers	2.087 qt.

Basket = 1 peck

Liquid Measures

	Kor	Bath	Hin	Kab	Log
Kor	60 gal.				
Bath (measure)	10 baths	6 gal.			
Hin	60 hins	6 hins	1 gal.		
Kab	120 kabs	12 kabs	2 kabs	2 qt.	
Log	480 logs	48 logs	8 logs	4 logs	1 pt.